EDUARD MEYER

Leben und Leistung
eines
Universalhistorikers

MNEMOSYNE

BIBLIOTHECA CLASSICA BATAVA

COLLEGERUNT

A.D. LEEMAN · H.W. PLEKET · C.J. RUIJGH

BIBLIOTHECAE FASCICULOS EDENDOS CURAVIT

C.J. RUIJGH. KLASSIEK SEMINARIUM. OUDE TURFMARKT 129, AMSTERDAM

SUPPLEMENT CENTESIMUM DUODECIMUM

WILLIAM M. CALDER III

UND

ALEXANDER DEMANDT

(HGG.)

EDUARD MEYER

Leben und Leistung
eines
Universalhistorikers

Eduard Meyer (1855–1930).

EDUARD MEYER

Leben und Leistung eines

Universalhistorikers

HERAUSGEGEBEN VON

WILLIAM M. CALDER III

UND

ALEXANDER DEMANDT

E.J. BRILL

LEIDEN · NEW YORK · KØBENHAVN · KÖLN

1990

Gedruckt mit Unterstützung der Deutschen Forschungsgemeinschaft

Library of Congress Cataloging-in-Publication Data

Eduard Meyer : Leben und Leistung eines Universalhistorikers /
herausgegeben von William M. Calder III und Alexander Demandt.
    p.   cm. -- (Mnemosyne, bibliotheca classica Batava.
Supplement, ISSN 0169-8958 ; 112.)
    Papers presented at a meeting held Nov. 10-14, 1987, in Bad
Homburg.
    Chiefly in German with 3 papers in English and 1 in Italian.
    ISBN 9004091319
    1. Meyer, Edward, 1855-1930--Congresses. 2. Historians--Germany-
-Biography--Congresses.   I. Calder, William M. (William Musgrave).
1932-   . II. Demandt, Alexander, 1937-   . III. Series:
Mnemosyne, bibliotheca classica Batava. Supplementum : 112.
D15.M45E38   1990
943'.007202--dc20   80-38588
                                            CIP

ISSN 0169-8958
ISBN 90 04 09131 9

PRINTED IN THE NETHERLANDS

INHALT

VORWORT

Den Historikern geht es ähnlich wie anderen Literaten: ihr Ansehen bei den Zeitgenossen und der Ruhm bei der Nachwelt sind nicht immer ausgewogen. Bei Ranke und Droysen war es der Fall; die Namen von Mommsen und Burckhardt haben an Klang gewonnen, die von Treitschke und Haller haben verloren. Letzteres gilt auch für Eduard Meyer (1855–1930). *The most eminent living historian, the one final authority*—so der Evanston Index 1910—war Meyer gewiß nie, aber er war einer der wenigen, von denen man das behaupten konnte. Wenn er diesen Rang eingebüßt hat, so beruht das, wenigstens unter anderem, auf seiner politischen Haltung. Ähnlich wie Treitschke dachte Meyer national und hielt sich selbst für fortschrittlich. Spätestens seit dem Sturz der Hohenzollerndynastie stimmte das nicht mehr überein. Meyer wurde auf die konservative, ja reaktionäre Seite geschoben und als überholt abgetan.

Ist ein solcher Stimmungswechsel schon für sich ein Grund, Meyers zu gedenken, so kommt hinzu, daß die Verbindung von Politik und Geschichte bei einem Historiker des Deutschtums wie Treitschke sehr viel enger ausfallen muß als bei einem Altertumsforscher wie Meyer. Sein wissenschaftliches Werk ist von politischen Anschauungen weniger gefärbt und in der Substanz überdies so gehaltvoll, daß noch immer viel aus ihm zu lernen ist. Beide Gründe lassen es bedauern, daß Meyer von der Wissenschaftsgeschichte bisher vernachlässigt worden ist. Es gibt keine Biographie über ihn, wie sie manchen Fachkollegen durchaus minderen Ranges zuteil geworden ist.

Insofern war es eine begrüßenswerte Idee von William Calder III, nach den Studien über Wilamowitz nun einmal Meyer vorzunehmen. Meyers enge, später von ihm so brüsk gelöste Verbindung zu Amerika hat dort das Interesse an ihm beflügelt. Auf Calders Anregung fand vom 10. bis 14. November 1987 in den gastlichen Räumen der Reimers-Stiftung zu Bad Homburg eine Tagung statt, deren Ergebnis wir hier vorlegen. Auch an dieser Stelle sei Herrn Konrad von Krosigk, dem Vorstand der Stiftung, für sein wohlwollendes Entgegenkommen gedankt. Zu danken ist ebenso Winfried Gebhardt (Bayreuth), Beat Näf (Zürich) und Edgar Pack (Köln), die Sektionen der Diskussion geleitet haben, und Jaap Mansfeld, der die Verbindung zum Verlagshaus Brill hergestellt hat. Äußere Gründe haben es verhindert, daß die Beiträge von Brian Croke (Melbourne), Gustav Adolf Lehmann (Köln), und Leandro Polverini (Rom) hier gleichfalls vorgelegt wurden. Sie werden gegebenenfalls an anderem Ort erscheinen.

Der Reiz und die Schwierigkeit bei der Organisation des Kolloquiums lag in der Vielseitigkeit von Meyers Werk. Es erwies sich als unmöglich, alle Aspekte seines Lebens und seiner Schriften zu behandeln. Insbcson- dere bedauerlich ist es, daß wir die orientalistischen und ägyptologischen Forschungen—nach einer Reihe von Absagen—zurückstellen mußten. Was blieb, war mehr als genug. Das spiegelt nicht nur die Herkunft, son- dern auch die Fachrichtung der Teilnehmer: es waren Altphilologen, Philosophen und Theologen, Neuhistoriker, Wissenschaftshistoriker, Religionshistoriker und Althistoriker. Letztere überwogen nach der Zahl, entsprechend Meyers eigener Profession. Unsere Fragestellung galt einerseits der Stellung Meyers in seiner Zeit und andererseits seiner Be- deutung für uns. Insofern waren biographische und forschungskritische Ansätze zu verbinden, um aus Leben und Leistung ein Ganzes zu machen.

William M. Calder   Alexander Demandt

Berlin/"Salerno", 4. Jan. 1990

ABKÜRZUNGEN FÜR DIE HAUPTWERKE ED. MEYERS

Amerika   : Die Vereinigten Staaten von Amerika, 1920

Caesar   : Caesars Monarchie und das Principat des Pompeius, 1918/22

England   : England. Seine staatliche und politische Entwicklung und der Krieg gegen Deutschland, 1915

Forschungen : Forschungen zur Alten Geschichte I 1892/1966
                                           II 1899/1966

GdA   : Geschichte des Altertums (jeweils letzte Auflage)

Hannibal   : Hannibal und Scipio, In: Meister der Politik, I 1922, S. 65ff

Heimstätten : Die Heimstättenfrage im Lichte der Geschichte, 1924

Hellenismus : Blüte und Niedergang des Hellenismus in Asien, 1925

Kl. Schr.   : Kleine Schriften, 1910
Kl. Schr. I/ II : ''   ''   2 Aufl. I/ II, 1924

Marohl   : H. Marohl, Eduard Meyer—Bibliographie, 1941

Mormonen   : Ursprung und Geschichte der Mormonen, 1912

Nordamerika : Nordamerika und Deutschland, 1915

Staat   : Staat und Wirtschaft, In: Von Altertum und Gegenwart. Die Kultur- zusammenhänge in den Hauptepochen und auf den Hauptgebieten, 2. Aufl., 1920, S. 80–100 (1. Aufl. 1919)

Theorie   : Zur Theorie und Methodik der Geschichte, 1902

UAC   : Ursprung und Anfänge des Christentums I–III, 1921

Weltgeschichte: Weltgeschichte und Weltkrieg. Gesammelte Aufsätze, 1916

E. BADIAN

EDUARD MEYER'S AMERICAN PARALIPOMENA*

When the editors first suggested to me that I should deal with Meyer's interpretation of Alexander the Great, I wondered whether, after Professor A. Demandt's exemplary treatment of the Wilhelmine interpretation in general,[1] there was enough left to be said. But there was what appeared to be an interesting question: that of the genesis of the paper in his *Kleine Schriften* ([1]1910, 283–332; Marohl item 205), which is his only substantial statement on Alexander.

At first glance, the answer seemed easy enough. It was in 1904 that Julius Beloch produced the second part of his idiosyncratically divided treatment of Alexander, with a dedication to Meyer, "in alter Freundschaft."[2] In this, although avoiding absurd extremes, he denied Alexander's personal genius as a commander and expressed views that happened (as later appeared) to run counter to Meyer's as yet unpublished ideas in other respects. It seemed obvious that it was under this stimulus that Meyer sorted out his own thoughts and presented them in an academic lecture in 1905 (as set out in the introduction to the published paper)—of course, without explicit contradiction of his friend. It might seem all the more obvious since, as we shall see, it is very likely that his first treatment of an Alexander topic was similarly stimulated. It all goes to show how, even in quite recent history, a rational argument can be shown to be totally wrong, or at least grossly oversimplified, as soon as a real fact turns up.

---

* I owe thanks to many for help at various stages. First, to Professor M.H. Chambers for inspiring this research, as detailed in my text; to Dr. Edgar Pack, for drawing my attention to Herman Volrath Hilprecht as an editor of the *Sunday School Times*, thus enabling me to penetrate part of the mystery surrounding Meyer's first American publication; to Dr. Chr. Hoffmann, for readily sending me information regarding Meyer's correspondence; to Professor Calder, for trying to get information for me from the University of Jena; to Professor Kevin Graffagnino, Curator of Special Collections at the University of Vermont, for finding out as much as he could for me regarding Richardson and Stetson; and to the staff of the Congregational Library in Boston. As always, the staff of the Zentrales Archiv der Akademie der Wissenschaften der DDR has made work in that Archive both pleasant and profitable. Further debts are acknowledged at various points below.

[1] *Archiv für Kulturgeschichte* 54 (1972) 325–363. (On the particular topic, pp. 334–338.)

[2] *Griechische Geschichte* III 1 (1904). Beloch's discussion of Alexander is oddly divided between II (1897) and III 1, in the second edition between III[2] 1 (1922) and IV[2] 1 (1925). Beloch objects to Alexander-worship, but also to extreme hostility to Alexander, for which he cites Grote.

Meyer's "history" of the paper (p. 284) describes it as "Nach einem auf der Hamburger Philologenversammlung am 5. Oktober 1905 gehaltenen Vortrag und einem für eine amerikanische Zeitschrift niedergeschriebenen Manuskript." This implies that the lecture was the original version, followed by the manuscript; and it makes no allusion to publication of that manuscript.[3] It was Professor Chambers who discovered (and turned over to me, with an indication that he did not want to make further use of it) what, on inspection, turned out to be nothing less than the version written for an American magazine; it had indeed been published, in English, and that long before the Hamburg lecture. He also drew my attention to Meyer's first appearance in print in America: an article in the *Sunday School Times* (a weekly magazine published by the influential American Sunday-School Union) in 1890. After this, it did not take me long to discover that there was indeed a third, and perhaps even more striking, publication by Meyer in America. His essay "Der Gang der Alten Geschichte" (*Kl. Schr.*[1] 231–282) is described as "Geschrieben 1902 für eine in Amerika geplante Universalgeschichte:" it turned out that that essay had been written for a work that had indeed not merely been "planned", but that was one of the most ambitious and most striking American historical publications of the beginning of this century.

It is these three works, one of them never mentioned by Meyer (though apparently known to Marohl: his item 74) and two implicitly denied by what appears to be deliberately misleading language, that I propose to rescue in this contribution.[4] They are not only interesting in connection with Meyer's own ideas and their development, but they contribute to a sketch of American *Kulturgeschichte* of about a century ago.

The evidence on how Meyer came to be invited to write these three essays becomes progressively less explicit and must increasingly be supplemented by conjecture. It is to be hoped that future work in archives will turn up precise information on the second and third, as my own search in the Zentrales Archiv der Akademie der DDR surprisingly yielded the evidence for the very first invitation, which I am now allowed, with the gracious permission of the Director of the Archive, to publish here for the first time. But hypotheses based on probability and on circumstantial evidence are only too familiar to the practising ancient historian: as we have

---

[3] We shall come back to this and another, similar, case in *Kleine Schriften* below.

[4] When discussing the Alexander essay, I shall incidentally deal with Meyer's interpretation of Philip and Alexander at least in some important respects—thus in part fulfilling the task the organizers had set me. I shall also (more briefly) touch on some of the ideas in his other major American essay. But it is the chief purpose of this contribution to draw attention to these "lost" papers and to set them in the background which Meyer did not wish us to know.

seen, the first real fact may overturn them. Yet these early contacts with America, later (long before the First World War) denied by Meyer, are worth pursuing as, in their different ways, attesting the connection of American academic life with German and the admiration of American intellectuals for German scholarship, in which many of them had been trained. It is particularly striking that, although Meyer had formed an early connection with England, and had in fact visited England and Scotland in 1876–77, while he did not visit the United States until 1904, his British connections did not result in any contribution to a British publication until 1899: and that only an encyclopaedia entry,[5] as indeed are all his later British publications. By contrast, by the time of his first visit to the United States he had already published the works here set out in America, on very different topics and in very different types of publication—all of this before the Chicago lecture (also first published in America) which was later the first and only such item that he chose to acknowledge.

I

The *Sunday School Times*, a weekly magazine aimed at Sunday School teachers and students of Divinity, and mainly devoted to practical and homiletic matters for their benefit, seems to have made it one of its main aims to demonstrate to its public (which, at the time, was immensely powerful in moulding the opinions of children and of congregations) how modern scientific advances helped to confirm the words of Scripture and how they could be worked into instruction. Distinguished outsiders were invited to contribute: Hilprecht, on whom we shall have more to say, mentions men like Delitzsch and Driver, Max Müller, Sayce and Rawlinson, and in Philadelphia Peters and himself. He is only concerned with scholars. More widely known, perhaps, than any of these was Mr. W.E. Gladstone, who produced learned, but intelligibly written, articles on a variety of biblical topics and was singled out for editorial praise, in view of his eminence and impeccable orthodoxy. It is against this background that we must ask how the editors came to want an article on Egyptian religion from Eduard Meyer.

The answer fortunately came to light in the letters from H.V. Hilprecht, the distinguished German-American Orientalist,[6] to Eduard Meyer

---

[5] See Marohl item 137. It should be added that, technically, *The Historians' History* (see below) might count as a British publication, since it was published in London as well as in New York. But the impulse and all the work came from America.

[6] On Hilprecht, see the *National Cyclopaedia of American Biography* X, p. 380, showing

which are preserved in the Eduard Meyer archive in Berlin.[7] As several
of the letters show, the two had known each other well at Leipzig: on May
19, 1893, Hilprecht offers to put his unpublished results at Meyer's dis-
posal "wie in alten Tagen zu Leipzig;" and even though they had later
lost contact, owing to a lung disease (tuberculosis?) which took Hilprecht
to Davos for two years with little hope for recovery, Meyer had sent him
a copy of the first volume of *Geschichte des Altertums*. Hilprecht's first letter
to Meyer (written from Philadelphia, on *Sunday School Times* letterhead
paper, on September 30, 1886) thanks him for it and sketches the events
of his life since they parted. After his recovery, unable to get a proper position in Germany, he accepted an offer of a chair at the University of
Pennsylvania, where he was to build up the Department of Oriental
Studies. At the same time (so he writes), he also accepted the editorship
of the Semitic Department of the *Sunday School Times*, and he praises the
academic excellence of that magazine.[8] He now invites Meyer to contribute an article of 1500 – 2000 words, and (what is more) he specifies precisely what is wanted: the title is to be "Egyptian learning and Egyptian
religion at their best" (!), and it is to be a demonstration ("ein Nachweis") of the excellence of the culture and the religion of the ancient
Egyptians, to make it possible to argue that this influenced the Israelites.
He would like the article by February 1887, and he promises a honorarium of 100 marks (an impressive amount) for it.

A second letter, of March 25, 1887, shows that the article has been
received and expresses effusive thanks to Meyer for overcoming his dislike

---

that he was still associated with the magazine as an editor in 1909 (the date of publication
of that volume); also *NDB* IX (1972) 160 and other biographical repertoria. There is a long
obituary in the Proceedings of the Society for Biblical Literature and Exegesis for December 1925, in *Journal of Biblical Literature* 45 (1926) pp. iii – iv, where not a word is said about
the controversy that ended his career (see below). The biographies differ on whether it was
the University of Pennsylvania or the *Sunday School Times* that brought him to America.
His letter to Meyer, cited below, should settle that question.

[7] American archives, which may contain further information relevant to this, have not
been as helpful as the Academy Archive in Berlin (see above). There is information on
Hilprecht at the University of Pennsylvania, which I have not succeeded in obtaining.
There is also likely to be information on the editors of the *Sunday School Times* in the archive
of the American Sunday-School Union, which published the magazine. A portion of the
archive (not relevant to this) is available on microfilm, but the Librarian of the Presby-
terian Church Office of History in Philadelphia, where the archive is kept, refused to give
me information on what else may be there. The University of Jena reports that it has
nothing relevant.

[8] See text above, for some of the contributors he lists. In his second letter, he gives the
number of subscribers as 108,000, the number of readers as half a million, and the number
of persons influenced by the magazine as 15 million ("statistisch festgestellt"). The figures
must be taken seriously and throw light on the background of American life and thought
at the time.

for publishing in religious magazines: more is said on the excellence, wide audience, and influence of the *Sunday School Times*, and Meyer is promised that the article will be printed in a few weeks ("in nächsten Wochen") and that he will receive 3 copies of the issue.

At this point something clearly went wrong. The article appeared in volume 32, no. 38, on September 20, 1890 (pp. 595 – 596), i.e. two and a half years later. And it was not the one that Meyer had been explicitly directed to write. It starts by commenting on the difficulty felt by the layman in understanding Egyptian religion: "once led within the circle of the Egyptian gods, (he) receives from these strange figures only the impression of a general confusion." The author proposes to explain the mysteries by applying "the historic method, carefully separating one period from another" in order to gain a picture of the actual development.

The trouble with this, of course, was that there was no evidence at all on primitive Egyptian religion. Meyer starts by sketching, *a priori*, a development that leads from animistic and totemistic religion ("a conception which . . . prevailed . . ., in general, in each primitive religion") to a period when, with developing civilization, "an inclination towards speculation was awakened, and a theology was evolved within the priesthood;" this he then traces from the first actual evidence, that of the Pyramids. Down to the age of the Pyramids, the argument proceeds entirely by analogy; and it cannot even be argued: the general nature of "primitive religion" is presumed to be known. By then, a large array of evidence on the religion of contemporary primitive peoples had been collected. J.G. Frazer's first little study, *Totemism*, had appeared in 1887, based (with similar work by others) on the famous articles by M'Lennan in the *Fortnightly Review* of 1869 and 1870. The analogy from these known facts to unknown antiquity was unquestioned in scientific circles.

Needless to say, it was not lightly accepted by the *Sunday School Times*. There is no longer any question of the Israelites: far more fundamental principles appear to be at stake. The article is dogged by several editorial footnotes, devoted to demolishing the foundations of the eminent contributor's case. On the argument from analogy, the editor is silent, only observing (with literal truth):

> This suggestion of "totem worship" as the earliest form of religion among primitive peoples, is a favorite assumption of theorists in the realm of science, but it rests only on a theory that has as yet found no supporting proof *in the earliest monuments of the human race* [my emphasis].

A second note is more insistent:

> There is nothing known of Egypt, either by its records or in its traditions, that goes to show a history that antedates a high state of civilization.

Meyer's own book, *Geschichte des Alten Ägyptens* (Marohl item 51: published in Oncken's series of general history in 1887), on which the essay is based, is adduced in evidence for the strange suggestion that Egyptian civilization was apparently created out of nothing:

> This very writer himself says on this point: "Whoever undertakes to study the ancient history of China or of Egypt expecting to receive information about the gradual improvement of civilization, or to become acquainted with monuments that throw light upon its development, will be gravely disappointed. It is a complete, yea even a superior, standard of development of government, of art, and of religion, that we meet with in the ancient monuments of Eygpt ... It is therefore only speculation, that speculations about religion had their spontaneous origin in the days of a ruder civilization in Egypt.

On Meyer's sketch of theological development after the time of the Pyramids, there is the following comment:

> Earliest among the monuments of Egypt stand the pyramids; and those monuments furnish proof that the religion of Egypt was at that date purer and simpler than in the centuries that followed. See the article of Dr. Osgood, following.

Finally, on a statement by Meyer on magic as creating the concept of the unity of human and divine essence:

> ... there is no record of any practice or theory of magic at any time when the conception of the Divine Spirit was not already developed.

The annotated article was indeed followed by one by Professor Howard Osgood, D.D., of the Rochester Theological Seminary, one of the magazine's house theologians. Entitled "The Newer History of the Older World," it essentially makes these points:

that the earliest monuments of both Babylon and Egypt show language and religion already fully formed;

that their earliest art is the best;

and that it is at the earliest time that we find widespread trade and exchange.

It follows that "Historical criticism ... is a contradiction of the history by monuments." An editorial note completes the lesson, pointing out that this applies to what calls itself "historical criticism" (obviously Meyer's "historic method"), but not to "true historical criticism ... as a means of Bible knowledge"—as demonstrated by Dr. Osgood.

This is not the place to debate the merits of the case. Modern anthropologists would not accept the naive argument from analogy; though they would unanimously reject what appears to be the argument for cultural and religious creationism. There had clearly been a great deal of discussion when Meyer's article was seen by the editorial board: not only had Meyer ignored the "instructions" he had received, but he had submitted what was clearly an unacceptable view of the origin of civilization and of the knowledge of God. The delay in publication had not been foreseen by Hilprecht in March 1887: presumably he himself had not perceived the reaction that his colleagues would show to the article. (Hilprecht, as a trained Orientalist and old friend of Meyer's, must have been familiar with Meyer's book, and although perhaps miffed at having his instructions ignored, cannot have been surprised by Meyer's basic interpretation.) We must conjecture that there had been resistance to publishing it at all; and in the end it had been agreed to publish it with notes and an invited comment by Osgood: Meyer was to be turned into a striking moral lesson, an opportunity to refute "pseudo-science" for the greater glory of God.

In view of Hilprecht's initial comments on the article, it is inconceivable that this treatment of Meyer, and the editorial comments, are due to him. I have not been able to find out who were his colleagues on the Editorial Board, and in particular, who was the Editor of the magazine at that time. But it looks as though Hilprecht was overruled and, in a way, lost face over the affair. He nonetheless continued to be associated with the magazine, but he did not explain to Meyer what had happened—at least, not as far as our record shows. There is now a long break in the correspondence. When it resumed (letter of May 19, 1893, on University of Pennsylvania stationery), more than two and a half years had passed since the publication of the article, more than six years since it was received and acknowledged. The letter apologizes for long silence ("Lang, lang ist es her") and now makes a new start, again sketching his life from his lung trouble to his appointment at Philadelphia, and continuing to describe his work as Assyriologist to the Nippur expedition and an attack of typhus, which again brought him close to death. He also announces his first results and publication of the first volume, and he asks Meyer to insert a notice of it in a professional journal. He promises to visit Meyer on his forthcoming visit to Germany, and in summer of 1893 the two men met, for the first time since Leipzig. It would be interesting to know what they talked about, and whether it included the article in the *Sunday School Times*: there is no reference to it in Hilprecht's letter. Meyer presumably received the promised three copies; but he clearly did not keep them, since Marohl did not see the actual article among his papers. Nor (it seems) did he bother to reply. His reluctance to deal with religious publications had clearly been justified.

As for his relations with Hilprecht, contact fitfully continues, with occasional visits. The last communication in the file is a postcard of April 2,

1907, which promises to return later on to a topic of major interest to both of them. We can only wonder whether this was the notorious controversy that started with an attack on Hilprecht's integrity by his ex-fellow student (at Leipzig) and ex-colleague (at Philadelphia: Peters had been in charge of the expedition for which Hilprecht acted as Assyriologist) John P. Peters in 1905, went on over several years in professional journals and general magazines, did not end with an investigation in 1908 by the University, in which Hilprecht was cleared, and finally led to his resignation of his post in 1911. During this controversy, Hilprecht was opposed by nearly all his professional colleagues in the United States and supported by most of his colleagues in Europe. In 1908–9, a *Festschrift* with over thirty contributions was presented to him, only one (by his pupil Hugo Radau) American. Meyer's name is rather conspicuously absent. He had apparently lost contact with Hilprecht, for in May 1908, he asks Charles Lanman, with whom he had established contact some time before, for the latest news of the affair, and Lanman replied in a letter of June 3. Meyer was clearly interested, but did not want to get involved. His opinion on the merits of the case is not on record.[9] We cannot tell to what extent the memory of his first experience of publishing in America played a part in his view of Hilprecht and the controversy.

II

We must next look at the Alexander article. It was miserably translated by a Professor C.B. Stetson, who had received A.B. and A.M. degrees from Colby College in Maine, had then (we are told in an obituary) "studied" at Harvard (where he does not appear on any alumni list I have

---

[9] Charles R. Lanman, the eminent Harvard Indologist, like most American Orientalists at this time, had studied at Leipzig and could still lecture in German many years later. He does not seem to have met Meyer at Leipzig. In 1905, Meyer sent him a copy of "Die Mosesagen und die Lewiten" (Marohl item 171), and the formality of the reply suggests this was the first contact. (Letter kindly communicated to me by Dr. Hoffmann, who is not responsible for the interpretation.) Lanman's letter of June 1908 informs Meyer of the letter by various eminent American Orientalists acknowledging Hilprecht's acquittal and self-justification (*The So-Called Peters-Hilprecht Controversy*): the letter, kindly communicated to me by Dr. Pack from the Handschriften-Abteilung of the University Library at Hamburg, is rather ambivalent as to the merits of the case, but hopes it will fade away. In fact, it did not, and in the end led to a confrontation between European supporters and American opponents that developed national overtones. We can only speculate whether Meyer's enquiry, precisely at that point, was possibly connected with a request (which he must surely have received) to contribute to the Hilprecht *Festschrift* (see text). Dr. Pack informs me that he is at present working on the controversy, which greatly needs a new assessment.

seen), and after teaching at Colby College was appointed to the University of Vermont as Professor of German in 1902—a post which he held until his death in 1912. I have given details of the translation, which show Stetson's knowledge of German below what one might expect of a respectably taught undergraduate, in Appendix I, which also contains an analysis of the relationship of the article to the essay in *Kleine Schriften*.

What is more interesting is the nature of the magazine for which it was written, and (again) the question of how Meyer may have come to be invited to contribute to it. The magazine was the personal creation of an extraordinary young man, Frederick A. Richardson, of Burlington, Vermont. After getting a degree at his local university, he went on to take a further A.B. at Harvard, under Josiah Royce, long one of America's leading philosophers. On receiving the degree in 1897, he seems to have gone back to Burlington, which at the time was the home of a number of quite varied publications, apparently planning to make Burlington into a centre of international culture. He devoted himself to organizing local music and inviting famous singers (including artists at the Metropolitan Opera) and lecturers; while he himself, at the time only in his twenties, in the space of two years set up an elaborate and ambitious framework for a new magazine that should contain the latest available information in all important fields of intellectual and artistic activity. He found the co-operation of a major New York publisher, but himself retained the editorship and the copyright; and he made sure that every issue was marked as having been published at 148 College Street, Burlington.

The magazine was called *International Monthly*. Right from the start, it gave a list of very eminent specialists in the various fields covered as editorial advisers and provided a varied and interesting list of contents. Richardson himself, of local industrial-commercial background (his father's considerable fortune was in part based on patent medicines), must have provided much of the money that kept it going. But as things became more and more difficult, the increasing strain can be followed through the publication history. The first monthly issue appeared in January 1900, and for over two years there was one issue per month. But in 1902, without any announcement, the title was changed to *International Quarterly*; and even that was optimistic. Right from the start, the new magazine appeared twice a year, nominally in double issues. But the panel of eminent outside editors was retained (see the photocopy attached), as was the note informing readers that their post was no sinecure. How a man of not more than twenty-six, with a Harvard A.B. as his highest degree, was able to organize such a network of academic support is a puzzle that cannot at present be solved (and will not be unless family papers survive): how did those gentlemen take him seriously? At any rate, there is nothing shodddy about the *International Quarterly*.[10] The contributors are men of both quality and qualifications. Meyer's essay stands between one by William Morton Payne on "The American Scholar in the 20th Century" and one by a psychologist at Geneva on "The Consciousness of Animals." Obviously, execution could not always be guaranteed. Editors learn to live with that. Stetson, as it turned out, was an absurd choice. But Richardson presumably wanted to use local Burlington talent, and since the man was Professor of German at the University, he must have seemed formally qualified. Richardson himself would have neither the time nor the knowledge to check the product.

The real question is: how did Meyer get this assignment? Here we are not as well off as in the case of the *Sunday School Times*, but we have an obvious indication. Since we must no doubt believe Richardson's statement regarding the real responsibilities of his Editorial Board, we must take it that one of the major responsibilities, in "the work assigned to" each of them, would be to mediate in finding suitably eminent persons to write for the magazine. Hence the invitation must have come from one of the History editors. Seignobos, in Paris, surely need not be considered: there is no evidence, or probability, of his having any contacts with Meyer, or being interested in reading any of his work. At first sight, Robinson and Lamprecht do not seem suitable either. It is clear that Richardson, who had no doubt read some recent historical work at Harvard, had decided ideas about the kind of history he wanted. All three of his editorial advisers may be said to represent what in Robinson's famous phrase one might call the "New History"—a kind of historical writing that went well beyond concentration on political, military and diplomatic history. The battle had been fought in Germany in the recent past, and the issue was very much alive. In his lecture on the Emperor's birthday in 1897, Wilamowitz seized the occasion to point out that the dispute did not really concern ancient history: its practitioners had always taken "das ganze Leben des Volkes" as their subject.[11] Presumably James Harvey Robinson had picked up the "new" ideas when studying at Freiburg (PhD 1880), and he certainly kept up his contacts when he moved (ultimately) to Columbia, where he became a Professor in 1895. Richardson and his talent

---

[10] There is unfortunately no doubt about its fast decline, clearly for financial reasons. Volume VIII no. 2 (1903) shows that Richardson had found a New York publisher to collaborate with him: he remains editor and the Burlington address continues. By vol. IX no. 2 another New York firm has completely taken over and claims the copyright. In vol. X, although Richardson remains as Editor, there is no more mention of Burlington. Publication ceased with the end of vol. XII (December 1905).
[11] *Reden und Aufsätze*[4] (1926) 13: delivered a few months after Lamprecht's salvo against Ranke and his school in *Alte und neue Richtungen* (see p. below).

scouts had had the right instincts: Robinson was to go on to reform the teaching and writing of history in America.[12]

We know of no contact between Robinson and Meyer, and none can easily be presumed. At most, as an educated historian, Robinson would have read parts of the *Geschichte des Altertums* when it began to appear in 1884 (Marohl item 24). But no correspondence between the men is on record. On the other hand, it was probably Robinson who led Richardson to Lamprecht. Their contact, and Robinson's admiration for the German scholar, is attested by the fact that, when Lamprecht visited the United States as one of the German scholars invited to the International Exposition at St. Louis, he received an honorary degree at Columbia and, on that occasion, delivered (in German) his programmatic lectures *Moderne Geschichtswissenschaft*.[13]

We arrive, by the Holmesian process of exclusion of the impossible, at Lamprecht as the only scholar who can have been responsible for the invitation to Meyer. At first sight, their well-known opposition regarding the theory of historiography (on which more below) makes the suggestion seem improbable. But that opposition, especially at this early period, should not be overstressed. We can see that personal relations were good, and in spite of theoretical differences, the two men had much in common.

Karl Lamprecht[14] had been trained by Herbst to be an admirer of Thucydides, and in his early career was looked after by his old teacher. In this, he would obviously agree with Meyer whose admiration for, and fascination with, Thucydides hardly needs documentation.[15] The two men may well have met in Leipzig, even though they did not quite overlap. Meyer was doing his military service in 1877/88, when Lamprecht was a member of the historical seminar there. But we know that Meyer was in close touch with his university, for it was precisely at this time that his mentor Ebers wrote to him, strongly urging him to return and

---

[12] On Robinson, see (best in short compass) the entry in *NCAB* (cited n. 6 above) C (1930) 28–29, written a few years before his death; also (short but after his death) *Webster's American Biographies* (1974) 882. He is prominently discussed in all English-language histories of historiography.

[13] Translated into English as *What is History?* (London/New York 1905). It is worth mentioning that Columbia owed a great part of its reputation to a German historian and disciple of Niebuhr who became a Professor there: Francis Lieber.

[14] On Lamprecht see (best) the careful discussion in *NDB* XIII (1983) 467–472, doing full justice to his stature within the profession in his day and describing his search for historical laws as "zeitgebunden". (My references to his life are based on this article).

[15] It clearly goes back to his schooldays, but I have first found it explicitly stated in *Forschungen zur Alten Geschichte* II (1899: Marohl item 79). It culminates in the well-known eulogy of Thucydides in his *Antrittsrede* of 1919 (*Kl. Schr.* II 549 ff.), which made Momigliano say that Meyer wanted to be the Thucydides of Germany's defeat.

practically promising him, in due course, a *Dozentur*.[16] They also regularly met at the newly instituted Versammlungen deutscher Historiker. Lamprecht was a member from the start, at the first congress in Munich in 1893. Meyer first appears at the second congress (Leipzig 1894), and henceforth is regularly listed as a Theilnehmer, as is Lamprecht. Both are among the founding members of the Verband deutscher Historiker, which was founded at the third congress (Frankfurt 1895). Since the number of participants, in those days, was small (between about 140 and 170), it can safely be presumed that they all knew one another. But there is more to be said. At the Frankfurt congress Meyer delivered the main address, in fact his lecture "Die wirtschaftliche Entwicklung des Altertums" which was to make professional history. It is at that same congress that we find Lamprecht as Outgoing President (i.e., President during the previous year), delivering the opening address.[17] It is surely evident that the choice of Meyer as speaker for that congress must have been largely Lamprecht's doing.

It was in this address, incidentally, that the man who was making a name for himself as searching for historical laws explicitly stated that history was not an exact but a descriptive science. Even in his first major methodological disquisition, *Alte und neue Richtungen in der Geschichte* (1896), although his principal theses would not meet with Meyer's approval, he said much that must have been acceptable to Meyer. Meyer, at this time, was deeply interested in social and economic history. He was practically the only ancient historian who contributed to the *Handwörterbuch der Staatswissenschaft*; his contribution to the major *Jubiläumsschrift* of his University of Halle was his "Untersuchungen zur Geschichte der Gracchen" (Marohl item 82: 1894); finally, his Frankfurt lecture was complemented by "Die Sklaverei im Altertum" (Marohl item 127: 1898), completing his exposition of his main ideas on the ancient economy, on which he never again did any comparable work.[18]

---

[16] Letter of February 3, 1878, in K. 5 of the Eduard-Meyer-Nachlaß in the Staatsbibliothek (Preuß. Kulturbesitz) in West Berlin. My thanks are due to the Library, where I was allowed to go over the archive.

[17] Details of these congresses and lists of members and participants can readily be consulted in the published proceedings (*Berichte*) of the meetings.

[18] For the *Handwörterbuch* see Marohl item 77 (1891), continuing through the second edition (items 119–121, 136–139, 140, 143: two articles—202–203—were later revised for the third edition). In the second edition, there are in fact only two articles on ancient subjects not by Meyer: one by Max Weber, on "Agrarverhältnisse im Altertum", and one by Beloch on (unexpectedly) "Zinsfuß im Altertum." (One suspects he had to take the place of someone who had dropped out.) Lamprecht, incidentally, contributed five articles, all on agrarian matters. Meyer was clearly regarded as the only ancient historian regularly working on such topics. Some of the ideas expressed at this period were, of course, developed in detail later, e.g. for Attica in *Forschungen* (Marohl item 79) II, and

We happen to have two letters, closely related, from this period, shedding light on the nature of their relationship. In a letter of January 27, 1897 (the year is corrected from 1896, which guarantees that it is right), Meyer thanks Lamprecht for sending him his recent as well as earlier offprints (presumably they had not been exchanging before, or at least not for some time), expresses firm, but polite, disagreement with his basic theses regarding "psychologische Entwicklungsstufen" and indicates his own view that "die wissenschaftliche Periodisierung der Geschichte" must be based on major political events, adding that, for the present and future as well, he sees the major political problems facing Europe as more important than even the most ardently debated social problems. (He signs "mit bestem Gruß und Dank.")[19] A letter in the Eduard-Meyer-Nachlaß in the Archiv of the Akademie der Wissenschaften der DDR shows Lamprecht replying either to this letter or to another in the same series, trying to minimise the differences that Meyer has pointed out.[20] Perhaps equally important for our present purpose: at the end of 1895 Lamprecht writes to Meyer, inviting him to contribute to a new journal which he is editing. This, as we saw, was precisely the time when Meyer, no doubt at Lamprecht's nomination, had delivered the main address at the congress of German historians at Frankfurt.

Whether Meyer's rather intemperate attack on Lamprecht in his lecture on historiography in 1902 (Marohl item 145, expanded and reprinted in *Kleine Schriften* 1 ff.) made a difference to their personal relations, I do not know. But in any case, that was much later. Although we cannot tell precisely when Meyer was asked to write his contribution for Richardson's magazine, we have a secure *terminus ante quem*: in the actual issue, published late in 1903, he is listed as "Professor Publicus Ordinarius at the University of Halle, Wittenburg" (*sic*: one wonders whether Stetson composed the title). He had obviously not only written the essay before he moved to Berlin, in the autumn of 1902, but he had not even informed the Editor of the move—which suggests that the essay was written quite a while before and then dismissed from his mind. In view of the change in publication schedule, precisely in 1902, from a monthly to a (*de facto*) semi-annual magazine, the editor must have had some stock on his hands which gradually had to be worked into the new format. I would suggest that Meyer was asked to write it several years earlier (perhaps even before

others had to be defended later on. But he published no major new thoughts in this field after this short period of intense activity and production.

[19] The letter is in the Lamprecht-Nachlaß in the Handschriftenabteilung of the University of Bonn (Sign. S. 2713, Korr. 37). I thank the University for permission to use it and my friend, Professor Gerhard Wirth, for mediating.

[20] I thank the Director of the Archiv for permission to refer to this letter.

the first issue of the journal as a monthly, in January 1900). It must, in
any case, precede his public attack on Lamprecht.[21] In view of his eminence, and his acquaintance with Lamprecht, Meyer may have been
among the first to be asked when the magazine was planned.

We might next consider why, when he had not published a major work
on Alexander (and in fact he was never to do so), he was asked to write
on Alexander in particular; if indeed he was. Strictly speaking, we cannot
tell whether the subject was suggested to him, or whether he chose it himself, after a general invitation to contribute. Either explanation seems to
make sense, although I think a specific invitation more probable.

He had, in fact, quite recently written a short note on an Alexander
topic: entitled ''Arrians Geschichte Alexanders des Grossen'' (*Hermes* 33
(1898) 648–652: Marohl item 132), it attacks Schwartz's recent treatment of Arrian in *RE* (II, 1895, 1243 ff.) on a particular point. Although
of some interest to students of Meyer, the note shows no sign of being a
precursor of a major study: it merely supplies a *terminus ante quem non* for
the conception of the essay. Schwartz, in a study that is still important,
had synthesized a great deal of work on various aspects of Arrian; i.a.,
he had tried to reexamine the chronology of his works. Against Nissen,
who thought the *Anabasis* the crowning achievement of Arrian's life,[22]
Schwartz saw it essentially as one in a series of ''Übungen'', by which
Arrian was training himself for a worthy account of his native country,
to be produced at a later stage. Dividing Arrian's life into distinct periods
of activity, he put the composition of the *Anabasis* soon after 130, after his
putative retirement from public service to live in Athens. Meyer, essentially, returned to Nissen's view.[23] But against Schwartz's cautious statement that Arrian—a retired soldier and civil servant, who had done an
honest job of writing as best he could—left Alexander history for us in
a state where ''wenigstens die Umrisse klar hervortreten'' (col. 1247)
Meyer set his own encomium: ''Arrian verdanken wir es, dass wir über
wenige Epochen der Geschichte bis zum Ausgang des Mittelalters so gut

---

[21] The article must also, obviously, precede the contributions to *The Historians' History*
(see below), which according to Meyer were written in 1902. The later date implied in *Kl.
Schr.* must be deliberately misleading.

[22] *RhM* NF 43 (1888) 236–251.

[23] The debate continues inconclusively, like all such essentially subjective debates;
new dates are from time to time suggested, or old ones endorsed, but there is no decisive
evidence and none has been found since Nissen wrote. For a selective bibliography of the
debate, and argument for a very early date, see F. Reuss, *RhM* NF 54 (1899) 45 ff., not
yet aware of Meyer's note; recently revived by A.B. Bosworth, *A Historical Commentary on
Arrian's History of Alexander* I (1980) 8 f. For a late date, based on a psychological interpretation of Arrian's development, see G. Wirth, *Studii Clasice* 16 (1974) 199 ff. (support for
Meyer p. 200 n. 128).

unterrichtet sind, wie über die Geschichte Alexanders des Grossen'' (652). Arrian towers high above the rest of the Alexander tradition: unlike even some modern scholars, he showed true historical judgment (surpassed, in antiquity, only by that of Thucydides) in rejecting, often without even a mention, the stories made up by most of the writers on Alexander. Ptolemy, as saved for us by Arrian, is the sole firm foundation for Alexander history.

What had moved Meyer to write this (as it nowadays seems) rather naive note? In a list of about 75 previous items in Marohl (if we ignore duplicates and encyclopaedia contributions) there is not a single item relevant to Alexander. Perhaps more interesting still: when the note appeared, why did it follow Schwartz's treatment after an interval of three years? We may surely posit that the 1890s did not know long delays in publication. Perhaps the delay is only further proof of Meyer's essential lack of interest in Alexander, which allowed him to wait some years either before reading the article by an acknowledged master or in reacting to it. But we should consider a possible motive.

It was precisely in 1897 that Julius Beloch, Meyer's close friend, published the second volume of his *Griechische Geschichte*, containing the first part of his treatment of Alexander. That was one volume which Meyer would certainly at once receive, and read. At the end of it, however, there is in fact a short survey of the Alexander sources (658 f.). Beloch propounds a balanced judgment: Arrian is often negligent; Diodorus can be used to supplement him on military matters, and Curtius, in particular, is a "sehr willkommene Ergänzung" to Arrian in this respect; and he regards as "ganz besonders wertvoll" Curtius' transmission of the view of a supposed Macedonian "Oppositionspartei". He concludes that the excessive cult of Arrian ("jener unbedingte Arriankultus") that has been fashionable until recently is in need of judicious limitation. In outline (though not in detail), the judgment is one that would be widely shared today.[24] But it clearly could not be further from Meyer's own views; and, coming in such an authoritative work, it might seem to call for a reply. An attack on his friend's views was unthinkable as such: it is often obvious that these two firm friends, neither of them one to avoid polemics (or to suffer them without rancour), maintained their friendship by simply ignoring each other's professional views where they were incompatible. I would say, in an untranslatable German idiom: "Sie schrieben an einander vorbei."

---

[24] See, e.g., Bosworth in *Entretiens sur l'Antiquité classique* 22 (Genève 1976) 1–33, i.a. showing the connection between unquestioning acceptance of Arrian and unquestioning Alexandrolatry. Beloch objected to both of these.

The suggestion that Schwartz had to stand in for Beloch can be rein-
forced. Schwartz had essentially accepted Arrian as far the best source,
and there was little need to refute him (technically) on a minor matter of
biography. But Meyer in fact went further and used this occasion for a
vicious attack on Schwartz and his methods. He accuses Schwartz of
thinking entirely in terms of stylistic training and ignoring the need for
historical training, in order to achieve the "Schärfung und Sicherheit des
Urteils" shown in the *Anabasis* (650):

> Man möchte wünschen, dass Schwartz' . . . Äusserung nur einer momenta-
> nen Flüchtigkeit entsprungen wäre; aber ich fürchte, sie ist nur zu bezeich-
> nend für die weitverbreitete Neigung unserer Zeit, romanhafte Constructio-
> nen an die Stelle geschichtlicher Thatsachen zu setzen.

Schwartz, in fact, is typical of the "philologists" who do not understand
the profession of the historian, ancient or modern.

In a sense, this points to Meyer's later attempt (for which see Professor
Calder's analysis) to formulate a basic difference between philologists and
historians. That attempt, however, was to proceed along totally different
lines. The naive charge that philologists, through ignorance of historical
method, substitute romance for fact and cannot understand an ancient
writer's need for historical training seems dragged in here, and does not
correspond to or foreshadow anything in the essay on historical method.

It becomes intelligible, however, on the (perhaps) "romanhafte Construction" that Meyer's aim was to set the record straight against Beloch,
whose recently expressed view was much further from his own than
Schwartz's. The essentially slight correction in Schwartz's conception became a vehicle for reasserting the absolute primacy of Arrian and the un-
blemished excellence of what he gives us, which Beloch had shrugged off
as an outmoded misconception. To avoid giving offence to his friend, the
reassertion of the old "truth" was garbed in a needless attack on a target
that would not only deflect attention from the real aim, but would actually
delight Beloch. His contempt for "philologists" far surpassed Meyer's
(normally) polite and scholarly disagreement.

The note is of no importance whatsoever in Alexander scholarship. But
in an age where reading was much less specialised than today, it must have
helped to draw attention to Meyer as to one who had thought about
Alexander and who might be induced to write about him. We may regard
it as certain that Lamprecht received an offprint. We see in Marohl
(no. 132 note) that offprints were in fact produced, and we have seen that,
by the beginning of 1897, Meyer and Lamprecht may be presumed to
have been exchanging publications. Once the thought occurred, Meyer
might appear to be singularly qualified for the task. What had always been

needed (and still is) for a proper interpretation of Alexander history was a combination of philological training in the use of sources with a good knowledge of the history and institutions of the various Near Eastern civilizations. That combination, even then rare, is by now almost unattainable. But Meyer was the one man fully qualified. Trained in the Classics at school and chiefly as an Orientalist at Leipzig, he had intensively studied the Near Eastern languages and cultures; and he had shown his mastery of that (even then) complex field in his *Geschichte des Altertums*, as well as in continuing specialist studies, while at the same time making the Classical field his main preoccupation. Where else was there such an opportunity to practise that *Universalgeschichte* that he had long regarded as his aim, and who else was there who could practise it? Meyer was at this time writing what is still much the best account of the Achaemenid kingdom (unfortunately never translated into English);[25] it must have been widely known that he was engaged on this task. In fact, it was no doubt assumed that he would before long reach the history of Alexander. No one could have foreseen that he would put the end of Greek history at the defeat of Athens in the Social War,[26] and for the rest of his life refuse to continue.

The Alexander essay, as it appeared in its American guise, was reduced to nonsense. An incompetent translator, too lazy to look up what he did not know, made it difficult (at times) to disengage even the main lines of the argument. (See Appendix I.) Any competent reader (and the magazine must have had many) must have wondered what to think of Meyer. Meyer himself, had he seen it, would have been shocked and dismayed, for his own English was good. But there is reason to think that he did not see it.[27] His failure to inform the editor of his move to Berlin shows that he was simply not concerned about what went on in America. Had he received a copy, one would have expected a letter of protest, and later comments.

Comparison between what can be reconstructed of the earliest version through the obfuscation of C.B. Stetson and the later essay in *Kleine Schriften* is not as fruitful as it might be. We cannot be certain whether

---

[25] Volume III of *GdA* appeared in 1901. (For the complicated bibliography of the work see Marohl item 24.) In Stier's rather heavy-handed reorganization, that section is in IV² 1.

[26] Vol. V Book 4, "Der Ausgang der griechischen Geschichte" (1902). Meyer ended at the point where the Greek city states proved unable to fulfil their *Kulturaufgabe*, so that monarchy hat to take over and do it for them (see below).

[27] I at one time thought that this might be his reason for refusing to acknowledge the work. But I soon found that this is refuted by the fact that he acted in the same way in the case of his contributions to *The Historians' History* (see below), where the translation is adequate.

some of the additional material found later was merely omitted owing to
a limitation on space or because it had not yet occurred to the author. And
we cannot be certain what was added in the German lecture of 1905 and
what only in the final printed version, since the lecture was not printed
as such. But I think we may take it that the main work of revision was
indeed undertaken for the lecture, and we may perhaps guess why it was
never printed at the time.

   We may start by asking why Meyer, asked to address a major
Philologenverein, in 1905, dug up an old manuscript in which he had (as
we saw) lost interest and reused it. After all, ''Der Gang der Alten
Geschichte,'' written in 1902, was never thus used at all. The only reason
I can see is one that I mentioned at the outset, and that can now be supported by reference to the note on Arrian. Just as Beloch's excursus on
the sources had (I suggest) stimulated Meyer to a resounding reaffirma-
tion of the primacy of Arrian, so his friend's interpretation of Alexander,
in the volume of 1904 dedicated to Meyer, must have sent Meyer back
to his forgotten manuscript as a vehicle for revision and expansion. It is
suggestive that, precisely as the *Hermes* article followed Beloch's second
volume after one year, so the Hamburg lecture followed Beloch's third
volume after the same interval. We may take it that, when we find points
that needed restating, against an authoritative view that Meyer found
quite unacceptable, in the printed version of 1910, they were inserted into
the lecture in 1905, and I shall henceforth treat them as such. Had the lecture been as anodyne as the American essay, there is no reason why the
author should not have printed it for private circulation. But appearance
of polemic against his friend had to be carefully avoided. By 1910, it would
no longer look like a direct attack.

   That Beloch was in Meyer's mind in 1905 can be seen from comparison
of the two versions. (See Appendix I.) Apart from the long story of Alexander's fatal quarrels with his officers and with Callisthenes, for which I
see no good reason (except perhaps to give more background to the unin-
formed), there are two and only two major expansions.

   The first is the history of the Macedonian kingdom, centred on foreign policy and leading up to the first enunciation of what was to remain
Meyer's characterization of the difference between Philip's policy and
Alexander's: while Philip's was anchored in Europe, and even the attack
on Asia served only to secure his control over the Aegean, Alexander from
the start planned the total conquest of the Persian kingdom, if not more.
This, with the corresponding difference between Augustus and Caesar,[28]

----

[28] This difference I have not found suggested before ''Kaiser Augustus'' (Marohl item
151) of 1903. It at once reappears as the striking climax to his Chicago lecture (Marohl

was to become the King Charles's Head of Meyer's construction of historical turning-points in terms of accident and individual will. For him, Philip planned to wage war in Asia Minor as Agesilaus had done in the 390s. It was only Alexander, "von einer ganz anderer Gedankenwelt erfüllt als sein Vater," who changed this.

Beloch's treatment of Philip, of course, was in the 1897 volume. At that time, however, Meyer had not yet thought seriously about Alexander. For Beloch, there was no doubt that Philip intended to conquer the Persian Empire—a task which was not even very difficult (!). Meyer only seems to have clarified his thinking about this some time after he had written the Alexander essay (which does not go into it), perhaps when reading Beloch's treatment of Alexander in the next volume. The long history of Macedon, inserted into the revision, has the sole purpose of leading up to his argument on this point.

Beloch (incidentally) was not convinved. Of course, he never attacked his friend. But in the extensive reorganization that, at this point, went into the making of III² 1 (1922)—it involved treating the reconquest of the Empire by Artaxerxes Ochus earlier, to allow more coherent treatment of Philip later—he entirely rewrote this section. He had changed his mind on Philip. Now Philip is said (601 f.) to have had wider plans; but what they were would have to emerge in the course of the campaign. In other words, his Philip is (correctly, I would add) seen as a pragmatist, seizing his chance when he found it and going as far as events would let him. Philip certainly never showed any signs of deliberate self-limitation, such as Meyer imposes on him.

Beloch had not forgotten Meyer. Indeed, one of the points of major personal interest in this study is the way in which it illustrates the preservation of the friendship between these two irritable giants by well-covered polemics, designed to avoid public offence. In a footnote stressing that even Jason of Pherae had intended to conquer the Empire, he continues:

> Es gibt freilich Leute, die ganz genau wissen, dass Philip solche Pläne nicht hatte, und daraufhin, *in maiorem Alexandri gloriam*, einen Gegensatz zwischen

---

item 169: slightly corrected version—the corrections demonstrably by Meyer himself—in *Kl. Schr.* 213 ff.). It is then fully developed into the basis of *Caesars Monarchie* (Marohl item 342). We must note that it is conspicuously absent at the end of the Alexander essay, where Meyer's formulation, that Caesar's plan for world unification *had* to be abandoned ("aufgegeben werden mußte") preserves the wording rendered by Stetson *c.* 1900. This, of course, contradicts the later, final, view that Augustus freely *chose* to give up Caesar's plan. We can therefore trace Meyer's first development of the idea to within fairly narrow limits—*c.* 1900–1903. Fortunately, he did not eliminate the discrepancy in his revision of the Alexander essay for *Kl. Schr.* If his statement on Augustus' "Willensentschluß" is part of his original historiographic lecture (I know it only from *Kl. Schr.* 61), we may narrow the limits down to between 1900 and 1902.

dessen Politik und der Politik seines Vaters konstruieren, ohne auch nur
einen Schatten eines Anhalts in unserer Überlieferung.

He had waited more than a decade to say this; but now it had to be said.
It is surprising what a different Beloch we meet here: far from the comba-
tive bully he so often showed himself, he is here a man who, irritated
beyond bearing by his friend's misconceptions, and by groundless distor-
tion of important historical connections (as he saw them), not only never
withdrew his friendship (or the dedication of his book), but was as meticulous in keeping Meyer's name out of the well-aimed attack as Meyer had
been in avoiding offence to him.

Yet this matter of Philip's plans was a relatively minor difference. There
was something more important: Alexander's deification. In Meyer's view
(following Kaerst, who later claimed his priority, barely admitted by
Meyer in a footnote[29]), deification has nothing to do with Oriental ideas:
he rightly points out that nowhere in the East, except in Egypt, was the
king regarded as a god. Meyer derives the deification from Greek sources:
the "individualism" which he saw climactically personified in Alexander,
and the supposed Greek tradition of obscuring the boundaries between
human and divine, for which he claims Aristotle as a witness.[30] And he
here first advances the idea that the god-king, as the embodiment of the
Law, stands above the cities and the citizens and thus has a fully legal basis
for giving them orders: Augustus' refusal of divine honours can then be
said (oddly, in view of the partial nature of that refusal) to show that he
was a "Beamter" and not a king (312). With the recognition of the ruler
as a god "hören seine Willenserklärungen auf Willkür zu sein und werden
rechtliche und rechtschaffende Akte." Alexander, basing himself on the

---

[29] *Kl. Schr.*[1] 330 n. 2; Kaerst, *Gesch. d. Hell.* I (1917) 479 n. 4, and again in his review
of Meyer in *Gnomon* 2 (1926) 34. Meyer's lack of generosity is certainly striking.

[30] *Kl. Schr.*[1] 307. Significantly, no reference is given. He is certainly thinking of the
discussion of monarchy in *Politics* III (1284a f.; 1288a; *et al.*). Unfortunately—the more
so because the argument has often been repeated, with reference to Meyer—he had not
read the context. Aristotle is concerned to show that men of perfect *aretē* cannot be fitted
into a city state, since (*ex hypothesi*) they could not be treated as equals by the other citizens.
The discussion moves on an entirely theoretical level; but such superior *aretē* is carefully
distinguished from mere superiority in wealth or power, which poses no problems. Above
all, *it is never confined to one person.* For the sake of the discussion, there may always be more
than one such, e.g. a whole *genos.* In 1284a and b and 1288a, the plural, perhaps deliberately, alternates with the singular in the discussion of such men: monarchy is simply not
the issue. (Indeed, *pambasileia*, a term dragged into this discussion by Meyer as applying
to the rule of the perfect man, merely means "absolute monarchy" and nowhere appears
as a term of approval.) Nor is there anywhere in Aristotle (as far as I know) any suggestion
that such men—who are in any case theoretical constructs—should be deified: we are
merely told (twice) that they would not fit into a human city any more than a god
would.—It is time this flagrant misuse of Aristotle, introduced into the debate by Meyer's
slipshod reading, were discontinued.

Greek tradition of the rights of superior *aretē*, had found the only way of reconciling city and empire. The *Rechtsstaat* "soll durch die neue Monarchie nicht aufgehoben, sondern gesteigert werden" (311). Above all, he goes on to derive the Christian idea of kingship *Dei gratia* from Alexander's divine kingship—an idea with which I see no quarrel.

For Beloch, needless to say, things looked different. In his view, although Greek tradition did not oppose deification, it was essentially an Oriental idea, which Greeks could accept. It comes from Egypt (48), where, especially on his visit to Ammon, Alexander picked it up; and it is generally Oriental (50 f.). Beloch does not know whether Alexander demanded deification, but he rightly thinks this of little importance; it would, of course, be fatal to Meyer's view to admit the possibility that he did not. For Beloch, Alexander needed it chiefly to gain legitimacy—an idea that, as Beloch reminds us, he had hinted at over a decade earlier, in his book on Athenian politics.[31] However, the result, in Beloch's view, was the beginning of an Orientalization which ultimately destroyed the Greek spirit (51):

> Zum ersten Male hatte der Orient auf die Sieger politisch zurückgewirkt; es war der erste Schritt auf jener Bahn, die das freiheitsstolzeste aller Völker im Laufe der Jahrhunderte zum Byzantinismus geführt hat.

It will now be clear that Meyer could not leave it at that. The appearance of the volume (and its dedication to himself must have made the whole affair positively embarrassing!) was bound to have a powerful effect. It became necessary to take the negelected old manuscript out of its drawer and to build up what had there only been hinted at into a full and (he might hope) decisive statement of his view. The idea that deification of the ruler was essentially evidence of Hellenistic corruption—that, in fact, modern monarchy went back to Oriental infiltration of Greek character and tradition—was intolerable. It had to be at once refuted.

We have now seen that the two major additions (the third long addition, as we noted, is in no way major, or indeed important) to the original Alexander are directly relevant to Beloch's views. Once more, it can be shown that Beloch noticed; but in this case, he clearly did not greatly care. In the second edition (III^2 1 46 ff.), not a word of the original is changed. There

---

[31] *Attische Politik seit Perikles* (1884) 233, where he still believes in the order for deification. Study of the sources, obviously, later led him to see that it is unattested. (It must be suggested, and it is pleasant to think, that reading the despised Niese is likely to have made him change his mind.) His view—that the point essentially does not matter, since it is in any case clear that Alexander liked and wanted deification—has been convincingly reargued by E. Bickerman (*Athenaeum* NS 41 (1963) 70 ff.). We must, however, repeat that for Meyer's thesis the possibility that there was no such order is inadmissible.

is only one addition: in a list of scholars who, in the first edition, had been cited as dealing with the matter of deification (48 n. 1), a reference to Meyer's *Kleine Schriften* is now added (46 n. 2), without any comment whatsoever. The retention of the dedication must have made this even more embarrassing for his old friend.

I do not propose to review Meyer's ideas on Alexander in the context of Alexander research, or even of his own age. Suffice it to say that the two leading ideas which he chose to elaborate and to stress in his revision have turned out to be wrong, indeed (as Beloch hinted in one case) wrongheaded. Beloch is certainly right in stressing that we cannot gauge Philip's intentions, had he lived. *Of course* Alexander's nature was very different from his father's: so was his early education and his early life. But it will simply not do to take the attitude of (say) Parmenio or Philotas to Alexander's continuing ambition, or even to his coming to see himself as a god, as typical of Philip's. The case does even less than that of Caesar and Augustus (which does not concern us here) to justify the far-ranging conclusions as to the factors that shape history which Meyer drew from it. Whether Philip would have settled for Darius' offer of half the empire (had he got far enough to receive it) would have depended on his calculation of whether he could expect to get more; and the chances are that such calculation would have produced the same result that Alexander's heroic impulse reached without it.[32]

The case of deification is, in a sense, even worse. Greek opposition to it is far too well attested to be lightly dismissed, or turned into its opposite. One is tempted to quote Meyer's statement on another scholar, in the context of this argument (330 n. 2 (331)): "Aber die historischen Probleme werden dadurch nicht aus der Welt geschafft, daß man die Augen vor ihnen verschließt." I have dealt with this issue at length and do not want to reopen discussion of it here.[33] But the shoddy use of sources, from the intricate matter of the *proskynesis* affair to the misuse of Aristotle, proclaims the will to force the evidence into the mould of preconceived theory. And the strange notion that the arrogation of divinity would in

---

[32] I must make it clear that I am not arguing against Meyer's stress on the importance of personality and of accident in many historical situations—a view which, in general, I share. I am merely arguing that this illustration, one of Meyer's favourites, should be discarded.

[33] See *Ancient Macedonian Studies in Honor of Charles F. Edson* (Thessaloniki 1981) 27–71. Meyer's reference is to Hogarth's article in *EHR* 3 (1887) 317 ff., denying the order for deification. Meyer's reference helped to condemn the article (unread) to infamy and oblivion, from which it was only rescued by J.P.V.D. Balsdon in a classic discussion of the problem, *Historia* 1 (1950) 364 ff. Unlike Meyer, Hogarth had at least carefully read the sources.

some sense supersede the oaths the king had sworn as *hegemon* of the Hellenic League and authorize him to issue commands and laws to its members, and that the ruler's status as a god was in some sense a development of Greek freedom and not a negation of it, casts light chiefly on Meyer's own views regarding monarchy. Beloch, in this case, knew better. Meyer pursued his misuse of sources into positing that the decree to restore the exiles was the first command legitimately issued by the new god. This view did not meet with much success in Germany, where it was finally demolished by Wilcken.[34] But it was eagerly accepted by W.W. Tarn, whose chief concern was to acquit Alexander of the charge that he had broken his oaths; and it became so orthodox in the English-speaking tradition that Charles Alexander Robinson—who accepted many of Tarn's fancies, but, to his credit, balked at this one—could describe it as "generally assumed." After its meticulous destruction by Balsdon, I called it (in 1961) one of the curiosities of scholarship. But, as though to prove the axiom that no error is so convincingly disproved that it will not be revived by someone who simply ignores evidence and argument, this one was revived by Meyer's devoted disciple H.E. Stier, in his Academy lecture on Alexander in 1973—even more oddly, without mention of Meyer (or, for that matter, Tarn, who can be shown to be the immediate source).[35]

Let this suffice, as a small demonstration of the powerful influence, for better or worse, of a major scholar's minor works. That the Alexander essay is, as a whole, disappointing is unfortunately clear. As I have said: it might have been hoped and expected that a well-qualified Orientalist would at last be able to do what had long needed to be done: to tie Alexander's arrival in with the history and society of the various Eastern provinces, at least as far as Egypt and Iran. Meyer never even attempted it; and it seems clear that, in this respect at least, the article may indeed be called a preview of what his treatment might have looked like, had he come to this point in his *Geschichte.* If it is indeed, as his encomiast called it, "von ganz besonderem Wert," that value must be taken as limited to this function and not thought of as describing intrinsic merit.[36] In fact, Meyer was interested only in the early stages of Near Eastern history. His

---

[34] *Alexander der Große* (1931) 200. Kaerst and others had earlier expressed disagreement.

[35] C.A. Robinson, *Alexander the Great* (1947) 240; Balsdon, art. cit. (n. 33) 386 f.; Badian, *JHS* 81 (1961) 29; H.E. Stier, *Welteroberung und Weltfriede im Wirken Alexanders des Großen,* Rhein.-Westf. Akad. d. Wiss., Vorträge G 187 (1973). Cf. my characterization of that strange performance in *Entretiens* (cit. n. 24) 290 ff., i.a. demonstrating its dependence on Tarn.

[36] For that assessment see Wilcken *ap.* Marohl, p. 127.

often-reiterated view that the Orient was essentially unchanging, locked
up in sterile tradition, prevented him from taking the later periods seriously as objects of historical enquiry. A preconceived opinion—like all
heresies, not wholly devoid of truth, of course—deprived him of the ability
of seeing Alexander as interacting with, and in part disrupting, living
native cultures, most of them trying to adapt themselves to a variety of
outside influences that had long been peacefully irradiating much of the
region. If he ever (as a trained Egyptologist) knew that the Egypt of
Nectanebo II differed from that of Ramses II, or how Persians, Jews and
Elamites (to name no others) had affected life in southern Mesopotamia
by the late fourth century, he showed no sign of caring. In a sense, for the
man who had begun his career as a major scholar by writing a history of
Egypt, the Near East had no history; it was an inert object, waiting for
living Hellenism to act on it.[37]

For Meyer, indeed, the essay may be taken to have been an opportunity
to formulate, still in a sketchy form, some of the general ideas that were
to be the mainsprings of his historical thought: the importance of the
individual, and of accident, in history, as we have seen; the origin of legitimate monarchy; and the expansion of a superior *Kultur* at the expense of
its inferiors. The first of these (expanded, perhaps chiefly with an eye on
Beloch's very different treatment, as we have seen, in his final version)
was developed in his essay on historical method within a year or two of
the original Alexander essay. The second (the basis and legitimation of
monarchy) was always of great personal importance to him. Even as a
student, he expresses firm belief in the right of the monarch, in an extraordinary letter to his father, of July 2, 1872, in which he expresses his deep
reverence ("tiefe Ehrfurcht") for the monarch who has pardoned, and
even given office to, his rebellious subjects who ought to have been
brought to him "in Ketten oder womöglich geköpft."[38] The middle-aged
professor and publicist encouraged the soldiers of the Fatherland in
November 1915 by assuring them that a strong German monarchy was

---

[37] There is no point in collecting Meyer's abundant references to this *topos*. But see,
e.g., the statement in the Chicago lecture (*Kl. Schr.*[1] 218), where he notes, but does not
face, the problem (for him) of visible change in those civilisations. Much of the evidence
that we have on (e.g.) Achaemenid Babylonia was not yet available to him; but he knew,
and referred to, the evidence for change in Egypt, and there was enough to document the
mingling of cultures in Mesopotamia. As the evidence to the contrary began to accumulate
during his lifetime, there is no sign of any abandonment of his preconceived opinion on
the stagnation of the East. For a splendid recent synthesis on the development of cultural
life in Persian-ruled Asia Minor, and its disruption by the Macedonian invasion, see
Chester G. Starr, *Iranica Antiqua* 11 (1976) 39–99 and 12 (1977) 49–116. (This important
monograph is unfortunately split between two issues of a journal not usually seen except
by specialists in Iranology.)

[38] Meyer-Nachlaß (cit. n. 15) K. 1: "Briefe aus der Studienzeit."

not only the basis for the future of the German people, but that it would secure "damit zugleich auch die Möglichkeit des Fortbestandes und der fortschreitenden Weiterentwicklung der modernen Kultur;"[39] and he assured an unlikely audience of Church Women, whom he addressed on the nature and organization of the State in February 1916, that after Germany's victory Germany's enemies would have to adopt her system of monarchy.[40] The institution of monarchy, which alone can ensure the success of a nation and its *Kultur*, clearly held a life-long fascination for him; and it was the commission to write on Alexander, and later the need to justify and thus expand his views, that gave him the opportunity to formulate those views on its first appearance in its "modern" form.

That his view, as expounded here and elsewhere, regarding Alexander's deification rests, essentially, on misinterpretation of the sources—of the sources on Alexander and, worse still, of Aristotle's *Politics*: it is perhaps significant that he gives no actual reference to the passages he is using—has already been said, and cannot be argued here at full length. He is right only in insisting that Oriental kings, except for the Pharaoh, were not deified. Ammon may well have supported Alexander's later aspirations to divinity, but there can be no doubt as to the personal background of Alexander and its contribution. As it happens, this had recently been stressed in an assessment of Alexander that strongly contrasts with the standard Wilhelmine interpretation. In *RhM* 47 (1892) Nissen wrote a long article on Aristotle's political writings ("Die Staatsschriften des Aristoteles": pp. 161–206), which combines the stimulatingly unconventional with the merely odd, in a way most uncharacteristic of German scholarship of the period. (He makes Aristotle into a Macedonian agent in Athens.) Among his *obiter scripta* are some realistic allusions to Alexander, which would fit well into a post-World War II context (see, e.g., 176 f., 191 f.). As we now know from Professor Calder's contribution to this colloquium, they seem to have aroused the ire of Wilamowitz: "wol aber haben Alexandros und Caesar erstrebt was zu schön für sterbliche ist, und nach denen werfen freilich leute wie Nissen mit ihrem dreck" (Calder, at n. 100).[41] In

---

[39] "Die Entwicklung der römischen Weltherrschaft," in *Weltgeschichte und Weltkrieg* (Marohl item 319: 1916) p. 80 of book.

[40] "Der Staat, sein Wesen und seine Organisation" (Marohl item 326), ibid. p. 166.

[41] The idea that great men are above human judgment—often supported by a common inaccurate interpretation of Nietzsche, but in Wilamowitz an aspect of the same psychological need for heroes that led to his idealization of ancient Greece—is basic to Wilamowitz's attitude. It is probably this attitude that Meyer was trying (a little clumsily) to define and to differentiate from that of the historian, in his remark on "Philologie" (*Kl. Schr.*[1] 65 f.). If the historian ought to be free of hero worship, Meyer was hardly the one to say so. For a striking illustration of Wilamowitz's intoxication with heroes, see his statement at the end of his Alexander lecture (*Kl. Schr.* V 1, 202) that a great man is like

particular, Nissen (204) characterized the desire for deification as "ein
Ausfluss persönlicher Eitelkeit"—a view that would have been as shock-
ing to Meyer as it was to Wilamowitz, had he cared to notice it. But a
historical, like a scientific, formulation that is not of its own time is likely
to moulder unnoticed. Nissen was not even refuted.[42]

Connected with the admiration of monarchy is the first glimpse of
Meyer's view that only monarchy is capable of fulfilling the
Kulturaufgabe[43] of its age and circumstances: the Macedonian monarchy
had undertaken the task which the Greek city states had been unable to
fulfil. Alexander embodied the "Drang ins Ungemessene, der jeder auf-
strebenden Kultur anhaftet" (297)—a formulation that Stetson, for once,
cannot be blamed for finding impossible to translate. A different translator (probably checked by Meyer himself) was to convey the idea a little
later, in the Chicago lecture (229):

> It was the Macedonian kingdom which took up the task, in which Greece
> had failed, and conquered the East for Greek civilization. In Alexander the
> development of Greek civilization reached its climax.

It is difficult, in a more sober age, to see what Meyer meant by "aufstre-
bende Kultur" and above all by the "Aufgabe" set for it. Self-confidence
and arrogant assumption of superiority seem to be important constituents
(297):

> Die hellenische Kultur fühlte ihre volle Überlegenheit über alle Völker der
> Erde, die sie insgesamt als eine minderwertige Masse unter dem Barbaren-
> namen zusammenfasste.

This can be amply documented, much later, from the wartime writings.

But what is a *Kulturaufgabe*? Meyer did not believe in predestination or
in historical laws. It is clear that the "Aufgabe" could be undertaken or
ignored, and undertaken either successfully or unsuccessfully. Free will
was essential in his methodological view. Yet does not the very term
"Aufgabe" imply an agency that sets the task?[44] Who, in Meyer's view,

---

a great work of art, and "bleibt uns ein Wunder . . . Und das reine, stille Anschauen des
Göttlichen ist allen Strebens Ziel, *in der Wissenschaft wie im Leben*" (my emphasis). To
Meyer, at least, Alexander was not an object of mystical contemplation.
[42] His challenging wording made it difficult for men like Wilamowitz or Meyer to take
him seriously; and, of course, his views are only part of the answer. But in what I have
before now called our post-imperialist age, a restatement (in more solid fashion) of this
view by E. Bickerman (see n. 31) has found much acceptance.
[43] The term (not translatable into English) is used *Kl. Schr.*[1] 299, and then frequently
throughout Meyer's work, e.g. strikingly in the title of a wartime lecture (Marohl item
312, repr. *Weltgeschichte* (cit. n. 39) 1 ff.) The hint of this view in the original magazine
article was considerably expanded in the theoretical discussion of 1910 (*Kl. Schr.*[1] 309).
It was clearly developed in the years after 1900.
[44] The English word "task" (the nearest equivalent) is perhaps more non-committal.

was the "Aufgeber"? And what precisely was the "Aufgabe" itself? The answer to the latter question seems amply clear, even in the Alexander essay: it was, most simply, expansion. It was this that the city states were unable to do and the Macedonian kings did for them. One cannot help being reminded of the enthusiasm of a later writer, in a purple patch of ideologically inspired prose, which I have quoted in a similar context, and with which Meyer's view of the "Kulturaufgabe" would undoubtedly have agreed: opposed by the "verengte Polisgeist" of the fourth century, Alexander had the mission,

> dem eingeengten Griechentum ein weites, neues Feld zu eröffnen, seinen herrlichen Geist sieghaft gegen die Barbaren vorzutragen als eine die Waffen heiligende Idee.[45]

Armed conquest as the fulfilment of the *Kulturaufgabe* is precisely what Meyer was to propound in his Chicago lecture, clarifying the rather nebulous formulation in some other places as far as it could be.[46]

As to who or what sets the "Aufgabe", Meyer is not as clear in his answer as he ultimately is on the contents. It is unlikely that the author of a long methodological essay never considered the language he used: he had much to say about the terminology of others. But the only answer I have found, in the light of hints in some of Meyer's own works, is that he must have thought the task inherent in the development (the "Aufstreben") of a "Kultur" itself, so that it provided what in Toynbeean language might be called a "challenge", to which there might or might not be an adequate "response". That the idea of a task ("Aufgabe") being set by the actual development of a process is perilously close to one

---

[45] H. Berve, *Griechische Geschichte* I (1933) 167 ff. The volume appeared, as it happened, in the very year that saw Berve's entry into the NSDAP. (See Volker Losemann, *Nationalsozialismus und Antike* (1977) 207.)

[46] I do not want to be misunderstood as implying that the idea of armed diffusion of one's superior civilisation is solely a German one. Its spirit is that of the Conquistadores, that of the Crusades, and perhaps that of the White Man's Burden. It is merely the actual realisation of this idea which, in modern Germany, has turned up the most striking example since the Conquistadores of the effect of taking the view to extremes. Nor do I want to argue that Meyer was, or would have been, a Nazi. His firm denial of the importance of biological race in cultural development (see especially his lecture on the Italian Nation, *Weltgeschichte* (cit. n. 39) 113) would have prevented it. And we might remember *Caesars Monarchie* 532: "Aber nur zu leicht vergißt man dabei, daß oft gerade die unheilvollsten Taten aus den reinsten Motiven hervorgegangen sind." It is doubtful whether his belief that all means might be permissible to ensure national survival would have sufficed to overturn his academic convictions. In this insistence on the unimportance of race, incidentally, he strongly contrasts with his father's (at least early) views, as attested by his scurrilous libel against Heine and Börne ("Gegen L. Börne, den Wahrheit-, Recht- und Ehrvergeßnen Briefsteller aus Paris" (Altona 1831)—a very early instance of purely racial anti-Semitism, which at the time aroused a great deal of opposition.

of those historical laws which, at the very time when he was formulating this terminology, Meyer claimed never to have found in a long career as a historian (*Kl. Schr.* 32) will be obvious to the most superficial reader. It might be added that it will also be obvious how close that model, which seems to have been implied by Meyer, was to some of the thinking of Karl Lamprecht.[47]

III

The two essays which Meyer chose to combine into "Der Gang der Alten Geschichte" are of even greater interest in the history of his writing, since they were to serve as a quarry from which many later lectures and essays are mined, at times without any change even in actual wording. We must again mainly say a few words about how they came to be written; though there is no more certainty to be obtained than in the case of the Alexander essay.

The Historians' History of the World is, in conception and execution (if not in academic quality) an imposing work; and the man who, with very little help, conceived, wrote and edited all of it was an extraordinary man, even by the standards of contemporary America, although he is not listed in any biographical reference-work.[48]

I have given some basic information on Henry Smith Williams elsewhere, and there is no need to repeat it here.[49] He was an extraordinary "Renaissance man" who attained professional skill, and in part even eminence, in fields ranging from psychiatry and bird ethology to horticulture and eugenics (he edited the manuscripts of Luther Burbank[50] in twelve

---

[47] That he did intend this model seems to be fully confirmed (e.g.) by *Vorläufer des Weltkriegs* (Marohl item 347) 522: "... die von Grund aus veränderte Weltlage *forderte gebieterisch* die Zusammenfassung der Kräfte der Nation zu einer Einheit ... Diese *Aufgabe* hat das griechische Volk nicht lösen können ..." (my emphasis).

[48] All my information, apart from what is available in *Who's Who in America* (last 1942/43), is taken from a rambling and chatty autobiography-cum-biography entitled *We Three: Henry, Eddie and Me*, by his sister, Harriet Williams Myers. A bound copy of this, reproduced from her typescript (she admits she was "never a good speller"), was presented by her to Harvard College, with the (to me) unintelligible dedication: "To Harvard College from the Granddaughter of the 2nd President, Rev. Chales [*sic*] Chauncey—Sincerely—Harriet Williams Myers." The coat of arms on the title-page bears a Latin and a Welsh text. That her facts may not be reliable is shown by her ascribing a PhD to her brother. He had an LL.D. and an M.D., but nowhere (in *Who's Who* or in his books) claims a PhD.

[49] See *Quaderni di Storia* 29(1989) 23–29, where I have sketched the background and set out the main facts I could find, in an introduction to Professor Canfora's very welcome republication of the "lost" contributions of Diels and Wilamowitz.

[50] On Luther Burbank see *NCAB* XXXIII, pp. 149–150. Another unusual New Englander, he grew up a poor farm boy, ultimately moved to Southern California, and, without any formal study or training, became "the greatest breeder of plants in history"

volumes), from wrestling to painting. Above all, he was an indefatigable writer, who in a life of eighty years published 120 books, as well as innumerable articles in journals and magazines ranging from *Good Housekeeping* and *Harper's* to respected medical publications. At the very time when he was organizing *The Historians' History*, which appeared in 1904/05, he was also engaged in several other multi-volume works. Yet the *History* remained the pride of his life, called by a friend (Myers p. 141) "his master achievement in the realm of history." (He adds that "every student worthy of the name pores over its annals.")

Originally commissioned by the *Encyclopaedia Britannica*, it was intended as a world history told from the sources, with some evaluative chapters added. Ancient and modern historians appear in extracts cheek by jowl, and the impression it gives is not unlike that of Pliny's *Natural History* with the original sources quoted in full. But a distinguished list of academic advisors and contributors was collected, chiefly (it seems) during a trip to Europe in 1898–1902, when (we are told by his biographer) he visited hospitals and libraries in London, Paris and Berlin.[51] In fact, the scholars that grace his list, prefixed to each volume in the set of twenty-five, come from precisely those three countries, plus Austria-Hungary (which he may or may not have actually visited), indeed from only one or two cities in each. Six (by the second (?) edition, seven) men are from Berlin, and it is clear that Berlin was his main recruiting ground. His method seems to have been to invite scholars whom he met, or others whom they recommended: this is the only hypothesis that will account for the pattern we find. Most of them, incidentally, were specialists on the ancient world or on the Near East—the earlier volumes must have been preoccupying him at the time—and he never changed the list, except for slight corrections and an occasional addition or deletion between editions. It would be interesting to know whether he met Meyer in Berlin—and important, in view of what followed. But no evidence appears to have survived.

Most of the academics whom he put on his list were asked to write one article each, to be inserted at a suitable point. Not all seem to have performed in time, and it can be shown that emergency measures had to be taken.[52] But many did; and this leads us to the real puzzle: of those whose work I have checked, not one later acknowledged his contribution to this series. Of Classical scholars readily checked, Hirschfeld reused his

---

and creator of innumerable varieties of (chiefly) domesticated plants. (He has, i.a., a plum, a cherry, a potato, and a city in Southern California named after him.) He advocated the application of selective breeding techniques to humans (see *The Training of the Human Plant* (1900)). Henry Smith Williams seems to have found him congenial.

[51] For discussion of this tour and its importance for the *History*, see *Quaderni* (cit.).

[52] For this and what follows, see again *Quaderni* (cit.).

article, explicitly calling it unpublished; Meyer reused his in expanded form, with the misleading "acknowledgment" we have noted; Wilamowitz, Diels and Harnack neither reused theirs nor kept copies or listed them; not one appears in the relevant scholar's bibliography, except for a mistaken reference to Wilamowitz's, under wrong title and date, and based only on a carbon copy of one of his letters. A possible guess is that, if they had not done anything about it until 1915, they then refused to acknowledge any American involvement. But that is contradicted by Hirschfeld, whose denial of previous publication, of what is an almost unchanged reprint of his article, was made in 1913. It must be presumed that copies of the set—lavishly published though it was in America and in Britain, reaching at least two editions (available at Harvard) and perhaps more—were never put in German libraries; a conjecture that should be readily verifiable by our German colleagues.

However, Meyer's case is very peculiar. The set was certainly widely available in America, in universities and no doubt also in large public libraries. Its use for teaching undergraduates, even though exaggerated by an encomiastic friend, must be taken as genuine, indeed obvious. Of the two editions at Harvard, one seems to have been presented some time after Meyer's visit, by a Professor of History (Albert Bushnell Hart) who had had it in his own library. The other (the 1908 edition) had no donor's bookplate, but merely one stating "Gratis"! The chances are that it was presented by the editor or the publisher.

That set was probably on the library shelves when Meyer lectured at Harvard. In any case, some of his colleagues were bound to have their own copies, of a work that had by then seen at least two editions in five years. Did Meyer never look at the General History shelves? Did none of his colleagues mention seeing his essays in that well-known teaching work? Yet it was precisely at Harvard that he completed preparing his essays for the first edition of the *Kleine Schriften*, therefore precisely at Harvard that he must have written those misleading words disguising the fact that he had written for Henry Smith Williams's work. One cannot help suspecting that he deliberately suppressed his connection with a work that perhaps did not seem to him academically respectable. If that was his aim, he certainly succeeded. Henry Smith Williams probably never saw *Kleine Schriften*: it was not his type of reading, and in any case he had by then moved on to scores of other things. And neither Marohl nor any other bibliographer later cared to look.

It seems that the two essays were conceived as a unit from the start, even though they appear in different volumes and under different titles: the first introduced volume III and by implication extended to IV, which treated Greek and Hellenistic history; the second introduced the foreign relations of the Roman Republic in volume V. Yet, although not a word has been changed at the point of transition in *Kl. Schr.* ([1]p. 258), they fit together so perfectly that no reader unaware of the publication history would notice a fissure. The transition from the Aegean area to the Western Greeks and from them to the Italian tribes is smooth and natural. But the facts remain, that Meyer did write two separate essays; that he was the only scholar who did; and that his Roman essay, in volume V, was immediately followed by one written by Soltau and dealing with rather similar matters, with a great deal of overlap. It must follow that Meyer was asked to write a single essay (as all his colleagues had been), covering Greece through the Hellenistic age down to its being overpowered by the Roman Republic, and that the essay had to be divided by the editor, no doubt because it had turned out too long, yet he did not want to offend the eminent Professor. As the length was presumably due to additional detail on the Roman Republic, the nature of the division was obvious; and it accounts for the overlap with Soltau, who no doubt kept to his assignment. No other reconstruction (I think) will accommodate the facts; and it is supported by the further fact that although there is an introduction at the beginning and a conclusion at the end of the compound article in *Kl. Schr.*, there is no trace of either at the point where they join.

Republication of the essay was almost certainly not envisaged. It is really not suited for separate publication, as the topic treated is visibly incomplete. In fact, as we have seen, Meyer did not republish it until (presumably) he thought it might as well be saved from oblivion when his *Kleine Schriften* were first collected. There was then the problem of finding a title for it. It obviously would not do to call it, e.g., "Der Gang der Alten Geschichte bis zur Errichtung der römischen Hegemonie über die griechische Welt" (which would accurately describe it). So a short and pretentious title was found, and at the end of the whole essay the admission that the author could not follow further developments "an dieser Stelle," which was legitimate and obvious in its original context, had to be retained, negating the promise of the title for no reason explained to the reader. The whole makeshift solution shows conclusively that Meyer had not originally intended to publish the work in this form after its original use. The essay is a fragment, and Meyer's lack of candour about the origin and first use of it—the impression that it had not been published, and probably also that he, Eduard Meyer, had had the sole responsibility of providing a discussion of Ancient History for the American universal history—makes its oddity stand out all the more starkly. It is surprising that its genesis has never aroused a scholar's curiosity.

I have already indicated that it is nevertheless important in the study of Meyer's views. Indeed, this is probably why he finally wanted it republished, for a German academic public. Again and again it contains ideas that we keep coming across in his later work: to take some at random: that Hannibal's failure was the turning-point of ancient history,[53] when the development of a society based on nations became impossible; that the consequent universal empire of Rome had a "levelling" effect and thereby abolished the possibility of progress. It would not be suitable, and was not intended, to pursue them here.

The recovery of Meyer's earliest *Americana* is variously interesting. It throws light on American *Kulturgeschichte* precisely at the level between the academic and the popular, which was (and perhaps always is) the level of the chief bearers and developers of national culture and which is nonetheless often the least studied by professional historians. In spite of his interest in much that was American, it seems to have been uncongenial to Meyer when he came across (at least) these more popular levels of American "Kultur". Had he chosen to attend to what he found (and had he not allowed it to be further distorted by the bitterness developed during the World War), he would not so easily have equated the decline (as he saw it) from "Kultur" to "Zivilisation" with "Amerikanisierung".[54] That again cannot be developed here, but any study of it will henceforth have to take the *International Quarterly* and *The Historians' History* into account.

We must also, unfortunately, raise disturbing questions regarding Meyer's credibility in his autobiographical statements where we cannot check them.[55] The fact will have to be faced that, as in other cases, autobiographical reminiscence is not a fully reliable source for the historian.

Above all, however, we here find Meyer at a formative period of his historical thinking. The difference between the original Alexander essay and its later form (perhaps, as I have suggested, in reaction to Beloch), as well as the persistent use of the material of what became "Der Gang der Alten Geschichte" throughout his later life, cannot but draw attention to the importance, to Meyer himself, of the opportunities provided by the invitations to write the studies that he later chose not to acknowledge.

E. Badian   Harvard University

---

[53] This, with some of the development that follows, is repeated *verbatim* in "Vorläufer des Weltkriegs" (cit. n. 47) 42 ("den Wendepunkt der Geschichte des Altertums"); and so is the other idea, regarding the effect of the Roman Empire.

[54] For this idea see *Blüte und Niedergang des Hellenismus in Asien* (Marohl item 420), written in 1925, under the long-lasting influence of the First World War: Spengler's formulation is approvingly cited p. 61.

[55] Professor Chambers, in his paper, has had occasion to throw doubt on this, in connection with his statement that he tore up and sent back "all" his honorary diplomas from universities in the English-speaking world.

Appendix I

Meyer in Stetson's Translation: the First Alexander

Where there are no additions by Meyer in his published essay, the wording is practically unchanged, and the translation can be checked from the published German. It is possible that occasional annotation was omitted (perhaps deliberately) by Stetson, but Meyer may have added one or two small comments, e.g. the two lines "während bei Diodor . . . erhalten ist—" (pp. 286 – 7), in revision. I shall ignore these very minor changes in what follows. The following passages are added in Meyer's own publication (all page numbers from *Kl. Schr.* 1st edition):

289 – 294 "Das makedonische Reich . . . erfüllt als sein Vater." This, the first major addition in Meyer's revision, is merely a brief summary of the earlier history of Macedonia, with special emphasis on Philip II, centred on foreign policy. It is no more than background, and added chiefly in order to stress Meyer's interpretation of Philip as uninterested in Asia and major expansion. (See text.)

306 – 307 "und so können die Verhältnisse . . . und haben ihn ermordet." What is added is the quotation from Plato and a brief account of Plato's attempt to put his theory into practice in the cases of the younger Dionysius and of Dio. The passage (moving from Plato's recognition of the fact that the ideal state was "only for gods and the sons of gods" and that in modern terms, constitutional monarchy would have to be substituted for enlightened despotism, back to his support for Dio's attempt to introduce the "ideal state" in Syracuse) is confused and ill organized and clearly an attempt to find a place, *post scriptum*, for one of Meyer's favourite ideas. The place of this longish exposition is taken by a single sentence in the original English: "As is well known [I wonder how well known it was to readers of the magazine], he made two attempts in Sicily, —first, through the instrumentality of the younger Dionysius, and then through Dion." This is clear, coherent and adequate.

307 n. 1 is not in the original. (But see just below.)

308 The passage on Isocrates ("Auch Isokrates . . . als Gott zu werden") is added.

308 – 313 The whole theoretical discussion, leading up to Meyer's idea that Alexander's divine monarchy is the ancestor of monarchy by the grace of God, and hence of modern absolute monarchy, is added ("Herbeigeführt ist sie . . . im Reiche Alexanders des Grossen"). In the original, there is a sentence quoting "the true king, as a god, stands above his subjects, and his will is for them an inviolable law like the command of God." To this Meyer attached the reference to Aristotle's heroization of

Hermias and his altar to Plato, which he later slightly expanded, with a few lines of generalization added, into p. 307 n. 1. The reference to *Aristoteles und Athen* appears, characteristically for the translator, as *Aristotle in Athens*.

313 – 328 The original version states that "It is not our task to set forth the particulars in the course of these catastrophes" [Alexander's conflicts with Greeks and Macedonians: "the most serious conflicts with his nearest environment (cf. p. 316)"]. Meyer's full treatment adds the influence of Oriental forms, which he interestingly compares with "orientalisms" that have survived to modern manifestations of courtesy (316). The rest consists of detailed accounts of the individual conflicts, mostly plain narrative with occasional sketches of analysis. It is-not clear why Meyer thought he had to add this. Hamburg philologists surely did know it.

330 – 332 Slightly expanded, but not significantly, except that the polemic against Hogarth (330 n. 2) is even longer than in the original version and that the Greek note (331 n. 1) is omitted, with a sentence of English summary substituted.

332 Two phrases found in the original must have been deleted by Meyer in his final version:

(a) Before "dass er nicht unter dem Gesetze stehen kann" there appears an expansion of that idea by anticipation: "that he could not be measured by the same standard."

(b) At the end of the last but one paragraph, Meyer omitted a long phrase, no doubt since the idea it expresses had been much more fully treated in one of the added passages: "only *slightly* modified by Christianity, then into the place of the king who is god, steps the king by God's grace." ["then" must be a mistranslation, as what follows applies only to the "civilization . . . of modern times," not to that of antiquity.]

332 The final phrase ("bis auch sie durch die ansteigende orientalische Reaktion, die im Islam ihren letzten Ausdruck fand, überflutet worden ist") was added by Meyer, no doubt under the influence of what later became an obsession with the "Reaktion des Orientalismus:" it is interesting to find it developing in the years between these two versions.[1]

As was stated initially, places where there seems to have been merely verbal revision, or where perhaps one sentence was added, have been

---

[1] Cf. the end of "Der Gang der Alten Geschichte," written at the same time, for *Kleine Schriften*: the fact that here too the sentence is not in the original shows that it must in both cases be a new reflection. Later, of course, it occurs at the end of every general survey of ancient history, under any title. It is amusing to note that Wilamowitz, in his lecture on Alexander a few years later (1916/17), also stresses the Oriental reaction which in the end overwhelmed the West as well; but he identifies it with Christianity (192 f.). Did he get the basic idea from Meyer's revised Alexander essay?

ignored. But all significant changes between the two versions are indicated above. It will be seen that most of the changes are by no means essential: the narration of Alexander's conflicts with his Macedonians and with Callisthenes offers nothing of any value (it is quite inadequate, indeed sketchy and at times misleading, in what source analysis is attempted); the lengthy discussion of earlier Macedonian foreign policy is otiose, and again mostly mere narrative, except for the statement about the difference between Philip's aims and Alexander's, for which a sentence would have sufficed. The discussion of divine and absolute monarchy (pp. 308–313) is in fact the only important addition (indeed, a very important part of the essay in its final form). Presumably Meyer had not yet clearly formulated it when he wrote the original version, although a hint of it ("but only of the relationship between divine monarchy and monarchy by the grace of God") is given at the end of the original essay. Most of the difference in length between the two versions is accounted for by the addition of long narrative passages.

The translator's performance can only be characterized as incompetent. He clearly did not know nearly enough German to undertake such an ambitious task, and one at times wonders whether he knew enough English either. (I have not been able to discover any original work by him, or indeed what his own specialty was.) There would be no point in giving a complete listing of even those mistranslations that essentially change the sense of the original (or produce nonsense), but a few should be adduced, to justify our verdict. (All emphasis added.)

The second line contains a warning example: "Among the mighty personalities which ... have *laid a disturbing hand* upon the course of the world's history ..." ("... deren Eingreifen in den Gang der Weltgeschichte ..."). But worse soon follows, characteristic of how nonsense can be created out of what Meyer had carefully chosen to say. A few lines further down, we find, "It is universally conceded that *the power of the Greek mind*, when left to itself, never again could attain even a tolerable condition." What can this mean? Meyer, clearly enough, wrote "die griechischen Gemeinwesen." Soon after, the omens "welche alle wichtigen Entscheidungen voraus verkünden" become omens "which herald in advance important *verdicts*"—a splendid example of brainless use of a dictionary. 286 n. 1 Meyer condemns certain of the vulgate anecdotes: "Man begreift nicht, wie manche Neuere derartige absurde Erfindungen für Wahrheit haben nehmen können." This becomes "... how such *new and absurd inventions* could have been regarded as true"—turning Meyer's polemic into nonsense. P. 288, claiming that Alexander's aims are clear beyond doubt: "Über die Ziele Alexanders herrscht freilich auch Streit, aber es sollte keiner herrschen:" "Concerning the aims of Alexander there is evidently a difference of opinion, *but this should influence no one.*"

Nonsense may "influence no one," but when the opposite of what is in the original is said, misunderstanding is bound to result. In the same context (p. 294), Meyer makes Alexander set out for Asia after securing his rear against the barbarians: "nachdem er ... seinen Rücken gegen Thrakien und Illyrien gedeckt ... hatte:" "Alexander ... turned his back upon Thrace and Illyria!" Or, when the pro-Persian tyrants are said to have been "den Städten zur Bestrafung übergeben," we find "the [Greek] cities were given over to punishment." The non-specialist reader must be misled, and the specialist could not help wondering about Meyer's own competence. Similarly, Meyer compares the practical advice given to Alexander by Aristotle in a "popular" essay sent to him with the theoretical exposition "in seiner Staatslehre" (the *Politics*). But not for Stetson: "in a work composed in his popular style ... and sent to Alexander ... *he had maintained theoretically as a state doctrine* ..." Meyer's most important ideas (as he saw them) can thus be obscured and made unintelligible. Caesar at the time of his death was about "die grosse Kulturaufgabe zu erfüllen, die Rom als dem Erben von Hellas gestellt war" [on this, see text]; for Stetson, he was "to solve the *great problems of culture* ..." Subjects and objects are freely interchanged: the ideas of Aristotle no longer sufficed for Alexander, who had outgrown them ("Nicht mehr Aristoteles Ideale waren es, die Alexander erfüllen konnten"); this, by obvious transposition, becomes "Nor was it *merely* the ideals of Aristotle *that Alexander could carry out.*" Misunderstanding of words, such as use of a dictionary (despite its dangers: see above) could have forestalled, is comparatively trivial, though often serious enough in itself; as when "offiziös" becomes "obsequious" and "Umsturz" becomes "subjugation", all within a few sentences, or when the importance of *Ämterwechsel* as characteristic of a free state is turned into almost its opposite as "government control." In one case, we must surely assume inability to read German handwriting (plus, needless to say, complete indifference to sense): when Meyer speaks of "Callisthenes and the [Greek] idealists" (p. 313), Stetson writes "Callisthenes and the Socialists!"

It is clear from these few and almost random examples that the American reader could not get a very clear idea of what Meyer was trying to say: filtered through the ignorant stupidity of the translator, it too often emerges as trivial, nonsensical, or even as the opposite of what was intended.[2] Unfortunately, this must be generalized from the specific

---

[2] Stetson's use of his own language is not such as to inspire confidence in the first place. Although this is of no importance in our case, a few instances ought to be given, in addition to what will have been incidentally gathered from the specimens of translation.

instance. The art of scholarly translation has not improved since Stetson's day, as those of us who have had their work translated, or who have checked translation of other people's, can confirm. Worse still: for most scholarly work, which is not translated at all, the language skills of a Stetson form—as again many of us can confirm—an insuperable barrier to any truly international scholarship. Understanding is in no way superior to actual translation.

Appendix II

The two essays and "Der Gang der Alten Geschichte"

I here list the chief places where the two essays written for *The Historians' History* were significantly expanded for *Kleine Schriften*. The differences do not seem to me as important for the development of Meyer's thought, and even for his intellectual biography, as those in the Alexander essay. I shall therefore take even less account of minor changes than in Appendix I, but shall try to indicate all the major changes. All references, again, are to the 1st edition of *Kleine Schriften*. I have indicated the division between the two essays by giving the original volume numbers to introduce the citations.
III. There is no significant change through the top of p. 249 (the first generation of the Successors). After this, there is a good deal of expansion, which I shall merely indicate.
249–250 The effect of depopulation and the destruction of Philip's firm European kingdom by expansion are new ideas.
251 Most of the details on the state of Greece are new.
252–253 The emphasis on the absence of race mixture in the Ptolemaic kingdom is added.
253–257 This is the most significant expansion. The analysis is largely new, especially (and not surprisingly) in the importance of deification of the ruler ("der Weg, den Alexander gewiesen hat"—254). The other basic ideas are already in the original.
V. 262 Interestingly, the comparison between Rome and the USA ("Es ist eine Entwicklung . . . Staaten Europas") has been added: it would no doubt have been tactless to state it in these terms in an American publication. What is perhaps most striking, in the light of later developments, is his contrast between Presidential power in America and

---

"With his position as king [incidentally, also mistranslated: see Meyer p. 294] corresponded the regulations which he adopted . . ."
"Thus the Macedonian king steps for the time quite into the background."
"Alexander . . . was created of different material than his father."
"Modern critics . . . who, because of the trees, cannot see the forest.[!]"

the "schroffe Gegensatz" of this to parliamentary regimes. We would nowadays say the opposite.

268–269 The discussion of the whole Saguntum affair has been greatly expanded. In part the reason for this is the need to reply to Kromayer (269 n. 1). The discussion continues, in precisely the same terms.

273–274 Nearly everything on Antiochus III has been added: a transitional phrase ("instead of taking action there"—before mentioning his turning east: Achaeus is ignored) in the original version makes addition certain.

274–275 The paragraph "Für die kleineren Mächte ..." is new, as is the insertion of the Sicilian war. A transitional phrase in the English again makes expansion certain here.

277 ("die Regierung empfand," near end of second paragraph)—279 end of first paragraph is new.

279–280 There are more details about Roman expansion; on p. 280, one or two sentences have been retained, surrounded by new material. The end of the long paragraph on p. 280 ("Indessen ... verfuhr es weiterhin völlig planlos ...") is unchanged.

281 Details on Antiochus IV are added, as is the parenthesis on Arsacid "philhellenism."

282 The striking phrase about Orientalisation ("während der Osten ... um sich greift") is new.

The translation, in both these essays, is very adequate. I did not look through it in detail, as it at once becomes clear that this translator knew his trade and did not seriously distort the meaning. Discrepancies can, on the whole, confidently be ascribed to Meyer's revision.

In one case (266) "hellenistischen Staaten" is mistranslated as "Hellenic states:" the translator was apparently not a professional ancient historian. The only serious mistranslation I noticed was (241) "nationale Aufgabe," which appears in a note on III p. 5 as "national *destiny.*" (The term, a favourite of Meyer's—see text—is correctly rendered elsewhere, e.g. "the political tasks" of Athens (239 middle).) Meyer might have objected to this, had he seen it. But his own term, "Aufgabe", is not free from objection.

The International Quarterly

ADVISORY BOARD

History
J. H. Robinson, *Columbia University*; Karl Lamprecht, *University of Leipzig*; Ch. Seignobos, *Paris*.

Literature
William P. Trent, *Columbia University*; Richard Garnett, *London*; Gustave Lanson, *Paris*; Alois Brandl, *University of Berlin*; Anatole Le Braz, *Rennes*.

Fine Art
John C. Van Dyke, *Rutgers College*; Georges Perrot, *Ecole Normale, Paris*; Adolph Furtwängler, *University of Munich*.

Science of Religion
C. H. Toy, *Harvard University*; Jean Réville, *University of Paris*; F. B. Jevons, *University of Durham*; Ths. Achelis, *Bremen*.

Sociology
Franklin H. Giddings, *Columbia University*; Gabriel Tarde, *College of France*; Georg Simmel, *University of Berlin*; J. S. Mackenzie, *Cardiff, Wales*.

Philosophy and Psychology
Josiah Royce, *Harvard University*; Xavier Léon, *Paris*; Paul Natorp, *University of Marburg*; Th. Ribot, *Paris*.

Biology
Charles O. Whitman, *University of Chicago*; Raphael Blanchard, *University of Paris*; E. B. Poulton, *University of Oxford*; Wilhelm Roux, *University of Halle*.

Medicine
D. B. St. John Roosa, *Pres. Graduate School of Medicine*; Carl von Noorden, *Frankfurt a. M.*; Photino Panas, *University of Paris*.

Geology
N. S. Shaler, *Harvard University*; Sir Archibald Geikie, *London*; Hermann Credner, *University of Leipzig*; Chas. Barrois, *University of Lille*.

Economics and Commerce
J. W. Jenks, *Cornell University*; Eugen Schwiedland, *University of Vienna*; André Lebon, *Paris*; Baron Kentaro Kaneko, *Tokio*.

International Politics
John Bassett Moore, *New York*; Emil Reich, *London*; Salvatore Cortesi, *Rome*; Theodor Barth, *Berlin*.

The use of the names of the Editorial Staff is not merely formal and honorary, but each one is responsible for the work assigned to him.

$4.00 *A YEAR.*　　　　　*SINGLE NUMBERS,* $1.25.

Illustration I

Contributors, and Editorial Revisers

Prof. Adolf Erman, University of Berlin.

Prof. Joseph Halévy, College of France.

Prof. Thomas K. Cheyne, Oxford University.

Prof. Andrew C. McLaughlin, University of Chicago.

Prof. David H. Müller, University of Vienna.

Prof. Alfred Rambaud, University of Paris.

Capt. F. Brinkley, Tokio.

Prof. Eduard Meyer, University of Berlin.

Dr. James T. Shotwell, Columbia University.

Prof. Theodor Nöldeke, University of Strasburg.

Prof. Albert B. Hart, Harvard University.

Dr. Paul Brönnle, Royal Asiatic Society.

Dr. James Gairdner, C.B., London.

Prof. Ulrich von Wilamowitz Möllendorff, University of Berlin.

Prof. H. Marczali, University of Budapest.

Dr. G. W. Botsford, Columbia University.

Prof. Julius Wellhausen, University of Göttingen.

Prof. Franz R. von Krones, University of Graz.

Prof. Wilhelm Soltau, Zabern University.

Prof. R. W. Rogers, Drew Theological Seminary..

Prof. A. Vambéry, University of Budapest.

Prof. Otto Hirschfeld, University of Berlin.

Dr. Frederick Robertson Jones, Bryn Mawr College.

Baron Bernardo di San Severino Quaranta, London.

Dr. John P. Peters, New York.

Prof. Adolph Harnack, University of Berlin.

Dr. A. S. Rappoport, School of Oriental Languages, Paris.

Prof. Hermann Diels, University of Berlin.

Prof. C. W. C. Oman, Oxford University.

Prof. W. L. Fleming, Louisiana State University.

Prof. I. Goldziher, University of Budapest.

Printed in the United States.

Prof. R. Koser, University of Berlin.

Illustration II

WILLIAM M. CALDER III

"CREDO GEGEN CREDO; ARBEIT GEGEN ARBEIT; ANSCHAUUNG GEGEN ANSCHAUUNG" ULRICH VON WILAMOWITZ – MOELLENDORFF CONTRA EDUARD MEYER

"gerade der universalhistoriker stöbert nicht nach alten inschriftsteinen in den fußböden der tempel, sammelt keine sprüchwörter und macht keine topographischen studien, nicht nur weil er keine zeit hat, sondern weil seine geistesrichtung ins weite geht."

Ulrich von Wilamowitz-Moellendorff, *Aristoteles und Athen* I (1893) 306.

I. The Problem

Ulrich von Wilamowitz-Moellendorff (1848 – 1931) and Eduard Meyer (1855 – 1930) knew each other from at least October 1886 until Meyer's death 31 August 1930.[1] They were colleagues in the same university, and later in the same complex-institute, 1902 – 1930. They were never friends in the sense that Wilamowitz was a friend of Lüders, Kaibel, Kießling, or Wellhausen: or Meyer of Beloch, Crusius, Norden, Pietschmann, or Wissowa. They did not share a common past. Meyer knew Hamburg not Posen, the Johanneum not Schulpforte, Bonn only for one disappointing semester then Leipzig, which Wilamowitz could only disapprove,[2] but where Meyer both promoted and habilitated. Nor had Meyer attended the German Institute in Rome. Of course there were good reasons for all

---

[1] The earliest preserved letter of Wilamowitz to Eduard Meyer is dated 31 October 1886. Its formal tone suggests that if not the first letter written by Wilamowitz to Meyer, it was one of the first. I have no indubitable evidence that Wilamowitz ever met Meyer before Meyer's appointment to Berlin in 1902. One may compare his correspondence with Gilbert Murray. The earliest letter is dated October 1894. They met first at Oxford in 1908. Hugh Lloyd-Jones' assertion in his Oxford inaugural that Murray had earlier studied under Wilamowitz at Göttingen is fiction: see William M. Calder III and E. Christian Kopff, *CP* 72 (1977) 53 – 54 and Duncan Wilson, *Gilbert Murray OM 1866 – 1957* (Oxford 1987) 128, 416 n. 8.

[2] There the despised Friedrich Ritschl (1806 – 1876) had taught and the faculty had granted the undeserving Friedrich Nietzsche an honorary degree to secure him the Basel chair. For Meyer's activity at Leipzig see Ulrich Wilcken. "Das Seminar für Alte Geschichte," *Festschrift zur Feier des 500 jährigen Bestehens der Universität Leipzig* IV.1 (Leipzig 1909) 145. Not until April 1906 was there an Ordinarius for ancient history at Leipzig (*ibid.*, 146).

this but a shared common past of a sort that often caused a lasting friendship with Wilamowitz was lacking. Except for the bizarre coincidence that both studied Sanskrit under the dull and incompetent Gildemeister, they shared no teacher. Meyer had been taught the *Odes* of Horace at school by their later commentator, the attractive but superficial colleague of Wilamowitz at Greifswald, Adolph Kießling (1837–1893). One doubts that they spoke of him often.

Nor can one underestimate the difference in class. There was no aristocracy in Hamburg and Meyer was bourgeois through and through, the son of a schoolmaster, industrious, goodhumored, horrified at the premarital pregnancy of his daughter. Leo Baeck in a letter to Ernst-Ludwig Ehrlich, dated London, 17 December 1946 compared Meyer with Friedrich Meinecke:[3]

> Sie haben durchaus recht in Bezug auf Meinecke. Männer wie er sind geschichtlich die Schuldigsten; er und seinesgleichen haben gelehrt, sich vor jeder Macht, die massiv wurde, d.h. Macht auch bedenkenlos ausübte, gehorsam und schliesslich bewundernd zu beugen. Er ist ein reiner Typus auch des professoralen Kleinbürgers, der immer davon erzählen muss, welch 'feinen' Verkehr er gehabt hat, welch feine Leute mit ihm gesprochen haben. Ich hatte ein paar Mal Gelegenheit, von der Zuschauer-gallerie zu beobachten, *wie* Professoren sich vor hohen Herrschaften verbeugten; besonders das Bild von Eduard Meyer, wie sein Rückgrat sich in ein Reptil zu verwandeln schien,—schade, dass ich nicht zeichnen konnte—ist mir in einer lebhaften Erinnerung. Dabei sind alle diese Männer wirkliche Gelehrte und zum Teil Männer von Geist. Aber der Kleinbürger kommt immer wieder zum Vorschein; vielleicht müssen sie deshalb Antisemiten sein und darüber schliesslich auch ihren Geist verlieren ...

Wilamowitz contrarily was the rebellious aristocrat, arrogant, always assured, amused that his daughter married a homosexual (*unser Hauseunuchus*). Meyer's American students (James Breasted and Henry A. Sill) addressed him with *Du*. No student of Wilamowitz, other than his son Tycho, or his son-in-law, Carl Friedrich, ever dared that. That Wilamowitz, in June 1914, aged sixty-six and rector elect of the Friedrich-Wilhelms-Universität, pursued two young ladies into the upper branches of a cherry tree at a reception in Meyer's Lichterfelde garden, was surely done on impulse; but the conviction that Meyer would be discomfited must have delighted Wilamowitz.[4] His Berlin salary of 15,000 gold

---

[3] I cite Dr. Christhard Hoffmann's transcription of Leo Baeck to Ernst-Ludwig Ehrlich, London, 17 December 1946: Archiv des Leo-Baeck-Institutes, New York (Leonard Baker Collection). I am grateful to Dr. Hoffmann for knowledge of the document.

[4] See Gottlieb Haberlandt, *Erinnerungen Bekenntnisse und Betrachtungen* (Berlin 1933) 196–197. For another such garden party see Charles Breasted, *Pioneer to the Past: The Story*

marks would have far exceeded that of Meyer.[5] That Wilamowitz and not Meyer was the close confidant of Althoff was expected.

There were two differences in the way they worked. Eduard Meyer, like a closer friend of Wilamowitz, Eduard Schwartz (1858–1940), wrote Pauly-Wissowa articles. Wilamowitz only advised Wissowa to whom he should assign them.[6] This was a drudge's chore. Meyer also wrote many articles for the *Encyclopaedia Britannica*, especially the great eleventh edition, whereas the thought would never have occurred to Wilamowitz. Although he recognized their value, he was too impatient to participate. To this impatience of Wilamowitz is owed another more telling difference. Meyer knew as early as the end of June 1873[7] that he wished to write a universal history of antiquity. As a school boy he laid the linguistic foundation that later allowed him to read Greek, Latin, Hebrew, and Arabic sources in the original. The first volume of his *Geschichte des Altertums* appeared in 1884 when he was 29 years old. He died 47 years later revising volume II.2. There were important volumes not strictly included within the history but in fact of the nature of supplement volumes, e.g., *Ägyptische Chronologie* (1904), or volumes that might be called anticipatory, e.g., those concerned with Roman history or Christianity. His political writings aside, only very rarely did Meyer write a volume on impulse. *Der Papyrusfund von Elephantine* (1912) and *Caesars Monarchie und das Principat des Pompeius: Innere Geschichte Roms von 66 bis 44 v. Chr.* (1918: reprinted 1919) are the obvious exceptions.

---

of *James Henry Breasted Archaeologist* (Chicago 1943; reprinted 1977) 128–129. For Meyer's students addressing him with *Du* see M.H. Chambers, *infra*. Lewis R. Farnell, the son of a failed businessman, declared that Wilamowitz was not "a gentleman:" see Lewis R. Farnell, *An Oxonian Looks Back* (London 1934) 95. So much for the parochialism of Edwardian Oxford. Theodor Gomperz' view of Wilamowitz is a different story.

[5] The salary is attested in the Althoff papers. In 1896 the highest salary for an Ordinarius in Prussia was 12,000 marks: see W. Lexis, *Academische Revue* III, 28.4 (1897) 193–198 (Bernhard vom Brocke).

[6] For the letters of Wilamowitz to Wissowa see Francesco Bertolini, *Quaderni di Storia* 4 (1976) 47–54.

[7] The evidence is his letter from Bonn of that date to his father published by Christhard Hoffmann, *Die Darstellung von Juden und Judentum im Werk deutscher Althistoriker des 19. und 20. Jahrhunderts* (Diss. T.U. West Berlin 1986) 112. Meyer confirms this in his autobiographical sketch available in Heinrich Marohl, *Eduard Meyer Bibliographie mit einer autobiographischen Skizze Eduard Meyers und der Gedächtnisrede von Ulrich Wilcken* (Stuttgart 1941) 9–10. For biographical details I depend on the valuable but necessarily brief life by Karl Christ, "Eduard Meyer (1855–1930)." *Von Gibbon zu Rostovtzeff: Leben und Werk führender Althistoriker der Neuzeit*[2] (Darmstadt 1979) 28 333 and "Eduard Meyer," *Römische Geschichte und deutsche Geschichtswissenschaft* (Munich 1982) 93–102. The latter is a revision of the former. I shall cite them Christ (1) and Christ (2). For Meyer's early decision on his life work see Christ (1) 287, after the autobiography. A book-length biography of Meyer resting on the extensive *Nachlaß* is needed. His sketch is cited *Skizze* within. See recently J. Irmscher, "Eduard Meyer," *Das Altertum* 33 (1987) 99–103.

Wilamowitz could not have worked more differently. In the foreword to this *Erinnerungen*,[8] he states:

> Fast alles, was ich geschrieben habe, ist durch einen äußeren Anlaß hervor-gerufen, der mir dies und jenes Objekt in die Hände warf.

Scrutiny of Wilamowitz' bibliography confirms that this was the case. The discovery of a new inscription (*Isyllos*) or a papyrus (*Aristoteles und Athen*: *Timotheus*), his friendship with Wellhausen (*Untersuchungen*) or with Schwartz (*Heimkehr*), the request of Althoff (*Lesebuch, Kultur der Gegenwart*), the appearance of a pornographic novel (*Sappho*), or a deep personal involvement with the subject matter (*Hippolytos, Herakles, Platon, Glaube*), called forth his great books. By 1931 he had treated Greek literature from Homer to Libanius but never systematically. To someone like Meyer this must have seemed slapdash. The advantage was that his books are fresh, urgent, bubbling with ideas some of which he will later withdraw, and utterly delightful to read. Meyer contrarily is solid and, so far as I know, rarely withdrew a thesis, not least because so much was invested in it. But how interesting can a book be that one has planned for 50 years? We have the verdict of the highest mortal judge. In January 1894 Theodor Mommsen (1817–1903) loyally read *Aristoteles und Athen* and *Geschichte* II. He writes his son-in-law:[9]

---

[8] See Ulrich von Wilamowitz-Moellendorff, *Erinnerungen 1848–1914*[2] (Leipzig 1929) 7. Henceforth cited: *Erinnerungen*[2].

[9] I cite *Mommsen und Wilamowitz: Briefwechsel 1872–1905*, edd. Friedrich und Dorothea Hiller von Gaertringen (Berlin 1935) 485–486, No. 388 (3 January 1894). Mommsen did not automatically write letters of praise to his son-in-law. He disapproved *Hippolytos* and said so in a way that in 1891 deeply hurt Wilamowitz: see *Antiqua* 27 (Naples 1984) 172–175. I do not know whether Meyer sent his book to Mommsen as he did to Wilamowitz or whether correspondence on the book between them survives. Hans Erich Stier, *GdA* III[2] vi, observes:

> EDUARD MEYER pflegte bis in seine letzten Lebenstage hinein gern darauf hinzuweisen, daß er in seinem langen Forscherleben—anders als der in diesem Zusammenhange mit Vorliebe von ihm genannte große ULRICH V. WILAMOWITZ-MOELLENDORFF—nur ganz wenige seiner wissen-schaftlichen Thesen habe zurücknehmen müssen ..."

For a contemporary opinion similar to Mommsen's and from a friendly source see Max Dessoir, *Buch der Erinnerung* (Stuttgart 1947) 193 [of Meyer]:

> Von seinen Büchern hatte ich den Eindruck, daß er nicht nur erkunden und aufhellen, sondern auch zusammenfassen und gestalten wollte; er war gleichzeitig Tatsachenfinder und Wert-deuter; die sprachliche Meisterschaft eines Herder, Ranke, Burckhardt, Mommsen war ihm jedoch versagt.

Even his loyal student and friend Victor Ehrenberg had to admit that his books were dull. See V. Ehrenberg, *HZ* 143 (1931) 510:

> ... obwohl doch diese Bücher garnicht faszinierend waren, weniger als das "Römische Staats-recht" und erst recht als die "Römische Geschichte" ...

Ich sollte Index zum C.I.L. machen, aber statt dessen lese ich Deinen Aristoteles und E. Meyers zweiten Band. Über Dein Buch habe ich mich aufrichtig gefreut; die ruhige Klarheit der bei weitem meisten Partien wirkt vortrefflich und insbesondere die erzählenden Abschnitte scheinen mir in hohem Grade geglückt. Von Meyers Buch kann ich das nicht so sagen, wie bewundernswert auch die Wissensweite und die Kombinationskraft ist. Daß der Pelion auf den Ossa gesetzt, der Horizont von Babylon nach Gades erstreckt wird, ist wohl grandios; aber ich fürchte, im Grund falsch, und die Handbuchform für ein Geschichtswerk ist für mich kaum erträglich. Das *narrare* versagt ganz bei diesem *capitulatim* geschriebenen Buch.

One could have thought the author of *Staatsrecht* and the admirer of Harnack more charitable toward handbooks. But the future winner of the Nobel prize for literature requires that an historian be a writer, not only a compiler, however learned or industrious he may be. Mommsen found Meyer dull. Meyer, again like Eduard Schwartz, never founded a school.[10] He lacked, as his student Ehrenberg admitted, the gift of charisma, a gift that Wilamowitz knew he possessed.[11]

These were the differences. There were similarities. Even the unsatisfactory biographical material available in print on Meyer allows us to discern some of them. First their remarkable schooling. Both became scholars not because of their university teachers. The die was cast at school; for Wilamowitz at Schulpforte and for Meyer at the Johanneum. This caused an early professional commitment that never left the slightest room for self-doubt and provided an ease with Greek and Latin (also for Meyer Hebrew) denied men who must learn the languages in later life. Meyer's inclination to history presumably owed much to the coincidence that the two Hellenists at his school ranked among the leading nineteenth century Thucydidean scholars. Franz Wolfgang Ullrich (1795 – 1880) was the father of the "Thucydidean Question"[12] and Johannes Classen

---

Julius Wellhausen (cited by Christhard Hoffmann, *infra*) called him "Kaffer und Kulturpauker." Wilhelm Dilthey was kinder. See Dilthey to Graf Paul Yorck von Wartenburg (spring 1895), "Briefwechsel zwischen Wilhelm Dilthey und dem Grafen Paul Yorck v. Wartenburg 1877 – 1897," edited by Sigrid v. d. Schulenburg, *Philosophie und Geisteswissenschaften* 1 (Halle 1923) 181 (No. 116):

> Zu den älteren Griechen las ich den zweiten Band von Meyer in den entsprechenden Parthien mit großer Förderung durch sein ächtes geschichtliches Denken. Zumal die orphische Bewegung ist historisch gesehen.

He continues to contrast Meyer favorably with Erwin Rohde, *Psyche* which he found disappointing.

[10] See Christ (1), 333: "Eine Schule im engeren Sinne hat Meyer nicht gebildet . . ."
[11] For Wilamowitz on charisma see his remarkable letter of 12 August 1921 on the teacher to Ernst Krieck: *Volk im Werden* 9 (1941) 18 – 20. Contrast V. Ehrenberg, *HZ* 143 (1931) 510 (Meyer lacked "Charisma").
[12] See Franz Wolfgang Ullrich, *Die Entstehung des Thukydideischen Geschichtswerkes*, ed.

(1806–1891) wrote what remains today in the revisions of Julius Steup and Rudolf Stark the authoritative philological commentary on all of Thucydides. As a young man (1827–1831) Classen was *Hauslehrer* in the home of Barthold Georg Niebuhr (1776–1831). Certainly to Classen is owed the influence of Niebuhr on the young Meyer.[13] One reason why Wilamowitz later underestimated Thucydides was because he was neglected at the Pforte. The decision for Meyer was far easier than for Wilamowitz. The elder Meyer was on the staff of the Johanneum, a scholar in his own right, a student of Gottfried Hermann and August Böckh,[14] who retired early in order to turn his two gifted sons into prodigies. One may compare him with James Mill.[15] Wilamowitz' choice to become a scholar required the painful repudiation of his father and his class. He courageously made his public declaration at Schulpforte in September 1867.[16] Meyer was spared this agony.

The *Wanderjahre* differed for both but for both in different ways profoundly affected their later work. The importance of Wilamowitz' sojourn

---

Hans Herter (Darmstadt 1968). For the emphasis on Thucydides at the Johanneum in the 1860's see O. Crusius, *Erwin Rohde: Ein biographischer Versuch* (Tübingen/Leipzig 1902) 5–6. As a Bonn student, Wilamowitz read privately Thuc. I–IV and VIII. For Meyer's admiration of Thucydides see especially *Forschungen* II. 368–400 and *Kl. Schr.* 67. Of the former Arnaldo Momigliano, *Studies in Historiography* (London 1966) 86 remarks: "Eduard Meyer expounded his historical method by an analysis of Thucydides."

[13] See Johannes Classen, *Barthold Georg Niebuhr: Eine Gedächtnissschrift zu seinem hundert-jährigen Geburtstag den 27. August 1876* (Gotha 1876) 2–3 and Wilcken, *apud* Marohl, 118–119. For the influence of Niebuhr on the schoolboy Meyer see Eduard Meyer, "Geschichte des wissenschaftlichen Vereins von 1817 an der Gelehrtenschule des Johanneums zu Hamburg," *Festschrift zur Feier seines hundertjährigen Bestehens* (Halle 1923) 48–49 (*non vidi*), cited at Christ (1), 287 n. 3. For his later praise of Niebuhr see *GdA* III².226–227. He was not immune to Niebuhr's faults: see *ibid.*, 473 n. 1.

[14] For the elder Meyer see Christ (1), 286 with n. 1. He had been an examiner of Wilamowitz' enemy, Erwin Rohde (1845–1898): see Crusius, *op. cit.* (*supra*, n. 12) 6 n. 1 (Christhard Hoffmann).

[15] *The Autobiography of John Stuart Mill*, ed. John Jacob Coss (New York 1944) 3: "And to this is to be added, that during the whole period, a considerable part of almost every day was employed in the instruction of his children: in the case of one of whom, myself, he exerted an amount of labour, care, and perseverance rarely, if ever, employed for a similar purpose, in endeavouring to give, according to his own conception, the highest order of intellectual education."

[16] See *Antiqua* 27 (Naples 1984) 134:

> Ich will ein Jünger der Wissenschaft werden, freiwillig, scheel angesehen von Verwandten, Nahestehenden, verstossen aus den vermeintlich höheren Kreisen, in welche die Geburt mich gestellt hat.

His marriage to a bourgeois woman in a ceremony which all his family boycotted continued this trend. An important and overlooked testimony are the words of the Baron Bunsen to Agricola on the death of Christian Gottlob Heyne (1729–1812) in his letter of 13 July 1813: "... he was too great for a mere philologer ...:" see Frances Baroness Bunsen, *A Memoir of Baron Bunsen* I (London 1868) 38.

in Italy and·first visit to Greece is well known.[17] By good luck Meyer became tutor in the family of the British consul general in Constantinople, Sir Philip Francis (1822 – 1876), where he lived for some eighteen months and accompanied the bereaved family to England.[18] He experienced the *bios politikos* intimately as a young scholar only rarely can. His observation of the dogs of Constantinople convinced him that in the history of mankind the state preceded the individual, a *Leitmotiv* of the *GdA*.[19] The

---

[17] See Wolfgang Schindler, *Wilamowitz nach 50 Jahren*. edd. William M. Calder III, Hellmut Flashar and Theodor Lindken (Darmstadt 1985) 246–252 (henceforth cited *Wilamowitz*).

[18] Meyer, *Skizze*, 10. Sir Philip Francis was a descendant of Sir Philip Francis (1740–1818), reputed author of "Junius' letters" and the friend of Robert Wood (1717?–1771): see *The Times* 12 August 1876, p. 11, a reference owed E. Badian. Meyer cites these letters at *England: Its Political Organization and Development and the War against Germany* (Boston 1916) 46. Meyer calls him (*ibid.*, 40): "a highly educated man who had studied in Germany and . . . a member of the radical reform party." He edited the letters of Boswell to W.J. Temple, etc. (1857) and published on Common Law. Meyer knew English well and roared with laughter at Johannes Vahlen's inability to converse in the language: see Henry Rushton Fairclough, *Warming both Hands* (Stanford 1941) 229 (Berlin 1910).

[19] The *locus classicus* is *GdA* I.1².7. Other travelers remarked upon self-government among the dogs of Constantinople. See Charles White, *Three Years in Constantinople; or domestic manners of the Turks in 1844* 3 (London 1845) 291:

> Although living in a sort of federal community, or republic—worthy emblem of that mode of government—the dogs appear to be divided into tribes, and to obey distinct chiefs. So tenacious are they of their peculiar territory and feeding-ground, that none can with impunity intrude upon the filth-heaps of others. When females produce young, they also breed up their whelps within their own district: so that the puppies soon learn to know their own territory, and to distinguish the dogs of their tribe, before they are compelled to shift for themselves.

Compare Josiah Brewer, *A Residence at Constantinople in the Year 1827* (New Haven 1830) 122:

> Like another class of privileged quarrelers, they are also not a little careful to maintain the *balance of power*. Should a stranger dog, trespass on territories not belonging to him, and threaten to become too formidable to those in his vicinity; the weaker party retires upon his neighbors, until they collect sufficient strength to drive back the intruder.

See further Lady Hornby, *Constantinople during the Crimean War* (London 1863) 48–49 and Anonymous, "The Dogs of Constantinople," *Chambers' Journal* NS 5 (26 April 1856) 267–268; esp. (268):

> . . . into this space there bounded one morning two dogs, giving chase to another which was wounded. Half-a-dozen dogs . . . sprang up upon witnessing this invasion of their frontiers, and threw themselves upon the enemy, which, after a furious conflict, they put to flight; the wounded dog meanwhile, shrinking into a corner and tremblingly awaiting his fate. The victors drew round him, and each smelt him in turn, and then they withdrew together, and appeared to be holding a council. One of them then left the others, and went up to the stranger, to which he put some questions, and being apparently satisfied with his answers, led him away to headquarters, where he was regaled with a bone. On the evening of the same day, he was enrolled as a member of the society.

For the final destruction of the dogs by trapping them and releasing them onto an island without water see *Forty Years in Constantinople: The recollections of Sir Edwin Pears 1873–1915 with 16 Illustrations* (New York 1916) 312. I am grateful to Mr. Ian Jackson (Berkeley) for

48 WILLIAM M. CALDER III

chance to learn English speech and manners fostered an "English [later American] connection" that made the sense of betrayal in 1914 all the more acute.[20] It was easier for Wilamowitz, whose favorite foreign country was neutral Denmark. Early marriage and his preference to use holidays for work limited Meyer's travel in the lands whose history he wrote and taught.[21] Wilamowitz never lectured on Thucydides VI–VII because he had never been to Syracuse.[22] Meyer wrote the history of Egypt and Palestine, lands he saw only in old age. Topography was decisive for the philologist. Both learned from their military service. Meyer less. He never served in wartime, detested drill and the monotony of service. Neither ever killed a man.

Finally they were joined by two great bonds. Wilamowitz could only have admired Meyer's utter devotion to his work. For both men scholarship formed the undisputed center of their lives. Their published bibliographies are proof of their industry. Before 1914 neither took more than an intelligent citizen's part in politics.[23] Wilamowitz in fact declined the offer of two parties to run for elective office in Greifswald in 1877. He thought the matter a joke.[24] The outbreak of World War I in August

---

these canine references. G. Huxley (Athens) adds Capt. Charles Colville Frankland, *Travels to and from Constantinople in the Years 1827 and 1828* I (London 1829) 106–108 for complaints of the dogs. Plato cites the analogy of dogs in explaining the nature of man: see *Rep* 2. 375e with Adam *ad loc.* (E. Schütrumpf).

[20] A moving reconciliation is recorded in Meyer's old age (autumn 1925) with James Breasted: see Charles Breasted, *op. cit.* (*supra*, n. 4) 386–387, where Meyer should be seventy years old and not seventy-two. Charles Breasted describes Meyer in 1904/05 (128) as "a wiry, inflexible giant with a brown beard, massive head, thick gold-rimmed spectacles, frock coat, bull-of Bashan voice and Olympian laughter—at heart a kindly and engaging human being ..." For Meyer's stentorian voice compare Dessoir, *op. cit.* (*supra*, n. 9) 193: "Da rief Meyer mit seiner Bärenstimme." For Meyer in the context of German historians of the time see Charles E. McClelland, "The End of Anglophilia," *The German Historians and England: A Study in Nineteenth-Century Views* (Cambridge 1971) 159–236; for Eduard Meyer: 226. The Oxford ancient historian, G.B. Grundy, whose guest at Corpus Meyer had been shortly before the war, alleges that Meyer in print "accused all the women of England of being prostitutes:" see G.B. Grundy, *Fifty-five Years at Oxford: An Unconventional Autobiography* (London 1945) 152. I have been unable to find the passage and suspect slander. The great document for divided loyalties during World War I remains: Evelyn, Princess Blücher, *An English Wife in Berlin: A Private Memoir of Events, Politics, and Daily Life in Germany throughout the War and the Social Revolution of 1918*[8] (London 1920).

[21] Meyer, *Skizze*, 11; cf. Christ (1), 289–290.

[22] Wilamowitz, *Erinnerungen*[2], 168.

[23] In this as in other matters I see Wilamowitz' friendship with Meyer similar to his with Eduard Schwartz: see William M. Calder III and Robert L. Fowler, "The Preserved Letters of Ulrich von Wilamowitz to Eduard Schwartz Edited with Introduction and Commentary," *Sitzungsberichte der Bayerischen Akademie der Wissenschaften philos.-hist. Klasse* Heft 1 (1986) 12–18 ("What drew Wilamowitz to Schwartz?"). That Schwartz had attended Wilamowitz' lectures in Greifswald added an element of loyalty and concern for Schwartz' career obviously lacking for Meyer.

[24] Wilamowitz, *Erinnerungen*[2], 192–193.

1914 immediately politicized both scholars. Their war speeches were published and never retracted.[25] One must not forget that each was rector at what from hindsight were unfortunate years. Wilamowitz declined[26] to be rector for the Jubilee Year 1909/10 and urged Erich Schmidt (1853 – 1913), the Germanist and Pforte Old Boy, on the pretext that he was *salonfähig* and an eloquent speaker. But he could not avoid the task forever and served 1914/15. This required official speeches which he would not have made otherwise. One should perhaps recall the picture of his weeping as his students went off to war.[27] Meyer was rector (1919/20) during the most difficult year in the University's history until the equally difficult rectorship of Johannes Stroux (1886 – 1954) in 1946/47. Their official duties necessarily intensified a nationalistic tendency that already was there.[28] Each lost his eldest son and Meyer his younger in the struggle. After the armistice Wilamowitz naturally supported Meyer's founding of the *Notgemeinschaft*.[29] He did not, however, like Meyer refuse to have any further dealings with Americans or Englishmen. The philologist was more forgiving than the historian.[30]

---

[25] See Eduard Meyer, *Weltgeschichte* and Ulrich von Wilamowitz-Moellendorff, *Reden aus der Kriegszeit* (Berlin 1915). For discussion of these writings and an Italian translation of some of them see Luciano Canfora, *Cultura classica e crisi tedesca: Gli scritti politici di Wilamowitz 1914–1931* (Bari 1977) with the review of Wolfgang Buchwald, *Gnomon* 51 (1979) 780–782. It is instructive to recall that even a theologian (rector 1918/1919) contributed to the genre: see Reinhold Seeberg, *Geschichte, Krieg und Seele: Reden und Aufsätze aus den Tagen des Weltkriegs* (Leipzig 1916). The Delphic inscription on the monument for Berlin university graduates fallen in World War I (*invictis victi victuri*), dedicated 10 July 1926, was not composed by Wilamowitz as Reinhart Koselleck, "Kriegerdenkmäler als Identitätsstiftungen der Überlebenden," *Identität, Poetik und Hermeneutik* 8, edd. Odo Marquardt and Karlheinz Stierle (Munich 1979) 263, holds, but by Seeberg: see Bux-Schöne-Lamer, *Wörterbuch der Antike* (Leipzig 1933) 347 and Günther Brakelmann, *Protestantische Kriegsideologie im Ersten Weltkrieg: Reinhold Seeberg als Theologe des deutschen Imperialismus* (Bielefeld 1974) with a useful bibliography at pp. 208–222. The inscription is cited by Friedrich Zucker, *Klassisches Altertum und deutsche Bildung* (Jena 1934) 5 with the remark "Ist diese Inschrift etwa undeutsch, weil sie lateinisch ist?" For Seeberg's funeral oration for Meyer see Reinhold Seeberg, *Rede gehalten bei der Beerdigung Eduard Meyers am 3. September 1930* (Stuttgart 1930).

[26] Unpublished letter of Wilamowitz to Hermann Diels (15 January [1909?]) in the Archive of the Akademie der Wissenschaften der DDR (NL-Diels Nr. 3). This will be included in the forthcoming edition edited by Calder-Ehlers.

[27] For Wilamowitz weeping as students leave the university to do battle on 3 August 1914 see Agnes von Zahn-Harnack, *Adolf von Harnack*[2] (Berlin 1951) 345 and for his weeping uncontrollably at the suicide of a young officer in November 1918 see Alois Brandl, *Zwischen Inn und Themse: Lebensbeobachtungen eines Anglisten Alt-Tirol/England/Berlin* (Berlin 1936) 331–332.

[28] I draw attention to the beautiful publication: *Die Rektoren der Humboldt-Universität zu Berlin*, edd. Friedrich Herneck et al. (Halle 1966) 176–177 (Wilamowitz), 184–185 (Meyer).

[29] See the authoritative discussion of W. Unte, *infra*.

[30] Meyer made his view absolutely clear to both Breasted and Grundy: see Breasted,

I have tried to sketch the similarities and differences between the two men. I have avoided the question what precisely distinguished the philologist from the ancient historian. Wilamowitz and Meyer were colleagues for almost thirty years. Wilamowitz was the greatest Hellenist of modern times. Meyer—if one excludes Mommsen as a "Roman historian"—the greatest German historian of antiquity. How did they differ in their approaches to their subject? From a modern point of view Wilamowitz is far more an historian than what American classicists call "a literary critic." The *locus classicus* for his historicism is in his edition of *Lysistrate*.[31] The critic must become a member of the play's original audience. "Endlich muß das Gedicht, das für eine Stunde bestimmt ist, erst als das verstanden sein, was es in diesem Momente sein wollte, ehe man es auf seinen absoluten Wert hin betrachtet." My teacher, Werner Jaeger (1888–1961), wrote of Eduard Meyer:[32]

> Eduard Meyer war zwar kein Humanist, der der eigenen Zeit die idealen Geisteswerte der Vergangenheit in Kunst und Philosophie als höchste Maßstäbe vorhält. Er war ganz historischer Realist, und die Quellen lesen, das hieß für ihn: rücksichtslos die geistige Form, in der die Geschichte überliefert ist, wie eine Maske abstreifen und sie in die Realität des noch gärenden Lebensvorgangs zurückübersetzen.

---

op. cit. (supra, n. 20) 325, 386 and Grundy, *op. cit. (supra,* n. 20) 152 (December 1919). For Wilamowitz' forgiveness of Americans see his noble letter of 29 October 1920 to his American student Edward Fitch at *Antiqua* 23 (1983) 82–83, a remarkable contrast to Meyer's curt note to Breasted. Meyer was as *borniert* as Paul Shorey while Wilamowitz shared the magnanimity of B.L. Gildersleeve. Scholarship must be above politics. The Pindaric belief of the aristocrat in the supranational chivalry of his class was also a factor. Recall Wilhelm II's bewilderment when King George V, yielding to the demagogues, removed his cousin from the Order of the Garter: see Tyler Whittle, *The Last Kaiser: A Biography of Wilhelm II German Emperor and King of Prussia* (New York 1977) 277–278. Comparable is Wilamowitz' rage when the French expelled him from their Academy: see *Erinnerungen*[2], 316.

In June 1920 my teacher, the New Testament scholar, Henry Joel Cadbury (1883–1974), then part of a Friends relief group in Germany, met Adolf Harnack in Berlin. I cite Margaret Hope Bacon, *Let This Life Speak: The Legacy of Henry Joel Cadbury* (Philadelphia 1987) 60:

> Adolf von Harnack asked gruffly, "Why do Americans want to talk with us before they have made peace?" He was affable to Henry Cadbury, however, asking about his Harvard colleagues and saying that the Quaker work was making a deep impression on German hearts and minds. He also praised Henry Cadbury's article "The Basis of Early Christian Antimilitarism."

[31] Ulrich von Wilamowitz-Moellendorff, *Aristophanes Lysistrate* (Berlin 1927) 5 and see his letter to Stenzel of 26 February 1931 at *Antiqua* 23 (Naples 1983) 277–278, the last proclamation of his unrepentant historicism.

[32] Ulrich Wilcken and Werner Jaeger, *Eduard Meyer zum Gedächtnis: Zwei Reden* (Stuttgart/Berlin 1931) 27. Jaeger did not chose to have this address reprinted in his *Humanistische Reden und Vorträge*.

Jaeger wrote of Ulrich von Wilamowitz-Moellendorff:[33]

> Zwei Seelen rangen in seiner Brust unaufhörlich miteinander: der Historiker, der nichts anderes wissen will als was gewesen ist, und der Humanist und Philologe, der anbeten und verkünden muß was groß und ewig ist.

Is Jaeger right? What did Wilamowitz and Meyer themselves say? I think that several new documents may clarify their differences. I shall edit these and then draw attention to what they said of each other publicly during their lifetimes. I shall then try to summarize the differences.

II. The New Documents

Forty-one letters of Ulrich von Wilamowitz-Moellendorff, dated 1886–1926, to Eduard Meyer are preserved in the Eduard Meyer *Nachlaß* in the archive of the Akademie der Wissenschaften der DDR in Berlin. Four personal letters, one of Wilamowitz to Meyer and three of Marie Mommsen to Rosine Meyer, are preserved in West Berlin.[34] One letter of Meyer to Wilamowitz is preserved in the Wilamowitz *Nachlaß* in Göttingen.[35] The 41 letters in the Academy are distributed in eight files within the *Nachlaß*.[36] The most important are the 26 filed under No. 1354.

---

[33] Werner Jaeger, *Humanistische Reden und Vorträge*[2] (Berlin 1960) 219.

[34] Of Marie to Rosine there are: 1. 18 February 1915 (congratulations on the engagement of her daughter, Mathilde); 2. 8 May 1915 (sympathy for Herbert missing in action); 3. 23 May 1915 (sympathy for Mathilde's broken engagement). All letters have a black border because of the death of Tycho. On 17 May ⟨1915⟩ Wilamowitz wrote a letter of sympathy to Meyer on the death of Herbert in battle.

[35] Wilamowitz *Nachlaß* No. 853. One letter of Meyer to Wilamowitz (1921) survives. The others were presumably destroyed by thieves in winter 1945/46: see *Antiqua* 23 (1983) 7 with n. 37.

[36] Wilamowitz' 41 letters and postcards to Meyer are divided within the *Nachlaß* as follows:

No. 130: one postcard (6 November 1912): thanks for *Ursprung und Anfänge des Christentums*.

No. 160: one postcard (18 February 1912): thanks for *Der Papyrusfund von Elephantine*.

No. 255: three letters (12 August ⟨1915⟩; 31 December ⟨1915⟩; 1 January 1916): Unterlagen des archäologischen Seminars der Universität Berlin.

No. 276: two letters (1922–1923): requests for financial support through the *Notgemeinschaft* for Hiller's index to Dittenberger ed.[3]. I was unable to find the originals in November 1987.

No. 307: two letters, two postcards, an undated list of program suggestions (10 July 1907; 4 April 1908; 17 April 1908; 27 April 1908): International Historical Congress.

No. 328: one undated letter (1915?): Meyers Stellung zum 1. Weltkrieg (thanks for *England*).

No. 330: two letters (25 July 1916; 7 July 1917).

No. 1354: 26 letters (31 October 1866–7 June 1927).

They are written to Meyer the scholar and are more revealing, although
never intimate, than those on academic business. Five of them are undated.[37] With "business letters" I am not concerned. Of the 26 I edit
here three which I think are of more than specialist interest. I am grateful
to Professor Dr. Joachim Herrmann, Director of the Zentralinstitut für
Alte Geschichte und Archäologie, Akademie der Wissenschaften der
DDR (*per litt.* 7 March 1988), for owner's permission to publish the following three letters and to the late Dr. Wolfgang Mommsen for permission to publish his uncle's letters.

1. Hochgeehrter herr college,

Ihr freundlicher brief über mein buch[38] war so inhaltreich, und ich fühle
das lebhafte verlangen, darüber mit Ihnen zu disputiren; das ist leider
nicht möglich, aber ein par worte möchte ich doch erwidern.

  Zuerst daß ich alles was Sie über Staatsrecht und Geschichte sagen,
vollkommen unterschreibe; es ist sehr schön formulirt, und daß es in
betreff Roms ausgeführt würde, wünschte ich dringend.[39] wir müssen,
weil wir den ewigen fluß der dinge in der geschichte verfolgen, auch
darüber hinweg kommen: das recht ist in der geschichte was die analogie
in der grammatik ist. wir wissen ja, daß sie für die concrete sprachgeschichte und ihre erzeugnisse nicht ausreicht, aber was wären wir ohne
sie? in der griechischen geschichte fehlt zur zeit noch die einfachste grammatik. ein einzelbeamter in dem Athen des 5. jhdts, cumulirung diverser
bürgerrechte, confundirung deliberativer und executiver gewalten sind
an der tagesordnung. da meine ich, muß erst die grammatik geschaffen
werden, und dabei sind wir, die wir jetzt leben, ganz wesentlich beschäftigt. Sie, gott sei dank, auch.[40] eine einfache bemerkung, wie daß

---

[37] Letters 22–26 are undated. No. 22 is a postcard whose cancellation is illegible on
the photocopy. Dated ca. 1922/23, it concerns the *Notgemeinschaft* and inflationary sums
of money. No. 23 supplements No. 21 (7 June 1927) and may be dated June 1927. No. 24
mentions Tycho's wounded eye and hence is dated January 1908: see Calder-Fowler,
op. cit. (*supra*, n. 23) 77 n. 354. A letter of Grenfell is included. No. 25 is thanks for Meyer's
Die Israeliten und ihre Nachbarstämme. Alttestamentliche Untersuchungen (Halle 1906) and should
therefore be dated to that year. No. 26 ends with "gutes Glück für Belgien" but I do
not know when or if Meyer visited that country. It answers queries of Meyer (largely
Homeric). It is written from Eichenallée and should therefore be pre-1914 but post-1898.
[38] The situation is presumably that Meyer has received a review copy of *Aristoteles und
Athen* 2 vols (Berlin 1893) and has begun to read it. He writes Wilamowitz praising the
work and sends him a copy of *Forschungen* I. Wilamowitz' letter consists largely of his reaction to Meyer's book.
[39] Here Wilamowitz refers to the lost letter of Meyer. He is in full agreement with
everything that Meyer writes about public law and history. He would much like to see that
it be done for Rome.
[40] No book of Greek laws is preserved. The Greeks never developed legal scholarship:

die ephoren zunächst richterliche beamte sind, braucht man ja nur zu verfolgen, um gott weiß wie viele tollheiten los zu werden.[41] mit dem heftesten interesse habe ich Ihre behandlung der lokrischen bronzen[42] gelesen, über die ich auch schreiben wollte; teils haben Sie dasselbe gesagt, teils besseres: es ist fast zu viel, was Ihre behandlung der kleinen[43] lehrt, aber ich kann noch nichts gegen Sie finden. (bei der anderen habe ich einige stärkere einwände, aber ich muß es erst neu durchdenken). daß Sie zur exegese geführt sind, hat mir gerade die überzeugung gestärkt, daß wir in denselben bahnen wandeln,[44] und wie Sie das staatsrecht beurteilen, bin ich eben ganz Ihrer meinung.

Daß Ephoros kenntlich wäre und reconstruirbar, habe ich vor 20 jahren geglaubt,[45] und vor 15 auch.[46] damals hieß es, daß Müllenhoff[47] ihn herstellen lassen wollte. jetzt gestehe ich, auch Ihrer zusicherung gegenüber skeptisch zu sein. diese frage heißt wol in wahrheit Diodor: und wenn ich die habe an buch IV–V angreifen lassen, so schrecke ich vor XI–XX immer mehr zurück.[48] wenn jemand Ephoros anpacken wollte, gewiß würde er vieles finden, aber an dem den ich einst zu haben meinte, bin ich irr geworden, und einen anderen habe ich nicht.[49]

Was Thukydides anlangt, so habe ich zwar noch einen trumpf in der

---

see *Aristoteles*, I. 380 ("Eine Rechtswissenschaft fehlt den Athenern und den Hellenen überhaupt freilich …"). Philologists made up for the lack. Things were better by 1923 because of systematic classification of literary evidence (Schoemann-Lipsius) and the accumulation of epigraphic (e.g., Gortyn) and papyrological material: see Wilamowitz, *Staat*².213.

[41] A reference to Meyer, *Forschungen* I. 252 n. 1.

[42] A reference to Meyer, *Forschungen* I. 287–316 ("Drei lokrische Gesetze"). Meyer elucidates and translates three difficult early Locrian inscriptions, 362 Schwyzer (291–305) and 363 Schwyzer (307–316). The detailed work is more philological than historical. See *infra*, n. 109.

[43] That is 363 Schwyzer. Wilamowitz never published a separate discussion of these texts but in 1927 discussed a newly discovered one: see *KS* 5.1.467–480.

[44] It was axiomatic for Wilamowitz that philology was interpretation. That is what Meyer is doing and, therefore, he is a fellow philologist. See *Aristoteles*, I. vi: "denn die schönste aufgabe der Philologie ist das interpretiren."

[45] See n. 47 *infra*.

[46] Wilamowitz, *Kydathen*, 115 n. 27, where he reassigns *FGrHist* 70 F 97.

[47] Apparently a reference to Karl Müllenhoff, *Tacitus, Germania antiqua. Libellum post Maur. Hauptium cum aliorum veterum auctorum locis de Germania praecipuis* (Berlin 1873). *non vidi* but the book appeared in 1873 ("vor 20 jahren"), Wilamowitz shared in it (*Praefatio*, iv) and Müllenhoff is mentioned by name.

[48] The numerical references are to the books of Diodorus not to the lost books of Ephoros. *angreifen* is difficult but is what Wilamowitz wrote.

[49] "If anyone should want to tackle Ephoros, he would certainly find a lot; but I have lost my confidence in the Ephoros I once thought I had; and I don't have another." For later views of Ephoros see especially Wilamowitz' student, Felix Jacoby on *FGrHist* 70 and G.L. Barber, *The Historian Ephorus* (Cambridge 1935), a book innocent of both Meyer and Wilamowitz.

hand; ich bin vor dem fund des Aristoteles schon zu meiner ansicht gekommen,[50] aber wahrscheinlich ist es nur der ausdruck, in dem wir differiren. und die litterarische schätzung kommt wol bei mir stärker, vielleicht störend, bei der historischen dazu.[51]

Natürlich bin ich äusserst gespannt auf Ihren zweiten band,[52] die religionsgeschichte (ich habe mich bisher nur mit dem plane getragen, die religion des VI/V jhdts darzustellen, weil ich den Götter krimskrams der "mythologie" nicht ausstehen kann)[53] und die differenzen—oder vielmehr das bild, das Sie von der ältesten zeit,[54] der völkerwanderung, zeichnen werden. Ich habe doch auch da eine basis der gemeinsamen ansicht 1) die griechische geschichte bis 500 hat ihr centrum in Asien, dort sind die collectiven stammbegriffe entstanden, auch die der Hellenen.[55] 2) die wirkliche überlieferung ist in den Epen und zwar allen, bis zu den jungen ausläufern, Danais und Alkmeonis herab[56] 3) staat und religion

---

[50] Wilamowitz triumphantly refers to "Die Thukydideslegende," *Hermes* 12 (1877) 328 n. 1 = *KS* 3. 3 n. 1: "Platon und Aristoteles ignorieren ihn geflissentlich." With this compare *Aristoteles* I. 99: "Den Thukydides nennt die Politie nirgend. ich hatte schon früher darauf hingewiesen, daß die übrigen schriften des Aristoteles ebensowenig wie die des Platon ... eine spur seiner benutzung zeigen, von der viel gefabelt worden ist und trotz dem augenschein gefabelt wird." See further *Greek Historical Writing and Apollo* (Oxford 1908; repr. Chicago 1979) 19: ... "he [Plato] never read Thucydides." This is only true if one denies the authenticity of *Menexenus*: see Charles H. Kahn, *CP* 58 (1963) 220 – 234. Wilamowitz' contention that Plato nowhere reveals knowledge will not bear scrutiny: see Schmidt-Stählin, *GGL* I.5.2. 208 – 211; Vincenzo Costanzi, "Una probabile concordanza tra Tucidide e Platone," *RFIC* 32 (1904) 225 – 230 (reference owed E.C. Kopff); Max Pohlenz, *Platons Werdezeit* (Berlin 1913) 238 – 256; Paul Shorey, *What Plato Said* (Chicago/London 1933; repr. 1968) 2 – 3, 8, 447 (with literature there cited). The most obvious citation is Th. 3.82.4 – 5 at Pl. *Rep* 8.580c – d. Eckart Schütrumpf would compare Pl. *Rep* 6.488d4 with Th. 2.40.2. He further suggests at Arist. *AthPol* 34.2 an echo of Th. 8.24.5.

[51] Contrast Wilamowitz, *Aristoteles*, I.99 – 120 with Meyer, *Forschungen* I. 120 – 123.

[52] In the lost letter Meyer announced the imminent appearance of *GdA* II, which indeed within a fortnight he sent to Wilamowitz (see letter 2 *infra*).

[53] For Wilamowitz' long preoccupation with *Religionsgeschichte* see the exemplary study of Albert Henrichs, *Wilamowitz*, 263 – 305. His publications of 1870 – 1885 contain almost nothing on the subject (Henrichs, 269); but his most important and persistent ideas ripened during the Göttingen period (Henrichs, 273). This explains his keen interest in anything that Meyer might say. The reference to "mythologie" is polemic against Max Müller and Usener: see especially *Herakles* I³.xv – xvi with the remarks of Henrichs, 282 with nn. 97, 98.

[54] Wilamowitz is especially interested in the prehistoric period, which Meyer with his knowledge of the oriental languages presumably controlled. Except for Schliemann of whom Wilamowitz was highly sceptical (see *Antiqua* 27 [1984] 229 – 234), the great sites (e.g., Knossos) were not yet excavated. This meant a far greater dependence on epic than one would allow today.

[55] By 1923, largely because of archaeological discoveries, Wilamowitz' views had broadened: see *Staat*².4 – 27.

[56] Similarly the new discoveries modified Wilamowitz' view of the uniqueness of Homer. Homer became just part of the evidence. One sees the change clearly in *Das homerische Epos* (Berlin 1927).

gehören unlösbar zu sammen.[57] sonst wollen wir nur ruhig unsere gebiete
neben einander stellen: anders geht es zur zeit nicht. daß man aber sich
ein ganzes gebiet errichtet, nicht bloss mit trümmerbrocken hantiert, das
ist die hauptsache. und gerade wenn wir ganz weit auseinander gehen
oder so scheinen, hoffe ich, wird es der wissenschaft am besten frommen.
ganz soweit wie Sokrates bin ich noch nicht, zu sagen ἐγὼ μέν εἰμι τῶν
ἡδέως μὲν ἐλεγχόντων ἥδιον δὲ ἐλεγχορένων,[58] aber ich weiß, daß das das
ziel ist, zu dem man kommen soll. und da ich eben über Herodot vor-
trage, sehe ich, daß ich mich, wesentlich durch Ihre schärfe und klarheit,
ganz artig dazu anschicke, alte eingewurzelte meinungen mit den wurzeln
auszuroden.[59]

> und so fortan
>   mit besten grüßen
>   Ihr sehr ergebener

Gött. 4 XI 93.   UvWilamowitz

2. Hochgeehrter herr college,

Ihr buch habe ich erhalten,[60] gleich mich darin verbissen, so daß ich
ganz dumm im kopfe im colleg und bei den mahlzeiten erschien und auch
im schlafe immer davon occupirt war. dann hab'ichs zum buchbinder
geschickt, um zu atem zu kommen. und doch kann ich Ihnen nur danken,
nicht eigentlich etwas sagen. das synchronistische prinzip ist vortrefflich:
daß Sie dafür eintreten und schon hier das Italien des VI jahrhunderts
zeichnen, ist dem wesen so überraschend wie erfreulich.[61] vom aufbau
sonst habe ich deshalb keine klare vorstellung, weil ich da zu viel an dem
einzelnen haften blieb.[62] aber daß Sie mit dem schema brechen würden,

---

[57] This view Wilamowitz retained until his death, although allowing place too for "the
individual religion of the heart." The *locus classicus* is *Glaube* I[2].12–17.

[58] A paraphrase of Pl. *Gorgias* 458a3 ff.

[59] The reference is to Meyer, *Forschungen* I. 151–202. In WS 1893/94 he lectured on
"Quellenkunde der griech. Geschichte:" see Hiller-Klaffenbach, *Bibliographie*, 78. There
he must have treated Herodotus. The sentiment is a further example of Wilamowitz'
famous "umzulernen stets bereit:" see *KS* 1. 466 = *DLZ* 47 (1926) 854 and compare
(1931) "und da ich dankbar bereit zu lernen" at *Antiqua* 23 (1983) 278. It recalls his
definition of the philologist as "uir bonus discendi peritus:" see *AJP* 108 (1987) 168–171.

[60] Meyer has sent Wilamowitz *GdA* II (Stuttgart 1893): see *supra*, n. 52. I cite the later
edition = *GdA* III[2] (Stuttgart 1937). Wilamowitz' enthusiasm is undisguised. For receipt
of an exciting book (Cairo Menander) that caused Wilamowitz to interrupt his lectures
and discuss it see Eduard Frankel, *apud* Friedrich Leo, *Ausgewählte kleine Schriften* I (Rome
1960) xxxii n. 1. The script reveals that the letter was hurriedly *j*written.

[61] Wilamowitz refers to *GdA* III[2].451–491 ("Anfänge der Geschichte Italiens").

[62] Quintessentially philological, preference for detail over the whole; but I wonder
whether Wilamowitz is not being ironic.

wusste ich zwar,[63] und ich würde wol auch so disponiren. Die gewalt, mit der Sie das detail bezwungen haben, und die entschiedene erklärung, daß der moderne nicht breite und kürze von der zufällig erhaltenen über-lieferung abhängig machen darf (wie Niese[64] jetzt wieder so erzählt, daß man Diodor darunter spürt) hat meinen beifall um so mehr, als ich be-stimmt weiß, daß ich's nicht übers herz bringen würde.

Ich sehe das ganze an als ein buch mit dem ich immer rechnen werde, teils mich freuend gemeinsamer anschauung, wie über das epos und die hinter ihm liegende realität, teils damit ringend, sicher bald zu überwin-den, bald überwunden zu werden—ζυνὸς Ἐνωάλιος.[65] ein unterschied wird bleiben: Sie halten die gegenwart für fähig, eine griechische geschichte zu schreiben. ich habe das negirt.[66] wo man von der zukunft keine vermehrung der kenntnis hoffen kann, weder durch zuwachs noch durch forschung, wie z.b. in Sparta.[67] nur da kann man's eben jetzt so gut wie später. aber selbst über Rom würde ich nicht zur inneren beru-higung kommen, wenn ich nicht von der chronologie etwas zuverläs-

---

[63] *zwar* has been inadvertantly almost entirely blotted out.

[64] Benedictus Niese, "Geschichte der griechischen und makedonischen Staaten seit der Schlacht bei Chaeronea I. Teil: Geschichte Alexanders des Grossen und seiner Nach-folger und der Westhellenen bis zum Jahre 281 v. Chr.," *Handbücher der Alten Geschichte II. Serie. Zweite Abteilung: Geschichte der griechischen und makedonischen Staaten seit der Schlacht bei Chaeronea 1. Teil* (Gotha 1893).

[65] *Iliad* 18.309.

[66] The irony and, therefore, the excitement with which Wilamowitz greets Meyer's book derive from the fact that it appeared in the same year that Wilamowitz published his view that it was not yet time to write a history of Greece. A Greek historian could not write a history of institutions as Th. Mommsen had of Rome. *Staatsrecht* did not exist for the Greeks. "das recht der Hellenen steckt in der philosophie" (*Aristoteles*, I.380). One must reconstruct Greek constitutional history (403–322), which means the reconstruction of Aristotle's lost constitutions, from the orators and inscriptions "mit allen mitteln" (Welcker's *Totalitätsideal*) and go forwards from them and backwards from Rome ending in the attempt to reconstruct the constitutions and bureaucracies of the Hellenistic monar-chies. His negation is (*Aristoteles*, 379–380): "wenn das ergebnis der kritik ist, daß es keine verfassungsgeschichte Athens gibt, so sollte man doch meinen, daß es sehr überflüssig wäre, athenische geschichte zu treiben." See further on this theme the important intro-ductory pages at *Staat*².1–4. Compare Ettore Pais' (1856–1939) doubt at "La storia antica negli ultimi cinquant'anni," *Rivista d'Italia* 14 (1911) 707–708, that an exact his-tory of ancient peoples could be written. I cite the translation of Ronald T. Ridley, "Ettore Pais," *Helikon* 15/16 (1975/76) 522:

> It is debatable if, in the present state of our knowledge, we can today write a real, exact history of ancient peoples. What has come down to us is often not synchronous material, has too frag-mentary a nature, and represents in many cases partisan bias. The historical evidence we pos-sess does not in fact have direct relationship with its essential importance, but with artistic, for-mal, or even purely chance causes which have determined its preservation.

[67] Wilamowitz could not foresee the importance of the British excavations at Sparta and Laconia (especially the Temple of Artemis Orthia) begun in 1906 but not fully published until 1929: see Helen Waterhouse, *The British School at Athens: The First Hundred Years* (London 1986) 105–107.

sigeres wüßte.[68] denn bloß Diodors ämterliste, das ist mir zu wenig. es ist aber gut, daß die temperamente und die begabungen verschieden sind,[69] und so begrüße ich Ihr buch mit freude und werde den erfolg, den es haben muß, fördern so viel ich kann, auch durch dissens.

Ich will aber keine einzelfrage anrühren; sehr gern würde ich's mündlich[70] tun, schriftlich würde es endlos und wahrhaft fördernd könnte doch nur ein διαλέγεσθαι sein, das in den wichtigsten stücken auf die grundprinzipien zurückgriffe. Mich zieht es mächtig zu den poeten, die ich so lange habe fallen lassen müssen;[71] wenn ich aber wieder mal zur historie zurückkehre, sollen Sie sehen, wie viel ich bei Ihnen gelernt haben werde.

Ihr dankbar ergebener

UvWilamowitz

Gött. 13 XI 93

3. Hochgeehrter herr college,

Schönen dank für die freundlichen zeilen, mit denen Sie mir Ihre besprechung zusenden.[72] wenn jemand ehrlich ausspricht, was er von mir und meiner arbeit hält, der sache zu liebe, so wie ich selbst es tue, so wird mir nie in den sinn kommen, es ihm zu verübeln. ist es vollends ein ebenbürtiger, der eine ansicht sich selbst erworben hat, so ist es mir sehr lieb, wenn er diese ansicht der meinen gegenüberstellt. ich werde mir's gewiß auf das gewissen nehmen, was er an dem aussetzt, was und wie ich schrieb. also daß Sie es so gemacht haben, weil Sie so urteilen, das weckt mir nur die sympathie, oder erhöht sie: denn ich habe sie längst empfunden.[73]

---

[68] For progress see A.H. McDonald, "Fifty Years of Republican History," *JRS* 50 (1960) 135–148; for chronology, 138–139, culminating in the work of the Canadian-American, T.R.S. Broughton.

[69] He does not specify the differences which (see *Grundprinzipien, infra*) he considers largely methodological, that is, the way in which evidence is treated. But he greets what he sees as an Hegelian progression.

[70] That he would prefer an oral exchange of views could suggest that by 1893 they had met.

[71] The discovery of the *AthPol* and the need to teach ancient history at Greifswald (*Erinnerungen*², 192) and to examine in it at Greifswald and Göttingen (*Erinnerungen*², 195) have long kept Wilamowitz from his first love, the poets. The production of the ensuing years documents his return to them, the tragedians, Callimachus, Bacchylides, and others.

[72] Wilamowitz acknowledges receipt of Meyer's review of *Aristoteles und Athen* in *Literarisches Centralblatt für Deutschland* 45 (1894) 75–81. This letter is Wilamowitz' rebuttal. He had received the review 13 January: see *Briefe-Mommsen*, 486.

[73] The chivalrous *captatio benevolentiae* welcomes the honest criticism of an equal who is

Sachlich dagegen meine ich in meinen stiefeln leidlich fest zu stehen und höre nur eine abweichende und nach meiner ansicht falsche meinung vorgetragen. nicht selten ist es eine, die mich, ehe ich der sache tiefer auf den grund gegangen war, auch gelockt hatte; eine solche kann mich wirklich nicht schrecken. ob die worte des Theramenes nicht ein apophthegma sein könnten, habe ich wirklich auch überlegt: aber die interpretation der parallelen stellen gestattet es nicht.[74] wenn ich im dritten capitel σημεῖον ἐπιφέρουσι lese, so weiß ich, daß dieses raisonnement von Aristoteles andern entlehnt ist, die also die von Ihnen gespendeten lobsprüche für sich fordern. von seinem standpunkte ist die erweiterung der macht des archons nicht 'νεωστί' geschehen.[75] Wenn Sie den anfangsteil herstellen, à la bonheur: ich kann nicht mehr geben als die fragmente und muß abwarten, wo mehr material steckt.[76] Auf das siebente jahrhundert habe ich außer der beamtenliste die Atthis nicht erstreckt, vielmehr das zeitliche verhältnis von Kylon und Drakon offen gelassen, das Sie in Ihrer geschichte fixiren.[77] also bezieht sich II 40 auf die zustände, auf die verfassung; Sie haben in Ihrer geschichte dem gecken Beloch[78] sehr viele auf

---

stating his opinion openly. Wilamowitz will remove his gloves but without ill feeling. A contrast is implied: see *Erinnerungen*², 196, especially: "Es ist jetzt einerlei, was damals wider mich geschrieben und noch mehr geredet worden ist, aber dazu zu schweigen kostete Überwindung." We must remember that if it had been up to the colleagues the greatest Greek scholar of Germany would never have been professor at Greifswald, Göttingen or Berlin! For the scandalous circumstances of the Göttingen appointment see *SIFC* NS 3, 3 (1985) 136–160. Only Sauppe behaved honorably. Wilamowitz named his second son after him: see *Philologus* 129 (1985) 286–298.

[74] Wilamowitz at *Aristoteles*, I.165 writes of the citation of Theramenes at *AthPol* 36.2: "es kann sich immer noch um ein apophthegma handeln, das im gedächtnis geblieben war." But he dismisses the possibility because of the context of its reappearance at X. *Hell.* 2.3.19. He prefers that the source is an oligarchic pamphlet by Theramenes. Meyer at *LCB* 45 (1894) 76 suggests that both Xenophon and Aristotle's source heard Theramenes say it. That is that it was a remembered apophthegma and one need not postulate the pamphlet. Wilamowitz trumps him with a philological appeal to parallels.

[75] Wilamowitz cites *AthPol* 3.3 [= 2.9–10 Kaibel-Wilamowitz (ed.1)]. In their third edition (1898) they read τεκμήριον δ'ἐπιφέρουσιν with the later editors. The verbal change does not affect his point, i.e. that Aristotle's proof is borrowed from his source. The second philological difficulty is to how remote a time may the temporal adverb νεωστί (*AthPol* 3.3 = 2.7 Chambers) refer. The change could not possibly be "recent" to Aristotle and so the adverb must derive from his source.

[76] The lost beginning of the *AthPol* would have occupied four to six pages of the Berlin papyrus: see M.H. Chambers, *TAPA* 98 (1967) 63–65 and for an attempt at reconstruction based on the preserved fragments see P.J. Rhodes, *A Commentary on the Aristotelian Athenaion Politeia* (Oxford 1981) 65–79 (henceforth cited: Rhodes). Wilamowitz' complaint is that the historian underestimates the difficulty of any convincing reconstruction.

[77] At *Aristoteles* II. 55–56, Wilamowitz leaves the chronological relationship of Cylon and Draco open with the implication that Draco followed Cylon. Meyer, *GdA* III².591 with n. 1 sets the exile of Cylon "etwa 636 oder 632." He dates Draco's revision of the laws (*ibid.*, 593) to 624 BC. The canonical Greek date for Draco was 621/0: for details see Rhodes *ad AthPol* 4.1.

[78] The chief source for the life of Karl Julius Alwin Beloch (1854–1929) is his autobio-

seiner profunden ignoranz beruhenden behauptungen geglaubt, darunter die verwerfung von Peisistratos dreifacher tyrannis:[79] für diese kritik gibt es überhaupt keine begründung als *car tel est mon plaisir*. Sie beloben Schäfers chronologie der Pentekonta⟨e⟩tie, die mit wiederholten änderungen der archontennamen verbunden ist, und von zahlen bei Thukydides, die Ephoros gelesen hat.[80] Unmöglich kann mir da der einwurf eindruck machen, daß ich im vierten capitel des Aristoteles eine Zahl ändere.[81] Wie Schäfer, m. Er. ein sehr reputirlicher Philologe,[82] aber mit dem geschichtlichen Urteil und der Fähigkeit Menschen und Verhältnisse zu durchschauen, wie sie nur die schulstube erzeugt—wie A. Schäfer dazu kommt, die historische Methode zu repraesentiren, das bin ich begierig zu vernehmen:[83] Ihre behauptung, daß Aristoteles seine

---

graphy: Karl Julius Beloch, *apud Die Geschichtswissenschaft der Gegenwart in Selbstdarstellungen*, ed. Sigfrid Steinberg 2 (Leipzig 1926) 1–27. For the authoritative bibliography of his work see Leandro Polverini, "Bibliografia degli scritti di Giulio Beloch," *AnnPisa* NS 3, 9 (1979) 1429–1462 with *addendum* at *ibid.*, NS 3, 11 (1981) 825–827. There is a brief, informative life at Christ (1), 248–285: see also Hermann Bengtson, *NDB* 2 (Berlin 1955) 31–32 and Arnaldo Momigliano, *Terzo contributo alla storia degli studi classici e del mondo antico* I (Rome 1966) 239–265. On 14 January 1894 Wilamowitz writes to Mommsen (*Briefe-Mommsen*, No. 389, p. 487):

> In Italien scheint Beloch die Köpfe zu verwirren; der ist gewiss gescheit und findig, aber gewissenlos und *rerum novarum studiosus*. Ich mag mit ihm nichts zu tun haben.

His violent anti-semitism (attributed to his Jewish origin: see Otto Th. Schulz, *BiogJahr* 264 [1936] 63) and that he was a student of Rohde's friend Ribbeck, would not have endeared him to Wilamowitz. One letter of Wilamowitz to him, dated Greifswald 25 September 1884, is known to me through the kindness of Professor Polverini (*per litt.* 18 June 1985). It is a polite note of thanks for a not yet read copy of *Die attische Politik seit Perikles* (Leipzig 1884). Similarly antisemitic Jewish classical scholars were Th. Gomperz, Jacoby, and Leo. On Leo's antisemitism see Christhard Hoffmann, "Antiker Völkerhass und Moderner Rassenhass: Heinemann an Wilamowitz," *Quaderni di storia* 25 (1987) 149 with n. 29. *Geck* is *fool* not *dandy*. Momigliano's view that Meyer was partially Jewish is based on a dubious interpretation of the name of Meyer's maternal grandfather (Dessau): see Arnaldo Momigliano, *Settimo contributo alla storia degli studi classici e del mondo antico* (Rome 1984) 215. If Meyer's grandfather had been called *Dessauer*, he would probably have been Jewish: cf. *Hamburger, Frankfurter* (U.K. Goldsmith). Momigliano later alleges (*ibid.*, 238) on no evidence that either Ernst Kapp or Kurt von Fritz was Jewish.

[79] A reference to Meyer, *GdA* III².715 n. 1. For Wilamowitz' discussion of the chronology see *Aristoteles*, I.21–22.

[80] Meyer bases his chronology on an antiquated book for schoolboys: see Arnold Schaefer, *Abriß der Quellenkunde der griechischen Geschichte bis Polybius* (1867). The book was frequently reprinted certainly until 1967.

[81] Wilamowitz after Henri Weil at *Aristoteles* I.80 emends 10 to 200 at *AthPol* 4.2. Kaibel-Wilamowitz, *Aristotelis AthPol³* (Berlin 1899) 3 confine the emendation to the apparatus. In their first edition (Berlin 1891) they had suggested changing 100 to 5 at *AthPol* 3.2: see *apparatus criticus ad loc*. Meyer exaggerates the change at *LCB*, 75.

[82] Compare Wilamowitz, *Geschichte³*.69: "Die sauberste Gelehrtenarbeit hat A. Schäfer in seinem Demosthenes geliefert, aber es ist philologische Arbeit, möchte man sagen."

[83] For Arnold Schaefer (1819–1883) see Roderich Schmidt, "Arnold Schaefer 1819–

chronologie bestätigt hätte, ist in jedem einzelnen Punkte falsch.[84] Aristoteles gibt entweder Daten, die bei Schäfer gar nicht vorkommen konnten, oder er gibt andere Daten, von Themistokles zu schweigen. Ich aber werde die änderung von Φαίδων in 'Αψεφίων für eine unmethodische, philologisch wie historisch gleich verwerfliche spielerei zu halten fortfahren.[85] Ich kann mir nicht denken, daß Sie diese Untersuchung auf grund der quellen geführt haben.

'Αθῆναι von 'Αθήνη zu sondern oder gar das verhältnis umzudrehen ist eine Zumutung, die mir mein grammatisches gewissen verbietet. mit allen Ihren vier gründen schlagen Sie nur ins wasser.[86] 'Αθάνη, wie der name außer Athen und nachbarschaft (Megara mit colonien, Korinth) lautet, und 'Αθήνη, wie er im epos überwiegend lautet, für eine verkürzung zu erklären ist erst dann erlaubt, wenn γαλήνη aus γαληναίη verkürzt ist. und wenn 'Αθῆναι ein guter stadtname ist ὡς Μυκῆναι, so ist es ein guter frauenname auch ὡς 'Αλκμήνη Κυρήνη. daß keine stadt in alter zeit nach einem gotte heisse, ist erstens falsch, 'Ηραῖα,[87] und zweitens gilt es umgekehrt erst recht: welcher gott heisst nach der stadt? bei Kyrene,

---

1883," *150 Jahre Rheinische Friedrich-Wilhelms-Universität zu Bonn 1818–1968: Bonner Gelehrte: Beiträge zur Geschichte der Wissenschaften in Bonn: Geschichtswissenschaften* (Bonn 1968) 170–189. Before becoming professor at Bonn in 1865, Schaefer had been schoolmaster at Dresden and Grimma. At Dresden he had begun his chronological studies. Hence Wilamowitz' remark.

[84] "Your assumption that Aristotle has confirmed Schaefer's chronology in each and every instance is not true." A devastating verdict. Meyer had heard Schaefer at Bonn: see *Skizze*, 10: "A. Schäfer als Historiker bot mir kaum etwas." In a letter of 21 June 1872 to his parents Meyer describes Schäfer as "sehr gelehrt und vernünftig, aber sehr trocken und langweilig: das Ideal eines guten, einfachen Gelehrten" (E. Badian).

[85] For Phaidon, Athenian archon in 476/75, attested DS 11.48; Plu. *Theseus* 36; and elsewhere: see Johannes Kirchner, *RE* 19 (1938) 1538 *s.n.* Phaidon. 1). R. Bentley, *Dissertations upon the Epistles of Phalaris, Themistocles, Socrates, Euripides and upon the Fables of Aesop,* ed. Wilhelm Wagner (Berlin 1874) 301–302 emended Φαίδωνος to 'Αφεψίωνος [*sic*] accepted by Gotthold Ephraim Lessing, *Gesammelte Werke* 4, ed. Paul Rilla (Berlin 1955) 494–495: see *contra* Henrici Clintonis *Fasti Hellenici civiles et litterarias graec-orum res ab OI.LVᵐᵃ ad CXXIVᵐᵃᵐ explicantes,* translated from the second English edition by C.G. Krueger (Leipzig 1830) 34 and Wilamowitz, *Aristoteles* 1.146 n. 41. The reference is to the conquest of Eion (Th. 1.98.1) regarding which Schaefer emended a scholiast to Aeschines: see Busolt. *GrG* III.1. 103 n. 1.

[86] Did Athene take her name from Athens or Athens hers from the goddess? Meyer (*GdA* II.115) argued the former. Beloch (*GrG* I.1² 155 n. 1) followed his friend. Wilamowitz (*Aristoteles* 2.35–36) independently and in the same year argued the latter. His view has prevailed: see Martin P. Nilsson, *Geschichte der griechischen Religion* I²: *Die Religion Griechenlands bis auf die griechische Weltherrschaft* (Munich 1955) 434 n. 2: Hermann Usener, *Götternamen: Versuch einer Lehre von der religiösen Begriffsbildung³* (Frankfurt/Main 1948) 232 (without mention of Wilamowitz); Curt Wachsmuth, *RE* Supp. 1 (1903) 159 (with mention of Meyer and not of Wilamowitz). Recently Walter Burkert has returned to the view of Meyer: see Walter Burkert, *Greek Religion,* translated by John Raffan (Cambridge, Massachusetts 1985) 139: "the goddess most probably takes her name from the city."

[87] A city in west Arcadia: see Felix Bölte, *RE* 8 (1912) 407–416.

wo stadt und heroine (göttin?) homonym sind, ist die priorität unzweifelhaft, und bei Πριήπος dürfte erst der gott als barbar das gegebene sein,[88]
wenn Sie 'die Athenen' für absurd halten: ja, was sind dann 'die Philip-
pi?' heisst Philip auch nach Φίλιπποι? was ist Ἀρχίλοχοι Αἶτναι?[89] der
plural mag grammatisch sehr sonderbar sein,[90] aber eine grammatische
schwierigkeit löst man nicht, indem man einen fall mit gewalt eliminirt.
geschichtlich betrachtet ist Ihre annahme unmöglich, da Sie selbst ad hoc
erfinden, daß Athen eine so große macht einmal gehabt habe, seine
eponymos als göttin ganz Hellas zu octroyiren. nehmen Sie mir's nicht
übel—das geht über Timaios.[91]

Natürlich würde ich, wenn ich über Ihre beurteilung von Thukydides,
Themistokles, Perikles urteilen sollte, auch sagen, daß Sie sie falsch
auffassten; bei Perikles würde ich sagen, daß Sie auf einem standpunkte
beharrten, den wir alle erst verpflichtet sind zu teilen, weil wir ihn bei
Thukydides finden. aber man kommt darüber hinweg, sobald man die
bilanz seiner staatsverwaltung zieht.[92] dazu gehört freilich, daß man die
entwickelung der institutionen, das staatsrecht, eingehender durchdenkt
als ich das bei Ihnen finde. Ihr buch zeigt mir das und auch Ihre stellung
zu dem meinen. wenn Sie oder wer sonst die unechtheit der drakontischen
verfassung inhaltlich dartun wollen, so sind die redensarten von den

---

[88] A city on the Asia Minor coast of the Propontis: see Eckart Olshausen, *RE* Supp.
14 (1974) 482 – 484, esp.: "Es ist nicht zu entscheiden, ob dieser Ortsname oder der Name
des Gottes Priapos der primäre ist" (482.47 – 49).

[89] See Wilamowitz, *Herakles* I³.57 n. 14; *Interpretationen*, 242 n. 1; *KS* 6.246 n. 4.

[90] Regarding feminine plural placenames (e.g., Thebai, Mykenai) Wilamowitz suggested at *Herakles* I³.56 n. 14 that the singular was earlier but "als man aber die epony-
men Nymphen lebhafter persönlich empfand, drangen die Pluralbildungen durch."

[91] "This goes even beyond Timaios." A reference to Polybius' criticism of Timaios
(= *FGrHist* 566): see Truesdell S. Brown, *Timaeus of Tauromenium* (Berkeley/Los Angeles
1958) 99 – 106. As Timaeus wildly overvalued Sicily so Meyer, if he believes what he
writes, must overvalue Athens.

[92] Wilamowitz repeats his rather unflattering remark that Meyer's misinterpretations
are understandable as those of one who has devoted insufficient attention to the evidence.
Meyer remained unrepentant. See *GdA* IV.1⁸ 699 n. 1: "Wilamowitz' Beurteilung des
Perikles Arist. II 99 f. u. a. scheint mir recht verfehlt; wie man zur Illustration seines
Verhältnisses zu Phidias das Friedrich Wilhelm III. zu Schinkel heranziehen kann, ver-
stehe ich nicht." And so with Aspasia: see Meyer, *Forschungen* 2. 55: "Wie über Perikles'
Persönlichkeit hat Wilamowitz, Arist. II,99 über Aspasia ein Urtheil gefällt, welches mir
auf völliger Verkennung der Thatsachen zu beruhen scheint." Wilamowitz had early pro-
tested against "die antike und moderne überschätzung des Perikles" at *Hermes* 14 (1879)
319, a view queried by Jacob Bernays: see *Antiqua* 23 (1983) 26 with n. 31. At *Forschungen*
II. 412, Meyer writes of Wilamowitz:

Es ist natürlich, dass man zunächst so urtheilte; auch ich habe, wie ich offen bekennen will, das
lange genug nachgesprochen, da ich keinen andern Ausweg sah.

Wilamowitz was not amused: see *KS* 4.125: "Mein Urteil, das freilich gegenüber dem
geschulten Historiker inferior ist . . ."

strategen ganz unkräftig. jeder muß das einsehen, der sich klar macht, was die bedeutung eines durch direkte wahl hervorgegangenen amtes ausmacht, und nicht leugnet, daß Peisistratos durch die strategie tyrann geworden ist.[93] wol aber hängt alles an den prytanen, an der frage also, wie ist der rat entstanden und gebildet. wer bloss die historiker li⟨e⟩st, der kann freilich Kleisthenes in seiner bedeutung unter Themistokles stellen: aber phyle demos rat zehner collegien: das macht den attischen staat, den wir kennen.[94] jetzt hat Keil den nachweis geliefert, daß auch das jahr eine Kleisthenische schöpfung ist;[95] Sie mögen seine tätigkeit tadeln oder beklagen: daß er die verfassung geschaffen hat, die in ihren grundzügen nur mit Athen vergehen konnte, ist eine tatsache, und die verkennen Sie, m. Er., durchaus. meine ansichten über das recht des geschlechterstaates habe ich mir erworben wesentlich durch das studium Mommsens[96] und dann des rechtes, das die urkunden geben mit verwertung des epos. Ich habe die freude, daß Wellhausens arabische forschungen,[97] wie er versichert, genau die selben formen zeigen, nicht wie in

---

[93] Wilamowitz defended the authenticity of the Constitution of Draco at *Aristoteles* 1.76–98; 2.55–56. Meyer attacked it at *Forschungen* 1.236–239. For the history of the controversy see Georg Busolt, "Das Problem der drakontischen Verfassung," *Griechische Staatskunde* 1 (Munich 1920) 52–58 with the valuable bibliography at 53 n. 2. For Meyer on the *strategoi* see *LCB*, 77;

[94] For the contribution of Kleisthenes see Busolt, *GrG* 2².400–449 ("Die Verfassung des Kleisthenes"). Only a scholar who confines his reading to the ancient historians could consider Themistocles more important than Kleisthenes. Contrast Meyer, *GdA* III².743 n. 1: "Die Bedeutung des Kleisthenes und seines Werkes ist neuerdings mehrfach auf Kosten Solons stark überschätzt worden, namentlich von Wilamowitz …" For Wilamowitz' sentiment compare *Aristoteles* 1.381: "wer in griechischer geschichte zu hause sein will, der muß, was die alte zeit anlangt, in Homer und Pindar, was die spätere anlangt, in Platon und Aristoteles zu hause sein: bei denen lernt er denken und empfinden wie die leute, deren staat und geschichte er verstehn soll."

[95] See Busolt, *GrG* 2².432 n. 2: "Die Einführung eines vom bürgerlichen Jahre verschiedenen Amtsjahres durch Kleisthenes hat B. Keil, Hermes XXIX (1894), 32–81 und 321–372 zweifellos nachgewiesen …" For a recent discussion of the vexed subject of the Athenian calender see Alan E. Samuel, *Greek and Roman Chronology: Calendars and Years in Classical Antiquity* (Munich 1972) 57–64.

[96] See Wilamowitz' letter to Mommsen of 23 November 1892 (*Briefe-Mommsen*, No. 370, p. 464) written while composing *Aristoteles*:

> Bei meiner eigenen Arbeit ist mir außer Böckh ganz allein Dein Staatsrecht und die Röm. Forsch. I eine merkliche Hilfe: zu lernen, wie man aufpassen soll, und daß die Institutionen ihre innere Logik haben, die es zu fassen gilt.

[97] For Wilamowitz' admiring view of Julius Wellhausen (1844–1918) see Calder-Fowler, *op. cit.* (*supra*, n. 23) 78–84 with literature there cited. For Wellhausen's Arabic work (he concentrated on the pre-Islamic and early Islamic periods) see the exemplary discussion of Kurt Rudolph, "Wellhausen as an Arabist," *apud* "Julius Wellhausen and his *Prolegomena to the History of Israel*," ed. Douglas A. Knight, *Semeia* 25 (Chico 1985) 111–155, especially 116–121 ("Methodology"), where one immediately sees how similar their approach to ancient texts was. Soon Meyer's *Die Entstehung des Judentums* (Halle 1896) would elicit a highly critical review by Wellhausen, *GGA* 159 (1897) 89–98, to which

Rom, sondern wie ich sie Herm. XXII gezeichnet habe:[98] jetzt meine ich die phratrie erläutert zu haben. Ich sehe, daß Ihnen diese arbeiten gleichgültig erscheinen, wenigstens für die historie gleichgültig. Sie werden es wol begreiflich finden, daß ich dann die ansichten, die Sie über den ältesten staat vortragen, wo gastrecht und clientel kaum vorkommen, als auf einem zu schmalen fundamente errichtet betrachte. Was schließlich die moralischen und historischen werturteile anlangt, so führen diese immer, wenigstens bei menschen, die eigne urteile fällen, auf die innerste überzeugung von göttlichen und menschlichen dingen zurück, über die sich nicht disputiren läßt. ich bekenne mich zu dem glauben, daß der größte staatsmann keine schmutzigen hände haben darf, also ist Themistokles keiner.[99] wol aber haben Alexandros und Caesar erstrebt was zu schön für sterbliche ist, und nach denen werfen freilich leute wie Nissen mit ihrem dreck, wie Beloch nach allem was über seinen Heine captus[100] moralisch hinausgeht (wie Sappho, der Sie nicht unrecht haben tun

---

Meyer replied with *Julius Wellhausen und meine Schrift Die Entstehung des Judentums. Eine Erwiderung* (Halle 1897). The controversy is authoritatively treated by Christhard Hoffmann, *Juden und Judentum im Werk Deutscher Althistoriker des 19. und 20. Jahrhunderts* (Leiden 1988) 159 ff. Meyer was bewildered by the unexpected virulence of the attack and in a letter of 25 IV 1897 to his teacher Georg Ebers (see Hoffmann, 160 n. 39) remarks: "Ich fürchte, es ist die berüchtigte Göttinger Luft, die sich dabei in recht wenig erfreulicher Weise geltend macht." Ebers replied on 16 V 1897 (Hoffmann, *ibid.*): The Göttingen air has "für die dortigen Olympier etwas Berauschendes. Die Selbstüberhebung und das Unfehlbarkeitsbewußtsein gedeihen dort üppiger als irgend wo anders in Deutschland." Wilamowitz presumably was one of the Olympians. On 25 XII 1896 Wellhausen wrote to Adolf Harnack (Hoffmann, *ibid.*):

> Ich habe eine Abh. über den Josippus geschrieben und bin eben dabei, dem Eduard Meyer die Haare etwas gegen den Strich zu kämmen. Er macht sich gar zu wichtig mit seinem gesunden Menschenverstand, mit seiner orientalist. Gelehrsamkeit, und mit seiner Kunst dick zu unterstreichen was andere Leute gesagt haben. Sonst ist er nicht übel, sehr fleißig, und klar. Er erinnert etwas an Stade, dem freilich die siegesgewisse Naivetät fehlt.

In old age Meyer accepted Wilamowitz' view of Wellhausen as presented in *Erinnerungen*. See Eduard Meyer, *DLZ* 51 (1928) 2491: "Tief und wie ich glaube durchaus zutreffend erfaßt ist die Persönlichkeit Wellhausens ..."

[98] Ulrich von Wilamowitz-Moellendorff, "Demotika der attischen Metöken. I. II.," *Hermes* 22 (1887) 107–128; 211–259 = *KS* 5.1.272–342: see *Briefe-Mommsen*, 309–311.

[99] For Wilamowitz' highly critical view of Themistokles see *Aristoteles* I.138–149. For the same reason he dispised Demosthenes: see William M. Calder III, *CW* 72 (1978/79) 239–240. The denial of greatness to Themistokles could only offend Meyer, who thought him one of the greatest men in the history of the world: see Eduard Meyer, *Kl. Schr.* 227 (the Chicago address of 1904).

[100] *Heine* is a XIX century variant for *Heini*. *Heini* (diminutive of Heinrich) is an archaic *Schimpfwort*, meaning a dolt, who irritates those who meet him. *captus* is the substantive, "capacity, ability, potentiality" (*OLD*). The whole then refers to Beloch's "irritatingly stupid mentality." This is consistent with Wilamowitz' attested view of Beloch. A. Demandt suggests *mente captus* but this does not fit the *ductus litterarum*. With Nissen Wilamowitz refers to *RhM* 47 (1892) 161–206 (E. Badian).

wollen, aber hoffentlich noch einmal abbitte tun werden):[101] aber nur durch das streben ins übermenschliche sind sie herren geworden.[102]

Credo gegen credo: arbeit gegen arbeit: anschauung gegen anschauung. ich habe zwei briefe zerissen, eh ich diesen schrieb, und täte es auch mit diesem lieber.[103] aber ich musste doch irgend wie Ihnen persönlich gegenüber meine stellung wahren. Zarnckes[104] aufforderung, Ihr buch zu besprechen, hatte ich abgelehnt, und antworten tue ich prinzipiell nicht. Seien Sie versichert, verehrter herr college, daß ich so nicht geschrieben hätte, wenn ich nicht wissenschaftlich und menschlich Ihnen in hochschätzung und sympathie aufrichtig zugetan wäre.

der Ihre

UvWilamowitz

Göttingen 18 I 94

---

[101] Meyer, *GdA* III^2.588–589 with n. 1 treats briefly the exile and dating of "die adlige Dichterin;" but says not a word about her poetry. Wilamowitz was particularly sensitive to any criticism of Sappho and in 1896 would rise to her defense against Pierre Louys: see *GGA* 158 (1896) 623–638. For his view of Sappho and its source in Welcker see William M. Calder III, "F.G. Welcker's *Sapphobild* and its Reception in Wilamowitz," *Friedrich Gottlieb Welcker Werk und Wirkung*, edited by William M. Calder III, Adolf Köhnken, Wolfgang Kullmann, Günther Pflug, *Hermes Einzelschrift* 49 (Stuttgart 1986) 131–156, especially 154–156.

[102] An echo of Goethe, *Faust* II.11934–37 (Christhard Hoffmann). For the conviction that Meyer was able to grasp the greatness of Alexander in contrast to Beloch compare Ulrich von Wilamowitz-Moellendorff, "Eduard Meyer," *Süddeutsche Monatshefte* 22 (1924/25) Heft 4, 55 (henceforth cited *Meyer*): "Ein Aufsatz in seinen kleinen Schriften beweist, daß er den großen Könige [sc. Alexandros] das Verständnis entgegenbringt, das vielen modernsten Historikern fehlt, weil der große Mann ihnen unbehaglich ist." Wilamowitz refers to Meyer, *Kl. Schr.*, 283–332. For Wilamowitz' view of Alexander see *KS* 5.1.181–203, especially 200–203 (on understanding great men). For a critical discussion of Beloch's *Alexanderbild* see J. Kromayer, *HZ* 100 (1908) 11–52. Beloch consistently underestimates the greatness of the man. See further Alexander Demandt, "Politische Aspekte im Alexanderbild der Neuzeit: Ein Beitrag zur historischen Methodenkritik," *Archiv für Kulturgeschichte* 54 (1972) 325–363.

[103] Such selfdoubt is remarkable for Wilamowitz, who normally wrote for keeps. The earlier two versions presumably were less restrained than the third. He had had five days to think the review over: see *supra*, n. 72. Meyer's sharp criticism was unexpected after the "freundlicher brief über mein buch" to which Wilamowitz' letter of 4 November 1893 was the answer. Nor was Wilamowitz amused by any implied or actual comparison with Beloch. Obviously, just because Wilamowitz respected Meyer, the criticism hurt.

[104] Eduard Zarncke was editor of the *Literarisches Centralblatt für Deutschland*, where Meyer had reviewed *Aristoteles*. In fact when at *Forschungen* 2.537–541, Meyer attacks Wilamowitz and Kaibel, he is answered in the sharpest of terms: see Wilamowitz, *KS* 4.124–126. In a letter of 16 October 1900 to Wilamowitz, F.G. Kenyon accepts *pen]te* at *AthPol* 13.2 and refers to *CR* forthcoming [= *CR* 14 (1900) 413]. Generally Wilamowitz avoided polemic: see *KS* 4.193: "Ich pflege die Leute reden zu lassen und mich an die Sachen zu halten."

III. Wilamowitz contra Meyer

A biographer soon learns that letters about people often reveal more than letters to people. Wilamowitz wrote to Mommsen about Meyer's review before he mailed the third version of his letter to Meyer. On 14 January 1894 he wrote to his father-in-law:[105]

E. Meyer, dessen Rezension ich gestern erhalten habe, ist durchaus Weltgeschichtler, und ich hoffe doch, die Freude an dem Detail, der Einzeluntersuchung, wird ihm noch kommen; seine Forschungen zur alten Geschichte zeigen den Ansatz. Aber er perhorresziert die Bestrebungen, irgendwo die Dinge rechtlich systematisch[106] zu nehmen, ganz und gar. Und diese Manier greift überhaupt um sich. Ich glaube nicht, daß sein Buch im einzelnen sehr viel Bedeutendes neu hinzugewonnen hat, allein die Energie, mit der er das Ganze wie auch immer bewältigt, imponiert mir doch; es ist doch einer, der etwas will und etwas kann. Auf viele Partien seines Buches hat Robert[107] (nicht immer glücklich) eingewirkt.

Wilamowitz' chief criticism of Meyer in both letters is that the worldhistorian disdains detail. He is, like Ephorus, superficial. In 1893 the work of Wilamowitz and of Meyer was based largely on the critical, that is philological, examination of literary sources with archaeology providing

---

[105] *Mommsen-Briefe*, No. 389, pp. 486–487.

[106] One cannot avoid comparing Meyer's *credo* at *Kl. Schr.*, 3: "Die Geschichte ist keine systematische Wissenschaft." This in turn recalls Wilamowitz' conviction (1919) that there was no hard and fast philological method: see *Antiqua* 23 (1983) 258 and the German original at Wolfgang Schadewaldt, *Hellas und Hesperien: Gesammelte Schriften zur Antike und zur neueren Literatur in zwei Bänden*, edd. Klaus Bartels, Reinhard Thurow and Ernst Zinn II² (Zürich/Stuttgart 1970) 606–607:

> ... Aber diese gepriesene "Philologische Methode:" die gibt's doch gar nicht, die gibt es so wenig wie eine Methode, Fische zu fangen. Der Wal wird harpuniert, der Hering im Netz gefangen. Der Butt wird getreten, der Lachs gespießt, die Forelle geangelt. Wo bleibt da *die* Methode, Fische zu fangen?—Und überhaupt die Jägerei! Vielleicht gibt's da so etwas wie Methode. Aber, meine Damen und Herren (mit schalkhaft blitzenden Augen): es ist doch schließlich ein Unterschied, ob man Löwen jagt oder Flöhe fängt.

The reference to trampling flounder is from Ael. *HA* 14.3: see my note at *RhM* NF 126 (1983) 191. The source of the simile is Ov. *AA* I.763–764, a passage brought to my attention by J. Mejer (Copenhagen). The closing reference to hunting fleas provides a remarkable anticipation of Housman's comparison in 1922 of textual criticism to a dog's hunting fleas: see *The Classical Papers of A.E. Housman*, collected and edited by J. Diggle and F.R.D. Goodyear III 1915–1936 (Cambridge 1972) 1059. Both similes reveal impatience with tiresome blithering about method. Wellhausen to his credit shared this impatience: see Rudolf, *op. cit.* (*supra*, n. 97) 117: "... he preferred to keep to the material, and thereby made his own method more concrete."

[107] For Wilamowitz' critical view of his old friend and "first student," Carl Robert (1850–1922): see *Dichtung* 2.232 and Calder-Fowler, *op. cit.* (*supra*, n. 23) 90. In his review of *Erinnerungen*, Meyer would claim that Wilamowitz underrated Robert: see *DLZ* 50 (1928) 2492: "... während ich für Robert auf wärmere Töne gehofft hatte." Perhaps *Halle-Solidarität*! Meyer dedicated a volume of *GdA* to him.

the trimmings.[108] Expert familiarity with the ancient languages was indispensable. On this there could be no disagreement. Both historian and philologist seek to understand as precisely as possible what the source is saying. What they do with what they extract from the source differs but the method of extraction is for both the same, that is philological. Wilamowitz never forgot Meyer's exegesis of the archaic, dialectal inscriptions of Locris.[109] But while Wilamowitz admired Meyer's ease with oriental languages he could not himself control,[110] he is curiously oblivious to the plea that Meyer could not control eight ancient languages with the same exactitude that Wilamowitz did two. The price Meyer paid, Wilamowitz implies, was imperfect knowledge of Greek. Meyer's erroneous assumption that Athena took her name from Athens revealed precisely this. Their disagreement concerning a remark of Theramenes arises from Meyer's limited reading in Greek literature. On the other hand Meyer's history was not based on translations from the Greek as were those of lesser ancient historians.[111] Kurt Rudolph has remarked of Julius Wellhausen:[112]

---

[108] Wilamowitz, *Meyer*, 56:

> Berlin brachte Meyer durch den Eintritt in die Akademie und die Verbindung mit den Museen äußerlich und auch innerlich eine Erweiterung seiner Tätigkeit. Die Verwertung der immer wachsenden Schätze der Museen verlangte das Studium der monumentalen neben der schriftlichen Überlieferung.

Cf. supra, n. 55.

[109] Wilamowitz, *Meyer*, 58: "Seine Interpretation der alten lokrischen Bronzen, Inschriften in einem wenig kenntlich Dialekt, ist unübertrefflich."

[110] Wilamowitz, *Meyer*, 55 (of early Meyer):

> Er erfaßte seine Lebensaufgabe, und erfaßte sie richtig. Er mußte die Sprachen des Orients lernen, und wirklich sind ihm Ägyptisch, die semitischen Sprachen, und Persisch so vertraut wie das Griechische.

I doubt that there is irony here. On the other hand Goethe's scepticism regarding oriental studies had prejudiced Wilamowitz: see Goethe, *Maximen und Reflexionen* Nr. 763:

> Chinesische, indische, ägyptische Alterthümer sind immer nur Curiositäten; es ist sehr wohlgethan, sich und die Welt damit bekannt zu machen; zu sittlicher und ästhetischer Bildung aber werden sie uns wenig fruchten.

See Ernst Grumach, *Goethe und die Antike: Eine Sammlung* I (Potsdam 1949) 417 and *Quaderni di storia* 18 (1983) 282.

[111] Wilamowitz, *Meyer*, 58:

> Das bleibt die Hauptsache, daß dieser Historiker imstande ist, die Urkunden, die er benutzt, alle selbst zu interpretieren. Es gibt auch alte Historiker, die auf Übersetzungen aus dem Griechischen angewiesen sind; die sind aber auch danach.

[112] Kurt Rudolph, *op. cit.* (*supra*, n. 97) 117. See earlier Otto Eissfeldt, "Julius Wellhausen," *Kleine Schriften* I edd. Rudolf Sellheim and Fritz Maass (Tübingen 1962) 56–71, especially 57: "Wellhausen war Historiker ... So ist er zugleich ein großer Philologe gewesen."

Wellhausen was a philologian at heart, and as such also a historian; for in his day philology meant not only the study of languages but immersion in the history and culture associated with the language one studied. All the great philologians of Wellhausen's day were to a greater or lesser extent also historians ...; or, conversely, there is strictly speaking no historian who must not practice philology, for which reason one speaks of the philological-historical method as *the* method of the nineteenth century. Wellhausen once gave brief expression to this insight: "Philology takes revenge on those who treat her with disdain."[113] Yet Wellhausen was never willing to stop there but placed all his philological learning and ability at the service of history; and in this too he showed himself a true historian, a historian indeed of the highest caliber. One sensed repeatedly that it was the historical question which was at stake in all his investigations and that it always formed the criterium of judgment in his critical reviews.

Rudolph might have been writing about Wilamowitz. One sees that a philological approach to antiquity was one of the bonds that drew the two friends together. That Meyer neglects details does not only cause him to make errors of detail. The historian is limited because he only reads historians and indeed he does not read them with care. His *Periklesbild* is that of the hurried reader of Thucydides. He underestimates literature. "Wir lernen also griechisch ausschließlich, um griechische Bücher zu lesen."[114] But Meyer does not. Because Sappho played no role in military or political history other than being exiled, her poems do not exist for Meyer. Solon's elegies are something else. On the other hand he will write[115] "historisch ist, was wirksam ist oder gewesen ist." A poem of Sappho *is* more real than the battle of Issus *is*. If he had read Aristophanes, the orators, or Plato, he would never think Themistokles more important than Cleisthenes. One must learn to think as the Greeks thought. To do this one must read and reread the preserved literature.

Meyer, from Wilamowitz' point of view, improved with age. This was due in part to his increased interest in the history of religion at the expense of traditional constitutional history. In the final version of his essay on method of 1910 he defines the importance of an event and therefore interest in it by the extent of its influence. That means that "religion and the creations of literature and art" become most important "because their effects are most universal."[116] To speak with authority about such

---

[113] Julius Wellhausen, *Muhammed in Medina: Das ist Vakidi's Kitab alMaghazi in verkürzter deutscher Wiedergabe herausgegeben* (Berlin 1882; repr. Berlin 1970) 26 (against A. Sprenger). I owe the reference to Rudolph but in the citation have replaced the translator's *it* with *her* to preserve the effective personification.

[114] Ulrich von Wilamowitz-Moellendorff, *Griechisches Lesebuch* I[13] (Zürich/Berlin 1965) iv.

[115] Meyer, *Kl. Schr.*, 43.

[116] Meyer, *Kl. Schr.*, 45–46.

matters requires familiarity with more than Thucydides. The historian
has embraced the *Totalitätsideal* of the philologist. A *Realhistoriker* is on the
way to becoming a *Kulturhistoriker*. Wilamowitz in a famous passage formulated the latter's task:[117]

> Die Aufgabe der Philologie ist, jenes vergangenen Leben durch die Kraft der
> Wissenschaft wieder lebendig zu machen, das Lied des Dichters, den
> Gedanken des Philosophen und Gesetzgebers, die Heiligkeit des Got-
> teshauses und die Gefühle der Gläubigen und Ungläubigen, das bunte
> Getriebe auf dem Markte und im Hafen, Land und Meer und die Menschen
> in ihrer Arbeit und in ihrem Spiele.

In his famous essay, translated into Japanese and Russian, but never into
English or French, "On the Theory and Method of History," Meyer
devotes the closing pages to an attempt to clarify the difference between
what an historian and a philologist do. He states that he has Wilamowitz
in mind.[118] It is no coincidence that the address was delivered, expanded
and published in the same year that Meyer was leaving an historical institute at Halle to become part of what would become an Institute for *Altertumswissenschaft* under the hegemony of Wilamowitz at Berlin. He goes
under protest. He writes the following:[119]

> As is well known many attempts have been made to bring the two [*sc.* history
> and philology] together under one definition or possibly to identify them
> completely ⟨with one another⟩. But these attempts have provided no useful
> result. It is obvious that for modern history such an identification is utopian.
> But even in antiquity the tasks of an historian are essentially different from
> those of the classical philologist. No matter how close the two disciplines
> frequently are to each other—each is one of the most important auxiliary dis-
> ciplines for the other—fundamentally they are separate from one another;
> and a fusing of the two, i.e., merging them under the concept of "Altertums-
> wissenschaft", is unjustified and leads to confusion. Indeed for the treat-
> ment of ancient history it is already disastrous enough. It[120] has led to a

---

[117] Ulrich von Wilamowitz-Moellendorff, *Geschichte der Philologie*⁴ (Leipzig 1959) 1.

[118] Meyer, *Kl. Schr.*, 64–65: "Es ist diejenige, welche ich nach ihrem Hauptvertreter
[*sc.* Wilamowitz] als die philologische bezeichnen möchte." The essay was first published
as a separate volume: Eduard Meyer, *Zur Theorie und Methodik der Geschichte: Geschichtsphilosophische Untersuchungen* (Halle 1902). The revision of 1910 has modernized spelling
with minor revisions and addenda in the footnotes. I cite the edition of 1910 with occasional references to the earlier one. Note too Eduard Meyer, *Humanistische und geschichtliche
Bildung: Vortrag gehalten in der Vereinigung der Freunde des humanistischen Gymnasiums in Berlin
und der Provinz Brandenburg am 27. November 1906* (Berlin 1907).

[119] Meyer, *Kl. Schr.*, 65. On the Wilamowitzian ground that a translation is the best
commentary I have sought to provide an English one. I am grateful for help to the
Germanist, Professor Ulrich K. Goldsmith. At *Theorie*, v, Meyer alludes to "die Verhandlungen, welche zu meine Berufung nach Berlin geführt haben . . .," a passage omitted in
1910.

[120] The *Sie* is ambiguous. Does it refer to *Verquickung* or to *Behandlung*? I think the

tearing apart of what belongs together and the isolating of the individual parts of a discipline, to specialization; and the much praised scholarly division of labor, of which our time is as proud as any nation or any individual could be proud of his weakness, has been artificially enhanced.

He adds an uneasy footnote:[121]

> I consider it theoretically wrong and damaging that at many a German university the teaching of ancient history is not found in departments of history, joined with modern history; but rather it is made one with classical philology in "Institutes for Altertumswissenschaft." On practical grounds such an arrangement, at least in large universities such as Berlin, is unavoidable, because the necessarily large library here would have to be duplicated. At universities where smaller reference libraries suffice the situation differs.

The conclusion seems to be that only at universities with inadequate libraries can ancient historians be correctly housed. He never changed his mind.[122] But he is simply elevating a personal inclination into a principle. He enjoyed writing books on modern history. Earlier Leopold Ranke (1795 – 1886), Johann Gustav Droysen (1808 – 1884) and Jacob Burckhardt (1818 – 1897) had done so. His contemporary, Hans Delbrück (1848 – 1929), did both. A great ancient historian such as Sir Ronald Syme with books on Ammianus Marcellinus, Ovid, Sallust, *Scriptores Historiae Augustae*, or Tacitus, has far more in common with philologists. So earlier Theodor Mommsen. It is simply wrong to assert that classical philology and the history of Greece and Rome are fundamentally separate from one another. Contrarily they are indissolubly joined. I can barely conjecture what Meyer means when he laments the disastrous influence of philology on ancient history. Could he mean the naive homilies of Ernst Curtius? Wilamowitz would agree.[123] But that was long ago. Wilamowitz did as much as anyone to free Greek history from classicism. Did he mean Georg Busolt, whose vast compilations resembled the variorum editions

---

former. But how fusing can lead to a "tearing apart of what belongs together" is beyond me. Dr. Renate Schlesier *per litt.* writes: "Ich würde vermuten, 'Sie' bezieht sich auf "Altertumswissenschaft" (wofür auch die Argumentation in der Fußnote spricht)." *certent grammatici*!

[121] Meyer, *Kl. Schr.*, 65 n. 1. In 1902 (*Theorie*, 55 n. 2) he wrote: "Ich halte es für durchaus unrichtig und schädlich." Eight years later he modified his statement to "Ich halte es für theoretisch unrichtig und schädlich ..." The remark on libraries was also added in 1910, after he had used the Berlin one for eight years!

[122] *Cf.* Meyer, *Skizze*.

[123] For Wilamowitz on Curtius see *Aristoteles* I.377; *cf.* Hermann Bengtson, *Griechische Geschichte von den Anfängen bis in die römische Kaiserzeit* (Munich 1950) 5, who (5 n. 1) cites Wilamowitz' opinion with approval. The letters of Curtius to his brother Georg reveal his rage at Wilamowitz' criticism in *Kydathen*. Vain and unforgiving, he consistently opposed, against Mommsen, Wilamowitz' Berlin appointment. The way was cleared with his death in 1896.

of philological exegetes?[124] Their abiding value cannot be denied. Outside of Germany certainly the history of Busolt has outlived that of Meyer.
Jaeger called Meyer a realist. Part of Wilamowitz was precisely that. An
ancient was a "Mensch wie Du und ich."[125] Gundolf would dismiss his
Platon as "Platon für Dienstmädchen" just because of its realism.[126]

In Germany ancient history has generally followed Meyer's lead with
ancient historians in history departments and indeed archaeologists in art
history departments. In the United States universities differ with many
preferring that archaeology, ancient history, and philology be united in
a department of classics. Ancient historians, therefore, take their degrees
in classics. This insures expertise in the ancient languages, the first pre-
requisite for any ancient historian, and relieves candidates from examinations in areas far removed from their professional interests. Neither solution is satisfactory; and the tiresome debate will go on interminably.

Meyer, desperate to establish a difference between philology and history, argued a paradoxical and unexpected distinction:[127]

> I should like to define the essence of philology as that it transposes the results
> of history into the present and treats them as contemporary and, therefore,
> relevant. That holds first and above all for products of literature and art,
> which still exert a continuing direct influence on the present and require a
> discipline which unlocks their correct understanding for the present. In this
> way we can treat a language, civic and religious institutions, customs and
> viewpoints, and at the end the whole culture of an epoch grasped as a
> unity:—in short what is covered by the term "antiquities". Philology treats
> her subject not as developing nor functioning historically but as still existing.
> Here there is a place for a thorough treatment which history has no business
> dealing with, in a word, for an exhaustive interpretation of an individual
> creation. This always forms the true center of philology.

The paradox is that the historian, who, according to Meyer, deals with
what was "real and has existed," in fact deals with what has vanished and

---

[124] Busolt at last will receive his due in the forthcoming biography with letters by
M.H. Chambers, the *sospitator Busoltii*.

[125] See Ada Hentschke and Ulrich Muhlack, *Einführung in die Geschichte der klassischen
Philologie* (Darmstadt 1972) 102:

> Realismus und Aktualisierung—der Alltag des antiken Menschen und dieser Mensch als
> "Mensch wie du und ich"—sind die hervorstechenden Merkmale aller großen Interpretationen
> Wilamowitz'.

[126] Friedrich Gundolf quoted by K. Hildebrandt, *Erinnerungen an Stefan George und seinen
Kreis* (Berlin 1965) 55 n. 11; see *contra* E.R. Dodds, *Plato Gorgias: A Revised Text with
Introduction and Commentary* (Oxford 1959) 31 n. 2.

[127] Meyer, *Kl. Schr.*, 65–66; compare *GdA* I.1².189:

> Die Geschichte sucht das Sein einer Gegenwart zu erfassen, indem sie es als ein Werden aus
> einer Vergangenheit betrachtet. Ihre Aufgabe ist daher nicht die Schilderung von Zuständen,
> sondern die Darstellung einer Entwicklung.

is only with great effort perceived as relevant, while the philologist who deals with poetry and ideas rather than armies and politics in fact deals with the tangible, visible, and extant: a vase or a poem. I say "a vase" because archaeology derived from philologists like F.G. Welcker, Otto Jahn and Carl Robert, who called what they did "monumental philology." Of course the distinction does not work when pressed. The most obvious exception, as Wilamowitz himself noted,[128] is the *Iliad* which can only be understood in terms of its growth. Meyer next commends to philologists that step-child of historians, biography:[129]

> Biography also belongs to the philological disciplines. In our time (in antiquity it was different) certainly it is predominantly, if not exclusively, treated by historians. But it is not really an historian's job. Its object is the personage concerned in his totality as an individual, not as a factor affecting history. That he was that is here only a premise, the reason why a biography is devoted to him. Hence there is room in a biography for all the details of the person, his appearance, the outer and inner life of the hero, with which the historian cannot concern himself. By the same token no biography, so long as it really remains biography and is not merely another name for the history of its hero's time, can ever attain what is the real task of an historical work, a comprehensive and exhaustive description of an historical process.

Meyer's view that biography is interpretation and a philologist's task appealed deeply to Wilamowitz, who was both a philologist and a biographer. He begins his great biography of Plato with an unnoticed echo of Meyer's words:[130]

---

[128] See Wilamowitz, *Meyer*, 57:

> Das ist ja gerade des Fortschritt, daß wir die Ilias nicht mehr als ein gegebenes Kunstwerk analysieren, hinnehmend oder auflösend, sondern ihr Werden aus der Geschichte der epischen Dichtung und aus dem ganzen Leben ihrer Zeit und Vorzeit verstehen wollen.

He might also have adduced the Bible, which Meyer inexplicably overlooks. See *Goodenough on the History of Religion and on Judaism*, edited by Ernest S. Frerichs and Jacob Neusner (Atlanta 1986) 34:

> No one will expect that a single paper will appraise a body of literature in which, with the single exception of the first century B.C., experts find original compositions of every century from the thirteenth or twelfth century B.C. to the first or second century A.D. The sources of ideas in the biblical writings add to these many more centuries indeed ...

[129] See Meyer, *Kl. Schr.*, 66 and for the role of the great man in history: *ibid.*, 59 ff.

[130] Ulrich von Wilamowitz-Moellendorff, *Platon* I² (Berlin 1920) 4, where *Seele* is mind and not *soul*, as taken by Harold Cherniss, *Selected Papers*, ed. Leonardo Taran (Leiden 1977) 5. Compare his later approval at *Meyer*, 57:

> Es ist sehr richtig, daß er in der Interpretation den eigentlichen Kern der Philologie sieht, und wie weit er diese faßt, zeigt sich darin, daß er ihr die Biographie zuweist, ein Satz, der zuerst befremdet und vielen anstößig ist, aber eine große Wahrheit in sich schließt.

He defines a true biography at *Herakles* I³.1: "eine Entwicklungsgeschichte des Individuums innerhalb der Kreise, in die es gestellt war."

> Der Philologe ist nun einmal Interpret, Dolmetsch, aber nicht nur der
> Wörter; die wird er nicht voll verstehen, wenn er nicht die Seele versteht,
> aus der sie kommen. Er muß auch der Interpret dieser Seele sein. Denn weil
> sie ihre ganze Kunst im Interpretieren bewährt, ist die Biographie recht
> eigentlich Philologenarbeit, nur in höherer Potenz. Und doch stellt sich
> wieder die Aufgabe nicht höher als zu verstehen, wie dieser Mensch gewor-
> den ist, was er gewollt, gedacht, gewirkt hat.

In the end differences were far less than common ties. Wilamowitz and
Meyer were allies rather than competitors, both seeking to create new
facts out of facts in order to understand the ancient world and both doing
this from the unsatisfactory sources that have survived. Each had different
priorities. Persians were closer to Meyer's heart than *Persae*.

I shall end with a glance at the next generation.[131] We know Wilamowitz' disgust with the Third Humanism.[132] We can only imagine Meyer's
views. Its founder thought there was nothing worth hearing in Meyer's
lectures when a student at Berlin; and, although he called Wilamowitz
Master,[133] he only visited Greece once briefly in old age and found the
visit wasted time. Ancient Greece was *gegenwärtig*. Jaeger was almost as
different from Wilamowitz as he was from Meyer. The split between
ancient history and philology in Germany widened considerably to the
detriment of both disciplines in Jaeger's generation. How many great
German philologists of the period 1919–1939 wrote books of history?
Felix Jacoby (1876–1959) was a philologist who wrote philological books
about historical texts. Jaeger's *Demosthenes* is an exception. But it is in concept autobiographical, as Hans Lietzmann saw in February 1940[134] and
is antihistorical in its humanistic argument that the personal tragedy of
Demosthenes' defending a lost cause is of more interest than the progress
of world history.

On the other hand Wilamowitz never wavered. An historical philologist who expected ancient historians to know their place, *Philologia
ancilla historiae* was never for him. At age eighty with Meyer's words of

---

[131] The most revealing contemporary document for the break is Paul Friedländer's letter to Wilamowitz of 4 July 1921: see my "The Credo of a New Generation: Paul Friedländer to Ulrich von Wilamowitz-Moellendorff," *Antiqua* 23 (1983) 127–139 and more
generally Ernst Vogt, "Wilamowitz und die Auseinandersetzung seiner Schüler mit
ihm," *Wilamowitz*, 613–631.

[132] See, e.g., *Antiqua* 23 (1983) 257–263, 310.

[133] *Antiqua* 23 (1983) 190.

[134] Werner Jaeger, *Demosthenes: The Origin and Growth of His Policy* (Berkeley 1938).
Hans Lietzmann in his letter of 7 February 1940 already saw what Jaeger was doing: see
*Glanz und Niedergang der deutschen Universität: 50 Jahre deutscher Wissenschaftsgeschichte in Briefen
an und von Hans Lietzmann (1892–1942) mit einer einführenden Darstellung herausgegeben von* Kurt
Aland (Berlin 1979) 989. The letter is written with the knowledge that censors would read
it and must be so read.

26 years before unforgotten, he wrote his last proud words on the matter:[135]

Und wie läppisch ist der Dünkel gewisser Historiker, die meinen, Philologie, Archäologie usw. wären ancillae historiae, wie ehedem die Theologen von der weltlichen Wissenschaften meinten. Mir hat einer zu sagen gewagt: ''Ihr bratet das Beefsteak, das wir essen.'' Ich will das Bild nicht weiter ausführen, denn was würde denn aus dem Braten im Magen des Historikers? Man kann den Unterschied machen, daß der Historiker das Einzelne für das Ganze verwendet, der Philologe es umgekehrt macht. Aber in Wahrheit kommen beide in den Fall beides zu tun, und die Biographie, also die Erfassung eines einzelnen Menschen in seiner Zeit erfordert die Vereinigung des historischen und des philologischen Denkens und Darstellens.[136]

---

[135] Wilamowitz, *Erinnerungen*[2], 101-102.

[136] I am grateful to the Akademie der Wissenschaften der DDR in Berlin for permission to publish the three letters edited here and for their kindness in allowing me access to the Meyer *Nachlaß*. I owe especial thanks to two friends whose expert help has much improved my paper. Dr. Christhard Hoffmann (West Berlin) worked with me on the first transcription of Wilamowitz' difficult hand. His unique knowledge of the life of Meyer has strengthened my case and saved me from frequent error. Professor Dr. Albert Henrichs during a visit to the Villa Mowitz in June 1987 recovered the text in some 15 places and in several important passages elucidated conclusively what Wilamowitz was saying. I am grateful as well to Ernst Badian (Harvard); Bernhard vom Brocke (Marburg/Lahn), M.H. Chambers (Los Angeles); Ulrich K. Goldsmith (Boulder, Colorado), George Huxley (Athens), Ian Jackson (Berkeley), L. Polverini (Rome); Renate Schlesier (West Berlin), Eckart Schütrumpf (Boulder, Colorado) and Wolfgang Schindler (Humboldt Universität).

LUCIANO CANFORA

EDUARD MEYER TRA CRATIPPO E TEOPOMPO

1. Cratippo potrebbe definirsi un incubo incombente sugli studi di storiografia greca. Il pochissimo che le fonti superstiti ci dicono di lui ha indotto anche grandi storici, come Eduard Schwartz, ad auspicare che di lui non si sapesse nulla affatto, addirittura un suo "precipitare nel buio:" "wer ihn ans Licht zieht, trägt nur Schaden davon!"[1].

Come mai un così sconfortato pessimismo? Due dei tre "frammenti" conosciuti figurano in due opuscoli la cui formazione e natura è alquanto oscura: le *Vite dei dieci oratori* comprese tra i *Moralia* di Plutarco e la cosiddetta *Vita di Tucidide* di Marcellino. In entrambi i casi siamo di fronte a stratificazioni compositive, ad accumuli di materiale erudito di varia provenienza, amalgamato con annotazioni di tipo scoliastico e con notizie tra loro divergenti sulla stessa materia, messe tutte insieme forse proprio perché divergenti. In due contesti particolarmente tormentati e tormentosi dei due complicati opuscoli (*Vita di Andocide* 834 CD e Marcellino 31-33) figurano appunto i due rinvii a Cratippo.[2] Non trattandosi di citazioni vere e proprie ma di semplici cenni ad argomenti che Cratippo avrebbe trattato—in un caso la responsabilità dei Corinzi nella mutilazione delle Erme, nell'altro la tesi secondo cui Tucidide sarebbe morto in Tracia e non in Atene—, è comunque difficile trarre significative deduzioni dai due passi. Restano invece, per la delizia degli interpreti, le due relativamente ampie notizie fornite da Dionigi di Alicarnasso (*Su Tucidide* 16) e Plutarco (*Sulla gloria degli Ateniesi* 1 = *Moralia* 345 D).

Da Dionigi apprendiamo che Cratippo si esprimeva come persona all'incirca "coetanea" di Tucidide, ed era in grado di dare informazioni sul principale mutamento stilistico verificatosi nella stesura dell'opera tucididea, e cioè sulla rinuncia a inserire nel racconto discorsi diretti dei personaggi. In Plutarco abbiamo una specie di sommario piuttosto dettagliato del contenuto dell'opera di Cratippo. Tale "sommario" si estende da eventi dell'anno 411 a.C. alla ricostruzione della flotta ateniese per merito di Conone nel 394/3 a.C.[3] Sono entrambe date significative: il

---

[1] Ed. Schwartz, *Die Zeit des Ephoros*, "Hermes", 44, 1909, p. 502.

[2] Qui non potremo tentarne una analisi, che riserviamo ad altra sede: cfr. comunque, *infra*, *Epimetron*, § 4.

[3] Dirò in seguito (*Epimetron*, §§ 1-3) delle discussioni intorno alla identificazione degli episodi ricordati da Plutarco. Comunque tale discussione non intacca il dato generalmente

411 è l'anno in cui si interrompeva il racconto tucidideo (un anno assunto come *inizio* da due storici del IV secolo: Senofonte e Teopompo), il 394/3 è l'anno in cui si incrina, con la sconfitta di Cnido e la rinascita delle mura di Atene, il predominio spartano instauratosi dieci anni prima (Teopompo concludeva appunto col 394 le sue *Elleniche*).

Nel medesimo contesto del *De gloria Atheniensium*, Plutarco accenna, prima di parlare di Cratippo, al contenuto dell'opera tucidea, ma ne dà una descrizione che può apparire disordinata;[4] nel caso di Cratippo invece racchiude tra il 411 e il 394 una ordinata serie di eventi. Anche questo induce a ritenere che il sommario dedicato a Cratippo sia un vero e proprio riassunto dell'opera mirante a dare un'idea esatta del contenuto. E' ovvio che si tratta pur sempre di indicazioni approssimative. In particolare non si deve perdere di vista l'impianto e la finalità del *De gloria Atheniensium*. Qui Plutarco elenca grandi gesta di personaggi ateniesi: perciò "Conone che riporta Atene sul mare" sta bene a conclusione della lista delle imprese ateniesi narrate dall'ateniese Cratippo, ma va da sé che il racconto poteva comprendere, ad esempio, anche le conseguenze politiche di Cnido, magari fino alla sistemazione generale rappresentata dalla pace di Antalcida. Il profilo plutarcheo dell'opera di Cratippo resterebbe, anche in tal caso, sostanzialmente valido.

Il termine iniziale (il 411) deve comunque considerarsi certo, dal momento che Dionigi, quando presenta Cratippo, oltre a definirlo "coetaneo" di Tucidide, mette anche in relazione la sua opera con il completamento di quella tucidea.

Quale immagine di Cratippo danno queste due testimonianze? Quella di uno storico ateniese vicino all'ambiente di Tucidide, autore di un'opera storica comprendente gli anni tra il 411 e, all'incirca, il 394/3. Dinanzi ad un così notevole ma, al tempo stesso, così dimenticato e quasi evanescente storico, Karl Müller, il grande editore dei *Fragmenta Historicorum Graecorum*, fu indotto a formulare una ipotesi, che tentava di tener conto appunto e del rilievo dell'opera di Cratippo (recante tratti così simili alle *Elleniche* di Senofonte e di Teopompo) e, insieme, della sua quasi totale scomparsa dalla successiva tradizione: pensò che Cratippo fosse colui che aveva pubblicato, insieme, un Tucidide 'completo' e le *Elleniche* di Teopompe. Ecco la sua, non limpidissima, formulazione: "Nimirum ita rem sese habere suspicor: Edidit Cratippus opus historicum quod Thucydidis historias una cum Hellenicis Theopompi complectebatur: ita tamen, ut postrema

---

accolto: che cioè gli 'estremi' deducibili dal riassunto plutarcheo sono, appunto, il 411 e il 394/3.

[4] Pone prima l'impresa di Demostene a Pilo e la cattura, da parte di Cleone, dei quattrocento spartani (425 a.C.) e poi la vittoria di Mironide a Enofita (457 a.C.).

Thucydidei operis retractaret simulque e suo penu adderet quae deinceps gesta sunt, usque ad finem belli Peloponnesiaci" (*FHG* II, 1848, p. 78). Così, Cratippo prendeva corpo e di colpo scompariva: era essenzialmente editore di opere altrui. Questo rendeva, certo, meglio tollerabile la singolarità propria di Cratippo: di essere presentato dall'unica fonte (Plutarco) che ne parli compiutamente come un autore di grande spicco, subito accanto a Tucidide, e di risultare, nondimeno, completamente ignorato, quasi svanito nel nulla, di non essere, anzi, utilizzato nemmeno dallo stesso Plutarco che pure mostra per lui tanta considerazione.[5] L'ipotesi di Müller dev'essere apparsa appagante (non si citano, per i decenni successivi, altri studi su Cratippo), finché Ernst von Leutsch, l'editore, con Schneidewin, dei *Paroemiographi* e direttore, dopo Schneidewin, di "Philologus", in uno dei suoi ultimi scritti, una brevissima nota su "Philologus" (33, 1874), compì un ulteriore passo—in fondo, il tassello mancante—sulla strada indicata da Müller: rilevò la notevole rassomiglianza tra la formula con cui Dionigi definisce Cratippo continuatore-editore di Tucidide (τὰ παραλειφθέντα ὑπ'αὐτοῦ συναγαγών) e quella con cui Diogene Laerzio riferisce (II,57) che editore delle inedite carte tucididee sarebbe stato Senofonte. E concluse perciò che "Cratippo" altro non era che lo pseudonimo sotto cui Senofonte aveva pubblicato *Elleniche* I – IV.[6]

Che, comunque, nella importante testimonianza di Plutarco (*Glor. Athen.* 345 D) disturbasse la mancanza—nella rassegna degli storici ateniesi—di un cenno alle *Elleniche* di Senofonte era stato rilevato da Daniel Albert Wyttenbach nel II volume di *Animadversiones* all'edizione commentata dei *Moralia* (Oxonii 1810, p. 137): "Quom Thrasybuli et Cononis res sint pars *Hellenicorum* Xenophontis, horumque mentio a Plutarcho praetermittatur, facile quis in eam suspicionem incidat, aliquid hoc loco excidisse, quod mentionem illius operis xenophontei continuerit; praesertim cum aliis in libris Plutarchus illius auctoritate et testimonio

---

[5] Il *locus classicus* è, a questo proposito, Plutarco, *Alcibiade*, 32. Qui Plutarco elenca—per confutare Duride—Teopompo Eforo e Senofonte: "Das sind also die grundlegenden Quellen für diese Zeit; Kratippos dagegen ist nicht unter ihnen" (Meyer, *Theopomps Hellenika*, Halle, 1909, p. 127); cfr. H. Weil, *L'historien Cratippe continuateur de Thucydide*, "REG", 13, 1900, p. 5.

[6] Von Leutsch pensava ai libri I–IV, che si concludono appunto con la vittoria di Conone a Cnido e le sue conseguenze. Che in tale prima parte (o meglio prima edizione) delle *Elleniche* rientrasse però anche quello che—nella divisione in libri prevalsa—è V,1, sembra certo: lo conferma la indiscutibile citazione di V,1,36 in Isocrate, *Panegirico* 139 (che meriterebbe una discussione a parte, che qui debbo omettere; ma cfr. comunque K. Münscher, *Xenophon in der griechisch-römischen Literatur*, Leipzig 1920, p. 7). Che d'altra parte con τὰ ὑπὸ Θουκυδίδου παραλειφθέντα Dionigi intenda riferirsi a ciò che manca, negli otto libri tucididei, del racconto della guerra peloponnesiaca, è chiaro da un altro passo dell'opuscolo dionisiano (*Su Tucidide*, 19,1: πολλὰ καὶ μεγάλα πράγματα παραλιπών).

utatur.'' Müller, il quale inizialmente aveva trascurato questa nota di
Wyttenbach, la segnalò tra gli *Addenda* posti al termine del IV volume dei
Fragmenta Historicorum Graecorum (Paris 1851, p. 654).

L'ipotesi, alquanto attraente, di von Leutsch suscitò l'interesse di
Arnold Schaefer, il quale ne fece cenno in un'opera di larga consultazione
e di orientamento generale, la terza edizione (1882) dell'*Abriß der
Quellenkunde der griechischen und römischen Geschichte* (p. 31). Reagì Franz
Rühl sugli ''Jahrbücher für klassischen Philologie'' del 1883 (pp.
738–739), 'allarmato'—come si dichiarava—per l'accoglienza riservata
all'ipotesi di von Leutsch dall'autorevole manuale di Schaefer; e la polemica non ebbe seguito. Peraltro le due obiezioni che Rühl moveva a von
Leutsch non erano particolarmente stringenti. Plutarco e Dionigi—osser-
vava—mostrano altrove di conoscere il vero autore delle *Elleniche*;[7] e
quanto ai discorsi diretti, la loro presenza nelle *Elleniche* senofontee fa sì
che di tale opera non possa essere considerato autore colui—Cratippo
appunto—che definì ''molesti per gli ascoltatori'' i discorsi tucididei. Col
che il Rühl apriva quella nutrita schiera di studiosi i quali hanno creduto
di leggere nelle parole di Cratippo riferite da Dionigi non già—come si
dovrebbe—un giudizio sull'insuccesso dei discorsi tucididei, bensì una
condanna *in generale* dei discorsi diretti nelle opere storiografiche.

La proposta di von Leutsch non riscosse—a parte Schaefer—adesioni.
Rimaneva perciò l'ingombro dell'imbarazzante Cratippo, coevo, continuatore e critico di Tucidide ma ignorato fino all'età di Augusto
(Dionigi) e di Plutarco. Non a caso il tentativo più radicale di sgomberare
il campo dalla sua presenza venne da un notevole studioso della biogra-
fia e del testo di Tucidide, Johann Matthias Stahl. Egli propose di modi-
ficare il testo della testimonianza di Dionigi al fine di spostare Cratippo
dall'età di Tucidide a quella di Augusto. Suggeriva di scrivere ὁ
συνακμάσας⟨σοι⟩αὐτῷ in luogo di ὁ συνακμάσας αὐτῷ. Trasformava
così Cratippo in coetaneo non già di Tucidide ma del destinatario, Elio
Tuberone, dell'opuscolo di Dionigi, cioè in pratica di Dionigi medesimo:[8] e lo identificava senz'altro con il filosofo Cratippo di Pergamo,
buon amico di Pompeo e più volte ricorrente negli scritti di Cicerone. (Col

---

[7] L'obiezione ha meno efficacia di quanto sembri, se si considera che anche
Temistogene, lo pseudonimo di Senofonte per l'*Anabasi*, ha finito col diventare, nella
tradizione erudita, un autore a sé (Suda, s.v.). Col nome ''Cratippo'' poté circolare una
parte delle *Elleniche*, preceduta da una *Praefatio* (cfr. *infra*, *Epimetron*, § 3).

[8] J.M. Stahl, *De Cratippo historico*, Münster 1888, p. 14. Ma se riesce ad eludere la difficoltà sollevata qualche anno prima da Justus Hermann Lipsius (''Leipziger Studien,''
4, 1881, p. 153) contro Schaefer, il quale suggeriva un nome proprio in luogo di αὐτῷ,
non si sottrae però alla obiezione di Schmid (''Philologus'', 52, 1894, p. 128): non ha senso *attestare* qualcosa su Tucidide invocando un autore vissuto quattro secoli dopo.

che Stahl si spingeva troppo oltre: dal contesto di Plutarco è chiaro che Cratippo dev'essere un ateniese).

Si apriva così una nuova fase della discussione su Cratippo, nel corso della quale si affrontarono, su ''Philologus'', da un lato Stahl (50, 1891) e dall'altro Wilhelm Schmid (49, 1890 e 52, 1894), lo storico della letteratura greca (morto quasi centenario nel 1951). Allo Schmid si debbono alcuni rilievi miranti a confermare l'appartenenza di Cratippo all'epoca di Tucidide. In particolare Schmid poneva l'accento sulla espressione— che Dionigi ricavava, probabilmente, dallo stesso Cratippo—, secondo cui ἐν τοῖς τελευταίοις Tucidide aveva trascurato i discorsi diretti: una espressione, notava Schmid (e aveva già notato W. Roscher, *Leben Werk und Zeitalter des Thukydides*, Göttingen 1842, p. 561), che non sembra presupporre ancora la alessandrina suddivisione in otto libri dell'opera di Tucidide. Schmid notava anche che al diradarsi dei discorsi diretti aveva corrisposto, in Tucidide, un intensificarsi dei discorsi indiretti. Fenomeni tra loro congruenti, e conformi alle osservazioni di Cratippo su questa materia. Stahl ebbe un insigne e rigoroso sostenitore in Henri Weil (REG 1900, pp. 1 – 9), il quale teorizzò, in certo senso non a torto, che la modifica ⟨σοι⟩αὐτῷ era assolutamente necessaria per risolvere il rompicapo della plurisecolare eclisse di un Cratippo ''coetaneo'' di Tucidide.

2. Eduard Meyer ha affrontato dapprima il tema Cratippo nella *Geschichte des Altertums* (III[1], 1901, p. 276), nella parte di quel volume dedicata alla discussione delle fonti. Qui Meyer non prende posizione, si limita a prospettare le due possibilità: Cratippo contemporaneo di Tucidide, ovvero dotto di ''età romana,'' ed a rinviare ai saggi principali di Schmid e di Stahl, assertori rispettivamente delle due tesi. E dice ''di età romana'' appunto perché intende riferirsi alla veduta di Stahl, sorretta dalla ben nota congettura.

Pochi anni più tardi furono pubblicati gli ampi frammenti delle cosiddette *Elleniche di Ossirinco* (*The Oxyrhynchus Papyri*, V, London 1908, a cura di Bernard P. Grenfell e Arthur S. Hunt). I frammenti riguardavano gli anni 396/395 e risultavano internamente databili, dal punto di vista della composizione, tra il 356 e il 346. Ma erano privi di una esplicita indicazione d'autore: il che metteva in moto la *vexata quaestio* della loro attribuzione, e perciò riproponeva all'attenzione dei dotti il nome di Cratippo. Si era in presenza di un frammento adespoto, che trattava di eventi rientranti nell'ambito cronologico sia delle *Elleniche* di Teopompo che dell'opera di Cratippo (quale risulta dal riassunto plutarcheo).[9] Perciò fu

---

[9] Ovviamente anche delle *Storie* di Eforo. Ma la candidatura di Eforo parve subito alquanto debole, nonstante venisse riproposta con forza da Walker, perché il sistema

prudente, da parte degli editori principi, intitolare l'edizione ''Theopompus (or Cratippus) *Hellenica*,'' ma la ipotesi preferita era che si trattasse delle *Elleniche* di Teopompo. Ipotesi che ottenne prontamente il consenso dei tre 'grandi': Wilamowitz, Meyer e Schwartz. Per Cratippo si era espresso invece Blass: il che spingeva quasi automaticamente il suo disistimatore Wilamowitz a sostenere la veduta contraria.[10]. Isolata voce di dissenso, nell'*entourage* dei tre grandi, quella del loro scolaro Jacoby, allora trentenne e appena all'inizio dell'immane lavoro sui *Frammenti degli storici greci*.[11]

In particolare Meyer e Wilamowitz erano stati consultati da Grenfell e Hunt *prima* dell'edizione. Era il momento di massima collaborazione scientifica anglo-tedesca; Wilamowitz, editore dei *Bucolici Graeci* nella ''Bibliotheca Oxoniensis,'' teneva ad Oxford la lezione, poi ampiamente rielaborata, *Greek Historical Writing*; si percepiva nei pur notevolissimi studiosi inglesi un senso di rispettosa 'inferiorità' rispetto a questi *leaders* della filologia classica mondiale. Il legame era antico, risaliva per lo meno all'inizio del secolo precedente, quando Niebuhr veniva pubblicato, in lingua inglese, nel ''Philological Museum'' di Cambridge (1832) e la *Storia della letteratura greca* di Karl Otfried Müller usciva (postuma) a Londra (1840), quindi a Breslau (1841).

Grenfell e Hunt elencavano (pp. 129 sgg.) dieci ''buone ragioni'' per cui il nuovo papiro doveva considerarsi parte delle *Elleniche* di Teopompo e chiarivano subito che si trattava di argomenti approvati, o 'concordati', con Wilamowitz e Meyer (p. 129). Si trattava di considerazioni relative all'orientamento politico (atteggiamento nei confronti di Atene) a di stile e di lessico (κατᾶραι nel senso di ἐλθεῖν, che *Anecd. Bekk.* p. 104,15, considera tipico di Teopompo, e ricorre un paio di volte nei frammenti: col. XVIII,39 e VIII,22) o di natura schiettamente contenutistica (descrizioni geografiche: col. VI,45 e XV,17 ~ Teopompo, fr. 385 e 391 Jacoby), o infine di orientamento narrativo (puntigliosa polemica implicita e constante rettifica nei confronti di Senofonte). L'anno dopo, su ''Hermes'' (1909, p. 496), Schwartz commentava: ''Gli argomenti di Grenfell e Hunt sono talmente forti che non vedo come potrebbero essere confutati.''

La reazione—a dir vero un po' saccente—venne dagli scolari. Jacoby

---

cronologico dell'autore delle ''Elleniche di Ossirinco'' risultava chiaramente essere quello tucidideo (''annalistico'' e ''per estati e inverni''), il che non si adatta a quanto sappiamo dell'impianto narrativo di Eforo.

[10] Per una tavola sinottica delle varie proposte di attribuzione avanzate tra il 1908 e il 1939, *cf.* H. Bloch, *Studies in Historical Literature of the Fourth Century B.C.*, ''Harvard Studies in Classical Philology,'' Suppl. I, 1940, pp. 306–307.

[11] *Die Entwicklung der griechischen Historiographie*, ''Klio'', 9, 1909, p. 97, nota.

nell'articolo programmatico in cui annunciava il piano dei *Fragmente*
("Klio", 1909) dichiarava in tono sconsolato: "Mi è incomprensibile
come proprio i nostri giudici più competenti, Meyer e Wilamowitz, abbia-
no potuto seriamente raccomandare l'identificazione con Teopompo"
(p. 97, nota). Jacoby toccava l'argomento solo marginalmente, e si schie-
rava senz'altro per l'ipotesi di Blaß (Cratippo autore del nuovo testo).
Meyer reagì in tono alquanto piccato. Nel volume in gran parte dedicato
ai nuovi frammenti (*Theopomps Hellenika*, Halle 1909) riprese le stupefatte
parole di Jacoby (p. 125: "qualcuno ha dichiarato incomprensibile che
Wilamowitz ed io abbiamo ritenuto evidente l'attribuzione a Teopompo
ecc.") e gli dedicò una efficace confutazione (nota 2). L'altro dissenso
venne da Paul Maas.[12] Come al solito, Maas partiva da alcuni luoghi di
Ateneo. Prendeva spunto da citazioni teopompee presenti in Ateneo e
metteva l'accento sulla diversità di stile rispetto ai nuovi frammenti. Anni
dopo[13] Jacoby presenterà questo intervento di Maas come risolutivo e
definitivamente letale nei confronti dell'ipotesi Teopompo. Eppure, visti
da vicino, gli argomenti di Maas rivelano una certa fragilità e soprattutto
una portata molto limitata: egli stesso del resto si mostra consapevole del
carattere anomalo degli esempi teopompei che adduce, scelti da un autore, Ateneo, il quale è andato a caccia di aneddoti singolari e di *excursus*
etimologico-antiquari ("gerade solche curiosa ausgewählt hat"). Il che
significa che quegli esempi non sono un sufficiente campione stilistico.

Maas notava che, comunque, le attestazioni da lui raccolte (in Ateneo,
appunto) erano tali da dimostrare la sostanziale identità dello stile del
giovane (*Elleniche*) e del maturo (*Filippiche*) Teopompo, e che d'altra parte
l'abisso tra lo stile del papiro e quello di Teopompo era "tiefer als jener,
den der Wechsel der Vorbilder und der Lauf der Jahre bei einem Schriftsteller hervorruft;" e dichiarava in conclusione di "sentire" ("fühle
ich"), nel caso del papiro e di Teopompo, "den Gegensatz zweier Volksstämme, des attischen und des jonischen." Osservazioni alquanto im-
pressionistiche. Nelle lezioni bonnensi, quasi un secolo prima, Niebuhr
aveva notato che un dato *oggettivo*—l'ampiezza dell'opera, il numero dei
libri—può orientare (aggiungo: ben più dell'analisi di singole frasette)
nella valutazione del divario che intercorreva tra le *Elleniche* e le *Filippiche*:
"Ausser Xenophon setzte auch Theopompus den Thukydides in seinen
Helleniken fort. Er führte die Geschichte von dem Ende des Thukydides
bis zur Schlacht von Knidus fort. Dieses Werk mag sein bestes gewesen

---

[12] *Stilistisches zum Historiker Theopomp*, "Berliner Philologische Wochenschrift," 1912,
col. 1845 (= *Kleine Schriften*, München 1973, pp. 74–75).
[13] *Der Verfasser der Hellenika von Oxyrhynchos*, "Nachrichten von der Gesellschaft der
Wissenschaften zu Göttingen," Phil.-Hist. Klasse, 1924, pp. 13–18 (= *Gesammelte
Abhandlungen*, Leiden 1956, pp. 316–321).

sein, *als Werk von beschränkten Umfange* und ohne Ansprüche, und da *seine Persönlichkeit hier aus dem Spiele blieb.*"[14] L'osservazione relativa all'ampiezza delle due opere (12 libri le *Elleniche* per gli anni 411 – 394, e quali anni!, 58 libri le *Filippiche* per gli anni 359 – 336) è illuminante. Oltre tutto con le *Filippiche* Teopompo passava alla storia contemporanea; col che tutto cambiava, a cominciare dal modo di scrivere, che è in stretta relazione con la materia e con il tipo di informazione. Bene scriveva Niebuhr che nelle *Elleniche* la personalità di Teopompo "restava fuori del gioco:" si indeboliscono molto le lamentele di coloro che, da Meß ("Rheinisches Museum" 1908, p. 372) a Beloch (citato alla nota 35), hanno denunciato la mancanza, nelle *Elleniche di Ossirinco* del "Feuergeist" o della "Feuerseele" di Teopompo, nonché le più caute ma analoghe osservazioni di Maas.

E' appena necessario soggiungere che l'attribuzione dei nuovi frammenti a Cratippo si fondava sul consueto fraintendimento della testimonianza di Dionigi: Cratippo era un "odiatore" dei discorsi nelle opere storiche, nei frammenti conservatisi mancano discorsi diretti (il che non è del tutto esatto, se si considera l'esortazione di Dorimaco in colonna XI, 20 – 23), *ergo* l'autore dei frammenti è Cratippo. Qui, come sappiamo, è errata la premessa: a stare a Dionigi, infatti, Cratippo non attaccava *in generale* l'uso, così diffuso nella storiografia classica, di inserire discorsi diretti nelle opere storiche,[15] notava piuttosto che quelli tucididei non avevano avuto successo. E azzardata era anche l'altra premessa del 'sillogismo': che cioè nell'opera *tutta* da cui provengono i frammenti di Ossirinco mancassero discorsi diretti. (Se di Tucidide avessimo soltanto frammenti della "Pentecontetia" o dell'VIII libro o di buona parte del V o del VII, diremmo che Tucidide, "autentico scienziato in senso moderno ecc.ecc.," aborriva i discorsi diretti). E' impressionante la coerenza con cui è stato applicato il postulato della "assenza di discorsi diretti nello storico di Ossirinco." Quando nel 1968 fu pubblicato il Pap.Michigan inv. 5982 (scoperto a Karanis nel '30), gli editori principi (Merkelbach e Youtie) accantonarono immediatamente l'ipotesi, in sé più che legittima, che il nuovo frammento appartenesse alle "Elleniche di Ossirinco," con

---

[14] *Vorträge über alte Geschichte*, II.2, Berlin 1848, pp. 43 – 44.
[15] Su questo punto la confusione è massima: non c'è scritto riguardante Cratippo in cui non venga ripetuto, in barba al testo di Dionigi (*Th.* 16), che Cratippo era "ostile ai discorsi nelle opere storiche:" ciò serve a bollarlo come mentecatto lontanissimo cronologicamente dall'età classica della storiografia greca. Un caso limite di fraintendimento del capitolo 16 del *Tucidide* di Dionigi è G. De Sanctis (*L'Attide di Androzione*, "Atti dell'Accad. d.scienze di Torino," 1908, p. 339), secondo cui Cratippo avrebbe sostenuto che Tucidide "non aveva dato termine alla sua storia distoltone dalla ineguaglianza che risultava da questo tardivo ravvedimento [*scil.* di Tucidide sull'opportunità di inserire discorsi diretti nell'opera storica]."

l'argomento che nelle "Elleniche di Ossirinco" mancano i discorsi diretti
mentre nel nuovo frammento ce n'è uno!.[16] Ragionamento inconsistente
per molte ragioni (come rilevò due anni più tardi Max Treu),[17] e, tra
l'altro, per l'uso approssimativo della nozione stessa di "discorso diretto."
Non è del tutto esatto infatti che lo storico del Pap.Michigan dia la parola
a Teramene per un "discorso diretto." Lí Teramene non pronuncia un
discorso del genere di quelli che Tucidide fa pronunciare ai suoi personaggi (fuor che nell'ottavo libro), bensì un paio di frasi, conclusive di un
pensiero che incomincia in forma indiretta al rigo 12 della I colonna[18] e
prosegue, appunto, con un paio di frasi dette in forma diretta: esattamente come accade nell'VIII di Tucidide (53,2 – 3)—il libro, come si
suol dire, "privo di discorsi diretti!"—, dove le parole di Pisandro sono
riferite dapprima in forma indiretta (53,2), quindi, per circa sette righi
oxoniensi, in forma diretta (53,3); ed è quello l'unico, brevissimo, "discorso diretto" dell'VIII libro: di estensione identica all'intervento di
Teramene nel Pap.Michigan. (Se di un Tucidide altrimenti perduto
ritrovassimo vari frammenti dell'VIII[19] e ad un certo punto anche
VIII,53, diremmo che quest'ultimo appartiene a un altro autore giacché
presenta un discorso diretto?)

3. La scoperta delle "Elleniche di Ossirinco," prontamente identificate
con quelle di Teopompo, spinsero Meyer ad una completa riconsiderazione dell'intero problema. Nacque così *Theopomps Hellenika*, che fornisce
anche una nuova edizione dei frammenti vecchi e nuovi.

I nuovi testi sbilanciavano, per così dire, la posizione di Meyer. Ora
era meno facile lasciare impregiudicata la questione Cratippo. L'esistenza
di un'opera storica non identificabile con le *Elleniche* di Senofonte, ma
palesemente dovuta ad uno storico (quale lo "storico di Ossirinco" cer-
tamente è) piuttosto vicino ai fatti narrati, imponeva di *scegliere* una delle
immagini sin lì prospettate di Cratippo. Vediamo perché. Fare di Cratippo un autore di IV secolo, non molto lontano, nel tempo, da Tucidide,
e dunque un autorevole candidato alla paternità delle nuove "Elleniche",
significava scontrarsi più che mai con la difficoltà della singolare eclissi di
un'opera così importante: un'opera di cui ci si sforzava di dire, sulla base

---

[16] "ZPE" 2, 1968, pp. 161 – 162: "Man denkt zunächst an die Hellenika von Oxyrhynchos; aber die bisher gefundenen Teile dieses Werkes enthalten keine direkte Rede,
während der neue Text ausführlich eine Rede des Theramenes referiert." Che Hell.Oxy.
potesse contenere discorsi diretti, in parti non conservate, è ovvio: cfr. Meyer, *Theopomps
Hellenika*, pp. 122 – 123.

[17] "Studi Clasice" 12, 1970, p. 31, nota 46.

[18] Dove non si integrerà [τὸ] ma [ὅτι]: infatti ci sono tre spazi.

[19] Effettivamente ne sono venuti fuori tre (Pack² 1532 – 1534).

di indiscutibili coincidenze, che era stata usata da Eforo e di cui si riscontravano 'tracce' in Diodoro. D'altra parte, trasportare *manu militari* Cratippo in età romana (per esempio tenendosi alla congettura di Stahl, che ancora nel 1901 Meyer mostrava di apprezzare) era bensì giovevole per escluderlo dalla corsa alla paternità delle ''Elleniche di Ossirinco''—che non possono certo essere opera di un autore di età romana—, ma si scontrava con la difficoltà non piccola della insostenibilità sintattica della congettura di Stahl.

La scelta di Meyer (*Theopomps Hellenika*, pp. 125–129) fu quella di proclamare Cratippo ''unbedeutender Autor der hellenistischen Zeit [sec. III] der sich an einem Stoff der älteren Geschichte versucht hat'' (p. 128), senza peraltro spiegare come mai Dionigi ne parlasse come di un ''coetaneo'' di Tucidide.[20]

Fu Schwartz a compiere, nello stesso anno, nel saggio su Eforo, l'ulteriore passo: quello di proclamare Cratippo un ''falsario'', il quale ''durch die Maske eines Zeitgenossen seinem Elaborat Ansehen verschaffen wollte''.[21] La teoria del falsario, però, era piuttosta rovinosa. A rigore, il falsario poteva (forse doveva) fingere che l'impero persiano fosse ancora in piedi! Il riferimento all'impero persiano come tuttora in vita è l'argomento con cui si pongono con certezza nel IV secolo le ''Elleniche di Ossirinco:'' le quali dunque potrebbero essere anch'esse opera di un falsario . . . .

Meyer dal canto suo è talmente insensibile al fatto che non solo Dionigi ma lo stesso Plutarco (quando nel *De gloria Atheniensium* colloca Cratippo tra Tucidide e Senofonte) pongono chiaramente, e concordemente, Cratippo in età tucididea, da giungere, trascinato dal proprio ragionamento, ad auspicare che un giorno vengano fuori, a risolvere l'annosa questione, ''ganz authentische Angaben über sein Leben oder sein Werk'' (p. 129)!

Liberatosi di Cratippo, Meyer può, senz'altro, 'dare' a Teopompo le ''Elleniche di Ossirinco,'' riprendendo e arricchendo i ben noti argomenti elaborati da Grenfell e Hunt.

4. Il molesto dilemma dal quale non facilmente uscivano sia Meyer, per un verso, che Blaß e i sostenitori dell'attribuzione a Cratippo, per l'altro, era, detto in breve, il seguente: optare per Teopompo come autore dei

---

[20] Sulla vicinanza cronologica di Cratippo rispetto a Tucidide conviene insistere: essa è esplicitamente affermata da Dionigi, ma si ricava chiaramente da Plutarco, il quale colloca Cratippo tra Tucidide e Senofonte. In ''RFIC'' 102, 1974, pp. 133–139 avevo suggerito una spiegazione (συνακμάζω = rivaleggiare) che, pur suffragata da attestazioni, non bene si adatta a quanto sappiamo di Cratippo.

[21] *Die Zeit des Ephoros*, ''Hermes'', 44, 1909, p. 500.

nuovi frammenti comportava un preliminare declassamento di Cratippo ad autore tardo contro la concorde testimonianza di Dionigi e Plutarco; optare per Cratippo significava lasciare inspiegata la dimenticanza in cui una così importante opera era vissuta presso la successiva tradizione storiografica ed erudita.

Com'è chiaro, il miglior contributo alla denunzia della poca credibilità di una tale eclissi veniva proprio dagli studiosi come Meyer e Schwartz (ma anche Weil e altri ancora), i quali miravano a presentare Cratippo come autore tardo (o addirittura falsario). I migliori e più convincenti argomenti sono proprio quelli di Meyer. Egli non si limitava a valorizzare il molto citato passo di Plutarco (*Alcibiade* 32) in cui il biografo discute il resoconto di Duride sul trionfale rientro di Alcibiade in Atene nel 408. L'assenza, in tale discussione plutarchea, del nome di Cratippo è stata più volte messa in rilievo (*supra*, nota 5): è infatti un bell'esempio di uso «sano» dell'*argumentum ex silentio*. Però Meyer chiama in causa anche altre fonti, ed il quadro che traccia è di estrema efficacia. Oltre all'intero corpus delle *Vite* di Plutarco e di Cornelio Nepote riguardanti gli anni 411 – 394,[22] ci sono—egli osserva—autori e repertori, irti di citazioni erudite e rare della più varia provenienza, quali Ateneo, Stefano di Bisanzio, la cosiddetta "Suda", nonché lessici specialistici come quello di Arpocrazione,[23] dai quali (e dalle cui fonti) è davvero incredibile che il nome di Cratippo rimanesse sistematicamente fuori; vi è poi—seguita Meyer—un più specifico genere di fonti, 'specializzate', per così dire, nel catalogare i "continuatori di Tucidide" (Diodoro, XIII,42; XIV,84 e 89;[24] Marcellino, 45; Vita anonima di Tucidide, 5): e anche qui si parla unicamente di Senofonte e Teopompo. E si potrebbe aggiungere che anche il rude Polibio, il quale elargisce pedantescamente lodi e biasimi alla storiografia precedente, di Cratippo non fa mai il nome.

Sono silenzi piuttosto impressionanti. Ma una speciale considerazione la merita proprio il caso Plutarco. Plutarco infatti non si limita a mostrare conoscenza dell'opera di Cratippo: nel *De gloria Atheniensium* si esprime come se per lui Cratippo fosse "*der klassische Autor* für die Jahre, die

---

[22] Alcibiade, Lisandro, Agesilao, Trasibulo, Conone.

[23] Meyer dice propriamente: "bei Suidas und wo man sonst literar-historische Angaben sucht" (p. 127, nota 1).

[24] Si potrebbero indicare anche altri passi (es. XII,37) e aggiungere una considerazione sulla *provenienza* di queste notizie diodoree dalla tradizione cronografica (Apollodoro di Atene), molto attenta alle notizie storico-letterarie. Alcuni di questi silenzi erano stati segnalati da Henri Weil, in un articolo che ebbe risonanza ("REG", 13, 1900, pp. 1 – 9): tanto più interessante, in quanto precedente la scoperta dei frammenti di Ossirinco (che Weil ritenne senz'altro di Teopompo), e perciò non condizionato dal dilemma 'Cratippo o Teopompo.'

Thukydides übrig gelassen hatte.''[25] Lì Cratippo figura subito accanto a Tucidide; e la sua opera è rievocata in un ben ordinato riassunto che è il più lungo di tutta la tirata plutarchea sugli storici ateniesi (345 CE); ed è citata come quella *ad hoc* per la conoscenza del periodo dopo-Tucidide, così come quella tucididea lo è per il periodo precedente; le *Elleniche* di Senofonte non sono neanche nominate (Senofonte è nominato subito dopo, ma per l'*Anabasi*, o meglio per l'abile trovata di diffondere l'*Anabasi* con uno pseudonimo). Tanto più, perciò, sorprende che colui che qui appare a Plutarco come *lo storico per eccellenza dell'età 411–394* non sia poi stato da lui adoperato assolutamente mai quando di quegli anni ha parlato, anni assai spesso ritornanti nelle *Vite* e in tanti riferimenti nei *Moralia*.

Tentando di spiegare questa non lieve difficoltà (a far emergere la quale forse nessuno ha contribuito così efficacemente come Meyer), Eduard Schwartz escogitò questa strana formulazione: "Dionys und Plutarch haben sich täuschen lassen [*scil*. dal falsario Cratippo], doch hat dieser [Plut.] ihn [Cratippo] bezeichnenderweise in seinen *Viten* nie benutzt, sondern nennt ihn nur einmal in einer rhetorischen Schrift, wo es ihm auf eine effectvolle Antithese ankam: die wahren 'attischen' Geschicht-schreiber sollen den hellenistischen (...) gegenübergestellt werden" (pp. 501–502). E' però lecito chiedersi perché mai, per fissare una tale "antitesi", fosse necessario annoverare, tra gli altri, l'altrimenti mai nominato Cratippo e 'saltare' le *Elleniche* di Senofonte.[26]

5. In realtà, la soluzione che consente di superare questi dilemmi e queste aporie è l'ipotesi intravista da Müller e meglio prospettata da von Leutsch: ipotesi che, tra l'altro, consente di restituire serenamente a Teopompo le "Elleniche di Ossirinco." "Cratippo"—un nome che ben si addice a Senofonte, autore di un *Ipparco* e di un trattato *Sull'equitazione*—, a stare a quanto di lui riferiscono Dionigi e Plutarco ("il raccoglitore-editore del *Nachlaß* tucidideo" lo definisce Dionigi, mentre Plutarco mostra che l'opera di lui andava ben oltre il 404), corrisponde pienamente alla figura storico-letteraria di Senofonte.

Plutarco sembrerebbe consapevole di ciò che si cela sotto il nome "Cratippo", e perciò subito dopo sfodera Temistogene, e fa in modo, con sottile artificio, di determinare la successione di parole Κράτιππος Ξενοφῶν, divise unicamente dal verbo.[27]

---

[25] Come scrisse molto efficacemente Carl Peter, *Wahrheit und Kunst*, Leipzig 1911, p. 123, nota 1.

[26] Un po' affannoso e strumentale è anche il tentativo di squalificare l'opuscolo plutarcheo ed il significato del panorama storiografico lì tracciato ("una sola volta, in uno scritto retorico" ...).

[27] Ma poco dopo, nel raccontare le gesta dei cavalieri ateniesi a Mantinea, parafrasa con tutta chiarezza le *Elleniche* senofontee: cfr. *infra*, *Epimetron*, § 3.

La 'scomparsa', per tanti secoli, di Cratippo trova così, nell'ambito di
questa ipotesi, la più ragionevole spiegazione. In età augustea, quando
scrive Dionigi, saranno tornati alla luce vecchi esemplari di quella edizione parziale, poi superata. Non è azzardato pensare alla biblioteca di
Apellicone di Teo—cioè a quella di Aristotele—come al probabile veicolo
di questa "resurrezione".[28] Nella biblioteca di Aristotele quella edizione
parziale delle *Elleniche* ci sarà stata, con tutta probabilità (Luciano,
Adv.indoct., 4, attesta che nella biblioteca di Apellicone c'erano esemplari tucididei di IV secolo a.C.): è stato da tempo osservato che nella
Costituzione di Atene (a proposito dei Trenta) Aristotele presuppone e
parafrasa formulazioni tratte appunto dalle *Elleniche* senofontee.[29]
Questo tipo di eclissi e di ricomparsa spiega anche il diverso modo in cui
Dionigi—che è il primo a darne notizia—e Plutarco parlano di Cratippo.
Quando scrive Dionigi, Cratippo à una "novità": e perciò il critico gli
dedica uno spazio amplissimo, uno spazio che non concede altrove quando riferisce pensieri altrui (di altri 'critici', e qui Cratippo gli serve in tale
veste); e proprio perché è una novità, non vi è stato ancora un 'accumulo
di dottrina' su di lui, non si è ancora appurato cosa veramente fosse quel-
l'opera (a complicare le cose, a rendere meno ovvia l'identificazione c'era,
oltre alla diversa divisione in libri ed al proemio, la diffusa pratica del
plagio, che induceva alla prudenza prima che si proclamasse che due
opere fossero la stessa opera).[30] Un secolo più tardi, invece, Plutarco
sembra già consapevole del gioco pseudonimico, e parla di Cratippo e,
insieme, di Temistogene.

D'altra parte è evidente che le considerazioni relative al silenzio della
tradizione successiva valgono anche per il cosiddetto "anonimo" delle

---

[28] Notare che la biblioteca di Apellicone rimase a lungo possesso privato di Silla e di
suo figlio, il quale la vendette molto dopo la morte del dittatore. Anche il lavoro di
Andronico di Rodi sul testo aristotelico incominciò in età augustea.

[29] Non è l'unico segno di attenzione di Aristotele per Senofonte. Basti pensare al dialo-
go *Grillo*, che prende nome appunto dal figlio di Senofonte caduto a Mantinea nella
cavalleria ateniese, e destinatario, secondo Aristotele, di innumerevoli encomii postumi.

[30] Per esempio Didimo, quando considera il caso della cosiddetta *Filippica XI* di
Demostene (*Risposta alla lettera di Filippo*), dice prudentemente che "alcuni pensano" che
essa sia di Anassimene, giacché "si ritrova identica nel VII libro dei *Philippikà*" (*Commento
a Demostene*, colonna XI,10–14). Qui l'assurdo (per noi) è che non basti una constatazione
del genere per affermare senz'altro che dunque il brano è di Anassimene! Un altro
esempio è Filisto. Teone diceva che Filisto "aveva trasferito di peso nella sua opera il
racconto tucidideo della guerra attica" (*RhGr* II, p. 63,25 Spengel = 556 T 14 Jacoby):
ma ci si guardava bene dal sospettare—per le parti identiche—che si trattasse di un unico
autore. I primi paragrafi del discorso di Lisia *Sui misteri* ricalcano l'inizio di Lisia XIX
(o viceversa). Il tema dei "furti dei Greci," talora enfatizzato al massimo, è presente in
Clemente, Eusebio ecc. Era insomma del tutto usuale constatare che due opere avessero
molto in comune: la prudenza con cui Didimo ragiona è un effetto di tale diffusa confusione.

"Elleniche di Ossirinco." La volta che non lo si identifichi con un autore già noto, anche di questo splendido anonimo è lecito chiedersi come mai lo ignorino le fonti che catalogano i continuatori di Tucidide o quelle che trattano dello stesso periodo storico ecc. L'identificazione di "Cratippo" con Senofonte e dell' "anonimo" con l'altro continuatore di Tucidide, cioè con Teopompo, rende giustizia alle non lievi aporie.

Per quel che riguarda le "Elleniche di Ossirinco," non si dovrebbe trascurare il punto di partenza materiale: il papiro come oggetto concreto. Da questo punto di vista i dati si sono di molto arricchiti rispetto al momento in cui scriveva Meyer. Sono affiorati alla luce altri due frammenti che è ormai sensato ritenere appartenenti alla medesima opera storica riemersa primamente nel 1907. Il primo nel 1934 (= PSI 1304), il secondo nel 1976 (Pap.Cairo, inv. provv. 26/6/27/1 – 35). E dovremmo, a rigore, parlare anche di un terzo frammento, se consideriamo, secondo il suggerimento di Max Treu [*supra*, nota 16], anche il Pap.Michigan inv. 5982 derivante dalle "Elleniche di Ossirinco." Ciò che mette conto rilevare è che i tre (o quattro col Pap.Michigan) spezzoni provengono, di sicuro, da altrettanti differenti rotoli: infatti il primo, i cosiddetti frammenti londinesi (1907), è scritto, in piena età antonina, sul *verso* di un registro di proprietà agricole, nel sud-ovest del nomo egizio Arsinoite; il secondo proviene invece da un rotolo librario non riutilizzato sul *verso*, trovato da Evaristo Breccia nel Kôm Abu-Teir di Ossirinco; il terzo, che risale al I secolo d.C., è sul *verso* di un papiro documentario (lista di spese) in demotico. La presenza in area egizia di tre (o quattro) diversi esemplari della medesima opera, in un relativamente ristretto lasso di tempo, attesta la notevole diffusione di tale opera tra le persone alfabetizzate. Questi papiri ci fanno intravedere dei privati che riutilizzano vecchi registri o libri di conti per copiarsi quell'opera, biblioteche (forse private) per le quali quell'opera veniva allestita. Ciò dimostra—ha osservato opportunamente Ludwig Koenen—che difficilmente si tratterà "di un anonimo completamente dimenticato dagli storici successivi:" si tratterà piuttosto "di uno storico citato da altri e perciò ben conosciuto,"[31] e tale quindi da suscitare la curiosità dei più vari lettori. Non è del tutto irrilevante osservare che, per lo stesso torno di tempo (I/II secolo d.C.), disponiamo soltanto di tre frammenti papiracei delle *Elleniche* di Senofonte.

Il fatto poi che anche il terzo (e anche il quarto, se si include nel ragionamento anche il Pap.Michigan) rinvenimento casuale riguardi pur sempre avvenimenti posteriori al 411 conferma che non può che trattarsi di un

---

[31] L. Koenen, *Papyrology in the Federal Republic of Germany*, "Studia Papyrologica" 15, 1976, p. 65.

continuatore di Tucidide.[32] Sarebbe ben strano che solo per caso i frammenti che via via riemergono con le nuove scoperte capitano tutti nel periodo successivo a quello trattato da Tucidide, o, per esser più precisi, tra il 411 e il 394. Dunque non si trattava né di uno storico universale alla Eforo, né di un attidografo, e tanto meno di un Daimaco (forse plateese, candidato da un certo momento in poi prediletto da Jacoby), un autore del quale tutto può immaginarsi—dato che nulla o quasi si sa di lui—tranne che fosse, lui storico della Beozia, un continuatore di Tucidide.

Si torna dunque a Teopompo, il cui nome riaffiora prontamente nel saggio di Koenen. E' merito di G.A. Lehmann aver indicato, in dissonanza col vezzo di chi trova poco ''isocrateo'' e quindi poco teopompeo lo stile delle ''Elleniche di Ossirinco,'' un interessante nesso tra quest'opera ed il *Panatenaico* e il *Filippo* di Isocrate[33] ed aver quindi documentato lo stretto nesso che lega i frammenti di Ossirinco con quanto sappiamo delle *Elleniche* di Teopompo.[34] Sarebbe facile ironizzare sugli effetti del pregiudizio secondo cui un autore scriverebbe sempre allo stesso modo. Un po' comiche sono, in questo campo, le vedute riguardanti Teopompo: esse hanno oscillato tra l'immagine di un autore ''phrasenhaft'' perché levigatamente ''isocrateo'' (Maas) e l'immagine torbido-romantica di un ''Feuergeist'' (Beloch).[35] Immagini dunque entrambe arbitrarie. Sommari e immotivati giudizi, che prescindono da fattori primari, tra i quali i seguenti: a) dello stile di un autore, come Teopompo, noto soltanto attraverso citazioni ci si fa un'idea falsata perché filtrata e selezionata dal gusto e dai fini di chi cita; b) da Tucidide in poi, in una narrazione storiografica si alternano lunghe parti espositive e pezzi di bravura (oratoria politica ed epidittica, ma anche *ekphraseis*). Non solo Omero, anche Teopompo (e Tucidide e in genere i narratori di grande lena) *quandoque dormitat*. E poi un torrenziale scrittore-letterato come

---

[32] Il nuovo rinvenimento mi ha dimostrato l'infondatezza dei dubbi che manifestavo nel 1970 (*Tucidide continuato*, Padova, pp. 211–217) in merito alla attribuzione alla medesima opera di P.Oxy. 842 e PSI 1304.

[33] ''ZPE'' 28, 1978, pp. 109–126. Anche Koenen (*art.cit.* p. 65, nota 42) trovava difficoltà a proposito dell'attribuzione a Teopompo: ancora una volta per il solito φανήσεται ''phrasenhaft''.

[34] ''ZPE'' 55, 1984, pp. 18–44; cfr. anche Ruschenbusch, ''ZPE'' 39, 1980, pp. 81–90 e 45, 1982, pp. 91–94. Non bisognerebbe dimenticare, in ogni caso, che, con tutta probabilità, Teopompo, nelle *Elleniche*, si sarà adeguato allo stile tucidideo, come del resto già Senofonte nelle sue. I frammenti superstiti delle *Elleniche* teopompee sono così pochi, e di tal fatta, da non consentire alcun giudizio stilistico. L'imitazione tucididea nelle *Elleniche* teopompee era data per ovvia dal Wilamowitz, *Greek Historical Writing*, Oxford 1908, p. 8.

[35] *Griechische Geschichte*, III,2² (1923), p. 3. Con la consueta tracotanza, Beloch liquidava con una battuta la questione dell'evoluzione stilistica di Teopompo: ''Er war kein Privatdozent, der auf eine Professur wartete.''

Teopompe è un 'universo' che non si caratterizza con un unico tratto, un universo di cui è arduo delineare lo stile in modo unitario.

Ma c'è dell'altro. Nei frammenti "fiorentini" (PSI 1304, fr.A, col. II, linea 23) si legge chiaramente il nome di Pedarito, l'armosta spartano morto nel 411 (Tucidide, VIII,55,3); il contesto è guasto, ma è chiaro che di Pedarito qui si parla "al di fuori dell'ordine strettamente cronologico degli avvenimenti"[36] (la colonna I parla di fatti del 409): esattamente come nelle *Elleniche* di Teopompo, dove il nome di Pedarito veniva fatto, evidentemente in un riepilogo di avvenimenti precedenti riguardanti Chio, nel II libro (Arpocrazione, s.v. Πεδάριτος). Non può essere casuale questa coincidenza, già rilevata dal Bartoletti e successivamente dal Bruce,[37] così come è degno di nota che Arpocrazione (il quale attinge largamente agli storici, in ispecie a Teopompo) dedichi una voce a Pedarito: evidentemente si trattava, nel racconto teopompeo, di un episodio di un certo rilievo. Ed è anche notevole che, proprio in connessione con Pedarito, si leggano, nel frammento fiorentino (col. A II, linee 30 – 31) le parole περὶ ἧς καὶ Θουκυδίδης: Teopompo era un continuatore il quale nominava esplicitamente Tucidide al principio delle sue *Elleniche* (lo si ricava anche da Polibio VIII,13,3) e puntigliosamente contrapponeva, nel corso del lavoro, la superiorità delle proprie indagini rispetto ai dati forniti dai suoi predecessori (lo si ricava dalla sua auto-esaltazione nel proemio delle *Filippiche*, riferita da Fozio, cod. 176, p. 121 a 1 – 7 = fr. 25 Jacoby).

6. Alla fine della sua vita, ricorda Hans Erich Stier, Eduard Meyer soleva dire di aver cambiato ben poche volte veduta, sul piano scientifico, "diversamente dal grande Wilamowitz."[38]

Se dunque nella riedizione postuma della *Geschichte des Altertums* Stier ha lievemente ritoccato (IV,1, p. 258) ciò che Meyer aveva scritto nel 1901 e si è giovato a tal fine di quanto Meyer aveva scritto nel volume del 1909 *Theopomps Hellenika*, possiamo esser certi che un tale procedimento rispecchia l'autentica volontà di Meyer, se non addirittura il suo "Handexemplar".[39]

---

[36] Così Bartoletti, *PSI*, XIII,1 (1948), p. 66.

[37] *Historical Commentary on the "Hellenika of Oxyrhynchos,"* Cambridge 1967, p. 32.

[38] *Geschichte des Altertums*, III², 1937, p. VI. Di questo insistente ritornare sul medesimo tema era consapevole lo stesso Wilamowitz, quando ad esempio notava, nel '26, in *Hellenische Geschichtschreibung*: "Ho lavorato tutta la vita su Tucidide ed ho schizzato nel mio *Platone* (II,13) come concepisco la sua evoluzione."

[39] Un indizio in tal senso può considerarsi anche il breve cenno dello stesso Meyer, nel *Vorwort* alla ristampa (1912) del volume III¹ (= IV,1 dell'edizione postuma), dove è indicata, tra le grandi novità di cui si si dovrebbe tener conto in un aggiornamento dell'opera, — oltre ai papiri aramaici di Elefantina— "la recente scoperta di frammenti delle *Elleniche* di

Nel giudizio su Cratippo, all'espressione "... oder vielmehr der römischen Zeit angehört" Stier sostituisce, nell'edizione postuma: "... der
vielmehr der hellenistischen Zeit angehört," in coerenza appunto con la
veduta espressa da Meyer nel saggio del 1909.[40] Quanto a Teopompo,
invece, si limita ad aggiungere in nota un riferimento a *Theopomps Hellenika*, dove i frammenti londinesi delle "Elleniche di Ossirinco" sono
senz'altro incorporati nell'edizione teopompea e suddivisi tra i vari libri.
Ma a rigore tale riferimento contrasta alquanto con la frase, che pure è
rimasta nel testo: "Nachrichten, die auf sein Werk [= di Teopompo]
zurückgehen, besitzen wir nur sehr wenige" (*GdA* III,1[1], pp. 275–276
= IV,1[3], p. 258). Fino ai suoi tardi anni, Meyer ha conservato—ne fa
fede lo scrupolo editoriale di Stier—il convincimento della attribuzione a
Teopompo delle "Elleniche di Ossirinco:" ipotesi cui, come si è visto, i
nuovi ritrovamenti hanno portato non piccola conferma.

Messi in soggezione dai 'giovani' Maas e Jacoby furono, invece,
Wilamowitz e Schwartz. Maas, col fascino della sua prosa einsteiniana,
aveva sentenziato nel '12 che, se in un frammento delle *Elleniche* (21
Müller = 20 Jacoby = Ateneo, XII,543 B) ricorre "das phrasenhafte
φανήσεται," lo stile delle *Elleniche* non poteva che essere tutto "phrasenhaft", dal principio alla fine. Jacoby tre anni prima aveva affermato sec-
camente che Cratippo e lo storico di Ossirinco "sono un'unica persona,"
ma nel '24 aveva 'lanciato' Daimaco, e rimproverato Meyer di dimenticare la "Dürftigkeit unserer Kentnisse."[41] Nello stesso periodo prospetta-
va la medesima ipotesi nel nuovo volume (II A, nr. 66) dei *Fragmente
der griechischen Historiker*. Queste prese di posizione risultarono efficaci
forse soprattutto per il prestigio via via acquisito da coloro che le avevano
espresse: Maas nell'ambito della stilistica greca; Jacoby per la insuperata
competenza nel campo della storiografia greca. Così, ritornando nel '26
sul suo vecchio saggio-conferenza letto a Oxford nel 1908 (*Greek Historical
Writing*), nel quale attribuiva senz'altro a Teopompo le nuove *Elleniche*,
Wilamowitz scriverà con la consueta decisione: "der Historiker von Oxyrhynchos, von dem wir zwar wissen, daß er Theopomp, Ephoros und
Kratippos nicht ist, aber mit Zuversicht können wir ihm keinen Namen
geben."[42] Di Cratippo, invece, Wilamowitz non sembra essersi

---

Teopompo." Ancora in *Caesars Monarchie* (1919[2]), p. 617, Teopompo è citato come
autore del "Bruchstück aus Oxyrhynchus."

[40] Che comunque Meyer non provasse grande simpatia per il problema Cratippo si
può ricavare dal fatto che, proprio in un contesto dove il richiamo a Cratippo è d'obbligo
(i discorsi in Tucidide e la loro assenza nell'ottavo libro) il nome di Cratippo non viene
mai fuori (*Forschungen zur Alten Geschichte*, II, Halle, 1899, pp. 379–406).

[41] Cfr. *supra*, nota 13. Nel 1950 Jacoby scriverà un lungo saggio per suggerire che
l'autore delle "Elleniche di Ossirinco" è un anonimo.

[42] *Reden und Vorträge*, II[4], Berlin, 1926, p. 224.

occupato mai. Forse ha aderito alla veduta di chi, come Schwartz, lo considerava un falsario: dichiara infatti che i continuatori di Tucidide furono *tre*: Senofonte, Teopompo e le "Elleniche di Ossirinco" (*ibid.*): Cratippo, pur nominato da lui nello stesso contesto, si è volatilizzato.

Quanto a Schwartz, che nel 1909, nel saggio su Eforo, si chiedeva come si potesse anche solo pensare di confutare gli argomenti in favore dell'identificazione con Teopompo, nel '28, in un saggio di sintesi per la nuova rivista vagamente 'georgeana' diretta da Jaeger, "Die Antike," optava inopinatamente (e senza dare argomenti) per Eforo: "der sogenannte Historiker von Oxyrhynchos den Ephoros zu nennen ich seit geraumer Zeit kein Bedenken mehr trage . . . ."[43] E' una veduta che Schwartz ripropone in modo ancor più deciso in uno degli ultimi suoi scritti, *Die messenische Geschichte bei Pausanius*,[44] nonostante il sistema annalistico tucidideo "per estati e inverni," bene attestato nei frammenti londinesi (P.Oxy. 842, col. III,9–11 = p. 9 Bartoletti), sia il meno conciliabile con l'ordinamento narrativo κατὰ γένος, mirante a far coincidere un argomento compiuto con ciascun libro, caratteristico di Eforo (*FGrHist* 70 T 11 = Diodoro V,1,4).[45]

7. La lunga discussione su Cratippo, Teopompo e le "Elleniche di Ossirinco" ha anche un rilievo metodologico. Per esempio costituisce un interessante indizio dell'arbitrio con cui alcune opinioni, del tutto infondate, si affermano, ed altre, che hanno il vantaggio della chiara verosimiglianza, si perdono sempre più nei meandri di una discussione ipercritica.

Nel caso delle "Elleniche di Ossirinco" l'andamento è stato sconcertante: subito i termini della questione sono stati chiari, poi si sono andati via via obnubilando. Quei frammenti—fu subito osservato—non potevano che spettare, dato il sistema cronologico adoperato, ad un continuatore di Tucidide, che peraltro non era, ovviamente, Senofonte. E invece l'ingombrante fantasma di Cratippo ha insidiato, sin dal principio, l'ovvia attribuzione all'altro continuatore, cioè a Teopompo, e aperto la strada alle attribuzioni piu inverosimili: Daimaco, o, più stravagante ancora, l'*Atthis* di Androzione. Quest'ultima ipotesi, pur così cara a

---

[43] *Geschichtschreibung und Geschichte bei den Hellenen* (= *Gesammelte Schriften*, I, Berlin 1937, p. 77).

[44] "Philologus", 92, 1937, p. 21, nota 3 (= *Ges. Schriften*, II, Berlin 1956, p. 210, nota).

[45] Questo argomento contro l'attribuzione a Eforo è sorretto da una attestazione esplicita. Dionigi (*Su Tucidide*, 9 = I, pp. 337–338 UR) nota che il sistema "tucidideo" fu abbandonato "da tutti gli storici successivi:" dunque là dove (come in P.Oxy. 842) esso figura si può esser certi che siamo in presenza di un continuatore di Tucidide, un continuatore che, appunto perché tale, ne assume il sistema cronologico.

Gaetano De Sanctis, appare quasi inspiegabile, se solo si considera lo spazio che il presunto attidografo dedicherebbe alle campagne in Asia del re di Sparta;[46] a tacere poi della ironica considerazione di Jacoby: "This thesis is marred at once because its author [= De Sanctis] overlooked a fragment of Androtion, missing in Mueller's collection, which proves (what in fact does not stand in need of proof) that the Attidographer used the Athenian archon-year, not the Thucydidean war-year."[47] Ma audace, a ben vedere, è anche la scelta, apparentemente iperprudente, di inventare un anonimo: che è quanto dire, nel nostro caso, *un nuovo storico* rilevantissimo ma per tutta l'antichità completamente dimenticato. (Solo il reiterato rinvenimento di altri frammenti ha scosso tale ipercritica prudenza).

In realtà era proprio la disturbante figura di Cratippo, questa specie di "doppio" delle *Elleniche* di Teopompo (come in fondo lo considerava Müller) a creare impaccio. Il modo stesso in cui si è tentato di liquidarlo (togliendolo in un modo o nell'altro dall'epoca in cui concordemente le fonti lo collocano) sta a significare che era lui il "disturbatore". Imbarazzante a tal punto che un onnipresente come Wilamowitz, il quale ha cercato di dire la sua su tutta la grecità, ha finito col non parlarne mai, mentre Schwartz auspicava che tornasse "in dem verdienten Dunkel," e Wachsmuth, nella monumentale *Einleitung in das Studium der alten Geschichte* (1895) evitava anche solo di nominarlo.

La riconsiderazione approfondita di Cratippo è invece il punto ineludibile dell'indagine sulla storiografia del IV secolo.[48] Averlo ignorato ha spinto su false piste: è dal chiarimento della natura dell'opera che circolò sotto quel nome che dipende una corretta visione dell'opera di Teopompo (e dei frammenti di *Elleniche* man mano affioranti), nonché dell'opera stessa di Tucidide e delle sue vicende editoriali. "Cratippo", se si evita la strada di togliere valore a quanto ci viene detto di lui da Dionigi, è in realtà un perno della questione tucididea.

Nel suo intervento del 1924 (quello in cui avanzava il nome di Daimaco), Jacoby rimproverava a Meyer un difetto di metodo: di avere cioè perso, nella questione delle "Elleniche di Ossirinco," la consapevolezza di quanta parte, anche influente, della tradizione sia andata persa: ". . . wie wenig wir von sehr vielen Autoren wissen, die nicht nur zu ihrer Zeit

---

[46] Ma è il modo stesso di raccontare che contrasta con quanto di Androzione riusciamo a capire, per esempio dalle citazioni di Didimo.

[47] *The Authorship of the Hellenica of Oxyrhynchos*, "Classical Quarterly" 44, 1950, p. 2 (= *Ges. Abhandlungen*, p. 324).

[48] Sulla centralità di Cratippo nella 'questione' tucididea: F. Lasserre, "RFIC" 100, 1972, pp. 246–247.

bedeutend waren; wie vollständig uns ganze Schichten der Tradition verloren sind, deren Einfluß ein nicht geringer war und deren Fortwirkung
wir konstatieren können." Nel caso delle "Elleniche di Ossirinco,"
Meyer avrebbe immotivatamente scartato "beachtenswerte Namen, wie
die der Boioter Anaxis und Dionysodoros (*Theopomps Hellenika*, 124),"
pur essendosi in altra circostanza mostrato consapevole, per esempio a
proposito della tradizione sulla Seconda Punica, della "Dürftigkeit" della
nostra tradizione.[49] Oggi questo ammonimento astratto di valore generale mi sembra sempre meno giovevole ad illuminare concreti casi di
storia della tradizione. Che il continuatore di Tucidide (oltre Senofonte)
letto in età antonina fosse Teopompo è l'ipotesi più sensata, *proprio dal
punto di vista della storia culturale*. Avrà pur un peso il fatto che siano appunto
Senofonte e Teopompo gli unici due continuatori noti ad una tradizione
(il "cronografo" di Diodoro) che disponeva dei repertori di Alessandria
e di Pergamo, o che tracciava profili della storiografia greca che andavano
ben oltre le immediate esigenze della *institutio oratoria* (Cicerone, *De oratore*,
II,55–58; *Brutus*, 287; *Orator*, 30; Quintiliano, X,1,73–75).[50] Così come
fa una certa impressione constatare che, alla fine dell'età antonina o
all'inizio di quella severiana, proprio in Egitto, Teopompo sia lo storico
di gran lunga più citato nei *Deipnosofisti* di Ateneo di Naucrati: il quale è,
tra l'altro, l'autore cui dobbiamo gli unici brani di senso compiuto delle
Elleniche di Teopompo noti da tradizione indiretta.[51] E non è superfluo
ricordare infine che tra I e II secolo d.C. Teopompo è ben presente
nell'opera di letterati e uomini di cultura che operano nelle più varie parti
dell'impero: da Plutarco (Vite di Lisandro, Agesilao, Alcibiade ecc.) a
Luciano (*Come si scrive la storia*, 59) all'autore del *Sublime* (cap. 31) a Gellio
(X,18,6) a Frontone (115 T 22 Jacoby) a Dione di Prusa (or.
XVIII,10)[52] ed è adoperato assiduamente da Plinio (115 F 316–320
Jacoby).

---

[49] *Der Verfasser der Hellenika von Oxyrhynchos*, "NGG" 1924, p. 14 (= *Ges. Abhandlungen*,
p. 317).

[50] Ovviamente ci sarà sempre chi dirà che, "mancando nelle Elleniche di Ossirinco i
discorsi diretti," i teorici dell'oratoria, di quell'opera non si occupavano. Si è già detto
prima quanto sia infondata la premessa.

[51] A. Koerte ("Archiv für Papyrusforschung," 6, 1920, p. 243) già formulò
chiaramente l'osservazione secondo cui una "copia privata," ad Ossirinco, intorno al 200
d.C., di un autore del IV secolo a.C. non può che provenire da un "klassisch anerkannter
Historiker." Onde, conclude Koerte, Teopompo si impone, escluso Eforo per le ragioni
illustrate da Laqueur ("Hermes" 46, 1911, p. 353–354).

[52] Quest'ultimo è un brano per certi versi simile, per impianto e finalità, ai profili della storiografia in relazione all'oratoria tracciati da Cicerone e Quintiliano.

Epimetron

1.

Nell'opera di Cratippo campeggiava Trasibulo liberatore dai Trenta: καὶ Θρασύβουλον καὶ ᾽Αρχῖνον καὶ τοὺς ἀπὸ Φυλῆς ἑβδομήκοντα dice Plutarco. Oltre che in "Cratippo", la cifra di settanta uomini originariamente al fianco di Trasibulo ricorre *soltanto* in Senofonte *Elleniche* II,4,2. *Tutte* le altre, numerose, fonti danno altre cifre: Pausania (I,29,3) sessanta; *Rhetorica ad Alexandrum*, 8, cinquanta; Cornelio Nepote, *Thrasyb.* 2,1, trenta; Elio Aristide, *Panatenaico* (I, p. 271 Dindorf), "poco più di cinquanta;" scolio ad Aristofane *Pluto* 1146, ottocento; il più veridico sembra però Eschine (III,187 – 190), il quale sulla base di un documento parla di circa cento uomini. Dunque tra Senofonte e "Cratippo" non solo vi è coincidenza contro tutte le altre, assai numerose, fonti, ma, si direbbe nella critica testuale, "coincidenza in errore."

2.

"Le gesta di Trasillo a Lesbo." Sembra escluso—nonostante gli argomenti di Friedrich (*Zum Panegyrikos des Isokrates*, "Jahrbücher für klassische Philologie," 147, 1893, p. 22)—un riferimento alle Arginuse: per la semplice ragione che nessuna descrizione della battaglia delle Arginuse attribuisce a Trasillo speciali meriti nella vittoria, e inoltre perché si parla, nelle fonti, di battaglia ἐν ᾽Αργινούσσαις (cfr., oltre Senofonte *Elleniche*, I,6 e 7, Diodoro XIII,97,3, Pausania VI,7,7 ecc.) e non Περὶ Λέσβον. Oltre tutto il nome di Trasillo come "comandante di turno" nel giorno dello scontro è congettura su di un testo guasto di Diodoro (XIII,97,6, cfr. XIII,74,1). Sarà più semplice pensare alla cattura ἐν Μηθύμνῃ τῆς Λέσβου di navi siracusane e di molti prigionieri, da parte di Trasillo, narrata da Senofonte *Elleniche* I,2,11 – 13: 'coda' positiva dell'infelice attacco contro Efeso. E' infatti un episodio tutt'altro che trascurabile, che prelude alla riconciliazione tra Alcibiade e Trasillo (*Elleniche* I,2,17), e ben noto a Plutarco (*Alcibiade*, 29,3 – 4). Se, come credo, l'identificazione dell'episodio "cratippeo" relativo a Trasillo con *Elleniche* I,2,13 – 14 è esatta, si può osservare che i primi due episodi citati da Plutarco quando parla di "Cratippo" (gesta di Alcibiade in Ellesponto e gesta di Trasillo a Lesbo) sono, nell'ordine, i primi due episodi delle *Elleniche* senofontee.

3.

Se Cratippo è il falso nome che figurava in testa ad una edizione delle

Elleniche, il quasi totale eclissarsi, nelle fonti più recenti, di tale nome è del tutto comprensibile. Lo stesso è successo per "Temistogene". E' sintomatico il comportamento di Plutarco: nel *De gloria Atheniensium* discorre in modo circostanziato di "Cratippo" e lo colloca subito dopo Tucidide; ma nelle *Vite* non lo cita mai pur trattando spesso dei fatti che "Cratippo" narrava.

4.

Nel tormentato passo della *Vita di Andocide* (= *Moralia* 834 CD) relativo agli ermocopidi, Cratippo è citato come autorità sulla vicenda. Il testo è stato variamente sollecitato e corretto. Si è pensato ad interpolazioni di primo e di secondo grado (si vedano ad esempio la presentazione del testo e l'apparato di Jacoby *FGrHist* 64 F 3, e l'apparato di Mau, nell'edizione "BT" dei *Moralia*, V,2,1, 1971, pp. 6 – 7); in genere si è concordi nel ritenere che le frasi in cui viene fatto il nome di Cratippo, poiché sono omesse da Fozio nella parafrasi di questa *Vita* (*Bibl.* 261, p. 488 a 25), debbano considerarsi uno scolio: scolio che viene a sua volta variamente corretto per ottenere che dia un senso. L'altra difficoltà percepita dagli studiosi è ancora più sostanziale: che infatti Cratippo (qualunque idea si abbia della sua identità) *raccontasse* la vicenda degli ermocopidi non è affatto ovvio. Per trovare un posto al *racconto* (non era una semplice menzione, a stare al testo della *Vita* andocidea) del celebre episodio del 415 in un'opera che partiva dal 411 si sono tentate le ipotesi più varie: Krüger pensava che se ne parlasse a proposito del rientro di Alcibiade (408), Jacoby pensava invece che Cratippo se ne occupasse a proposito del processo di Andocide (399). Ipotesi davvero stravagante quest'ultima, giacché è difficile che un processo privo di riflessi generali, riguardante unicamente la persona di Andocide, potesse diventare materia di Ἑλληνικά. In realtà non è affatto facile immaginare dove mai un racconto sugli ermocopidi potesse trovar posto in un'opera del genere. A me sembra perciò lecito il dubbio sulla correttezza del nome Κράτιππος: si può osservare, del resto, che all'incirca in una trentina di casi, nel giro delle poche pagine delle *Vite dei dieci oratori*, i nomi propri appaiono sfigurati. Esempi clamorosi e interessanti sono *Erodoto* in luogo di *Erode* in 833 D, *Senofonte* in luogo di *Cherefonte* in 843 E; ma c'è anche *Clearco* in luogo di *Cleocrito* ecc. Ovviamente in casi del genere, anche a causa della genesi composta del testo, è lecito chiedersi se si tratti di errori nati nel corso della tradizione o dovuti all'ignoranza o scarsa informazione di coloro cui si debbono i materiali (note erudite, redazioni alternative ecc.) confluiti a costituire l'opuscolo.

La difficoltà che sorge dalla presenza del nome Κράτιππος può forse sanarsi pensando che il nome da ripristinare sia, in questo caso, Κρατερός, e che il riferimento sia alla *Raccolta dei decreti* di Cratero, la quale, come si sa, comprendeva, tra l'altro, documenti (verdetti di tribunali, liste di beni confiscati) riguardanti la vicenda degli ermocopidi (U. Köhler, *Hermokopideninschriften*, "Hermes", 23, 1888, pp. 396 – 401), e forniva anche, per ciascun documento, un prezioso commento illustrativo (Plutarco, *Vita di Aristide*, 26; Jacoby, "RE", s.v. *Krateros*, 1618, 23 – 30). Ritengo anzi (ne parlerò altrove) che in *Moralia* 834 CD noi abbiamo, del verdetto relativo ad Andocide, citazioni dal testo e dal commento, e che proprio questa ipotesi consenta di intendere il testo tramandato, così com'è, senza necessità di ritoccarne la sintassi. La derivazione da Cratero (attraverso Cecilio di Calatte) è generalmente riconosciuta nella subito precedente *Vita di Antifonte* (833 E: decreto di Andron; cfr. Arpocrazione, s.v. Ἄνδρων).

MORTIMER CHAMBERS

THE "MOST EMINENT LIVING HISTORIAN, THE ONE FINAL AUTHORITY": MEYER IN AMERICA

The title of this paper is taken from a newspaper, the Evanston (Illinois) Index of February 12, 1910. Even earlier, in announcing that Eduard Meyer would soon give three lectures at Northwestern University, the Index had declared:

> The Meyer lectures at the university will be the literary event of the year. These lectures are on the Harris foundation and will be given by Prof. Eduard Meyer, the greatest living historian, professor of ancient history at the University of Berlin. His contributions to historical literature are many and authoritative; his is usually the last word on any subject that he discusses.[1]

The Index was perhaps a little naive in stating that the word of any historian is ever the last one, but this respectful article shows the immense esteem that Meyer enjoyed in America in the years before the Great War. The enthusiastic welcome that he received in the new world makes it all the sadder that his relationship with America was to collapse in misunderstanding and bitterness, as he stood by his principles and his fatherland and, also influenced by personal tragedy, could not preserve the collegiate spirit that had marked his two voyages across the sea.

I. First Contacts with England and America

Meyer completed the first stage of his academic career with his doctoral thesis at age 20.[2] He then obtained the post of tutor to the children of Sir Philip Francis (1822 – 1876), the British Consul General in Constantinople from 1867 to 1876.[3] This first contact with English-speaking society lasted a year and a half. On the sudden death of Sir Philip aboard HMS Antelope,

---

[1] January 29, 1910, p. 2.

[2] Set-Typhon. Eine religionsgeschichtliche Studie, Leipzig 1875.

[3] A jurist, Sir Philip wrote, e.g., The New Common Law of Procedure, London 1854. In Meyer's autobiographic sketch in H. Marohl, ed., Eduard Meyer, Bibliographie, Stuttgart 1941, 10, he does not explain how he got this post: "Ein Zufall wirkte dann...." For details, see Ch. Hoffmann, in this volume infra. Sir Philip was a descendant of the Sir Philip Francis (1740–1818) who was the reputed author of the famous letters of "Junius": see the letter signed W.H.R. (probably Sir William Howard Russell [1820–1907], the noted war correspondent) in the Times, August 12, 1876, 11. He was buried in the British cemetery at Scutari; for a report of his military funeral, see ibid. Aug. 22, 6.

August 9, 1876, Meyer accompanied the family back to England and spent
the winter of 1876/7 in Bournemouth, thus deepening his knowledge of
English and of Great Britain. He got to know the British Museum, visited
Edinburgh, and during these months wrote his Geschichte von Troas.[4]

He published some work in English in the form of articles in English
journals and encyclopedias.[5] He also issued one longer paper in America
in 1903,[6] a broad essay on Alexander the Great, which contains some
ringing statements. His declaration that ''The impulse toward the un-
fathomed, which clings to all aspiring culture, and is ever conscious of its
own vitality, displayed itself in Alexander,''[7] could have been written by
Spengler and reminds us of Meyer's support for that historical philosopher. Again, his conclusion, ''No longer could there exist Greeks and barbarians in sharp contrast to[8] rulers and subjects, but all the forces of the
realm must be assimilated and all peoples ascend into the one Hellenic
civilization,''[9] resembles Droysen's vision of Alexander the harmonizer
of East and West.[10] It is also within reach of the romantic theory that
W.W. Tarn was to launch, thirty years later, namely that Alexander's
purpose was to blend all humanity together as in a loving cup.[11]

Meyer evidently continued to visit England; he signed the preface to
vol. III of his Geschichte des Altertums in New Brighton in Cheshire,

---

[4] Leipzig 1877.

[5] Beginning with ''The Development of Religion in Egypt,'' in: Sunday School
Times, Philadelphia, vol. 32, September 20, 1890, 595–596 [non uidi]; see Professor
Badian's illuminating discussion of this and Meyer's other writings published in America,
in this volume supra; note also Marohl (n. 3 supra), nos. 137, 146, 147, 161–164.

[6] ''Alexander the Great and Universal Monarchy'' [trans. C.B. Stetson], in: The
International Quarterly 8 (1903/4) 280–295 (not in Marohl). This was expanded in
''Alexander der Große und die absolute Monarchie,'' in: Kl. Schr. [I], Halle 1910, 283–
332 = I², ibid. 1924, 265–314. Marohl records (see his no. 205) that the manuscript of
this paper was ''urspr. für eine amerik. Zeitschrift'' (evidently Intern. Quart.).

[7] Op. cit., 285.

[8] The German text shows that ''as'' should be written: ''Nicht mehr Hellenen und
Barbaren in scharfem Gegensatz von Herrschern und Beherrschten durfte es geben . . . ,''
Kl. Schr. I 300 = I² 282. On Stetson's difficulties in translating Meyer, see Professor
Badian, in this volume.

[9] P. 287.

[10] For Droysen, Alexander's aim was ''politisch die Völker des Ostens und Westens
zu Einem Reich, zu einer Weltmonarchie zusammenzufassen,'' which would thus achieve
''die Verschmelzung des hellenischen Wesens mit dem der Völker Asiens, die Schaffung
eines neuen westöstlichen Culturlebens, die Einheit der geschichtlichen Welt in der
hellenischen Bildung:'' Geschichte des Hellenismus, 2. Teil, Geschichte der Diadochen²,
2. Halbband, Gotha 1878, 358.

[11] W.W. Tarn, ''Alexander the Great and the Unity of Mankind,'' in: Proc. British
Academy 19 (1933) 123–166; the necessary reply, identifying one of the crucial ''sources''
for this hypothesis as an innocent rhetorical flight in Plutarch: E. Badian, Historia 7 (1958)
425–444. Further criticism, A.B. Bosworth, Ancient Society Resources for Teachers 13
(1983) 131–150.

October 10, 1901. His brother Kuno (1858 – 1919) was professor of Teutonic languages in the University of Liverpool and was later to marry an American nurse.[12] Such were at least some of his connections with the English-speaking nations before 1904.

II. Meyer in Chicago, 1904

In the autobiography in Marohl, written at the time of his retirement from Berlin in 1923, Meyer reports that "[g]rößere Reisen habe ich . . . nur wenige ausführen können." But among them he lists his two journeys to America, "im Frühjahr 1904, auf Einladung der Universität Chikago [sic], und im Wintersemester 1909/10 als Austauschprofessor der Harvard-Universität nach Amerika."[13] The origin and background of these two journeys are well investigated and documented by B. vom Brocke, to whose work I am deeply indebted.[14]

The first president of the University of Chicago, William Rainey Harper (1856 – 1906), was a Semitic scholar with a high respect for German scholarship.[15] In his new university there were several professors on the faculty who held German doctorates, and Harper looked further to Germany to nourish his new institution. In 1891, for example, he offered a chair in classical philology to Friedrich Blass (1843 – 1907), then at Kiel, but the death of Eduard Hiller (1844 – 1891) opened a chair in Halle, to which Blass moved.[16]

In fall 1903, while in Berlin, Harper began to explore the possibilities of closer collaboration with German scholars and universities.[17] One of his hopes was that German students might come to study in America: we may recall that precisely in that same fall 1903 the first five German Rhodes Scholars arrived in Oxford, to be followed by those from America and the British Empire in 1904—a prelude to the decline in the number

---

[12] Kuno Meyer was Professor of Teutonic languages, 1894 – 1903; Professor of German, 1903 – 1911; and Hon. Professor of Celtic, 1908 – 1911 and 1913 – 1914. The nurse had cared for him as he recovered from an accident; see Eduard Meyer's necrology of him, Irische Korrespondenz 2 (October-November 1919) 2 – 5 (reference from W.M. Calder III).

[13] Marohl 11.

[14] "Der deutsch-amerikanische Professorenaustausch," in: Zeitschrift für Kulturaustausch 31 (1981) 128 – 182.

[15] On Harper: T.W. Goodspeed, William Rainey Harper, Chicago 1928; P. Shorey in: Dict. Amer. Biogr. IV.2, New York 1932, 287 – 292; R.J. Storr, Harper's University, The Beginnings: A History of the University of Chicago, Chicago 1966 (omits the conference of 1904).

[16] W. Crönert, in: Bursian's Jahresbericht 145 (1909) 7.

[17] On his travels and negotiations in Germany, 1903, see Goodspeed (n. 15 supra), 197 – 198.

of Americans who went to Germany for advanced training in classics.[18] Harper thus set about organizing a conference, to coincide with the 50th Convocation of the University of Chicago, at which German scholars would appear, receive honorary degrees, and give talks. The general theme of the conference was to be the recognition of the influence of the ideals of German scholarship on the development of American universities.[19] The conference and its attendant ceremonies represent one of the highest points ever reached in harmony and enthusiasm among intellectuals of the two nations. The nearly unique nature of the gathering justifies a detailed narrative.

A committee in Chicago chose scholars representing the four traditional faculties in German universities. From the philosophical faculty came Meyer of Berlin and the Indo-European linguist Berthold Delbrück (1841–1922) of Jena;[20] from the faculty of law, Josef Kohler (1849–1919) of Berlin; from the faculty of medicine, Paul Ehrlich (1854–1915) of Frankfurt.[21] The representative from the faculty of theology was to be Friedrich Loofs (1858–1928) of Halle (but see *infra*). On January 9, 1904, Harper sent a letter formally inviting Meyer,[22] who accepted within the month. A draft of the reply survives, saying in part,

> If I have had the good luck and the great pleasure to assist several American students during their stay at the University of Halle [1889–1902], and if I am proud to count some of them among my special pupils,[23] I never could have imagined that it would bring me such a reward.[24]

James H. Breasted (1865–1935), the great Chicago Egyptologist, was then in Berlin, and when he heard that Meyer would go to Chicago he wrote him on January 31 in German, setting forth an estimate of his expenses.[25] His transatlantic fare, for example, would be 760 marks. His stipend from Chicago, $500, would raise 2075 marks; four weeks in America, at 20 marks a day (and this would be "reichlich"), would bring

---

[18] On this theme see E.C. Kopff in: Wilamowitz nach 50 Jahren, ed. W.M. Calder III-H. Flashar-T. Lindken, Darmstadt 1985, 558–580, esp. 558–563.

[19] Meyer was inaccurate about the occasion for the conference in *Kl. Schr.* I[2] iv, assigning it "zur Feier ihres [the university's] zehnjährigen Bestehens in vollausgebauter Gestalt." The decennial celebrations for the University of Chicago actually took place on June 14–18, 1901, and led to 28 volumes of Decennial Publications: see T.W. Goodspeed, A History of the University of Chicago, Chicago 1916, 399–405.

[20] A lively portrait of him at Jena: B. Litzmann, Im alten Deutschland [etc.], Berlin 1923, 247 f.

[21] Ehrlich was to win the Nobel Prize in 1908. His work on immunization was celebrated in the Hollywood film "Dr. Ehrlich's Magic Bullet," 1940. Hermann Credner, the geologist, was also invited: see n. 38 *infra*.

[22] Akademie der Wissenschaften der DDR [here: AkdW, DDR], NL Ed. Meyer 217.

[23] That is, for whom he was the "Doktorvater."

[24] AkdW, DDR, *loc. cit.*

[25] *Ibid.*

the total costs to about 1660 marks, thus leaving a pleasant surplus.[26] He suggested several good staterooms on Meyer's intended ship, the Blücher. Breasted also wrote, February 28, three letters of introduction for Meyer ("my dear friend"), pointing in one of them to Meyer's interest in agricultural development: "If you could go out on a country trolley line with him . . . he would be very grateful."

As news of Meyer's coming reached America, he began to hear from acquaintances, especially former students, who expressed their joy at the prospect of seeing him again. On February 16 William Kelly Prentice (1871 – 1964)[27] wrote,

> Enno[28] and I are perfectly delighted. You need not worry about where to meet us: you will find us on the dock when you arrive. It does not occur to me to recommend a hotel to you, for I want you to stay with me at my father's house.[29] . . . I do not think that you will be able to spend any money in New Jersey.[30]

On February 18 another pupil at Halle, Henry A. Sill (1869 – 1917), then assistant professor of ancient history at Cornell University, wrote to say that President J.G. Schurman (1854 – 1942) of Cornell wanted Meyer to give a lecture during his visit to America; the honorarium would be $50.[31] Sill went on in a highly emotional style, calling Meyer "you, my master and dearest friend;" but,

> Eigentlich habe ich durch undankbares und rüppelhaftes Benehmen so schwer an Dir gesündet, dass ich mir kein Recht mehr auf Deine Freundschaft anmassen darf . . . .[32]

---

[26] Harper wrote Meyer on February 4, summarizing the program and confirming his stipend as $500: *ibid.*

[27] Prentice, professor of classics at Princeton, was a Ph.D. from Halle (De Bacchylide Pindari artis socio et imitatore, Halle 1900); though a pupil of Blass, he also thanks Meyer in his preface.

[28] Enno Littmann (1875 – 1958) was Ph.D. Halle, in Abyssinian linguistics. He was assistant professor at Princeton, 1901 – 1906. Owing to the generosity of Robert Garrett (winner of the discus contest and a jumping event in the Athens Olympics, 1896), he was able to travel to Abyssinia for research. He also worked with Prentice on the Princeton expeditions to Syria and was professor in Tübingen, 1921 – 1958. See his autobiography in: The Library of Enno Littmann, Catalogue 307, E.J. Brill, Leiden 1959, xiii – xx. "Ganz besonderen Eindruck machte auf mich der geniale und vielseitige Historiker Eduard Meyer, der mir bis zu seinem Tode (1930) ein väterlicher Freund blieb" (xv).

[29] Prentice's father lived at 9 W. 16th St., New York.

[30] AkdW, DDR, *loc. cit.*

[31] $50 was the usual honorarium for Meyer's lectures. Baedeker's Guide to the United States[4], Leipzig etc. 1909, 12, reports that a room in New York at the Waldorf-Astoria or the Plaza then cost $2.50. A man's shirt commonly cost $1.50. If honoraria for lectures had kept pace with inflation over 80 years and more, they would now be several thousand dollars ($100 – 150 is often paid today). Note too that some, at least, of the full professors at the new University of Chicago were paid $7000 a year in 1892.

[32] AkdW, DDR, *loc. cit.* Sill wrote his dissertation, Untersuchungen über die pla-

Preparations for the conference were well under way when, on February
29, Harper learned by cable that the representative from the faculty of
theology, Loofs, was ill. He cabled Camillo von Klenze (1865–1943),
professor of Germanic philology at Chicago, who was then in Berlin, and
asked him to consult with Breasted and Adolf Harnack (1851–1930),
professor of church history in Berlin, to choose another theologian. Von
Klenze replied, in a letter that I publish in full because it shows the Prussian system in operation:[33]

Berlin March 3d. 1904

My Dear Pres. Harper—:
When I received your cable I went to see Harnack who proved very kind
and much interested. He suggested my going to Giessen to see Krüger.[34]
I was just going to start when I happened to meet Mr. Wever, the brother
of our consul who is "assistant Secretary of State" in the Department of
the Interior.[35] When he heard of my errand, he begged me to wait a day,
because he believed the German government was taking great interest in
this celebration & he was anxious to help me. He said he would talk it over
with Althoff,[36] who, as you probably know, is in charge of all university
matters in Prussia. The next day he reported having seen Althoff and the
latter's proposing Herrmann[37] from Marburg. He said Althoff would
write to Harnack and make it all right with him. I might use Althoff's
name, he said, in discussing the matter with Herrmann. I knew what a
powerful lever that would be & therefore started that same evening for
Marburg. The name of Althoff worked like a charm & after some hesitation
Herrmann accepted, although his wife was ill & he ought to finish a book
before May. Perhaps a line of acknowledgement to "Herrn Unterstaats-

---

tonischen Briefe, I. Teil: Prolegomena, Halle 1901, under Meyer. It is one chapter ("Die
Tyrannis und die Theorie") of a larger work, Prolegomena zu einer Untersuchung über
die Echtheit der platonischen Briefe, that was accepted as his dissertation and was to be
published by Niemeyer in Halle in 1901. This work did not appear, and Sill felt guilty
about not completing his book. Nevertheless, he and Meyer traveled together during the
week beginning March 13.

[33] University of Chicago Archives, President's papers, 16:11.

[34] Gustav Krüger (1862–1940), professor of church history in Giessen.

[35] Walther Wever (1859–1922) was the German consul in Chicago. His brother
Hermann, whom von Klenze met, was Unterstaatssekretär in the Prussian Ministerium
des Innern.

[36] Friedrich Althoff (1839–1908) was Vortragender Rat in the Prussian Kultusministerium and was the powerful administrator who in effect made the university appoint-
ments in Prussia. See B. vom Brocke, "Hochschul- und Wissenschaftspolitik in Preußen
und im Deutschen Kaiserreich 1881–1907: das 'System Althoff,'" in: Bildungspolitik in
Preußen zur Zeit des Kaiserreichs, ed. P. Baumgart, Stuttgart 1980, 9–118; A. Sachse,
Friedrich Althoff und sein Werk, Berlin 1928.

[37] Wilhelm Herrmann (1846–1922), professor of church history.

sekretär Wever, Unter den Linden 4 Berlin.W.'' without whom the whole matter would have been much more difficult, might not be amiss.

When I found that Wever was so much interested I telegraphed to ask if you cared for a substitute for Credner,[38] for I knew he could get me one.

I may add that I did my best to induce Credner to go. I wrote to him a second time & offered to work him up again, but he said, much to his regret, he would have to stay by his decision of not going.

I hope the celebration will go off smoothly. The programme, every one agrees, is splendid and all the men are looking forward to it with anticipation. There is more interest in this matter in Germany than one might imagine. It is regarded as unique and as a fine proof of American appreciation of German scholarship. I immensely regret my inability to be present.

I just heard of your recent illness. I sincerely hope you will have completely recovered by the time this letter reaches you.[39]

I remain, with kindest regards,

Very respectfully

yours

Camillo von Klenze

Before departing Germany, Meyer had an audience with the German Emperor.[40] He arrived in New York on the Blücher on March 14 and received mail at the home of Prentice's father. On March 8, for example, Bernadotte Perrin (1847 – 1920), the translator of Plutarch for the Loeb series, wrote from New Haven, inviting Meyer to lecture at Yale University.[41] Ernest Bynum, another pupil from Halle, wrote on March 11, urging Meyer to visit Allegheny College (Meadville, Pennsylvania), where he was professor of modern languages.[42] On March 13 John Henry Wright (1852 – 1908) of Harvard invited Meyer to Cambridge, and on March 14 Woodrow Wilson, then President of Princeton University, invited him to Princeton.[43]

---

[38] Hermann Credner (1841 – 1913) was professor of geology and palaeontology, Leipzig. He had traveled widely in America in the 1860s and was on the original list of those invited; thus the plan was to have six Germans in the conference rather than the five who actually came.

[39] It was learned that Harper had cancer. He continued to lead the university until the end.

[40] Wilhelm II, ruled 1888 – 1918 (lived 1859 – 1941); Schurman's letter to Roosevelt: n. 74 infra.

[41] Meyer lectured there in German on April 18.

[42] Ernest Taylor Bynum (1873 – ?) wrote, under Meyer, Das Leben des M. Junius Brutus bis auf Caesars Ermordung, Halle 1897. I cannot confirm whether Meyer went to Allegheny.

[43] All these papers are in AkdW, DDR, loc. cit.

It had been expected that Meyer would come directly to Chicago from New York, but, as he was to prove again in 1909/10, he was a passionate traveler with a hunger to sweep the length and breadth of America. He evidently went to Cornell University, probably on March 15, for his lecture[44] and then traveled with Sill to the Niagara frontier, staying at the Iroquois Hotel, Buffalo, on March 16–17, and reached Chicago on Friday, March 18, the first day of the program at the university.[45]

While von Klenze and Althoff were occupied in negotiating with Herrmann, Harper carried his preparations to the highest level, writing to the White House to secure the participation of President Theodore Roosevelt:[46]

Mr. William Loeb,[47]

White House, Washington, D.C.

My dear Mr. Loeb:—

When in Washington last, the president very kindly consented to prepare a letter which might be read on the occasion of the celebration in honor of the contribution of German scholarship to higher education in the United States ... I have received a telegram from Ambassador Tower[48] saying that the German Emperor will send a communication direct to the University in connection with this occasion.

President Roosevelt suggested that I should prepare the draft of the statement which he might revise and amend according to his pleasure . . . .

The whole purpose of this meeting is to create good fellowship between American citizenship and German citizenship, especially in view of the fact that in our City of Chicago we have the third German city of the world.[49] . . .

Yours very sincerely,
[stamped] W.R. Harper

The German professors stayed at the Windermere Hotel, still elegant today, a little east of the university. The first event in the program was

---

[44] On "The Emergence of the Individual in History;" he also gave this talk on March 21 in Chicago.

[45] On this day Sill wrote to him, reporting that President Benjamin I. Wheeler (1854–1927) of the University of California, who had heard Meyer in Leipzig (he was Ph.D. Heidelberg, 1885), wanted him for three lectures in Berkeley (honorarium, $150): *ibid*.

[46] President's papers, 35:7.

[47] Loeb (1866–1937), a New York businessman, was secretary to President Roosevelt, 1903–1909.

[48] Charlemagne Tower (1848–1923) was American ambassador to Germany. He received an honorary degree (in absentia) during the ceremonies of 22 March.

[49] Baedeker's Guide (n. 31 *supra*), 369, estimated the number of Germans in Chicago at 550,000. Only Berlin and Hamburg clearly had more German inhabitants.

a dinner for about 50 men, with Harper as host, at the Chicago Club on Friday, March 18. On Saturday came a dinner at the university, followed by a reception.[50]

On Sunday, March 20, Rabbi Emil G. Hirsch presided at a service in Leon Mandel Hall, the main assembly building of the university. The building was crowded long before the set hour of 11:00, and hundreds were locked out by the city's safety laws. Rabbi Hirsch hailed the German scholars as "exponents not of the new Germany of industrial success and power but of German ideals, and the spirit of searching for more light, deeper information, greater wisdom." There followed a stupendous reception, from 3:00 to 6:00, in the Auditorium in downtown Chicago.[51] Some 5000 people attended, including members of various German clubs in the city and graduates of German universities. The guests entered to a march from *Tannhäuser* and later heard music from the organ and from the 600-member Männerchor; the North American Turnerbund performed exercises. All the speeches were in German. The principal speaker was Professor Alexander R. Hohlfeld (1865–1956) of the University of Wisconsin, a state with a long tradition of German culture (not least the breweries of Milwaukee). He paid special tribute to German universities as "die im edelsten Sinne des Wortes demokratischste Institution der Neuzeit."[52] Delbrück replied for the honored guests, also stressing that the fundamental ideas and principles of the German people were democratic despite a monarchic form of government.[53] In the only departure from the German language, the choir and the whole audience closed the meeting by singing "America."

On Monday, March 21, the scene returned to the university, where the five Germans were received into the "congregation" of the university.[54] The morning was completed by lectures given by each visiting scholar.[55]

---

[50] The dinner was open to students and faculty for $.50; about 600 were present. All the events were reported in the student newspaper, the Daily Maroon, as well as in the Chicago press, above all the Chicago Daily Tribune.

[51] The Auditorium included a hotel and a famous theater. Built 1887–1889, it still stands, one of the architectural masterpieces of Louis Sullivan and the German Dankman Adler along Chicago's lake shore.

[52] Hohlfeld's oration was published in: German American Annals 6 (1904) 242–251.

[53] His "Antwort im Namen der deutschen Gäste" was published in: University Record [of the University of Chicago] 8 (1903/4) 385–387.

[54] That is, the faculty and graduates of the University of Chicago. The ceremonies are reported in University Record, *loc. cit.* 364–368; Meyer was introduced by Benjamin Terry (1857–1931), professor of history.

[55] Kohler spoke on "Die Quellen des Strafrechts und Hammurabi," published *ibid.* 371–373; Ehrlich on "Die Bindungsverhältnisse zwischen Toxin und Antitoxin:" see *ibid.* 9 (1904/5) 65–76; the talks by Herrmann (listed as "On the Study of Theology") and Delbrück ("On Conditional, Concessive, and Temporal Clauses in German and English") were apparently not published.

Only Meyer spoke in English, in the chapel of Cobb Lecture Hall, at
12:00. His topic had been announced only as "On some subject connected with history." In fact he treated "The Development of Individuality in Ancient History."[56] He showed that the old civilizations of Egypt
and the Orient were so dominated by tradition that individualism could
hardly arise: we lack from them any literary work bearing the name of an
author. Individualism and radically independent thought arise with the
prophets of Israel and, even more, in the many Greek states once the
influence of the East over them had waned. Here he is true to one of the
main themes in his Geschichte des Altertums, namely that Greek civilization is the central subject of antiquity.[57] Toward the end Meyer rather
loses his theme in choosing to contemplate the growth of the power of the
state, especially in Macedonia[58] and in Rome. But he closes with the
observation that both America and Germany speak Teutonic languages,
the very existence of which is a legacy of a decision made by an individual,
Augustus: not to try to subdue Germany, as Caesar surely would have
done if he had lived longer.

The guests were received that evening at private dinners; Meyer dined
with the historian J. Franklin Jameson (1859–1937) at his residence.

The final academic exercise took place at 3:00 on Tuesday, March 22,
at the 50th Convocation of the university in Mandel Hall. The hall had
again been crowded to the legal limit long before the hour. German and
American flags stood on the proscenium; the university's military band
played two Marches Militaires of Schubert as the processional and reces-
sional music. After the presentation of degrees to students, John Merle
Coulter (1851–1928) spoke for the university and Meyer replied for the
German guests. The German ambassador, Hermann Freiherr Speck von

---

[56] First printed in University Record 9 (1904/5) 56–65, then in *Kl. Schr.* I 213–230.
It was not published in German. See further p. 126 *infra*. (The Chicago Daily Tribune,
March 22, gave the title of Meyer's talk as "A Dominant Factor in the Development of
History.") It is not clear how good Meyer's English was. His many lectures to clubs at Har-
vard show that it was fluent in conversation. My friend Professor Badian points out that
Meyer revised the English version of this talk for publication in *Kl. Schr.*, always for the
better; but this does not show whether he wrote the original or corrected the work of his
translator. See further p. 118 *infra* on his hazardous pronunciation.

[57] Compare "Das Zentrum der Geschichte des Altertums bildet die Geschichte der
griechischen Kultur," in: "Der Gang der alten Geschichte: Hellas und Rom," *Kl. Schr.*
I 233 = I² 215. (Professor Badian points out to me that this essay, divided in two parts,
was published in English in vols. 3 and 5 of The Historians' History of the World, New
York-London 1904, although Marohl describes it at "bisher ungedruckt" and Meyer
himself refers to it as written for an "in Amerika geplante Universalgeschichte," thus implying that it had not in fact been published. For details, see Appendixes II–III to Professor Badian's paper in this book.)

[58] "In Alexander the development of Greek civilization reached its climax," *Kl. Schr.*
I 299.

Sternburg, read a message of congratulation from the Emperor; H.P. Judson (1849–1927), dean of the faculty, read a like message from Theodore Roosevelt. Degrees of Doctor of Laws were conferred on the German scholars, as well as on the respective ambassadors. The citation for Meyer, read out by Jameson, said:

> for writings in ancient history evincing mastery of technical detail, yet marked by originality and breadth of view, and especially for his brilliant and comprehensive History of the Ancient World.[59]

Harper then announced the foundation, by a German-American, Mrs. Catherine Seipp, of the Conrad Seipp prizes for essays on "The German Element in the United States, with Special Reference to its Political, Moral, Social, and Educational Influence."[60] The festivities concluded that night with a banquet, once more downtown in the Auditorium; after other speeches Kohler spoke for the guests.

On Wednesday March 23 the German scholars went to the northern suburb, Evanston, to visit Northwestern University, where they were welcomed in a large assembly of students and faculty in Fisk Hall.[61] Acknowledging Northwestern's welcome, Meyer (according to the Index) "responded with a few words in broken English, praising Evanston and alluding to the kindly receptions he had met with in his journey through America."

The visit to Evanston included a highly amusing scene. On the previous day, in Chicago, the students of the University of Chicago had offered a reception, with music, for the German guests. Presiding was Arthur E. Bestor (1879–1944),[62] then a graduate student. After speeches, including one in German by Eduard Prokosch (1876–1938),[63] another student, Meyer replied for the visitors. With bluff good humor, he praised the convivial beer-drinking ways of German students. His own happiest recollections of university life were of evenings in a *Kneipe* with "a stein on the table and a good song ringing clear."[64] Now, in Evanston, Kohler spoke briefly in German at the reception. "Do not follow the advice of

---

[59] The fifth and last volume of the first edition of Meyer's Geschichte had appeared in 1902.

[60] Mrs. Seipp acted on the suggestion of Wever, the German consul in Chicago. The prizes were to be $3000, $2000, and $1000, and the best essay was to be published by the University of Chicago. The first prize went to A.B. Faust for The German Element [etc.], 1909.

[61] The visit is reported in the Evanston Index, March 26, p. 8, with a photograph of the group wearing silk top hats.

[62] Later a prominent public speaker and president of the Chautauqua Institute; father of the historian A.E. Bestor.

[63] Prokosch was later professor of German at Yale University.

[64] Chicago Daily Tribune, March 23.

Professor Meyer, but leave strong drink strictly alone.''[65] The Tribune
also noted this incident, under a headline, ''DENIES MERITS OF BEER,''[66]
reporting Kohler as saying that ''for many years he had abstained absolutely from drinking beer, and that he especially advised temperance for
students.''

That this little debate took place in Evanston was significant, for that
city has long been the national home of the Women's Christian Temperance Union, which could only abhor Meyer's endorsement of beer. Indeed, the President of the WCTU, Lillian M.N. Stevens, took note in the
official journal[67] of Kohler's warning, which (she said)

> was received with applause, and Professor Meyer did not take issue with his
> compatriot . . . . We may well quote from a leading Chicago daily which . . .
> says: ''In a very large proportion of cases the evils of beer drinking are
> manifest at the first glance.''[68]

Northwestern University itself was a Methodist foundation, and the life
style in Evanston (population then some 21,000) was conservative. An
official of Northwestern said that if Meyer had recommended beer at that
university he might have been mobbed.

Meyer's advising Chicago's students to drink beer, and the public replies, did not take place in a total vacuum. The WCTU was always
vigilant, and just at that time legislation was under consideration in the
American Congress (the Hepburn-Dolliver Bills) that would have re-
stricted access to liquor. C.J. Hexamer (1862–1921), President of the
National German American Alliance, had appeared before the Judiciary
Committee of the House of Representatives to protest against this ''en-
croachment of the personal liberty guaranteed to every citizen.'' Another
witness was Mrs. Fernande Richter, who suggested that prohibition of
liquor in the home would estrange men from their families; as a German-
American woman, she had a good knowledge of ''Lebensfreude'' and tes-
tified that ''beer and light wines, even if taken regularly by women, are
conducive to their general health.''[69]

Meyer's remarks even reached high places in Berlin. From a letter
of his to Althoff we can see that the latter had reproached him for his

---

[65] Evanston Index, *loc. cit.*
[66] March 24.
[67] The Union Signal 29 (1903/4), no. 50, pp. 8–9.
[68] The reference is to The Chicago Record-Herald, March 23, p. 6. Another mild
rebuke to Meyer: Harper's Weekly 48, April 9, 1904, 539. See also Clara Eve Schieber,
American Sentiment Toward Germany: 1870–1914, Boston/New York 1923, 257 f.
[69] The remarks of Hexamer and Mrs. Richter were printed in Mittheilungen des
Deutsch-Amerikanischen National-Bundes, in: German American Annals 6 (1904) 128–
132, 199–205.

forthright praise of students' drinking; Meyer replied on May 15, 1904,

> ... Sollte ich sagen, dass in Deutschland nicht gekneipt wird? Oder sollte ich aus Rücksicht auf die Temperanceweiber und das Muckerthum mein Bedauern darüber aussprechen? Ich hätte damit ja nicht nur meine überzeugung, sondern geradezu mein Deutschthum verläugnet.[70]

The Chicago conference now being over, some of the visitors returned to Germany, but Meyer continued his exploration of America. He went to the Universities of Illinois[71] and Wisconsin, then across the country to speak at the University of California, where Edward B. Clapp (1856–1919), professor of Greek, received him.[72] On either the outward or the return journey he visited Salt Lake City, Utah, the headquarters of the Mormon church, for research on his history of the Mormons.[73] Returning to the East, he attended a meeting of the American Oriental Society on April 7–8 in Washington, where he received the privileges of the Cosmos Club for five days. On April 10 he dined with the German ambassador in the German embassy. He may also have met President Roosevelt.[74] On April 12 he lectured at Princeton (fee, $50); on April 14 he visited the Oriental Club in Philadelphia. At some time during this period he visited Harvard University. On April 18 he spoke at Yale. On April 19 he stayed at the University Club, New York, whose privileges were offered to him for a week. On April 20 he visited Columbia University at the invitation of Vladimir G. Simkhovitch (1874–1959) of the University library, for lunch and then dinner at the Century Club, whose privileges he was also offered.[75]

---

[70] The letter goes on, "Ich bin allerdings der Überzeugung ... dass unser studentisches Leben, unsere Fähigkeit zu trinken und Trinklieder zu singen und uns von den Sorgen des Tages einmal frei zu machen, eine Hauptwurzel unserer Kraft ist, und dass es einen schweren Verlust an geistiger Cultur bedeuten würde, wenn bei uns die extremen Bestrebungen des Temperanzlerthums siegen würden." In another letter from July 7, 1904, Meyer assures Althoff that his first letter was not meant as an attack: he simply wanted to be judged fairly. Both letters are in Zentrales Staatsarchiv, Dienststelle Merseburg (DDR), Rep. 29 Althoff B 131, 1. Althoff had previously consulted Meyer about various other scholars, but their correspondence was henceforth sharply reduced.

[71] I have not been able to confirm Meyer's visit to Illinois in 1904, but that he did speak here is shown from the fact that Oldfather, Pease, and others sent him Christmas cards when he was at Harvard in 1909: this seems to attest that they had met him on his trip in 1904. See n. 106 infra.

[72] On March 30 he spoke on "The Emergence of the Individual in Ancient Times," in effect his Chicago lecture; on March 31, "Socrates".

[73] He records the journey in Ursprung und Geschichte der Mormonen, Halle 1912, repr. Hildesheim 1970, 4.

[74] On March 30 President Schurman of Cornell wrote Roosevelt to introduce Professors Sill and Meyer: "Professor Meyer is undoubtedly the greatest living authority on the history of classical antiquity, so that I feel you will be pleased to know him for his own sake:" Jacob Gould Schurman Papers, Cornell University, 3/4/6, vol. 14.

[75] On these activities, the documents are in AkdW, DDR, NL Ed. Meyer 217.

As he was about to leave, his pupil Sill wrote him a letter of farewell on April 20, pointing out that Meyer had made an impression on eight universities.[76] Soon afterward Meyer concluded his first trip to America and returned to Germany.[77]

III. Meyer at Harvard, 1909/10

In 1909 Meyer returned, this time as the professor from Berlin in the Harvard-Berlin exchange program, in which each university supplied a visitor to the other, usually for one semester, rarely for a year.[78] He and his wife reached New York, probably on September 21. After spending a few days on the Niagara frontier they arrived in Cambridge on September 29.[79] They lived in the same apartment that the last two exchange professors had occupied, in a building known as Washington Court, at No. 51 in Cambridge's stately Brattle Street.[80]

The year was to include a rare event, the inauguration (October 6–7) of a new president of Harvard University: Abbott Lawrence Lowell (1856–1943), scion of a great Boston family, was to succeed Charles William Eliot (1834–1926), of no lesser pedigree, who had been president for 40 years. At the inaugural ceremonies, October 6, Meyer received an honorary degree of D.Litt., with the citation,

> Eduard Meyer, classical historian, unsurpassed by any living man; doubly welcome here, as delegate from the University of Berlin; and as our fellow teacher and comrade for the coming year.[81]

Meyer thus represented Berlin at the ceremonies and spoke after the final

---

[76] Apparently Chicago, Harvard, Yale, Princeton, California, Wisconsin, Illinois, Cornell: AkdW, DDR, *loc. cit.* On the same day an American, Ernest Gordon, wrote Meyer a less approving letter from Stockholm, about his recommendation of beer: "American students are first gentlemen. They have little in common with German students. In fact they look upon these latter as hopeless barbarians ...," *ibid.*

[77] I do not know on what ship; the Blücher sailed for Hamburg on April 28.

[78] On the history of this program, see B. vom Brocke (n. 14 *supra*). In fact, not all the Germans came from Berlin.

[79] These dates: The Harvard Crimson, September 29. The Crimson had Meyer arriving on the 22nd, but the 21st may be right: the Friedrich der Große and the Kaiser Wilhelm II both arrived then, both having left Bremen on September 14.

[80] It still stands, now containing doctors' offices. Meyer had three rooms and a small kitchen, paying no rent. But the Prussian Kultusministerium paid him a "Wohnungsgeld-zuschuß" as well as 2200 marks to replace his "Kolleghonorare": AkdW, DDR, NL Ed. Meyer 218.

[81] The diploma itself was in Latin. The text, written by E.K. Rand (1871–1945), Ph.D. Munich, 1900, and professor of Latin, read: "Eduardum Meyer, antiquitatis scriptorem nemini viventium concedentem, cum Universitatis Berolinensis legatum tum in hunc annum collegam nostrum comitemque dupliciter nobis acceptum:" Harvard Graduates Magazine 18 (1909/10) 278, 280.

banquet on October 7.[82] On October 10 the Harvard History Club elected him its honorary president, and he spoke at its first meeting on November 9.[83] On that day he was told by Lowell that he had been appointed a regular member of the faculty, a status not usually awarded to visitors.

Normally the professors lectured in their native language, but Meyer spoke in English: the only German, so far as I know, to do so.[84] For the fall semester he offered three courses: History 3a, History of the Ancient World from Alexander the Great to Augustus, Monday, Wednesday, and Friday at 9, "assisted by Mr. Blake;"[85] History 45, History and Monuments of the Ancient East, Monday and Wednesday at 3:30,[86] again with Blake (this was open to the public without charge); and History 20k, a research course, The Origin and Opening of the Second Punic War, Thursday at 1:30. Good fortune has preserved at Harvard a well written set of notes to the first course,[87] taken by Samuel H. Cross (1891 – 1946),[88] which enables us to see what Meyer said to his pupils in the new world.

The course was announced as beginning with Alexander, but Meyer devoted several lectures to a survey of Greek civilization down to Philip II and then treated the emergence of Macedonia. For this portion it was natural for him to draw on his own Geschichte des Altertums, but since the Geschichte ends in 350 B.C. it is interesting to look at his treatment of the following period and compare it with, for example, his long essay on Alexander in Kleine Schriften I.[89]

---

[82] On June 20 Georg Wissowa (1859–1931), the Rector of the University of Halle and authority on Roman religion, had writen Meyer (as "Du") to ask him, as an old Halle colleague, to represent Halle as well: AkdW, DDR, NL Ed. Meyer 219.

[83] *Ibid.* He spoke on the subject of the World Empire. "In an interesting discussion he traced the idea from ancient days down to the 19th century:" History Club record book, 1904–1917, Harvard University Library HUD 3453.510.

[84] George Foot Moore (1851–1931), the Harvard professor of theology, went to Berlin on the exchange in 1909. He wrote Meyer on June 3 to ask advice about his courses, then on July 21, to ask whether he ought to deliver one of these in German: AkdW, DDR, NL Ed. Meyer 219.

[85] Robert Pierpont Blake (1886–1950) was later professor of Byzantine history at Harvard and an expert in Caucasian languages; he was also director of the Harvard University Library, 1928–1937.

[86] The catalogue of courses listed this at 12:00, but the list of those enrolled records the time as 3:30.

[87] Some 50 enrolled for this course, including H.W. Bell, who was later to act as editor of Sardis, Vol. XI, Coins, Part I, 1910–1914, Leiden 1916.

[88] Harvard University Library HUC 8909.338.3.15. Cross had a career in public service and returned to the Harvard faculty in 1928. An eminent medievalist, he was also professor of Slavic languages and in 1942 acted as interpreter for President Roosevelt in a conference with V.M. Molotov.

[89] "Alexander der Große und die absolute Monarchie," in: *Kl. Schr.* I 283–332 =

At the outset Meyer states his loyalty to Greek civilization as the main force of progress. "No race in the east [I draw on Cross's notes] has ever been an agency of development or had a national existence until the Turks, because dominating empires have succeeded one another." As for Carthage, it "had good political organization, but no ideas of culture or innovation came from Carthaginians .... Carthage cannot be considered as a bearer of civilization." Within the survey of the Greeks and their states, we learn of the growing influence of trading classes:

> By the development of trading classes, the agricultural classes and great nomarchs ⟨were⟩ thrown into ⟨the⟩ background. In Athens, the dominant position of tradespeople and ⟨the⟩ laboring class was increased by ⟨the⟩ prevalence of town influence and naval skill.

Agrarian interests were opposed to trading interests; thus "the tradespeople were responsible for Greek imperial policy—though repressed by Pericles, it was favored by Cleon and Alcibiades, and led to ⟨the⟩ Sicilian expedition." Even though these ideas have behind them the authority of the published version in the Geschichte des Altertums, we may well wonder whether this schematic analysis of Athenian politics, with its confrontation of economic classes and rival motives, is to be accepted.[90]

Continuing with our brief sample, we come to the Macedonians, who, for Meyer, "were probably a branch of the Greek race, coming from Thessaly & Dorians." As for Philip II, he "tried to insure peace and add territory:" this latter was, in Meyer's opinion, the ultimate duty of the state.[91] Moreover, Philip was not "the perfidious politician that Demosthenes paints him."[92] His son Alexander was

> filled with ⟨the⟩ Greek idea that Greeks ought to conquer and rule the

---

I² 265–314. As we have seen, Meyer published a shorter essay on Alexander in 1903 (n. 6 supra).

[90] Meyer develops this view of the change in Greek political forces above all in Geschichte des Altertums III, Stuttgart 1901, 542–564. I recognize that we depend on the notes of an undergraduate for our knowledge of what Meyer said, but Cross's notes are coherent and inspire confidence; and he became a distinguished scholar. Since any of Meyer's opinions merit attention, the notes should perhaps be published in full.

[91] At least, up to a certain point. In "Der Gang der alten Geschichte," Kl. Schr. I 275 ff., Meyer approves of the "Gleichgewicht der Staaten und der in ihnen organisierten Nationen," which enforces healthful competition on all leading states. By contrast, after the Punic Wars Rome was the only dominant power, and from that moment began "der Stillstand und dann der Rückgang der Kultur."

[92] Admiration for Philip, and a tendency to compare his Athenian opponents, who really ought not to have resisted him, with ineffective British parliamentarians, emerge in the writings of other German historians: for a survey, see J.R. Knipfing, "German Historians and Macedonian Imperialism," in: Amer. Historical Rev. 26 (1920/1) 657–671. The same criticism of Philip's opponents is found in K.J. Beloch's Die attische Politik seit Perikles, Leipzig 1884.

world, and no longer be dependent on barbarians, who should by rights be subjects. Philip felt as a Macedonian, Alexander as a Greek.[93]

Alexander "came into hostility with his father, became partially reconciled, and then caused Philip's murder, removed those who stood in his way to ⟨the⟩ throne, and seized the power in Macedonia." This remarkable statement differs from the formulation in Kleine Schriften: "Nachdem er ... die Mörder seines Vaters und die gefährlichsten Prätendenten beseitigt ... hatte," he opened the "Nationalkrieg gegen das asiatische Weltreich."[94]

But, on the whole, the portrait of Alexander is harmonious with that in the German essay. His marriage with Roxane "symbolized ⟨the⟩ union of conquering Greece with Asia." He "aimed to make the world wholly civilized." The nearest comparison is with Charlemagne: as the latter "aimed to restore ⟨the⟩ unity of the Christian world, Alex⟨ander⟩ wanted to establish ⟨the⟩ unity of mankind and ⟨the⟩ supremacy of Greek civilization." Thus he "granted liberty to all Greek towns in Asia Minor and Cilicia."[95]

Finally, what was Alexander's legal position as ruler? The "world ruler had to stand above all men, all local powers, and all law. Not ⟨the⟩ abolishment of law, but merely the power of ⟨the⟩ monarch to be a law unto himself alone." This rather terrifying statement, which seems to sweep aside such basic Greek ideas as respect for the individual, whom the law protects from abuse, is consistent with Meyer's perception of the higher demands of the state. In his Chicago lecture of 1904, he had said,

> In the theory of Greek politics there dominates the same fundamental error which has thrown so much confusion into the political discussions of the past century, especially in liberal, but also in conservative, parties. They were inclined to consider their constitutional ideal as the final aim of a state, whereas even the idea of liberty and the rule of law is nothing but a means for reaching the highest aim, for developing and securing the power and greatness of a state.[96]

Since Alexander, in Meyer's view, had successfully transcended any such

---

[93] "Aber Alexander war aus anderem Stoffe als sein Vater. In noch ganz anderer Weise als dieser fühlte er sich als Hellene," *Kl. Schr.* I 297 = I² 279. That barbarians should by rights be subjects is good Aristotelian doctrine: see Politics I 1252 a24–b12.

[94] *Kl. Schr.* I 294 = I² 276. This is one point at which we may wonder whether Cross recorded Meyer rightly: was Meyer perhaps reviewing the opinions of various historians, some of whom accused Alexander of contriving Philip's murder?

[95] A view that others have also held, but for critical discussion see E. Badian, "Alexander the Great and the Greeks of Asia," in: Ancient Society and Institutions, Studies ... Ehrenberg, Oxford 1966, 37–69.

[96] *Kl. Schr.* I 227–228.

obsession with "the ideal of liberty and the rule of law," little could be said against his uncontrolled use of supreme power as he saw fit. Indeed, Meyer's consistent monarchism, strengthened by his loyalty to his country in the Great War, was to lead him to this definition of the ideal of liberty as seen by a German:

> er will regiert sein, und zwar in allen Schichten des Volkes, nicht selbst regieren. Die Regierung aber soll die Interessen der Gesamtheit vertreten. ... Der Pflichtbegriff steht dem Deutschen höher als der der politischen Rechte.[97]

He went on to a detailed narrative of the Hellenistic period and the Republic. Like many university teachers, he did not attain the final point originally announced, but ended with the battle of the Metaurus River in the second Punic War, 207 B.C. He thus did not reach the age of the great Roman personalities, about whom his judgments would have been stimulating to his hearers and instructive to us. Even Hannibal sweeps by so quickly in the last lecture that no picture of the great commander emerges.

Meyer now entered the full social life of the Havard-Boston community, and we cannot follow up all the invitations that he and his wife received.[98] The historian of the American constitution, James Ford Rhodes (1848 – 1927), invited him to a dinner for Lowell on October 26 (at which Meyer spoke), to dinner at the Tavern Club on October 29, and to a luncheon meeting of the Saturday Club (at the Union Club) on October 30.[99] On November 18 Meyer spoke to the Harvard Cosmopolitan Club; the president was John Reed (1887 – 1920), A.B. 1910, who was to become the famous Communist and observer of the Russian revolution (Ten Days that Shook the World, New York 1919).[100]

In December 1909 began another round of lectures and trips.[101] Old pupils and hearers pressed Meyer to renew acquaintances, while university presidents and secretaries of learned societies joined the queue. Bernadotte Perrin of Yale arranged a lecture for December 9: "We should

---

[97] Die Vereinigten Staaten von Amerika etc., Frankfurt a.M. 1920, 245.

[98] At some time during this early period Meyer gave an interview in which he criticized the methods of teaching in English universities. A column, "Ex Cathedra," in the Liverpool Courier, November 6, rebuked him for his view that "England has great scholars, but in England they do not teach ... careful seminary work, which is so much more important than the best lectures, is lacking." (I thank Miss Angela Durkin for identifying the newspaper; a clipping of the column is in the Meyer papers, AkdW, DDR, NL Meyer 219.)

[99] AkdW, DDR, NL Meyer 219.

[100] *Ibid.* The club existed from 1908 to 1925; two-thirds of the active members had to be of foreign birth.

[101] Chronicled in summary form in the Addendum.

rather prefer to hear you in German, and I think your audience would be quite as large in that case."[102] During the Christmas vacation Meyer spent several days in Philadelphia. Knowing of his plans, Caroline L. Ransom (1872–1952) wrote from Bryn Mawr College, asking him to lecture there: "Ich habe oftmals Sehnsucht nach Berlin."[103] Among the audience would be Tenney Frank (1876–1939), the historian of Rome, who was to be in Berlin to hear Meyer in 1910/1. The main academic event in Philadelphia was to be the annual meeting of the American Historical Association, and already on May 13 W.L. Westermann (1873–1954) at the University of Wisconsin had written Meyer, enlisting him to read a paper to the Association.[104] While in New York Meyer also received an invitation to lunch from Mary L. Adams (Mrs. John Quincy Adams), the wife of the Assistant Secretary of the Art Commission of New York City. The couple had been in Halle in winter 1889/90, and now she wrote, "I want to hear you laugh again!"[105]

The Christmas/New Year's season having passed, Meyer returned to Cambridge.[106] The time for his leaving Harvard was approaching, and on January 19, 1910, the Boston Evening Transcript said, "[h]is departure will be deeply regretted by all who have come to know him, and his brief service to Harvard will long be remembered." The Outlook was

---

[102] AkdW, DDR, *loc. cit.* Meyer spoke on "Kaiser Augustus," for which he could draw on his paper originally delivered at the Heidelberg Versammlung deutscher Historiker = Hist. Zeitschr. 91 (1903) 385–431 = *Kl. Schr.* I 441–492 = I² 423–474; in this he tried to uphold the theory that Augustus' "restoration of the Republic" was sincere and that he was no "Heuchler". Meyer had spoken in English at Yale in 1904. It was at least a slight lapse from academic courtesy to deliver a lecture that had been published some years earlier: Meyer would not have done this in Germany.

[103] AkdW, DDR, *ibid.* Ransom, head (1905–1910) of the department of archaeology at Bryn Mawr, had studied under Erman in Berlin, 1900–1903, and had published "Reste griechischer Holzmöbel in Berlin," in: Jahrb. deut. Arch. Inst. 17 (1902) 125–140 (the first publication there by a woman), leading to her Couches and Beds of the Greeks Etruscans and Romans, Chicago 1905.

[104] AkdW, DDR, *ibid.* The paper was "The Papyri from Elephantine;" compare the full publication, Der Papyrusfund von Elephantine etc., Leipzig 1912 (in English: Papyri at Elephantine etc., New York 1912).

[105] AkdW, DDR, NL Meyer 218. On Meyer's famous laugh, compare Charles Breasted's sketch of Meyer in Berlin, 1904: "a wiry, inflexible giant with a brown beard, massive head, thick goldrimmed spectacles, frock coat, bull-of-Bashan voice and Olympian laughter:" Pioneer to the Past, The Story of James Henry Breasted, Archaeologist, New York 1947, 128. See also p. 119 *infra*.

[106] Prosopographically fascinating is a list of some 68 names, in Mrs. Meyer's hand, recording the persons from whom the Meyers received Christmas cards or bouquets; most are checked off, suggesting that acknowledgments had been sent. Among the names are Breasted, Pease, Oldfather, Westermann, President Harris of Northwestern, Bynum, Sill, Gildersleeve, and the whole Cambridge circle of Lowell, Ferguson, Kuno Francke (see p. 123 *infra*), and others: Staatsbibl. Preuß. Kulturbesitz, West Berlin, NL 213 (Ed. Meyer) 3.

equally complimentary, recording that he was given a silver loving-cup on the eve of his departure:

> It is no exaggeration to say that no other of the eminent teachers from abroad who have visited Harvard since the system of professorial interchange was established some years ago has made so profound an impression both on members of the faculty and on the student body. . . . Professor Meyer entered freely into the undergraduate life, giving numerous informal talks to departmental clubs, and invariably leaving on his hearers' minds the impress of a vigorous, stimulating, and really fascinating personality.[107]

To say goodbye and to reciprocate for Harvard's hospitality (for their lodgings were not suited to elegant dinners), the Meyers hosted a large dinner at the Colonial Club, Cambridge, on Sunday January 23.[108] The replies[109] could be the basis for a prosopography of Cambridge-Boston academic society: the expected guests attended, Blake, Ferguson, Lowell, Francke, and so on. James Ford Rhodes was ill but wrote on January 24,

> Our intercourse has been a source of great pleasure to me and I shall always remember its many agreeable episodes. I hope that you will soon come to Cambridge-Boston again for I would like to renew the friendship already formed . . . . As we say in our slang we shall keep your memory green . . . .[110]

We may also record that Mrs. Meyer was asked to pour with Mrs. Lowell at the final College Tea of the semester on January 29.

On Sunday January 30 the Meyers received the Lowells in their apartment, and later that day Meyer wrote Lowell an affectionate letter.

Jan. 30st [sic] 1910

Dear President Lowell,

I am very sorry that you and Mrs. Lowell found it so uncomfortabl[e][111] with us this morning. There were a few things which I wanted to tell you, but forgot under these circumstances. The first is, that there appears to be some contradiction in what my wife and I myself told you a week ago about a prolongation of the Exchange Professor's stay to a whole year. I certainly have occasionally said that a stay of four months is rather short for real work; but I think that is really inevitable, and the decisive argument seems to me, that you would scarcely find a German professor, who could come to America for a whole year.

---

[107] The Outlook 94 (1910), Feb. 5, 277–278.

[108] This was a men's club founded in 1880. The Harvard Faculty Club, built in 1931 on Quincy Street, occupies its former site.

[109] Staatsbibl. Preuß. Kulturbesitz, West Berlin, *loc. cit.*

[110] AkdW, DDR, NL Meyer 219.

[111] "uncomfortably" is written: a reference to the Meyers' small apartment, or to the unwelcome news that Meyer could not remain for the whole year?

The second thing is, that I wanted to inform you that I have taken the liberty of using your and Mr. Rhodes' name in the dedication of a volume of Essays which has been printed during the winter and will be published in a few weeks. I wanted to leave by that a longer lasting remembrance of my stay in Cambridge and the great pleasure I derived from it.[112]

Finally my wife and I would ask you and Mrs. Lowell for your portrait. Can you send us your photographs [[for]] to Chicago?

(c/o Prof. J.H. Breasted

5545 Lexington Avenue

Hyde Park, Chicago Ill)

We shall arrive there about the middle of February and would with great pleasure send you our portraits from there.[113]

And so once more: good bye!

With best greetings from us both to Mrs. Lowell and you

Yours very sincerely

Eduard Meyer[114]

This letter permits us to ask whether Meyer had acted with complete candor regarding the length of his stay at Harvard: was he really supposed to remain for a year, and did he curtail his visit for his own convenience? On April 26, 1909, the Harvard faculty met and (among other business) announced his appointment, recording that "Professor Meyer's term of service will fall in the first half-year,"[115] and this was indeed the usual period.[116] On the other hand, the Board of Overseers appointed him a regular member of the faculty "for one year from September 1, 1909,"[117] and the citation for his honorary degree called him a colleague "for the coming year."[118] It appears that the appointment was originally

112 Meyer signed the preface to the *Kl. Schr.* "Harvard University, Cambridge Mass. Weihnachten 1909," as "Abbott Lawrence Lowell, President of Harvard University, und James Ford Rhodes, dem Geschichtsschreiber der Union, zugeeignet." The first acknowledgment I have found for a copy is from Prentice, February 28: AkdW, DDR, NL Meyer 219. Lowell sent his thanks for the book on April 25: "I feel that I have not only made a friend, but come into closer contact with German scholarship than one does through books:" Harvard University Archives, Lowell papers, UAI.5.160, 1909–14, no. 1180.

113 Meyer also sent his picture to the Cosmopolitan Club (p. 114 *supra*), for which John Reed thanked him, February 2: "You have been a fine and inspiring member and we shall miss you much in the Spring; but your portrait will adorn a prominent place on our wall:" AkdW, DDR, *loc. cit.*

114 Harvard University Archives, Lowell papers, *loc. cit.*

115 Harvard University Gazette, April 30, 1909.

116 Of the 11 exchange professors, only Eugen Kühnemann (1868–1946), professor of philosophy at Breslau, stayed a year (1908/9), on his second visit: see B. vom Brocke (n. 14 *supra*), 142.

117 On December 8: *ibid.*, December 10, 1909.

118 P. 110 *supra*.

foreseen as lasting one term, but that, after his arrival, the authorities at Harvard hoped he would remain for a year. Meyer's statement, that a German professor could hardly remain for a year, is only partly convincing. Professor Badian has pointed out to me that, if he had stayed at Harvard for the spring term, his lectures would have been over within May, an assistant would have marked his examinations, and he could have returned to Berlin only a short time after the beginning of the German summer semester, which the University of Berlin would surely have accepted.[119] He apparently preferred to spend some ten weeks traveling and lecturing in America; but there is no firm evidence showing that his decision breached any agreement with Harvard.

In any case, on January 31 Meyer left Cambridge for New York and gave several lectures, including one to the Germanistic Society of America.[120] After a visit to Princeton, where he dined with President Wilson, he began his second exploration of America. He stayed with his old pupil Sill at Cornell and gave three lectures; he then reached Chicago on February 13, where he stayed with Breasted.

There followed six lectures, for $1000, at Northwestern, funded by the Norman W. Harris Foundation.[121] We have already noted the euphoria with which the Evanston Index hailed the arrival of the one final authority, and we also have the Index's impression of the first lecture.[122] The originally scheduled room in Annie May Swift Hall was filled to overflowing, so the audience had to scramble across the fresh snow to Fisk Hall, where all could be seated. Meyer then entered and spoke in a fairly clear voice, "but some words in our vernacular resisted his most strenuous efforts to articulate them. One of these words was 'think', others 'rule' and 'ruler'." But "the lecturer's evident knowledge of the things spoken of was of the most inspiring kind." The lectures were all well attended and approvingly reviewed in The Northwestern, the student newspaper.[123]

On February 15, the University Guild offered a reception for the Meyers, attended by nearly the whole faculty. The Index reported that

---

[119] The summer semester at the University of Berlin in 1910 ran from April 16 to August 15.

[120] "Die Kultur und die Denkmäler der Pyramidenbauer" (originally delivered to the Deutsche Orientgesellschaft, published Leipzig 1908). On the Society and its secretary, Rudolf Tombo, who arranged the lecture, see B. vom Brocke (n. 14 supra), 148–149. The invitation: AkdW, DDR, NL Meyer, loc. cit.

[121] Harris was a prominent Chicago banker, benefactor of Northwestern, and member of its trustees, 1890–1916. The lectures are still given annually and many sets have been published, but Meyer's were not. The topics were: The earlier forms of Greek constitutions, The constitution of Sparta, The constitution of Athens, The reaction against democracy, Plato and Dionysios of Sicily, The absolute monarchy of Alexander the Great.

[122] Evanston Index, February 19, 1910, p. 4.

[123] February 16, 18, 21.

Mrs. Meyer, who spoke only German and French, said, on being asked her opinion of America, "I think the waste of food is something startling and that the American women are spoiled." Meanwhile, "occasionally through the rooms could be heard a rumbling noise like that from the lion house in Lincoln park [the home of the Chicago zoo]. It was found to be Prof. Meyer laughing . . . ."[124] On February 16 Meyer lunched with the Cliff Dwellers, a Chicago dining club. On February 18, there was no lecture, but Meyer met students at an afternoon reception at the Sigma Chi fraternity house. In a survey of German university life, he restated his conviction that "more German convivialities" would improve American college life.[125] Two lectures on Saturday, February 19, closed the series.

Meyer remained with Breasted in Chicago for several days, delivering three lectures at the University of Chicago, and dining on February 23 with the wealthy Mr. and Mrs. Harold McCormick at 1000 Lake Shore Drive on Chicago's "Gold Coast."[126] He then visited the University of Wisconsin for three lectures (fee, $200).[127] For the first, "[t]he auditorium of University Hall was completely filled and nearly all standing room was taken. Professor Meyer held the attention of his audience for two hours."[128]

Meyer now began an energetic sweep of the states of the middle west and south, not only to give lectures but also to investigate agricultural and social conditions. The tight schedule he sometimes followed is seen in the events of March 3 – 4.[129] His longest stay was in Urbana, Illinois, where he stayed with Arthur Stanley Pease (1881 – 1964), the eminent Latinist, who taught the courses in ancient history at the University of Illinois. Here between March 9 and 15 Meyer delivered the same six lectures he had given at Northwestern (fee, $300).[130] After stopping at the University of Oklahoma in Norman, where his old pupil Bynum was now teaching, he reached the University of Texas in Austin to lecture on March 18.[131]

---

[124] Evanston Index, February 19, p. 5.

[125] The Northwestern, February 21, p. 1

[126] Cyrus H. McCormick (1809–1884), McCormick's father, had invented the agricultural reaper, and Robert R. McCormick (1880–1955) was to become publisher of the conservative Chicago Tribune.

[127] Egyptian Civilization in the Time of the Pyramid Builders, February 23; The Origin and Development of the State, Feb. 28; The Emperor Augustus, March 2.

[128] The Daily Cardinal, February 26.

[129] Having finished his lectures at the University of Wisconsin, Meyer left there at 9:05 and reached Beloit College, Wisconsin, at 12:00. He lunched with President Edward D. Eaton (1851–1942), spoke on "The Importance and Value of the Study of Classical History" at 2:00, and left Beloit for Oberlin College, Ohio, at 3:30: AkdW, DDR, NL Meyer 218. He had been invited to Oberlin by Charles R. Martin ("My own memory of your lectures during the year 1906–1907 is vivid and abiding," December 9); Meyer gave two lectures in Oberlin on March 4: AkdW, DDR, NL Meyer 219.

[130] AkdW, DDR, NL Meyer 218.

[131] J.R.S. Sterrett (1851–1914) of Cornell had written him on February 22, informing

That same afternoon he moved on to San Antonio, arguably the most interesting city in Texas, and went to New Orleans on Sunday, March 20.

Now came the most adventurous part of his tour. On February 24, Alfred H. Stone, the owner of a plantation at Dunleith, Mississippi, had written him to invite him for a visit.[132] After seeing an American plantation at work, Meyer visited the Tuskegee Normal and Industrial Institute in Tuskegee, Alabama, which was a pioneering college for black Americans.[133] Its founder and Principal was the great Booker T. Washington (1856–1915), who had been born a slave.[134] In the invitation to Tuskegee it was suggested that Meyer might like to visit Mound Bayou, Mississippi, a "Negro town" of some 5000 inhabitants built in the Yazoo delta along the Illinois Central Railroad.[135]

Meyer had also been invited to visit Fisk University, a mainly black institution in Nashville, Tennessee, by President George A. Gates (1851–1912), who was aware that he was "making a special study of the race problem in America."[136] After two lectures at Richmond College, in Virginia, Meyer reached Baltimore on March 30, where he stayed with Hermann Collitz (1855–1935), the German-born scholar of Greek dialects, now professor at the Johns Hopkins University. Basil L. Gildersleeve (1831–1924), the great Hopkins classicist and Ph.D. from Göttingen (1853), had arranged for two lectures on March 31 and April 1.[137] On April 4 Meyer lunched with Johann Heinrich Graf von Bernstorff

---

him that he would be invited to Texas. He urged Meyer to see Austin, San Antonio, Houston, and Galveston, but "Dallas is a modern town and may be omitted:" AkdW, DDR, NL Meyer 219.

[132] Stone published much on the races in America, e.g., Studies on the American Race Problem, New York 1908. He recommended that Meyer travel on the Yazoo and Mississippi Railroad from New Orleans to Leland, Mississippi, about four miles from the plantation. The trip will have taken place about March 22: AkdW, DDR, NL Meyer 218. Meyer cites Stone's book in his Die Vereinigten Staaten von Amerika, Frankfurt 1920, 93; cf. 126 ("der Besitzer einer großen Baumwollenplantage").

[133] In Meyer's papers is a copy of the Tuskegee Student, the college paper, for March 26: AkdW, DDR, NL Meyer 219.

[134] On March 25 Washington wrote Meyer, regretting that he could not be in Tuskegee for the historian's visit: AkdW, DDR, NL Meyer 218. Meyer notes Tuskegee and Washington with approval, though within a generally dismal picture of the position of black citizens, op. cit. 95–96.

[135] This was the railroad along which thousands of black Americans migrated northward. On Mound Bayou, a town founded by black Americans in 1887, see H. Tong, "The Pioneers of Mound Bayou," in: Century Illustrated Monthly Magazine 79 (1909/10) 390–400; Janet S. Hermann, The Pursuit of a Dream, New York-Oxford 1981, 219–245, with full bibliography.

[136] AkdW, DDR, loc. cit. Ann Allen Shockley, University Archivist at Fisk University, reports that she cannot confirm a visit by Meyer.

[137] Meyer spoke on the Oriental Seminary (as the Department of Near Eastern Studies was formerly known) on "The Egyptians at the Time of the Pyramid Builders" and on "Augustus."

(1862 – 1939), the German ambassador; for the period April 4 – 8 he had a ticket to the visitors' gallery of the United States Senate, and on April 7 he visited the University of Virginia.[138]

He remained in the east until his departure. He had originally planned to sail on March 29, but for the sake of his long trip through the Midwest and South he postponed the date. On March 27 Perrin wrote from Yale, thanking him for a copy of Kleine Schriften and saying,

> I hope the postponement of your date of sailing has not been a trial to you or to Mrs. Meyer. You are in the most gratifying demand here in America! ... I shall hope to see you in New York before you sail on April 16.[139]

On April 16, therefore, Meyer left New York for Hamburg.[140] We need be in no doubt that he enjoyed the adulation and the competition for his presence all over America, but what did he think of American life and society? His visits created an interesting confrontation between a convinced monarchist and the flourishing, still expanding democracy of the new world.

Among Meyer's strongest points as a scholar and thinker are his frankness and clarity of expression. In one of his first talks at Harvard, to the members of the graduate schools on October 15, he touched on the history of various states and found that war was "one of the great factors in the growth of nations and in the advancement of civilizations . . . . War he assigned as the cause of the tremendous growth of the United States." As between the United States and Germany, war was not desirable, but "intellectually the keenest rivalry should be cultivated. Here also the strife of strong powers tends to the highest development."[141] He repeated his endorsement of war as the medium by which a state can achieve its true purpose, namely expansion, on January 15, in a talk to the Harvard Graduate Club. The United States was "the greatest conquering nation of the nineteenth century, as a glance at a map will show." He also criticized one of the bases of American foreign policy, the Monroe Doctrine, and suggested that if it were violated the United States would turn at once to war rather than to the world court. The New York Times took exception to his conception of American foreign policy on January 24;[142] and even in Germany the visitor's remarks were a little disturbing. The Frankfurter Zeitung, February 9, entitled a short article "Vereinigte

---

[138] *Ibid.*
[139] AkdW, DDR, NL Meyer 219.
[140] He sailed for Hamburg on the Kaiserin Auguste Victoria.
[141] Harvard Crimson, October 16.
[142] "The United States is not a 'conquering nation,' nor animated by 'land hunger,' as Prof. Meyer asserts," p. 8.

Staaten. Ein unvorsichtiger Austauschprofessor,'' and said in part,

> ... muß man sich billig darüber wundern, daß die Herren Austausch-Professoren so wenig geneigt sind, die Empfindlichkeiten Amerikas zu berücksichtigen.[143]

But, if he complimented America on its successful expansion through war—probably not praise that his hearers wholly enjoyed—, he found material for criticism in its government. Speaking to the Men's League of Newton, Massachusetts on January 25,[144] he observed that, in America, the individual takes the initiative in everything, but this can lead to incompetent or dishonest rule by men who happen to have the support of the majority. In Germany, the government takes the initiative in all things that affect the public welfare; and Germans cared less than Americans for majority opinion. ''Why should we respect the opinion of those who have not the knowledge to form judgment? We respect their rights and have regard to their needs, but care nothing for their opinions.'' Notorious pilfering could not happen in a German city: ''A mayor is chosen because of his fitness and for the term of 12 years, and when his term is up he is usually chosen again, so that he has a life post.''[145] On the international scene, Germany, unlike America, could not go on expanding, for she was held back by warlike states. ''And it is her august emperor who has held back the warring elements of Europe and maintained peace for more then 20 years.'' Meyer also praised the customs of the German, ''who sits an hour over a glass of beer with his family and neighbors around him,'' in contrast to the American bar with its hurried drinking. The talk, which was well received for its logic and arguments, ended with the modest reflection that we cannot say which of the two systems is superior: ''That may be judged 2000 years hence.''

Meyer's Platonic view of the right social organization also informed his second lecture to the University of Wisconsin on February 28, ''The Origin and Development of the State.'' Monarchy was ''perhaps a better form of government than democracy.'' The weakness in the American system was that offices are filled by men who are not trained for the positions. In ancient Rome, too, ''every child was taught the essentials of a

---

[143] On March 4, in Chicago, Meyer drafted a letter, addressed to ''Ew. Excellenz'' (the ambassador to America?), defending himself and referring to the misrepresentations often found in journalism: AkdW, DDR, NL Meyer 219.

[144] His address was reported in the Newton Center Circuit, January 28.

[145] I rely on Meyers Konversations-Lexikon[5], vol. 3, Leipzig-Vienna 1905, s.v. Bürgermeister, p. 710, for the following information. Mayors could be either elected or appointed by the state. The term of office could be a fixed one, as in Prussia, or for life, as in Saxony, or for life after re-election, as in Bavaria. They had to be confirmed by the national government.

particular administrative office and therefore when he became of age he was capable to carry the responsibilities of the office.''[146] Thus in America we lack a trained body of men. As for the Germans, most of them

> would not be willing to do away with the monarchical form of government because they wanted a responsible leader who could not throw his responsibility upon laws which bind him as they do the president of this country.[147]

In effect, this statement—the German emperor is fortunately not bound by laws—returns us to his approval of the position of Alexander, the world ruler who "had to stand above all men, all local powers, and all law."[148]

IV. Later Relations with America

Meyer's first tour of America was brief, but warmly greeted by his friends and colleagues; the second was a veritable triumphal parade. We must now look at the sequel. My friend Professor Sösemann surveys his political writings elsewhere in this book, but the personal emotions and strains of his break with America have their place here.

After the outbreak of the Great War, Woodrow Wilson, no longer president of Princeton University but of the United States, proclaimed America's neutrality. Yet he sponsored the selling of arms to the allies, but not to Germany-Austria.[149] It is impossible to reconcile these two policies. And it is easy to understand the frustration of Germans, in both Europe and America, with Wilson's moralizing posture. When Harvard itself, as Meyer thought, took a stand against Germany, he unleashed a furious article, "Der Geist von Harvard."[150]

The cause was this. An American congressman, Richard Bartholdt (1855–1932),[151] called in 1915 for a meeting of protest in Washington against Wilson's policy and for the re-establishment of true neutrality. Among those from whom he sought support was Kuno Francke (1855–1930), born in Kiel and since 1884 instructor, then professor, at

---

[146] It is not clear whether Meyer or the report in the Daily Cardinal, March 1, is responsible for this exaggeration.

[147] Reported in the Milwaukee Sentinel, March 1; small wonder that the column is headed, "PROF. MEYER SCORES RULE BY DEMOCRACY."

[148] Cross's notes, p. 113 supra.

[149] For a thorough discussion of Wilson's dilemma, see Arthur S. Link, Wilson [vol. III], The Struggle for Neutrality 1914–1915, Princeton 1960, especially 161–170 on the anger of German- and Irish-Americans over Wilson's policy.

[150] Vossische Zeitung, Berlin, March 7, 1915, no. 121, pp. 1–2; not reprinted, but summarized in the New York Times, March 13.

[151] Bartholdt, born in Germany, was editor of the St. Louis Tribune, 1885–1892, and a Republican congressman from Missouri, 1893–1915. He wrote From Steerage to Congress. Reminiscences and Reflections, Philadelphia 1930.

Harvard. Francke declined to attend the meeting and gave his reasons in the New York Times[152] and elsewhere. Francke's position at Harvard was painful beyond Meyer's knowledge. He thought Germany was in the right and said so; this cost him friendships in America and is even said to have caused his private mail to be opened.[153] In the Times, he declared that "[m]y sympathies . . . in this war are wholly and fervently on the German side." But, as a naturalized American citizen, he saw his duty as supporting the policy of "neutrality" as currently interpreted, largely because an embargo on arms to the allies "might drive us into war with England." Thus Francke stood by the national policy, even though to his regret it was harming his native country.

This reasoning enraged Meyer, who inferred that Francke's position

> ist ihm von der Universität, an der er angestellt ist, und vermutlich von deren Präsidenten, dem Staatsrechtler Lowell, suppeditiert.

I seriously doubt that this was true. But Meyer also pointed to Harvard's withdrawal of invitations to German professors to give lectures, while Frenchmen were still welcomed. Lowell had further invited to Harvard professors from Louvain, whose library German bombardment had destroyed; he had also signed a paper sent to Wilson, warning against any interruption of the trade in weapons with England, on the interesting ground that such an embargo would breach the policy of neutrality. Such being, in Meyer's eyes, the new "spirit of Harvard," he concluded that "der Professorenaustausch mit Harvard aufhören muß, jetzt und für alle Zukunft."[154]

Some six weeks after this short pamphlet appeared, Meyer's son Herbert fell at Ypres (April 22, 1915). Only superhuman tolerance could have prevented this tragedy from deepening his antipathy toward America. Among the many letters of condolence he received was one from George Chatterton-Hill (1883 – ?);[155] even more notable is one from

---

[152] February 3, p. 10; reprinted in Francke's A German-American's Confession of Faith, New York 1915, 35 – 42.

[153] See Francke's Deutsche Arbeit in Amerika, Leipzig 1930, 64 – 75, and cf. previous note. See also G.H. Genzmer in: Dict. Amer. Biogr. III.2, New York 1931, 584 – 585, and in: Neue Deut. Biogr. 5 (1961) 328 – 329.

[154] Meyer's brother Kuno was then the exchange professor in Celtic philology. He resigned on April 26, 1915. There was but one more exchange professor, Adolph Goldschmidt (1863 – 1944) of Berlin, who served in 1927 and 1930. See B. vom Brocke (n. 14 supra), 142; and, on Goldschmidt and his dates of service, H. Kauffmann in: Neue Deut. Biogr. 6 (1964) 613 – 614.

[155] Staatsbibl. Preuß. Kulturbesitz, West Berlin, NL 213 (Ed. Meyer) 3. He was the author of Irland und seine Bedeutung für Europa, Berlin 1916; Meyer, to whom the Irish rebellion against England was welcome, contributed an approving foreword. Elsewhere Meyer praised German-Irish cooperation in America, recording that Irish and Germans

the Irish revolutionary, Sir Roger Casement (1864–1916), writing from Limburg/Lahn, May 18: "may God comfort your hearts and those of the innumerable others who have given their sons for Germany."[156]

A list of names is preserved, in Mrs. Meyer's hand, evidently of those to whom the family had sent a notice of Herbert's death.[157] One of the entries is "Chicago: Breasted." But even this old friendship was to suffer. We may recall Breasted's affectionate letters ("Du") when he heard that Meyer was first coming to America. A little later, in July 1904, Meyer approached Breasted in Berlin and asked him whether he might consider accepting a chair in Germany when one became open.[158] Moreover, Breasted's home was Meyer's headquarters in spring 1910. But after the war, in 1922, as Breasted returned to Germany for the first time since 1907, Meyer declined to see him, sending a message through Adolf Erman (1854–1937), Breasted's colleague in Egyptology, that he could have no relations with any American.[159]

But there was to be another meeting, aboard ship in Genoa, in October 1925. Breasted and his family were traveling to Egypt, and by chance he had been assigned a deck chair next to one marked "Professor Eduard Meyer." Meyer saw this and pointed it out to his wife. Charles Breasted goes on,

> My father was standing at the rail in conversation with friends when Frau Meyer approached him and gently touched his arm. He turned. She held out her hand and said in German, "I want to greet you and give you my hand!—and so does my husband! May he also come to you?"
>
> "There were tears in her eyes," my father wrote afterwards. "Meyer was standing in the background. I stepped forward at once and he likewise. He

---

had raised money to assist some towns in East Prussia; houses to be built there would bear the name of Kuno Meyer, whom the Irish respected for his "der Rettung der irischen Sprache und der Ideale des irischen Volkes gewidmete Lebensarbeit:" Zeit- und Streitfragen. Korrespondenz des Bundes deutscher Gelehrter und Künstler 1 (1917), No. 4.

[156] *Ibid.* Casement had come to Germany in 1914, seeking military aid for an Irish rebellion. Meyer concluded his preface to Chatterton-Hill's book with an encomium to Casement. He was then (May 1, 1916) a prisoner of the British, who executed him for treason on August 3, 1916. See Sir Roger Casement's Diaries: His Mission to Germany and the Findlay Affair, ed. Charles E. Curry, Munich 1922.

[157] Staatsbibl. Preuß. Kulturbesitz, West Berlin, NL 213 (Ed. Meyer) 3.

[158] Charles Breasted, *op. cit.* (n. 105 *supra*), 129.

[159] *Ibid.* 325. Meyer's enmity toward America, which he justified with the logic of war, also appears in his pamphlet (two sides of a single sheet of paper) "Amerika und unser Krieg" (March 1916). Here he argued for unrestricted U-boat warfare (this came to pass in February 1917), largely as a way of weakening Wilson's position and preventing his re-election in 1916. "Die Möglichkeit, daß es mit Amerika zum Krieg kommt, müssen wir hinnnehmen."—This pamphlet, written in March (Marohl 324), came out earlier than "Denkschrift über den U-Bootkrieg" (Marohl 320), which was the same text followed by the names of 316 supporters of Meyer's position.

seized my hand in both of his, and his face glowed with his old friendliness. With glistening eyes and all his one-time heartiness, he said, 'Es freut mich ungemein Dich wieder zu sehen!' . . . "It was the old Meyer, now a kindly, *gentle* old man of seventy-two [actually 70]. I confess I was deeply touched by the 'Dich'. Good Frau Meyer beamed with joy through her tears. *She* had done it. Well—it is better so.''[160]

One year before this moving reconciliation, Meyer had issued a two-volume edition of his Kleine Schriften; thus volume I now went into a second edition. The new preface includes a denunciation of Woodrow Wilson and American policy in the war; the lecture in English, delivered in Chicago 20 years earlier, is "jetzt natürlich weggelassen;" the original dedication, to Lowell and Rhodes of Harvard, is recalled only in pain. Meyer records that, in winter 1919/20, after the postwar demand for the extradition of the German Emperor was lodged, he had torn up his honorary degrees from Oxford, Liverpool, St. Andrews,[161] Harvard, and Chicago, had sent them back in pieces, and had proclaimed his action.[162]

There survives, however, a small notebook, compiled by one or more of his children, with the title "Verzeichniß der Ehrendiploma von Papa."[163] Along with notes on many other honors, the book records that the honorary doctorates from Oxford and Harvard are indeed "nicht vorhanden." Only the cover (Hülle) from the St. Andrews degree is registered; Liverpool is not mentioned.

His honorary memberships in the Society for the Promotion of Hellenic Studies (1908)[164] and in the Massachusetts Historical Society (1910)

---

[160] *Ibid.* 386–387.

[161] Oxford: D.Litt., October 22, 1907; Liverpool: Litt.D., May 8, 1909; St. Andrews: LL.D., September 14, 1911 (with his brother Kuno). Kuno Meyer was no less a German patriot, not to say chauvinist, than Eduard. On his career, see n. 12 *supra*. On December 3, 1914, he wrote the Vice-Chancellor of Liverpool, evidently (the letter is lost) saying he would give the remainder of his lectures when England was conquered. The University of Liverpool interpreted this haughty message as a letter of resignation from his chair. He apparently also wrote A.L. Smith (1850–1924), Master of Balliol College, Oxford, offering his protection when Germans should occupy Oxford. See Thomas Kelly, For Advancement of Learning, The University of Liverpool 1881–1981, Liverpool 1981, 174–176.

[162] *Kl. Schr.* I² vi; so too his autobiography in Marohl, 11. His proclamation was published in Berliner Lokalanzeiger 38, February 5, 1920, no. 65. In June 1920 he also contributed a foreword to the German version of a bizarre book, England gegen Amerika: Der kommende Kampf (Berlin 1921), by Daniel F. Cohalan (1867–1946), a member of the Supreme Court of New York, 1911–1924, and a tireless champion of Ireland. He praised this work for its analysis of the "englische Weltherrschaft," which threatened the whole world and above all the United States; the latter nation in turn practiced "eine ebenso rücksichtslose, brutal zugreifende Interessenpolitik," etc.

[163] Staatsbibl. Preuß. Kulturbesitz, West Berlin, *loc. cit.*

[164] Walter Leaf (1852–1927), president of this society, referred in his presidential

were found. So was the honorary doctorate from the University of Chicago, 1904. Meyer said he had torn it up. He had not.

V. Meyer's Impact on America

What effect, then, did this universal historian have on American academic life and scholarship? It would appear, little. The pupils whom he had already taught in Halle—Bynum, Sill, Prentice—were faithful adherents. His assistant at Harvard, Robert Blake, did follow him back to Berlin in 1910 and recorded that he changed his field from classics to history under Meyer's influence.[165] But Meyer encouraged him to pursue his interest in oriental languages, and Blake became professor of Byzantine history; he was Ph.D. Harvard (1916), not Berlin. He also recorded that it was M.I. Rostovtzeff who persuaded him to stay in history rather than in linguistics. Another North American who studied under Meyer in Berlin in 1912–1914 ("I was Eduard Meyer's student," he said to me in 1956) was the Canadian A.E.R. Boak (1888–1962), a specialist on the later Roman Empire and long a professor at the University of Michigan; but he took his doctorate at Harvard under Ferguson.

The Great War and its aftermath did not cause a wave of students to seek out Berlin; a potential following for Meyer may thus have been stifled. His antipathy to American policy could have been a further discouragement. Moreover, the study of German as a spoken language was now less strong than it had been in the 1890s, and Rhodes Scholarships offered a classical student a broadening experience after which one could return to America for a Ph.D.

Meyer's convinced Germanness, his commitment to monarchy, his imperiousness, might also have turned Americans away. But even in Germany the master did not have many pupils. Among his disciples,[166] only Ulrich Kahrstedt (1888–1962)[167] and Hans Erich Stier (1902–

---

address, June 24, 1919 (see Journ. Hell. Stud. 39 [1919] xxvii), to the famous manifesto, "An die Kulturwelt!" which 93 German scholars, including Meyer, had issued through many newspapers on October 4, 1914. The manifesto rejected all accusations of German responsibility for the war and for the shattering of Belgium's neutrality. On the manifesto and other aspects of the political stance taken by German scholars of the time, see B. vom Brocke, "Wissenschaft und Militarismus," in: Wilamowitz nach 50 Jahren (n. 18 *supra*), 649–719 (a reproduction of the manifesto, 718). Leaf observed, "Some of these names still stand on our list of honorary members. It is not for me to say how they should be treated." No action appears to have been taken: Meyer, Wilamowitz, and other Germans remained honorary members.

[165] On Blake see Harvard University Gazette, October 28, 1950 (a necrology by Ferguson and others).

[166] I have identified 24 men who wrote dissertations under Meyer in Berlin.

[167] Kahrstedt succeeded Georg Busolt in Göttingen, 1921–1952. His political views

1979)[168] received chairs in Germany. In America, again, some of Meyer's ideas have taken root. Boak[169] and Lily Ross Taylor (1886–1969)[170] endorsed his theory that Caesar wanted to found a divine monarchy, while Mason Hammond (1903–) accepted that Augustus sincerely restored the Republic.[171] But these ideas radiate from Meyer's writings, not necessarily (save in Boak's case) from the personal influence of the master. It rather seems that Meyer came to America at the height of his powers and reputation and, we may hope, inspired his many hearers to try to emulate his colossal knowledge and energy. But after 1910 his personal influence on the study of ancient history in America was—considering his status in the history of the subject—surprisingly modest.

---

were surely sympathetic to Meyer. They were both "Mitarbeiter" of the Eiserne Blätter, a distinctly conservative journal to which Meyer contributed a despairing article, "Ein Amerikaner über den Zusammenbruch Deutschlands," vol. 1 (1919/20) 804–807. Kahrstedt's short, strange book on America, Pax Americana, Munich 1920, a kind of Polybian essay about the coming American domination, is in Meyer's style.

[168] Professor in Münster as successor to Friedrich Münzer, 1936–1968, and editor of the latest editions of the Geschichte des Altertums.

[169] A History of Rome, New York 1921, 179–180, and later editions.

[170] The Divinity of the Roman Emperor, Middletown 1931.

[171] The Augustan Principate, Cambridge 1933, e.g. "Augustus was sincere in his claim that he had restored the Republic," 5. Further, "Meyer's view that Augustus harked back to Cicero and Pompey rather than to Caesar for his inspiration in shaping his own position still has great verisimilitude," 111, referring to Cäsars Monarchie 174–191.

Addendum

A Meyer Calendar, 1904

Jan. 9	Is invited to Chicago
March 5	Departs from Hamburg
March 14	Arrives in New York
March 15?	Lectures at Cornell: "The Emergence of the Individual in History"
March 16–17	At Niagara frontier with Sill
March 18	Arrives in Chicago
March 18–22	Ceremonies at University of Chicago
March 23	Visits Northwestern University
ca. March 28?	Visits Salt Lake City
March 30–31	Lectures at University of California, Berkeley: "The Emergence of the Individual in Ancient Times," "Socrates"

ca. April 4 – 5	Visits Universities of Illinois, Wisconsin
April 7	In Washington, D.C.
April 10	Dines at German Embassy
April 12	Lectures at Princeton University: "The Athenian Democracy"
April 14	In Philadelphia
ca. April 17	Lectures at Harvard University
April 18	Lectures at Yale University: "The Athenian Democracy"
April 19	In New York
April 20	Lectures at Columbia University
?	Departs for Germany

* * * * * * *

A Meyer Calendar, 1909/10

Sept. 14?	Departs from Bremen (?)
Sept. 21?	Arrives in New York
Oct. 6 – 7	Represents Universities of Halle and Berlin at inauguration of Lowell
Oct. 8	Lectures to graduate students of classics
Oct. 11	Elected Hon. President, Harvard History Club
Oct. 15	Speaks to Harvard graduate schools on history of states
Nov. 11	Speaks at first meeting of History Club; appointed regular member of faculty
Nov. 18	Speaks to Harvard Cosmopolitan Club
Dec. 6	Speaks to Seminary of Economics, Harvard: "Some Problems in the Economic History of Ancient Times"
Dec. 9	Lectures at Yale University: "Kaiser Augustus"
ca. Dec. 15	Lectures at Bryn Mawr College
Dec. 16	Lectures to Oriental Club, Philadelphia
Dec. 17	Lectures to graduate school, University of Pennsylvania: "The Greek Colonization of the East after Alexander the Great;" and to American Philosophical Society: "The Story of the Wise Ahikar"
Dec. 30	Speaks to American Historical Association: "The Papyri from Elephantine"
Jan. 15	Speaks to Harvard Graduates Club, Cambridge

Jan. 21	Speaks at Classical Conference, Harvard: "Hesiod's Ages of Man"
Jan. 22	Speaks to the College Club, Boston
Jan. 23	Hosts dinner, the Colonial Club, Cambridge
Jan. 25	Speaks to Men's League, Newton, Mass.
Jan. 31	Leaves Cambridge. Dines in Greenwich House, New York
Feb. 1	Lectures to Phi Beta Kappa Assn., New York: "The Earliest Civilizations of the East"
Feb. 2	Lectures at Columbia University
Feb. 3	Lectures to Germanistic Society of America, New York: "Die Kultur und die Denkmäler der Pyramidenbauer"
Feb. 4	Speaks to Graduate Students' Association, Princeton University: "University Life and Scholarship Ideals in Germany;" dines with Woodrow Wilson
Feb. 5	Lectures at Princeton: "Recent Discoveries in Ancient Oriental History"
Feb. 8–10	Lectures at Cornell University: "The Athenian Democracy," "Alexander the Great," "Origin and Development of Mormonism Compared with the Beginning of Islam"
Feb. 13	Arrives in Chicago, stays with Breasted
Feb. 15–19	Six Harris lectures at Northwestern University
Feb. 21	Lectures to Germanistic Society at Art Institute, Chicago: "Aegypten zur Zeit der Pyramidenbauer"
Feb. 23–24	Lectures at University of Chicago: "Alexander the Great and Absolute Monarchy," "Papyri of the Jewish Colony at Elephantine," "The Greek Colonization of the East after Alexander"
Feb. 25	Lectures at University of Wisconsin: "Egyptian Civilization in the Time of the Pyramid Builders"
Feb. 26–27	Visits Minneapolis-St. Paul, Minnesota
Feb. 28	Lectures at Wisconsin: "The Origin and Development of the State"
March 2	Lectures at Wisconsin: "The Emperor Augustus"
March 3	Lectures at Beloit College: "The Importance and Value of the Study of Classical History"
March 4	Two lectures at Oberlin College
March 9–15	Six lectures at University of Illinois
March 17?	Visits University of Oklahoma

March 18	Lectures at University of Texas: "The Development of the State"
March 20	In New Orleans
March 22?	Visits Dunleith, Miss.
March 25?	Visits Mound Bayou, Miss.
March 26?	Visits Tuskegee Institute
March 28 – 29	Lectures at Richmond College, Virginia: "The Origin and Development of the State," "The Foundation of the German Empire"
March 31 – April 1	Lectures at Johns Hopkins University: "The Egyptians at the Time of the Pyramid Builders," "Augustus"
April 6?	Lectures at University of Virginia
April 11	In Philadelphia
April 16	Sails from New York

JÜRGEN DEININGER

EDUARD MEYER UND MAX WEBER

Der erste Eindruck, den man vom Verhältnis zwischen Eduard Meyer und Max Weber (1864 – 1920) empfängt, ist in vieler Hinsicht der einer ausgesprochen einseitigen Beziehung. Ed. Meyer hat Arbeiten Webers, die seine unmittelbaren Interessengebiete betrafen, zwar im allgemeinen zur Kenntnis genommen, Weber gelegentlich—und fast immer mit ausgesprochener Hochachtung—zitiert und manchmal auf ihn einzugehen versucht; aber eine tiefere Bedeutung hat Max Weber für Ed. Meyer offensichtlich nicht gehabt. Es gibt in diesem Verhältnis nichts, was sich z.B. mit der engagierten Auseinandersetzung Ed. Meyers mit den "modernen" Historikern Lamprecht, Breysig usw. oder auch später mit Oswald Spengler vergleichen ließe. Ed. Meyers so oft zitiertes "Streben nach Gewinnung einer einheitlichen, historisch begründeten Weltanschauung," welche die "innerste Triebfeder" bei der Ergreifung seines Berufes gewesen sei,[1] hat speziell von dem neun Jahre jüngeren Max Weber nichts profitiert. Ganz anders und ungleich intensiver stellt sich dagegen umgekehrt die Beziehung Max Webers zu Ed. Meyer dar: Für Weber war Ed. Meyer nicht nur einer der maßgebenden Historiker des Altertums, sondern einer der Hauptvertreter der zeitgenössischen Historie insgesamt.[2] Rein stofflich verdankte Weber seinem Werk vor allem für den Alten Orient, die antike jüdische und die griechische Geschichte teilweise sehr viel. Freilich wäre es wiederum falsch, wollte man Weber in seinem Verhältnis zu Ed. Meyer einseitig als Nehmenden und Ed. Meyer als den Gebenden sehen. Denn neben der 'Rezeption' Ed. Meyers steht immer auch—wie könnte es anders sein?—die selbständige Auseinandersetzung Max Webers mit ihm, deren Zentrum nicht etwa, wie man zunächst vielleicht vermuten könnte, das Verhältnis von Sozial- und Wirtschaftsgeschichte und politischer Geschichte, sondern Webers Insistieren auf einer sorgfältigen (im Falle Ed. Meyers vor allem ökonomischen) Begriffsbildung der Historiker und überhaupt auf theoretischer Klarheit über ihr Tun bildet. Demgegenüber bleiben die in jüngster Zeit mehrfach aufgestellten Hypothesen eines starken Einflusses Ed. Meyers auf Weber, geradezu als eine Art heimlicher Anreger oder Ideenvermittler, proble-

---

[1] Ed. Meyer, GdA I² 1, IX.
[2] Vgl. unten, S. 146 f.

matisch.[3] Wichtig erscheint indes, daß bei allen ins Auge fallenden Divergenzen zwischen Max Weber und Ed. Meyer es doch eine Reihe wichtiger Gemeinsamkeiten in ihrem Erkenntnisinteresse wie in ihren Grundanschauungen gab, aus denen sich—neben dem rein stofflichen Interesse Max Webers—dessen besondere Aufmerksamkeit und Aufgeschlossenheit für Ed. Meyers wissenschaftliche Arbeiten zu einem beträchtlichen Teil erklären dürften.

I

Welches sind, so ist zuerst zu fragen, die wichtigsten für das Verständnis der Beziehungen zwischen Eduard Meyer und Max Weber in Betracht kommenden Arbeiten? Die Grundlage für Max Webers intensives Interesse für Eduard Meyer bildeten selbstverständlich Webers eigene Schriften zum Altertum, das bekanntlich vom Beginn seiner wissenschaftlichen Laufbahn an eine besondere Bedeutung für ihn hatte. Weber, der selbst im engeren fachlichen Sinn nie ein "Historiker" war und sich nie als solcher gesehen hat, sondern 1882–1886 ein juristisches Studium absolviert hatte, veröffentlichte 1891 als sein erstes der Antike gewidmetes Werk "Die römische Agrargeschichte in ihrer Bedeutung für das Staats- und Privatrecht," das ihm als römischrechtliche Habilitationsschrift für die 1892 in Berlin vollzogene Habilitation für Römisches und Handelsrecht diente.[4] In diesem Buch versuchte er vor allem, ursprünglich in der mittelalterlichen und neuzeitlichen Agrargeschichte entwickelte Fragestellungen mit der Untersuchung der Rechtsverhältnisse von Grund und Boden in der römischen Antike zu verbinden, um so zu vertieften Einsichten in die sozial- und wirtschaftsgeschichtliche Entwicklung des römischen Agrarwesens zu gelangen. Dabei stand er stark unter dem Einfluß des Berliner Agrarhistorikers August Meitzen (1822–1910), von Theodor Mommsen (1817–1903) sowie des Nationalökonomen Johann Karl Rodbertus (1805–1875), der in seinen in vielem überaus scharfsichtigen Arbeiten zur antiken Ökonomie schon in den 60er Jahren des 19. Jhdts. den 'Oikos', das (geschlossene) 'Haus', in seiner Bedeutung als wesentliche wirtschaftliche Struktureinheit in der Antike erkannt hatte.

Insofern markiert bereits die Römische Agrargeschichte, noch vor den großen Arbeiten zur ostelbischen Landarbeiterproblematik in den unmittelbar folgenden Jahren, Webers Weg von der Jurisprudenz hin zur Nationalökonomie, der 1894 zu seiner Berufung auf einen nationalöko-

---

[3] Vgl. unten, S. 154 ff.
[4] M. Weber, Die römische Agrargeschichte in ihrer Bedeutung für das Staats- und Privatrecht, Stuttgart 1891; jetzt in: Max Weber-Gesamtausgabe I/2, Tübingen 1986.

nomischen Lehrstuhl in Freiburg i.B. führte. Wichtig war, daß die Antike
für Max Weber auch weiterhin ein deutlicher Interessenschwerpunkt
blieb—zweifellos eine Folge seiner ganzen bisherigen Entwicklung und
nicht nur der auch in der damaligen deutschen Nationalökonomie herrschenden historischen Orientierung. So hatte die Antike auch ihren Platz
in Webers großer Vorlesung "Theoretische Nationalökonomie," die er
unter diesem und etwas variierten Titeln zunächst in Freiburg und später
in Heidelberg zu halten pflegte. 1896 erschien der bekannte Vortrag "Die
sozialen Gründe des Untergangs der antiken Kultur,"[5] 1897 und 1898
folgten die ersten beiden Fassungen des Artikels "Agrarverhältnisse im
Altertum" im Handwörterbuch der Staatswissenschaften, von denen die
erste neben Rom auch Griechenland, die zweite außerdem den Alten
Orient, d.h. Ägypten und Mesopotamien, umfaßte.[6] 1904 griff Weber in
dem Aufsatz "Der Streit um den Charakter der altgermanischen Sozialverfassung in der deutschen Literatur des letzten Jahrzehnts" wiederum
Fragen auf, die schon im Umkreis seiner Römischen Agrargeschichte
eine Rolle gespielt hatten.[7] Fünf Jahre danach, 1909, brachte die umfangreiche letzte Version der "Agrarverhältnisse im Altertum" in der 3.
Auflage des Handwörterbuchs Webers bedeutendste Abhandlung über
die sozialen und wirtschaftlichen Strukturen der Alten Welt.[8] Besondere
Beachtung im vorliegenden Zusammenhang verdient ferner der Teil
"Das antike Judentum" der zunächst als Aufsatzreihe erschienenen
"Wirtschaftsethik der Weltreligionen" aus den Jahren 1917–1919;[9]
doch spielte die Antike auch sonst vielfach eine nicht geringe Rolle in den
späteren Werken Webers, insbesondere in wichtigen Partien von "Wirtschaft und Gesellschaft" sowie in der unvollendeten, wohl nur anfänglich
für "Wirtschaft und Gesellschaft" bestimmten Untersuchung "Die
Stadt," in deren Mittelpunkt eine 'idealtypisch' vergleichende Gegenüberstellung von mittelalterlicher und antiker Stadt steht.[10]

---

[5] M. Weber, Die sozialen Gründe des Untergangs der antiken Kultur (1896); hier zitiert nach: ders., Gesammelte Aufsätze zur Sozial- und Wirtschaftsgeschichte (= GASW),
Tübingen 1924, 289–311.
[6] M. Weber, Agrarverhältnisse im Altertum, in: Handwörterbuch der Staatswissenschaften, hsgg. v. J. Conrad u.a., 2. Suppl.-Bd., Jena 1897, 1–18; dass., Bd. I, 2. Aufl.
1898, 57–98.
[7] M. Weber, Der Streit um den Charakter der altgermanischen Sozialverfassung
(1904), in: GASW (wie Anm. 5) 508–556.
[8] M. Weber, Agrarverhältnisse im Altertum, in: Handwörterbuch der Staatswissenschaften (wie Anm. 6), Bd. I, 3. Aufl. 1909, 52–188; hier zitiert nach GASW (wie
Anm. 5) 1–288.
[9] M. Weber, Das antike Judentum (1917–1919; 1921), abgedruckt in: Ges. Aufsätze
zur Religionssoziologie, Bd. III, Tübingen 1921, 1–442.
[10] M. Weber, Die Stadt. Eine soziologische Untersuchung, zuerst in: Archiv für
Sozialwissenschaft und Sozialpolitik 47, 1920–1921, 621–772; hier zitiert nach: ders.,

Soweit der Überblick über Webers hauptsächlichste Arbeiten zum Altertum, die rein. quantitativ natürlich nur einen Bruchteil seines Gesamtwerkes darstellen. Nicht überraschend, aber auch nicht unwichtig für die Gesamtbeurteilung des Verhältnisses von Max Weber zu Ed. Meyer ist, wie sich noch zeigen wird, daß Webers erste Studie zur Antike, die Römische Agrargeschichte, in der bereits viele der späteren Themen Webers in ersten Ansätzen zu erkennen sind, noch keinerlei Berührung mit Ed. Meyer zeigt. Ed. Meyer war es dann, der in dem 1893 erschienenen II. Band seiner "Geschichte des Altertums," wo er auch kurz auf die "Anfänge der Geschichte Italiens" einging, erstmals ausdrücklich auf Max Weber und dessen Römische Agrargeschichte Bezug nahm. Dabei hielt er Weber einerseits die Ignorierung der Ergebnisse der historischen Kritik am Alter des ager publicus, "wie das bei den Juristen Brauch ist," vor, hob aber andererseits die anfängliche Besiedelung des Landes in Rom "nicht nach Geschlechtern, sondern genossenschaftlich" als zutreffende Erkenntnis hervor.[11] In seinem wenig später, 1895, publizierten berühmten Vortrag "Die wirtschaftliche Entwicklung des Altertums" erwähnte Ed. Meyer das Werk Max Webers dann gleich dreimal lobend für wesentliche Einsichten in Mängel der Rodbertusschen Oikentheorie sowie in die Entstehung des spätrömischen Kolonats.[12] Diese Arbeit Ed. Meyers wurde ihrerseits offenbar der Hauptanlaß für eine grundsätzliche Stellungnahme Webers in Gestalt seines Vortrags über die sozialen Gründe des Untergangs der antiken Kultur.[13] Die gleichzeitig bzw. kurz danach entstandenen beiden ersten Fassungen der "Agrarverhältnisse im Altertum" sind in den nichtrömischen Partien, insbesondere in dem Griechenland betreffenden Teil, Ed. Meyer in beträchtlichem Maße verpflichtet, während die Arbeit über die altgermanische Sozialverfassung naturgemäß keinen Einfluß vonseiten Ed. Meyers aufweist. Dagegen läßt die dritte Version der "Agrarverhältnisse" wiederum klar die besondere Bedeutung von Meyers Forschungen für Max Weber sowie den Umfang, in dem er diese verarbeitete, erkennen: Ed. Meyer ist hier der mit Abstand am häufigsten zitierte moderne Autor. Natürlich zog Weber Ed. Meyers

---

Wirtschaft und Gesellschaft, 5. rev. Aufl. hsgg. v. J. Winckelmann, Tübingen 1976, 727–814.

[11] Ed. Meyer, GdA II¹ (1893) 518. (So bestreitbar Webers Hypothesen zum Ursprung des ager publicus im einzelnen auch sein mögen, macht es sich Ed. Meyer, der diesen als Produkt erst der Eroberungen seit dem späten 4. Jhdt. v. Chr. erklärt, doch wohl zu einfach.)

[12] Ed. Meyer, Die wirtschaftliche Entwickelung des Altertums, in: Jahrbücher f. Nationalökon. u. Statist. 3.F. 9, 1895, 696–750; hier zitiert nach ders., *Kl. Schr.* I 79–168.

[13] Vgl. J. Deininger, "Die sozialen Gründe des Untergangs der antiken Kultur:" Bemerkungen zu Max Webers Vortrag von 1896, in: Alte Geschichte und Wissenschaftsgeschichte, Festschrift f. K. Christ, Darmstadt 1988, 95–112, hier 101 ff.

einschlägige Arbeiten auch für seine Abhandlung über das antike Judentum heran, und noch in "Wirtschaft und Gesellschaft" findet sich Ed.
Meyer namentlich mehrfach genannt. Bei all dem ist noch nicht der aufs
Ganze gesehen eigentliche Höhepunkt in Webers Beschäftigung mit dem
Werk Ed. Meyers erwähnt worden, Webers Abhandlung über Fragen der
Definition des Gegenstandes der historischen Forschung und die Kausali-
tät in der Geschichte in den "Kritischen Studien auf dem Gebiet der kul-
turwissenschaftlichen Logik" aus dem Jahre 1906, deren I. Teil den Titel
trägt: "Zur Auseinandersetzung mit Eduard Meyer," wobei den Anlaß
Ed. Meyers kleine, aber aufschlußreiche Programmschrift von 1902 bot,
"Zur Theorie und Methodik der Geschichte."[14]

II

Schon das bisher Gesagte dürfte zeigen, daß es in erster Linie Max Weber
war, der Arbeiten Ed. Meyers rezipiert hat bzw. dem sie Anlaß zu
kritischer Auseinandersetzung wurden, während das Echo, das Max
Weber seinerseits bei Ed. Meyer fand, vergleichsweise schwach geblieben
ist. Wenn man nun fragt, worauf sich die Rezeption Meyers durch Weber
inhaltlich bezieht, so ist in erster Linie das ganze Gebiet der griechischen
Geschichte in allen drei Fassungen der "Agrarverhältnisse im Altertum"
zu nennen, daneben, wenn auch in deutlich geringerem Maße, der Bereich des Alten Orients (Ägypten, Mesopotamien). Während für diese
Teile des Handwörterbuchartikels Ed. Meyers "Geschichte des Altertums" für Weber am wichtigsten war, zog er für die erst in der letzten
Fassung der "Agrarverhältnisse" behandelte nachexilische Zeit des
Judentums vor allem die "glänzende Arbeit" Meyers "Die Entstehung
des Judentums" von 1896 heran;[15] in Webers "Antikem Judentum"
von 1917–1919 spielt dann außerdem das 1906 erschienene Werk Meyers
"Die Israeliten und ihre Nachbarstämme" eine bedeutende Rolle.[16]
Was Weber Ed. Meyer in all dem stofflich und sachlich verdankt, ist bisher noch kaum eingehend untersucht worden und würde auch einen
peniblen Vergleich der umfangreichen einschlägigen Texte Webers wie
Meyers erfordern, der im Rahmen dieses Beitrags nicht geleistet werden
kann.[17] Naheliegend, wenn auch nicht direkt beweisbar ist, daß bei der

---

[14] M. Weber, Kritische Studien auf dem Gebiet der kulturwissenschaftlichen Logik
(1906), in: ders., Ges. Aufsätze zur Wissenschaftslehre, 4. Aufl. hsgg. v. J. Winckelmann,
Tübingen 1973, 215–290; Ed. Meyer, Theorie (danach zitiert); spätere Fassung in: ders.,
Kl. Schr. 1–78 (= *Kl. Schr.* I 1–78).

[15] GASW 282; die positive Charakterisierung in: Das antike Judentum (wie oben,
Anm. 9) 3, Anm.

[16] Ed. Meyer, Die Israeliten und ihre Nachbarstämme, Halle 1906.

[17] Vgl. die Hinweise bei H. Liebeschütz, Das Judentum im deutschen Geschichtsbild

Einbeziehung des Alten Orients bereits in der zweiten Fassung der "Agrarverhältnisse" das Vorbild von Ed. Meyers "Geschichte des Altertums" eine ausschlaggebende Rolle gespielt hat. In großen Zügen läßt sich dann immerhin z.B. erkennen, daß Max Weber in seiner Auffassung der inneren—politischen, sozialen und wirtschaftlichen—Entwicklung der griechischen Poleis besonders stark von Ed. Meyer beeinflußt ist; neben Konzepten wie dem der 'Geschlechterpolis' scheint Weber vor allem ihm die Erkenntnis der Bedeutung der militärischen Strukturen und speziell der Konsequenzen des Prinzips der militärischen "Selbstausrüstung" in der Polis zu verdanken. Während sich Weber zumal in der Einleitung der letzten Fassung der "Agrarverhältnisse" mit den ökonomischen Kategorien Meyers kritisch auseinandersetzt, worauf noch näher einzugehen sein wird, verdankt sein dort dargelegtes Schema der politischen Strukturen der antiken Welt und ihrer Entwicklung einige wichtige Elemente offenbar ebenfalls Ed. Meyer.[18] In dem ausführlichen bibliographischen Anhang der "Agrarverhältnisse" von 1909 findet sich eine umfangreiche Liste der hier von Weber herangezogenen Meyerschen Arbeiten.[19] Bei allen direkten Nennungen Meyers im Text des Artikels handelt es sich freilich in aller Regel um historische Detailfragen, die hier nicht zu diskutieren sind und bei denen Weber z.T. gegen Meyer Stellung nimmt, z.T.—mit ebenso eigenständigem Urteil—der Auffassung Ed. Meyers folgt.[20] Auch wenn in dem ganzen Bereich inhaltlicher Übereinstimmungen bzw. Abhängigkeiten Webers von Ed. Meyer noch vieles zu klären bleibt, gibt es über die Ursachen der intensiven Rezeption Meyers durch Weber wohl kaum einen Zweifel: Abgesehen davon, daß Weber auf den genannten Gebieten nicht wie in der römischen Geschichte auf eigene Forschungen und Quellenstudien zurückgreifen konnte, war es vor allem die Tatsache, daß Ed. Meyer die sozial- und wirtschaftshistorischen Aspekte in erheblichem Maße berücksichtigte, was Weber selbst auch immer wieder hervorgehoben hat: "Für Hellas ist für die soziale Entwickelung am reichsten an allgemeinen Gesichtspunkten Ed. Meyer's 'Geschichte des Altertums,' Bd. II (in dieser Beziehung dem I. Bande weit voranstehend)," heißt es in der ersten Fassung der "Agrarverhältnisse" von 1897;[21] von "Ed. Meyers ausgezeichnetem, in Würdigung der Wirt-

---

von Hegel bis Max Weber, Tübingen 1967, 272 ff.; 303 ff.; außerdem Ch. Schäfer-Lichtenberger, Staat und Eidgenossenschaft im Alten Testament, Berlin-New York 1983, z.B. 71; 128.

[18] Vgl. J. Deininger, Die politischen Strukturen des mittelmeerisch-vorderorientalischen Altertums in Max Webers Sicht, in: W. Schluchter (Hsg.), Max Webers Sicht des antiken Christentums, Frankfurt/M. 1985, bes. 77; 81 f.; 104, Anm. 53.

[19] GASW 279–287.

[20] Vgl. ebd. 82; 101; 105 f.; 111; 121, Anm. 1; 127; 136; 150; 154; 193; 198; 200; 218; 240.

[21] Weber, Agrarverhältnisse¹ (wie Anm. 6) 18.

schaft dem ersten Bande weit voranstehenden Band II der 'Geschichte des Altertums'" ist in der zweiten Fassung von 1898 die Rede,[22] und als "für die Sozialgeschichte mit jedem folgenden Bande ergiebiger werdend" charakterisiert Weber schließlich in der dritten Fassung von 1909 die bis dahin erschienenen fünf Bände des Werkes.[23]

Ähnlich rühmt er dort auch Ed. Meyers "Entstehung des Judentums" gegenüber den 'großen Werken' Julius Wellhausens ausdrücklich wegen ihrer starken Berücksichtigung der Sozialgeschichte.[24]

Wo liegen nun aber Differenzen zwischen Ed. Meyer und Max Weber? Neben den später zu erörternden allgemeinen Fragen der Geschichtstheorie geht es zunächst um die grundsätzliche Beurteilung der wirtschaftlichen Verhältnisse des Altertums. Den Hauptausgangspunkt bildet dabei der erwähnte Vortrag Eduard Meyers von 1895, "Die wirtschaftliche Entwicklung des Altertums," mit dem dieser dezidiert gegen die von dem Leipziger Nationalökonomen und Wirtschaftshistoriker Karl Bücher vertretene Lehre von der geschlossenen Hauswirtschaft als grundlegender Wirtschaftsform des Altertums Stellung nahm und zugleich eine heftige, in vielem bis heute bedeutsame Auseinandersetzung auslöste, die sog. "Meyer-Bücher-Kontroverse," der Streit, wie man z.T. später auch sagte, zwischen "Modernisten" und "Primitivisten" in der antiken Wirtschaftsgeschichte, also Verfechtern eines mehr "modernen" bzw. "primitiven" Charakters der Wirtschaftsentwicklung im Altertum.[25] Meyer trat der Vorstellung vom Dominieren einer geschlossenen Oikoswirtschaft im Altertum mit Vehemenz entgegen und versuchte durch eine Fülle von Einzelzeugnissen die "modernen", durch entwickelten Handel, Verkehr, Geldwirtschaft, "Fabriken" usw. bestimmten Züge des Wirtschaftslebens im Altertum, vom Alten Orient bis in die Zeit des römischen Imperiums, herauszuarbeiten. Er glaubte in der antiken Wirtschaftsentwicklung, die er insgesamt als einen "Kreislauf" von eher primitiven Anfängen über hochentwickelte Formen der Geldwirtschaft und mobiler Arbeitskräfte (Kaufsklaven) zurück zu Naturalwirtschaft und Hörigkeit am Ausgang des Altertums verstand, eine unmittelbare Analogie zur mittelalterlich-neuzeitlichen Wirtschaftsentwicklung in Europa zu sehen und setzte in seinem Vortrag sogar die Zeit vom 7. bis zum 3. Jhdt. v. Chr. in eine direkte Parallele zum 14.–18. Jhdt., also zu Spätmittelalter und Früher Neuzeit.[26] An einer Stelle heißt es ausdrück-

[22] Dass.² (wie Anm. 6) 84.
[23] GASW 279.
[24] Ebd. 282.
[25] Dazu ausführlich H. Schneider, in diesem Band.
[26] Vgl. Meyer, *Kl. Schr.* I 118 f.; 141 f.

lich, man könne sich Handel und kommerzielle Interessen in der hellenistischen Zeit "in jeder Hinsicht nicht modern genug" (gemeint: entsprechend den Verhältnissen des 17. und 18. Jhdts.) vorstellen.[27] Max
Webers gegen Rodbertus gerichtete Feststellung in seiner Römischen
Agrargeschichte, die "Autarkie" des Oikos sei nicht für den gesamten
Gang der antiken Wirtschaftsgeschichte bestimmend, sondern erst ein
spätes Entwicklungsprodukt am Ende der Antike, zitierte er als eine
willkommene Stütze seiner eigenen Argumentation gegen Bücher.[28] Als
allgemeine Ursache des schließlichen Untergangs des römischen Reiches
nannte Meyer dann im Schlußteil seines Vortrags einen auf zahlreichen
Lebensgebieten sich geltend machenden inneren "Zersetzungsprozeß",
der durch die "Steigerung und allgemeine Verbreitung der antiken Kultur," speziell auch die langfristig "korrumpierende Wirkung" der Stadt
hervorgerufen worden sei.[29] Verbindungen zur Sicht der eigenen Gegenwart, auch wohl zum späteren Interesse Ed. Meyers für Spenglers
"Untergang des Abendlandes" sind dabei deutlich.

Zweierlei an der Auffassung Ed. Meyers stand nun in starkem Widerspruch zu dem eigenen Bild Webers, das sich diesem aus seinen Forschungen zur römischen Agrargeschichte ergeben hatte, nämlich die grundsätzlich 'modernisierende' Sicht Meyers sowie die Vernachlässigung der
'sozialen' Faktoren im Niedergangsprozeß des antiken Kulturlebens, und
gegen beides wandte er sich denn auch in seinem Vortrag "Die sozialen
Gründe des Untergangs der antiken Kultur" von 1896 wie in allen drei
Fassungen der "Agrarverhältnisse im Altertum" von 1897 – 1909, wobei
deren letzte Version z.T. eine leichte Annäherung an einige Positionen
Meyers bzw. der "Modernisten" aufweist.

Was zunächst Webers Abhandlung über den Untergang der antiken
Kultur betrifft, so kann hier nur gesagt werden, daß darin—als Folge der
Vortragsform—der Name Ed. Meyer so wenig wie irgendein anderer
genannt wird, daß aber dennoch offenkundig ist, daß Meyers Vortrag
über die Wirtschaftsentwicklung des Altertums den eigentlichen Anstoß
zu Webers Stellungnahme bildete und—ungeachtet einer Reihe von
Übereinstimmungen—Meyer in dieser Arbeit gewissermaßen der Haupt-
kontrahent Webers ist.[30] Weber hatte in der Römischen Agrargeschichte
eine Anzahl sozialer und wirtschaftlicher Wandlungen herausgearbeitet,
durch die er den wirtschaftlichen Niedergang der Städte und damit letztlich auch des Reiches zu erklären versuchte, wobei er nicht zuletzt auf

---

[27] Ebd. 141.
[28] Ebd. 83, Anm. 1.
[29] Ebd. 146 f.; 156.
[30] Vgl. Deininger (wie Anm. 13), 101 ff.

Rodbertus und dessen Theorie vom Gegensatz zwischen dem natural-
wirtschaftlichen 'Unterbau' und den damit verbundenen Transport-
problemen und dem notwendigen (und nach Rodbertus durch teilweise
Sprengung des autarken Oikos in der Spätzeit entstandenen) geldwirtschaftlichen 'Überbau' des spätrömischen Weltreiches fußte.[31] Bald nach
dem Erscheinen der Römischen Agrargeschichte, in den Jahren 1893 und
1894, hatte dann Karl Bücher Rodbertus' Theorie von der grundlegenden Bedeutung der geschlossenen Oikoswirtschaft in der Antike erneuert,
womit er zwar die heftige Reaktion von Ed. Meyer 1895 auslöste, Max
Weber dagegen in dessen eigenen Anschauungen offenkundig be-
stärkte.[32] So setzte Weber in seinem Vortrag von 1896 den eher pauscha-
len Vorstellungen Meyers über Kulturverfall durch Kulturverbreitung
eine sozial- und wirtschaftsgeschichtliche Erklärung entgegen, die auf
genau definierten Begriffen und Kategorien beruhte, in denen zugleich
der spezifische (und im wesentlichen ''unmoderne'') Charakter der
antiken Kultur erfaßt war, die Weber als Stadt-, Sklaven- und Küstenkultur charakterisierte.[33] Insofern sie städtische Kultur war, stand die
Antike in einer gewissen tatsächlichen Nähe zur mittelalterlich-neuzeitlichen Kultur; aber als Sklaven- und Küstenkultur war sie in den Augen
Max Webers sozial und ökonomisch fundamental verschieden davon. Die
''sozialen Gründe'' des Untergangs der Kultur des Altertums lagen daher
für Weber auch nicht etwa in der 'Kulturverbreitung' als solcher, sondern
in dem Scheitern der Übertragung der antiken städtischen Sklaven- und
Küstenkultur und ihrer besonderen sozialen und ökonomischen Strukturen auf die gewaltigen binnenländischen Territorien des römischen
Reiches der Kaiserzeit.[34] Die antike Wirtschaft war nach ihrer ganzen
Entwicklung, so könnte man sagen, im Gegensatz zur Auffassung Ed.
Meyers gerade nicht 'modern' genug, um dies zu leisten: die städtische
Entwicklung der europäischen Binnengebiete blieb für Weber daher der
in vielem grundsätzlich andersartigen mittelalterlich-neuzeitlichen Ent-
wicklung vorbehalten.

   Die anonyme, jedenfalls implizite Auseinandersetzung mit Ed. Meyer
in Webers ''Sozialen Gründen'' nimmt im Prinzip schon alle wesentlichen Differenzen vorweg, wie sie dann in den ''Agrarverhältnissen''
explizit und mit ausdrücklicher Namensnennung zur Sprache kommen,
wobei die Differenzen dort dann freilich nicht mehr der speziellen Frage

---

[31] Ebd. 105 ff.
[32] K. Bücher, Die Entstehung der Volkswirtschaft. Sechs Vorträge, Tübingen 1893
(bes. 15–44, 76 ff.); ders., Die diokletianische Taxordnung vom Jahre 301, in: Zeitschr.
f. d. ges. Staatswissensch. 50, 1894, 189–219; 672–717 (bes. 673 ff.; 696 f.).
[33] GASW 291–293.
[34] Ebd. 295 ff.

nach dem Untergang der antiken Kultur, sondern den durch die Meyer-Bücher-Kontroverse bezeichneten allgemeineren Problemen gelten. So formuliert Weber in den beiden ersten Fassungen der Agrarverhältnisse ausdrücklich, daß die Entwicklung zur "lokalen und interlokalen Verkehrswirtschaft" in der Antike nicht weit gediehen sei, und zwar "zufolge des Anschwellens des Sklavenunterbaues der antiken Gesellschaft"[35]: Diese Entwicklung, so Weber, sei "auch schon wegen dieser steigenden Bedeutung der unfreien Arbeit an sich eine ganz andersartige Erscheinung, als das unter äußerlich ähnlichen Begleiterscheinungen sich vollziehende Emporwachsen des freien Gewerbes in den mittelalterlichen Städten, der Niedergang der Geschlechterherrschaft, der Kampf zwischen Stadtwirtschaft und Grundherrschaft und die Zersetzung der Grundherrschaft durch die Geldwirtschaft im Mittelalter und der Neuzeit." Ed. Meyers Name wird auch an dieser Stelle nicht eigens genannt, aber es besteht wohl kein Zweifel, daß der ganze Passus in erster Linie auf ihn gemünzt ist: "Die Analogien mit mittelalterlichen und modernen Erscheinungen, scheinbar auf Schritt und Tritt vorhanden, sind eben wegen jener ganz andersartigen Unterlagen gänzlich unverläßlich und oft deshalb direkt schädlich für die unbefangene Erkenntnis."[36] Wichtig ist dabei, daß Weber sich in seiner Sicht der mittelalterlichen Verhältnisse nicht nur auf die Nationalökonomen bzw. K. Bücher berufen, sondern vor allem auch auf die durch seine juristische Dissertation von 1889 gewonnenen eigenen Erkenntnisse über die Betriebsformen des Handels in italienischen Städten des Mittelalters zurückgreifen konnte.[37] In der ersten Fassung von 1897 stellt er daher in den abschließenden Bemerkungen zur Literatur, in denen er u.a. auf Rodbertus und Bücher verweist, fest, die Schärfe der ökonomischen Begriffe Ed. Meyers lasse "zu wünschen übrig," und für die römische Zeit—mit der sich Weber in seiner Habilitationsschrift befaßt hatte—werde er seine Auffassung "noch stark modifizieren müssen," wobei er ohne Zweifel die Ausführungen Ed. Meyers in seinem Vortrag von 1895 im Auge hat.[38] In der zweiten Version von 1898 heißt es, die Stellungnahme zu der "neuerdings heftig gewordenen" Kontroverse zwischen Bücher und Ed. Meyer müsse an dieser Stelle unterbleiben; doch verweist Weber dafür ausdrücklich auf seinen Aufsatz über die "Sozialen Gründe"[39]).

Was er 1898 unterlassen hatte, hat Weber dann aber elf Jahre später,

---

[35] Weber, Agrarverhältnisse[1] (wie Anm. 6) 2 (= dass.[2] 59).
[36] Ebd.
[37] M. Weber, Zur Geschichte der Handelsgesellschaften im Mittelalter. Nach südeuropäischen Quellen, Stuttgart 1889.
[38] Weber, Agrarverhältnisse[1] 18.
[39] Dass.[2] 85.

anläßlich der dritten Auflage des "Handwörterbuchs", in vieler Hinsicht
nachgeholt. Die wichtige, mehr als 40 Spalten füllende Einleitung der
dritten Fassung seines Artikels, "Zur ökonomischen Theorie der antiken
Staatenwelt," läuft zu einem beträchtlichen Teil auf eine Auseinandersetzung mit den durch die Meyer-Bücher-Kontroverse aufgeworfenen
Fragen und insofern mit Ed. Meyer hinaus. Im Prinzip wird man dabei
feststellen können, daß die Position Max Webers unverändert geblieben
ist; im einzelnen unterscheiden sich seine Darlegungen von den beiden
älteren Versionen aber nicht nur durch ihre viel größere Ausführlichkeit
und Detailliertheit, sondern auch, wie schon angedeutet, durch ein teilweise leichtes Näherrücken an Auffassungen Eduard Meyers.

Es würde freilich den Rahmen dieses Beitrages bei weitem sprengen,
wollte man dies im einzelnen verfolgen. Weber betont auch hier den
Grundcharakter der antiken Kultur als Küstenkultur sowie den bei all
seiner sozialen und ökonomischen Bedeutung quantitativ begrenzten
Umfang des Handels, wobei er eine ganze Reihe von Einzelbeispielen
heranzieht, die prinzipiellen Unterschiede gegenüber der Entwicklung im
Mittelalter und in der Neuzeit hervorhebt und auch des längeren auf den
Gegensatz der Theorien von Rodbertus und Bücher auf der einen und
Ed. Meyer auf der anderen Seite eingeht.[40] Was dagegen die antike Kul-
tur als 'Sklavenkultur' betrifft, so konstatiert Weber eine gewisse Überschätzung der Rolle der Sklaverei für "erhebliche Teile und Zeiträume
der Antike" (Alter Orient, Griechenland, Hellenismus) wie auch eine
Überschätzung des geldwirtschaftlichen Charakters der Oikenwirtschaft
mit Sklaven in den "klassischen Zeiten des Altertums" nicht nur durch
Rodbertus, sondern z.T. auch bei sich selbst und eine zu niedrige Ein-
schätzung der quantitativen Bedeutung der freien Arbeit.[41] Für diese
Modifikation seiner Auffassung verweist er namentlich auf Ed. Meyer
(wobei er offenbar vor allem an dessen 1898 publizierten Vortrag "Die
Sklaverei im Altertum"[42] denkt) sowie (neben U. Wilcken) auf Herman
Gummerus, einen aus Finnland stammenden Schüler Meyers, dessen
Arbeit über den römischen Gutsbetrieb 1906 erschienen war.[43] In diesem
Werk, das zweifellos wesentlich durch das letzte Kapitel von Webers
Römischer Agrargeschichte und Meyers Auseinandersetzung mit der

---

[40] GASW 3–10.
[41] Ebd. 7; 11 f.
[42] Ed. Meyer, Die Sklaverei im Altertum (1898), wiederabgedruckt in: *Kl. Schr.* I
169–212.
[43] H. Gummerus, Der römische Gutsbetrieb als wirtschaftlicher Organismus nach
den Werken des Cato, Varro und Columella, Leipzig 1906.—Zu ihm vgl. P. Aalto,
Classical Studies in Finland 1828–1918, Helsinki 1980, bes. 131–137 (freundlicher Hinweis von W. Calder III).

"Bücherschen Schule" angeregt war, betonte Gummerus, wenn auch im allgemeinen im Einklang mit Weber, im ganzen doch stärker die verkehrswirtschaftliche Verflechtung der römischen Gutswirtschaft und die Rolle der freien Arbeiter in ihr.[44] Doch warnt Weber zugleich vor jeder Unterschätzung der Bedeutung der Sklaverei im Altertum[45] und bleibt ungeachtet solcher 'Zugeständnisse' bei seiner grundsätzlichen Kritik der für ihn anachronistischen ökonomischen Begrifflichkeit Meyers. Während dieser etwa für die hellenistische Epoche festgestellt hatte, daß sie "in jeder Hinsicht nicht modern genug" gedacht werden könne,[46] formuliert Weber pointiert und umgekehrt, es sei "nichts gefährlicher, als sich die Verhältnisse der Antike 'modern' vorzustellen."[47] Dies wird von ihm im einzelnen an den von Meyer verwendeten Begriffen "Fabrik" und "Fabrikarbeiter" sowie für die Rolle von Handel und Banken gezeigt, und zwar anhand eingehender ökonomischer Begriffsanalysen, die Weber zu den Ergebnis führen, daß in allen diesen Bereichen die Antike allenfalls einen dem frühen Mittelalter, jedenfalls der Zeit vor dem 13. Jhdt., entsprechenden Entwicklungsgrad aufzuweisen habe (ebd. 10)[47a]. Auch hier spielen—neben dem offenkundigen Einfluß Büchers—sichtlich Webers eigene Forschungen zu den mittelalterlichen Handelsgesellschaften eine wesentliche Rolle. Seine Überlegungen zur 'ökonomischen Theorie der antiken Staatenwelt' spitzen sich schließlich auf die Frage zu, ob es im Altertum einen "Kapitalismus" gegeben habe. Seine nachdrückliche Bejahung dieser Frage versucht Weber in genauen Begriffsbestimmungen zu begründen, wobei er jedoch zugleich die grundlegenden Unterschiede zwischen antikem und modernem Kapitalismus herausarbeitet (ebd. 13 – 33). Dies führt zwar über Ed. Meyer, für den das Kapitalismus-Problem keine besondere Rolle spielte, erheblich hinaus, verdeutlicht aber doch zugleich Webers eigene Position Ed. Meyer gegenüber in doppelter Hinsicht: Einmal gewinnt Weber auch mit dem "antiken Kapitalismus" einen bei ihm genau definierten ökonomischen Begriff im Gegensatz zu der von ihm bemängelten Unklarheit (und Unangemessenheit) der ökonomischen Begriffe Meyers, und zum andern gipfelt in Max Webers Verständnis des antiken Kapitalismus in vieler Beziehung auch seine Stellungnahme im Meyer-Bücher-Streit: Einerseits lehnt er die Modernismen Ed. Meyers ab und schreibt dem Oikos "im Rodbertusschen Sinn" bzw. der—idealtypisch interpretierten—Oikenwirtschaft im Sinne Büchers im

---

44 Vgl. ebd. 94 ff.
45 GASW 272; vgl. auch z.B. Die Stadt (wie Anm. 10) 798.
46 Vgl. oben, Anm. 27.
47 GASW 10 (danach auch die folgenden Zitate im Text).
47a Ganz anders Ed. Meyers Auffassung, vgl. oben, S. 138 (m. Anm. 26).

Gegensatz zu Meyer eine "höchst bedeutungsvolle Rolle" in der antiken
Wirtschaft zu (ebd. S. 10); andererseits betont er neben der Rolle des
geschlossenen Oikos vor allem in der Früh- und Spätzeit der Antike die
zwischen beidem erfolgte starke Entwicklung des Verkehrs. So gelangte er
zu der von ihm mit Entschiedenheit vertretenen Vorstellung eines bereits
in der Alten Welt—vom Alten Orient bis zum römischen Weltreich—
teilweise erheblich ausgeprägten "Kapitalismus", der sich allerdings in
wesentlichen, von Weber im einzelnen analysierten Besonderheiten vom
Kapitalismus neuzeitlicher Prägung unterscheidet (ebd. 15 ff.) und insofern—trotz des "modernen" Charakters des Kapitalismusbegriffs selbst
—dem Vorwurf des Modernismus entgeht, den sich die ökonomische
Begrifflichkeit Ed. Meyers von Max Weber gefallen lassen mußte. In
gewisser Weise nimmt Weber in der Meyer-Bücher-Kontroverse also eine
mittlere Position ein, die jedoch letztlich, in ihrem Beharren auf der
Verwendung "besonderer ökonomischer Kategorien für das Altertum"
(ebd. 8) und in der allgemeinen Orientierung auf die Oikos-Theorie hin,
dem "nationalökonomischen" bzw. Rodbertus-Bücherschen Ansatz klar
näher stand als der Meyerschen Interpretation der antiken Wirtschaft.
Ed. Meyer, der im übrigen mit seiner Anschauung von der antiken Welt
als einem in vieler Hinsicht zum mittelalterlich-neuzeitlichen Europa
parallelen 'Entwicklungskreis' mit Sicherheit Arnold Toynbee,[48] möglicherweise aber auch Oswald Spengler nachhaltig beeinflußt hat,[49] hat
also Max Weber wesentlich mit zur Formulierung von dessen eigener,
dezidiert abweichender Auffassung herausgefordert. Meyer selbst hat
immerhin—im Einklang mit Webers Sicht—ausdrücklich den Unterschied in der politischen Entwicklung mit der Ausbildung der universellen
Herrschaft Roms auf der einen und dem neuzeitlichen Staatenpluralismus Europas auf der anderen Seite hervorgehoben;[50] Weber dagegen
erfaßte von Anfang an die grundlegende Differenz auch in der sozialen
und ökonomischen Entwicklung, die sich für ihn am stärksten in der
neuen Art des Kapitalismus in der Moderne manifestierte. Doch läßt
wohl noch ein Begriff Webers wie der der 'beiden Entwicklungskreise' für
die antike und die mittelalterlich-neuzeitliche Welt in den "Agrarverhältnissen" von 1909 die ursprüngliche Bedeutung der Vorstellungen Ed.
Meyers und der Auseinandersetzung mit ihm für Weber erkennen.[51]

---

[48] A.J. Toynbee, A Study of History, Bd. X: The Inspirations of Historians, London
1954, 233.
[49] Vgl. dazu A. Demandt, in diesem Band.
[50] Ed. Meyer, *Kl. Schr.* 275 f. (= *Kl. Schr.* I 257 f.).
[51] GASW 257. (Vgl. außerdem noch die Bemerkung in "Die Stadt" (wie Anm. 10)
788 über den "Kreislauf" in der Entwicklung der italienischen Städte.)—Eine Kritik der
entsprechenden Äußerungen Meyers auch noch bei Weber: Roscher und Knies (1903),
in: ders., Wissenschaftslehre (wie Anm. 14) 22, Anm. 3.

—Wenn Weber in seinen Arbeiten von 1896 bis 1909, von den "Sozialen Gründen" bis zur letzten Fassung der "Agrarverhältnisse", in einzelnen Details dieser Kontroverse sich dennoch Ed. Meyer eher genähert als sich weiter von ihm entfernt hat, so konnte er andererseits in der abschließenden Literaturübersicht der "Agrarverhältnisse" von 1909 darauf hinweisen, daß die "Fortschritte der Erkenntnis der Historiker" gerade auch dort, wo sie gegenüber Rodbertus und Bücher Recht behalten hätten, dadurch erzielt worden seien, "daß sie (erfreulicherweise) mit dem Kalbe der verachteten ökonomischen 'Theoretiker' zu pflügen begannen und so zu klaren Begriffen kamen."[52] Weber denkt dabei wohl nicht zuletzt an den erwähnten Herman Gummerus, der seine Untersuchung über den römischen Gutsbetrieb mit längeren Überlegungen zur Oikentheorie der Nationalökonomen einleitet, sich um eine genuin wirtschaftsgeschichtliche Erfassung 'typischer' Verhältnisse im römischen Landwirtschaftsbetrieb bemüht und übrigens u.a. zu dem Ergebnis gelangt, daß der catonische Gutsbetrieb "ganz im Zeichen des Kapitalismus" stehe.[53]

III

Wenn somit im Verständnis der antiken wirtschaftlichen Verhältnisse ein deutlicher Dissens zwischen Max Weber und Eduard Meyer zu konstatieren ist, so gilt Ähnliches auch für ein ganz anderes Gebiet, nämlich die Theorie der Geschichte, und hier insbesondere für eine Grundfrage, nämlich die nach dem Gegenstand der Geschichtswissenschaft, wozu Ed. Meyer in der schon genannten Schrift "Zur Theorie und Methodik der Geschichte. Geschichtsphilosophische Untersuchungen" aus dem Jahre 1902 Stellung genommen hatte.[54] Ähnlich wie sein Vortrag von 1895 in erster Linie eine polemische Funktion gegen die nationalökonomischen Theorien eines Rodbertus und Bücher zum Altertum gehabt hatte, war auch diese Abhandlung primär gegen bestimmte 'neue Theorien,' konkret vor allem gegen K. Lamprecht und K. Breysig, gerichtet. Diese 'modernen Theorien' stellten sich Meyer dar als eine Sicht der Geschichte, die den Zufall, den freien Willen sowie die Kraft von Ideen für historisch bedeutungslos erklärte, für die das "eigentlich historisch Bedeutsame" die "Massenerscheinungen" und das "Typische" waren, nicht aber das Individuelle, und die insbesondere auch auf die Erkenntnis angeblicher 'Gesetzmäßigkeiten' in der Geschichte gerichtet waren (ebd. 4 f.). Dagegen wendet sich Meyer in großer Schärfe. "Die Geschichte ist keine systematische Wissenschaft" lautet gleich der erste Satz seiner Schrift (1).

---

[52] GASW 279.
[53] Vgl. Gummerus a.O. (wie Anm. 43) 94.
[54] Vgl. oben, Anm. 14.

Für Meyer kann es keinen prinzipiellen Vorrang von 'Massenerscheinungen' vor dem Individuellen in der Geschichte geben und ebensowenig "Gesetze" oder "gesetzmäßige" (z.B., wie bei Lamprecht, sozialpsychologische) Entwicklungsstufen. Er betont demgegenüber die "ungeheure" Bedeutung des "Zufalls" (21; vgl. 17 ff.) und des freien Willens (13 ff.) als nicht zu eliminierender Kategorien der historischen Betrachtung sowie den Primat der politischen Geschichte (38 f.). Das historisch Bedeutsame ist für Meyer nun allerdings nicht etwa das Individuelle im Gegensatz zu den von den modernen Theoretikern in den Vordergrund gerückten Massenerscheinungen und dem Typischen, sondern vielmehr das "Wirksame", unabhängig davon, ob es sich dabei im einzelnen um Massen- oder individuelle Erscheinungen handelt: "Historisch ist, was wirksam ist oder gewesen ist." (36),[55] wobei der Historiker immer erst von der historischen Wirkung ausgehen und von dorther zu den Ursachen fortschreiten müsse. Insofern ist das "historische Leben" für Meyer immer nur ein begrenzter, eben der "wirksam" gewesene Ausschnitt aus dem "allgemeinen Leben der Menschen." Das am stärksten wirksame einzelne Moment aber ist für Meyer der Staat— "das Wort im weitesten Sinne genommen"—, denn dieser stellt "die maßgebende äußere Organisation des menschlichen Lebens" dar; von den politischen Ereignissen, so Meyer, ist "in letzter Linie jede andere Lebensbethätigung des Menschen abhängig" (38). Gegen die Ansprüche der Kulturgeschichte wie der Wirtschaftsgeschichte formuliert Meyer: "Die politische Geschichte wird das Centrum der Geschichte bleiben, so lange das menschliche Leben sein Wesen nicht von Grund aus ändern sollte" (39); und wenn es im Schlußsatz der Abhandlung heißt, das unerreichte Vorbild für die "Behandlung historischer Probleme" bleibe auch weiterhin Thukydides (56), so denkt Meyer gewiß nicht zuletzt an den Vorrang der politischen Geschichte.

   Mit dieser Schrift Ed. Meyers, mit der dieser gleichsam einige Grundelemente der von ihm erstrebten "historisch begründeten Weltanschauung" darzulegen unternahm, setzte sich Weber 1906 in den erwähnten "Kritischen Studien" auseinander.[56] Er stellt dabei von vornherein klar, daß Ed. Meyer kein Erkenntnistheoretiker vom Fach sei und es sich bei seinen Darlegungen gewissermaßen um den "Krankheitsbericht" des "Patienten" und nicht des Arztes handle, der aber, da Ed. Meyer "einer

---

[55] Vgl. auch die Formulierung in GdA I² 1, 186: "Historisch ist derjenige Vorgang der Vergangenheit, dessen Wirksamkeit sich nicht in dem Moment seines Eintretens erschöpft, sondern auf die folgende Zeit weiter wirkt und in dieser neue Vorgänge erzeugt."
[56] Vgl. oben, Anm. 14. Zu Webers Positionen in dieser Auseinandersetzung vgl. neuerdings auch Tenbruck (wie Anm. 80) 338–352.

unserer ersten Historiker'' sei, dadurch nichts von seiner Bedeutung einbüße.[57] Die kürzlich von M.I. Finley getroffene Feststellung, Ed. Meyers ''Ausflug in die Geschichtstheorie'' sei von Max Weber ''verrissen'' worden,[58] wird der tatsächlichen Reaktion Webers allerdings kaum gerecht. Schon rein äußerlich wird Ed. Meyer, zumal im Vergleich zu anderen Kontrahenten wie R. Stammler und K. Knies, von Weber geradezu auffällig schonend behandelt. Ed. Meyer ist für Weber ein Hauptrepräsentant der zeitgenössischen Geschichtswissenschaft, mit dem sich eine methodologische Auseinandersetzung lohnt. Bei allen sachlichen Differenzen rühmt Weber ausdrücklich die ''durchsichtige Verständlichkeit'' von Meyers Abhandlung (216); auch bleibt immer zu beachten, daß Weber eine Reihe von grundsätzlichen Übereinstimmungen mit Meyer hervorhebt, so etwa, daß die Ermittlung von ''Gesetzen'' nicht die Aufgabe der Geschichtswissenschaft sein könne (228 f.), aber auch, daß das ''Individuelle'' als solches nicht den Gegenstand der Geschichte bilde (232); gelten läßt Weber nicht zuletzt, daß man mit Ed. Meyer die politischen Verhältnisse als das ''eigentliche Rückgrat des Historischen'' betrachten könne (256). Weber geht es im übrigen nicht einfach um eine Parteinahme für die eine oder andere Seite, also die ''modernen'' Historiker wie Lamprecht bzw. die Historiker des ''Gepräges'' (231) von Ed. Meyer selbst, sondern anhand der Ausführungen Meyers um Fragen der (kulturwissenschaftlichen) ''Logik'', hier um die Frage, was ''unter 'historischer' Arbeit im logischen Sinne verstanden'' werden könne (217; vgl. 218 f.). Bei aller Kritik an logischen Unvollkommenheiten, Inkonsequenzen, Widersprüchen usw. in zahlreichen Formulierungen Meyers—denen freilich nicht wenige Hinweise auf 'höchst treffende Bemerkungen,' 'durchaus Korrektes,' 'den berechtigten Kern,' 'das Richtige,' usw. gegenüberstehen (223; 239; 263; 267)—läßt Weber nie einen Zweifel daran, daß er die Praxis der historischen Forschungen Ed. Meyers, um deren theoretische Rechtfertigung es sich für diesen handelt, grundsätzlich bejaht (vgl. 215; 232; 255; 265).

Es ist hier wiederum nicht daran zu denken, die umfangreiche, vielfach überaus subtile Auseinandersetzung Max Webers mit Ed. Meyers Abhandlung von 1902 in allen Einzelheiten und gar unter Einbeziehung aller Schriften Webers zur ''Wissenschaftslehre'' zu verfolgen. Weber kritisiert zunächst an Meyers Behandlung der Rolle der auch von ihm selbst für grundlegend gehaltenen Willensfreiheit in der Geschichte, daß Meyer

---

[57] Vgl. auch die ''unlimitierte Bewunderung'' Webers für Ed. Meyers Gelehrsamkeit, von der Paul Honigsheim berichtet (in: Köln. Zschr. f. Soziol. u. Soz.-Psychol., Sonderh. 7, 1963, hier 206 f.).

[58] M.I. Finley, in: HZ 239, 1984, 271. Anders mit Recht auch Tenbruck (wie Anm. 80) 350 f.

dabei ethische Momente und Werturteile ins Spiel bringe und dies von
der kausalen Betrachtung nicht klar scheide, obwohl beides logisch klar
getrennten Sphären angehöre (223; 225). Damit ist bereits ein Haupteinwand Webers genannt, den er dann ausführlich vor allem an einer zentralen These Meyers demonstriert, nämlich an dessen Definition des Objekts
der Geschichtswissenschaft als des "Wirksamen", wobei die auch dann
notwendige "Auswahl" des Historikers von diesem nach dem "historischen Interesse, welches die Gegenwart an irgend einer Wirkung,
einem Ergebnis der Entwicklung hat," vorgenommen würde. Da die
Gegenwart des Historikers aus keiner Geschichtsdarstellung ausgeschieden werden könne, sei—so Ed. Meyer—"niemals eine absolute
und unbedingt gültige" Erkenntnis der Geschichte möglich.[59]
    Weber hält dem im wesentlichen zwei Einwände entgegen. Einmal
fehlt nach ihm bei Ed. Meyer jede klare Trennung zwischen 'Wert'- und
'Kausalanalyse'. Die primäre Konstituierung des historischen Objekts
bzw. 'Individuums' geschieht nach Weber—im Prinzip subjektiv—über
eine "Wertbeziehung" des Historikers zu seinem Objekt (259), die
Weber im einzelnen sorgfältig analysiert, wobei die betreffenden Werte
"jenseits des Historischen" (249) angesiedelt sind.[60] Erst mit dieser
Abgrenzung des historischen Objekts wird die Voraussetzung geschaffen
für die Kausalanalyse der 'historischen Tatsachen,' die auf einer anderen
Ebene verläuft, aber ihrerseits der Leitung durch die Wertbeziehung
bedarf, da diese ihr die entscheidenden Gesichtspunkte liefert, gleichsam
den "Kompaß" der historischen Deutung darstellt (251). Insofern ist
beides, Wertbeziehung und Kausalanalyse, auch unlöslich miteinander
verbunden. Während die Bestimmung des primären historischen Gegenstandes, des "gewerteten Kulturindividuums," wie sich Weber ausdrückt (261), selbst ein wesentlich subjektives Moment enthält, kann im
Gegensatz dazu die historische Analyse im engeren Sinn, also die Tat-
sachen- bzw. Ursachenermittlung, für Weber prinzipiell zu intersubjektiv
gültigen Ergebnissen gelangen und ist in dieser Hinsicht nur durch die
Existenz bzw. den Umfang des entsprechenden Quellenmaterials, nicht
jedoch 'logisch' in irgendeiner Form begrenzt (261); grundsätzlich und
auch abweichend von Meyers Behauptung von der generellen Unmöglichkeit einer 'absoluten und unbedingt gültigen' Erkenntnis der Geschichte besteht in diesem Bereich für Weber kein Unterschied zur natur-

---

[59] Ed. Meyer, Theorie 37; 45 (= *Kl. Schr.* I 44; 54).
[60] Weber greift hier seinerseits bekanntlich nicht zuletzt auf Heinrich Rickert zurück;
doch muß die vielerörterte Frage der Gemeinsamkeiten und der Unterschiede zwischen
beider Auffassungen hier beiseite bleiben.

wissenschaftlichen Kausalanalyse und auch keine spezifische 'Irrationalität' der Geschichte (vgl. 221–230). Der Unterschied zu den Naturwissenschaften (jedenfalls, soweit sie in die Richtung der Mechanik orientiert seien) besteht vielmehr in der primären Wertbeziehung, durch die in den Kulturwissenschaften bzw. der Geschichte das Objekt der Betrachtung erst bestimmt wird.

Neben der von Ed. Meyer nicht erfaßten Differenz von Wertbeziehung und Kausalanalyse, ihrer Bedeutung und fehlenden Zuordnung zum Begriff des "Wirksamen" und des "historischen Interesses" tritt dann als zweiter Haupteinwand Webers gegen Ed. Meyer die zu große Enge des auf das (kausal) Wirksame begrenzten Gegenstandes der Geschichtswissenschaft, die Meyer z.B. zum Ausschluß nicht nur jeglicher Zustandsbeschreibungen aus dem Bereich der "Geschichte" veranlaßt, sondern speziell auch der Biographie, weil deren Objekt die Persönlichkeit "in ihrer Totalität, nicht als historisch wirksamer Faktor" sei.[61] In der Tat ist für Ed. Meyer auch immer wieder eine eigentümlich hohe Bewertung der Wirkung einzelner (politischer und militärischer) Ereignisse kennzeichnend, so z.B. des Ausgangs der Perserkriege für die Entfaltung des gesamten griechischen (bzw. okzidentalen) Denkens, der Politik Artaxerxes' I. für die 'Entstehung des (nachexilischen) Judentums' oder des II. Punischen Krieges für die politische Gesamtentwicklung der antiken Welt.[62]—Weber argumentiert nun, daß zur historischen Kausalanalyse nicht nur die "Realgründe", sondern auch die "Erkenntnisgründe" gehörten, d.h. es komme nicht nur auf den realen, ursächlichen Zusammenhang mit der Gegenwart des Historikers an (234 ff.). Ebenso wichtig seien vielmehr die "Erkenntnismittel" zur Erhellung der Eigenart bestimmter historischer Zustände ohne Rücksicht auf deren kausale Bedeutung für die Gegenwart, insbesondere—ein bezeichnender Gedanke Max Webers—zur Bildung "kulturtheoretischer" bzw. historischer Begriffe (237; 258). An einer Reihe von Einzelbeispielen, so einem Aufsatz von K. Breysig über die Entstehung des Staates bei den Indianerstämmen der

---

[61] Ed. Meyer, Theorie 47 ff.; 55 f. (= *Kl. Schr.* I 57 ff.; 66).

[62] Vgl. Meyer, GdA III 1 (1901), 444 ff.; ders., Die Entstehung des Judenthums, Halle 1896, bes. 239 ff. (vgl. den Schlußsatz, 243: "Das Judenthum ist im Namen des Perserkönigs und kraft der Autorität seines Reichs geschaffen worden, und so reichen die Wirkungen des Achämenidenreichs gewaltig wie wenig anderes noch unmittelbar in unsere Gegenwart hinein"); GdA III 1 (1901), 167 ff., bes. 203; 206 (dazu auch unten, S. 151); *Kl. Schr.* 275 ff. (= *Kl. Schr.* I 257 ff.).—Umgekehrt dagegen erkennt Meyer der Geschichte der "Kleinstaaten Griechenlands und Italiens" nur ein begrenztes Interesse zu, denn: "Nicht nur ihr innerer Wert ist gering, sondern auch ihre geschichtliche Wirkung" (GdA I^2 1 (1907), 191, wobei hier die Berücksichtigung des "inneren Wertes" wohl bereits auf die Lektüre von Webers Aufsatz von 1906 deuten dürfte, vgl. auch unten, S. 153).

Tlinkit und Irokesen, an den Maya und Azteken, an Goethes Briefen an
Charlotte von Stein sowie an verschiedenen Arten des modernen Interesses am Altertum sucht Weber die beiden neben der Ermittlung von
"Realgründen" wesentlichen Aspekte historischen Arbeitens zu verdeutlichen, d.h. die "Wertbeziehung" des Historikers und die Gewinnung
von historischen "Erkenntnismitteln" (234 f.; 241 ff.; 264 f.). Letzteres
kann z.B. im Fall der Goethebriefe nach Weber in Erkenntnissen über
die "historische Eigenart" Goethes oder seiner Gesellschaftsschicht bestehen; auch aus den Briefen abzuleitende kultur-, sozial- oder allge-
meinpsychologische Gattungsbegriffe könnten u.U. für die "Kontrolle
der historischen Demonstration" wichtig werden (244). Beim Altertum
nennt Weber zwei zu seiner Zeit aktuelle, aber durchaus gegensätzliche,
mögliche Wertbeziehungen zur antiken Kultur sowie die ebenfalls von
Meyer nicht beachtete und gerade hier bedeutsame Möglichkeit der
Gewinnung "allgemeiner Begriffe, Analogien und Entwicklungsregeln
für die Vorgeschichte nicht nur unserer eigenen, sondern 'jeder' Kultur"
(265). Freilich sieht die Praxis Ed. Meyers denn doch anders aus als seine
all dies außer Acht lassende Theorie. Auch er kann, so Weber, nicht
ernstlich daran denken, "alles vom Standpunkt der Gegenwart aus historisch nicht mehr 'Wirksame' aus der Geschichte des Altertums ausmerzen" zu wollen (265); "eitel Selbsttäuschung" sei die Vorstellung
einer Geschichte des Altertums, die nur kausal auf die gegenwärtige Kultur wirksame Tatsachen enthielte (258 f.). Das "Historische" besteht in
der Tat nicht in den "Massenerscheinungen", auch nicht im "Individuellen", aber auch nicht einfach im kausal "Wirksamen"; es beruht
vielmehr zunächst auf einer Wertbeziehung, und der Begriff des "Wirksamen" kann in diesem Zusammenhang allenfalls meinen, so Weber, daß
"wir Gegenwartsmenschen Wertbeziehungen irgendwelcher Art" zu den
antiken Kulturinhalten besitzen, unabhängig von ihrem kausalen Zusammenhang mit der Kultur der Gegenwart. Jede Geschichte ist nach Weber
vom Standpunkt von Wertinteressen der Gegenwart geschrieben und enthält schon deswegen immer auch "schlechthin 'vergangene'," d.h. nicht
kausal wirksame "Kulturbestandteile" (259).[63]

Wenn demnach für Max Weber Ed. Meyers Begriff des "Historischen"
in mehrfacher Beziehung unhaltbar ist: in sich unklar, durch die Ver-
mengung heterogener Elemente wie Wert- und Kausalbeziehungen, des
'kausal Wichtigen' und des 'Wertvollen', widersprüchlich und darüber-

---

[63] Vgl. dagegen die Formulierung Ed. Meyers, Theorie 38 (= *Kl. Schr.* I 45), wonach
keines der ('ausgewählten') Objekte des historischen Interesses "rein um seiner selbst
willen" interessiere, "sondern lediglich um der Wirkung willen, die es ausgeübt hat und
noch ausübt." Dazu auch oben, S. 146.

hinaus durch die Beschränkung auf das kausal Bedeutsame entschieden
zu eng, wenn ferner Weber mit der Bestimmung der subjektiven und
objektiven Momente in der historischen Arbeit durch Meyer nicht einverstanden ist, so bieten auch Meyers gegen die Annahme historischer
Gesetzmäßigkeiten gerichtete Ausführungen Weber Anlaß zu eigenen
Überlegungen, die z.T. bereits in der "Auseinandersetzung mit Eduard
Meyer," vor allem aber im II. Teil der "Kritischen Studien" von 1906
enthalten sind. Meyer hatte in seiner Schrift von 1902 eigene frühere
Äußerungen über "allgemeine Gesetze" in den "Grundzügen" der historischen Entwicklung ausdrücklich widerrufen und ein entsprechendes
Beispiel—die deutsche Einigung im 19. Jhdt.—für falsch erklärt.[64] Bei
ihm spielt hier u.a. die 1896/97 ausgefochtene Kontroverse mit Wellhausen über die Herausbildung des (nachexilischen) Judentums eine
Rolle, die von Wellhausen "immanent evolutionistisch," als eine folge-
richtige innere Entwicklung aufgefaßt und dargestellt worden war,
während für Ed. Meyer ein äußerer Umstand, die—in dieser Beziehung
zufällige—Rolle des Perserreiches für das Auftreten und das Werk von
Esra und Nehemia das Entscheidende war.[65] Weber (der in der Sache
auf der Seite Meyers stand) setzt sich mit den daran deutlich werdenden
logischen Problemen der Entwicklung, der angeblichen historischen Notwendigkeit und historischer Gesetze im II. Teil der "Kritischen Studien"
auseinander: "Objektive Möglichkeit und adäquate Verursachung in der
historischen Kausalbetrachtung." Unter "adäquater Verursachung"
versteht Weber die Summe solcher Elemente aus der jeweils unendlichen
Zahl kausal wirkender Momente, die nach "allgemeinen Erfahrungsregeln" eine bestimmte (historische) Wirkung hervorzubringen pflegen,
im Gegensatz zur "zufälligen" Verursachung, bei der solche Regeln nicht
zu erkennen sind (276; vgl. 287). Hier geht es nicht so sehr um eine "Auseinandersetzung" mit Ed. Meyer als um die Untersuchung von logischen
Problemen, die auch bei diesem eine kennzeichnende Rolle spielen, und
Weber knüpft daher auch im einzelnen wiederholt an charakteristische
Beispiele Ed. Meyers an, wie z.B. dessen These über die welthistorische
"Tragweite" des Ausgangs der Perserkriege für die Kulturentwicklung
des Okzidents (273 ff.). Dabei wird eine andersartige Entwicklung der
griechischen und späteren europäischen Welt nach einem persischen Sieg
über die Griechen angenommen, d.h., logisch betrachtet, durch die Konstruktion unwirklicher Kausalzusammenhänge eine "adäquate Folge"
eines persischen Sieges erdacht, deren Gegenüberstellung mit den tat-

---

[64] Meyer, Theorie 24 f. (= *Kl. Schr.* I 29 f.)
[65] Vgl. Weber a.O. 230, dazu ders., Antikes Judentum (wie Anm. 9), 53 f., Anm. 2;
Ed. Meyer, *Kl. Schr.* 55, Anm. 2.

sächlichen 'adäquaten' Folgen die Tragweite jener Ereignisse erkennen läßt. Weber hat die Erörterung über die logische Natur der adäquaten Verursachung nicht zu Ende geführt. Doch hat er insgesamt noch die Schlußfolgerung festgehalten, daß in der Geschichte durchaus "Entwickelungstendenzen" existierten, wobei alles auf ein bestimmtes Ergebnis hindränge und dieses in dem Sinne wahrscheinlich mache, daß es nach den erwähnten "allgemeinen Erfahrungsregeln" eher erreicht werde als ein anderes, prinzipiell-logisch nicht auszuschließendes Resultat. Von historischen "Gesetzen" dagegen kann für Weber—auch hier—keine Rede sein; wenn man sich jedoch der genannten logischen Strukturen bewußt bleibe, seien Begriffe wie "Entwicklungstendenz", "treibende Kräfte," "Hemmungen" einer Entwicklung usw. "unbedenklich" (290).

Weber geht es im Ganzen seiner "Studien" nicht zuletzt um den Nachweis, daß die Geschichte—obwohl die "Fachhistoriker" selbst zu diesem Vorurteil nicht wenig beigetragen hätten—nicht nur eine deskriptive bzw. materialsammelnde Disziplin sei, sondern daß sie neben der letztlich "wertenden" primären Abgrenzung ihrer Objekte in ihrer praktisch wichtigsten Arbeit, der Erforschung von Kausalzusammenhängen, einen durch und durch wissenschaftlichen Charakter besitze.[66] Dabei ist Ed. Meyer aber nicht nur, wie es leicht scheinen könnte, eine Art "Wetzstein" für die Formulierung von Webers höchst eigenen Erkenntnissen bzw. Auffassungen. Wohl bestehen nicht unerhebliche Differenzen zwischen beiden, wobei es paradox erscheinen mag, daß ausgerechnet der bedeutendste neuere "Universalhistoriker" des Altertums durch seine Begrenzung auf das "Wirksame" einen viel beschränkteren theoretischen Begriff vom "Historischen" hat als Max Weber, der auch ein Interesse an der Vergangenheit 'rein' als solcher und unabhängig von ihrer kausalen Bedeutung anerkennt, der ferner die "systematische" Behandlung von "Zuständen" in die Geschichte mit einbezieht, der Herausarbeitung von "historischen Eigenarten" einen wichtigen Platz zuweist und für den die Geschichte nicht zuletzt auch eine bedeutende Funktion für die wissenschaftliche Begriffsbildung besitzt. Neben der mit den Weberschen Kategorien der Wertbeziehung, der Real- und Erkenntnisgründe in der Geschichte zusammenhängenden unterschiedlichen Zuordnung von subjektiven, rationalen und 'irrationalen' Elementen in der Geschichtsforschung, auch der andersartigen Bestimmung des Verhältnisses von Geschichts- und Naturwissenschaft ist ferner festzustellen, daß Weber zwar mit Eduard Meyer historische "Gesetzmäßigkeiten" ablehnt, aber doch "Regeln" und "Entwicklungstendenzen" eine

---

[66] Weber a.O. 216 f. Vgl. auch Tenbruck (wie Anm. 80) 344 ff.

größere Bedeutung beimißt als jener. Andererseits muß man sehen, daß Max Weber nicht nur die Praxis des Historikers Ed. Meyer ausdrücklich positiv bewertet, sondern auch eine ganze Reihe von dessen theoretischen Positionen teilt, wobei außer dem schon Erwähnten auch noch die grundsätzliche Bedeutung der Gegenwart des Historikers für die historische Perspektive bei Weber und Meyer genannt werden kann.

Die Reaktion Ed. Meyers auf die ''Auseinandersetzung'' Webers mit ihm ist bezeichnend sowohl für die hier immer wieder konstatierte Einseitigkeit ihrer Beziehung wie auch für die bei allen von Weber artikulierten Differenzen eben doch nicht minder großen Gemeinsamkeiten zwischen beiden. Bereits in der Einleitung zur 2. Auflage der ''Geschichte des Altertums'' von 1907, den ''Elementen der Anthropologie,'' fallen einzelne wahrscheinlich auf Webers Kritik zurückzuführende Formulierungen auf, auch wenn Weber dabei nicht namentlich erwähnt wird.[67] In der 1910 erschienenen Neubearbeitung seiner methodologischen Schrift spricht Meyer dann ausdrücklich von der ''eingehenden, sehr dankenswerten Kritik,'' die diese durch Max Weber erfahren habe,[68] wobei er konkret an mehreren Stellen darauf zu sprechen kommt.[69] Zu den ''Wirkungen'' auf die Gegenwart z.B. gehört für ihn, wie es jetzt—in einer Anmerkung—heißt, ''selbstverständlich auch der Wert (. . .), den wir einem Vorgang oder einem Erzeugnis der Vergangenheit um seiner selbst willen beimessen, etwa einem Kunstwerk, einer Heldentat oder einem eigenartigen Kulturzustand oder Staatsmann.''[70] Damit bleibt freilich (ganz abgesehen davon, daß Meyer diesen einer Erscheinung der Vergangenheit um ihrer selbst willen beigemessenen ''Wert'' in seiner Schrift tatsächlich nicht berücksichtigt hatte)[71] unbeachtet, daß es sich bei einem solchen ''Wert'' um eine ganz andere Art von ''Wirkung'' handelt als bei einem ursächlichen historischen Zusammenhang und daß schon die Verwendung des einen Begriffs der ''Wirkung'' für derart ''heterogene Elemente'' fragwürdig wäre.[72]

---

[67] Meyer, GdA I² 1, 186 f.; 189 f. (mit der Verwendung von Begriffen wie ''Wert'', ''innerer Wert,'' ''Werturteil'', freilich in deutlich anderem Sinn als bei Weber).

[68] Meyer, *Kl. Schr.* 21, Anm. 1.

[69] Ebd. 44, Anm. 2; 55, Anm. 2.

[70] Ebd. 45, Anm. 1.

[71] Vgl. ders., Theorie 36 f. (= *Kl. Schr.* I 43 f.).

[72] Gegenüber dem in der Diskussion von E. Badian vorgebrachten Einwand, das von Ed. Meyer geltend gemachte ''historische Interesse'' entspreche durchaus Webers ''Wert''-Begriff, sei also nochmals betont, daß Meyers ''Interesse'' außer der eigentlichen ''Wert''-Beziehung auch die nach Weber scharf davon zu trennende Kausalität (Meyer: ''Wirkung''), bei der nach Weber wiederum Real- und Erkenntnisgründe zu scheiden sind, ohne klare Differenzierung mit umfaßt (vgl. bes. Meyer, Theorie a.O.). Das historische ''Interesse'' etwa an dem preußischen König Friedrich Wilhelm IV. ist—so

IV

Die Hauptlinien im Verhältnis von Eduard Meyer und Max Weber dürften damit umrissen sein. Man hat zwar in neuester Zeit mehrfach wesentlich über das hier Gesagte hinausgehende Einflüsse Ed. Meyers auf Weber vermutet; doch scheint dabei durchweg Vorsicht geboten. Wenn z.B. E. Narducci Webers Interesse für die ''Bürokratisierung'' in der Spätantike mit Ed. Meyer in Verbindung bringt,[73] so wäre erstens zu fragen, an welche Arbeiten Meyers (außer den wenigen Bemerkungen dazu in dem Vortrag von 1895) dabei überhaupt zu denken wäre, und zweitens auf entsprechende Äußerungen Webers bereits in der Römischen Agrargeschichte, also in der Zeit vor seiner Rezeption Ed. Meyers, zu verweisen.[74] Wenn Narducci außerdem die Vorstellung einer in der Antike gehemmten und erst in der Neuzeit wieder aufgenommenen und vollendeten Entwicklung bei Weber von der Konzeption der parallelen Entwicklungskreisläufe in Antike und Neuzeit bei Ed. Meyer herzuleiten versucht, so ist dem die viel zu große grundsätzliche, von vornherein bestehende Verschiedenheit beider Ansätze entgegenzuhalten, abgesehen davon, daß auch hier der Gedanke sowohl des Vergleichs wie der Andersartigkeit antiker und mittelalterlicher Verhältnisse bei Max Weber in nuce bereits am Schluß der Römischen Agrargeschichte zu erkennen ist.[75] A. Momigliano hat seinerseits darauf aufmerksam gemacht, daß, nachdem Weber zunächst von der Betrachtung der agrarischen und ländlichen Verhältnisse ausgegangen sei, mit der Rezeption Ed. Meyers mehr und mehr die Stadt in den Mittelpunkt seines Interesses gerückt sei, bis hin zu der Abhandlung ''Die Stadt.''[76] Es ist zweifellos eine zutreffende und wichtige Beobachtung, daß vor allem in den Partien der ''Agrarverhältnisse im Altertum,'' in denen Weber stofflich stärker auf Ed. Meyer angewiesen war, die agrarischen Verhältnisse wiederholt hinter der Erörterung von Fragen der allgemeinen Sozial- und Wirtschaftsgeschichte zurücktreten, die mit den Agrarverhältnissen allenfalls lose in Verbindung stehen. Aber man wird dies doch mehr als Folge einer ungenügenden Bearbeitung der agrarischen Probleme der vorrömischen Welt

---

Weber a.O. 234 ff.—auch seiner logischen Struktur nach grundsätzlich verschieden von dem (denkbaren) an den Schneidern seiner Röcke (dies ist das berühmte, auch von Ed. Meyer zitierte Beispiel Heinrich Rickerts).

[73] E. Narducci, Max Weber fra antichità e mondo moderno, in: Quaderni di storia 14, 1981, 31–77, hier 35.

[74] Vgl. etwa Weber, Römische Agrargeschichte (wie Anm. 4) 291.

[75] Ebd. 352.

[76] A. Momigliano, Max Weber and Eduard Meyer (1977), in: ders., Sesto contributo alla storia degli studi classici e del mondo antico, Rom 1980, hier 288 f.; vgl. auch ders., Max Weber di fronte agli storici dell'antichità (1981), in: Settimo contributo ... (1984), hier 250 f.

in der Weber vorliegenden modernen Literatur denn als Ausdruck eines
erst durch Ed. Meyer veranlaßten Interessenwandels Webers verstehen
müssen, zumal auch für die Bedeutung der Stadt in Webers Untersuchungen gilt, daß sie sehr deutlich bereits in der Römischen Agrargeschichte erkennbar ist.[77] Eine andere Feststellung Momiglianos, nämlich daß Weber sich durch Ed. Meyer von dem "juristischen Ansatz"
Mommsens "befreit" habe,[78] kann leicht zu Mißverständnissen führen:
Für die nichtrömischen Bereiche der "Agrarverhältnisse" konnte Weber
einfach deswegen nirgends mehr auf Mommsen zurückgreifen, weil dessen Forschungen nur der römischen Welt galten, während bezeichnenderweise die römischen Partien der "Agrarverhältnisse" sich auch später
immer eng an das durch die Römische Agrargeschichte, damit also auch
wesentlich mithilfe der Mommsenschen Arbeiten gelegte Fundament
anschlossen. Im übrigen wird man sich im klaren darüber sein müssen,
daß Mommsens Einfluß auf Weber nur zu einem Teil juristische Aspekte
(des Staatsrechts) betraf und umgekehrt die nichtjuristischen, sozialen
und ökonomischen Interessen Webers schon in seiner römischrechtlichen
Habilitationsschrift, also wiederum vor der "Rezeption" Ed. Meyers,
z.T. gerade unter dem Einfluß Mommsens, unübersehbar zutage-
traten.[79]

Obwohl das Gesagte schon darauf hindeuten dürfte, daß weitergehende
Einwirkungen Ed. Meyers auf Weber schwerlich greifbar sind, hat jüngst
Friedrich H. Tenbruck in einer sehr engagierten Abhandlung den Versuch unternommen, eine noch viel erheblichere Dimension der Rolle Ed.
Meyers für Max Weber zu erschließen.[80] Er hat die These aufgestellt,
daß Webers Interesse für die außerokzidentale Welt, Indien und China,
von Ed. Meyers "Elementen der Anthropologie" von 1907 inspiriert
worden sei, d.h. dem I. Teil des I. Bandes der "Geschichte des Altertums" in dessen zweiter Auflage,[81] und daß dies sogar das eigentliche
Vorbild von "Wirtschaft und Gesellschaft" gewesen sei, durch das
Weber erst zu dessen Konzeption gelangt und überhaupt die Entstehung
von "Wirtschaft und Gesellschaft" zu erklären sei;[82] speziell gehe auch
ein zentraler Begriff beim späteren Max Weber, das Charisma, zwar
nicht dem Wort, aber doch seinem wesentlichen Gehalt nach auf das II.
Kapitel, "Die geistige Entwicklung," der "Anthropologie" Ed. Meyers

---

[77] Vgl. MWG I/2 (wie Anm. 4) 47 f.
[78] A. Momigliano, Sesto contributo (wie Anm. 76), ebd.
[79] Vgl. dazu MWG a.O. 22 ff.
[80] F.H. Tenbruck, Max Weber und Eduard Meyer, in: W.J. Mommsen—W.
Schwentker (Hsg.), Max Weber und seine Zeitgenossen, Göttingen-Zürich 1988, 337–
379.
[81] Ebd. 351.
[82] Ebd. 353 ff.

und außerdem auf sein (Ende 1912 erschienenes) Mormonenbuch zurück.[83] An eine nähere Auseinandersetzung mit diesen weitreichenden Behauptungen ist im vorliegenden Rahmen nicht zu denken. W. Hennis hat Tenbrucks Auffassung unter Hinweis auf die in gänzlich andere Richtung weisenden Randbemerkungen Webers in dessen Handexemplar der "Elemente der Anthropologie" bereits zurückgewiesen.[84] Die direkten Belege für die von Tenbruck angenommene Bedeutung der "Anthropologie" Ed. Meyers für Max Weber sind überaus vage und erscheinen in keiner Weise beweiskräftig.[85] Daß gerade Ed. Meyer, der selbst Indien und China bewußt immer außerhalb seiner Forschungen—auch der "Anthropologie"—gelassen hat, Webers Interesse darauf gelenkt haben sollte, ist besonders unwahrscheinlich; viel näher liegt hier in jedem Fall die umfangreiche vergleichend-religionswissenschaftliche Literatur der Zeit, die Weber kannte und in der die Berücksichtigung jener Gebiete vielfach üblich war. Wiewohl der Name Ed. Meyers in der gesamten Religionssoziologie Webers an keiner Stelle genannt wird und die Erwähnungen der Mormonen in "Wirtschaft und Gesellschaft" ebenfalls ganz vereinzelt und unbedeutend sind, soll nicht ausgeschlossen werden, daß einzelne Elemente des Kapitels über die "geistige Entwicklung" in Meyers "Anthropologie", auch seines Buches über die Mormonen in Max Webers Religionssoziologie eingeflossen sind; doch läßt sich vor einer systematischen Prüfung sowohl von "Wirtschaft und Gesellschaft" wie der in Frage kommenden zeitgenössischen religionswissenschaftlichen Arbeiten nichts Abschließendes sagen und vor allem nicht "der Grundgedanke" der Weberschen Religionssoziologie[86]—und womöglich noch die Grundidee von "Wirtschaft und Gesellschaft"[87]—genetisch mit Ed. Meyers "Anthropologie" verbinden.

Ohne daß hier das Ergebnis einer genauen Untersuchung der Thesen Tenbrucks vorweggenommen werden könnte, bleibt doch insgesamt festzuhalten, daß weiterreichende konzeptionelle Einflüsse Ed. Meyers auf

---

[83] Ebd. 360 ff.

[84] W. Hennis, Max Webers Fragestellung. Studien zur Biographie des Werkes, Tübingen 1987, 163, Anm. 79.

[85] Vgl. Weber, GASW 279; dazu Tenbruck a.O.—Nicht exakt ist die Feststellung Tenbrucks (a.O. 365, Anm. 94), das "universalgeschichtliche Interesse, mit dem Ed. Meyer begann," sei bei Weber "ein später Erwerb" gewesen. Vielmehr manifestiert sich dieses—ganz im Sinne Ed. Meyers verstandene und wahrscheinlich auch von ihm wesentlich mit angeregte—Interesse bei Weber bereits seit 1898 (vgl. oben, S. 136 f.), wahrscheinlich aber schon einige Jahre früher, wenn er nämlich den Alten Orient in seiner oben, S. 134 erwähnten und im WS 1894/95 zum ersten Mal gehaltenen nationalökonomischen Vorlesung von Anfang an (wenn auch nur am Rande) mit berücksichtigte.

[86] Vgl. Tenbruck a.O. 366.

[87] Vgl. Tenbruck a.O. 357 ff.

Weber, wie sie die zuletzt genannten Autoren für möglich halten, durchweg fraglich bleiben und vor allem auch nicht dem allgemeinen Bild entsprechen, das sich aus dem mit einiger Sicherheit zu erschließenden
Verhältnis zwischen Ed. Meyer und Weber ergibt. Ein Hauptkenn-
zeichen dieses Verhältnisses ist zwar die starke einseitige, wenn auch
durchaus kritische Rezeption des Historikers Ed. Meyer durch Weber,
während umgekehrt der Einfluß Webers auf Ed. Meyer, wie er sich in den
wenigen Zitierungen Webers vom II. Band der "Geschichte des Altertums" bis zur zweiten Fassung der Theorieschrift von 1910 spiegelt,
minimal und eher diffus bleibt. Aber abgesehen wohl von der Einbeziehung des Alten Orients in die "Agrarverhältnisse im Altertum" handelt
es sich bei der "Rezeption" Ed. Meyers durch Weber nicht um die Übernahme von eigentlichen Interessenschwerpunkten bzw. Interessenrich-
tungen, sondern um eine ganz andere Art von "Rezeption": Auf der
einen Seite steht die weitergehende, aber im einzelnen auch immer wieder
kritische Übernahme von Forschungsergebnissen Ed. Meyers zur alt-
orientalischen, israelitisch-jüdischen, griechischen und z.T. römischen
Geschichte; zum andern handelt es sich um die Kritik an der fehlenden
begrifflichen Präzision Ed. Meyers, zumal im Bereich der ökonomischen
bzw. wirtschaftsgeschichtlichen Begriffe, und überhaupt an Meyers
Auffassung der wirtschaftlichen Verhältnisse des Altertums, dazu zumindest an Teilen von Ed. Meyers theoretischen Positionen. Wenn es dabei
einen wirklich wesentlichen Gegensatz zwischen dem Historiker Ed.
Meyer und Max Weber gibt, dann liegt er in der Bedeutung, die Weber
der begrifflich klaren Durchdringung der Welt des Altertums, ihrer
Strukturen und ihrer Geschichte beigemessen hat, worin er gegenüber
Ed. Meyer zweifellos neue Maßstäbe gesetzt hat und worin vor allem
auch eine fortwirkende Bedeutung Max Webers bestehen dürfte. Andererseits ist aber die intensive kritische Rezeption gerade der Arbeiten Ed.
Meyers durch Weber neben den rein stofflichen Gesichtspunkten gewiß
auch auf dem Hintergrund fundamentaler Gemeinsamkeiten hinsichtlich
der spezifischen Inhalte und Aufgaben der historischen Wissenschaft zu
sehen. Es ist nicht nur allgemein die Kombination von authentischem
Gespür für wesentliche historische Fragen mit der Leidenschaft für die
Vielfalt und zugleich Exaktheit des Details, was die beiden Zeitgenossen
Ed. Meyer und Max Weber miteinander verband. Neben allen schon
genannten Übereinstimmungen in wichtigen Grundfragen wird man vielmehr insbesondere an das ausgeprägte Interesse beider an sozial- und
wirtschaftsgeschichtlichen Fragen, an der Religion als bewegender
historischer Kraft und an grundlegenden allgemeinen und theoretischen
Fragen der historischen Disziplin denken müssen wie auch, was speziell
die Geschichte des Altertums betrifft, an die Überwindung der isolieren-

den Betrachtung einzelner Völker, sei es der Ägypter, Juden, Griechen oder Römer, auch dies eine Aufgabe, die von ihrer Wichtigkeit seither nichts eingebüßt hat. Insofern ist, wenn man alles Gesagte kurz auf einen Nenner bringen will, Max Webers Verhältnis zu Ed. Meyer letztlich durchaus bestimmt durch das, was man mit guten Gründen als die—nach wie vor—''modernen'' Züge Eduard Meyers bezeichnen kann.

ALEXANDER DEMANDT

EDUARD MEYER UND OSWALD SPENGLER. LÄSST SICH GESCHICHTE VORAUSSAGEN?*

Immanuel Kant[1] stellte 1784 die Frage, "wie es unsre späten Nachkommen anfangen werden, die Last von Geschichte, die wir ihnen nach einigen Jahrhunderten hinterlassen möchten, zu fassen?" Die Antwort gab Friedrich Nietzsche[2] 1874 in seiner Zweiten Unzeitgemäßen Betrachtung. Er forderte, daß die Geschichte nur soweit betrieben werden sollte, als sie dem Leben diene. Dies leiste sie in drei Formen: als monumentalische Historie, die das Große bewundert, als antiquarische Historie, die das Alte um seiner selbst willen liebt, und als kritische Historie, die das Brauchbare vom Unbrauchbaren trennt, um aus der Vergangenheit Baustoff für die Zukunft zu gewinnen.

1. Diese drei Zugänge zur Allgemeingeschichte eröffnen uns auch drei Seiten der Wissenschaftsgeschichte. Die monumentalische Wissenschaftshistorie wurzelt in der Totenehrung. Sie zeigt uns die Heroen unseres jeweiligen Faches von ihrer besten Seite, und das mit Recht. Denn durch sie zeichnen sich die Größen ja gerade aus. Das Mittelmäßige und Alltägliche können wir überall studieren, nicht zuletzt an uns selbst. Die echten Leistungen aber sollten im Bewußtsein bleiben, um uns als Maßstab und Anreiz zu dienen. Sie sind Muster für die Zukunft.

Daß Meyer und Spengler zu den großen Autoren unseres Faches zählen, bezweifelt nur, wer sie nicht gelesen hat. Meyer ist der neben Theodor Mommsen bedeutendste deutsche Althistoriker. Während Mommsen sich ganz auf die römische Geschichte konzentrierte und in einem von ihm selbst erkannten und beklagten Spezialistentum endete,[3] hat Meyer gegen den Zug der Zeit einen universalhistorischen Ansatz gewählt und diesen durch theoretische Überlegungen vertieft. Er hatte zwar nie eine solch große Leserschaft wie Mommsen, dennoch hat er das Geschichtsverständnis von Max Weber, Michael Rostovtzeff und, wie wir sehen werden, von Arnold Toynbee und Oswald Spengler entscheidend beeinflußt.

---

* Der Text wurde als öffentlicher Vortrag entworfen und während der Tagung am 12.XI.1987 in Homburg gehalten. Für den Druck wurde er leicht überarbeitet. Anregung verdanke ich den Teilnehmern und Dr. E. Flaig.
[1] I. Kant, Sämtliche Werke in sechs Bänden (Insel), 1921, I 239.
[2] F. Nietzsche, Werke in drei Bänden, 1960, I 219 ff.
[3] Th. Mommsen, Reden und Aufsätze, 1905, 198.

Spengler hingegen ist vielleicht stärker durch seine Wirkung als durch sein Werk bemerkenswert. Vom "Untergang des Abendlandes" hat der Verlag C.H. Beck in München inzwischen über 300 000 Exemplare verkauft. Spengler vertritt die einflußreichste nach- und nichthegelianische Geschichtsphilosophie, eine kulturmorphologische Zyklustheorie, die das Denken einer ganzen Generation geprägt hat.

Die antiquarische Wissenschaftshistorie bringt uns die Forscher als Menschen näher und zeigt uns die Tradition, in der wir stehen. Nietzsche (I 227) spricht vom "Wohlgefühl des Baumes an seinen Wurzeln." Der Zukunftsaspekt dieses Ansatzes liegt in der Forschungsökonomie. Wenn eine Forschung nichts mehr zu erforschen hat, kann sie immer noch die Forschung erforschen und findet in sich selbst einen unerschöpflichen Stoff. Das führt indes leicht ins Pittoreske und Pikante. Um das zu vermeiden, verzichte ich darauf, die Äußerungen des Rathenau-Biographen Harry Graf Kessler[4] zu zitieren, der Spengler nach einer Begegnung in Weimar 1927 als einen "halbgebildeten Scharlatan" und "Nietzsche-Pfaffen" bezeichnete. Ebenso versage ich es mir, meinen ersten Besuch in der Mommsenstraße von Groß-Lichterfelde zu beschreiben, wo im verlassenen Arbeitszimmer Eduard Meyers hinter grauen Fenstern dick bestaubte Bücher und Papiere sich auf Tisch und Boden türmten, die ganze Etage bewohnt von einer neunzigjährigen Nichte (?) des Historikers und einer hundertjährigen Schildkröte, die sich friedlich und niedlich von Meyers letzten Briefen und Tagebüchern ernährte . . . .

Für die kritische Wissenschaftshistorie ist derartiges Klatsch. Sie fragt nicht nach dem Unterhaltsamen, sondern nach dem Verwendbaren. Sie bemüht sich um abwägende Bestandsaufnahme in der Absicht, erreichte Einsichten zu vertiefen und begangene Fehler zu vermeiden. Dazu bedarf es freilich der Fachkompetenz des Kritikers und seiner Bereitschaft, den Gelehrten aus seiner Zeit zu verstehen. Wissenschaftsgeschichte ohne Fachkompetenz bleibt belanglos für die Wissenschaft; Wissenschaftsgeschichte ohne Willen zum Verständnis verfehlt die Geschichte. Das führt zur ideologischen Schulmeisterei. War einst jede Epoche unmittelbar zu Gott, so ist nun jede Epoche mittelbar zu Hitler. Meyer und Spengler bieten dafür Angriffspunkte. Beide gehören wie Gottfried Benn, Carl Schmitt und Ernst Jünger zu den Rechtsintellektuellen. Sie haben den Vorzug, weniger Illusionen als die Linksintellektuellen zu hegen, müssen sich aber von diesen sagen lassen, zur Bestätigung ihrer pessimistischen Weltsicht beigetragen zu haben.

Die monumentalische, die antiquarische und die kritische Fragestellung verbindend, werde ich nun zweitens einiges zu Meyer, drittens

---

[4] H. Graf Kessler, Tagebücher 1918–1937, 1961, 543 ff.

einiges zu Spengler sagen, viertens die Beziehungen der beiden skizzieren und fünftens das Problem der Prognose anreißen.

2. Eduard Meyer[5] wurde 1855 als Sohn eines bedeutenden Gymnasiallehrers geboren. Als zwölfjähriger Schüler der Hamburger Gelehrtenschule des Johanneums verfaßte er eine Tragödie über Caesars Tod in fünf Akten (Den Text fanden wir zwischen den von der Schildkröte verschonten Papieren), in der Prima entwarf er seine spätere Habilitationsschrift.[6] Während des Studiums lernte er die orientalischen Sprachen, die er wie kein zweiter seines Fachs vor oder nach ihm beherrschte. Mit zwanzig Jahren promoviert, wurde Meyer Hauslehrer beim englischen Gesandten in Konstantinopel, leistete ein Jahr Wehrdienst, habilitierte sich mit 24 Jahren in Leipzig und übernahm dann Professuren in Breslau, Halle und seit 1902 in Berlin, wo er bis 1923 lehrte. Reisen in die Mittelmeerländer (1884, 1887/88, 1925/26),[7] nach England (1876) und Rußland (1925, 1928) sowie zwei Gastprofessuren in den Vereinigten Staaten (1904 Chicago, 1909/10 in Harvard) rundeten sein Weltbild. Meyers zweite Amerikareise 1909/10 glich einem Triumphzug. Die Presse feierte ihn als den *most eminent living historian*.[8] Meyer bekleidete leitende Stellungen im Deutschen Archäologischen Institut, im Kartell der Deutschen Akademien, in der deutschen Orient-Gesellschaft und seit 1902 in der Römisch-Germanischen Kommission, der er 1927 in Frankfurt die Geburtstagsrede hielt. Meyer war siebenfacher Ehrendoktor, Geheimrat und trug den Pour le Mérite der Friedensklasse. 1919 wurde er Rektor der Friedrich-Wilhelms-Universität. Damals entstanden Einrichtungen, die uns heute selbstverständlich sind: die Mensa, eine Unterstützungskasse für arme Studenten, der Allgemeine Studentenausschuß und die Vorläuferin der Deutschen Forschungsgemeinschaft.[9]

Meyers Schriftenverzeichnis umfaßt 570 Titel,[10] darunter die achtbändige >Geschichte des Altertums<, ein Gesamtbild der Antike vom ältesten Orient bis zur Alexanderzeit. Es folgten Bücher über die Entstehung des Judentums (1896), über die Mormonen (1912), über Caesar und Pompeius (1918) und über die Ursprünge des Christentums (1921/23). Im Weltkrieg verfaßte er historisch-politische Werke über Nord-

---

5 K. Christ, Von Gibbon zu Rostovtzeff, 1972, 286 ff. Dazu die autobiographische Skizze bei Marohl 1941.

6 H. Marohl, Eduard Meyer—Bibliographie, 1941, 9.

7 Polverini hierzu anderen Ortes (s. S. VII).

8 Chambers in diesem Bande S. 97 ff.

9 Unte in diesem Bande S. 505 ff.

10 S.o. Anm. 6.

amerika und England, letzteres nach Friedrich Meinecke[11] eher ein
"Werk der Leidenschaft als der Wissenschaft." Besonders wirksam wur-
den Meyers theoretische Schriften, die in der Nachfolge von Droysens
Historie stehen. Sie wurden ins Japanische und Russische übersetzt.

Meyers Umgang mit der Geschichte gehört nach der Typologie
Nietzsches in die kritische Historie. Denn Meyer suchte in der Geschichte
Bausteine für eine "einheitliche, historisch begründete Weltanschauung."[12] Er besaß die von Novalis[13] am echten Gelehrten bewunderte
"Universaltendenz". Das Altertum schien Meyer aus zwei Gründen
wichtig. Zum ersten habe es die Grundlagen gelegt für alle weitere Entwicklung. Athen sei der "Ort, dem wir alles verdanken, was wir an
geistiger Kultur, an wahrer Bildung besitzen, ohne den wir Barbaren sein
würden."[14] Gleichwohl war Meyer kein Klassizist: die Antike wird nicht
verklärt, sondern mit all ihren Schattenseiten wiedergegeben. Zum zweiten liefert die griechisch-römische Geschichte ein Modell, weniger ein
Vorbild als ein Schaubild, das verkleinert, aber maßstabgetreu das
Schicksal der romanisch-germanischen Völker vorwegnimmt (England
210). Zwischen beiden Kulturen glaubte Meyer eine "Parallelität der
Entwicklung" (Weltgeschichte 39) zu erkennen. Diese Ansicht hat er
schon 1895 auf dem Frankfurter Historikertag ausgeführt (Kl. Schr. I
79 ff.). Dort beschrieb er die griechisch-römische Antike als zyklische
Einheit, die nach seiner Ansicht von einer primitiven Frühzeit über eine
fortschreitende Modernisierung zu einer dekadenten Spätphase führte
und abermals in der Primitivität endete.

Als Leitfaden wählte Meyer die Wirtschaft. Den Grund für diese Wahl
bot die damals verbreitete These von Karl Bücher, der die Wirtschaftsgeschichte nach dem hegelianischen Fortschrittsprinzip in drei Stufen von

---

[11] 23.V.1915 an Dove. F. Meinecke, Werke VI 1962, 61.
[12] GdA I 1, S. IX. Meyer nennt dies die "innerste Triebfeder" bei der Ergreifung
seines Berufes. Aus ihr erklärt sich auch sein Interesse an Religionsgeschichte. Gleichwohl
geht es kaum an, Meyers Universalgeschichte als eine Ersatzreligion zu bezeichnen. Das
widerlegt der Kontext der zitierten Stelle, wo sich Meyer gegen das "Überwuchern
moderner Konstruktionen und phantastischer Systeme" wendet, "welche gegenwärtig
unserer Zeit als gesicherte Endergebnisse der Wissenschaft ausgeboten werden." Meyer
benutzt die Wissenschaft einerseits als kritisches Werkzeug gegenüber vorgegebenen
Weltanschauungen und andererseits als Instrument zur Gewinnung einer eigenen. Er
rechnet mit dem "bewußt und unbewußt in einem jeden arbeitenden Bestreben, zu einem
einheitlichen Gesamtbilde der menschlichen Entwicklung zu gelangen," und unterscheidet dafür zwischen einem unwissenschaftlichen und einem wissenschaftlichen Vorgehen. Im Gegensatz zu den "ewigen" Wahrheiten der Religion betonte Meyer, "daß
die wissenschaftliche Discussion ihrem Wesen nach unendlich ist, und daß, wo eine
Generation schon geglaubt hat, fast am Ziele zu sein, die nächste in ihrem Resultat nur
neue Probleme erkennt" (Sitzungsber. Berl. Akad. 104, 1013).
[13] Novalis, Werke und Briefe, Insel 1942, 410.
[14] Meyers Brief vom 10.IV.1884. Dazu Polverini demnächst.

der Haus- zur Volks- zur Weltwirtschaft dargestellt hatte, wobei der ''unermeßliche Rückschritt, der in der Zeit von Hadrian bis auf Karl den Großen sich vollzogen hat'' (Kl. Schr. I 174), nicht in Erscheinung trat.[15] Die Zeit von Homer und Hesiod sah er geprägt einerseits durch einen ritterlichen Adel, der mit seinem höfischen Leben und den epischen Sängern, mit seinem Gefolgschaftswesen und seinen Fehden so sehr an das europäische ''Mittelalter'' erinnert, daß Meyer diesen Begriff auf die frühgriechische Zeit übertrug.[16] Durch aufkommendes Städtewesen, durch fortschreitende Arbeitsteilung und vor allem durch die beginnende Geldwirtschaft gewannen Handwerk und Handel an Bedeutung. Ohne Export und Import konnten die Städte gar nicht mehr leben. Das 7. und 6. Jahrhundert v. Chr. in Griechenland entsprächen dem 14. und 15. Jahrhundert, das 5. dem 16. und die Folgezeit dem Hellenismus. Den Höhepunkt der antiken Kultur erblickte Meyer im klassischen Athen, namentlich in der Person des Sokrates (GdA. IV 2, 150 ff.). Gegenüber der Aufgabe einer nationalen Einigung hätten die Griechen allerdings versagt.[17] Die letzte Chance verspielten die Tyrannen von Syrakus, so daß die Randmacht Makedonien die Führung übernahm und die Polisautonomie beendete. In den Großreichen des Hellenismus mit seiner Weltkultur erreichte die griechische Geschichte ihren Abschluß.[18] Schon Droysen[19] hatte den Hellenismus als die ''moderne Zeit des Altertums'' bezeichnet, und dem folgte Meyer. Als dauernde Errungenschaft des freien Griechentums betrachtete er die Entwicklung des Individualismus. Sie führte zum Gottkönigtum Alexanders, der wiederum die griechische

---

[15] Ob diese Wahl glücklich war, ist zu bezweifeln. Denn man kann zwar den Aufstieg der antiken Wirtschaft mit dem im europäischen Mittelalter vergleichen, doch fehlt hier die ökonomische Dekadenzphase, die in der Völkerwanderungszeit am Ende des Altertums zu beobachten ist, als die Naturalwirtschaft wiederum die Geldwirtschaft verdrängte, die Arbeitsteilung zurückging und der Fernhandel an Bedeutung verlor.

[16] Meyer, Theorie 27. Ebenso betonte Wilamowitz, Reden und Vorträge, 1902 S. 127, daß die frühgriechischen Jahrhunderte ''auf fast allen Gebieten überraschende Analogien zu dem Mittelalter der christlichen Periode bieten'' (1897).

[17] GdA IV 2, 150 ff.; *Kl. Schr.* I 267. Die Vorstellung, daß die Geschichte bestimmten Völkern und Männern bestimmte Aufgaben stelle (vgl. 281; 272 f.), dürfte Meyer indirekt von Hegel haben, während seine Annahme, daß diese Aufgabe die Gewinnung der nationalen Einheit sei, eine Rückblendung eigener Ideale auf die Griechen zu sein scheint. 1919 stellte Meyer (Caesar S. X) fest, daß das deutsche ''Volk der großen weltgeschichtlichen Aufgabe, die ihm gestellt war, nicht gewachsen ist,'' womit er anscheinend die Selbstbehauptung als Kultur- und Machtstaat meint.

[18] Wenn Meyer seine Geschichte des Altertums mit dem Scheitern der nationalen Einigung im großgriechischen Westen beendet, so ist dies weniger abrupt, als bisweilen behauptet wird. Denn Meyer endet in der Zeit ''wo die griechische Kultur ihr Höchstes geleistet hat und reif geworden ist, zur Weltkultur zu werden.'' Dieses Resultat empfindet Meyer insofern als tragisch, als fortan ''die Nation politisch alle Bedeutung verloren'' habe (GdA V 514).

[19] 1843 im unterdrückten Vorwort zur Geschichte des Hellenismus II: J.G. Droysen, Historik 1960, 384.

"Vollfreiheit" beendete. So erscheint der Weg von Askra über Athen nach Alexandria als Modernisierungs- und Erschöpfungsprozeß. Die Kultur wurde breiter, flacher, anfälliger.[20] Der als Heilmittel gegen den Bürgerzwist gedachte Absolutismus erwies sich als Gift (Hellenismus 60). Die Kriege zwischen den hellenistischen Mächten ermöglichten es der Randmacht Rom, ihr Universalreich aufzurichten.

Rom hat nach Meyer, wenn auch verspätet, so doch eine ganz ähnliche Entwicklung wie Griechenland durchgemacht, von einer bäuerlichen, kleinräumigen Gesellschaft zum kapitalistischen Universalsystem. Den mit dem Abzug des Pyrrhos erreichten Idealzustand eines geeinten Italien[21] habe man leichtfertig zugunsten immer weiterer Expansion geopfert. Das Imperium Romanum der Kaiserzeit habe Frieden und Wohlstand gebracht, wie es das nie zuvor, nie hernach gegeben habe. Dennoch war das eine "Friedhofsruhe". Mit dem Verlust der politischen Selbständigkeit hätten die Völker ihre Schaffenskraft und ihre kulturellen Eigenarten eingebüßt. Seit Augustus herrschten Geldgier und Lebensgenuß bei den Oberschichten, Stumpfsinn und Erlösungsbedürfnis bei den Unterschichten. Es ist für uns heute schwer begreiflich, aber die Pax Romana ist durch namhafte Autoren entschieden abgelehnt worden. Mommsen[22] verkündete am 24.III.1881: "Der ewige Friede ist unter allen Umständen nicht bloß ein Traum, den heute auch Kant nicht träumen würde, sondern nicht einmal zu wünschen." Am 11.X.1916 kritisierte Eduard Schwartz den "entnationalisierten Schematismus" und den "rein animalischen Lebensgenuß" im Weltreich des Augustus. Schwartz sagte: "So etwa sah der einzige Weltfriede aus, der einmal Wirklichkeit geworden ist, die Pazifisten haben schwerlich Ursache, mit diesem Paradigma besonders zufrieden zu sein."[23]

---

[20] Ernst Badian nannte dies die "Flaschentheorie" der Kultur: Für wenige reicht sie aus; läßt man zu viele teilhaben, lohnt es für keinen. Die Reduzierung der Kultur auf eine begrenzte Menge an geistigen Konsumgütern ist in der Tat merkwürdig. Diese Vorstellung übernahm Michael Rostovtzeff, Gesellschaft und Wirtschaft im römischen Kaiserreich II 1925/29, S. 247. Er erklärte den Verfall der antiken Kultur durch die "allmähliche Absorbierung der gebildeten Schichten durch die Massen," forderte eine Massenkultur, aber endete in der Frage: "Ist nicht jede Kultur zum Verfall verurteilt, sobald sie die Massen zu durchdringen beginnt?"

[21] Meyer (Weltgeschichte 97) kritisiert Mommsen darin zu Recht, daß dieser den Römern die Einigung der italischen Nation zugute gehalten habe, da eine solche doch erst durch die Romanisierung Italiens geschaffen worden sei. Dennoch betrachtet auch Meyer den Übergang nach Sizilien 264 v. Chr. als Verrat am nationalen Prinzip. Wer, wie Meyer, Völker als zusammengewachsene Gruppen betrachtet, dürfte zwischen einer nationalistischen und einer imperialistischen Außenpolitik nicht den scharfen Unterschied machen, den Meyer betont.

[22] Th. Mommsen, Reden und Aufsätze, 1905, 106.

[23] Ed. Schwartz, Weltreich und Weltfriede (Rede 11.X.1916). In: ders., Gesammelte Schriften I 1938/1963, S. 173 ff.; 192.

Mit Augustus begann für Mommsen[24] der Abend, für Schwartz[25] der Herbst, für Meyer (Staat 97) das Greisenalter. Endlich sei das ganze System auf Grund seiner inneren Fäulnis unter dem Ansturm der Germanen zusammengebrochen. Die Kultur sank zurück in die Barbarei. Die Hauptschuld maß Meyer, ganz wie Mommsen, politisch dem Imperialismus, ökonomisch dem Kapitalismus, sozial dem Großstadtleben zu. Letztlich scheiterte die antike Kultur an moralischem Versagen. Man widerstand den Verlockungen der Macht und des Wohlstandes nicht. Den darin klassisch ausgeprägten Kreislauf—die Figur übernahm Max Weber 1896[26]—erachtete Meyer als ein allgemeines Modell der Kulturentwicklung, das schon der arabische Historiker Ibn Chaldun um 1400 erkannt habe (GdA I 1, 83). Meyer gewann die Überzeugung, daß die von Hegel und den Hegelianern vertretene Annahme eines steten Fortschreitens der menschlichen Kultur "ein Postulat des Gemütslebens, nicht eine Lehre der Geschichte" sei (GdA I 1, 181 f.).

Wie Mommsen betonte Meyer, "daß die Geschichtsbetrachtung immer von der Gegenwart ausgeht."[27] Geschichte und Gegenwart stehen durch Kausalitäten und Analogien in Verbindung. So wird erst in wechselseitiger Beleuchtung die Geschichte für die Gegenwart bedeutsam und die Gegenwart durch die Geschichte verständlich. Dieser Zusammenhang wurde blitzartig klar mit dem Ausbruch des Ersten Weltkrieges. Er bedeutet für die Geschichtsphilosophie eine Kehre. Zahlreiche, nicht nur deutsche Denker gewannen jetzt die Überzeugung, daß der Niedergang der antiken Kultur sich an uns wiederhole. Zu diesen Autoren gehören nicht nur Toynbee und Spengler, sondern auch Eduard Meyer. 1902 hatte er noch gemeint, der Gleichtakt zwischen Antike und Abendland höre im 16. Jahrhundert auf. Denn das Altertum sei in eine Universalmonarchie gemündet, in der Moderne dagegen behaupteten sich die Staaten nebeneinander und entfalteten in bald friedlichem, bald kriegerischem Wettstreit ihre Kultur (Kl. Schr. I 258). Denselben fundamentalen Unterschied zwischen Antike und Moderne verfocht Friedrich Meinecke[28] noch 1915.

---

[24] Th. Mommsen, Römische Geschichte III 1856/1909, 630.
[25] S.o. Anm. 23, S. 185.
[26] M. Weber, Die sozialen Gründe des Untergangs der antiken Kultur (1896), in: ders., Soziologie, weltgeschichtliche Analysen, Politik, 1968 S. 3. Weber spricht vom "Kreislauf der antiken Kulturentwicklung" infolge ihrer "inneren Selbstauflösung." Auch bei ihm spielen ökonomische Entwicklungsfehler die Hauptrolle.
[27] GdA I 1, 191; *Kl. Schr.* II 585. Meyer behauptet nicht, daß die Vergangenheit nur soweit interessant sei, als sie zur Gestaltung der Gegenwart entscheidend beigetragen habe, sondern meint, daß die Vergangenheit nur soweit erforschbar ist, als sie in der Gegenwart erhaltene Spuren hinterlassen habe; GdA I 1, 188.
[28] F. Meinecke, Nach der Revolution, 1919, 72.

Die optimistische Ansicht von der offenen Zukunft Europas, so konstatiert Meyer, habe der Kriegsausbruch widerlegt.[29] Nun habe der Kampf um die Universalhegemonie ebenfalls Europa erfaßt. Meyer parallelisierte seine Zeit mit der Hannibals. So wie damals die antike Kultur, habe jetzt die moderne ihren Zenit überschritten, gleichgültig, wer siegen werde.[30] Europa hätte seine Weltgeltung verloren und sei nach einer archaischen und einer klassischen Periode in die Spätzeit eingetreten. Der letzte Akt hätte begonnen, unklar war lediglich die Verteilung der Rollen. Am Anfang des Krieges glaubte Meyer noch, Deutschland spiele die Rolle Roms; sollte Deutschland jedoch unterliegen, übernähme Rußland die Führung auf dem Kontinent. Käme es zu einem Erschöpfungsfrieden, würde die Entscheidung bloß vertagt. Lachender Dritter sei heute wie damals letztlich Asien.

Gegen Ende des Krieges gab Meyer den Glauben an Deutschlands römische Rolle auf. Nun wurden Hannibal und Hindenburg verglichen, beide als heroisch gescheiterte Vorkämpfer des Staatenpluralismus gegen die neue Weltmacht (Kl. Schr. II 543). Bei der Gleichsetzung von Deutschland und Karthago, die später Bertolt Brecht übernahm, ließ Meyer sich auch dadurch nicht stören, daß die Karthager keine eigene Kultur besaßen und zudem Semiten waren, die Meyers Neigung nicht genossen (Hannibal 79 f.; GdA I 2, 415 f.).

Die Rolle Roms übertrug Meyer den Vereinigten Staaten. Innen- wie außenpolitisch sah er zwischen Rom und Amerika "die schlagendste Analogie."[31] Dafür gab es Gründe. Innenpolitisch: Völkermischmasch, Pazifismus, Landflucht, Plutokratie, Sektenwesen. Außenpolitisch: Internationaler Friede, homogene Zivilisation. Den alten Vorwurf gegen die Römer, ihre gerechten Kriege seien selbstgerechte Kriege, wendete Meyer gegen Amerika, dessen Politik zugunsten des Weltfriedens und der Völkerverbrüderung pure Heuchelei sei (Amerika 250; 253; 288). So wie die Randmacht Rom kulturell hellenisiert worden war, um dann die Ökumene politisch zu romanisieren, so würde die Randmacht Amerika kulturell europäisiert, um jetzt die Welt zu amerikanisieren. Das war für Meyer das Ende der europäischen Kultur. Kulturelle Leistungen seien nur von freien Völkern zu erwarten, die mal friedlich, mal kriegerisch

---

[29] Daß Meyer schon sehr früh pessimistischen Anwandlungen unterlag, zeigt der von Hoffmann in diesem Bande publizierte Auszug aus dem Vortrag von 1874.

[30] Diese Parallelisierung findet sich bereits in dem 1902 verfaßten, später "an einigen Stellen" erweiteren Artikel über den >Gang der Alten Geschichte<, *Kl. Schr.* I 214; 256; II 537; 576; England 200 ff. Zu Meyers Pessimismus im Weltkrieg vgl. Meinecke (o. Anm. 11) S. 76 von 1915.

[31] Nordamerika 37; Weltgeschichte 71; 103; Caesar 5; Heimstätten 50; Hellenismus 73.

miteinander konkurrierten, nicht bei Satelliten von Weltmächten, die—
damals Rom, heute Amerika und Rußland—nie aus der Halbbarbarei
herausgekommen seien. Die Schuld am Ende der Antike treffe Rom, die
Schuld am Ende Europas treffe England beziehungsweise Amerika.[32]
Trotzdem wäre Roms Aufstieg ebensowenig zu verhindern gewesen, wie
der Aufstieg Amerikas.[33] Den Übergang zur Weltmacht sah Meyer bei
den Römern im Griff nach Sizilien während des Ersten Punischen
Krieges 264, bei den Amerikanern im Griff nach Kuba und den Philippinen 1898 (Hannibal 70). Eine letzte Chance hätten die europäischen
Mächte vielleicht dann gehabt, wenn sie im amerikanischen Sezessions-
krieg die Südstaaten unterstützt und damit eine Teilung herbeigeführt
hätten (Kl. Schr. I 256).

Die römische Rolle der Angloamerikaner ist nach dem Ersten Weltkrieg mehrfach, unter anderem durch Meyers Schüler Ulrich
Kahrstedt[34] und durch Meyers Kollegen Friedrich Meinecke hervorgehoben worden. Meinecke sah, analog zur Pax Romana, eine Pax Anglo-
saxonica kommen, deren Macht wirtschaftlicher Natur war. Unter der
"Glasglocke der angelsächsischen Weltherrschaft" könnten die Nationalstaaten Europas vielleicht in einer "Scheinautonomie" fortbestehen, so
wie die Griechenstädte im Römerreich. Gewiß aber erwarte uns eine "allgemeine Mischmaschkultur unter angelsächsischen Vorzeichen," vor der
es Meinecke schauderte. Mit der "Autonomie der Staaten und Nationen
ist es, weltgeschichtlich gesehen, nun doch einmal vorbei."[35] Meinecke
hegte dieselben Befürchtungen wie Meyer (Weltgeschichte 23) gegenüber
der kulturellen "Einförmigkeit eines entnationalisierten Weltreichs."

Preußen-Deutschland parallelisierte Meinecke nicht, wie Meyer, mit
Karthago, sondern wie Kahrstedt mit Makedonien-Griechenland, fraglos
eine ergiebigere Analogie. Sie entspricht der schon im 16. Jahrhundert
aufkeimenden Wahlverwandtschaft zwischen Deutschen und Griechen,
die dann von Winckelmann und Herder, von Schiller, Hölderlin und
Wilhelm von Humboldt angenommen wurde. Für Meinecke hat das
Ende der griechischen Freiheit 168 v. Chr. bei Pydna den Niedergang der

---

[32] England 204; 212; Weltgeschichte 52; Hellenismus 73; *Kl. Schr.* I S. V.

[33] Unklar ist bei Meyer das Verhältnis zwischen Notwendigkeit und Moral. Auf der
einen Seite betrachtet er die Entwicklung zur Großraumordnung als notwendig, da die
Kleinstaaten sich als politisch unfähig erwiesen hätten. Er wirft sogar den Römern vor,
diese Politik nicht hinreichend energisch verfolgt zu haben, die er gleichwohl kriminali-
siert.

[34] U. Kahrstedt, Pax Americana 1920. Unabhängig von der antiken Parallele erörtert
das Bewußtsein vom Niedergang Europas zwischen den Flankenmächten: G. Barraclough,
Europa, Amerika und Rußland in Vorstellung und Denken des 19. Jahrhunderts, Hist.
Zeitschrift 203, 1966 S. 280 ff.

[35] Meinecke (s. Anm. 28) S. 98 ff.

antiken Kultur besiegelt. "Nur der Geist," ruft Meinecke seinen Lesern zu, "der kein unentrinnbares Fatum über sich anerkennt, kann dieses Fatum unwirksam machen."[36]

So wenig wie Meinecke war Meyer ein Fatalist. Das zeigt sich schon in seinen scharfen Moralurteilen. Anders als später Spengler sah Meyer im Kulturkreislauf bloß eine Erfahrungstatsache, kein "blindwirkendes Naturgesetz."[37] Regenerationen hielt er 1902 (Theorie 26 f.) noch für möglich. Die Parallelität zwischen Antike und Moderne verstand er wie Geschichte überhaupt als Folge von drei Faktoren: von verantwortlichen Entscheidungen Einzelner, von zeitbestimmenden Ideen und von unberechenbaren Zufällen (Kl. Schr. II 576). Meyer glaubte, Geschichte liefere nicht nur Bausteine für die Erkenntnis der Welt, sondern auch Werkzeuge zu ihrer Gestaltung, und hat darum im Weltkrieg publizistisch zu wirken versucht.[38] Wilamowitz nannte Meyer 1925 einen der "tapfersten Kämpfer für die Ehre unseres Vaterlandes."[39]

Zutiefst überzeugt von Deutschlands Recht auf einen "Platz an der Sonne," sah Meyer (Weltgeschichte 13 f.) ganz wie Meinecke in Deutschland das letzte Bollwerk des Nationalismus und der Völkervielfalt gegenüber dem Internationalismus der Angloamerikaner, die allen Völkern ihre Demokratie, ihren Kapitalismus, ihre Zivilisation aufzwingen wollten. Annexionen schienen ihm zeitweilig zur außenpolitischen Defensive nötig, ohne daß er ihren innenpolitisch korrumpierenden Charakter verkannt hätte. Das lehrte ihn Rom. In seinen patriotischen Schriften hat

---

[36] a.O. 78 ff.; 106. Die Parallelisierung mit dem späten Griechenland zog auch der von Meyers Gegner G.F. Nicolai (Die Biologie des Krieges 1919, 13) und Albert Einstein im Oktober 1914 verfaßte >Aufruf an die Europäer<. Dort wird befürchtet, daß "Europa infolge seiner mangelhaften Gesamtorganisation dasselbe tragische Geschick erleide, wie einst Griechenland."

[37] GdA I 1, 84. Meyer verband mit dem Begriff des Naturgesetzes die Vorstellung einer Notwendigkeit im Geschehen, die zwar das Leben von Pflanzen und Tieren, nicht aber das Handeln des Menschen regiere. Eine solch strikte Fassung des Gesetzesbegriffs macht diesen indes ebenfalls für die Naturwissenschaften unbrauchbar, da deren "Gesetze" auch nur Ereignisfolgeregeln sind, die auf Erfahrung beruhen. Insofern besteht zwischen den Gesetzen, die Meyer für die Geschichte ablehnt, und den Entwicklungstendenzen bzw. Kreislaufmodellen, die er anwendet, nur ein gradueller Unterschied. Daneben hat er freilich bisweilen die unbedingte Geltung von Gesetzen in der Geschichte—wenn auch unbegründet—behauptet, so seine These, daß "jede Idee, die sich verwirklicht, in ihr Gegenteil umschlägt" (GdA I 1 § 103 S. 182). Zwei Beispiele dafür:

1. Nachdem die griechische Freiheit den Individualismus ermöglicht hat, zerstört das höchste Individuum, der Gottkönig Alexander, wiederum die Freiheit.

2. Nachdem die griechisch-okzidentale Kultur in Alexanders Siegeszug ihre Überlegenheit gegenüber dem Orient bewiesen hat, erliegt sie selbst der inneren Orientalisierung (Kl. Schr. I 297 f.).

[38] Hierzu Sösemann in diesem Bande S. 446 ff.

[39] U.v. Wilamowitz-Moellendorff, Eduard Meyer, Süddeutsche Monatshefte 22, Januar 1925, S. 55 ff.

Meyer sich zu Ausfällen gegen die Westmächte hinreißen lassen, die der alliierten Greuelpropaganda gegen die deutschen "Hunnen" nicht nachstehen.[40] Als die Entente 1919 die Auslieferung und Aburteilung des Kaisers und der sogenannten Kriegsverbrecher verlangte, ging über Deutschlands Hochschulen ein Sturm der Entrüstung. Meyer gab damals bekannt, er habe die Ehrendoktordiplome von Oxford, Liverpool, St. Andrews, Chicago und Harvard zerrissen (Kl. Schr. I S. VI). Durch den Frieden von Versailles habe Amerika eine "unübersehbare Folge weiterer vernichtender Kriege" programmiert und die Kultur Europas "rettungslos dem Untergang überantwortet" (Amerika 288 f.). Noch 1929 schrieb er an Spengler, Amerika sei ihm "mit seiner inneren Verlogenheit und salbungsvollen Überhebung" der "widerwärtigste unserer Feinde."[41]

Mit Weimar fand sich Meyer nur schwer ab. Sein Einwand gegen die parlamentarische Demokratie war, daß sie "dem einzelnen die Verantwortung abnimmt und sie durch Uniformierung und Reglementierung zu ersetzen sucht."[42] Der Parlamentarismus sei die "elendste aller Staatsverfassungen," aber die amerikanische Präsidialdemokratie imponierte Meyer (Amerika S. VII). 1924 fürchtete er, daß ein Volk, das der Demokratie "einmal verfallen ist, davon nicht wieder loskommt."[43] Immerhin konstatierte Meyer schon in seiner Rektoratsrede 1919, "daß eine gefallene Monarchie sich nicht wieder aufrichten läßt. Das deutsche Kaiserreich sei "nicht, wie wir geglaubt haben, ein Abschluß, sondern nur ein Durchgangspunkt der Entwicklung gewesen" (Kl. Schr. II 584). Nur scheinbar habe Deutschland mit der Demokratie die Staatsform der Feinde angenommen. In Wahrheit lebe selbst in der deutschen Sozialdemokratie ein Pflichtbewußtsein und ein Idealismus, der mit dem angelsächsischen Individualismus und dem französischen Materialismus nichts zu tun habe (a.O. 557 ff.). In ihrem Kampf gegen die "furchtbare Gestalt des seelenlosen, rein mechanischen Kapitalismus" hätte die Sozialdemokratie allerdings versagt—so Meyer in seinem Brief an Spengler vom 25.VI.1922,[44] in dem er den Mord an Rathenau beklagte. Meyer, der in seiner Jugend Sympathie für den Sozialismus erkennen ließ,[45] trat 1924 für eine Bodenreform ein. Meyers innenpolitische Haltung entspricht Spenglers Auffassung von "Preußentum und Sozialismus."

---

[40] Dazu: A.J. Toynbee, The German Terror in Belgium 1917; ders., The German Terror in France 1917 (das Exemplar dieser Kampfschrift in der Universitätsbibliothek der FU Berlin trägt den Stiftungsvermerk der World Brotherhood).
[41] O. Spengler, Briefe 1913–1936, hg. v. A.M. Koktanek, 1963, S. 533.
[42] Vossische Zeitung 19.IX.1915.
[43] 7.VI.1924 an Spengler, s.o. Anm. 41, S. 327 ff.
[44] S.o. Anm. 41, S. 202 ff.
[45] So im Brief vom 26.I.1872. Hoffmann in diesem Bande S. 208 ff.

1925 war Meyer (Rußland 101 ff.) zusammen mit Max Planck und Heinrich Lüders Ehrengast der Sowjetunion zur 200-Jahrfeier der russischen Akademie der Wissenschaften in Leningrad und Moskau. Obwohl Meyer überzeugt war, daß "das russische Reich nicht in den Kreis der europäischen Kultur gehört" (Weltgeschichte 10), bewunderte er das neue Rußland. Der Zarismus sei unheilbar verrottet gewesen, die Revolution habe kommen müssen, und Lenin sei der größte Staatsmann seit Bismarck gewesen. Den Spekulationen auf einen Zusammenbruch des kommunistischen Regimes trat er entgegen. Rußland sei innerlich gefestigt und könne nicht erobert werden. Seine Macht überrage nicht nur die europäischen Staaten. Meyer lehnte den Marxismus ab, er prophezeite in der NÖSPL Glasnost, eine allmähliche Abkehr von Dirigismus und Dogmatismus und eine Rückwendung zur bürgerlichen Normalität. Ohne Geld, ohne Eigentum, ohne Polizei könne ein Staat nicht bestehen. Eine außenpolitische Anlehnung Deutschlands an Rußland schien Meyer im Sinne Bismarcks sympathisch, da Rußland sich Deutschland gegenüber kulturell offen zeige. Deutsch sei die einzige für alle Studenten der Sowjetunion obligate Fremdsprache. Über die Hälfte der zur Feier delegierten Gelehrten war aus Deutschland gekommen, nur ein einziger aus Amerika.

Meyer steht in der Tradition der national-konservativen Sympathie für Rußland, die in der Ablehnung Napoleons wurzelt. Schon Fichte[46] stellte 1807 die "russische Kraft" den "ein wenig entnervten europäischen Nationen" gegenüber. Das Fazit zog Meyer in einem Brief vom 1.X.1925 an Spengler:[47] Rußland böte Deutschland "gewaltige Aussichten sowohl auf wirtschaftlichem Gebiet wie auf dem der internationalen Politik." Auf der "Russischen Historikerwoche" 1928 in Berlin hielt Meyer die Festrede beim Empfang der Deutschen Gesellschaft zum Studium Osteuropas.[48] In seinen letzten Jahren löste sich Meyer von der Untergangsstimmung der Nachkriegsjahre. 1926 betonte er, "daß zu pessimistischer Auffassung nicht der mindeste Grund vorliegt." Der "deutsche Idealismus" werde sich behaupten.[49] 1930 ist Meyer gestorben. Nun zum dritten Punkt, zu Spengler!

3. Spengler ist 1880 in Blankenburg am Harz geboren. In seinem Elternhaus trafen eine artistische und eine kleinbürgerliche Tradition

---

[46] J.G. Fichte, Machiavell, 1807/1918, 23.

[47] S.o. Anm. 41, S. 417 ff.

[48] H. Jonas, Die russische Historikerwoche und die Ausstellung "Die Geschichtswissenschaft in Sowjetrußland." Osteuropa 3, 1927/28, S. 751 ff.; 762.

[49] So Meyer in seiner Antwort auf die durch Karl Alexander von Müller in den Süddeutschen Monatsheften (Nr. 24, Dez. 1926, S. 169 ff., S. 195 f.) publizierte Frage über die > Deutsche Zukunft <. Meyer betonte die Leistungen der Notgemeinschaft und den Leistungswillen der jüngeren deutschen Gelehrten.

aufeinander. Spenglers Vater war Postsekretär, seine Mutter die Tochter eines Solotänzers und Ballettmeisters, Enkelin einer Berliner Jüdin. Als Schüler erfand Spengler Kontinente, Völker und Staaten, konstruierte deren Verfassung, Religion und Geschichte über Jahrtausende.[50] Spengler studierte Biologie und Mathematik und promovierte in Philosophie über Heraklit. 1908 wurde er Oberlehrer in Hamburg, seit 1911 wohnte er in München und lebte von seiner mütterlichen Erbschaft, später auch von seinen literarischen Einkünften. Im Weltkrieg schrieb er den ersten Band seines Hauptwerkes > Der Untergang des Abendlandes <. Am 11. Mai 1918 schickte er ein Exemplar an Rathenau, der am 15. respektvoll antwortete. 1922 erschien der zweite Band. "Das gottlose Werk einer gottlosen Zeit" schrieb die > Frankfurter Zeitung <.[51]

Spengler eröffnete sein Buch, das er eine "Formenlehre" der Weltgeschichte nannte, mit dem Satz: "In diesem Buche wird zum ersten Male der Versuch gemacht, Geschichte vorauszubestimmen. Es handelt sich darum, das Schicksal einer Kultur, und zwar der einzigen, die heute auf diesem Planeten in Vollendung begriffen ist, der westeuropäisch-amerikanischen, in den noch nicht abgelaufenen Stadien zu verfolgen." Die Möglichkeit hierzu fand Spengler in der Zyklusgestalt der Hochkulturen. Er bestritt nicht nur wie Meyer den Fortschritt, sondern auch die Einheit der Weltgeschichte. Die von Meyer zwischen griechisch-römischer und romanisch-germanischer Geschichte angenommene Analogie weitete Spengler aus auf die Geschichte von insgesamt acht selbständigen Hochkulturen, die sich ohne nennenswerten äußeren Einfluß nach einem inneren Gesetz aus einem primitiven Frühstadium zu einem kulturellen Höhepunkt erhoben hätten, um von dort unweigerlich in eine zivilisatorische Spätphase herabzusinken. Der Kreislauf vollende sich in etwa tausend Jahren. Wie lange die Spätzeit dauere, sei unberechenbar und unerheblich. Während Meyer (Mormonen 12) die Analogie als heuristisches Instrument betrachtete, um die Besonderheiten der einzelnen Erscheinungen zu ermitteln, diente sie Spengler dazu, eine Schema zu entwickeln, in das sich alles einordnen ließ. Spengler betrachtet die Kulturen als höhere Organismen, die einem strengen Determinismus gehorchen. Die abendländische Kultur befinde sich in ihrer alexandrinischen Schlußperiode und verbreite ihre Zivilisation über die Welt wie einst der Hellenismus.

Spenglers Bild der Zukunft ähnelt demjenigen Meyers. Die Gegenwart verlegte Spengler allerdings nicht mit Meyer in die Zeit von Cannae 216

---

[50] A.M. Koktanek (ed.), Oswald Spengler in seiner Zeit, 1968, 29 ff.
[51] S.o. Anm. 41, S. 101 f.; P. Reusch (ed.), Oswald Spengler zum Gedenken, 1937, 91.

v. Chr. oder mit Meinecke in die Zeit von Pydna 168 oder mit Kahrstedt in die Zeit nach Kynoskephalai 197 v. Chr., in der es um die Entscheidung zwischen Staatenpluralismus und Hegemonialprinzip ging, sondern in die Periode von Actium 31 v. Chr., als nur noch zur Debatte stand, welcher Typ von Weltstaat gewänne. So wie die späte römische Republik zwischen Optimaten und Popularen zerrieben wurde, so stünde Europa die Auseinandersetzung zwischen einem liberal-demokratisch verbrämten Kapitalismus und dem preußisch-sozialistischen Militarismus bevor. Spenglers Sympathie gehörte letzterem. Anders als Meyer und Meinecke glaubte er, daß die Westeuropäer zu dekadent seien, um eine römische Rolle spielen zu können. Sie erhoffte er für die siegreichen Deutschen, "die letzte Nation des Abendlandes."[52] Die Schrift >Preußentum und Sozialismus< sollte zunächst >Römer und Preußen< heißen, wie ein Brief vom 1.IX.1918 bezeugt.[53]

Freilich fürchtete Spengler schon am 25.X.1914, mit Deutschlands Sieg werde "ein vollkommen seelenloser Amerikanismus zur Herrschaft gelangen."[54] Deutschland als Träger des Amerikanismus? Deutschlands Gleichsetzung mit Rom durch Spengler oder auch mit Karthago durch Meyer zeigt weniger Entsprechungen als die mit Makedonien-Griechenland durch Meinecke und Kahrstedt. Einig war man sich im Ruf nach dem Retter. "Nur eine ganz starke diktatorische Gewalt auf demokratischer Basis und mit sozialistischer Tendenz" könne Deutschland noch retten, schrieb Meinecke 1919.[55] Und bei Spengler heißt es 1921:[56] "Zu einem Goethe werden wir Deutschen es nicht wieder bringen, aber zu einem Cäsar."

Spengler bemühte sich bis 1925 um politischen Einfluß. Er suchte ohne Erfolg Kontakt zu Militärs wie Seeckt und Ludendorff, mit Erfolg Verbindung zu Männern der Wirtschaft, zu Albert Vögler und Paul Reusch, dem Vorstandsvorsitzenden der Gutehoffnungshütte. Wolfgang Kapp hatte Reusch 1920 zum Wirtschaftsminister,[57] möglicherweise auch Eduard Meyer als Mitglied seiner Revolutionsregierung ausersehen.[58] Spengler verehrte Reusch eine Totenmaske Napoleons.[59] Er träumte

---

[52] O. Spengler, Der Untergang des Abendlandes. Umrisse einer Morphologie der Weltgeschichte, II 1923, 129.
[53] S.o. Anm. 41, S. 108.
[54] S.o. Anm. 41, S. 29.
[55] S.o. Anm. 28, S. 104.
[56] O. Spengler, Reden und Aufsätze, 1938, 79.
[57] B. Herzog, Die Freundschaft zwischen Oswald Spengler und Paul Reusch, In: A.M. Koktanek (ed.), Spengler-Studien, Festgabe für Manfred Schröter, 1965, S. 77 ff., 82.
[58] E.J. Gumbel, Vier Jahre politischer Mord, 1922, 99.
[59] S.o. Anm. 57, S. 85.

von einem "Direktorium", einer "nationalen Loge" und hoffte auf einen deutschen Mussolini.[60]

Gegenüber Hitler empfand Spengler wenig Sympathie, dennoch hat er ihn 1932 *faute de mieux* gewählt. Am 25. Juli 1933 kam es in Bayreuth zu einem von Spengler ersehnten Gespräch zwischen beiden, das jedoch umschlug in einen Monolog des Führers über die Führungslosigkeit der evangelischen Kirche.[61] Angebote zur Propagandaarbeit durch Goebbels lehnte Spengler ab, ebenso wie die ihm im gleichen Jahre angetragenen Lehrstühle im Leipziger Lamprecht-Institut und an der Marburger Philipps-Universität.[62]

Die Abrechnung des Nationalsozialismus mit Spengler vollzog der Berliner Philosophieprofessor Alfred Baeumler im November 1933. Baeumlers Vortrag im Schinkelsaal der Deutschen Hochschule für Politik in Berlin entlarvte Spengler als Aristokraten und Verächter der Arbeiterschaft, als einen "umgekehrten Marxisten," dessen extremer Individualismus und undeutscher Ästhetizismus keinen Sinn für Volk und Rasse habe. Spenglers übernationaler Cäsarismus sei mit dem nationalen Führertum Hitlers unvereinbar. Punkt für Punkt widerspreche Spenglers Theorie dem Nationalsozialismus, der nach dem Zeitalter des Imperialismus ein Zeitalter der "Volkskonzentration" heraufführe. Spengler gehöre in die "Rumpelkammer der Geistesgeschichte." Baeumlers Vortrag wurde in der >Deutschen Allgemeinen Zeitung< vom 29.XI.1933 und im >Völkischen Beobachter< vom 1.XII.1933 referiert, blieb aber anscheinend ungedruckt. Der Autor hat sich 1965 nochmals über Spengler geäußert,[63] nun in etwas anderem Sinne kritisch, ohne seinen Vortrag von 1933 zu erwähnen.

Spengler ignorierte die innerdeutschen Vorgänge, er blickte über Europas Grenzen hinaus. Im Januar 1936, im Jahr seines Todes, publizierte eine amerikanische Zeitung, >Hearst's International Cosmopolitan<, Spenglers politisches Testament.[64] Es ist seine als Kabeltele-

---

60 Koktanek (s.o. Anm. 57), S. 221; 331 f. Spengler sandte Mussolini seine Schriften, die jener mehrfach zitierte: B. Mussolini, Opera omnia XXVI 122 f. (zu dem Buch Spenglers >Jahre der Entscheidung< in der Zeitung >Popolo d'Italia< 15. Dez. 1933); XXIX 426; XXXII 188. 1928 erschien die Arbeit von Richard Korherr über den Geburtenrückgang (1927) mit Vorworten von Spengler und Mussolini in der >Libreria del Littorio< Rom, auf italienisch (freundlicher Hinweis von L. Canfora). Vgl. Spengler (s.o. Anm. 56). S. 135 ff.; ders. (s.o. Anm. 41), S. 559.

61 Koktanek (s.o. Anm. 50), S. 439 f. Wenn H.R. Trevor-Roper, Hitlers letzte Tage, 1985, S. 58 zutreffend berichtet, warnte Spengler Hitler vor seiner "Prätorianergarde" und betrachtete ihn somit als deutschen Caesar.

62 Koktanek (s.o. Anm. 50), S. 452.

63 Koktanek (s.o. Anm. 60), S. 99 ff.

64 Spengler (s.o. Anm. 56), S. 292 f.

gramm eingegangene Antwort auf die von der Zeitung erhobene Umfrage: >Ist Weltfriede möglich?< Darin schrieb Spengler, wenn die weißen Völker des Krieges müde sein sollten, "dann würde die Welt das Opfer der Farbigen sein, wie das römische Reich den Germanen zufiel."

Als Vormacht der Farbigen betrachtete Spengler stets Asien und Rußland. Die petrinische und die marxistische Europäisierung erschienen ihm oberflächlich, die Verlegung der Hauptstadt von Petersburg nach Moskau sei die Rückwendung nach Asien. "Das Russentum ist das Versprechen einer kommenden Kultur, während die Abendschatten über dem Westen länger und länger werden."[65] "Wir sind nicht mehr der führende Staat in Mitteleuropa, sondern der Grenzstaat gegen Asien."[66] All das lag nicht auf Hitlers Linie. Erst am 19.III.1945 kam Hitler zu der Einsicht, daß die Zukunft nicht den Deutschen, sondern den Slawen gehöre, dem "stärkeren Ostvolk."[67] Spengler ist 1936, als unverbesserlicher Schwarzseher von der Partei verfemt, in seiner Münchener Wohnung gestorben. Soweit Spengler, nun zum vierten Punkt, zu den Beziehungen zwischen ihm und Meyer!

4. Spengler hat den ersten Band seines "Untergangs" an zahlreiche Männer in Wirtschaft und Gesellschaft verschickt, unter anderem an Meyer. Dieser hat zunächst jedoch nicht reagiert. Erst als Spengler auch den zweiten Band sandte, antwortete Meyer am 25. Juni 1922. Trotz "schärfstem Widerspruch" gegen die "Halbwahrheiten" der Parallelen, insbesondere gegen Spenglers Idee einer (römisch-)arabischen Kultur in der Spätantike, stimmte Meyer im Blick auf die Gegenwart zu.[68] Es entwickelte sich eine Korrespondenz; am 25. März 1923 besuchte Spengler Meyer in Groß-Lichterfelde. Weitere Besuche folgten. Daraus entstand eine Freundschaft, die angesichts der unterschiedlichen Charaktere nicht leicht zu verstehen ist. Meyer, der positivistische, ja pedantische Professor, der stets dem Historismus verpflichtet blieb—Spengler, der dilettierende, systematisierende Prophet mit seinem Kasernenhofkommandoton ...

1924 erschien zum Historikertag—wieder in Frankfurt—eine Sondernummer (45) der >Deutschen Literaturzeitung<, in der sich Meyer (S. 1759 ff.) mit Spengler auseinandersetzte. Während die Fachwelt die "Spenglerei" überwiegend ablehnte, war Meyer im Prinzip einverstan-

---

[65] Ders., Preußentum und Sozialismus, 1924, 93. Zu Spenglers Verhältnis gegenüber Rußland: G.L. Ulmen in: P. Ch. Ludz (Hg.), Spengler heute, 1980, S. 123–173, und X. Werner (Hg.), Der Briefwechsel zwischen Oswald Spengler und Wolfgang E. Groeger 1987.

[66] Ders., Politische Schriften, 1932, S. VIII.

[67] A. Speer, Erinnerungen, 1969, 446.

[68] S.o. Anm. 41, S. 202 ff.

den. Die abendländische Kultur zeige die gleichen Rhythmen wie die Antike und lasse das gleiche Ende erwarten. Der Untergang Roms sei seit dem 19. Jahrhundert ein Menetekel auch für uns. Die kulturellen Interessen seien den materiellen gewichen. Europas große Leistungen in Kunst und Musik, in Literatur und Philosophie lägen unwiderruflich in der Vergangenheit, alle wirtschaftlichen und technischen Fortschritte böten dafür keinen Ersatz. Im Weltkrieg hätten die Völker Europas ihre Führungsrolle verspielt und seien in ihr zivilisatorisches Endstadium eingetreten. Das könne nun Jahrhunderte so weitergehen, bliebe aber ein Leben der Kultur- und Geschichtslosigkeit. Schon 1923 hatte Meyer bei seinem Vortrag in Upsala über den ''Niedergang des Hellenismus in Asien'' (Hellenismus 61) Spenglers Begriff der Amerikanisierung für die normale Endphase einer Kultur übernommen.

Meyers Kritik an Spengler betraf zunächst die angebliche Eigenständigkeit der Hochkulturen. Diese seien in Wahrheit keine geschlossenen, sondern durchlässige Systeme von vielfältiger Wechselwirkung. Ohne den Einfluß des Orients wäre die griechische Kultur nicht entstanden,[69] ohne das antike und christliche Erbe wäre auch die faustische Kultur nicht zu denken. Allzu spekulativ erschien Meyer Spenglers Quasibiologismus und die Annahme von Kulturseelen, die den kulturellen Erscheinungen vorausgingen. Meyer erklärte die innere Einheit der antiken, arabischen und der okzidentalen Kultur aus Angleichungsprozessen innerhalb der jeweiligen Kulturkreise (SB Berlin 1924, 156). Auch Spenglers Fatalismus fand Meyers Beifall nicht. Er glaubte an eine individuelle Handlungsfreiheit der Völker, die zwar selbst Ergebnisse historischer Entwicklung seien, damit aber wiederum zu Triebkräften weiterer historischer Entwicklung würden (Theorie 31). Die Priorität der Kultur bei Spengler ersetzte Meyer durch die Priorität der Staaten. Waren die Völker bei Spengler bloß mehr oder weniger zufällige Gewächse auf der sie tragenden Kultur, so sah Meyer umgekehrt in den freien, staatlich verfaßten Völkern den Wurzelboden kultureller Leistung (Weltgeschichte 7). Gleichwohl schrieb er am 19.IX.1915 in der Vossischen Zeitung: ''Das höchste Erzeugnis der geschichtlichen Entwicklung ist das, was wir Kultur nennen.''

Spengler hat diese Kritik hingenommen (Koktanek 1968, 360). Er ließ sich darüber hinaus von Meyer für ein Museumsprojekt gewinnen—es ging um die Turfan-Funde und den Hellenismus in Mittelasien.[70] Der Plan zerschlug sich trotz Spenglers Bereitschaft, aber die Verbindung blieb bestehen. Meyer nahm Spengler als Wissenschaftler ernst. Er

---

[69] Dies ist das Leitmotiv in Meyers >Geschichte des Altertums.<
[70] S.o. Anm. 41, S. 327.

warnte ihn vor historischen Phantasten (Briefe 501; 562) und widersprach seinen abwegigen Ideen mit großer Nachsicht, so der Vorstellung, daß die minoische Kultur auf Kreta ihre Anregungen aus Spanien empfangen habe.[71]

Meyers Einfluß auf Spenglers Konzeption ist bisher nicht erkannt. Das liegt nicht zuletzt an Spenglers Zitierweise. Während er über die Herkunft seines Stoffes bereitwillig Auskunft gab, hat er die Ursprünge seiner Gedanken verheimlicht. Spengler nennt als seine Inspiratoren nur Goethe und Nietzsche. Von Goethe habe er die Methode, die Erscheinungen mit Hilfe einer "exakten sinnlichen Phantasie" zu erfassen, Nietzsche verdanke er die Fragestellungen, insbesondere meint er wohl den Begriff Kultur als "Einheit des künstlerischen Stiles in allen Lebensäußerungen eines Volkes"[72] und das Gespür für *décadence*. In der Hochschätzung Goethes stimmt Spengler mit Meyer überein, nicht jedoch im Urteil über Nietzsche, den Meyer (Weltgeschichte 36 f.) den "undeutschesten" aller Philosophen nannte.

Eduard Spranger[73] und Hans Joachim Schoeps[74] haben gezeigt, daß wichtigere Voraussetzungen für Spenglers Lehre bei Herder, Vollgraff und Lasaulx liegen, die Spengler nicht anführt. Ob er sie überhaupt gelesen hat, wissen wir nicht. Als nächstliegender Vermittler ist Eduard Meyer zu vermuten, dessen Kreislaufmodell demjenigen Spenglers so weitgehend entspricht, daß Spenglers Abhängigkeit von Meyer in der Konzeption in die Augen springt.[75] Das ist um so wahrscheinlicher, als Spengler seine Abhängigkeit im Material selbst ausgiebig dokumentiert. Unter den Autoren, die Spengler zitiert, steht Meyer mit großem Abstand an der Spitze. Er hat nicht nur Stoff, sondern auch Ideen geliefert. Offener urteilte Arnold Toynbee, er räumte ein, daß Meyers Schrift über den >Gang der Alten Geschichte< von 1902 seiner Konzeption von geschlossenen Kulturen zugrundeliege. Toynbees Übereinstimmungen mit Spengler beruhen wesentlich auf der Abhängigkeit beider von Meyer.[76]

---

[71] Spengler, Briefe (s.o. Anm. 41) 557 ff. Dazu noch eine mit Bleistift geschriebene Postkarte (jetzt im Meyer-Nachlaß der Staatsbibliothek in Berlin-West) vom 18.IV.1928 aus Sevilla an Meyer: "Ihnen und Ihrer Frau Gemahlin die besten Grüße aus dem schönen Andalusien (von wo die minoische Kultur stammt). Darf man zur Vollendung von GdA II schon gratulieren? Oswald Spengler." Auf der Bildseite, die den Alcazar darstellt: "Grundriß mit Hof und Durchblicken wie in Knossos." Eine zweite Karte (ebenda) vom 2.X.29 aus Ballenstedt kündigt Spenglers Besuch bei Meyer an.

[72] Nietzsche (s.o. Anm. 2) I 140.

[73] E. Spranger, Die Kulturzyklentheorie und das Problem des Kulturverfalls. In: ders., Gesammelte Schriften V, 1969, S. 1 ff.

[74] H.J. Schoeps, Vorläufer Spenglers, 1953.

[75] Welchen Anregungen wiederum Meyer das Kreislaufmodell verdankt, ist ebenso unklar. Auch er nennt seine Inspiratoren nicht.

[76] Meyer, *Kl. Schr.* I 1924, 213 ff.; A.J. Toynbee, A Study of History X 1954, S. 233;

Meyers Tod 1930 hat Spengler tief getroffen. Er verehrte in ihm eine Vatergestalt. Meyer sei der einzige, der ihn ganz begriffen habe. Soweit zum Verhältnis zwischen Meyer und Spengler, und nun zum fünften und letzten Punkt, dem Problem der Prognose!

5. Bei Novalis[77] lesen wir den Satz: "Echt historischer Sinn ist der prophetische Visionssinn, erklärbar aus dem tiefen unendlichen Zusammenhange der ganzen Welt." Für Novalis schließt die Geschichte den Blick auf die Zukunft ein. Demgegenüber heißt es bei Schelling:[78] "Der Mensch hat nur deswegen Geschichte, weil, was er tun wird, sich nach keiner Theorie zum Voraus berechnen läßt." Für Schelling schließt die Geschichte den Blick auf die Zukunft aus.

Spengler vertrat die Auffassung von Novalis, Meyer hielt es mit Schelling. Mehrfach hat Meyer (Kl. Schr. I 35; II 538) die prognostische Kompetenz des Historikers ebenso energisch bestritten, wie Spengler dieselbe behauptet hat. Wenn Meyer trotzdem Prognosen gestellt hat und sich dabei von Spengler weder in der Methode (der Analogie) noch im Resultat (der Dekadenz) unterschied, fragt sich, wieso er davor zurückschreckte, sich zu dem zu bekennen, was er tat.

Der Grund liegt im herkömmlichen Wissenschaftsverständnis des Historikers. Für ihn ist nur das Wirkliche erforschbar. Die Kunst des Möglichen bleibt Sache der Politik. Die Historiker unterscheiden sich von den Politikern unter anderem darin, daß sie in die Vergangenheit, nach hinten blicken, nicht nach vorne, nicht in die Zukunft. Ihr Wahlspruch lautet: "Lehrst du wen historisch sehen, mußt du ihm den Kopf verdrehen."

Auf die Gefahr hin, die Gebote meiner Zunft zu verletzen, werde ich nun den Gegensatz zwischen erforschbarer Vergangenheit und unergründbarer Zukunft ein wenig abschwächen. Natürlich stimmt die Behauptung, daß wir nicht in die Zukunft vorausblicken können. Aber die entsprechende Annahme, daß uns die Vergangenheit offen stehe, ist mindestens irreführend.

Ich sehe hierbei ab von unserer jeweils eigenen Lebensgeschichte. Über das, was wir selbst erfahren haben, können wir verläßliche Aussagen machen, jedenfalls sofern wir unserer Erinnerung trauen dürfen. Ähnliches gilt aber auch für unsere eigene Zukunft. Über das, was wir tun werden, können wir Versprechungen abgeben. Das wußte schon Kant,[79]

---

ders., Experiences 1969, 109: *Eduard Meyer combined a mastery of Greek and Latin sources for the pre-modern history of the western end of the Oikoumene with some first-hand knowledge of the Sumerian, Akkadian and Egyptian languages and scripts. He pushed his mental horizon as far eastward as the Bactrian Greeks pushed their conquests in India.*

[77] S.o. Anm. 13, S. 417.

[78] F.W. Schelling, System des tranzendentalen Idealismus, 1800, 416.

[79] S.o. Anm. 1, I 631.

als 1797 er schrieb, eine Geschichte a priori sei dann möglich, "wenn der Wahrsager die Begebenheiten selber macht."

Soweit unser Handeln Einfluß auf das hat, was überhaupt geschieht, ist es von der allgemeinen Zukunft nicht sauber abzugrenzen. Das Maß für diesen Einfluß ist unsere Macht, und sie ist zugleich das Maß für unser Vermögen, Aussagen über die allgemeine Zukunft in eigener Verantwortung zu machen. Zu den Mitteln der Zukunftsgestaltung gehört die Zukunftsvorhersage. Die Soziologen[80] sprechen von *self fulfilling prophecy* und von *self destroying prophecy*. Wenn die Aussage über einen Sachverhalt diesen beeinflußt, dann wird es schwierig, ihre Richtigkeit festzustellen. Denn dazu müßte man beantworten, ob das vorausgesagte Ereignis auch dann eingetreten wäre, wenn es nicht vorhergesagt worden wäre. Eine solche Antwort gibt der griechische Mythos, wo Oedipus das Orakel gerade deswegen erfüllt, weil er ihm ausweicht. Hier sind die Vorhersage und ihre Erkenntnis Bedingungen der Erfüllung. In der Geschichte ist der Zusammenhang dagegen meist ambivalent, weil sich die Vorhersage positiv oder negativ auswirken kann, so daß sich beide neutralisieren. Als Spengler ein Zeitalter des Cäsarismus prophezeite, hat das Anhängern dieser Idee wie Ludendorff und Reusch Mut gemacht und Gegner wie Rathenau und Graf Kessler zur Wachsamkeit gerufen.

Jedermann glaubt, der Unterschied zwischen Voraussicht und Rückblick liege darin, daß die Zukunft uns bestenfalls Möglichkeiten zeige, die Vergangenheit hingegen unumstößliche Tatsachen enthalte. Jedermann hätte damit recht, wenn jedermann wüßte, was eine historische Tatsache ist. Voltaire wußte das, als er die *histoire* 1764 eine *fable convenue* nannte. Tatsachen sind tatsächlich bloß Inhalte von Hypothesen, auf die man sich geeinigt hat, d.h. Vermutungen, mit denen wir uns abgefunden haben. So wie wir in Unkenntnis künftigen Geschehens mehrere Möglichkeiten bedenken müssen, so müssen wir ebenso in Unkenntnis vergangenen Geschehens mehrere Möglichkeiten einkalkulieren. Der Kautel "Es kann so, kann aber auch anders kommen" entspricht die Kautel "Es kann so, kann aber auch anders gewesen sein." Die Wißbarkeit des Vergangenen wird leicht überschätzt, die Vermutbarkeit des Künftigen oft unterschätzt. In beiden Fällen können wir nur Grade von Wahrscheinlichkeit erreichen.

Die Behauptung einer historischen Tatsache steht unter doppeltem Vorbehalt. Der erste ergibt sich aus der veränderbaren Quellenlage. Meinungsänderungen dieses Typs gehorchen im allgemeinen dem Gesetz des wissenschaftlichen Fortschritts. Der zweite Vorbehalt liegt in der

---

[80] Vgl. hierzu die einschlägigen Aufsätze bei E. Topitsch (Hg.), Logik der Sozialwissenschaften, 1968.

Deutungsproblematik. Die veränderte politische Einstellung verändert das Bild der Vergangenheit ohne das Hinzutreten neuer Quellen. Derartiges hängt vom Zeitgeist ab, der hin- und herschwankt. Wie fest eine historische "Tatsache" steht, merken wir, wenn wir an ihr rütteln.

Zwischen dem Schluß auf Vergangenes und dem Schluß auf Künftiges besteht eine logische Symmetrie. Beidemale gehen wir von der Gegenwart aus, beidemale urteilen wir nach Erfahrungsregeln. Vergangene Tatsachen erschließen wir, indem wir von einer gegenwärtig vorliegenden, als Wirkung interpretierten Quelle über Erfahrungsregeln auf ein als Ursache interpretiertes, in der Vergangenheit liegendes Ereignis folgern. So lesen wir bei Meyer (GdA I 1, 188): "Historisch ist derjenige Vorgang, der ... erkennbar weiter wirkt."

Genau derselbe, nur im umgekehrter Richtung beschrittene Weg erlaubt uns Schlüsse auf die Zukunft. Wir sehen gegenwärtige, als Ursachen interpretierte Indizien, nehmen unsere Erfahrungsregeln zu Hilfe und folgern auf die Konsequenzen. Wenn wir die Indizien richtig deuten und zutreffende Erfahrungsregeln richtig anwenden, dann müßten wir mit derselben Sicherheit, mit der wir auf Vergangenes schließen, Künftiges vorhersagen können.

Die Erfahrungsregeln des historischen Schließens bestehen darin, daß wir Entwicklungen verlängern und Konstellationen übertragen. Ersteres ist eine lineare, letzteres eine zyklische Argumentationsfigur. Beide gehören zusammen. Spenglers Beispiel ist der wachsende Baum. Er war einmal kleiner, wird einmal größer, doch ist dafür gesorgt, daß er nicht in den Himmel wächst. Wir beobachten den Vorgang und schließen ein Stück weit in die Vergangenheit, ein Stück weit in die Zukunft. Ein Stück weit, denn die Prozesse in unserer Erfahrungswelt haben Anfang und Ende; die Dauer übertragen wir von bekannten auf unbekannte Fälle.

Das lineare wie das zyklische Argument sind Analogieschlüsse. Bei der linearen Analogie übertragen wir Information von einer Zeit auf die andere, bei der zyklischen Analogie übertragen wir Information von einem Gegenstande auf den anderen. Letzteres setzt voraus, daß beide Gegenstände zur selben Gattung gehören. Dies ist bei Bäumen einfacher auszumachen als bei politischen Konstellationen oder gar bei Hochkulturen. Spenglers These,[81] die einzig verläßliche Technik des Parallelisierens gefunden zu haben, ist kaum haltbar. Zu jedem historischen Vorgang gibt es eine unbestimmbare Zahl von Analogien. Sie differieren im Grade der Ähnlichkeit, d.h. in der Zahl der Entsprechungen. Man wende gegen eine Parallele nicht ein, sie liege weit ab. Schon eine einzige Über-

---

[81] S.o. Anm. 52, I 4 ff.

einstimmung rechtfertigt die Suche nach einer zweiten. Darin besteht der
heuristische Wert von Analogien. Ohne diesen Schlüssel können wir in
den Bereich fremden Geschehens nicht vordringen. Von der
heuristischen gehen wir zur typologischen Analogic über, indem wir
Begriffe bilden. Ohne sie können wir das Selbsterlebte nicht verstehen.[82]

Spenglers Anspruch, als erster die Geschichte vorauszusagen, ist unbegründet. Dies tat schon Scipio Africanus, als er beim Untergang Karthagos an den Untergang Trojas erinnerte und den Untergang Roms
prophezeite (Polyb. 38, 22); das tat schon Seneca (NQ. VI 5,3; VII
25,4 f.), als er einen endlosen Fortschritt der Wissenschaften voraussagte.
Die beiden Grundfiguren geschichtsphilosophischer Prognose, Linearität
und Zyklik, waren bereits im Altertum ausgebildet. Sie vertragen sich
insofern, als sie sich auf unterschiedliche Sachbereiche beziehen. Die
Wissenschaften wachsen. Die politischen Mächte kommen und gehen.
Fortschritts- und Kreislaufidee dürfen sich, je auf ihre Weise, als bestätigt
erachten.

Natürlich sind unserem Blick in die Zukunft Grenzen gesetzt. Die Warnung Meyers ist berechtigt, da wir es hier nicht mit strenger Wissenschaft
zu tun haben, die zu sicheren Resultaten führt. Das beweisen schon die
zahlreichen Fehlprognosen: Denken wir an den römischen Glauben an
das *imperium sine fine*, an die christliche Erwartung des nahen Jüngsten
Gerichts, an die Vision Marxens von der Weltrevolution. Wer aus dem
Nebeneinander von eingetretenen und ausgebliebenen Prognosen folgert,
daß Schelling gegen Novalis Recht behalten habe, historische Prognosen,
samt und sonders unseriös sind, der müßte auch auf die Medizin verzichten, weil nicht alle Kuren gelingen.

Es gibt drei Schwierigkeiten bei Aussagen über Künftiges. Es sind
erstens unsere Ängste und Wünsche. Wir geben Meyer und Spengler
gern zu, daß wir uns vor den Illusionen des Fortschritts hüten müssen,
aber auch Schwarzseher sind keine Hellseher. Unsere Emotionen müssen
wir kontrollieren. Die Zukunft erscheint im Spiegel der Vergangenheit
nur, sofern wir uns selbst durchschauen. Zum andern geschieht dauernd
Neues. Unsere Erfahrungen müssen ständig verbessert und erweitert

---

[82] Das beste über die Analogie als Erkenntnismittel findet sich bei Goethe (Ausgabe
letzter Hand 50, 147): "Jedes Existirende ist ein Analogon alles Existirenden; daher
erscheint uns das Dasein immer zu gleicher Zeit gesondert und verknüpft. Folgt man der
Analogie zu sehr, so fällt alles identisch zusammen; meidet man sie, so zerstreut sich alles
in's Unendliche. In beiden Fällen stagnirt die Betrachtung, einmal als überlebendig, das
anderemal als getödtet." Grundlage für die Bedeutung der Analogie in der neueren
Theoriediskussion ist J.G. Droysen, Historik 1937, S. 88; 159 f. Zur ideologischen Komponente in der Verwendung von Analogien vgl. L. Canfora, Analogia e storia. L'uso
politico dei paradigmi storici, 1982.

werden. Neues passiert überwiegend im Speziellen, während sich im Generellen zumeist Altes wiederholt. Aussagen über Kommendes sind desto verläßlicher, je allgemeiner sie sind, je mehr sie den unberechenbaren Zufall einkalkulieren. Umgekehrt sind Aussagen über Vergangenes desto sicherer, je spezieller sie sind, je mehr sie die Deutungs- und Verallgemeinerungsproblematik vermeiden. Zum dritten verändern neue Ereignisse alte Begriffe. Für uns heute klingen Wörter wie Volk und Rasse, Nationalismus und Sozialismus anders als für Meyer und Spengler. Das hat zur Folge, daß bei manchen Prognosen hinterher nicht klar ist, ob der Prognostizierende Recht oder Unrecht hatte, weil unklar ist, ob er das Eingetretene gemeint hat oder nicht.

Wer den historischen Visionssinn eines Novalis besitzt und dennoch die Warnung von Schelling berücksichtigt, lernt aus den Fehlern der anderen. Meyer und Spengler haben die Entwicklung in Umrissen richtig vorausgesehen. Meyers Urteil über das Ende der politischen Weltgeltung Europas war richtig, richtig war zudem die darin enthaltene Prognose, daß der Versuch, sie wiederherzustellen, scheitern würde. Hitler war kein Caesar; darin irrte Spengler. Treffend war dafür seine Einsicht in den Übergang von der Kultur in die Zivilisation. Große Leistungen sind seither in Technik und Naturwissenschaft, kaum in Literatur und Kunst zu verzeichnen. Beide Denker täuschten sich in Einzelheiten und Wertungen. Diese sind gewöhnlich von der opti- oder pessimistischen Stimmung des Autors abhängig. Denn selbst wenn wir das künftige Geschehen klar vor Augen hätten, wüßten wir noch lange nicht, was die künftigen Menschen dabei empfinden werden. Über Politik und Kultur, über Wirtschaft und Gesellschaft lassen sich Prognosen begründen, nicht aber über das Glück der Nachwelt. Das hat etwas Enttäuschendes, aber auch etwas Tröstliches. Soweit die Optimisten Recht behalten haben, haben sie weniger Grund zum Stolz auf den Fortschritt, als sie meinten. Soweit die Pessimisten Recht behalten haben, haben sie weniger Grund zur Klage über den Verfall, als sie meinten. Bisher haben wir die von Meyer befürchtete Amerikanisierung Europas und den von Spengler befürchteten Untergang des Abendlandes ganz gut überstanden.

ALBERT HENRICHS

ALTE UND NEUE PROPHETEN ALS STIFTER VON OFFENBARUNGSRELIGIONEN: DER URSPRUNG DER MORMONEN NACH EDUARD MEYER

Meinen mormonischen Gast-
gebern von 1978 gewidmet.

America ist wahrhaftig nicht zu verachten, und für den, der das Studium des Menschen und seiner Ideen zu seiner Lebensaufgabe gemacht hat, ebenso interessant wie die alte Welt. Denke nur an die großen, wunderbaren religiösen Bewegungen, z.B. die Mormonen![1]

Vor 75 Jahren, im Spätherbst 1912, ließ der damals 57jährige Eduard Meyer (1855–1930), der als Verfasser der monumentalen "Geschichte des Altertums" und als engagierter Universalhistoriker der antiken Welt längst auf der Höhe seines Ruhmes stand, nach mehrjährigen Vorarbeiten ein ungewöhnliches Buch erscheinen, das man gerade aus seiner Feder am wenigsten erwartet hätte: "Ursprung und Geschichte der Mormonen".[2] Darin werden die Entstehung des Mormonentums und die sukzessiven Phasen seiner Ausbreitung von Ohio und Missouri über Illinois bis zur endgültigen Niederlassung im "gelobten Land" Deseret, dem späteren Bundesstaat Utah auf der anderen Seite des amerikanischen Kontinents, unter ständiger Berücksichtigung der politischen Geschichte mit kritischem Blick und seltener Anschaulichkeit geschildert. Die Dar-

---

[1] Aus einem Brief Eduard Meyers vom 11.2.1877 an seine Mutter; herausgegeben in diesem Band von C. Hoffmann, "Die Selbsterziehung des Historikers. Zur intellektuellen Entwicklung des jungen Eduard Meyer (1855–1879)," Nr. 8.

[2] Für die in unserem Zusammenhang relevanten Arbeiten Meyers einschließlich der Meyer-Bibliographie werden folgende Abkürzungen benutzt: *Anthropologie = Geschichte des Alterums*, 1. Bd. 1. Hälfte: *Einleitung. Elemente der Anthropologie*, 3. Aufl. Stuttgart/Berlin 1910 (zuerst 1884), Nachdr. Darmstadt 1953; Marohl = H. Marohl, *Eduard-Meyer-Bibliographie. Mit einer autobiographischen Skizze Eduard Meyers und der Gedächtnisrede von Ulrich Wilcken*, Stuttgart 1941; UAC = *Ursprung und Anfänge des Christentums*, Bd. I–III, Stuttgart/Berlin 1921–1923; *Mormonen = Ursprung und Geschichte der Mormonen. Mit Exkursen über die Anfänge des Islâms und des Christentums*, Halle a. S. 1912, Nachdruck Hildesheim/New York 1970. Die beiden wichtigsten kanonischen Schriften der Mormonen werden nach den Standardausgaben der Church of Jesus Christ of Latter-day Saints wie folgt zitiert: *Doctrine and Covenants = The Doctrine and Covenants of the Church of Jesus Christ of Latter-day Saints*, Containing Revelations Given to Joseph Smith, the Prophet, with some Additions by his Successors in the Presidency of the Church (1835), nach Abschnittsnummern; *The Book of Mormon. An Account Written by the Hand of Mormon upon Plates Taken from the Plates of Nephi, translated by Joseph Smith, Jr.*, (1830), nach den Titeln und Unterteilungen der einzelnen Bücher (vgl. unten Anm. 8).

stellung endet mit dem Manifest von 1890, in dem sich die mormonische Kirche offiziell von der Polygamie lossagte, und mit der Eingliederung des Mormonenstaates in die Union (1896). Was Meyers Buch jedoch eine besondere Note gibt, ist die enge Vorbindung der historischen mit der religionsgeschichtlichen Perspektive, vor allem der direkte Vergleich zweier zeitlich, räumlich und herkunftsmäßig weit voneinander entfernten Religionsstifter, Joseph Smith und Mohammed.

Die 279 Bücher, Aufsätze und Miszellen Meyers, die der Monographie über die Mormonen vorausgehen, beschäftigen sich auf breitester Basis mit der politischen und geistigen Entwicklung der großen Kulturvölker des Vorderen Orients und des daran angrenzenden Mittelmeerraums. Der geographische Horizont erstreckt sich von Persien und dem Zweistromland bis nach Griechenland und Italien; der zeitliche Rahmen ist weit gespannt, vom 3. Jahrtausend bis 350 v. Chr., wobei das chronologische Gerüst über lange Perioden zuerst einmal aus den Quellen mühsam erstellt werden mußte. Von diesem gewaltigen, ganz auf das Altertum bezogenen Œuvre hebt sich das Buch über die Religion der Mormonen auf den ersten Blick wie ein Fremdkörper ab.[3] Die "Church of Jesus Christ of Latter-day Saints", wie die Mormonen mit Stammsitz in Salt Lake City offiziell heißen, ist eine moderne Gründung relativ

---

[3] Die Literatur über die Geschichte der Mormonen ist sehr umfangreich. Die spärliche deutschsprachige Literatur ist verzeichnet bei D.L. Ashliman, "Mormonism and the Germans: An Annotated Bibliography, 1848–1966," *Brigham Young University Studies* 8, 1967/68, 73–94. Jüngste Bibliographien und bibliographische Essays aus mormonischer Sicht: J.B. Allen und G.M. Leonard, *The Story of the Latter-day Saints*, Salt Lake City 1976, 639–700; R.L. Bushman, *Joseph Smith and the Beginnings of Mormonism*, Urbana/Chicago 1984, 189–192 ("Writings on Mormon history ... suffer from a division between the works of believers and nonbelievers"); L.J. Arrington, *Brigham Young: American Moses*, New York 1985, 500–509. Die fundiertesten und interessantesten Darstellungen des Mormonentums aus der Sicht von Nichtmormonen, und zwar jeweils von soziologischer bzw. religionsgeschichtlicher Warte, sind T.F. O'Dea, *The Mormons*, Chicago 1957, und J. Shipps, *Mormonism: The Story of a New Religious Tradition*, Urbana/Chicago 1985. Ob man das Mormonentum als "Religion", als "Sekte" oder als "religious movement" (so z.B. O'Dea) bzw. "Bewegung" (U. von Wilamowitz-Moellendorff, *Süddeutsche Monatshefte* 22, 1924/25, Heft 4, 56, in einer Würdigung Meyers) bezeichnet, hängt vom Standpunkt des Betrachters ab. Christentum und Manichäismus (unten IV) haben bekanntlich als Sekten, d.h. als Splittergruppen bereits bestehender Religionsgemeinschaften, begonnen und sind beide zu Weltreligionen geworden, wenn auch nur eine davon überlebt hat. Die bisherige Entwicklung des Mormonentums weist vergleichbare Stufen auf, z.B. das Schisma von 1852/53, das zur Gründung der "Reorganized Church of Jesus Christ of Latter Day Saints" in Independence, Missouri führte (im Gegensatz zu der "Church of Jesus Christ of Latter-day Saints" von Salt Lake City), und die inzwischen weltweite Missionstätigkeit. Meyer stuft denn auch das Mormonentum in seiner ursprünglichen Form ausdrücklich als "neue Offenbarungsreligion" ein, die allerdings später "zur Sekte herabsinkt" (*Mormonen* 1, zitiert unten S. 184, u. 272). Die Selbstbezeichnung der Mormonen lautet "Kirche".

jungen Datums; als Gründungstag gilt der 6. April 1830.[4] Meyer selbst spricht von einer "religiösen Neubildung", und einer seiner Rezensenten von "einer Episode der neueren Religionsgeschichte".[5] Wäre Joseph Smith (1805 – 1844), der Stifter und "First Prophet" des Mormonentums, nicht vorzeitig eines gewaltsamen Todes gestorben, so hätte sich seine Lebenszeit mit der Eduard Meyers (1855 – 1930) vermutlich noch um ein oder zwei Jahrzehnte überschnitten.[6] Wie kam der große Althistoriker dazu, sich so intensiv mit einer modernen und damals noch sehr umstrittenen Religion zu befassen, die erst ein Vierteljahrhundert vor seiner Geburt in der Neuen Welt entstanden war?

Die ausführliche Antwort, die er selbst in seiner Einleitung gibt, ist symptomatisch für sein umfassendes, Vergangenheit und Gegenwart einschließendes Geschichtsverständnis:

> Unter den religiösen Neubildungen unserer Zeit hat schon früh das Mormonentum mein Interesse erregt, vor allem wegen der überraschenden und bis ins einzelnste gehenden Analogie sowohl der grundlegenden Antriebe und Erscheinungsformen, wie seiner geschichtlichen Entwicklung mit dem Islâm: ließen sich doch hier bedeutsame Aufschlüsse für das richtige Verständnis Mohammeds und seiner Religion erhoffen. Aber auch an sich ist das Mormonentum eine der lehrreichsten Erscheinungen auf dem Gebiet der Religionsgeschichte. . . . Die einzigartige Stellung des Mormonentums, durch die es sich von allen andern auf christlichem Boden erwachsenen Bildungen unterscheidet, besteht darin, daß es nicht etwa eine neue Sekte ist, wie es deren unzählige gibt, sondern eine neue Offenbarungsreligion. Diese neue Religion hat sich inmitten des neunzehnten Jahrhunderts gebildet, und wir können daher ihre Entstehung und Geschichte an der Hand einer außerordentlich reichen, zeitgenössischen Überlieferung von Anhängern und Gegnern und zahlreicher nach Jahr und Tag genau datierter Dokumente bis ins einzelnste hinein verfolgen; was die historische For-

---

[4] *Doctrine and Covenants* 20 – 21; Meyer, *Mormonen* 35 f.; Bushman (Anm. 3) 143 – 149. Die Gründungsversammlung fand in Fayette statt, einem kleinen, im Nordwesten des Bundesstaats New York gelegenen Ort; nicht weit davon entfernt befindet sich Palmyra mit dem Hügel Cumorah, wo Smith die ersten Engelserscheinungen erlebte und die goldenen Tafeln erhielt.

[5] *Mormonen* 1 (zitiert im folgenden); E. Lehmann, *Göttingische gelehrte Anzeigen* 175, 1913, 317.

[6] Joseph Smith, der damals mitten im Wahlkampf um die Präsidentschaft der Union stand, und sein Bruder Hyrum wurden am 27. Juni 1844 im Gefängnis von Carthage, Illinois, von einem starken Aufgebot mormonenfeindlicher Milizsoldaten überfallen und nach einem kurzen Kugelwechsel erschossen. Vgl. Meyer, *Mormonen* 173 – 184; O'Dea (Anm. 3) 66 – 69; K. Huntress (Hrsg.), *Murder of an American Prophet*, San Francisco 1960; D.H. Oaks und M.S. Hill, *Carthage Conspiracy: The Trial of the Accused Assassins of Joseph Smith*, Urbana, Illinois, 1975; D.C. Jessee, "Return to Carthage: Writing the History of Joseph Smith's Martyrdom," *Journal of Mormon History* 8, 1981, 3 – 19. Was den Historiker Meyer an den Umständen, die zum "Martyrium" des Religionsstifters führten, besonders interessierte, war die dichte Überlagerung religiöser und politischer Faktoren.

schung bei andern Offenbarungsreligionen mühselig und unvollkommen erschließen muß, wird ihr hier unmittelbar in zuverlässigen Zeugnissen geboten. Dadurch gewinnt die Entstehung und Geschichte des Mormonentums für den Religionshistoriker einen außerordentlich großen Wert, der dadurch nur noch erhöht wird, daß es unter den geoffenbarten Religionen eine der rohesten, ja vielleicht die intellektuell am tiefsten stehende ist: eben dadurch treten die elementaren Faktoren, welche das religiöse Leben beherrschen und den Aufbau einer großen, nach Weltherrschaft strebenden Religion ermöglichen, nur um so greifbarer hervor.[7]

Drei Gesichtspunkte sind es demnach, die Meyers Interesse an diesem Gegenstand bestimmten und mit denen wir uns im folgenden zu beschäftigen haben: die für Meyer selbstverständliche, aber für heutige Begriffe überraschende Einbeziehung der Religionsgeschichte in die allgemeine Geschichtswissenschaft, die dazu führt, daß der Historiker von Amts wegen auch Religionshistoriker ist (I–IV); der Rekurs auf eine moderne, quellenmäßig unmittelbar zugängliche Religionsgemeinschaft, d.h. einer bekannten Größe, zum Verständnis einer antiken Religion (I und III); und drittens, damit eng zusammenhängend, der Begriff der "historischen Analogie", der es Meyer ermöglicht, eine direkte Verbindungslinie von Joseph Smith zu Mohammed zu ziehen (IV). Dazu kommt das biographische Moment (II), ohne das die Existenz des Buchs über die Mormonen unverständlich bliebe: Woher rührte Meyers frühes Interesse an den Mormonen, das offenbar mit einem übergeordneten Interesse an Mohammed und dem Islam ursächlich zusammenhing?

I. Meyer und die Mormonen: Konvergenz von Altertum und Neuer Welt

Meyer trat nicht nur als Historiker an die Mormonen heran, sondern auch als Ägyptologe und Kenner des Judentums. Beim Studium der mormonischen Schriften und der an Joseph Smith ergangenen Offenbarung, der sie ihre angebliche Wiederentdeckung und Entzifferung verdankten, mußten ihm zahlreiche Züge der Überlieferung vertraut vorkommen. Das Mormonentum ist nämlich eine Buchreligion mit heiligen Schriften, darunter der jüdisch-christlichen Bibel und dem "Book of Mormon", in dem die Geschichte der ersten Bewohner Nordamerikas in enger Anlehnung an den Stil und die Erzählformen des Alten Testaments als christliche Heilsgeschichte konzipiert und dargestellt ist.[8] Demnach waren die

---

[7] *Mormonen* 1 f.

[8] Zum "Book of Mormon" vgl. Meyer, *Mormonen* 19–28, 33–43; G. Lanczkowski, *Heilige Schriften*, Stuttgart 1956, 148–153; O'Dea (Anm. 3) 22–40. Meyer übersetzte den Titel der mormonischen Hauptschrift wortgetreu mit "das Buch Mormons", d.h. "ein Bericht, geschrieben von der Hand Mormons auf Platten, den Platten Nephis entnommen"

frühesten Siedler weiße Einwanderer jüdischer Herkunft, die aus Babylonien und Judäa zu verschiedenen vorchristlichen Zeiten auf dem Seeweg nach Amerika gelangt waren. Sie und ihre Nachkommen gelten als die eigentlichen Empfänger des ursprünglichen "Evangeliums", d.h. derselben doppelten Offenbarung, auf die auch das Alte und Neue Testament zurückgehen. Die christlichen Evangelien sind aber nicht die endgültige Offenbarung. Christus war nämlich nach seiner Auferstehung nicht nur in Jerusalem und Emmaus erschienen, sondern auch auf dem nordamerikanischen Kontinent, wo er erneut predigte, Wunder wirkte, die Taufe und Eucharistie einsetzte, zwölf Jünger berief und eine Kirche gründete.[9]

Die Geschichte der amerikanischen Ureinwanderer, ihrer Propheten und der ihnen von Jahwe und Christus zuteil gewordenen Offenbarungen wurde in alter Zeit auf Goldplatten aufgezeichnet, die um 400 n. Chr. vergraben wurden und unzugänglich blieben, bis sie Joseph Smith am 22. September 1827 von einem Engel übergeben wurden. Der Engel hieß Moroni und war ein auferstandener Sohn Mormons, eines der letzten weißen Ureinwohner Amerikas. Smith übersetzte dann die in einer seltsamen Zeichenschrift, die er "reformed Egyptian" nannte, beschriebenen Platten mit göttlicher Hilfe ins Englische und veröffentlichte diese Offenbarung im März 1830 als "The Book of Mormon". Danach gab er die Goldplatten dem Engel zurück. Die Existenz der Platten ist durch die eidesstattliche Erklärung von elf Augenzeugen verbürgt, wird aber von Meyer und der Mehrzahl der nichtmormonischen Forscher bezweifelt. Abschriften der rätselhaften Zeichen wurden sogar dem Polymath und Herausgeber lateinischer Schultexte Charles Anthon (1797–1867), Professor an der Columbia University, vorgelegt, über dessen Verdikt widersprüchliche Aussagen vorliegen.[10]

(so der Untertitel). Vorbild für den Titel waren jedoch die entsprechenden englischen Bezeichnungen alttestamentlicher Bücher, z.B. "the Book of Job" ("das Buch Hiob"), in denen die präpositionale Wendung nicht possessiv ist, sondern definitorisch. In der offiziellen, von der mormonischen Kirche verbreiteten deutschen Übersetzung lautet daher der Titel "Das Buch Mormon". Die Rolle Mormons wird folgendermaßen dargestellt (*Das Buch Mormon*, 15. Auflage, 1964, IV): "Der Hauptteil des Buches, von Mosiah bis einschließlich Mormon, Kapitel 7 [nämlich 320 von insgesamt 492 Druckseiten der deutschen Übersetzung; "Mormon" bezeichnet hier ein Einzelbuch des Gesamtwerkes], ist von den von Mormon abgekürzten Platten Nephis übersetzt worden. Der letzte Teil des Buches, vom Anfang des 8. Kapitels in Mormon bis zum Ende [48 Druckseiten], wurde von Moroni, dem Sohne Mormons, geschrieben, der zuerst den Bericht seines Vaters fertigstellte und dann eine Abkürzung des jareditischen Berichtes anfertigte, die als das Buch Ether bekannt ist. Später fügte er die Teile hinzu, die heute das Buch Moroni bilden." Zu dieser komplizierten, in den Text der Schrift eingebauten "antiken Redaktionsgeschichte" äußert sich Meyer selbst da, wo man es am ehesten erwartet hätte (*Mormonen* 40 f.), mit keinem Wort.

[9] 3 Nephi 11–28.

[10] Meyer, *Mormonen* 37 f.; vgl. S. Newmyer, "Charles Anthon: Knickerbocker Scholar", *Classical Outlook* 59, 1981–82, 41–44.

Dieses eklatante Zurückgreifen auf drei der markantesten Gattungs-
merkmale antiker Offenbarungsliteratur, nämlich die Aufzeichnung
eines religiösen Textes auf unzerstörbarem Schreibmaterial, die Über-
bringung durch einen himmlischen Boten und schließlich die Übersetzung aus einer unzugänglichen Sprache, mußte Meyers Interesse erre-
gen.[11] Die entscheidenden Impulse für eine gründlichere Beschäftigung
mit den Mormonen waren jedoch teils biographischer und teils wissen-
schaftstheoretischer Natur. Zwei ausgedehnte Amerikareisen ermöglichten es Meyer, sich ein genaueres Bild von den Mormonen zu machen und
die einschlägige Literatur einzusehen (unten II). Der so gewonnene Eindruck von der neuen Offenbarungsreligion war ein integraler Bestandteil
von Meyers intensivem Amerikaerlebnis, das weit über die fachlichen
Kontakte hinausging und auf lange Zeit nachwirkte. Es blieb jedoch nicht
bei bloßen Reiseeindrücken. Für Meyer gehörte die Gegenwartserfah-
rung zum unabdingbaren Rüstzeug jedes Historikers und bestimmte dessen Vorstellung von der Vergangenheit.[12] Entsprechend stellte Meyer
die Entstehungsgeschichte der Mormonen mit Hilfe des theoretischen
Konzepts der "historischen Analogie" in einen größeren Zusammenhang. Denn mit der Person des Religionsstifters und dem Typus der
Buch- und Offenbarungsreligion waren zwei unverkennbare religionsgeschichtliche Grundphänomene gegeben, denen sich unschwer analoge
Erscheinungen aus dem Altertum zur Seite stellen ließen. Diese Analogie
kommt dann auch im Untertitel von Meyers Mormonenbuch deutlich
zum Ausdruck, der lautet: "Mit Exkursen über die Anfänge des Islâms
und des Christentums". Es werden also zwei der ältesten und bekann-
testen Offenbarungsreligionen mit dem strukturell verwandten
historischen Nachkömmling verglichen (unten IV). Mit dieser universalhistorischen Einordnung wurden die Mormonen auch für die Wissenschaft vom Altertum relevant.

   Neben die biographische und wissenschaftstheoretische Komponente
trat ein dritter Faktor, ohne den die beiden anderen nicht zum Zuge gekommen wären, nämlich Meyers ausgeprägtes Interesse an den antiken

---

[11] W. Speyer, *Bücherfunde in der Glaubenswerbung der Antike*, Göttingen 1970, 23–42 (zu
den "Himmelsbriefen" und "Büchern vom Himmel") u. 107–110 (zu Joseph Smith)
sowie "Angebliche Übersetzungen des heidnischen und christlichen Altertums", *Jahrb. f.
Antike u. Christentum* 11/12, 1968/69, 26–41; A. Henrichs u. L. Koenen, *Zeitschr. f. Pap.
u. Epigr.* 19, 1975, 49 Anm. 89 (Stein und Metall als unverwüstliche Schreibmaterialien,
welche die Erhaltung von Offenbarungsschriften sicherstellen sollten).
[12] Vgl. Meyer, "Zur Theorie und Methodik der Geschichte" (1902), *Kl. Schr.* I 1–78,
bes. S. 54: "Die Gegenwart des Historikers ist ein Moment, das aus keiner Geschichtsdarstellung ausgeschieden werden kann, und zwar ebensowohl seine Individualität wie die
Gedankenwelt der Zeit, in der er lebt. Zu allen Zeiten ist es nur unsere Erkenntnis der
Geschichte, zu der wir gelangen können, niemals eine absolute und unbedingt gültige."

Religionen, an der Religionsgeschichte und selbst an der Religionswissenschaft. Schon als Student und als junger Gelehrter besaß er einen scharfen Blick für religionsgeschichtliche Zusammenhänge und für die Religion seiner eigenen Umwelt.[13] Auch in seinen reifen Jahren verließ er immer wieder die beiden damaligen Zentralbereiche der historischen Forschung, die Chronologie und die politische Geschichte, um sich mit der ägyptischen und griechischen Religion, dem Judentum und schließlich dem Christentum zu befassen. Die Reihe der einschlägigen Arbeiten Meyers beginnt mit der Leipziger Dissertation zum Thema ''Set-Typhon. Eine religionsgeschichtliche Studie'' (1875). Es folgten bis 1912 in unregelmäßigen Abständen kürzere oder längere Arbeiten über semitische Götter (1877), ägyptische Religion (1887 u. 1890) einschließlich Isis (1891), griechischen Heroenkult (1895), die Entstehung des Judentums (1896), Adonis (1899), ägyptische Kulte (1904) und zoroastrische Religion (1908), von den zahlreichen religionsgeschichtlichen Abschnitten in der ''Geschichte des Altertums'' ganz abgesehen.[14] Das Buch über die Mormonen fügt sich organisch in diese Entwicklungslinie ein. Es ist von der Konzeption und nicht zuletzt vom Titel her ein Vorläufer des abschließenden religionsgeschichtlichen Werks über ''Ursprung und Anfänge des Christentums'' (1921 u. 1923), in dem die Visionen, welche Joseph Smith für sich in Anspruch nahm, mehrmals im Sinne der ''historischen Analogie'' (unten IV) als ''Parallelerscheinungen'' zur Visionsfreudigkeit des Urchristentums herangezogen werden.[15]

Religion galt Meyer als eine der Grundmanifestationen der Geschichtlichkeit des Menschen und als Maßstab seiner ''geistigen Entwicklung''.[16] Universalgeschichte zu betreiben, ohne die Religionsentwicklung auf Schritt und Tritt miteinzubeziehen, wäre für ihn unvorstellbar gewesen. Dabei wird Religion nicht bloß als politische oder soziale Realität aufgefaßt und in ihrem äußeren Ablauf dargestellt. Vielmehr versuchte Meyer, wenn auch nur in tastenden und zumindest aus heutiger Sicht nicht immer geglückten Ansätzen, über die ''geschichtlichen Tatsachen'' hinausgehend die innere Motivation, das ''innere Agens'', des individuellen Religionsträgers zu bestimmen. Allerdings hielt er die ''psychologische Analyse einzelner Persönlichkeiten und Völker'' ledig-

---

[13] Vgl. den Beitrag von C. Hoffmann in diesem Bande.

[14] Marohl Nr. 4, 51, 74 (''The Development of Religion in Egypt'', *Sunday School Times* Bd. 32, Nr. 38, Nov. 1890, 585 f.; vgl. dazu den Beitrag von Ernst Badian), 78, 100, 107, 137 (vgl. 157a), 168 u. 191.

[15] UAC I 153 f., II 418 f., III 353. Vgl. den Beitrag von Eckhard Plümacher (''Eduard Meyer und das frühe Christentum'').

[16] So lautet die Überschrift des der Religion gewidmeten Kapitels in *Anthropologie* 87–183.

lich für "ein mit Vorsicht zu benutzendes Hilfsmittel" der Geschichtswissenschaft,[17] hat aber dann gerade in seiner Beurteilung des Stifters der
Mormonen diese Vorsicht nicht in genügendem Maße walten lassen
(unten IV).

II. Ursprung und Geschichte der Mormonen: *Entstehung und Rezeption*

Eduard Meyer hat sich schon sehr "früh", d.h. lange vor seiner ersten
Amerikareise, für die Mormonen interessiert; bereits in einem Briefe des
22jährigen Hauslehrers werden sie als Beispiel der "großen, wunderbaren religiösen Bewegungen" Amerikas erwähnt.[18] Woher der erste
Anstoß kam, läßt sich allenfalls vermuten. Waren es Bücher, die den
jungen Meyer auf die Mormonen aufmerksam gemacht hatten, oder war
es die Bekanntschaft mit in Hamburg oder England missionierenden bzw.
ansässigen Mitgliedern der Kirche?[19] In diesem Zusammenhang ist daran zu erinnern, daß Meyer nach seinem eigenen Zeugnis an den Mormonen nicht um ihrer selbst willen interessiert war, sondern auf dem Weg
über Mohammed und den Islam zu ihnen geführt worden ist.[20] Zum
Islam, und zwar dem modernen, hat sich Meyer aber erst im letzten
Kriegsjahr geäußert, sechs Jahre nach dem Erscheinen seines Buches.[21]
Seine ersten Arabischkenntnisse erwarb er jedoch bereits als Gymnasiast
auf dem Hamburger Johanneum und vertiefte sie später während seiner
Studentenzeit in Bonn und Leipzig, wobei die Koranlektüre sicher als
Grundlage diente.[22] Das Interesse an den Mormonen muß demnach
spätestens in den Jahren 1872–1877 aufgekeimt sein.

Für ein ernsthaftes Studium des Mormonentums und seiner Literatur war jedoch die Zeit noch nicht reif. Erst drei Dezennien später,
während der beiden Amerikareisen der Jahre 1904 (Frühjahr, University

---

[17] Meyer, *Anthropologie* 203 f.

[18] *Mormonen* 1 (aus der Einleitung, zitiert oben S. 184); Brief Meyers vom 11. Februar
1877 (ediert von Christhard Hoffmann [Anm. 1], zitiert oben S. 182).

[19] Die erste deutsche Übersetzung des "Book of Mormon" erschien 1852 in Hamburg,
der Heimatstadt Meyers. Dort wurde auch im selben Jahr die erste Mormonengemeinde
Deutschlands gegründet; dazu K. Hutten, *Seher, Grübler, Enthusiasten. Sekten und religiöse
Sondergemeinschaften der Gegenwart*, 3. Aufl. Stuttgart 1953, 427–429. Vgl. Meyer, *Mormonen*
204 Anm. 1: "In Deutschland ist die mormonische Mission, sobald sie zur Kenntnis der
Behörden kam, immer unterdrückt, die fremden Missionare ausgewiesen worden, und
auch gegenwärtig [1912] wird mit Recht [!] daran festgehalten." Der erste Tempel der
Mormonen in Deutschland wurde erst kürzlich in Friedrichsdorf/Taunus, nicht weit von
Bad Homburg, eingeweiht; vgl. *Die Zeit*, 13. Nov. 1987, 87.

[20] *Mormonen* 1 (zitiert oben S. 184).

[21] "Die islamische Welt seit dem XVI. Jahrhundert" und "Deutschland und die
islamische Welt", beide von 1918 (Marohl Nr. 352 f.)

[22] Vgl. Meyers undatierte autobiographische Skizze im *Almanach d. Akad. d. Wiss.
Wien* 82, 1932, 207–213 = Marohl 9–12, hier S. 10.

of Chicago) und 1909/10 (Wintersemester, Harvard University), mit
denen ein Jugendtraum Meyers in Erfüllung ging, wurde aus der gelegentlichen Beschäftigung mit diesem Thema ein mehrjähriges Forschungsprojekt.[23] Meyer selbst erklärt die Genese seines Buchs mit dem
Hinweis auf seine Amerikaerfahrung:

> In Deutschland hätte ich nie an eine Abhandlung über die Mormonen
> denken können; dazu fehlte ebensowohl die Zeit wie die Hilfsmittel. Aber
> als ich 1904 zum ersten Mal nach Amerika kam, habe ich die Gelegenheit
> benutzt, um mich etwas genauer zu unterrichten, und habe wenigstens
> einen Tag in Salt Lake City zubringen und dadurch einige, wenn auch recht
> unzureichende, unmittelbare Anschauung gewinnen können. Der Gegen
> stand reizte mich immer mehr; und so habe ich, als ich fünf Jahre darauf
> als Austauschprofessor mehrere Monate in Amerika lebte, meine spärlich
> bemessene Mußezeit vorwiegend auf diesen Gegenstand verwandt. Was mir
> die schöne Bibliothek der Harvard University an Literatur bot, habe ich
> möglichst auszunutzen gestrebt; und die reiche in der Bibliothek der Univer
> sität von Wisconsin in Madison befindliche, von A.T. Schroeder, einem
> Gegner der Mormonen, zusammengebrachte Sammlung habe ich wenig
> stens durchsehen können. Dagegen ist es mir leider unmöglich gewesen, die
> größte derartige Sammlung, die Berrian Collection in der New York Public
> Library, zu benutzen.[24]

Dem Vorwort läßt sich entnehmen, daß nicht nur die unmittelbare
Vorarbeit an dem Buch, sondern auch dessen erste Ausarbeitung
während der mit Lehrverpflichtungen, Vorträgen und sonstigen Einladungen ohnehin schon reichlich ausgefüllten Monate der Gastprofessur
in Harvard begonnen wurde.[25] Eine reine "Ferienfreude", wie es einer

---

[23] Für alle Einzelheiten der Amerikareisen verweise ich auf die umfassende Chronik
von Mortimer Chambers ("The 'Most Eminent Living Historian, the One Final Authority:' Meyer in America"). Vgl. Meyers Brief vom 11.2.1877 (Anm. 1): "Wenn ich hinaus
könnte in den Orient oder nach Italien in die alte Welt, oder nach Nordamerica in die
neue, ich wollte alle Bücher hinter mir lassen, wenn es sein müßte, und ich wirklich frei
leben und sehen könnte" (es folgen die Sätze über Amerika und die Mormonen, die oben
S. 182 zitiert sind).
[24] Einleitung zu Meyer, *Mormonen* 4 f. Vgl. Meyers autobiographische Skizze (Anm.
22) in Marohl 11: "Dabei habe ich die Vereinigten Staaten nach allen Richtungen bereisen und gründlich kennenlernen können, was gerade für den alten Historiker sehr lehrreich ist und die Anschauung wesentlich fördert. Außerdem konnte ich dort das Material
für eine religionsgeschichtlich außerordentlich lehrreiche Erscheinung, die Geschichte der
Mormonen, sammeln."
[25] *Mormonen* III: "So will ich hier nur noch erwähnen, daß ich die Ausarbeitung vor
drei Jahren [d.h. im Herbst 1909] in Amerika begonnen habe, dann aber infolge von
Überhäufung mit Geschäften die Fortsetzung lange habe liegen lassen müssen; erst in diesem Sommer ist es mir möglich geworden das Buch zu vollenden." Zu Meyers Gastsemester in Harvard vgl. Chambers (Anm. 23) 12 – 14. Für diejenigen Leser, die Harvard
kennen, sei vermerkt, daß Meyer die hiesigen Bücherbestände noch in der neugotischen
Gore Hall benutzte, die Anfang 1913 der Widener Library weichen mußte. Die heutige
Bibliothek wurde am 24. Juni 1915 eingeweiht und ist nach Harry Elkins Widener (1885 –

der Rezensenten nennt,[26] war also dieses Projekt keineswegs, wohl aber eine Art Neigungsarbeit, im Gegensatz zur Pflichtarbeit.

Im Frühjahr 1910, nach dem Abschluß des Gastsemesters, bereiste Meyer zwei Monate lang die Ostküste, den Mittleren Westen sowie die Südstaaten und hielt Dutzende von Vorträgen über zahlreiche Themen aus der vorderorientalischen, griechischen und römischen Geschichte. Neben dem Historiker der Alten Welt kam aber auch der in seiner Offenheit immer wieder provozierende politische Denker zu Wort, der zu akuten Zeitfragen Stellung nahm, etwa zum Staatsbegriff, zum Wert des Studiums der Alten Geschichte oder zur Gründung des Deutschen Reiches. *Ein* Vortrag, gehalten Anfang Februar an der Cornell University, unterschied sich jedoch thematisch von allen anderen: "Mormonism and Mohammedanism".[27] Es ist für Meyers erstaunlich schnelle und energische Arbeitsweise charakteristisch, daß er auch sein jüngstes Forschungsprojekt gleich in sein Vortragsprogramm einbezog—bei ihm gingen Forschung und Lehre immer Hand in Hand—und damit als Religionshistoriker vor einem amerikanischen Publikum eine direkte Brücke zwischen Vergangenheit und Gegenwart, zwischen der Alten und der Neuen Welt, schlug.

Das Buch über die Mormonen erschien dann ganz unerwartet im Herbst 1912. Verständlicherweise wurde es von Althistorikern und Klassischen Philologen bestenfalls als bibliographisches Kuriosum oder als Beweis für Meyers weiten Blick zur Kenntnis genommen.[28] Sein Haupttitel, der nicht einmal den Bezug auf das Christentum und den Islam erkennen läßt, mußte auf weite Kreise geradezu abschreckend wirken. Wer in Europa konnte sich um 1912 schon etwas unter den Mormonen vorstellen oder war an ihnen ernsthaft interessiert?[29]

1912) benannt, der am 29. April 1912 mit der "Titanic" unterging (das Vorwort von Meyers "Mormonen" ist auf den 6. Oktober 1912 datiert); vgl. W. Bentinck-Smith, *Building a Great Library: The Coolidge Years at Harvard*, Cambridge, Mass. 1973, 28–103.

[26] H. Weinel, *Theologische Literaturzeitung* 39, 1914, 659.

[27] Die einzelnen Vorträge sind mitsamt ihren Titeln, soweit sie bekannt sind, aufgeführt bei Chambers (Anm. 23) 30–32.

[28] Im letzteren Sinne äußerten sich in ihren Nachrufen bzw. Gedenkreden etwa Walter Otto (*Zeitschr. d. Deutschen Morgenländ. Gesellsch.* 85, N. F. 10, 1931, 20: "hier sogar die Grenzen des Altertums kühn weitüberschreitend"), Ulrich Wilcken (*Sitzungsber. Berliner Akad. d. Wiss.*, Phil.-hist. Kl. 1931, CXXXIX u. Marohl 127) und Wilamowitz (Anm. 3) 56 ("Wer konnte das von dem Historiker des Altertums erwarten?").

[29] Vgl. F. Kattenbusch, *Theologische Rundschau* 19, 1916, 40: "Gemeinhin weiß man von den Mormonen kaum etwas anderes, als daß sie die Polygamie hegten." Zur Polygamie vgl. Anm. 36. Zeph Stewart verweist mich auf Arthur Conan Doyles ersten Sherlock-Holmes-Roman, *A Study in Scarlet* (1887), dessen zweiter Teil ("The Country of the Saints") in Utah zur Zeit der ersten mormonischen Einwanderung spielt. Die Charakterisierung Brigham Youngs und seines Regimes ist durchweg negativ, unter Betonung

Die ersten Stellungnahmen beschäftigten sich denn auch vornehmlich nicht mit der eigentlich historischen, sondern mit der religionsverglei-chenden Seite des Buchs und stammen durchweg nicht von Althistori-kern, sondern von namhaften Religionshistorikern, Arabisten, Theo-logen und Kirchenhistorikern.[30] Meyers Darstellung der Geschichte der Mormonen und ihrer Verzahnung mit der gleichzeitigen politischen Ent-wicklung wurde von den Rezensenten, die von dieser Materie viel weni-ger verstanden als der Autor, kritiklos gutgeheißen. Neben seinem his-torischen Urteil imponierte ihnen der fesselnde und anschauliche Stil, dem sich wohl kein Leser entziehen kann. Die Berechtigung des Ver-gleichs des Propheten Smith mit Mohammed, der keineswegs neu war, wurde grundsätzlich akzeptiert, wenn auch mit gelegentlichen Modifi-kationen (unten IV). Dagegen stieß seine eigenwillige Beurteilung Jesu als eines religiösen Lehrers, dem der Status eines Propheten abzusprechen sei, weithin auf Ablehnung.[31]

In den dreißiger Jahren setzte sich dann der französische Islamforscher Georges-Henri Bousquet (1900–1978) als erster und meines Wissens bisher einziger Nichtmormone mit dem Mormonenbild Meyers kritisch auseinander.[32] Bousquet war im Zusammenhang mit seinen Islamstu-dien auf Meyers Buch und damit auf die Mormonen gestoßen. Er reiste 1934 eigens in die Vereinigten Staaten, wo er sich längere Zeit am Stammsitz der Mormonen in Salt Lake City, Utah, aufhielt und Spezial-bibliotheken in New York und an der Harvarduniversität besuchte, um sich so an Ort und Stelle über das Mormonentum und seine Schriften zu informieren. Obwohl nicht eigentlich ein Spezialist auf diesem Gebiet,

---

der Polygamie und der von der Kirchenführung angeordneten Fememorde. Entsprechend hat man sich das Bild vorzustellen, das man sich noch um die Jahrhundertwende und selbst darüberhinaus in Europa und Amerika (s. Anm. 38) von den Mormonen machte.

[30] U.a. von Edvard Lehmann (1862–1930), Alfred Loisy (1857–1940) und Nathan Söderblom (1866–1931) als Religionshistoriker; Carl Brockelmann (1868–1956) und Johannes Pedersen (1883–1977) für die Arabistik; dem Theologen Ferdinand Katten-busch (1851–1935) und dem Kirchenhistoriker Albert Werminghoff (1869–1923). Zu den zwischen 1912 und 1916 erschienenen Rezensionen vgl. Marohl 97, Nr. 280.

[31] So etwa bei A. Loisy, *Revue d'histoire et de littérature religieuses* n.s. 4, 1913, 568; N. Söderblom, *Deutsche Literaturzeitung* 35, 1914, 1289; Weinel (Anm. 26) 661; Wilamowitz (Anm. 3) 56.

[32] Ich beziehe mich vor allem auf Bousquets Aufsatz "L'église mormone et ses livres sacrés", *Revue de l'histoire des religions* 113, 1936, 219–255, der in Salt Lake City verfaßt worden ist. Von Meyer, der nicht nur keine mormonischen Primärquellen eingesehen, sondern lediglich einen Tag in der Hauptstadt Utahs verbracht hatte, heißt es (S. 219 Anm. 3): "Il a aussi passé moins de jours à Salt Lake City, que l'auteur de cet article de mois." Weitere einschlägige Arbeiten Bousquets: "Une théocratie économique, l'église mormone", *Revue d'économie politique* 50, 1936, 126–145; *Les Mormons. Histoire et institu-tions*, Paris 1949; "Observations sociologiques sur les origines de l'Islam," *Studia Islamica* 2, 1945, 61–88.

war Bousquet doch über die Mormonen weitaus besser unterrichtet als die eigentlichen Rezensenten von Meyers Buch. Er kam zu dem zutreffenden, wenn auch etwas paradoxen Schluß, daß Meyer trotz seiner unzureichenden Quellenforschungen den bis dahin eindringlichsten Beitrag zur Geschichte der Mormonen geliefert habe.[33] Bousquet bemängelte jedoch, daß Meyer bei der historischen Beurteilung der Mormonenkirche, einer "théocratie économique", und ihrer schnellen Ausbreitung die wirtschaftlichen Faktoren, die in der Tat ganz erheblich waren und es auch weiterhin sind, völlig außer acht gelassen habe.[34]

An Bousquets Kritik lassen sich die ersten Ansätze zu einer bedeutsamen Verschiebung der historischen Perspektive ablesen: an die Stelle des "Adlerblicks", den Meyer noch für sich in Anspruch nehmen durfte, ist in steigendem Maße die mikroskopische Inspektion der Details durch den "social historian" getreten. Dagegen verstand Meyer Geschichte noch ganz im Sinne des 19. Jhdts. als ein mehr oder minder zufälliges und in der jeweiligen Konstellation unwiederholbares Zusammenspiel von Menschen und Ereignisketten. Die "Individualität der wollenden Persönlichkeit" und die Faktizität der "historischen, d.h. wirkenden Vorgänge oder Tatsachen", sind die beiden Grundgegebenheiten, die im Mittelpunkt seiner Geschichtsauffassung stehen.[35] Sozial- und wirtschaftsgeschichtliche Faktoren, die gerade in den jüngsten Behandlungen der Geschichte der Mormonen stark betont werden, waren für ihn von untergeordneter Bedeutung.[36]

Die Reaktion von Seiten der Mormonen ließ lange auf sich warten.

---

[33] "L'église mormone" (Anm. 32) 219: "Les modifications seront assez peu nombreuses: il est presque extraordinaire de constater que Meyer n'a le plus souvent consulté les sources que de la façon la plus imparfaite [vgl. unter III], même lorsqu'il s'agit de publications bien facilement accessibles, et que pourtant son ouvrage est de tous le plus profond sur l'histoire du Mormonisme."

[34] Zur Wirtschaftsstruktur der mormonischen Gemeinden aus historisch-anthropologischer Sicht vgl. M.P. Leone, *The Roots of Modern Mormonism*, Cambridge, Mass. 1979, der von einer "consciously materialist religion" spricht.

[35] Meyer, *Anthropologie* 173–211 (Zitat S. 185 u. 200).

[36] Meyer hatte sich in Vorträgen mit der "Wirtschaftlichen Entwicklung des Altertums" (1895) und der "Sklaverei im Altertum" (1898) beschäftigt (vgl. dazu den Beitrag von Helmuth Schneider). Bei seiner Behandlung der Mormonen fällt dagegen beispielsweise auf, daß er die wirtschaftlichen Grundpfeiler der frühen Kolonisation Utahs, die Landverteilung und das Bewässerungswesen, kaum berührt (*Mormonen* 203 u. 205 f.; anders O'Dea [Anm. 3] 189–205) und die von 1852 bis 1890 offiziell praktizierte Polygamie ("plural marriage") ausschließlich vom sexuellen (Triebhaftigkeit von Joseph Smith) und theologischen (Lehre von der "celestial marriage" bzw. den "spiritual wives") Standpunkt beurteilt, ohne ihre wirtschaftlichen und demographischen Auswirkungen ernsthaft zu berücksichtigen (Meyer, *Mormonen* 158–168, 216–219; differenzierter z.B. O'Dea 245–249, Bousquet [Anm. 32] 245–250 und L. Foster, *Religion and Sexuality. Three American Communal Experiments of the Nineteenth Century*, New York/Oxford 1981, 123–225).

Deren Desinteresse erklärt sich einmal daraus, daß Meyers Monographie erst ein halbes Jahrhundert nach ihrem Erscheinen ins Amerikanische übersetzt worden ist. Diese Übersetzung existiert lediglich in maschinen-schriftlicher Form in einigen Universitätsbibliotheken im Staate Utah und ist damit praktisch unzugänglich.[37] Dazu kommt, daß Meyer aus seiner geringen Meinung von Joseph Smith und der von ihm gegründeten Religion keinen Hehl machte.[38] Das tat seinem Urteilsvermögen als Historiker wenig Abbruch, zumal für ihn historische Wirksamkeit und überragende Persönlichkeit zwei getrennte Größen waren, was sie ja auch sind.[39] Trotzdem mußte seine kritische, ja bisweilen sarkastische Einstellung gerade auf mormonische Leser abstoßend wirken.

In der bisher ausführlichsten Stellungnahme zu Meyer aus mormonischer Sicht, die mir bekannt ist, fehlt jedes Eingehen auf die eigentlich historischen Teile des Buchs. Die Auseinandersetzung beschränkt sich auf Meyers Vergleich von Joseph Smith mit Mohammed (unten IV), der als "facile generalization" verurteilt und kategorisch abgelehnt wird: "In such a *Weltanschauung* as Meyer's there are few heroes; there are mainly lumps of human clay molded by the forces of history."[40] Wer nach

---

[37] *The Origin and History of the Mormons, with Reflections on the Beginnings of Islam and Christianity*, translated by Heinz F. Rahde and Eugene Seaich, Salt Lake City, University of Utah, 1961 (bereits der Titel enthält einen Übersetzungsfehler, nämlich "reflections" zur Wiedergabe von "Exkurse"). Der Übersetzung ist keinerlei Kommentar beigegeben, nicht einmal in Form einer Einleitung der Übersetzer. Eine schwedische Fassung erschien 1914 (Marohl Nr. 295).

[38] Hier eine Auswahl: "Vielleicht kann man den Mahdi von Khartûm auf dieselbe Stufe mit Joseph Smith stellen; aber z.B. Mohammed steht ... weit höher, um von Zoroaster oder etwa Mani [dazu unter IV] und Bâb ganz zu schweigen" (*Mormonen* 2 Anm. 1); "nur trägt bei Smith alles ein noch weit groteskeres Gewand [als bei Mohammed], sein Auftreten ist viel cynischer, so daß hier der Prophet vom Charlatan garnicht mehr zu scheiden ist" (59); "sich von Andern Geld zu verschaffen hat Smith immer verstanden" (19); "der stark entwickelte sinnliche Trieb des Propheten" (158); "die Kirche is durch die Ermordung des Propheten nicht vernichtet, sondern erhalten worden. Durch die blutige Tat war die Farce jäh in eine Tragödie umgeschlagen." (183); "so steht das Machwerk [das "Buch Mormon"] noch weit unter dem Qorân, der doch auch an Monotonie und Trivialität schon schlimm genug ist; kein Mensch, es sei denn ein Gläubiger, wird sich überwinden können, das ganze durchzulesen" (43, vgl. 81 f.). Meyers ablehnende Einstellung gegenüber dem Mormonentum (s. Anm. 19 u. 56) entspricht der damaligen öffentlichen Meinung in Deutschland und Amerika. Zur überwiegend negativen Beurteilung des "Mormon way of life", bei aller Anerkennung der sozialen und wirtschaftlichen Leistungen, des Erziehungssystems sowie der strikten Moralvorschriften, durch die amerikanischen Zeitschriften zwischen 1904 und 1912 vgl. D.L. Lythgoe, *The Changing Image of Mormonism in Periodical Literature*, Diss. University of Utah 1969, University Microfilms, Ann Arbor, Mich., 1969 (Nr. 69–21051) 54–64, 162–166, 205–207.

[39] Meyer, *Anthropologie* 178: "Es ist ein Irrtum, wenn man glaubt, daß die wirksame Individualität eine an sich durch ihre geistigen Eigenschaften bedeutende Persönlichkeit sein müsse—darauf beruht der Heroenkult Carlyles" (dem bekanntlich auch Wilamowitz huldigte).

[40] A.H. Green u. L.P. Goldrup, "Joseph Smith, an American Muhammad? An

Geistesheroen sucht, ist bei Meyer allerdings an der falschen Adresse; den romantischen "Heroenkult" eines Thomas Carlyle hat er ebenso verurteilt wie die Heroisierung von Smith durch die Mormonen.[41] Zwischen Meyer und den Mormonen ist keine Verständigung möglich. Deshalb schenkt die offizielle mormonische Geschichtsschreibung dem "heidnischen" ("Gentile"), d.h. nichtmormonischen, Historiker des Mormonentums auch weiterhin keine Beachtung.

III. Offenbarung und Geschichte

Meyers Darstellung gibt sich als durchgehender historischer Bericht, der lediglich von dem Exkurs über den "Ursprung des Islâms und die ersten Offenbarungen Mohammeds" unterbrochen wird (S. 67–83). Der Exkurs steht an einschneidender Stelle und teilt das Buch in zwei ungleiche Hälften. Diese Dichotomie hat sich im Titel niedergeschlagen: "*Ursprung* und *Geschichte* des Mormonentums". Der erste Teil (S. 14–66) beschäftigt sich nämlich mit dem Propheten des Mormonentums und seinen ersten, grundlegenden Offenbarungen, die zur Niederschrift des "Book of Mormon" und zur Kirchengründung führten. Der zweite, weitaus umfangreichere Teil (S. 84–276) behandelt dann in chronologischer Abfolge die wichtigsten Phasen der Kirchengeschichte von der Gründung bis zur Eingliederung des mormonischen "Kirchenstaates" in die Union.

Der erste Teil ist mehr religionsgeschichtlich, der zweite naturgemäß mehr historisch orientiert, aber beide Betrachtungsweisen überlagern sich häufig. Der Vergleich von Joseph Smith mit Mohammed, der von außen herangetragen ist und die eigentliche Geschichte der Mormonen nicht berührt, zieht sich wie ein roter Faden durch das ganze Buch. Die doppelte Perspektive von Offenbarung und Geschichte, oder von einer Offenbarung, die Geschichte machte und sich damit als eine historische Erscheinung bekannten Typs erwies, entspricht den beiden zentralen Fragestellungen, die für Meyers Geschichtsdenken charakteristisch sind, nämlich der universalhistorischen und der religionsgeschichtlichen. Auf das Verhältnis dieser beiden Perspektiven werde ich zurückkommen. Zuvor möchte ich jedoch Meyers Zuverlässigkeit als Historiker des Mormonentums an einem konkreten Beispiel kurz beleuchten.

Im Gegensatz zu seinen Forschungen zur Alten Welt bezog Meyer bei der Vorbereitung seines Mormonenbuchs seine Dokumentation auf lange

---

Essay on the Perils of Historical Analogy", *Dialogue: A Journal of Mormon Thought* 6, Spring 1971, 46–58, bes. 56 f.

[41] Vgl. Anm. 39.

Strecken lediglich aus zweiter Hand.[42] Nur wenige bereits publizierte
Primärquellen waren ihm zugänglich. Daß ihm bei dieser Arbeitsweise
Fehlurteile unterlaufen mußten, war unvermeidlich. Zu einer kritischen
Prüfung der historischen Substanz von Meyers Darstellung ist es allerdings bisher nicht gekommen. Das in der gegenwärtigen Situation zu tun,
wäre ein schwieriges und wohl auch müßiges Unterfangen, das mir am
wenigsten zusteht. Denn der Zuwachs an historischen Quellen ist gerade
für die von Meyer behandelte Periode (1830–1890) beträchtlich und
kann wichtige Personen und Episoden sehr leicht in einem anderen Licht
erscheinen lassen. Der Zugang zu diesen Quellen, soweit sie sich in den
mormonischen Kirchenarchiven befinden, wird dadurch erschwert, daß
die Kirchenleitung jeder vorurteilslosen Geschichtsschreibung, selbst der
aus den eigenen Reihen, seit Jahren mit immer größerem Mißtrauen begegnet und das Einsehen der Dokumente einer strengeren Zensur unterworfen hat.[43] Abgesehen von dem Zuwachs an Quellenmaterial haben
sich aber auch die der historischen Kritik zur Verfügung stehenden
Fragestellungen, Interpretationsmodelle und Methoden inzwischen so
sehr gewandelt, daß Meyers Behandlung im Vergleich mit der hochspe-
zialisierten Einzelforschung oft abfällt. Trotzdem wünscht man dem Buch
auch in Zukunft zahlreiche Leser. Denn zumindest im deutschsprachigen
Raum ist es als erste Informationsquelle noch immer unentbehrlich und
als historische Erzählung von unvergleichlicher Frische.

Als Beispiel dafür, wie sich die Forschungslage in der Zwischenzeit
geändert hat, wähle ich Meyers packenden Bericht über das "Massacre
von Mountain Meadows" (1857), eine der blutigsten Episoden der an
Gewalttaten reichen Frühgeschichte der Mormonen. Bei diesem Vorfall
wurden an die hundert nichtmormonische Auswanderer auf ihrem Treck
nach Kalifornien von der lokalen Mormonenmiliz, die sich mit Indianern
zusammengetan hatte, im südlichen Utah auf hinterhältige Weise ermordet:

> So ging man am nächsten Morgen, dem 11. September, ans Werk.
> Während die Indianer abzogen und sich verbargen, ging ein Mormone ins

[42] *Mormonen*, Vorwort u. S. 7. Meyers Hauptinformationsquelle war das umfassende,
aber mormonenfeindliche Geschichtswerk von W.A. Linn, *The Story of the Mormons: From
the Date of their Origin to the Year 1901*, New York/London 1902.
[43] Shipps (Anm. 3) 89–91, 106 f.; D.B. Davis, "Secrets of the Mormons", *The New
York Review of Books*, 15. August 1985, 15–19. In dieselbe Richtung weist auch eine
ungewöhnliche Bemerkung in Arrington (Anm. 3) xii: "Latter-day Saint authorities have
not screened this volume for its suitability for Mormon readers. In short, this has been
a private, not a church project." Der mormonische Historiker, der 1982 seines Amtes als
"Church Historian" enthoben wurde, gilt als der Begründer einer neuen, mehr objektiven und professionellen Kirchengeschichtsschreibung, die von den kirchlichen Behörden
abgelehnt wird.

Lager der Emigranten, wo er mit Freuden begrüßt wurde, da sie von der wahren Sachlage keine Ahnung hatten und von den Mormonen Rettung erhofften. Es wurde ihnen vorgeschlagen, das Lager zu räumen und in Cedar City unter mormonischer Deckung Schutz zu suchen; Lee erhielt den Auftrag, für die Ausführung zu sorgen. Er erzählt, daß ihm bei dem feigen Verrat geschaudert habe; er habe gewünscht, daß die Erde ihn verschlingen möge. Aber es gab keine Wahl: er mußte gehorchen und Gottes Willen vollziehen. Die Kinder und Verwundeten wurden auf zwei herbeigeschaffte Wagen geladen, desgleichen die Waffen; dann folgten die Frauen, zum Schluß die Männer, geleitet und scheinbar beschützt von bewaffneten Mormonen. Als man an den für die Tat ausgewählten Ort gekommen war, erscholl der Befehl: Tut eure Pflicht! Die Männer wurden von ihren Begleitern erschossen, die Weiber und Kinder von den Indianern niedergehauen, die Verwundeten in den Wagen abgeschlachtet; die wenigen, die zu entkommen versuchten, wurden eingeholt und erbarmungslos umgebracht, darunter mehrere junge Mädchen und Knaben. Verschont blieben nur die Kinder unter sechs Jahren, von denen man annahm, daß sie noch nichts erzählen könnten; von allen andern, über 120 Männern und Frauen, ist kein einziger am Leben geblieben. Die Leichen wurden notdürftig bestattet, die beträchtliche Beute weggeschleppt, die Kinder in die benachbarten Ortschaften verteilt; im Jahre 1859 sind sie von der Unionsregierung befreit und in den Osten gebracht worden.[44]

Dieses unmenschliche Vorgehen hat schon immer einen dunklen Schatten auf die frühe Geschichte der Mormonen geworfen. Dem Historiker geht es bei der Behandlung dieses "tragic incident"[45] nicht nur um die Hintergründe und den Ablauf der Tat, sondern auch um die Schuldigen. Gerade hier, in der Beurteilung der Schuldfrage, hat sich Meyer jedoch ein herrschendes Vorurteil zu eigen gemacht und die Grenze dessen, was nach der heutigen Quellenlage historisch vertretbar ist, nachweislich überschritten.

An der Spitze des Mormonenstaates stand damals Brigham Young (1801 – 1877), Nachfolger von Joseph Smith als Kirchenpräsident, Erbauer von Salt Lake City, erster Gouverneur des Staates Utah und die eindrucksvollste Erscheinung der Gründerzeit. Meyer war überzeugt, daß dieses Blutbad wenn nicht auf ausdrückliche Anordnung, so doch unter stillschweigender Zustimmung von Young stattgefunden habe, der drei Tagereisen vom Ort des Geschehens entfernt war: "daß [es] gegen

---

[44] Meyer, *Mormonen* 237–245, Zitat S. 239 f. Meyers Darstellung gibt das eigentliche Massaker sachlich richtig wieder, aber die Farben sind noch kräftiger aufgetragen (z.B. "erschossen ... niedergehauen ... abgeschlachtet", ein Trikolon mit Crescendo) als bei Linn (Anm. 42) 517–534, dem Meyer sonst oft bis in die Formulierung folgt. Die tatsächliche Zahl der Opfer läßt sich nicht mehr feststellen, lag aber vermutlich unter hundert; vgl. J. Brooks, *The Mountain Meadows Massacre*, 4. Aufl., Norman, Oklahoma 1970, XIII ff.

[45] So Arrington (Anm. 3) 258.

seinen Willen geschehen sei, wie er selbst später behauptet hat und die
Mormonen ihm nachsprechen, ist völlig ausgeschlossen.''[46] Nach An-
gabe eines maßgeblich beteiligten Mormonen soll Young jedoch angeordnet haben, die Auswanderer unbehelligt ziehen zu lassen. In einer
Fußnote tut Meyer diese Order als Scheininstruktion ab, die absichtlich
nicht zur Ausführung gekommen sei.[47] Meyer sah also mit der Mehrzahl
seiner nichtmormonischen Zeitgenossen in Young einen der Hauptschul-
digen an dem Massaker.

In diesem Fall läßt sich jedoch zeigen, daß Meyer aus Unkenntnis der
Primärquellen zu einem vorschnellen Urteil verleitet worden ist. Der
jüngste Biograph Youngs und profilierteste mormonische Historiker der
Gegenwart hat nämlich auf einen Brief Youngs vom 10. September 1857
hingewiesen, der an Isaac C. Haight, den ranghöchsten Mormonen von
Cedar City und Ortskommandanten der "Iron County Militia", gerichtet ist und von dessen Existenz Meyer ohne Einsicht in die Kirchenarchive
nichts ahnen konnte. Young wird durch dieses Dokument im entscheidenden Punkt entlastet.[48] Denn aus diesem Brief geht eindeutig hervor,
daß Young zwar den Indianern in ihrem Umgang mit den durchziehen-
den Aussiedlern freie Hand lassen wollte, aber seinen eigenen Leuten jed-
wede Einmischung strikt verbat.[49] Der Tenor des Briefs läßt an der
Aufrichtigkeit von Youngs Haltung keinen Zweifel. Der Bote kam jedoch

---

[46] *Mormonen* 240 f.
[47] *Mormonen* 240 f. Anm. 1: "Vermutlich haben Young und die übrigen Leiter die Tat
geschehen lassen, sich aber zugleich nach Möglichkeit durch derartige nicht ausgeführte
Instruktionen decken wollen."
[48] Arrington (Anm. 3, vgl. Anm. 43) 258 f., vgl. 279–281 u. 385 f., der im wesentlichen Brooks (s. Anm. 44) 60 ff. u. 110 ff. bestätigt, wo Youngs Brief ebenfalls abgedruckt
ist. Er existiert wie so viele Briefe Youngs anscheinend nur in amtlicher Kopie und gehört
zu einer umfangreichen Sammlung von Youngs offizieller Korrespondenz in Form von
"letterpress copies", die sich seit seiner Amtszeit in den Kirchenarchiven von Salt Lake
City befinden.
[49] Die ausschlaggebenden Sätze lauten: "In regard to the emigration trains passing
through our settlements, we must not interfere with them until they are first notified to
keep away. You must not meddle with them. The Indians we expect will do as they please
but you should try and preserve good feelings with them. There are no other trains going
south that I know of. If those that are there will leave, let them go in peace. While we
should be on the alert, on hand, and always ready, we should also possess ourselves in
patience, preserving ourselves and property, ever remembering that God rules." Der
Brief bestätigt allerdings Meyers Verdacht, daß Young die Indianer, die ebenso wie die
Mormonen mit der Bundesregierung in Fehde lagen, nur allzu gern gewähren ließ,
solange sie die Mormonen und deren Besitz verschonten. Er ändert auch nichts an der
Tatsache, daß Young die offizielle Verantwortung für das Massaker auf die Indianer
abwälzte und die schuldigen Mormonen nicht zur Rechenschaft zog. Einer der Haupt-
beteiligten, John D. Lee, wurde 1870 exkommuniziert, erst 1876 von den Bundesbehör-
den vor Gericht gestellt, zum Tode verurteilt und am 23. März 1877 "an der Stätte seiner
Tat vor seinem Sarge erschossen" (Meyer, *Mormonen* 242; vgl. Brooks [Anm. 44] 207 ff.).
Young starb fünf Monate später im Alter von 76 Jahren.

trotz eines Parforceritts um zwei Tage zu spät. Hätte Meyer dieses Dokument gekannt, wäre seine Beurteilung Youngs vermutlich anders ausgefallen. Daß Meyer unzulänglichen Zugang zu den Primärquellen hatte, macht sich auch an anderen Stellen unangenehm bemerkbar.[50]

Als wirklich autoritatives Geschichtswerk kann Meyers Buch nicht gelten. Die selbständige Erforschung der Geschichte des Mormonentums reizte ihn offensichtlich nicht in demselben Maße wie das religionsgeschichtliche Problem, das sich mit dem Prophetentum von Joseph Smith stellt und dem der erste Teil des Buchs gewidmet ist. Hierbei kam ihm seine Vertrautheit mit den alttestamentlichen Propheten und mit Mohammed zu Hilfe. Propheten stehen in einem seltsamen Verhältnis zur Geschichte: sie sind in den geschichtlichen Prozeß wie jedes andere Individuum einbezogen und weisen doch durch den Anspruch höherer Eingebung und durch ihre Zukunftsoffenbarungen ganz bewußt über die Geschichte hinaus. Gleichzeitig repräsentieren sie aber auch eine religiöse Sonderform des historischen Bewußtseins. Prophetie und Offenbarung bilden sich nämlich jeweils ihren eigenen Zeitbegriff, der von den Zeitkategorien des Historikers grundverschieden ist.[51] Deshalb gelten sie seit der Antike als autonome Weisen des Geschichtsverständnisses. Für den Historiker sind die Propheten allerdings eine ständige Herausforderung; denn sie berühren sich gerade wegen ihres betonten Geschichtsbewußtseins ganz eng mit seinem Metier.[52] So erklärt sich Meyers lebenslanges Interesse an diesen Prophetengestalten, denen wir uns abschließend zuwenden.

IV. Der Begriff der ''historischen Analogie'': Joseph Smith, Mohammed und Mani

Der junge Smith wuchs in einer religiösen Umwelt auf, die einen starken Hang zur Superstition und zu okkulten Praktiken hatte. Er selbst beschäftigte sich ganz ernsthaft mit Magie und Schatzsuchen, wobei er einen ''Seherstein'' benutzte, ja anscheinend sogar mit Nekromantie und Geisterbeschwörungen, und zog sich in die Einsamkeit zur Kontemplation zurück, wie es unzählige Visionäre der verschiedensten religiösen

---

[50] So in seiner Schilderung der Ermordung von Smith (vgl. Anm. 6), die der offiziellen Version von 1856 folgt, obwohl darin zwei unabhängige, aber widersprüchliche Augenzeugenberichte willkürlich kontaminiert sind. Beide Berichte waren zu Meyers Zeit längst publiziert (vgl. Jessee [Anm. 6] 14–17), ihm aber anscheinend nicht zugänglich.
[51] Vgl. z.B. A. Henrichs, ''The Timing of Supernatural Events'' in the Cologne Mani Codex'', in L. Cirillo u. A. Roselli (Hrsg.), *Codex Manichaicus Coloniensis. Atti del Simposio Internazionale (Rende-Amantea 3–7 settembre 1984)*, Cosenza 1986, 183–204.
[52] Dazu A. Momigliano, ''Prophetie und Geschichtsschreibung'', in J. Petersohn (Hrsg.), *Prophetie und Geschichtsschreibung. Ehrenpromotion Arnaldo Momigliano*, Schriften der Universitätsbibliothek Marburg 27, Marburg 1986, 13–21.

Färbungen vor ihm getan hatten.[53] Dieser religionssoziologische Befund wird in der jüngsten Forschung zur Erklärung der Visionsfreudigkeit des jungen Smith immer wieder mit Recht herangezogen.[54]

Auch Meyer stellte die überspannte Religiosität, von der Smith umgeben war, als äußeren Einfluß in Rechnung: "ein völlig ungebildeter, aber eben darum '[!] durchaus gläubiger Junge, aufgewachsen in einer Umgebung voll wüstesten Aberglaubens und wirrster religiöser Phantasie."[55] Aber er sah darin wie im Mormonentum überhaupt lediglich das "Fortleben ganz primitiver Vorstellungen und Denkformen"[56], also eines jener "survivals", nach denen die evolutionistische Religionstheorie seiner Zeit ständig suchte. Dieser Primitivismus war für ihn ein Zeichen ursprünglicher, unverfälschter Religiosität. Seine abfälligen Bemerkungen über die vermeintliche Naivität des "Book of Mormon" und des Korans sind also in seinem Munde nicht nur Ausdruck überlegener akademischer Distanz, sondern kommen aus der damaligen religionshistorischen Sicht einem Echtheitszeugnis gleich.

Den wirklichen Schlüssel zum Verständnis von Smiths Prophetentum suchte Meyer jedoch in der Religionspsychologie, die zu Beginn dieses Jahrhunderts in Deutschland und Amerika sehr populär war. Erinnert sei nur an William James (1842–1910), der im Zusammenhang mit seiner religiösen Typenlehre bereits zehn Jahre zuvor Mohammed und Joseph Smith als Repräsentanten einer "exalted sensibility", bei denen die Inspiration zur zweiten Natur geworden war, nebeneinandergestellt hatte.[57] Die für Meyer entscheidende Anregung kam aber nicht von James, sondern von Isaac Woodbridge Riley (1869–1933), der in seiner "Psychological Study of Joseph Smith" den Gründer des Mormonentums als einen Epileptiker und Psychopathen eingestuft hatte; dieser Diagnose schloß sich Meyer gerne an.[58]

Mit einer so ausschließlich psychologisch motivierten Bestimmung von Smiths Persönlichkeitsbild war aber die Gefahr gegeben, daß sich der Fall Smith der Kompetenz des Historikers ganz entzog. Um sich dagegen abzusichern und den Kompetenzbereich des Historikers von dem des

---

[53] Vgl. F.M. Brodie, *No Man Knows My History: The Life of Joseph Smith, the Mormon Prophet*, 2. Aufl. New York 1971, Nachdruck 1982, 16–33.

[54] Bushman (Anm. 3) 64–76, 184; Shipps (Anm. 3) 6–8.

[55] *Mormonen* 14–19, 28–33, Zitat S. 28.

[56] *Mormonen* 8. Die Mormonen sind deshalb "so besonders instruktiv, weil es sich hier um die tiefstehendsten Volksschichten handelt" (UAC II 418).

[57] W. James, *The Varieties of Religious Experience* (1902), in F. Burkhardt u. F. Bowers (Hrsg.), *The Works of William James*, Bd. 15, Cambridge, Mass., 1985, 376–380.

[58] I.W. Riley, *The Founder of Mormonism: A Psychological Study of Joseph Smith, Jr.*, New York 1902; dagegen z.B. O'Dea (Anm. 3) 24. Vgl. Meyer, *Mormonen* 7, 11 f. u. 33 (Smith hatte "die erbliche Anlage zu Visionen und ähnlichen Krankheitserscheinungen").

Psychologen abzugrenzen, berief sich Meyer auf den Begriff der "historischen Analogie", den er bereits in seinen geschichtstheoretischen Schriften von 1884 bzw. 1902 entwickelt hatte und dessen er sich vor allem in seinen zeitpolitischen Stellungnahmen mit Vorliebe zur Parallelisierung von Gegenwart und Antike bediente:

> Der Historiker ist kein Psychologe. Die Bedingungen und Formen des Seelenlebens sind ihm gegebene Voraussetzungen für die Erkenntnis der geschichtlich wirksamen Momente. Er hat daher keine Untersuchungen über geistige Anomalien, über Visionen und Halluzinationen, Suggestionen und "magnetische" Heilkraft, Hypnotismus, Neuropathie, Hysterie, Epilepsie usw. anzustellen; aber ebensowenig darf er diese Dinge aus der Welt hinwegdeuten, sondern er hat sie und die gewaltige Bedeutung, die sie im geschichtlichen und speziell im religiösen Leben jederzeit ausgeübt haben und ausüben, als Tatsachen anzuerkennen und als solche bei der Erklärung der historischen Erscheinungen zu verwerten. *Dabei steht ihm ein für alle historische Forschung bedeutungsvolles Mittel zur Verfügung, die historische Analogie. Gleichartige Ereignisse erläutern sich gegenseitig, und ihre Vergleichung führt zu einem tieferen Verständnis des Einzelfalls.* Diesen in seiner historischen Eigenart zu erfassen, bleibt immer die letzte Aufgabe der Geschichte; wenn die Psychologie aus der Vergleichung die allgemeinen Formen eines seelischen Vorgangs zu ermitteln sucht, hat die Historie umgekehrt zu zeigen, wie diese allgemeinen Formen sich unter der Einwirkung der Sonderbedingungen des Einzelfalls gestaltet haben und wie daraus ihre individuelle Erscheinungsform und ihre geschichtliche Wirkung erwächst.—Soviel Licht von der Genesis des Mormonentums auf die verwandten Erscheinungen ausstrahlt, vor allem auf das Verständnis der Einzelgestaltung, ebensoviel Licht strahlt von diesen auf jene für das Verständnis des letzten Grundproblems zurück.[59]

Meyer betont wiederholt, daß die blinde Anwendung des Konzepts der historischen Analogie auf wichtige Einzelpersönlichkeiten der Geschichte unweigerlich zu einer Nivellierung führen würde, die den Blick für die spezifischen Unterschiede und damit für die Vielfalt der geschichtlichen Erscheinungen verstellt. Aber ebensosehr steht für ihn fest, daß sich gerade beim Vergleich mehrerer Vertreter desselben Typus, etwa des Reli-

---

[59] *Mormonen* 12 f. (die Hervorhebung stammt von mir). Zu Meyers theoretischer Rechtfertigung des Konzepts der "Analogie" vgl. *Anthropologie* 174, 203 (wo jedoch im Gegensatz zu den anderen Stellen von einem "Analogieschluß auf uns selbst" die Rede ist) u. 206 f. sowie den Beitrag von Renate Schlesier; zur praktischen Anwendung bei Meyer vgl. die Beiträge von Alexander Demandt, Jürgen von Ungern-Sternberg und Helmuth Schneider. Mit weitgespannten historischen Analogien operierten nicht nur B.G. Niebuhr (1776–1831) und Gustav Droysen (1838–1908), sondern nach Meyer gerade in Anwendung auf die Religionsgeschichte auch Max Weber (1864–1920). In Jürgen Deiningers Beitrag wird die Möglichkeit eines Einflusses von Meyers Mormonenbuch auf Webers Religionssoziologie erwogen. Konkrete Anzeichen dafür gibt es nicht. In Webers "Gesammelten Aufsätzen zur Religionssoziologie" werden die Mormonen nur einmal genannt, und zwar an ganz untergeordneter Stelle (Bd. I, 1920, 171 Anm.-3). Zur Behandlung des Islam ist Weber nicht mehr gekommen.

gionsstifters oder Propheten, die individuellen Züge am deutlichsten vom
Gattungsbegriff abheben.

Das historische Analogon, das Meyer heranzog, war nun Mohammed
(ca. 570–632). Durch diese "historische Parallele" wurden Smith und
die Mormonen in einen universalhistorischen Zusammenhang gestellt
und dem Historiker wieder in seinem eigenen Bereich zugänglich gemacht. Die Parallelisierung von Smith und Mohammed bot sich aufgrund des ähnlich gelagerten Persönlichkeitsbilds an: Meyer hielt beide
für eine "Mischung von Schwärmer und Schwindler".[60] Die Vergleichsbasis war also im Ansatz wiederum psychologisch, nicht historisch bestimmt. Dazu kam Meyers frühe Vertrautheit mit dem Koran und sein
Interesse am Islam (oben II). Der Vergleich zwischen Joseph Smith und
Mohammed war jedoch keineswegs neu; er ist seit dem 14. Oktober 1838
immer wieder gezogen worden. An diesem Tag hielt der Prophet der
Mormonen nämlich in Far West, Missouri, eine feurige politische Rede,
in der er sich als einen "second Mohammed" bezeichnete:

> If the people will let us alone, we will preach the gospel in peace. But if they
> come on us to molest us, we will establish our religion by the sword. We will
> trample down our enemies and make it one gore of blood from the Rocky
> Mountains to the Atlantic Ocean. I will be to this generation a second
> Mohammed, whose motto in treating for peace was "the Alcoran or the
> Sword." So shall it eventually be with us: "Joseph Smith or the Sword."[61]

Smith kannte Mohammed und den Islam nur vom Hörensagen. Anders
als Meyer ging es ihm bei diesem Vergleich gerade nicht um Offenbarungen und Glaubensinhalte, sondern ausschließlich um eine Religionspolitik, die selbst vor dem Heiligen Krieg nicht zurückschreckte. Es war
der Kämpfer Mohammed, nicht der Visionär, der Smith als Vorbild
diente.

Mit einer so vagen und dazu noch mehr politisch als religiös konzipierten Parallelisierung konnte sich aber die Religionswissenschaft nicht
zufriedengeben. Die zahlreichen Berührungspunkte zwischen Smith und
Mohammed bzw. zwischen Mormonentum und Islam, die von Meyer
und der späteren Forschung hervorgehoben worden sind, konzentrieren
sich auf drei eng zusammenhängende Themenbereiche: die Persönlichkeit und das Prophetentum der beiden Religionsstifter, die sich auf göttliche Offenbarungen beriefen; die Aufzeichnung dieser Offenbarungen in

---

[60] So mit Bezug auf Mohammed der junge Meyer in einem Brief an den Studien-
freund Richard Pietschmann vom 8.11.1876; zitiert von Hoffmann (Anm. 1) Anm. 73.
Genauso urteilte Meyer auch über Joseph Smith (vgl. Anm. 38).

[61] Der von einem Augenzeugen verbürgte Text ist zitiert nach Brodie (Anm. 53)
230 f.; vgl. Meyer, *Mormonen* 119. Zur Geschichte des Modells Smith/Mohammed vor
Meyer vgl. Green und Goldrup (Anm. 40) 46–48.

einer heiligen Schrift, die zur kanonischen Grundlage der jeweiligen Buchreligionen wurde; und schließlich der universale Anspruch der beiden Religionen, der zu expansiver Missionierung und zur Errichtung von militanten Theokratien mit politischen Ambitionen führte.[62]

Abschließend sei anhand des ersten der drei genannten Themenbereiche die Probe aufs Exempel gemacht. Welche Rolle spielte die Offenbarung in der Selbstauffassung der beiden Propheten? Neben Smith und Mohammed möchte ich jedoch noch den Stifter einer weiteren Offenbarungsreligion in den Vergleich miteinbeziehen, nämlich Mani (216 bis ca. 276), nach dem der Manichäismus benannt ist. Auch bei Mani waren die Offenbarungen die treibende Kraft, die ihn zum Religionsstifter werden ließen. In den letzten zwei Jahrzehnten sind neue Texte bekanntgeworden, darunter vor allem der Kölner Mani-Codex, die unsere Kenntnis des jungen Mani und der Frühzeit des Manichäismus auf eine ganz neue Basis stellen. Hätte Meyer diese Texte gekannt, so hätte er Mani vermutlich berücksichtigt, zumal er ihn in einer Anmerkung des Mormonenbuchs neben Mohammed und Smith ausdrücklich nennt.[63]

Der Anstoß zu Joseph Smiths Sendung als Prophet eines reformierten Christen- bzw. Judentums ging von einer Serie von Visionen aus, die ihm seit dem Frühjahr 1820, als er 14 Jahre alt war, in immer kürzer werdenden Abständen zuteil wurden; im Herbst 1823 erschien ihm zum ersten Mal der Engel Moroni: "Not only was his robe exceedingly white, but his whole person was glorious beyond description, and his countenance truly like lightning."[64] Die sukzessiven Jugendvisionen von Smith kulminier-

---

[62] Vgl. Meyer, *Mormonen* 67–83 ("Exkurs: Der Ursprung des Islâms und die ersten Offenbarungen Mohammeds"); J. Pedersen, Rezension von Meyer, *Mormonen* (vgl. Anm. 30), in *Der Islam* 5, 1914, 110–115; H. Thimme, "Mormonism and Islam", *The Moslem World* 24, 1934, 155–167; apologetische Zusammenfassung aus mormonischer Sicht bei Green und Goldrup (Anm. 40).

[63] *Mormonen* 2 Anm. 1 (zitiert oben Anm. 38).

[64] J. Smith, Jr., *History of the Church of Jesus Christ of Latter-day Saints: Period I, History of Joseph Smith, the Prophet*, hrsg. von B.H. Roberts, 2. rev. Aufl., Salt Lake City, Utah, 1955, I 11 f. (die offizielle, dem Gründer zugeschriebene Kirchengeschichte); abgedruckt im Vorspann des *Book of Mormon*. Die lichte, blitzartige Engelserscheinung hat eine lange Vorgeschichte in der antiken Offenbarungsliteratur; vgl. Meyer, *Mormonen* 280 u. 288 sowie Henrichs/Koenen (Anm. 11) 82 Anm. 98. Smith selbst machte über das Jahr (1820 bzw. 1822) und den Inhalt (Lichtsäule mit einer bzw. zwei göttlichen Personen) seiner ersten Offenbarung widersprüchliche Angaben, die aus der Zeit von 1831/32 bis 1839 stammen; mehrere seiner engsten Verwandten verwechselten die Erstoffenbarung mit dem ersten Erscheinen des Engels Moroni, das dreieinhalb Jahre später stattfand. Zur umstrittenen Erstoffenbarung und den ersten Visionen insgesamt vgl. D.C. Jessee, *The Early Accounts of Joseph Smith's First Vision*, Brigham Young University Studies IX 3, 1969 (Edition neuer autobiographischer Texte von Smith); Brodie (Anm. 53) 24 f., 405–412 (beste Zusammenfassung); Bushman (Anm. 3) 49–64 (vom Standpunkt einer akademisch verbrämten mormonischen Orthodoxie); Shipps (Anm. 3) 1–23 (aus nichtmormonischer Sicht).

ten in der Übergabe der goldenen Tafeln (oben I). In den Jahren 1829 bis 1831, also vor, während und nach der Kirchengründung von 1830, häuften sich die Offenbarungen (''"revelations"''), die wie bei Mohammed die Form von inneren Eingebungen ohne Engelserscheinungen annahmen und ganz bewußt als Instrument der Kirchenführung eingesetzt wurden.[65] Das Einsetzen der eigentlichen Offenbarungsvisionen in der Pubertätszeit und ihre allmähliche Intensivierung sind auch für Mani bezeugt.

Mohammed war im Vergleich mit Smith und Mani ein Spätentwickler, der seine erste Vision im Alter von ungefähr 40 Jahren hatte.[66] Von nur zwei Visionen wird im Koran berichtet: "Er stand aufrecht da, (in der Ferne) ganz oben am Horizont. Hierauf näherte er sich und kam (immer weiter) nach unten und war (schließlich nur noch) zwei Bogenlängen(?) (entfernt) oder (noch) näher (da). Und er gab seinem Diener (d.h. Mohammed) jene Offenbarung ein.—Er hat ihn ja auch ein anderes Mal herabkommen sehen, beim Zizyphusbaum."[67] Neben der Selbstaussage im Koran stehen sekundäre Traditionen aus Mohammeds Umgebung, die im Zusammenhang mit seiner ersten Offenbarung von einer Stimme bzw. von einer Engelserscheinung reden.[68] Der Übergang von der Stimme zur Personifikation, d.h. vom Hören zum Sehen, ist bei visionären Erfahrungen oft fließend.[69] Danach hatte Mohammed anscheinend keine Visionen mehr, auch darin Smith vergleichbar, sondern Einge-

---

[65] In den 136 Abschnitten der von Smith redigierten *Doctrine and Covenants* (Anm. 2) ist der Inhalt von insgesamt 123 ausgewählten Offenbarungen verzeichnet, die sich folgendermaßen auf die Jahre 1823 bis 1843 verteilen: 1823 (1), 1828 (2), 1829 (13), 1830 (19), 1831 (37), 1832 (16), 1833 (13), 1834 (4), 1835 (2), 1836 (3), 1837 (1), 1838 (7), 1841 (3) und 1843 (2).

[66] Zu Mohammed habe ich die folgende Literatur benutzt: Meyer, *Mormonen* 67–83; M. Rodinson, ''A Critical Survey of Modern Studies on Muhammad,'' in M.L. Swartz (Hrsg.), *Studies on Islam*, New York/Oxford 1981, 23–85; W. Montgomery Watt, ''Muhammad'', *The Encyclopedia of Religion* 10, New York/London 1987, 137–146.

[67] *Der Koran. Übersetzung von Rudi Paret*, Stuttgart/Berlin 1979, 372 (Sure 53,5–10); vgl. Meyer, *Mormonen* 72 f. u. bes. R. Bell, ''Muhammad's Visions,'' *The Moslem World* 24, 1934, 145–154 = R. Paret (Hrsg.), *Der Koran*, Darmstadt 1975, 93–102.

[68] Ob der Engel ihm auch wie im Falle von Smith den Text des heiligen Buchs überbrachte, das dann sozusagen präexistent gewesen wäre, ist umstritten. Bei dieser Kontroverse geht es um die Übersetzung von Sure 96,3 (''lies'', ''rezitiere'' bzw. ''trag vor''), vgl. Meyer, *Mormonen* 75–80; Pedersen (Anm. 62) 111–115; Lehmann (Anm. 5) 323–325, bes. 323: ''Beide [Mohammed und Smith] reden von einem imaginären Buch, das als Bürgschaft für die absolute Zuverlässigkeit ihrer Offenbarung dient.''

[69] Zum Alternieren von Schauen und Hören in Offenbarungstexten vgl. F. Lentzen-Deis, *Die Taufe Jesu nach den Synoptikern. Literarkritische und gattungsgeschichtliche Untersuchungen*, Frankfurter Theologische Studien 4, Frankfurt a. M. 1970, 99–127; zur ''hypostatic voice,'' d.h. der zur Person gewordenen Stimme, in antiken Offenbarungsberichten vgl. J.H. Charlesworth (Hrsg.), *The Old Testament Pseudepigrapha*, New York 1985, I 693, II 406 u. 408.

bungen, die er "in seinem Herzen fand." Im Gegensatz zu Smith und Mani hat Mohammed seine Visionen und Offenbarungen allerdings nicht datiert.

Manis erste Visionen fielen in seine Kindheit; bereits im Alter von vier Jahren begann er, überirdische Stimmen zu vernehmen und Engelserscheinungen zu sehen.[70] Diese Visionen nahmen im Laufe der Zeit an Intensität zu. Als er zwölf Jahre alt war, erschien ihm zum ersten Mal sein himmlisches Alter Ego bzw. höheres Ich, der sogenannte Syzygos, in Engelsgestalt: "Als es meinem Vater gefiel und er mir sein Erbarmen und seine Fürsorge erwies, da sandte er von dort meinen Gefährten (Syzygos), der höchst zuverlässig, der die umfassende Frucht der Unsterblichkeit ist, damit mich dieser aus den Irrungen der Anhänger jenes Gesetzes loskaufte und erlöste."[71] Diese Erscheinungen des Syzygos, die meist mit Offenbarungen verbunden waren, wiederholten sich dann in regelmäßigen Abständen im Verlauf von Manis Sendung. Im Gegensatz zu Mohammed datierte Mani die wichtigsten Offenbarungen sorgfältig.[72] Darin berührte er sich mit Smith.

Es ist an der Zeit, das Fazit aus diesem keineswegs erschöpfenden Vergleich zu ziehen, was Meyer merkwürdigerweise versäumt hat. Folgende Übereinstimmungen im Offenbarungsmodus lassen sich feststellen:

(1) Kindheits- bzw. Jugendoffenbarungen (Mani und Smith; nicht Mohammed);
(2) wachsende Häufigkeit und zunehmende Intensität der Offenbarungen (Mani und Smith; unklar bei Mohammed);
(3) genaue Datierung der einzelnen Offenbarungen (Mani und Smith; nicht Mohammed);
(4) Engelserscheinungen (Mani, Mohammed, Smith);
(5) Vermittlung eines heiligen Textes durch einen himmlischen Boten (Smith, möglicherweise Mohammed; nicht Mani).

Es zeigt sich also, daß die Affinitäten zwischen Mani und Smith zahlreicher sind als die zwischen Mani und Mohammed. Wie nicht anders zu erwarten, muß man bei der Anwendung der historischen Analogie auf Gradunterschiede gefaßt sein: nicht jeder Fall ist gleich instruktiv. Deshalb sollte man sich nie damit begnügen, nur zwei Fälle zu vergleichen, wie es Meyer getan hat.

---

[70] Vgl. den Kölner Mani-Kodex (CMC) 2–4, ediert von Henrichs/Koenen (Anm. 11) 4–7.
[71] CMC 69,9–20 bei Henrichs/Koenen (Anm. 11) 68 f.
[72] Henrichs (Anm. 51) 199–203; W. Sundermann, "Mani's Revelations in the Cologne Mani Codex and in Other Sources," in Cirillo/Roselli (Anm. 51) 205–214.

Die Vergleichsmöglichkeiten sind damit keineswegs erschöpft. Es sei daran erinnert, daß über den Inhalt der ersten Offenbarung in allen drei Fällen widersprüchliche bzw. unklare Zeugnisse vorliegen, was wohl bedeutet, daß die drei Religionsstifter mit ihrem jeweiligen Berufungserlebnis im Rückblick ziemlich frei verfahren sind. Gemeinsam ist jedoch allen drei Erstoffenbarungen, daß sie für den Empfänger den Bruch mit seiner bisherigen religiösen Umwelt markierten und daß diese Wende auch im Offenbarungsinhalt deutlich zum Ausdruck kam. Es gibt noch weitere Berührungspunkte. So verstreicht immer eine geraume Frist zwischen der ersten Offenbarung und dem ersten öffentlichen Auftreten: zwölf Jahre bei Mani (228 – 240), etwa drei Jahre bei Mohammed (ca. 610 – 613) und zehn Jahre bei Smith (1820 – 1830). Die Verbreitung der Offenbarung nimmt ebenfalls einen ähnlichen Verlauf: zuerst werden Mitglieder der unmittelbaren Familie bzw. des engsten Bekanntenkreises für den neuen Glauben gewonnen; dann wird die Mission ausgedehnt; und schließlich folgt eine Emigration (Hijra des Jahres 622 bei Mohammed; Auswanderung aus Ohio und Missouri, dann Gründung der Mormonenstadt Nauvoo, Illinois im Jahre 1831 bei Smith), die allerdings bei Mani der eigentlichen Missionstätigkeit voraufgeht (Trennung von den Täufern und Auswanderung im Jahre 240).

Abschließend sei noch auf einen wichtigen Unterschied hingewiesen. Mani und Mohammed betrachteten sich als letztes Glied in einer langen Kette von Prophetengestalten, als ''Siegel der Propheten''. Die Offenbarung hatte mit ihnen ihren Höhepunkt erreicht, der gleichzeitig ein endgültiger Abschluß war. Das ist anders bei den Mormonen. Joseph Smith verstand sich als der ''Erste Prophet'' der Neuzeit, der in früheren Zeiten zahlreiche Vorgänger hatte; aber anders als Mani und Mohammed gab er das Prophetenamt an seine Nachfolger weiter, womit die Offenbarung zur Institution wurde.[73]

Die historische Analogie ist zweifellos ein legitimes und instruktives Verfahren, vor allem wenn die Vergleichsbasis breit genug ist. Am Beispiel der Offenbarungstypologie hat sich gezeigt, daß Meyer die in dieser Methode liegenden Möglichkeiten nicht voll ausgeschöpft hat und ein unzureichendes Gesamtbild vermittelt. Was sich hier am Einzelfall demonstrieren ließ, gilt auch für das Buch über die Mormonen insgesamt: das Gespür für historisch relevante Zusammenhänge ist meisterhaft; die Weite des Blicks ist erstaunlich; die Darstellungsweise ist lebendig und packend; die methodischen Ansätze sind anregend, zumindest aus damaliger Sicht; aber die Ausführung läßt im einzelnen sehr zu wünschen

---

[73] Vgl. z.B. Leone (Anm. 34) 30.

übrig, und die Synthese von Geschichte und Religionsgeschichte ist nicht ganz geglückt.[74]

---

[74] Für kritische und bibliographische Hinweise danke ich Ernst Badian, Christiane Baum, Jan Bremmer, William M. Calder III, William A. Graham, Jr., Zeph Stewart und Jeffrey Wills.

CHRISTHARD HOFFMANN

DIE SELBSTERZIEHUNG DES HISTORIKERS. ZUR INTELLEKTUELLEN ENTWICKLUNG DES JUNGEN EDUARD MEYER (1855–1879)*

"Es ist eine gefährliche und schädliche Illusion, wenn der Professor der Geschichte meint in derselben Weise bilden zu können, wie Philologen und Mathematiker allerdings auf der Universität ausgebildet werden können. Mit mehr Recht als von diesen kann man es von dem Historiker sagen, daß er nicht gebildet wird, sondern geboren, nicht erzogen wird, sondern sich erzieht."

Theodor Mommsen, Rektoratsrede (1874)[1]

Als der siebzehnjährige Abiturient Eduard Meyer im Frühjahr 1872 sein Elternhaus in Hamburg verließ und zum Studium der Philologie und Geschichte an die Universität Bonn zog, notierte der drei Jahre jüngere Bruder Kuno in sein Tagebuch. "[wir] bekamen wieder eine Correspondenzkarte von Edu aus Cöln. [. . .] Ich bekomme alle Briefe, die Edu schreibt und wenn Edu später mal ein berühmter Mann wird, so gebe ich seinen Briefwechsel mit uns heraus."[2]

Es gab Gründe für die Erwartung, Eduard werde einmal ein berühmter Mann. Zunächst waren es einfach die überragenden schulischen Leistungen, die der etwas langsamere Kuno—der später gleichwohl ein berühmter Professor der Keltistik wurde—mit ungläubiger Bewunderung registrierte. Kurz vor Eduards Abitur heißt es z.B. lakonisch: "mehrere Primaner, unter ihnen Edu, haben einen lateinischen Aufsatz geschrieben; wer den besten macht bekommt ein Stipendium von 80 fl. Edu machte den besten."[3]

Eduard Meyer war der weitaus jüngste Abiturient seines Jahrgangs, das Abgangszeugnis der renommierten Hamburger Gelehrtenschule des Johanneums verzeichnet nicht nur in Geschichte ein "vorzüglich", sondern auch "sehr gute" Leistungen im Lateinischen, Griechischen, Deutschen, Hebräischen und in Mathematik—im Englischen und Französischen allerdings ein "nicht befriedigend."[4]

---

* Den Teilnehmern des von der Werner-Reimers-Stiftung im November 1987 veranstalteten Kolloquiums über Eduard Meyer danke ich für ihre Hinweise und Anregungen.
[1] Theodor Mommsen, *Reden und Aufsätze*, Berlin 1905, 11.
[2] Kuno Meyer, *Tagebuch*, Bd. 2: 1872 und 1873, 46 (Staatsbibliothek Preußischer Kulturbesitz (StPK) Berlin, NL Kuno Meyer).
[3] Ebd., 11.
[4] Reifezeugnis Eduard Meyers (AdW der DDR—Archiv—Sign.: NL Ed. Meyer Nr. 4).

Als Eduard Meyer das Johanneum verließ, besaß er nicht bloß eine gründliche Kenntnis der klassischen Sprachen, er hatte darüber hinaus auch Hebräisch und die Anfänge des Arabischen gelernt. Über so zentrale althistorische Themen wie "die Ermordung Cäsars und ihre Hintergründe" (1868), den "Hellenismus" (1870), den "Untergang des Altertums" (1871), "Cornelius Tacitus und seine Zeit" (1871/72) und die "Geschichte des Königsreiches Pontos unter den Achaemeniden" (1872) hatte er Vorträge und Aufsätze ausgearbeitet, die weitgehend auf selbständiger Quellenforschung beruhten.

Wie zuverlässig Meyer schon als Schüler arbeiten konnte, beweist die Tatsache, daß er seine in Pennälerzeiten begonnene und im 1. Semester ausgearbeitete "Geschichte des Königreiches Pontos" 1878 nur wenig umzuarbeiten brauchte, um sie als Habilitationsschrift einzureichen.

Angesichts dieser Leistungen waren es nicht nur der jüngere Bruder und der Vater, sondern auch die Lehrer—allen voran der damalige Direktor und Thukydidesforscher Johannes Classen—, die große Hoffnungen in Eduard Meyer setzten. Meyer enttäuschte diese Hoffnungen nicht—aber er erfüllte auch nicht einfach die Erwartungen, die auf ihm lagen. Schon bald verließ er die ausgetretenen Pfade eines Philologie- und Geschichtsstudiums und wandte sich—weitgehend autodidaktisch—ganz dem Alten Orient, der Urgeschichte des Menschen und der allgemeinen Religionsgeschichte zu. Er schloß sich keiner bestehenden Schule an und ließ sich von althistorischen Forschungsprogrammen wenig beeindrucken, sondern verfolgte mit Konsequenz—und gegen manche Widerstände— seine eigenen weitgespannten Interessen. Dadurch gewann er sein unverwechselbares Profil in einer weitgehend von der Mommsenschule bestimmten Historikerlandschaft.

In meiner biographischen Skizze werde ich die wichtigsten Stufen der intellektuellen Entwicklung des jungen Eduard Meyer nachzeichnen und dabei die Frage in den Mittelpunkt stellen, durch welche Einflüsse und Erfahrungen seine historischen Interessen und Anschauungen geprägt wurden. Ich kann mich auf umfangreiches unveröffentlichtes Quellenmaterial stützen, da fast alle Jugendwerke und zahlreiche Jugendbriefe Meyers erhalten sind.[5] Eine Auswahl besonders aufschlußreicher Briefe des jungen Eduard Meyer wird im Anhang erstmals veröffentlicht (*Dokumente* 1 – 9).

---

[5] Die meisten Jugendwerke befinden sich im Nachlaß Ed. Meyer im Archiv der Akademie der Wissenschaften (AdW) der DDR in Berlin. Von den Jugendbriefen sind die an die Eltern (StPK Berlin) und die an Richard Pietschmann (SUB Göttingen) am wichtigsten.

Meyers Jugend- und Studentenzeit gliedere ich in drei Abschnitte:
(1) Elternhaus und Gelehrtenschule (1855 – 1872), (2) Studium in Bonn
und Leipzig (1872 – 1875), (3) Hauslehrer in Konstantinopel und Bournemouth, Militär, Habilitation (1875 – 1879). Das Jahr 1879 bildet einen
natürlichen Einschnitt in Meyers Biographie: zum einen wurde er durch
die Habilitation zum Hochschullehrer, zum anderen erhielt er in jenem
Jahr von Cotta den Auftrag zur *Geschichte des Altertums*—eine Aufgabe, die
ihn bis zu seinem Tode 51 Jahre später in Anspruch nehmen sollte.

(1) Elternhaus und Gelehrtenschule (1855 – 1872)

Eduard Meyer wurde am 25. Januar 1855 in Hamburg geboren. Der
Vater, nach dem Eduard benannt wurde, hatte anderthalb Jahre zuvor,
49jährig, in zweiter Ehe die erst 17jährige Henriette Dessau geheiratet.
Auf Eduard folgten noch drei weitere Kinder: Kuno (1858), Albrecht
(1860) und Antonie (1864).

Eduard Meyer senior war ordentlicher Lehrer am Johanneum in Hamburg, er hatte die Gelehrtenschule bereits Anfang der 20er Jahre unter
dem reformfreudigen Direktor Johann Gottfried Gurlitt (1754 – 1827)
als Schüler besucht. Anschließend hatte er in Leipzig (bei Gottfried
Herrmann) und in Berlin (bei August Böckh) klassische Philologie studiert. Finanzielle Schwierigkeiten zwangen den Sohn eines Weinkauf-
mannes 1827 für ein Jahr eine Lehrerstelle in der Schweiz zu übernehmen, bevor er sein Studium dann in München fortsetzen und in Erlangen
mit der Promotion 1829 abschließen konnte.[6]

Am Johanneum, in dessen Lehrkörper er 1830 eintrat, unterrichtete
Meyer die klassischen Sprachen, Geschichte und Deutsch. Auch schrift-
stellerisch trat er in Erscheinung. Die beiden Flugschriften, die er 1831
und 1832 gegen Ludwig Börne richtete,[7] zeigen ihn beeinflußt von dem
Ideengut der Romantik und des entstehenden deutschen Nationalismus,
verbunden mit einer deutlichen antijüdischen Komponente.[8] In seinen

---

[6] Zu Eduard Meyer senior vgl. den Kasten 10 im Nachlaß Ed. Meyer (StPK Berlin).
[7] Ed. Meyer [sen.], *Gegen L. Börne den Wahrheit-, Recht- und Ehrvergeßnen Briefsteller aus
Paris*, Altona 1831; ders., *Nachträge zu der Beurteilung der Börne'schen Briefe aus Paris*, Altona
1832.—Gabriel Riesser hatte auf Meyers erste Schrift repliziert: Gabriel Riesser, *Börne
und die Juden. Ein Wort der Erwiderung auf die Flugschrift des Herrn Dr. Eduard Meyer gegen Börne*,
Altenburg 1832.
[8] Vgl. zu diesem Aspekt: Mosche Zimmermann, *Hamburgischer Patriotismus und deutscher
Nationalismus. Die Emanzipation der Juden in Hamburg 1830 – 1865*, Hamburg 1979, 61 – 67;
Hans Liebeschütz, *Das Judentum im deutschen Geschichtsbild von Hegel bis Max Weber*, Tübingen 1967, 290; Christhard Hoffmann, *Juden und Judentum im Werk deutscher Althistoriker des
19. und 20. Jahrhunderts*, Leiden 1988 (Studies in Judaism in Modern Times 9), 174 f.

wissenschaftlichen Arbeiten behandelte Meyer Themen der alten[9] und
vor allem der Hamburger Geschichte,[10] er war auch der erste Verfasser
eines Kommentars zu Goethes *Faust*[11] und schrieb selbst Gedichte, von
denen er 1876 eine Auswahl veröffentlichte.[12]

Die Lebens- und Weltanschauung des alten Meyer war ganz und gar
durch das humanistische Ideal geprägt, wie es sich in der deutschen Klassik ausgebildet hatte. Demnach liegt das Ziel des Menschen darin, sich zu
"bilden", d.h. durch Aneignung und Auseinandersetzung mit der Welt
der Kunst, Literatur und Geschichte seine unverwechselbare Persönlichkeit zu entwickeln. Die Selbstentfaltung des Individuums in Freiheit und
sittlicher Verantwortung bildet den höchsten Wert menschlichen Seins.
Dieser Geist einer deutschen "Bildungsreligion"[13] bestimmte auch die
Erziehung der Kinder.

Das hatte vor allem zwei Konsequenzen: Das klassische Ideal des
selbstbestimmten Individuums prägte einen Erziehungsstil, in dem schon
die Kinder als Persönlichkeiten ernstgenommen und ihrer Entfaltung ein
erheblicher Freiraum gewährt wurde. Man erwartete geradezu von den
Kindern, daß sie ihren eigenen Weg gingen, eigene Interessen entwickelten und ihr Leben zunehmend selbst verantworteten. Deshalb gab es
keinen Drill, keine Gängelei oder Verbote, und auch ein bürgerliches
Prestigedenken spielte offenbar keine Rolle. Ob die Kinder in die Schule
gingen oder mal einen Tag zu Hause blieben, war weitgehend ihrer
eigenen Entscheidung überlassen, und als Kuno sich in den Zwang der
Schule (an der sein Vater immerhin jahrzehntelang unterrichtet hatte)
immer schlechter einfügen konnte, hatten die Eltern Verständnis für seine
Lage und nahmen eine Gelegenheit wahr, ihn der täglichen Reibereien
zu entziehen, indem sie ihn als Amanuensis für zwei Jahre zu einem blinden deutschen Gelehrten nach Edinburgh gaben.[14]

Die ausgesprochen liberale Atmosphäre, in der die Kinder aufwuch-
sen, wurde vielleicht durch den Altersunterschied der Eltern noch begünstigt. Eduard Meyer senior war gegenüber seinen Kindern eher im Alter
eines Großvaters, er mischte sich wenig in die Erziehung, bildete aber in
seiner Abgeklärtheit, Distanz und Gelehrsamkeit eine besondere Autori-

---

[9] Ed. Meyer [sen.], *Der Freiheitskrieg der Bataven unter Civilis*, Hamburg 1856.
[10] *Geschichte des Hamburgischen Schul- und Unterrichtswesens im Mittelalter*, Hamburg 1843;
Das Einbeckische Haus in Hamburg, Hamburg 1868.
[11] *Studien zu Goethe's Faust*, Altona 1847.
[12] *Poetisches Vermächtnis*, Hamburg 1876.
[13] Vgl. dazu allgemein: Thomas Nipperdey, *Deutsche Geschichte 1800–1866. Bürgerwelt
und starker Staat*, München 1983, 440 ff.
[14] Vgl. Ed. Meyer, Nachruf auf seinen Bruder Kuno, *Irische Korrespondenz* 2. Jg.
Nr. 9/10 (Oktober/November 1919), 2–5, hier 2.

tät. Die Kinder lebten vor allem im intensiven Umgang mit der jungen Mutter, die Meyer später in ihrer Lebensklugheit und Schlagfertigkeit mit der "Frau Rath" (Goethes Mutter) verglichen hat.[15]

Hinzu kam ein reiches kulturelles Leben, welches die materiell eher bedrückten Verhältnisse zu kompensieren vermochte. Eduard Meyer wurde in einer Atmosphäre groß, in der Hausmusik und Theaterspielen, Tagebuchschreiben und klassische Dichtung, eigene schriftstellerische Bemühungen und Wissenschaft, dazu die Antike in allen ihren Ausdrucksformen, zum selbstverständlichen Alltag gehörten.

Dieser spezifische Anregungsgehalt verfehlte seine Wirkung nicht. Der fünfjährige Eduard gratulierte dem Vater mit einem deutschen Gedicht zu Weihnachten, der sechsjährige schrieb zum selben Anlaß bereits Lateinisch, der zwölfjährige überraschte die Familie mit einer selbstverfaßten Tragödie in 5 Akten *Brutus oder die Ermordung Cäsars*.[16] Darin folgte Meyer zwar im großen und ganzen der dramatischen Disposition des Stoffes bei Shakespeare, die Einzelheiten verraten aber eine genaue Kenntnis der antiken Quellen. In der Tat hatte der Obertertianer für eine gleichzeitige Prosafassung, die er in der Schule über die Umstände von Cäsars Ermordung vortrug, die entsprechenden Biographien Plutarchs im griechischen Urtext erarbeitet.[17] In dieser Zeit (1867) ließ sich der Vater pensionieren, um sich ganz seinen wissenschaftlichen Neigungen und dem Unterricht der Kinder widmen zu können. Durch häusliche Lektüre mit dem Vater wurde Eduard so mit den klassischen Sprachen immer mehr vertraut, und er hatte—im Gegensatz zur Schule—den Vorteil, solche Texte auszuwählen und studieren zu können, die ihn gerade interessierten. Noch als Geheimrat führte Eduard Meyer seine guten Griechischkenntnisse auf den häuslichen Unterricht durch den Vater zurück.[18] Die Anregung zu eigenständigen Arbeiten ging von dem Versuch aus, historische Landkarten zu zeichnen. Meyer stieß dabei auf Strabo, verfolgte dann die Geschichte einzelner Städte und Landschaften und wurde so immer mehr in die antike Literatur geführt.[19]

Hinzu kamen die Anregungen der Schule. Die Gelehrtenschule des Johanneums, eine Eliteschule, deren vorrangiges Ziel darin lag, das wissenschaftliche Denken und selbständige Arbeiten zu fördern und die

---

[15] Ebd.

[16] Das Manuskript befindet sich in StPK Berlin, NL Ed. Meyer.

[17] Vgl. Ed. Meyer, *Geschichte des wissenschaftlichen Vereins von 1817 an der Gelehrtenschule des Johanneums zu Hamburg. Festschrift zur Feier seines hundertjährigen Bestehens*, Halle 1923, 44 (Anm. 1).

[18] Vgl. Liebeschütz, *Geschichtsbild*, 292.

[19] Ed. Meyer, Autobiographische Skizze, in: *Marohl*, 9–11, hier 9.

Schüler so auf ein Universitätsstudium vorzubereiten, zeichnete sich in den sechziger Jahren des 19. Jahrhunderts noch durch den Geist hanseatischer Liberalität und humanistischer Gelehrsamkeit aus.[20] Zwei Jahre nachdem Eduard Meyer, siebenjährig, in die Sexta eintrat, wurde Johannes Classen zum Direktor berufen, ein Thukydidesforscher wie F.W. Ulrich und L.P. Herbst, die bereits an der Schule lehrten. Ohne Übertreibung kann man sagen, daß der Fortschritt der Thukydidesstudien damals in der Prima der Gelehrtenschule stattfand.[21] Von den Lehrern wurde nicht nur erwartet, daß sie sich auf der Höhe der Wissenschaft hielten, sondern daß sie auch durch eigene Veröffentlichungen im *Programm* der Schule oder anderen gelehrten Zeitschriften zur Forschung beitrugen. Dafür ließ man ihnen erhebliche Freiheiten: es gab Lehrer, die niemals eine Klassenarbeit korrigierten. Auch der individuelle Freiraum der Schüler war beträchtlich, der Schulbesuch nicht immer regelmäßig. Eduard Meyer hat selbst darauf hingewiesen, daß das Johanneum zu seiner Schulzeit—im Unterschied zu den späteren, vom preußischen System beeinflußten Jahren nach 1874—keine ''ängstliche Bevormundung'' oder gar ''Kontrolle des Privatlebens oder des Umgangs'' seiner Schüler kannte.[22] Nicht Reglementierung und Zwang, sondern Anregung zu eigenem Denken und wissenschaftlichen Arbeiten, hieß das Rezept, dessen Erfolg offenbar nicht gering war. Die Anforderungen waren besonders in den klassischen Fächern ausgesprochen hoch und entsprachen in der Prima denen der Universitäten. Das Lehrangebot war vielfältig. Wer—wie Meyer—wollte, konnte während seiner Schulzeit sechs Sprachen lernen: in der Sexta wurde mit Latein und Französisch begonnen, in der Quinta kam Griechisch, in der Tertia Englisch und (fakultativ) Hebräisch hinzu, und schließlich gab es noch die Möglichkeit, am

---

[20] Zum Johanneum und seiner Entwicklung vgl. Walter Jens, Auf ein humanistisches Gymnasium, in: ders., *Ort der Handlung ist Deutschland. Reden in erinnerungsfeindlicher Zeit*, München 1981, 107–125, hier bes. 117; Ludwig Martens, Erziehung zur Selbständigkeit. (Erinnerungen aus der eigenen Schulzeit.), *Monatsschrift für höhere Schulen* 3 (1904), 641–647; zu Classen vgl. *Johannes Classen. Gedächtnisschrift der Gelehrtenschule des Johanneums*, Hamburg 1892, bes. der Beitrag von F. Schultess, 1–34; zu Meyers Beurteilung der eigenen Schulzeit vgl. seine Antrittsrede in der Preussischen Akademie der Wissenschaften, *Sitzungsberichte der Kgl. Pr. ADW* 34 (1904), 1012–1015, bes. 1014 f.: ''wenn ich aber an dem heutigen Tage einen Dank aussprechen darf, so gilt er der Erziehungsanstalt, aus der ich hervorgegangen bin, der Hamburger Gelehrtenschule, einer Anstalt, die in ihren Vorzügen und auch in den Gebrechen, die nach menschlicher Art damit verbunden waren, der jüngeren Generation schon jetzt als unverständlich und als ein Mythus erscheinen wird. Sie wollte eine Vorbereitungsschule sein für das Universitätsstudium, nicht mehr, aber auch nicht weniger. Was ihre Schüler ihr verdanken, ist die Erziehung zu ernster wissenschaftlicher Arbeit und zu früher Selbständigkeit und geistiger Unabhängigkeit.''
[21] Jens, *Ort der Handlung*, 108.
[22] Meyer, *Verein*, 11.

akademischen Gymnasium beim alten Professor Redslob Arabisch zu
lernen.[23]

Das dabei erreichte Niveau wird an den Beispielen deutlich, die Meyer
aus seiner Schulzeit anführt: bei Classen wurden in der Oberstufe lateinische Schriftsteller—Nepos, Cäsar, Sallust und schließlich Tacitus—ins
Griechische übersetzt, bei Kießling auf Lateinisch über Horazoden dispu-
tiert, bei Mumssen schließlich neutestamentliche Perikopen ins Hebräische gebracht und in der Schlußprüfung der Psalm im Buch Jona ohne
weitere Präparation zur Übersetzung gegeben.[24]

Von den Lehrern übte Johannes Classen den größten Einfluß auf Eduard
Meyer aus. Classen, ein Schul- und Studienkollege von Meyers Vater,
hatte während seines Studiums in Bonn eine Hauslehrerstelle bei Barthold Georg Niebuhr angetreten und mit dem Begründer der modernen
althistorischen Wissenschaft auch an der Edition byzantinischer
Geschichtsschreiber zusammengewirkt. Nach Niebuhrs Tod hatte er den
3. Band von Niebuhrs *Römischer Geschichte* herausgegeben.

Über Classen kam der junge Meyer mit dem Werk Niebuhrs in
Berührung, durch Niebuhr, besonders durch seine an Pompeius Trogus
orientierten *Vorträge über alte Geschichte* wurde ihm eine Sicht der alten
Geschichte vermittelt, die nicht durch die klassizistische Verengung auf
Griechenland und Rom beeinträchtigt und wesentlich universalhistorisch
ausgerichtet war. Man hat vermutet, daß Meyers Interesse an alter Geschichte im allgemeinen und seine spätere universalhistorische Perspektive im besonderen durch Niebuhr—via Classen—geprägt wurden.[25]

Auch nach dem Abitur blieben Classen und Meyer in Kontakt. Es war
Classen, der Meyer immer wieder die alte Geschichte in Erinnerung rief,
als dieser sich völlig in orientalistischen und religionsgeschichtlichen
Studien vergraben—bzw. aus Classens Sicht: verzettelt—hatte. Wenn
überhaupt, dann ist Meyer in erster Linie als Classen-Schüler anzu-
sprechen.[26]

---

[23] Ebd., 45.

[24] Ebd., 42 ff.

[25] Vgl. Ulrich Wilcken, Gedächtnisrede auf Eduard Meyer, in: *Marohl*, 115–130, hier
119; Hermann Bengtson, *Einführung in die Alte Geschichte*, 8. Aufl. München 1979, 17;
Arnold Toynbee, Die ''Alte Geschichte'' und die Universalhistorie, *Saeculum* 12 (1970),
91–105; Joseph Vogt, *Orbis. Ausgewählte Schriften zur Geschichte des Altertums*, Freiburg,
Basel, Wien 1960, 269 f.

[26] Auch von den Mitschülern wurde Meyer als ''Spezialschüler Classens'' angesehen,
vgl. die Beiträge verschiedener Verfasser zu Meyers 75. Geburtstag, in: *Das Johanneum.
Mitteilungen des Vereins ehemaliger Schüler der Gelehrtenschule des Johanneums* Heft 10 (März
1930), 275–280, bes. 277: ''Direktor Classen beschäftigte sich besonders mit ihm [Ed.
Meyer]; es war deutlich zu merken, daß er Classens Spezialschüler war, und schon als

Daneben standen A. Kießling und L. Herbst in den klassischen Sprachen, G.H. Bubendey in Mathematik und W. Mumssen in Deutsch, Religion und Hebräisch. Schon früh entwickelte Meyer eine Abneigung gegen eine Überfrachtung des altsprachlichen Unterrichts durch philologische Detailstudien, durch Textkritik und Konjekturen, wie sie v.a. Classen und Herbst betrieben. Dagegen verstand es Mumssen, der ein undogmatisches, liberales Christentum vertrat, der "ein Sucher und daher ein Anreger" war, die Schüler zu fesseln und in die Grundfragen der Philosophie einzuführen.[27] Auch die historischen Vorlesungen A. Wohlwills, der am akademischen Gymnasium lehrte, wurden von Meyer regelmäßig besucht und übten einen anregenden Einfluß aus.[28]

Der Unterricht war darauf ausgerichtet, das selbständige Arbeiten und Forschen der Schüler zu fördern, und zu diesem Zwecke diente die Einrichtung von jeweils einstündigen Vorträgen zu einem selbstgewählten Thema, die dann von der Klasse diskutiert wurden. Hier lagen Meyers besonderen Stärken: Obwohl er der jüngste und leistungsmäßig nicht der Primus, sondern ungefähr der Zwölfte seiner Klasse war, verstand er es aufgrund seiner umfangreichen Privatstudien, die Mitschüler zu inspirieren und ihnen Impulse zu geben.[29]

Noch stärker als im Schulunterricht wurde das eigenständige wissenschaftliche Arbeiten durch den "Wissenschaftlichen Verein von 1817" angeregt. Die Mitglieder des Vereins, in der Regel besonders begabte Schüler der letzten beiden Jahrgangsstufen, trafen sich wöchentlich, um die Abhandlungen der Mitglieder zu besprechen. Auf den Vortrag folgte eine ausgearbeitete Kritik durch ein anderes Mitglied, dann eine allgemeine Diskussion. Die Aufnahme in den Verein war streng und von der positiven Beurteilung einer Probearbeit abhängig. Die aufgegriffenen Themen behandelten überwiegend wissenschaftliche Probleme, z.B. "Das System des Kopernikus," "Der jetzige Stand der Homerfrage," "Darstellung des theurgisch-empirischen Zeitalters in der Geschichte der Medizin," "Die Wellenbewegungen tropfbar flüssiger Körper," "Über Anfänge und Entwicklung der Schrift."[30]

Eduard Meyer hat sowohl in seinen Vorträgen für die Schule als auch

---

Primaner arbeitete er unter Classens Leitung an der Geschichte der Kunde der trojanischen Landschaft, über die er später die ähnlich betitelte Schrift herausgab."
[27] Vgl. Meyer, *Verein*, 42 u. 44.
[28] Ebd., 45.—Zu Adolf Wohlwill, dem ersten jüdischen Lehrer am Johanneum, vgl. Peter Freimark, Juden auf dem Johanneum, in: *450 Jahre Gelehrtenschule des Johanneums zu Hamburg*, Hamburg 1979, 123–129 u. 224–226, hier 128.
[29] Vgl. *Das Johanneum* Heft 10 (März 1930), 277.
[30] Vgl. Meyer, *Verein*, 45 ff.; außerdem das *Verzeichnis der im Wissenschaftlichen Verein von 1817 gelieferten Aufsätze und ihrer Beurteiler nebst einem Mitgliederverzeichnis 1817–1903*, Hamburg 1903, 66 f.

in seinen Abhandlungen für den "Wissenschaftlichen Verein" ausschließlich Themen der alten Geschichte behandelt. Vor der Prima sprach Meyer (jeweils zweistündig) über *Der Hellenismus: Entwicklungsgeschichte, allgemeiner Charakter und kulturhistorischer Zustand der einzelnen hellenistischen und halben hellenistischen Länder* (1871) und über *Cornelius Tacitus. Mit einer Darstellung der Entwicklung der römischen Kaisergeschichte bis auf Tacitus Zeit* (1872).[31] Als Probearbeit für den "Wissenschaftlichen Verein" lieferte er eine umfassende Darstellung der Geschichte Kleinasiens bis zur römischen Unterwerfung. Die Abhandlungen beschäftigten sich mit *Alexander d. Großen* (1870), *Tiberius* (1871) und dem *Untergang des Alterthums* (1871).[32]

Besonders der letzte Vortrag, dessen Manuskript vollständig erhalten ist, gewährt einen aufschlußreichen Blick in die Welt- und Geschichtsauffassung des jungen Meyer und soll deshalb im folgenden ausführlicher betrachtet werden.

In seiner Abhandlung diskutiert Meyer zunächst die traditionelle Epocheneinteilung in Altertum, Mittelalter und Neuzeit und läßt allein den Unterschied zwischen Altertum und Neuzeit gelten, da der Übergang vom Mittelalter zur Neuzeit nicht durch einen Bruch, sondern durch eine "regelmäßige Weiterentwicklung" gekennzeichnet sei: "die Völker treten nicht in einen neuen Culturzustand, sie verändern nicht ihren Charakter, ihre Nationalität" (1). Zwischen Altertum und Neuzeit dagegen gebe es einen deutlichen Epocheneinschnitt. Meyer definiert die Unterschiede folgendermaßen (2 f.): Das Altertum repräsentiert die "natürliche Entwicklung" der Völker, die Nationen der Neuzeit sind dagegen erst "durch einen geschichtlichen Proceß" entstanden, in der alten Welt löst ein Volk das andere ab, "um dann selbst von einem neuen gestürzt und verschlungen zu werden," während in der Moderne "die Völker eine harmonische Verbindung anstreben und miteinander sich fortentwickeln," in der Antike nimmt jedes Volk eine "gesonderte Culturstufe" ein, dagegen herrscht in der Neuzeit "eine allgemeine Cultur," bei den Alten schwanken die politischen Anschauungen und Verhältnisse hin und her, während sie in der Jetztzeit "durch lange Erfahrung ausgebildet und geordnet einen festeren Charakter und eine ruhigere Entwicklung angenommen haben," schließlich—und darauf kommt es Meyer an—hat das Altertum "in seinen noch ungezügelten socialen und sitt-

---

[31] Die Manuskripte befinden sich in der AdW der DDR—Archiv—Sign.: NL Ed. Meyer Nr. 193 (Hellenismus) und Nr. 112 (Tacitus).
[32] AdW der DDR—Archiv—Sign.: NL Ed. Meyer Nr. 193 (Alexander) und Nr. 194 (Untergang); das Manuskript über Tiberius ist offenbar verlorengegangen.

lichen Anschauungen den Ernst und die würdigeren und erhabeneren
Bestrebungen der Neuzeit nie erreicht." Hier wird bereits deutlich, auf
welcher Seite Meyer steht. In dem alten, seit Perraults *Querelle des Anciens
et des Modernes* immer wieder diskutierten Kulturvergleich zwischen Antike und Moderne, verteidigt Meyer die Errungenschaften der Neuzeit:

> "Wir sind gewohnt, das Alterthum als die ideale Zeit aufzufassen, in
> welcher das Schöne und Edle verkörpert gewesen sei. Seine einfachen und
> doch großartigen Zustände, die herrlichen Werke, die es geschaffen, die
> unnachahmlichen Thaten, die es vollbracht hat, das Tragische seines Unter-
> gangs, vor allem aber die unbeschreibliche Anmuth, welche über dasselbe
> ausgegossen ist und alle seine Erscheinungen durchdringt, üben einen
> ewigen Reiz auf uns aus und gewähren dem Betrachtenden höchsten Genuß.
> Wir sind daher geneigt, dem Schicksale zu zürnen, welches jene Zeit ver-
> gehen ließ und so völlig von uns trennte. Und wenn wir nun die Zustände
> des Mittelalters betrachten, wenn wir sehen, wie auch die letzten Jahrhun-
> derte sich nur allmählich [...] zu dem herausgebildet haben, was sie sind,
> so lassen wir uns wohl dazu hinreißen, dem Geschick Laune und Ungerech-
> tigkeit vorzuwerfen, wir betrachten den Untergang des Alterthums als ein
> Werk blinden Zufalls, als einen Rückschritt in der Entwicklungsgeschichte
> der Menschheit.
>   Doch nichts ist sonst der Geschichte ferner, als ein Rückschritt: langsam
> aber ohne zu ruhen führt sie die Menscheit ihrer Vollendung entgegen, för-
> dert jedes Geschlecht weiter als seine Ahnen; in ihr herrscht nicht der Zufall,
> sondern das Geschick" (3 f.).

Diese beiden Prämissen—die Annahme eines sinnvollen historischen
Geschehens und der Glaube an einen unaufhaltsamen Fortschritt—
führen Meyer geradewegs zu seiner zentralen These: Der Untergang des
Altertums ist weder blinder Zufall noch ungerechter Rückschritt, sondern
eine notwendige Folge der der antiken Welt innewohnenden "Fehler und
Mängel."

Die langfristig wirkenden Ursachen des Verfalls liegen für Meyer vor
allem auf moralischem und politischem Gebiet: Die Lebensauffassung
des Altertums war allein auf den "Egoismus" gegründet, das Lebens-
ziel des Einzelnen lag im "Streben nach Lebensgenuß," in der "Befriedigung der Lüste." Ausdruck für den "fehlenden sittlichen Ernst" ist
u.a. die Unterdrückung der Sklaven und Frauen. Die Staatsverfassung
zeige zwar bei den europäischen Völkern mit dem Streben nach Freiheit
positive Ansätze, die politische Mitbestimmung wurde aber auf die Frei-
geborenen beschränkt. Das Fehlen einer Repräsentativverfassung und
das Schwanken zwischen verschiedenen Verfassungsformen trugen
außerdem zur Instabilität bei.

Zu diesen allgemeinen Defiziten der Antike kamen dann konkrete Entwicklungen, die den Untergang des Altertums veranlaßten: Die wach-

sende Macht des Staates, die sich im "Despotismus" des Hellenismus und der römischen Kaiserzeit äußerte, hatte zur Folge, daß der Einzelne sich nicht mehr für das Gemeinwesen interessierte und den Militärdienst vernachlässigte. Der wachsende Wohlstand führte zu einem vollständigen Sittenverfall und zu allgemeiner "Schlaffheit". Schließlich trugen Weltherrschaft und Völkermischung dazu bei, daß die Freiheit und Individualität der Völker unterdrückt wurden, so daß "etwas Kräftiges" unmöglich mehr geschaffen werden konnte.

Hellenismus und Romanismus stellen für den jungen Meyer denn auch deutliche Verfallserscheinungen dar:

> "Der Charakter des Hellenismus ist zusammengesetzt aus dem knechtischen Sinn der Asiaten und der äußerlichen Bildung der Hellenen. Er ist begründet auf Despotismus und Weltmonarchie—wenn ich so die Herrschaft über mehrere verschiedenartige Völker nennen darf. Beide unterdrücken die Selbständigkeit und Freiheit des einzelnen wie des Volks vollkommen. Das höchste Gut des Europäers, die Freiheit, mußte daher verloren gehn, er sank zum Asiaten herab. Höchstmöglicher sinnlicher Lebensgenuß wird daher mehr und mehr sein höchstes Gut; daher kann die alte Bildung wohl äußerlich bestehn bleiben, aber sie hat keinen geistigen Werth mehr, sie dient gleichfalls nur zur Befriedigung der Sinnlichkeit" (17).

Die Abwärtsbewegung war nicht mehr aufzuhalten: Die Reformversuche der römischen Kaiser blieben erfolglos, die Bildung der breiten "Volksmasse" sank immer tiefer, und die Verhältnisse führten "mehr und mehr zur Durchführung eines vollkommen orientalischen Despotismus hin" (26)—wenn sich nicht mit dem Christentum und den Germanen "neue Elemente" gezeigt hätten, die die Antike umgestaltet und überwunden hätten.

Meyers Bewertung des Christentums ist ambivalent. Positiv beurteilt er die "neuen Lehren der Moral," die die Defizite der antiken Lebensanschauung behoben (29); als negative Folgen der Christianisierung erkennt er den "Untergang des heiteren Sinnes, für den ernstes Grübeln und finstere Betrachtungen eintreten" (29) und vor allem den dogmatischen Rigorismus, der sich im christlichen Glaubens- und Bekehrungseifer und schließlich in der Inquisition zeigte (30). Gegenüber seinen Kritikern nimmt Meyer das Christentum aber in Schutz:

> "Wenn wir uns vom Christenthum befreien, wenn wir eine noch höhere Stufe einzunehmen suchen als dieses, so ist es nur das Dogma, welches wir verwerfen; die Moral erkennen wir nicht nur an, sondern betonen sie sogar falschen Vertretern des Christenthums gegenüber. In ihr ruht der große Fortschritt vom Alterthum zur Neuzeit; um aber wirken zu können, mußte sie, wenn ich so sagen darf, mit etwas Materiellem verbunden sein, dem sie sich zunächst unterordnete" (29).

Selbst das christliche Dogma war in Meyers Sicht zunächst notwendig, um dem Volk einen "Halt" zu geben und das Christentum bei der "Masse" zu verankern. Nur so konnten "die socialen Übelstände des Alterthums beseitigt" und "zuerst eine wahre Humanität geschaffen" werden (39). Auch den weiteren Geschichtsverlauf hat das Christentum positiv beeinflußt: Das Unabgeschlossene und Unsystematische des Christentums gab immer wieder Anlaß zu Meinungsverschiedenheiten und übte dadurch einen "geistig belebenden Einfluß" aus (40). Deshalb konnte das Christentum auch zum Motor "jeder geistigen Bewegung, jedes neuen Aufschwungs der Neuzeit" werden. Reformation und Aufklärung trugen dazu bei, die "Mißbräuche der Kirche" zu beseitigen und die "reinere Auffassung" durchzusetzen. Philosophie und Wissenschaft befreiten sich aus der Vorherrschaft der Kirche und vermochten so, "das Vergängliche am Christenthum zu besiegen, seinen höchsten, ewigwahren Inhalt aber zu verwirklichen" (41).

Auch die politischen Verhältnisse der Neuzeit spiegeln in Meyers Sicht einen entscheidenden Fortschritt wider. Der Einzelne ist weniger 'politisiert' als in der Antike, er trägt eine Freiheit in sich selbst und findet im "innigen Familienleben" vollkommenen Ersatz für politische Aktivitäten. Die allgemeine Entwicklung verläuft—umgekehrt als im Altertum —vom Despotismus zur Republik. Der Übergang zur politischen Selbständigkeit des Einzelnen findet in der Neuzeit aber in gemäßigten Formen statt, es fehlt die "Leidenschaftlichkeit" der Antike. Die "neu geschaffene constitutionelle Monarchie" verhindert durch das "Staatsbürgerthum," die "Volksvertretung" und die "Fürsorge für eine allgemeine Volksbildung" eine radikale Entwicklung, verhindert vor allem, daß "die wild erregte Demokratie des Alterthums jemals wiederkehre" (41).

Meyers Fazit faßt den Grundgedanken seiner Abhandlung noch einmal prägnant zusammen:

> "Ich glaube erwiesen zu haben, daß die Entwicklung vom Alterthum zur Neuzeit ein Fortschritt war, daß das Alterthum große, jetzt überwundene Mängel hatte. Wir haben Recht, wenn wir das Alterthum als eine ideale Zeit betrachten, insofern dort hohe geistige Blüthe, heiterer Sinn und freies Leben bei den vom Glück begünstigten herrschten; aber vergessen wir nicht, wenn wir uns in einzelnen Stunden nach ihm sehnen, wie viel höher wir stehn und wie groß der Fortschritt ist von ihm bis zu unserer Zeit." (42)

Meyers Aufsatz ist vor allem biographisch ein interessantes Dokument. Es zeigt, daß bereits für den Sechzehnjährigen Geschichte mehr bedeutete als eine bloße Ansammlung von Fakten und Ereignissen, daß er bemüht war, "auf Grund der Geschichte zu einer umfassenden und einheitlichen Weltanschauung zu gelangen."[33] Die Weltanschauung, die in Meyers

---

[33] Meyer, Autobiographische Skizze, in: *Marohl*, 9.

Geschichtsinterpretation deutlich wird, bewegt sich ganz im traditionellen
Rahmen dessen, was im deutschen säkularisierten Bildungsbürgertum
seit dem Beginn des 19. Jahrhunderts repräsentativ war. Die wesentlichen
Elemente dieses Welt- und Geschichtsbildes sind: ein (im Reichsgrün-
dungsjahr 1871 vielleicht besonders) ungebrochener Fortschrittsglaube,
der Stolz auf die Errungenschaften der Neuzeit: auf Kunst, Wissenschaft
und Bildung; die Anerkennung der christlichen Moral bei gleichzeitiger
Ablehnung der christlichen Dogmatik; die Hochschätzung der konstitu-
tionellen Monarchie als Idealstaat, die Angst vor der Demokratie und die
Vorstellung, daß sich der Bürger in politischen Dingen mäßigen und
zurückhalten müsse; die nationale Perspektive in der Betonung von nationaler Eigenheit und Freiheit gegenüber Kosmopolitismus und ethnischer
Pluralität in einem Gemeinwesen; schließlich die bürgerliche Moral, die
in Reichtum und mangelnder Sittenstrenge bereits einen ersten Schritt
zur Dekadenz erkennt.

Dazu kommen die Topoi der historischen Deutung: die Konzentration
auf Griechen und Römer, die ausgesprochen okzidentalische Perspektive,
die den Orient nur als Gegenbild und Gefahr wahrnimmt, die entsprechend negative Wertung des Hellenismus als Verfallserscheinung, die
Akzentuierung von Christentum und Germanen als Überwinder der Antike etc.

Der Versuch des jungen Meyer, ''das größte der weltgeschichtlichen
Probleme, den Untergang des Altertums,''[34] zu erklären und zu bewer-
ten, ist in seinen wesentlichen Aussagen, Argumenten und Deutungen
sicherlich wenig originell, sondern von dem Bildungshintergrund (u.a.
Herder, Goethe, v. Ranke) beeinflußt, der für Meyers Entwicklung
prägend war. Wir gewinnen hier aber einen authentischen Einblick in das
Weltbild des Schülers Meyer. Von diesem Ausgangspunkt kann nun die
weitere Entwicklung verfolgt werden.

(2) Studium in Bonn und Leipzig (1872 – 1875)

Für die Wahl Bonns als Studienort sprachen verschiedene Gründe. Hier
hatte B.G. Niebuhr gewirkt, Classen studiert und auch die damaligen
Professoren der Philologie (Usener, Bücheler und Bernays) und der
Geschichte (Sybel, Schäfer) versprachen ein hohes Niveau. Hinzu kam
die rheinische Landschaft, die auf dem jungen Hamburger, der bisher
nur seine engere Heimat kannte, einen starken Reiz ausübte. Nicht
zuletzt spielte eine Rolle, daß noch fünf weitere Schüler seines Jahrgangs

---

[34] Meyer, *Verein*, 94.

mit ihm nach Bonn gingen; andere, wie Johannes Mordtmann, studierten bereits dort. Meyers Vorfreude war groß. Von unterwegs schrieb er an die Eltern: "[ich bin] recht vergnügt und möchte am liebsten der ganzen Erdkugel um den Hals fallen; wie froh werde ich erst sein, wenn ich am Rhein bin."[35]

Bonn wurde jedoch, was das Studium betrifft, eine ziemliche Enttäuschung. Keiner der Professoren vermochte Meyer in seinen Bann zu ziehen oder auch nur wesentlich anzuregen. Dies lag nicht nur an der mangelnden Ausstrahlungskraft einzelner Lehrer, sondern vor allem an Meyers spezifischen Interessen, die im Bereich der klassischen Philologie immer weniger befriedigt wurden. Fachliches und Persönliches kamen zusammen. Wer als Professor anregend war wie z.B. Usener, Bücheler oder Sybel, las über Gebiete, die Meyer weniger interessierten. Auf den Gebieten aber, wo er weiterkommen wollte, wie z.B. in griechischer Geschichte oder Orientalistik, stieß er mit Schäfer und Gildemeister auf Lehrer, die "zwar sehr gelehrt und ganz vernünftig, aber sehr trocken und langweilig" waren und ihm deshalb letztlich wenig bieten konnten (*Dok* 1).

Angesichts dieser Situation zögerte Meyer nicht lange, sondern zog Konsequenzen: er gab das Studium der klassischen Philologie ganz auf. Wie er dem Vater auseinandersetzte, besaß die Philologie in ihrer Konzentration auf "Textkritik und Conjekturenmachen" keinen Reiz mehr für ihn, lediglich mit der Grammatik wollte er sich auch noch in Zukunft beschäftigen (*Dok* 2).

Eine zweite Konsequenz lag darin, daß Meyer bereits nach einem Semester Bonn den Rücken kehrte. Der Plan sah zunächst vor, zusammen mit Mordtmann nach Berlin zu gehen. Dort werde ihm mit Mommsen, Droysen und Curtius in Geschichte, Weber in Sanskrit, mehreren hebräischen Kollegien und Arabisch wissenschaftlich "unendlich viel mehr" als in Bonn geboten (*Dok* 2). Im Laufe der Semesterferien änderten Meyer und Mordtmann jedoch ihre Pläne und immatrikulierten sich zum Wintersemester 1872/73 an der Universität Leipzig, dem damaligen Zentrum der Orientalistik.

Meyers Wechsel von Bonn nach Leipzig war sicherlich durch die gleiche Entscheidung Mordtmanns mitbeeinflußt, er war jedoch vor allem folgerichtiger Ausdruck des eigenen Studieninteresses. In einem Brief an den Vater, der Eduards Eifer für die orientalischen Sprachen nicht recht verstehen konnte, formulierte Meyer sein Studienziel. Dieser

---

[35] Kuno Meyer, *Tagebuch* Bd. 2: 1872 und 1873, 46 (StPK Berlin, NL Kuno Meyer).

Brief ist ein Schlüsseldokument für das Forschungsinteresse und die Gegenstandsbestimmung der Althistorie durch den jungen Meyer (*Dok* 3). Nicht allein die Geschichte der Griechen und Römer, sondern die Erforschung des *gesamten* Altertums "in allen Richtungen" hat er sich vorgenommen. Dabei resultiert die Bedeutung der alten Geschichte für ihn nicht aus ihrer Vorbildlichkeit und Klassizität, sondern liegt vor allem in der Tatsache, daß es sich hier um die "erste Epoche der Entwicklung des menschlichen Geistes" handelt, daß sich von hier aus Antworten geben lassen auf die grundlegenden anthropologischen Fragen nach Herkunft und Urgeschichte des Menschen, nach der Entstehung von Sprache, Religion, Kultur und Moral. Meyer zeigt sich hier deutlich von den Fragestellungen beeinflußt, die die Darwinsche Evolutionslehre für die frühe Menschheitsgeschichte aufgeworfen hatte. Er will von historischer Seite zu ihrer Klärung beitragen. Meyers Konzept der Alten Geschichte als historischer Anthropologie läßt sich nicht auf bestimmte Nationen oder Epochen einschränken, sondern ist notwendig universalistisch. Es setzt bei den frühen Manifestationen gesellschaftlichen Lebens, bei Sprache und Religion, an und zeigt enge Berührungspunkte mit der entstehenden Ethnologie (Völkerpsychologie), der Vergleichenden Sprachwissenschaft und der Religionsgeschichte. Aus den Worten des jungen Meyer sprechen das Selbstbewußtsein und der Optimismus desjenigen, der davon überzeugt ist, mit den Methoden positivistischer Forschung Klarheit in ein Gebiet bringen zu können, das bisher im Halbdunkel religiöser oder philosophischer Spekulation lag bzw. durch beschränkte Perspektive verzerrt wahrgenommen wurde.

Die Weite von Meyers Fragestellung sprengte die traditionellen Fächergrenzen. Meyer wurde denn auch nicht eigentlich zum "Orientalisten", obwohl er sich in Leipzig so gut wie ausschließlich dem Studium möglichst zahlreicher orientalischer Sprachen widmete. Es war nicht der Orient als Orient, der ihn interessierte, sondern die orientalische Welt als Frühform menschlicher Geistesentwicklung, von der er Aufschluß für seine umfassendere anthropologische Fragestellung erwartete. Neben dem Studium an der Universität, das weitgehend dem Spracherwerb gewidmet war, stand so auch immer das Selbststudium, in dem Meyer—ganz autodidaktisch—seine 'eigentlichen' Interessen verfolgte. Beide Bereiche verdienen eine nähere Betrachtung.

Zunächst das Statistische, wie es sich aus der Studienbescheinigung ergibt:[36] In den fünf Semestern seines Leipziger Studiums belegte Eduard

---

[36] AdW der DDR—Archiv—Sign.: NL Ed. Meyer Nr. 4.

Meyer 40 Lehrveranstaltungen, 35 davon sind der Orientalistik zuzurechnen, nur jeweils eine der klassischen Philologie (Curtius: "Griechische Grammatik"), der Geschichte (Dove: "Deutsche Kaisergeschichte"), der Philosophie (Windelband: "Geschichte der neueren
Philosophie"), der allgemeinen Sprachwissenschaft (Merkel: "Physio-
logie der menschlichen Sprache") und der Völkerkunde (Peschel: "Anthropologie und Ethnographie"). In der Orientalistik hörte Meyer bei
Heinrich Leberecht Fleischer (12 Veranstaltungen: Arabisch, Persisch,
Islam), Otto Loth (9 Veranstaltungen: Persisch, Türkisch, Islam), Ernst
Kuhn (6 Veranstaltungen: Sanskrit), Ludolf Krehl (4 Veranstaltungen:
Semitische Philologie, Syrisch), Georg Ebers (3 Veranstaltungen: Ägyp-
tisch) und Bernhard Stade (2 Veranstaltungen: Altes Testament und
phönizische Inschriften).

Darüber hinaus scheint Meyer auch gelegentlich Vorlesungen bei
Hermann Brockhaus (Orientalistik) und Wilhelm Roscher (Nationalökonomie) gehört zu haben.[37]

Die wichtigsten Lehrer waren zweifelsohne Fleischer, Loth, Ebers und
Kuhn. Besonders Fleischer, der Nestor der deutschen Orientalistik, der
zu Meyers Studienzeit schon fast 40 Jahre ununterbrochen in Leipzig
lehrte, war in seinem fesselnden Unterrichtsstil und seiner herzlichen
unkomplizierten Art anziehend für Meyer.[38] Allerdings hat Meyer
Fleischers Konzentration auf die formale Seite der Sprache, auf Grammatik, Lexikon und Sprachgebrauch, im Laufe der Zeit immer kritischer
beurteilt. Das "völlige Fehlen historischen Sinnes" empfand er gerade in
der Behandlung des Koran als problematisch.[39] Hier konnte Otto Loth
eine "höchst wertvolle Ergänzung" bilden. Vom Typus her war Loth das
genaue Gegenteil von Fleischer: schüchtern, zurückhaltend, mit "Mühe
aus sich herauszugehn." "Das beste," schreibt Meyer über ihn, "was er
vortrug, kam immer nur in Nebensätzen heraus, oft verlegen genug."
Aber er besaß ein "wirklich lebendiges Verständnis sowohl für die

---

[37] Meyers Vorlesungsnachschrift von Roschers "Geschichte der politischen und soci-
ierten Theorien" befindet sich im Nachlaß (AdW der DDR—Archiv—Sign.: NL Ed.
Meyer Nr. 43).

[38] Meyer an seinen Vater, Leipzig 22.1.1873 (StPK Berlin, NL Ed. Meyer).

[39] Meyer an Theodor Nöldeke, Berlin 18.5.1925 (UB Tübingen, NL Nöldeke): "Daß
ich Ihrem Urteil über Fleischer vollkommen zustimme, brauche ich wohl nicht erst zu
sagen. Die Einseitigkeit seiner Richtung und das völlige Fehlen historischen Sinnes habe
ich durchaus auch damals schon empfunden—z.B., daß er beim Choran (Badhawi) niemals auch nur mit einem Wort auf die zahllosen damit verbundenen Probleme kam—und
für seine Schüler ist sie ja in der Tat vielfach verhängnisvoll gewesen, die die wirklichen
Aufgaben überhaupt nicht zu sehen vermochten. Aber eine große segensreiche Wirkung
hat er doch geübt; denn ohne streng grammatische Interpretation ist ja alles Treiben nur
ein äußerer Dilettantismus."

Geschichte wie für das Geistesleben,"[40] und Meyer war interessiert genug, um aus seinen Vorlesungen Gewinn zu ziehen.

Georg Ebers stand während Meyers Studienzeit auf dem Höhepunkt seines wissenschaftlichen Schaffens. 1872/73 hatte er auf einer Forschungsreise nach Ägypten zwei wichtige Papyri entdeckt, erworben und später herausgegeben. Ebers war einer breiteren Öffentlichkeit als Verfasser zahlreicher historischer Romane ("Professorenroman") bekannt und zog in seinen Vorlesungen viele Hörer an. Er verstand es, seine Schüler am Forschungsprozeß zu beteiligen und lehrte Ägyptologie nicht als etwas "Fertiges und Abgeschlossenes," sondern als Lernender, der die "zahlreichen Probleme, die hier noch der Lösung harrten" nicht beschönigte und der sich mit seinen Schülern auch an die "schwierigsten Texte" wagte, "bei denen nur zu oft bekannt werden musste, dass ein vollständiges, allseitig gesichertes Verständnis noch nicht erreicht sei."[41] Das war natürlich nach Meyers Geschmack. Er trat zu Ebers auch dadurch in engere persönliche Beziehungen, daß er dem Sohn Hausunterricht erteilte. Auch nach seiner Promotion blieb Meyer mit Ebers in engem Kontakt.[42]

Ernst Kuhn war zu Meyers Studienzeit noch Privatdozent, arbeitete aber gerade in jenen Jahren an seinen grundlegenden Forschungen zur heiligen Sprache des Buddhismus, die er 1875 in seinem Buch *Beiträge zur Pali-Grammatik* veröffentlichte.[43] Meyer nahm auch an diesen Untersuchungen regen Anteil.

Hinzu kam der Fortschritt der Assyrologie, die Entzifferung der Keilschriften durch Eberhard Schrader, die Hinwendung von Friedrich Delitzsch zu diesem neuen Forschungsgebiet und seine Habilitation 1874 in Leipzig. Für den Studenten Meyer kam diese Entwicklung allerdings zu spät. Erst nachdem er bereits selbst Privatdozent geworden war, fand er Zeit, sich intensiv mit den Keilschriften zu beschäftigen und besuchte die Übungen Delitzschs.[44]

Die orientalistische Wissenschaft war gerade in Meyers Studienzeit eine sich sehr rasch entwickelnde Disziplin, fast jährlich kam es mit neuen

---

[40] Ebd.

[41] Ed. Meyer, Nachruf auf Ebers, in: *Biographisches Jahrbuch und deutscher Nekrolog* 3 (1898), 86–99, hier 91; zu Ebers' literarischem Werk vgl. Elisabeth Müller, *Georg Ebers. Ein Beitrag zum Problem des literarischen Historismus in der zweiten Hälfte des neunzehnten Jahrhunderts*, Diss. phil. [masch.] München 1951, zum Urteil Ed. Meyers über Ebers' Romane vgl. 162–165.

[42] Dies dokumentiert der Briefwechsel: die Briefe Meyers an Ebers in StPK Berlin, NL Ebers; diejenigen von Ebers an Meyer in AdW der DDR—Archiv—Sign.: NL Ed. Meyer Nr. 557.

[43] Zu Kuhn vgl. Friedrich Wilhelm, *NDB* 13 (1982), 256 f.

[44] Vgl. Wilcken, Gedächtnisrede auf Ed. Meyer, in: *Marohl*, 119.

Entdeckungen und Funden zu großen Veränderungen und Fortschritten, erschlossen sich durch die Entzifferung von Sprachen ganz neue Welten und Studiengebiete. Meyer war gerade von den vielen ungelösten Problemen auf dem Gebiet der Orientalistik fasziniert und angeregt, und er sah zunehmend, daß er sein Ziel, die Sprachen und Kulturen des Orients zu studieren, an der Leipziger Universität in idealer Weise verwirklichen konnte. Deshalb widerstand er auch 1873/74 den drängenden Ermahnungen Classens und seines Vaters und lehnte einen Wechsel nach Berlin ab. Beide hofften offenbar, Meyer werde sich durch den Kontakt mit den renommierten Althistorikern der Berliner Universität wieder stärker den traditionellen Gegenstandsgebieten der alten Geschichte zuwenden. Meyer blieb jedoch an diesem Punkt völlig unbeirrt: er sei mit den orientalischen Sprachen noch nicht so vertraut wie dies für seine "Zwecke" notwendig sei, werde sie deshalb auf jeden Fall—wenngleich nicht so gut—auch in Berlin weiterstudieren müssen, und werde folglich überhaupt keine Zeit haben, in Berlin "historische Collegien" zu besuchen. Außerdem—und das ist bezeichnend für Meyers damaligen Interessenschwerpunkt—sei es doch "Sünde" in Berlin zu studieren und dann nicht einmal Bastian und Steinthal hören zu können.[45]

Man muß sich diesen Satz einmal klar machen: nicht um die Koryphäen althistorischer Geschichtsschreibung, nicht um Curtius, Droysen und Mommsen ist es Meyer leid, sondern um zwei Gelehrte, die damals eher unbekannt waren und als umstritten galten: die Begründer der modernen Völkerpsychologie Adolf Bastian und Heymann Steinthal.[46]

In den Augen Classens ging Meyers Begeisterung für das Orientalische allmählich ein bißchen zu weit: Hymnen des Rigveda anstelle von Oden des Horaz, obskure ägyptischen Totenbuchtexte und nicht Homer oder Thukydides, Pali-Grammatik statt griechischer Stilübungen—kein Wun-

[45] Meyer an seinen Vater, Leipzig 3.3.1874 (StPK Berlin, NL Ed. Meyer). Außer inhaltlichen Gründen führte Meyer auch finanzielle Argumente an, um seinen Vater davon zu überzeugen, daß es am besten sei, wenn er sein Studium in Leipzig beendete. Die Studiengebühren und vor allem die Promotionskosten lagen in Berlin wesentlich höher als in Leipzig. Bei den bescheidenen finanziellen Verhältnissen der Familie Meyer kam diesem Argument eine entscheidende Bedeutung zu.
[46] Meyers Kommilitone Richard Pietschmann hatte von 1870–1872 in Berlin bei Bastian und Steinthal gehört, vgl. Georg Leyh, Richard Pietschmann zum Gedächtnis, *Zentralblatt für Bibliothekswesen* 43 (1926), 213–235, hier 215. Es ist zu vermuten, daß Meyer über Pietschmann mit den Werken Steinthals und Bastians in engere Berührung kam. Zu Bastian vgl. Annemarie Fiedermutz-Laun, *Der kulturhistorische Gedanke bei Adolf Bastian*, Wiesbaden 1970; Klaus-Peter Koepping, *Adolf Bastian and the Psychic Unity of Mankind. The Foundations of Anthropology in Nineteenth Century Germany*, St. Lucia, London, New York 1983. Zu Steinthal vgl. Waltraud Bumann, *Die Sprachtheorie Heymann Steinthals*, Meisenheim am Glan 1965; Ingrid Belke (Hrsg.), *Moritz Lazarus und Heymann Steinthal. Die Begründer der Völkerpsychologie in ihren Briefen*, 3 Bde. Tübingen 1971–1986.

der, daß der Thukydidesforscher seinen Schüler auf Abwege geraten sah.
Um Meyer einen Restkontakt zur griechischen Geschichte zu erhalten,
gab Classen ihm den Auftrag, eine Abhandlung über *Ethnographie, Religion
und Geschichte der alten Troas* zu schreiben und damit eine Grundlage zur
Beurteilung der Schliemannschen Ausgrabungen zu liefern.[47] Meyer
entledigte sich dieser Aufgabe Ende 1873 mit Routine und Fleiß, jedoch
ohne große Begeisterung. Classen fand die Arbeit denn auch für den
Druck nicht ausgereift genug.[48]

Meyers eigentliches Interesse lag in diesen Jahren völlig auf den sprach-
und religionsgeschichtlichen Studien, denen er sich innerhalb und außerhalb seines Universitätsstudiums widmete.
    Kaum in Leipzig angekommen, stürzte er sich zunächst ganz auf die
Sprachgeschichte. Ob es darum ging, himjarische Inschriften zu entziffern
und er dazu ein Lexikon der himjarischen Sprache zusammenstellte, oder
ob er sich allgemein mit Problemen der semitischen Grammatik auseinandersetzte und ganze Abhandlungen über die "Entwicklung der semitischen Deklination" oder die "Verwandtschaft des semitischen mit dem
indogermanischen Sprachstamm" schrieb[49]—immer ging Meyers Intention über den bloßen Spracherwerb und Übungszweck hinaus, immer
versuchte er, größere Zusammenhänge aufzuzeigen, die Sprachgeschichte zur Wesensbestimmung von Völkern und Völkergruppen her-
anzuziehen und so die frühe Menschheitsgeschichte aufzuhellen. Zielsetzung, Methode und Ergebnisse seiner sprachgeschichtlichen Studien hat
Meyer 1874 in einem Vortrag vor dem Leipziger "Philosophischen
Verein" über *Die Anfänge menschlicher Entwicklung* näher ausgeführt.[50]
    Meyers Ausgangspunkt ist dabei die Darwinsche Entwicklungslehre,
deren Ergebnisse er als richtig hinstellt: es könne keinen ernsthaften
Zweifel daran geben, daß sich der Mensch aus den unteren Tierformen
entwickelt hat (4). Das Unterscheidungsmerkmal zwischen Mensch und
Tier bildet die Vernunft. Diese ist ohne Sprache nicht denkbar, ja, die
Vernunft wird sich erst durch Sprache bewußt (8). Somit bietet die
Sprache ein Mittel, "die historische Entwicklung der Vernunft zu verfol-
gen" (14):

    "Indem nämlich die Etymologie eines Wortes nachweist, von welchem ein-
    fachen Worte dasselbe abgeleitet ist, zeigt sie zugleich, welche Seite des zu

---

[47] Manuskript in AdW der DDR—Archiv—Sign.: NL Ed. Meyer Nr. 116.
[48] Classen an Meyer, Hamburg 16.1.1874 (AdW der DDR—Archiv—Sign.: NL Ed.
Meyer Nr. 487).
[49] Manuskript in AdW der DDR—Archiv—Sign.: NL Ed. Meyer Nr. 117.
[50] Ebd., Nr. 195.

bezeichnenden Gegenstandes dem Verstand als die wichtigste erschien, so daß er von ihr die Bezeichnung wählte. Indem ferner die Bedeutungen desselben Wortes fortwährend sich ändern, sich weiterentwickeln, während der Laut unverändert bleibt, können wir sehen, von welchem Ausgangspunct aus ein Begriff sich entwickelt hat" (14).

Auf diese Weise versucht Meyer, sprachliche "Urwurzeln" zu isolieren, die nicht weiter reduziert werden können. In der Frage, wie diese Lautwurzeln entstanden seien, wodurch eine Verbindung von Laut und Bedeutung zustande kam, schließt sich Meyer weitgehend den Thesen von Lazarus Geiger und Heymann Steinthal an.[51]

Danach sind "Gesichtseindruck", "Reflexbewegungen" und "Onomapoiie" die entscheidenden Faktoren. Meyer ist sich aber darüber im klaren, daß sich die Einzelheiten dieser Entwicklung nicht mehr vollständig rekonstruieren lassen. Dazu sei die empirische Forschung noch zu wenig fortgeschritten; außerdem bleibe immer ein unaufklärbarer Rest als natürliche Folge davon, "daß die Spracherzeugung den Übergang darstellt vom Unbewußten zum Bewußtsein, vom Unbegreiflichen zum Begreiflichen. Den Vorgang *mitzuerleben*, dazu sind wir daher nicht im Stande" (21). Meyer selbst kam aufgrund seiner vergleichenden Sprachstudien zu der Hypothese, daß die Übereinstimmungen zwischen indogermanischen, semitischen und ägyptischen Spracheigentümlichkeiten nicht zufällig seien und man einen einheitlichen Ursprung der Sprache annehmen müsse (22).

Interessanter als diese weitgehend spekulativen Einzelheiten ist die Tatsache, daß Meyer seine sprachgeschichtlichen Untersuchungen als Beitrag zu einer umfassenden "Wissenschaft vom Menschen" verstanden wissen wollte, ja, daß er eine solche Anthropologie geradezu als neue Leitwissenschaft begriff, die allein in der Lage sei, die aktuellen Fragen nach der Herkunft und dem Wesen des Menschen zeitgemäß und befriedigend zu beantworten. Über die begrenzte Wirkung eines solchen wissenschaftlich fundierten Menschenbildes auf die breite Öffentlichkeit machte er sich jedoch keine Illusionen:

"Ich habe versucht, in kurzen Zügen ein Bild zu entwerfen von dem, was die Sprachwissenschaft zu leisten im Stande (aber auch verpflichtet) ist für die Anfänge der menschlichen Entwicklung. Doch nicht nur auf diese beschränkt sie sich. Indem sie auch die weitere Entwicklung der Begriffe und Anschauungen sowie der Sprachgeister zeigt, indem dann die Religionswissenschaft und vergleichende Mythologie, die vergleichende Ethnographie

---

[51] Vgl. z.B. Bumann, *Sprachtheorie Steinthals*, 56 ff.; später lehnte Meyer den Versuch, durch die Erforschung der geschichtlichen Entwicklung eines Sprachstamms zu einem historischen Einblick in den Ursprung und die Anfangsstadien der Sprache überhaupt zu gelangen, als "Illusion" ab, vgl. Meyer, *GdA* I 1, 4 f.

sich zu ihr gesellen, indem dann schließlich mit den Anfängen historischer
Kunde auch die Völkergeschichte hinzu tritt, wird uns die Möglichkeit gegeben zu einer zusammenhängenden Geschichte des menschlichen Geistes von
seinem Einen beschränkten Ausgangspunct bis zu seiner reichen und mannigfachen Entfaltung, bis zu seiner unendlichen Ausbildung und Vertiefung
in den begabtesten Völkern der Geschichte. Was bisher unzusammenhän-
gend und zwecklos erschien in den einzelnen Wissenschaften, erhält so seine
Stellung in einem großen Ganzen: es wird ein Glied der Wissenschaft vom
Menschen und seiner Entwickelung, seinem Werden. Daß diese Wissenschaft zugleich das einzige Mittel ist, zu einer unsern jetzigen Bedürfnissen,
der jetzigen Ausbildung unseres Verstandes genügenden Auffassung und
Beurteilung der menschlichen Verhältnisse zu gelangen, ist meine feste
Überzeugung. Daß man auf diesem Wege zu einem System gelangen muß,
ist sicher; ob es aber allgemein durchführbar ist, d.h. von einem größern
Theil des Volkes angeeignet und zur Basis einer neuen Entwicklung, zum
Rettungsanker in dem gegenwärtigen Zusammensturz aller Verhältnisse
gemacht werden kann, ist wohl mehr als zweifelhaft'' (25).

Im Laufe des Studiums verlagerte sich Meyers Interesse dann immer
mehr von der Sprachwissenschaft zur *Religionsgeschichte*. Auch hier lag der
große Reiz darin, Neuland zu betreten und durch vergleichende Forschung zu einem "System" der Religionsentwicklung zu gelangen. Dazu
kam das Motiv der Polemik: Meyer war davon überzeugt, daß gerade auf
dem Gebiet der Religionswissenschaft die Forschung durch falsche Rücksichtnahme auf theologische und philosophische Dogmen beeinträchtigt
wurde, und er gefiel sich in der Rolle des Aufklärers, der den "von den
biederen Vorfahren und Mitarbeitern aufgefahrenen Schutt [wegräumt]
und die einfache klare Wahrheit ans Licht [zieht]," dabei "die auf den
Pfaden theologisierender Thorheit herumirrenden Menschen verspottend" (*Dok* 5).

Der religionskritische Zug ist beim Studenten Meyer sehr ausgeprägt:
für ihn stellt sich die Geschichte der Religionen als der "interessanteste
Theil der Geschichte der Illusionen" dar,[52] wie sein Freund Pietschmann
ist er davon überzeugt, "daß in der genetischen Entwicklung der Religionen ihre vernichtendste Kritik liegt,"[53] und nach einem Besuch eines
englischen Gottesdienstes bricht es geradezu aus ihm heraus:

"Neulich wohnte ich einem Church of England service bei, der denn in der
That vielleicht der höchste Schwindel ist, den die Religion hervorgebracht
hat. [...] Die Predigt war the most disgusting and stupid nonsense I ever
heard; [...] Wäre es nicht der Mühe wert, einmal ein paar Predigten mit

[52] Meyer an Pietschmann, Hamburg 20.8.1874 (SUB Göttingen, MS Pietschmann
25, 620).
[53] Pietschmann an Meyer, Breslau 21.1.1876 [vermutlich: 31.1.1877] (AdW der
DDR—Archiv—Sign.: NL Ed. Meyer Nr. 1052).

Commentar herauszugeben, wie man doch indische, avestische und To-
dtenbuchtexte herausgibt? Man hätte ja die Sache viel näher; und dasselbe
Zeug ist es doch: Mythologie, Gottvater und Gottsohn, mystischer Einfluß
des Wortes, des Gebets, der Zauberformeln des Abendmahls, und alle die
Scheinheiligkeit Verlogenheit und Immoralität, welche die Religion ins
menschliche Geschlecht gebracht hat—oder vielmehr deren Ausdruck sie
immer gewesen ist. [. . .]''[54]

Grundlage für Meyers religionskritische Wertungen bildet seine durch
Aufklärung und Idealismus geprägte philosophische Weltanschauung,
die den höchsten Wert menschlicher Entwicklung in der Selbstentfaltung
und Freiheit des Individuums, in sittlicher Verantwortung und kritischer
Verstandestätigkeit erkennt. Derselbe Maßstab liegt zugrunde, wenn
Meyer z.B. die ''großartigen philosophischen Systeme des Buddhismus''
anerkennt und in Parallele zu Kants Vernunftkritik stellt.[55]

Für Meyers religionsgeschichtliche Studien ist dann sehr wichtig geworden, daß er im Laufe seines Leipziger Studiums mit Wilhelm Spitta und
Richard Pietschmann zwei Kommilitonen und Gesprächspartner traf, die
seine Interessen teilten. Spitta, der Sohn des protestantischen Kirchen-
lieddichters Philipp Spitta, beschäftigte sich vor allem mit dem Koran,
promovierte auch über ein Thema der Islamwissenschaft und wurde
anschließend Bibliothekar in Kairo.[56] Pietschmann promovierte wie
Meyer bei Ebers in Ägyptologie und schlug später auch die Bibliotheks-
laufbahn ein.[57]

Die Themen, die Meyer und seine Freunde in ihren religionsgeschichtlichen Untersuchungen und Debatten aufgriffen, waren vielfältig und
entsprachen der Weite der sprachlichen Studien. Ein systematisches
Vorgehen ist nicht zu erkennen, auch eine methodische Anleitung fehlte.
Meyer war hier weitgehend Autodidakt, und gerade das reizte ihn. Man
könnte seine Vorgehensweise mit dem Motto 'Urtext und Spekulation'
charakterisieren. Meyer las alles durcheinander—aber jeweils in der Ori-
ginalsprache: arabische und phönizische Inschriften, das Totenbuch und
das Alte Testament, avestische und persische Texte usw. Die extensive
Lektüre führte ihn dann zu weitreichenden universalen Fragestellungen
und Spekulationen. So stellte er z.B. Vergleiche zwischen dem Monothe-

---

[54] Meyer an Pietschmann, Bournemouth 26.1.1877 (SUB Göttingen, MS Pietschmann 25, 640). Der vollständige Text bei Hoffmann, *Judentum im Werk deutscher Althistoriker*, 136, Anm. 10.
[55] Meyer an seinen Bruder Kuno, Buyukdere 20.7.1875 (StPK Berlin, NL Ed.
Meyer).
[56] Vgl. Ed. Meyer, Wilhelm Spitta (Nekrolog), *Zentralblatt für Bibliothekswesen* I (1884),
1–7.
[57] Zu Pietschmann vgl. Leyh, *Zentralblatt für Bibliothekswesen* 43 (1926), 213–235.

ismus der Ursemiten und dem Glauben der Indianer an den großen Geist
an, um die These zu überprüfen, daß es bei primitiven Völkern eine
monotheistische Entwicklung noch nicht gegeben habe.[58] Das Ziel der
Forschung lag für Meyer darin, zu einer Systematik der Religionen und
der Religionsentwicklung zu gelangen. Meyer interessierte sich deshalb
auch schon früh für die Mormonen, weil er glaubte, hier den Prozeß der
Entstehung einer Religion aufgrund der guten Quellenlage genau rekonstruieren und die Ergebnisse für die antike Religionsgeschichte fruchtbar
machen zu können (*Dok* 8).

In seinen Leipziger Studienjahren konzentrierte Meyer sich vor allem auf
die vergleichende Mythenforschung, namentlich beschäftigte er sich mit
der Göttin Astarte und ihren indogermanischen, semitischen und ägyptischen Erscheinungsformen.[59] Ursprünglich plante Meyer auch, über
Astarte seine Dissertation zu schreiben, dann wählte er aber doch ein rein
ägyptisches Thema: *Set-Typhon. Eine religionsgeschichtliche Studie.*[60] Darin
polemisierte Meyer gegen die traditionelle Forschungsmeinung, nach der
Set im alten ägyptischen Reich hoch verehrt worden und erst infolge der
Hyksosherrschaft zum bösen, verabscheuten Gott geworden sei. Meyer
versuchte, die ''Grundanschauung des Gottes'' aus den religiösen und
mythologischen Texten (besonders dem Totenbuch) abzuleiten und kam
so zu dem Ergebnis, daß Set von Anfang an eine ''finstere, vernichtende
Macht [darstellte], welche den Lichtgöttern Verderben und Tod droht,
und mit der sie fortwährend zu kämpfen haben'' (24).
Die Art und Weise, wie Meyer seine Dissertation fertigstellte, ist nicht
ganz untypisch für seine Persönlichkeit und seinen damaligen Arbeitsstil:
Nachdem er den Januar 1875 infolge mehrerer studentischer Feste in
einem Zustand verbracht hatte, von dem er selbst nicht wußte, ''ob er
Rausch oder Kater war,''[61] faßte er am 1. Februar ''den heroischen
Entschluß,'' mit der Abfassung der Dissertation, deren Disposition er
bereits im Kopf hatte, zu beginnen. Er schrieb ''natürlich gleich ins
Reine'' und konnte das 88 Seiten starke Manuskript bereits am 18.
Februar zum Buchbinder bringen—nach nur 15 Tagen Arbeit (''da die

---

[58] Meyer an Pietschmann, Hamburg 20.8.1874 (SUB Göttingen, MS Pietschmann
25, 620).
[59] Meyer an Pietschmann, Hamburg 2.9.1874 (SUB Göttingen, MS Pietschmann 25,
621); Meyer an Pietschmann, Leipzig 9.11.1874 (SUB Göttingen, MS Pietschmann, 25,
623).
[60] Leipzig 1875; vgl. die überwiegend positiven Rezensionen von Pietschmann, *Jenaer
Literaturzeitung* 3 (1876), 216 f. und Diestel, *Theologische Literaturzeitung* 2 (1877), 29 f.
[61] Meyer an Pietschmann, Leipzig 25./28.2.1875 (SUB Göttingen, MS Pietschmann
25, 626).

beiden Carnevalstage vollständig, ein anderer Tag, an dem wir mit Fleischer, Kuhn, Loth usw. zusammen kneipten, fast vollständig ausfielen''[62].

Von dem Ergebnis war Meyer selbst keineswegs völlig begeistert— ''die Grundanschauung ist, glaube ich, unzweifelhaft richtig, aber die Ausarbeitung flüchtig und nicht gründlich genug;''[63] zudem mußte er fürchten, daß Ebers—dem ''die Bekanntschaft mit der Mythenforschung und -erklärung abgeht''[64]—für seine spezifische Vorgehensweise wenig Verständnis hatte. Doch es kam anders: Ebers zeigte sich ''sehr zufrieden,'' stimmte ''in allen wesentlichen Puncten'' Meyer bei, und zwar selbst dort, wo Meyer gegen Eberssche Ansichten polemisiert hatte.[65] Der Rest war reine Formalität. Am 11. März 1875 bestand Meyer das Rigorosum bei Ebers, Fleischer und Brockhaus ''in aller Gemütlichkeit''[66] und beendete damit sein Studium.

Betrachtet man Meyers Entwicklung in den Studienjahren, so fällt auf, wie selbstbestimmt und konsequent er seine eigenen Ziele verfolgte. Äußere Einflüsse und Moden spielten so gut wie keine Rolle. Selbst die akademischen Lehrer waren—außer in Fachfragen—weniger wichtig für Meyer als die gleichaltrigen Freunde, mit denen er seine Forschungsinteressen teilte, mit denen er sich auseinandersetzte und dadurch seine eigenen Anschauungen immer weiter entwickelte.

Natürlich war Meyer nicht völlig unbeeinflußt von den Fragen seiner Zeit, schon sein Konzept einer umfassenden ''Wissenschaft des Menschen'' als Antwort auf die durch die Evolutionstheorie aufgeworfenen anthropologischen Probleme beweist dies. Aber gerade dieser Ansatz Meyers war durchaus originell und innovativ, besonders was die Weite der Fragestellung und die angestrebte interdisziplinäre Zusammenarbeit betrifft. Meyer dachte schon als Student über die Fächergrenzen hinaus und paßte seine Methoden und Lernprogramme dem Untersuchungsgegenstand an. Er gehörte gerade nicht zu denen, die er nur als ''große Kleingeister'' belächeln konnte, ''die ihre Carriere machen, Schritt, vor Schritt, ihren Fuß dahinsetzend, wo ihr Vorgänger ihn weggenommen,

---

[62] Meyer an seine Eltern, Leipzig 26.2.1875 (StPK Berlin, NL Ed. Meyer).
[63] Meyer an Pietschmann, Leipzig 25./28.2.1875 (SUB Göttingen, MS Pietschmann 25, 626).
[64] Meyer an Pietschmann, Buyukdere 20.6.1875 (SUB Göttingen, MS Pietschmann 25, 630).
[65] Meyer an Pietschmann, Leipzig 25./28.2.1875 (SUB Göttingen, MS Pietschmann 25, 626).
[66] Meyer an Pietschmann, Hamburg 22.3.1875 (SUB Göttingen, MS Pietschmann 25, 627).

ohne je die Linie zu verlassen, ohne Extravaganzen, ohne Gedanken''
(*Dok* 7).

Meyers Ethos des Lernens machte auch vor den eigenen liebgeworde-
nen Anschauungen nicht halt. Im vierten Semester (1874) kam es zu
einen deutlichen Umbruch, zu Ansätzen einer Adoleszenzkrise (*Dok* 4),
die vom Vater durchaus ernst genommen wurde.[67] Das Welt- und Geschichtsbild, welches der Schüler in seiner Abhandlung über den Untergang des Altertums vertreten hatte, verlor für den Studenten jetzt an Gültigkeit. Vor allem der naive Fortschrittsglaube der Schülerzeit wich einer
betont ''realistischen'' und ''illusionslosen'' Weltanschauung, die von
pessimistischen Zügen nicht frei war. Für Meyer zeigte die Geschichte
jetzt, ''daß die Menschen immer vergeblich Illusionen nachgejagt haben
und nachjagen werden'' und ''daß alles Hoffen auf Besserung Wahnsinn
ist'' (*Dok* 4). Diese skeptische Sicht wollte Meyer jedoch nicht als Ausdruck einer pessimistischen Lebensanschauung verstanden wissen. In
einem Brief an Pietschmann grenzte Meyer sich von der philosophischen
Modebewegug des ''Pessimismus'', die v.a. durch die Schriften Schopen-
hauers, Nietzsches und Ed. v. Hartmanns in der zweiten Hälfte des 19.
Jahrhunderts gerade in bürgerlichen Kreisen starken Einfluß gewonnen
hatte, deutlich ab:[68]

---

[67] Vgl. Meyer sen. an Meyer, Hamburg 11.7.1874 (StPK Berlin, NL Ed. Meyer):
''[...] Also auch *du* birgst den alten Faust im Herzen? und er thut sich in den Worten
kund, die der tieffühlende, Welt, Leben und Menschenherzen so innig kennende Goethe
ihm in den Mund legt, die aber aus des Dichters eigenem Inneren stammen. Selbst dieser
große Geist erkannte früh und spät, daß kein menschlicher Verstand Gott und die Schöpfung begreifen könne und ins Innere derselben dringen. Wähne aber nur nicht, daß ich
hier den Wagner spielen und dir pedantisch und lehrsam gegenüber treten werde. Aber
folgende Betrachtungen möchte ich doch bei dieser Gelegenheit dir mittheilen, da ich ihre
tröstliche und lebensregelnde Kraft an mir selbst erprobt und, ach wie gern! noch mehr
bethätigt hätte. [...] Es ist nicht wahr, daß die Menschen immer *vergeblich Illusionen* nachgejagt. Ist nicht Amerika und Australien entdeckt? [...] Unsere Zeit ist nicht *herrlich*, wir
haben es nicht *herrlich* weit gebracht. Wer sagt das? Nicht daß wir's schon errungen hätten,
wir jagen ihm aber nach. Nicht alles Hoffen auf Besserung ist Wahnsinn. Sind wir nicht
schon tausenderlei Vorurtheile los geworden? Aber das ist wahr, die Weltverbesserung
geht einen sehr langsamen Weg. 'Laß die Zeit gewähren,' sagte schon im J. 1817 Platen
in seinen trefflichen Lebensregeln [...].—Mir scheint's als wenn der, vom höchsten
Wesen mit Vernunft als höchster Kraft begabte Mensch, dem ganzen unermeßlichen
Schöpfungsräthsel, besonders den Problemen der Erde gegenüber gestellt sei, um an
diesen seine Kraft zu versuchen, zu stärken, und daß die Art und Weise wie er das thut,
und die Energie welche er dabei entwickelt, seine künftige überirdische, geistige Fort-
dauer bedingen wird, denn den Glauben an Geistesunsterblichkeit kann ich mir nicht
rauben lassen, weil mir sonst das ganze Leben als sinnlos erscheinen würde und der Idee
einer Gottheit unwürdig und nicht entsprechend eingesetzt und angeordnet. Völlige
Ergebung in den höchsten Willen ist jedoch erste Lebensbedingung, und Streben und
Wirken von innen nach außen höchste Lebensaufgabe. Wohl dem, der darin am Mächtig-
sten und Ausdauerndsten sich zeigt und zeigen kann [...].''
[68] Meyer an Pietschmann, Buyukdere 20.6.1875 (SUB Göttingen, MS Pietschmann
25, 630).

"[...] Denn was ist der gewöhnliche Pessimismus: Krankheit, weiter nichts als Krankheit: Übersättigung in Folge einer schiefen Cultur und des ihr gebotenen Luxus, Schwachheit des Charakters, Energielosigkeit und Feigheit. Sie wagen nicht, gegen sich selbst aufzutreten, sich zu ändern und zu bessern, ihre Phantasiebilder zu zerstören weil sie falsch sind. Stattdessen schimpfen sie auf die Welt, die Lebensbedingungen, die Lebensgenüsse usw., erklären alles für Unsinn und—leben und genießen ruhig weiter!

Wer das Leben nicht ertragen kann, schieße sich todt! Damit raubt er die Berechtigung Pessimist in dem gewöhnlichen Sinn des Wortes zu sein. Sonst aber lasse er das Leben wie es ist und füge sich darein statt es zu schelten [...]. Dies ist kein Optimismus, sondern ethischer Realismus, und das ist Deine Anschauung auch. [...] Unsere Anschauungen über das Geschick des Menschen und das Leben der Menschheit im allgemeinen, bleiben unverändert diesselben; aber sie mag ich nicht mehr Pessimismus nennen, seit ich gesehen habe, was man meist darunter versteht. Auch Göthe war kein Pessimist, und doch hatte er ganz ähnliche Anschauungen.''

Meyers moralische Invektive gegenüber dem Pessimismus zeigt deutlich, daß die im Elternhaus vermittelte Lebens- und Weltanschauung—trotz mancher Modifikationen und Umbrüche—insgesamt für ihn ihre Gültigkeit behielt, sie zeigt sein grundsätzliches Einverständnis mit der bestehenden Gesellschaft und Kultur. Obwohl Meyer manchmal davon sprach, daß alles menschliche Tun sinnlos und "Wahnsinn" sei, blieb er in seinen grundlegenden Anschauungen, z.B. was den Wert und die Erkenntnisfähigkeit der Wissenschaft betrifft, doch von wirklichen Selbstzweifeln frei. Nur so war er auch in der Lage, das gewaltige Arbeitspensum, das er sich in seinem Studium auferlegt hatte, zu bewältigen.

(3) Hauslehrer in Konstantinopel und Bournemouth, Militär, Habilitation (1875–1879)

Ein Zufall führte dazu, daß Meyer den Orient bald persönlich kennenlernen konnte. Von Professor Zarncke erfuhr er, daß der englische Gesandte in Konstantinopel, Sir Philip Francis, einen deutschen Hauslehrer für seine beiden Kinder suchte. Meyer bewarb sich auf die Stelle und erhielt sie. Ende April traf er in Konstantinopel ein.

Die anderthalb Jahre, die Meyer im Orient zubrachte, waren für ihn eine willkommene Abwechslung nach den Schul- und Studienjahren, sie bedeuteten für ihn eine Bekanntschaft mit der "große[n] freie[n] Welt," mit dem "große[n] Leben [...], wo man lernt aus dem was man sieht und hört und nicht aus Büchern" (*Dok* 8).

Es waren vor allem drei Bereiche seiner neuen Umgebung, durch die Meyer "lernte": Zunächst die *Atmosphäre im Haus des englischen Generalkonsuls*, die "große" Welt von Politik und Diplomatie, von Wohlstand und aristokratischem Flair, die dem zwanzigjährigen Bürgersohn aus Hamburg bisher so ganz fremd war und die ihn faszinierte. Sir Philip, der in den 40er Jahren in Bonn und München studiert hatte, erwies sich als aufgeschlossener Gesprächspartner, der gern seine Anschauungen über Politik, Philosophie oder Religion mit dem jungen Doktor aus Deutschland austauschte. Meyer war denn auch begeistert:[69]

> "Sir Philip Francis ist ein ganz ausgezeichneter Mann, und wird unzweifelhaft einen langen nachhaltigen Eindruck bei mir hinterlassen. Durchaus bestimmt und klar, dabei aber leicht und fein in seinem Benehmen. Sein ganzes Wesen hat etwas außerordentlich aristokratisches im besten Sinne des Worts, ebenso wie das ganze Haus. Alles hat einen feinen Anstrich, nie findet sich das Renommieren mit Reichthum und Stellung, das Prunken usw., was man so häufig—auch hier—bei reichen Leuten findet. Es wird nichts gesucht, sondern alles versteht sich von selbst. So fühlt man sich nicht eingeengt und bedrängt, sondern frei unter dem wohltätigen Zwange der Sitte. Ich habe mich denn auch, wie ich glaube, in alles rasch und ohne Anstoß oder Zwang hineingefunden.
> Sir Philip ist sehr liebenswürdig, aber auf dem ganzen Verkehre mit ihm ruht die angenehme Zurückhaltung, die keinen alles sagen, sich ganz aussprechen läßt und daher etwas zu denken übrig läßt. [...] In religiösen Dingen ist er sehr freisinnig. [...] Kurz und gut, er ist ein treffliches Beispiel der Art der Engländer, zu der ein Locke, D. Hume, Stuart Mill, Darwin, Lewes gehören: ausgebildeten Geistes, klar denkend und darin rücksichtslos, aber praktisch und gewandt, ihr Ziel im Auge habend und verfolgend."

Dann die *politischen, sozialen und religiösen Verhältnisse* im immer mehr zerfallenden Osmanischen Reich: 1875 war der türkische Staat vollkommen zahlungsunfähig geworden, so daß der Staatsbankrott verkündet werden mußte. Dazu kamen Unruhen in der Herzegowina. Die Situation führte zu innenpolitischen Turbulenzen: 1876 wurde der Sultan 'Abd ül-Asis in einer Revolte entthront und beging Selbstmord, nach einer kurzen Zwischenregierung des geistesschwachen Murad V. (Mai–August 1876) folgte 'Abd ül-Hamid II., der unter dem Druck von Studentenunruhen und der allgemeinen Unzufriedenheit im Dezember 1876 eine (allerdings dann nie in Kraft getretene) Verfasung einführte.

Meyer hat diese politischen Vorgänge auf seinen Streifzügen durch die Stadt hautnah miterlebt, ja, er besaß durch seine Kontakte zu europäischen Diplomaten und Journalisten und nicht zuletzt zu Mordtmanns Schwiegervater, der Leibarzt des Thronfolgers war, sogar interne Informationen. Kurz vor seinem gewaltsamen Tod sah Meyer noch einmal den alten Sultan, als dieser zur Moschee ausritt. Meyer benutzte die

---

[69] Meyer an seine Eltern, Buyukdere 30.6.1875 (StPK Berlin, NL Ed. Meyer).

Schilderung dieser Szene dazu, seinem Bruder Albrecht die korrupten politischen Verhältnisse der Türkei zu verdeutlichen:[70]

"Um halb 12 Uhr morgens war ich unten am Palais von Dolmabagtsche. Große Menschenmassen, Equipagen voll von Fremden, vornehmen Türken, jungen Beys, wohl auch Armeniern oder Griechen; eine Menge schaulustiger Reiter in allen Farben, junge Nubier und Neger treiben sich auf den Straßen herum. Überall stehen Soldaten bereit; Offiziere, Palastbeamte, Eunuchen usw. stehen an den Toren. Niemand weiß, in welche Moschee der Sultan heute geht, denn das macht er erst kurz vorher bekannt. Endlich um halb eins wird es angezeigt: nach Beshiktasch! Schleunigst fahren die Sandkarrenführer welche den Weg zu bestreuen haben, damit der Padisha sanft reiten könne; unbekümmert ob sie vielleicht ein Pferdebahngeleise zuwerfen, beschütten sie den ganzen Weg. Die Regimenter marschieren auf mit Musik, um auf der ganzen Route an einer Seite Spalier zu bilden; vornehme Beamte fahren zur Moschee und Haremsdamen in Masse in fest verschlossenen Wagen. Unzählige Pferde werden herumgeführt und weit über hundert kostbar gekleidete Reitknechte des Palastes sind auf den Beinen. Endlich erscheinen die höchsten Beamten des Reichs: Pashas, Minister, der Großvezir; endlich der älteste Sohn des Sultans, Jusuff 'Izz eddin, ein junger gänzlich entnervter und blasser Bengel von 16 oder 17 Jahren, der sich kaum auf dem Pferde halten konnte. Alle steigen auf, grüssen sich feierlich, und warten; die Straßen werden gereinigt, das Volk zurückgedrängt. Und warum das alles?—*Dem großen Vieh zu Ehren*, das jetzt langsam unter Kanonendonner aus dem Palast hervorreitet. Der Sultan war in seinen schwarzen seidenen Mantel gehüllt, und sah in Folge dessen sehr dick und unförmig aus. Er ritt langsamen Schritt, die Augen starr vor sich gerichtet und mit souveräner Verachtung nichts sehend nichts bemerkend. Seine Züge sind etwas schlaff und alt; sonst ist sein Gesicht nicht uninteressant. Man erzählt, daß er alle paar Monate Anfälle von tagelanger Raserei habe, anstatt dessen natürlich jedesmal eine andre Krankheit angegeben wird.

Hier und da begrüßen ihn die Soldaten mit Geschrei,—arme Kerle; vielleicht schickt er sie den nächsten Tag nach der Herzegowina, um dort wenn nicht in Engpässen niedergeschossen zu werden, durch die Schurkerei gewinnsüchtiger Lieferanten, die Mangelhaftigkeit der Lazarethe, die Unfähigkeit der Officiere, zu Tausenden zu verhungern, zu erfrieren, zu versiechen [...]"

Meyer glaubte, daß die politischen Verhältnisse der Türkei nicht mehr reformbar seien, er erwartete ein baldiges Zerfallen des Osmanischen Reiches; einen Krieg zwischen Rußland und der Türkei (der dann ja auch wirklich 1877/78 eintrat) hielt er für "unvermeidlich und höchst heilsam."[71]

---

[70] Meyer an seinen Bruder Albrecht, Constantinopel 6.4.1876 (StPK Berlin, NL Ed. Meyer).
[71] Meyer an Ebers, Bournemouth 27.12.1876 (StPK Berlin, NL Ebers). Meyer hat seine Ansichten über die politischen Situation der Türkei auch in einem Zeitschriften-

Schließlich die *Begegnung mit den Überresten antiker Kulturen*, die Meyer sowohl in Konstantinopel als auch auf seinen Exkursionen in die kleinasiatische Umgebung, nach Bithynien (Prusa, Apameia, Nikaia, Nikomedeia) und vor allem nach Troja kennenlernte.

Der unmittelbare Kontakt führte Meyer zu einer Wiederaufnahme seiner Studien über die kleinasiatische Geschichte, Arbeiten, die ihm "in den letzten Jahren ziemlich fremd und kalt geworden waren."[72] Unter dem Eindruck der persönlichen Anschauung überarbeitete er seine Untersuchung zur Ethnographie und Religion des alten Troja, die er in seiner Studienzeit für Classen angefertigt hatte und publizierte sie 1877 unter dem Titel *Geschichte von Troas*. Darin setzte er sich u.a. kritisch mit den Hypothesen Schliemanns auseinander und wies nach, daß der sogenannte "Schatz des Priamos" bzw. auch der "Palast des Priamos" unmöglich zu der Stadt gehört haben können, deren Mauern Schliemann in Ilion ausgegraben hatte.[73] Meyers Versuch, die historischen Fakten der troischen Geschichte aus der Sagenüberlieferung herauszuschälen und die nationalen und religiösen Eigenheiten dieses Volkes zu ermitteln, erschien zu einem Zeitpunkt, wo das öffentliche Interesse an Troja durch die Ausgrabungen Schliemanns besonders groß war. Meyers Beitrag ist in der Fachwelt jedoch überwiegend mit Enttäuschung aufgenommen worden. Besonders kritisiert wurden der unangemessen selbstsichere Ton, "der mit einer gewissen kühlen, allem Excentrischen abgewendeten, vornehmen Art über die schwierigsten Fragen glatt hinweg[geht],"[74] die mangelnde Quellenkritik (z.B. bei Strabo) und die Nichtberücksichtigung der modernen Literatur.[75]

Neben den troischen Untersuchungen blieb die Religionsgeschichte auch in Konstantinopel Meyers Hauptarbeitsgebiet. Er hatte den Kopf voller Pläne und Projekte, die er "gerne endlich einmal herunterwälzte in der Gestalt von Büchern" (*Dok* 8). Gegenüber Ebers bot Meyer sich an, "eine

---

artikel niedergelegt: Anonym. [Ed. Meyer], Türkische Zustände. Von einem Augenzeugen, *Im neuen Reich* 6 (1876), 681–692 u. 726–739.

[72] Meyer an Ebers, Constantinopel 5.12.1876 (StPK Berlin, NL Ebers).

[73] Meyer, *Geschichte von Troas*, Leipzig 1877, 51–55. In Briefen an Pietschmann äusserte sich Meyer sehr negativ über Schliemann, z.B. Meyer an Pietschmann, Hamburg 8.11.1875 (SUB Göttingen, MS Pietschmann 25, 638): "Sybels Vortrag [über Schliemann] ist sehr gut; nur fürchte ich, daß auch Schliemann ein Beispiel jener Mischung von Schwärmer und Schwindler ist, die in Mohammed u.a. auf andern Gebieten so oft hervortritt."

[74] Stark, *Jenaer Literaturzeitung* 4 (1877), 665–678, hier 674.

[75] Ebd.; vgl. außerdem die Rezension im *Literarischen Zentralblatt* 1877, 1429 f. Positiver äußerten sich die Gelehrten, denen Meyer ein Exemplar zugesandt hatte, in Dankesschreiben an ihn, so z.B. Georg Ebers, Johann Gustav Droysen und Adolf v. Gutschmid (AdW der DDR—Archiv—Sign.: NL Ed. Meyer).

Reihe kleiner Hefte 'Religionsgeschichtliche Studien' heraus[zu]geben, als deren erste mein 'Set-Typhon' zu bezeichnen wäre. Ich habe noch mehrere andere Themata in Aussicht genommen, und würde das Ganze mit meinem Aufsatz über Religion, ihr Wesen und ihre Entwicklungsgeschichte im allgemeinen abschließen.''[76]

Wie der Briefwechsel mit Pietschmann und Spitta zeigt, beschäftigte sich Meyer in dieser Zeit mit den unterschiedlichsten Fragen der Religionswissenschaft: er entwarf ein Schema der Religionen, welches von den Freunden lebhaft diskutiert und kritisiert wurde,[77] er griff die Studien zu Astarte wieder auf und brachte sie zu einem gewissen Abschluß,[78] er vergrub sich immer wieder ins Totenbuch und plante die Herausgabe einzelner Kapitel mit religionsgeschichtlichem Kommentar,[79] oder er interessierte sich für Einzelprobleme, so für die religiösen Hintergründe von Kastration und Beschneidung oder die Bedeutung des Hakenkreuzsymbols.[80]

Gelegentlich kamen ihm jetzt Zweifel, ob seine Arbeitsweise die richtige sei, und er begann zum ersten Mal, auch an seine wissenschaftliche Zukunft zu denken: ''Wie eine Biene überall den Honig sammeln ist doch etwas zu gefährlich um es gerade weg als Ziel hinzustellen; und heute Aristophanes, morgen Göthe, übermorgen das Todtenbuch, und dann den Rigveda oder Hafiz oder Macaulay lesen ist doch keine Beschäftigung, die Aussicht auf eine sichere Lebensstellung eröffnet'' (*Dok* 6). Aber im Grunde hielt Meyer den von ihm eingeschlagenen Weg, sich nicht von Karrieregesichtspunkten bestimmen zu lassen, sondern zu treiben, wozu man sich getrieben fühlt und ''ein Specialstudium sich später von selbst ergeben [zu lassen],'' auch weiterhin für den allein richtigen, wie sein 'Wissenschaftliches Credo' im Brief an Kuno (*Dok* 7) zeigt.

Im Laufe der Zeit wurde Meyers Arbeitseifer ohnehin immer mehr

---

[76] Meyer an Ebers, Buyukdere 29.7.1876 (StPK Berlin, NL Ebers).

[77] Meyers Konzept im Brief an Pietschmann, Constantinopel 24.11./4.12.1875 (SUB Göttingen, MS Pietschmann 25, 633). Darin unterscheidet Meyer zwischen ''nationalen Religionen'' und ''Weltreligionen''. Unter die nationalen Religionen subsumiert er ''Volksreligionen'' (Fetischismus, Ahnenkult, amerikan. Religion, Veda, Griechen und Römer etc.) und ''theologische Religionen,'' die auf einen philosophischen Stifter zurückgehen wie der Brahmanismus, Zoroastrismus, Judentum, Konfucius etc. Unter Weltreligionen versteht Meyer allein Buddhismus, Christentum und Islam.—Die Reaktion seiner Freunde: Pietschmann an Meyer, Greifswald 8.2.1876 (AdW der DDR—Archiv—Sign.: NL Ed. Meyer Nr. 1052); Spitta an Meyer, Cairo 29.2.1876 (Ebd. Nr. 171).

[78] Veröffentlicht unter dem Titel: Über einige semitische Götter, *ZMG* 31 (1877), 716–741.

[79] Meyer an Ebers, Constantinopel 5.12.1875 und Buyukdere 29.7.1876 (StPK Berlin, NL Ebers).

[80] Vgl. v.a. die Briefe an Pietschmann, Hamburg 21.10.1876 und 6.11.1876, Bournemouth 14./20.2.1877 (SUB Göttingen, MS Pietschmann 25, 637.638.641).

gebremst, selbst ihn holte der orientalische Schlendrian ein; die Hitze tat ein übriges; "Ich bin ziemlich Epicuräer geworden, und von der Wahrheit, daß man den Augenblick genießen muß, und höchstens das Genossenhaben einen Werth hat, aber nicht das Pläne in die Zukunft bauen—, mehr als je überzeugt."[81]

Der plötzliche Tod von Sir Philip am 10. August 1876 bedeutete ein jähes Ende der Konstantinopeler Zeit. Meyer versuchte zunächst, noch im Orient zu bleiben und fragte bei Spitta an, ob es in Kairo vielleicht eine Hauslehrer- oder Bibliothekarstelle für ihn gebe.[82] Da dies jedoch völlig aussichtslos war, ging Meyer mit der Familie des Verstorbenen nach Europa zurück und blieb bis zum Frühsommer 1877 in Bournemouth, wo er weiterhin Hausunterricht erteilte.

Die Zeit in der englischen Provinz wurde ihm durch das Fehlen von Gesprächspartnern und von wissenschaftlichen Arbeitsmöglichkeiten besonders lang, und er sehnte sich nach dem 'unzivilisierten' Konstantinopel zurück: "Hier herrscht wie überall in Europa das Philisterium vor und wenn ich nicht wieder hinauskomme, so werde ich ihm unfehlbar auch verfallen [. . .]. Nur so lange man frisch und frei und unter fortwährend neuen Anregungen lebt, wie dort draußen, erhält man sich die Ungebundenheit und Schwungkraft des Geistes."[83]

Am englischen Leben interessierten Meyer besonders die religiösen und politischen Verhältnisse. Er ging in die Kirche, "um Culturstudien zu treiben"[84] und hörte vor allem die Prediger der Independenten, "die ein höchst bedeutendes Leben und Kraft haben."[85] Was die politischen Verhältnisse betrifft, zeigte sich Meyer gegenüber dem parlamentarischen System der Engländer eher kritisch. Der "extreme Parlamentarismus," der in England herrsche, sei vor allem in der Außenpolitik schädlich, weil er eine klare Entscheidungsfindung beeinträchtige.[86] Über Meyers allgemeine politische Orientierung in diesen Jahren informiert eine Bemerkung gegenüber Pietschmann über die

---

[81] Meyer an Pietschmann, Buyukdere 4.8.1876 (SUB Göttingen, MS Pietschmann 25, 635).
[82] Vgl. Spitta an Meyer, Cairo 6.9.1876 (AdW der DDR—Archiv—Sign.: NL Ed. Meyer Nr. 171) Die Briefe Meyers an Spitta sind offenbar verlorengegangen.
[83] Meyer an Pietschmann, Bournemouth 26.1.1877 (SUB Göttingen, MS Pietschmann 25, 640).
[84] Ebd.
[85] Meyers an Pietschmann, London 28.5.1877 (SUB Göttingen, MS Pietschmann 25, 645).
[86] Meyer an Pietschmann, Bournemouth 14./20.2.1877 (SUB Göttingen, MS Pietschmann 25, 641).

Ergebnisse der deutschen Reichstagswahlen von 1877:[87]

"Der Ausfall der deutschen Wahlen hat mich sehr interessiert, und der Erfolg der Socialdemokraten durchaus nicht überrascht. Du weißt, daß ich im allgemeinen mit ihnen sympathisiere. Es war mir eine große Freude, daß auch Sir Philip [...] mir hierin im allgemeinen völlig beistimmte, und es nicht nur als etwas wahrscheinliches und natürliches, sondern als etwas wünschenswerthes betrachtete, daß die Gesellschaft sich im Laufe der Jahrhunderte auf socialistischer Basis umgestalte."

Als Pietschmann daraufhin widersprach und das kulturpessimistische Bild eines tyrannischen sozialistischen Staates, der "weiter nichts ist, wie die absolute Verwirklichung der numerischen Majorität, für die es keine Toleranz, keine Schonung einer Sonderstellung gibt,"[88] an die Wand malte, konnte Meyer dieser negativen Sicht nicht beistimmen. Für ihn zeichnete sich die Gegenwart neben der Tendenz zur Vermassung auch immer durch eine "auf Emancipation der Individualität hinlaufende Entwicklung" aus, "die den modernen Menschen von vielen Fesseln der Vergangenheit befreit" und positiv bewertet werden müsse.[89]

Nach dem Abschluß seiner Hauslehrertätigkeit verbrachte Meyer noch vier Wochen im Britischen Museum, bevor er nach Hamburg zurückkehrte. Hier hatte er zunächst seiner Wehrpflicht zu genügen. Vom 1. Oktober 1877 bis zum 30. September 1878 diente er als Einjährig-Freiwilliger bei der 1. Kompanie des 76. hanseatischen Infanterieregiments.[90] Die Militärzeit wurde für Meyer zum Albtraum, er kam so gut wie gar nicht mehr zu seinen wissenschaftlichen Arbeiten, obwohl er auch sonst nichts Richtiges zu tun hatte und unter der "entsetzlichen Bummelei und Trödelei" litt.[91]

"[.] in Wirklichkeit ist der Militärdienst doch nichts anderes als Sklaverei:

---

[87] Meyer an Pietschmann, Bournemouth 26.1.1877 (SUB Göttingen, MS Pietschmann 25, 640).
[88] Pietschmann an Meyer, Breslau 21.1.1876 [vermutlich 31.1.1877] (AdW der DDR—Archiv—Sign.: NL Meyer NR. 1052).
[89] Meyer an Pietschmann, Bournemouth 14./20.2.1877 (SUB Göttingen, MS Pietschmann 25, 641). Meyers jugendliche Schwärmerei für die Sozialdemokratie hat sich nicht zu einem politischen Engagement verfestigt, sie zeigt aber, daß Meyer auch in politischen Fragen um ein unabhängiges Urteil bemüht war. An den Grundlagen des Bismarckschen Reiches, dessen Gründung Meyer als Primaner bewußt miterlebt hatte, zweifelte er aber keinen Augenblick. Zur politischen Mentalität von Meyers Generation, der Generation der "Wilhelminer", vgl. Martin Doerry, *Übergangsmenschen. Die Mentalität der Wilhelminer und die Krise des Kaiserreichs*, 2 Bde. Weinheim und München 1986,
[90] Vgl. Meyers militärisches Führungszeugnis (AdW der DDR—Archiv—Sign.: NL Ed. Meyer Nr. 4).
[91] Meyer an Pietschmann, Hamburg 20./27.1.1878 (SUB Göttingen, MS Pietschmann 25, 650).

denn wer nicht Nein sagen darf ist ein Sklave. [. . .] es ist ja bekannt beim
Commiss wird jeder 'faul dickfällig und gefrässig' und mir geht es gerade
ebenso. Alles Ehrgefühl wird ja systematisch ausgetrieben.''[92]

Immerhin hatte Meyer jetzt ausreichend Zeit, sich über seine wissenschaftliche Zukunft Gedanken zu machen. Der unermüdliche Classen,
mit dem Meyer jetzt wieder stärkeren Kontakt hatte, drängte ihn, sich
möglichst bald zu habilitieren, und zwar natürlich in Geschichte und
natürlich in Berlin; ein Stipendium von 1500 Reichsmark hatte er für
seinen Schüler bereits organisiert.[93] Meyer hatte keine Wahl: mit Religionswissenschaft ließ sich wenig anfangen, die Orientalistik war ihm zu
trocken, also blieb nur die Geschichte, wo er zudem seine kleinasiatischen
Studien ausbauen konnte. Vor Berlin schreckte Meyer aber zurück. Er
habe, schrieb er an Ebers, ''ein gewisses Mißtrauen gegen die dortigen
Verhältnisse,'' wisse auch nicht, ''ob die Bedingungen so coulant sind
wie in Leipzig'' und fürchte, daß dort ''eine lateinische Dissertation''
verlangt werde: ''und mir ist nichts mehr zuwider, als lateinisch schreiben.''[94] Auch die Befürchtung, daß er mit seiner orientalistischen
und religionsgeschichtlichen Ausrichtung—ohne tiefere Kenntnisse der
Rechtsgeschichte und der römischen Geschichte—in Berlin, und namentlich bei Mommsen, keine Gnade finden könnte, dürfte bei Meyers Überlegungen eine Rolle gespielt haben. In Leipzig dagegen ließ sich alles ein-
richten: Ebers nahm Kontakt zu dem Fachvertreter der Geschichte v.
Noorden auf und empfahl seinen Schüler wärmstens.[95] Meyer konzentrierte sich nach Abschluß der Militärzeit ganz auf die Habilitation,
arbeitete seine Schülerarbeit über die *Geschichte des Königreichs Pontos* zügig
um und reichte sie bereits Ende 1878 ein. Die Probevorlesung über den
Hellenismus in Babylonien[96] und das Kolloquium am 23. April 1879 ver-
liefen ohne Schwierigkeiten.[97] Zum Sommersemester konnte der junge
Privatdozent schon Kollegien anbieten.

---

[92] Meyer an Pietschmann, Hamburg 21.4.1878 (SUB Göttingen, MS Pietschmann
25, 643).
[93] Meyer an Ebers, Hamburg 16.1.1878 (StPK Berlin, NL Ebers).
[94] Ebd.
[95] Meyer an Ebers, Hamburg 22.4.1878 (StPK Berlin, NL Ebers). Im selben Brief
legte Meyer auch seine Pläne für die ersten Kollegien dar: ''Wegen der Collegien bin ich
nicht in Verlegenheit. Ich beabsichtige zunächst über die Geschichte Alexanders des
Großen und der hellenistischen Zeit zu lesen, dann eine Geschichte des alten Orients, die
wie ich denke sich über zwei Semester erstrecken wird. Dann hoffe ich so weit zu sein,
daß ich einen meiner liebsten Gegenstände, ältere griechische Geschichte, behandeln
kann, ohne allzu unverschämt zu sein. Wenn es dann sein muß, bringe ich wohl auch ein
Colleg über römische Geschichte, wenigstens die der Kaiserzeit, fertig. An andere Dinge,
die mir sehr am Herzen liegen, darf ich natürlich fürs erste noch garnicht denken.''
[96] Manuskript in AdW der DDR—Archiv—Sign.: NL Ed. Meyer Nr. 181.
[97] Meyer an Pietschmann, Hamburg 6.3.1879 (SUB Göttingen, MS Pietschmann 25,
655).

Ein anderes Ereignis dieses Frühjahrs sollte für seine wissenschaftlichen Arbeiten, ja für sein ganzes weiteres Leben bestimmend werden: Der Cotta-Verlag wandte sich an Meyer mit der Anfrage, ob er grundsätzlich bereit sei, ein Hand- und Lehrbuch der Geschichte des Altertums zu bearbeiten, welches für Schüler höherer Unterrichtsanstalten gedacht sei.[98] Durch wen Cotta gerade auf den 24jährigen Privatdozenten in Leipzig aufmerksam geworden war, ist nicht bekannt. Es ist jedoch zu vermuten, daß Meyer empfohlen worden ist. Meyer lehnte zunächst ab, wies aber gleichzeitig darauf hin, daß nach seinen Vorstellungen ein solches Werk —wenn es auch wissenschaftlichen Maßstäben genügen wolle—der universalhistorischen Tradition des Heerenschen Handbuchs verpflichtet sein und besonders auch die orientalische Geschichte ausführlich einbeziehen sollte.[99] Auf erneute Aufforderung Cottas hin entwarf Meyer dann doch einen vorläufigen Plan (*Dok* 9). Dieser führte noch im Laufe des Sommers zum Abschluß eines Vertrages, in dem Meyer sich verpflichtete, die drei ersten Teile des Handbuchs—die orientalische, griechische und hellenistische Geschichte—zu übernehmen; auf die römische Geschichte wollte er sich allerdings nicht einlassen.

Cottas Auftrag veränderte Meyers Leben grundlegend: fortan widmete er jede freie Minute diesem Projekt und den notwendigen umfangreichen Vorarbeiten. Das breit gestreute Interesse der Studienzeit wurde nun gebündelt und auf ein einziges Ziel hin ausgerichtet. Dieses bedeutete zweifellos eine Verengung: die meisten der religionswissenschaftlichen Ideen und Pläne blieben unausgeführt, die umfassenden anthropologischen Fragestellungen gingen in der Routine der historischen Kleinarbeit mehr oder weniger unter.

Man kann jedoch auch die andere Seite akzentuieren, und die ist hier vielleicht noch wichtiger: gerade weil Eduard Meyer nicht den Weg eines 'normalen' Historikers gegangen war, weil er nicht einer bestimmten Schule angehörte, sondern sich in bemerkenswerter Unabhängigkeit und 'Selbsterziehung' in die verschiedenen Disziplinen hineingearbeitet hatte, war er in der Lage, das zu werden, was in einer Zeit zunehmender Spezialisierung und Fächerdifferenzierung der Wissenschaft paradox und provokativ erscheinen mußte und was auf jeden Fall singulär war: er wurde zum *Universalhistoriker* des Altertums.

---

[98] Cotta an Meyer, Stuttgart 28.5.1879 (AdW der DDR—Archiv—Sign.: NL Ed. Meyer Nr. 504).
[99] Meyer an Cotta, Leipzig 22.6.1879 (Schiller-Nationalmuseum/Deutsches Literaturarchiv Marbach a.N., Cotta-Archiv).

Dokumentenanhang: Unveröffentlichte Briefe des jungen Eduard Meyer[100]

1. An der Vater   *Bonn, d. 21. Juni 1872*

Ich bin jetzt lange genug hier um die hiesigen Zustände beurtheilen zu
können, und so will ich versuchen Dir einiges darüber zu schreiben. In
meinen Erwartungen sehe ich mich in einer Beziehung ziemlich
getäuscht; es ist hier bis jetzt wenigstens kein Professor, dem—ich meine,
dessen Fach und Behandlungsweise—ich mich enger anzuschliessen
wünschte, der mich in höherem Grade anzöge. Zwar schadet das nichts,
denn ich kann allein völlig genügend arbeiten und weiß auch, wie ich
meine Ziele zu verfolgen habe; aber doch würde es angenehmer sein,
wenn hier ein Professor wäre, der auf mich einen bedeutenden Eindruck
und Einfluß ausübte. Vielleicht würde dies *Usener* nach dem, was ich von
ihm gehört habe: sein Hauptfach ist Mythologie und alte Cultur-
geschichte, und er ist ein sehr geistreicher gelehrter und anziehender
Mann; aber unglückseligerweise liest er dies Semester Thukydides (ab
VI) und habe ich ihn daher nicht belegt. Nur als er die Urgeschichte
Siciliens behandelte, hospitirte ich einige Male: er bot hier sehr gute
Sachen und hatte vor allen Dingen richtige Anschauungen. Aber sonst
gibt er fast nur grammatische und kritische Anmerkungen und die sind
natürlich langweilig und bieten wenig. Er wird im nächsten Jahre Mythologie lesen; ich bedaure sehr, daß ich ein Jahr zu früh gekommen bin.

Mein Hauptmann ist also *Schäfer* (gr. Gesch. 4std.). Schäfer ist nun
zwar sehr gelehrt und ganz vernünftig, aber sehr trocken und langweilig:
das Ideal eines guten, einfachen Gelehrten. Doch bieten seine Vorlesungen für mich wenig. Denn das Material kann man—oder wenigstens
ich—hier ja leicht sammeln, und so ganz unbekannt ist mir griechische
Geschichte auch nicht. Anregend aber ist Schäfer recht wenig.

Ganz anders ist da natürlich *Sybel* (deutsche G. 5st.). Er behandelt die
deutsche Geschichte von Anfang an und will in die Neuzeit hinein. In
Folge dessen gab er von Anfang an nur die Resultate seiner Forschungen,
nur seine Ansichten, seine Auffassung der Begebenheiten; aber für mich
wenigstens schadete das nichts. Es war einmal etwas ganz anderes; von
der auf den Schulen leider üblichen Methode nur Schlacht auf Schlacht,
Eroberung auf Eroberung zu reihen, die inneren Zustände aber, das
wichtigste von allem, zu übergehn—natürlich, weil man selbst nichts
davon weiß—bis sie dann, wo es unumgänglich nothwendig ist, mit einem

---

[100] Quellennachweis: Nr. 1–4, 7 und 8: StPK Berlin, NL Ed. Meyer; Nr. 5 und 6:
SUB Göttingen, MS Pietschmann 25, 631.632; Nr. 9: Schiller-Nationalmuseum/
Deutsches Literaturarchiv Marbach a.N., Cotta-Archiv. Ich danke Frau Barbara Meyer,
der Enkelin Eduard Meyers, sowie den Handschriftenabteilungen der o.a. Bibliotheken
für die Publikationsgenehmigung. Außerdem danke ich Dr. E. Pack (Köln) für die Entzifferung einiger schwer lesbarer Stellen in den Briefen Eduard Meyers.

"so ist (resp. war) es" unklar und möglichst verworren geschildert werden, ohne daß man weiß, woher es so ward und was daraus ward: von alle dem ist natürlich bei Sybel keine Spur. Mit klarer Anschaulichkeit entwickelt er die Verhältnisse von Anfang an, zeigt das allmähliche Entstehen der Adelsmacht und die Unterdrückung der Gemeinfreien, das Entstehen eines Nationalgefühls, die Entwickelung der Herzogthümer, ferner die Stellung von Staat und Kirche zu einander u.s.w. Freilich fehlt ihm eins—und darauf machte Heylbut mich zuerst aufmerksam—die Begeisterung für die Geschichte; ich meine nicht, daß er für das Mittelalter begeistert sein sollte, sondern für die Geschichte als Geschichte; man merkt ihm nicht an, daß er ganz in seinem Studium lebt, daß er überall mit dem Geiste dabei ist, und das ist allerdings ein großer Fehler. Doch, er bietet unendlich viel, und man (d.h. ich) gewinnt durch ihn zuerst eine klare Anschauung vom Mittelalter. Aber seitdem er, wie Ihr Euch erinnern werdet, zu Pfingsten sehr lange Ferien hat machen müssen, rennt er ganz furchtbar und streicht überall die Hälfte von dem was er sagen wollte resp. sollte. Und da kommen denn namentlich die inneren Verhältnisse sehr zu kurz; er ist schon bei den Hohenstaufen und hat noch fast garnicht von der Entwickelung der Städte geredet. Hoffentlich kommt er hierauf noch zurück. Sonst habe ich hier zum Glück vom vorigen Sommer her Wohlwills Städtegeschichte, die mir dann eine Ergänzung zu Sybels Vorträgen bildet.—Nichtsdestoweniger, hätte ich hier nur jemanden, der die alte Geschichte in Sybels Weise behandelt, ich würde mich sehr freuen. Freilich will ich nicht läugnen, daß es auch sehr angenehm ist, seine Anschauungen so viel wie möglich durch sich selbst zu erhalten.

Was nun das historische *Proseminar* (1 Std. unter Schäfer) angeht, so habe ich wenig davon. Wie ich schon schrieb, wird hier der Sachsenaufstand gegen Heinrich IV behandelt; jedes Mitglied hält in einer Stunde einen Vortrag—Mittwoch vor 8 Tagen ich—und später wird debattiert. Es ist mir ganz angenehm, auf die Weise auch einmal einen Abschnitt der mittleren Geschichte genau kennen zu lernen und selbst darin zu arbeiten. Sonst habe ich wenig davon, und Schäfer behandelt die Sache ganz evident partheiisch, für Heinrich; natürlich, allzustark kann man ihm nicht widersprechen, zumal da er die Quellen genauer kennt; aber seine Parteilichkeit ist doch ganz klar.

Ich komme zu den classischen Philologen:

Bücheler (Plauti Truculentus, 4stdg) ist ein ganz genialer Kerl und behandelt seine Sache ganz vorzüglich, mit schlagender Kürze und colossalem Scharfsinn. Nichtsdestoweniger glaube ich kaum, daß ich ihn im nächsten Semester hören werde. Man hat immer ein großes Vergnügen bei jeder seiner Vorlesungen; aber an der classischen Philologie selbst habe ich kein grosses Interesse und sie werde ich wohl im nächsten Semester ganz aufgeben. [. . .]

Bernays (Aristot. Politik, 4stdg) ist zwar ein grundgelehrter Kenner des Aristoteles,—vielleicht gegenwärtig der bedeutendste—und sehr geistreich und scharfsinnig, aber er behandelt uns, als ob wir Secundaner wären—freilich, die Rheinländer erfreuen sich keines guten Rufs und sind auch nicht mehr werth, aber nichtsdestoweniger sollte er doch auf sie keine Rücksicht nehmen ebenso wie die anderen. Er behandelt seinen Gegenstand mit unausstehlicher Breite, bringt neben vielem sehr guten das allergewöhnlichste u.s.w.; ein Extract aus seinen Vorlesungen würde vorzüglich sein, so sind sie kaum genießbar. Noch schlimmer ist sein publicum: Staatslehren der Griechen 1stdg. Wenn ich ihn im nächsten Semester wieder höre, werde ich es nur thun, weil er Oberbibliothekar ist und man durch ihn, wenn man eine Stunde täglich für die Bibliothek arbeitet, eine ganz freie Benutzung der Bibl. erhält.

Kekulé (Grundzüge der Archäologie 3stdg, und Erklärung des Kunstmuseums 1stdg) ist sehr tüchtig, ein gründlicher Kenner seines Faches und dabei erfüllt von einer einfachen, ungekünstelten Begeisterung für alte Kunst. Nur ergeht er sich leider in seinen Vorlesungen etwas zu sehr in Citaten und manchmal auch in Details, und ihm fehlt ein anregender Vortrag.—Nebenbei, das Kunstmuseum ist hier ganz außerordentlich reichhaltig und ganz vorzüglich.

Schließlich *Gildemeister* ist zwar grundgelehrt, aber recht trocken und garnicht anregend; er langweilt sich natürlich furchtbar und läßt diese Langeweile fortwährend erkennen.—Das Sanskrit ist ungeheuer interessant, nimmt aber unendlich viel Zeit weg; wir haben jetzt angefangen zu übersetzen.

Willst Du schließlich noch wissen, was ich bis jetzt hier gethan habe? Sanskrit und Arabisch haben mir sehr viel Zeit weggenommen, ferner die Ausarbeitung und Copie meiner Arbeit über Pontos, die ich nächstens an Schäfer bringe. Seit ich damit fertig bin habe ich nur—größtenteils alte Schriftsteller—gelesen; ich muß hier bedeutend nachholen, da ich von der alten Literatur noch recht wenig kenne.

Nun erwarte ich aber das nächste Mal mit Bestimmtheit auch von Dir einen Brief. Vale!

2. An den Vater   *Bonn, 1. und 2. Juli 1872*

Das letzte Mal schrieb ich, ich würde wahrscheinlich zum Winter hier bleiben: seitdem habe ich mir jedoch die Sache genauer überlegt und sie auch mit Mordtmann eifrig besprochen und finde, daß es doch bedeutend besser ist, hier wegzugehn. Ich habe hier doch verhältnismäßig weit weniger als an andern Universitäten, und es ist daher eigentlich Zeitverschwendung, wenn ich hier bleibe. Von Schäfer habe ich eigentlich garnichts, und auch trotz aller seiner Gelehrsamkeit von Gildemeister nicht. Buecheler geht höchstwahrscheinlich nach Heidelberg. Und des Seminars wegen hier zu bleiben, hat eigentlich keinen Sinn; ein Seminar habe ich anderswo auch. Ich denke daher nun doch, hier wegzugehn, und zwar wahrscheinlich mit Mordtmann nach Berlin. In Berlin ist außer dem unschätzbaren Mommsen und dem trotz aller seiner Fehler doch nicht zu verachtenden Ernst Curtius der alte Droysen, der noch immer ganz gut sein soll, und der ja die Geschichte des Hellenismus behandelt hat, womit ich mich bisher (d.h. in Hamburg) meistentheils beschäftigt habe. Also das sind drei bedeutende Historiker. Sanskrit liest der berühmte Weber, der, wie mir jemand,—Adr. Mordtmann—der es erst bei Gildemeister, dann bei Weber und jetzt wieder bei Gildemeister treibt, erzählt hat, es namentlich für Anfänger viel praktischer behandelt. Ferner sind in Berlin, was für mich ganz unentbehrlich ist, mehrere hebräische Collegien. Denn ich kann noch zu wenig hebräisch um allein darin gut fortzukommen, und brauche es doch nothwendig. Schließlich ist dort auch arabisch gut vertreten. Und nun, in der classischen Philologie sind dort Kirchhoff und Haupt. Kirchhoff werde ich wohl hören, wenn ich Zeit übrig behalte. Wissenschaftlich bietet Berlin mithin unendlich viel mehr als Bonn. [...]

Meine Äußerung, ich wolle die classische Philologie wahrscheinlich ganz aufgeben, hast Du mißverstanden. Die eigentliche classische Philologie besteht—jetzt wenigstens—im wesentlichen in Textkritik und *Conjecturenmachen*, und mich hierin weiter zu versenken, habe ich sowohl wenig Lust als auch keine Zeit. Dagegen der Grammatik bin ich durchaus nicht abgeneigt. Nur glaube ich, ohne Anmaßung sagen zu können, daß ich in griechischer und lateinischer Grammatik so weit bescheid weiß, daß ich einen Schriftsteller lesen kann. Und stößt mir etwas Neues auf, so kann ich es ja in der Grammatik nachsehn und auch selbst bei der Lectüre weiter darauf achten. Für mich hat eine gute syntaktische Beobachtung, die Erklärung einer sprachlichen Erscheinung und die Darlegung, wie sich dieselbe allmählich entwickelt hat und bis wie weit sich dieselbe erstreckt, viel mehr Interesse als ein ganzer Haufen Conjecturen. [...]

3. An den Vater   *Ohne Datum [ca. Mitte Juli 1872]*

Zunächst sehe ich, daß ich mich in meinem letzten Brief entweder schlecht ausgedrückt habe oder Du mich mißverstanden hast. Meine Meinung war jedenfalls nur, ich hätte mich bisher fast nur mit hellenistischer und älterer römischer Kaisergeschichte beschäftigt, nicht, diese wären mein Hauptstudium. Mein Studium ist die Geschichte des Alterthums, die Erforschung desselben in allen Richtungen, in seiner Entwickelung und seinem Verfall, in seinem geistigen Leben und den Anschauungen, den Bestrebungen, die jede Periode desselben bewegten, kurz, die möglichst genaue Erkenntnis dieser ersten Epoche der Entwickelung des menschlichen Geistes. Es umfaßt also die ältesten Zeiten ebensogut wie die späteren. Die Entwickelung der ersten Anschauungen des Menschen, die Entstehung und Ausbildung der Sprache, der Beginn und die Entwickelung geistigen Lebens, die Anfänge und die Ausbildung der religiösen und der sittlichen Anschauungen, die Entstehung und allmähliche Ausbildung und Fixierung der Moral, sind Fragen an deren Beantwortung zu arbeiten ebensogut meine Aufgabe ist, wie die Untersuchung über die Anfänge, die Blüthe und den Verfall der einzelnen Nationen, über die Denkweise und die Ideale, über das Leben der Alten, über die allmähliche Veränderung der alten Anschauungen, die Entstehung neuer, den Verfall und den Untergang der alten Welt, die Keime der neuen; die Erforschung der ältesten Thaten und Schicksale der Nationen ist ebensogut meine Aufgabe wie die der späteren.

Wenn Du also die Erkenntnis des gesammten Alterthums als meine Aufgabe betrachtest, so wird Dir auch klar sein, wie unentbehrlich dazu die Kenntnis des Sanskrit, des Arabischen, des Hebräischen ist. Das Hebräische zunächst bedarf ich, um das alte Testament, d.h. die Geschichte der Juden und ihre Anschauungen kennen zu lernen; dies ist also unumgänglich nothwendig. Das Arabische aber ist der Schlüssel zu den semitischen Sprachen; es ist nothwendig zu einer genaueren Erkenntnis der semitischen Sprachen, und damit eines wesentlichen Theils des semitischen Geisteslebens. Doch dies ist nicht der einzige Grund, aus dem ich arabisch treiben muss; nur durch eine Kenntnis der bekannten semitischen Sprachen wird die Erkenntnis der unbekannten ermöglicht. Nur durch sie sind die Keilschriften zu lesen, nur durch sie wird das Urtheil darüber möglich ob ein Volk arisch oder semitisch war.

Ebenso wichtig wie das Arabische ist das Sanskrit, das allein die Erkenntnis des Wesens der indogermanischen Sprache ermöglicht, das ein Haupthülfsmittel bietet zur Frage nach dem Ursprunge der sprachlichen Bildungen, oder eigentlich das einzige; das ferner für die Vergleichende Mythologie von so colossaler Wichtigkeit ist—denn die Veden in einer Übersetzung zu lesen ist doch kein ordentliches Lesen—; das drittens den praktischen Nutzen hat, daß durch dasselbe die Erlernung des Persischen sehr erleichtert wird—und dies zu kennen ist schon um der in ihm erhaltenen Denkmäler willen nothwendig.

Was nun die Grammatik, vor allem die Syntax angeht, so hat sie für mich ein grosses Interesse, weil sie zeigt, wie der Geist der einzelnen Völker die verschiedenen Verhältnisse aufgefaßt hat, weil sie, wenn man die verschiedenen Syntaxen der einzelnen Völker vergleicht, ein deutliches Bild gibt von den Anschauungen und dem Geistesleben derselben. Doch da nicht alles möglich ist, werde ich eingehendere grammatische Studien wohl kaum treiben können.

Altdeutsch und Gothisch werde ich vorläufig auf sich beruhen lassen;

wenn ich sie für mein *Studium brauche*, werde ich sie lernen müssen. [. . .]

4. An die Familie *Leipzig, d. 26. Juni 1874*

Ich hatte versprochen, Euch Ende voriger Woche einen ausführlichen Brief zu schreiben. So will ich ihn denn wenigstens nicht später als Ende dieser Woche abgehen lassen und stelle hier kurz meine letzten Erlebnisse zusammen.

Da aus unserm Anthropophagenverein[101] nichts geworden war, wie ich glaube ich schon geschrieben hatte, sind Pietschmann und ich seit einiger Zeit in den hiesigen philosophischen Verein eingetreten (Pietschmann ist früher schon einmal Mitglied desselben gewesen). Hier habe ich dann am Donnerstag vor 8 Tagen einen Vortrag gehalten über die Anfänge der menschlichen Entwickelung und den Ursprung der Sprache, der einen recht guten Eindruck gemacht zu haben scheint. Ich hatte schon lange vorgearbeitet, schon im vorigen Winter einiges niedergeschrieben und kurz nachdem ich wieder hierhergekommen war, die Sache ausgearbeitet; behufs des Vortrags habe ich es dann noch einmal völlig umgearbeitet.

Wahrscheinlich werde ich in 14 Tagen eben daselbst noch einen zweiten Vortrag halten über einzelne Puncte aus der Entwickelungsgeschichte der Sprache. Genaues weiß ich selbst noch nicht was ich geben werde; es wird wohl mehr eine Zusammenstellung einzelner interessanter Puncte als ein einheitliches Ganzes werden. Wenn man sich nur mehr Bücher anschaffen könnte! Ich habe nun behufs dieser Arbeiten mehrere Bücher schon 4 Monate von der Bibliothek und mich in manche sehr hineingearbeitet; es wird mir schwer werden, sie wieder zurückzugeben. [. . .]

Neulich habe ich auch—mit Boeddicker zusammen—die schöne Helena gesehn. Wir amüsierten uns sehr gut. Es ist der tollste Wahnsinn zusammengehäuft, und man kommt aus dem Lachen garnicht heraus. Und Ihr wißt, daß Wahnsinn sehr nach meinem Geschmack ist.

Dabei fällt mir natürlich Kuno ein. Geschrieben habe ich ihm noch nicht, will es aber nächstens thun. Ich werde ihm dann auch den Ulfilas schicken, den ich ihm seit langem versprochen habe. Ich werde es wirklich sehr vermissen, daß er in den Sommerferien nicht da ist. Ich war selten so froh, als wenn wir beide zusammen uns im tollsten Unsinn ergingen. Und doch könnte ich es jetzt am meisten brauchen. Denn jemehr man einsieht, daß die ganze Geschichte eigentlich nichts anderes zeigt als ''daß überall die Menschen sich gequält und hie und da ein glücklicher gewesen,'' daß die Menschen immer vergeblich Illusionen nachgejagt haben und nachjagen werden; jemehr man alle die Begriffe los wird, die einem durch Erziehung und Unwissenheit eingeimpft und liebgeworden waren,

---

[101] Gemeint ist ein wissenschaftlicher Verein der Anthropologen.

je mehr man erkennt, wie denn eigentlich "unsere herrliche Zeit" beschaffen ist, "wie wir es jetzt so herrlich weit gebracht," und wie alles Hoffen auf Besserung Wahnsinn ist,—desto trüber gestimmt wird man, desto mehr verliert man die alte Frische und Lust. Es mag sein, daß ebenso wie ich allmählich immer weiter gekommen bin, wie ich mich an eins nach dem andern gewöhnt habe, einen Pfeiler des alten Gebäudes nach dem andern weggehauen habe, ich mich so auch jetzt gewöhnen, zufrieden geben und die alte Stimmung wieder gewinnen werde. Aber für jetzt ist es mir natürlich sehr hinderlich, und ich sehe, daß es andern Leuten, wie z.B. Pietschmann, genau ebenso geht. [...]

5. An Richard Pietschmann   *Buyukdere, 9.9.1875*

[...] Die Zeit läuft hier fabelhaft rasch, und beschickt habe ich diesen Sommer wirklich recht wenig. Meine geistige Thätigkeit beschränkte sich fast ausschließlich auf Ausbrütung einiger Anideen, die vielleicht mit Deinen wirklich genialen Distinctionen 'ob die Civilisation der Hemmschuh der Cultur oder diese der Wurm der Civilisation sei usw.' eine gewisse Analogie ausweisen dürften. Es handelt sich um das wahnsinnige Unternehmen, die Menschheitsgeschichte und das Wesen der Menschheit auf einige bestimmte Formeln zu reduciren, den Gesichtspunct aufzufinden, von dem die ganze Vergangenheit und Zukunft zu betrachten und in ein System zu bringen ist. Es thäte da wahrlich noth, daß Du alter Scepticus da einmal über mich herführest und mir eine große Strafpredigt hieltest.

Das beste bei der ganzen Geschichte ist, daß mir alle derartigen Untersuchungen auf die Dauer höchst trocken und langweilig werden, und ich mich eigentlich nur für sie erwärme wenn ich zu polemisiren und sie zu vertheidigen habe, oder mit den ins System gehörigen Phrasen um mich werfen kann, vom hohen Pfade der Weisheit und Lunarkenntnis herunter die auf den Pfaden theologisirender Thorheit herumirrenden Menschen verspottend. Eigentliches Vergnügen—und deshalb beschäftigt man sich ja damit—finde ich immer nur bei specielleren, handgreiflicheren, reellen Dingen, wo man den von den biederen Vorfahren und Mitarbeitern aufgefahrenen Schutt wegräumen und die einfache klare Wahrheit ans Licht ziehn kann—ein Grund weshalb mich auch die religionsgeschichtlichen Forschungen länger festhalten als die zu abstracten sprachlichen. Und doch ruhe ich nie eher, als bis ich alles in ein deutliches System gebracht, in die Weltformel eingeordnet und mir dadurch selbst das Vergnügen von eingehender Forschung provozirt[102] habe.

Dies soll indessen—bis jetzt wenigstens—nicht von meinem Dir zuge-

---

[102] Auch die Lesart "prorogirt" ist möglich.

schickten System der aeg. Mythen gelten; denn hier gibt es in der That noch des interessanten in Masse zu thun. [...]

6. An Richard Pietschmann   *Buyukdere, 16. u. 18.10.1875*

[...] Was nun mich selbst angeht, so ist wenig neues zu berichten. Ich habe im Tb.[Todtenbuch] herumgeblättert und wie ich glaube schon einiges ganz interessante herausgebracht, und es dann wieder liegen lassen und griechisch oder englisch gelesen oder garnichts gethan. Worauf ich hinaussteuere weiß ich noch viel weniger als Du. Allerdings wenn man ad libitum leben könnte, arbeiten wann, was und wie man Lust hat, ohne zu veröffentlichen als wann und was man Lust hat, ohne daß die große Masse der Weisen und besonnenen Leute etwas von einem Plane merkte und einen für verrückt, toll, von wahnsinnigen Ideen besessen erklärte, bis man dann endlich—wahrscheinlich doch nicht zu dem erstrebten Ziele käme und die Leute äußerlich wenigstens doch recht behielten. Indes wer weiß? Verloren wenigstens habe ich meine Hoffnungen noch nicht, und eigentlich kann ich ja jetzt ganz so leben wie ich eben geschildert, und das kann ja wohl auch noch einige Jahre fortgehn. [...]

Wenn mir nur ein Gott sagte, ob es eigentlich irgend welchen Sinn hat, sich mit den Ägyptiacis weiter abzugeben! Allerdings kann ich wohl sagen daß ich aus der ägyptischen Religion sehr viel gelernt habe, daß die ägyptische Mythologie vielleicht eben so instructiv ist wie die indische, daß die Grundzüge der Religion vielfach in sehr klarer Weise hervortreten. Aber nirgends ein höheres geistiges Leben, eine weiterschreitende Entwickelung, eine Vertiefung der Anschauung, wie sie die Inder, die Perser, die Griechen darbieten, von dem gänzlichen Mangel einer belebenden Persönlichkeit ganz zu schweigen. Z.B. ist es für eine gründliche Erforschung oder zur Darstellung der äg. Religion durchaus nothwendig, das Tb. mit der größten Akribie durchzuarbeiten, und die Sache hat ja auch immer viel Reiz, namentlich in Folge der vielen Räthsel der Schrift und Sprache; aber dann kommt wieder so viel Dummes, Abgeschmacktes, Sinnloses, daß ich mich schon oft gefragt habe ob nicht das räthselhafte das einzig Fesselnde ist: und Räthsel lösen macht man doch nicht gern zu seiner Hauptbeschäftigung.

Du siehst meinen schwankenden status des Geistes; ich weiß jetzt wahrhaftig nicht, was thun. Wie eine Biene überall den Honig sammeln ist doch etwas zu gefährlich um es gerade weg als Ziel hinzustellen; und heute Aristophanes, morgen Göthe, übermorgen das Todtenbuch, und dann den Rigveda oder Hafiz oder Macaulay lesen ist doch keine Beschäftigung die Aussicht auf eine sichere Lebensstellung eröffnet. Und daran muß man doch auch einmal denken, und diese Frage liegt mir jetzt eigentlich zum ersten Male im Leben herum.

Für solche Lagen ist der philosophische Verein oder etwas ähnliches ein
höchst nützliches Institut: denn da der Ehrgeiz einen immer zu Vorträgen
antreiben wird, greift man immer neue Gebiete unter einem Gesichtspunct zusammen und sucht sie möglichst zu verarbeiten. Hier aber flat-
tert der Geist immer ohne Halt hin und her. [. . .]

7. An den Bruder Kuno   *Constantinopel d. 12. Februar 1876*

Diesmal will ich mit der Antwort auf Deine zwei lieben langen Briefe nicht
länger zögern. Du kannst Dir denken, daß mir Deine Zukunft oft durch
den Kopf gegangen ist, und ich stimme im wesentlichen ganz dem bei,
was mir als Deine Ansicht erscheint. Eins vor allem, was ich Dir nicht
genug predigen kann: folge nur Dir selbst und Deinen eigenen Impulsen,
und laß Dich durch keinen andern irre machen. Schließlich ist es doch
immer nur man selbst, der über die Lage der Dinge das richtige und entscheidende Urtheil fällen kann.

So wird Dir zwar vielleicht großer Widerspruch entgegentreten, wenn
Du es versuchen willst, gleich nach Oberprima zu kommen; aber es ist
immer meine Meinung gewesen, daß Du nur so kurze Zeit wie irgend
möglich die Schule wieder besuchen solltest, zumal soweit wie ich sehen
kann garkeine Aussicht vorhanden ist, daß Du in eine gute, gebildete und
Dir zusagende Classe kommen wirst, wie durch einen der glücklichsten
und leider namentlich jetzt auch für Hamburg seltenen Zufälle die
meinige war. Auch die Lehrer werden Dir in Folge der alles zersetzenden
Borussomania nicht viel bieten können. So wird es nur darauf ankommen, ob der Direktor nichts dagegen hat; denn bei Examen ect. (!) und
in der Classe, und namentlich bei den Dir unentbehrlichen Stipendien
hängt von ihm alles ab. Daher will ich Dir rathen, Dich nicht eher zu entscheiden, als bis Du ihn gesprochen hast.

d. 22. Febr.

Wenn Du nun aber von Deinem vielen Hin- und Herschwanken sprichst,
so kann ich Dich sehr wohl verstehn; habe doch auch ich das gleiche
gethan, je weiter ich vorwärts kam, und weiß jetzt eigentlich garnicht
mehr wohin mich nicht nur im äußeren sondern auch im inneren Leben
die Wogen tragen oder verschlagen werden. Eins habe ich immer gesehn
und empfinde es noch immer: das Interessante, Anregende, Erforschens-
werthe ist zwar unendlich, aber doch sind wir im Stande, uns einen
großen Theil desselben anzueignen, und das Eine hier das andere da
auflesend, bald flüchtig etwas betrachtend bald tiefer eindringend uns
eine allgemeinere Anschauung zu gewinnen. Du bist vielleicht unzufrie-
den, noch nicht zu einem tiefen Studium vorgedrungen zu sein, aber sei

unbesorgt. Ein Jahr ist eine sehr lange Zeit, namentlich aber ein Universitätsjahr; und Du hast garkeine Ahnung, was sich darin thun läßt, wie sich Anschauungen und Kenntnisse tagtäglich erweitern. Mein Rath ist also der: fahre fort, wie Du angefangen, laß Dich durch keinen Menschen beirren, treibe, wozu Du Dich getrieben fühlst, und laß ein Specialstudium sich später von selbst ergeben, wenn Du ein solches findest—ich habe bisher noch keines, und bin immer in Verlegenheit, wenn mich Jemand fragt, was mein Fach sei, was ich studiert habe u.s.w. Nur eines binde ich Dir aufs Gewissen, wovon Du *nie* abweichen mögest: Gehe immer an die erste Quelle. Alles Studieren, Lesen, Auswendiglernen abgeleiteter Werke ist werthlos für Deine wissenschaftliche Ausbildung, ja meist für Deine geistige Entwicklung im allgemeinen: ein kleines Stück Original ist fast immer zehnmal mehr werth als alles was darüber gesagt worden ist.

Dieser mein Rath läuft nun schnurstracks dem entgegen, was Dir von *allen* Menschen dieser Zeit gepredigt werden wird; Groß wie Klein: concentrire Dich. Allerdings, das "sich so frühzeitig wie möglich concentriren" gibt sehr schöne "große" Klein-Geister, es gibt ausgezeichnete Fachmänner, die ihre Carriere machen, Schritt vor Schritt, ihren Fuß dahinsetzend, wo ihr Vorgänger ihn weggenommen, ohne je die Linie zu verlassen, ohne Extravaganzen, *ohne Gedanken.* Wir aber, meine ich, sollten streben, etwas mehr zu sein; wir sollen uns ein hohes Ziel nehmen, wenn wir es auch nicht erreichen; wir sollen uns um die Regel wenig kümmern, aber um die Ausnahmen. Diese Weisheit nun aber behalte fein für Dich, und laß keinen Menschen Deine Geheimnisse wissen, bis Du findest, daß Du sie bei ihm nicht profaniren wirst. Mir hat jeder Mensch gesagt: "Was willst Du denn eigentlich? Bist Du denn verrückt? Du bildest Dir doch nicht ein, das alles thun zu können?" Bis ich endlich seit meinem vierten Semester Menschen traf, die desselbigen Weges wandelten. Darum noch einmal: Laß Dich nicht beirren, sondern vertraue Dir und nur Dir allein.

Was soll nun aber Dein Hauptaugenmerk sein? Auch da kann ich Dich nur Dir selber überlassen. Du bist in dem Alter, wo man noch träumt von Berühmtheit und Menschenbeglückung. Es gibt Illusionen, ohne die man sich das Leben werthlos denkt, und die nur langsam wieder dahinsinken. Nachher steht man auf einem Standpunct, der einem früher entsetzlich erschien, und findet ihn ganz natürlich und in der Ordnung, ja wohl sogar heilsam. So ist es jedem denkenden Menschen gegangen, so wird es auch Dir gehn. Ich will darüber nicht weiter schreiben, wenn ich Dich sprechen könnte, würde uns dieser Punct Stoff genug zu Gesprächen bieten. Und es ist vielleicht besser, auch Du gehst ganz Deinen eigenen Weg.

Also nur eins: nicht in dem, was für andere dabei abfällt an Brocken

von Wissen und Phrasen der Weisheit, sondern in dem, was sie Dir selbst
bietet, besteht der Werth der Wissenschaft. Das erste, das eigentliche
Hauptmotiv Deines Studirens bist Du selbst, ist Dein Forschungs- und
Erkenntnistrieb. Du studirst, um zu klaren Anschauungen zu gelangen
über die Welt, den Menschen, Dich selbst;
   Soweit für diesmal. [. . .]

8. An die Mutter   *Bournemouth, d. 11. Februar 1877*

Es werden nun schon drei Wochen, daß Ihr den letzten Brief von mir
erhalten habt; da muß ich mich wohl einmal wieder hinsetzen und Euch
schreiben. Ich bin noch nie so schreibfaul gewesen wie diesen Winter, was
wohl auch daher kommt, daß ich wenig zu erzählen habe. Im allgemeinen
freue ich mich, daß die Hälfte meines hiesigen Aufenthalts vorüber ist; es
ist doch so gar einsam und ich brauche Umgang und muß mich gelegentlich einmal mit andern aussprechen können. Ich habe immer große Sehnsucht danach gehabt, und wo ich ihn so reichlich genossen habe, entbehre
ich ihn doppelt.
   Doch ist es auch so ganz heilsam, und wer weiß in welche Lagen mich
das Schicksal noch verschlägt. Nur fehlt zum Arbeiten manchmal die
Lust, und oft bedrängen mich wieder die vielen verschiedenartigen
Sachen, die alle auf meiner Seele lasten und mir lieb geworden sind und
die ich gerne endlich einmal herunterwälzte in der Gestalt von Büchern.
Wenn ich nur einmal wieder ein Jahr oder auch nur ein Halbjahr für mich
allein hätte, arbeiten könnte wann und was und wie ich wollte, in ähnlicher Weise wie in den vier Wochen in Hamburg: das würde schaffen!
   Entweder das: oder hinaus in die große freie Welt, ins große Leben, wie
ich es in Constantinopel kennen gelernt habe, wo man lernt aus dem was
man sieht und hört und nicht aus Büchern. Wenn ich hinaus könnte in
den Orient oder nach Italien in die alte Welt, oder nach Nordamerica in
die neue, ich wollte alle Bücher hinter mir lassen, wenn es sein müßte,
und ich wirklich frei leben und sehen könnte. America ist wahrhaftig nicht
zu verachten, und für den, der das Studium des Menschen und seiner
Ideen zu seiner Lebensaufgabe gemacht hat, ebenso interessant wie die
alte Welt. Denke nur an die großen, wunderbaren religiösen Bewegungen, z.B. die Mormonen!
   Ich habe dieser Tage viel Göthe gelesen, d.h. immer wieder das alte.
Es gibt doch nichts was uns den Faust, den Wilhelm Meister, Wahrheit
und Dichtung auch nur annähernd ersetzen könnte, und je öfter man
liest, desto wunderbarer, theurer und reichhaltiger werden einem die
Werke.
[. . .]

9. An den Verleger Cotta   *Leipzig, 9.7.1879*

Sehr geehrte Herr!

Ihrem Wunsche gemäß gestatte ich mir Ihnen im folgenden die Haupt-
gesichtspuncte mitzutheilen, die mich bei der Bearbeitung eines Handbuchs der alten Geschichte leiten würden. Ich muß übrigens gleich bemerken, daß ich an eine Bearbeitung der römischen Geschichte, die ja ein
völlig in sich abgeschlossenes Gebiet bildet und mir noch längere Vorarbeiten nöthig macht, fürs erste noch nicht denken kann. Ich würde also
zunächst nur eine Bearbeitung der orientalischen und griechischen Geschichte geben.

Ich schrieb Ihnen schon, daß mir für die Ausführung im einzelnen die
Anlage des Heerenschen Handbuchs vorschwebt, nur daß natürlich in
Folge des Fortschritts der Wissenschaften überall eine völlige Umar-
beitung nöthig ist. Auch möchte ich den Plan insofern erweitern, daß die
Staatsverfassung und Staatsverwaltung eingehender berücksichtigt und
überall ein Abriß der Cultur- und Literaturgeschichte mit aufgenommen
wird. Auch würde die Religionsgeschichte kurz zu verfolgen und namentlich bei den orientalischen Völkern eine kurze Skizze der Religiösen Systeme zu geben sein.

Im allgemeinen scheint es mir die Aufgabe eines wissenschaftlichen
Handbuchs der alten Geschichte zu sein, den der es benutzt nicht nur
über die neuesten Ergebnisse der Forschung zu orientiren sondern ihm
auch ein selbstständiges Arbeiten auf dem betr. Gebiete zu ermöglichen;
außerdem aber auch dem Gelehrten als ein Buch zum Nachschlagen über
ihm fernerliegende Gegenstände zu dienen.

Es würde daher neben einer kurzen Darstellung der bekannten Ereignisse auch ein Eingehn auf die weniger bekannten Gegenstände geboten
sein, ohne die ja ein lebendiges Bild nicht zu gewinnen ist, z.B. die
Geschichte der kleineren griechischen Städte, der kleineren asiatischen
Staaten nach Alexander u.s.w., wie diese ja auch von Heeren gegeben
sind. Zu diesem Zwecke wäre es vielleicht manchmal rathsam, die Haupt-
stellen der griechischen und lateinischen Schriftsteller kurz anzuführen.

Ferner ist überall eine kurze Übersicht und Kritik der Quellen sowie
ein Nachweis der wichtigsten neueren Schriften zu geben.

Vor der Geschichte eines jeden Staates ist die Organisation desselben
zu schildern.

Am Ende jeder Periode folgt eine kulturgeschichtliche Übersicht.

Der Stoff, soweit ich ihn zunächst behandeln würde, zerfällt in drei
Theile:

1, Geschichte des Orients bis auf Alexander;
2, Griechische Geschichte bis auf Alexander;

3, Geschichte der hellenistischen Zeit.

Jeder würde, soweit ich es bis jetzt beurtheilen kann, etwa fünfzehn Bogen umfassen und wohl am besten gesondert erscheinen. Vielleicht dürfte der erste Theil etwas umfangreicher werden.

Um Ihnen von meinem Plane ein deutlicheres Bild zu geben, füge ich eine Skizze des dritten Theiles bei, die ich, da ich mich mit dieser Zeit gegenwärtig gerade eingehender beschäftige, sofort entworfen habe. In ähnlicher Weise wären dann die beiden anderen Theile zu behandeln.

Wenn Ihnen der angedeutete Plan im allgemeinen zusagt, so bitte ich Sie, mir Ihre Bedingungen anzugeben: Da ich einem derartigen Unternehmen natürlich meine ganze Arbeitszeit, soweit sie nicht durch meine akademische Thätigkeit in Anspruch genommen ist, widmen müßte, müssen natürlich die genaueren Bedingungen für mich von größerer Bedeutung sein, als mir selbst wünschenswerth ist. [. . .]

J. MANSFELD

GREEK PHILOSOPHY IN THE *GESCHICHTE DES ALTERTUMS*

1. The 'Ideen'

In the final version of his *Zur Theorie und Methodik der Geschichte* the mature
Eduard Meyer, maintaining his rejection of economically or sociologically
inclined theories involving the concept of historical laws and a certain
degree of historical determinism, lists the three interrelated factors which
in his view bring about historical developments, viz. (1) chance as connected with events; (2) the free will of human agents; and (3) "Ideen".
Ideas he defines as the dominant

> "Vorstellungen und Forderungen, welche die Menschen einer gegebenen
> Epoche in weitem Umfang beherrschen und Denken, Ziele und Handeln der
> einzelnen Individuen bestimmen."[1]

Ideas are found both with society, or societies, and with individuals, and
the ideas of some individuals may be different from those that are pre-
dominant in the society in which they live. Examples of ideas provided by
Meyer are the idea of the religious and political unity of humanity,[2] that
of the promises of socialism,[3] and that of nationality.[4] Appealing to
Ranke, Meyer points out that he has always looked for the essence of what
he calls living history "in dem Gegensatz von Individuum und Gemeinschaft (den typischen Formen) und dem Kampfe zwischen beiden ...,"[5]
which of course is very much a battle of Meyeran ideas. Appealing to the
Neokantian philosopher Heinrich Rickert (1863 – 1936) and quoting him
at some length, Meyer sticks to his view that history deals with the par-

---

[1] *Kl. Schr.* I, 8. Cf. *GdA* I.1, 173 ff. (= I.1, Stuttgart [2]1907, §§ 99 – 100), also for what
follows.—Unless otherwise indicated, references to *GdA* will be to the reprint, Darmstadt
1953 – 80; in this ed., only vols. III – V have been to some extent revised by H.E. Stier
[first published in this form 1936 – 58: notes (occasionally reduced) instead of concluding
passages of paragraphs in *petit*, references to more recent editions of sources quoted, and
occasional additions from marginalia in Meyer's private copies]. Meyer himself had only
published a much expanded edition of the original vol. I, which became vols. I.1 + I.2
+ II; a further revision of the first part of II was after his unexpected death published from
the *Nachlass* by Stier as II.1, who then reprinted the unrevised remaining part of this vol.
as II.2.
[2] *Kl. Schr.* I, 35 n. 1.
[3] *Ibid.*, 35.
[4] *Ibid.*, 40 f.
[5] *Ibid.*, 30, correctly referring to *GdA* I, Stuttgart [1]1884, § 15.

ticular rather than the universal (a view already promoted in ch. 9 of
Aristotle's *Poetics*, but this is by the way), and adds that in his whole career
as a historian he has never discovered a single historical law even remotely
comparable to those of physics.[6] Both political[7] and economical developments, he states, are determined by chance and the creative activity of
individual persons.[8] The ideas embodied in a society at a certain moment
of its history may prove stronger than those of such individuals as want
to change it, but they also may not, and in the long run the ideas of individuals may prevail. Some ideas however, according to Meyer, will never
gain the upper hand:

> "Es ist ein Wahn, wenn die Theoretiker des Altertums, vor allem die
> Sokratiker, *und ihre moderne Nachfolger* glaubten, ein Gesetzgeber könne, wenn
> er nur neben dem vollen Besitz der Staatsgewalt auch die richtige Einsicht
> gewonnen habe, die Gesinnung und das ganze Leben der Bürger seines
> Staates von Grund aus umwandeln."[9]

The ground for this statement, presumably, is that not even a follower of
Socrates would be able to abolish chance, free will, and the battle of ideas.
We may believe that the history of this century to some degree has taught
us otherwise (that perhaps we feel that those who, albeit not genuine
Socratics, succeeded in changing their societies—in some cases only tem-
porarily—in this way did not possess the "richtige Einsicht" is not to the
point insofar as those concerned thought they *did* possess it). In our present context, however, it is more important to note that Meyer's interest
in what he calls ideas is of crucial importance to his concept of history.
Although political history remains "das Zentrum der Geschichte,"[10] history in the full sense of the word should include "alle Zweige der Kulturgeschichte."[11] By no means all ideas are originally political, yet any
number of them (as for instance those of the founders of religions) may
influence history and so become political in that they become part of political history. This, again, explains why the history of Greek philosophy
looms large in the *Geschichte des Altertums*. This is so not merely because,
in a general way, philosophy is part of cultural history but, so Meyer
argues, because the emergence of philosophy in the Greek world gave a

---

[6] *Ibid.*, 31 ff. Meyer's references are to Rickert's *Die Grenzen der naturwissenschaftlichen
Begriffsbildung*, Tübingen 1896–1902 [²1913]. For history as a scientific discipline.
Rickert used the term *Kulturwissenschaft* not *Geisteswissenschaft*.

[7] Bismarck's career got started by chance (*Kl. Schr.* I, 61).

[8] *Ibid.*, 37.

[9] *Ibid.*, 62 (my italics). Cf. also *infra*, text to n. 14.

[10] *Ibid.*, 46.

[11] *Ibid.*, 42. Conversely, the individual disciplines belonging with cultural history
should in his view be firmly placed in the context of general history (cf. *infra*, n. 33).

decisive turn to Greek history and caused its development to differ sharply from that of the peoples of the ancient Middle East which he had studied and described at length with admirable originality and insight.

However, before we turn to Meyer's treatment of the history of philosophy at various places in the body of the *GdA*, we should cast a brief glance at vol. I.1 pp. 182 f.,[12] which treats of "die Idee" at some length. Ideas are created by individuals (they are "das höchste, was die Individualität zu schaffen vermag"). Pessimistically and somewhat oddly, he affirms that "jede Idee, die sich verwirklicht, in ihr Gegenteil umschlägt" (we shall note that this is a principle he did not consistently apply). The preachings of Jesus produce the inquisition, the ideals of the French revolution produce the Terror, or the despotism of modern socialism,[13] and

> "der Reformversuch Platos und Dios in Syrakus (führt) zur Usurpation der Staatsgewalt und zur Zersetzung des Staates, die man retten will."

This, of course, is one of the reasons why in the passage quoted above[14] he says that the Socratics were fools to believe their ideas could be converted into reality.

Among the ideas produced by philosophy those specifically concerned with the state, i.e. involving a theory pertaining to political realities, are understandably enough very much on Meyer's mind, and among these the political ideas of Plato which, so he believed, produced a disastrous chain of events in Sicily, occupy a key position. Plato's Sicilian adventure illustrates two of Meyer's own favourite topics, viz. the impact of ideas on history and the "Tragik der Geschichte" or the fact that ideas, once realized, invariably turn into their opposites. Accordingly, the account of the history of Sicily in what was to remain the final volume of the *GdA* allows Meyer to provide a unique blend of political and cultural history. It should be noted, however, that he omits to draw the same moral and historical lesson from the perhaps even more drastic catastrophe that befell the Pythagoreans a century earlier, and fails to provide a unified picture of Phythagorean politics in theory and practice.

We may conclude this paragraph with the remark that although Meyer

---

[12] = I.1, Stuttgart-Berlin ²1907, § 103; This volume, published after the 1st ed. of the concluding one (V, Stuttgart-Berlin 1902), contains the very much enlarged revision of the slim general introduction to ¹I (*supra*, n. 5), §§ 1–27, pp. 1–25.

[13] The "Despotismus des sozialdemokratischen Systems." In a later volume, IV.2, 172, he intelligently defends the "Sozialdemokratie, der die öffentliche Meinung und die Staatsmänner die Lehren und die Verbrechen des Anarchismus in die Schuhe schieben, obwohl sie dessen konsequentester prinzipieller Gegner ist." The German socialists turned out to be staunch supporters of the state, see S. Haffner, *Von Bismarck zu Hitler*, München 1987, 130 ff.

[14] Text to n. 9.

refused to speak in terms of historical laws, his view of history is dominated by two law-like descriptive rules, of which the first is concerned with
the opposition between individual and society and the second with the
impact of ideas upon society. His pessimistic suggestion that every idea
that is realized necessarily turns into its opposite moreover resembles a
form of piecemeal soft determinism. Furthermore, his view of historical
developments is often teleological; the position of Socrates, for instance,
is a sort of logical sequel to all that came before. From a purely theoretical
point of view Meyer's position is not fully consistent.

2. Orphic Theology and the Birth of Philosophy

We may now turn to *GdA* III,[15] and more especially to the chapter
"Geistige Entwicklung des sechsten Jahrhunderts. Theologie und
Philosophie."[16] Meyer begins with the ethical ideals of the epoch of the
Seven Sages and interestingly finds the first glimmerings of rationalism
in the remains of the poet Stesichorus. Stesichorus in individual cases
criticizes and modifies the religious tradition on rational grounds both
ethical and physical. "Die individuelle Überzeugung ist fortan die
Grundlage des religiösen Glaubens."[17] We may infer that for Meyer
Stesichorus' attitude represents the "Idee" of an individual which conflicts with the prevailing "Ideen" of the community. He then turns to
what he calls religious mass movements concerned with personal immortality or personal liberation: the mysteries of Eleusis; Bacchic and other
cults. He argues that the difference from the rationalism represented by
Stesichorus is only apparent, because in each case you have the same purpose or need, viz. to swap the old religion which can no longer be of service for a new one, and the same root, viz. individualism (here called "der
Individualismus").[18] Interestingly enough, the parallel constructed by
Meyer runs counter to his professed semi-theoretical view that in history
one does not find necessary developments.

The most important section of this chapter[19] is his consecutive but

---

[15] I have compared the same section in the 1st ed., *GdA* II, Stuttgart 1893; there are
no differences as to the text and the content of the notes.

[16] *GdA* III, 661–706.

[17] *Ibid.*, 672.

[18] *Ibid.*, 673–4. See further below, n. 24.

[19] Note that the theme is taken up again at *GdA* IV.1, 398–419. For the crucial difference between theology on the one hand and philosophy or science on the other see *ibid.*,
405.

parallel treatment of Orphism[20] and early Milesian philosophy.[21] Orphic religion, which intends to replace the old religion, is "Offenbarung" and "notwendig ... pseudepigraph wie die Thora."[22] As we shall see, the comparison with the Thorah is not a mere metaphor. Orphic literature is the product of a plurality of anonymous poets masquerading as Orpheus or Musaeus and stretching over several generations. The most important Orphic god is Dionysus. Orphism, according to Meyer, is a purely native Greek phenomenon, "ein *notwendiges* Produkt der einheimischen religiösen Entwicklung,"[23] as necessary, presumably, as the religious drive behind the mystery cults. One would like to know in which sense of the word "necessary" Meyer describes these developments as inevitable. Does he mean that, when something is no longer satisfactory, you simply have to look for something else? Or does he mean that, inevitably, Greek society was moving toward individualism which then had to assume some shape or other? Then the question why this movement occurred becomes inescapable, and Meyer's heuristic model of ideas in conflict as the prime movers of historical developments turns out to be superficial, or rather to be only a rather external descriptive device which is unable to cope with those historical necessities he feels bound to acknowledge. For in the period at issue, individualism is not an "Idee" in Meyer's sense of the word, i.e. a view people know they are holding. It clearly is an anachronistic notion (a theoretical or meta-concept, just as the concept of the "Idee" itself) used as a convenient tool by the historian in order to grasp in a cognitive way a plurality of historical phenomena that would otherwise seem unrelated and inexplicable.[24] Without individualism in one form or another you would have no conflict of ideas, no living history. This becomes

---

[20] *GdA* III, 679–693. Meyer points out that his account of the mystery cults and of Orphism is dependent on that of Lobeck's *Aglaophamus* (1829), and criticizes both Lobeck and Rohde (in *Psyche*) for not paying sufficient attention to the religious background, i.e., presumably, to the historically necessary desire to replace the old religion by religions that cater to the needs of the individual.

[21] *Ibid.*, 693 ff.

[22] *Ibid.*, 681.

[23] *Ibid.*, 684; my italics. If Orphism is purely Greek, its Dionysiac component must be Greek too. Among Meyer's contemporaries and near-contemporaries, only Nietzsche, although he had Dionysus arrive from Asia, believed that the "Triebe" at issue came "aus der tiefsten Wurzel des Hellenischen," *Die Geburt der Tragödie* § 2, in: G. Colli—M. Montinari (eds.), Friedrich Nietzsche. *Sämtliche Werke. Kritische Studienausgabe* Bd. I, Berlin 1980, 32.19.

[24] Note that at *GdA* I.1, 176 (= ²I.1, § 100), Meyer, arguing against Jakob Burckhardt's view "dass die Individualität erst mit der Renaissance erwacht sei" defends his own heuristic application of the concept. In a later volume, he is sharply critical of individualism, depicting it as a destructive rather than a liberating force (see *infra*, § 4).

even more clear when we compare Meyer's description of Orphic thought
with his analysis of the main ideas of early Milesian philosophy.

Orphism, according to Meyer,[25] is concerned with two main problems: (1) the essence of the divinity and its relation to the world, and
(2) the essence and fate of the human soul.[26] In the seventh century
BCE, the Zeus of traditional religion had come to represent the idea of the
supremely reigning divinity. Rather questionably, he argues that the
Bacchic religion had made Bacchus the divinity which penetrates and
gives life to the whole world. Orphism in his view combines these ideas.
Among other things, Meyer aptly quotes[27] the Orphic lines preserved ap.
ps. Arist. *Mu.* 7 [= F21a Kern], some among which have since turned
up in the Derveni papyrus, and which (like the other samples quoted by
him) he appears to date to the mid-sixth century BCE[28] and attributes to
what he calls the 'great epical poem' later called the "rhapsodische Theo-
gonie." The Dionysus-Zagreus myth, he argues, has been interpreted in
a cosmological way: the dispersed ashes of the Titans convey the Dio-
nysian spark to all living things. Thus, a plurality of rather crude myths
is subjected to reinterpretation and then combined in a *systematical* way by
the Orphic poets, just as the Indians, Iranians, Egyptians and Hebrews,

> "als ihre Religion in das theologische Stadium trat, die alten Mythen
> umgewandelt und in den Dienst neuer sittlicher und religiöser *Ideen* gestellt
> (haben)."[29]

Meyer finds other novel views in Orphism, such as that of the moon as
another inhabited earth, and apparently considers this to be an early
notion as well. He sums up his account of Orphism as follows:

> "So hat sich die Dionysosreligion in der Orphik *zum vollen Pantheismus* ent-
> wickelt."[30]

Meyer's pages on Orphism are admirable in many ways, but the gist of
his interpretation is not religious but allegorical, i.e. philosophical. The
term pantheism may of course be used in relation to F21a K., but there

---

[25] *GdA* III, 684.

[26] Note that subsequently he can only accommodate the first of these problems for his
parallel with the earliest philosophy, and that Pythagoras, Empedocles, and Plato in his
view are *influenced* by the Orphic doctrine of the soul.

[27] *Ibid.*, 685.

[28] *Ibid.*, 691: "Die ersten Ansätze der orphischen Lehre mögen noch dem 7. Jahrhundert angehören; zu voller Ausbildung ist sie erst um die Mitte des 6. Jahrhunderts
gelangt." This makes Orphism the to some extent older contemporary of the new learning
of Ionia (cf. also *ibid.*, 695).

[29] *Ibid.*, 688 (my italics). I assume "Ideen" here has its full Meyeran sense.

[30] *Ibid.*, 687 (my italics). Meyer illustrates this analysis with other quotations as well.

remains a nagging doubt in my mind as to whether these famous lines really are the expression of an original religious belief; rather, they convey a thinly veiled philosophical (or scientific) notion by religious and poetical means. Meyer's cosmological and pantheistic interpretation of the Dionysus-Zagreus myth, itself of doubtful antiquity, is even more dubious. In *GdA*, however, this *interpretatio philosophica* of a number of Orphic fragments serves a definite purpose, viz. the comparison with the early philosophy (or, as I would prefer to say, science[31]) of Ionia. Meyer affirms that somewhat later figures such as Xenophanes Pherecydes Pythagoras Heraclitus (he could have added his Empedocles) have all been influenced by Orphism. The relation with the earliest philosophy, however, is of a subtler nature than would be conveyed by the word influence:

> "Mit den Anfängen der Philosophie steht [die orphische Lehre] in Wechselwirkung: gleichzeitig mit ihr und aus denselben Wurzeln ist sie erwachsen."[32]

Another instance of soft determinism, or at the very least one of what one may call convergence. This time, philosophy is added to the various attempts to replace the old by the new. What is more, Meyer finds striking similarities between the main idea of Orphism and that of early Milesian philosophy. Yet philoshopy according to him is crucially different from the religious movements with which, viewed from the historical vantage-point concerned with its origins, it belongs.[33]

Meyer's *Geschichte* deals with the Orient as well as with Greece. At the beginning of his account of "Die ionische Philosophie," he permits himself a backward glance. With the creation of the systematical Orphic theol-

---

[31] See my paper *Myth Science Philosophy: A Question of Origins*, in: W.M. Calder III—U.K. Goldsmith—P.B. Kenevan (eds.), *Hypatia*. Festschrift H.E. Barnes, Boulder, Colorado 1985, 45 ff.

[32] *GdA* III, 691. One may compare *GdA* I.1, 162 (= [1]I.1, § 90), where he states this view in more general terms: "Beide [viz., philosophy and religion] *behandeln dieselben Probleme, sie können oft genug auch zu den gleichen oder sehr ähnlichen Ergebnissen gelangen*; der Unterschied besteht darin, dass Philosophie und Wissenschaft prinzipiell—in der Praxis können oft genug andere Momente einwirken—lediglich die Denknotwendigkeiten des Verstandes anerkennen ..." (my italics).

[33] In a footnote (III 696 f. n. 1 = [1]II, § 462 *ad fin.*) he cites some literature. He praises Zeller but criticizes him for not putting the history of philosophy in its general historical context ("der Versuch, die Entwicklung der Philosophie im Zusammenhang der gesamten geistigen und politischen Entwicklung Griechenlands zu begreifen, ist hier nicht unternommen"). He praises H. Berger's *Geschichte der wissenschaftlichen Erdkunde der Griechen*, Leipzig I 1886, II 1889, III 1891, IV 1893 [today to be consulted in Leipzig [2]1903, repr. Berlin 1969], as "mustergültig" because it puts the history of geography in its proper setting. For the parallel between Orphism and philosophy he appeals to J. Freudenthal, *Über die Theologie des Xenophanes*, Breslau 1886, and to "Kern, Diels u.a.," but argues that the correspondences involved are "spontan", not derived from philosophy.

ogy, he contends, Greek cultural history had reached the stage which for
the Oriental cultures, without exception, was the final phase of their
development. Revealed religion is in possession of unchanging truth.
What is more, as soon as a revealed religion has achieved its accomplished
form, the priests take over and throttle new ideas. That in Early Greece
no trace of a dominant priestly class is to be found is irrelevant, for exist-
ing priesthoods, powerless before, tend to usurp the ecological niche a
revealed religion prepares for their benefit. There were priests in early
Israel, but no powerful independent priesthood; yet the religion of the
prophets brought the priests to power, who simply appropriated the ideas
of others. Parallel phenomena can be pointed out elsewhere in the Orient.
It could have happened in Greece, where the local priests of Athena or
Zeus or whatever divinity could have joined in a common cause and
appropriated the Orphic theology. But things never got that far:

> "hier ist *der entscheidende Wendepunkt der griechischen Geschichte*. Gleichzeitig mit
> der Orphik entsteht eine Gegenströmung, welche die religiöse Bewegung
> durchbricht und *in langem Ringen* zu Boden wirft und so die Einzigartigkeit
> der griechischen Entwicklung begründet . . . Ionien (hat der Nation) . . . ein
> letztes und höchstes Geschenk dargebracht, das, worauf für alle kommende
> Generationen der Menschen die befreiende Kraft der griechischen Kultur
> beruht, *die Philosophie*."[34]

These are strong words; one doesn't know that a modern ancient historian
would care to express himself in this way. Note that Meyer speaks of a
turning-point in Greek *history* not cultural history. The impact of
philosophy is perhaps his prime example of the influence of the "Ideen"
of individual persons on what he elsewhere calls "das Leben der
Geschichte."[35] Science and philosophy, moreover, have a social effect in
that they create a class which is analogous to the priestly class created by
systematical theology, viz. the "Gelehrtenzunft".[36] Scientists as a class
may be as conservative as a priestly class can be, but science cannot,
"ihrem Wesen nach," be the conservative ally of the powers that be:

> "Denn die Wissenschaft ist auf das Prinzip der Freiheit der geistigen Bewe-
> gung gegründet."[37]

Meyer's succinct characterization of early philosophy is in fact one of
early scientific thought: the study of celestial and geographical phenomena (the latter stimulated by the new knowledge brought by travellers),

---

[34] *GdA* III, 695 (my italics).
[35] *Kl. Schr.* I, 30.
[36] *GdA* I.1, 163 f. (= ²I.1, § 91). Cf. also IV.1, 840 (= ¹IV, Stuttgart—Berlin 1901,
§ 498).
[37] *GdA* I.1, 164.

the discovery of natural laws and of the necessary link between cause and effect which is sharply opposed to the ancient religious view which holds the personal gods acting in arbitrary ways responsible. Meyer adds that also "die Orphik . . . diese Probleme behandelt (hat),"[38] thus insisting again on the parallel between this systematical theology and philosophy. The Orphics speak of a moon that is inhabited and even seem to have thought that the sun also shines underneath the earth. Several Orphic doctrines.

> "decken sich fast völlig mit den Spekulationen der ältesten Philosophen: beide sind ja Erzeugnisse derselben Zeit und suchen dieselben Problem zu lösen."[39]

Historical determinism again, or at least a kind of *Zeitgeist* . . . . At this stage, Meyer is not yet clear about the correspondences that are involved, but it is certain that he is mentally comparing his Orphic pantheism ("all things are Zeus-Dionysus") with the handbook view of the speculations of the Milesian philosophers of nature ("all things are water," see below on Thales,[40] or "air").[41] But he clearly insists on the difference between Orphism and philosophy. (Milesian) philosophy is fundamentally *ir*religious[42] and the result of the

> "Nachdenkens des Einzelnen; das Individuum wahrt sich seine Rechte, es tritt mit seiner eigenen Autorität der Tradition entgegen."[43]

---

[38] *GdA* III, 697.

[39] *Ibid.*

[40] Cf. also his account of Anaximander's "Urprinzip" as "das, was aller Materie gemeinsam ist, also dasselbe was die [orphische] Theologie in Chaos und Äther zu erfassen sucht. Es ist der Träger alles Lebens . . .," *ibid.*, 699. He surprizingly finds Orphic "Anklänge" in the idea of cosmic retribution in Anaximander's famous fragment (*Vorsokr.* 12B1), although he translates ἀλλήλοις.

[41] See *GdA* IV.1, 853 (= ¹IV, § 504), on "Thales, Anaximander, Anaximenes:" "Eine lebendige Substanz von ewiger Dauer was ihnen die Welt, nicht geschieden in Stoff und Kraft [. . .]. Hinzu kommt . . . das Postulat von der Einheit alles Stoffs, sei es nun das Wasser, oder das Grenzenlose [*scil.*, Anaximander's ἄπειρον], das alles umschliesst und durchdringt, . . ., oder die Luft, oder was sonst." Meyer's enthusiastic unifying vision has him put Anaximander's principle on a par with that of Anaximenes, which is of course most dubious. As to Thales, most probably he only said all things are from water, not that in some sense of the word they still are; see my paper *Aristotle and Others on Thales, or the Beginnings of Natural Philosophy*, Mnemosyne 38 (1985), 109 ff.

[42] Cf. also *GdA* IV.1, 854: "die milesische Physik ist im Grunde atheistisch, auch wenn sie das Leben der Materie göttlich nennt und ihre Ursubstanz und deren Erscheinungen mit den Göttern des Volksglaubens identifizieren möchte." Meyer could of course have exploited the fact that Anaximander and Anaximenes provided their principle with divine attributes for his parallel with pantheistic Orphism. Presumably, the fact that Thales said that all things are full of gods (note the plural) and that Anaximenes seems to have implied that the traditional gods are descendants of Air keeps him back.

[43] *GdA* III, 697.

The formula recalls Meyer's rule of the conflict of "Ideen" as motive forces in history. Somewhat unhistorically (think e.g. of Nicias before Syracuse) he adds that Thales' successful prediction of a solar eclipse "mit den mythischen Anschauungen gründlich aufräumt."[44] Yet Thales' element or principle, viz. water, will have penetratated all things as a "belebende Macht;"[45] thus for him too all things are full of gods, just as for the (pantheistic) Orphics[46]—but, Meyer adds, they are so in a totally different sense.

We need not follow Meyer's account in this chapter much further. He speaks intelligently of the importance of prose as the vehicle of rationalist and empiricist thought.[47] Hecataeus is the first rationalist (or, to paraphrase Meyer more precisely, the first impersonation of rationalism) to attack religious beliefs in an explicit way, but his rationalisation of myths does not find much favour with Meyer who argues that early Greek rationalism "ist ebenso platt wie der des 18." [the first edition reads "vorigen"] "Jahrhunderts", although equally influential,[48] i.e. equally important from a historical point of view (ideas in history again). The chapter ends with the description of the "Vermittlungsversuche" between religion and philosophy of Pherecydes and Xenophanes. The latter is for Meyer more important than the former:

> "Sein ganzes Denken ist beherrscht von der *Idee* der einheitlichen, die Welt durchdringenden göttlichen Macht. Darin berührt er sich mit der Orphik; aber er verschmäht ihren Mystizismus und ihre kosmogonischen Phantastereien . . . ."[49]

To conclude, it should be stated as clearly as possible that Meyer (unlike others, who have insisted on the resemblances they believe can be pointed out) never says philosophy in some way or other *derives from* religion, not even from the in many respects according to him so remarkably similar

---

[44] *Ibid.*, 698. Meyer rhetorically anticipates the *actio in distans*. See further the next paragraph.

[45] *Ibid.*, 699.

[46] Cf. however above, n. 42.

[47] One should add that at *GdA* IV.1, 838 (= ¹IV, § 497), he anticipates much of today's discussion about oral culture: "Aber zunächst ist überall, wie in der Dichtung so in den Lehren der Philosphen und Techniker, das gesprochene Wort die Hauptsache; das Buch sucht es nur festzuhalten und weiteren Kreisen in Mit- und Nachwelt zu übermitteln."

[48] *GdA* III, 702. This does not entail a rejection of rationalism in favour of religious thought; his point is that this kind of rationalism fails to take account of religion as an important historical phenomenon. Although Hecataeus is the first Greek historian, he apparently is not, in Meyer's view, a good one.

[49] *Ibid.*, 704 (my italics). Cf. also *ibid.*, 761 f.

Orphic theology.[50] There is no trace in Meyer of the miraculously popular notion, widespread even today, of a development "Vom Mythos zum Logos"[51] (to quote the title of a well-known book by W. Nestle).[52] Developments in early Milesian philosophy and in the Orphic religion are parallel, cross-fertilizations between the ensuing currents apparently occurring only later (Pherecydes, Xenophanes, Pythagoras, Plato).

Finally, it should be noted that Meyer in this chapter pays little attention to Pythagoreanism. To some extent, he makes up for this omission in the next.[53] This is because he places Pythagoras in the context of the history of the Greek West (more often than not, Meyer's insistence that philosophy be treated in its proper historical setting boils down to treating it in its local context). Pythagoras in his view provides an eclectic[54] blend of Orphic mysticism and various parts of Ionian science which however is geared to a practical end, viz. to save the soul. In the case of Pythagoras, Meyer speaks of Orphic *influence* ("aufs stärkste beeinflusst"), especially as to the "Lehre von der Seelenwanderung und von den Strafen im Jenseits, ferner die Askese . . . ."[55] Just as the Orphics, he is the founder of a sect. A blend of "Ideen" deriving from the Orphics and from Anaximander is unmistakable:

> [Orphic:] "Die grosse Eins ist der Urgrund der Dinge, die Gottheit und zugleich das Weltall, der Himmel;" [Anaximandrean:] "jenseits desselben liegt das Unbegrenzte, aus dem der Himmel den Atem und die Zeit und das Leere einatmet . . . ."[56]

In his zeal to attribute pantheist so-called Orphic ideas to Pythagoras, Meyer provides an interpretation of the early Pythagorean 'One' that is patently false.

The treatment of Pythagoras is wound up with a few words about the sect as a factor in the political history of the Greek cities of Southern Italy;

---

[50] A different view is taken by his younger contemporaries: K. Joël, *Der Ursprung der Naturphilosophie aus dem Geiste der Mystik*, Basel 1903, Jena [2]1906, and A. Diès, *Le cycle mystique. La divinité, origine et fin des existences individuelles dans la philosophie antésocratique*, thèse Paris 1909.

[51] For instance, in G.S. Kirk—J.E. Raven, *The Presocratic Philosophers*, 2nd. ed. revised by M. Schofield, Cambridge 1983, the so-called "Forerunners of Philosophical Cosmogony," among them the Orphic cosmogonies, are allowed more space than Leucippus and Democritus.

[52] Stuttgart 1940, Darmstadt [2]1966. Much earlier, J. Dörfler published a book with the same title, Freistadt 1914 (*non vidi*).

[53] *GdA* III, 757 ff. (there are no differences with [1]II §§ 502 f.). See further below.

[54] *Ibid.*, 759 and n. 1, he translates and quotes *Vorsokr.* 21B129.

[55] *Ibid.*, 758.

[56] *Ibid.*, 759.

historically, this account is remarkably accurate,[57] anticipating that of von Fritz.[58] In a later volume, however, Pythagoreanism will stand out in stronger relief.

3. The Historical Impact of Early Philosophy

We have noticed that Meyer in GdA III argues that the birth of philosophy changed the course of Greek history because, among other things, it prevented the priests from taking over. To the best of my knowledge, this argument is not sustained in the volumes that follow. In order to prevent the priests from taking things in charge, the social and political impact of philosophy should have occurred rather quickly, because the systematical Orphic theology, according to Meyer, was fully developed by the mid-sixth century BCE. In GdA IV, however, Meyer does not fail to point out several times that philosophy and science did not reach the general public for a long time, and in some sense perhaps not at all. His conviction that Thales' prediction of a solar eclipse "mit den mythischen Anschauungen gründlich aufräumt,"[59] although correct from the theoretical vantage-point of pure science, is premature from a historical point of view. In GdA IV.1 he affirms, more correctly:

> "Völlig lokal sind noch Jahrzehntelang die Anfänge der Philosophie; in Milet,[60] in Elea,[61] in Ephesos[62] sammeln die Weisen einen Kreis von Schülern um sich, der ihre Lehren bewahrt und weiterbildet, während in das grössere Publikum[63] nur unbestimmte und verzerrte Kunde von ihrem seltsamen Treiben dringt."[64]

One wonders how such isolated small groups would have been able to compete with the systematic theology of Orphism. In his discussion of Sicilian culture in the fifth century BCE, Meyer even points out:

---

[57] Ibid., 761. Cf. also IV.1, 627 f.

[58] K. von Fritz, Pythagorean Politics in South Italy: an analysis of the sources, New York 1940.

[59] Cf. above, n. 44.

[60] Scil., Thales, Anaximander, Anaximenes.

[61] Scil., Xenophanes, Parmenides, Zeno.

[62] Scil., Heraclitus.

[63] Cf. ibid., 883 (= ¹IV § 517): "Dem grösseren Publikum ... waren ihre Schriften notwendig so gut wie unverständlich."

[64] GdA IV.1, 406 (= III, Stuttgart—Berlin 1901, § 247). The anachronistic notion of early philosophical schools is probably derived from H. Diels, Ueber die ältesten Philosophen-schulen der Griechen, in: Philosophische Aufsätze Ed. Zeller gewidmet, Leipzig 1887, 241 ff. (not reprinted in his Kleine Schriften, ed. W. Burkert, Darmstadt 1969). Actually, the first philosopher of whom we know that he practised teaching (presumably, to the happy few) is Anaxagoras, see the decree of Diopeithes ap. Plut. Per. 32 = Vorsokr. 59A17.

"Der reine Rationalismus genügt wohl einzelnen Denkern, aber niemals einem Volk. [. . .] Einzig der Glaube vermag die Erlösung und den versöhnenden Abschluss zu bieten.''[65]

Elsewhere, he mentions the traditional religion in this context and speaks of the "an der überlieferten Religion festhaltenden Massen.''[66]

This would entail that the priests, having appropriated the systematical Orphic theology, could have taken over after all—or would the masses rather than the intellectuals have offered resistance? Although Meyer, "bis in seinen letzten Lebenstage hinein,'' often said that he hardly ever had to change his views,[67] he actually does so this time within the body of the *GdA* itself, perhaps without noticing the inconsistency. Infatuated with his counterfactual based on the parallel with the priestly classes of the Orient, he apparently never questioned his supposition that the Orphic theology constitutes a unified whole. What he could have pointed out is that we do not have one single and systematical Orphic theology, but a plurality of Orphic theologies or rather theogonies,[68] and that the plurality of cults and beliefs which constitute what he calls the traditional religion were still a living force. In other words, Meyer's principles of individualism and the ensuing conflict of ideas as the motive forces in Greek history in the seventh and sixth centuries BCE would have been able to serve him rather well. He would for instance have been in a position to argue that the plurality of Orphisms prevented the formation of a systematical theology which would definitely have replaced the old religion, and so blocked the rise to power of a priestly class.

Actually, Meyer has it both ways, for he (quite correctly) also insists once again that the development of philosophy and the sciences introduces

"ein neues Element in das geistige Leben der Menschheit, *das der Orient nie . . . gekannt hat*: der Gelehrte . . . tritt mit seinen eigenen Überzeugungen an die Öffentlichkeit. [. . .] So eröffnet sich *die wissenschaftliche Diskussion*, die

---

[65] *Ibid.*, 621 (= ¹III, § 659). I can point out only in passing that Meyer discusses Empedocles in this geographico-historical context, *ibid.* 622 ff., i.e. after Xenophanes and before—again—Pythagoras, Heraclitus, and the Eleatics whose doctrines according to Meyer he used for the formation of his own views. The account is remarkable enough. Meyer states that Empedocles (like others) has been strongly influenced by Orphism, and—unlike Diels and Bidez—finds no real contradiction between the *Katharmoi* and the physical poem: ". . . so übersieht man, dass der Gegensatz nur ein logischer, aber kein psychologischer ist. Die Tendenz beider Gedichte ist ganz die gleiche, praktische: die Begründung der Stellung des inspirierten Wundermanns'' (625, n. 1). A verdict which I, for my part, feel bound to accept to a large extent, only adding that the logical opposition is one between physics and ethics.

[66] *GdA* IV.1, 886 (= ¹IV, § 518).
[67] Cf. Stier in his editorial preface to *GdA* III, p. VI.
[68] See now M.L. West, *The Orphic Poems*, Oxford 1983.

zunächst zwischen den Fachgenossen geführt wird,[69] aber in letzter Instanz das gesamte Publikum zur Entscheidung aufruft.''[70]

But apparently the general public more often than not did not respond to this appeal. Yet Meyer puts a date to philosophy's going public:

"So wird etwa um die Mitte des fünften Jahrhunderts das Publikum allmählich reif für theoretische Diskussionen,''[71]

that is to say about a century later than his date for the final form of the systematical Orphic theology. His arguments[72] are rather weak. Diogenes of Apollonia and Anaxagoras no longer use what Meyer calls mystical, half prophetical language, but write in such a way that their doctrines are "jedem Laien fassbar." This is to ignore that Anaxagoras is notoriously difficult and that already Anaximenes is said to have used a "simple, uncluttered Ionic diction" (Vorsokr. 13A1). He believes, I know not on what grounds, that Anaxagoras read from his book on public occasions and explained it in "öffentlichen Vorträgen," and argues that Parmenides and Zeno even came to Athens to give public lectures—which entails not only that he accepts the dramatical setting of Plato's Parmenides as historical truth,[73] but also that he forgets that according to Plato's novella Zeno read from his book to a small circle of cognoscenti. He argues that Melissus, a politician from Samos, tried to popularize the Eleatic doctrines, which again entails ignoring how difficult Melissus really is. He also refers to Euripides, who, he somewhat hyperbolically affirms, was interested in each and every system, but whose main plays, one should say, were composed at a later date and who presumably does not represent the general public of his time anyway. He correctly refers to medical tracts to be found in the Corpus Hippocraticum we still possess that are addressed to the general public, but these do not provide the required parallel, because, at the earliest, they are to be dated to the last decades of the fifth

---

[69] Cf. GdA IV.1, 882 f. (= ¹IV, § 517): "Zunächst haben die Weisheitslehrer unmittelbar nur auf einen engen Schülerkreis gewirkt, ..., daneben aber ... ununterbrochen eine rege Wechselwirkung aufeinander geübt, der zu immer neuen Systembildungen Anlass gab. Dem grösseren Publikum dagegen waren ihre Schriften notwendig so gut wie unverständlich.''

[70] Ibid., 840 (my italics). For another "Gegensatz zum Orient" see ibid., 846, where Meyer opposes Greek rational and empirical medicine, which has been influenced by philosophy but also in its best representatives constitutes a reaction to philosophy, to Oriental medicine.

[71] Ibid., 883.

[72] Ibid.

[73] Cf. the explicit argument ibid., 866 n. 1. Plato's implied chronology is still accepted by many scholars but cannot be right; see my paper Aristotle, Plato, and the Preplatonic Doxography and Chronography, in: G. Cambiano (ed.), Storiografia e dossografia nella filosofia antica, Torino 1986, 41 ff.

century BCE and because, moreover, the general public of course was much more interested in medical matters than in the highly speculative theories of the natural philosophers. What Meyer does not know is that such general knowledge of these abstruse theories as was conveyed to the general public in the later fifth century as a rule derived from the popularizing teachings of the Sophists.[74] Some doctors, of course, did study some of the original philosophical books; so did other professionals and, one may assume, one or two interested laymen.

Another remarkable phenomenon in *GdA* IV.1 (note that this account is nowhere different from that in [1]1901) is that Meyer to some extent retracts his earlier privileged treatment of Orphism and points out the importance of Pythagoreanism:

> "Für das volle Verständnis der *geistigen* Entwicklung des Griechentums ist die richtige Beurteilung des Pythagoreismus von derselben Bedeutung wie die der Orphik. In Bd. III² S. 758 ff." [[1]IV, § 504 *ad fin.*, refers to "Bd. II, 502 f."] "habe ich die *wissenschaftliche* Bedeutung des Pythagoras noch zu gering geschätzt."[75]

Presumably he means that Pythagoreanism, insofar as it is a revisionist or even revolutionary religious movement concerned with the well-being of the soul, may be placed on a par with Orphism, and that it is perhaps even superior to Orphism (and to the philosophy of Miletus) because of the decisive and highly influential mathematical[76] and scientific discoveries—such as, e.g., that the earth is a globe and does not occupy the centre of the solar system—he attributes to Pythagoras and his immediate pupils. At any rate, Pythagoras brought things much further than the Milesians had because of the religious element in his thought:

> "unverkennbar ist es, dass ... das ... System ... des Pythagoras viel weiter gekommen ist, obwohl oder vielleicht gerade weil es an der Religion festhält und sich ganz dem Mystizismus und der Erlösungslehre in die Arme wirft. Denn es hat eine unerschütterliche Grundlage in die Mathematik. Diese lenkt das Denken nicht auf die Substanz, sondern auf die Form der Dinge."[77]

Pythagoras, moreover, laudably distinguishes himself from the *physikoi* of Miletus because

---

[74] See my paper (*supra*, n. 73), 1 ff., 36 ff.

[75] *GdA* IV.1, 855 f. n. 1 (my italics). Note that in the earlier volume philosophy, not Orphic theology, is claimed to have had historical consequences. Orphism therefore remained a "geistiges" phenomenon, and so may be put on a par with Pythagoreanism. On the political impact of Pythagoreanism Meyer is remarkably reticent; see below.

[76] *Ibid.*, 843 f., 854 f.

[77] *Ibid.*, 854.

"die *ethischen* und *politischen* Fragen ... für ihn ein ebenso wesentlicher
Bestandteil der Welterkenntnis (sind) wie die kosmischen Gesetze."[78]

But exactly what this ethics and politics resemble we do not learn from
these pages of *GdA*; and a subsequent reference is rather jejune.[79] What
is more, most surprisingly Meyer, in his treatment of the political vicissi-
tudes of the Pythagorean school culminating in the catastrophe of ca. 450
BCE,[80] omits to speak of "das Tragische in der Geschichte," or of ideas
that are converted into their opposites. Yet he could have dealt with the
historical fate of Pythagoras' ethical and political ideas in exactly the same
way as, in the final volume, he deals with that of Plato's abortive attempt
to introduce a measure of philosophy into the politics of Syracuse.
Presumably this is because, when modifying his evaluation of the importance of Pythagoras' philosophy, he stuck to the philosophy itself and
failed to integrate his modified view of Pythagoreanism as a whole into the
plan of his work. Furthermore, it is a definite possibility that only when
he had finished planning or even writing the chapters dealing with Plato
and Sicily in the final volume the notion that an "Idee" necessarily
produces its opposite dawned on his mind. But it is odd that even in this
section of the final volume he fails to draw attention to the obvious parallel
between Pythagorean ethico-political theory and its actual historical
results on the one hand and Platonic ethico-political theory and its actual
historical results on the other. Note, moreover, that both these disasters
took place in Magna Graecia.

Meyer also discusses what he calls the "Bankrott der Naturphiloso-

---

[78] *Ibid.*, 855. At 855 n. 1 (= ¹IV, § 504 *ad fin.*) Meyer refers to "neuere Werke" on
the history of Greek philosophy: P. Tannéry, *Pour l'histoire de la science hellène de Thalès à
Empédocle*, Paris 1887; "Windelband im Handbuch der klass. Altertumsw. V, 1888;" and
H. Gomperz, *Griechische Denker* I, Berlin—Leipzig 1896 [last revised edition ⁴1922]. The
reference to Windelband is to the latter's *Geschichte der alten Philosophie*, in: *Handb.* V, Nord-
lingen 1888, 115–237 (in this vol., S. Günther, *Mathematik, Naturwissenschaft (inclusiv
Medizin) und wissenschaftliche Erdkunde* is at pp. 1–114); rather remarkably, Meyer does not
refer to the "zweite, völlig durchgesehene Auflage," München 1894, where Windelband's monograph is at pp. 1–228 and Günther's has become an "Anhang" (224–306).
For Windelband's views on Early Pythagoreanism see 134 f., 171 ff. = 2nd. ed., 21 f.,
59 ff. Meyer's modified view of Pythagoreanism presumably owes a lot to the studies of
Tannéry and Windelband. Note that he praises Gomperz (whom Wilamowitz disliked and
who was also by others at the time considered to be too much of a positivist) because he
"die Erkenntnis des Werdens und Wachsens der Gedanken und Probleme [. . .] durch
vortreffliche moderne Parallelen belebt."

[79] *Ibid.*, 886, he speaks of the mystical system of Pythagoras which simultaneously
strived to attain practical ends.

[80] See above, text to n. 58. In *GdA* IV, the philosophy and the practical politics of the
Pythagoreans are treated in different sections. Note, however, that in *GdA* IV.2, 144, he
compares the destruction of the Pythagorean *synedria* with the burning on stage of Socrates'
phrontisterion inclusive of its inmates in Aristophanes' *Clouds*.

phie."[81] Before looking at these interesting pages, we should say something about his treatment of Heraclitus, Parmenides, and others. There is a weak attempt to put Heraclitus in a political context, i.e. to provide him with an idea that conflicts with another idea, in that he apparently has him react to the democratic regime of Ephesus.[82] Heraclitus is a favourite with Meyer: he translates numerous fragments,[83] a treatment no other Presocratic receives at his hands. Heraclitus is the individual par excellence:

"Er ist einer von den wenigen Menschen, dessen individuellste Gedanken fortleben durch alle Zeiten."[84]

We recall Meyer's use of the explanatory notion of individualism and understand how pleased he is that one of his players almost seems to be conscious of the role he is made to play. What in these pages Meyer does not do is discuss Heraclitus' ethical and political philosophy; rather, he has him withdraw unto himself as a reaction to the hated democracy. About twenty pages further down, however, he speaks of Heraclitus' "Sonderstellung" among the philosophers of nature, because he also touches—albeit unsystematically—on "die ethischen, sozialen, religiösen Fragen."[85]

Meyer's pages on Parmenides[86] are perceptive. He dwells on his physics at appropriate length, arguing[87]—with Gomperz as an ally—against Diels that the "zweite Teil des Lehrgedichts ebenso ernsthaft gemeint (ist) wie der Erste" because the hypothetical explanation of the world of Seeming is as necessary as the explanation of the world of Truth. He admits that there is a snag in that Parmenides does not say how the former could arise from, or is related to, the latter, but posits that this simply was

---

[81] *GdA* IV.1, 884 ff. (= ¹IV, § 517).

[82] *Ibid.*, 856.

[83] *Ibid.*, 857–862, are a cento of fragments, with comments. Note that Meyer of course could not avail himself of Diels' *Fragmente der Vorsokratiker*, first published as a single vol. without critical apparatus Berlin 1903, or of Diels' monograph *Herakleitos von Ephesos*, Berlin 1901 [²1909]. At *GdA* IV.1, 857 n. 1 *ad fin.*, Meyer added a reference to the monograph: "[Vgl. jetzt Diels, . . . , 1901, der manches anders auffasst als ich]". In the revised ed., Stier added the references to the numbering of *Vorsokr.*

[84] *Ibid.*, 864. Cf. 857: "In Heraklit tritt uns zum erstenmal das Selbstbewusstsein der denkenden Persönlichkeit in seiner ganzen Wucht entgegen."

[85] *Ibid.*, 886–887. Cf. Windelband, *o.c.* (*supra*, n. 78), 150 = 2nd. ed., 37, who interprets Heraclitus' philosophy in a similar way. Cf. also the remarkable account by J. Owens, *A History of Ancient Western Philosophy*, Englewood Cliffs N.J. 1959, 44 ff.

[86] *Ibid.*, 865 ff.

[87] *Ibid.*, 866 f. n. 2, where the references to Diels (*Parmenides' Lehrgedicht*, Berlin 1897) and Gomperz are given. Note that Windelband, *o.c.* (*supra*, n. 78), 154–6 = 2nd. ed., 41–3, argues on much similar lines.

impossible for him.[88] There is today still no scholarly consensus as to the status of Parmenides' *doxa*, but Meyer's intuition that the physics is totally serious is shared, among others, by the present writer.[89] There is an interesting corollary to this interpretation of Parmenides. Diogenes Laertius IX 29 (*Vorsokr.* 29A1) puzzlingly attributes to Parmenides' pupil Zeno, the author of the famous paradoxes—which are not discussed by Meyer— a theory of four elementary forces. Meyer brilliantly interprets this as a minor modification of the Parmenidean *doxa*.[90] There is of course nothing to be said of Parmenides' or Zeno's ethical or political thought. Elsewhere, Meyer is entirely skeptical even as to the stories about Zeno's attempt [one should add: as a citizen, not as a philosopher] to overthrow the tyrant of Elea, but inclined to believe the remark attributed to Speusippus (fr.1 Lang) that Parmenides [again as a citizen, not as a philosopher] gave Elea a code of laws.[91]

Skipping Anaxagoras[92] and Leucippus,[93] we may now turn to the bankruptcy of natural philosophy, as Meyer calls it. This was caused by the plurality of rival and mutually exclusive scientific systems:

> "Wissenschaftlich standen alle diese Erklärungen auf gleicher Linie; die Probleme, die man lösen wollte, waren für die Zeit noch nicht lösbar, ja oft kaum formulierbar."[94]

Thus, the next epoch is one of salutary reactions against speculative natural philosophy (an instance, presumably, of the ideas of individuals in conflict with the ideas of other individuals). The reaction is represented on the one hand by Hippocrates[95] [i.e. in this case the author of *De vetere*

---

[88] Cf. also *ibid.*, 871.

[89] I believe one can also reconstruct Parmenides' explanation for the origin of the world of Seeming, but cannot enter into this question here.

[90] *GdA* IV.1, 867 n. At 620 f. n. 1 he accounts for the theory of sensation reliably attributed to Gorgias (*Vorsokr.* 82 B4, B5) in precisely the same way.

[91] *Ibid.*, 629 n. 2. This information about Parmenides and Zeno is to be found in their *bioi* in Diog. Laert. IX 21–3 and 25–8; the stories about Zeno's heroism are also to be found in other sources (such behaviour is attributed to Anaxarchus as well, e.g. Diog. Laert. IX 59).

[92] *Ibid.*, 874 ff. His cosmology is said by Meyer to be old-fashioned compared with those of the Pythagoreans and Parmenides.

[93] *Ibid.*, 876 ff. Treatment of Democritus is postponed as in Windelband, to whom Meyer here refers [*o.c.*, *supra*, n. 78, 169 ff. = 2nd. ed., 55 ff. (Leucippus), and 207 ff. = 2nd. ed., 93 ff. (Democritus); on Democritus' ethics see *ibid.*, 215 ff. = 2nd. ed., 103 ff.], since he is better understood in a chronologically later context. This is because of his ethics: "Die ältere Naturphilosophie kennt eben eine Ethik als selbständige Wissenschaft noch nicht" (877 n. 1). Democritus' epistemomology, moreover, has been influenced by Protagoras (879).

[94] *Ibid.*, 884. Cf. also *GdA* IV.2, 156.

[95] *GdA* IV.1, 885.

medicina] and his empiricist colleagues, and by the Sophists[96] on the other. Meyer adds that science, in order to survive, was bound to give priority to securing its foundations. Two instruments which would serve this purpose were available:

> "auf der einen Seite die pythagoreische Mathematik, auf der anderen die systematische Untersuchung der Begriffe auf der Grundlage der eleatischen Ontologie, aber belebt von dem zündenden Feuer der Gedanken Heraklits."[97]

Meyer does not say whom he is thinking of, but it is an easy guess: Plato. Before we get to Plato, however, we have to study the Sophistic movement, and of course Socrates. Meyer points out that the natural philosophers (with the mystical Pythagoreans and Empedocles and the unsystematical Heraclitus as exceptions) as a rule had paid no attention to moral and political questions.[98] The interior development of society and politics, especially in sophisticated Athens, had created new needs which natural philosophy because of its abstruseness and state of bankruptcy and for its lack of suggestions that would be useful for political and moral purposes was unable to satisfy. Hence the Sophistic movement, which became influential from ca. 450 BCE: "Neue Bedürfnisse erzeugen auch die Mittel, sie zu befriedigen."[99] The teachings of the Sophists are a reaction and an alternative to those of the natural philosophers, and the development of political history gives them elbow room. With the doctrines of the Sophists moreover, individualism (as in Protagoras' relativism[100]) reaches a new climax.

The picture painted by Meyer is a familiar one, and there is much truth in it. One should point out, however, that the early phase of the Sophistic movement (Protagoras, Gorgias, Prodicus and others) is contemporary with the final phase of creative Presocratic natural philosophy (Anaxagoras, Leucippus, Melissus, Democritus). We have noticed above that Meyer elsewhere affirms that from 450 BCE, i.e. from the date which he assigns to the first impact of the Sophistic movement, the general public became interested in the theoretical questions posed by natural philosophy.[101] The term "Bankrott", and the date assigned to it, should be taken *cum grano salis*. Natural philosophy, apart from the exceptions also singled out by Meyer, never catered for the needs of practical life, and its

---

[96] *Ibid.*, 890 ff. Cf. also *GdA* IV.2, 136, 156 f.
[97] *GdA* IV.1, 885.
[98] *Ibid.*, 886 f.
[99] *Ibid.*, 890 (opening sentence of the chapter "Die Sophistik").
[100] *Ibid.*, 892 f., 897.
[101] Cf. above, text to n. 71.

reception by the doctors is more diverse and complicated than Meyer allows. It was criticized in some circles and by some persons, but continued to flourish nevertheless. Democritus and Diogenes of Apollonia are contemporaries of Socrates, and both Socrates and Diogenes are satyrized in Aristophanes' *Clouds*. Although it remains correct to say that the epistemology of Protagoras and others is highly critical of the epistemic claims made by the natural philosophers, and also to affirm that Gorgias and others exploit their doctrinal disagreements, one should point out that in other respects the Sophistic movement is the successor of the moralizing and counseling poets (cf. Plato, *Protagoras* 316d). What is more, in the early fifth century BCE Sicily produced predecessors of the Sophists in the persons of the rhetoricians Corax and Tisias, on whom Meyer dwells elsewhere[102] without suggesting that they, too, reacted to a natural philosophy they believed to be bankrupt. Consequently, his favourite dynamic scheme of the conflict of ideas occasionally results in oversimplification.

4. Socrates and Plato

We may now move on to the next volume of the *GdA*. Meyer discusses the "Wirkungen des Krieges," i.e. the Ten Years War (431–421 BCE) or first instalment of the Peloponnesian War. He states, somewhat unpalatably:

> "Ein Krieg im grossen Stil entfesselt neben den niedrigsten auch die höchsten Kräfte und Triebe des Menschen."[103]

The Peloponnesian war was most destructive, but the "schöpferische Kraft des Krieges hat sich auch diesmal gezeigt." It provided the decisive impulse for Herodotus' universal history, for the great political comedy of Eupolis and Aristophanes, and for the more important tragedies of Euripides. However the most important effect of the war is that it propels individualism toward its peak ("vollendete Emanzipation des Individuums ... im guten wie im Schlimmen"[104]). In a way, this period of Greek history provides the culmination of the conflict of ideas which serves Meyer to write a living history of Greece:

> "All die Gegensätze, welche die Entwicklung der griechischen Kultur geschaffen hat, rüsten sich zum entscheidenden Kampf. Innerhalb Athens

---

[102] *GdA* IV.1, 619 f.
[103] *GdA* IV.2, 135. I know what Heraclitus said (*Vorsokr.* 22B53) but still do not like what Meyer said.
[104] *Ibid.*

steht auf der einen Seite das Alte, die homogene, in sich geschlossene Kultur,[105] auf der anderen der Subjektivismus des modernen Denkens,[106] die wissenschaftliche Aufklärung und der Unglaube, das freie Recht des einzelnen, die neuen Formen in Literatur und Kunst."[107]

Meyer no longer sees individualism in an entirely favourable light; on the contrary, it now appears to be a force that more often than not is destructive. It is not false to say that, in a way, he holds the Sophists at least in part responsible for the excesses that were committed by the Athenian democracy during the Ten Years War—a perspective that reminds one of Plato's point of view in his earlier, anti-sophistic dialogues, and which seems to be more in agreement with the intellectual's prejudice (i.e. the assumption that intellectuals are far more important than they really are) than with the historian's coolness and impartiality.

However this may be, Meyer proceeds to describe a battle of ideas and to provide a blend of cultural and political history. On the one hand you have the "revolutionären Ideen" of the Sophists and, to some extent, of the natural philosophers, which attract the young, on the other the "alte Glauben der Väter."[108] The social opposition involved is one between conservative, even reactionary democracy on the one hand, which only wants to reap the material benefits of individualism, or the spoils of empire and of war, and the essentially undemocratic "moderne Bildung;" the morally unscrupulous Cleon is the declared enemy of the modern arts of disputation and argument.[109] Comedy (Cratinus and especially Aristophanes) satyrizes the hypothesis of the natural philosophers and the education provided by the Sophists; Aristophanes attacks Euripides for being too modern.[110] The "Kampf um die Politik des Staates" actually gets to be more and more a "Kampf um seine Kultur;"[111] for the first time, Meyer really is in a position to shore up his conviction that ideas help to shape political history. Both reactionaries and revolutionaries, however, being equally modern,[112] are equally wrong,[113]

---

[105] Of which Meyer had argued up till now that it was not all that "geschlossen". Elsewhere, he is aware that the noble culture of ancient Athens is very much the imaginary creation of his conservatives of the closing decades of the fifth century.

[106] Protagoras (cf. IV.1, 136) and the Sophistic movement in general (this also holds for the enlightenment, cf. below, text to n. 115).

[107] *Ibid.*

[108] *Ibid.*, 136.

[109] *Ibid.*, 137–9.

[110] *Ibid.*, 146 f.

[111] *Ibid.*, 136.

[112] *Ibid.*, 149: "der moderne Geist ... hat sich, mag man es sich eingestehen oder nicht, Staat und Gesellschaft bereits vollständig unterworfen."

[113] *Ibid.*

and Athens seems to be on the brink of self-destruction; indeed, it is

"in vollem Zuge, ganz der [*scil.* modernen] Zeitströmung anheimzufallen, wie die Städte Ioniens und Siziliens . . . ."[114]

But this disaster was averted:

"Das es anders gekommen ist, dass *die sophistische Aufklärung* nicht das letzte Wort der *geistigen* Entwicklung von Athem und Hellas geblieben ist, ist nicht das Werk der um die Herrschaft ringenden Parteien, die den politischen Kampf auch auf *geistigem* Gebiet ausfechten wollten, sondern das Werk des unscheinbaren Mannes, in dem jene recht eigentlich die Inkarnation der modernen *Ideen* zu erkennen glaubten, des Sokrates."[115]

Meyer's picture of Socrates, set out at considerable length,[116] is in many ways a conventional one. It is based on what are assumed to be the convergences between the sources: Aristophanes (who has him profess several tenets that actually were quite foreign to him),[117] Xenophon, Plato, and the Minor Socratics. Rather amusingly, Meyer says that in view of the infinitely large body of secundary literature dealing with Socrates, he feels bound, more than ever, to stick to the facts.[118] He accepts that Socrates studied the writings of the experts, and dwells on his disappointment with natural philosophy.[119] Consequently, Socrates' doctrine "geht von denselben Voraussetzungen aus"[120] as the teachings of the Sophists, but the

---

[114] *Ibid.*, 150. For the moment, Meyer forgets about Plato's intervention in Sicilian politics seventy years later. It was a Sicilian city, not Athens, which seemed to give him a break.

[115] *Ibid.*, (my italics).

[116] *Ibid.*, 150–175.

[117] *Ibid.*, 143 f.

[118] *Ibid.*, 151 f. n. 1. According to Meyer, Xenophon is more faithful, but Plato saw deeper and used Socrates as his mouthpiece right from the beginning, giving a faithful portrait of the historical Socrates in the *Apology* only. For a recent study of the *Ap.* in this sense see K. Döring, *Der Sokrates der platonischen Apologie und die Frage nach dem historischen Sokrates*, Würzburger Jahrbücher für die Altertumswissenschaft, N.F. 13 (1987), 75 ff. The practically finished *Commentary on Plato's Apology* on which the regretted É. de Strycker had laboured for years and on which he worked until a few weeks before his untimely death has not yet been published from his *Nachlass*; hopefully, the Belgian government will be able to finance publication in the near future. De Strycker has told me that in his view even in the *Apology* Socrates has been transformed in a Platonic sense to a far greater extent than is commonly assumed [for part of the argument involved see his paper *The Oracle given to Chaerephon about Socrates*, in: J. Mansfeld—L.M. de Rijk (eds.), *Kephalaion*. Studies . . . de Vogel, Assen 1975, 39 ff.].

[119] *GdA* IV.2, 154–6, where he also briefly resumes the theme of the bankruptcy of natural philosophy and of the subjectivism of the Sophists as filling the gap.

[120] *Ibid.*, 157. I note in passing that Windelband, who treats Socrates after the Sophists and before the Minor Socratics, expresses a similar view: "Sokrates, der zwar mit seinen [*scil.*, sophistischen] Gegern auf dem gemeinsamen Boden der Aufklärung stand und wie sie das selbständige Nachdenken über alles durch Herkommen und Gewohnheit Gegebene zum Prinzip erhob . . .," *o.c.* (*supra*, n. 78), 198 = 2nd. ed., 77.

results are of course much different. According to Meyer (who here presents a Platonic rather than a historical figure, which is odd because he believes—a belief also open to objections—that Plato is historically reliable only in the *Apology*)[121] Socrates was convinced that the general concepts on which human value judgements are based are real ("das Reale schlechthin"), eternal, unchangeable, and divine, a description which however makes them virtually indistinguishable from Plato's Forms.[122] It is not the case that man is the measure of all things, but conversely: the eternal truths are the measure of man. Socrates' logic is not a science but a method.[123] This is what opposes his doctrine to the subjectivism and relativism of the Sophists. Socrates changes the course of philosophy from the study of nature to that of the laws of human life and thought. However, this does not yet turn him into the person required by Meyer's historical vision, the man who single-handedly prevented the moral ruin of Athens. Socrates is not merely a most important figure in the history of thought:

> "Alle diese Probleme sind ihm wie seiner Schule, auch für Plato, nur Mittel zum Zweck: . . . die Erziehung zum wahren Menschen, d.h. zum wahren *Staats*bürger . . . ."[124]

Only Socrates is the "wahre Lehrer der politischen Kunst" and a "politischer Reformator:"[125]

> "Auf der Tugend . . . beruhen die Ordnungen der menschlichen Gemeinschaft, des *Staates*."[126]

But Meyer's is not only a Platonic Socrates, but also a Kantian one: he introduces the "kategorischen Imperativ, den Begriff der sittlichen Pflicht."[127] Oddly enough, Meyer still calls this individualism;[128] pre-

---

[121] Cf. *supra*, n. 118. In *GdA* V, 337, moreover, he knows that the dialogues of Aeschines reputedly gave the most reliable picture of Socrates: see now the excellent paper of K. Döring, *Der Sokrates des Aischines von Sphettos und die Frage nach dem historischen Sokrates*, Hermes 112 (1984), 16 ff.

[122] Cf. *GdA* IV.2, 169: the "allgemeinen Begriffe, . . . was dann Plato die ewigen Ideen genannt hat." But note that *ibid.*, 174, Meyer is more aware of the crucial difference between Socrates who ignores the importance of Eleatic ontology and Plato who makes up for this omission: "Die Begriffe, die sittlichen Werturteile, die Sokrates als das Ewige, als den Masstab aller Dinge empfand, sind ihm [*scil.*, Plato] *etwas an sich Existierendes, Reales* . . . ." (my italics).

[123] *Ibid.*, 160–2; cf. *ibid.*, 175: "eben das erst ist seine volle Grösse, dass er nicht Glauben verlangte, sondern nur Prüfung . . ."

[124] *Ibid.*, 162 (my italics).

[125] *Ibid.*, 158–9.

[126] *Ibid.*, 164 (my italics).

[127] *Ibid.*

[128] I note in passing that M. Hossenfelder, *Die Philosophie der Antike, 3: Stoa, Epikureis-*

sumably, this is because he believes Socrates, although a deeply religious person and one not even averse to participation in the traditional cults, to be yet, from a theoretical point of view, as much in conflict with traditional religion as, say, the physicists of Miletus:

> "Das Entscheidende ist, dass die Moral[129] innerlich von der Religion vollkommen losgelöst und ganz auf sich selbst gestellt ist. Es ist der vollkommene Sieg des *Individualismus* über die in der Religion verkörperten Mächte der Tradition; soweit diese noch anerkannt wird, herrscht sie nicht mehr, sondern muss sich umwandeln nach den Postulaten der Moral."[130]

At any rate, according to Meyer Socrates represents a third answer to the spirit of modernity beside the democratic and the aristocratic reactions. It is through Socrates that

> "die *Staats*idee die theoretische Forschung (zwingt), ihre zentrale Stellung anzuerkennen. Seit ihm steht ein Jahrhundert lang das Problem der richtigen Gestaltung des *Staates* im Mittelpunkt des griechischen Denkens . . ."[131]

One may doubt that for Socrates the idea of the state did have the importance it was to acquire for Plato or, for that matter, for a German of Meyer's generation and political hue, and certainly feel unhappy with the implied suggestion that the historical Socrates would have been in favour of an authoritarian rather than a democratic regime.[132] Meyer, who of course describes the unfortunate way Socrates was dealt with by the majority in his own days, again anticipates *actio in distans*. He criticizes Socrates for neglecting that the state is not merely a moral ideal, but also

---

mus und Skepsis = W. Röd (ed.), *Geschichte der Philosophie*, III, München 1985, in his "Einleitung", 11 ff., argues that the Hellenistic philosophies are characterized by the "Primat der praktischen Vernunft" and concentrate on the individual person. But the individual in Hellenistic moral philosophy is a standardized one, and so is that of Socrates' philosophy as depicted by Meyer.

[129] Just as physics in the sixth century BCE.

[130] *GdA* IV.2, 165 (my italics). There is an interesting footnote (165, n. 1): "Die überspannten Lehren der christlichen Moral von Sokrates oder Plato zu fordern, würde meines Erachtens diese Männer herabsetzen."

[131] *Ibid.*, 169 (my italics). One should not, in my view, tacitly assume with Meyer that πόλις is equivalent with "Staat".

[132] R. Kraut, *Socrates and the State*, Princeton N.J. 1984, which consists for the most part of an investigation of the *Crito*, argues that the idea of the state was important for Socrates and that the ideal state of the *Politeia* would certainly have been acceptable to him. K. Döring, in his review of this book, Gnomon 58 (1986), 206 ff., correctly points out that the Socrates of the *Crito* is much closer to the *persona* of the *Apology* than to that of Plato's other early dialogues, which of course entails the corollary that there is a capital difference between the views which *perhaps* one may attribute to the historical Socrates on the one hand and those of Plato in the *Politeia* on the other. For Socrates' preference for the institutions of democratic Athens see G. Vlastos, *The Historical Socrates and Athenian Democracy*, Political Theory 11 (1983), 495 ff.

"zugleich Macht."[133] Meyer constructs the Socrates he needs for his cultural history as involved with political history, because he wants to preserve the central position in the development of Greek thought traditionally ascribed to him. The unique position of Greece in the history of humanity is based on Socrates, who

> "die Summe der ganzen bisherigen Entwicklung ihres [scil., der griechischen Geschichte] Denkens gezogen und das Ergebnis so hingestellt (hat), dass es der Menschheit nicht wieder verlorengehen konnte. [. . .] Nicht in eine neue Religion konnte die Entwicklung des griechischen Geistes einmünden, sondern nur in die Schöpfung der Wissenschaft. So ist denn diese mit Sokrates' Person untrennbar verbunden."[134]

In the next volume, the final one of the GdA, Meyer has to admit that what he has called the modern spirit remained a living force for much of the fourth century. Euripides replaces Homer the way Goethe replaced the Bible in Germany, and the rhetoricians, first of all Isocrates, are the successors of the Sophists.[135] Isocrates, moreover, wants "die Schüler vom Schlechten abzulenken" and to educate them as "tüchtige Staatsbürger—so his aims are not that much different from those of Meyer's Socrates—, and the "historische Wirksamkeit" of his panhellenic pamphlets is singled out for special mention.[136] The true philosophers, or the inheritors of Socrates, only occupy a position "neben" these other intellectuals.[137] He also modifies his previous picture of science's going public from the mid-fifth century (see above, § 3) and now puts this firmly in the fourth.[138] Democritus is treated in the same chapter as the (minor) Socratics and Plato,[139] although, if only for chronological reasons, he should have been discussed in the previous volume.[140] Finally, the individualistic morality ("ebenso individualistisch") of two of Socrates' three important pupils

---

[133] GdA IV.2, 174.

[134] Ibid., 175. Cf. 169: "Nicht erst für Plato und Aristoteles, sondern schon für Sokrates ist der Mensch das ζῷον πολιτικόν, das staatenbildende" [sic] "Wesen".

[135] GdA V, 321–30. For the present paragraph, I have throughout compared ¹V, Stuttgart—Berlin 1902; there are no differences apart from occasional abridgement of footnotes.

[136] Ibid., 329–30.

[137] Ibid., 326.

[138] Ibid., 331.

[139] Ibid., 330–52.

[140] For Meyer's motive for postponing treatment of Democritus see above, n. 93. What he has to say about him is interesting. As to the variety and quantity of his output, he rightly compares him to Aristotle (333). He criticizes his lack of mathematical acumen ("tief unter Plato," 334), and his ethics is "durchwegs und ausschliesslich individualistisch und daher im Grunde ziemlich quietistisch" (336, my italics; note that this is another kind of individualism than that attributed to Socrates). He fails to dwell on Democritus' influence on the ethical doctrines of the great Hellenistic schools.

according to Meyer (the third being Plato), Aristippus and Antisthenes, of which the first founded a school and the second was later claimed to be the archegete of the Cynic movement, is not inaccurately described;[141] but Meyer is silent about the fact that their total lack of interest in the state is at variance with his account of Socrates in the previous volume. To some extent, he makes up for this omission by proclaiming Plato to be the "wahre Erbe und Fortbildner des Sokrates."[142] But this, of course, begs the question.

For the biography of Plato,[143] Meyer already in this chapter uses the *Seventh Letter*, which he accepts as genuine much earlier than Wilamowitz did.[144] He also accepts the *Fifth*, the *Eighth*, the *Ninth*, and even the mystagogic and virtually Neopythagorean *Second*. His analysis of Plato's career much resembles that which later was advocated by Wilamowitz: early disappointment with politics, the decision to switch to philosophy as the foundation for politics, the hope to realize this ideal in real life, the disappointment and catastrophe in Sicily. Meyer's anachronistic account of Plato's epistemology as ultimately intuitive[145] is heavily indebted to the *Second* and *Seventh*, and colours his interpretation of comparable passages in the dialogues (the vision of the Beautiful in the *Symposium*; "der Ausgang des Theaetet, der bis an die Schwelle führt").[146] But he believes that with the famous remark in the *Second*—addressed to Dionysius and today unanimously considered a much later document, certainly not by Plato—, viz. "there is no writing by Plato, and there never will be, but only by a Socrates grown young and beautiful" (314c), the author—according to Meyer, Plato—is indulging in a private joke: in the dialogues of Plato's old age, Socrates is the one who is taught, not the one who teaches.[147]

Meyer's account of the Forms in relation to the world curiously enough recalls his earlier description of Orphic pantheist theology and Milesian physics and its early aftermatch:

"Das *lebendige Prinzip, welches die Welt gestaltet und bewegt*, ist ewig und unvergänglich und hat allein eine reale Existenz."[148]

Plato's doctrine of the soul, he argues, is heavily indebted to Orphism; he

[141] *Ibid.*, 338–42.
[142] *Ibid.*, 342.
[143] *Ibid.*, 342 ff.
[144] Compare my paper *Wilamowitz' Ciceronian Philosophy*, in: W.M. Calder III—H. Flashar—Th. Lindken (eds.), *Wilamowitz nach 50 Jahren*, Darmstadt 1985, § 8, 217 ff.
[145] *GdA* V, 344.
[146] *Ibid.*, 344, 347.
[147] *Ibid.*, 351.
[148] *Ibid.*, 345 (my italics). For the Orphics and Milesians see above, § 2.

combines the influences of Socrates, of Pythagoreanism (which gives him mathematics and reinforces his Orphic tendencies), and of Eleatic ontology in a grandiose synthesis. But his writings are almost without exception either "nur ... propädeutischer Art" or "logische und ethische Einzeluntersuchungen." However:

> "In das innerste Heiligtum seiner Gedanken führen nur Andeutungen, namentlich in der Politik. [...] der Kern seiner Lehre, die Erkenntnis der Ideen, ist eben durchaus intuitiv."[149]

This very much anticipates the tenor of Wilamowitz' *Platon*, and again shows to which extent his whole interpretation of Plato's philosophy is coloured by his acceptance of the letters.

Meyer, in a justificatory addendum,[150] adds that "in der Chronologie der platonischen Schriften" he "im Wesentlichen" accepts the stylometric results of Lutoslawski.[151] But he adds:

> "Entscheidend sind für mich die inneren Gründe ...; dass die stilistischen dazu stimmen, ist eine sehr willkommene Bestätigung."

Lutoslawski however did not include the *Letters* in his synopsis and amplifications of the stylometric studies of Plato (to which he added a substantial account of the development of the doctrines). "Internal grounds," of course, tend to be subjective, as the history of Plato studies in the nineteenth century (as in others) makes abundantly clear. We shall have more to say about Meyer's use of the *Letters* shortly, but this perhaps is the place to say that the present writer wants to be included among the skeptics. My main point is that the *Seventh*, which is supposed to have been written by Plato in his old age (a "Greis von 76 Jahren" according to Meyer's chronology[152]), provides an epistemology which is incompatible with that of the *Theaetetus*, *Sophist*, and other late works[153] (Meyer promised to treat these in a subsequent volume but as we know never did), and which harks back to the period of the *Politeia*. In the *Seventh Letter*, knowledge is by acquaintance; in the works of Plato's old age dealing with problems in epistemology, knowledge is propositional knowledge, or 'knowledge that ...;' and there is nothing intuitive about the deduction

---

[149] *Ibid.*, 350, with reference to *Ep.* II 314b and quotation of *Ep.* VII 341d.

[150] *GdA* ¹V, 360–1. Lamentably abridged out of the footnote by Stier in the revised ed. of V, 352 n. 1.

[151] W. Lutoslawski, *The Origin and Growth of Plato's Logic*, London 1897 (repr. Dubuque, Iowa, ca. 1965). Wilamowitz kept aloof from stylometry.

[152] *GdA* V, 313.

[153] I accept Owen's relative date for the *Timaeus* as being close to the *Politeia*; see G.E.L. Owen, *The Place of the Timaeus in Plato's Dialogues*, now in: G.E.L. Owen, *Logic, Science, and Dialectic*. Collected papers in Greek Philosophy, London 1986, ²1987, 65 ff.

of the "most important kinds" in the *Sophist*. The author of the *Seventh Letter* seems to have missed, or wilfully and whimsically have preferred to ignore, the main achievements of Plato's ripest thought. His mystagogic utterances belong with, indeed cap, comparable intimations from the period of the *Politeia*, (*Symposium*, and *Timaeus*)—as, indeed, does his politics, or rather political philosophy. Another reason for suspicion are the relative ages of the *dramatis personae*, which appear to be based on the same pre-Apollodorean system as the relative ages of Parmenides Zeno Socrates in the *Parmenides*.[154] Plato's first visit to Sicily according to the *Letter* is in the year of his ἀκμή, and there he meets Dion who at the time is twenty years old: the ideal age for the ideal pupil. Again, at the time of his second visit, Plato is slightly over sixty and Dion about forty (ἀκμή).[155]

The story of Dionysius II, Dion, and Plato is the tragic climax of the final volume of the *GdA*.[156]

"Hauptquelle sind Platos Briefe 13.2.3.7.8,[157] die von Plutarch im Dio (von ihm wie von seiner Quelle) eingehend benutzt sind . . . ."[158]

---

[154] For the latter, cf. my paper cited above, n. 73, § 6, "Plato and the Origins of the ἀκμή-method," 41 ff. I should add that I feel sorry for those who hate to lose the account by [Plato] at the beginning of *Ep.* VII of the regime of the Thirty, and of Socrates' courageous (or, according to I.F. Stone, *The Trial of Socrates*, New York 1988, not sufficiently courageous) behaviour when the tyrants tried to get him involved in their dirty business.

[155] The literature on the *Letters* is, of course, enormous. E. Bauer, *Die historischen Angaben der Platonbriefe VII und VIII im Urteil der modernen Forschung seit Eduard Meyer*, typewritten diss. Berlin 1957, is most useful. Important later contributions are L. Edelstein, *Plato's Seventh Letter*, Leiden 1966 (rejects the *Seventh*); K. von Fritz, *Platon in Sizilien und das Problem der Philosophenherrschaft*, Berlin 1968 (accepts the *Seventh* and rejects the *Eighth*); M. Isnardi Parente, *Filosofia e politica nelle lettere di Platone*, Napoli 1970 (accepts the *Seventh*); W.K.C. Guthrie, *A History of Greek Philosophy*, V: *The Later Plato and the Academy*, Cambridge 1978, 399 ff. (accepts the *Sixth*, *Seventh*, and apparently several others). See also A. Wörle, *Die politische Tätigkeit der Schüler Platons*, Darmstadt 1981, esp. 69 ff. (accepts both the *Seventh* and *Eighth*), and F.L. Vatai, *Intellectuals in Politics in the Greek World from Early Times to the Hellenistic Age*, London etc. 1984, esp. 83 ff. (accepts both these letters). Wörle and Vatai provide further bibliographical information. H. Tarrant, *Middle Platonism and the Seventh Epistle*, Phronesis 28 (1983), 75 ff., argues *ex silentio* that the puzzling philosophical digression (*Ep.* VII 340–345c) is a Middle Platonist interpolation because Plutarch (*De E* 389F ff. and *De def. or.* 427A ff.)—or should we say, as I believe, the tradition followed by Plutarch?—, in his listings of pentadic series in Plato in which every passage that can be somehow used is pressed into service, omits the pentad of the excursus (ὄνομα, λόγος, εἴδωλον, ἐπιστήμη, and the πέμπτον). But this argument fails; Plutarch also both times omits to mention the pentad of the mathematical sciences *Rep.* VII 522–31.— The new Teubneriana, *Platonis epistulae* rec. J. Moore-Blunt, Leipzig 1985, is most useful for its upper apparatus.

[156] *GdA* V, 487–512; no differences with ¹V, 500–25.

[157] Elsewhere (*ibid.*, 500 n. 2), he adds the *Fourth* and the *Tenth*.

[158] *Ibid.*, 487 f. n. 4.

Remarkably enough, Meyer—apart from occasional exclamations[159]—
provides no arguments, let alone proofs, for the *Letters* being genuine;[160]
his facts turn out to be factoids. That Plutarch believed them to be genuine
is not to the point, because in his *Alexander* he relied on the *Correspondence*
between Alexander and Aristotle. However, for the political historian it
should be irrelevant whether or not the letters (esp. the *Seventh* and *Eighth*)
are genuine; he is perfectly entitled to use them with caution, in different
ways, as historical documents even if they were fabricated by later Plato-
nists, the *Seventh* and the *Eighth* presumably by a member (or two different
members) of the Old Academy, some of the others most certainly at a
much later date. But Meyer clearly *wants* practically the whole corpus to
be genuine, because only the assumption that it is permits him to describe
from a privileged vantage-point (i.e. using the accounts of an eye-witness)
the impact of "Ideen" on political history and their tragic conversion into
their opposite.[161] From now on "hat die Nation politisch alle Bedeutung
verloren;"[162] this sad statement constitutes Meyer's verdict on the history of Greece as pronounced on the final page of what was to remain his
final volume.

There is need to follow out the familiar story of the Sicilian disaster in
detail. One or two points may be mentioned. Heraclides' murder on
Dion's orders is said to be in accordance with Platonic morality:

---

[159] *Ibid.*, 496 n. 2: "Die entscheidende Szene hat Plato ep. 3, 318c. 319.7, 348. 349
mit lebendigster Anschaulichkeit geschildert: das soll ein Fälscher erfunden haben!" Why
not? Plato's dialogues (just as the Homeric epics, for instance, or any number of Greek
tragedies) are full of splendid and lively scenes that are entirely fictional and, qua fiction,
entirely convincing. The author of the *Letter* may have learned the trick from Plato, and
he may have used Plato the way Plato used Socrates.

[160] In *Caesar*, "Beil. II" (558 ff.), "Sallusts politische Broschüren an Caesar," we at
least find an extensive argument in favour of authenticity on internal and historical
grounds: the two pamphlets could only have been written at the moment they purport to
have been written. E. Norden, moreover, assured Meyer that he could prove them
genuine on purely philological grounds (*ibid.*, 560 n. 1). Note that Meyer puts these two
pieces on a par with the *Correspondence* between Cicero and Brutus and Plato's *Letters*
("*ibid.*, 559: ... das Problem liegt vielmehr ebenso wie bei der jetzt glücklich überwundenen Anzweiflung des Briefwechsels zwischen Cicero und Brutus oder bei den Briefen
Platos ..."). Another interesting case is provided by his somewhat reluctant acceptance
of the fragments of the *Letters* of Cornelia which earlier he had rejected as spurious; see
H.U. Instinsky, *Zur Echtheitsfrage der Brieffragmente der Cornelia, Mutter der Gracchen*, Chiron 1
(1971), 177 ff., also for references to Meyer's utterances. Instinsky's paper is important
for its acute and subtle analysis of the intricacies of the general question concerned with
the being genuine or spurious of documents of this nature. I am grateful to Professor
J. von Ungern-Sternberg for the references to *Caesar* and to Instinsky's paper.

[161] Cf. above, text to n. 9 and to n. 14.

[162] *GdA* V, 154.

"den unverbesserlichen Bürger aus der menschlichen Gesellschaft hinwegzutilgen, ist die Pflicht des wahren Staatsmanns."[163]

Meyer admits that this highly ethical act did not strengthen Dion's political position:

"es mag ihm [*scil.*, Dion] zum Bewusstsein gekommen sein, dass die Kluft zwischen der Theorie und der Praxis unüberbrückbar sei."[164]

The *Seventh Letter* in which [Plato] gave the murdered Dion's idealistic followers the advice they had allegedly asked for,[165] according to Meyer, is an "offener Brief."[166] Such a justificatory open letter need not have been written by its presumed author. At any rate, because Meyer's grounds for accepting most or even all of the Platonic *Letters* as genuine clearly are ideological and private rather than historical or scholarly, the appeal to the authority of the great ancient historian in favour of their authenticity in my view does nothing to further the cause of those who want to accept one of them, or even more than one.

---

[163] *Ibid.*, 508. Against this absurd suggestion see J.H. Thiel, *Rond het Syracusaanse experiment*, Med. Kon. Ned. Ak. Afd. Lett. N.R. 4.5, Amsterdam 1941. It makes for even more painful reading today.

[164] *Ibid.*, 509.

[165] *Ibid.*, 510.

[166] *Ibid.*, 511. So Meyer, not Wilamowitz invented this caption. R. Thurnher, *Der siebte Platonbrief. Versuch einer umfassenden philosophischen Interpretation*, Meisenheim am Glan 1975, 9 n. 43, is mistaken.

BEAT NÄF

EDUARD MEYERS GESCHICHTSTHEORIE. ENTWICKLUNG UND ZEITGENÖSSISCHE REAKTIONEN[1]

Im Frühjahr 1879 erhielt Meyer vom Cotta-Verlag die Anfrage, ob er bereit sei, ein Handbuch der Alten Geschichte zu schreiben. Nach anfänglichem Zögern sagte Meyer zu: Es schwebe ihm die "Anlage des Heerenschen Handbuchs" vor, die freilich zu erweitern und umzuarbeiten sei. Es kann sein, dass der Ansatz Arnold Hermann Ludwig Heerens, von den materiellen Bedürfnissen der Menschen auszugehen, dazu beitrug, dass Meyers Interesse sich auf die in der Einleitung angesprochene Anthropologie richtete. Entscheidender war wahrscheinlich die Auseinandersetzung mit Darwin, dessen Entwicklungslehre Meyer akzeptierte, und mit der Sprachgeschichte, wie sie sich in einem 1874 gehaltenen Vortrag über "Die Anfänge menschlicher Entwicklung" zeigt.[2]

In seiner Einleitung zur "Geschichte des Alterthums" geht Meyer von diesen Überlegungen aus. An den Anfang setzt er das Vorhandensein des Menschen, der Sprache hat und niemals isoliert lebt, weil er als φύσει πολιτικὸν ζῷον nur in einem grösseren staatlichen Verbande leben kann. Nachdem Meyer die These von der Priorität des Staates ausgeführt hat, skizziert er die Entstehung des Kultus, der Religion, der Bedeutung der Tradition, der Kriegführung, des Rechts, des Adels, des nationalen Staates, der moralischen Anschauungen und der Wirtschaft. Von besonderer Bedeutung ist seine Theorie von der Entstehung der Religion. Die Religion sei entwicklungsgeschichtlich jünger als der Staat. Ihre Wurzeln lägen im Kultus. Der Kultus wiederum habe sich daraus ergeben, dass der Mensch allmählich versucht habe, seine Aussenwelt zu beeinflussen: "Da nun die Menschen überall von der Aussenwelt abhängig sind, suchen sie diese in ihr herrschenden Mächte zu beeinflussen (...). So entstehen die Anfänge des religiösen Cultus, Zauberformeln, Opfer, Gebete." (4) Diese ganze Skizze nennt Meyer "Elemente der Anthropologie." Sie hat offenbar zunächst einmal die Aufgabe, diejenigen Zeiten zu beschreiben, die Meyer in seiner "Geschichte des Alterthums"

---

[1] Dieser Aufsatz entstand auf Anregung der Eduard-Meyer-Tagung in Bad Homburg. Der Text wurde dort nicht diskutiert.
[2] Christhard Hoffmann: "Die Selbsterziehung des Historikers. Zur intellektuellen Entwicklung des jungen Eduard Meyer (1855–1879)," Beitrag zum Eduard-Meyer-Colloquium.

nicht behandelt, weil sie dieser vorausliegen. Darüber hinaus aber werden hier anthropologische Konstanten und überall vorkommende Entwicklungsstufen gezeichnet.

Das Verhältnis zwischen Geschichte und Anthropologie wird folgendermassen definiert: "Während die Anthropologie die allgemeinen Grundzüge menschlicher Entwickelung zu erforschen, die ihn ihnen herrschenden Gesetze darzulegen sucht, setzt die Geschichte ihre Ergebnisse als gegeben voraus. Die Geschichte beschäftigt sich niemals mit dem Menschen, dem Staate, dem Volke im allgemeinen, sondern stets mit einem räumlich und zeitlich bestimmten Volke, das unter dem Einfluss nicht allgemeiner Gesetze, sondern bestimmter, für den einzelnen Fall gegebener Verhältnisse steht. Daher hat die Geschichte zunächst das Vorhandensein einer Überlieferung zur äusseren Voraussetzung. Nach den Anfängen eines Volkes hat die Geschichte niemals zu fragen; da, wo die Kunde beginnt, setzt sie ein ..." (11). Weil sich die Geschichte also mit bestimmten Menschen, Staaten oder Völkern befasst, hat sie einen anderen Gegenstand. Obwohl sie nicht Gesetze darlegen will, müssen aber die anthropologischen Konstanten und Entwicklungsstufen auch in der Geschichte zu bezeichnen sein.

Für Meyer ist Geschichte die Beschäftigung mit dem Individuellen. Das macht, wie er schreibt, das "innere Wesen der Geschichte" aus. Mit Individuellem sind Menschen oder Völker gemeint. Das Individuelle differenziere sich in der Geschichte fortwährend. Dabei stünde es im Konflikt mit der Macht der Tradition und mit den Entwicklungsgesetzen (14). Es würden sich drei Typen der geschichtlichen Entwicklung zeigen: Erstickung der Individualität und Ende der Geschichte; Ausbildung eines festen Typus—Meyer denkt an die Geschichte der Ägypter und an den Islam—; übermässiger Durchbruch der Individualität wie in der französischen Revolution, was alle Bedingungen individuellen Lebens aufhebe und die Nation der "Herrschaft des Naturgesetzes" unterwerfe. Innerhalb der Grenzen, die durch diese extremen Typen der Entwicklung gegeben sind, sieht Meyer die unendliche Mannigfaltigkeit der Geschichte, wie sie sich durch das Zusammenwirken von Zufall und freiem Willen ergibt.

Nach einem Abschnitt über quellenkundliche Fragen äussert sich Meyer zum Charakter der Geschichtsschreibung. "Alle Geschichtsschreibung ist nothwendig subjectiv ..." (19). Objektiv seien nur die ungeordneten Tatsachen und das wirkliche Leben der Gegenwart. Deshalb müsse der Historiker von der Gegenwart ausgehen, d.h. der Gegenwart die für die Darstellung notwendigen Ideen und leitenden Gesichtspunkte entnehmen. Geschichtsschreibung sei "Darstellung und Beurtheilung der Vergangenheit im Lichte der Gegenwart" (19).

Den Schluss der Einleitung bildet eine Epochengliederung. Von den zwei grossen Kulturkreisen des ostasiatischen Raumes und der Mittelmeervölker wendet sich Meyer dem zweiten zu. In der Geschichte der Mittelmeervölker werden eine vorderasiatisch-ägyptische Gesamtkultur und eine griechisch-römische Kultur unterschieden. Das Schicksal der vorderasiatisch-ägyptischen Kultur sei politisch das Misslingen eines Gesamtstaates und geistig der Stillstand gewesen. Hellas habe es nicht zu politischer Dauerhaftigkeit gebracht, das sei Rom vorbehalten gewesen, in dem freilich in der späten Kaiserzeit nach einer ''zweihundertjährigen kaum getrübten Friedensperiode'' das nationale Leben in der Nivellierung und Interesselosigkeit erstickt sei.

Diese geschichtstheoretische Konzeption blieb im grossen und ganzen erhalten. Ihre Geschlossenheit und Einfachheit vertrug sich ausgezeichnet mit der grossen Arbeitskraft Meyers; sie scheint den schöpferischen Bedürfnissen genügend Raum gegeben zu haben und zugleich den pädagogischen Intentionen, aber auch dem Rationalismus Meyers entsprochen zu haben. Die Reaktionen der Zeitgenossen waren eher zurückhaltend. Auf allgemeine Anerkennung stiess die ''Geschichte des Alterthums'' als ganzes, obwohl Ulrich von Wilamowitz-Moellendorff später geschrieben hat, dass die Form des Werkes, das in Paragraphen gegliedert war, ungünstig gewirkt habe.[3] Aber das änderte nichts am gesamthaft positiven Urteil, das sich beispielsweise in Curt Wachsmuths ''Einleitung in das Studium der alten Geschichte,'' aber auch bei einem Althistoriker wie Robert von Pöhlmann zeigt, der gegenüber einer typologischen Betrachtung sehr viel aufgeschlossener war, mit Meyer aber in der ''universalgeschichtlichen'' Auffassung, der Gegenwartsbezogenheit und der Ablehnung der philologisch-antiquarischen Auffassung übereinstimmte.[4] Die geschichtstheoretische Einleitung wurde in den meisten Rezensionen vermerkt, jedoch ohne sonderliche Begeisterung. Als überflüssig erachtete sie Heinrich Gelzer.[5] Kritisch äusserte sich Jakob Mähly, der an die Theo-

---

[3] Süddeutsche Monatshefte 22 (1924/25) 55.

[4] Curt Wachsmuth: Einleitung in das Studium der alten Geschichte, Leipzig 1895, 66, 363, 402, 463, 564. Robert von Pöhlmann: Aus Altertum und Gegenwart. Gesammelte Abhandlungen, München 1895, 34, Anm. 1;—: Griechische Geschichte und Quellenkunde, 5. Aufl., München 1914 (Handbuch der Altertumswissenschaft, Bd. 3, 4. Abt.), 8 f.

[5] HZ 61 (1889) 116 (die einleitenden Abschnitte seien nur ein ''Tribut'' an die ''Handbuchmanier''); Neue Jahrbücher für Philologie und Pädagogik 55 (1885) 1 f. (''hat nicht vielleicht Duncker den richtigern weg eingeschlagen, welcher uns ohne anthropologische und prähistorische vorbetrachtungen gleich mit der ägyptischen geschichte auf den boden der thatsachen stellt?''). Eher positive Nennungen der Geschichtstheorie dagegen bei Georg Ebers, einem wichtigen Lehrer Meyers, im Literarischen Centralblatt (1884) 1664, und bei Adolf Holm in der Berliner philologischen Wochenschrift 4 (1884)

rie vom Primat des Staates nicht glauben wollte. Auch über den Ausschluss der indischen Geschichte zeigte er sich nicht ganz glücklich.[6]
Adolf Bauer, der im übrigen Meyers Werk hoch einschätzte, setzte sich
für eine Ausweitung der Geschichte gegen rückwärts ein: Die Begrenzung
der Geschichte gegen die Anthropologie und Vorgeschichte sei zu eng.[7]
Auch der Rezensent der "Allgemeinen Zeitung," vermutlich Friedrich
Ratzel, kritisierte die Abgrenzung zur Anthropologie, wobei er dem Verfasser zubilligte, das Bedenkliche gespürt zu haben und sich nicht streng
an seinen engen Begriff der Geschichte gehalten zu haben.[8]

Gründe für die Formulierung der Geschichtstheorie von 1884

Ein unbekannter Rezensent glaubte, die Einleitung stütze sich auf Johann
Gustav Droysen.[9] Das trifft nicht zu, auch wenn man davon ausgehen
darf, dass Meyer Droysens Historik kannte. Die Annahme ist nur gerade
verständlich, weil Droysen der einzige aus der Altertumswissenschaft
stammende Autor war, der eine viel gelesene und einigermassen akzeptierte geschichtstheoretische Arbeit vorgelegt hatte. Was Johann Jakob
Bachofen, Jacob Burckhardt oder Friedrich Nietzsche unter "Geschichte" verstanden, wurde von den Althistorikern mit Misstrauen zur Kenntnis genommen. 1858 erschien für die Hörer seiner Vorlesung bestimmt
Droysens 27 Seiten zählendes Heftchen "Grundriss der Historik," das
1862 noch einmal gedruckt wurde, 1868 dann der Öffentlichkeit vorlag
und in zweiter Auflage 1875, in dritter Auflage 1882 publiziert wurde.
Grob gesehen bestehen zwischen Droysen und Meyer zwar Gemeinsamkeiten, was die hohe Wertschätzung der Staatlichkeit und die Betonung
des Individuellen in der Geschichte betrifft. Bei beiden Autoren macht
sich auch der Versuch bemerkbar—trotz ihrer Vorbehalte gegenüber
Gesetzmässigkeiten—, von bestimmten Konstanten in der Geschichte zu
sprechen. Für Droysen gibt es neben der Methodik (Heuristik, Kritik, Interpretation) auch eine Systematik, in der die geschichtliche Arbeit nach
ihren Stoffen, Formen, Arbeitern und Zwecken dargestellt wird.
Bei Droysen hat Geschichte sogar die Züge eines geordneten Systems.
Droysens "Systematik" lässt sich aber nicht mit Meyers "Anthropologie" vergleichen. Sie ist nicht vom Staat her aufgebaut, und Meyer betont

---

1510 (interessante Einleitung, zu allgemein, bei einigen Dingen Übereinstimmung, An-
deutung von Vorbehalten). Keine Nennung der Geschichtstheorie z.B. bei Eberhard
Schrader in: Zeitschrift für Assyriologie 1 (1886), 71–84.
  [6] Blätter für literarische Unterhaltung 1 (1885) 125 f.
  [7] GGA (1884) 1003.
  [8] (Erste) Beilage zur Allgemeinen Zeitung, Nr. 286, 14.10.1884, 4217 f.
  [9] Grenzboten (1884) 386.

die subjektiven Voraussetzungen der Geschichtsschreibung viel stärker.

Zu den wenigen grundlegenden Werken aus der Zeit vor 1884, die einen breiteren Konsens fanden, und mit dem man Meyers Einleitung vergleichen könnte, gehört auch August Boeckhs (1785–1867) "Encyclopädie und Methodologie der philologischen Wissenschaften," die auf jahrzehntelangen Vorlesungen beruht, aber erst 1877 erschien—sie wurde von Ernst Bratuschek herausgegeben. Obwohl Boeckhs "Encyclopädie" Platz für alle Lebensäusserungen einer Kultur hat, konnte sie jedoch nicht alle Althistoriker ganz befriedigen, denn Boeckh ging von der Philologie aus, die er als "Erkenntnis des Erkannten" verstand. Das meint zwar die Rekonstruktion sämtlicher bisherigen Vorstellungen des menschlichen Geistes und erlaubt eine universale Geschichte, wie sie von den meisten Althistorikern angestrebt wurde, aber nicht unter dem Gesichtspunkt historischer Entwicklung. Auch wollte sich die Alte Geschichte von der Philologie lösen, und das gilt ebenfalls für Meyer (v.a. in seiner Auseinandersetzung mit Wilamowitz). Wichtiger für sie waren deshalb die Arbeiten von Historikern, auch wenn diese primär historischen, und nicht theoretischen Charakter hatten. Theodor Mommsen war dabei die wohl einflussreichste Gestalt.

Die Besprechungen von Meyers Einleitungen sahen grösstenteils die Notwendigkeit methodologischer Studien nicht ein. Andererseits bestanden aber Bedürfnisse nach solchen Studien, und sie wurden auch gefordert. 1889 erschien Ernst Bernheims "Lehrbuch der Historischen Methode." Bernheim konstatierte dort für die ganze Geschichtswissenschaft: "Die theoretische Darstellung der Methode hat nicht Schritt halten können mit dieser rapiden Entwicklung des Jahrhunderts, welche wir zu schildern hatten, geschweige dass sie derselben wie zu anderen Zeiten vorausgeeilt wäre." (148)

Das Bedürfnis nach theoretischer Darstellung der Methode war vorhanden, nahm zu und führte auch zur Publikation zahlreicher theoretischer Werke sowie von Werken, welche die Entwicklung der Geschichtswissenschaften zeichneten. Die Gründe für dieses zunehmende Bedürfnis sind vielfältig und sicher nicht nur davon abhängig, dass wenig theoretische Literatur vorhanden war. In diesem Zusammenhang ist auch die Einleitung Meyers zu sehen.

Zunächst ging mit der Entfaltung der Altertumswissenschaften und der Alten Geschichte ein Unbehagen einher, das sogar von Theodor Mommsen formuliert wurde und sich nicht nur bei Aussenseitern wie Friedrich Nietzsche oder Jacob Burckhardt findet. 1895 klagte Mommsen: "Aber die Besten von uns empfinden es, dass wir Fachmänner geworden sind." Zeitlich voraus gingen die zahlreichen Unmutsbekundungen gegen eine allzu formalistische Philologie, wie sie in der Nachfolge Gottfried

Hermanns, Karl Lachmanns und Friedrich Ritschls ausgeübt wurde.
1852 meinte Wilhelm Herbst: ''. . . die classische Periode der Altertumswissenschaft gehört der Vergangenheit an . . .'' 1860 konstatierte Adolf
Kirchhoff in seiner Antrittsrede an der Berliner Akademie, das Streben
nach dem Grossen und Ganzen habe einer Forschung Platz gemacht,
welche sich an das Detail zu verlieren drohe. Ein Zeitalter der Epigonen
habe begonnen: ''Ich, meine Herren, gehöre zu diesen Epigonen!'' 1888
mahnte Rudolf Hirzel die Philologen: ''Die Zeit hat sich von den Philologen abgewandt, weil die Philologen sich von der Zeit abgewandt haben.''
Adolf Bauer warnte in einem Forschungsbericht, der 1899 erschien,
Übersicht und Anschaulichkeit des Vergangenen könnten durch die
positivistische Forschung ''ertötet'' werden.[10]   .

Dieses Unbehagen hing nicht nur mit dem Wachstum der Wissenschaft
zusammen, sondern auch mit der zunehmenden Erschütterung der Stellung der klassischen Bildung. Hingegen besteht wohl kein Zusammenhang mit dem Kulturpessimismus des ausgehenden Jahrhunderts. Die
Vorgänge im Bildungswesen waren Gegenstand tiefer Beunruhigung und
zahlreicher Diskussionen unter den Altertumswissenschaftlern. Gymnasien und Universitäten wandten sich mehr und mehr von der Antike ab.
Wilhelm II. sah 1890 in der klassischen Bildung keinen Garanten einer
vaterländischen Erziehung mehr: ''Wir müssen als Grundlage das
Deutsche nehmen; wir sollen junge Deutsche erziehen, und nicht junge
Griechen und Römer.''[11]

Die Altertumswissenschaftler selbst waren zwar teilweise bereit, das
''Dogma vom klassischen Altertum'' aufzugeben. Nicht zufällig erschien
Paul Nerrlichs Kritik an diesem Dogma im Jahre 1894 (''Das Dogma
vom klassischen Altertum in seiner geschichtlichen Entwicklung''). Dafür
suchte man aber nach neuen Möglichkeiten, die Beschäftigung mit dem
Altertum aufzuwerten.

Zu diesem Anliegen mischte sich eine weitere Auseinandersetzung.

---

[10] Theodor Mommsen: Reden und Aufsätze, Berlin 1905, 198. Wilhelm Herbst: Das
classische Alterthum in der Gegenwart. Eine geschichtliche Betrachtung, Leipzig 1852,
13. Kirchhoff zit. nach O. Schroeder, in: Jahresbericht über die Fortschritte der klassischen Altertumswissenschaft 141 (1908) 166. Rudolf Hirzel: Ueber die Stellung der classischen Philologie in der Gegenwart. Akademische Antrittsrede gehalten in Jena am 5.
Mai 1888, Leipzig 1888, 34. Adolf Bauer: Die Forschungen zur griechischen Geschichte
1888–1898 verzeichnet und besprochen, München 1899, 413 f.
[11] Friedrich Paulsen: Geschichte des gelehrten Unterrichts auf den deutschen Schulen
und Universitäten vom Ausgang des Mittelalters bis zur Gegenwart. Mit besonderer
Rücksicht auf den klassischen Unterricht, 2. Aufl., Bd. 2, Leipzig 1897, 592. Georg G.
Iggers vertritt die Auffassung, dass der Kulturpessimismus sehr wohl einen Einfluss auf
die Geschichtswissenschaft ausübte und dort ein Krisenbewusstsein erzeugte (vgl. Georg
G. Iggers: Deutsche Geschichtswissenschaft. Eine Kritik der traditionellen Geschichtsauffassung von Herder bis zur Gegenwart, München 1971).

Mehr und mehr hatte man sich mit den Ideen mehrerer Wissenschaften und theoretischer Ansätze zu befassen, die mit eigenen Ansprüchen konkurrierten. Dieser Konkurrenz gemeinsam war die Orientierung an Modellen, welche den Naturwissenschaften nahestanden. Bereits Johann Gustav Droysen hatte sich mit Henry Thomas Buckle auseinandergesetzt, wobei Buckle aber in aussichtsloser Position stand. Doch das Verhältnis änderte sich. Es ist bezeichnend, dass Ernst Bernheims 1889 erschienenes "Lehrbuch" das Verhältnis der Geschichtswissenschaft zur Soziologie, Anthropologie, Ethnographie, Ethnologie und Naturwissenschaft eindringlich untersucht und dabei einleitend bemerkt: "Es ist wiederum der Mangel an eindringender Beschäftigung mit den Grundbegriffen unserer Wissenschaft seitens der Historiker selbst und die daher rührende Lauheit und Unsicherheit in der Vertretung derselben nach aussen hin, wodurch verschuldet wird, dass die Geschichtswissenschaft sich den übergreifendsten Grenzverletzungen von seiten benachbarter und fernstliegender Disciplinen ausgesetzt sieht. Die einen rechnen die Geschichte zur Philologie, die anderen erklären sie für eine Naturwissenschaft" (59). Nachdem die Auseinandersetzung der Neukantianer um Wilhelm Windelband und Heinrich Rickert sowie der Lamprechtstreit begonnen hatten, und nachdem auch der Einfluss des westeuropäischen Positivismus mehr und mehr sichtbar wurde, fühlte sich die traditionelle Geschichtswissenschaft angegriffen. Eine Flut von Artikeln wurde ausgelöst, auch die Alte Geschichte beteiligte sich an den Diskussionen. Ähnliche Diskussionen spielten sich in anderen Fächern ab, erinnert sei nur an den "Methodenstreit" in der deutschen Volkswirtschaftslehre.

Meyers Antwort war formuliert, von den Zeitgenossen 1884 in ihrer Bedeutung aber nicht erkannt, wie man es anhand der Rezensionen ersehen kann. Für Meyer nicht entscheidend war das Unbehagen über die Erstarrung der Wissenschaft in Lebensferne, Spezialistentum, erdrükkender antiquarischer Stoffülle oder abwegigen philologischen Fragen. Hingegen waren die Begründungen für eine universale Geschichtswissenschaft auf historischer Basis aufrechtzuerhalten und zu erneuern, und das gegenüber den Ansprüchen der Philologie, den an den neuen generalisierenden Modellen ausgerichteten Vorstellungen sowie den Anforderungen der Gegenwart auf die Brauchbarkeit der Geschichte. Meyer schuf sich mit der Verankerung der Geschichtsdarstellung in der zugleich die Gegenwart spiegelnden Subjektivität des Historikers den Freiraum, um objektiv wirkende Historie zu entwerfen und zu schreiben. Die Geschichtskonzeption Meyers gründet auf diesem Paradox, das sich freilich auch bei vielen anderen Historikern findet. Es ist die Konzeption einer hauptsächlich vom Politischen ausgehenden Geschichte, in der zwar dem Individuellen der Vorrang gegeben wird, die aber auch mit Hilfe generalisierender Vorstellungen—der Anthropologie—dargestellt wird. Entscheidend ist trotz aller Quellenkritik der Glaube an das Vorhandensein von erkennbaren Fakten, die vom Historiker gemäss ihrer historischen Bedeutsamkeit in einen Entwicklungszusammenhang gestellt werden können. Der Entwicklungszusammenhang ist für Meyer zwar ein Resultat der Subjektivität, in der Darstellung ist von dieser Einschränkung aber gar nichts zu merken.

So entsteht eine gegenüber der Philologie einerseits und den neuen sozialwissenschaftlichen Ansätzen andererseits klar abgegrenzte Geschichtswissenschaft, die sich als "universal" bezeichnet—ohne es freilich zu sein; und die den Anspruch erhebt, die Alte Welt so darstellen zu können, dass die Darstellung richtig ist und auch ohne den Glanz des nun verpönten Klassizismus Bedeutung für die Gegenwart hat.

Die Geschichtstheorie von 1902: Weiterentwicklung im Schatten des Lamprechtstreites

Von den bisherigen Feststellungen her ist es nicht erstaunlich, mit welcher Selbstsicherheit Meyer in der Kontroverse mit dem Nationalökonomen Karl Bücher über die Einordnung der antiken Wirtschaft in die allgemeine Wirtschaftsgeschichte 1895 und 1898 behauptete, die antike Wirtschaft habe moderne Züge getragen.[12] Am 14. Juni 1902 referierte Meyer dann im Hallischen Vortrags-Kränzchen zu einem Thema, das in erweiterter Form unter dem Titel "Zur Theorie und Methodik der Geschichte. Geschichtsphilosophische Untersuchungen" im selben Jahr erschien. Die Publikation besteht aus drei Teilen, von denen der erste der längste ist: Es ist eine Polemik gegen den nun im Unterschied zu 1884 deutlich erkannten Gegner, welcher—gemäss Meyer—der Geschichte die Aufgabe stellen würde, Gesetze zu entdecken und in den Einzelvorgängen nachzuweisen und sie so dem glänzenden Vorbild der Naturwissenschaften anzugleichen.

"Geschichte ist keine systematische Wissenschaft." So heisst der apodiktische erste Satz. Es brauche keine Vereinheitlichung der historischen Methode, vielmehr folge die Praxis des Historikers eigenen Geboten. Wohl könne man das Äusserliche der historischen Technik methodisch einüben, die Hauptsache aber, werde nur "aus dem Innern des Forschers heraus geboren" (2). Ernst Bernheims Lehrbuch geht Meyer zu weit, erst recht Paul Barth, Kurt Breysig, Hans Ferdinand Helmolt, Friedrich

12 Die Texte der Kontroverse enthält auch Moses I. Finley (ed.): The Bücher-Meyer Controversy, New York 1979. Vgl. v.a. Mario Mazza: "Il dibattito sull'economia antica nella storiografia tedesca tra otto e novecento," in: Società e storia 29 (1985) 507–546.

Ratzel, und Karl Lamprecht, gegen den sich der Hauptangriff richtet. Lamprecht wird vorgeworfen, den Reichtum der Geschichte in Formeln zu zwängen. Statt mit den Individuen beschäftige er sich mit den Massen, um danach mit den falschen Gesetzmässigkeiten der Massenpsychologie zu operieren; dafür verkenne er die bestimmende Potenz des freien Willens und die Bedeutung des Zufalls. In Lamprechts Stufentheorie sieht Meyer die falschen vereinfachenden Schemen, die er bereits in der Bücher-Kontroverse den Nationalökonomen vorgeworfen hatte. Schliesslich kritisiert er, dass Lamprecht in den Nationen die massgebenden gesellschaftlichen Einheiten sieht, denn Nationen seien Produkte der Geschichte und nichts Gegebenes.

Bereits im ersten Teil entwickelt Meyer seine Auffassung vom Zufall und vom freien Willen. Zufall ist für Meyer eine Kategorie für Erscheinungen, die zu kompliziert sind, als dass sie bezüglich all ihrer kausalen Verursachungen erklärt werden können. Der freie Wille setze die Zwecke, nach denen Vorgänge zu gestalten seien. Er ist verknüpft mit den ''Ideen'', den ''bestimmten dominirenden Vorstellungen und Forderungen, welche die Menschen einer gegebenen Epoche in weitem Umfang beherrschen und Denken, Ziele und Handeln der einzelnen Individuen bestimmen'' (5).

Im zweiten Teil sollen Wesen und Aufgabe der Geschichte theoretisch genauer erfasst werden. Die erste Aufgabe des Historikers sei die ''Ermittelung von Thatsachen'' (35). Untersuchungswürdig ist das Historische: ''. . . historisch ist, was wirksam ist oder gewesen ist.'' (36) Die Auswahl beruht somit auf einem von der Gegenwart ausgehenden Interesse (37). Als historisch nicht wirksam bezeichnet Meyer die Geschichte primitiver Völker—''mancher Negerreiche u.s.w.'' (47). Bei der Bedeutung der historischen Persönlichkeiten unterscheidet er historische Bedeutsamkeit und geniale Grösse. Beides decke sich selten (49–54).

Zudem sei Geschichte nur möglich in Beziehung auf eine menschliche Gemeinschaft. Weil aber der politische Verband, der Staat, die massgebende Organisation sei, müsse die politische Geschichte das ''Centrum der Geschichte bleiben'' (39).

Die historische Forschung müsse von den Wirkungen auf die Ursachen schliessen. Meyer betont aber die Bedeutung, welche dabei der ''historische Sinn'' (43) habe. Die Komplexität der Kausalreihen könne nicht ohne subjektive Elemente dargestellt werden, das Primäre sei das erkennende Individuum—wie sogar in den Naturwissenschaften (45). Psychologische Erklärungen will Meyer nicht zulassen, weil für ihn der Wille des Individuums nicht weiter analysierbar ist.

Der letzte Abschnitt grenzt die Geschichte von der Philologie ab, denn diese behandle ''ihr Object nicht als werdend und historisch wirkend, sondern als seiend" (55). Aus dem gleichen Grunde wird die Biographie von der Geschichte getrennt.

Die Reaktionen auf Meyers Buch waren geteilt. "Unter den zahlreichen über diesen Gegenstand erschienenen Aufsätzen ist dieses . . . Schriftchen eines der besten, wenn nicht überhaupt das beste," schrieb der Althistoriker Adolf Bauer und erklärte vor allem seine vollkommene Zustimmung zu den über die "modernen Theorien" vorgetragenen Ansichten.[13] Georg von Below, der 1898 in der "Historischen Zeitschrift" Meyer wegen seiner Rede von "geschichtlicher Notwendigkeit" kritisiert hatte, nahm die Publikation mit Sympathie zur Kenntnis.[14] Zu weit in der Verteidigung des Individuellen in der Geschichte ging Meyer Carlo Cipolla ("Parmi che qui si vada da un eccesso all'altro.") und Alfred Vierkandt, der Meyer als Verfechter des "Individualismus und des Irrationalismus in der Geschichte" bezeichnete, wobei aber das "letzte Wort" damit "schwerlich" gesprochen sei (das Urteil von Vierkandt über Meyers Einleitung zur 2. Auflage der "Geschichte des Altertums" fiel dann positiver aus, wohl weil ihm das dort entworfene Netz der allgemeinen kulturgeschichtlichen Begriffe besser gefiel).[15] In der fünften und sechsten Auflage von Ernst Bernheims "Lehrbuch der Historischen Methode und der Geschichtsphilosophie" (1908) wird Meyer mehrfach kritisiert: Meyer wolle sich auf das historisch Wirksame beschränken (in diesem Punkt treffe Friedrich Ratzels, vor allem aber Max Webers Kritik zu), er habe wegen seiner Konzentration auf das Individuelle, den Staat und die sogenannten Kulturvölker einen zu engen Geschichtsbegriff und er sehe die Geschichte als Kunst statt als Wissenschaft.[16] Friedrich Ratzel, auf den sich Bernheim unter anderem bezog, und dessen Ansatz von Meyer abgelehnt wurde, äusserte seine Verwunderung über den ihm wissenschaftlich nicht verständlichen Ausschluss der kulturarmen Völker vom historischen Interesse.[17]

Karl Julius Beloch begann ähnlich wie Meyer seine eigene "Griechische Geschichte" mit einer geschichtstheoretischen Einleitung, die sich auch mit Meyer auseinandersetzt. Kürzlich, schreibt Beloch, habe "einer unserer bedeutendsten Geschichtsforscher gesagt, die Gestaltung, welche Augustus im Jahre 27 v. Chr. dem römischen Reiche gege-

---

[13] Berliner philologische Wochenschrift 24 (1904) 560.
[14] HZ 94 (1905) 449–453 (die Kritik von 1898 im Bd. 81, S. 238, Anm. 1).
[15] Carlo Cipolla in: Rivista Storica Italiana 20 (1903) 289–293, zit. 289. Alfred Vierkandt in: Zeitschrift für Socialwissenschaft 6 (1903) 479 f.; Archiv für die gesamte Psychologie 17 (1910) 81 f.
[16] Ernst Bernheim: Lehrbuch der Historischen Methode und der Geschichtsphilosophie, Leipzig 1908, v.a. 7 mit Anm. 1, 50 mit Anm. 1, 64 mit Anm. 1, 149 mit Anm. 2.
[17] HZ 93 (1904) 21–23.

ben hat, sei 'ausschliesslich ein Ausfluss seines Willens und seiner Individualität' gewesen ....''[18] Belochs geschichtstheoretische Überlegungen gehen einher mit einer massiven Polemik gegen solche personale Geschichtsbetrachtung. Meyer hatte sich in einer Rezension der "Griechischen Geschichte" Belochs bereits 1894 gegen die "starke Betonung der materiellen Grundlagen des Lebens" gewehrt und sich zur umgekehrten Ansicht bekannt, dass die "grosse Entscheidung den "Verlauf der ganzen Culturentwicklung der Welt" bestimmt habe.[19] Die Polemik zwischen den beiden Autoren darf zwar nicht darüber hinwegtäuschen, dass sie viele gemeinsame Auffassungen hatten. Beide formulierten eine Theorie, die besagt, dass persönliche Grösse und historische Wirksamkeit nicht identisch sind. Für beide steht das historisch Wirksame im Vordergrund, wobei für Beloch die kausalen Aspekte noch viel wichtiger sind als für Meyer. Beide bestreiten den Vorrang der Philologie in der Altertumswissenschaft. Hingegen fehlen bei Beloch der Zufall—alles sei kausal erklärbar—und ebenso der freie Willensentscheid, weil auch das Individuum—so Augustus—kausal bedingten Motiven folge. Vor allem auch stand Beloch dem westeuropäischen Positivismus und quantifizierenden Methoden näher, als es Meyer lieb war.

Mit der Bemerkung "Gegenschrift" verzeichnet Marohls Meyer-Bibliographie die Besprechung des Berliner Literaturhistorikers Richard M. Meyer, der sich in einem Aufsatz mit dem Titel "Über die Möglichkeit historischer Gesetze" äusserte.[20] R.M. Meyer sah Natur- und Geisteswissenschaften viel näher beisammen als Ed. Meyer. Zufall und Gesetze gebe es in beiden Bereichen. Einen Unterschied stelle er hinsichtlich der Experimente und der Anwendbarkeit der statistischen Methode fest. Messbarkeit in den Geisteswissenschaften sei aber erreichbar, Gesetzmässigkeiten habe man verschiedentlich nachgewiesen. So hätten die Literaturgeschichte mit den Motiven, Heinrich Wölfflin mit gleichbleibenden Werten in der Kunstgeschichte oder die Massenpsychologie Beispiele dieser Art gegeben. Schliesslich sei zu erwarten, dass man bei der Entwicklung historischer Ideen Gesetzmässigkeiten zeigen könne. Die Philologie verteidigte R.M. Meyer, weil dieser die Induktion und die naturwissenschaftliche Methode des Sammelns, Sichtens und Verarbeitens von alters her näher stünden als der Geschichte. Gerade deshalb fühle er als Philologe sich berufen, auf diesen Weg zu verweisen.

---

[18] Karl Julius Beloch: Griechische Geschichte, 2. Aufl., Bd. 1, 1. Abt., Strassburg 1912, 14.
[19] Literarisches Centralblatt (1894) 109–114, zit. 112 f.
[20] Historische Vierteljahresschrift 6 (1903) 161–174. Vgl. aber die positivere Besprechung der erweiterten Einleitung für die "Geschichte des Alertums" von 1907 in der Zeitschrift für Volkskunde 18 (1908) 226 f. (gesunde Nüchternheit).

Max Webers Kritik an Meyer

Die ausführlichste Auseinandersetzung mit Ed. Meyer stammt von Max Weber.[21] Weber hatte bei der Übernahme des "Archivs für Sozialwissenschaft und Sozialpolitik" als Hauptaufgabe formuliert, die unzählig gewordenen wissenschaftlichen Arbeiten durch eine "wissenschaftliche Synthese gleichsam zu beseelen." Theoretischen Gesichtspunkten sollte besonderes Gewicht zukommen, insbesondere auch der klaren Begriffsbildung: "Denn soweit wir von der Meinung entfernt sind, dass es gelte, den Reichtum des historischen Lebens in Formeln zu zwängen, so entschieden sind wir davon überzeugt, dass nur klare eindeutige Begriffe einer Forschung, welche die spezifische Bedeutung sozialer Kulturerscheinungen ergründen will, die Wege ebnen."[22] Für Weber war die Antike seit seiner römisch-rechtlichen Habilitationsschrift ein wichtiges Interessengebiet. Bereits im Rahmen der Bücher-Meyer Kontroverse hatte sich Weber mit Meyer auseinandergesetzt und—ohne Meyer zu bekämpfen—die grundsätzlich modernisierende Haltung Meyers sowie auch dessen Vernachlässigung sozialer Faktoren abgelehnt. In der Besprechung von Meyers "Theorie und Methodik der Geschichte" zeigen sich ebenfalls grosse Differenzen zwischen Meyer und Weber, die davon herrühren, dass Weber an Meyer sein Programm der klaren Begriffsbildung exemplifiziert, dabei hauptsächlich eine Analyse der Wertbeziehung vornimmt und im wissenschaftstheoretischen Streit eine von Meyer unterschiedliche Position bezieht. Trotz dieser Differenzen bewertet Weber in seinem Aufsatz Meyers Buch als die Äusserung eines "unserer ersten Historiker" (143) oder—an anderer Stelle—eines "hervorragenden Schriftstellers" (144, Anm. 1).

Der Aufsatz beginnt mit der Feststellung, dass Meyer den Bereich seiner Disziplin überschritten und das Gebiet erkenntnistheoretischer Betrachtungen betreten habe. An verschiedenen Formulierungen müsse Anstoss nehmen, wer von der Logik und Erkenntnistheorie her komme. Es sei Meyer zwar zuzustimmen, dass methodologische Studien für die Praxis einen beschränkten Wert hätten, der gegenwärtige Umbruch in der Praxis aber erfordere sie (145). Die Auseinandersetzung Meyers mit Lamprecht wird beiseite gelassen, um gleich zur Kritik von Meyers Theorie zu kommen. Dabei geht es gleich von Beginn an um das Aufzeigen

---

[21] Max Weber: "Kritische Studien auf dem Gebiet der kulturwissenschaftlichen Logik," in: Archiv für Sozialwissenschaft und Sozialpolitik 22 (1906) 143–207 (auch in: Gesammelte Aufsätze zur Wissenschaftslehre, hrsg. von J. Winckelmann, Tübingen 1973, 215–290).

[22] Archiv für Sozialwissenschaft und Sozialpolitik, Neue Folge des Archivs für Soziale Gesetzgebung und Statistik 19 (1904) VI.

von Widersprüchen und Unklarheiten in den Begriffen Meyers. Es ist im folgenden nicht möglich, diese Kritik im Detail zu verfolgen, es können nur ihre allgemeinen Züge herausgearbeitet werden.

Ein erster Kritikpunkt betrifft den Begriff des "Zufalls" (146–148). Während dieser von Meyer aber nicht absolut gedachte Begriff des Zufalls ("Zufall" umfasst auch kausale Bedingtheiten) für die Praxis genügen könne, genüge Meyers Begriff des freien Willens nicht, weil in diesem Begriff ethische Momente und Werturteile nicht klar von der kausalen Betrachtung geschieden seien. Meyer verbinde Willensfreiheit und Verantwortlichkeit des Einzelnen für seine Willensbetätigung. Damit aber— und auch auf Grund von Formulierungen—müsse man annehmen, Meyer wolle Werturteile über die historisch handelnde Persönlichkeit gewinnen. Solche Urteile seien denkbar als Beurteilung des Zwecks, der einem Entschluss zugrunde lag oder als Analyse des Entschlusses im Hinblick auf die Frage, warum der Entschluss im entsprechenden Moment geeignet war, seinen Zweck zu erreichen. In eine Argumentation über historische Kausalität, wie sie Meyer eigentlich wolle, passe freilich nur letzteres (150).

Auf alle Fälle würden bei Meyer Wertung und Erklärung ineinanderfliessen (151). Damit komme er auch zur irrtümlichen Auffassung, dass zugleich einerseits die Willensfreiheit die Geschichte zum Bereiche des Individuellen mache und er andererseits das Handeln der Menschen kausal und rational als notwendig gegeben zu deuten wisse (152 f.).

Bedenklich seien auch die Formulierungen über das Verhältnis zwischen "Allgemeinem" und "Besonderem". In ihnen vermag Weber mehrere Widersprüche aufzuzeigen. Die damit verbundene Ablehnung der Entwicklungstheorien könne Meyer nicht konsequent durchführen (155 f.). Wenn Meyer behaupte, in der Geschichte sei nur das Individuelle konkret, so erscheine aber trotzdem der abstrakte Begriff der "Regel", bei Meyer ein Synonym für "Allgemeines", als konkrete wirkende Kraft (156).

Stark kritisiert wird von Weber Meyers Definition des Objekts der Geschichte: historisch sei, "was wirksam ist und gewesen ist." Meyer berücksichtige zu wenig, dass das historische Interesse Interesse an "Realgründen" und "Erkenntnisgründen" sein könne (159), d.h. an der Wirkung eines Phänomens auf weitere geschichtliche Ereignisse und an dem, was man aus einem Phänomen lernen und auf andere Phänomene übertragen könne. "Erkenntnisgründe" seien gerade so wichtig wie "Realgründe". An verschiedenen Beispielen wird das verdeutlicht, so an den Briefen Goethes an Charlotte von Stein, an denen man in folgender Hinsicht Gehalt zu gewinnen vermöge (167): a) die Briefe könnten als Exemplar einer Gattung und deshalb als Erkenntnismittel ihres generel-

len Wesens genommen werden, b) sei es möglich, sie als charakteristi-
schen Bestandteil eines Kollektivum und deshalb Erkenntnismittel seiner
individuellen Eigenart oder c) als kausalen Bestandteil eines historischen
Zusammenhangs und (168 f.) schliesslich d) als Objekt der Interpretation
und Bewertung zu sehen. Immerhin halte sich Meyer nicht an das, was
er in der Theorie vorbringe, er interessiere sich in der Praxis auch für
Dinge, denen keine historische Wirksamkeit zukomme (163).

Die Stellung der Geschichte im Spannungsfeld zwischen Natur- und
Geisteswissenschaften zeichnet Weber in diesem Zusammenhang so, dass
für die Geschichte zwar individuelle Tatbestände Erkenntnismittel und
Erkenntnisobjekt sind, kausale Beziehungen hingegen nicht Erkenntnis-,
sondern nur Realgrund (162). Meyers Abgrenzungen gegenüber der
Philologie werden genauso abgelehnt wie seine Abgrenzungen gegenüber
der Naturwissenschaft, denn die Geschichte brauche sowohl Zustandsbeschreibungen, wie sie die philologische Methode gibt (170 f., 182), als
auch die Anwendung allgemeiner Sätze auf die historischen Vorgänge
nach Art der Naturwissenschaften. Die Unterschiede zur Naturwissenschaft liegen für Weber in der Untersuchung der Wertbezogenheit.

Webers wissenschaftstheoretische Analyse wird hier zur Analyse der
Wertbeziehung, d.h. der wissenschaftstheoretischen Bedeutung des wis-
senschaftlichen Interesses, das sich durch die Beziehung zu Werten der
Kultur konstituiert. Meyers Ansatz wirft er vor, den Unterschied
zwischen Wert- und Kausalanalyse nicht zu machen und sich zudem auf
die kausale Analyse zu beschränken. Meyer habe einen zu engen Begriff
des historischen Interesses, wenn er dieses nur von dem, was in der
Gegenwart noch wirksam sei, ausgehen lasse. Freilich tue er das in der
Praxis auch nicht (176–181, vgl. auch 184 f.). Meyers Begriff des
Historischen als des Wirksamen fehle die logische Scheidung des "primä-
ren" historischen Objekts, des von einem wertenden Interesse ausgewählten individuellen Kulturindividuums und der "sekundären" historischen
Tatsachen, der Ursachen, welche diesem Individuum im kausalen
Regress zugerechnet würden (181).

Diese Zurechnung erfolge mit dem prinzipiellen Ziel, " 'objektiv' als
Erfahrungswahrheit gültig zu sein" (181)—damit lehnt Weber Meyers
Auffassung von der subjektiven Historie klar ab, auch wenn die Wertbeziehung Subjektives an sich hat. Weber geht es offensichtlich auch um
den Nachweis, dass das Fach Geschichte einen wissenschaftlichen Charakter hat.

In einem zweiten Teil seines Aufsatzes widmet sich Weber dem Thema
"Objektive Möglichkeit und adäquate Verursachung in der historischen
Kausalbetrachtung" (185–207). In diesem Teil geht es weniger um eine
direkte Auseinandersetzung mit Meyer, obwohl bei Beispielen aus dem

Werk Meyers angeknüpft wird. Einsicht in die kausalen Zusammenhänge
gewinne man dadurch, dass man mögliche Kausalzusammenhänge kon-
struiere und unter diesen diejenigen aussuche, durch die das Ereignis
"adäquat" ausgelöst worden wäre. Mehrfach wird in diesem Abschnitt
auch darauf verwiesen, dass die historische Wirklichkeit kategorial konstituiert wird.

Die überarbeitete Geschichtstheorie

Als Meyer 1910 seine methodologische Untersuchung in seinen "Kleinen
Schriften" neu herausgab (zitiert wird im folgenden die 2. Aufl. von
1924), brachte er, wie er es selbst im Vorwort formulierte, mehrere
Zusätze und kleinere Korrekturen an: "Dagegen konnte es nicht meine
Absicht sein, den Gegenstand neu und erschöpfend zu bearbeiten oder zu
den zahlreichen in den letzten Jahren über diese Fragen erschienenen
Untersuchungen, wie etwa dem grossen Werk von XÉNOPOL, la théorie de
l'histoire (1908), Stellung zu nehmen." Der Ort der Publikation war
dafür wohl weniger ausschlaggebend (vgl. dazu auch S. 51, Anm. 1) als
Meyers in der Hauptsache gleichgebliebene Meinung. Die im Vorwort
als Hauptänderung angekündigte Neufassung des Abschnittes über den
freien Willen wollte diesen nur "klarer fassen" und blieb unbeschadet der
Kritik Webers in der Substanz gleich.

Meyer anerkannte zwar den Wert von Webers "eingehender, sehr
dankenswerten" Kritik (21, Anm. 1), ja fühlte sich teilweise sogar sehr
gut von ihm verstanden (55, Anm. 2). Im allgemeinen ist die Antwort
Meyers auf die Einwände von Weber, er meine eigentlich das von jenem
Gesagte. So habe Weber recht, wenn er bei der Erwähnung der Verantwortlichkeit im Zusammenhang der Willensfreiheit ein ethisches Moment
sehe; es sei aber eigentlich nur darum gegangen, die Freiheit des Willens
mit dem Verweis auf die Verantwortlichkeit zu betonen (21, Anm. 1). Er
gibt auch zu, dass die Darstellung von Werten ihren Platz in der
Geschichtsschreibung habe, denn auch Werte hätten ihre Wirkungen auf
die Gegenwart (45, Anm. 1). Doch alle diese Formulierungen kommen
den Anliegen Webers nicht entgegen. Meyer hält nach wie vor am Vorrang des Individuellen, des Singulären, des Politischen und der Ideen
fest, und er bleibt bei einer auf die Ereignisse konzentrierten politischen
Geschichte, die sich zudem der Werturteile nicht enthält.

Immerhin sind noch in "Die Aufgaben der höheren Schulen und die
Gestaltung des Geschichtsunterrichts" (1918) in einem Abschnitt über
"Wesen und Bedeutung der Geschichte" gewisse Einflüsse der Kritik
Webers spürbar, wenn Meyer von der historischen Begriffsbildung
schreibt, die auch mit dem Vorstellungsleben in der Gegenwart im

Zusammenhang steht (47), oder wenn er darauf hinweist, mit welchen
Urteilen scheinbar empirische Begriffe verbunden seien (48). Allerdings
wirken sich diese Einflüsse auch hier nicht auf das Wesentliche der Konzeption aus.

Im grossen und ganzen behielt Meyer die 1884 formulierte Konzeption
bei. Bevor diese Feststellung an der überarbeiteten Einleitung für die
"Geschichte des Altertums" belegt werden soll, müssen aber noch ein
paar wichtige nuancierende Zusätze in der in den "Kleinen Schriften"
(1910/1924) neu aufgelegten "Theorie und Methodik der Geschichte"
(1902) genannt werden: Verteidigt wird die Abgrenzung der Geschichtsschreibung gegenüber der Biographie (66, Anm. 1). Hingegen werden die
Vorbehalte gegen Wilamowitz und die Einrichtung von Instituten für
Altertumswissenschaft etwas vorsichtiger formuliert (65, Anm. 1). In der
Auseinandersetzung mit Breysig findet man Argumente gegen dessen
Beispiele für historische Gesetze (S. 32, Anm. 1). Die Berechtigung der
Kulturgeschichte wird—wie auch in der neu formulierten Einleitung für
die "Geschichte des Altertums," auf die verwiesen wird,—neu zugege-
ben, wobei es auch in ihr um das Individuelle gehen müsse (46, Anm. 1).
Neu sind die im Anhang (vgl. auch 7, Anm. 1) beigefügten (ursprünglich
1908 veröffentlichten) Überlegungen zum Verhältnis zwischen Naturwissenschaft und Geschichte, die dann freilich zu eher forschungsgeschicht-
lichen Informationen über neuere Funde übergehen: Meyer betont hier
die Ähnlichkeiten zwischen der Geschichte und naturwissenschaftlichen
Fächern, welche die Entwicklung der Natur erforschen: Bei beiden würden aufgestellte Hypothesen mit Neufunden überprüft. Damit will er das
feste, wissenschaftliche Fundament der Geschichte betonen, was insofern
ungewöhnlich ist, als er sonst gerade die subjektive Grundlage der Geschichtsschreibung betont.

Die Reaktionen auf die Neuauflage von Meyers "Zur Theorie und Methodik der Geschichte" im Rahmen seiner "Kleinen Schriften" waren
bescheiden, denn es handelte sich nun nur noch um einen Aufsatz unter
mindestens so interessanten Texten, und einige der Rezensenten hatten
sich auch schon früher geäussert. Interessant ist die Reaktion Wilhelm
Webers aus dem Jahre 1928. Obwohl er Meyer einer älteren Generation
zurechnete, die ihm zu nüchtern erscheint, nennt er ihn den "Führer auf
dem weiten Gebiet der Alten Geschichte." Sympathien findet Meyers
Universalgeschichte und die Betonung der Verwurzelung der Geschichtsschreibung in der intuitiven Schöpferkraft des Individuums.[23]

Die Einleitung zur zweiten Auflage der "Geschichte des Altertums"

---

[23] Orientalistische Literaturzeitung 31 (1928) 257–262, zit. 259 f.

von 1907 (im folgenden nach der 3. Aufl. zitiert, die im wesentlichen nur Ergänzungen zu den Paragraphen 10 und 11 enthält) gibt eine starke Erweiterung und Überarbeitung der ersten Auflage von 1884.[23a] In den Grundzügen ist jedoch die Konzeption von 1884 vollständig erhalten. Bereits im Vorwort bekennt Meyer, dem allenfalls erhobenen Vorwurf, nicht modern genug und rückständig zu sein, gelassen entgegenzusehen: "... in den Jahrzehnten, die ich als Lernender und Mitarbeitender auch in ihrer Einzelgestaltung überschauen kann, habe ich so viele Theorien und Systeme kommen und gehen sehen, die alle bisherige Erkenntnis umstossen und eine neue gesicherte Wahrheit an ihrer Stelle aufpflanzen zu können glaubten, dass mich derartige Einwände nicht mehr beirren können." (IX f.) Schon die Verankerung in der Subjektivität bedeutet eine gewisse Resistenz der Konzeption, die als "historisch begründete Weltanschauung" (IX) bezeichnet wird. Immerhin ist die Betonung der subjektiven Verankerung etwas schwächer; an einer Stelle scheint sie auch vor allem auf die Darstellung bezogen zu sein, so dass sie nicht für den Prozess der Forschung gelten würde: "... die auf der Einzelpersönlichkeit des Historikers beruhende Individualität der Darstellung (steht) keineswegs im Gegensatz zu der Forderung historischer Objektivität ..." (210).

Die Einleitung trägt neu den Untertitel "Elemente der Anthropologie," was darauf schliessen lassen müsste, dass für Meyer die Gegensätze zwischen Anthropologie und Geschichte kleiner geworden seien. Nun behaupten jedoch alle diesbezüglichen Textstellen das Gegenteil: An der 1884 vorgenommenen Abgrenzung werde festgehalten (184–187). Dennoch gilt aber nach wie vor Webers Kritik, dass Meyer in dieser Beziehung nicht konsistent ist und sich vor allem in der Praxis nicht an seine Theorie halte. Die Inkonsistenzen sind dadurch verstärkt, dass Meyer wie dann auch 1910 die politische der Kulturgeschichte gegenüberstellt, wobei er freilich nur den Unterschied von den Objekten her zulässt. Es sei ein "Wahn", dass in der Kulturgeschichte die individuellen Momente zurücktreten würden (195). Auch komme der politischen Geschichte die "dominierende Stellung" zu (197). Erklären lässt sich dieser Tatbestand wohl hauptsächlich aus dem Wirken der historischen Tradition und dem Bedürfnis, die Geschichte gegen die aufkommende Sozialwissenschaften zu verteidigen. Es kam hinzu, dass diese Sozialwissenschaften auch im Zusammenhang mit dem Erstarken politischer Strömungen gesehen wurden, die Meyer—wie die meisten Historiker—ablehnte. Die Gleichset-

---

[23a] Vgl. auch Eduard Meyer: Humanistische und geschichtliche Bildung. Vortrag, gehalten in der Vereinigung der Freunde des humanistischen Gymnasiums in Berlin ... am 27. Nov. 1906, Berlin 1907.

zung sozialgeschichtlicher Tendenzen mit der politischen Linken war verbreitet. Auch die ''Einleitung'' verweist an einer Stelle darauf, dass der ''moderne Liberalismus'' von dem Streben beherrscht sei, ''wie in der Praxis die Macht, so in der Theorie die Bedeutung des Staats herabzudrücken und demgegenüber einerseits die Rechte des Individuums auf freie Bewegung, andererseits die Bedeutung der teils in Wirklichkeit, teils wenigstens scheinbar nicht vom Staate gebildeten und abhängigen Verbände und Genossenschaften zu betonen.'' (16)

Die Abgrenzung gegenüber der Philologie wird ebenfalls aufrecht erhalten. Ähnlich wie die Anthropologie biete die Philologie nur ''Hilfsarbeit'', denn beide Wissenschaften würden nur Zustände beschreiben, während es der Geschichte darum gehe, das Sein einer Gegenwart als Werden aus einer Vergangenheit zu betrachten (187, 189). Immerhin ist zu bemerken, dass die Formulierungen von 1907 wie bei der Anthropologie auch den Wert der Philologie höher einschätzen als das in der Schrift von 1902 der Fall war. Dort hiess es noch, in der Philologie sei ''Raum für eine allseitige Behandlung, mit der sich die Geschichte nicht abgeben darf ...'' (1902, 55).

Bei der Konzeption der Geschichte als Universalgeschichte fällt auf, dass nach wie vor nicht von einer tatsächlichen Universalgeschichte die Rede ist. Nur wenige Völker hätten es zu höherer Kultur gebracht (84), bei den Völkern mit niederer Kultur fehle der Fortschritt, und über allem liege die Monotonie der Vorgänge (175, 192). ''Niemals kann die Geschichte des alten Orients das gleiche Interesse erwecken, wie die Griechenlands oder Roms; und dasselbe gilt von der Geschichte zahlreicher islamischer Dynastien oder von den ephemeren und in ihrem Umfang beschränkten Staatenbildungen des Mittelalters und der ersten Jahrhunderte der Neuzeit, oder z.B. auch von der der Kleinstaaten Griechenlands und Italiens. Nicht nur ihr innerer Wert ist gering, sondern auch ihre geschichtliche Wirkung.'' (193)

Die Darstellung der anthropologischen Elemente verteilt sich über die beiden (ersten) Abschnitte ''Die staatliche und soziale Entwicklung'' und ''Die geistige Entwicklung.'' Von eminenter Bedeutung ist die Theorie von der Priorität des Staates. Gegenüber der Fassung von 1884 ist sie stark ausgebaut. Ihren apodiktischen Charakter verliert sie trotzdem nicht, und ihre Abstützung auf das persönliche Erlebnis mit dem Hundestaat in Konstantinopel gibt ihr eher skurrile Züge. Zur gleichen Frage äusserte sich Meyer auch in der ebenfalls 1907 erschienenen Akademierede ''Über die Anfänge des Staats und sein Verhältnis zu den Geschlechtsverbänden und zum Volkstum.'' Die Behandlung der anthropologischen Elemente hat verschiedene Funktionen. Einmal soll die Vorgeschichte übersichtsmässig dargestellt werden. Dann geht es um die

Erarbeitung von generalisierenden Erkenntniskonzepten. Schliesslich aber sind die geschaffenen Begriffe auch das Fundament für die geschichtstheoretischen Konzepte des dritten Teils "Die Geschichte und die Geschichtswissenschaft," wobei die Gleichsetzung der in der Geschichte erkannten Strukturen mit den erkenntnistheoretischen Strukturen der Geschichtstheorie der als subjektiv ausgegebenen Historie ihren objektiven Charakter gibt. So bedeutet die Priorität des Staates auch den Vorrang der politischen Geschichte. Der Kausalitätstrieb, der als Grundlage von allem menschlichen Denken ausgegeben wird (87), sowie der Analogieschluss, nach Meyer das einzige Mittel, das dem Menschen zur Verfügung steht, um äussere Vorgänge begrifflich zu erfassen (87), bedeuten über ihren Gehalt als anthropologische Begriffe hinaus zentrale geschichtstheoretische Konzepte. Die Darstellung der Entstehung der Religion (ihren Ausgang nimmt sie bei den Versuchen des Menschen, die Wirklichkeit zu erklären und zu beeinflussen) bedeutet die für Meyer ohnehin selbstverständliche Liquidierung einer religiösen Geschichtsauffassung.

Die anthropologischen Faktoren gelten Meyer als Allgemeinheiten. Mit Allgemeinheit verbindet er die Macht äusserer Faktoren, der Tradition und der universellen, von der Masse getragenen Tendenzen. Nur den Staat sieht Meyer verbunden mit dem Gegensatz des Allgemeinen, mit inneren Bedingungen und Motiven, Freiheit und Individualität bzw. individuellen Tendenzen (173). Gesetzmässigkeiten will Meyer in der Geschichte nicht zulassen. Immerhin gibt es aber immer wieder die Gegensätze der beschriebenen allgemeinen und individuellen Faktoren. Die Wirksamkeit der Individualität hängt von ihnen ab (175). Bei der Wirksamkeit der Individualität kommt Meyer auch wieder darauf zu sprechen, dass die innere Grösse einer Persönlichkeit nicht zwingend mit ihrer historischen Wirkung einherläuft (178). Trotz der Betonung der fehlenden Gesetzmässigkeiten in der Geschichte zeichnet Meyer aber so etwas wie Lebensgesetzlichkeiten der Kulturen. Kulturforschritt verdanke sich der Individualität; wenn die allgemeinen Faktoren stärker würden, komme es zur Stagnation (180 f.). Die menschliche Kultur müsse nicht ständig fortschreiten (181), Meyer vertritt—verbunden mit der Ablehnung geschichtsphilosophischer Entwicklungstheorien—eine Kreislauftheorie, die beim jüngeren Meyer in etwas anderer Form vorlag (nur zwei Kulturkreise). Eine solche formuliert er auch bei den Ideen, das "höchste, was die Individualität zu schaffen vermag," die sobald sie verwirklicht seien, in ihr Gegenteil umschlügen (182).

Zum Bereiche des Individuellen wird die Geschichte durch das Wirken des freien Willens und des Zufalls, Begriffe an denen Meyer trotz Webers Kritik festhält (sie seien "vollständig klare, von der Erfahrung gegebene Begriffe," 187). Festgehalten wird auch an der Definition des Historischen: ''. . . historisch wirksam ist derjenige Vorgang der Vergangenheit, dessen Wirksamkeit sich nicht in dem Moment seines Eintretens erschöpft, sondern auf die folgende Zeit erkennbar weiter wirkt und in dieser neue Vorgänge erzeugt.'' (188) Immerhin gibt Meyer aber jetzt zu: ''Sie (die Geschichte) setzt die Kenntnis der bestehenden Zustände ebenso voraus, wie die der allgemeinen Formen menschlichen Lebens überhaupt . . .'' (189). Die Kritik Webers wird auch dort aufgenommen, wo es heisst, dass das Ausgehen von der Gegenwart auf einem Werturteil beruhe (191). Auch dass der Historiker, wenn er von der Gegenwart ausgehe, von dem ausgehe, was ''für unsere Gegenwart noch inneren Wert'' besitze und in ihr als ''bedeutsamer Faktor'' weiter wirke, berücksichtigt Webers Aufsatz. Alles in allem kommt Meyer so zu einem weniger engen Geschichtsbegriff, der sich nicht allein auf die kausale Herleitung des politisch wirksam Gewordenen beschränken will.

Auch die Nennung der Analogie als Mittel des historischen Schlusses erweitert den ursprünglichen Geschichtsbegriff. Mit Hilfe der Analogie sollen nämlich nicht nur die äusseren Kräfte, sondern auch die inneren psychologischen Momente untersucht werden (203). Man verfahre so, dass man eine allgemeine Tendenz anhand eines Tuns herausnehme und in anderen Lebensäusserungen eine Bestätigung suche, die gefundene Tendenz aber auch für Erklärungen brauche (203 f.). Allerdings kommen nach dieser Erweiterung wiederum Vorbehalte, die das Gesagte einschränken.

Die Reaktionen auf Meyers geschichtstheoretische Darlegungen waren sehr verschieden. Viele der in Marohl verzeichneten Rezensionen akzeptieren sie, weil sie von einer anerkannten Autorität stammen; wer sich aber mit ihnen auseinandersetzt, bringt meist auch Vorbehalte an. Zu berücksichtigen ist, dass viele Autoren sich in erster Linie für die historische Darstellung, nicht aber für die geschichtstheoretischen Fragen interessierten. Rezensionen, welche hauptsächlich die geschichtstheoretischen Grundgedanken referieren wollen, sind in der Minderzahl, obwohl vorhanden (so von Heinrich Swoboda und Carl Winkelsesser— beide zustimmend[24]). Wichtig für sie ist letztlich nur der Punkt, den Thomas Lenschau (oder auch Maurice Croiset) in seiner Besprechung sehr deutlich hervorgehoben hat: ''Allein auch wer Meyers Theorie nicht billigt, wird in der Praxis meist mit ihm übereinstimmen, und jene Schärfe der Theorie rührt wohl nur daher, weil der Verf. den Gegensatz seiner Geschichtsauffassung gegen Lamprechts Auffassung und gegen den histo-

---

[24] Heinrich Swoboda in: Zeitschrift für die Österreichischen Gymnasien 60 (1909) 232–238. Carl Winkelsesser in: Mitteilungen aus der historischen Literatur 37 (1909) 257–260.

rischen Materialismus möglichst scharf herausarbeiten wollte."[25] Oft kritisiert wurden die als verkürzt empfundenen Formulierungen (so Friedrich Cauer).[26] Eher wenig Zustimmung fanden die Ausführungen über die Religion, insbesondere natürlich bei den Theologen, wobei sich die Kritik, aber in Grenzen hält, wofür als Beispiel das Urteil des evangelischen Alttestamentlers Hugo Gressmann bezeichnend sein dürfte: "Ueberhaupt vermisst man in den Partien, die von den Religionen der verschiedenen Völker handeln, das Gemüt ..."[27]

Ernst Troeltschs "Der Historismus und seine Probleme" weist mehrfach zur Illustration von Tendenzen auf Meyer hin, wobei dieser ihm in seinen Absichten oft entgegenkommt, zwar nicht in der Betonung des Vorranges des Staates, aber in der Auffassung der Geschichte als realer Prozess, in der universalgeschichtlichen Auffassung oder in der Bevorzugung der europäischen Geschichte.[28]

Dem ebenfalls stark an der Geschichtsphilosophie interessierten Julius Kaerst ging Meyer zu wenig weit. Die Abhandlung sei zu summarisch, und das entscheidende Moment komme nicht genügend zur Geltung, nämlich dass—wie er in einem späteren Aufsatz ausführte—Antike und Moderne zwei Kulturkreise seien, die charakteristische Stufen einer Entwicklung bilden würden, und dass der Kreislauf nicht die Grundform geschichtlichen Lebens sei. Kaerst kritisierte auch Meyers Zurückdrängung des Gesellschaftlichen, seinen engen Geschichtsbegriff und die Unterschätzung der "tieferen Bedeutung der Religion für die geistige und sittliche Kultur."[29]

Die Vertreter der Anthropologie zeigten sich im allgemeinen erfreut über das Interesse, das sie durch Meyer von seiten der Geschichtswissenschaft erfuhren.[30]

Emile Durkheim besprach Meyers Buch in einer von Marohl nicht erfassten Rezension im "L'Année sociologique."[31] Insgesamt 8 Seiten

---

[25] Thomas Lenschau in: Berliner philologische Wochenschrift 30 (1910) 274; vgl. Maurice Croiset in: Revue critique d'histoire et de littérature 32. année, n.s. 66 (1908) II, 124 f.

[26] Wochenschrift für klassische Philologie 25 (1908) 1161–1173, 1166.

[27] Die christliche Welt 25 (1911) 467–470, zit. 470.

[28] Ernst Troeltsch: Der Historismus und seine Probleme. Erstes Buch: Das logische Problem der Geschichtstheorie (Gesammelte Schriften, Bd. 3), Tübingen 1922, v.a. 43, 53, 376, 704.

[29] HZ 104 (1910) 139–145, zit. 144. Für die Anschauung von Kaerst vgl. dessen Aufsätze in der HZ 83 (1899) 193–225; 106 (1911) 473–534; 111 (1913) 253–320 sowie in den Neuen Jahrbüchern für das klassische Altertum 9 (1902) 32–53.

[30] So wird im Korrespondenzblatt der deutschen Gesellschaft für Anthropologie 39 (1908) 85 von Johannes Ranke mit Genugtuung auf Meyers Einleitung als "Anerkennung des Wertes unserer Bestrebungen von seiten einer Nachbardisziplin" hingewiesen.

[31] L'Année sociologique 11 (1906–1909) 5–13.

widmete er der Publikation, was im Rahmen der Zeitschrift recht viel
bedeutete. Meyer wird als Autorität dargestellt; für Durkheim ist er ein
bedeutender Repräsentant einer Geschichtswissenschaft, der er kritisch
gegenüberstand. Von seiner Lektüre hatte er einen zwiespältigen Eindruck, denn einerseits musste er Meyers Anthropologie—''Soziologie''
wäre treffender, korrigierte Durkheim—vom Ansatz her begrüssen,
andererseits fand er eine individualisierende und auf das Politische
bezogene Geschichtsauffassung vor, wie er sie intensiv bekämpfte.

Die Auseinandersetzung mit Spengler. Ausblick

Der Erste Weltkrieg und der deutsche Zusammenbruch trugen viel dazu
bei, dass ein bereits früher vorhandenes mehr oder weniger latentes Unbehagen zur ''Krisis des Historismus'' wurde, wie es der bezeichnende
Titel eines 1932 erschienenen Buches von Karl Heussi oder bereits der
Titel des ersten Kapitels von Ernst Troeltschs Buch ''Der Historismus
und seine Probleme'' (1922) sagen. Die Krise betraf nicht die historische
Produktion, sondern die weltanschaulichen Grundlagen der Geschichtsschreibung. Georg G. Iggers sieht in seinem den Historismus kritisieren-
den Werk ''Deutsche Geschichtswissenschaft'' den Grund der Krise in
den Zweifeln an der Möglichkeit rationalen und objektiven Wissens:
''Damit war der Historismus als Theorie an seinem logischen Schlusspunkt angelangt. Wenn alle Wahrheiten und Werturteile individuell und
historisch sind, dann gibt es keinen festen Punkt mehr in der Geschichte,
weder für historische Kräfte im Sinne Rothackers noch für das Leben in
Diltheys Sinn. Übrig blieb nur der subjektive einzelne. (...) Damit
erreichte der Historismus—in philosophischer, nicht in historiographi-
scher Hinsicht—das Ende seines Weges: die letzten Werte und Sinngebungen hatten sich verflüchtigt.''[32]
Iggers behandelt die theoretischen Auffassungen von Meyer leider
nicht. Man kann aber annehmen, dass die bisher behandelten geschichtstheoretischen Schriften Meyers bei Iggers noch einiges vor dem ''logischen Schlusspunkt'' des Historismus als Theorie angesiedelt wären,
denn zwar findet man bei Meyer die Subjektivität jeder Geschichtsschreibung, aber Werte und Sinngebungen haben sich bei ihm noch keineswegs
verflüchtigt. Es stellt sich die Frage, ob Meyer seine geschichtstheoretischen Auffassungen nach dem Ersten Weltkrieg revidierte und ob sich
dann aus ihnen jene Folgerungen ergeben hätten.

---

[32] Georg G. Iggers: Deutsche Geschichtswissenschaft. Eine Kritik der traditionellen
Geschichtsauffassung von Herder bis zur Gegenwart, München 1971, 316 und 317.

1924 rezensierte Meyer mit grossem Engagement Oswald Spenglers
"Der Untergang des Abendlandes" in Hinblick auf den Frankfurter
Historikertag.[33] Meyer und Spengler kannten sich persönlich. Spengler
hatte Meyer sein Werk zugeschickt und auf den zweiten Band hin eine
briefliche Antwort von Meyer bekommen, aus der sich ein Briefwechsel
entspann, der wiederum zu mehreren Besuchen Spenglers führte. Sogar
für ein gemeinsames Museumsprojekt wollte Meyer Spengler gewinnen.[34] Meyers Besprechung beginnt mit pessimistischen Feststellungen.
(Am Schluss schreibt er sogar, pessimistischer als Spengler zu sein.) Die
Kräfte der Gegenwart, die für den weiteren Ausbau und die Erhaltung
der modernen Kultur gebraucht würden, seien erschöpft. Demokratische
Allgemeinbildung und materielle Interessen statt geistiger trügen zur
Nivellierung bei. Jede Kultur zeuge, wenn sie ihre Höhe erreiche, die
Mittel, durch die sie sich untergrabe. Vor dem Ersten Weltkrieg habe
man noch den Glauben haben können, die Kräfte für den Fortschritt der
Kultur seien vorhanden, nun aber sei das anders: "Wer wie der Referent
diesen Glauben hegte, ist durch den Ausbruch des Weltkriegs jäh aus
seinen Träumen gerissen worden: seit dem 4. August 1914 steht es fest,
dass die moderne europäische Kultur in den letzten Jahrzehnten des
neunzehnten Jahrhunderts ihren Höhepunkt überschritten hat ...''
(1760). In Spengler sieht Meyer seine jetzige Sicht bestätigt, wobei er
Spengler zubilligt, bereits 1911 das Bevorstehen der Katastrophe erkannt
zu haben. Meyer fühlt sich aus einem zweiten Grund zu Spengler hin-
gezogen, er erkennt in ihm nämlich ähnliche Auffassungen vom Wesen
der Geschichte. Spenglers Werk ziele nämlich darauf ab, das "Wesen des
weltgeschichtlichen Lebens in seiner Tiefe zu erfassen" (1762). Mit
diesem Wesen meint Meyer offenbar sowohl gewisse Gesetzmässigkeiten
als auch die grundsätzliche Einsicht in die Rolle der Individualitäten, des
freien Willen, des Zufalls sowie in deren Verhältnis zum Gesetzmässigen.
Deshalb schreibt er unmittelbar an das Zitierte anschliessend, Spenglers
Werk arbeite korrekt den Gegensatz zwischen der Welt als Natur und der
Welt als Geschichte heraus. Schliesslich habe Spengler auch die Bedeutung der "Intuition" erkannt (1763).

Ein für Meyers Geschichtstheorie neues Element ist die Auffassung
vom Schicksal: "Jede Kultur und jede ihrer einzelnen Epochen, so
möchte ich Spenglers Gedanken fassen, fühlt sich durch dies Schicksal
gebunden, es setzt ihr die Grenzen, die sie nicht überschreiten kann; ob
sie die Möglichkeiten die ihr innerhalb dieser Grenzen bleiben, voll erfüllt

---

[33] Deutsche Literaturzeitung 45 (1924) 1759–1780.
[34] Alexander Demandt: "Eduard Meyer und Oswald Spengler. Lässt sich Geschichte
vorhersagen?" Beitrag zum Eduard-Meyer-Colloquium.

oder nicht, das hängt dann von dem Zufall ab, der überall die Einzelgestaltung bestimmt'' (1764).

Es sei richtig, bei der Betrachtung der Weltgeschichte kein lineares
Modell anzunehmen und statt der traditionellen Epocheneinteilung von
der Gliederung nach den hohen Kulturen auszugehen (1765). Zustimmung erhält auch Spenglers Gedanke, die Parallelen der Entwicklung der
Kulturen mit der Analogie zu überschauen (1768). Hingegen wehrt sich
Meyer gegen den Versuch, die Geschichte vorauszusagen (1780). Kritisiert wird die Zusammenfassung der ''unerschöpflichen Mannigfaltigkeit
der Einzelerscheinungen als seelische Einheit'' (1777)—bewährt sei vielmehr der Begriff der Kulturkreise (1778). Auch bezweifelt Meyer die Ho-
mogenität von Spenglers Kulturen (1770) und die Priorität der Kultur.

Grundsätzlich blieb Meyer bei seiner bereits vor dem Ersten Weltkrieg
formulierten geschichtstheoretischen Konzeption. Man mag zugeben,
dass Meyer den Gedanken der Kulturkreise und der Parallelen zwischen
den Kulturkreisen aufgewertet hat sowie mit dem Begriff des Schicksals
in Verbindung sieht. Erstaunlich ist die Tatsache, dass Meyer bei einem
Autor zu einem positiven Urteil kommt, den man einer von Meyer abgelehnten Richtung zuordnen würde. Zunächst will es nicht einleuchten,
wie ein Autor von Meyer geschätzt werden kann, der doch von quasibio-
logischen Gesetzmässigkeiten ausgeht. Doch in Meyers Geschichtstheorie
sind genügend Ansatzpunkte für Verbindungen enthalten. Gegenüber
dem nicht zu Vereinbarenden grenzt er sich deutlich ab. Die Haupt-
gemeinsamkeit und das auslösende Moment zugleich dürfte Spenglers
Einschätzung der Gegenwart sein. Die Kritik an der demokratischen
Nivellierung und an der materialistischen Wirtschaftsgesinnung, vor
allem aber die Erfahrung, dass die europäischen Kulturwerte den Weltkrieg nicht zu verhindern mochten—das wird von Meyer an Spenglers
Buch herausgehoben. Sein Pessimismus übertrifft nach eigenem Urteil
denjenigen Spenglers. Im Hintergrund steht die Enttäuschung über die
deutsche Niederlage und die Weimarer Republik.

Die geschichtstheoretischen Grundlagen sind es ganz eindeutig nicht,
welche Meyers Pessimismus auslösen. Für Meyer war das subjektive Fundament der Geschichtswissenschaft nie ein Problem, sondern im Gegenteil eine Stütze. Meyer trägt seine Geschichtstheorie nach wie vor mit der
ihm schon früher eigenen Selbstsicherheit vor, klar, einfach und mit
einem Ton natürlicher Autorität. Meyers Pessimismus ergibt sich vielmehr aus der Beobachtung der Gegenwart. Ein englischer Kritiker konstatierte ganz zu recht, dass Meyers Sympathie für Spengler mit seinem
konservativen Nationalismus zusammenhängt: ''But if in so many vital
respects Professor Meyer sees Spengler to be wrong, what does it mean
that he expresses agreement with his 'basic ideas' and welcomes his work

as a great contribution? One can hardly doubt that the answer to this question is that Professor Meyer is not only a great Ancient Historian, but a passionate German nationalist . . .''[35] Meyers Geschichtsschreibung erhob den Anspruch, für die Gegenwart eine Bedeutung zu haben. Sie dachte an ihre belehrende und bildende Wirkung, und sie wollte gemäss der Theorie aus der Gegenwart entworfen sein. Der Vorrang des Politischen, die Vorliebe für den starken Staat, die Bewunderung des schöpferischen Individuums, der Ausschluss der verachteten Massen und der ''niederen'' Kulturen, der Glaube an die gestaltende Kraft der europäischen Kultur—das alles war auf einmal in Frage gestellt. Historiker anderer Nationen mögen in jenen Jahren ähnlich gedacht haben. Aber die hintergründige Verbindung mit der Frustration des Nationalismus gibt den deutschen Stimmen eine besondere Note. Bei den Reaktionen auf Meyers Spenglerbesprechung fällt auf, dass auch sie davon bewegt sind, wie die Gegenwart aussah oder wie es weitergehe: Julius Kaerst zeigte sich durch die ''packenden Bildern'' Spenglers von der ''modernen Verbindung von Demokratie und Kapitalismus'' beeindruckt; Adolf Grabowsky glaubte, in der Wesenschau könne der Anfang der Selbstbesinnung enthalten sein.[36]

In Meyers geschichtstheoretischen Schriften frappiert der Gegensatz zwischen dem Bekenntnis zur Subjektivität und dem selbstgewissen zupackenden Rationalismus. Ebenso erstaunlich ist die Verbindung einer generalisierenden mit einer individualisierenden Geschichtsauffassung. Sowohl die Verankerung in der Subjektivität als auch die Betonung des Individuellen schufen Meyer einen Spielraum für eine schöpferische Intelligenz, die einen ausgeprägten Sinn für die Beherrschung weiter Forschungsgebiete besass, und die in hohem Masse die Fähigkeit besass, Geschichte als Geschichte von Tatsächlichem zu zeigen. In diesem Punkt entpuppt sie sich als positivistisch. Die Geschichtsschreibung Meyers hat auch in anderer Hinsicht eine Tendenz zur Willkür einer zu selbstsicheren Ratio. Sie erhebt den Anspruch, universal zu sein, schliesst aber ganze Kulturen aus[37] und distanziert sich von sozialgeschichtlichen Fragestellungen allzustark. Sie enthält im teilweisen Widerspruch zu ihrem Hinweis auf ihre Subjektivität die stillschweigende Implikation, die der Geschichte angemessenen Interpretationsmuster zu bieten. Jedoch muss es Meyer auch positiv angerechnet werden, dass seine Geschichts-

---

[35] Journal of the Hellenic Studies 47 (1927) 289.
[36] Julius Kaerst in: Gnomon 1 (1925) 219. Adolf Grabowsky in: Zeitschrift für Politik 15 (1926) 191.
[37] In einem gewissen Sinne kann man in Meyers Geschichtsbild das Nachwirken des Dogmas vom klassischen Altertum sehen.

theorie den Hinweis auf die subjektive Verankerung enthält und seine
Geschichtstheorie damit eine nützliche Warntafel vor der Beschäftigung
mit dem Werk Meyers darstellt—eine Beschäftigung, welche sich dann
oft nur umsomehr lohnen kann. Bedenken sind m.E. jedoch gegen eine
Meyer-Lektüre anzubringen, die von der Voraussetzung ausgeht, Meyers
Ansatz biete eine umfassende Geschichtsschreibung, die alle heutigen
Bedürfnisse erfüllen könne.[38]

Ähnliche Beobachtungen liessen sich bei den geschichtstheoretischen
Äusserungen anderer Althistoriker jener Zeit machen, insbesondere bei
Julius Beloch, obwohl Beloch vorgab, von einem ganz anderen Ansatz
auszugehen und vor allem keine personale Geschichtsbetrachtung zu
bieten. M.E. stellt sich aber überhaupt die Frage, ob die bisherige
Historismuskritik nicht einen wichtigen Punkt zu wenig hervorstreicht.
Die Konzentration auf die Kritik an der individualisierenden stark auf
die politische Geschichte ausgerichteten Betrachtungsweise und auf die
staatstreue Konservativität hat vergessen lassen, welche zwiespältigen
Folgen die bis in die Gegenwart durchgehende Tradition hat, in der
Geschichtswissenschaft dem subjektiven Faktor zu viel Raum zuzubilli-
gen. Diese Tendenz zeigt sich vor allem darin, dass die Originalität und
die wissenschaftliche Produktion überbewertet werden. Einerseits müssen
wissenschaftliche Arbeiten Neues bieten, andererseits stehen Wissenschaftler unter dem Druck zu publizieren, ohne aber immer Neues zu wissen. Die wissenschaftlichen Moden und der immer wieder von neuen
Standpunkten ausgehende Forschungszugriff gewährleisten wohl Fruchtbarkeit. Allzuoft sind sie aber mit dem—die Forschung natürlich
erleichternden—Selbstverständnis verbunden, das Richtige zeigen zu
können. Dass mehr und mehr die Rezeption der Forschung leidet, hängt
nicht nur mit der Fülle des Geschriebenen, sondern auch mit dem vorschnellen und selbstsicheren Urteilen zusammen.

---

[38] Es ist paradox, dass diese Hoffnung gerade im Zusammenhang mit geschichtstheoretischen Überlegungen auftaucht, so bei Peter Hassel: Der Untergang Westroms aus der
Sicht neuerer marxistischer Forschungen im deutschen Sprachraum, Marburg/Lahn
1980, II.

WILFRIED NIPPEL

PROLEGOMENA ZU EDUARD MEYERS *ANTHROPOLOGIE*

Eduard Meyer hat 1884 den 1. Band seiner *Geschichte des Altertums* mit einer 25-seitigen Einleitung in 27 Paragraphen eröffnet. Die Überschriften der einzelnen Abschnitte "Elemente der Anthropologie"; "Anthropologie und Geschichte"; "Inneres Wesen der Geschichte"; "Äußere Bedingungen der Geschichte. Das historische Material"; "Allgemeiner Charakter der Geschichtsschreibung"; "Chronologie"; "Geschichte des Altertums" lassen erkennen, daß diese Einleitung grundsätzliche Aussagen zur Geschichts- und Sozialwissenschaft enthält und erst gegen Schluß eine speziellere Einführung in bestimmte Probleme des vorliegenden Werks gibt. Dies ist in verschiedenen Hinsichten bemerkenswert genug; noch erstaunlicher und erklärungsbedürftiger ist aber, daß Eduard Meyer in der Neubearbeitung seines Werkes 1907 diese allgemeine Einleitung unter dem Titel *Elemente der Anthropologie* zu einem eigenen Halbband gemacht hat, der schließlich (nach einigen Ergänzungen hauptsächlich bibliographischer Natur) in der Auflage von 1910 insgesamt 252 Seiten bzw. 147 Paragraphen umfaßte. Gegliedert ist dieser Einleitungsband in drei große Teile mit den Überschriften "Die staatliche und soziale Entwicklung"; "Die geistige Entwicklung"; "Die Geschichte und die Geschichtswissenschaft". Dieser Ausweitung liegt, von der äußeren werkgeschichtlichen Seite gesehen, die Eingliederung von zwei umfangreichen Abhandlungen zugrunde, der Schrift zur *Theorie und Methodik der Geschichte* von 1902 sowie der Berliner Akademie-Abhandlung von 1907, *Über die Anfänge des Staats und sein Verhältnis zu den Geschlechtsverbänden und zum Volksthum.* Auf die erste Schrift, Meyers explizite Stellungnahme zum Methodenstreit in der deutschen Geschichtswissenschaft, der sich am Werk Lamprechts entzündet hatte,[1] hat Max Weber bekanntlich mit seinen *Kritischen Studien auf dem Gebiet der kulturwissenschaftlichen Logik* (1906) geantwortet.[2] Auch Meyers Akademie-Abhandlung von 1907 steht in einem

---

[1] Vgl. dazu aus der jüngeren Literatur M. Viikari, Die Krise der "historistischen" Geschichtsschreibung und die Geschichtsmethodologie Karl Lamprechts, Helsinki 1977; L. Schorn-Schütte, Karl Lamprecht. Kulturgeschichtsschreibung zwischen Wissenschaft und Politik, München 1984; K.H. Metz, Grundformen historiographischen Denkens, München 1979, 424 ff.; ders., Der Methodenstreit in der deutschen Geschichtswissenschaft (1891–99), Storia della storiografia 6, 1984, 3–20; G.G. Iggers, The "Methodenstreit" in International Perspective, ebd. 21–32.

[2] Gesammelte Aufsätze zur Wissenschaftslehre, Tübingen ⁴1973, 215–290; vgl. J. Deininger (in diesem Band).

polemischen Kontext gegenüber der Rezeption bestimmter sozialwissen-schaftlicher Theoreme in der Geschichtswissenschaft.

Obwohl Meyers elaborierte Theorie in großen Teilen unverkennbar aus der Auseinandersetzung mit vorherrschenden Strömungen der Sozial- und der Geschichtswissenschaft seiner Zeit entstanden ist, so ist doch eine Einordnung in diese Zusammenhänge dadurch erschwert, daß Meyer nur selten Diskussions- und Gesprächspartner nennt,[3] bei seinen erratischen Literaturangaben verschiedentlich Werke geringeren Rangs nennt, die ihm gerade bekannt geworden sind, die grundlegenden Arbeiten aber nicht anführt, oder daß er sich ganz pauschal auf neuere Tendenzen der Forschung beruft. Hinzu kommt der Umstand, daß er sämtliche seiner Aussagen, mögen sie nun auf eingehenden eigenen Untersuchungen basieren oder mehr aus zweiter Hand geschöpft sein bzw. schlicht auf Alltagswissen beruhen, im stets gleichen Duktus unbeirrbarer Gewißheit, mit der Autorität des inzwischen international hochangesehenen Univer-salhistorikers vorträgt.

Es gibt nur wenige Untersuchungen zu Eduard Meyers Theorie. In der Althistorie hat man, wie sich schon in den Nachrufen von 1930/31 zeigt, schon bald mit ihr nicht mehr allzuviel anfangen können;[4] in Werken zur Theorie und Geschichte der Geschichtswissenschaft,[5] der Soziologie und Sozialanthropologie[6] wird Ed. Meyer mit wachsendem zeitlichen Ab-stand immer weniger berücksichtigt,[7] sei es, daß die größer gewordene Distanz zwischen den wissenschaftlichen Disziplinen auch die Retrospek-tive bestimmt, sei es, daß gerade in diesen Disziplinen der Abstand zur deutschen Wissenschaftradition stark gewachsen ist. Erst in den letzten Jahren sind einige Beiträge zu Ed. Meyers Theorie im Kontext des derzeit starken Interesses (besonders in Italien) an der kritischen Aufarbeitung der deutschen altertumswissenschaftlichen Tradition erschienen.[8]

---

[3] Vgl. A. Momigliano, Premesse per una discussione su Eduard Meyer, in: Settimo Contributo alla storia degli studi classici e del mondo antico, Rom 1984 (215–231), 224.

[4] Kritische Anmerkungen zu seiner Theorie finden sich bei M. Gelzer, Gnomon 6, 1930, 624; W. Otto, Eduard Meyer und sein Werk, Zs. d. deutschen morgenländischen Gesellschaft 85, 1931 (1–24), 23; E. Täubler, ZRG 51, 1931, 605; V. Ehrenberg, HZ 143, 1931 (501–510), 507 f.

[5] Vgl. nur die (kritischen) Hinweise bei E. Bernheim, Lehrbuch der historischen Methode und der Geschichtsphilosophie, München/Leipzig ⁶1914, 7, A.1. 9, A.2. 113, A.1. 149, A.2. 181, A.2.

[6] S. die Erwähnungen bei W.E. Mühlmann, Geschichte der Anthropologie, Wies-baden ³1984, 122.170 f.241; W. Krauss, Zur Anthropologie des 18. Jahrhunderts, München 1979, 15.

[7] Fehlanzeigen z.B. in den Werken von A.C. Haddon, History of Anthropology, London 1934; R.H. Lowie, The History of Ethnological Theory, New York 1937; M. Harris, The Rise of Anthropological Theory, London 1968.

[8] Momigliano (wie A.3); L. Capogrossi Colognesi, Eduard Meyer e le teorie sull'ori-

Mit den folgenden Ausführungen soll versucht werden, die Theorie Meyers in die Historiographie und Gesellschaftstheorie der Zeit um die Wende vom 19. zum 20. Jahrhundert in einigen Hinsichten einzuordnen. Angesichts der schon erwähnten Eigenarten von Meyers Präsentation wie des augenblicklichen Forschungsstands kann es sich hierbei nur um Präliminarien handeln.

Das Schwergewicht des Interesses liegt hier auf seinen Positionen gegenüber der Sozialanthropologie seiner Zeit, nicht auf den allgemeinen Aussagen zur Geschichtstheorie. Meyer hat ''Anthropologie'' definiert als ''Wissenschaft von der Entwicklung des Menschen'' bzw. als ''Lehre von den allgemeinen Formen menschlichen Lebens und menschlicher Entwicklung''. In beiden Fassungen seiner Einleitung heißt es gleichlautend, daß die Anthropologie durch ''die Forschungen der neueren Zeit eine festere Gestaltung erhalten und ... aus dem Bereiche logischer Deduktionen auf den Boden gesicherter Tatsachen gestellt worden'' sei (GdA I^1, 1. I^3, 3). Konkret bezieht er sich auf die Disziplinen der Sprachwissenschaft, der Prähistorie, der vergleichenden Ethnologie und der allgemeinen Entwicklungstheorie; allerdings hat sich die Gewichtung dieser Teildisziplinen in den beiden unterschiedlichen Fassungen erheblich verschoben.

Meyers Anthropologie gilt mit Recht als Unikat innerhalb der althistorischen Literatur und zudem als äußerst seltener Fall der Vorlage einer theoretischen Grundlegung durch einen empirisch arbeitenden Historiker überhaupt. Es stellt sich deshalb zunächst die Frage, was Ed. Meyer eigentlich veranlaßt hatte, seinem Geschichtswerk eine Einleitung dieser Art vorauszuschicken. Dies gilt besonders für die erste Fassung von 1884. Sie ist später als eine ihrer Zeit vorauseilende Stellungnahme zur Theorie der Geschichtswissenschaft und zur Abgrenzung zwischen Geschichtswissenschaft und nomologischer Sozialwissenschaft verstanden worden.[9] Meyer selbst hat diese Deutung verbreitet, so in der Schrift von 1902, in der es heißt, der Grund für die Einleitung von 1884 habe in dem praktischen Bedürfnis gelegen, ''die Geschichte in ihren Anfängen gegen verwandte Wissensgebiete, vor allem gegen die allgemeine Wissenschaft

---

gine dello stato, Quaderni Fiorentini 13, 1984, 451–469; L. Canfora, Intelletuali in Germania tra reazione e rivoluzione, Bari 1979, pass.; ders., Die Kritik der bürgerlichen Demokratie durch Eduard Meyer, in: R.W. Müller/G. Schäfer (Hgg.), Arthur Rosenberg zwischen Alter Geschichte und Zeitgeschichte, Politik und politischer Bildung, Göttingen 1986, 46–58; F.H. Tenbruck, Max Weber and Eduard Meyer, in: W.J. Mommsen/J. Osterhammel (Hgg.), Max Weber and his Contemporaries, London 1987 (234–267), 244 ff.
[9] G. v. Below, Rez. Meyer, Theorie, HZ 94, 1905, 449; ähnlich urteilt Tenbruck (wie A.8), 245.247.

vom Menschen, für die mir nach wie vor der Name Anthropologie der richtige scheint—andere mögen sie Soziologie oder wie sonst immer nennen—scharf und prinzipiell abzugrenzen'' (Kl. Schr. 5 f.). Damals habe man sich nur vereinzelt mit diesen Fragen befaßt, die inzwischen ausführlich diskutiert worden seien und bekanntlich zu dem Versuch geführt hätten, eine neue Art der Geschichtsbetrachtung zu schaffen, die einen Exklusivanspruch auf Wissenschaftlichkeit erhebe, diese Qualität dagegen der herkömmlichen historiographischen Praxis abspreche, weil sie nicht die Aufdeckung von Gesetzmäßigkeiten in Analogie zur Natur- wissenschaft betreibe. Im Vorwort zum Einleitungsband von 1907 heißt es schließlich: ''daß ich meinem Werk eine derartige Einleitung voran- gestellt habe, hat ehemals, wo das Interesse der meisten Historiker diesen Fragen völlig abgewandt war, bei manchen Beurteilern Verwunderung und Tadel erfahren; gegenwärtig, wo derartige Fragen an der Tages- ordnung sind, wird eine Rechtfertigung nicht mehr erforderlich sein'' (GdA I³, IX).

Diese Selbstauslegung enthält jedoch eine retrospektive Verzeichnung der Zusammenhänge. Daß der 29jährige Meyer die Grundsatzdebatte über das Verhältnis von Natur- und Sozialwissenschaft sowie den Methodenstreit innerhalb der Geschichtswissenschaft so klar antizipiert haben sollte, erscheint bei Kenntnis seiner intellektuellen Entwicklung[10] von vornherein kaum wahrscheinlich; dies wird noch unwahrschein- licher, wenn man die beiden Fassungen seiner theoretischen Einleitung vergleicht. Natürlich hat Meyer—eine seiner Stärke wie Schwäche zugleich ausmachenden Eigenschaften—an manchen einmal gefaßten Ideen unbeirrt festgehalten; deutlich ist jedoch, daß er gerade in der hin- sichtlich des Methodenstreits entscheidenden Frage der Geset- zeskategorie in der ersten Fassung noch bei weitem nicht die eindeutige Ablehnung des Gesetzesbegriffes für die Geschichtswissenschaft ver- fochten hat, die für seine spätere Position charakteristisch wurde. So heißt es 1884: ''Die Geschichte lässt sich daher, obwohl sie allgemeinen Geset- zen unterworfen ist, doch niemals auf solche reduciren oder einfach in Formeln auflösen. Sie ist nothwendig mannigfaltig, kein Abschnitt dem anderen gleich. Während die Anthropologie sich beschränkt, das Gesetz- mäßige und Allgemeine aufzuweisen, herrscht in ihr (scil. der Geschichte) *daneben* (Hervorhebung W.N.) der Zufall und der freie Wille des Einzel- nen'' (GdA I¹, 15). Und weiter gilt hier als Aufgabe der Historie, ''die allgemeinen Gesetze und Formen historischen Lebens zu erforschen und die Verkettung von Ursache und Wirkung im Einzelvorgang nachzu-

---

[10] Vgl. Ch. Hoffmann (in diesem Band).

weisen'' (ebd.). Below hat notabene 1898 kritisiert, daß Eduard Meyer dem Element der Notwendigkeit noch zu große Bedeutung eingeräumt habe.[11]

Meyer zeigt also 1884 durchaus noch nicht diese Berührungsangst vor dem Gesetzesbegriff, wie sie sich in der späteren Theoriediskussion auf Seiten der Historiker manifestierte. Er bewegt sich eben auch noch in einem anderen Diskussionskontext. Die Namen, die 1884 fallen, August Schleicher, Heymann Steinthal, Johannes Schmidt und Lazar Geiger verweisen auf den Kontext der Sprachwissenschaft und der daraus abgeleiteten Völkerpsychologie. Inhaltlich schließt sich Meyer den jüngeren Tendenzen an, für die der Name Johannes Schmidt steht, der gegen die Annahmen der frühen Indogermanistik und gegenüber einer sich als Naturwissenschaft verstehenden Sprachwissenschaft (Schleicher)[12] betont hatte, daß sich eine indogermanische Ursprache bzw. ein Urvolk nicht rekonstruieren ließen.[13] Meyer hat entsprechend auch in seinen späteren Äußerungen zu allen um den Rassegedanken gruppierten Ideen der Identifizierung von Abstammungs- und Sprachgruppen[14] deutliche Distanz gehalten.[15]

Von einer Auseinandersetzung mit den bahnbrechenden ethnosoziologischen Werken der Dekade nach 1860—Morgan, Tylor, McLennan— zeigt Meyers Diskussion von 1884 ebensowenig erkennbare Spuren wie von einer Rezeption der Werke von Bachofen, Maine oder Fustel de Coulanges, die auf der Basis klassischer Quellen die anthropologische Diskussion über die Entstehung sozialer und politischer Strukturen maßgeblich beeinflußten.

Der Anstoß zur Einleitung von 1884 wird somit in anderen Gründen zu suchen sein als denjenigen, die Meyer selbst später angeführt hat. Ein beachtliches Indiz dafür, daß man in eine ganz andere Richtung zu

---

[11] G. v. Below, Die neue historische Methode, HZ 81, 1898 (193–273), 237 f.; vgl. Weber (wie A.2), 229 f.

[12] Vgl. v.a. A. Schleicher, Die Darwinsche Theorie und die Sprachwissenschaft. Offenes Sendschreiben an Dr. Ernst Häckel, Weimar (1863), ²1873; dazu H. Arens, Sprachwissenschaft. Der Gang ihrer Entwicklung von der Antike bis zur Gegenwart, Freiburg/München 1955, 224 ff.; E.F.K. Koerner, Schleichers Einfluß auf Häckel: Schlaglichter auf die wechselseitige Abhängigkeit zwischen linguistischen und biologischen Theorien im 19. Jahrhundert, Zs. f. vgl. Sprachforschung 25, 1981, 1–21.

[13] GdA I¹, 2.8; I³, 3–5; zu J. Schmidt, Die Verwandtschaft der indogermanischen Sprachen, 1872 vgl. Arens (wie A.12), 279; A. Borst, Der Turmbau von Babel. Geschichte der Meinungen über Ursprung und Vielfalt der Sprachen und Völker, III, 2, Stuttgart 1961, 1725 (ebd. 1727 zu Ed. Meyer); R. Girtler, Kulturanthropologie, München 1979, 67 f.; R. Römer, Sprachwissenschaft und Rassenideologie in Deutschland, München 1985, 55 ff.

[14] Vgl. dazu allgemein L. Poliakov, Der arische Mythos, Wien 1977; Römer (wie A.13).

[15] S. GdA I³, 73 ff.

schauen habe, stellt eine Rezension Heinrich Gelzers von 1889 dar, der diese Einleitung nicht als avantgardistisch, sondern als antiquiert emp-fand. Die Einteilung in Paragraphen gehöre einer "vergangenen Epoche an", die Einleitung selbst sei ein "Tribut an diese Handbuchmanier", auf die "übliche Metaphysik über die Anfänge des Staates und der Reli-gion, über die Macht der Tradition, das Erwachen des Nationalgefühls, die ersten Ansätze zu Mythologie und Ethik usf" hätte man auch ver-zichten können, "das durchaus auf realhistorischem Boden stehende Werk" hätte dieser "mystischen Vorhalle" nicht bedurft.[16]

Wenn man dieser Spur folgt, dann ist es durchaus möglich, die Meyersche Einleitung von 1884 in einigen Hinsichten in den Kontext äl-terer Traditionszusammenhänge zu stellen. So wie die *Geschichte des Alter-tums* als Ganze die Tradition der aufklärerischen Universalhistorie,[17] die eigentlich durch die Entwicklung neuer Standards der Quellenkritik und das Anwachsen von Spezialwissen veraltet schien, unter gänzlich verän-derten Bedingungen zu wiederholen suchte, so kann auch eine Einleitung dieses Typs zur Tradition dieser Gattung von Werken[18] in Beziehung gesetzt werden. Heerens Werk *Ideen über die Politik, den Verkehr und den Handel der vornehmsten Völker der alten Welt*, das zwischen 1793 und 1812 erst-mals erschienen und bis in die 1820er Jahre mehrfach nachgedruckt wor-den war, hatte bekanntlich das Vorbild für Meyers Konzipierung einer Universalgeschichte des Altertums abgegeben,[19] die die orientalische

---

[16] HZ 61, 1889 (114–125), 116.

[17] Vgl. v.a. H. Wesendonck, Die Begründung der neueren deutschen Geschichts-schreibung durch Gatterer und Schlözer, Leipzig 1876; W. Dilthey, Das achtzehnte Jahrhundert und die geschichtliche Welt, in: Gesammelte Schriften III, Stuttgart [3]1959, 209–275; E. Schaumkell, Geschichte der deutschen Kulturgeschichtsschreibung von der Mitte des 18. Jahrhunderts bis zur Romantik im Zusammenhang mit der allgemeinen geistigen Entwicklung, Leipzig 1905; T. Benz, Die Anthropologie in der Geschichtswis-senschaft des 18. Jahrhunderts, Diss. Bonn 1932; H.L. Stoltenberg, Geschichte der deut-schen Gruppwissenschaft (Soziologie), Leipzig 1937, 248 ff. (bibliographische Nach-weise); J. Streisand, Geschichtliches Denken von der deutschen Frühaufklärung bis zur Klassik, Berlin [2]1967; P.H. Reill, The German Enlightenment and the Rise of Histori-cism, Berkeley 1975; ders., Die Geschichtswissenschaft um die Mitte des 18. Jahrhun-derts, in: R. Vierhaus (Hg.), Wissenschaften im Zeitalter der Aufklärung, Göttingen 1985, 163–193; H.W. Blanke/J. Rüsen (Hgg.), Von der Aufklärung zum Historismus, Paderborn 1984; H. Möller, Vernunft und Kritik. Deutsche Aufklärung im 17. und 18. Jahrhundert, Frankfurt 1986, 144 ff.; H.E. Boedeker et al. (Hgg.), Aufklärung und Geschichte, Göttingen 1986; die Artikel zu Gatterer (P.H. Reill), Schlözer (U.A.J. Becher), Heeren (H. Seier) in: H.U. Wehler (Hg.), Deutsche Historiker, Göttingen 1980–1982, VI, 7–22; VII, 7–23; IX, 61–80.

[18] H.W. Blanke/D. Fleischer/J. Rüsen, Historik als akademische Praxis, Dilthey-Jahrbuch 1, 1983 (182–255), 197 f. mit dem Hinweis auf Ed. Meyers Einleitung von 1884 als einem "späten Versuch, diese Tradition fortzusetzen."

[19] GdA I[1], 25; I[3], 250.—Die Orientierung an Heeren ist schon öfter erwähnt worden; so bei F. Cauer, Wochenschrift f. klass. Philologie 25, 1908, 1161; M. Gelzer, Gnomon 6,

Geschichte einbezog, dafür aber nur bis in die Mitte des 4. Jahrhunderts v. Chr. reichte. Heeren war in seiner Zeit ein hochangesehener Historiker gewesen, dann aber seit den 1830er Jahren namentlich auf Grund schärfster Kritik von seiten Niebuhrs und Gervinus', die ihm unkritische Quellenbehandlung und eine Vernachlässigung der politischen Geschichte vorgeworfen hatten, in Vergessenheit geraten.[20]

Die Aufklärungshistorie hatte endgültig den Rahmen eines durch die Bibel begrenzten Geschichtsbildes samt der damit vorgegebenen Chronologie überwunden.[21] Die neue universalhistorische Betrachtungsweise, ob nun in der Form erzählter Geschichte oder in Entwürfen möglicher Geschichte (wie sie in der *conjectural history* der schottischen Aufklärung vorlagen oder in Werken vom Typus der Kantschen und Herderschen "Ideen" zur Geschichte der Menschheit), erforderte nun inhaltliche Aussagen über die Einheit der Gattungsgeschichte;[22] ob man einen Naturzustand annehmen wollte oder nicht; wie die in der Gegenwart lebenden sogenannten Naturvölker in die Geschichte der Gattung und der Zivilisation einzuordnen seien; es ging auch um die Frage nach dem zeitlichen und räumlichen Kontext, der von Universalhistorie zu behandeln sei, ob z.B. China oder auch die Naturvölker einzubeziehen seien oder nicht.

Für die schottische Sozialphilosophie, die allgemein in Deutschland sehr beachtet worden war[23] und die speziell auch auf die Historiographie der deutschen Spätaufklärung gewirkt hatte,[24] hatten Modelle im Vordergrund gestanden, mit denen man die Gesellschaftsentwicklung als Fortschritt im Sinne der Entfaltung der materiellen Zivilisation in Stufenfolgen gebracht hatte, ohne damit notwendig eine gesetzmäßige Abfolge

---

1930, 624; J. Vogt, Geschichte des Altertums und Universalgeschichte, Institut f. Europäische Geschichte Mainz, Vorträge Nr. 24, Wiesbaden 1957; A. Toynbee, Die "Alte Geschichte" und die Universalhistorie, Saeculum 21, 1970 (91–105), 93.100 f.; sie wird jetzt dokumentarisch belegt durch den von Ch. Hoffmann publizierten Brief Meyers an den Verleger Cotta (in diesem Band).

[20] Siehe H.W. Blanke, Verfassungen, die nicht rechtlich, aber wirklich sind. A.H.L. Heeren und das Ende der Aufklärungshistorie, Berichte zur Wissenschaftsgeschichte 6, 1983, 143–164; J.N. Ryding, Alternatives in Nineteenth-Century German Ethnology, Sociologus 25, 1975 (1–28), 20.

[21] A. Klempt, Die Säkularisierung der universalhistorischen Auffassung. Zum Wandel des Geschichtsdenkens im 16. und 17. Jahrhundert, Göttingen 1960.

[22] G. Scholtz, "Geschichte, Historie," Historisches Wörterbuch der Philosophie 3 (1973), 353.357 f.; R. Koselleck, "Geschichte", Geschichtliche Grundbegriffe 2 (1975), 663 f.670.688; H.E. Boedeker, "Menschheit", ebd. 3 (1982), 1088 f.; vgl. auch H. Dreitzel, Die Entwicklung der Historie zur Wissenschaft, Zs. f. hist. Forschung 8, 1981 (257–284), 279 ff.

[23] N. Waszek, Bibliography of the Scottish Enlightenment in Germany, Studies on Voltaire and the Eighteenth Century 230, 1985, 283–303.

[24] Blanke (wie A.20).

zu postulieren.[25] Hier wurden zuerst die Schemata Sammler und Jäger
—Hirten—Ackerbauern—Stadtbewohner bzw. solche wie Wildheit—
Barbarei—Zivilisation entwickelt. Auch Ed. Meyer widmet in beiden
Fassungen seiner Einleitung einen Abschnitt den Folgen der Seßhaftwer-
dung, dem Übergang zum Ackerbau und schließlich zur städtischen
Zivilisation. Anders als bei den Aufklärungstheoretikern und -historikern
dienen bei ihm diese "Stufen des Wirtschaftslebens und der Kulturentwicklung" jedoch nicht als zentrale Kategorien, mit denen sich die Gattungsgeschichte insgesamt strukturieren ließe.[26]

Die Übernahme bestimmter Darstellungsformen der Universalhistoriker der Aufklärung bedeutet somit nicht, daß Meyer hier auch ihre inhaltlichen Annahmen übernehmen will. Im Gegenteil: Mit Meyers Verständnis, daß der Staat die Zentralkategorie menschlicher Gesellschaft
sei, lag eine deutliche Abwendung von der Aufklärungstheorie vor. Denn
diese hatte ja überhaupt erst postuliert, daß es eine vom Staat getrennte,
sich nach eigenen Regeln entwickelnde, deshalb auch den Gegenstand
einer eigenständigen Wissenschaft ausmachende Gesellschaft gebe; das
setzte die Überwindung des aristotelischen Politikverständnisses voraus,
wie sie schon in den Theoremen des Naturzustands und des Gesellschafts-
vertrags impliziert gewesen war.

Gegen diese Tradition stellt sich Ed. Meyer explizit: "der isolierte
Mensch, den das Naturrecht und die Lehre vom *contrat social* an den
Anfang der menschlichen Entwicklung stellte, ist eine Konstruktion ohne
jede Realität und daher für die theoretische Analyse der menschlichen
Lebensformen eben so irreführend wie für die geschichtliche Erkenntnis"
(GdA I[3], 6). Demgegenüber postuliert Meyer eine Universalität des
Staates als der zu allen Zeiten und an allen Orten fundamentalen Form
menschlicher Vergesellschaftung. Diese Theorie wird auf verschiedenen
Ebenen hergeleitet. Zum einen durch den Rückgriff auf die aristotelische
Kategorie des *zoon politikon*. Nun sind die Ausführungen von Aristoteles
vielschichtig und stammen aus unterschiedlichen Diskussionskontex-
ten.[27] Meyer greift den Punkt bei Aristoteles heraus, daß nämlich der

---

[25] H. Medick, Naturzustand und Naturgeschichte der bürgerlichen Gesellschaft, Göttingen 1973; ders., Einleitung zu A. Ferguson, Versuch über die Geschichte der bürgerlichen Gesellschaft, Frankfurt 1986; J. Rohbeck, Die Fortschrittstheorie der Aufklärung,
Frankfurt 1987 (jeweils mit Lit.).

[26] GdA I[1], 6 f.; I[3], 63 ff.; vgl. F. Cauer, Wochenschrift f. klass. Philologie 25, 1908,
1168: "Die Fortschritte in der Verwertung der Natur werden von Eduard Meyer nicht
sehr beachtet; er unterscheidet zwar einige Stufen des wirtschaftlichen Lebens, aber diese
Stufenfolge erhebt sich nicht über den Eintritt des Rindviehs und des Getreides in das
menschliche Leben."

[27] W. Kullmann, Der Mensch als politisches Lebewesen bei Aristoteles, Hermes 108,
1980, 419–443; 423 zu Ed. Meyer.

Mensch als *zoon politikon* sich in dieser Hinsicht nicht grundsätzlich von den Bienen und den Herdentieren unterscheide, die grundsätzliche Differenz zu diesen politischen Tieren vielmehr in der Sprache bestehe. Meyer illustriert dieses Argument mit einem aus Autopsie gewonnenen Beispiel aus seiner Zeit als Hauslehrer beim englischen Gesandten in Konstantinopel, als er die Formierung der Straßenhunde in abgegrenzten Quartieren beobachtet habe, die sozusagen "räumlich umgrenzte Hundestaaten" dargestellt hätten.[28]

Die aristotelische Kategorie des *zoon politikon*, die aus dem Kontext eines naturwissenschaftlichen Denkens stammt, das eine invariante Natur voraussetzt, wird nun bei Ed. Meyer in Verbindung gebracht mit den modernen Einsichten in die Geschichtlichkeit der Natur. Entwicklungsgeschichtlich habe sich der Mensch aus einem höheren Tier entwickelt. Dies sei nur aufgrund seiner besonderen geistigen Entwicklung—physiologisch gesprochen infolge der Ausbildung der Großhirnrinde—möglich gewesen; diese geistige Entfaltung habe wiederum das Bestehen abgegrenzter Gruppenverbände zur Voraussetzung; Sprache habe nur aus der Kommunikation zwischen Gleichstehenden mit gemeinsamen Interessen entstehen, sich nicht aus der Eltern-Kind-Beziehung ergeben können; dies gelte um so mehr für die weitere zivilisatorische Entwicklung, die Erfindung von Werkzeugen, die Gewinnung des Feuers, die Züchtung der Haustiere, die Ansiedlung in Wohnstätten usw. und natürlich erst recht hinsichtlich der Entstehung von Sitte, Recht, Religion, geistiger Kultur. "Somit ist die Organisation in solchen Verbänden (Horden, Stämmen), welche wir empirisch überall antreffen, wo wir Menschen kennen lernen, nicht nur eben so alt, sondern weit älter als der Mensch: sie ist die Voraussetzung der Entstehung des Menschengeschlechts überhaupt. Aus dieser Betrachtung erhellt zugleich der innere Widerspruch, den die aus mythischen Vorstellungen entstandene Ableitung des Menschengeschlechts als Ganzen oder gar die eines einzelnen Volks von einem einzelnen Paare enthält" (GdA I³, 8).

Meyer führt seine Argumentation schließlich noch auf der Ebene der empirischen Evidenz weiter. Überall da, wo man etwas über menschliche Organisationsformen wisse, zeige sich zwar eine Vielfalt von Verbänden, erweise sich jedoch zugleich, daß jeweils einer dieser Verbände vorrangig sei und sich gegebenenfalls auch durch Zwang gegenüber konkurrierenden Anforderungen durchsetzen könne. "Diese dominierende Form des sozialen Verbandes, in deren Wesen das Bewußtsein einer vollständigen,

---

[28] GdA I³, 7: ebenso SB Berlin 1907, 509, A.1; das Beispiel wird (mit dem Hinweis, daß die Hunde inzwischen aus der Stadt vertrieben seien) noch einmal im Kriegsvortrag von 1916 angeführt; Weltkrieg 144 f.

auf sich selbst ruhenden Einheit enthalten ist, nennen wir den Staat. Wir müssen daher den staatlichen Verband nicht nur begrifflich, sondern auch geschichtlich als die primäre Form der menschlichen Gemeinschaft betrachten, eben als denjenigen sozialen Verband, welcher der tierischen Herde entspricht und seinem Ursprung nach älter ist als das Menschengeschlecht überhaupt, dessen Entwicklung erst in ihm und durch ihn möglich geworden ist.'' Und dies sei wiederum ''im Grunde identisch mit der berühmten Definition des Aristoteles, daß der Mensch ein von Natur staatenbildendes Wesen und der Staat der alle anderen umfassende und an Leistungsfähigkeit überragende soziale Verband ... ist, der anders als die übrigen durch sich selbst bestehen kann ...'' (ebd. 11). Die Herleitung des Staates aus den natürlichen Geschlechts- und Verwandtschaftsverbänden, wie sie die moderne Ethnologie vertrete, aber wie auch Aristoteles an der Stelle, an der er die Polis historisch aus dem Haus und dem Dorf ableite, sei demgegenüber unhaltbar (ebd. 15).

Meyers Konstruktion seiner These von der Universalität des Staates durch eine Kombination von phylogenetischer Betrachtung, Aristoteles-Rezeption, historischen Beobachtungen und Alltagswissen ist methodisch mehr als problematisch, der Versuch der Wiedergabe gerät schnell in die Nähe der Parodie. Die von Meyer einzeln angeführten Punkte sind jedoch nicht einfach abzutun. So ist die Anführung von Aristoteles als Kronzeuge für ein Konzept von Vergesellschaftung, das keine Trennung zwischen Staat und Gesellschaft anerkennt, gewiß keine Idiosynkrasie Meyers. Vielmehr hatte der politische Aristotelismus im 19. Jahrhundert gerade bei deutschen Historikern eine Heimstatt gefunden; so ist die aristotelische Tradition z.B. bei Treitschke für den Vorrang der politischen Geschichte einerseits, gegen die Berechtigung einer eigenständigen wissenschaftlichen Disziplin Soziologie andererseits ins Feld geführt worden.[29]

Grundsätzlich läßt sich auch eine These von der Universalität des Staates im Sinne einer Ubiquität von Herrschaft verfechten. Dies ist bis heute eine in Soziologie und Anthropologie vertretbare Gegenposition zu der Auffassung, daß es akephale Gesellschaften gebe, die sich allein durch Reziprozitätsmechanismen regulieren.[30]

---

[29] H. v. Treitschke, Die Gesellschaftswissenschaft. Ein kritischer Versuch, Leipzig 1859; M. Riedel, Der Staatsbegriff der deutschen Geschichtsschreibung des 19. Jahrhunderts in seinem Verhältnis zur klassisch-politischen Philosophie, Der Staat 2, 1963, 41–63; F. Jonas, Geschichte der Soziologie II, Reinbek 1968, 128 f.

[30] Vgl. R.H. Lowie, The Origin of the State (1927), New York 1962, 2; L. Krader, Formation of the State, Englewood Cliffs, N.J. 1968, 12 ff. und für Hinweise auf neuere Theorien dieser Art U. Wesel, Frühformen des Rechts in vorstaatlichen Gesellschaften, Frankfurt 1985, 23 ff.

Methodisch inakzeptabel ist jedoch, wie Meyer seine Auffassung von der Allgegenwart staatlicher Strukturen als empirisch gesicherte Tatsache hinstellt. Mit seiner Kenntnis der Hochkulturen des mediterranen und vorderasiatischen Raums kann er legitimerweise allgemeine Annahmen z.B. über die Entwicklung staatlicher Strukturen aus denen von Verwandtschaftsgruppierungen überprüfen und in ihrer Allgemeingültigkeit verwerfen. So wendet er sich gegen die Auffassung, die politischen Strukturen Roms ließen sich aus der *patria potestas* herleiten[31] oder gegen die Auffassung, daß Verbände wie Phylen, Phratrien, Gentes Überreste tribaler Strukturen seien; statt dessen handle es sich, wo immer man sie historisch erkennen könne, bereits um künstliche Untergliederungen des Staates.[32] Manche Irrwege der Forschung hätten vermieden werden können, wenn man diese Auffassung ernster genommen hätte.[33] Unzulässig ist nur, wie Meyer nun seinerseits diesem negativen Befund hinsichtlich der antiken Hochkulturen universalhistorische Geltung zuschreibt. Und unbefriedigend ist auch, daß er für seinen weitgefaßten Staatsbegriff keine weiteren Differenzierungen vornimmt, sondern sich allein auf die Verwerfung des Kriteriums der Territorialität als Wesensmerkmal des Staates[34] schlechthin beschränkt. Für eine Differenzierung zwischen den von ihm angeführten locker gefügten Verbänden, die sich leicht zu größeren Einheiten zusammenschließen, genauso leicht aber auch wieder auseinanderfallen können, und z.B. modernen Staaten werden so keinerlei Kriterien angeboten.

Die an rezenten Primitiven gewonnenen ethnosoziologischen Theorien an Materialien aus den antiken Hochkulturen zu überprüfen, war angesichts der Tendenzen des zeitgenössischen Evolutionismus, Entwicklungsgesetze am Werk zu sehen, die für sämtliche Gesellschaften galten,[35] nicht nur legitim, sondern geradezu notwendig. Meyers Neigung, die so gewonnenen Befunde seinerseits zu verallgemeinern, reproduziert dann

---

[31] Schon 1884 hatte sich Meyer gegen—nicht beim Namen genannte—''neuere Forscher'' gewendet, die den Ursprung des römischen Staats in einer Vereinigung von Familienhäuptern sahen (GdA I¹, 3). Meyers eigene These von der Uranfänglichkeit des Staates ist später in der italienischen Diskussion gegen Bonfante ins Spiel gebracht worden; A. Momigliano, New Paths of Classicism in the Nineteenth Century, Middletown 1982 (History & Theory, Beiheft 21), 24 ff.; Capogrossi Colognesi (wie A.8); M. Kaser, Das Römische Privatrecht, München 1971, I, 55.

[32] GdA I³, 13 f.; vgl. auch Meyers Replik auf die Kritik an seiner Anwendung dieser Konzeption auf die griechische Geschichte (durch Wilamowitz u.a.); Forschungen II, 512 ff.

[33] D. Roussel, Tribu et Cité, Paris 1976; F. Bourriot, Recherches sur la nature du genos, 2 Bde., Lille/Paris 1976.

[34] Meyer wendet sich gegen Ratzel; GdA I³, 11.

[35] J.W. Burrow, Evolution and Society, Cambridge 1966 zeigt, daß diese Vorstellungen älter als der Darwinismus sind.

fatalerweise unter umgekehrten Vorzeichen unhaltbare, jedenfalls empirisch zumindest nicht beweisbare Positionen und steht der Entwicklung
von Typologien zu Vergleichszwecken im Wege.

Meyers kritische Kompetenz einerseits, seine methodisch fragwürdige
und im Ergebnis enttäuschende Theoriebildung andererseits zeigen sich
deutlich bei seinen Stellungnahmen zu den großen ethnosoziologischen
Theorien seiner Zeit. Die Diskussion wurde beherrscht von den Fragen
nach den ursprünglichen Strukturen von Verwandtschaftsgruppen einerseits und nach dem Ursprung der Religion andererseits. Beide Fragen-
komplexe konvergierten an einem Punkt, nämlich in der Theorie des
Totemismus, wenn man in den Gruppen, die eine heilige Beziehung zu
einem Totem-Tier unterhielten, zugleich die exogamen Clans erkannte.
In der Übernahme der Ideen von McLennan[36] hat dann W. Robertson
Smith—auf Grund der Annahme evolutionär zwingender Stufenfolgen—
survivals von matrilinearen Clans und Totemismus auch bei den alten
Arabern und Israeliten finden wollen, und andere sind ihm darin ge-
folgt.[37] Mit den Berichten über die australischen Ureinwohner (bei denen
man die älteste Zivilisationsstufe vorzufinden glaubte), die gegen Ende
des Jahrhunderts die ethnologische Diskussion entscheidend prägten,
wurde zwar dieser enge Zusammenhang in Zweifel gezogen, daß nämlich
Totemgruppen und exogame Clans identisch seien, doch schien sich
zugleich zu bestätigen, daß der Totemismus die ursprünglichste Form der
Religion sei.[38]

---

[36] Primitive Marriage, Edinburgh 1865; wieder in: Studies in Ancient History, London 1876; The Worship of Animals and Plants, Fortnightly Review 6, 1870, 407–427;
562–582; 7, 1870, 194–216; J.G. Frazer, The Origins of Totemism, Fortnightly Review
n.s. 68, 1899, 647–665; 835–852.

[37] W. Robertson Smith, Animal Worship and Animal Tribes Among the Ancient
Arabs and in the Old Testament, Journal of Philology 9, 1880, 75–100; Kinship and Marriage in early Arabia 1885, ND Beirut 1973; Lectures on the Religion of the Semites,
Edinburgh 1889 (auch deutsch 1899); s. weiter J. Jacobs, Are There Totem-Clans in the
Old Testament? Archaeological Review 3, 1889, 145–164.—Meyer verweist zum einen
auf die Matriarchatsthese, die auch G.A. Wilken 1884 vertreten hat (GdA I³, 29), zum
anderen darauf, daß sich die Faszination modischer Thesen auch daran erkennen lasse,
daß "ein so trefflicher Gelehrter wie B. Stade im Anschluß an R. Smith sogar die israelitische Religion auf Ahnenkult und Totemismus zurückgeführt" habe (ebd. 122). Vgl.
u.a. B. Stade, Biblische Theologie des Alten Testaments, Tübingen I, 1905.—Zu Leben
und Werk von Robertson Smith s. T.O. Beidelman, W. Robertson Smith and the Socio-
logical Study of Religion, Chicago 1974; für eine kritische Bewertung seiner (durch die
Wirkung auf Durkheim und Freud folgenreichen) Religionssoziologie E.E. Evans-
Pritchard, Theorien über primitive Religionen, Frankfurt 1968, 89 ff.

[38] Die Arbeiten von L. Fison/A.W. Howitt, Kamilaroi and Kurnai, Melbourne 1880
(non vidi); B. Spencer/F. Gillen, The Native Tribes of Central Australia, London 1889
standen im Zentrum des Interesses; vgl. zur Einschätzung ihrer Bedeutung J.G. Frazer,
Observations on Central Australian Totemism, Journal of the Royal Anthropological
Institute n.s. 1, 1899, 281–286.

Anstatt sich nun auf die Kritik dieser problematischen Theorien (und die Auseinandersetzung mit den älteren Theorien über den Ursprung der Religion im Ahnenkult, im Animismus oder im Naturmythos) zu beschränken, bietet Meyer nun seinerseits Steinthals[39] Theorie von der mythischen Weltsicht des primitiven Menschen, der die Erscheinungen der ihn umgebenden Welt kausal aus den Handlungen von Wesen erklären wolle, als die definitive Lösung an.[40] Zeitgenössische Kritiker Meyers haben Anstoß daran genommen, daß dieser sich in religionssoziologischen Fragen ohne ausreichende Kenntnis der einschlägigen Forschung als Dilettant verbreitet habe.[41] Nun sind die von Meyer nicht angemessen aufgearbeiteten Forschungen (einschließlich der Durkheimschen Totemismus-Theorie) in empirischer Hinsicht längst und endgültig ad acta gelegt;[42] die kritische Distanz des Dilettanten hat sich den kühnen Theoriebildungen der Spezialisten gegenüber als nur zu berechtigt erwiesen.[43] Dem steht auf der anderen Seite die Neigung zur Grenzüberschreitung im Hinblick auf die eigene fachliche Kompetenz und auf die Reichweite der eigenen empirischen Feststellungen gegenüber.

---

[39] Mythos und Religion, Berlin 1870 (Sammlung gemeinverständlicher wissenschaftlicher Vorträge Heft 97).

[40] GdA I³, 91; vgl. schon I¹, 4.

[41] K. Th. Preuss, Religion der Naturvölker (1906–1909), Archiv für Religionswissenschaft 13, 1910 (398–465), 417 ff.; E. Durkheim schließt seine freundliche Besprechung von Meyers Anthropologie, ohne auf die Ausführungen zur Religion einzugehen: "On trouvera dans le livre une théorie de la religion, de ses origines et de son évolution, dont nous n'avons rien dit parce qu'elle n'est qu'un cas particulier des idées qui viennent d'être exposées. D'autre part, prise en elle-même, elle est d'un simplisme vraiment excessif. Il est surprenant qu'un savant qui sait combien il est difficile de faire l'histoire d'une religion ait pu croire possible d'esquisser en une cinquantaine de pages une sorte d'histoire explicative de la religion en général;" L'Année Sociologique 11, 1910; zit. nach E. Durkheim, Textes I: Éléments d'une théorie sociale, hg. v. V. Karady, Paris 1975 (391–399), 399. (Auf Durkheims Rezension hat mich W. Gebhardt hingewiesen).—Vgl. weiter die kritischen Anmerkungen in den Rez. von F. Cauer, Wochenschrift f. klass. Philologie 25, 1908, 1170 und J. Kaerst, HZ 104, 1910, 144 (der eine Auseinandersetzung mit Usener vermißt).

[42] Evans-Pritchard (wie A.37); C. Lévi-Strauss, Das Ende des Totemismus, Frankfurt 1965.—Die Kritik an Durkheims, von Robertson Smith beeinflußter, auf höchst selektiver Auswahl australischer Materialien basierender Religionssoziologie hat bald nach Erscheinen von Les Formes élementaires de la vie religieuse, 1912, eingesetzt; vgl. A.A. Goldenweiser, The Views of Andrew Lang and J.G. Frazer and E. Durkheim on Totemism, Anthropos 11, 1916, 948–970; ders., Religion and Society: A Critique of Émile Durkheim's Theory of the Origin and Nature of Religion, The Journal of Philosophy, Psychology and Scientific Methods 14, 1917, 113–124; W.E.H. Stanner, Reflections on Durkheim and Aboriginal Religion, in: M. Freedman (Hg.), Social Organization. Essays Presented to Raymond Firth, Chicago 1967, 217–240; S. Lukes, Émile Durkheim. His Life and Work, Harmondsworth 1973, 237 ff.450 ff.; Evans-Pritchard (wie A.37), 95 ff.; ders., A History of Anthropological Thought, New York 1981. 153 ff.

[43] Ähnlich urteilt schon R.M. Meyer, Zeitschrift des Vereins für Volkskunde 18, 1908, 226.

Ähnliches läßt sich für Meyers Umgang mit den Thesen zur Entwicklung der Geschlechtsverbindungen und Verwandtschaftsstrukturen feststellen. Hier stand das Stufenschema von der ursprünglichen Promiskuität über die Gruppenehe, den matrilinearen und den patrilinearen Clan bis zur patriarchalischen Kleinfamilie im Vordergrund der Diskussion. Meyer setzt sich explizit zunächst nur mit Bachofen auseinander, dessen Beobachtungen am antiken Quellenbefund nachträglich zur Stützung der primär ethnologisch fundierten Theorien von Morgan und McLennan benutzt worden waren.[44]

Er diskutiert die von Bachofen herangezogenen Quellenzeugnisse ausgiebig und kommt dann zu der (sicherlich zutreffenden) Einschätzung, daß mit der Kategorie Mutterrecht eine Vielzahl unterschiedlicher Phänomene unzulässig zusammengefaßt werde (GdA I^3, 21 ff.).

Pauschaler geschieht dagegen die Auseinandersetzung mit den "ethnologischen Kulturhistorikern." (Die Bezeichnung dürfte mit Bedacht gewählt, eine Anspielung darauf sein, daß in der—bekämpften—Kulturgeschichte bestimmte sozialanthropologische Konzepte rezipiert worden waren.) Auch hier ist die Schlußfolgerung durchaus plausibel: "So tritt uns eine bunte Fülle oft diametral entgegengesetzter Ordnungen entgegen. Es ist eine Willkür und *petitio principii*, wenn eine von ihnen als die ursprünglich allgemein herrschende, alle anderen als spätere Umwandlungen angesehen werden, wie es von den ethnologischen Kulturhistorikern bald mit dieser, bald mit jener versucht ist . . . ." Es sei "verkehrt, so oft es auch geschehen ist, die uns roher erscheinende Form als die ältere zu betrachten, die einmal allein geherrscht habe und dann durch fortgeschrittenere Formen verdrängt sei; die umgekehrte Entwicklung ist ebensogut möglich" (GdA I^3, 26.27).

Meyer nennt in seiner Diskussion der ethnosoziologischen Theorien über den Ursprung von Familie und Staat keine Namen; der von Morgan, der dank seiner Heranziehung durch Engels und Bebel zum Kronzeugen des Sozialismus geworden war,[45] fällt nie. Zur Kritik von Thesen unver-

---

[44] In Ancient Society (1871) hat Morgan auf Bachofen verwiesen; McLennan diskutiert Bachofen, der ihm erst nachträglich bekannt geworden sei, in: Studies in Ancient Society 1886, 319–325. Bachofen hat sich seinerseits später ausgiebig mit Ethnologie befaßt, ist in Korrespondenz mit Morgan, Adolf Bastian, J. Kohler eingetreten und hat seine Studien schließlich in den Antiquarischen Briefen 1880/1886 partiell publiziert; vgl. M. Schuster, Bachofen, Das Mutterrecht und die Ethnologie, in: Johann Jakob Bachofen (1815–1887). Eine Begleitpublikation zur Ausstellung im Historischen Museum Basel 1987, 91–105.

[45] F. Engels, Der Ursprung der Familie, des Privateigentums und des Staates, 1884; zu Engels Umgang mit Morgan vgl. E. Lucas, Die Rezeption Lewis H. Morgans durch Marx und Engels, Saeculum 15, 1964, 153–176; A. Bebel, Die Frau und der Sozialismus, hat zwischen 1879 und 1909 fünfzig Auflagen (und verschiedene Übersetzungen) erfahren. Morgans Werk ist unter dem Titel: Die Urgesellschaft. Untersuchungen über den

kennbar Morganscher Provenienz beruft Meyer sich allein auf das Buch von Heinrich Schurtz, Altersklassen und Männerbünde (1902), das einen Beitrag zur endgültigen Überwindung von Morgan leisten wollte.[46] Schurtz stellte auf einer breiten Basis ethnologischer Materialien fest, daß die Existenz von Junggesellenhäusern und die Möglichkeit freier sexueller Beziehungen für Heranwachsende als Formen, die neben bzw. vor der monogamen Ehe bestehen, nicht als Relikte urgesellschaftlicher Promiskuität verstanden werden können. Bedeutsamer war wohl noch sein positiver Beitrag, die Bedeutung von Initiationsriten und von Vereinigungen, die nicht auf Verwandtschaftsbindungen beruhen, zu betonen.[47]

Für eine fundierte Stellungnahme zum Gesamtkomplex der Entstehung gesellschaftlicher Strukturen kann aber die Anführung von Schurtz' Buch allein—wenn man eine Stellungnahme zur Forschungslage, nicht nur ein Urteil auf der Grundlage von *common sense* abgeben will—nicht befriedigen. Eine vielfältige und weitverzweigte Diskussion hatte z.B. Eduard Westermarck's *History of Human Marriage* (1891) ausgelöst.[48] Dieser auf eine Fülle von ethnographischen Daten gestützte Generalangriff auf die Theorien in der Tradition Morgans wurde von vielen als Todesstoß für die evolutionistischen Modelle dieser Art angesehen;[49] andere—darunter gerade auch die Repräsentanten der deutschen "ethnologischen Jurisprudenz"—verwarfen Westermarck's Werk als Materialkompilation ohne theoretische Relevanz.[50] Eine informierte und

---

Fortschritt der Menschheit aus der Wildheit durch die Barbarei zur Zivilisation 1891 im Parteiverlag der Sozialdemokraten (Dietz, Stuttgart) in einer von W. Eichhoff und K. Kautsky besorgten Übersetzung erschienen. Die Morgan-Rezeption in Deutschland war somit von Anfang an dadurch geprägt, daß dieser "unter die sozialdemokratischen Bildungsmittel aufgenommen" worden war; so F. Ratzel, Lewis Morgans Forschungen über die Entwicklung des Staates (1894), in: Kleine Schriften II, 1906 (269–283), 269; vgl. zur Attraktivität der Matriarchatskonzeptionen für die sozialistische Theorie E. Fromm, Die sozialpsychologische Bedeutung der Mutterrechtstheorie, Zs. f. Sozialforschung 2, 1935, 196–227.

[46] "Auch die letzte große Gesellschaftstheorie, als deren Vertreter Morgan gelten kann, ist in ihren Grundfesten erschüttert"; Schurtz 1; vgl. auch E.K. Winter, Bachofen-Renaissance, Zs. f. d. ges. Staatswissenschaft 85, 1928 (316–342), 317.

[47] Lowie (wie A.7), 58.99 f.

[48] Vgl. die Hinweise bei Lowie (wie A.7), 96 f.; Mühlmann (wie A.6), 103.105. und Westermarcks eigene Bilanz, Neueres über die Ehe, Zs. f Socialwissenschaft 11, 1908, 553–559.

[49] S. Tax, From Lafitau to Radcliffe-Brown. A Short History of the Study of Social Organization, in: F. Eggan (Hg.), Social Anthropology of North American Tribes, Chicago 1955 (445–481), 465 f.

[50] A.H. Post, Grundriss der ethnologischen Jurisprudenz, 2 Bde., Oldenburg 1894/95, ND Aalen 1970; J. Kohler, Zur Urgeschichte der Ehe. Totemismus. Gruppenehe. Mutterrecht, Stuttgart 1897; vgl. auch G. Schmoller, Die Urgeschichte der Familie: Mutterrecht und Gentilverfassung, Schmollers Jahrbuch 23, 1899, 1–21. Nicht über-

informierende Stellungnahme zur Forschungslage hätte diese Diskussion nicht ignorieren dürfen.

Meyer dürfte sich auch weniger für die neuere Entwicklung in der Ethnologie selbst interessiert haben, als dafür, daß manche Theorien aus der Sozialanthropologie in die Geschichtswissenschaft selbst eindrangen. Gerade in einer Zeit, in der der Evolutionismus in der Ethnologie deutlich an Boden verlor (im deutschen Sprachraum besonders gegenüber der Kulturkreislehre),[51] wurde er in der "Kulturgeschichte" rezipiert. So wurde das Mutterrecht auch bei den Germanen entdeckt,[52] ist die Mutterrechtsthese (ebenso wie die Konzeption des Animismus) für die germanische Zeit von Lamprecht[53] aufgenommen worden. Kurt Breysig hat 1904 einen Aufsatz über "die Entstehung des Staates aus der Geschlechterverfassung bei Tlinkit und Irokesen" vorgelegt (Schmollers Jahrbuch 28, 483–527), der sich auf Morgan stützte; man geht sicherlich nicht fehl in der Annahme, daß Meyers eigene Akademieabhandlung von 1907 (auch) eine Replik auf diesen Aufsatz darstellt.[54] Die für den Streit um die Kulturgeschichte typische Verknüpfung von wissenschaftlichen und politischen Argumenten wird auch bei Meyer verschiedentlich deutlich.

So wird bei ihm die Betrachtungsweise *der* Ethnologie, die den Staat aus

---

raschend ist Westermarck—wie auch C.N. Starcke (Die primitive Familie in ihrer Entstehung und Entwicklung dargestellt, Leipzig 1888)—von sozialdemokratischer Seite angegriffen worden; so bei H. Cunow, Die Verwandtschaftsorganisation der Australneger. Ein Beitrag zur Entwicklungsgeschichte der Familie, Stuttgart (Dietz-Verlag) 1894; Bebel im Vorwort zur 25. Auflage von Die Frau und der Sozialismus, 1895 (S. 4 f. der Ausgabe Berlin 1946).

[51] F. Ratzel, Geschichte, Völkerkunde und historische Perspektive, HZ 93, 1904, 1–46; W. Schmidt, Die moderne Ethnologie, Anthropos 1, 1906, 134–163; 318–388; 592–644; 950–997; A. Vierkandt, Die historische Richtung in der Völkerkunde, HZ 101, 1911, 70–80; E. Rothacker, Zur Methodenlehre der Ethnologie und der Kulturgeschichtsschreibung, Vierteljahresschrift für wissenschaftliche Philosophie und Soziologie 36, 1912, 85–106; Tax (wie A.49), 469 ff.; P. Leser, Zur Geschichte des Wortes Kulturkreis, Anthropos 58, 1963, 1–36 (19 ff. zu Ed. Meyers Verwendung des Begriffs); R. Heine-Geldern, One Hundred Years of Ethnological Theory in the German-Speaking Countries: Some Milestones, Current Anthropology 5, 1964, 407–418.—Auch Below hatte (in seiner Kampfschrift gegen Lamprecht) die innere Krise des Evolutionismus konstatiert, HZ 81, 1898, 232 f.

[52] L. Dargun, Mutterrecht und Raubehe und ihre Reste im germanischen Recht und Leben, Breslau 1883; vgl. die Rez. von v. Below, HZ 71, 1893, 489–492.

[53] K. Lamprecht, Deutsche Geschichte I, Berlin [5]1912, 111 ff.; weitere Nachweise aus den Schriften Lamprechts bei Viikari (wie A.1), 212.272 f.; vgl. die Kritik bei v. Below, HZ 71, 1893, 489 ff.

[54] Vgl. die Kritik an Breysig, Der Stufenbau und die Gesetze der Weltgeschichte, 1905, Kl. Schr. 32, A.2; ferner Meyers Stellungnahme gegen Breysigs Institutswünsche (1908); dazu B. vom Brocke, Kurt Breysig. Geschichtswissenschaft zwischen Historismus und Soziologie, Husum 1971, 93 ff.; F. Hampl, Universalhistorische Betrachtungsweise als Problem und Aufgabe, in: ders./I. Weiler (Hgg.), Kritische und vergleichende Studien zur Alten Geschichte und Universalgeschichte, Innsbruck 1974 (121–155), 128 ff.— Auf Breysigs Aufsatz von 1904 nimmt auch Max Weber (wie A.2) 234 ff. Bezug.

den Verwandtschaftsverbänden erwachsen läßt, in Gegensatz gesetzt zu der Sichtweise *der* Historiker, für die der Staat im Vordergrund stehe; die Perspektive der modernen Ethnologen decke sich mit der des Liberalismus, der die Bedeutung des Staates herabmindern wolle: "Der moderne Liberalismus ist von dem Streben beherrscht, wie in der Praxis die Macht, so in der Theorie die Bedeutung des Staates herabzudrücken . . . Er verwirft die Auffassung der Historiker von der zentralen Bedeutung des Staats für das menschliche Leben und stellt statt dessen den Begriff der menschlichen Gesellschaft und ihrer Wandlungen in den Vordergrund: die Anthropologie tritt daher vielfach unter dem Namen der Soziologie auf. Die starke Bedeutung des wirtschaftlichen Lebens, das sich dem äußeren Anschein nach im wesentlichen selbständig, unbekümmert um staatliche Regelung, entwickelt, ja den Staat, wenn er den Versuch macht, einzugreifen, vielmehr umgekehrt in seine Bahnen zu zwingen scheint, hat diese Auffassung mächtig gefördert. In mannigfachen Variationen, bei denen oft der tatsächliche Zusammenhang mit den dennoch ihren Ausgangspunkt bildenden liberalen Prinzipien ganz in den Hintergrund tritt, hat sie die Theorien der Gegenwart gestaltet. Die Ergebnisse der vergleichenden Ethnologie schienen damit aufs beste übereinzustimmen. So gilt es in weiten Kreisen als ein erwiesener und unbestreitbarer Lehrsatz, daß der Staat eine junge Bildung der menschlichen Entwicklung ist, und daß ihm eine Zeit vorhergegangen ist, in der die aus der physischen Blutsverwandtschaft und dem Verkehr der Geschlechter mit einander entstandenen sozialen Verbände die maßgebende Gestaltung der menschlichen Gesellschaft bildeten und das Leben der einzelnen Individuen bestimmten" (GdA I[3], 16).

Die wissenschaftliche wie politische Richtigkeit seines Staatskonzepts hat Eduard Meyer dann durch die Erfahrung des Weltkriegs bestätigt gesehen. Sein Kriegsvortrag *Über den Staat, sein Wesen und seine Organisation* (1916) bietet einen Rundumschlag gegen Liberalismus, Kulturgeschichte, materialistische Geschichtsauffassung und Soziologie zugleich.

Meyers eigene ideologische Fixierung (man beachte auch sein Selbstzeugnis, es sei ihm um die Gewinnung "einer einheitlichen, historisch begründeten Weltauffassung" gegangen)[55] hat sicherlich wesentlich bedingt, daß seine mit ungewöhnlichem Aufwand betriebene und—was immer an kritischen Einwänden im einzelnen vorgebracht werden kann und muß—in vielen Hinsichten beachtliche Auseinandersetzung mit der Anthropologie seiner Zeit in eine fruchtlose Antithese von Geschichts- und Sozialwissenschaft mündet, die dann eine gänzlich theorielose

---

[55] Vorwort zur 2. Auflage, GdA I[3], IX; sowie das Selbstzeugnis von 1923 bei Marohl 9.

Historie zurückläßt. Für die Geschichte des eigenen Kulturzusammenhangs hat der Universalhistoriker Ed. Meyer mit seinen Analogien und Kreislaufmodellen bestenfalls hilflose Konzepte, in einigen Fällen—man denke an seine Stellungnahmen zur antiken Ökonomie[56]—aber auch geradezu fatale Fehldeutungen anzubieten.

Die Konstellation des Methodenstreits, in dem die Historiker glaubten, ihr Terrain gegen die Sozialwissenschaften verteidigen zu müssen, hat im Verein mit der Neigung Meyers, zu allen ihn interessierenden Fragen autoritative Urteile auch jenseits der Grenzen der eigenen Kompetenz abzugeben, bewirkt, daß seine *Anthropologie* Dokument einer verpaßten Chance geworden ist.[57]

---

[56] Charakteristisch für seine Auseinandersetzung mit Bücher ist, daß er dessen spätere Klarstellungen nicht akzeptiert, statt dessen ihn auf ein deterministisches Stufenschema festlegen will und die Chance zu einem typisierenden Verfahren (die M. Weber, Agrarverhältnisse im Altertum, in: Gesammelte Aufsätze zur Sozial- und Wirtschaftsgeschichte, Tübingen 1924, 7 f. gewiesen hatte) ignorierte; vgl. zur Bücher-Meyer-Kontroverse H. Schneider (in diesem Band).

[57] Vgl. schon das Urteil in der Rezension von Walter, Zentralblatt für Anthropologie 1909, 100: "Im ganzen bleibt der Eindruck eines wohldurchdachten Systems, aber entgegenstehende Ansichten sind doch gar zu oft nicht als Stufen der Erkenntnis benutzt, sondern mit allgemeinen Wendungen als unbrauchbar abgetan ... Dem ruhigen Fortschritt der Erörterung ist überhaupt die durchgehende Polemik nicht gerade förderlich geworden".

FAUSTO PARENTE

DIE ENTSTEHUNG DES JUDENTHUMS: PERSIEN, DIE ACHÄMENIDEN UND DAS JUDENTUM IN DER INTERPRETATION VON EDUARD MEYER

Zum Andenken Elias J. Bickermans

1. Im Jahre 1896 gab Ed. Meyer die Schrift in Druck, die bis heute zu seinen bedeutendsten zählt: *Die Entstehung des Judenthums. Eine historische Untersuchung.*[1] Wie er selbst im Vorwort sagte, stellte die Untersuchung eine Vorarbeit für den 3. Band der *Geschichte des Alterthums* dar: ''Die vorliegende Arbeit ist zunächst aus Vorarbeiten für die Geschichte des Perserreichs im dritten Bande meiner Geschichte des Alterthums erwachsen.''[2] Der 2. Band der *Geschichte des Alterthums*, *Geschichte des Abendlandes bis auf die Perserkriege* war drei Jahre zuvor erschienen (1893); der 3., *Das Perserreich und die Griechen* sollte fünf Jahre später veröffentlicht werden (1901).[3]

Der Blickwinkel, aus dem das Problem angegangen wird, ist schon im erwähnten Vorwort klar ausgesprochen: die Wiederherstellung Israels nach dem Exil muß als Teil des Gesamtkomplexes der Geschichte des Nahen Orients im Altertum zwischen der Mitte des VI. und der Mitte des V. Jahrhunderts gesehen werden, denn nur in diesem Zusammenhang kann sie richtig interpretiert werden; mit anderen Worten, die Wiederherstellung der jüdischen Gemeinschaft von Jerusalem ist wohl eine Episode—wenn auch von großer Bedeutung—für die jüdische Geschichte, aber sie ist zugleich auch ein wichtiges Zeugnis für die Politik der Achämeniden, einer Politik, die nicht nur das jüdische Volk betrifft.[4]

Um diese Problemstellung von Meyer genau zu erfassen, müssen wir uns folglich die Teile des dritten Bandes der *Geschichte des Alterthums* vergegenwärtigen, in dem das Problem im historischen Gesamtkontext der

---

[1] *Die Entstehung des Judenthums. Eine historische Untersuchung* von Eduard Meyer, Halle a.S. 1896 (*Eduard Meyer. Bibliographie* von H. Marohl, Stuttgart 1941, n. 107).

[2] Meyer, *Entstehung*, III.

[3] *Geschichte des Alterthums* von Ed. Meyer. *Zweiter Band. Geschichte des Abendlandes bis auf die Perserkriege*, Stuttgart 1893 (Marohl, *Bibl.*, n. 81); 2. vollig neubearb. Aufl. 1. Abt. 1928; 2. Abt. 1931 (Marohl, *Bibl.*, n. 434). *Dritter Band. Das Perserreich und die Griechen.* 1. Hälfte. *Bis zu den Friedensschlüssen von 448 u. 446 vor Chr.*, Stuttgart 1901 (Marohl, *Bibl.*, n. 141); 2. Aufl. [Anast. Neudr.] 1912 (Marohl, *Bibl.*, n. 275).

[4] Meyer, *Entstehung*, III–IV. Über Meyer als Historiker des jüdischen Volkes vgl.: *Das Judentum im deutschen Geschichtsbild von Hegel bis Max Weber* von H. Liebeschütz, Tübingen 1967, 269–301; *Juden und Judentum im Werke deutsche Althistoriker des 19. und 20. Jahrhunderts* von Chr. Hoffmann, Leiden-New York-København-Köln 1988, 133–189.

Epoche wiederaufgenommen wird, und zwar vor allem den § 8 über die
jüdischen Quellen für die persische Geschichte (*Jüdische Quellenkunde*);[5]
die §§ 56 und 57 über die Religionspolitik der Achämeniden (*Die Reichs-
politik und die Religion*)[6] und die §§ 103–138 über die Entstehung des
Judentums (*Die Anfänge des Judenthums*).[7]

Aber das ist nicht alles. Nach 1901 wurden Entdeckungen gemacht und
Texte wieder veröffentlicht, die entscheidend waren für die Beurteilung
der Religionspolitik der Achämeniden und damit für die Erforschung des
Problems, wie es der Sicht Meyers entsprach. 1907 machte Ed. Sachau
drei der in Elephantine entdeckten aramäischen Papyri bekannt[8] und
veröffentlichte 1911 das gesamte Corpus mit Übersetzung und Kommentar.[9] Meyer machte es gleich zum Gegenstand eines Beitrages an die
Preußische Akademie der Wissenschaften *Zu den aramäischen Papyri von
Elephantine*[10] und eines Buches, das im Jahr darauf erschien, *Der Papyrusfund von Elephantine. Dokumente einer jüdischen Gemeinde aus der Perserzeit und
das älteste erhaltene Buch der Weltliteratur.*[11] 1911 veröffentlichte F.H. Weissbach in Transliteration und übersetzte den sogenannten "Rassam-Zy-
linder" (B.M. 90920)[12] 1909 von H.C. Rawlinson im 5. Band von *The
Cuneiform Inscriptions of Western Asia* herausgegeben.[13] 1914 wieder veröffentlichte W. Spiegelberg die sogenannte "Demotische Chronik" des
Papyrus 215 der Bibliothèque Nationale von Paris;[14] im Rückseite waren
verschiedene Texte eingeschrieben, und zwischen diesen ein Kambyses'

---

[5] *Geschichte*, III, 1, 13–15 (§ 8). Vgl. VIII und Anm. 1 über die Polemik gegen
Wellhausen (im Vorwort zum ersten Auflage).

[6] *Geschichte*, III, 1, 93–95 (§§ 56–57).

[7] *Geschichte*, III, 1, 167–233 (§§ 103–138).

[8] *Drei Aramäische Papyrusurkunden aus Elephantine*, von Ed. Sachau, "Abhandl. der
königl. preuss. Akademie der Wissenschaften" vom Jahre 1907; Neudruck 1908; *Ein alt-
amäischer Papyrus aus der Zeit des Aegyptischen Königs Amyrtaeus* in *Florilegium ou recueil de travaux
d'érudition dédiés à Monsieur le Marquis Melchior De Vogüé à l'occasion du quatre-vingtième anniver-
saire de sa naissance*, Paris 1909, 529–541.

[9] *Aramäische Papyrus und Ostraka aus einer jüdischen militär-Kolonie zu Elephantine. Altorien-
talische Sprachdenkmäler des 5. Jahrhunderts vor Chr.* bearbeitet von Ed. Sachau, Leipzig 1911.

[10] *Zu den aramäischen Papyri von Elephantine*, "Sitzungsberichte der königl. preuss.
Akademie der Wissenschaften" Jahrg. 1911 (zweiter Halbband), 1026–1053 (Marohl,
Bibl., n. 241).

[11] *Der Papyrusfund von Elephantine. Dokumente einer jüdischen Gemeinde aus der Perserzeit und
das älteste erhaltene Buch der Weltliteratur* von Ed. Meyer, Leipzig 1912; 1912²⁻³ (Marohl,
Bibl., n. 278).

[12] *Die Keilinschriften der Achämeniden* bearbeitet von F.H. Weissbach (Vorderasiatische
Bibliothek, 3), Leipzig 1911, XI und 2–9.

[13] *Cuneiform Inscriptions of Western Asia* V. *A selection from the Miscellaneous Inscriptions of
Assyria and Babylonia.* Prepared for publication ... by ... Sir H.C. Rawlinson ...,
London 1909, 35. Vgl. schon: H.C. Rawlinson, *Notes on a newly-discovered Clay-Cylinder of
Cyrus the Great*, "Journal of the Royal Asiatic Society" N.S. 12 (1880), 70–97.

[14] *Die sogenannte demotische Chronik des Pap. 215 der Bibliothèque Nationale zu Paris, nebst den
auf der Rückseite des Papyrus stehenden Texten*, herausg. und erklärt von Wilhelm Spiegelberg
(Demotische Studien, Heft 7), Leipzig 1914.

Erlass über die Renten der ägyptischen Tempel, von dem Meyer sofort einen umfassenden historischen Kommentar in den Sitzungsberichten der Berliner Akademie herausgab.[15]

Die Thematik geht also weit über das Buch von 1896 hinaus, aber ich werde mich im wesentlichen mit ihm beschäftigen, weil das historische Problem der Entstehung des Judentums darin eingeführt und auch in methodologischer Hinsicht diskutiert wird. Meyer hat oft beiläufig oder ausführlich πῶς δεῖ ἱστορίαν γράφειν[16] behandelt, und unter diesem Gesichtspunkt ist die *Entstehung des Judenthums* wirklich von außerordentlichem Interesse.

Das Buch verdankt seine Entstehung einer Polemik, die eingangs geklärt werden muß, damit die Neuheit, die es auf dem Gebiet der Geschichtsschreibung des Nahen Orients im Altertum darstellt, ins rechte Licht gerückt werden kann. Diese Polemik ist zwar direkt gegen einige Historiker gerichtet, die sich in jenen Jahren mit der Erforschung der Wiederherstellung Israels nach dem Exil beschäftigten, zielt jedoch auf eine gesamte Tendenz in der Geschichtsschreibung, und zwar auf jene "historische Theologie," die aufgrund ihrer nie wirklich überwundenen ideologischen Grundlagen dazu neigt, die genaue Analyse der Urkunden einer weiter gefaßten Interpretation der Vorgänge unterzuordnen. "Der Historiker," erklärt dagegen Meyer, "hat zunächst feste Thatsachen zu suchen, ganz unbekümmert um jede Theorie, die er sonst irgendwie von den Begebenheiten gewonnen haben mag."[17] Wenn in diesem Fall die "Theorie" dazu geführt hatte, daß man die in den Kapiteln 4–7 des *Esra* Buches enthaltenen persischen Urkunden für spätere jüdische Fälschungen hielt, so ermöglichte jedoch deren konkrete Analyse den Beweis ihrer Echtheit und damit ihre Verwendung als glaubhafte Quellen für die Rekonstruktion nicht nur der jüdischen sondern auch der persischen Geschichte. Ihre Echtheit bedeutet nämlich, daß die Wiederherstellung und die Gliederung der jüdischen Gemeinschaft nach dem Exil von der Haltung des persischen Hofes abhing. Folglich erklärt Meyer gegen die Interpretation, das Judentum sei ein einfaches Produkt der inneren Entwicklung der jüdischen Geschichte, "das Judenthum ist innerhalb des persischen Reichs entstanden, es ist nur möglich geworden durch ein energisches Eingreifen des Perserkönigs, dadurch daß die Autorität des Reichs hinter Nehemia und Ezra stand," und er fährt fort: "so ist die

---

[15] *Ägyptische Dokumente aus der Perserzeit*, "Sitzungsberichte der königl. preuss. Akademie der Wissenschaften" Jahrg. 1915, 287–311 (Marohl, *Bibl.*, n. 306) = *Kleine Schriften* II, Halle 1924, 67–100 (Marohl, *Bibl.*, n. 410).

[16] Ed. Meyer, *Zur Theorie und Methodik der Geschichte*, Halle 1902 (Marohl, *Bibl.*, n. 145) = *Kleine Schriften zur Geschichtstheorie und zur wirtschaftlichen und politischen Geschichte des Alterthums*, Halle 1910, 1–78 (Marohl, *Bibl.*, n. 205).

[17] Meyer, *Entstehung*, 4.

Entstehung des Judenthums nur zu begreifen als Product des Perserreichs.''[18] Das nicht begriffen zu haben, ist die direkte Folge der Tatsache, daß er der in eine Art eifersüchtige "Exclusivität" eingeschlosse-
nen theologischen Forschung nicht gelingt, einen wirklich historischen
Standpunkt einzunehmen: "auch hier rächt sich die Exclusivität der
modernen Forschung, wenn sie das nicht beachtet.''[19]

Und so ist das Kernstück von Meyers Buch der erste Teil, nämlich der
genau und eigensinnig geführte Beweis von der Echtheit der in Esra, 4–7,
enthaltenen aramäischen Urkunden, was die notwendige und unabding-
liche Voraussetzung für diese These ist und was die spätere Kritik trotz
anhaltender Gegenstimmen bestätigt hat. Aber—und das muß energisch
unterstrichen werden—die Kritik hat nicht allein diese Voraussetzung der
Meyerschen These bestätigt: das was in der Folgezeit immer deutlicher
geworden ist, ist die Fruchtbarkeit seiner Grundthese. H.H. Schaeders
Buch über Esra (Esra der Schreiber, 1930, zusammen mit Die Komposition von
Esra 4–6 in Iranische Beiträge, I, aus demselben Jahr)[20]—meiner Meinung
nach der bedeutendste Beitrag nach dem von Meyer zur Rekonstruktion
der Geschichte der Wiederherstellung Israels nach dem Exil—setzt Die
Entstehung des Judenthums voraus und füllt gewissermaßen die größte und
augenfälligste Lücke, und zwar die fehlende Charakterisierung der Gestalt Esras, die bei Meyer unbestimmt und flüchtig bleibt, was sich auch
an der Tatsache erweist, daß er gezwungen ist, auf psychologische Kategorien zurückzugreifen.[21] Das von R. de Vaux gezeichnete Bild von der
Religionspolitik der Achämeniden als Voraussetzung für seine Widerlegung der Argumenten gegen die Echtheit der aramäischen Dokumente[22] ist schon ganz und gar im Keim in Die Entstehung des Judenthums
enthalten. Aber das ist nicht alles. Der Gott der Makkabäer von E.J. Bickerman stützt sich gänzlich auf die Voraussetzung einer offiziellen Verkündung des "Gesetzes des Himmelskönigs," das auch Gesetz des Königs
von Persien wird (Esra, 7.26), Grundtheorie von Schaeders Buch, aber
schon von Meyer formuliert.[23] Und von Meyer hat Bickerman selbst

---

[18] Meyer, Entstehung, 4; 71.

[19] Meyer, Entstehung, 71.

[20] Esra der Schreiber von Hans Heinrich Schaeder (Beiträge zur historischen Theologie,
5), Tübingen 1930; Iranische Beiträge I von Hans Heinrich Schaeder (Schriften der königs-
berger Gelehrten Gesellschaft. Geisteswiss. Klasse 6. Jahr, Heft 5), Halle (Saale) 1930,
212–225. Vgl. Omeljan Pritsak, Hans Heinrich Schaeder (31 Jan. 1896–13 März 1957),
ZDMG 108 (NF 33) (1958), 21–40 bes. 31–32.

[21] Meyer, Entstehung, 239–241.

[22] R. de Vaux, Les décrets de Cyrus et de Darius sur la reconstruction du temple, RB 46 (1937),
29–57 = R. de Vaux, Bible et Orient, Paris 1967, 83–113.

[23] Der Gott der Makkabäer. Untersuchungen über Sinn und Ursprung der makkabäischen Erhebung
von Elias Bickermann, Berlin 1937: "Jerusalem war also eine heilige Stadt; aber nicht aus

gelernt, Urkunden zu analysieren und ihre Bedeutung als historische Quelle zu beurteilen: auch er polemisiert gegen die "Exclusivität" der Theologen. Selbst der mißlungene Versuch Bickermans, auch die Echtheit des (in hebräischer Redaktion bewährten) Edikts des Kyros bei *Esra*, 1.1–4 zu beweisen, bestätigt die Richtigkeit der Meyerschen Analyse der offiziellen, im Buch *Esra* enthaltenen aramäischen Urkunden.

2. Die Positionen der Kritik, die Meyer vorfand, können folgendermaßen zusammengefaßt werden. Im Jahre 1867 hatte Eberhard Schrader bemerkt, daß die Behauptung des Chronisten bei *Esra* 3.8, wonach im zweiten Jahr nach der Rückkehr (537) zur Zeit der Herrschaft des Kyros mit dem Tempelbau begonnen worden sei, unvereinbar war mit der gleichzeitigen Aussage des *Haggai* (1.1), wonach im zweiten Jahr der Herrschaft des Darius (520) damit begonnen worden sei.[25] 1887 behauptete Th. Nöldeke, das Dekret des Artaxerxes bei *Esra*, 7.12–26 sei unecht.[26] Das ist die erste radikale Athetese eines im Buch *Esra*, 4–7 enthaltenen Dokuments: vorher betrafen die Zweifel im wesentlichen die Form, in der sie vom Chronisten überliefert worden waren. Hinsichtlich des Edikte des Darius (*Esra*, 6.3–12) zum Beispiel hatte Schrader in der achten Auflage der *Einleitung* von de Wette (1869), Bertheau zitierend, geschrieben: "Daß das Edikt VI, 3–12 schwerlich in seiner ursprünglichen Gestalt uns überkommen ist, dürfte auch aus der Incongruenz zwischen VI, 3–5. und 6–12. erhellen."[27] Die Verkettung der Ereignisse, so wie sie in den Büchern *Esra* und *Nehemia* erzählt werden (was auf eine gleichzeitige Anwesenheit der beiden Persönlichkeiten in Jerusalem hindeutet) wurde auf jeden Fall grundsätzlich akzeptiert. 1890 jedoch meinte Albin van Hoonacker beweisen können, daß die Ankunft Esras in Jerusalem und die im Buch *Esra* 7–10 berichteten Ereignisse nicht ins siebte Jahr (*Esra*, 7.7) von Artaxerxes Longimanus (458) zu datieren

---

eigener Machtvollkommenheit der Judenheit, sondern kraft eines königlichen Befehls, der 'die Gesetze der Vorfahren' bestätigte und dadurch ihre Ausübung sicherte," 53.

[24] E. Bickerman, *The Edict of Cyrus in Ezra I*, JBL 65 (1946), 249–275 = *Studies in Jewish and Christian History*. Part one, by Elias Bickerman (Arbeiten zur Geschichte des Antiken Judentums und des Urchristentums IX), Leiden 1976, 72–108; Meyer, *Entstehung*, 49.

[25] Eb. Schrader, *Die Dauer des zweiten Tempelbautes. Zugleich ein Beitrag zur Kritik des Buches Esra*, ThSK 40 (1867), 460–504. Ein guter *status quaestionis* in *Einleitung in die Bücher Alten Testaments* von Wolf Wilhelm Grafen Baudissin, Leipzig 1901, 279–300 (§§ 74–76).

[26] In der Besprechung zur *Grammatik des Biblisch-Aramäischen* ... von E. Kautsch, Leipzig 1884, GGA 1884, n. 26, 1014–1023: 1015, Anm. 3.

[27] *Lehrbuch der historisch-kritischen Einleitung in die kanonischen und apokryphischen Bücher des Alten Testaments sowie in die Bibelsammlung überhaupt* von Wilhelm Martin Leberecht de Wette. Neu bearbeitet von Eberhard Schrader ... Achte ... Ausgabe ..., Berlin 1869, 387; *Die Bücher Esra, Nehemia und Esther* erklärt von Ernst Bertheau (Kurzgefasstes exegetisches Handbuch zum Alten Testament. Siebenzehnte Lieferung), Leipzig 1862, 82.

seien, sondern ins entsprechende Jahr von Artaxerxes II. Mnemon (398): Esra sei damit in eindeutig späterer Zeit als Nehemiah in Jerusalem tätig gewesen.[28] Die herkömmliche These wurde von Abraham Kuenen in einem Bericht wiederaufgenommen, die im selben Jahr (1890) vor der Holländischen Akademie der Wissenschaften gegen van Hoonacker vorgetragen wurde.[29] Dieser bestand jedoch in einem zweiten, zwei Jahre später veröffentlichten Aufsatz auf seiner These, die heute allgemein akzeptiert wird.[30]

Im Jahre 1893 veröffentlichte W.H. Kosters, der Nachfolger Kuenens († 1891) auf dem Lehrstuhl in Leiden, *Het Herstel van Israël in het Perzische Tijdvak*,[31] ein Buch, das, wie A.R.S. Kennedy bemerken sollte, "has made more noise in the critical world than almost any book since Wellhausens *Prolegomena.*"[32] Das Buch Kosters' ging von der Voraussetzung aus, daß es keine Rückkehr von Exilanten zur Zeit des Kyros gegeben habe, weshalb der Tempel von den Nachkommen der in Jerusalem verbliebenen Bewohner zur Zeit der Herrschaft des Darius Hystaspis (521 – 485) wiederaufgebaut worden sei. Zerubabel und Josua hätten nicht an der Spitze der zurückgekehrten Exilanten gestanden, sondern derer, die geblieben seien, die unter der Leitung Nehemiahs die Mauern wieder aufgebaut hätten. Die erste Rückkehr von Exilanten habe mit Esra stattgefunden, der nicht im siebten, sondern im zweiunddreißigsten Jahr der Herrschaft von Artaxerxes Longimanus (433) während der zweiten Statthalterschaft von Nehemiah in Jerusalem angekommen sei. Dieser habe die Gemeinschaft nicht auf der Grundlage des Priesterkodex sondern einer vorhergehenden Gesetzgebung neu organisiert. Kosters behauptete als erster, daß alle im Buch *Esra*, 4 – 7, enthaltenen Urkunden ausnahmelos unecht und daher als historische Quellen gänzlich wertlos seien.

---

[28] A. van Hoonacker, *Néhémie et Esdras. Une nouvelle hypothèse sur la chronologie de l'epoque de la Restauration*, "Le Muséon" 9 (1890), 151 – 184; 317 – 351; 389 – 401.

[29] A. Kuenen, *De Chronologie van het Perzische Tijdvak der Joodsche Geschiedenis*, "Verslagen en Mededeelingen der Koninklijke Akademie van Wetenschappen Afdeeling Letterkunde," Amsterdam R. III; D. VII (1890), 273 – 322 = *Die Chronologie des persischen Zeitalters der jüdischen Geschichte* in *Gesammelte Abhandlungen zur biblische Wissenschaft* von Dr. Abraham Kuenen. Aus dem Holländischen übersetzt von K. Budde, Freiburg i.B. und Leipzig 1894, 212 – 251.

[30] A. van Hoonacker, *Zorobabel et le second temple*, "Le Muséon" 10 (1891), 72 – 96; 232 – 260; 379 – 397; 489 – 515; 634 – 644; Ders., *Néhémie en l'an 20 d'Artaxerxès I, Esdras en l'an 7 d'Artaxerxès II. Résponse à un Mémoire de A. Kuenen*, Gand et Leipzig 1892; Ders., *Nouvelles études sur la Restauration juive après l'exil de Babylone*, Paris-Louvain 1896.

[31] *Het Herstel van Israël in het Perzische Tijdvak. Eene studie van W.H. Kosters*, Leiden 1893 = *Die Wiederherstellung Israels in der persischen Periode*. Eine Studie von … W.H. Kosters … Mit Genehmigung des Verfassers übersetzt von A. Basedow, Heidelberg 1895. Kosters' Buch entsteht aus einer Polemik gegen van Hoonacker.

[32] A.R.S. Kennedy, *Did the Jews return under Cyrus?*, ET 8 (1896–1897), 268a – 271a: 269b.

Im März des folgenden Jahres las J. Wellhausen vor der Gesellschaft der Wissenschaften von Göttingen ein Bericht mit dem Titel *Die Rückkehr der Juden aus dem babylonischen Exil*, eine gewissenhafte Diskussion von Kosters' Buch, wo die darin vertretene Grundthese, daß es zur Zeit des Kyros keine Rückkehr gegeben habe, vollständig untergraben wurde. Diese These, stellte Wellhausen fest, gründe sich auf die Bemerkung Schraders, aber dazu sei zu sagen, daß dem Bericht im Buch *Esra*, 3.8, von *Haggai*, 1.1 widersprochen wird, er im Buch *Jesaja*, 44.28 dagegen bestätigt wird.[33] Wellhausen wirft Kosters also vor, sich eine These zu eigen gemacht zu haben und die gesamte spätere Forschung ihr untergeordnet zu haben, was gegen die guten Regeln der historischen Kritik verstößt. "Alle diese Aufstellungen Kosters' laufen schließlich zurück auf seine primäre Annahme, vor Ezra sei überhaupt keine Gola aus Babylonien nach Judäa zurückgewandert. Diese Annahme spielt überall ein und beeinflußt die Beweisführung, im Widerspruch zu der methodischen Grundregel aller nicht spekulativen Wissenschaft, daß man die Untersuchung für jeden einzelnen Punkt möglichst unabhängig führen müsse."[34]

In einigen Punkten stimmt Wellhausen immerhin Kosters bei; vor allem darin, daß er die im Buch *Esra*, 4–7 enthaltenen aramäischen Dokumente für unecht hält. "Darin hat er jedenfalls Recht, daß die Urkunden, die in 4, 11–22 mitgeteilt werden, der Brief der samarischen Beamten an Artaxerxes und das Antwortschreiben des Königs, gefälscht und wertlos sind."[35] Und weiter unten, "Mit der Tatsache, daß persische Beamte über den Tempelbau Zerubabels bei Hofe angefragt haben, mag es seine Richtigkeit haben; im Übrigen ist der aramäische Briefwechsel in Esd. 5.6 nicht mehr wert als der vorhergehende in Kap. 4," und er fügt bezeichnenderweise hinzu: "Kosters sucht hier merkwürdiger weise durch Quellenscheidung einen historischen Kern herauszuschälen."[36]

Diesen Auseinandersetzungen verdankt Meyers Buch seine Entstehung. Als Wellhausen es rezensiert, beginnt er seinen Text mit folgenden Worten: "Dies Buch ist wesentlich gegen mich gerichtet, nämlich dagegen, daß ich nicht gewagt habe die Echtheit der im Buche Esdrae mitgeteilten Urkunden den Angriffen Kosters' gegenüber aufrecht zu erhal-

---

[33] *Die Rückkehr der Juden aus dem Babylonischen Exil* von J. Wellhausen, "Nachrichten von der königl. Gesellsch. der Wissenschaften zu Göttingen" Phil.-hist. Klasse aus dem Jahre 1895, 166–186. Kosters' Antwort: *Het Tijdvak van Israëls Herstel*, "Theol. Tijdschrift" 29 (1895), 549–575; 30 (1896), 489–504; 31 (1897), 518–554.

[34] Wellhausen, *Rückkehr*, 175.

[35] Wellhausen, *Rückkehr*, 169.

[36] Wellhausen, *Rückkehr*, 176.

ten.''[37] Er hatte deutlich wahrgenommen, daß die schon zitierte Äußerung Meyers ''der Historiker hat zunächst feste Thatsachen zu suchen,
ganz unbekümmert um jede Theorie, die er sonst irgendwie von den
Begebenheiten gewonnen haben mag'' nur die Umschreibung des methodologischen Vorbehalts war, den er selbst gegen Kosters geäußert hatte.

In Wirklichkeit waren die Gründe für die Gegnerschaft Meyers Wellhausen gegenüber sehr viel tiefer und auf den historischen Zusammenhang bezogen. Wellhausen selbst hatte gegen Kosters (und gegen
Schrader) *Jesaja* 44.28 zitiert.[38] Aber wenn Kyros in einem zweifellos
zeitgenössischen Stelle ''mein Hirte'' genannt wird, insofern er dazu bestimmt ist, den göttlichen Willen zu erfüllen und ''von Jerusalem sagt, es
möge wieder aufgebaut werden! und vom Tempel: du wirst gegründet
werden,'' kann sein Edikt, das den Tempelbau genehmigt (*Esra*, 6.3 – 5)
höchstens verändert, aber nicht ''historisch wertlos'' sein, und auch noch
so, daß es nicht einmal einer genauen und ausführlichen Analyse für
würdig befunden wird. Und Wellhausen hatte tatsächlich Kosters' Verwerfung der überlieferten Lesart einfach hingenommen und sich außerdem gewundert, daß dieser aufgrund des Umstands, daß die in Babylon
gesuchte Urkunde in Ecbatana gefunden worden war (*Esra*, 6.1 und 2),
angenommen hatte, daß zwei verschiedene Originalurkunden existierten.
''Jeder Fälscher hätte Kyros' Erlaß in Babylon suchen und finden lassen,'' hält Meyer ihm ohne Schwierigkeit entgegen.[39] Der Gegensatz ist
jedoch, wie ich es schon angedeutet habe, viel tiefer und umfassender.

Wenn man die *Prolegomena zur Geschichte Israels* (*Geschichte Israels* I, 1878)
von Wellhausen wiederliest, und vor allem das letzte Kapitel *Die Theokratie
als Idee und Anstalt*,[40] so läßt sich die These klar verfolgen, daß die Entwicklung vom alten Israel zum Judentum hin zu einer Institutionalisie-
rung (und Verknöcherung) der Ideen und Auffassungen geführt hat, die
früher im Volksleben wurzelten. ''Das Judentum, welches die mosaische
Verfassung verwirklicht und konsequent fortgebildet hatte, ließ für die
Individualität keinen Spielraum: im alten Israel war das göttliche Recht
nicht bei der Institution, sondern bei dem Creator Spiritus, bei den Individuen.''[41] Die neue Wirklichkeit ist ein ''unpolitisches Kunstprodukt,''

---

[37] Wellhausens Besprechung zu Meyer, ''Gött. Gelehrte Anzeigen'' 1897, 2, 89 – 98:
89. Meyers Antwort: *Julius Wellhausen und meine Schrift Die Entstehung des Judenthums*, Halle
1897.
[38] Wellhausen, *Rückkehr*, 175.
[39] Meyer, *Entstehung*, 47.
[40] *Prolegomena zur Geschichte Israels* von J. Wellhausen, Berlin 1883, 409 – 424. Erste
Auflage: *Geschichte Israels* von J. Wellhausen. Erster Band, Berlin 1878, 426 – 442. Vgl.
R. Smend, *Julius Wellhausen and his Prolegomena to the History of Israel*, ''Semeia'' 25 (1982),
1 – 20.
[41] Wellhausen, *Prolegomena*, 410; *Geschichte* I, 428.

das nur im Bereich eines fremden Staates leben kann: "Die mosaische Theokratie, das Residuum eines untergegangenen Staates, ist selbst kein Staat, sondern ein unter ungünstigen Bedingungen durch eine ewig merkwürdige Energie geschaffenes, unpolitisches Kunstprodukt; sie hat die Fremdherrschaft zur notwendigen Ergänzung."[42]

"Das Gesetz," so behauptet dagegen Meyer, indem er sich auf das von Esra erlassene Gesetz bezieht, "ist nicht eine private Abmachung zwischen den Mitgliedern eines religiösen Conventikels, sondern das rechtlich bindende Grundgesetz einer vom Staate anerkannten Gemeinde."[43] Das Gesetz ist "Gesetz deines Gottes und Gesetz des Königs," *dātā' dī-'elohak wĕdātā' dī malkā'*, dem "das ganze Volk im 'Abarnahra'", *kāl-'ammā' dī ba 'abar-naharāh* unterworfen ist (*Esra*, 7.25–26). "Daß unter 'Volk' hier nur das isrealitische Volk, d.i. die jüdische Gemeinde verstanden werden kann ... ist klar."[44] Das Edikt von Antiochus III. (Josephus, *ant.* XII, 142) ist die eindeutige Bestätigung dieser Rechtslage: πολιτευέσθωσαν δὲ πάντες οἱ ἐκ τοῦ ἔθνους κατὰ τοὺς πατρίους νόμους. Wie Bickerman gezeigt hat, ist ἔθνος hier ein *terminus technicus* der seleukidischen Kanzlei,[45] aber *'ammā'* gab es schon für den persischen Hof.

3. Mehrere Historiker hatten die "israelitische Färbung" der aramäischen Urkunden im Buch *Esra*, deren Echtheit sie übrigens nicht bestritten, hervorgehoben. Schon Ewald hatte in Bezug auf das Edikt des Kyros diesen Ausdruck verwandt;[46] Stade hatte geschrieben: "Äußerungen wie Cap. 5, 11 ff., Cap. 6, 11 ff. verraten die jüdische Denkungsart und können nicht wohl von einem Perser geschrieben worden sein."[47] Nach Kuenens Ansicht spricht Artaxerxes im Erlaß an Esra im Buch *Esra* 7.12–25 nicht wie ein Anhänger von Ahura-Mazda, sondern wie ein frommer Israelit.[48]

---

[42] Wellhausen, *Prolegomena*, 421; *Geschichte* I, 428.

[43] Meyer, *Entstehung*, 66.

[44] Meyer, *Entstehung*, 66–67.

[45] Bickermann, *Der Gott*, 53 ff.; Ders., *La charte séleucide de Jérusalem*, REJ 100 (1935), 4–35: 26 = *Studies in Jewish and Christian History*. Part two (Arbeiten zur Geschichte des Antiken Judentums und des Urchirstentums IX), Leiden 1980, 44–85: 70.

[46] *Geschichte des Volkes Israel von Heinrich Ewald. Vierter Band. Geschichte Ezra's und der Heiligherrschaft in Israel bis Christus*. Dritte Ausgabe, Göttingen 1864, 65.

[47] *Geschichte des Volkes Israels von Berhard Stade. Zweiter Theil. I Geschichte des vorchristlichen Judenthums bis zur Griechischen Zeit* (Allgemeine Geschichte in Einzeldarstellungen ... herausg. von W. Oncken, Erste Hauptabteilung, sechster Theil), Berlin 1881, 122, Anm. 1 (von Seite 120 ab).

[48] *Historisch-critisch Onderzoek naar het ontstaan en de Verzameling van de Boeken des Ouden Verbonds*, door A. Kuenen. Tweede ... Uitgave. Eerste Deel. *De Thora en de historische Boeken des Ouden Verbonds*, Leiden 1887, 496 (§ 33), Anm. 5 = *Historisch-kritische Einleitung in die Bücher des alten Testaments hinsichtlich ihrer Entstehung und Sammlung* von A. Kuenen. Autorisierte deutsche Ausgabe von Th. Weber. Erster Theil. Zweites Stück. *Die historischen Bücher*

Meyer analysiert besonders aufmerksam diese Seite des Problems. Eine derartige Bemerkung wäre richtig gewesen, bezogen auf vorhergehende Epochen: "Seit wir wissen, wie Kambyses und Darius in den ägyptischen Inschriften als treue Diener der einheimischen Götter auftreten, wie Kyros in seiner Proclamation an die Babylonier sich als den eifrigsten Verehrer und den erklärten Liebling des Marduk einführt."[49] Dies ist jedoch nicht der Fall für Artaxerxes: "Für ihn ist der Himmelsgott von Jerusalem nur ein mächtiger Gott, dessen Zorn man zu meiden hat, dessen Cult er daher nach dem Beispiel seiner Vorgänger mit reichen Gaben und Privilegien ausstattet,"[50] aber es ist nicht "sein" Gott; denn er verwendet den Ausdruck: "euer Gott, der in Jerusalem ist," 'elāhakōm di biyrušlem (Esra, 7.17).

Nach Meyer ist also eine klare Entwicklung in der Einstellung der achämenidischen Herrscher gegenüber den fremden Gottheiten erkennbar: "Für Darius—und das gleiche dürfen wir von Kyros annehmen—ist die Connivenz gegen die fremden Götter nur ein Ausfluß seiner Politik," persönlich sei er—das gehe aus den persischen Inschriften hervor, "ein überzeugter Mazdajasnier." Für seine Nachfolger dagegen "sind die fremden Götter wirkliche Mächte, mit denen es rathsam ist, auf gutem Fuße zu stehen."[51]

Diese Behauptung scheint darauf hin zu deuten, daß bei den frühen Achämeniden die Religion ein bloßes instrumentum regni gewesen ist, aber im weiteren liefert Meyer eine Charakterisierung der Veränderung, die der Mazdaismus in den Religionen der zum persischen Reich gehörigen Völker hervorgebracht habe (sie wird übrigens im 3. Band der Geschichte des Alterthums sehr ausführlich wieder aufgenommen),[52] die mit einer solchen Behauptung nicht ganz vereinbar scheint.

In Bezug auf Charakter und Tendenzen des Priesterkodex, d.h. des Gesetzes, das zur Perserzeit das religiöse Leben der jüdischen Gemeinschaft regelt und dem die achämenidischen Herrscher Autorität verliehen hatten, indem sie es als das "Gesetz des Königs" empfingen, äußert Meyer, es sei ein Gesetz, das nicht allein für die Juden in Palästina "sondern für alle Jahveverehrer in der ganzen Welt" gültig sei. Der Grund dafür sei in der Tatsache zu suchen, daß "die Entwicklung, aus der das Judenthum hervorgegangen ist" nicht allein der jüdischen Religion eigen sei, sondern allen Religionen des Orients während der Perserzeit gemein-

---

des alten Testaments, Leipzig 1890, 165 (§ 33), Anm. 5. Vgl. Chronologie, 235: "Nach einem in aramäischer Sprache mitgeteilten Erlass (Esra 7, 12–26), der stark jüdisch gefärbt ist."
[49] Meyer, Entstehung, 64.
[50] Meyer, Entstehung, 64.
[51] Meyer, Entstehung, 64.
[52] Meyer, Entstehung, 221–222; Geschichte des Alterthums, III, 167–174 (§§ 103–106).

sam sei, als aufgrund des Verschwindens der Nationalstaaten die Religion ihren ursprünglichen Charakter verloren habe. "Staat, Nation und Religion sind nicht mehr unlösbar mit einander verwachsen," sondern gehen auseinander, ein jedes seinen eigenen Weg und "die Religion lebt für sich allein weiter als Selbstzweck, als ein Institut für sich." Damit hat die Religion keine politische Funktion mehr; das Individuum als Sonderwesen hat eine direkte Beziehung zur Gottheit, welche ihrerseits dazu neigt, eine kosmische Kraft mit universellen Forderungen zu werden.[53]

4. Ich habe nicht die erforderliche Sachkenntnis, um die Entwicklung der persischen Religion zur Zeit der Achämeniden beurteilen zu können, wo nicht einmal die Spezialisten auch nur teilweise übereinzustimmen scheinen. Einige von ihnen sprechen hinsichtlich der frühen Achämeniden von einer Verwendung der Religion als *instrumentum regni*.[54] Das ist

---

[53] Meyer, *Entstehung*, 221.

[54] Besonders H.S. Nyberg, *Das Reich der Achämeniden* in *Historia Mundi. Ein Handbuch der Weltgeschichte* ... herausg. von F. Vajavec ..., III, Bern 1954, 56 – 115: "Pietät gegen die Verordnungen von Kyros bewegte ihn dabei wahrscheinlich weniger als die politische Notwendigkeit, die Juden wegen des bevorstehenden Feldzuges gegen Ägypten ruhig und loyal zu erhalten," 82. Ueber die Religion der Achämeniden: E. Dhorme, *La religion des Achéménides*, RB N.S. 10 (1913), 15 – 35 = *Recueil Edouard Dhorme. Etudes bibliques et orientales*, Paris 1951, 619 – 641: E. Herzfeld, *Die Religion der Achämeniden*, RHR 113 (1936), 21 – 41; *The Avestan Hymn to Mithra*. With an Introduction, Translation and Commentary by Ilya Gershevitsch (University of Cambridge Oriental Publications, 4), Cambridge 1959, 16 ff.; J. Duchesne-Guellemin, *La religion de l'Iran ancien* ("Mana" Introduction à l'histoire des religions, 1), Paris 1962, 157 – 170; M.A. Dandamaev, *Iran pri pervych Achemenidach* (*VI v. do n.e.*) (Akademija Nauk SSSR—Institut Narodov Azii), Moskwa 1963, 102 ff.; 182 ff. = *Persien unter den ersten Archämeniden* (*6. Jahrhundert v. Chr.*), übersetzt von Heinz-Dieter Pohl (Beiträge zur Iranistik, herausg. von G. Redard, 8), Wiesbaden 1976, 91 ff.; 166 ff.; J. Duchesne-Guillemin, *Die Religion der Achämeniden*, "Acta Antiqua" (Budapest) 19 (1971), 25 – 35; Ders., *La religion des Achéménides*, "Historia", Einzelschriften, 18. *Beiträge zur Achämenidengeschichte* herausg. von G. Walser, Wiesbaden 1972, 59 – 82; Ders., *Le Dieu de Cyrus*, "Acta Iranica" 3 (1974), 11 – 21; Heidemarie Koch, *Die religiösen Verhältnisse der Dareioszeit. Untersuchungen an Hand der Elamitischen Persepolistäfelschen* (Göttinger Orientalforschungen ... III. Reihe: Iranica, Band 4), Wiesbaden 1977; Cl. Herrenschmidt, *La religion des Achéménides: état de la question*, "Studia Iranica" 9 (1980), 325 – 339; M. Boyce, *Persian religion in the Achemenid Age* in *The Cambridge History of Judaism* edited by W.D. Davies and L. Finkelstein. Volume One, Cambridge 1984, 279 – 307; 439 – 441 (Bibliogr.); R.N. Frye, *The History of Ancient Iran* (Handbuch der Altertumswiss. III. Abhandl. 7), München 1984, 120 – 124; über ihre Religionspolitik: Hildegard Lewy, *Babylonian background of the kay kâûs legend*, "Archiv Orientální" 17 (1949) (*Symbolae ad studia orientis pertinentes Frederico Hrozný dedicatae*. Pars secunda), 28 – 109: 56 ff.; J. Duchesne-Guillemin, *Religion et politique de Cyrus à Xerxès*, "Persica" 3 (1967 – 68), 1 – 9; G. Gnoli, *Politica religiosa e concezione della regalità sotto gli Achemenidi* in *Gururāja-mañjarikā. Studi in onore di Giuseppe Tucci*, Napoli 1974, I, 24 – 88 = *Politique religieuse et conception de la royauté sous les Achéménides*, "Acta Iranica" 2 (1974), 118 – 190; R.J. Littman, *The Religious policy of Xerxes and the Book of Esther*, JQR 65 (1974 – 75), 145 – 155; M. Dandamaev, *La politique religieuse des Achéménides*, "Acta Iranica" deuxième série 1 (1975) (*Monumentum H.S. Nyberg*), 193 – 200, P. Tozzi, *Per la storia della politica religiosa degli Achemenidi: distruzione di templi greci agl'inizi del V secolo*, "Rivista Storica Italiana" 89 (1977), 18 – 32.

eine Behauptung, die mir grundsätzlich fragwürdig erscheint. In diesem besonderen Fall habe ich zudem den Eindruck, daß das unterschiedliche Verhalten, das die Achämeniden im Vergleich zu den Assyrern und Neu-babyloniern den unterworfenen Völkern gegenüber an den Tag legen, auch wenn sie es klug einsetzen, um Aufstände zu vermeiden und das Reich zu sammenzuhalten, notwendigerweise von einer anderen religiö-sen Perspektive abhängt und ein völlig anderes Begriffsschema voraus-setzen muß, und das interessiert uns ja letzten Endes. Abgesehen von den Problemen dieser Art erscheint es uns nützlich, diesen Seiten Meyers einige Bemerkungen zu widmen, denn ihre Bedeutung steht, wie mir scheint, ganz außer Frage.

Vor allem ist für mich die Behauptung, "die Entwicklung, aus der das Judenthum hervorgegangen ist, ist nichts der Jahvereligion Eigenthüm-liches, sondern der Ausdruck einer Bewegung, die seit der Perserzeit alle Religionen des Orients erfaßt hat,"[55] nicht haltbar. Wenn der jüdische Universalismus seinen höchsten und folgerichtigsten Ausdruck in dem unbekannten Verfasser der Kapitel 40 – 55 des Buches *Jesaja*, also in der Zeit nach dem Exil, findet, so kann der sogenannte "Deuterojesaja" nicht von der vorangehenden Prophetentradition getrennt werden, die einen Gott mit zweifellos noch naturalistischen und ethnischen Merkmalen in einen Gott verwandelt hat, der Gerechtigkeit fordert und der, wenn sein Volk sie nicht verwirklicht, nicht zögert, sich eines fremden Herrschers zu bedienen, um es zu strafen. Auf diesem Wege hat der Universalismus in Israel Eingang gefunden, so daß der "Deuterojesaja" Kyros zum "Ge-salbten" Jahvehs erklären kann. Aus diesem Grund hat der Gott Israels seine ethnischen Züge stark abgeschwächt und in einigen Fällen ganz verloren.

Der persische Universalismus hat einen völlig verschiedenen Ursprung und eine ganz andere Bedeutung und hat mit dem Umwandlungsprozeß der jüdischen Religion nichts zu tun. Das haben Wellhausen und Duhm sicher viel klarer erkannt als Meyer, der wenigstens in diesen Jahren zeigt, daß er den spezifischen Faktoren, die die Entwicklung der jüdischen Religion bestimmt haben, wenig Aufmerksamkeit geschenkt hat. Das wird von seiner Äußerung bestätigt (die nur in einer Anmerkung er-scheint), in der es heißt: "ganz falsch ist es aber, eine directe Beeinflus-sung des Judenthums durch den Parismus oder umgekehrt anzunehmen, so oft das auch bis auf LAGARDE hinab geschehen ist."[57] Als Meyer

[55] Meyer, *Entstehung*, 221.
[57] Meyer, *Entstehung*, 239, Anm. 1. P. de Lagarde betrachtete Purimfest als aus der iranischen "Totentagenfest" (*farvardigān*) abgeleitet: *Purim. Ein Beitrag zur Geschichte der Religion*, "Abhandl. der königl. Gesellschaft der Wiss. zu Göttingen" 34 (1887), vgl.

später (1921) das Buch über den Ursprung des Christentums schreibt und sich das Problem der jüdischen Religion in persischer und griechischer Zeit stellen muß, hat sich seine Position in dieser Hinsicht auf jeden Fall deutlich verändert und er gewährt dualistischen Auffassungen persischen Ursprungs breiten Raum.[58]

Ähnlich bedeutet die Äußerung, daß ''daraus folgt, daß die Religion fortan keine politischen Aufgaben mehr hat, daß die Verbindung des einzelnen mit seinem Gotte nicht mehr im Staat und auf der Basis der Nationalität in der Heimath sich vollzieht, sondern das einzelne Individuum als Sonderwesen, losgelöst von dem heimathlichen Verbande, überall hin begleitet,''[59] daß dem persischen Reich eine Situation zugesprochen wird, die erst für das römische und spätrömische Reich zutreffen wird.[60] Damit der Mensch als Sonderwesen eine direkte Verbindung mit der Gottheit wahrnehmen kann, ist es nötig, daß sich universell die Überzeugung durchsetzt, etwas Göttliches in sich zu haben, das heißt, daß der griechische Gedanke von der Unsterblichkeit der Seele universell akzeptiert wird. Zur Zeit der Entstehung des Judentums ist nichts fremder als eine ''personal religion.''

Während der jüdische Universalismus, wenigstens da, wo er bei den Propheten seinen höchsten Ausdruck findet, zu einem reinen Monotheismus führt—die anderen Götter sind ''Menschenwerk aus Holz und Stein'' (*Jesaja*, 37.19), deuten zweitens die Ausdrücke, die in den persischen Urkunden den Gott Israels charakterisieren, auf eine ungelöste Spannung zwischen einer himmlischen und einer lokal und ethnisch bestimmten Natur der Gottheit hin. Jahveh ist der ''Gott des Himmels,'' *'elāh šmayin* (*Esra*, 6.9 und 10; 7.12, 21 und 23; vgl. *Dan.*, 2.18), aber zugleich ist er auch ''euer Gott, der in Jerusalem ist'' (*Esra*, 7.14). Ich glaube nicht, daß zwischen diesen beiden Charakterisierungen der Gottheit ein realer Widerspruch besteht: denn spätestens beginnend mit Darius neigt die Religion des achämenidischen Reiches dazu, eine Art himmlische Gottheit mit lokalen Gottheiten zu verbinden, wofür Mithra ein typisches Beispiel ist. Man könnte glauben, daß ein ähnlicher synkretischer Mechanismus zur Anerkennung der Götter der verschiedenen Völker geführt hat, die zum Reich gehörten, eine Anerkennung, aus

---

Meyer, *Ursprung* (volg. Anm.), II, 94, Anm. 1. Ueber *farvardigān*: *The Religious Ceremonies and Customs of the Parsees* by Ji.Ja. Modi, Bombay 1922, 465–479.

[58] *Ursprung und Anfänge des Christentums* von Ed. Meyer. Zweiter Band. *Die Entwicklung des Judentums und Jesus von Nazaret*, Stuttgart und Berlin 1921, 41–57 und 95 ff. (*Das Eindringen des Dualismus ins Judentum*).

[59] Meyer, *Entstehung*, 221.

[60] Meyer, *Entstehung*, 222: ''Universalismus und Individualismus sind in die Signatur der religiösen Entwickelung, welche unter den Achämenidenreich beginnt und in der Religionsconcurrenz des römischen Kaiserreichs ihren Höhepunkt erreicht.''

der nicht nur folgte, daß der Kult gestattet war, sondern die ihn auch gewährleistete, was dazu führen mußte, daß auch in politischer Hinsicht sich Unabhängigkeit im Keim herausbildete, und dies ist ersichtlich aus der Tatsache, daß die vom achämenidischen Hof begünstigte Form der Selbstregierung für die unterworfenen Völker eben die hierokratische war.

Gerade in dieser Hinsicht jedoch ist noch eine Bemerkung zu Meyers Buch am Platze. Nach Wellhausen hat sich im Israel nach dem Exil eine Art hierokratische Regierung durchgesetzt, weil die Theokratie, wenn sie sich institutionalisiert, die natürliche Tendenz hat, sich in Hierokratie zu verwandeln: "Theokratie als Verfassung ist Hierokratie."[61] Nach Meyer ist die Tatsache dagegen, daß sich die Priesterklasse in Israel nach dem Exil als "Regierungsschicht" durchsetzt, die Folge einer bewußten Politik der Achämeniden. Er betont jedoch diese Seite des Problems nicht; er greift in dieser Sache Wellhausen nicht an, und auch Wellhausen sagt in seiner Rezension kein Wort darüber, auch wenn das von Meyer dargelegte Ergebnis besonders darin gänzlich und radikal seiner Ansicht von der Entstehung des Judentums, wie er sie in den *Prolegomena* dargelegt und gewissermaßen in der Jugendschrift von 1874 über den Pharisäismus vorausgenommen hatte, widersprach.[62] Nur das Buch von Schaeder mit der darin vorgenommenen Deutung des Titels "Schreiber", *safrā'* (*Esra*, 10.10 und 16; *Neh.*, 8.2 und 9), wie er von Esra angeführt wird, hat wirklich Meyers Interpretation des Judentums als eines Ergebnisses der persischen Politik völlig verdeutlicht. Das macht jedoch vielleicht eine Neueinschätzung der These erforderlich, nach der die Achämeniden die Religion als *instrumentum regni* benutzt hätten. Diese Frage scheint komplexer und umfassender zu sein, als sie üblicherweise dargelegt wird.

5. Trotz der Bedeutung des Werks hat *Die Entstehung des Judenthums* zu Beginn einen eher schwachen Widerhall gefunden. Die Rezensionen beschränken sich bestenfalls auf die Darlegung der Argumente Meyers und der polemischen Erwiderungen Wellhausens, und wahrscheinlich ist in der unbestrittenen Autorität dieses letzteren der Grund für die Vorsicht vieler Rezensenten zu suchen.[63] Der Akzent liegt jedenfalls auf der Analyse der armäischen Urkunden, und die von Meyer vorgenommene historische Rekonstruktion der Entstehung des Judentums bleibt eindeutig im Hintergrund. W. Staerk[64] schreibt vor dem Erscheinen von Meyers

---

[61] Wellhausen, *Prolegomena*, 420; *Geschichte* I, 438.
[62] *Die Pharisäer und die Sadduzäer. Eine Untersuchung zur inneren jüdischen Geschichte* von J. Wellhausen, Greifswald 1878; Hannover 1924[2].
[63] Anweisung der verschieden Besprechungen in Marohl, *Bibl.*, 92, n. 107; vgl. auch n. 117.
[64] ZWTh 40 (1897), 151–154.

Buch ebenfalls, man habe sich nicht klargemacht, welche Schätze in diesem Teil des Werks des Chronisten begraben lägen und er fügt hinzu: dank einer zum erstenmal methodologisch korrekten Analyse der im Buch *Esra* 4 – 7 enthaltenen offiziellen Urkunden "hat Meyer bewiesen, daß die traditionelle Anschauung über die Genesis des Judentums im wesentlichen völlig richtig ist,"[65] ein zumindest überraschendes Urteil.

Wenn wir jedoch vom Ende des 19. Jahrhunderts, als *Die Entstehung des Judenthums* geschrieben wurde, zu unserer Gegenwart übergehen, erscheint uns das Gesamtbild wesentlich verändert. Von denen, die behaupten, die im Buch *Esra* enthaltenen aramäischen Urkunden seien unecht, gibt es nur noch wenige.[66] "The authenticity of these Texts, partly or totally, has been disputed, but Eduard Meyer demonstrated that they were genuine" hat Widengren 1977 geschrieben;[67] "Cyrus issued a decree ordering the restoration of the Jewish Community and cult in Palestine. The Bible gives two reports of this . . . the latter is part of a collection of aramaic documents . . . the authenticity of which need not be questioned" schreibt Bright in seiner *History of Israel* (1959).[68] Aber was noch wichtiger ist—wir können sagen, daß die Deutung der Entstehung des Judentums von Meyer eindeutig den Vorrang hat gegenüber der zur Zeit der Veröffentlichung des Buches vorherrschenden von Wellhausen. Wenn wir in der *Einleitung* von Eissfeldt aufmerksam das Kapitel von *Esra* und *Nehemiah* lesen, stellen wir fest, daß die Analyse der Texte Meyers Deutung voraussetzt und bestätigt, auch wenn der am meisten zitierte Name der von Schaeder und nicht der von Meyer ist.[69]

Meyers Buch bleibt jedenfalls das bei weitem wichtigste Werk, das je über die Entstehung des Judentums geschrieben worden ist. Es ist das Werk eines Historikers, der das Problem nicht theologisch sondern historisch gestellt und gelöst hat. So hat auch Willy Staerk in der eben erwähnten Rezension geschrieben: "Es ist das Verdienst des Historikers, hier die Fehler . . . der Theologen aufgedeckt und verbessert zu haben."[70]

---

[65] W. Staerk, ZWTh 40 (1897), 151.

[66] Zum letzten: G. Garbini, *Storia e ideologia nell'Antico Israele*, Brescia 1986, 208 – 235.

[67] G. Widengren, *The Persian Period* in *Israelite und Judaean History* edited by John Hayes and J. Maxwell Miller, London 1977, 489 – 538: 496.

[68] J. Bright, *A History of Israel*, London 1960², 342.

[69] *Einleitung in das Alte Testament . . . Entstehungsgeschichte des Alten Testaments* von Otto Eissfeldt. 3., neubearbeitete Auflage, Tübingen 1964, 734 – 756 (§ 73).

[70] W. Staerk, ZWTh 40 (1897), 151.

ECKHARD PLÜMACHER

EDUARD MEYERS "URSPRUNG UND ANFÄNGE DES CHRISTENTUMS." VERHÄLTNIS ZU FACHWISSENSCHAFT UND ZEITGEIST

I

"Ursprung und Anfänge des Christentums geschichtlich zu begreifen und in den Zusammenhang der historischen Entwicklung einzureihen ist eine der größten Aufgaben, die dem Geschichtsforscher gestellt ist"—mit diesem als programmatische Erklärung zu verstehenden Satz hat Eduard Meyer das Vorwort zu seiner Darstellung des Urchristentums begonnen. Meyer zufolge haben die Fachgenossen die große Aufgabe freilich sämtlich vernachlässigt; "mit ängstlicher Scheu sind bisher alle Historiker ihr aus dem Wege gegangen."[1] In der Tat war ihr Theodor Mommsen "sichtlich ausgewichen"—dies kein Urteil des stets zu scharfen Verdikten neigenden Meyer, sondern Meinung des sehr viel abgewogener urteilenden Kirchenhistorikers Hans Lietzmann;[2] erinnert sei hier auch an das offenherzige Eingeständnis Otto Seecks: "Alle Fragen, die sich auf die Entstehung des Christentums beziehen, sind so schwierig, daß wir uns freuen, ihnen aus dem Wege gehn zu dürfen."[3] Nicht so Meyer; ausdrücklich erklärt er, "daß ich, falls es mir beschieden sein würde, meine Geschichte des Altertums bis in diese Zeiten [sc. die der Anfänge des Christentums] fortzuführen, ganz anders verfahren müsse, ist mir nie zweifelhaft gewesen" (UAC I, S. VII). Die Aufgabe einer in die Universalgeschichte eingebetteten Darstellung des Urchristentums, vielleicht auch das von Meyer den Fachgenossen unterstellte Versagen gegenüber dieser Aufgabe, müssen ihn dann derart gereizt haben, daß er sich entschloß, sie auch unabhängig von der in den Jahren des 1. Weltkriegs stecken gebliebenen "Geschichte des Altertums" in Angriff zu nehmen. Möglich ist, daß Anstöße von außen hinzu kamen, Anregungen aus dem

---

[1] Ursprung und Anfänge des Christentums (= UAC) I, S. VII.
[2] HZ 127 (1923) 98.—Ein Beispiel für Meyers Verdikte ist sein Urteil über Julius Wellhausen: dessen Ansichten erklärten sich "nur aus seiner tiefgewurzelten eigenwilligen Abneigung, auf Anschauungen einzugehn, die er nicht selbst gewonnen hatte" (UAC II 384, A.1).
[3] Geschichte des Untergangs der antiken Welt 3, Stuttgart ²1921, 173. Der Gleichklang mit Meyers oben zitierter Passage legt die Vermutung nahe, daß es gerade Seecks Bekenntnis gewesen sein könnte, das Meyer zu seiner Äußerung veranlaßt hat.

Schülerkreis; eine entsprechende Bemerkung, die sich allerdings lediglich auf Meyers Beschäftigung mit der Apostelgeschichte bezieht, findet sich im Vorwort (S. VII f.). Einen weiteren Grund für die Beschäftigung mit dem Urchristentum nennt Meyer dann noch an versteckter Stelle, in einer Anmerkung des zweiten Bandes: die Absicht, den Anschauungen der sog. ''Religionsgeschichtlichen Schule'' über das Verhältnis von Christentum und Hellenismus zu widersprechen; sein ganzes Buch diene der Widerlegung dieser Ansichten und versuche stattdessen die wirklich für die Entwicklung maßgebenden Momente darzulegen (UAC III 316, A.1).[4]

Meyers Buch—ein monumentales Werk von drei Bänden mit insgesamt über 1400 Seiten—erschien in den Jahren 1921 bis 1923. Das Echo war lebhaft. Die Berliner Theologische Fakultät verlieh Meyer, der, wie ein Rezensent bemerkte, ''über seinem Werke zum Theologen geworden'' sei,[5] die Würde ihres Ehrendoktors; die Rezensenten allerdings, durchweg Theologen, urteilten, mit einziger Ausnahme Hans Lietzmanns,[6] überwiegend negativ. Einer von ihnen, der Mitbegründer der ''Formgeschichtlichen Schule,'' Karl Ludwig Schmidt, suchte seine Rezension des Meyerschen Werkes sogar als ''den Protest der Wissenschaft gegen den unwissenschaftlichen Schritt eines gefeierten Wissenschaftlers'' verständlich zu machen;[7] ein anderer, Hans von Soden, konstatierte: ''So, wie uns hier die Ursprünge und Anfänge des Christentums dargestellt werden, ist es—mit Ranke zu reden—eben einfach nicht

---

[4] Dazu Martin Dibelius, DLZ 45 (1924) 1641 f.; Rudolf Bultmann, Literaturblatt. Beilage zur Frankfurter Zeitung, No. 21 vom 23. Mai 1926.

[5] Hermann Strathmann, Neue kirchl. Zeitschrift 35 (1924) 559.

[6] HZ 127 (1923) 98–104.—Fast uneingeschränkte, allerdings nie publizierte Zustimmung fand Meyer auch bei Adolf von Harnack. Vgl. die Dankschreiben, die Harnack am 22. Dezember 1920, 6. November 1921 und 16. Oktober 1923, jeweils nach Erhalt der einzelnen Bände von Meyers Werk, an diesen geschickt hat (den Hinweis auf diese jetzt im Archiv der AdW der DDR [Nachlaß Ed. Meyer 130] aufbewahrten Schreiben—eine Postkarte, zwei Briefe—verdanke ich Frau Johanna Jantsch/Marburg). Harnacks Beifall kann nicht überraschen—fußte Meyers Werk, wie unten gezeigt werden wird, doch ganz auf den Ergebnissen der liberalen Theologie des 19. Jhdts., die Harnack wesentlich mitgestaltet hatte.

[7] Die Christliche Welt 35 (1921) 120.—Durch den scharfen Ton, den Schmidt anschlug, handelte er sich eine nicht minder scharfe Zurechtweisung Lietzmanns ein (aaO [wie A.6] 99); ein Briefwechsel mit diesem schloß sich an (Schmidts Briefe sind abgedruckt in: Kurt Aland [Hg.], Glanz und Niedergang der deutschen Universität. 50 Jahre deutscher Wissenschaftsgeschichte in Briefen an und von Hans Lietzmann, Berlin/New York 1979, 460–462). Meyer selbst empfand ''Urteile wie die von Schmidt'' als ''naiv'', sie hätten ihn ''nur belustigt'' (Brief an Lietzmann vom 3. Dezember 1922; abgedruckt in: Aland, aaO 459 f.). Ganz ähnlich äußerte sich der Berliner Kirchenhistoriker Karl Holl: Schmidts ''famose Besprechung'' wirke auf ihn ''unsagbar komisch, bloß ein Zeichen mehr, wie tief unsere neutestamentliche Wissenschaft heruntergekommen ist'' (Brief vom 24. März 1921 an Lietzmann, s. Aland, aaO 441).

gewesen.''[8] Am häufigsten begegnet indes der Vorwurf, Meyer biete—
im Gegensatz zu der hohe Erwartungen weckenden Ankündigung seines
Vorworts, im Bereich der Geschichtsschreibung über das Urchristentum
liege "ein sehr reiches Material von höchster Bedeutung vor, das der
geschichtlichen Behandlung [erst noch] harrt" (UAC I, S. VII)—nur
allzu oft nichts Neues, sondern lediglich "lauter bekannte und von anderen besser begründete Dinge,"[9] ja, seine Arbeit bedeute sogar "einen
Rückschritt hinter das schon Erreichte."[10] Verübelt wurde Meyer auch
die hartnäckige Weigerung, in hinreichendem Maße von neueren Forschungsergebnissen Kenntnis zu nehmen; die diesbezügliche salvatori-
sche Klausel des Vorworts (S. IX) hatte die Kritiker offensichtlich nicht
besänftigen können.[11] Einspruch gegen solche Kritik erhob allerdings
Victor Ehrenberg. In seinem Nachruf auf Meyer schrieb er, den universalhistorischen Anspruch des Meyerschen Werkes würdigend: "Große
schöpferische Werke bleiben von solchem Vorwurf, der nur die wissenschaftliche Kleinarbeit zu Recht treffen kann, unberührt."[12]

Um entscheiden zu können, wer hier richtig geurteilt hat, bedarf es
allererst eines Blickes auf das Bild selbst, das Meyer von Ursprung und
Anfängen des Christentums entworfen hat. Freilich kann dies Bild als
Ganzes hier nicht nachgezeichnet werden, nicht einmal in groben Zügen
—handelt es sich doch, Meyers Anspruch gemäß, um ein weit ausgreifen-
des Panorama, in dem ebenso ausgedehnte wie minutiöse Untersuchungen zur Quellenkritik der Evangelien oder der Apostelgeschichte genauso
ihren Platz gefunden haben wie z.B. eine ganze, keineswegs knapp gehaltene Geschichte der politischen und religiösen Entwicklung des nachexilischen Judentums, in deren Kontext dann sogar noch eine umfäng-
liche Darstellung der Religion Zoroasters als einer wesentlichen
Vorbedingung für die Entstehung des Frühjudentums begegnet. Will
man angesichts der Überfülle des von Meyer Gebotenen nicht überhaupt
darauf verzichten, in einer begrenzten Studie wie der vorliegenden ein
Urteil über Geist und Zeitgemäßheit von Meyers monumentaler Darstel-

---

[8] Zeitschr. f. Kirchengeschichte 43 (1924) 440; vgl. Adolf Jülicher, Theolog. Lit.ztg
49 (1924) 338: "In Wahrheit ist bei dem Zustande unsrer Quellen auch Meyer nicht im
Stande, die Anfänge des Christentums so vorzustellen wie sie wirklich waren."
[9] Johannes Behm, Orientalist. Lit.ztg 25 (1922) 212. Vgl. z.B. noch Dibelius, DLZ
42 (1921) 226 f.; Julius Kögel, Theol. Lit.bericht 44 (1921) 105; Johannes Leipoldt, Hi-
stor. Vierteljahresschr. 21 (1922/23) 341.
[10] Bultmann, Literaturblatt Nr. 8. Beilage zur Frankfurter Zeitung vom 13. April
1921; vgl. Schmidt, aaO (wie A.7) 118.
[11] Vgl. Dibelius, aaO (wie A.9) 227 f.; Schmidt, aaO (wie A.7) 116 ff.; Kögel, aaO
(wie A.9) 106; Behm, Orientalist. Lit.ztg 27 (1924) 474; von Soden, aaO (wie A.8) 430
f.; selbst Lietzmann, aaO (wie A.6) 100.
[12] HZ 143 (1931) 506.

lung zu gewinnen, bleibt lediglich ein Ausweg, nämlich den Teil für das Ganze zu nehmen und durch die Betrachtung einer einzelnen—freilich wesentlichen!—Facette des Riesenwerks zum, Ziel zu gelangen. Die Facette, die mir für unsere Zwecke am tauglichsten erscheint, ist das Bild, das Meyer von Jesus gezeichnet hat. Dessen Gestalt besaß für ihn, der ohnehin von der geschichtsbestimmenden Kraft überragender Persönlichkeiten überzeugt war (UAC III 219 f.), zentrale Bedeutung, denn: "auf dem Zusammenströmen der Entwicklungsreihen, die an Sokrates und an Jesus anknüpfen, teils gegensätzlich, teils sich verbindend, beruht im letzten Grunde die gesamte weitere Entwicklung des geistigen Lebens der abendländischen Menschheit" (ebd. 200).

II

Zur Zeichnung seines Jesusbildes haben auch Meyer keine anderen Quellen zur Verfügung gestanden als allein die Evangelien. Ihrer—mit den herkömmlichen Methoden der Literarkritik durchgeführten—Analyse dient der gesamte erste Band des Werkes. Das Ergebnis der Analyse findet sich knapp zusammengefaßt in einer Anmerkung zu Beginn von Meyers Jesuskapitel: "Die hier gegebene Darstellung der Anschauungen und Lehren Jesu beruht auf ... Marcus, dessen Angaben, soweit nicht die Eschatologie und die Lehre vom leidenden Messias hineinspielt, als durchaus zuverlässig gelten können; daneben ist Q[13] mit Vorsicht, die Sonderstücke des Matthaeus und Lukas nur ausnahmsweise benutzt" (UAC I 425, A.2). Meyer hat sich freilich nicht auf die Darstellung von Jesu "Anschauungen und Lehren" beschränkt; die eben skizzierte Quellenbasis schien ihm auch dafür auszureichen, einen Blick in Jesu Leben zu tun, d.h. zumindest die Chronologie seiner Wirksamkeit festzustellen sowie ein Bild von der Entwicklung seiner Persönlichkeit zu malen. Insbesondere dem Markusevangelium glaubte er entnehmen zu dürfen, "daß wir für die Erkenntnis der Geschichte Jesu keineswegs lediglich mit Aufzeichnungen der zweiten, nachapostolischen Generation zu rechnen haben, sondern weit darüber hinaus mitten in die erste Generation hineingeführt werden, die ihn [sc. Jesus] persönlich genau gekannt hat und noch eine lebendige Erinnerung bewahrte ... So liegt gar kein Grund vor, diese ältesten Überlieferungen nicht in allem Wesentlichen, auch in der chronologischen Anordnung seiner Geschichte, für historisch zuverlässig zu halten" (I 146 f.; vgl. ebd. 125). Beispiele dieser von Meyer freilich verdächtig oft allein aufgrund ihrer Anschaulichkeit als

---

[13] D.h. die sog. Spruchquelle, die fast ausschließlich "Worte" Jesu enthält und neben dem Mk.-Ev. die zweite durchlaufende Quelle für Lk. und Mt. gewesen ist.

authentisch erkannten "lebendigen Erinnerung"[14] sind etwa die Notiz vom Fortgang Jesu aus Kapernaum (1,35–38), die Geschichte von Petri Verleugnung (14,27–31.54.66–72), die Gethsemaneszene (14,32–42) und insbesondere die Überlieferung von Petri Messiasbekenntnis (8,27–33) mit der unmittelbar anschließenden Erzählung von Jesu Verklärung (9,2–8).[15] Meyer zufolge verdankte der älteste Evangelist alle diese Stücke dem Petrus, dessen Dolmetscher Markus gewesen sei: an der Zuverlässigkeit der entsprechenden Papiasnotiz hegt Meyer keine Zweifel (I 158 f.). Zwar vermag er an anderer Stelle einzuräumen: Im Markusevangelium sei "alles . . . beherrscht von den Anschauungen des [Ur-] Christentums und daher in der Auffassung und Gestaltung von der geschichtlichen Grundlage schon beträchtlich abgerückt." Doch folgt dieser Erkenntnis sogleich wieder die Feststellung: "Aber daneben treten die der ältesten Tradition angehörigen menschlichen und individuellen Züge Jesu noch so anschaulich hervor, daß sie ermöglichen, von seiner Entwicklung und seiner Lehre ein zuverlässiges Bild zu gewinnen" (I 123).

Man kann sagen, daß Meyer diese Möglichkeit, so wie er es verstand, zu nutzen gewußt hat. Ein charakteristisches Beispiel dafür ist seine Interpretation der knappen Perikope Mk 1,35 ff. Sie berichtet, wie Jesus sich nach einer Reihe von Krankenheilungen am frühen Morgen des folgenden Tages aus Kapernaum hinaus in die Wüste zurückzieht, um dort zu beten. Die Jünger suchen ihn und teilen ihm mit, daß alle Welt ihn vermisse. Darauf geht Jesus jedoch nicht ein; er antwortet lediglich: "Laßt uns anderswohin in die benachbarten Ortschaften ziehen, damit ich dort predige; denn dazu bin ich ausgesandt." Meyer: "Ein sehr wertvolles Selbstzeugnis Jesu: in dem Drange, zu predigen, die erkannte Wahrheit der Welt zu verkünden, hat er, offenbar erst vor wenigen Tagen, seine Heimat Nazaret verlassen, und zur Vorbereitung auf sein Werk bedarf es immer aufs neue der inneren Sammlung in der Einsamkeit und der Stärkung durch Gebet. Wir erkennen in dieser Scene die inneren Kämpfe und Anfechtungen, die er zu bestehen hat, wenn er als Wanderprediger mit der vollen Autorität . . . des gottgesandten Verkünders des Evangeliums auftreten will" (I 147).

Im Vorwort seines Werkes hatte Meyer verheißen, daß er "in dem Verständnis des Evangeliums des Marcus sehr viel weiter" gekommen sei (S. VIII). Die Interpretation von Mk 1,35 ff. lehrt indes das Gegenteil—

---

[14] Vgl. UAC I 114.117.155.166.188. Von Soden, aaO (wie A.8) 432: "Ein Hauptkriterium der Geschichtlichkeit ist für Ed. Meyer die 'Anschaulichkeit'." Siehe Meyer selbst, UAC III 40. Zur Kritik: Von Soden, aaO und Roland Schütz, Eisenacher Kartell Akademisch-Theologischer Vereine. Kartellzeitung 1921, 64 f.

[15] UAC I 147–152 sowie 114.117.

steht sie doch ganz in den überholten Traditionen der Leben-Jesu-Forschung alter Schule. Zum Beweis dessen braucht man sich nur die entsprechenden Passagen aus einem jener Leben Jesu, dem 1864 von Daniel Schenkel veröffentlichten und seinerzeit vielbeachteten "Charakterbild Jesu,"[16] vor Augen zu führen. Hier heißt es: "Die Nacht, welche auf jenen thaten- und ereignißreichen Sabbathtag folgte, brachte ihm [sc. Jesus] weder körperliche noch geistige Ruhe. Noch ist der Morgen nicht angebrochen, wie der zweite Evangelist mit der unverwelklich frischen Färbung der Ursprünglichkeit erzählt, und schon erhebt sich Jesus von seinem Lager, um nicht nur die Stadt Kapernaum, sondern den Schauplatz seiner gestrigen Thätigkeit überhaupt zu verlassen. Von den Menschen und ihrem Treiben reißt er sich los; er sucht die Stille der Einsamkeit auf und überläßt sich ernster Sammlung im Gebete ... Wozu hatte Jesus in so auffallender Weise die Flucht ergriffen? Zunächst, um dem lästigen Andringen und Hülfesuchen der Menschen aus dem Wege zu gehen, aber im Weiteren doch hauptsächlich deßhalb, um einer Thätigkeit sich zu entziehen, die er nicht als eine seiner Bestimmung angemessene betrachten konnte ... er war in Gefahr gekommen, seine Gabe zweckwidrig und darum zum Nachtheile des von Gott ihm zugewiesenen Berufes anzuwenden. Aber gegen diese Versuchung hatte ihn der Kern seines Charakters geschützt: seine lautere Demuth vor Gott und vor Menschen. Ohne solche Einfalt des Herzens hätte er ihr kaum zu widerstehen vermocht" (71 f.). "Ernste Sammlung," "lautere Demuth vor Gott und vor Menschen" hier, "innere Sammlung" sowie "innere Kämpfe und Anfechtungen" dort—es sind moderne, psychologischem Empfinden entsprungene Ingredienzien, die Meyers Jesusbild noch genauso prägen wie das fast 60 Jahre zuvor entstandene Schenkels, Ingredienzien, über deren Anwender Albert Schweitzer bereits 1906 in seiner Bestandsaufnahme der liberalen Leben-Jesu-Forschung ätzenden Spott ausgegossen hatte, weil mit ihrer Hilfe nicht der historische Jesus, sondern ein Phantom porträtiert wurde,[17] eine ganz und gar "moderne Gestalt mit allen Zügen der Erhabenheit, der Humanität und manchmal auch des Kitsches," die allererst dem Persönlichkeitsideal des 19. Jhdts entsprach.[18] Darüber hinaus verbindet Meyer mit Schenkel—und das heißt: mit der ganzen liberalen Leben-Jesu-Forschung des 19. Jhdts, die "alles von einer fortschreitenden methodischen Ausdeutung des

---

[16] Eine 4. Aufl. erschien bereits 1873. Zu Schenkel vgl. Albert Schweitzer, Geschichte der Leben-Jesu-Forschung, Tübingen [2]1913 (= [6]1951), 207–210.

[17] 2. Aufl. 193–221; 207 zu Schenkel: "Der geschilderte Jesus ist so, daß er auf jeder Pastorenkonferenz alsbald in die Debatte eingreifen könnte."

[18] Walter Schmithals, Einleitung in die drei ersten Evangelien, Berlin/New York 1985, 200.

Markusdetails'' erwartete[19]—auch das fast naiv anmutende Zutrauen zu dem *historischen* Überlieferungswillen der synoptischen Quellen und insbesondere des Markusevangeliums; waren doch Meyer wie Schenkel beide gleichermaßen der Ansicht, sich aus den Evangelien Aufschlüsse selbst über Jesu intimste Seelenregungen verschaffen zu können. Auch hier sind neue Ansätze bei Meyer nirgends spürbar. Wo er sich mit solchen von anderer Seite konfrontiert sieht, sucht er bei den wohlvertrauten Autoritäten der liberalen Orthodoxie Schutz. Gegen Wellhausens Urteil, ''daß dem Evangelium Marci im ganzen die Merkmale der eigentlichen Historie abgehn,'' zitiert er aus Jülichers Einleitung: ''im großen und ganzen hat sich Jesu Leben so entwickelt, wie Marcus es darstellt.''[20]

Hätte Meyer es besser wissen können oder gar müssen? Die Einsichten der ''Formgeschichtlichen Schule,'' der z.B. auch die Erkenntnis zu verdanken ist, daß es sich bei dem eben ausführlicher traktierten Stück Mk 1,35–38(39) nicht um alte Jesusüberlieferung, sondern um eine redaktionelle Bildung des Evangelisten handelt, mit der dieser den Übergang Jesu zu dauerndem Wirken darstellen bzw. motivieren will,[21] sind in ihren klassisch gewordenen Werken nicht sehr lange vor Meyers ''Ursprung und Anfängen'' publiziert worden. Karl Ludwig Schmidts Untersuchung über den ''Rahmen der Geschichte Jesu'' erschien 1919, im gleichen Jahr auch Martin Dibelius' ''Formgeschichte des Evangeliums;'' Rudolf Bultmanns ''Geschichte der synoptischen Tradition'' folgte 1921. Daß Meyer sich mit diesen Arbeiten nicht mehr ausführlich beschäftigen konnte, ist verständlich. Eine der grundlegenden Einsichten der formgeschichtlichen Untersuchung der Evangelien, die Erkenntnis, ''daß sie Sammelgut enthalten'' und die Evangelisten ''in der Hauptsache Sammler, Tradenten, Redaktoren'' gewesen sind,[22] war freilich schon lange vor Schmidt, Dibelius und Bultmann erarbeitet worden, etwa von Julius Wellhausen, dessen einschlägige Untersuchungen Meyer, wie die häufigen Verweisungen auf sie zeigen, auch durchaus bekannt gewesen sind.

---

[19] Schweitzer, aaO (wie A.16) 220.—In diesem Bereich, in der (methodisch freilich antiquierten) Quellenanalyse des Mk., liegt bezeichnenderweise auch der von den Kritikern noch am ehesten als originell empfundene Forschungsbeitrag von Meyers erstem Band, s. Schmidt, aaO (wie A.7) 116; Schütz, aaO (wie A.14) 65; Dibelius, aaO (wie A.9) 229–231.

[20] UAC I 121; Julius Wellhausen, Einleitung in die drei ersten Evangelien, Berlin [2]1911, 43; Adolf Jülicher, Einleitung in das Neue Testament, Freiburg i.B./Leipzig 1894, 196 f.

[21] Bultmann, Die Geschichte der synoptischen Tradition, Göttingen [4]1958, 167. Vgl. aber immerhin schon Theodor Keim, Geschichte Jesu von Nazara 2, Zürich 1871, 166–169.

[22] Dibelius, Die Formgeschichte des Evangeliums, Tübingen [6]1971, 2.

Ja, gelegentlich ist sogar Meyer selbst zu Erkenntnissen gelangt, wie sie
zunächst Wellhausen und dann die Formgeschichtler in ihren Arbeiten
begründet haben. "Es kann nicht zweifelhaft sein," äußert er einmal,
"daß die Erzählungen von Jesu Aussprüchen und Wundertaten zunächst
größtenteils isoliert und zeitlos überliefert waren." Doch sogleich heißt es
dann wieder: "In der Hauptsache gibt Marcus eine kontinuierlich fort-
laufende Erzählung, in der äußerlich wie innerlich ein ständiges Fortschreiten, eine geschichtliche Entwicklung sehr deutlich hervortritt. Der
Verfasser ... ist nichts weniger als ein bloßer Kompilator; vielmehr hat
er diese Entwicklung mit vollem Bewußtsein und großem Geschick herausgearbeitet" (UAC I 102). Das bedeutet nun allerdings nichts anderes,
als daß, wie Dibelius mit Recht gegen Meyer einwandte, "aus der Rechtfertigung des literarischen Zusammenhangs im Markus fast unvermerkt
die Behauptung, dieser Zusammenhang sei auch geschichtlich," geworden ist.[23] Die richtige Konsequenz hatte Wellhausen gezogen: aus der
von ihm beobachteten Tatsache, daß die einzelnen Stücke des Markus-
stoffes "meist anekdotisch neben einander" stünden, folgerte er: "Sie
reichen nicht aus als Stoff für ein Leben Jesu."[24] Das hätte auch Meyer
wissen können, wenn er nur seine eigenen Einsichten nach dem Vorbild
Wellhausens zuende gedacht haben würde. Anstoß dazu hätte ihm aber
vor allem die bereits 1901 erschienene epochemachende Markusanalyse
William Wredes sein müssen.[25] Wrede hatte in ihr gezeigt, daß der
Zusammenhang des Markusevangeliums von einer dogmatischen Überzeugung des Evangelisten, dem theologischen Gedanken der durch Jesus
geheimgehaltenen Messiaswürde, beherrscht wird. Es ist also ein "Zusammenhang des Gedankens, nicht der geschichtlichen Entwicklung,"
der das Evangelium zusammenhält (132). "Markus hat keine wirkliche
Anschauung mehr vom geschichtlichen Leben Jesu" (129), "nur blasse
Reste einer solchen sind in eine übergeschichtliche Glaubensauffassung
übergegangen" (131). Mit Wredes Buch war die bereits 1874 von
Harnack aufgestellte These "vita Christi scribi nequit"[26] wissenschaftlich begründet und jede Leben-Jesu-Forschung alten Stils ein für allemal
ad absurdum geführt. Die Geschichte der synoptischen Tradition konnte
von nun an nur noch "als die eines Glaubens verstanden werden."[27] Dies

---

[23] AaO (wie A.9) 233.
[24] AaO (wie A.20) 43.
[25] Das Messiasgeheimnis in den Evangelien, Göttingen [4]1969.
[26] Disputationsthese Harnacks bei seiner Habilitation, vgl. Agnes von Zahn-Harnack,
Adolf von Harnack, Berlin [2]1951, 46.
[27] Von Soden, aaO (wie A.8) 433.—Das Mk. will eben *nicht* dazu "dienen, der Masse
der Gläubigen in zuverlässiger Fassung die *Tatsachen* zugänglich zu machen, auf denen
ihr Seelenheil und ihre Lebensführung beruht" (UAC I 237, Hervorhebung E.P.).

jedoch, "die Grundfrage, was denn die Evangelien ihrer eigenen Absicht
nach und für ihre ursprünglichen Leser sein wollen,"—Kundgabe des
Glaubens, auf den sich die Rückfrage nach der Historie zwar nicht ein-
zulassen braucht, durch dessen Anschauungen sie aber stets wie durch
einen Filter hindurch muß—"wird von Ed. Meyer gar nicht ernstlich
berührt. Für ihn bedeutet Kritik immer noch: die vorliegende Tradition
durch operative Kürzungen auf Geschichte zu reduzieren."[28] Das Wesen
der Evangelien als Urkunden des Glaubens an Jesus als den Christus
schließt indes einen solch direkten Zugang zur Historie, hier: zur Historie
des Lebens Jesu, prinzipiell aus. Dadurch, daß Meyer von dieser grundlegenden, zum Zeitpunkt der Abfassung seiner Geschichte des Urchristentums längst vorhandenen Einsicht keine Notiz nahm und statt dessen
bei den abgelebten Traditionen der liberalen Leben-Jesu-Forschung
verharrte, hat er sein Jesusbild, jedenfalls insoweit es Aspekte eines
"Leben Jesu" enthält, selbst um allen wissenschaftlichen Wert gebracht.

III

Nun zu Meyers Darstellung der "Anschauungen und Lehren" Jesu!
Hervorgewachsen sind sie aus dem Weltbild des zeitgenössischen Judentums, genauer: dem der Pharisäer (UAC II 425 f.). Was sie hiervon unterscheidet, ist allererst Jesu "Auffassung des inneren Wesens des
Gesetzes und des durch dasselbe begründeten Verhältnisses zu Gott"
(ebd. 427): dort "immer weitere Ausspinnung ausgetüftelter Gebote"
(ebd.), hier "innere Freiheit auch gegenüber dem Gesetz selbst; es soll
dazu dienen, durch volle Hingabe in den göttlichen Willen ein festbe-
gründetes dauerndes Verhältnis des Menschen zu Gott zu schaffen, aber
ihn nicht durch mechanische Abrichtung innerlich von Gott zu entfrem-
den" (429). Befolgung des Gesetzes muß "aus der inneren Gesinnung"
erwachsen, denn "nur auf die Gesinnung kommt es an" (428). Diese
"innere Freiheit, die er ... dem Gesetze gegenüber gewonnen hat, " ist
es, die Jesus "weit hinaushebt über alle jüdischen Vorgänger." Denn
"erst bei Jesus vollzieht sich wirklich seine [sc. des Gesetzes] Umwandlung in eine religiöse Ethik, die von seinen jüdischen Vorläufern wohl
erstrebt ... wird, die sie aber nicht zu erreichen vermochten, weil sie
nicht die Kraft und den Mut hatten, den Ritualismus abzustreifen"
(430).
   Wie Johannes der Täufer ruft auch Jesus zur Umkehr auf; anders
als beim Täufer bedarf sie jedoch keiner äußeren Riten und Manifestationen wie Taufe und Fasten mehr; "die Erneuerung des Menschen

---

[28] Von Soden, aaO (wie A.8) 433.

soll von innen aus erfolgen" (433). "Wer aber die innere Gesinnung, die Bekehrung gewonnen hat, der hat ... auch den Eintritt in das Gottesreich errungen" (436). Dieses ist zuvörderst "eine rein innerliche Größe, es wächst ... aus der Ethik Jesu in jedem [für Jesu Wort] Empfänglichen."[29] Jesus versucht, "das außerweltliche Gottesreich in der geistigen Gemeinde, die er schaffen will, zu verwirklichen" (I 164). "Vorbedingung für den Eintritt in das Gottesreich" ist der Glaube; "er schafft die innere Gewißheit" der "unmittelbaren Verbindung mit Gott," verlangt aber ebenso "die unbedingte Hingabe in den Willen Gottes in unerschütterlichem Vertrauen auf seine väterliche Fürsorge für alle Kreatur" (II 438). Durch solche "unbedingte Hingebung an Gott gelangt das mit seinem [sc. Gottes] inneren Wesen identische sittliche Postulat zu voller Verwirklichung" (439).

In der Eschatologie steht Jesus freilich noch "ganz auf dem Boden der pharisaeischen Religion"—wie z.B. Jesu Rede von der hundertfältigen Vergeltung zeigt, die die Gläubigen im ewigen Leben für ihr Leiden in dieser Welt zu erwarten haben (ebd.). "Daß durch die Verinnerlichung des Begriffs des Gottesreichs ... diese ganze Eschatologie im Grunde aufgehoben ist"—ist doch für Jesus selbst "das Gericht in Wirklichkeit ins Innere jedes einzelnen Menschen verlegt" (436)!—hat Jesus nur nicht gemerkt (440): das Empfinden für logische Widersprüche ging ihm ab (441). Erst das Christentum hat diese Vorstellungen dann wieder breit ausgeführt und damit erhebliche Erfolge erzielt (440).

Eine vom Kanon der "beiden Grundgebote der Gottesliebe und der Nächstenliebe" (430) normierte Gesinnungsethik für das durch Gesinnungswandel zu dieser Ethik befreite Individuum, das Gottesreich als ideales Reich der Sittlichkeit und die väterliche, allen Menschen zugewandte und jeder juridischen Komponente entblößte Gottheit als Prinzip des sittlichen Postulats: das sind die wesentlichen Merkmale der Verkündigung Jesu. Sein Selbstverständnis entspricht dieser Verkündigung; die "Überzeugung von der untrüglichen Wahrheit seiner Erkenntnis, das Bewußtsein der innigen Gemeinschaft mit Gott dem Vater, erzeugt in Jesus den Glauben, daß er in der Tat der seinem Volk verheißene ... Messias ist" (444). "Damit aber verschiebt sich für ihn der Begriff des Messias in derselben Weise wie der des Gottesreichs. Nicht als Vollzieher des Strafgerichts über die heidnischen Reiche und Aufrichter der Weltherrschaft des auserwählten Gottesvolkes kommt der Messias, sondern als der Führer zum seligen Leben, der Erlöser eines jeden, der Wille und Kraft hat, dem Satan zu widerstehn ... Die Seelsorge um

---

[29] Friedrich Büchsel, Zum Jesusbilde Eduard Meyers, Neue kirchl. Zeitschrift 33 (1922) 269–282, 273 zu Meyer, UAC II 433.

jeden einzelnen Menschen und damit der religiöse Individualismus ...
gelangt so zu voller Alleinherrschaft'' (445). Das heißt: ganz wie die
Vorstellung vom Gottesreich bei Meyer zu einer bloßen Chiffre für das
Reich der Sittlichkeit geworden ist, hat er auch den Messiasbegriff zu
einer ''façon de parler'' entleert[30]—Messiassein bedeutet nichts anderes
mehr als die Aufgabe, alle Menschen guten Willens in jenes Reich des
Guten, Wahren, Schönen zu leiten, in welchem Gott als sittliches Prinzip
herrscht. Schließlich ist es auch Jesu apokalyptischer Überzeugung von
der Nähe des Gottesreichs nicht besser ergangen. Aus der zeitlichen Nähe
wird bei Meyer eine ethische: überall dort, wo das wahre Wesen der
Gottheit—das mit dem sittlichen Postulat identisch ist!—begriffen, der
Mensch von ihm durchdrungen wird, da ist das Gottesreich ''bereits jetzt
auf Erden im Anzug'' (444).

Meyers Bild von Jesu ''Anschauungen und Lehren'' ist nun freilich in
keiner Weise eigenständig. Punkt für Punkt läßt sich zeigen, daß es nichts
anderes bietet als eine Nachzeichnung jenes Bildes, das die liberale Theologie des 19. Jhdts schon lange zuvor von Jesu Verkündigung und Selbstbewußtsein entworfen hatte, eines Bildes, das dann über den Kreis der
Fachgelehrten hinaus auch von der Welt des gebildeten Bürgertums,
der Adressatin zahlreicher allgemeinverständlicher Darstellungen zum
Thema, weithin akzeptiert worden war. Meyers Abhängigkeit von diesem
Strom theologischen Denkens sei durch eine kurze Wiedergabe einschlä-
giger Passagen zunächst aus Heinrich Julius Holtzmanns ''Lehrbuch der
Neutestamentlichen Theologie''[31]—keinem ''eigenen Entwurf'' sondern
Darstellung des ''Höhepunkts liberaler theologischer Forschung''[32]—,
dann aus Harnacks ''Wesen des Christentums''[33]—einem, wenn nicht
gar: dem Höhepunkt der haute vulgarisation liberal-theologischen Ge-
dankenguts—sowie dessen ''Lehrbuch der Dogmengeschichte''[34] und
schließlich aus Wilhelm Heitmüllers populärem Jesusbuch[35] illustriert.

In der ''Loslösung vom Formalprincip des Pharisäismus'' sah auch
Holtzmann den Ausgangspunkt von Jesu Predigt (I, 139). ''Darin liegt
das folgenreichste und fruchtbarste Ergebniss der sittlichen Arbeit Jesu
vor: es ist die Entdeckung eines inneren Schauplatzes aller sittlichen Vorgänge, die Klarstellung eines in Gesinnung und Charakter wurzelnden
... Ernstes der Gesetzesbefolgung'' (151). In solcher ''jeder Vermittlung
durch cultische Weitläufigkeiten und Schwierigkeiten sich entschlagen-

---

[30] Strathmann, aaO (wie A.5) 569.
[31] 2 Bde., Freiburg i.B./Leipzig 1897.
[32] Otto Merk, Art. Holtzmann, in: TRE 15 (1986) 519–522, 520.
[33] Leipzig 1900.
[34] 3 Bde., Freiburg i.B. 1886–1890 (= DG).
[35] Jesus, Tübingen 1913.

den, niemals willkürlich erfundene und ausgeklügelte, überall dagegen unmittelbar sittliche Aufgaben stellenden, Auffassung des Verhältnisses zwischen Gottheit und Menschheit liegt der Grund für die nachhaltige Kraft" von Jesu Auftreten (344). Sein Bekenntnis zum Vater-Gott, in welchem er "sein Innerstes zum Ausdruck brachte" (169), ist "Mittelpunkt einer neuen religiös-ethischen Weltanschauung. Das Gottesbild kennzeichnet sich nirgends durch metaphysische Merkmale, wohl aber durch ethische Beziehungen zur Menschenwelt. Denn je reiner die Vateridee durchgeführt wird, desto nachdrücklicher wird das ganze religiöse Verhältniss unter den Gesichtspunkt einer sittlichen Aufgabe gestellt, die dadurch gelöst werden kann, dass der Mensch in der Kräftigkeit dieses von ihm an- und aufgenommenen Gottesbewusstseins zur Vollkommenheit heranwächst" (170 f.). So wird "das Gottesbild ... zum unentrathsamen Coefficienten des Vollzugs sittlicher Vorgänge im Selbstbewusstsein" (171 f.). Jesu "Idee vom Reiche Gottes" weist eine Reihe alttestamentlicher wie frühjüdischer Komponenten auf, namentlich den "die jüd[ische] Religiosität charakterisirenden Lohnbegriff;" dies, obwohl "die Vertiefung seines [sc. Jesu] Gottesbegriffes, seine ganze Fassung des religiösen Verhältnisses denselben nicht mehr recht vertrug" (339). "Das Himmelreich im Sinne der Verkündigung Jesu ist ... die vom Himmel her in die gegenwärtige Wirklichkeit eintretende, diesseitig werdende, göttliche Ordnung der Dinge" (191). Jesu "'Sohnesbewusstsein' ... bildet die treibende Kraft einer geradlinig fortschreitenden Entwicklung des [sc. seines] religiös-sittlichen Charakters" (344). "Und so ist auch für die Selbstbezeichnung Jesu als 'Sohn' nicht bloss der religiöse, sondern auch der sittliche Gesichtspunkt maassgebend" (267). "Sein Messiasthum war demnach [nur] die geschichtlich gebotene, die unvermeidliche Anschauungsform, in welche sich für seine Vorstellung der Erfahrungsgehalt seines religiösen Lebens, also sein Sohnesbewusstsein, gekleidet hat" (345 f.).

Von dem Holtzmannschen unterscheidet sich Harnacks Jesusbild allenfalls durch Nuancen. Wieder ist Jesus derjenige, der "mit scharfem Schnitte die Verbindung der Ethik mit dem äußeren Kultus und den technisch-religiösen Übungen" löst (Wesen 45) und "überall in den sittlichen Fragen auf die Wurzel, d.h. auf die Gesinnung" zurückgeht (ebd. 46). "Das definitive Geschick des Einzelnen" macht Jesus "von dem Glauben, der Demuth und der Liebe abhängig" (DG I 51, A.2). Dem korrespondiert, daß "erst durch Jesus Christus ... der Wert jeder einzelnen Menschenseele in Erscheinung getreten" ist (Wesen 44); "das Individuum wird erlöst, nicht das Volk oder der Staat" (ebd. 39). "Der Gedanke des unschätzbaren Werthes, den jede einzelne Menschenseele besitzt, tritt in der Verkündigung Jesu deutlich hervor und bildet das

Complement zur Botschaft von dem in der Liebe sich verwirklichenden
Reiche Gottes'' (DG I 53). Dieses "kommt, indem es zu den einzelnen
kommt, Einzug in ihre Seele hält, und sie es ergreifen" (Wesen 36).
"Es hat die Natur einer geistigen Größe, einer Macht, die in das Innere
eingesenkt wird und nur von dem Innern zu erfassen ist" (ebd. 39). Apo-
kalyptische Vorstellungen vom Kommen des Reiches hat Jesus, in ihnen
groß geworden, nur "beibehalten" (35). Die "Sphäre der Gottessohn-
schaft" Jesu ist seine Gotteserkenntnis; er "ist überzeugt, Gott so zu kennen, wie keiner vor ihm, und er weiß, daß er den Beruf hat, allen anderen
diese Gotteserkenntnis . . . mitzuteilen" (81). Jesus fordert die Menschen
auf, "sich ihm anzuschliessen, weil er sich als den von Gott berufenen
Helfer und desshalb als den verheissenen Messias erkannt hatte" (DG I
49).

Jesu Sohnesbewußtsein ist schließlich auch Heitmüller zufolge Konsequenz aus dem Anspruch, "allein Gott erkannt zu haben und allein ihn
offenbaren zu können" (70 f.). Und ganz wie Holtzmann, Harnack (und
Meyer) bestimmt auch Heitmüller den Unterschied zwischen jesuani-
scher und pharisäischer Ethik als den zwischen Gesinnung und Kasuistik.
"Die Schriftgelehrten und Pharisäer legen Wert auf die einzelnen Handlungen und Leistungen: Jesus drängt auf die Gesinnung; sie erst bestimmt den sittlichen Charakter einer Handlung" (131). "Mit kühner
Hand schiebt Jesus diese [sc. der Schriftgelehrten] scharfsinnigen, haar-
spaltenden Unterscheidungen, d.h. im Grunde das Feilschen und Sich—
drücken um die Pflicht beiseite: er verkündet die Unbegrenztheit, die
Unbedingtheit der sittlichen Verpflichtung" (132). Jesu Reich-Gottes-
Predigt hat so "vor allem sittlichen Charakter" (145). Darüber hinaus ist
als "Grundzug der Ethik Jesu zu beachten: der Individualismus" (135).
Endlich findet sich bei Heitmüller auch die Einsicht, daß Jesus kein Sy-
stematiker war: Seine Erkenntnisse gewann er nicht "auf dem Wege
des Nachdenkens;" sie sind vielmehr "unwillkürliche, unvermeidliche
Ausstrahlung seines eigenen Erlebens" (144).

Aus dem Voranstehenden sollte, auch ohne daß ein Punkt-für-Punkt-
Vergleich der beiderseitigen Ansichten erfolgt wäre, deutlich genug her-
vorgegangen sein, in welchem Ausmaß sich Meyers Darstellung von Jesu
Anschauungen und Lehren dem Bilde verdankt, das liberale Theologen
wie Holtzmann, Harnack und Heitmüller schon lange vor ihm von Jesu
Verkündigung gezeichnet hatten. In allem Wesentlichen geht Meyers
Darstellung auf das von der liberalen Theologie entworfene Jesusbild
zurück.[36] Hier wie dort findet sich die Vorstellung von Jesu Ethik als

---

[36] Vgl. z.B. schon Lietzmann, aaO (wie A.6) 104 und Behm, Orientalist. Lit.ztg 26
(1923) 337.

einer auf das Individuum zielenden Gesinnungsethik, hier wie dort die Auffassung vom Gottesreich als eines inneren, immanent wachsenden bzw. zu verwirklichenden Reiches der Sittlichkeit, hier wie dort die Überzeugung, Jesus habe Gottesbezug und Sittlichkeit miteinander verknüpft, hier wie dort die Verdrängung des Apokalyptikers Jesus, hier wie dort die Deutung des Messias- bzw. Sohnesbegriffs als bloße Chiffre für Konsequenzen, die Jesus aus seinen Erkenntnissen, Erfahrungen oder Aufgaben zog.

So verbreitet dieses liberale Jesusbild seinerzeit auch war und so wenig es, anders als die liberale Leben-Jesu-Forschung, in den beiden ersten Jahrzehnten des 20. Jhdts als überholt begriffen werden konnte, hatte sich doch schon schwerwiegende Kritik gegen es erhoben. Sie betraf die gänzliche Enteschatologisierung von Person und Verkündigung Jesu, wie sie hier gang und gäbe geworden war. Bereits 1892 und nochmals im Jahre 1900, in einer weiteren Auflage seines Buches über "Die Predigt Jesu vom Reiche Gottes," hatte Johannes Weiß die Ansicht vorgetragen, "dass das Reich Gottes nach der Auffassung Jesu eine schlechthin überweltliche Grösse ist, die zu dieser Welt in ausschliessendem Gegensatze steht. Damit ist aber gesagt, dass von einer innerweltlichen Entwicklung des Reiches Gottes im Gedankenkreise Jesu die Rede nicht sein kann."[37] Hinzu kam die weitere Feststellung, "dass Jesus kraft seines Tauferlebnisses der religiösen Ueberzeugung lebte, dass er zum Richter und Herrscher im Reiche Gottes ausersehen sei,"[38] was bedeutete, "dass auch das Messiasbewusstsein Jesu, wie es sich im Namen 'Menschensohn' ausdrückt, an dem durchaus transcendentalen, apokalyptischen Charakter der Reich-Gottesidee Jesu teilnimmt und nicht von ihr losgelöst werden kann."[39] In die gleiche Kerbe hieb dann auch, kurz nach der Jahrhundertwende, Albert Schweitzer. Seiner und Weiß' Einsicht sollte die Zukunft gehören; noch heute geht "jeder ernst zu nehmende Theologe von einem wie auch immer näher zu bestimmenden positiven Verhältnis Jesu bzw. der Jesusüberlieferung zur Apokalyptik aus."[40] Hätte Meyer mehr historisches Gespür besessen, wäre er an den neuen Erkenntnissen vielleicht nicht so unbeeindruckt vorübergegangen, wie er es getan hat. Das, freilich, ist Spekulation.

Nicht spekulativ ist indes die Beobachtung, daß es, Meyers Klage über die Scheu aller Historiker vor der Beschäftigung mit dem Urchristentum (I, S. VII) entgegen, doch zumindest einen Historiker gegeben hatte, der

---

[37] 1. Aufl., 49 f.
[38] Ebd. 60.
[39] Ebd. 61.
[40] Schmithals, Jesus und die Apokalyptik, in: Jesus Christus in Historie und Theologie (FS Hans Conzelmann), Tübingen 1975, 59–85, 60.

es im Rahmen seiner—noch dazu gleichfalls universal angelegten—
Geschichtsschreibung durchaus nicht verschmäht hatte, den Blick auch
auf das Urchristentum zu richten: Leopold von Ranke. Seine Weltgeschichte enthält, im Zuge der Darstellung des ''altrömischen Kaiser-
thums,'' ein entsprechendes Kapitel,[41] das sich auch, keineswegs nur
marginal, mit Jesus beschäftigt. Ranke fußte, nicht anders als später
Meyer, auf den Anschauungen der liberalen Theologie, so daß, wie
Albert Schweitzer spöttisch bemerkte, ''der Jesus der Schenkel, Keim,
Hase und Holtzmann einen Ehrenplatz in Leopold von Rankes Weltgeschichte'' bekam.[42] In der Tat lassen sich bei Ranke alle wesentlichen
Bestandteile des liberalen Jesusbildes wiederfinden. Da heißt es: ''Von
der strengen und strafenden Gottheit, die jede Abweichung von dem
Gesetze unnachsichtig heimsucht, ging Jesus zu der Lehre von der väter-
lichen Liebe Gottes über, welche alle Menschen umfaßt ... Jesus verkün-
digte ein Gottesreich, zu welchem nur die Sittlichreinen, die wahren
Kinder Gottes, sich vereinigen sollten. Und wenn die Juden durch den
vermeinten Messias, den sie erwarteten, zur Herrschaft über alle Nachbarn erhoben zu werden hofften, so faßte Jesus eben diese Idee in ihrer
geistigen Bedeutung ... Darin, dies Reich [sc. das Gottesreich] zu ver-
kündigen zugleich und zu stiften, sah er seinen göttlichen Beruf,''[43] ein
Reich, ''welches ... der Menschheit eine allgemeine Vereinigung rein
geistiger Art in Aussicht stellte.''[44] Meyer hat also nicht nur insofern
wenig Originalität bewiesen, als er, statt selbständig ein Jesusbild zu entwerfen, kritiklos dasjenige der liberalen Theologie übernahm, sondern
war auch darin nicht originell, dieses Jesusbild in den größeren Rahmen
der Universalgeschichte hineingestellt zu haben.

IV

Im folgenden sei danach gefragt, *wie* Meyer das Phänomen Jesus in den
Zusammenhang der (Religions-)Geschichte eingeordnet hat. Da Meyer
Zentrum und Gewicht der Verkündigung Jesu in dessen Ethik bestehen
sah, liegt es nahe, jene Frage im Horizont von Meyers Anschauungen
über das Verhältnis von Religion und Moral, wie er sie im ersten Bande
seiner ''Geschichte des Altertums''[45] dargelegt hat, zu beantworten.

---

[41] Weltgeschichte. Dritter Theil. Das altrömische Kaiserthum. Erste Abtheilung,
Leipzig [4]1886, 151–194 (= Fünftes Capitel. Ursprung des Christenthums).
[42] AaO (wie A.16) 221.
[43] AaO (wie A.41) 165 f.
[44] AaO (wie A.41) 166.
[45] Bd. 1, erste Hälfte. Einleitung. Elemente der Anthropologie, Stuttgart [3]1910
(= GdA).

Danach ist die Moral "ihrem Ursprung nach völlig selbständig und ihr Gebiet wird erst allmählich, beim Fortschreiten der Kultur und der religiösen Idee, von dieser erobert" (GdA 135). In diesem Prozeß steht die Moral freilich "in fortwährendem, kaum je vorübergehend ausgeglichenen Konflikt mit der Religion und ihren Geboten;" die Moral erweist sich in diesem Kampfe jedoch "in der Regel als die stärkere Macht" (136). So "entsteht das ethische Postulat, die Forderung, daß die Götter sittliche Mächte sind, daß sie die Welt nach den Grundsätzen der sittlichen Ordnung geschaffen haben und regieren, daß zwischen dem Tun des Menschen und seinen Schicksalen ein gerechter Ausgleich bestehen soll" (142). "Die tatsächlichen Schicksale der Menschen und die Gewalten, welche für die Gestaltung ihres Lebens ausschlaggebend sind," stehen indes "in schroffem Gegensatz zu den Forderungen des ethischen Postulats. Und doch ist das Gefühl unüberwindlich, daß die sittlichen Gebote der sozialen Gemeinschaft etwas Absolutes sind." Allerdings, "der Glaube, . . . daß die von den Göttern geschaffene Welt dem Ideal entspricht und den Ausgleich wirklich enthält, den dieses erfordert, kann immer nur vorübergehend zur Herrschaft gelangen und einzelnen Persönlichkeiten . . . zum festen Glaubenssatz werden. Vielfach sucht man sich, unter Einwirkung des durch die Steigerung der Individualität ausgebildeten Unsterblichkeitsglaubens durch die Annahme einer zukünftigen, besseren Welt zu helfen, in der das Ideal zur Alleinherrschaft gelangt" (143). "Oder . . . das Weltregiment der Gottheit wird für ein Rätsel erklärt, . . . dessen Verständnis . . . die Gottheit dem Menschen verschlossen hat: das religiöse Bewußtsein muß sich begnügen mit der Anerkennung ihrer Allmacht, die über jede Verantwortung erhaben ist (so im Buch Hiob). Am tiefsten ist das Problem von Plato und den späteren ethischen Philosophen der Griechen erfaßt, welche den Ausgleich allein in das Innere der Menschenbrust verlegen, in die freiwillige Unterordnung unter das Sittengesetz, dem gegenüber alle äußeren Schicksale völlig irrelevant sind" (144).[46]

In dem Prozeß der—je und dann gelungenen—Behauptung der Moral gegenüber der Religion und ihren Geboten, etwa dem Ritualismus, bezeichnet Jesus für Meyer einen seltenen Höhepunkt. Indem Jesus das zeitgenössische Judentum, d.h. die pharisäische Gesetzlichkeit, "innerlich überwunden" hat, erweist sich gerade auch in diesem Fall wieder "die Ethik stärker als alle überkommene Religion" (UAC II 432). Ja, Meyer sieht in Jesu Ethik sogar "nichts anderes als eine Umsetzung des kategorischen Imperativs in ein praktisches Gebot: 'Handle so, daß die

---

[46] Vgl. UAC III 529.

Maxime deines Willens jederzeit zugleich als das Prinzip einer allgemeinen Gesetzgebung gelten könne.' ... Da fehlt auch der ethische Rigorismus Kants nicht: 'wenn ihr die liebt, die euch lieben, was ist da euer Verdienst? ... Vielmehr liebt eure Feinde''' (431). Das Christentum hat
diese einsame Höhe sittlichen Bewußtscins dann freilich wieder verlassen.
Denn "das Leben im Gottesreich, das Jesus in die Welt bringt, setzt sich
[im Christentum] um in das zukünftige Leben im Jenseits, in die volle
Loslösung von dieser Welt, während Jesus gerade durch die Höhe seines
sittlichen Bewußtseins mitten in dieser steht." Verantwortlich für solche
"Verengung" der Botschaft Jesu ist die im Urchristentum vorgenommene "Verknüpfung der Erlösung und des Glaubens mit dem Weltgericht und der Auferstehung." Damit fällt nun der Eschatologie, und
das heißt: mythischen Vorstellungen—Jesu Predigt kam Meyer zufolge
ohne solche aus (I 155, A.1)—wieder eine "maßgebende Rolle" zu, wie
z.B. die Argumentation des Paulus in 1. Kor. 15,17 ff. zeigt: Wenn die
Verheißungen nicht wahr wären, "wenn es keine leibliche Auferstehung
der Toten gäbe, so wäre der Glaube und die Erlösung eitle Torheit ...
Damit tritt, trotz aller Ethik, ... doch schließlich ein materielles, welt-
liches Interesse in den Vordergrund und damit ist die freie Sittlichkeit,
wie sie die griechischen Philosophen und Hiob ebensogut verkündet
haben wie Jesus, tatsächlich untergraben" (III 398).
   "Für die Wirkung der Missionspredigt freilich war das ein gewaltiger
Gewinn." Denn "was die Massen verlangten, war die Erlösung von dem
Elend dieser Welt ... und die Aussicht auf ein seliges Leben im Jenseits"
(398 f.). Die "weit tieferen Gedanken, wie sie Jesus verkündet hat, ...
sind [so] verhüllt unter einem viel primitiveren, roheren Gewande, das
durch die Materialisierung das selbstsüchtige Interesse wieder in den
Vordergrund stellt. Nur um diesen Preis"—den Preis der Verbindung
von Eschatologie und Ethik—"hat sich die Ethisierung der Religion für
die Massen erreichen lassen" (373; vgl. 322 – 324.333). "Auf die Höhe
der ethischen Anschauungen Hiobs oder Platos" und, wie in Meyers Sinn
hinzuzufügen ist, Jesu, "vermag sich die Menge nicht zu erheben, sie
können niemals populär werden" (II 319). Immerhin kann Meyer Jesu
und des (Ur-)Christentums ethische Anschauungen gelegentlich auch
einmal zusammenfassen: *beider* Lehre sucht die Erlösung—anders als etwa
die Gnosis—nicht auf dem Gebiet der "Spekulation", sondern "auf dem
der Sittlichkeit und damit des Gewissens" (III 286; vgl. 292). Allerdings
—einzig "in der Durchführung der sittlichen Gebote und der Kirchen-
zucht" leben die "Grundgedanken Jesu" noch fort. "Sein Evangelium
hat darin die Verwirklichung gefunden, soweit das überhaupt möglich ist,
wenn eine durchaus auf das Innenleben des einzelnen Menschen gestellte
Idee durch eine die Massen umfassende und ihr Verhalten normativ

regelnde Organisation in die Praxis des Alltagslebens umgesetzt werden soll'' (619). ''Das Wesentliche'' ist im Christentum jedoch die eschatologische Aussicht, ''die Herrlichkeit des ewigen Lebens bei Gott; um dieses Gewinns willen nimmt der Gläubige alle Lasten des Sittengesetzes und alle Leiden des Daseins geduldig auf sich. Wohl tritt . . . bei tiefer empfindenden Naturen dieser äußere Vorteil der Zukunftsverheißung vor der sittlichen und religiösen Pflichterfüllung in den Hintergrund; aber für die Massenwirkung bildet der materielle Gewinn, der so gesichert wird, doch ein wesentliches Moment, das im Lauf der Entwicklung umso fragwürdiger wird, je mehr die mechanische Annahme der Glaubenssätze, d.h. die Knechtung des selbständigen Denkens, und der von der Kirche immer systematischer ausgebildete Apparat der formalen Gesetzeserfüllung mit dem Ritual der Bußübungen und Kasteiungen die innere sittliche Freiheit erstickt'' (322).

Welchen Einflüssen Meyer bei der Konzipierung seiner Vorstellungen von Verlauf und Charakter der Religionsgeschichte unterlag, ist nicht zu übersehen; es sind Kant und wohl mehr noch die durch seine Schule gegangenen Theologen und Philosophen, die nachwirken.

Mit Kant verbindet Meyer zunächst die Überzeugung von der Autonomie des Sittengesetzes; seine Rede von der ''freien Sittlichkeit,'' wie sie bei Plato, Hiob oder Jesus zu beobachten sei (vgl. z.B. III 398), ist nichts anderes als ein matter Abglanz des IV. Lehrsatzes der Kritik der praktischen Vernunft (''Die Autonomie des Willens ist das alleinige Prinzip aller moralischen Gesetze und der ihnen gemäßen Pflichten.'').[47] Dessen Wirkung auf Meyer ist allerdings keineswegs ungewöhnlich: war doch Kants Ethik seinerzeit derart omnipräsent, daß man allen Ernstes den Gedanken hegen konnte, ''die Kantsche Moral'' stehe u.a. ''wegen ihrer Konzentration auf das eigentlich praktische Problem der persönlichen Sittlichkeit in einem sehr nahen Verhältnis zu unserer deutschen populären Moral überhaupt.''[48] Weiter: die auch von Meyer geteilte Überzeugung, ''dass Religion und Moral in keinem ursprünglichen Zusammenhang gestanden, sondern spät erst mit einander verbunden worden seien,'' ließ sich—gewissermaßen als Versuch der Übertragung jenes Lehrsatzes auf das Feld der Geschichte—gut mit diesem verknüpfen und war jedenfalls, wie Otto Pfleiderer 1896 in der dritten Auflage seiner ''Religionsphilosophie'' mißmutig einräumte, eine ''jetzt oft gehörte Behauptung'' (367). Einer, der dies behauptete, war der Ritschlschüler und—als solcher—Neukantianer Hermann Schultz. Seine 1883 erschie-

---

[47] A58 (Kant, Werke hg. Wilhelm Weischedel, Bd. 4, 1956, 144).
[48] Martin Rade, Art. Sitte, Sittlichkeit, Sittengesetz, in: Realenc. für prot. Theol. u. Kirche[3] 18 (1906) 400–410, 403, Z. 24 ff.

nene Abhandlung über ''Religion und Sittlichkeit in ihrem Verhältnis zu einander''[49] gelangte zu dem Ergebnis: ''Die Sittlichkeit beginnt ganz ohne religiösen Charakter. Sie wird zuletzt vollständig von der Religion getragen und empfängt ihr oberstes Prinzip und ihre Motive aus der Offenbarung Gottes,'' sie ''kennt dann keinen anderen Richter [mehr] als die Gewissensstimme in der eigenen Brust, die zugleich Stimme Gottes ist'' (127).

Auf Kant—vgl. dessen Anthropologie I § 2—geht auch Meyers kritisches Urteil über den religiösen Eudämonismus zurück. Ihn abzulehnen war im Zeitalter des Neukantianismus freilich längst guter Brauch geworden: ''Heute ist die Ansicht weit verbreitet, daß eine sittliche Gesinnung und Handlungsweise, welche solcher Stützen''—gemeint ist der ''Glaube an die Strafgerechtigkeit der Gottheit''—''bedarf, welche nicht rein aus dem Gefühl von der verpflichtenden Kraft des sittlichen Ideals hervorgeht, geringen Werthes sei,'' heißt es z.B. in Julius Kaftans 1881 publiziertem ''Wesen der christlichen Religion'' (144).[50] Aus der Tatsache, daß Meyer diese Ansicht teilte, resultiert sowohl sein negatives Urteil über die Eschatologie des Paulus und insbesondere über die christliche Auferstehungshoffnung als auch sein Verständnis der Ethik Jesu als einer ''Umsetzung des kategorischen Imperativs in ein praktisches Gebot'' (UAC II 431). Schließlich hatte es ja Kant selbst schon so gesehen: ''Jenes Gesetz aller Gesetze''—das doppelte Liebesgebot Jesu—''stellt . . ., wie alle moralische Vorschrift des Evangelii, die sittliche Gesinnung in ihrer ganzen Vollkommenheit dar, so wie sie als ein Ideal der Heiligkeit von keinem Geschöpfe erreichbar, dennoch das Urbild ist, welchem wir uns nähern, und, in einem ununterbrochenen, aber unendlichen Progressus, gleich zu werden streben sollen.''[51] Die liberale Theologie vernahm diese Botschaft ebenso gern wie Meyer; ''in der That wurzeln die sittlichen Begriffe Kants in der Gesinnungsmoral Luthers, Pauli und *Jesu*,'' meinte z.B. Martin Rade, der freilich, aufgrund einer positiveren Bewertung des Christentums als Meyer sie vertreten konnte, folgerte: ''Und keine Ethik steht mit ihren allgemeinen Begriffen der *christlichen* Moral in unserm Volke näher als die Ethik Kants.''[52] Immerhin stimmte die vom Neukantianismus beeinflußte liberale Theologenschaft wenigstens insoweit mit Meyers Ansichten über die mangelnde Höhe des sittlichen Bewußt-

---

[49] In: Theolog. Studien u. Kritiken 56,1 (1883) 60–130.
[50] Vgl. Wilhelm Herrmann, Ethik, Tübingen/Leipzig ²1901, 142: ''Die Gesinnung, die uns erfüllen soll, ist also reine Hingabe an Gott in sittlicher Selbständigkeit.''
[51] Kritik der praktischen Vernunft A149 (Werke ed. Weischedel, Bd. 4, 205 f.).
[52] AaO (wie A.48) 403, Z. 17 ff. (Hervorhebungen E.P.)—Zum Problem der Entwicklung einer religiösen Moral im Idealismus selbst s. Otto Pfleiderer, Religionsphilosophie auf geschichtlicher Grundlage, Berlin ³1896, 388–395.

seins im Christentum überein, als sie bereit war, dem konfessionellen oder kirchenpolitischen Gegner entsprechende Vorwürfe zu machen. "Was für eine Rolle spielen nicht die kirchlichen Satzungen in der Frömmigkeit des katholischen Volkes, und wie leicht führt das nicht in den katholischen Christen zu einer Abstumpfung und Verschiebung des sittlichen Urtheils," klagte Kaftan;[53] und ganz ähnlich räsonierte Wilhelm Herrmann am Schluß eines populären, 1903 vor dem Evangelisch-sozialen Kongreß gehaltenen Vortrags: "Am wenigsten aber können die sittlichen Gedanken, d.h. die einheitliche Gesinnung Jesu, in ihrer Kraft die Kirchenmänner verstehen, die von dem Grundsatz der pharisäischen Sittlichkeit schwer loskommen, daß man das Gute aus irgend welchen Vorschriften ablesen könne, und daß der Wille als gut zu gelten habe, der bereit sei, sich durch solche Vorschriften einschnüren zu lassen."[54]

Schließlich: ganz wie Meyer in Jesu Ethik nur *einen* Gipfelpunkt der Entwicklung des sittlichen Bewußtseins erblickte, dem andere, vor allem Plato, an die Seite zu stellen waren, hatten auch die liberalen Theologen entsprechende Parallelen zu Jesus (bzw. zum Christentum) gelten lassen. Beispiele hierfür sind Heinrich Julius Holtzmann sowie Hermann Schultz. "Eine Analogie zu der nachgewiesenen Uebersiedelung der Religion aus der metaphysischen in die sittliche Sphäre als ihre eigentliche Heimath," wie solche in Jesu "nirgends durch metaphysische Merkmale, wohl aber durch ethische Beziehungen zur Menschheit" geprägtem Gottesbild vorliege, fand Holtzmann "in der Herabholung der Philosophie vom Himmel auf die Erde durch Sokrates oder in dem kühnen Griff, womit Plato die Idee des sittlich Guten zum Maassstab der Gottesidee erhob."[55] Schultz: indem der Christ "nicht als Knecht ein fremdes Gebot, sondern ... als Kind des Vaters Willen" erfüllt, "kann sich im Christentum ... die individuelle Gestalt der Sittlichkeit entfalten, wie sie sonst nur der hellenischen Philosophie als Ideal vorgeschwebt hat."[56]

V

Eines allerdings trennte Meyer von der zeitgenössischen liberalen Theologie: sein harsches, aus totaler Negation geborenes Urteil über das Christentum. Es bezieht sich auch keineswegs nur auf dessen Ethik, sondern betrifft das ganze Phänomen. Meyer zufolge begegnet im Christentum "eine Bewegung von unten, erwachsen aus der Religion und den von

---

[53] Das Wesen der christlichen Religion, Basel 1881, 137.
[54] Die sittlichen Weisungen Jesu, Göttingen ²1907, 72, vgl. 42 f.
[55] AaO (wie A.31) I 170 f.173.
[56] AaO (wie A.49) 124 f.

der Menge zäh festgehaltenen Vorstellungen des mythischen Denkens,"
eine Bewegung, die gar nicht anders kann als "prinzipiell irrational und
autoritätsgläubig" zu sein (UAC III 326). Die neue Religion steht in fun-
damentalem Gegensatz zu jeder philosophischen Aufklärung; hier "die
Herrschaft des Intellekts, der nur dem eigenen Gewissen folgt, unbekümmert darum, ob ihm nach dem Tode noch ein weiteres Dasein in Aussicht
steht," dort "ein kindischer Irrwahn, der die unwissenden Massen betört
und ihnen ein ewiges Fortleben in den Wonnen des Paradieses oder aber
in den Qualen des Höllenfeuers vorspiegelt" (529). Man vernimmt hier
die Tonart nicht des Historikers, sondern des Agnostikers Meyer,[57] der
gelegentlich auch einmal von der "Auferstehung der Toten (d.i. der
Leichen)" zu sprechen beliebt (374).[58] Stifter solcher Ausgeburt des
Aberglaubens ist nun freilich nicht Jesus (II 445); die Schöpfer der neuen
Religion sind "Petrus und seine Genossen," Paulus derjenige der christlichen Theologie (III 348)—einer weiteren Scheußlichkeit: ist jene doch,
jedenfalls soweit Paulus für sie verantwortlich ist, durch "Dogmatik" und
"eine spitzfindige rabbinische Theologie" geprägt (398).[59]

Wilhelm Boussets, des Göttinger Neutestamentlers und Zeitgenossen
Satz: "Eine von allem Kultischen und Zeremoniellen, von allem kleinlich
Gesetzlichen und Kasuistischen, von allen Neben- und Außendingen
gereinigte Moral verbindet sich im Evangelium mit der reinen von allen
Nebendingen befreiten Religion" hätte Meyer, bezöge man "Evangeli-
um" auf Jesu Verkündigung, möglicherweise mitsprechen können,
keinesfalls aber die aus der gleichen Feder stammende Feststellung, das
Christentum sei "im eminenten Sinn moralische Religion."[60] Wenn denn
Meyers Werk eine Botschaft enthält, so kann es sich dabei einzig um die
Anempfehlung von *Jesu* zwar religiöser, aber nicht mythisch begründeter
Ethik handeln, wie sich diese vornehmlich in seiner Reich-Gottes-Predigt
manifestiert hat—einer Ethik, die auf der gleichen Höhe stand wie analoge, "aus der Aufklärung, aus der Emanzipation des Geistes von den
traditionellen Vorstellungen der Religion" (III 325) erwachsene Ent-
würfe der griechischen Philosophie, einer Ethik, die sogar Kants kategorischen Imperativ schon in sich barg.

---

[57] Vgl. Ehrenberg, aaO (wie A.12) 505.

[58] Vgl. 274: "während die toten [!] Leichen wieder [!] zum Leben erwachen."

[59] Daß Meyer "sein letztes Ziel [eine Antwort auf die Frage nach dem Wesen des
Christentums zu finden] nicht erreicht, erkläre ich mir aus den Urteilen, die er über seinen
Gegenstand, die Religion, mitbringt. Er bemüht sich, ihr gerecht zu werden . . . , aber
weit überwiegt doch ein Zug aufklärerischer Geringschätzung: er sieht in ihr nur—und
zwar irrationale—Weltanschauung:" so zutreffend Jülicher, aaO (wie A.8) 344; ähnlich
Dibelius, DLZ 43 (1922) 1004 und von Soden, aaO (wie A.8) 438.

[60] Das Wesen der Religion, Halle 1903, 205 bzw. 239. Vgl. Paul Natorp, Religion
innerhalb der Grenzen der Humanität, Freiburg i.B./Leipzig 1894, 77.

Mit solcher Empfehlung rannte Meyer allerdings Türen ein, die bereits seit über einem Jahrhundert weit offen gestanden hatten—war doch der aus Jesu Verkündigung stammende Begriff des Reiches Gottes im 19. Jhdt völlig ethisiert und in dieser Fassung mehr und mehr zu einem Schlüsselbegriff der zeitgenössischen Theologie geworden.[61] Schon Kant hatte das Reich Gottes als den Begriff des höchsten Gutes verstehen wollen, "der allein der strengsten Foderung der praktischen Vernunft ein Gnüge tut,"[62] und in Albrecht Ritschls, des entschiedenen Kantianers und Gründers einer einflußreichen Schule 1875 erstmals publiziertem "Unterricht in der christlichen Religion" hieß es: "§ 5. Das Reich Gottes ist das von Gott gewährleistete höchste Gut ... allein es ist als das höchste Gut nur gemeint, indem es zugleich als das sittliche Ideal gilt, zu dessen Verwirklichung die Glieder der Gemeinde durch eine bestimmte gegenseitige Handlungsweise sich unter einander verbinden ... § 6. Das gerechte Handeln, in welchem die Glieder der Gemeinde Christi an der Hervorbringung des Reiches Gottes theilnehmen, hat sein allgemeines Gesetz und seinen persönlichen Beweggrund in der Liebe zu Gott und zu dem Nächsten."[63] Der Bereich, in dem diese Ansichten wirkten, war groß und umfaßte über die wissenschaftliche Welt hinaus auch das liberale protestantische Bildungsbürgertum. In einer in der "Christlichen Welt" abgedruckten Besinnung über Mt. 6,33 formulierte beispielsweise Martin Rade noch 1922 für das eben charakterisierte Publikum die Sätze: "Die homines bonae voluntatis (mit den Katholiken zu reden), libertatis christianae (mit den Protestanten zu reden), die Menschen des kategorischen Imperativs (mit den Philosophen zu reden): die alle sind Gottes Reichsgenossen, sind im Reiche Gottes ... Sie geben sich selber ohne Unterlaß das Gesetz, sind damit Könige und Untertanen zugleich im Reiche des Guten."[64] Der Gleichklang dieser und vieler ähnlicher in der "Christlichen Welt" und andernorts publizierter Auslassungen[65] mit entsprechenden Passagen Meyers ist nicht zu überhören. Er macht auch verständlich, weshalb Hans von Soden in seiner Rezension des Meyerschen Werkes die Erwartung äußern konnte, dieses werde "unfraglich ... die Vorstellungen vieler Gebildeter in unserem Vaterland

---

[61] Vgl. Johannes Weiß, Die Idee des Reiches Gottes in der Theologie, Gießen 1901, 82–155; Christian Walther, Typen des Reich-Gottes-Verständnisses. Studien zur Eschatologie und Ethik im 19. Jhdt, München 1961.

[62] Kritik der praktischen Vernunft A230/31 (Werke ed. Weischedel, Bd. 4, 259).

[63] Bonn ³1886, 3 f.; dazu Weiß, aaO (wie A.61) 110–155; Walther, aaO (wie A.61) 137–155.

[64] 36 (1922) 465.

[65] Vgl. z.B. [W. Classen, in:] Morgenandachten für das ganze Jahr. Dargeboten von den Freunden der Christlichen Welt, Tübingen 1909, 58 f.; Friedrich Naumann, Gotteshilfe, Göttingen ²1904, 530 f.

von der Entstehung des Christentums auf Jahre, vielleicht Jahrzehnte hinaus weithin bestimmen.''[66] Derlei zu hören und zu goutieren war man Jahrzehnte hindurch gewohnt gewesen, und insofern befand sich Meyer durchaus im Einklang mit dem Geist seiner, der wilhelminischen, Epoche.

VI

Von Sodens Erwartung—besser: Befürchtung—sollte indes nicht in Erfüllung gehen. Grund hierfür war, daß das Zeitalter der liberalen Theologie und des ihr inhärenten Ethizismus nach dem Ersten Weltkrieg, was freilich nur Nachgeborene leicht zu erkennen vermögen, immer schneller seinem Ende zueilte. Für das, was Meyers Anliegen ausgemacht haben mochte, war er schlicht zu spät gekommen. Die lebendigeren Geister unter den Theologen der Zwanziger Jahre suchten jetzt zunehmend nach neuen Konzeptionen und wandten sich insbesondere der von Karl Barth geprägten und zeitweise von Rudolf Bultmann mitgestalteten ''Dialektischen Theologie'' zu, die mählich auch in die Kreise der gebildeten Laien eindrang. Dadurch, daß vor allem ihre Anhänger es gewesen waren, die im Kirchenkampf während des ''Dritten Reiches'' Widerstand zu leisten versucht hatten, gewann sie nach 1945 ein geradezu kanonisches Ansehen. Nicht mehr der sittliche Fortschritt der vom gütigen Allvater beseligten religiösen Persönlichkeit, sondern die allein durch das Heilshandeln Gottes in Christus überbrückte Diastase von Gottes Gottheit und Sündersein des Menschen stand nunmehr im Mittelpunkt theologischen Denkens.

Doch auch unter den Fachwissenschaftlern sollte Meyers Werk kaum Wirkung erzielen. In Werner Georg Kümmels großem Standardwerk über die Geschichte der Erforschung des Neuen Testaments, das 1958 erschien,[67] sucht man den Namen Eduard Meyer vergebens.[68] In dem

---

[66] AaO (wie A.8) 429.

[67] Das Neue Testament. Geschichte der Erforschung seiner Probleme, Freiburg i.B./München 1958.

[68] Anders mag es freilich im Bereich konservativ-evangelikaler Exegese (insbesondere der angelsächsischen Welt?) stehen. Vgl. etwa Ward Gasque, A History of the Criticism of the Acts of the Apostles (Tübingen 1975), der Meyers für unerschütterlich gehaltene Autorität ''as one of the greatest masters of the whole range of ancient history which the world of scholarship has ever produced'' unreflektiert auch für Meyer als Historiker des Urchristentums in Anspruch nimmt, um auf diese Weise den eigenen (entsprechenden Anschauungen Meyers sehr ähnlichen) Ansichten über die Historizität der Apostelgeschichte verstärktes Gewicht verleihen zu können (158–163; Zitat: 158). S. noch Frank Fyvie Bruce, New Testament History, Garden City (N.Y.) 1980, 311; ders., Die Glaubwürdigkeit der Schriften des Neuen Testaments, Bad Liebenzell 1976, 19.

zwölf Jahre danach publizierten Forschungsbericht "Das Neue Testament im 20. Jahrhundert"[69] äußerte sich der Historiograph der neutestamentlichen Wissenschaft dann allerdings doch noch: Meyers Geschichte des Urchristentums könne "durch ihre kritiklose Übernahme der Darstellung der Apostelgeschichte und durch ihre Schilderung des Paulus als eines geschickten Politikers nur als rückschrittlich bezeichnet werden" (74 f.). Genauso, nur drastischer, hatte bereits von Soden über Meyers Paulusdarstellung geurteilt: Mit Meyers "energischer Umsetzung unseres Nichtwissens in Wissen wären wir bei den Anfängen der [sc. historischen] Kritik glücklich wieder angelangt."[70] Das heißt: auch aus dem Abstand von fast fünfzig Jahren betrachtet, erwies sich Meyers Arbeit als alles andere denn eine Förderung wissenschaftlicher Erkenntnis. Die Rezensenten—allen voran Karl Ludwig Schmidt, Martin Dibelius, Hans von Soden und, last not least, Rudolf Bultmann—hatten mit ihrem negativen Urteil über die Leistung Meyers Recht behalten. Konzilianter als Schmidt hatte Bultmann in ersichtlichem Bemühen, wenigstens etwas Positives zu äußern, zum ersten Buch von "Ursprung und Anfänge" geschrieben: "Für den gebildeten Laien, der sich über ein *früheres* Stadium der Evangelienforschung orientieren will, kann es ... immerhin empfohlen werden."[71] Positiveres läßt sich, jedenfalls soweit der Neutestamentler gefragt ist, über Meyers Werk—dieses Werk!—in der Tat nicht sagen. Zu den "großen schöpferischen Werken," zu denen Ehrenberg es zählen wollte, gehört es gewiß nicht.

Korrekturzusatz: Walter Schmithals verdanke ich den Hinweis auf zwei Briefe Rudolf Bultmanns an Hans von Soden, in denen ersterer sich u.a. auch zu seinen Besprechungen Meyers äußert. Die einschlägigen Passagen werden im folgenden mit freundlicher Genehmigung der den Nachlaß Bultmanns verwahrenden Universitätsbibliothek Tübingen abgedruckt.
Am 3.4.1921 schreibt Bultmann: "Für die Frankfurter Zeitung schrieb ich—auf Bestellung—eine Besprechung von Ed. Meyers Buch. Ich muß dem Urteil K.L. Schmidts Recht geben. Das Buch enthält—von beiläufigen Kleinigkeiten abgesehen—gar nichts Neues u. tritt mit unglaublicher Anmaßung auf. Das einzig Neue, die Quellenhypothese des Mk, ist in einigen Beobachtungen, die richtig sind[,] auch alt, in ihren Ausgestaltungen oberflächlich; kurz[,] das ganze Buch ist veraltet u. wäre besser ungeschrieben geblieben."
Am 30.4.1922: "Einen Abzug meiner Besprechung von Ed. Meyer II konnte ich Ihnen noch nicht schicken, weil sie noch nicht gedruckt ist. Übrigens ist die Besprechung (in der Frankf. Zeitung, mit einigen andern Büchern zusammen) ziemlich kurz. Das Buch ist ja besser als I, u. enthält in den Einzelheiten manches Gute, bringt aber im Ganzen doch nichts Neues u. gibt von der geistesgeschichtlichen Entwicklung doch nur ein unvollständiges u. flaches Bild. Von den Einzelheiten ist mir die (ja schon früher von Meyer vorgetragene) Datierung des Damaskustextes das Interessanteste."

---

[69] Stuttgart 1970.
[70] AaO (wie A.8) 436; vgl. Behm, aaO (wie A.11) 475.
[71] AaO (wie A.10); Hervorhebung R.B.

RENATE SCHLESIER

RELIGION ALS GEGENBILD.
ZU EINIGEN GESCHICHTSTHEORETISCHEN ASPEKTEN
VON EDUARD MEYERS UNIVERSALHISTORIE

Geschichtswissenschaft sei mit Notwendigkeit eine subjektive[1] Angelegenheit—das ist im Kern das Credo des Historikers Eduard Meyer (1855 – 1930), welches er zeitlebens unbeirrt vertreten hat. Ihm selbst verdanken wir den Hinweis auf eine literarische Quelle dieses wissenschaftlichen Glaubensbekenntnisses: Es leitet sich von Goethe her: ''. . . Es ist ein groß Ergetzen, / Sich in den Geist der Zeiten zu versetzen; / Zu schauen, wie vor uns ein weiser Mann gedacht, / Und wie wir's dann zuletzt so herrlich weit gebracht.'' (*Faust* I, 570 – 573) Fausts Replik auf diese Worte seines Famulus Wagner lautet: ''O ja, bis an die Sterne weit! / Mein Freund, die Zeiten der Vergangenheit / Sind uns ein Buch mit sieben Siegeln. / Was ihr den Geist der Zeiten heißt, / Das ist im Grund der Herrren eigner Geist, / In dem die Zciten sich bespiegeln.'' (574 – 579) Auf das ''Goethesche Wort vom Geist der Zeiten'' beruft sich Meyer in seiner Einleitung zur *Geschichte des Altertums* mit allem Pathos, freilich nicht ohne hinzuzufügen, daß dieses Diktum ''seiner ironischen Fassung entkleidet'' werden müsse.[2] Dürfen wir das so verstehen, daß Meyer sich nicht Fausts Skepsis, sondern eher die Überzeugung des fortschrittsgläubigen Famulus zueigen machen möchte? Und läßt sich denn das Selbstbewußtsein des Historikers ungebrochen bewahren, ohne daß es auf Schritt und Tritt von Faustschen Einwänden durchkreuzt wird? Wer Eduard Meyer die Gretchenfrage stellt, wird eines Besseren belehrt.

---

[1] Mit seiner Hochschätzung der Subjektivität in der Historie beruft sich Meyer auf Thukydides (s. Abschn. II). Freilich faßt er damit die Aufgabe des Historikers eher im Sinne Herodots, als ὡς ἐμοὶ ἐδόκει, auf—wovon sich Thukydides (I, 22) scharf abgrenzt. Thukydides fügt freilich hinzu, daß er selbst bei den von ihm in seine Geschichtserzählung eingebauten Reden so verfährt. Daß er mit diesem Kunstgriff Objektivität suggeriert, hat Meyer unterstrichen (*Forschungen* II, 380 f.).—Mit seinem Subjektivitätskonzept nimmt Meyer gegenüber der deutschen historischen Schule eine extravagante Position ein; denn er setzt sich damit sowohl gegen Ranke ab, der die Auslöschung des historischen Subjekts auf dem Wege der Einfühlung postulierte und die Geschichte im göttlichen Wissen aufgehen lassen wollte (vgl. Anm. 70 und 93), wie gegen Droysen, der ein Objektivitätsideal im Sinne der Historie als systematischer Wissenschaft verfocht (vgl. Anm. 35).

[2] *GdA* I/1[5], 207.

I. Das Problem einer anti-theologischen Universalgeschichte

Universalgeschichte dirigiert für Meyer die ersten und letzten Dinge der Historie: "Grundlage und Ziel aller Geschichtsforschung und aller historischen Arbeit auch im begrenztesten Detail kann immer nur die Universalgeschichte sein."[3] Diese Formulierung impliziert, daß nicht ein Schöpfergott oder die göttliche Vorsehung das Fundament der Historie, nicht Apokalypse, göttliches Weltgericht und Erlösung durch den Messias das Telos der Geschichte seien, sondern die Universalgeschichte selbst. Meyer stellt also keineswegs die Möglichkeit einer fundamentalistischen und teleologischen Geschichtsauffassung in Frage, sondern verlagert lediglich Grundlage und Ziel der Historie aus der Sphäre der Transzendenz in die der angenommenen Immanenz. Mit einer solchen Bestimmung von Universalgeschichte grenzt Meyer sich entschieden von jeglicher religiösen Auffassung von Geschichte ab und lokalisiert sein Unternehmen in der Tradition der Aufklärung des 18. Jahrhunderts, des Zeitalters, in dem, wie Ranke bemerkt hat, der "Begriff der Weltgeschichte (...) gleichsam säcularisirt"[4] wurde. Worin bestand die Säkularisierung? Weltgeschichte und Universalgeschichte, die bisher im Dienst der Theologie standen und sich an der religiösen Überlieferung orientierten,[5] wurden zu autonomen Abläufen erklärt. Mit dem selben Begriff wird also nun ein Verfahren bezeichnet, das in grundsätzlichem Widerspruch steht zu dem bisher so benannten Verfahren, nämlich der spätestens seit der Reformation auf Schulen und Universitäten getriebenen "Universal-Historie".[6]

Die theologisch bestimmte Universalgeschichte besaß ein heilsge-

---

[3] Kl. Schr. I, 41; vgl. GdA I/1[5], 199: "Alle Geschichte, die wirklich ihr Ziel erreichen will, muß ihrer Betrachtungsweise und Tendenz nach notwendig universalistisch sein, sei es, daß sie das Gesamtgebiet behandelt, sei es, daß sie ein Einzelobjekt mit dieser inneren Beziehung auf das Ganze darstellt."

[4] L. von Ranke, Weltgeschichte I.1 (1880), Leipzig 1886[4], Vorrede, VII.

[5] Zuerst um die Wende vom 3. zum 4. Jhdt.: Eusebios, Chronikon. Repräsentativ für die theologische Universalgeschichte in der Folgezeit blieb Augustinus, De civitate Dei (vgl. Anm. 36 und 106). Noch beim Bischof J.-B. Bossuet, Discours sur l'histoire universelle (1681), dominiert—im Dienst der anti-protestantischen Religionspolitik des Sonnenkönigs—die theologische Geschichtsauffassung. Dagegen trat Voltaire seit 1756 (Essai sur l'histoire générale et sur les moeurs et l'esprit des nations, depuis Charlemagne jusqu'à nos jours) mit einem anti-theologischen, fortschrittsgläubigen Konzept von Universalhistorie auf; im Widerspruch dazu plädierte von protestantischer Seite J.G. Herder seit 1774 (Auch eine Philosophie der Geschichte zur Bildung der Menschheit) für eine aufklärungskritische, wiederum theologische Auffassung von Universalgeschichte. Dieser Gegensatz zwischen Voltaire und Herder blieb grundlegend für die folgende geschichtsphilosophische Diskussion.— Zu Meyers Position s. Anm. 10.

[6] Vgl. A.L. von Schlözer, Kritisch-historische Nebenstunden, Göttingen 1797, IV (gegen Herder).

schichtliches Programm, das durch die Lehre von den vier Weltmonarchien[7] und eine biblizistische Zeitrechnung eschatologisch umgrenzt wurde. Die aufklärerisch umgedeutete Universalgeschichte konnte sich nicht auf ein Verdikt gegen Heilsgeschichte und Theologie beschränken, sondern war genötigt, die Eschatologie durch eine andere, ebenfalls einheitsstiftende Weltanschauung zu ersetzen.[8]

Dieser Nötigung war sich Meyer bei seinem universalhistorischen Unternehmen wohl bewußt.[9] Nach Reflexionen über die Problematik der Säkularisierung sucht man jedoch in seinem Werk umsonst, obwohl sich Meyer durchaus mit den daraus resultierenden geschichtsphilosophischen Fragen auseinandergesetzt hat.[10] Er scheint nicht daran gezweifelt zu haben, daß eine aufklärerisch umdefinierte Universalhistorie sich von der Theologie vollständig emanzipieren könne, also nicht mehr von theologischen Denkmodellen und Methoden geprägt wird. Ob dies überhaupt möglich ist,[11] muß hier dahingestellt bleiben. Es mag genügen, auf

---

[7] *Daniel* 2,27–45 (Daniels Deutung des Traums von Nebukadnezar).

[8] Zu den daraus resultierenden Aporien der Universalhistorie des 19. Jahrhunderts (im Sinne einer Teleologie ohne Telos) s. zusammenfassend H.-G. Gadamer, *Wahrheit und Methode. Grundzüge einer philosophischen Hermeneutik* (1960), Tübingen 1975⁴, 185–191 (sowie passim), zu Ranke, Droysen, Dilthey. Vgl. auch über *Die Säkularisierung der universalhistorischen Auffassung* seit dem 16. Jhdt. das gleichnamige Buch von A. Klempt (1960).

[9] Siehe Abschn. II (besonders Anm. 42).

[10] Meyer wandte sich polemisch gegen die von Hegel repräsentierte Tendenz, in der geschichtlichen Entwicklung "die Verwirklichung einer bestimmten transzendenten Idee zu suchen" (*GdA* I/1⁵, 182). Derartiges würde den Namen "Geschichtsphilosophie" nicht verdienen, womit nach Meyer "nur etwas total anderes genannt werden (kann), nämlich die theoretische Erörterung der grundlegenden Probleme der Geschichtswissenschaft" (ebd.). Allerdings gehört dazu für Meyer vorzüglich ein Thema, das Probleme der Geschichtstranszendenz aufwirft: die Frage nach den Anfängen der Religion, ein Motiv, dem Meyer spezialistische Werke gewidmet hat: *Die Entstehung des Judentums. Eine historische Untersuchung* (1896); *Ursprung und Geschichte der Mormonen. Mit Exkursen über die Anfänge des Islâms und des Christentums* (1912); *Ursprung und Anfänge des Christentums* I–III (1921–1923), s. dazu die Beiträge von Parente, Henrichs und Plümacher in diesem Band.—Vgl. auch Meyers Ausbau seiner Einleitung in die *Geschichte des Altertums* seit der 2. Aufl. (1907) zu einer *Anthropologie*, also, nach Meyer, der "Lehre von den allgemeinen Formen menschlichen Lebens und menschlicher Entwicklung," die man, wie er hinzufügt, "oft auch mißbräuchlich Geschichtsphilosophie genannt" habe (*GdA* I/1⁵, 3). Aus Meyers Perhorreszierung geschichtsphilosophischer Transzendenz-Annahmen (im Einklang z.B. mit Droysen) folgte indessen keineswegs, daß er auf solche Postulate ganz verzichtete, wie im folgenden gezeigt wird.

[11] Rigorose Zweifel daran: bei J. Taubes, *Abendländische Eschatologie*, Bern 1947, und K. Löwith, *Meaning in History* (1949), deutsch: *Weltgeschichte und Heilsgeschehen. Die theologischen Voraussetzungen der Geschichtsphilosophie* (1953); polemisch gegen Löwith: besonders W. Kamlah, *Utopie. Eschatologie. Geschichtsteleologie. Kritische Untersuchungen zum Ursprung und zum futurischen Denken der Neuzeit*, Mannheim 1969, und H. Blumenberg, *Säkularisierung und Selbstbehauptung. Erweiterte und überarbeitete Neuausgabe von "Die Legitimität der Neuzeit,"* erster und zweiter Teil, Frankfurt/M. 1974, 35–40, 267–269; Vgl. auch R. Koselleck, *Kritik und Krise. Eine Studie zur Pathogenese der bürgerlichen Welt*, Freiburg/München 1959.—Zur an

einige auffällige Berührungspunkte hinzuweisen zwischen den Leitlinien einer theologisch aufgefaßten Universalgeschichte und denjenigen, die der Universalhistoriker Eduard Meyer sich setzt. Ebenso wie in der traditionell theologischen Universalhistorie üblich, ist bei Meyer mit dem Begriff des Universalen nicht etwa die gesamte Welt der Erdkugel als physikalische Einheit gemeint, und Teile der Welt wie der Weltzeit werden paradigmatisch als pars pro toto behandelt. Freilich ist der Begriff des Universalen bei Meyer auf den ersten Blick nicht geschichtstranszendent, sondern geschichts-immanent bestimmt. Der Gegenstand von Meyers ehrgeizigstem universalhistorischen Projekt, der *Geschichte des Altertums*, ist örtlich auf den Mittelmeerraum und die geographisch an ihn angrenzenden Gebiete beschränkt.[12] Von einer über die abendländische Antike, über Griechenland, Rom und den Vorderen Orient hinausgreifenden Weltgeschichte der Menschheit kann bei Meyer—trotz seiner umfangreichen Beschäftigung mit weltpolitischen Phänomenen seiner Zeit —keine Rede sein. Seine "Universalgeschichte" ist vielmehr begrenzt auf einen antiken Begriff des Universums, im Sinne der von den mittelmeerischen Zivilisationen geprägten "Welt".

Räumlich und zeitlich universal ist Meyers Unternehmen also ebensowenig wie die theologische Universalhistorie, und ebenso wie sie ist es von einem geographischen und geistigen Mittelpunkt aus konzipiert, dem ein zeitlicher Index entspricht. Doch im Gegensatz zur theologischen Universalgeschichte heißt der Drehpunkt von Meyers Weltbild nicht Israel, sondern Griechenland, das Meyer als den Ursprungsort der Religionskritik erachtet, das er also gerade wegen seiner antitheologischen Funktion zum universalhistorischen Zentrum erklärt. Und in dem Maße, wie diese Qualität weiterwirkt und weiterwirken soll, tritt Griechenland unter umgekehrten Vorzeichen das Erbe des Heiligen Landes an.

Der von Meyer in Ionien und Athen zentralisierte zeitliche Index wird am Auftreten großer Repräsentanten der Individualität—Dichter, Politiker, Philosophen—gemessen. In ihnen sieht Meyer den okzidentalen Geist par excellence verkörpert. Wer oder was diesem Geist widerspricht, wird von Meyer dem Orient zugerechnet. Selbstverständlich handelt es sich dabei nur um den 'Orient', mit dem der 'Okzident' bis zum Ende seines Altertums in nähere politische und religiöse Verbindung

---

diese Differenz anknüpfenden Forschungsdiskussion siehe R. Koselleck/ W.-D. Stempel (Hg.), *Geschichte—Ereignis und Erzählung* (= *Poetik und Hermeneutik* 5), München 1973.

[12] Zeitlich bricht die *Geschichte des Altertums* ab mit dem "Ausgang der griechischen Geschichte" im 4. Jhdt., dem Ende der politischen Selbständigkeit Athens und dem Ende der Dominanz der Griechen in Sizilien; Meyers langfristigeres Konzept hat sich nicht realisieren lassen.

kam, d.h. die Länder des Fernen Ostens sind für diesen Orient noch irrelevant. Denn der Gegensatz zwischen Okzident und Orient ist bei Meyer ein polemisches Konzept. Er ist ihm gleichbedeutend mit dem Gegensatz zwischen Geistesfreiheit und Theologic. Den Ausgang der Perserkriege wertet er deshalb als "Entscheidung" darüber, "ob in der griechischen Welt eine theologisch gefärbte Kultur entstehen soll wie im Orient oder ob sich hier eine neue ganz andersartige Kultur auf dem Grunde freiester geistiger Bewegung erheben wird, wie sie die Welt bisher noch nicht gesehen hat."[13] Diese Frage hält Meyer auch nach dem von ihm günstig beurteilten Ergebnis der Perserkriege keineswegs für ausgestanden. Die Betroffenheit des Geschichtsschreibers rührt daher, daß er den Okzident auch nach den Perserkriegen wie zuvor durch die Machtansprüche orientalischer Theologie bedroht sieht. Diese Machtansprüche werden sich Meyer zufolge später tatsächlich langfristig durchsetzen, nämlich im Christentum, das er als die Vollendung einer orientalischen Religion, des Judentums, charakterisiert.[14] Das ausgeprägte Interesse für die verschiedensten Erscheinungsformen "theologischer Politik,"[15] das in Meyers Werk immer wieder durchschlägt, läßt sich durch seine Parteinahme für den Geist des Abendlandes erklären, der für Meyer mit der Religionskritik der alten Griechen unlösbar verbunden ist.

Doch auch unabhängig von Meyers anti-theologischen Motiven muß

---

[13] *GdA* III[2] (= *GdA* 5[8]), 768; vgl. *GdA* III[1], 444–448. Zu Meyers Abwertung des Orients s. auch *GdA* I/1[5], 193: "Niemals kann die Geschichte des alten Orients das gleiche Interesse erwecken, wie die Griechenlands oder Roms." Diese Überzeugung gehört zu den Stereotypen des deutschen Idealismus, namentlich bei Hegel und Humboldt (vgl. Anm. 19).

[14] Jesus wird von Meyer als "der Vollender des Judentums" bezeichnet (*UAC* II, 445); vgl. Meyers Beurteilung der Einführung des Gesetzbuches in Juda im Jahre 621: "auf ihm beruht das Judentum und damit auch das Christentum wie der Islam," *GdA* III[2] (= *GdA* 5[8]), 158. Zu Meyers Betonung der Gemeinsamkeiten zwischen Judentum und Christentum s. ebenso *Forschungen* II, 267, wo andererseits auch die Berührungspunkte zwischen den jüdischen Propheten und den zeitgenössischen griechischen Schriftstellern hervorgehoben werden. Zu Meyers Auffassung vom spezifischen "Wesen" des Judentums s. Anm. 30 und 31.

[15] Zum Begriff der "theologischen Politik" vgl. Ch. Meier, *Die Entstehung des Politischen bei den Griechen* (1980), Frankfurt/M. 1983, 222 f., n. 204. Meier lehnt sich hier an die Begrifflichkeit von C. Schmitt an (*Politische Theologie. Vier Kapitel zur Lehre von der Souveränität*, 1922, 1934[2], und *Politische Theologie II. Die Legende von der Erledigung jeder Politischen Theologie*, 1970), der nachzuweisen suchte, daß Begriffe der Staatslehre säkularisierte theologische Begriffe sind. Meiers Wendung "theologische Politik" soll im Vergleich dazu den Primat der Politik bei den alten Griechen herausstellen; vgl. auch "Die Entstehung einer autonomen Intelligenz bei den Griechen," in: S.N. Eisenstadt (Hg.), *Kulturen der Achsenzeit. Ihre Ursprünge und ihre Vielfalt, I: Griechenland, Israel, Mesopotamien*, Frankfurt/M. 1987, 109.—Ich verwende den Ausdruck "theologische Politik" hier freilich nicht mit einem solchen analytischen Anspruch, sondern deskriptiv zur Darstellung von Meyers Präjudizien.

festgehalten werden, daß theologisch intendierte und interpretierbare Politik von jeher ein adäquater Gegenstand der theologischen Universalgeschichte ist. So überrascht es nicht, daß Meyers parteilicher Unterschied zu ihr verblaßt, wenn er sich den historischen Erscheinungsformen einer Universalmonarchie und den theokratischen Implikationen von Weltherrschaftsansprüchen zuwendet. Die Erhebung des Herrschers zum Gott innerhalb einer Universalmonarchie, die er im Reich von Akkad zum ersten Mal verwirklicht sah[16] und die er Alexander dem Großen und Cäsar nachsagt, findet Meyer noch in den Verehrungsformen gegenüber dem christlichen Kaiser aufbewahrt.[17]

Freilich reichen Meyers Sympathien für die Monarchie ebensowenig wie die Sachzwänge der traditionellen hagiographischen Universalgeschichte aus, den Historiker seinem aufklärerischen, anti-theologischen Programm abspenstig zu machen. Denn sein Einblick in den Geschichtsverlauf zwingt ihn dazu, gegen die Weltmonarchie und für den okzidentalen Geist der Individualität Partei zu ergreifen. Die Individualität—auch der Staaten—, von der er sicher ist, daß sie schöpferische Rivalitäten bewirkt, sowie die durch den Individualismus ermöglichte Unabhängigkeit von Gottesglauben und Theokratie ist dem Universalhistoriker Meyer mehr wert als weltumspannende Universalität. Bezeichnenderweise macht er für Roms Niedergang "das nivellierende Weltreich und die Ersetzung der Volksindividualitäten durch eine homogene, entnationalisierte Menschheit" verantwortlich.[18]

Hier wird deutlich, worin sich Meyers Universalismus von einem politischen oder theologischen unterscheidet. Pointiert gesagt, zielt Meyers universalgeschichtlicher Impetus auf eine universelle Apotheose der Individualität. Das Pathos von Meyers Individualitätsbegriff speist sich aus einer idealistisch-historistischen Geschichtsauffassung, wie sie durch Wilhelm von Humboldt entwickelt wurde.[19] Auch bei ihm bilden die Griechen, nicht die Römer und das Christentum, die Ellipse des Altertums. Ähnlich wie bei Humboldt bleibt bei Meyer der Historismus huma-

---

[16] Vgl. *GdA* I/2³, 528.
[17] Vgl. *Alexander der Große und die absolute Monarchie*: *Kl. Schr.* I, 294.
[18] *Kl. Schr.* II, 537 (*Vorläufer des Weltkriegs im Altertum*).
[19] Zu bei Humboldt vorgeprägten universalhistorischen Leitgedanken Meyers s. besonders W. von Humboldt, *Über die Aufgabe des Geschichtschreibers* (1821), in: *Werke in fünf Bänden*, hg. von A. Flitner/F. Giel, I: *Schriften zur Anthropologie und Geschichte*, Darmstadt 1960, 585–606 (zum griechischen Individualitätsbegriff: 601 f.); zu Meyers Individualitätsbegriff vgl. vor allem: *Zur Theorie und Methodik der Geschichte* (1902), in: *Kl. Schr.* I, 3–67, sowie *The Development of Individuality in Ancient History*, *Kl. Schr.* (1910), 213–230.— S. auch zu Meyers Benutzung anderer Humboldtscher Zentralbegriffe der Historie (historisch Wirksames, Analogie usw.): Abschn. IV (besonders Anm. 97).

nistisch eingefärbt.[20] Zugleich wird dabei die Historisierung partiell aufgehoben durch die miteinander verknüpften Leitgedanken der Universalität und der Individualität.[21] Unter diesen Vorzeichen gewinnt gerade die griechische Historie eine normative Qualität, die scharf von derjenigen abgegrenzt wird, welche Judentum und Christentum beanspruchen: "So sind die Griechen die Schöpfer aller Geschichtsliteratur, und auch auf diesem Gebiete die Lehrmeister aller folgenden Zeiten geworden. Nachdem die Geschichtsschreibung einmal geschaffen war, ist sie nicht wieder untergegangen; und so ist sie auch zu Zeiten und Völkern gekommen, die aus eigener Kraft niemals eine Geschichtsüberlieferung geschaffen haben würden, wie die des früheren christlichen Mittelalters."[22] Bei aller Theologie-Kritik zwingt freilich eine normativ gefaßte Historie zur metaphysischen Transponierung ins Über- und A-Historische, nicht anders, als im Falle einer theologischen Geschichtsschreibung.

Mit seinem universalhistorischen Anspruch stellte sich Meyer gegen die zeitgenössische Tendenz des positivistischen Historismus, der das faktisch Abgelebte und nicht das überzeitlich Weiterwirkende der Geschichte betonte.[23] Würde man Auguste Comte's Dreistufenmodell der Geistesgeschichte—von der Theologie über die Metaphysik zur positiven Wissenschaft[24]—zugrundelegen, um Meyers geistigen Ort zu bestimmen, so fiele es schwer, ihn einer dieser Stufen eindeutig zuzurechnen oder abzusprechen. Wie es scheint, ist Meyer allen drei Tendenzen nicht allein durch Negation, sondern auch durch Anknüpfung verpflichtet.

Daß Meyers Werk sich gegen eine unzweideutige Klassifizierbarkeit

---

[20] Zu Humboldts humanistisch-normativem Historismus vgl. J. Bollack, in: H. Flashar/K. Gründer/A. Horstmann (Hg.), *Philologie und Hermeneutik im 19. Jahrhundert. Zur Geschichte und Methodologie der Geisteswissenschaften*, Göttingen 1979, 399 f., in kritischer Auseinandersetzung mit U. Muhlack, "Zum Verhältnis von Klassischer Philologie und Geschichtswissenschaft im 19. Jahrhundert," ebd. 225–239.

[21] Die Verknüpfung von Individualismus und Universalismus ist für Meyer gerade auch ein spezifisch religionsgeschichtliches Phänomen, s. *GdA* III[1], 225 (am Beispiel des Judentums).

[22] *GdA* I/1[5], 228.

[23] Zu Meyers dennoch vorhandener Nähe zum Positivismus s. W. Benjamin, Paralipomena zu den Thesen *Über den Begriff der Geschichte*, in: *Gesammelte Schriften*, hg. von R. Tiedemann/H. Schweppenhäuser, I/3, Frankfurt/M. 1974, 1230 f.: "Die Einfühlung ins Gewesene dient zuletzt seiner Vergegenwärtigung. Die Tendenz zu der letztern geht nicht umsonst mit einer positivistischen Vorstellung von Geschichte sehr gut zusammen (wie sich das bei Eduard Meyer zeigt). Die Projektion des Gewesenen in die Gegenwart ist im Bereich der Geschichte analog der Substitution identischer Konfigurationen für die Veränderungen in der Körperwelt. (...) Die falsche Lebendigkeit der Vergegenwärtigung, die Beseit[ig]ung jedes Nachhalls der 'Klage' aus der Geschichte, bezeichnet ihre endgültige Unterwerfung unter den modernen Begriff der Wissenschaft." Es muß freilich konzediert werden, daß Meyer die von Benjamin gemeinte "Klage" durch einen emphatischen Begriff von geschichtlicher "Tragik" zu erfassen suchte (vgl. Anm. 107).

[24] Vgl. A. Comte, *Discours sur l'esprit positif* (1844).

sperrt—auch im Sinne einer klaren Fortschrittlichkeit oder Rückschritt-
lichkeit—, erweist sich am deutlichsten an der Vehemenz, mit der Meyer
Religionsgeschichte aus religionskritischen Motiven betreibt. Die Ablehnung der Religion[25] als Weltanschauung und politischer Macht lenkte
Meyers Aufmerksamkeit keineswegs von der Religion ab. Im Gegenteil:
das Interesse für religionsgeschichtliche Fragen wirkt in seinem Gesamtwerk dominierend. Zur ägyptischen Religion, zum Judentum, zum
Christentum, zur prophetischen Sekte der Mormonen hat Meyer umfangreiche Bücher und engagierte Abhandlungen verfaßt.[26] Hervorstechen-
des Interesse an diesen Themen ist bereits für den Gymnasiasten und
Studenten dokumentiert.[27] Die Dissertation des Neunzehnjährigen, 1875
in Leipzig, widmet sich einem ägyptischen Gott, den Herodot mit einer
griechischen Mythenfigur gleichgesetzt hatte: *Seth-Typhon. Eine religionsgeschichtliche Studie.* Der 1877 veröffentlichte erste wissenschaftliche Aufsatz behandelt vorwiegend Astarte.[28] Ein bemerkenswert großer Teil der
zahlreichen gelehrten Abhandlungen und Handbuchartikel, die Meyer
im Laufe seines Lebens neben seinen universalhistorischen Großprojek-
ten und seinen nationalistischen Streitschriften schrieb, galt religionswissenschaftlichen Themen. Die *Geschichte des Altertums* ist von ausführlichen
Erörterungen religiöser Vorstellungen und ihrer Auswirkungen auf historische Prozesse leitmotivisch durchsetzt. Die religiöse Begründung der
Politik und die politische Rolle der Religion hat Meyers kritische, aber
nichtsdestotrotz bewundernde Aufmerksamkeit besonders in Gestalt der
Religionsstifter des Vorderen Orients und des Abendlandes auf sich gezogen, und große politisch-religiöse Zentren wie das delphische Orakel-
Heiligtum würdigt Meyer eingehender Analyse im Geschichtszusam-
menhang.

Beherrschend war und blieb dabei für Meyer die von Jugend an festge-
haltene Bewertung der Theologie als Feindbild, als Gefahr für geistige
Freiheit. Dies gilt gleichermaßen für den Orient, den geographisch-
geistigen Raum also, der ihm am ehesten theologie-adäquat erschien.
Zugleich übte das als bedrohlich und verwerflich, als unsinnig und ab-
scheulich Empfundene einen unwiderstehlichen Reiz auf ihn aus.[29] Von

---

[25] Vgl. Abschn. II.
[26] Siehe Anm. 10.
[27] S. dazu den Beitrag von Hoffmann in diesem Band.
[28] *Ueber einige semitische Götter*, in: *Zeitschrift der Deutschen Morgenländischen Gesellschaft* 31
(1877), 716–741.—Zu den religionshistorischen Schriften innerhalb von Meyers Oeuvre
s. H. Marohl. *Eduard Meyer. Bibliographie. Mit einer autobiographischen Skizze Eduard Meyers
und der Gedächtnisrede von Ulrich Wilcken*, Stuttgart 1941.
[29] Eine solche Ambivalenz gegenüber der Religion ist schon beim jungen Meyer ausgeprägt, vgl. dazu bei Hoffmann, Dok. 6: "Z.B. ist es für eine gründliche Erforschung
oder zur Darstellung der äg. Religion durchaus nothwendig, das Th. mit der größten

der Theologie, vom Orient, von der Religion in allen ihren Aspekten
fühlte Meyer sich, nach seinen biographischen und wissenschaftlichen
Zeugnissen zu urteilen, offensichtlich mindestens ebensosehr angezogen
als abgestoßen. Gegenüber dem Judentum, dem Meyer wohl, nimmt
man alles Publizierte zusammen, den überwiegenden Teil seiner religionshistorischen Arbeit gewidmet hat, zeigt sich die Ambivalenz von
Meyers Faszination durch religionspolitische Probleme besonders deutlich. "Nothwendiges Correlat" des Judentums seit dem Exil ist für Meyer
"der Judenhass," denn: "Nicht ihr Gott und ihre Religion an sich ist es,
was Spott und Hohn und Verfolgung der Heiden hervorruft, sondern die
hochmüthige Ueberlegenheit, mit der sie als alleinige Bekenner des
wahren Gottes allen anderen Völkern entgegentreten, jede Berührung
mit ihnen als befleckend zurückweisen, den Anspruch erheben, mehr und
besser zu sein als sie und berufen zu sein, über sie zu herrschen."[30]
Offenbar will Meyer damit freilich nicht sagen, daß staatlich sanktionierte
Missionierung anderer Völker die Juden vor Vertreibungen und Progro-
men bewahrt und selbst zu mörderischen Verfolgern gemacht hätte, wie
im Falle von Christentum und Islam. Denn zusammenfassend wird die
Ambivalenz auf die Juden selbst projiziert und dabei zu einer on-
tologischen Konstante ausgebaut: "Denn das ist überhaupt das Wesen
des Judenthums: Die höchsten und die abstossendsten Gedanken, das
Grossartige und das Gemeine liegen unmittelbar neben einander, untrennbar verbunden, das eine immer die Kehrseite des anderen."[31] Den
Schritt von einer solchen Rechtfertigung der Judenverfolgung mit dem
"Wesen des Judentums" und dem "Hochmut" der jüdischen Religion
zur systematischen Ausrottung der Juden hat Meyer nicht mehr erlebt.[32]

Akribie durchzuarbeiten, und die Sache hat ja auch immer viel Reiz, namentlich in Folge
der vielen Räthsel der Schrift und Sprache; aber dann kommt wieder so viel Dummes,
Abgeschmacktes, Sinnloses, daß ich mich schon oft gefragt habe ob nicht das Räthselhafte
das einzig Fesselnde ist" (Oktober 1875, Brief an Pietschmann). Zu Meyers Anziehung
und Abstoßung durch die Mythologie s. Abschn. IV.—Eine solche doppeldeutige Faszination war kennzeichnend für die akademisch akkreditierte Religionswissenschaft der
zweiten Hälfte des 19. Jhdts., s. dazu M. Detienne, "La mythologie scandaleuse" (1978),
deutsch: "Die skandalöse Mythologie (oder: Projekt einer Arbeit über das zweideutige
Wesen der sogenannten Mythologie)," in: Renate Schlesier (Hg.), *Faszination des Mythos.
Studien zu antiken und modernen Interpretationen*, Frankfurt/M. 1985, 13–34.
  [30] *GdA* III¹, 217.
  [31] Ebd. 218 f.—K. Christ (*Von Gibbon zu Rostovtzeff. Leben und Werk führender Althistoriker
der Neuzeit*, Darmstadt 1972, 313) kommentiert diese Meyersche Einschätzung des Judentums wie folgt: "(. . .) wahrte Meyer auch hier immer eine gewisse Distanz." Christ's
Understatement verzichtet wohlweislich auf Kritik an Meyers Position.
  [32] Solche Projektionen der Anlässe zur Judenverfolgung auf die Juden selbst waren für
einen beachtlichen Teil der deutschen Gelehrten spätestens seit Treitschke typisch und
wurden kaum differenzierter formuliert als im nationalsozialistischen Schrifttum vor und
nach 1933; vgl. dazu F. Stern, *The Politics of Cultural Despair: A Study in the Rise of the*

Meyers emotionales Engagement zeigte sich nicht allein in seinen deutschnationalen Aktivitäten.[33] Zugespitzt läßt sich sagen, daß Meyer gerade durch einen anti-religiösen Affekt immer wieder zu religionsgeschichtlichen Objekten getrieben wurde. Sein früh erwachtes Interesse für die in der zweiten Hälfte des 19. Jahrhunderts sprunghaft entwickelten Forschungsrichtungen Religionswissenschaft, vergleichende Mythologie und Sprachwissenschaft, Anthropologie und Ethnologie erkannte in ihnen wesentliche Ergänzungen der ''Völkergeschichte,'' um zu einer ''zusammenhängenden Geschichte des menschlichen Geistes'' zu gelangen.[34] Die Systematik der Religionsentwicklung, die sich der junge Meyer zur Aufgabe gestellt hatte, zielte auf eine geistige Überwindung des religiösen Denkens.

Verwirklicht hat Meyer diese selbstgestellte Aufgabe nicht. Der Historie insgesamt sprach er bald die Möglichkeit ab, eine systematische, eine objektive Wissenschaft zu sein[35] und näherte sie eher der Ästhetik, Psychologie und Ethik an. Desto mehr verdichtete sich ihm die Religion zum Gegenbild, in dem der individualistische, der anti-theologische Historiker sich spiegelt. Vielleicht wäre in der Auflösung der Religion das säkularisierte heilsgeschichtliche Programm von Meyers Universalhistorie zu erblicken. Denn Geschichte wird auch bei Meyer als via animae liberandae konzipiert wie bei Augustin[36]—freilich nicht im Sinne

---

Germanic Ideology, Berkeley/Los Angeles 1961, sowie F.K. Ringer, *The Decline of the German Mandarins* (1969), deutsch: *Die Gelehrten. Der Niedergang der deutschen Mandarine 1890–1933*, Stuttgart 1983.—Der sogenannte ''Historikerstreit'' in der Bundesrepublik Deutschland der achtziger Jahre zeigt, daß diese Gesinnung, in mindestens ebenso ''sachlichem'' Gewande wie bei Meyer (und freilich nicht unwidersprochen), weiterwirkt, s. z.B. die jüngste Publikation von E. Nolte, *Der europäische Bürgerkrieg 1917–1945. Nationalsozialismus und Bolschewismus*, Berlin 1987; zur unentlastbaren deutschen Verantwortung für den Holocaust s. Ch. Meier, *Vierzig Jahre nach Auschwitz. Deutsche Geschichtserinnerung heute*, München 1987.

[33] Siehe dazu B. vom Brocke, '' 'Wissenschaft und Militarismus.' Der Aufruf der 93 'An die Kulturwelt!' und der Zusammenbruch der internationalen Gelehrtenrepublik im Ersten Weltkrieg,'' in: W.M. Calder III/H. Flashar/Th. Lindken (Hg.), *Wilamowitz nach 50 Jahren*, Darmstadt 1985, 649–719; L. Canfora, ''Wilamowitz e Meyer tra la sconfitta e la 'Repubblica di Novembre,' '' in: *Quaderni di storia* 3 (1976), 69–94.—Zu Meyers ''unhistorischer'' Argumentation bei seiner Beurteilung des 1. Weltkriegs s. den Beitrag von v. Ungern-Sternberg in diesem Band. Vgl. auch Anm. 122.

[34] So Meyer 1874 als Student in einem Vortrag zum Thema *Die Anfänge menschlicher Entwicklung* vor dem ''Philosophischen Verein'' in Leipzig, zit. bei Hoffmann, in diesem Band.

[35] Siehe den ersten Satz von Meyers Programmschrift *Zur Theorie und Methodik der Geschichte* (*Kl. Schr.* I, 3): ''Die Geschichte ist keine systematische Wissenschaft.'' Meyer richtet sich damit gegen J.G. Droysens *Grundriß der Historik* (1858), der die ''Systematik des historisch Erforschbaren'' zu umfassen beanspruchte; zu Droysen vgl. Anm. 92 und 95.—Zu Meyers Gebrauch des Begriffs ''Geschichte'' s. Anm. 195.

[36] Augustinus, *De civ. Dei* X, 32: ''Haec est religio, quae universalem continet viam animae liberandae, quoniam nulla nisi hac liberari potest. Haec est enim quodam modo

einer Befreiung des Menschengeistes zu Gott sondern zu sich selbst, und nicht durch die Religion sondern von der Religion.

II. *"Weltanschauung": Das griechische Vorbild*

Die Frage, wie Eduard Meyer es mit der Religion hält, kann sich nicht auf seine Forschungsinteressen und -ergebnisse beschränken, sondern muß sich gerade an die professionellen Selbstzeugnisse des Forschers richten, der so unmißverständlich wie kaum ein anderer auf der entscheidenden Bedeutung der Subjektivität für die Arbeit des Historikers insistiert hat. Die Suche nach Meyers Antwort auf diese Frage ist keine Rätselaufgabe. Er macht kein Hehl daraus, daß er für seine Person keinem religiösen Erklärungsmodell der Wirklichkeit anhängt, ja mit jeglichem religiösen Herrschaftsanspruch auf Kriegsfuß steht. Denn das "eigentliche Charakteristikum einer religiösen Lehre" ist für ihn die Behauptung, "das Widersinnige und Absurde, das logisch Unmögliche" sei "dennoch wahr."[37] Auch die religiöse Rechtfertigung ethischer Normen stößt bei ihm auf Widerstand. Zumal der christlichen Moral bescheinigt er "überspannte Lehren."[38] Als einen "Grundirrthum der religiösen Weltanschauung" prangert er die Auffassung an, daß "alle sittlichen und staatlichen Ordnungen (...) auf dem Willen der Götter" beruhen.[39] Er selbst vertritt vehement die entgegensetzte Überzeugung: "Die Ethik ist so wenig ein Erzeugniss der Religion, dass sie diese vielmehr unter ihre Gebote zwingt, mag sie sich noch so heftig dagegen sträuben." Meyer hält fest daran, daß "die Religion nicht die Wurzel der Sitte" ist, "sondern umgekehrt das Erzeugnis und der Ausdruck einer sozialen Ordnung, des geregelten Zusammenlebens der Menschen."[40] Gegenüber

---

regalis via, quae una ducit ad regnum, non temporali fastigio nutabundum, sed aeternitatis firmitate securum. (...) quid hac historia vel inlustrius inveniri potest, quae universum orbem tanto apice auctoritatis obtinuit, vel fidelius, in qua ita narrantur praeterita, ut futura etiam praedicantur, quorum multa videmus impleta, ex quibus ea quae restant sine dubio speremus implenda?"

[37] *GdA* I/1[5], 158. Zu Meyers Polemik gegen spezifisch religiöse Unlogik vgl. Anm. 29 und 194.

[38] GdA IV[1], 452.—Andererseits rechnete Meyer (vgl. Plümacher in diesem Band, zu *UAC*) die Ethik im Sinne der vom Neukantianismus inspirierten liberalen Theologie seiner Zeit immerhin zu den Vorzügen des Christentums, im Unterschied etwa zur Apokalyptik; vgl. bei Christ (wie Anm. 31), 287, n. 3.

[39] *GdA* IV[1], 140 (am Beispiel des Sophokles).

[40] *GdA* I/1[5], 72. Meyers gesellschaftliche Erklärung der Religion blieb in Deutschland praktisch folgenlos. Im Unterschied dazu hat in Frankreich E. Durkheim mit einer ebenfalls religionssoziologischen Interpretation früher Gesellschaften schulbildend gewirkt, besonders durch sein Werk *Les formes élémentaires de la vie religieuse* (1912) (zu Durkheims Kritik an Meyer s. Anm. 118); zur Schulbildung vgl. M. Bloch/F. Braudel/L. Febvre u.a., *Schrift und Materie der Geschichte. Vorschläge zur systematischen Aneignung historischer Pro-*

dem jedoch, was eine Religion als heilige Gebote hinstellt, sei Argwohn angebracht, denn von ihnen "enthüllt sich nur zu vieles als Vorurtheil, ja als Hemmniss einer wahren Sittlichkeit."[41] Ausschlaggebend für Meyers Verdammung der "religiösen Weltanschauung" ist freilich kein ethischer Vorbehalt, sondern die Erfahrung, daß auf ihrer Grundlage keine akzeptable Erkenntnis der historischen Wahrheit zu gewinnen ist. Von den Unbeweisbarkeiten und Aporien, welche jede Religion charakterisieren, von der Unmöglichkeit, religiöse Vorstellungen historisch schlüssig zu begründen, konnte Meyer sich nur abgestoßen fühlen.

Folgerichtigerweise sah sich Meyer vom Beruf des Historikers angezogen, denn, so verrät er 1907 im Vorwort zur 2. Auflage seiner Einleitung in die *Geschichte des Altertums*: das "Streben nach Gewinnung einer einheitlichen, historisch begründeten Weltanschauung (ist) für mich überhaupt bei der Ergreifung meines Berufs die innerste Triebfeder gewesen."[42] Nicht eine Religion also, sondern allein die Historie schien ihm den sicheren Boden zu bieten, um Gewißheit über Prinzipien und Ganzheiten zu erreichen. Denn aus der Geschichte selbst sollte die als unabdingbar erachtete Weltanschauung abgeleitet werden. Meyers Berufsentscheidung verdankt sich dem Bedürfnis nach einem Religionsersatz, nach einer Weltanschauung, die dem Anspruch auf Einheitlichkeit verläßlicher als jede Religion genügt. Nach der Basis für eine solche Weltanschauung brauchte Meyer nicht umständlich zu suchen oder gar auf eigene Hand ein Denksystem zu entwickeln. Vielmehr glaubte er die benötigte ausreichende Grundlage—wie zahlreiche andere Gelehrte seiner Generation—in der Vergangenheit fertig vorzufinden: im religionskritischen Denken der alten Griechen, das von den ionischen Naturphilosophen zum ersten Mal systematisch ausgebildet wurde.[43] In diesem geistesgeschichtlichen Vorgang, und nicht in einem politischen oder wirtschaftlichen, hat Meyer den "entscheidende(n) Wendepunkt der griechischen Geschichte" angesiedelt: "In der zweiten Hälfte des 6. Jahrhunderts scheint es, als ob auch Griechenland in die Bahnen des Orients einlenken würde, als ob das Resultat der langen, tiefbewegten Entwicklung doch

---

zesse, hg. von Claudia Honegger, Frankfurt/M. 1977 ("Annales"-Schule), sowie J. Béguin u.a., *Cent ans de sciences religieuses en France à l'Ecole Pratique des Hautes Etudes*, Paris 1987.

[41] *GdA* IV¹, 141.

[42] *GdA* I/1⁵, X; vgl. auch Meyers *Autobiographische Skizze*, in: Marohl (wie Anm. 28), 9.—Meyers Bemühung, die Geschichtswissenschaft zur magistra vitae—und zwar des Historikers—zu machen, stellt in der Geschichte der "Geschichte" eine bezeichnende Akzentverschiebung dar; vgl. zum Traditionszusammenhang und Traditionsbruch dieses Problems: R. Koselleck, "Historia Magistra Vitae. Über die Auflösung des Topos im Horizont neuzeitlich bewegter Geschichte," in: H. Braun/M. Riedel (Hg.), *Natur und Geschichte. Karl Löwith zum 70. Geburtstag*, Stuttgart 1976, 196–219.

[43] Vgl. *GdA* III² (= *GdA* 5⁸), 206.

kein anderes sein würde als die Entstehung einer weiteren, in sich für alle
Zeiten abgeschlossenen religiösen Kultur. Aber es ist nicht dazu gekommen (...). Gleichzeitig mit der Orphik entsteht eine Gegenströmung,
welche die religiöse Bewegung durchbricht und in langem Ringen zu
Boden wirft und so die Einzigartigkeit der griechischen Entwicklung
begründet. Noch einmal hat Ionien seine führende Stellung im geistigen
Leben der Nation bewährt; es hat ihr ein letztes und höchstes Geschenk
dargebracht, das, worauf für alle kommenden Generationen der Menschen die befreiende Kraft der griechischen Kultur beruht, die Philosophie."[44] Von dieser vorwärtstreibenden quasi messianischen Kraft der
griechischen Weisheitslehre fühlt Meyer sich in höchstem Maße beflügelt.
Ebenso wie die mythenkritischen Naturphilosophen leitet auch ihn "das
Streben nach Universalität, nach theoretischer Verknüpfung der Einzel-
fälle," das er als "ein wesentliches Moment der Grösse wie der Einseitigkeit des griechischen Denkens" bezeichnet hat.[45]

Um an die Größe des griechischen Universalismus anzuknüpfen, ohne
in spekulative Einseitigkeit zu verfallen, wählte Meyer ganz bewußt nicht
die Philosophie zu seinem Betätigungsfeld, sondern die Geschichtswissenschaft. Denn den Beweis für die Gangbarkeit dieses Weges hatte ihm
zufolge kein griechischer Philosoph, wohl aber ein griechischer Historiker
erbracht, dessen Vorbild Meyer uneingeschränkt bewunderte, dessen
Vorgehensweise er für die absolut gültige historische Methode hielt und
dessen politisch-anthropologische Überzeugungen er zu teilen beanspruchte: Thukydides.[46]

In den ersten zwanzig Kapiteln des ersten Buches der *Geschichte des
Peloponnesischen Krieges* fand Meyer "alle die Grundsätze und Methoden
angewendet, nach denen wir verfahren oder wenigstens zu verfahren

---

[44] Ebd. 695; vgl. *GdA* I/1[5], 162.—Auf Meyers Einschätzung der Orphik als
philosophisch-theologisches Phänomen kann hier nicht eingegangen werden; vgl. dazu
den Beitrag von Mansfeld in diesem Band.

[45] *GdA* IV[1], 212.

[46] Zu Meyers weltanschaulicher und professioneller Berufung auf Thukydides vgl.
(neben *GdA*) seine Abhandlung *Thukydides*, in: *Forschungen* II, 269–436, besonders
369–379, sowie die Schlußsätze seiner geschichtstheoretischen Programmschrift (*Kl. Schr.*
I, 67).—Die im 19. Jhdt. (und bis heute) unter Althistorikern vorherrschende Bewunderung für Thukydides war nach A. Momigliano geprägt von Ranke, vgl. "History and
Biography," in: M.I. Finley (Hg.), *The Legacy of Greece. A New Appraisal*, Oxford/New
York 1984, 182. Meyer selbst war der Ansicht, daß es Niebuhr war, "der die Geschichtsforschung wieder auf Thukydides' Standpunkt zurückgeführt hat" (*Forschungen* I, 121).
Man kann davon ausgehen, daß Meyer durch den Niebuhr-Schüler J. Classen, Direktor
des Hamburger Johanneum und Thukydides-Forscher, während seiner Gymnasialzeit
auf den Weg seiner lebenslangen Thukydides-Verehrung gebracht worden ist.—Zu
Meyers Thukydides-Nachfolge in zahlreichen Einzelfragen vgl. Anm. 1, 47, 56, 60, 63,
70, 72, 94, 100, 122.

suchen—wobei wir uns im einzelnen dem Banne der Ueberlieferung oft genug ebenso wenig entziehen können wie Thukydides.''[47] Die Einschränkung zeigt deutlich, wie klar sich Meyer trotz aller Anerkennung für seinen Lehrmeister über die Probleme war, die aus der Bindung jedes Historikers an die Tradition herrühren und die eine kritische Interpretation jedes Textes der Geschichtsschreibung erforderlich machen, da es sich dabei immer um eine auch subjektiv gefärbte Geschichtsdeutung handelt. Freilich zweifelte er nicht daran, daß diese Schwierigkeiten wenn nicht in der Philologie[48] so doch in der strikt davon zu unterscheidenden Historie durch sichere Heilmitel überwunden werden können: die von Thukydides entdeckten Gesetze der historischen Kritik.[49]

Dazu gehört an erster Stelle die Beschränkung auf die ''nackten Thatsachen.''[50] Meyer macht sich keine Illusionen darüber, daß ein solches Auswahlverfahren in jeder Wissenschaft ein gewaltsames Unterfangen ist, das vom Willen des Forschers bestimmt wird und durchaus nicht auf Willkür verzichten kann. Gerade durch Thukydides, der die Grenze des historisch Bedeutsamen sehr eng gezogen hat und allgemeine Entwicklungsgänge schildert, ohne Einzelvorgänge bis ins Detail zu ermitteln,[51] sieht Meyer seine fundamentale Überzeugung bestätigt, daß die Darstellungsweise jedes, auch des noch so neutral erscheinenden Berichterstatters, subjektiv geprägt ist. Eine werturteilsfreie Feststellung von Tatsachen, so Meyer, gibt es nicht. ''Denn eben die Aussage, dass etwas eine 'Thatsache' sei, enthält schon ein Urtheil.''[52] Die Unvermeidbarkeit von

---

[47] *Forschungen* I, 121, n. 1; vgl. A. Momigliano, *Studies in Historiography*, London 1966, 86: ''Eduard Meyer expounded his historical method by an analysis of Thucydides.'' Siehe auch Momigliano (der selber über Thukydides promovierte) über den exemplarischen Charakter insbesondere von Thukydides' Geschichtsschreibung, ''Tradition and the Classical Historian'' (1972), in: *Essays in Ancient and Modern Historiography*, Oxford 1977, 161–177.

[48] Zu Meyers Auffassung von der Differenz zwischen Philologie und Geschichtswissenschaft (in Auseinandersetzung mit Wilamowitz) vgl. den Beitrag von Calder in diesem Band.—Gegen seine Intention hat Meyer das Postulat der methodologischen Trennbarkeit beider Gebiete durch seine eigene Arbeit gründlich falsifiziert: Die Stärken wie die Schwächen von Meyers Quellenkritik (vgl. Abschn. III) haben vorwiegend philologische Gründe und hängen davon ab, ob die historiographischen Quellen als Texte behandelt werden, auf die hermeneutische Interpretationskriterien anwendbar sind, oder nicht. Zum Problem der Textdeutung allgemein s. P. Szondi, ''Über philologische Erkenntnis'' (1962), in: *Schriften*, hg. von J. Bollack, I, Frankfurt/M. 1978, 263–286.—S. auch Anm. 63.

[49] Vgl. *Forschungen* II, 281.

[50] Ebd. 377.

[51] Vgl. *Forschungen* I, 121; II, 369.

[52] *Forschungen* II, 386; vgl. *GdA* I/1[5], 189. Eine entgegengesetzte Position dazu nahm bekanntlich Max Weber ein, der die Forderung nach der ''strengen Scheidung von Erfahrungswissen und Werturteil'' aufstellte, s. z.B. ''Die 'Objektivität' sozialwissenschaftlicher und sozialpolitischer Erkenntnis'' (1904), in: *Gesammelte Aufsätze zur Wissen-*

Werturteilen in der Geschichtsbetrachtung leitet Meyer davon ab, daß
niemals die Vergangenheit, sondern immer die Gegenwart Ausgangspunkt und Zielpunkt der Historie ist.[53] Infolgedessen steht für ihn fest,
"dass es eine objective Geschichtsschreibung im populären Sinne überhaupt nicht gibt."[54] Dem Historiker Thukydides hält Meyer zugute, daß
er es gerade durch die "Trockenheit" seines Berichtes verstanden habe,
seine Sichtweise aufzuzwingen, ohne sein Urteil direkt auszusprechen.
"In Wirklichkeit lässt er dem Leser gar keine Wahl: er muss so urtheilen
wie Thukydides will."[55] Ausnahmslos aber sei die von Meyer uneingeschränkt bejahte autoritative Subjektivität des Historikers in einem
politischen Werturteil verankert: "Zu allen Zeiten, die überhaupt eine
selbständige historische Literatur erzeugt haben, steht die Geschichtsschreibung bewusst oder unbewusst unter der Herrschaft und im Dienste
einer politischen Idee."[56] Für Meyer trifft es sich gut, daß er dem
Thukydides einen politischen Standpunkt nachrühmen kann, mit dem er
sich ohne Vorbehalte identifiziert: die Gegnerschaft zur "radikalen
Demokratie."[57]

---

schaftslehre von Max Weber, hg. von J. Winckelmann (1922), Tübingen 1985[6], 146, n. 1.
   [53] Vgl. z.B. GdA I/1[5], 191. Zur darin implizierten Idee der "historischen Wirksamkeit" vgl. Abschn. IV.
   [54] Forschungen II, 386; vgl. GdA I/1[5], 201 f.
   [55] Forschungen II, 386; zu Meyers Lob von Thukydides' "Trockenheit" s. ebd. 376.
   [56] Ebd. 228. Laut Meyer ist die von ihm behauptete Unvermeidlichkeit politischer
Leitideen in der Historie nicht unbedingt mit Parteilichkeit gleichzusetzen; von
Thukydides sagt er beispielsweise, "dass er wirklich ein unparteiischer, hoch über den
Dingen und den Leidenschaften des Tages stehender Historiker war" (ebd. 397). Einen
Historiker aber, dessen Standpunkt in Sachen Demokratie Meyer (im Unterschied zu
dem des Thukydides) nicht teilt, wie George Grote, tadelt er wegen dessen Parteilichkeit,
vgl. ebd. 353, n. 1, sowie GdA III[2] (= GdA 5[8]), 228.—Zu Meyers Verhältnis zu Grote
(freilich ohne Berücksichtigung des politischen Gegensatzes) s.U. Muhlack, "Die deutschen Einwirkungen auf die englische Altertumswissenschaft am Beispiel George
Grotes," in: Mayotte Bollack/ H. Wismann/ Th. Lindken (Hg.), Philologie und Hermeneutik
im 19. Jahrhundert II, Göttingen 1983 (376 – 393, sowie die Diskussion mit dem Korreferen-
ten A. Horstmann, 393 – 422), vor allem 405. Vgl. auch zu "George Grote and the Study
of Greek History" die gleichnamige Studie von Momigliano (1952), in: Studies in Historiography, London 1966, 56 – 74. Zustimmend auf Grotes Parteinahme für die attische
Demokratie reagierten in unserem Jahrhundert namentlich Wilamowitz, s. z.B. in:
U. von Wilamowitz-Moellendorff/ B. Niese, Staat und Gesellschaft der Griechen und Römer
(= Die Kultur der Gegenwart, II, Abt. IV,1), Berlin/ Leipzig 1910, 206 (Meyer griff
Wilamowitz deshalb scharf an), und M.I. Finley, Democracy Ancient and Modern, London
1973 (vgl. auch die folgende Anm.).—S. auch zum Problem des Historiker-Standpunktes:
Objektivität und Parteilichkeit in der Geschichtswissenschaft (= Theorie der Geschichte. Beiträge zur
Historik 1), hg. von R. Koselleck/ W.J. Mommsen/ J. Rüsen, München 1977.
   [57] Siehe Forschungen II, 373; vgl. L. Canfora, "Die Kritik der bürgerlichen Demokratie durch Eduard Meyer," in: R.W. Müller/ G. Schäfer (Hg.), "Klassische" Antike und
moderne Demokratie—Arthur Rosenberg zwischen Alter Geschichte und Zeitgeschichte, Politik und
politischer Bildung (= Zur Kritik der Geschichtsschreibung 4, hg. von H.-H. Nolte), Göttingen
1986, 46 – 58. Meyer hat auch in aktuellen politischen Zusammenhängen konsequent

Aus der politischen Gemeinsamkeit zwischen Meyer und Thukydides ergibt · sich zugleich eine willkommene Übereinstimmung in anthropologischen und religiösen Fragen. Unter Berufung auf Thukydides entwickelt Meyer eine These, der er universalhistorische Bedeutung zuspricht: Die radikale Demokratie krankt ihm zufolge an Gebrechen, die sich auf die prinzipielle Unvernünftigkeit jeglicher Masse zurückführen lasse. Die Masse ist für Meyer, immer und überall, per definitionem religiös.[58] Da er dies als ein unabänderliches Faktum erachtet und es nichtsdestotrotz nicht billigen kann, gibt es für ihn nur eine Staatsform, die sich rechtfertigen läßt: die von vernünftiger Machtpolitik geleitete Hegemonie über die Masse. Dem Diktat der Ratio und den notwendig opferreichen Erfordernissen der Außenpolitik fügt sich eine Masse, das ist für Meyer durch die Weltgeschichte bewiesen, nie aus eigenem Antrieb.[59] Das Heil des Staates liege allein in den Händen starker Führer-Persönlichkeiten, die der Masse ihren Willen oktroyieren, indem sie sich zwar der Religion bedienen mögen, jedoch niemals sich selbst religiösen Erwägungen unterwerfen und irrationalen Antrieben gehorchen.[60] An Stelle eines Gottes sind es bei Meyer der "vergötterte" Staat[61] und der

---

betont, daß die "glorreichen Erfindungen der Demokratie" gewöhnlich auf eine "Farce" hinausliefen, z.B. während der Weimarer Republik (s. dazu den Beitrag von Unte in diesem Band).—Zur Berufung von Nazis und von sich ans Dritte Reich anpassenden Historikern auf Meyers Antidemokratismus vgl. B. Näf, *Von Perikles zu Hitler? Die attische Demokratie und die deutsche Althistorie bis 1945* (= *Europäische Hochschulschriften*, Reihe III, 308), Bern/Frankfurt/M./New York 1986, z.B. 221 f. (zu H.E. Stier); 237. Bemerkenswert ist zumal das Beispiel des Meyer-Schülers Arthur Rosenberg, der—zunächst wie Meyer als Anhänger der rechtsextremen "Deutschen Vaterlandspartei," seit 1920 als KPD-Mitglied—an Meyers Ablehnung der bürgerlichen Demokratie anknüpfen konnte; vgl. dazu L. Canfora, "Moderne und antike Demokratie bei Arthur Rosenberg. Seine Ansicht über das Wesen der Demokratie," in: *"Klassische" Antike* . . . (wie oben), 34–45; s. auch Canforas Zustimmung zu Meyers Lenin-Lob, ebd. 58.—Zum Modell- und Gegenmodell-Charakter der attischen Demokratie in der modernen Geschichte und Geschichtsschreibung s. P. Vidal-Naquet, "Tradition de la démocratie grecque," Vorrede zur frz. Ausgabe von Finleys Demokratie-Buch (s. Anm. 56), *Démocratie antique et démocratie moderne*, Paris 1976, 7–44.

58 Vgl. z.B. *GdA* III¹, 240: Weil es den Massen so erscheint, als seien Entwicklungen "das Werk entweder des Zufalls oder höherer Mächte," sind sie nach Meyer "überhaupt unfähig (. . .), einen historischen Process (. . .) wirklich zu erfassen." Vgl. zu Meyers eigner Deutung der Rolle des Zufalls in der Geschichte, Anm. 107 und 114.—Zu Meyers Beurteilung der radikalen Demokratie als religiös konservativ s. *GdA* IV¹, 420; zur Religiosität der Masse überhaupt: *GdA* I/1⁵, 138.

59 Vgl. z.B. *Forschungen* II, 355 f.

60 Themistokles übte diese Führer-Rolle vorbildlich aus, so Meyer, der auch hier Thukydides (gegen Herodot) uneingeschränkt folgt (im Unterschied zu Wilamowitz), vgl. besonders *Forschungen* II, 223 f.; *GdA* III¹, 310 f.

61 Zu Aristoteles' *Politik* (vor allem: Beginn von Buch I) als theoretischem Fundament der "radikal staatsvergötternden Richtung" der deutschen Altertumswissenschaft im 19. und 20. Jhdt. s. L. Canfora, "Wilamowitz und die Schulreform: Das 'Griechische Lese-

heroisierte Führer, welche den Absolutheitsanspruch des Logos vertreten.

Meyer benutzt Thukydides' Geschichtswerk und seine eigenen universalhistorischen Schriften als politisches Werkzeug, um diese tiefempfundene Überzeugung zu untermauern und durchzusetzen. Die lehrhaft vorgetragenen Konsequenzen, die er aus ihr zieht, gehorchen einem geistigen wie praktischen Zweck: Mögen die Massen auch unbelehrbar an der Religion und anderen vernunftwidrigen Vorurteilen festhalten—der Politiker darf um keinen Preis dem Priester oder dem Theologen vertrauen, sondern muß dem Rat und dem Beispiel des autoritativen Historikers folgen, wenn es ihm um die Aufrechterhaltung und Erweiterung der Staatsmacht geht. Als Mittel der Unterweisung, als Vademecum für erfolgreiche Machtpolitiker, dient in erster Linie Thukydides' *Geschichte des Peloponnesischen Krieges*, die Meyer in apologetischer Manier interpretiert und rechtfertigt, also wie eine heilige Schrift behandelt. Meyer zollt diesem Werk die bedingungslos scheinende Verehrung und Gläubigkeit, die sein Autor dafür beansprucht hatte—als einem κτῆμά τε ἐς αἰεί, einem Monument mit Ewigkeitsanspruch, großzügig verschenkt als bleibender Besitz.[62] Mit derselben Entschlossenheit aber, mit der Meyer diese listige Werk-Mystifikation unbefragt übernimmt, bejaht er nicht minder naiv die dem Thukydides unterstellte Entmystifikation historischer Vorgänge.[63] Bei Thukydides findet er am reinsten das bereits durch Hekataios von Milet verfochtene Prinzip beherzigt, "jedes Wunder und jede Intervention höherer Mächte prinzipiell" zu streichen.[64] Welchen legitimatorischen Motiven Meyers Hermeneutik verpflichtet

---

buch,' " in: *Wilamowitz nach 50 Jahren* (wie Anm. 33), 648 (dort auch zu Meyer). Vgl. auch Anm. 118 und 119.

[62] Siehe Meyers Äußerungen dazu, *Forschungen* II, 391 (vgl. auch Anm. 46).—Zur Notwendigkeit, Thukydides' Anspruch auf überzeitliche "Monumentalität" und Gültigkeit in Frage zu stellen, um den Erfordernissen kritischer Althistorie gerecht werden zu können, s. Nicole Loraux, "Thucydide n'est pas un collègue," in: *Quaderni di storia* 12 (1980), 55–81.

[63] Diese Unterstellung beruht insbesondere auf der Einschätzung von Perikles' Leichenrede auf die Gefallenen (Thukydides, II, 35–46) als Dokument für Thukydides' eigene Geschichtsbetrachtung (so z.B. *Forschungen* II, 398).—Zur Widerlegung dieser communis opinio s. H. Flashar, "Der Epitaphios des Perikles. Seine Funktion im Geschichtswerk des Thukydides" (= *Sitzungsberichte der Heidelberger Akademie der Wissenschaften, Philosophisch-historische Klasse* 1969/1, 5–56), der mit H. Strasburger auch auf die religiöse Dimension im Werk des Thukydides aufmerksam macht (s. besonders 32 f.). Flashars Abhandlung erweist überzeugend die Notwendigkeit und Fruchtbarkeit einer philologisch-hermeneutischen Thukydides-Interpretation. Im gleichen Sinne jetzt: Loraux (vgl. Anm. 62 und 72). Vorläufer in dieser Richtung war F.M. Cornford, *Thucydides Mythistoricus* (1907).

[64] *GdA* III² (= *GdA* 5⁸), 207.—Zu Hekataios' Neuerung, Geschichtserzählung als deutende Geschichtserfindung zu konzipieren, vgl. M. Detienne, *L'invention de la mythologie*, Paris 1981, 134–154.

ist, wird überdeutlich, wenn er ein solches Verfahren ausdrücklich vom älteren und jüngeren Rationalismus unterscheidet. Meyer warnt davor, Thukydides als "Sophisten" zu betrachten, wie dies Wilamowitz getan hat.[65] Thukydides habe vielmehr mit den Mitteln der Historie den Rationalismus und zugleich den "Nihilismus" der Aufklärung überwunden, was Platon später mit den Mitteln der Philosophie nachvollzog.[66]

Der Sophistik und der attischen Aufklärung kreidet Meyer an, daß sie untrennbar mit der Demokratie verhaftet sind und sich als staatstragende Weltanschauungen nicht bewährt haben. Die aufklärerische Religionskritik wirkt auf Meyer inkonsequent und frivol, denn der von den Rhetorik-Lehrern propagierte Relativismus erlaubte auch demonstrative Frömmigkeit.[67] Die sophistische Leugnung der Möglichkeit eindeutiger Aussagen und Erkenntnisse verketzert er als Nihilismus. Der frühere, um Klarheit und Eindeutigkeit bemühte Rationalismus kann aber vor ihm ebensowenig Gnade finden, da hier das Irrationale immer noch zu ernst genommen ist, indem es durch seine Zurückführung auf Rationales glaubhaft gemacht wird.[68] Bei Thukydides dagegen findet Unerklärliches gar nicht erst statt. Nichts muß beglaubigt werden, alle Fakten und Faktoren scheinen Meyer auf wunderbare Weise unmittelbar einzuleuchten. Thukydides' heilige Nüchternheit entspricht ohne Abstriche Meyers weltanschaulichem Ideal.[69] Der im 19. Jahrhundert nach Christus geborene Adept des verehrten Weisheitsmeisters aus dem 5. Jahrhundert vor Christus erlaubt sich und niemandem sonst einen Zweifel daran, daß Thukydides berichtet, wie die Dinge wirklich gewesen sind,[70] und zwar als Mithandelnder und Mitleidender. Deshalb ist

---

[65] Vgl. Wilamowitz, *Aristoteles und Athen*, Berlin 1893, besonders: I, 99–120; II, 12 f.; Meyer gegen Wilamowitz' Thukydides-Bild: z.B. *Forschungen* II, 363 n. 2; 387.

[66] Siehe *Forschungen* II, 388; *GdA* III[2] (= *GdA* 5[8]), 212.

[67] Vgl. z.B. *GdA* IV[1], 269 (zu Gorgias); ebd. 260–265 (zu Protagoras).

[68] S. dazu Abschn. III.

[69] Vgl. *GdA* IV[1], 462 f. (sowie oben Anm. 55).

[70] Vgl. z.B. *Forschungen* II, 359. Diesem—nach Meyer: Thukydideischen—Prinzip entspricht Rankes Bestimmung der Aufgabe der Historie, auf die Meyer sich ausdrücklich beruft (insbesondere *GdA* I/1[5], 185; 210 f.): "(...) zeigen, wie es eigentlich gewesen," L. von Ranke, *Geschichten der romanischen und germanischen Völker* (1824), in: *Sämtliche Werke*, Leipzig 1874[2], Bd. 33, VII; bei Ranke ist damit freilich (im Unterschied zu Meyer) die Selbstbescheidung des Historikers verbunden, der sowohl verzichtet auf "das Amt, die Vergangenheit zu richten," wie darauf, "die Mitwelt zum Nutzen zukünftiger Jahre zu belehren."—Zu den Gemeinsamkeiten und Unterschieden zwischen dem Rankeschen Rezeptionskonzept und einer dialektischen Geschichtsauffassung s. W. Benjamin, "Eduard Fuchs, der Sammler und der Historiker," in: *Angelus Novus. Ausgewählte Schriften 2*, Frankfurt/M. 1966, 304: "Der historische Materialist (...) sprengt die Epoche aus der dinghaften *geschichtlichen Kontinuität* heraus, so auch das Leben aus der Epoche, so das Werk aus dem Lebenswerk. Doch der Ertrag dieser Konstruktion ist der, daß im Werke das Lebenswerk, im Lebenswerk die Epoche und in der Epoche der

Thukydides für Meyer der "unvergleichliche und unerreichte Lehrer
der Geschichtsschreibung,"[71] dem er Gefolgschaft leisten will. Denn
Thukydides, der Staatsmann, der Stratege, der von der Demokratie ver-
triebene Exultant, der den Peloponnesischen Krieg "geschrieben"[72] hat,
zeigte, daß historische Objektivität nichts anderes sein kann als nobi-
litierte Subjektivität.[73] Sie besteht darin, daß "der wissenschaftliche
Forscher die Dinge so zur Darstellung bringt, wie sie seinem Geiste als
wahr erscheinen."[74]
    Es liegt auf der Hand, daß die Übernahme einer solchen epiphanischen
Wahrheit Glaubensbereitschaft voraussetzt. Da Meyer aber trotz seines
buchstäblichen Bekenntnisses zu Thukydides niemals seinen wissenschaftlichen Anspruch aufgegeben hat, stellt sich die Frage, auf welche
Weise er seine vernunftreligiös gefärbte Weltanschauung mit historischer
Quellenkritik zu vereinbaren sucht.

III. "Rationalismus": Aporien der Quellenkritik als Forschungskritik

In schroffem Gegensatz zu seiner ehrfürchtig affirmativen Behandlung des
Thukydides steht Meyer allen anderen Geschichtsquellen außerordentlich skeptisch gegenüber. Den Schriftstellern vor Thukydides, aber auch
den meisten nach ihm—seien sie Dichter oder Historiker, Naturforscher
oder Theologen—bescheinigt Meyer eine naive rationalistische Vorgehensweise. Für Meyer sind bereits die ersten griechischen Dichter, deren
Werke uns überliefert sind, spätestens seit Hesiod zugleich Forscher,
die zum "Volksglauben" im Widerspruch stehen. Gerade deshalb aber

---

Geschichtsverlauf aufbewahrt und aufgehoben ist." Vgl. passim zum Historismus und zu
Ranke; s. auch W. Benjamin, "Geschichtsphilosophische Thesen," in: *Illuminationen.
Ausgewählte Schriften*, Frankfurt/M. 1961, 268–279. Zur Anwendbarkeit dieser Methode
s. P. Szondi, *Einführung in die literarische Hermeneutik* (= *Studienausgabe der Vorlesungen 5*, hg.
von J. Bollack), Frankfurt/M. 1975, 407 f.—Zu Meyers Verhältnis zu Ranke vgl. auch
Anm. 1 und 93.

[71] *Forschungen* II, 369.

[72] Meyer übersetzt ξυνέγραψε τὸν πόλεμον (Thukydides, I, 1) deskriptiv mit "hat den
Krieg beschrieben" (*Forschungen* II, 269), betont aber ansonsten den autoritativen Gestus
der Thukydideischen Historiographie, dem er sich apologetisch anschließt.—Zur Kritik
an dem von Thukydides intendierten autoritativen Schreiben s. Nicole Loraux, "Thucydide a écrit la Guerre du Péloponnèse," in: *Mètis. Revue d'anthropologie du monde grec ancien*
1/1 (1986), 139–161. Vgl. auch Anm. 62 und 195.

[73] Auch die objektiven Kriterien der Historie werden von Meyer aus den subjektiven
Überzeugungen des Historikers abgeleitet, vgl. *GdA* I/1⁵, 205.

[74] *Forschungen* II, 387. Anders als bei Meyer wurde mit diesem Argument seit Bodin
gerade die Möglichkeit von Wahrheitsfindung in der Historia humana (im Unterschied
zur Historia naturalis und zur Historia divina) angezweifelt, vgl. J. Bodinus, *Methodus ad
facilem historiarum cognitionem* (1566); ähnlich auch R. Descartes, *Discours de la méthode*
(1637), demzufolge jede historiographische Auswahl eine Verfälschung ist.

sei ihrer Glaubwürdigkeit gegenüber Mißtrauen angebracht. Die Ergebnisse dieser gelehrten dichterischen und historiographischen Arbeit seien nicht als verläßliche Zeugnisse weder über die Religion noch über die Geschichte brauchbar. In ausdrücklichem Widerspruch zur herrschenden Ansicht seiner zeitgenössischen Kollegen geht Meyer davon aus, daß in der "sagengeschichtlichen" Überlieferung der Griechen "der Bestand an wirklich volksthümlicher Tradition weit geringer (ist), an individueller Erfindung und Umgestaltung weit grösser, als man gewöhnlich glaubt."[75] Daran sei nichts Verwunderliches: "Die erwachende Forschung" ist "nothwendig rationalistisch;"[76] zugleich aber, und das sei schon eher erstaunlich, mitnichten unreligiös. Zwar enthalte die Entstehung des Rationalismus bereits den Keim zu philosophischer Reflexion, sei jedoch durch eine "Steigerung des religiösen Bedürfnisses"[77] zu erklären.

Die notorische Neigung der Forschung zum Rationalismus resultiert für Meyer quasi naturwüchsig aus der Tatsache, daß jedem Schriftsteller ältere Quellen vorlagen, die er nach Belieben benutzte, deren Unterschiede und Gegensätze er ausglich und an denen er Umdeutungen vornahm. Aus der Heterogenität des in den Quellen festgehaltenen Stoffes—der mythologischen Tradition—ergab sich die zunächst als Theologie auftretende rationalistische Nötigung, ihn zu vereinheitlichen. Das Ergebnis war freilich nicht eine zunehmende Uniformität, sondern im Gegenteil eine mehr und mehr wachsende Vieldeutigkeit und Unübersichtlichkeit des Stoffes, denn jeder Autor veränderte, ergänzte oder reduzierte in einer anderen Richtung, ohne sich an ein Dogma gebunden zu fühlen. Homer und Hesiod hatten die beiden Haupttendenzen des— sowohl anti-theologischen wie theologischen—Rationalismus schon entdeckt: die Wendung des Mythos ins Menschliche und ins Logische.[78] So verfügte die Folgezeit dank der Epiker über die grundlegenden Modelle

---

[75] *Forschungen* I, 4; auch diese Auffassung lehnt sich selbstverständlich an Thukydides (I, 20–21) an. Den Standpunkt, daß die Dichter und die Sänger "zugleich Gelehrte" waren, vertrat auch O. Gruppe, *Griechische Mythologie und Religionsgeschichte* (= *Handbuch der klassischen Altertums-Wissenschaft* V /2), München 1906, I, 7.—Zum Verhältnis zwischen griechischer Geschichtsschreibung und Mythos s. M.I. Finley, *The Use and Abuse of History*, London 1975, besonders 11–23.

[76] *Forschungen* I, 137, n. 1.

[77] *GdA* III² (= *GdA* 5⁸), 672.

[78] Vgl. Meyers Einschätzung der epischen Dichtung als "profan", ebd. 355 (sowie passim). Mit Hesiod freilich "beginnt" nach Meyer "die bewußte Umgestaltung und Systematisierung der Überlieferung, mit anderen Worten die Theologie" (ebd. 373). Vgl. *GdA* I/1⁵, 228 f.—Zur "Rückbindung an den Ursprung" als "Funktion der Genealogie im Mythos" vgl. den gleichnamigen Aufsatz in: K. Heinrich, *Parmenides und Jona. Vier Studien über das Verhältnis von Philosophie und Mythologie*, Frankfurt/ M. 1966, 11–28; 163–167. Siehe auch Anm. 166.

dafür, wie mit jeder Überlieferung, nicht allein der mythologischen, umgegangen werden kann, um sie "stimmig" zu machen.

Werden Quellen aber in Übereinstimmung gebracht, so bedeutet dies zugleich, daß jede einzelne von ihnen in ihrer Spezifität mißachtet, entstellt und verzerrt wird—das hat Meyer klar erkannt. Deshalb vermag er auch nicht daran zu glauben, daß in irgendeiner überlieferten Quelle von Homer bis Pausanias eine "volkstümliche" Tradition der griechischen Religion unverfälscht vorliegt. Von Anfang an, nicht erst bei den alexandrinischen Mythographen, haben wir es mit Forschungsergebnissen zu tun, mit Kombinationen und Fiktionen, mit Korrekturen und Irrtümern, also mit denkerischer Interessenpolitik. Eine vollständig verläßliche Quelle, so betont Meyer unermüdlich, gibt es nicht. Vielmehr müsse man sich darauf gefaßt machen, daß eine noch so wertungsfrei wirkende Quelle sich bei näherem Hinsehen als tendenziös herausstellt. Größte Vorsicht sei zumal gegenüber Chronologien und Genealogien geboten, denn mit diesen Mitteln werde in den Traditionsbestand besonders gewaltsam eingegriffen. Auch die Hoffnung auf historische Authentizität, welche die Urkunden und Aktenstücke zu versprechen scheinen, kann trügerisch sein. Gerade Urkunden erweisen sich nicht selten als tendenziöse oder gar fiktive Machwerke.[79] Meyer unterstreicht, daß dies bis auf den heutigen Tag so geblieben ist. Nur zu oft wird in einer Urkunde eine einzige Auffassung festgeschrieben, um alle anderen möglichen oder tatsächlichen Interessen auszuschließen.

Aus diesem kritischen Befund historischer Erfahrung zieht Meyer die Konsequenz, von vornherein die Autorität aller Quellen—mit der bezeichnenden Ausnahme des Thukydideischen Geschichtswerkes—grundsätzlich in Frage zu stellen.[80] Jeder Autor müsse als ein Übermittler älterer Angaben betrachtet und durch minutiöse Vergleiche auf seine Vorlagen, Neuerungen und Absichten hin untersucht werden. Unter dem Gesichtspunkt historischer Erkenntnis sei Hesiod ebensosehr ein Kompilator wie Ephoros. Angesichts des fragmentarischen Charakters der Überlieferung seien Justinus und Nepos nicht weniger wichtig zu nehmen als Plutarch und Diodor, zumal weil Thukydides, der vorbildlich strenge Meister, "keinen Nachfolger gefunden" habe.[81]

Meyer sieht also in den Quellen Subjekte der Kritik—oder auch der Kritiklosigkeit—am Werke. Die Forderung, keinem von ihnen unbesehen zuzustimmen, sondern sie allesamt zu Objekten der Kritik zu

---

[79] Vgl. *Forschungen* II, 422 f.; 436.
[80] Mit Irrtümern, die aus der Nichtbeachtung dieses Grundsatzes bei den "Modernen" folgen, hat Meyer sich engagiert auseinandergesetzt, s. z.B. *Forschungen* I, 19; 40.
[81] *Forschungen* I, 122; vgl. auch II, 24 f.; 67–69.

machen, ist also für Meyer keine triviale Selbstverständlichkeit, sondern ergibt sich aus seiner Einsicht in die unprotokollarische Färbung jeder Quelle. Kurz gesagt: Der Quellenkritiker findet in der Quelle bereits einen Kritiker vor. Am vollständigsten hat Meyer das dialogische Konzept einer entmystifizierenden Quellenkritik am Beispiel der Pelasgerfrage vorgeführt,[82] die spätestens seit Herodot bis ins 19. Jahrhundert heftig diskutiert wurde. Meyer weist nach, daß alles, was uns über die Pelasger überliefert ist, auf religiösen Hypothesen und ethnographischen Spekulationen beruht, die von "rationalistischen Kunststücken" durchgeformt sind. Dazu gehören moralisierende Umbildungen und etymologische Balanceakte, harmonisierende Ausflüchte und politisch motivierte Idealisierungen oder Verdammungsurteile. Um die jeweils vorgefaßte These durchzufechten, werden Versatzstücke der Tradition willkürlich zurechtgemodelt oder auf dürftige und durchsichtige Weise kombiniert. Hier erweist sich Meyers Quellenkritik nicht allein methodisch sondern auch erkenntnistheoretisch als unbestechlich. Bei der Prüfung dieses Materials kommt Meyer zu dem lapidaren Ergebnis: Das Problem der Pelasger, "welches länger als zwei Jahrtausende hindurch die wissenschaftliche Welt gequält hat," sollte "als ein Phantom anerkannt" werden.[83]

Ein solches Wunschziel, die Tabula rasa, ist freilich—nach Lage der Quellen—auf anderen Gebieten der Mythologie weniger leicht zu erreichen, dessen war Meyer sich bewußt. Die in der Pelasgerfrage entfaltete Radikalität seiner Quellenkritik konnte innerhalb des kühnen Projektes seiner *Geschichte des Altertums* nicht durchgehalten werden. Im Dienst seiner eigenen Geschichtserzählung griff Meyer ohne zu zögern auf Quellen zurück, deren Rationalismus—also deren Verzerrung der Wirklichkeit—er theoretisch und konkret nachgewiesen hatte, die er aber schließlich doch zu authentischen Geschichtszeugnissen deklarieren mußte, um sie ins Prokrustesbett seiner universalhistorischen Prämissen und Leitlinien einzuzwängen.[84] Die gebieterische Forderung nach Befreiung "vom Banne der Überlieferung" blieb in seinem Gesamtwerk weitgehend ein frommer Wunsch.[85] Zwar warnt Meyer immer wieder davor, den Alten unkritisch zu folgen und für "Volksglauben" zu halten, was bereits wissenschaftliches Arbeitsergebnis ist. Die Religionskritik der antiken Wissenschaftler macht Meyer sich jedoch vorbehaltlos zueigen, ohne nach der unverrechenbaren Spezifität religiöser Erfahrungen und

---

[82] Siehe: *Die Pelasger* (*Forschungen* I, 1–124).

[83] Ebd. 124; "rationalistische Kunststücke:" ebd. 45.

[84] Vgl. die Nachweise zu Abschn. I, II, IV und V.

[85] Das zeigt sich besonders an Meyers Umgang mit Thukydides, in dessen "Bann" (s. Anm. 47) er bei seiner Auslegung des Peloponnesischen Krieges tatsächlich steht; s. auch Abschn. II.

Erkenntnisse zu fragen. Die "Modernen"—eine von Meyer gern verwendete polemische Kollektivbezeichnung seiner Kollegen—sollten sich
nicht der Illusion hingeben, als sei durch die Quellen ein unmittelbarer
Zugang zu den Glaubensinhalten möglich, so gibt Meyer zu bedenken.
Daß aber ein vorbehaltloses Bündnis mit der anti-religiösen Erkennt-
nistendenz der Alten möglich sei, ohne daß kritische Umschweife nötig
wären, steht für Meyer außer Frage. Ihre gelehrten Konstruktionen seien
selten schlechter, vielmehr häufig fundierter als die gelehrten Konstruktionen der "Neueren".[86]

Unbeschadet der Globalität von Meyers Quellenkritik—und das hieß
riskanterweise für ihn: Forschungskritik—und trotz der mangelnden
Konsequenz ihrer Anwendung bleibt festzuhalten, daß Meyer einen entscheidenden Beitrag zur Überwindung des Autoritätsglaubens an die
Objektivität historischer Quellen geleistet hat. Tatsächlich kann seine Betonung der rationalistischen Tendenz—aus religiösen wie aus religionskritischen Motiven—, welche die gesamte antike Mythen-Tradition
kennzeichnet, bei der Arbeit mit den Quellen gar nicht ernst genug
genommen werden. Freilich hat Meyer die daraus resultierenden
Probleme keineswegs immer im Auge behalten. Von ihrer Lösung blieb
er weit entfernt. Nicht anders als die von ihm getadelten antiken und
modernen Forscher schwankt Meyer in seinem Verhältnis zu den Quellen
zwischen zwei entgegengesetzten Umgangsformen: Entweder wird die
Überlieferung als Beleg benutzt, da sie ins vorgefaßte Weltbild zu passen
scheint, oder sie wird ganz über Bord geworfen, da sie nicht bewiesen
werden kann.[87] Angesichts solcher ja nicht ungewöhnlicher Verfahren
wird zugleich deutlich, daß die methodische Befragung der Quellen nach

---

[86] Im übrigen verfahren nach Meyer die modernen Geschichtsforscher nach den
selben Methoden wie die antiken (s. *Forschungen* I, 183 f.), und auch die gegenwärtige
Philologie arbeite nicht anders als die von Aristarch geprägte alexandrinische, vgl. *GdA*
III² (= *GdA* 5⁸), 215.—Zur Unkonventionalität von Meyers eigenen hermeneutischen
Kriterien s. aber (gegen Wilamowitz'sche philologische Eingriffe): "Die alte Regel, dass
wer einen Text corrigirt, ihn nicht versteht, bewährt sich auch hier" (*Forschungen* I, 297,
n. 1). Vgl. auch (zum Text des Psephisma für Chalkis aus dem Jahre 446, *CIA* I, 27a,
über die Stelle zu den Fremden in Chalkis): "mir scheint der Satz zwar nicht grammatisch
correctes, wohl aber dem Sprachgebrauch nach völlig unanstössiges, ja vortreffliches
Griechisch zu sein" (*Forschungen* II, 146).
[87] Beide Vorgehensweisen können sogar kombiniert auftreten: z.B. geht Meyer (mit
Herodot u.a.) von der Historizität der Amazonen aus, und zwar als eines "Korps" von
Jungfrauen (gegen Herodot z.B.), mit der Begründung, ihre Physis hätte sie sonst zu
Untergebenen von Männern gemacht: "Denn die Unterordnung des Weibes unter den
Mann (...) ist nun einmal durch die physischen Eigenschaften des weiblichen Ge-
schlechts unabänderlich gegeben" (*GdA* I/1⁵, 21; vgl. ebd. 49).—Zur Analyse der Funk-
tion der Amazonen-Geschichten im Kontext der griechischen Polis-Gesellschaft s. Jeannie
Carlier, "Les Amazones font la guerre et l'amour," in: *L'Ethnographie* 74 (1980–1),
11–33.

ihren spezifischen Erkenntnisweisen, für die Meyer plädiert hat, und
seine Überzeugung von der Erreichbarkeit einer einheitlichen Weltanschauung sowie von der Möglichkeit einer eindeutigen Geschichtserkenntnis sich nicht in Einklang bringen lassen. Die Abfuhr, die Meyer
dem Autoritätsglauben erteilt hat, und die ihm dennoch unverzichtbare
Berufung auf der Kritik enthobene Autoritäten—nicht zuletzt die des
Thukydides—fallen sich in seinen Schriften unentwegt gegenseitig ins
Wort.

Meyers Versöhnungsversuch zwischen der rationalistischen Lügenhaftigkeit der mythologischen Quellen und der historischen Wahrheit, die
sie nichtdestotrotz transportieren, konnte nur mißlingen.[88] Die sich aus
diesem Versuch ergebenden Aporien versuchte er durch den Begriff der
"historischen Wirksamkeit" zu heilen. Dieses Konzept enthält die Erfahrung, daß geschichtliche Vieldeutigkeiten—auch und gerade die religiösen—nicht restlos in weltanschaulicher Eindeutigkeit auflösbar sind.

IV. "Historische Wirksamkeit" der Religion

Das Historische wurde von Meyer in seiner 1902 erschienenen Programmschrift *Zur Theorie und Methodik der Geschichte* wie folgt definiert:
"historisch ist, was wirksam ist oder gewesen ist."[89] Mit dieser Auffassung setzte sich Max Weber 1906 in seinen *Kritischen Studien auf dem Gebiet
der kulturwissenschaftlichen Logik* auseinander. Webers Ergebnis lautet, daß
sich in Meyers Werk gerade die Unanwendbarkeit einer solchen Bestimmung zeige, und er fügt am Schluß hinzu, daß ihre Anwendung auch gar
nicht wünschenswert wäre: "wenn (. . .) E.M. ernstlich alles vom Standpunkt der Gegenwart aus historisch nicht mehr 'Wirksame'[90] aus der
Geschichte des Altertums ausmerzen wollte, würde gerade er, in den
Augen aller derjenigen, welche im Altertum m e h r als nur eine historische 'Ursache' suchen, seinen Gegnern recht geben. Und alle Freunde
seines großen Werkes werden es erfreulich finden, daß er mit jenem
Gedanken gar nicht ernst machen k a n n, und hoffen, daß er nicht etwa
einer irrtümlich formulierten Theorie zuliebe auch nur den Versuch dazu
unternimmt."[91] Max Webers joviale Sympathie für Meyers wissen

---

88 S. zu einem vergleichbaren, ebenfalls mißlingenden Versöhnungsversuch: Renate
Schlesier, "Können Mythen lügen? Freud, Ödipus und die anstiftenden Mütter," in:
Barbara Schaeffer-Hegel/Brigitte Wartmann (Hg.), *Mythos Frau. Projektionen und Inszenierungen im Patriarchat*, Berlin 1984, 334–350.—Zu Freuds Bezug zu Meyer s. Anm. 135.

89 *Kl. Schr.* I, 43.

90 Weber unterschlägt hier, daß Meyers Bestimmung auch das historisch wirksam
Gewesene einschließt.

91 M. Weber, "Zur Auseinandersetzung mit Eduard Meyer," in: *Gesammelte Aufsätze*

schaftliche Verdienste sei hier dahingestellt; freilich bleibt, trotz Webers logisch-pragmatischem Einwand gegen Meyers Geschichtsbegriff, die Frage offen, von welchen geistigen Triebkräften das Pathos des Historikers und Geschichtstheoretikers Meyer gelenkt ist. Vorausgesetzt, Meyers Konzept der "historischen Wirksamkeit" ist tatsächlich unstimmig: warum konnte und wollte Meyer von ihm nicht Abstand nehmen?

Zunächst einmal und im allgemeinen deshalb, weil das Gebot der Stimmigkeit für Meyer keineswegs ein Dogma ist. Im Gegenteil: während seiner Quellenstudien hatte er die Erfahrung gesammelt, daß es sich dabei um einen Fallstrick des Rationalismus handelt. Er mußte konstatieren, daß hergestellte Stimmigkeiten, pointiert gesagt, verdeckte Unstimmigkeiten sind. Demgegenüber repräsentiert Meyers Konzept der "historischen Wirksamkeit" eine Vermittlungsinstanz zwischen der anzustrebenden Objektivität und den nicht aus dem Spiel zu lassenden Imponderabilien darstellerischer Subjektivität. In diesem Sinne läßt sich die Geschichtswissenschaft, laut Meyer, weder zu den philosophischen noch zu den naturwissenschaftlichen Disziplinen rechnen. Anders ausgedrückt: "alle Geschichtsdarstellung" ist in Meyers Augen "nicht nur Wissenschaft (...), sondern zugleich Kunst."[92] Wie es scheint, wirkte Meyer mit diesem sich an Ranke[93]—und natürlich an Thukydides[94]—anlehnenden Standpunkt innerhalb der Gelehrtenzunft anachronistisch, denn längst hatte mit Droysen die Angleichung der Historie an naturwissenschaftliche Systematik, ihre Entästhetisierung, begonnen.[95]

Meyer freilich beharrte auf dem Sonderweg der Geschichtswissenschaft. Ihr künstlerisches Element, die "schöpferische Phantasie," die er sich von keinem Positivisten abhandeln lassen wollte, besteht für ihn im produktiven Zugang des Historikers zur lebendigen Vergangenheit. Er könne sie nur verstehen, indem er sich in sie hineinversetzt, und über sie

---

... (wie Anm. 52), 265.—Zu den Divergenzen und Übereinstimmungen zwischen Weber und Meyer vgl. den Beitrag von Deininger in diesem Band.

[92] *GdA* I/1[5], 210; vgl. ebd. 186. Diese Ansicht Meyers steht im Gegensatz zum anti-ästhetischen Konzept Droysens (vgl. Anm. 35 und 95) sowie im Einklang mit Rankes Auffassung (s. Anm. 93).—Siehe auch jetzt, im Sinne eines philosophisch und historisch begründeten Programms: P. Feyerabend, *Wissenschaft als Kunst*, Frankfurt/M. 1984.

[93] Vgl. zu Rankes Konzept der Historie als Verbindung von Kunst und Wissenschaft: W. Hardtwig, "Die Verwissenschaftlichung der Historie und die Ästhetisierung der Darstellung," in: *Formen der Geschichtsschreibung* (= *Theorie der Geschichte. Beiträge zur Historik 4*), hg. von R. Koselleck/ H. Lutz/ J. Rüsen, München 1982, 147–191.

[94] Vgl. *Forschungen* II, 369; *GdA* III[1], 267 (Thukydides als "Künstler").

[95] Die Gattung der artes historicae, die seit dem 16. Jhdt. florierte und die die Historie als Kunstgattung, analog zur Dichtung, behandelte, endet praktisch mit G.G. Gervinus, *Grundzüge der Historik* (1837). Demgegenüber stellt Droysens *Historik* (vgl. Anm. 35) den Versuch dar, die Poetik als Analogon zur Historik auszuschalten. Vgl. dazu vor allem die Beiträge von J. Rüsen, W. Hardtwig, H.R. Jauss und U. Muhlack in: *Formen der Geschichtsschreibung* (wie Anm. 93).

nur berichten, wenn er sie zur Gegenwart macht. Vollständigkeit oder Untrüglichkeit des Nachvollzugs sei allerdings weder auf diesem noch auf irgend einem anderen denkbaren Wege zu erwarten. Der Historiker trifft in jedem Falle eine Auswahl, die immer nur relativ sein kann und auf die Erfahrungssphäre des Gegenwärtigen bezogen bleibt. Jeder Historiker müsse, ob er will oder nicht, ein Kriterium für seine Auswahl wählen. Meyers Kriterium ist das der "historischen Wirksamkeit:" "historisch ist derjenige Vorgang der Vergangenheit, dessen Wirksamkeit sich nicht in dem Moment seines Eintretens erschöpft, sondern auf die folgende Zeit erkennbar weiter wirkt und in dieser neue Vorgänge erzeugt."[96]

Die Idee der "historischen Wirksamkeit," unter deren Auspizien der Historiker, Meyer zufolge, als Künstler und Wissenschaftler zugleich agiert, verbindet Meyers Geschichtsauffassung mit dem Gedankengut des deutschen Dichters und Historikers Friedrich Schiller.[97] Die Antrittsvorlesung seiner Geschichtsprofessur, gehalten in Jena am 26. Mai 1789, hatte zum Thema: *Was heißt und zu welchem Ende studiert man Universalgeschichte?* Dort heißt es: "Aus der ganzen Summe (der) Begebenheiten hebt der Universalhistoriker diejenigen heraus, welche auf die h e u t i g e Gestalt der Welt und den Zustand der jetzt lebenden Generation einen wesentlichen, unwidersprechlichen und leicht zu verfolgenden Einfluß gehabt haben."[98] Nicht allein dieses Auswahlprinzip des Universalhistorikers, sondern auch dessen geschichtsphilosophische Begründung

---

[96] *GdA* I/1⁵, 188. So begründet Meyer auch das—ihm zufolge: notwendig dominierende—Interesse für das griechisch-römische Altertum (vgl. Anm. 13); zu Meyers dem auf den ersten Blick widersprechender ausgiebiger Beschäftigung mit dem "Orient" s. Abschn. I. Vgl. auch *Kl. Schr.* I, 68–78.

[97] Den Gedanken des historisch Wirksamen als Gegenstand der Historie hat nach Schiller W. von Humboldt 1821 programmatisch entwickelt, *Werke 1* (wie Anm. 19), 596 f.: "Zu den wirkenden und schaffenden Kräften hat sich der Geschichtschreiber zu wenden. Hier bleibt er auf seinem eigenthümlichen Gebiet. Was er thun kann, um zu der Betrachtung der labyrinthisch verschlungenen Begebenheiten der Weltgeschichte, in seinem Gemüthe eingeprägt, die Form *mitzubringen*, unter der allein ihr wahrer Zusammenhang erscheint, ist diese Form von ihnen selbst *abzuziehen*. Der Widerspruch, der hierin zu liegen scheint, verschwindet bei näherer Betrachtung. Jedes Begreifen einer Sache setzt, als Bedingung seiner Möglichkeit, in dem Begreifenden schon ein Analogon des nachher wirklich Begriffenen voraus, eine vorhergängige, ursprüngliche Uebereinstimmung zwischen dem Subject und Object. Das Begreifen ist keineswegs ein blosses Entwickeln aus dem ersteren, aber auch kein blosses Entnehmen vom letzteren, sondern beides zugleich. Denn es besteht allemal in der Anwendung eines früher vorhandenen Allgemeinen auf ein neues Besondres. Wo zwei Wesen durch gänzliche Kluft getrennt sind, führt keine Brücke der Verständigung von einem zum andren, und um sich zu verstehen, muss man sich in einem andren Sinn schon verstanden haben. Bei der Geschichte ist diese vorgängige Grundlage des Begreifens sehr klar, da Alles, was in der Weltgeschichte wirksam ist, sich auch in dem Innern des Menschen bewegt." Bemerkenswerterweise macht Humboldt hier die Weltgeschichte zu einem gleichzeitig psychischen Phänomen.

[98] F. Schiller, *Sämtliche Werke 4: Historische Schriften*, hg. von J. Perfahl/H. Koopmann, München 1975, 716.

waren noch für Meyer verbindlich. Um nämlich aus den "Bruchstücken" der Überlieferung Wissenschaft machen zu können, kommt der Weltgeschichte, so Schiller, "der philosophische Verstand zu Hülfe, und, indem er diese Bruchstücke durch künstliche Bindungsglieder verkettet, erhebt er das Aggregat zum System, zu einem vernunftmäßig zusammenhängenden Ganzen. Seine Beglaubigung dazu liegt in der Gleichförmigkeit und unveränderlichen Einheit der Naturgesetze und des menschlichen Gemüts, welche Einheit Ursache ist, daß die Ereignisse des entferntesten Altertums, unter dem Zusammenfluß ähnlicher Umstände von außen, in den neuesten Zeitläuften wiederkehren."[99] Damit ist ein methodisches Hilfsmittel gerechtfertigt, von dem Meyer intensiven Gebrauch gemacht hat: der Analogieschluß,[100] eine Verfahrensweise, deren gewissenhafte Benutzung Schiller dem Universalhistoriker ausdrücklich anempfiehlt: "daß also von den neuesten Erscheinungen, die im Kreis unsrer Beobachtung liegen, auf diejenigen, welche sich in geschichtslosen Zeiten verlieren, rückwärts ein Schluß gezogen und einiges Licht verbreitet werden kann."[101]

Wie verhält es sich nun aber mit der historischen Wirksamkeit in religiösen Dingen? Darf von "neuesten Erscheinungen" der Religion auf analoge Vorgänge "in geschichtslosen Zeiten" zurückgeschlossen werden? Meyer bejaht diese Frage ohne Einschränkung. Hier sieht er sich befugt, ein ihm unabweisbar scheinendes Objektivitätskriterium ins Feld zu führen: Es liegt "in den allgemeinen, immer sich gleich bleibenden Bedingungen des realen Lebens, den physischen wie den psychischen, der Vorstellung dessen, was überhaupt möglich und unmöglich ist, und deshalb wirklich gewesen sein kann, oder aber, mag die Überlieferung und der Glaube der Zeitgenossen scheinbar den Vorgang noch so sehr bestätigen, objektiv unmöglich ist—dieses Kriterium liegt außerhalb der

---

[99] Ebd. 717. Der "philosophische Verstand," der hier "zu Hülfe kommen" soll, ist selbstverständlich kein anderer als derjenige Kants, von dem Schiller auch die Perhorreszierung des "Aggregats" übernimmt, vgl. I. Kant, *Idee zu einer allgemeinen Geschichte in weltbürgerlicher Absicht* (1784), Neunter Satz.—Das von Schiller vertretene Konzept der historischen Wiederkehr ist freilich eher mit zyklischen (vgl. Anm. 106 und 113) als mit fortschrittsgläubigen Geschichtsauffassungen zu vereinbaren.

[100] Der Analogieschluß—von vergangenen Ereignissen auf die späteren—wurde ebenfalls bereits von Thukydides (I, 22) als probates Erkenntnismittel begründet. Zur theoretischen Rechtfertigung bei Meyer vgl. z.B. *GdA* I/1⁵, 203.—Meyer war sich bewußt, daß es sich dabei kaum noch um wissenschaftliche Erkenntnis, sondern eher um künstlerische Intuition handelt (s. ebd.; vgl. Anm. 92-94) und daß bereits das mythische Denken durch Analogieschlüsse gekennzeichnet ist (ebd. 35, 90 f.; s. auch Anm. 142). Im übrigen machte natürlich gerade die theologische Universalgeschichte (vgl. Anm. 5) von Analogieschlüssen kräftigen Gebrauch.—Zu Humboldts ontologischer Begründung der Unabdingbarkeit von Analogieschlüssen vgl. Anm. 97.

[101] Schiller (wie Anm. 98), 717.

Geschichte.''[102] Mit anderen Worten: Wunder gibt es nicht und kann es niemals gegeben haben. Daß höhere Mächte einen historischen Prozeß bestimmen, ist die fehlgeleitete Meinung der Massen, die eben deshalb, nach Meyer, zur Geschichtserkenntnis überhaupt unfähig sind.[103] Die Geschichte beruhe nicht auf übernatürlichen, sondern auf realen Vorbedingungen, die von Menschen beeinflußt, ja letztlich beherrscht werden können. Keineswegs dürfe die Religionsgeschichte daher unter einem ''religiös-theologischen Gesichtspunkt'' verfaßt werden. Denn ''hinter den geistigen Problemen'' verbergen sich ''materielle Zustände,'' aus denen jene ''vielfach erst erwachsen sind.''[104]

Religionsgeschichte motiviert sich demnach für Meyer durch das Ziel, die Verzauberungen der Welt,[105] welche von den Religionen vollzogen wurden, wieder rückgängig zu machen. Meyer ist überzeugt davon, daß in einer solchen Perspektive der geistige Fortschritt der Menschheit bestünde, auch wenn er sich die Entwicklung der Geschichte eher, nach antikem Denkmodell, zyklisch vorstellt und nicht an einen linearen Fortschritt zum Besseren glaubt.[106] Die in der griechischen Antike ermöglichte Abkehr von der Religion empfindet er freilich unzweideutig als Fortschritt und kann nur bedauern, daß die Menschheit diese Befreiung des Denkens nicht konsequent weitergetrieben habe. Es fehlt nicht viel, daß Meyer in solcher Hemmung ein außermenschliches Schicksal am Werke sieht. Die ''Tragik der Geschichte'' beruhe darin, ''daß jede Idee, sobald sie sich verwirklicht, in ihr Gegenteil umschlägt.''[107] Diese ''Tra-

---

[102] *GdA* I/1[5], 205. Man beachte die Verlagerung dieses Objektivitätskriteriums in eine geschichts-transzendente (objektive?) Sphäre.

[103] Vgl. Anm. 58.

[104] *GdA* III[1], 15.

[105] Von einer bereits erreichten ''Entzauberung der Welt'' scheint Meyer nicht ausgegangen zu sein, im Unterschied zu Max Weber: vgl. ''Wissenschaft als Beruf'' (1919), in: *Aufsätze* (wie Anm. 52), 612 und passim.

[106] Vgl. *GdA* I/1[5], 181.—Die zyklische Geschichtsauffassung geht auf die kosmologische Begründung der Weltgeschichte in Platons *Timaios* zurück; verknüpft mit Thukydides' historischem Analogieprinzip (vgl. Anm. 100): bei N. Machiavelli, *Discorsi sopra la prima deca di Tito Livio* (1532), der in folgenreicher Weise die skeptische Weisheit des Prediger Salomo damit kombiniert (''und geschieht nichts Neues unter der Sonne,'' *Pred. Sal.* 1,9); der Geschichtskreislauf als Ausdruck göttlicher Vorsehung: bei G. Vico, *Principi di una scienza nuova d'interno alla comune natura delle nazioni* (1725).—Meyer übernimmt sein zyklisches Geschichtskonzept ausdrücklich von Ibn Chaldûn, vgl. Anm. 113.—Von Augustin (*De civ. Dei* XII, 14) wurde die Kreislauftheorie als Irrlehre verdammt.

[107] *GdA* I/1[5], 182. Als besonders schlagenden Beleg für diese Erfahrung des Umschlags von Ideen führt Meyer die innere Entwicklung von Religionen an, vgl. ebd. 157–159.—Zu Meyers Konzept der historischen ''Tragik'' gehört auch seine Auffassung von der Rolle des Zufalls und des Schicksals in der Geschichte. Dafür sind folgende Etappen bemerkenswert: der Sechzehnjährige meinte, in der Geschichte ''herrscht nicht der

gik" zeige sich sowohl innerhalb der Religionsgeschichte selbst wie an den Auswirkungen religiöser Vorstellungen auf die Politik. Wenn in der Weltgeschichte der Fortschritt bedroht oder gar zeitweise aufgehalten wurde, dann war immer, so Meyer, religiöser Konservatismus mit im Spiel. Kulturfortschritt und "Steigerung der Religiosität" sind zwar nach Meyer phasenweise miteinander verknüpft,[108] doch sei jede Religon gezwungen, die einmal von ihr sanktionierte Tradition gegen einschneidende Veränderungen zu verteidigen. "Daher ist jeder Kampf um einen Forschritt zugleich ein Kampf mit der bestehenden Religion."[109] Die historische Wirksamkeit der Religion besteht also in ihrer Geschichtsfeindlichkeit. Ihre historische Unwirksamkeit zu befördern, sei die Aufgabe der Geschichte und, in ihrem Dienst, die des Historkers.

Zu einer solchen geharnischten Religionskritik und Fortschrittsgläubigkeit, zu dieser Berufung auf die Objektivität der Vernunft, in deren Lichte Mögliches und Unmögliches klar auseinandergehalten werden könne, stehen Meyers Verdikt gegen den reduktionistischen Rationalismus und sein Plädoyer für schöpferische Subjektivität in auffälligem Widerstreit. Ebenso schlecht vertragen sich damit seine zyklische Geschichtsauffassung und sein Bekenntnis zum universalhistorischen Konstanzprinzip, das zu Analogieschlüssen durch alle Geschichtsepochen hindurch, ja über diese hinaus, ermutigt. Die historische Wirksamkeit verwandelt sich auf religiösem Gebiet aus einem Bündnisfaktor der Historie in eine bedrohliche Kraft. Gerade weil Irrationalismus wie Rationalismus im Stoff der Historie weiterwirken, muß Meyer sie bekämpfen. Die Erkenntnis der religiösen und mythologischen Anfänge und Entwicklungsstufen wird so für ihn zur politischen Pflicht.

Zufall, sondern das Geschick" (zit. bei Hoffmann, in diesem Band); dreißig Jahre später zählt Meyer zu den historisch entscheidenden und "rein individuellen Momenten" an erster Stelle den Zufall, neben freiem Willen und "Ideen" (*Kl. Schr.* I, 8), während er als 69-Jähriger in seiner Spengler-Rezension das notwendige Zusammenwirken von "Schicksal" und "Zufall" in der Geschichte postuliert, in: *Deutsche Literaturzeitung* 45 (1924), 1764. Den τύχη-Begriff, der beides verbindet (vgl. auch Machiavellis Emphase der Fortuna, s. Anm. 106), fand Meyer bereits bei Thukydides vor (s. bejahend dazu: *Forschungen* II, 393).—Zum Problem des "Zufalls als Motivationsrest in der Geschichtsschreibung" s. den gleichnamigen Aufsatz von R. Koselleck, in: H.R. Jauss (Hg.), *Die nicht mehr schönen Künste. Grenzphänomene des Ästhetischen* (= *Poetik und Hermeneutik 3*), München 1968, 129–141.—Zum Verhältnis zwischen Spengler und Meyer s. den Beitrag von Demandt in diesem Band.

[108] Vgl. *GdA* I/1⁵, 126.

[109] Ebd. 137. Meyers leitmotivisches Beispiel dafür ist die Fesselung der geistigen Freiheit durch Theologie und Kirche im Judentum (und Christentum); s. im Vergleich mit der gegensätzlichen Entwicklung Griechenlands nach den Perserkriegen: *GdA* III¹, 446 (vgl. auch Abschn. I).

V. Drei Prioritäten: Der Staat. Das mythische Denken. Die Götter.

1. Der Staat als Ursprungsmacht

Meyers Definition des Historischen als des ''historisch Wirksamen'' wendet sich gegen eine antiquarische Behandlung der Geschichte:[110] Historische Ereignisse, Zusammenhänge und Entwicklungen können nicht nur um ihrer selbst willen Interesse beanspruchen. Geschichtsforschung müsse von der Gegenwart ausgehen, Geschichtsdarstellung fände in der Gegenwart den Endpunkt historischer Wirkungen.[111] Freilich ist für Meyer die Gegenwart kein endgültiges, sondern ein vorläufiges, ein heuristisches Geschichtsziel. Vom Standpunkt des Universalhistorikers aus besitzt die Gegenwart im Verhältnis zur Vergangenheit keineswegs eine Vorzugsstellung. Vielmehr löst sich die Spezifität der Gegenwart vor seinen Augen auf, und ebenso die der Vergangenheit: Die Gegenwart gleicht sich an die Vergangenheit an, die Vergangenheit an die Gegenwart—in dem Maße nämlich, wie die Vergangenheit in der Gegenwart weiterwirkt und die Gegenwart denselben Kausalitäten unterliegt wie die Vergangenheit. Meyers vieldiskutierter ''Modernismus'' ist keine bloße Darstellungstechnik oder gar lediglich eine Frage der Terminologie.[112] Vielmehr stützt sich Meyers Leugnung der Möglichkeit von fundamental Neuem in der Geschichte auf eine zyklische Geschichtsauffassung[113] und wäre vielleicht eher als ''Anti-Modernismus'' zu charakterisieren, denn er ist überzeugt davon, daß die heute geltenden Grundprinzipien der Geschichte immer gegolten haben. Meyer zufolge darf weder Früherem noch Aktuellem Eigengesetzlichkeit zugesprochen werden. Das bedeutet: Historische Veränderungen sind akzidentell,[114] und das historisch Unveränderliche ist das konstitutionelle Moment der Geschichte.

Diese fundamentale Autonomie—man könnte auch sagen: Unge-

---

[110] Z.B. *GdA* III² (= *GdA* 5⁸), 223; vgl. Abschn. I und IV.—Siehe wissenschaftsgeschichtlich dazu: A. Momigliano, ''Ancient History and the Antiquarian'' (1950), in: *Studies* ... (wie Anm. 56), 1–39.

[111] Siehe *GdA* I/1⁵, 208; 205–207.

[112] Zu den wirtschaftsgeschichtlichen Aspekten von Meyers ''Modernismus'' vgl. z.B. M. Austin/P. Vidal-Naquet, *Economies et sociétés en Grèce ancienne* (1972), deutsch: *Gesellschaft und Wirtschaft im alten Griechenland*, München 1984 (besonders: 3–5; 91), sowie den Beitrag von Schneider in diesem Band, gegen Meyers Analogisierung von moderner und antiker Wirtschaftsgeschichte.

[113] Meyer beruft sich dafür auf Ibn Chaldûn, den maurischen Historiker des 14. Jhdts.: *GdA* I/1⁵, 83 (s. auch Anm. 106).

[114] Zur Rolle des Zufalls und des freien Willens in der Geschichte, laut Meyer, vgl. (außer seinem Aufsatz *Zur Theorie und Methodik der Geschichte*, s. auch Anm. 107) ebenso *GdA* I/1⁵, 184.

schichtlichkeit—der Geschichte ist bei Meyer der Garant ihrer rationalen Erkennbarkeit. Erkenntnisweisen, die der gleichbleibenden Immanenz und Eigenständigkeit der Geschichte äußerlich sind oder sie in Frage stellen, werden damit ausgeschlossen: insbesondere die antiquarische Geschichtsbetrachtung, die sich in die Diffusität eines regellosen Konglomerats historischer Stoffe verliert, und die religiöse Auffassung, die der Geschichte äußere Ursachen unterstellt.

Daraus ergibt sich, daß sich für Meyer einzig und allein eine politische Geschichtsauffassung rechtfertigen läßt. Politik ist ihm die Substanz der Geschichte: Politik treibt die Geschichte an, liegt ihr zugrunde, dominiert sie.[115] Ist aber die—den Menschen definierende und durch ihn definierte—Politik die Universalie par excellence der Historie, so kann die Geschichte nicht von der Einwirkung übernatürlicher Mächte abhängen und kann ebensowenig die Konsequenz allgemeingültiger Naturgegebenheiten sein. Das von Meyer postulierte Dritte, das der Forderung genügt, weder übernatürlich noch nur natürlich zu sein, ist der Geist: Der Anstoß zur Geschichte muß von einem "rein geistigen Moment" ausgehen, "das zwar aus konkreten Bedürfnissen erwachsen, aber nicht sinnlich wahrnehmbar ist."[116] In diesem geistigen Moment lokalisiert Meyer die Geburtsstunde der Politik. Es besteht im Zusammenschluß "gleichartiger Einzelwesen" zu einer Gemeinschaft, die sich von anderen Gruppen absondert und einem Gesamtwillen unterordnet.[117] Eine solche Gemeinschaft bezeichnet Meyer als "sozialen Verband." Die "dominierende Form des sozialen Verbandes" sei aber derjenige, "in deren Wesen das Bewußtsein einer vollständigen, auf sich selbst ruhenden Einheit enthalten ist." Für Meyer ist dies der Staat: "Wir müssen daher den staatlichen Verband nicht nur begrifflich, sondern auch geschichtlich als die primäre Form der menschlichen Gemeinschaft betrachten, eben als denjenigen sozialen Verband, welcher der tierischen Herde entspricht und seinem Ursprung nach älter ist als das Menschengeschlecht überhaupt, dessen Entwicklung erst in ihm und durch ihn möglich geworden ist."[118]

---

[115] Vgl. z.B. *GdA* I/1[5], 197 f.

[116] Ebd. 6.—Zu Meyers Überzeugung von der "entscheidenden" Bedeutung des "Geistes" z.B. im Krieg vgl. ebd. 164.

[117] Siehe *GdA* I/1[5], 6.

[118] Ebd. 11; vgl. auch ebd. 34. Meyer beruft sich hier für seine Staatsauffassung auf Aristoteles' Definition (*Politik* I, 1253a 1). Zu Meyers Staatslehre s. ebenso *Über die Anfänge des Staats und sein Verhältnis zu den Geschlechtsverbänden und zum Volkstum* (= *Sitzungsberichte der Königlich Preußischen Akademie der Wissenschaften, Philosophisch-historische Klasse*, Berlin 1907, 508–538); *Der Staat, sein Wesen und seine Organisation* (Vortrag 1916 vor dem deutschevangelischen Frauenbund), in: *Weltgeschichte und Weltkrieg. Gesammelte Aufsätze*, Stuttgart/Berlin 1916, 132–158.—Meyers These vom Staat als Prius der Geschichte richtet sich vor allem gegen Hegels Lehre vom Staat als letzter und höchster Form historischer Vollen-

Meyers Postulat von der Priorität des Staates macht deutlich, daß seine politische Geschichtsauffassung gegen eine religiöse Geschichtsauffassung gerichtet ist.[119] Wenn nämlich die Entstehung des Menschengeschlechts den Staat voraussetzt, dann wird erstens ein Schöpfergott verzichtbar, und dann kann zweitens eine dem Menschen spezifische Institution wie die Religion nicht älter sein als der Staat. Dies impliziert, daß tierische Verbände dem Menschengeschlecht vorhergingen und zugleich, daß menschliche Verbände den tierischen zwar verwandt, aber überlegen sind: nicht durch die Religion, also durch etwas, das den Menschen vom Tier unterscheidet, doch auch nicht durch den Staat, denn er ist ja nach Meyer etwas, das beiden gemeinsam ist. Vielmehr seien die Menschen den Tieren durch die besondere Leistungsfähigkeit des menschlichen Staates überlegen. Ein göttliches Prinzip ist eskamotiert, und dennoch braucht ein geistiges Prinzip nicht aus der Welt geschafft zu werden. An die Stelle des demiurgischen Gottes tritt der soziale Verband, der Staat. Vermag der Staat aber ohne die Religion zu entstehen, so hat die Religion als etwas von ihm Abgeleitetes und für ihn auch in Zukunft nicht Unabdingbares zu gelten. Damit ist der Primat der Politik aufgerichtet—schon vor aller Geschichte und über die bisherige Geschichte hinaus. Nun erst kann Meyer guten Gewissens der Religionsgeschichte in der Historie den Platz einer Unterabteilung zuweisen.

Die Verabsolutierung der Politik hat freilich zur Folge, daß die Universalgeschichte nur einen geliehenen Triumph erzielt: Meyers Staatsauffassung tritt das Erbe der Religion an. Die religionskritische Universal-

---

dung und die daran anknüpfende marxistische Staatstheorie, die im Gegensatz zu Hegel freilich die Auflösung des Staates als Geschichtsziel propagierte: F. Engels, *Der Ursprung der Familie, des Privateigentums und des Staats* (1884). Aus Meyers Staats-Apologie ergab sich folgerichtig seine Ablehnung von Liberalismus und radikaler Demokratie (vgl. Anm. 56 und 57) sowie seine Rechtfertigung von nationaler Hegemonie und starken Führer-Persönlichkeiten (vgl. Abschn. II). Mit seiner Staatslehre befindet sich Meyer nicht zuletzt im Gegensatz zu Fustel de Coulanges, *La cité antique* (1864), der die Erzeugung des Staates durch die Religion (Ahnenkult) postulierte; vgl. dazu Momigliano, "The Ancient City of Fustel de Coulanges," in: *Essays . . .* (wie Anm. 47), 325–343. Durkheim (vgl. Anm. 40), Schüler von Fustel, setzte sich mit Meyers aprioristischem Staatskonzept in seiner Rezension der zu "Elementen der Anthropologie" ausgearbeiteten 2. Aufl. (1907) von *GdA* I/1 auseinander, in: *L'Année sociologique* 11 (1906–1909), 5–13, und wandte sich gegen Meyers individualisierende, politik-zentrierte Geschichtsauffassung, die typisch für die deutsche historische Schule war. Zum Problem vgl. auch V. Ehrenberg (zum Teil in Anknüpfung an Meyer, aber ohne Staats-Apologie), *Der griechische und der hellenistische Staat* (= *Einleitung in die Altertumswissenschaft*, hg. von A. Gercke/ E. Norden, III/3), Leipzig/ Berlin 1932, sowie *Der Staat der Griechen*, Stuttgart/ München 1965². —Vgl. auch Anm. 61 und 119.

[119] So bereits Aristoteles (s. Anm. 118); vgl. zu seiner Definition des ζῷον πολιτικόν: W. Kullmann, "Der Mensch als politisches Lebewesen bei Aristoteles," in: *Hermes* 108 (1980) 419–443 (kritisch zu Meyer: 426, n. 19).

historie erweist sich auch hier nicht allein als Konkurrenzunternehmen zur Theologie, sondern als Fortsetzung der Theologie mit anderen Mitteln, im Gewande der Ontologie.[120] Mittels des vormenschlich und präreligiös fundierten Staatsbegriffes werden unter der Hand die beiden Grundprinzipien der sozialdarwinistischen Evolutionstheorie in politische Theologie umgemünzt: das Recht des Stärkeren[121] und die Erhaltung der Art. Meyer glaubt unerschütterlich daran, "dass die Macht das eigentliche Wesen des Staates ist,"[122] und versucht unzählige Male, seinen Hörern und den Lesern seiner Schriften diese metaphysische Überzeugung einzuhämmern. In der Gerechtigkeit kann er demzufolge nur ein "Wahngebilde" erblicken: "Die Gestaltung eines jeden Staats zeigt, dass es kein Recht auf Erden gibt als das Recht des Stärkeren, als die unter blendenden Formeln verhüllte Gewalt."[123] Analog zum in der Natur herrschenden Gesetz von der Erhaltung der Art gehorche die Geschichte—auch die der Religion—dem Diktat der Erhaltung des sozialen Verbandes,[124] insbesondere seiner "dominierenden" Form, des Staates.

Dem Wesen des Staates, der Macht, sowie den Herrschaftsstrukturen, welche dieses Wesen ausdrücken und sichern, sind laut Meyer nicht allein die aktuellen politischen Entscheidungen unterworfen, sondern sämtliche gesellschaftlichen Einrichtungen: Auch und gerade die auf Dauerhaftigkeit angelegten Sitten und Gebräuche—nicht zuletzt die religiösen—

---

[120] Vgl. Abschn. I.

[121] Dieses Prinzip findet sich bekanntlich so nicht bei Darwin, sondern geht auf ältere (staatstheoretische) Konzepte zurück; s. besonders Machiavelli, *Il principe* (1532), sowie Th. Hobbes, *Leviathan* (1651).—Zur apologetischen Rechtfertigung des starken Souverän (eine Legitimation, die instrumentalisierbar war für den NS) s. C. Schmitt, *Der Leviathan in der Staatslehre des Thomas Hobbes*, Hamburg 1938. Vgl. auch Anm. 15.

[122] *GdA* V[1], 368; daraus leitet Meyer auch den Primat der Außenpolitik ab. Meyers Definition des Staates durch die Macht und das Recht des Stärkeren beruft sich wiederum auf Thukydides (und zwar ausdrücklich gegen die Staatsutopien von Platon und Aristoteles: *Forschungen* II, 393); damit begründet Meyer auch ex cathedra seine Propaganda für die Notwendigkeit einer hegemonialen deutsch-nationalen Weltpolitik, denn: "Machtstreben und Machterweiterung ist das Lebenselement jedes kräftigen und gesunden Staats, der in der Welt und in der Geschichte etwas bedeuten will," so Meyer in seiner *Rede beim Antritt des Rektorats der Friedrich-Wilhelms-Universität Berlin am 15. Oktober 1919* (= *Kl. Schr.* II, 539–567, hier: 551); daß diese Thukydides-Funktionalisierung auf einer Mißdeutung des Thukydideischen Standpunktes beruht, hat Flashar (wie Anm. 63, besonders 55 f., n. 105) gezeigt.—Vgl. auch die folgende Anm.

[123] *GdA* IV[1], 147. Die historischen Konsequenzen daraus—die "rücksichtslose Geltendmachung" der Interessen des "starke(n) Geist(es)", der die Dinge erkennt wie sie sind"—beurteilte Meyer freilich 1901 als "Verhängniss" (ebd.; s. aber Anm. 122; zu Meyers Schicksalsbegriff vgl. Anm. 107). Siehe auch Meyers Darstellung von Athens brutalem Vorgehen gegen Melos im Jahre 416, wobei man auf das "Recht des Stärkeren"—bei Menschen wie bei Göttern—rekurrierte: *GdA* IV[1], 494.

[124] Vgl. z.B. *GdA* I/1[5], 20 f.

haben dem Gesetz der Erhaltung des Staatsverbandes zu dienen und lassen sich nur durch staatliche Machtbefugnisse als etwas Allgemeinverbindliches durchsetzen. Ein schlagender Beleg dafür sei die Institution der Erbtöchter: "wenn kein Sohn, sondern nur eine Tochter da ist, greift der Staat ein und erhält die Familie künstlich, indem er ihre Hand und damit das Erbgut vergibt. Die Fiktion, daß dadurch dem Verstorbenen der Totenkult und die Fortexistenz seiner Seele gesichert wird, ist dabei durchaus nebensächlich und nur Einkleidung; die Erhaltung der Zahl der begüterten und leistungsfähigen Familien ist das, worauf es in Wirklichkeit ankommt, und eben deshalb ist die Erzeugung des fiktiven Nachkommen nicht der Pietät der Angehörigen überlassen—da würde das Pietätsgefühl oder die Furcht vor dem Zorn der Seele des Toten, in der die Modernen das Motiv sehen, sehr wenig erreichen, sondern in der Regel würden die Angehörigen das Erbgut für sich nehmen—, sondern wird vom Staat nach feststehenden Rechtssätzen erzwungen."[125] Das hier zum Ausdruck kommende Zutrauen in die Übermacht objektiver Staatsinteressen und in die Unmaßgeblichkeit religiöser Gefühle ist paradigmatisch für Meyers Religionsauffassung. Eine religiöse Begründung derjenigen Verhaltensnormen, die vor dem Richterstuhl des Universalhistorikers zu bestehen vermögen, beurteilt er als Nebensächlichkeit oder als Vorspiegelung falscher Tatsachen, durch die das "Wirkliche", das eigentlich Wirksame—die Staatsvernunft—verdeckt wird. So ist es nur konsequent, wenn Meyer die religiöse "Einkleidung" als einen überflüssigen Ballast erachtet, der abgestreift werden muß, damit die nackte Wahrheit sich enthüllt, welche aufklärerisches Entlarvungspathos allemal hinter den religiösen Masken vermutet. Im Unterschied zum Staat erscheint die Religion als Menschenwerk, als Fiktion. Meyer konzediert ihr im günstigsten Falle, daß sie der ihr zugrundeliegenden und von ihr verhüllten Wahrheit aufgesetzte, nachträgliche "Motivierungen"[126] liefert, die jedoch für sich genommen, also ohne die Gewalt der Staatsraison, keinerlei Macht ausüben könnten.

Denn aus der Priorität der Staatsentstehung vor der Religionsentstehung schließt Meyer auf eine zeitenübergreifende Priorität der Macht des Staates vor derjenigen der Religion: Da der Staat—wie die Gesellschaft, wie Recht und Moral, und wie "alle materielle Kultur"—"eine von der Religion völlig unabhängige Grundlage" besitzt,[127] ist und bleibt er der

---

[125] Ebd. 21.
[126] Meyer wirft Herodot vor, daß er eine Vorliebe für religiöse Motivierungen gehabt und diese nicht als taktische Manipulationen der Politiker durchschaut habe: vgl. z.B. *Forschungen* II, 255 f.
[127] *GdA* I/1⁵, 135.

Religion überlegen. Das, was am Anfang steht, der Ursprung, ist also auch in Meyers Denken, wie in theologischen Lehrgebäuden üblich, das tiefste und oberste Machtprinzip. Die Ersetzung des Schöpfergottes durch den Staatsgeist ermöglicht es Meyer, die aus der Ursprungsqualität abgeleitete Unvergänglichkeit des Gottes auf den Staat als solchen zu übertragen und der Religion Vergänglichkeit zu attestieren. Diese für ihn feststehende Glaubenswahrheit ermutigt ihn zu der lapidaren Formel: "Ewig ist nur der Verband an sich."[128]

2. Entstehung von Wissenschaft und Religion aus dem mythischen Denken

Meyer konnte sich nicht damit zufriedengeben, der Religion Ursprünglichkeit und Ewigkeit abzusprechen, denn die zum frühestmöglichen Zeitpunkt, seit Menschengedenken einsetzende historische Wirksamkeit der Religion war nicht zu leugnen. Er sah sich also gezwungen, in seiner Staatslehre der Religion eine Stelle zuzuweisen. Aus Meyers Auffassung vom Staat als einer Ursprungsmacht resultierte nämlich ein Problem, das ihn in höchstem Maße beunruhigen mußte: Wenn der Staat der Menschheitsgeschichte zugrundeliegt und daher, wie Meyer ontologisch folgert, unvergänglich ist, wie war es dann möglich, daß auf dem Boden des Staates die Religion, also eine konkurrierende Institution mit Ursprungs- und Ewigkeitsanspruch, sich bilden konnte?

Um dieses Problem zu lösen, griff Meyer auf bewährte Erklärungsversuche zurück, die sämtlich bereits von antiken Religionskritikern vorgeprägt worden waren.[129] Dabei handelt es sich im wesentlichen um die These von der Entstehung der Religion aus der ursprünglichen Ohnmacht und Unwissenheit—und deshalb Angst—des Menschen in seinem Verhältnis zur Natur.[130] Demzufolge führt der Fortschritt in der Naturbeherrschung und Naturerkenntnis den Untergang der Religion herbei. Diese aufklärerische Meinung war kennzeichnend für den Optimismus der religionskritischen Religionswissenschaft des 19. Jahrhunderts.[131]

---

[128] Ebd. 73; vgl. ebd. 19 f.

[129] Siehe dazu P. Decharme, *La critique des traditions religieuses chez les Grecs des origines au temps de Plutarque*, Paris 1904; W. Nestle, *Vom Mythos zum Logos. Die Selbstentfaltung des griechischen Denkens von Homer bis auf die Sophistik und Sokrates*, Stuttgart 1940; J.-P. Vernant, "Du mythe à la raison," in: *Mythe et pensée chez les Grecs. Etudes de psychologie historique* (1965), 1985[10], 373–410.

[130] Vgl. Demokrit, frg. 68 A 75, Diels-Kranz (= 111, Mansfeld). Wissenschaftshistorisch zur Erklärung der Religion aus der Angst s. Renate Schlesier, s.v. "Angst", in: *Handbuch religionswissenschaftlicher Grundbegriffe* I, hg. von H. Cancik/B. Gladigow/ M. Laubscher, Stuttgart 1988, 455–471.

[131] Vgl. dazu den Forschungsüberblick bei M.P. Nilsson, *Geschichte der griechischen Religion I: Die Religion Griechenlands bis auf die griechische Weltherrschaft* (= *Handbuch der Altertumswissenschaft* V /2.1), (1940) München 1967[3], 3–67.

Meyer räumt jedoch ein, daß dieser Fortschritt auf Tendenzen zurückgeht, die zunächst von der Religion selbst hervorgetrieben werden. Zu
eng sei deshalb Schleiermachers Definition der Religion als schlechthinni-
gen Abhängigkeitsgefühls,[132] die nur die Voraussetzung der Religion
bezeichnen könne, nicht aber ihr Wesen. "Dies besteht vielmehr," so
Meyer, "in dem persönlichen Verhältnis, in das eine Menschengruppe
und der einzelne Mensch zu den Mächten tritt, von denen er sich abhängig fühlt, in der unmittelbaren und unmittelbar wirksamen Verbindung,
die zwischen ihnen geschaffen wird und die daher nicht momentan, sondern dauernd und unauflösbar ist."[133] Aus einer solchen Bestimmung
des Wesens der Religion ergab sich die Frage nach den geistigen Bedingungen der religionsspezifischen Wechselwirkung zwischen den
Menschen und den übermenschlichen "Mächten". Zur Lösung dieses
Problems schien sich das Postulat zweier religionshistorischer Prioritäten
zu eignen: derjenigen des Kultus vor der Mythologie sowie derjenigen der
Geister und Götter vor den Heroen.

Die Auffassung von der Priorität des Kultus vor der Mythologie wurde
seit den achtziger Jahren des 19. Jahrhunderts insbesondere von den
"Cambridge Ritualists" (Robertson Smith, Frazer, Jane Harrison) vertreten.[134] Nach dieser Auffassung waren die Mythen als nachträgliche
Rechtfertigungen, anders gesagt: als ätiologische Rationalisierungen von
Kulthandlungen anzusehen. Dem lag die aufklärerische Überzeugung
von der Priorität der menschlichen Praxis vor dem—von Menschen
erdachten—Göttlichen zugrunde. Meyer, der diese Konzeption teilt,
wendet sich freilich gegen die namentlich in der Totemismus-Theorie von
Robertson Smith vorausgesetzte Priorität der Tat vor dem Wort. Smith's
These hingegen von der sakramentalen Qualität des Opfermahls als
"Kommunion" zwischen Mensch und übermenschlicher Macht übernimmt Meyer, ohne sich die aus der Totemismus-Theorie abgeleitete
Begründung, die Priorität des Totenkultes vor dem Götterglauben, zueigen zu machen.[135] Die Mythologie entsteht zwar, so Meyer, nach dem

---

[132] Vgl. F. Schleiermacher, *Über die Religion. Reden an die Gebildeten unter ihren Verächtern*
(1799); dazu Meyer: *GdA* I/1⁵, 93.

[133] *GdA* I/1⁵, 93.

[134] W. Robertson Smith, *Lectures on the Religion of the Semites* (1889); J.G. Frazer, *The
Golden Bough. A Study in Magic and Religion* (1890¹, 2 Bde.; 1901², 3 Bde.; 1911–1915³,
12 Bde.); Jane E. Harrison, *Mythology and Monuments of Ancient Athens* (1890), sowie *Prolegomena to the Study of Greek Religion* (1903). Zu den "Cambridge Ritualists" vgl. jetzt
Supplement II der *Illinois Classical Studies*, Urbana (im Druck).—Meyer setzte sich explizit
in seiner *Anthropologie* lediglich kurz mit Robertson Smith auseinander, teilt freilich
mit ihm und vor allem mit Frazer wesentliche religionstheoretische Konzepte (vgl. die
folgenden Anmerkungen); wie Frazer (und, im Anschluß an ihn und R. Smith, auch
Freud) versuchte Meyer ein irreligiöses Modell der Religion aufzustellen.

[135] Meyer polemisiert gegen "die totemistische Theorie" (*GdA* I/1⁵, 111) weitgehend

Kult, aber nur teilweise aus dem Kult und den in ihm entwickelten Ritualen. Sie habe eine vom Kult unabhängige Basis, nämlich in einem künstlerischen, also weder genuin metaphysischen noch genuin logischen Antrieb des Menschen. Meyer führt die Mythologie nicht auf ein produktives praktisches, sondern auf ein schöpferisches geistiges Moment zurück, die "Eingebungen der Phantasie."[136] Damit erweist sich Meyer eher als Gegner des Materialismus der ritualistischen Schule. Er bleibt von Mythentheorien der deutschen Klassik und der Romantik inspiriert.[137]

In diesem Sinne gehört die Mythologie für Meyer also strenggenommen nicht zur Religion. Denn die religiöse Bedingung des persönlichen Verhältnisses, der unmittelbar wirksamen Verbindung zwischen Menschen und außermenschlichen Kräften könne niemals von den Erzählungen der Mythologie, sondern nur von den Handlungen des Kultus erfüllt werden. Anders steht es mit dem "mythischen Denken," das Meyer strikt von der Mythologie—wie von der Kunst—unterscheidet und zum Ursprungsphänomen erklärt, von dem Religion und Wissenschaft ihren Ausgang nehmen. Mit dem von Steinthal geprägten Terminus des "mythischen Denkens"[138] bezeichnet Meyer den "prägnantesten Ausdruck"

---

ohne Namensnennung; gemeint sind natürlich vor allem Robertson Smith (s. Anm. 134) und Frazer, der seine Totemismus-Forschungen (ab 1887) später in einem vierbändigen Werk zusammenfaßte: *Totemism and Exogamy* (1910). Meyer wendet sich gegen die These, dem Götterglauben gehe in der Religionsgeschichte regelmäßig eine totemistische Phase voraus (*GdA* I/1⁵, 110 f.; vgl., mit Erwähnung von R. Smith, ebd. 122); s. aber die Übernahme (anonym) von Robertson Smith's sakramentaler Opfertheorie: ebd. 105.—Auf diese Opfertheorie stützt sich ebenfalls die psychoanalytische Erklärung der Totemmahlzeit durch Sigmund Freud, der freilich auch das religionsgeschichtliche Totemismus-Modell übernahm, siehe *Totem und Tabu* (1912/1913); *Der Mann Moses und die monotheistische Religion* (1937/1939). Im übrigen knüpft Freud im *Mann Moses* mit der These, daß Moses ein Ägypter war, explizit an Meyers Forschungen an.—Zum Totemismus vgl. den Versuch einer endgültigen Erledigung des Problems bei Cl. Lévi-Strauss, *Le totémisme aujourd'hui* (1962); zu Meyers theoretischen Gemeinsamkeiten mit Lévi-Strauss vgl. Anm. 138 ff.

[136] *GdA* I/1⁵, 172; vgl. Anm. 170.

[137] Siehe insbesondere K.Ph. Moritz, *Götterlehre oder Mythologische Dichtungen der Alten* (1791): Mythologie als Sprache der Phantasie; K.O. Müller, *Prolegomena zu einer wissenschaftlichen Mythologie* (1825): wegen seiner Betonung der Zusammenhänge von Mythos und Kultus hebt Meyer ihn lobend von der "vergleichenden Mythologie" der zweiten Jahrhunderthälfte ab, *GdA* I/2³, 872.

[138] Vgl. Heymann Steinthal, *Die Classification der Sprachen* (1850), sowie *Philologie, Geschichte und Psychologie* (1864). Meyer beschäftigte sich schon sehr früh mit Steinthals völkerpsychologischer Sprachtheorie und desgleichen mit der Lehre von den Elementargedanken, die A. Bastian, der Begründer der akademischen Ethnologie in Deutschland, entworfen hatte: *Der Mensch in der Geschichte. Zur Begründung einer psychologischen Weltanschauung*, 3 Bde. (1860). Zur spekulativen Völkerkunde dieser Zeit vgl. F. Kramer, *Verkehrte Welten. Zur imaginären Ethnographie des 19. Jahrhunderts*, Frankfurt/M. 1977.—Meyer bedauerte, seine Studienpläne nicht mit einem Besuch der Berliner Kollegien von Steinthal und Bastian vereinbaren zu können: s. dazu die Dokumentation von Hoffmann, in

der "Denkweise des primitiven Menschen."[139] In dieser Denkweise erblickt Meyer die "psychologische Grundlage" der Religion[140] wie zugleich der Überwindung der Religion. Denn das mythische Denken wird nach Meyer von einer fundamentalen anthropologischen Konstante beherrscht: dem praktischen und theoretischen Bedürfnis nach Beeinflussung und Erklärung der Wirklichkeit. Bereits im mythischen Denken findet Meyer "allgemeine, logische Formen" und die ihnen zugehörige Klassifikationstendenz am Werke. Das mythische Denken dient Meyer infolgedessen als Beleg dafür, daß der menschliche Denkprozeß außerhalb wie innerhalb der Religion überzeitlichen Gesetzen unterliegt.[141] Da jedoch das mythische Denken mit der "Übertragung menschlicher Analogien auf die Naturvorgänge"[142] operiert, sind seine Erkenntnismöglichkeiten sowie seine Entwicklungsfähigkeit begrenzt. Nur indem diese Analogien beseitigt werden, läßt sich nach Meyer "der Fortschritt des wissenschaftlichen Denkens" ungehemmt entfalten.[143]

Das mythische Denken ist demnach laut Meyer ebensowenig etwas Religionsspezifisches wie die Mythologie. Seine religionsspezifische Verwirklichung freilich findet ein solches Denken im Kultus. Dieser ist, Meyer zufolge, "der vollendetste Ausdruck der Kausalitätsidee, den das mythische Denken erzeugt hat."[144] Erst mit dem Kultus, der als dauerhafte und geregelte "Verknüpfung des menschlichen Verbandes mit der Gottheit" definiert sei und dem die "Vorstellung eines Vertragsverhältnisses" zu Grunde liege,[145] beginnt nach Meyers Auffassung die Religion. Was dem Kultus und damit der Gottesverehrung vorhergeht und

---

diesem Band.—Steinthals "mythisches Denken" gehört auch zu den Grundbegriffen von E. Cassirers *Philosophie der symbolischen Formen* (1925), Bd. 2: *Das mythische Denkens*, sowie von Lévi-Strauss' strukturaler Anthropologie (vgl. Anm. 141).

[139] *GdA* I/1⁵, 91.

[140] Ebd. 92.

[141] Diese Überzeugung vertritt heute Lévi-Strauss, s. besonders: *La pensée sauvage* (1962) sowie *Mythologiques*, 4 Bde. (1964–1971). Zur kritischen Rekonstruktion der Lévi-Strauss'schen Mytho-Logik vgl. Renate Schlesier, "Der bannende Blick des Flaneurs im Garten der Mythen," in: *Faszination des Mythos* (wie Anm. 29), 35–60, sowie "Ödipus, Parsifal und die Wilden. Zur Kritik an Lévi-Strauss' Mythologie des Mythos," in: R. Faber/R. Schlesier (Hg.), *Die Restauration der Götter. Antike Religion und Neo-Paganismus*, Würzburg 1986, 271–289.

[142] *GdA* I/1⁵, 90. Diese Auffassung liegt auch Frazers Magie-Theorie (vgl. Anm. 134 und 156) zugrunde, sowie dem Animismus-Konzept von E.B. Tylor, *Primitive Culture: Researches into the Development of Mythology, Philosophy, Religion, Art and Custom*, 2 Bde. (1871).—Zum Analogiebegriff bei Meyer vgl. Anm. 100.

[143] *GdA* I/1⁵, 90: dies entspricht Frazers Stufenlehre (magisches Analogiedenken als Vorstufe der Wissenschaft). Zu Meyers Fortschrittsbejahung und zugleich Skepsis gegenüber den Fortschrittsmöglichkeiten vgl. Abschn. IV.

[144] *GdA* I/1⁵, 103.

[145] Vgl. ebd. 103 f.

ebenso wie diese auf dem mythischen Denken beruht, ist in dieser religionsgeschichtlichen Konstruktion das "Zauberwesen". Meyer versteht darunter die "zwischen Menschen und Geistern für den einzelnen Moment geschaffenen Beziehungen."[146] Nicht anders als das mythische Denken gehört also das Zauberwesen für Meyer in die Vorgeschichte der Religion.

Auf diese Weise ist eine zu weit zurückreichende Frühzeitigkeit der Religion, die sie in die Nähe der Anfänge des Menschengeschlechts und vielleicht sogar des Staatsverbandes rücken könnte, wünschenswert beseitigt. Meyer sieht sich deshalb zu folgender Versicherung berechtigt: "Die Bedeutung der Religion für primitive Volksstämme wird von der modernen Forschung oft stark überschätzt."[147] Was bei den "Primitiven" im Unterschied zu den "Kulturvölkern" dominiere, seien vielmehr "Zauberei, blutige Opfer, wüster Aberglaube,"[148] also laut Meyer "die ursprünglichen Triebe und Anschauungen," aus denen die Religion zwar erwachsen ist, denen gegenüber jedoch der geordnete Kultus der "lebendigen Religion" einen begrüßenswerten Fortschritt darstellt.[149] Wie man sieht, neigt Meyer dazu, den Kultus erst der Kultur zuzurechnen.[150] Werden damit die Verbrechen der "Kulturvölker" exkulpiert? Keineswegs, denn bemerkenswerterweise verschließt sich Meyer nicht der Einsicht, daß "gerade der Beginn kulturellen Fortschritts in die wildeste Barbarei hineinführen" kann.[151] Der Geschichte entnimmt Meyer nämlich die regelmäßige Erfahrung, daß der kulturelle Fortschritt eine "Steigerung der Religiosität"[152] mit sich bringt und damit zugleich die Tendenz, in die Exzesse des präreligiösen Zauberwesens zurückzufallen.

Ähnlich argumentierten bereits Mythentheoretiker der französischen

---

[146] Ebd. 93; s. auch Meyers Rekurs auf die Theorie der Augenblicks- und Sondergötter von H. Usener, *Götternamen. Versuch einer Lehre von der religiösen Begriffsbildung* (1896); ebd. 103. Mit Useners religionsgeschichtlichen Forschungen wurde Meyer früh bekannt; zu seiner Enttäuschung las Usener ausnahmsweise während Meyers Bonner Studienzeit (1872) nicht über Mythologie. Vgl. zu Meyers Anschluß an Usener auch Anm. 177.

[147] *GdA* I/1[5], 127; das war auch die Meinung von Frazer, der die Magie für ein Stadium vor der Religionsentstehung hielt. Die Gegenposition vertraten insbesondere Durkheim (s. Anm. 40) sowie, im Zusammenhang mit seinen Forschungen, H. Hubert und M. Mauss, "Introduction à l'analyse de quelques phénomènes religieux," in: *Revue de l'histoire des religions* 58 (1906), 163–203.

[148] *GdA* I/1[5], 128. Hier trifft sich Meyer mit der Perhorreszierung der "Primitiven" durch die englische anthropologische Schule, vor allem durch Tylor (s. Anm. 142). Vgl. zu Tylors Konzept der Ausmerzung des "primitiven" Denkens: M. Detienne, *L'invention* . . . (wie Anm. 64), 33–36.

[149] Vgl. *GdA* I/1[5], 127.

[150] S. auch ebd. 104; 125 f.

[151] Ebd. 128.

[152] Ebd. 126.

Aufklärung des 17. und 18. Jahrhunderts. Fontenelle, Lafitau und de Brosses[153] schockierten ihre Zeitgenossen mit der realistischen Diagnose, daß die Zivilisierten ebenso roh sein können wie die "Wilden", und daß die "Wilden" sich in ihren Sitten, Institutionen und Denkweisen im Guten wie im Schlimmen den Zivilisierten ebenbürtig zeigen. Nicht anders als diese weltklugen Aufklärer war auch Meyer vom idealistischen Konzept des "guten Wilden" weit entfernt.[154]

Den Umschlag von der Kultur in die Barbarei wie den von der Barbarei in die Kultur führt Meyer wiederum auf ein subjektives Faktum zurück: auf den "ersten Berufsstand, den die Menschheit kennt."[155] Denn erfahrungsgemäß treten von Anfang an bei allen Völkern teils männliche, teils weibliche "Mittelspersonen" auf, "Medizinmänner, Fetischpriester, Seher, Propheten, Orakelverkünder," die Meyer unter dem Terminus Zauberer zusammenfaßt. Diesem Berufsstand spricht der Universalhistoriker eine nicht allein weit hinter die Religion zurückreichende, sondern auch über sie hinausweisende Rolle zu. Die Machtstellung der zauberkundigen Subjekte repräsentiert für Meyer jene unauflösliche Zweideutigkeit, welche das mythische Denken im Reiche des objektiven Geistes vertritt: Die Zauberer "sind im Besitz einer festen Tradition, die sie weitergeben und vermehren und die die Summe alles Wissens enthält, das der Stamm in seiner Entwicklung erworben hat. Darin besteht die kulturelle Bedeutung dieses Elements. Es übt, materiell wie geistig, einen furchtbaren Druck aus auf den Stamm und auf jede ihm zugehörige Persönlichkeit, und hemmt jede freie Entwicklung, da diese notwendig zu einem Bruch mit den alten Traditionen und den dominierenden mythischen Anschauungen führen muß; aber es umschließt und bewahrt auch alles, was ein primitiver Stamm von geistigem Leben besitzt. Die Anfänge des menschlichen Nachdenkens, so unbeholfen seine Äußerungen sind, werden in diesen Kreisen entwickelt und gepflegt, die ersten stammelnden Versuche, von den Einzelerscheinungen zu einem

---

153 B. Le Bovier de Fontenelle, *De l'origine des fables* (1724); J.-F. Lafitau, *Moeurs des sauvages amériquains comparées aux moeurs des premiers temps*, 2 Bde. (1724); Ch. de Brosses, *Du culte des dieux fétiches ou Parallèle de l'ancienne religion de l'Egypte avec la religion actuelle de la Nigritie* (1760). Vgl. dazu K.-H. Kohl, *Entzauberter Blick. Das Bild vom Guten Wilden und die Erfahrung der Zivilisation*, Berlin 1981.

154 Dieses Konzept steht bei Rousseau in dekadenz-theoretischem Zusammenhang: J.-J. Rousseau, *Discours sur l'origine de l'inégalité parmi les hommes* (1755); so auch, in Anknüpfung daran, bei Lévi-Strauss (vgl. Anm. 141). Siehe ebenfalls die vorige Anmerkung.

155 *GdA* I/1⁵, 94. Vgl. das Konzept eines lehrenden Priesterstandes als anthropologischer Konstante bei G.F. Creuzer, *Symbolik und Mythologie der alten Völker, besonders der Griechen*, 4 Bde. (1810–1812). Unter Berufung auf Creuzer entwickelte Hegel sein Konzept von der Zauberei als "unmittelbarer Religion," in den *Vorlesungen über die Philosophie der Religion* (1821 ff.), 2. Teil, 1. Abschnitt, I.

zusammenfassenden Weltbilde zu gelangen, und ebenso die Anfänge derjenigen Errungenschaften, durch welche die materiellen und sozialen
Zustände der Menschen zur Kultur gesteigert werden, der Heilkunst und
anderer nützlicher Künste, des Rechts und der Sitte—freilich immer ge-
hemmt und in Banden gehalten durch die Wucht der traditionellen Vorstellungen, in denen die Zauberer leben und auf denen ihre Machtstellung beruht.''[156]

Es ist unverkennbar, daß Meyers Charakterisierung dieser zwiespältigen Machthaber aus sachlicher Anerkennung und schaudernder Ehrfurcht gemischt ist. Doch daß sie seiner Theorie zu schaffen machen, hat
einen anderen Grund. Denn die heilsame und schädliche Gewalt, über
die die Zauberer verfügen, kann sich wohl in den Dienst der Religion und
sogar des Staates stellen, ist und bleibt aber beidem, nach Meyers Auffassung, fundamental fremd.[157] Aus diesem Widerspruch erklärt sich
Meyers Versuch, den Kultus strikt von Zauberwesen abzugrenzen. Bei
diesem Unternehmen verschieben sich freilich alsbald die Vorzeichen. In
dem Maße nämlich, wie der Kultus einen Fortschritt hin zur Religion,
über das Zauberwesen hinaus, bedeuten soll, wird das Zauberwesen zur
Verkörperung des Irrationalen, die Religion aber zur Maskierung der
Vernunft. Der Kultus, nicht die Magie, scheint sich als verhüllende Darstellung der Wahrheit und ihrer Macht, also der natürlichen Zusammenhänge und der politischen Interessen, zu erweisen.

Ein stichhaltiger Beleg für diese fundamentale nicht-religiöse Begründung der Religion ist laut Meyer insbesondere das religiöse Fest, das
er als Kultusform par excellence behandelt: Die Anfänge der Religion
kennzeichnen Festsitten, die ''aus dem Zusammenleben mit der Natur''
erwachsen sind.[158] Als Beispiel dafür nennt Meyer völker- und zeitenübergreifende rauschende Freudenfeste im Frühling und Trauerriten im
Sommer. Meyer hält es für selbstverständlich, daß das Fest, nicht die
Gottheiten, denen es gefeiert wird, das historisch Primäre und Dauerhafte ist. Aus dem Fest, so Meyer, entstehen die Gottheiten, nicht umge-

---

[156] *GdA* I/1⁵, 95. Diese Sätze wirken wie ein Résumé von Frazers Auffassung der
Zauberer; eine ähnliche Einschätzung vertrat noch Frazers Schüler B. Malinowski, *Magic,
Science and Religion; And Other Essays* (1925). Vgl. zum Problem (im Kontext der grie-
chischen Naturphilosophie): G.E.R. Lloyd, *Magic, Reason and Experience. Studies in the
Origin and Development of Greek Science*, Cambridge 1979.
[157] Ähnliches wie für die Zauberer und Priester gilt nach Meyer für das Verhältnis der
''Gelehrtenzunft'' zu ''den Mächten des Bestehenden und der äußeren Gewalt,'' nur daß
hier nicht der Zwang der Traditionsgebundenheit, sondern gerade die ''Freiheit der
geistigen Bewegung'' ein dauerhaftes und erfolgreiches Bündnis verhindere (vgl. *GdA*
I/⁵, 163 f.)
[158] Siehe *GdA* I/2³, 732. Diese ''natürliche'' Erklärung des Kultfestes findet sich auch
in Nilssons Standardwerk (s. Anm. 131).

kehrt: Die Gottheiten, heißt es im Anschluß an die Erörterung der Feste des Attis und als verwandt erachteter Figuren, haben sich vielmehr "erst in und aus den Festbräuchen entwickelt" und seien daher auch in den mythischen Erzählungen "mannigfach und schwankend genug."[159] Deshalb können sie Meyer zufolge aus den Festen verschwinden, ohne daß deren Sinn und Charakter sich ändern. Große Opferfeste wie beispielsweise die griechischen Hekatomben sind für Meyer "oft tatsächlich nichts als ein Volksfest, bei dem die Gesamtheit der Verbandsgenossen sich gütlich tun kann und an das sich ein Jahrmarkt anschließt; die religiöse Motivierung ist lediglich äußere Einkleidung."[160] Demnach drückt ein religiöses Fest also ebenso wie jedes nicht-religiöse Fest den Drang zum Wohlleben innerhalb des sozialen Verbandes aus. Auch die entgegengesetzte aggressive, nach außen gerichtete Tendenz, sei politisch begründet, ob sie sich im religiösen oder im nicht-religiösen Rahmen abspielt. Meyer geht davon aus, daß "die sakralen Bluttaten" häufig, wenn auch nicht immer, die Religion zum bloßen Vorwand nehmen: sie seien "oft genug nur ein Ausdruck des Volkscharakters und menschlicher Feindschaft, mit starken (bewußten oder unbewußten) politischen Motiven."[161]

Ein Spezialfall sind für Meyer die Menschenopfer, die er für eine im orientalischen und okzidentalen Altertum von Ägypten bis Rom oft geübte Praxis hält. Da er sie weder natürlich noch politisch rechtfertigen kann, behandelt er sie als einen Atavismus, dessen Herkunft ins vorreligiöse Zeitalter des Aberglaubens zurückreicht, und er hält fest daran, daß sie etwas Primitives, etwas Barbarisches seien. Der religiöse Fortschritt bestünde darin, die Menschenopfer durch "Darbringung von Puppen"[162]

---

[159] GdA I/2³, 732; die Priorität des Kultus vor den Göttern trifft nach Meyer allerdings erst für die Gottheiten "der zweiten Klasse" zu, die er zu den "Spukgestalten der Geisterwelt" (Dämonen, Gespenster usw.) rechnet und von der Gottheiten "der ersten Klasse" unterscheidet, die "ursprünglich wenig oder gar keinen Kult haben." Deshalb sieht sich Meyer in späteren Auflagen der Geschichte des Altertums genötigt, von seiner These der Priorität des Kultus vor den Göttern abzurücken, jedenfalls, was die Gottheiten der ersten Klasse betrifft, also, wie er hinzufügt, "oft die Götter κατ' ἐξοχήν" (GdA I/1⁵, 102 f.). Hat hier auf Meyer das Konzept eines ursprünglichen Hochgottglaubens eingewirkt, das Ende des 19. Jhdts. gegen evolutionistische Religionstheorien aufkam? Siehe z.B. A. Lang, The Making of Religion (1898).

[160] GdA I/1⁵, 105; vgl. ebd. 72 (die Religion als "Ausdruck einer sozialen Ordnung").

[161] Ebd. 105.

[162] Ebd. 139. Zu Menschenopfern bei Griechen, Römern, Phönikern und Ägyptern vgl. GdA I/2³, 97–100. Die Frage nach dem Vorkommen von Menschenopfern bei den Griechen—dazu auch Meyer in: Forschungen I, 56–60; GdA III² (= GdA 5⁸), 550 f.—ist heute umstritten; vgl. dazu A. Henrichs, "Human Sacrifice in Greek Religion: Three Case Studies," in: O. Reverdin/B. Grange (Hg.), Le sacrifice dans l'antiquité (= Entretiens sur l'Antiquité Classique 27, Fondation Hardt), Vandoeuvres-Genève 1981, 195–235.—Vgl. auch Anm. 183 und 185.

zu ersetzen. Allerdings fühlt Meyer sich zu der Feststellung genötigt, daß die historische Entwicklung wiederholt gegen dieses regelhafte Ideal verstößt, denn gerade für Kulturvölker gelte in Zeiten gesteigerter Religiosität: "Menschenblut fließt ihnen in Strömen."[163] Nichtsdestotrotz vertraut Meyer auf eine dem entgegenstehende hoffnungsvolle Gesamttendenz, welche die Opfer überhaupt zum Verschwinden bringen werde: "schließlich ist selbst das gesamte Opferwesen mit allem, was daran hängt, von der gesteigerten Kultur beseitigt worden, und lebt im Judentum, Christentum, Islam nur noch in vereinzelten rudimentären Gebräuchen und mystischen, fast unverständlich gewordenen Lehren weiter."[164]

Diese beruhigende Perspektive knüpft an den Optimismus antiker Religionskritik an. Aus ihr entnimmt Meyer, wie deutlich werden konnte, seine religionssoziologischen Überzeugungen und polemischen Absichten: die Einschätzung der Zauberei als Priesterweisheit, vorwiegend aber als Priestertrug; die Zurückführung der Göttervorstellungen auf natur- und gesellschaftsgemäße Festsitten und menschliche Analogien; die Aufspürung der religiös kamouflierten politischen Interessen. Nicht zuletzt aber entdeckt Meyer in der antiken Mythologie das früheste religionskritische Modell: Er beurteilt die Mythologie als Ätiologie, als rückwirkende Erläuterung und Begründung uralter Kultvorgänge, die in ihrem wahren Sinn nicht mehr verstanden werden. Es sei nicht daran zu zweifeln, "daß der Mythus, der den Brauch erklären soll, ganz sekundär und irrelevant ist."[165] Zugleich aber sind die Mythen, so Meyer, als rationalistische Distanzierung von der eigentlichen Religion und ihrem lebendigen Ausdruck, dem Kultus, zu verstehen.[166] Die mythologischen Erzählungen repräsentieren also für Meyer bereits eine Ablösung von der Religion. Ob notgedrungen, ob intentional: von dieser Ablösung bis zur Auflösung der Religion ist es nicht weit.[167] Aus diesem Grunde sei es kein Wunder, "daß das Studium der Mythologie rein religionsgeschicht-

---

[163] *GdA* I/1[5], 128.

[164] Ebd. 139.

[165] *GdA* I/2[3], 732; vgl. *GdA* I/1[5], 114; 194.—Unter den heutigen Mythologieforschern ist Lévi-Strauss am konsequentesten von der "Irrelevanz" der mythischen Aitien überzeugt (vgl. Anm. 141).

[166] Beispielhaft für diese rationalistische Religionskritik ist nach Meyer Aischylos, vgl. *Forschungen* I, 100 (sowie Abschn. III).

[167] Siehe z.B. *GdA* III[2] (= *GdA* 5[8]), 701: "Der Rationalismus, der bei Stesichoros und später bei Pindar und Äschylos die überlieferte Religion retten will, indem er die sittlichen und physischen Anstöße entfernt," wende sich bei den ionischen Philosophen "gegen die Religion selbst."—Vgl. dazu M. Horkheimer/Th.W. Adorno, *Dialektik der Aufklärung* (1944), die ebenfalls, wie Meyer, dem Umschlag von Mythologie in Aufklärung betonen, aber auch, im Unterschied zu ihm, die weiterwirkende Tendenz zum Umschlag von Aufklärung in Mythologie.

liche Forschung überhaupt nicht hat aufkommen lassen,''[168] wie Meyer im Zusammenhang mit der Orphik bemerkt.

In Meyers eigenen religionshistorischen Überlegungen ist es nun bezeichnenderweise gerade nicht die Mythologie, sondern der Kultus, mit dem er sich im Dienst einer kritischen Erkenntnis der Religion zu verbünden sucht. Denn die Legitimierung des Kultus durch den Historiker stellt sich als ein Konkurrenzunternehmen zur Tätigkeit der Mythologen heraus. Bei ihrer Kritik an der Religion gehen die Mythologen in Meyers Augen nicht weit genug. Trotz ihrer kritischen Tendenz entledigen sie nämlich die Mythologie keineswegs konsequent aller religiösen "Einkleidungen",[169] sondern fügen ihnen im Gegenteil anstößigerweise weitere Stoffe hinzu. Die den Mythologen unterstellte Intention, die Kultgebräuche zu erklären, muß nach Meyer scheitern, da die mythischen Geschichten keine wirklichkeitsgetreue überhistorische Historie sind, sondern willkürliche außerhistorische Erfindungen. Mag in ihnen auch ein "naiver Erkenntnistrieb" oder die "Lust zu fabulieren" am Werke sein:[170] im Gegensatz zur schöpferischen Phantasie des Historikers produziere die des Mythologen statt der Historie eine Geschichte, die meistens "bedeutungslos" ist.[171] Solche Geschichten, wie beispielsweise "die Sagen des Alten Testaments oder der griechischen Mythologie" seien "oft an sich höchst gleichgültig"[172] und können laut Meyer nur Interesse beanspruchen wegen des "ursprünglichen Sinnes," der sich in ihnen verbirgt und der erst nach dem mühsamen Durchgang durch sie, nach der Entledigung von ihren Fiktionen, aufgefunden werden kann.

3. Entgöttlichung der Götter

Durch die religionskritische Mythendeutung, so Meyer, wird endlich deutlich, daß die Götter, von denen die Mythen erzählen, tatsächlich

---

[168] *GdA* III² (= *GdA* 5⁸), 680, n. 2.
[169] Vgl. *GdA* I/1⁵, 105.
[170] Ebd. 92. Natürlich spielt Meyer hier an auf Goethes Selbstcharakteristik im 6. Buch der *Zahmen Xenien* (1823): "Vom Vater hab ich die Statur, / Des Lebens ernstes Führen, / Vom Mütterchen die Frohnatur / Und Lust zu fabulieren."—Nimmt man Meyers Anspielung daraufernst, so würde in seiner Bestimmung des mythischen Denkens als "Lust zu fabulieren" die seit Platons *Politeia* traditionelle Zuordnung der Mythenerzählungen zur Sphäre der Mütter und Ammen hindurchschimmern, welche durch den "Fortschritt" eines männlichen Logos-Konzepts philosophisch und historisch ersetzt und überboten werden sollte.
[171] Vgl. *GdA* I/1⁵, 110. Die Bedeutungslosigkeit der Mythen behauptet heute (in Anknüpfung an Platon) auch Lévi-Strauss, vgl. Anm. 141.
[172] *GdA* I/1⁵, 194.

gezeugt sind, nämlich aus dem "Kausalitätstrieb" des Menschen,[173] der
die Gesetze der Wirklichkeit zunächst nicht in ihrer tatsächlichen Ab-
straktheit, in ihrer nackten Wesenhaftigkeit erfassen kann, sondern welcher der sinnlich-übersinnlichen Verführung nachgibt, sie in die Außen-
welt und in außerweltliche Wesen zu "projizieren".[174] Die Unwahrheit
der Mythen besteht also nach Meyer nicht in der von ihnen ausgemalten
Annahme universeller Wirkungskräfte; darin liege vielmehr gerade ihr
wahrer Kern, der freigesetzt werden müsse. In dem Augenblick nämlich,
in dem auf dem Boden der ausgebildeten Religion der Glaube an Gottheiten erwacht, an universelle Persönlichkeiten also, die nicht zeitlich
oder räumlich begrenzt sind wie die Geister und Spukgestalten, an ver-
nünftige Wesen, mit denen ein Vertragsverhältnis abgeschlossen werden
kann, in diesem Augenblick, so verkündet Meyer, ist eine Entwicklungs-
stufe erreicht, die unmittelbar umschlagen könne in die Erkenntnis der
Naturgesetze, welche sich in den göttlichen Personen verpuppen.[175]

Die Mythologie indessen trägt nach Meyer mitnichten dazu bei, diesen
Fortschritt zu beschleunigen oder gar herbeizuführen. Im Gegenteil: sie
hält ihn auf und kehrt ihn um. Statt die universellen Wesen zu entkörper-
lichen, gleicht sie diese zunehmend den Menschen an[176] und verwandelt
so die Götter in Heroen. Den Prozeß dieser spezifisch mythologischen
Mystifikation der Wirklichkeit stellt Meyer sich wie folgt vor: "die heilige
Geschichte, der ausgebildete Mythus im engeren Sinne," so lautet das
idealhistorische Konstrukt, "entspringt immer aus den Kultushandlun-
gen (den δρώμενα), die er erläutern und motivieren will. Der ursprüngliche Sinn, aus dem er erwachsen ist, wird oft völlig unverständlich; aber
er wird von Generation zu Generation weiter überliefert, ebenso wie die
Kulthandlungen immer von neuem begangen werden. Dann setzt sich
der Mythus um in eine Erzählung von einem Vorgang, der sich in der
Urzeit einmal abgespielt hat, und der Festritus in eine Erinnerungsfeier.
Solche Erzählungen können dann als interessante Geschichten von
Stamm zu Stamm, ja von Volk zu Volk wandern, zu Menschen, die den
Gott und den Kultus nicht mehr kennen; aber auch für die Verehrer selbst
kann bei fortschreitender Kultur der Gott durch diesen Prozeß seiner
Göttlichkeit völlig entkleidet und zu einem sterblichen Menschen (einem

---

[173] Vgl. ebd. 131 f. Auch mit seiner Auffassung vom Götter-erzeugenden Kausalitätstrieb trifft sich Meyer mit Frazer.

[174] Vgl. *GdA* I/1⁵, 178.

[175] Vgl. ebd. 99–102.

[176] Zu Meyers Auffassung der Gottheiten als "zugleich sinnliche(n) und übersinn-
liche(n) Wesen" (ebd. 112) und als anthropomorphen Naturgewalten vgl. *GdA* I/2³,
88–90.—Zur kritischen Analyse einer solchen Konzeption siehe K. Heinrich, *anthro-
pomorphe. Zum Problem des Anthropomorphismus in der Religionsphilosophie* (= *Dahlemer Vorlesungen 2*), Basel/Frankfurt/M. 1986.

König oder Helden) werden, der nur in der Erinnerung und in den Festbräuchen fortlebt. Auf diese Weise ist die griechische und jede ähnliche
Heldensage entstanden.''[177] Dieser Prozeß ist laut Meyer auch die Ursache für ''die zahllosen Schwierigkeiten und Unmöglichkeiten, welche
die Sage bietet, sobald man sich die überlieferte Begebenheit in ihrem
ganzen Verlauf real und auf Grund der Verhältnisse und Anschauungen
der Gegenwart vorzustellen versucht,''[178] wie dies beispielsweise in den
Tragödien des Euripides[179] geschehe.

Doch nicht erst der letzte große Tragiker des 5. Jahrhunderts, auch die
homerische Dichtung sei ähnlich vorgegangen. Bereits das alte Epos habe
''seine Stoffe losgelöst von den lokalen Grundlagen,''[180] aus denen sie
entstanden sind. Das epische Weltbild, so Meyer, formt aus Lokalgöttern
raumübergreifende Wirklichkeitsmächte, deren Funktionen unterein-
ander ausgeglichen werden, oder deren Figuren, wo dies nicht möglich
ist, sich gänzlich in Menschen umbilden. Homers Götter sind für Meyer
universalisierte, Homers Heroen großteils ''degradierte Götter der alten
Volksreligion.''[181] So fügen sich die Unstimmigkeiten der Heroologie
aufs harmonischste zusammen: Die Entrückung der Heroen zum Beispiel
klärt sich auf als ''Nachklang der alten Göttlichkeit,''[182] und Gestalten
wie Lykaon,[183] Iphigenie und Io dürfen bedenkenlos in ihren Ursprüngen
mit Zeus, Artemis und Hera identifiziert werden, da sich diese Heroennamen ''aus Beinamen der Götter entwickelt''[184] haben.

---

[177] GdA I/1^5, 114. Mit diesem Konzept vom Heros als abgesunkenem Gott knüpft
Meyer an Frazer (s. Anm. 134) und Usener (s. Anm. 146) an. Bereits L. Preller vertrat
diese Meinung, Griechische Mythologie, 2 Bde. (1854). Gegen ein solches für die Schule der
vergleichenden Mythologie kennzeichnendes Konzept wandten sich z.B. Rohde (s. Anm.
185) und Wilamowitz (s. Anm. 186) wie überhaupt alle Forscher, die in den Mythen Erinnerungen an historische Tatsachen und Persönlichkeiten erkennen wollen, z.B. L.R.
Farnell, Greek Hero Cults and Ideas of Immortality, Oxford 1921, 280–285 (vgl. 326, n.a.:
vehement gegen Meyer), oder Nilsson (wie Anm. 131).
[178] Forschungen I, 149. Meyer bemerkt nicht, daß dieses Argument auch gegen seine
eigene Überzeugung von der Sinnlosigkeit der Mythen eingewendet werden könnte.
[179] Meyer schätzt Euripides als Religionskritiker ein (wie Wilamowitz), doch zugleich
auch als religiösen Denker, vgl. GdA IV^1, 151–162. Zur Auseinandersetzung mit diesen
beiden traditionellen Euripides-Bildern s. Renate Schlesier, "Daimon und Daimones
bei Euripides," in: Saeculum 34/3–4 (1983), 267–279, sowie "Götterdämmerung bei
Euripides?" in: H. Zinser (Hg.), Der Untergang von Religionen, Berlin 1986, 35–50.
[180] GdA III^2 (= GdA 5^8), 378.
[181] Ebd. 384; vgl. Anm. 177.
[182] Ebd. 385, n.
[183] Meyer hält es für erwiesen, daß im Kult des Zeus Lykaios Menschen geopfert wurden, vgl. Forschungen I, 56, sowie GdA III^2 (= GdA 5^8), 550. Siehe zu diesem Problem
W. Burkert, Homo necans. Interpretationen altgriechischer Opferriten und Mythen (= Religionsgeschichtliche Versuche und Vorarbeiten 32), Berlin/New York 1972, 98–108.—Vgl. auch
Anm. 162.
[184] GdA III^2 (= GdA 5^8), 385, n. 2.—Andererseits meint Meyer (im Gegensatz zu
Wilamowitz, vgl. Anm. 186), daß Götternamen (sowie manche Heroennamen) aus Stadt-

Durch seine These von der Priorität der Götter vor den Heroen und der Entstehung der Götter aus den Kultbräuchen setzt Meyer sich ausdrücklich von den religionshistorischen Postulaten zweier illustrer Vorgänger ab: Wilamowitz und Rohde. Rohde hatte den Heroenkult aus dem Totendienst abgeleitet und den Unsterblichkeitsglauben der Griechen im Seelenkult seinen Ursprung nehmen lassen.[185] Wilamowitz war von der Annahme ausgegangen, daß der Heros die ideale Übersteigerung eines realen Menschen oder Menschentyps sei, und hatte dementsprechend Herakles zur Verkörperung des Mannesideals im Stamme der Dorier erklärt.[186] Meyer ist, im Gegensatz zu Rohde und Wilamowitz, überzeugt davon, daß der Gott nicht jünger ist als der Heros, daß der Heros vielmehr angesehen müsse als ein "herabgesunkener" Gott.[187]

Die Gründe, aus denen Meyer die Idealisierung eines lebenden oder toten Menschen zum Heros, und ebenso die spätere Vergöttlichung des Heros, für religionsgeschichtlich ausgeschlossen halten muß, sind sozialgeschichtlicher Natur. Denn anders als Wilamowitz kann Meyer nicht den Geschlechtsverband als Keimzelle der Gesellschaft und damit als Voraussetzung der Religion betrachten, sondern den "Staatsverband des Stammes,"[188] welcher zunächst nicht seßhaft ist. Die ursprüngliche wandervölkische Universalität dieses Staatsverbandes wird nach Meyer durch die Tatsache bewiesen, daß "die Stämme nirgends in Griechenland eine geographische, geschweige denn eine politische Einheit bilden."[189]

---

und Stammesnamen entstanden sein können (vgl. dazu am Beispiel von Meyers Postulat, der Name Athene sei vom Namen Athen abgeleitet: den Beitrag von Calder in diesem Band).

[185] E. Rohde, *Psyche. Seelencult und Unsterblichkeitsglaube der Griechen* (1890–1894). Meyers Kritik an Rohdes Auffassung des Heroenkultes, in: *Hermes* 30 (1895); vgl. auch *Forschungen* II, 512, n. 2, sowie (ohne Nennung von Rohdes Namen) *GdA* I/1⁵, 121–123. Rohde verteidigte seinen Standpunkt gegen Meyer (ohne Namensnennung) in der 2. Aufl. der *Psyche* (1898), I, 148, n. 2; vgl. (mit Namensnennung) *Kl. Schr.* II, Leipzig/Tübingen 1901, 245–254, 287–292. Zur Auseinandersetzung zwischen Meyer und Rohde s. auch L. Canfora, *Ideologie del classicismo* (= *Piccola Biblioteca Einaudi* 396), Torino 1980; vgl. wissenschafts- und sozialgeschichtlich zu Rohde: H. Cancik, "Erwin Rohde— ein Philologe der Bismarckzeit," in: *Semper apertus. Sechshundert Jahre Ruprecht-Karls-Universität Heidelberg 1386–1986, Festschrift in sechs Bänden*, II, 436–505, zu Rohdes *Psyche*: 471–476; 498–501.—Meyer lehnte zwar Rohdes nicht-totemistische These von der Priorität des Totenkultes in der Religionsentwicklung ab, ging mit ihm freilich in vielen anderen Grundfragen konform, z.B. schätzen beide das homerische Epos als "rationalistisch" ein und hielten an der Historizität von Menschenopfern fest, vgl. zu Meyer Anm. 162 und 183; bei Rohde: *Psyche*², II, 78; 352.

[186] U. von Wilamowitz-Moellendorff, *Euripides Herakles* (1889), 1895², Bd. 2; s. Meyer, gegen Wilamowitz' Position, der Heros sei älter als der Gott (und dementsprechend das Adelsgeschlecht älter als Phratrie und Familie): *Forschungen* II, 512–530.

[187] *GdA* III² (= *GdA* 5⁸), 384; vgl. Anm. 177.

[188] *GdA* I/1⁵, 67; vgl. Anm. 186.

[189] *GdA* III² (= *GdA* 5⁸), 538, n. 1.

Demgegenüber sei die Geschlechtsverfassung "Ausdruck und (...)
Träger der Adelsherrschaft:"[190] In ihrer hierarchischen Gliederung und
in ihrer genealogisch begründeten Heroenverehrung spiegele sie also ein
jüngeres, bereits weit fortgeschrittenes, politisches und religiöses, Ent-
wicklungsstadium, das Meyer als "griechisches Mittelalter"[191] bezeichnet. Ihm müsse eine Urzeit vorausgehen, in der es weder Heroen noch
Adlige, sondern nur ein Stammesvolk und die aus dem Kultus entsprun-
genen, vom mythischen Denken mit Geschichten umrankten, ursprünglich tiergestaltigen[192] Götter gab.

So wird für Meyer der Kultus zum historischen missing link zwischen
dem menschheitserzeugenden Staat und der staatstragenden Religion.
Die Pointe dieser Hilfskonstruktion ist, daß Meyer die Priorität des
Staates gerade deshalb zu seiner Sanktionierung benutzen kann, weil
diese Sanktionierung vor aller Geschichte—sowohl der Menschheitsgeschichte wie der Religionsgeschichte—angesiedelt ist. So kann er
zugleich vermeiden, die beiden von ihm vertretenen spezifisch religionshistorischen Prioritäten—die des Kultus vor der Mythologie und die der
Götter vor den Heroen—theologisch legitimieren zu müssen. Unabhängig von der Triftigkeit oder Untriftigkeit dieser religionshistorischen
Stadientheorie[193] muß festgehalten werden, daß ihr im Rahmen von
Meyers universalhistorischem Denkgebäude die Rolle eine Stützpfeilers
für seine staatsgläubige Weltanschauung zugemutet wird. Gemessen an
der Priorität und Ewigkeit des Staates darf nach Meyer der Kultus ebenso

---

[190] *Forschungen* II, 518.

[191] Z.B. ebd. 514 und 516.—Zu Meyers "Modernismus" vgl. Anm. 112.

[192] Zu Meyers Konzept der tiergestaltigen Götter s. *GdA* I/1⁵, 108 (vgl. auch sein Auseinandersetzung mit dem Totemismus, Anm. 135). Zeus Lykaios z.B. ist nach Meyer
ursprünglich als Wolf verehrt worden, Artemis Kalliste als Bärin (*Forschungen* I, 60 f.),
Hera als Kuh (daher die Kuhgestalt der Io, ebd. 69). Diese Auffassung entspricht der von
S. Wide, *Lakonische Kulte* (1893) sowie von Jane Harrison (Zeus Meilichios ursprünglich
als Schlange usw.: *Prolegomena* ..., wie Anm. 134). Später hält sich Meyer mit solchen
Vermutungen zurück, rückt freilich nicht ab von der Meinung, die Heroen seien aus den
Beinamen der Götter entstanden, vgl. *GdA* III² (= *GdA* 5⁸), 384 f., n. 2 (s. auch Anm.
177), und verlegt die Tiergestalt der Götter (die er nach wie vor annimmt) in ein Entwick-
lungsstadium zwischen den als Naturmächte aufgefaßten Gottheiten und ihrer Ver-
menschlichung, vgl. *GdA* I/1⁵, 108–110.—S. auch Anm. 176.

[193] Weder für noch gegen eine solche Auffassung ist gegenwärtig ein Konsens unter
Religionshistorikern vorhanden. Von Prioritätsdiskussionen wird inzwischen (wie schon
bei J. Burckhardt, *Weltgeschichtliche Betrachtungen*) weitgehend Abstand genommen; stattdessen wird der Analyse von Simultaneität und Zusammenwirken des Götter- und
Heroenkults, der Mythen und der Riten größere Aufmerksamkeit geschenkt. Vgl. z.B.
W. Burkert, *Griechische Religion der archaischen und klassischen Epoche*, Stutt-
gart/Berlin/Köln/Mainz 1977; P. Vidal-Naquet, *Le chasseur noir. Formes de pensée et formes
de société dans le monde grec*, Paris 1981; F. Graf, *Nordionische Kulte. Religionsgeschichtliche
und epigraphische Untersuchungen zu den Kulten von Chios, Erythrai, Klazomenai und Phokaia*
(= *Bibliotheca Helvetica Romana 21*), Rom 1985.

wie die Mythologie, dürfen die Götter nicht anders als die Heroen kein
Recht auf überhistorische Sanktionierung beanspruchen. Nur historisch
partikular, nicht universalgeschichtlich, braucht den Religionsetappen so
allenfalls ein vorübergehender Wert zugebilligt werden, auf dem Wege
zum Geschichtsziel, der Abschaffung der Religion.

Was sich hier schließlich zeigt, mag überraschen: daß nämlich vor
den Augen des Universalhistorikers die Spezifitäten der Geschichte ins
letztlich Überflüssige verrinnen. Meyer hat einmal bemerkt, ''der Satz
credo quia absurdum trifft in der Tat das innerste Wesen der religiösen
Lehre.''[194] In ähnlich unstimmiger und metaphysisch wirkender Weise
freilich beschwört er selbst den Glauben an den Ursprung der Menschheit
aus dem Staat. Hat sich Meyer dabei ins für ihn modellhafte Denken der
alten Griechen, in die davon inspirierte Verehrung der Phantasie und der
Macht, der Analogie und des Logos, so sehr verstrickt, daß ihm die
kritische Distanz zu Geschichte und Geschichtsschreibung[195] abhanden
kam? Die Anstrengungen, die Meyer unternahm, um seine zyklische
Geschichtsauffassung mit dem Vernunftglauben der Aufklärung in Einklang zu bringen, um die Befreiung von der Religion als fortschrittliches
Geschichtsziel zu begründen und als Rezept dafür die Staatsverherr-
lichung anzubieten, ergeben ein atemberaubendes Schauspiel. Aber erweist sich der auf Suggestion erpichte Historiker nicht sowohl der von ihm
verkündeten Objektivität des mythischen Denkens wie seinen ehrwürdi-
gen subjektiven Vertretern, den Zauberern und Geschichtenerzäh-
lern,[196] auf verblüffende Weise wahrhaft ebenbürtig?[197]

---

[194] *GdA* I/1[5], 159, mit Anspielung auf einen dem Tertullian zugeschriebenen Satz;
vgl. *De carne Christi*, 5.

[195] Meyer trennt nicht terminologisch streng zwischen beiden Begriffen und verwendet oft das Wort ''Geschichte'' im Sinne von ''Geschichtsschreibung''. Zum Wort-
gebrauch s. die Analyse von Löwith: ''Die Problematik dieses Verhältnisses ist zunächst
schon dadurch verdeckt, daß die meisten europäischen Sprachen, mit Ausnahme der
deutschen, sowohl das historische Erkunden wie das erkundete Geschehen mit ein und
demselben Wort (*historia, storia, histoire, history*) bezeichnen, so daß die Geschichte selbst,
mit der Historie von ihr, nur mitbezeichnet, aber nicht eigens benannt wird. Dieses Fehlen einer Unterscheidung könnte ein Mangel bestimmter Sprachen sein oder auch darauf
hinweisen, daß Historie und Geschichte in der Tat zusammengehören und deshalb durch
ein Wort bezeichnet werden können'' (''Die Dynamik der Geschichte und der Historismus,'' 1952, in: K. Löwith, *Sämtliche Schriften 2*, Stuttgart 1983, 297 f.). Vgl. zu diesem
Problem auch M. de Certeau, *L'écriture de l'histoire*, Paris 1975.

[196] Vgl. Meyers Überlegungen zur funktionellen Beziehung zwischen Gelehrten und
Zauberern: Anm. 157.

[197] Eine erste Version dieses Textes war während der Bad Homburger Tagung vom
November 1987 Gegenstand einer teilweise heftigen und affektiven Debatte. Über diese
Erfahrung hinaus konnte ich sachliche Einwände und Fragen zum Anlaß nehmen, die
Materie erneut zu durchdenken. Resultat ist die vorliegende veränderte und ergänzte
Textfassung. Für kritische Hinweise danke ich besonders Alexander Demandt und
Helmuth Schneider.

HELMUTH SCHNEIDER

DIE BÜCHER – MEYER KONTROVERSE

Die Kontroverse zwischen dem Nationalökonomen Karl Bücher und dem Althistoriker Eduard Meyer über das Problem der Einordnung der antiken Wirtschaft in die allgemeine Wirtschaftsgeschichte[1] übte einen nachhaltigen Einfluß auf die Entwicklung der internationalen Althistorie aus und trug insbesondere in England zur Herausbildung des methodischen Selbstverständnisses jener Historiker bei, die Wirtschaft und Gesellschaft der Antike analysierten. So bedeutende Gelehrte wie W.L. Westermann oder M.I. Rostovtzeff übernahmen weitgehend die von Eduard Meyer 1895 und 1898 in zwei Vorträgen formulierten Thesen und legten sie ihren eigenen Arbeiten zugrunde.[2] Gleichzeitig aber wurde Meyers am Modell der neuzeitlichen Wirtschaft orientierte Darstellung der ökonomischen Verhältnisse der Antike einer dezidierten Kritik unterzogen; bereits 1896 lehnte L.M. Hartmann in einer Rezension die Ansicht ab, ''daß sich die antike Wirtschaft von der modernen nicht wesentlich unterschieden hat.''[3] J. Hasebroek, der in mehreren Aufsätzen und Monographien ein von der modernen Sichtweise unabhängiges Bild der griechischen Wirtschaft zu entwerfen suchte, sprach von der ''Anfechtbarkeit der Eduard Meyer-Belochschen Einstellung'' und betonte, daß die Quellen ''jenes stolze Gebäude der modernisierenden Richtung in keiner Weise zu tragen vermögen.''[4]

---

[1] Die wichtigsten Texte sind ediert in: M.I. Finley, ed., The Bücher-Meyer Controversy, New York 1979. Eine zusammenfassende Darstellung bietet M. Mazza, Meyer vs Bücher: Il dibattito sull'economia antica nella storiografia tedesca tra otto e novecento, Società e storia 29, 1985, 507–546. Unberücksichtigt bleiben im folgenden die Arbeiten von Max Weber, dessen Beziehungen zu Meyer Gegenstand einer eigenen Studie in diesem Band sind.

[2] W.L. Westermann, RE Suppl. VI (1935), 894–1068, s.v. Sklaverei. Vgl. außerdem ders., Die wirtschaftliche Grundlage des Niederganges der antiken Kultur, in: K. Christ, Hg., Der Untergang des Römischen Reiches, Darmstadt 1970, 109–137, bes. 124 f. M. Rostovtzeff, The Social and Economic History of the Roman Empire, Oxford 1926. Vgl. ders., Der Niedergang der alten Welt und seine wirtschaftlichen Erklärungen, in: K. Christ, Hg., Untergang. 228–253.

[3] L.M. Hartmann, Rez. Ed. Meyer, Die wirtschaftliche Entwicklung des Altertums, Zeitschr. f. Sozial- und Wirtschaftsgeschichte IV 1896, 153–157. Zu Hartmann vgl. den Nachruf von W. Lenel, HZ131, 1925, 571 ff. und jetzt K. Christ, Römische Geschichte und deutsche Geschichtswissenschaft, München 1982, 70 mit weiteren Literaturangaben.

[4] J. Hasebroek, Griechische Wirtschafts- und Gesellschaftsgeschichte bis zur Perserzeit, Tübingen 1931, X. Vgl. auch E. Pack, Johannes Hasebroek und die Anfänge der Alten Geschichte in Köln, in: Geschichte in Köln 21, 1987, 5–42.

Welche Bedeutung die Bücher-Meyer Kontroverse in der nach 1950
erneut einsetzenden Diskussion über die antike Wirtschaft besessen hat,
zeigt allein schon die Tatsache, daß sowohl E. Will als auch M.M. Austin
in ihren programmatischen Ausführungen über die griechische Wirtschaft die Arbeiten von Bücher und Meyer eingehend behandelten[5] und
daß M.I. Finley 1979 in den USA eine umfangreiche Dokumentation der
Kontroverse herausgab. Bei Will ist ebenso wie bei Austin die Tendenz
erkennbar, die Argumentation von Bücher wiederum stärker zu beachten; daneben hat gerade auch die Rezeption der Arbeiten Hasebroeks in
England zu einem Verständnis der griechischen Wirtschaft geführt, das
dem Büchers durchaus nahesteht.[6] Die Vorträge Eduard Meyers wurden
nach 1950 indessen sehr unterschiedlich beurteilt; während K. Christ
ihnen den "Rang einer verbindlichen Synthese" zuerkannte,[7] äußerte
sich Finley äußerst kritisch über Meyers Studie der antiken Sklaverei:
"In sum, Meyer's lecture on ancient slavery is not only as close to nonsense as anything I can remember written by a historian of such eminence, but violates the basic canons of historical scholarship in general
and of German historical scholarship in particular."[8] Dieses Verdikt blieb
freilich nicht unwidersprochen; E. Badian und zuletzt auch M. Mazza
halten eine differenziertere Bewertung der Auffassungen Meyers für
notwendig.[9]

Austin beschränkte sich nicht darauf, die Thesen von Bücher und
Meyer kritisch zu referieren, sondern er stellte darüber hinaus fest, daß
bereits der Ansatz der Diskussion insofern verfehlt war, als das Problem
der antiken Wirtschaft auf die einfache Alternative 'primitiv oder modern' reduziert und das grundlegende Problem der Anwendung moderner ökonomischer Theorien in wirtschaftshistorischen Untersuchungen
nicht erörtert wurde.[10] Der unglückliche Verlauf der Kontroverse war
auch eine Folge der schroff ablehnenden Haltung Meyers Bücher gegen-

---

[5] E. Will, Trois quarts de siècle de recherches sur l'économie greque antique,
Annales ESC 9, 1954, 7–22. M.M. Austin—P. Vidal-Naquet, Economic and Social History of Ancient Greece: An Introduction, London 1977, 3 ff.

[6] M.I. Finley, Classical Greece, in: Second International Conference of Economic
History, Vol. I, Paris 1965, 11–35. P. Cartledge, 'Trade and Politics' revisited: Archaic
Greece, in: P. Garnsey, ed., Trade in Ancient Economy, London 1983, 1–15.

[7] K. Christ, Von Gibbon zu Rostovtzeff, Darmstadt 1972, 293. Vgl. außerdem
J. Vogt, Die antike Sklaverei als Forschungsproblem von Humboldt bis heute, in: ders.,
Sklaverei und Humanität, Wiesbaden 1965, 97–111, bes. 103: "Eduard Meyer hat um
dieselbe Zeit in zwei großartigen Entwürfen der antiken Wirtschaftsgeschichte den Weg
gewiesen."

[8] M.I. Finley, Ancient Slavery and Modern Ideology, London 1980, 44–49.

[9] E. Badian, The Bitter History of Slave History, New York Review of Books, 22.
Oktober 1981. M. Mazza, aaO 542.

[10] M.M. Austin, aaO 5.

über, die Mazza mit der Situation der deutschen Geschichtswissenschaft in der Zeit zwischen 1890 und 1900 zu erklären versucht.[11] Die Fragestellung Mazzas scheint geeignet zu sein, die Position Meyers in der Kontroverse präziser als bislang zu erfassen. In den folgenden Überlegungen sollen daher nach einer kurzen Skizze der Theorie Büchers (I) zunächst die wissenschaftshistorischen Voraussetzungen der beiden Vorträge Meyers untersucht werden, wobei vier Problemkomplexe zu berücksichtigen sind: die Methodendiskussion der Historiker, die Stellung der Alten Geschichte innerhalb der Geschichtswissenschaften, die Frage einer modernisierenden Sicht der Antike und schließlich die Erforschung der antiken Wirtschaft vor Eduard Meyer (II); anschließend werden die Auffassungen Meyers systematisch dargestellt (III), während die Rezension Hartmanns und die Replik Büchers Thema des letzten Abschnittes (IV) sind.

I

Die von dem Leipziger Nationalökonomen Karl Bücher (1847 – 1930) in der Schrift 'Die Entstehung der Volkswirtschaft' (1893) vorgelegte Theorie der wirtschaftlichen Entwicklung war keineswegs originell, sondern stand in einer langen Tradition volkswirtschaftlicher Theoriebildung in Deutschland. In dem Augenblick, in dem das Werk von Adam Smith an den deutschen Universitäten rezipiert wurde, setzten auch die Bemühungen ein, die Abfolge verschiedener Wirtschaftssysteme theoretisch zu erfassen; die deutschen Ökonomen orientierten sich dabei zunächst am Vorbild des 'Wealth of Nations' und postulierten mehrere, einander ablösende gesellschaftliche Zustände, die durch die vorherrschende Subsistenzweise charakterisiert wurden (Hirten, Ackerbauern, Gewerbegesellschaft); später legte man solchen Stufentheorien andere ökonomische Kategorien zugrunde; so sprach B. Hildebrand von den Stadien der Natural-, Geld- und Kreditwirtschaft (1864), während bei Schmoller die Distribution der Güter im Zentrum steht und zwischen Haus-, Dorf-, Stadt-, Territorial- und Staatswirtschaft unterschieden wird.[12]

Die Aufstellung von Wirtschaftsstufen sah Bücher als ''unentbehrliches methodisches Hilfsmittel'' an, das dazu beitragen sollte, die konzeptionellen Schwächen der älteren Volkswirtschaftslehre zu überwinden; vor allem kritisierte Bücher, daß die historische Schule der Nationalökonomie ''fast unbesehen die gewohnten, von den Erscheinungen der modernen

---

[11] M. Mazza, aaO 539 ff.

[12] H. Winkel, Die deutsche Nationalökonomie im 19. Jahrhundert, Darmstadt 1977, 175 – 180. Zur Rezeption von Smith in Deutschland vgl. 7 ff.

*Volks*wirtschaft abstrahierten Kategorien auf die Vergangenheit übertragen, oder daß sie an den verkehrswirtschaftlichen Begriffen so lange her-
umgeknetet hat, bis sie wohl oder übel für alle Wirtschaftsepochen pas-
send erschienen."[13] Demgegenüber hat sich nach Meinung Büchers der
Wirtschaftshistoriker zunächst die Frage zu stellen, ob eine bestimmte
Wirtschaft der Vergangenheit überhaupt als Volkswirtschaft zu qualifi-
zieren ist: "Sind ihre Erscheinungen wesensgleich mit denjenigen unserer
heutigen Verkehrswirtschaft oder sind beide wesentlich voneinander
unterschieden?"[14] Die Einsicht in die Historizität der Volkswirtschaft,
die als "Produkt einer jahrtausendelangen historischen Entwicklung"
gesehen wird, führt schließlich zu der Überzeugung, daß die Menschheit
vor der Entstehung des modernen Staates "große Zeiträume hindurch
ohne Tauschverkehr oder unter Formen des Austauschs von Produkten
und Leistungen gewirtschaftet hat, die als volkswirtschaftliche nicht
bezeichnet werden können."[15]

Bei der Unterteilung der wirtschaftlichen Entwicklung in verschiedene
Stufen hält Bücher den Gesichtspunkt des Verhältnisses von Produktion
und Konsumtion für maßgeblich und gelangt zu den drei Stufen der
geschlossenen Hauswirtschaft, der Stadtwirtschaft und der Volkswirtschaft, die als System der reinen Eigenproduktion, der Kundenproduktion und der Warenproduktion gekennzeichnet werden;[16] zu seiner
Methode bemerkt Bücher, daß die theoretische Analyse der Wirtschaftsstufen darauf abziele, diese "in ihrer typischen Reinheit zu erfassen."
Dieses Vorgehen, das ansatzweise die Webersche Methode der Bildung
von Idealtypen vorwegnimmt,[17] abstrahiert von jeglichen "Übergangs-
bildungen" und von solchen Erscheinungen, "die als Nachbleibsel frü-
herer oder Vorläufer späterer Zustände in eine Periode hineinragen und
in ihr etwa historisch nachgewiesen werden können."[18]

In dem Kapitel über die Hauswirtschaft werden die allgemeinen Merkmale dieser Wirtschaftsstufe von Bücher klar herausgearbeitet: Das Haus
bildet den Rahmen für Produktion und Konsumtion, wobei die Güter-
erzeugung sich am Bedarf der Hausangehörigen orientiert. Die Erwerbs-
wirtschaft ist demnach mit der Produktion für die Bedarfsdeckung des
Haushaltes gleichzusetzen, Tauschgeschäfte sind "ursprünglich ganz

---

[13] K. Bücher, Die Entstehung der Volkswirtschaft, in: M.I. Finley, ed., The Bücher-
Meyer Controversy, New York 1979, 87.

[14] Ebd., 86.

[15] Ebd., 90 f.

[16] Ebd., 91.

[17] Ebd., 91. Vgl. dazu M. Weber, Gesammelte Aufsätze zur Sozial- und Wirtschaftsgeschichte, Tübingen 1924, 1–288, besonders 7.

[18] Bücher, aaO 91 f.

unbekannt.''[19] Die Arbeitsgemeinschaft ist unter diesen Bedingungen
wichtiger als die Arbeitsteilung; die vorherrschende soziale Organisa-
tionsform dieser Wirtschaftsstufe ist der Familienverband.[20]

Bücher entwirft nicht nur ein theoretisches Modell der geschlossenen
Hauswirtschaft, sondern er ordnet diese Wirtschaftsstufe gleichzeitig in
den Ablauf der allgemeinen Geschichte ein und identifiziert sie mit den
Epochen der Antike und des frühen Mittelalters.[21] In den folgenden Ausführungen zur griechischen und römischen Wirtschaft übernimmt
Bücher die Anschauungen von Johann Karl Rodbertus (1805 – 1875), der
den Begriff der Oikenwirtschaft (1864) geprägt hatte. Der Oikos, das
Haus, ist die Wohnstätte und darüber hinaus ''die gemeinsam wirt-
schaftende Menschengruppe.'' Als spezifisches Charakteristikum des
antiken Hauses wird der Besitz von Sklaven angeführt: ''In der *patria
potestas* ist die eheherrliche und väterliche Gewalt mit dem Herrenrecht
des Sklavenbesitzers begrifflich verschmolzen.''[22] Am Beispiel reicher
römischer Familien der frühen Kaiserzeit versucht Bücher nachzuweisen,
daß in der Antike die Selbstversorgung des Hauses als die grundlegende
wirtschaftliche Aktivität anzusehen ist; der Größe der einzelnen
Haushalte entspricht dabei die Differenzierung der Berufe, die die
Sklaven ausübten.[23] Auf dieselbe Weise wirtschaftet auch der Staat, der
wichtige Verwaltungsaufgaben Sklaven überträgt und diese wiederum
durch Staatsdomänen oder Tribute versorgen läßt.[24]

Die Existenz von Handel und Austausch in der Antike wie auch im
frühen Mittelalter wird von Bücher keineswegs geleugnet; dieser Handel,
der etwa durch eine ungleiche natürliche Ausstattung verschiedener
Regionen notwendig wurde, hat nach Bücher allerdings ''die geschlossene Hauswirtschaft nur an der Oberfläche'' berührt.[25] Die Funktion
des antiken Handels blieb insofern begrenzt, als ''Gegenstände des täglichen Bedarfs'' nicht regelmäßig ausgetauscht wurden. Allein für die
städtischen Bevölkerungszentren wird ein ''lebhafter Marktverkehr in

---

[19] Ebd., 92.

[20] Ebd., 94 ff.

[21] K. Bücher, Die Entstehung der Volkswirtschaft, Tübingen 1893, 15 f.: ''Die Periode der geschlossenen Hauswirtschaft reicht von den Anfängen der Kultur bis ins Mittelalter hinein (etwa bis zum Beginn des zweiten Jahrtausends unserer Zeitrechnung).''
Bücher hat diesen Satz in der 2. Auflage der Schrift gestrichen; vgl. dazu Ed. Meyer, Die
wirtschaftliche Entwicklung des Altertums, in: ders.: *Kleine Schriften* I, Halle ²1924,
87 Anm.

[22] K. Bücher, Entstehung, in: Finley, ed., Bücher-Meyer Controversy 98 f.

[23] Bücher, aaO 99 ff. Prononciert erklärt Bücher: ''Aus der wirtschaftlichen Autonomie des sklavenbesitzenden Hauses erklärt sich die ganze soziale und ein guter Teil der
politischen Geschichte des alten Rom'' (99).

[24] Bücher, aaO 103.

[25] Ebd., 109 ff.

Lebensmitteln'' angenommen, wofür das klassische Altertum und das Afrika des 19. Jahrhunderts Beispiele bieten. Trotz solcher Einschränkungen hält Bücher aber an der zentralen Aussage seiner Theorie fest: ''Anstoß und Richtung empfängt jede Einzelwirtschaft nach wie vor durch den Eigenbedarf ihrer Angehörigen; was sie zur Befriedigung desselben selbst erzeugen kann, muß sie hervorbringen.''[26] Damit ist eine deutliche Differenz zwischen der Hauswirtschaft und der Volkswirtschaft gegeben: ''Nach dem Gesagten wird es klar geworden sein, daß bei dieser Art der Bedürfnisbefriedigung die wesentlichen wirtschaftlichen Erscheinungen sich verschieden gestalten müssen von den Erscheinungen der modernen Volkswirtschaft.''[27] Diesen Unterschied verdeutlicht Bücher abschließend am Beispiel des Kreditwesens: Er weist darauf hin, daß Darlehen in der Periode der Hauswirtschaft vor allem konsumtiven Zwecken dienten und ein Produktivkredit nicht existierte.[28] Die geschlossene Hauswirtschaft wurde durch die Entwicklung eines direkten Austausches in den mittelalterlichen Städten überwunden, die Eigenproduktion wurde durch die Kundenproduktion abgelöst. Ansätze dieser Stadtwirtschaft hat es nach Bücher bereits in der Antike gegeben; gerade dieser Hinweis zu Beginn des Kapitels über die Stadtwirtschaft zeigt, daß Bücher neben der Hauswirtschaft noch mit anderen Formen der Bedarfsdeckung in der Antike rechnet.[29]

Die Theorie Büchers entwirft ein durchaus differenziertes Bild der antiken Wirtschaft; obgleich Bücher den Akzent seiner Analyse auf die Eigenproduktion legt, leugnet er keineswegs die Existenz von Austausch, Handel, Geldverkehr und Darlehensvergabe in der griechischen und römischen Wirtschaft; allerdings wird der geringe Umfang des Handels betont, der normalerweise auf seltene Naturprodukte und Luxusgüter beschränkt blieb. Daneben müssen aber auch die eklatanten Schwächen der Theorie Büchers gesehen werden, die zu Mißverständnissen Anlaß geben konnten. Die für die Antike und das frühe Mittelalter geltende Feststellung, daß es ''im regelmäßigen Verlauf der Wirtschaft auch keine Waren, keinen Preis, keinen Güterumlauf, keine Einkommensverteilung und demgemäß keinen Arbeitslohn, keinen Unternehmergewinn, keinen Zins als besondere Einkommensarten'' gegeben habe, steht in offenem Widerspruch zu einer Vielzahl von bekannten Fakten der antiken Wirtschaftsgeschichte,[30] und die Einschränkung der Aussage durch die Wen-

---

[26] Ebd., 111.
[27] Ebd., 113 f.
[28] Ebd., 115.
[29] Ebd., 116.
[30] Ebd., 114. Vgl. auch die kritischen Bemerkungen von L.M. Hartmann, Zeitschr. f. Sozial- und Wirtschaftsgeschichte IV 1896, 153.

dung "im regelmäßigen Verlauf" ist wenig hilfreich, weil damit die in den größeren antiken Städten üblichen Formen des Wirtschaftens nicht in die Theorie integriert, sondern einfach zur Ausnahme erklärt werden. Ein weiterer Gesichtspunkt ist hier noch erwähnenswert: Bücher entwirft ein statisches Modell der antiken Wirtschaft; die Quellen zur antiken Wirtschaftsgeschichte zeigen demgegenüber, daß es schon in der archaischen Zeit eine wirtschaftliche Entwicklung gab, als deren wichtigste Merkmale ein Bevölkerungswachstum, Urbanisation und eine Ausweitung des Handels angesehen werden können. Damit aber war für Eduard Meyer die Möglichkeit gegeben, Einspruch gegen die Thesen Büchers zu erheben.

II

Die Schärfe der Meyerschen Polemik gegen Bücher ist nur vor dem Hintergrund der Diskussion über Methodik und Fragestellung der Geschichtswissenschaft in den Jahren vor 1895 verständlich. Unter den führenden deutschen Historikern bestand ein Konsens darüber, daß die vor allem von Ranke entwickelte Konzeption der Historie gegenüber neuen Tendenzen zu bewahren sei; positivistische, sozialhistorisch orientierte oder sozialwissenschaftlich beeinflußte Ansätze wurden entschieden abgelehnt. Über nonkonformistische Arbeiten wurden Verdikte gefällt, die die Funktion besaßen, sich der eigenen, konventionellen Auffassung um so sicherer zu vergewissern. Es ist symptomatisch hierfür, daß Droysen seine Rezension von H.T. Buckles 'History of civilisation in England' im Anhang des 'Grundrisses der Historik' (1868) wiederum abdrucken ließ.[31] Droysen wendet sich entschieden gegen eine Geschichtsauffassung, die der Entwicklung der Zivilisation eine zentrale Rolle zugesteht und die darüber hinaus Gesetze zu formulieren sucht.[32] Der thematischen Beschränkung historischer Forschung auf das Gebiet der politischen Geschichte wurde allerdings auch widersprochen; so verteidigte E. Gothein in der Antwort auf D. Schäfers Tübinger Antrittsrede, in der die politische Geschichte als "das eigentliche Arbeitsgebiet" der Historiker bezeichnet wurde, die Kulturgeschichte, die anders als eine auf die politischen Ereignisse reduzierte Historie auch Massenerscheinungen behandele und "die Ereignisse auf Kräfte" zurückführe.[33]
Die Diskussion zwischen Schäfer und Gothein war jedoch nur das Vor-

---

[31] J.G. Droysen, Historik, hg. v. R. Hübner, ND Darmstadt 1974, 386–405.
[32] Ebd., 388.402. Zu den Gesetzen vgl. 396.
[33] D. Schäfer, Das eigentliche Arbeitsgebiet der Geschichte, Jena 1888. E. Gothein, Die Aufgaben der Kulturgeschichte, Leipzig 1889. Vgl. dazu G.P. Gooch, Geschichte und Geschichtsschreiber im 19. Jahrhundert, Frankfurt 1964, 609 ff. G. Oestrich, Die Fachhistorie und die Anfänge der sozialgeschichtlichen Forschung in Deutschland, HZ 208, 1969, 320–363, besonders 326 ff.

spiel zu einer größeren Debatte, die sich an der 'Deutschen Geschichte' von Karl Lamprecht entzündete.[34] G. Iggers hat die Positionen von Lamprecht und seinen Gegnern in folgender Weise umrissen: "Der grundlegende Unterschied zwischen Lamprecht und der traditionellen Methode bestand in der Frage, ob der Historiker sich mehr der sozialen oder der politischen Geschichte widmen sollte."[35] In diese Richtung zielt bereits die Kritik G. v. Belows, der die ersten drei Bände der 'Deutschen Geschichte' 1893 in der HZ als wissenschaftlich unzuverlässig bezeichnete. Zur Disposition des Stoffes bemerkt v. Below: "Die politische Geschichte ist nicht genug berücksichtigt worden. Wir wollen aus einem Geschichtswerk nun einmal lernen, was geschehen ist, uns über die politischen Ereignisse und Personen unterrichten lassen."[36] Auf die theoretischen Überzeugungen Lamprechts und auf die Rezeption seines Werkes in der deutschen Öffentlichkeit geht v. Below kurz zu Beginn der Rezension ein: "Doch wie dem auch sei, die zahlreichen Anpreisungen liegen vor, und ihr Chorus wird sich ohne Zweifel noch verstärken, nachdem Lamprecht sich neuerlich als Anhänger der jetzt blühenden materialistischen und physiologischen Geschichtsbetrachtung bekannt hat, deren Genossen sich freuen werden, in einem vielbelobten Historiker einen feurig vorausschreitenden Bannerträger für ihre Tendenzen gewonnen zu haben."[37] Below sieht sich an dieser Stelle genötigt einzugestehen, daß die kulturhistorisch orientierte Sicht der Geschichte bei Lamprecht weithin positiv beurteilt wurde; gerade diese Zustimmung scheint ihn—und später andere etablierte Historiker—dazu veranlaßt zu haben, sich scharf von Lamprecht zu distanzieren.[38] Es gibt Anzeichen dafür, daß in dieser Zeit das Ansehen der konventionellen Geschichtswissenschaft eher gesunken ist. G. Oestreich weist in diesem Zusammenhang auf Äußerungen Bernheims hin, der in einem Brief vom 16.7.1893 über den Rückgang des Interesses "an der politischen Geschichte" klagte und folgende Festellung über das Geschichtsstudium traf: "Eine seltsame Ironie der 'Geschichte' ist es, daß gerade jetzt, da überall die Seminare und Biblio-

---

[34] Zum Lamprecht-Streit vgl. Gooch, aaO 611 ff. Oestreich, Fachhistorie 346 ff. G.G. Iggers, Deutsche Geschichtswissenschaft, München 1971, 256 ff. K.H. Metz, "Der Methodenstreit in der deutschen Geschichtswissenschaft (1891–99):" Bemerkungen zum sozialen Kontext wissenschaftlicher Auseinandersetzungen, Storia della Storiografia 6, 1984, 3–20. G.G. Iggers, The "Methodenstreit" in International Perspective. The Reorientation of Historical Studies at the Turn from the Nineteenth to the Twentieth Century, Storia della Storiografia 6, 1984, 21–32.

[35] Iggers, Deutsche Geschichtswissenschaft, 258.

[36] G. v. Below, Rez. K. Lamprecht, Deutsche Geschichte I–III, HZ 71, 1893, 465–498. Vgl. dazu Oestreich, Fachhistorie, 347.

[37] Below, aaO 466.

[38] So etwa M. Lenz, Rez. Lamprecht, Deutsche Geschichte Bd. V, HZ 77, 1896, 385–447.

theken nebst Hilfsmitteln in üppigster Weise ausgestattet sind, das Studium so stark abnimmt. Ist man vielleicht zu lange Staats-Historiker gewesen?''[39] Während Bernheim aber für eine Öffnung der Geschichtswissenschaft den ''neuen Strömungen'' gegenüber plädierte, blieb die Mehrzahl der Historiker bei ihrer ablehnenden Haltung, die sich im Lamprecht—Streit schließlich auch durchsetzte.[40]

In einer schwierigen Situation befand sich nach 1890 gerade auch die Alte Geschichte, denn die dominierende Stellung der Altertumswissenschaften im Bildungssystem wurde zunehmend in Frage gestellt. Bereits in den Jahren vor 1890 wurde mit großem Nachdruck eine Schulreform gefordert; zu den Zielen der Bildungsreformer gehörte vor allem die Gleichstellung des Realgymnasiums mit dem traditionellen Gymnasium. Die Schulkonferenz, die auf Initiative von Wilhelm II. im Dezember 1890 in Berlin zusammentrat, um Vorschläge zu einer Neuordnung des Schulwesens auszuarbeiten, war vornehmlich gegen die Betonung der klassischen Sprachen im humanistischen Gymnasium gerichtet.[41] Der Kaiser, der in seiner Jugend ein Gymnasium in Kassel besucht hatte und seitdem eine tiefgehende, schon früh öffentlich geäußerte Abneigung gegen die Übersetzungsübungen in das Lateinische besaß, kritisierte in seiner Rede vor den Konferenzteilnehmern die zu starke Berücksichtigung der klassischen Antike in den gymnasialen Curricula und forderte zugleich eine eher an den nationalen Interessen ausgerichtete Erziehung: ''Es fehlt vor allem an der nationalen Basis. Wir müssen als Grundlage das Deutsche nehmen; wir sollen junge Deutsche erziehen, und nicht junge Griechen und Römer. Wir müssen von der Basis abgehen, die jahrhundertelang bestanden hat, von der klösterlichen Erziehung des Mittelalters, wo das Lateinische maßgebend war und ein bißchen Griechisch dazu. Das ist nicht mehr maßgebend.''[42] Das Resultat der Beratungen war eine Neufassung der Lehrpläne (1891/92), in denen die Stundenzahl

---

[39] Zitiert nach Oestreich, Fachhistorie, 337 Anm. 69.
[40] Die generelle Ablehnung wirtschaftshistorischer Arbeiten kommt auch in einem Brief von M. Lenz vom 20.10.1890 zum Ausdruck: ''Seinen 4 Bänden Wirtschaftsgeschichte stand ich schon mißtrauisch gegenüber; ich kannte sie nicht, mißbilligte sie aber'' (zitiert nach Oestreich, Fachhistorie, 331 Anm. 44).
[41] Zur Bildungspolitik in der wilhelminischen Zeit vgl. allgemein H.-U. Wehler, Das Deutsche Kaiserreich 1871–1918, Göttingen 1973, 122 ff. F. Paulsen, Geschichte des gelehrten Unterrichts II, Berlin-Leipzig [3]1921, besonders 576 ff. M. Kraul, Das deutsche Gymnasium 1780–1980, Frankfurt 1984, 100 ff. J.C. Albisetti, Secondary School Reform in Imperial Germany, Princeton 1983. L. Canfora, Wilamowitz und die Schulreform: Das Griechische Lesebuch, in: W.M. Calder III, Hg., Wilamowitz nach 50 Jahren, Darmstadt 1985, 632–648. Zur Position des Realschulmännervereins vgl. etwa F. Paulsen, Das Realgymnasium und die humanistische Bildung, Berlin 1889. Wichtige Hinweise zu diesem Themenkomplex verdanke ich meinem Kollegen Dr. W. Neugebauer.
[42] Zitiert nach Paulsen, Geschichte II, 597.

der klassischen Sprachen erheblich gekürzt wurde; der lateinische Aufsatz
entfiel als Ausbildungsziel, und innerhalb des Geschichtsunterrichts reduzierte man den Anteil der Alten Geschichte zugunsten der Geschichte der
Neuzeit.[43] Die pädagogischen Reformen, insbesondere die gewünschte
Politisierung des Geschichtsunterrichts, stießen allerdings auf den Widerstand der süddeutschen Historiker und trugen damit zu der Initiative für
die Einberufung des ersten Historikertages im Jahre 1893 bei.[44] Das
Problem der Stellung der Alten Geschichte im Unterricht wurde im folgenden Jahr auf dem zweiten Historikertag in Leipzig diskutiert, die Versammlung verabschiedete eine Resolution, die die humanistische Bildung
insgesamt würdigt und sich gegen die neuen Lehrpläne ausspricht. Dabei
ist bemerkenswert, daß die Maßnahmen der Kultusbürokratie durchaus
als populär eingeschätzt wurden.[45]

Die Debatte über die Curricula fand auch unter den Althistorikern
Beachtung; der Erlanger Ordinarius Robert Pöhlmann, der ein ausgeprägtes Problembewußtsein besaß, erkannte, daß mit den Äußerungen
Wilhelms II. die Berechtigung einer intensiven Beschäftigung mit der
Antike im Rahmen des Schulunterrichts generell in Frage gestellt war. In
einem bereits kurz nach der Schulkonferenz publizierten Aufsatz[46] geht
Pöhlmann auf die Kritik des Kaisers ein: "Unter der Fülle von Klagen,
welche in unserer Zeit über die humanistischen Studien hereinstürmen,
ist wohl keine schwerwiegender, für die höchsten Interessen der Nation
bedeutungsvoller, als die, welche wir neuerdings aus kaiserlichem Munde
vernommen haben, daß die humanistischen Gymnasien die zu maßge-
bendem Einfluß auf das Volksleben berufenen Kreise bisher nicht in der
Weise vorgebildet hätten, wie es im Interesse der Erhaltung des modernen Staates und der Durchführung seiner großen sozialen Aufgaben zu
wünschen wäre."[47] Ausdrücklich wird der in der Rede Wilhelms formulierte politische Anspruch an die Schule akzeptiert: "... soviel wird
wohl zuzugeben sein, daß der allgemeine Gedanke, der das leitende
Motiv für die Schulreform von 1892 war, unbedingte Geltung beanspruchen darf."[48] Pöhlmann kommt es in seinen Ausführungen darauf

[43] Paulsen, Geschichte II, 600 ff. Kraul, Das deutsche Gymnasium, 104 ff.
[44] P. Schumann, Die deutschen Historikertage von 1893 bis 1937, Diss. Marburg
1974, 36 ff.
[45] Ebd., 39 ff.
[46] R. v. Pöhlmann, Das klassische Altertum in seiner Bedeutung für die politische Erziehung des modernen Staatsbürgers, in: ders., Aus Altertum und Gegenwart, München
1895, 1–33. Zu Pöhlmann vgl. K. Christ, Von Gibbon zu Rostovtzeff, 201–247. Zur
Reaktion von Wilamowitz auf die neuen Lehrpläne vgl. Canfora, Wilamowitz und die
Schulreform, 637 ff.
[47] Pöhlmann, Aus Altertum und Gegenwart, 1.
[48] Ebd., 2.

an, den Vorwurf zu widerlegen, das Studium der Antike habe zur politischen Erziehung nichts beizutragen. Die Aktualität der Alten Geschichte wird am Beispiel der politischen Theorie des Aristoteles, an dem Problem des allgemeinen Stimmrechts und an der sozialen Frage verdeutlicht; Pöhlmann behauptet etwa, daß in der 'Politik' des Aristoteles dieselbe Auffassung über das Königtum zum Ausdruck gebracht wird wie in jenem preußischen Erlaß, in dem die Belehrung der Jugend "über die sozialpolitische Bedeutung der Monarchie als Verkörperung der ausgleichenden Gerechtigkeit" gefordert wird;[49] die "Betrachtung des antiken Massenelends" wiederum soll die Einsicht in die wirtschaftlichen und sozialen Ursachen von Revolutionen und folglich das Verständnis für Maßnahmen zugunsten der "leidenden Klassen" fördern.[50] Die Aktualisierung der Alten Geschichte war eine Antwort auf die Zweifel an dem Bildungswert der Antike; der Gegenwartsbezug der Historie entspringt bei Pöhlmann keineswegs einem progressiven politischen Bewußtsein, sondern dient vielmehr der Unterstützung des monarchischen Staates.

Für eine aktualisierende Darstellungsweise gab es in der deutschen Altertumswissenschaft durchaus Vorbilder. Das bedeutendste althistorische Werk, das eine modernistische Konzeption aufweist, ist ohne Zweifel Mommsens 'Römische Geschichte.' Es geht hier nicht allein um das Problem der Begrifflichkeit, wie Mommsen selbst 1854 in einem Brief an Henzen meinte: "es gilt doch vor allem, die Alten herabsteigen zu machen von dem phantastischen Kothurn, auf dem sie der Masse des Publikums erscheinen, sie in die reale Welt, wo gehaßt und geliebt, gesägt und gehämmert, phantasiert und geschwindelt wird, den Lesern zu versetzen—und darum mußte der Konsul ein Bürgermeister werden."[51] Für Mommsen war also die Aktualisierung der römischen Geschichte notwendig geworden, weil ein idealisiertes Bild der Antike nicht mehr akzeptiert werden konnte; die modernistische Begrifflichkeit sollte eine Wahrnehmung der realen Welt der Antike ermöglichen. Die Anpassung der historischen Darstellung an den intellektuellen Horizont der Leser ging tatsächlich aber weit über die Verwendung vertrauter Begriffe anstelle von Termini des römischen Staatsrechts hinaus. Da Mommsen glaubte, der Geschichtsschreiber habe "die Pflicht politischer Pädago-

---

[49] Ebd., 4.
[50] Ebd., 19 ff.
[51] Zu Mommsen vgl. A. Wucher, Theodor Mommsen—Geschichtsschreibung und Politik, Göttingen ²1968. A. Heuß, Theodor Mommsen und das 19. Jahrhundert, Kiel 1956. K. Christ, Von Gibbon zu Rostovtzeff, 84–118. Ders., Römische Geschichte und Wissenschaftsgeschichte III, Darmstadt 1983, 26–73. Ders.: Römische Geschichte und deutsche Geschichtswissenschaft, München 1982, 58 ff. Der Brief an Henzen ist zitiert nach K. Christ, Röm. Gesch. und Wissenschaftsgesch. III 45.

gik,''[52] hielt er es für legitim, seine politischen Überzeugungen in der
Darstellung der Entwicklung des römischen Staates ebenso wie in der
Beurteilung einzelner römischer Politiker explizit zum Ausdruck zu
bringen. Auf diese Weise wurde aber auch die Konzeption der 'Römischen
Geschichte' von modernen Strömungen politischen Denkens nachhaltig
beeinflußt: Die sozialen Unruhen und politischen Kämpfe in der späten
römischen Republik werden analog den inneren Konflikten europäischer
Staaten des 19. Jahrhunderts beschrieben, die römische Expansion in
Italien wird in Anlehnung an die Forderungen der Verfechter eines
deutschen Nationalstaates als Einigung ''des gesamten Stammes der
Italiker'' interpretiert.[53]

Gegen die modernistischen Tendenzen bei Mommsen wurden schon
kurz nach Erscheinen seines Buches gravierende Einwände erhoben;[54]
besonders negativ äußerte sich Bachofen in einer Reihe von Briefen an
den Züricher Philologen H. Meyer-Ochsner: ''Überhaupt handelt es sich
bei M. kaum um Rom und die Römer. Der Kern des Buches liegt in der
Durchführung der neuesten Zeitideen.''[55] Es existierte also durchaus
eine Sensibilität für die Problematik einer modernistischen Sicht der
antiken Geschichte. Dennoch gehörte Mommsens 'Römische Geschichte'
zu den erfolgreichsten Werken der deutschen Historiographie des 19.
Jahrhunderts; ihre Diktion übte auf die Historiker dieser Zeit bis hin zu
Pöhlmann, Beloch und Meyer einen großen Einfluß aus.[56]

Für die Entwicklung der klassischen Altertumswissenschaften in
Deutschland ist es nicht ohne Bedeutung gewesen, daß Mommsen in der
Römischen Geschichte die wirtschaftlichen und sozialen Verhältnisse
Roms ausführlich beschrieben hat; die wirtschaftshistorische Erforschung
der Antike begann zwar bereits mit August Boeckhs 'Die Staatshaushal-
tung der Athener' (Berlin 1817), aber erst Mommsen war es wirklich
gelungen, die Wirtschaftsgeschichte in die Darstellung der allgemeinen
Geschichte zu integrieren. In den folgenden Jahrzehnten setzte dann eine
intensive Erforschung der antiken Sozial- und Wirtschaftsgeschichte ein;
zu verschiedenen Themenkomplexen erschienen umfangreiche Mono-

---

[52] A. Wucher, Theodor Mommsen, in: H.-U. Wehler, Hg., Deutsche Historiker IV,
Göttingen 1972, 23.

[53] Th. Mommsen, Römische Geschichte, München 1976, 1, 22. Zum Problem des
modernistischen Geschichtsverständnisses bei Mommsen vgl. v.a. Wucher, Theodor
Mommsen 41 ff. und Christ, Röm. Gesch. u. Wissenschaftsgesch. III 45 f.

[54] Zur Resonanz der 'Römischen Geschichte' vgl. Wucher, Theodor Mommsen,
215 ff.

[55] J.J. Bachofen, Gesammelte Werke X, Basel-Stuttgart 1967, 262 (13.12.1862). Vgl.
außerdem 251 ff. 254 f. und Christ, Röm. Gesch. und deutsche Geschichtswiss. 75 ff.

[56] Zu Wilamowitz-Moellendorff vgl. U. Hölscher, Die Chance des Unbehagens,
Göttingen 1965, 17.

graphien, darunter 'Besitz und Erwerb im griechischen Altertum' von
A.B. Büchsenschütz (Halle 1869), H. Blümners handbuchartige Darstellung der antiken Technik 'Technologie und Terminologie der Gewerbe
und Künste bei Griechen und Römern' (4 Bde., 1875 – 1887) und schließlich die frühe Studie Pöhlmanns zur 'Übervölkerung der antiken Großstädte' (1884). Anschließend widmete sich Pöhlmann der Untersuchung
sozialer Bewegungen in Griechenland und Rom; die Ergebnisse seiner
Forschungen publizierte er in der zweibändigen 'Geschichte des antiken
Kommunismus und Sozialismus' (I 1893); der erste Band von Belochs
'Griechischer Geschichte' (1893) bietet ein längeres Kapitel zur Entwicklung der Wirtschaft in der archaischen Zeit. Beloch, der von einer
"Umwälzung im Wirtschaftsleben" spricht,[57] betont den teilweise
dramatischen ökonomischen Wandel in der Ägäis und überhaupt im
östlichen Mittelmeerraum. L.M. Hartmann schließlich, ein Schüler
Mommsens, behandelte 1894 in gedrängter Form die antike Sklaverei.[58]
Gleichzeitig begannen die Althistoriker auch, die Vorstellungen von
Sozialwissenschaftlern und sozialdemokratisch eingestellten Theoretikern
kritisch zu erörtern. So beschäftigte sich Pöhlmann in einem Aufsatz aus
dem Jahre 1894 mit den Thesen von Karl Kautsky, wobei er auch kurz
auf die Theorie eingeht, die Menschheit habe "in gesetzmäßiger Weise
bestimmte Stufen" durchlaufen. Für die Interpretation der Kritik, die
Eduard Meyer ein Jahr später auf dem Historikertag an dieser Auffassung übte, ist entscheidend, daß Pöhlmann die Stufentheorie politisch
einordnet und als Dogma der sozialistischen Wissenschaft ab-
qualifiziert.[59] Nach Pöhlmann konstruiert diese sozialistische Lehr-
meinung "für die Institution des Privateigentums eine Reihe von typischen Entwicklungsstadien ..., die mit den gleichfalls als notwendige
Durchgangsstadien der Völkergeschichte betrachteten Stufenfolgen der
volkswirtschaftlichen Produktion zusammenfallen sollen.''[60] Gegen eine
solche Konzeption wird eingewendet, alle Versuche, ''große geschichtliche Entwicklungen in ein enges Schema zu zwängen,'' könnten den Tat-

---

[57] K.J. Beloch, Griechische Geschichte I, 1893. Zur Wirtschaftsgeschichte bei
Mommsen vgl. Heuß, Theodor Mommsen 86.
[58] L.M. Hartmann, Zur Geschichte der antiken Sklaverei, Deutsche Zeitschrift f.
Geschichtswiss. 11, 1894, 1–17.
[59] R. Pöhlmann, Extreme bürgerlicher und sozialistischer Geschichtsschreibung, in:
ders., Aus Altertum und Gegenwart, 393. Kautsky, schreibt Pöhlmann, ''steht mit Marx
und Engels durchaus auf dem Boden jener Anschauungsweise, die—schon bei dem Kulturhistoriker Dikäarch, dem Schüler des Aristoteles, hervortretend und in neuerer Zeit
unter anderem durch Rousseau, Condorcet, List und besonders Morgan weitergebildet—
für die sozialistische Wissenschaft der Gegenwart zu einem geschichtlichen Dogma
geworden ist.''
[60] Pöhlmann, Aus Altertum und Gegenwart, 393.

sachen nicht gerecht werden, und die Theorie Morgans sei "wissenschaftlich ebenso wertlos . . . wie die seiner griechischen Vorgänger."[61]

Überblickt man die Entwicklung der Alten Geschichte in Deutschland
während der zweiten Hälfte des 19. Jahrhunderts, gewinnt man den Eindruck, daß die Althistoriker die Erforschung der antiken Sozial- und
Wirtschaftsgeschichte entschieden vorantrieben, dabei für unkonven-
tionelle Fragestellungen und Themen wie die Überbevölkerung der antiken Großstädte offen waren und gleichzeitig die Bereitschaft zeigten,
sozialwissenschaftliche Theorien—wenn auch sehr kritisch—zu diskutieren und einzelne Thesen selbst von Marx zu rezipieren, wie dies für
Pöhlmann belegt werden kann.[62] Einen uneingeschränkten Primat der
politischen Geschichte hat es in der klassischen Altertumswissenschaft vor
1895 nicht gegeben, die Einbeziehung der Sozial- und Wirtschaftsgeschichte in die historische Forschung wurde keineswegs als problematisch
empfunden. Zum Verhältnis von Staat und Gesellschaft bemerkt
Pöhlmann programmatisch in der Vorrede der 'Geschichte des antiken
Kommunismus und Sozialismus,' in Deutschland habe man "nach dem
epochemachenden Vorgang von Stein und Gneist längst gelernt, . . . die
Geschichte des Staates und seiner Verfassung auf der Geschichte der
Gesellschaft aufzubauen."[63] Aber gerade Pöhlmanns Hauptwerk, in
dem solche Begriffe wie Sozialismus und Kapitalismus auf die antiken
Verhältnisse übertragen werden, offenbart deutlich, daß vor 1895 auch in
Arbeiten zur antiken Sozial- und Wirtschaftsgeschichte modernistische
Tendenzen stark ausgeprägt waren.[64]

III

Eduard Meyer, der als erster Althistoriker auf einem Historikertag
sprach, hielt den Vortrag 'Die wirtschaftliche Entwicklung des Altertums'
am 20. April 1895 auf der dritten Versammlung deutscher Historiker in
Frankfurt; knapp drei Jahre später behandelte Meyer in Dresden die
antike Sklaverei, auf die er bereits im Anhang zu dem Frankfurter Referat
kurz eingegangen war.[65] In beiden Vorträgen, die thematisch eine Ein-

---

[61] Ebd., 394.

[62] Vgl. etwa K. Christ, Von Gibbon zu Rostovtzeff, 208 f.

[63] R. Pöhlmann, Geschichte des antiken Kommunismus und Sozialismus I, München
1893, V.

[64] Zu diesem Problemkomplex vgl. F. Oertel, Das Hauptproblem der 'Geschichte des
Sozialismus und der sozialen Frage' von R. v. Pöhlmann, in: ders., Kleine Schriften zur
Wirtschafts- und Sozialgeschichte des Altertums, Bonn 1975, 40 ff.

[65] Ed. Meyer, Die wirtschaftliche Entwicklung des Altertums, in: ders., Kleine
Schriften I, Halle ²1924, 81–168. Wieder abgedruckt in M.I. Finley, ed., The Bücher-
Meyer Controversy, New York 1979. Die Sklaverei im Altertum in: ders., Kleine
Schriften I, 171–212.

heit bilden, analysiert Meyer zentrale Probleme der antiken Sozial- und Wirtschaftsgeschichte; darüber hinaus nimmt er zu grundlegenden methodischen und theoretischen Fragen der Althistorie Stellung, wobei sich zahlreiche Wiederholungen ergeben, die es rechtfertigen, beide Texte im folgenden gemeinsam zu untersuchen.

Zu Beginn der Frankfurter Versammlung 1895 wurde noch einmal deutlich, daß die Althistoriker ihre eigene Position innerhalb der Geschichtswissenschaft als wenig befriedigend einschätzten. Wie aus Äußerungen von Julius Kaerst hervorgeht, glaubte man allgemein, die Althistoriker stünden "auf einem verlorenen Posten." Kaerst verlangte deswegen eine stärkere Beachtung der Beziehungen zwischen Altertum und allgemeiner Geschichte und führte exemplarisch Niebuhr und Ranke als Historiker an, die von der alten Geschichte ausgegangen oder zu ihr zurückgekehrt seien.[66] Unter diesen Bedingungen hatte Meyer sich bei der Wahl seines Themas von dem Wunsch leiten lassen, "einen Gegenstand möglichst universeller Art zu besprechen, bei dem die Bedeutung klar hervortreten könnte, die auch für unsere Gegenwart noch eine richtige Erkenntnis der Probleme besitzt, welche die alte Geschichte bewegen."[67] Außerdem weist Meyer darauf hin, daß seiner Meinung nach die vorherrschenden Anschauungen über die antike Wirtschaft falsch seien; er nimmt die kurz zuvor publizierte Schrift Karl Büchers über die Entstehung der Volkswirtschaft zum Anlaß, um "ein Bild des wirklichen Verlaufs der wirtschaftlichen Entwicklung des Altertums zu geben."[68] Dabei geht es Meyer um ein richtiges "Verständnis nicht nur des Altertums, sondern der weltgeschichtlichen Entwicklung überhaupt."[69] Auf diese Weise erhält der althistorische Diskurs wiederum Relevanz für das moderne Geschichtsbewußtsein. Das Bestreben, der Althistorie innerhalb der Geschichtswissenschaft erneut Gewicht zu verleihen, wird auch in der Schlußbemerkung des Vortrags deutlich, in der Meyer den Untergang des Altertums als "vielleicht das interessanteste und wichtigste Problem der Weltgeschichte" bezeichnet.[70]

Der Gegenwartsbezug der Althistorie wird in dem Referat über die antike Sklaverei noch deutlicher herausgearbeitet; Meyer stellt zunächst fest, die These Büchers, eine Volkswirtschaft habe in der Antike nicht existiert, lasse nur noch ein rein historisches Interesse an der antiken Wirtschaftsgeschichte zu. Nimmt man wie Bücher eine grundlegende

---

[66] Schumann, Historikertage, 190.
[67] Meyer, Wirtschaftl. Entwicklung, 81.
[68] Ebd., 89.
[69] Ebd., 81. Vgl. auch 89.
[70] Ebd., 160. Zur Krise der römischen Republik vgl. 142: "das alles sind Vorgänge, die ... noch für die Gegenwart eine tiefgreifende Bedeutung haben."

Differenz zwischen Altertum und Moderne an, kann man nach Meinung
Meyers aus der wirtschaftlichen Entwicklung des Altertums nichts mehr
lernen.[71] Da Meyer aber glaubt, daß in der Antike ''dieselben Einflüsse
und Gegensätze maßgebend gewesen sind, welche auch die moderne Entwicklung beherrschen,''[72] ist es für ihn möglich, direkte Bezüge
zwischen antiken und modernen Verhältnissen herzustellen. So wird die
Frage aufgeworfen, ob im Deutschen Reich nicht ebenso wie in den
antiken Großstädten ein erwerbsloses Hungerproletariat entstehen
könnte, wenn die Industrie ihre auswärtigen Absatzmärkte verlöre,[73]
und die Verdrängung der italischen Bauern durch Sklaven in Etrurien
während des 2. Jahrhunderts v. Chr. wird mit der Situation in der Lausitz
oder in Sachsen verglichen, wo viele deutsche Kleinbauern sich gezwungen sahen, ihr Land aufzugeben, während gleichzeitig ''gewaltige Scha-
ren polnischer Arbeiter'' auf den großen Gütern eingesetzt wurden.[74]
Meyer verzichtet zwar darauf, konkrete Maßnahmen zu empfehlen, aber
aus seinen Bemerkungen über die strukturelle Ähnlichkeit antiker und
moderner Verhältnisse konnten leicht politische Schlußfolgerungen gezogen werden.[75] Nur zu der Frage der Sklaverei in den deutschen Kolonien
hat Meyer offen seine Meinung geäußert; nach dem Hinweis darauf, daß
in den Kolonien ''die bestehenden Sklavereiverhältnisse . . . als rechtlich
bindend'' anerkannt werden, erklärt er, ''es würde wirtschaftlich ganz
verkehrt sein, wenn wir dort zur Zeit schon weiter, zur völligen Auf-
hebung der Sklaverei, vorschreiten wollten.''[76]

---

[71] Meyer, Sklaverei 175. Die hier von Meyer kritisierte Auffassung wurde kurz vor
dem Dresdner Vortrag explizit von Max Weber in der Rede 'Die sozialen Gründe des
Untergangs der antiken Kultur' (1896) vertreten: ''Es kommt dem Eindruck, den der
Erzähler macht, zugute, wenn sein Publikum die Empfindung hat: de te narratur fabula,
und wenn er mit einem dicite moniti! schließen kann. In dieser günstigen Lage befindet
sich die folgende Erörterung *nicht*. Für unsere heutigen sozialen Probleme haben wir aus
der Geschichte des Altertums wenig oder nichts zu lernen. . . . Unsere Probleme sind völlig anderer Art. Nur ein *historisches* Interesse besitzt das Schauspiel, das wir betrachten,
allerdings eines der eigenartigsten, das die Geschichte kennt: die innere Selbstauflösung
einer alten Kultur.'' Vgl. M. Weber, Gesammelte Aufsätze zur Sozial- und Wirtschaftsgeschichte, Tübingen 1924, 291.
[72] Meyer, Sklaverei 175.
[73] Ebd., 201.
[74] Meyer, Sklaverei 207 f. Auch an dieser Stelle wird betont, daß im 19. Jahrhundert
eine Arbeitslosigkeit großen Umfangs nur durch die Existenz einer für den Export
produzierenden Industrie verhindert wurde. Zur Frage der polnischen Landarbeiter
in dem deutschen Osten hatte sich seit 1892 wiederholt M. Weber geäußert. Vgl.
W. Mommsen, Max Weber, Gesellschaft, Politik und Geschichte, Frankfurt 1974, 24.
D. Käsler, Einführung in das Studium Max Webers, München 1979, 62 f.
[75] Später gab Meyer diese Zurückhaltung auf; zur Agrarfrage äußerte er sich in: Die
Heimstättenfrage im Lichte der Geschichte, 1924.
[76] Meyer, Sklaverei 178. Zur ''Antisklavereibewegung'' besaß Meyer ein eher distan-
ziertes Verhältnis; er wirft ihr vor, daß sie weder die antike noch die moderne Sklaverei
''richtig zu beurteilen vermag.'' Vgl. aaO 211.

Meyers Ablehnung der sozialwissenschaftlichen Auffassungen zur antiken Sozial- und Wirtschaftsgeschichte war nicht nur fachwissenschaftlich begründet, sondern auch geschichtsphilosophisch motiviert. Die Argumentation in beiden Vorträgen richtet sich gegen die Annahme eines universellen Fortschritts, gegen den "Wahnglauben, ... daß die Entwicklung der Geschichte der Mittelmeervölker kontinuierlich fortschreitend in aufsteigender Linie verlaufen sei."[77] Die Idee eines historischen Fortschritts beruht nach Ansicht Meyers wesentlich auf der konventionellen Einteilung der Geschichte in die drei Epochen Altertum, Mittelalter und Neuzeit: "Da man im Mittelalter ganz primitive Zustände findet, glaubt man für das Altertum wohl oder übel noch primitivere postulieren zu müssen."[78] Dieser These gegenüber insistiert Meyer darauf, "daß die Entwicklung der Mittelmeervölker bis jetzt in zwei parallelen Perioden verlaufen ist, daß mit dem Untergang des Altertums die Entwicklung von neuem anhebt, daß sie wieder zurückkehrt zu primitiven Zuständen, die sie einmal schon längst überwunden hatte."[79] Das Ende der Antike wurde weniger durch eine Zerstörung von außen als vielmehr "durch die innere Zersetzung einer völlig durchgebildeten, ihrem Wesen nach durchaus modernen Kultur" verursacht.[80] Da das Imperium Romanum in der Spätantike zur Bindung der auf dem Großgrundbesitz arbeitenden Pachtbauern an die Scholle und zur Naturalwirtschaft überging und somit zu Verhältnissen zurückkehrte, die bereits im frühen Griechenland bestanden, kann Meyer am Schluß seines Vortrages von einem "Kreislauf" der antiken Entwicklung sprechen.[81]

Voraussetzung für eine solche Periodisierung ist die bereits in der 'Geschichte des Altertums' formulierte Auffassung, die homerische Zeit sei als das griechische Mittelalter anzusehen; diese Epoche wird charakterisiert als eine "Zeit der Adelsherrschaft, des Ritterkampfs und des Heldengesangs, wo der Grundbesitz mit Viehzucht und Ackerbau zur vollen Entwicklung gelangt ist, wo die Form des Stadtstaats sich herausbildet, die von da an der typische Träger der antiken Kultur geblieben

---

[77] Meyer, Wirtschaftl. Entwicklung 88. Vgl. Sklaverei 173.

[78] Ebd., 89. Vgl. auch Sklaverei 173.

[79] Meyer, Wirtschaftl. Entwicklung 89. Vgl. die fast gleichlautenden Aussagen bei Meyer, Sklaverei 188. Hier gilt die Feststellung nicht mehr nur für den Mittelmeerraum.

[80] Meyer, Wirtschaftl. Entwicklung 89. 145. Sklaverei 175.

[81] Meyer, Wirtschaftl. Entwicklung 159 f. Vgl. Sklaverei 212. Die These vom "Kreislauf der antiken Kulturentwicklung" wurde von M. Weber rezipiert; vgl. Weber, Soziale Gründe, aaO 291. Diese hier noch vage formulierten Anschauungen hat Meyer später in Anlehnung an Ibn Chaldun zu einer Theorie der Kulturentwicklung ausgearbeitet; der Kreislauf "in den äußeren und inneren Schicksalen der Völker" wird von Meyer in den Elementen der Anthropologie (GdA 1, 6. Aufl. Stuttgart 1953, 82 ff.) auf das in jeder Kultur vorhandene "zersetzende Element" zurückgeführt.

ist.''[82] Die folgende Beschreibung der homerischen Gesellschaft orientiert sich dementsprechend eher an der mittelalterlichen Sozialstruktur als an den Aussagen der Epen Homers: ''Auf der einen Seite stehen die großen adligen Grundherren, die von der Arbeit ihrer Untergebenen leben und diese dafür beschützen, auf der andern eine zahlreiche, teils hörige, teils zwar freie, aber politisch ganz abhängige Bevölkerung von Kleinbauern, Pächtern, Tagelöhnern und Bettlern.''[83] In dem Dresdner Vortrag von 1898 präzisiert Meyer dann seine Thesen; er behauptet, im archaischen Griechenland hätten dieselben sozialen Verhältnisse wie im europäischen Mittelalter bestanden: ''Man sieht, es sind durchaus die Zustände des christlich-germanischen Mittelalters, die wir hier antreffen: eine scharfe Scheidung erblicher Stände, eine herrschende Stellung des grundbesitzenden Kriegeradels, eine stets zunehmende Abhängigkeit der Bauernschaft, von den mildesten Formen der Hörigkeit oder Untertänigkeit bis zu vollster Leibeigenschaft, ein zwar freies aber wenig geachtetes und entwickeltes Handwerk.''[84] Hieraus wird gefolgert, daß die Hörigkeit nicht nur ein Resultat der sozialen Entwicklung der Antike und der Sklavenwirtschaft gewesen ist, sondern bereits zu Beginn der Antike existierte und der klassischen Zeit vorausging.[85] Wenn aber die homerische Zeit dem Mittelalter entspricht, ist die klassische Epoche der Neuzeit gleichzusetzen; sozialhistorisch bedeutet dies, daß die Sklaverei der klassischen Epoche '''mit der freien Arbeit der Neuzeit auf gleicher Linie'' steht und ''aus denselben Momenten erwachsen'' ist.[86]

Diese Periodisierung der Geschichte ist für Meyers Darstellung der Wirtschaft des Altertums keineswegs bedeutungslos; mehrfach betont Meyer in der Rede auf dem Frankfurter Historikertag die Gleichartigkeit der wirtschaftlichen Entwicklung im archaischen und klassischen Griechenland einerseits und in der frühen Neuzeit andererseits; es werden sogar direkte Parallelen zwischen einzelnen Phasen beider Epochen kon-

---

[82] Meyer, Wirtschaftl. Entwicklung 99. Vgl. zum Begriff des griechischen Mittelalters auch Meyer, Geschichte des Altertums, 2. Bd. Stuttgart 1893, 291: ''Die Zeit, welche jetzt beginnt, bedarf eines zusammenfassenden Namens, der sie von der mykenischen Zeit wie von der folgenden, mit den Ständekämpfen beginnenden Epoche bestimmt scheidet; wir können sie mit einem der Geschichte der christlichen Völker entlehnten Ausdruck als das griechische Mittelalter bezeichnen.'' Vom ''hellenischen Mittelalter'' sprach auch R. Pöhlmann; vgl. Aus Altertum und Gegenwart 149 ff. Zur Kritik Belochs an der Verwendung des Ausdrucks 'griechisches Mittelalter' vgl. jetzt L. Polverini, Il carteggio Beloch-Meyer, in: K. Christ-A. Momigliano, Hg., L'Antichità nell'Ottocento in Italia e Germania, Bologna-Berlin 1988, 217.
[83] Meyer, Wirtschaftl. Entwicklung 101.
[84] Meyer, Sklaverei 187. Meyer hat seine Sicht der archaischen Zeit begründet in den Forschungen zur Alten Geschichte II, 1899, 512 ff.
[85] Meyer, Sklaverei 187 f.
[86] Ebd., 188. Vgl. außerdem 202.

statiert: "Das siebente und sechste Jahrhundert in der griechischen Geschichte entspricht in der Entwicklung der Neuzeit dem vierzehnten und
fünfzehnten Jahrhundert n. Chr.; das fünfte dem sechzehnten."[87] Folgerichtig wird der Hellenismus dann mit dem 17. und 18. Jahrhundert
verglichen,[88] und die Politik Karthagos ist nach Meyer ebenso wie die
"englische Politik des 18. und 19. Jahrhunderts" von ökonomischen Interessen bestimmt gewesen.[89] Der antiken Wirtschaft werden alle wichtigen Merkmale der Modernität beigelegt; dementsprechend häufig wird
das Attribut 'modern' verwendet, um bestimmte Erscheinungen des
antiken Wirtschaftslebens zu charakterisieren: So spricht Meyer von
den "modernen Verhältnissen" im spätarchaischen Athen oder vom
"modernen Charakter der antiken Sklaverei,"[90] und Xenophons Bemerkungen über die Arbeitsteilung werden mit den Worten kommentiert, diese Schilderung lasse sich "Wort für Wort . . . auf die Gegenwart,
auf die Verhältnisse . . . einer modernen Großstadt anwenden."[91] Die
Großstädte des Hellenismus, die an die Stelle der kleinen Landstädte
treten, werden als 'modern' bezeichnet und den Ackerbaustädten des
Mittelalters gegenübergestellt. Für Meyers Sicht der Antike ist gerade die
Beschreibung dieser hellenistischen Städte aufschlußreich: "Die neu-
gegründeten Städte werden systematisch angelegt und mit allem Komfort
der Neuzeit ausgestattet und bilden mit ihrer dichten Bevölkerung von Industriellen, Kaufleuten und Gewerbetreibenden das Zentrum für ein
großes Gebiet."[92] Resümierend stellt Meyer dann fest, daß der Hellenismus "in jeder Hinsicht nicht modern genug gedacht werden kann."[93]

Das modernistische Verständnis der antiken Wirtschaft wurde dadurch
begünstigt, daß die wirtschaftshistorische Forschung des 19. Jahrhunderts es versäumt hatte, eine hinreichend differenzierte Terminologie zu
entwickeln. Solche Begriffe wie 'Fabrik' oder 'Industrie' waren unscharf
und mehrdeutig;[94] sie konnten daher auch in Untersuchungen zur antiken Wirtschaftsgeschichte verwendet werden. Aber damit war weder bei

---

[87] Meyer, Wirtschaftl. Entwicklung 118 f.
[88] Ebd., 141.
[89] Ebd., 135.
[90] Ebd., 112. Vgl. auch Sklaverei 195. Zur Beurteilung der antiken Sklaverei vgl.
Sklaverei 211.
[91] Meyer, Wirtschaftl. Entwicklung 116.
[92] Ebd., 137.
[93] Ebd., 141. Gerade solche Bewertungen wurden in der Öffentlichkeit beachtet; vgl.
Schumann, Historikertage 59. Zur Modernität der Antike vgl. ferner Sklaverei 188: "die
Blütezeit des Altertums . . . ist . . . nach jeder Richtung eine moderne Zeit, in der die
Anschauungen herrschen, die wir als modern bezeichnen müssen."
[94] Vgl. D. Hilger, Fabrik, Fabrikant, in: Geschichtliche Grundbegriffe II, Stuttgart
1975, 229–252. L. Hölscher, Industrie, Gewerbe, Geschichtliche Grundbegriffe III,
Stuttgart 1982, 237–304.

Boeckh noch bei Büchsenschütz die Annahme verbunden, es habe im antiken Athen Betriebsformen gegeben, die unter dem Aspekt der Produktionstechnik mit den Fabriken der Industriellen Revolution verglichen werden könnten; Boeckh, der die Unterschiede zwischen antiker und neuzeitlicher Wirtschaft klar erkannt hat, weist in der 'Encyklopädie' nachdrücklich auf das Fehlen eines "complicirten Maschinenwesens" in der Antike und auf die "großartigen technischen Erfindungen der Neuzeit" hin.[95] Büchsenschütz definiert die antike Fabrik schließlich als einen Betrieb, der auf Sklavenarbeit beruht und dessen Erträge dem Besitzer zufließen, der selbst nicht als Handwerker tätig ist. Die Funktion des Besitzers beschränkt sich darauf, das Kapital für den Kauf der Sklaven sowie der Werkzeuge und des Arbeitsmaterials zur Verfügung zu stellen.[96]

Auch in Meyers wirtschaftshistorischen Arbeiten sind 'Fabrik' und 'Industrie' zentrale Begriffe, die zur Beschreibung der griechischen Wirtschaft von der Zeit der Kolonisation bis zum Hellenismus herangezogen werden. Die Modernität der Antike wird in dem Vortrag von 1895 darüber hinaus noch durch Begriffe wie Großverkehr, Großindustrie und Großkapital unterstrichen.[97] Neben dem Terminus Industrie erscheint eine Wendung wie "Industrialisierung der griechischen Welt,"[98] und eine Polis wie Megara wird als Industriestaat bezeichnet.[99] Erst 1898 reflektiert Meyer die von ihm verwendete Terminologie in zwei kurzen Abschnitten, in denen die Bedeutung von 'Fabrik' und 'Kapital' erläutert wird. Dabei wird deutlich, daß auch für Meyer eine Differenz zwischen Antike und Gegenwart besteht: "Gewiß, größere Maschinen hat das Altertum nicht gekannt, und die Riesenfabriken der Gegenwart sind ihm immer fremd geblieben." Dennoch hält Meyer am Begriff 'Fabrik' als Bezeichnung für die größeren Produktionsstätten der Antike fest; das entscheidende Kriterium ist für ihn dabei die Zahl der dort arbeitenden Sklaven; die Werkstatt des Demosthenes, in der 33 Sklaven Waffen produzierten, muß "auch nach dem Maßstab der Gegenwart" als Fabrik angesehen werden.[100] Trotz solcher Präzisierungen wird aber durch die

---

[95] A. Boeckh, Encyklopädie und Methodologie der philologischen Wissenschaften, Leipzig ²1886, 393.400.

[96] A.B. Büchsenschütz, Besitz und Erwerb im griechischen Altertum, Halle 1869, 193 f.

[97] Meyer, Wirtschaftl. Entwicklung 109, 127, 133, 154.

[98] Ebd., 116.

[99] Ebd., 117. An anderer Stelle spricht Meyer von "reinen Industriegebieten" (aaO 107) oder von "ausgeprägten Handels- und Industriestädten" (aaO 113).

[100] Meyer, Sklaverei 199. Zur Definition des Begriffs Kapital vgl. 205; als wesentliches Kennzeichen des Kapitals wird hier das "Bestreben der Geldmacht" genannt, ihr Vermögen durch den Kauf fremder Arbeitskraft "zu verwerten und zu vermehren."

von Meyer gewählte Begrifflichkeit eine strukturelle Übereinstimmung von antiker und neuzeitlicher Wirtschaft postuliert.

Der Diskussion von Büchers Thesen räumt Meyer in seinem Vortrag von 1895 nur wenig Platz ein; in der Einleitung werden die Auffassungen von Rodbertus und Bücher kurz skizziert, wobei die Festellung Büchers, es habe in Rom "keine produktiven Berufsstände, keine Bauern, keine Handwerker" gegeben, unter Hinweis auf die freien Bauern und Handwerker im klassischen Athen zurückgewiesen wird; die großen Haushalte der römischen Kaiserzeit wiederum läßt Meyer nicht als typisch gelten, sie werden vielmehr als singuläre Erscheinungen bewertet.[101] Immerhin ist bemerkenswert, daß Meyer an dieser Stelle Bücher konzedieren muß, die Selbstversorgung der bäuerlichen Familie im Prinzip richtig dargestellt zu haben. Der Einwand, die von Bücher zitierte Empfehlung Varros (I, 22), man solle nicht kaufen, was auf dem Gut hergestellt werden könne, habe "zu allen Zeiten im Altertum wie gegenwärtig für jede Bauernwirtschaft" gegolten, übersieht jedoch, daß die bäuerliche Wirtschaft in einer Industrienation des 19. Jahrhunderts eine wesentlich geringere ökonomische Bedeutung besitzt als im antiken Italien. Durchaus in Übereinstimmung mit der Theorie Büchers stellt Meyer fest, daß im homerischen Griechenland "die autonome Wirtschaft des Einzelhaushalts ... die maßgebende Lebensform" war,[102] aber er unternimmt keinen Versuch zu klären, ob der Oikos als Wirtschaftsform in den ländlichen Gebieten Griechenlands später fortexistierte und welche Rolle die Produktion für den Eigenbedarf in klassischer Zeit selbst in einer Polis wie Athen spielte.

Der folgende Überblick über die wirtschaftliche Entwicklung des Altertums reicht vom Alten Ägypten bis zum Untergang des Imperium Romanum. Den entscheidenden Fortschritt seiner eigenen Darstellung den älteren Arbeiten gegenüber sieht Meyer selbst darin, daß bislang "nirgends der Versuch einer historisch entwickelnden Betrachtung unternommen" worden ist, auf die es ihm gerade ankam.[103] Diese Einschätzung der Forschungslage ist insofern nicht überzeugend, als Büchsenschütz insgesamt zwar systematisch vorgegangen ist, die wirtschaftlichen Verän-

---

[101] Meyer, Wirtschaftl. Entwicklung 83 f. Die Kritik Meyers ist deswegen nicht gerechtfertigt, weil Bücher von Landwirten spricht, von Landbesitzern also, die für den Markt produzieren. Die Existenz einer kleinbäuerlichen, für den Eigenbedarf produzierenden Bevölkerung wird keineswegs geleugnet, wie aus den folgenden Bemerkungen hervorgeht: "Es gibt große und kleine Besitzer, Reiche und Arme. Drängt der Reiche den Armen aus dem Besitze des Grund und Bodens, so macht er ihn zum Proletarier." Vgl. Entstehung der Volkswirtschaft 99.

[102] Meyer, Wirtschaftl. Entwicklung 101.

[103] Ebd., 108 Anm.

derungen der archaischen und klassischen Zeit in den Kapiteln über
Gewerbe und Handel aber ausführlich behandelt hat.[104].

Die Ausführungen zur griechischen Wirtschaftsgeschichte lehnen sich
eng an entsprechende Passagen der 'Geschichte des Altertums' an und
wiederholen einfach ältere Auffassungen, ohne auf die Argumentation
Büchers einzugehen. Die homerische Zeit war nach Meyer von der Existenz der Einzelhaushalte adliger Familien geprägt. Daneben werden aber
bei Homer viele Handwerker erwähnt, die für die Gemeinde arbeiten;
mit Nachdruck weist Meyer darauf hin, daß der Seehandel dem jüngeren
Epos "bereits ganz geläufig" ist.[105] Mit der griechischen Kolonisation
setzte dann eine wirtschaftliche Entwicklung ein, die ihre Dynamik von
der Entstehung eines "ungeheuren Handelsgebiets" erhielt.[106] Die kommerzielle Beherrschung des Mittelmeerraumes hatte das Aufkommen
einer "für den Export arbeitenden Industrie" zur Folge.[107] Meyer illustriert dies an der Keramikproduktion, die es seiner Meinung nach ermöglicht, "die Konkurrenz der einzelnen Fabriken und die Wandlungen
der Handelsgeschichte" zu verfolgen. Nachdem Chalkis und Korinth
zunächst eine führende Position erworben hatten, eroberte im 6.
Jahrhundert dann Athen mit seinen Produkten alle wichtigen Absatzge-
biete, darunter auch Italien.[108] Im Gegenzug zu diesen Exporten wurden
Rohstoffe und Getreide eingeführt; gerade die "reinen Industriegebiete"
waren "auf überseeisches Korn" angewiesen.[109] Gleichzeitig gingen die
Griechen, die für die gewerbliche Produktion zusätzliche Arbeitskräfte
benötigten, zum Sklavenimport und zur Sklavenarbeit über.[110] Durch
den Aufstieg der Geldwirtschaft und des überregionalen Handels wurden
schließlich "die sozialen und ökonomischen Verhältnisse von Grund aus
umgestaltet."[111] Wesentliche Momente der daraus resultierenden sozialen Krise waren der Rückgang des Ertrags der Landwirtschaft[112] und die
Herausbildung eines neuen Standes "der städtischen Gewerbetreibenden." Die neuen sozialen Gruppen, die "Händler, Kaufleute, Matrosen
und ... freien Arbeiter" haben schließlich "vereint mit der Bauernschaft
... die Adelsherrschaft gestürzt und das Bürgertum an ihre Stelle
gesetzt."[113]

---

[104] Büchsenschütz, Besitz und Erwerb 316 ff. 356 ff.
[105] Meyer, Wirtschaftl. Entwicklung 101 ff. Vgl. GdA 2, 1893, 362 ff.
[106] Ebd., 105. Vgl. Sklaverei 188 f., wo die Entwicklung der archaischen Zeit ganz
ähnlich aufgefaßt wird, und außerdem GdA 2, 1893, 533 f.
[107] Meyer, Wirtschaftl. Entwicklung 105. Vgl. GdA 2, 1893, 547.
[108] Ebd., 106. Vgl. GdA 2, 1893, 548.
[109] Ebd., 107.
[110] Ebd., 108. Vgl. GdA 2, 1893, 549.
[111] Ebd., 109. Vgl. GdA 2, 1893, 549 ff.
[112] Ebd., 110. Vgl. GdA 2, 1893, 553.
[113] Ebd., 111. Vgl. Sklaverei 193. Wie stark Meyers Beschreibung der archaischen

Die wirtschaftliche Entwicklung der archaischen Zeit förderte nach Meyer den Aufstieg der Handels- und Industriestädte an den Küsten der Ägäis.[114] Zu diesen Städten gehörte schon früh Korinth,[115] später auch Athen, dessen Politik während des 5. Jahrhunderts "vollständig von den Handelsinteressen beherrscht" wurde.[116] Insgesamt gesehen kann Meyer von einer "Industrialisierung der griechischen Welt" und von einer "immer weiter fortschreitenden Arbeitsteilung" sprechen. Als treibendes Element dieser Entwicklung werden Handel, Export und die "Fabrikation für den Export" genannt.[117] Damit hatte Griechenland in klassischer Zeit jenes Niveau erreicht, das dem der frühen Neuzeit gleichkommt.[118]

Die Relevanz der Sklaverei für die griechische Wirtschaft darf nach Meyer nicht überschätzt werden, denn gerade in Athen haben auch viele freie Bürger im Handwerk gearbeitet.[119] Allerdings räumt Meyer ein, daß "die Arbeiter in der Großindustrie und in den Bergwerken ... meist Sklaven" waren;[120] dennoch ist anzunehmen, daß in Attika wesentlich mehr Bürger und Metoiken als Sklaven lebten.[121] Der Sklaverei wird deswegen eine "zersetzende Wirkung" zugeschrieben, weil die mit der Kapitalisierung der Landwirtschaft in die Städte gedrängte verarmte Landbevölkerung dort keine Arbeit finden konnte: "Dadurch entwickelt sich neben dem Großkapital ein immer stärker anwachsender Pauperismus."[122] Im Zeitalter des Hellenismus kam es schließlich zu einem "Rückgang des griechischen Mutterlandes," was im Fall von Athen auf die Verlagerung der Handelswege zurückgeführt wird.[123] Der neue Typus der Großstadt verdrängte in dieser Epoche die kleinen Land-

---

Gesellschaft von modernen Verhältnissen beeinflußt ist, zeigen besonders gut folgende Sätze in GdA 2, 1893, 555: "Sie alle bekämpfen das Adelsregiment. Die Landbevölkerung strebt nach Befreiung von dem unerträglichen ökonomischen Druck, die reich gewordenen Bürger nach Teilnahme am Regiment, die Nachkommen der Zugewanderten, welche an Zahl die Altbürger oft überragen mögen, nach Gleichberechtigung mit der erbgesessenen Bürgerschaft. Alle diese Elemente werden unter dem Namen des Demos zusammengefaßt wie zur Zeit der französischen Revolution unter dem des tiers état." Der Rekurs auf die Moderne als Erkenntnismodell verstellt den Blick für die Realität der Antike.
[114] Meyer, Wirtschaftl. Entwicklung 113.
[115] Ebd., 114. Zu Korinth vgl. jetzt die Analyse bei J.B. Salmon, Wealthy Corinth, Oxford 1984, bes. 157 f. Salmon spricht von "the overwhelming importance of agriculture in the Corinthian economy." Allein die Vernachlässigung des Agrarsektors macht es möglich, eine Stadt wie Korinth als Industriestadt zu bezeichnen.
[116] Ebd., 115. Vgl. Sklaverei 194.
[117] Meyer, Wirtschaftl. Entwicklung 116.
[118] Ebd., 118 f.
[119] Ebd., 121 ff.126.
[120] Ebd., 127.
[121] Ebd., 129.
[122] Ebd., 133.
[123] Ebd., 137.

städte,[124] der modernen Stadt dieser Zeit entspricht die hellenistische Monarchie, die "über alle Kräfte des modernen Lebens" frei verfügen konnte.[125]

Es folgen in dem Vortrag längere Ausführungen über das römische Kaiserreich, in denen aber weniger die wirtschaftliche Entwicklung als vielmehr der Niedergang der antiken Kultur thematisiert wird; als eine wesentliche Ursache des "Zersetzungsprozesses" wird die Tatsache angeführt, "daß auch auf politischem und militärischem Gebiet den Gebildeten die Führung entsinkt und auf die Massen übergeht."[126] Der schnell voranschreitende Verfall der Landwirtschaft, der zur Verödung ganzer Regionen führte,[127] hatte seine Ursachen in dem Anwachsen des Großkapitals: "Das Großkapital kauft den Grundbesitz auf und macht die Existenz eines kräftigen Bauernstandes unmöglich."[128] Mit dem "Ruin der Landbevölkerung" verloren aber auch die Städte ihre wirtschaftliche Basis. Der Wandel der ökonomischen Funktion der Städte wird von Meyer präzise erfaßt: "die Stadt, ursprünglich das Hauptförderungsmittel der Kultur und die Ursache einer gewaltigen Steigerung und Vermehrung des Wohlstandes, vernichtet schließlich Wohlstand und Kultur und zuletzt sich selbst." Die "Rückkehr zu den primitiven Lebensverhältnissen" bildet das Ende der antiken Kultur.[129]

Andere Akzente setzt der Vortrag über die Sklaverei insofern, als Meyer 1898 den sozialen und wirtschaftlichen Niedergang Roms auf die "Gewinnung der Weltherrschaft" in der Zeit der Republik zurückführt: Die Expansion hat den römischen Kleinbauern, "eben dem Stande," der die Weltherrschaft "errungen hatte, die Existenzbedingungen entzogen." Es kommt zu "einer furchtbaren und permanenten agrarischen Krisis," deren Nutznießer die Besitzer der großen Güter sind. "So ist es möglich gewesen, daß binnen wenigen Jahrzehnten in dem Hauptteil Italiens die freie Bauernschaft fast völlig vernichtet wurde, daß an ihre Stelle Latifundienwesen und Sklavenwirtschaft traten," die "in wenigen

---

[124] Ebd., 136.

[125] Ebd., 140.

[126] Ebd., 148. Vgl. A. Momigliano, Premesse per una discussione su Eduard Meyer, Riv. Stor. Ital. 93, 1981, 384–398, bes. 395. Erwähnenswert ist in diesem Zusammenhang auch die These Meyers, der Rückgang der Sklaverei sei auf das Ende jener "ununterbrochenen Kriege" zurückzuführen, "welche unter der Republik den Markt immer wieder mit neuem und billigem Menschenmaterial versorgten." Vgl. aaO 151. Von dieser Auffassung ist dann auch M. Weber in dem Vortrag 'Die sozialen Gründe des Untergangs der antiken Kultur' (1896) ausgegangen; vgl. aaO 299 ff. Zuvor war diese These schon von L.M. Hartmann, Zur Geschichte der antiken Sklaverei 8 f. formuliert worden.

[127] Meyer, Wirtschaftl. Entwicklung 152 ff.

[128] Ebd., 154 f.

[129] Ebd., 157 f.

Jahrzehnten ein blühendes Land nach dem andern verwüstet und entvölkert haben.'' Erst mit der Aufrichtung der Monarchie haben sich nach Meyer die Verhältnisse gebessert, die Situation der Sklaven "hat sich ständig gehoben.'' Schließlich beginnt die Sklaverei im 2. Jahrhundert zurückzugehen, "bis sie langsam und ohne Kampf abstirbt und als wirtschaftliche Institution bedeutungslos wird.'' Die Sklaverei wird aber nicht durch die freie Arbeit ersetzt, die vielmehr mit der Sklaverei zusammen zugrunde geht. An ihre Stelle tritt vielmehr der "Arbeitszwang in den erblich gewordenen Ständen . . . . Die Entwicklung kehrt auf den Punkt zurück, von dem sie ausgegangen war: die mittelalterliche Weltordnung tritt zum zweiten Male die Herrschaft an.''[130]

Meyers Darstellung der griechischen Wirtschaftsgeschichte folgt weitgehend den Thesen von Büchsenschütz, der die Entwicklung des griechischen Handels ausführlich beschrieben und dabei auch auf die von der Ausweitung des Handels ausgehenden Impulse auf die anderen Wirtschaftssektoren hingewiesen hat.[131] Büchsenschütz hat von einem "gewaltigen Umschwung in den Handelsverhältnissen Griechenlands''[132] während der nachhomerischen Zeit gesprochen und den Zusammenhang zwischen Kolonisation und Handel betont: "Der Einfluß dieser Colonien, welche den Bezug zahlreicher Naturprodukte aus den reichen Pontosländern und den Absatz griechischer Produkte und Industrieerzeugnisse an die dort wohnenden weniger civilisierten Völkerschaften in höchst gewinnbringender Weise sicher stellten, muß für die Entwicklung des ganzen griechischen Handels ein außerordentlicher gewesen sein.''[133] Auch die These, die Entstehung einer für den Export arbeitenden Industrie sei eng mit der Ausweitung des Handelsgebietes verbunden gewesen,[134] findet sich schon bei Büchsenschütz: "Mit der Entwicklung des Handels hielt die der Industrie gleichen Schritt, indem sie nicht allein durch die Erweiterung des Absatzes gesteigert wurde, sondern auch durch die in fremden Ländern gefundenen Vorbilder neue Anregungen empfing.''[135] Büchsenschütz hat außerdem den 'Fabriken' in Athen längere Ausführungen gewidmet; er nimmt an, daß solche 'Fabriken' "in den industriellen Städten sehr zahlreich'' waren und "für viele eine Quelle des Reich-

---

[130] Sklaverei 204 ff. Vgl. zur römischen Republik außerdem Wirtschaftl. Entwicklung 154 Anm. 3.
[131] Büchsenschütz, Besitz und Erwerb 356 ff. Aus GdA 2, 1893, 362 und 548 geht klar hervor, daß Meyer die Monographie von Büchsenschütz für die wirtschaftshistorischen Abschnitte von GdA benützt hat.
[132] Büchsenschütz, Besitz und Erwerb 366.
[133] Ebd., 376.
[134] Meyer, Wirtschaftl. Entwicklung 105.
[135] Büchsenschütz, Besitz und Erwerb 381.

tums'' darstellten;[136] weiterhin rechnet Büchsenschütz in Anlehnung an
einzelne Äußerungen von Xenophon und Platon mit einer ausgeprägten,
durch die Entwicklung des Gewerbes vorangetriebenen Arbeitsteilung im
städtischen Gewerbe.[137] Meyers Analyse der gewerblichen Produktion
gelangt Büchsenschütz gegenüber kaum zu neuen Einsichten.

Meyer hat aber nicht allein die Konzeption von Büchsenschütz übernommen, eine Vielzahl von einzelnen Fakten, auf die Meyer und später
auch Beloch[138] hinweisen, werden bereits in 'Besitz und Erwerb im griechischen Altertum' erwähnt, gleichgültig, ob es sich um die 'Fabriken'
einzelner Athener,[139] um die Textilproduktion von Megara[140] oder um
die Einfuhr von tausend Sklaven nach Phokis durch Mnason[141] handelt.
Neue Fakten oder Einsichten sind weder von Meyer noch von Beloch
in die Diskussion eingebracht worden; im Grunde argumentieren beide
nur mit dem von Büchsenschütz erarbeiteten Faktenmaterial, wobei sie
seine in vieler Hinsicht sehr differenzierten Überlegungen radikal verein-
fachen. So bleibt etwa die von Büchsenschütz vorgetragene Auffassung,
auf die gewerbliche Entwicklung hätten verschiedene Faktoren, darunter
das Fortbestehen einer weit verbreiteten Produktion für den Eigenbedarf
und die ''Mangelhaftigkeit der Transportmittel,''[142] hemmend eingewirkt, bei Meyer und Beloch bezeichnenderweise unbeachtet.

In auffallender Weise konzentriert sich Meyer in seinem Überblick
über die antike Wirtschaftsgeschichte auf den Handel und die Entwicklung der gewerblichen Produktion; die Landwirtschaft wird trotz ihrer
eminenten ökonomischen Bedeutung nicht näher untersucht.[143] Gerade
auch deswegen war es möglich, die Ausweitung des griechischen Handels
und das wirtschaftliche Wachstum sowie die generelle Tendenz der Urba-

---

[136] Ebd., 336.342.
[137] Ebd., 341 f.
[138] J. Beloch, Die Großindustrie im Altertum, Zeitschrift f. Socialwissenschaft 2,
1899, 18–26. Ders., Zur griechischen Wirtschaftsgeschichte, Zeitschrift f. Socialwissenschaft 5, 1902, 95–103.169–179 (ND bei Finley, The Bücher-Meyer Controversy).
[139] Büchsenschütz, Besitz und Erwerb 335 ff. Beloch, Großindustrie 21 ff.
[140] Büchsenschütz, Besitz und Erwerb 337. Meyer, Wirtschaftl. Entwicklung 117.
Beloch, Großindustrie 23. Zur griechischen Wirtschaftsgeschichte 177.
[141] Büchsenschütz, Besitz und Erwerb 325. Meyer, Wirtschaftl. Entwicklung 130.
Sklaverei 198. Beloch, Großindustrie 23. Die Beispiele lassen sich beliebig vermehren.
[142] Büchsenschütz, Besitz und Erwerb 316 f.
[143] Damit unterscheidet sich die Sicht Meyers völlig von Mommsens 'Römischer
Geschichte,' in der die Rolle der Landwirtschaft ausführlich behandelt wird; der Abschnitt über die Wirtschaft des frühen Rom beginnt mit folgender Feststellung: ''In der
Volkswirtschaft war und blieb der Ackerbau die soziale und politische Grundlage sowohl
der römischen Gemeinde als des neuen italischen Staates.'' Vgl. Röm. Gesch., München
1976, 1, 457. Zur Vernachlässigung der Landwirtschaft bei Meyer vgl. A. Momigliano,
Max Weber and Eduard Meyer: Apropos of City and Country in Antiquity, in: ders.,
Sesto Contributo alla Storia degli studi classici e del mondo antico I, Roma 1980, 289.

nisation als 'Industrialisierung' zu verstehen; an keiner Stelle unternimmt Meyer den Versuch nachzuweisen, daß in den von ihm als Handels- und Industriestädte bezeichneten Poleis das Gewerbe tatsächlich der wichtigste Wirtschaftszweig gewesen ist. Die knappen Bemerkungen zur griechischen Landwirtschaft beschränken sich auf die Behauptung, der Anbau habe sich nicht mehr rentiert, das Großkapital habe das Land aufgekauft und dann die Landbevölkerung verdrängt. Diese Entwicklung, die im Hellenismus durch die Expansion noch einmal aufgefangen werden konnte, wiederholte sich in römischer Zeit; die "volle Ausbildung des Kapitalismus" führte nunmehr zum Ruin der Landbevölkerung und zuletzt zur Zerstörung der antiken Kultur.[144]

Die politische Tendenz des Vortrags ist am ehesten in diesen Überlegungen zu erfassen: Die aus der uneingeschränkten Durchsetzung des Kapitalinteresses resultierende Umwandlung herkömmlicher sozialer und ökonomischer Strukturen besitzt nach Meyer letztlich einen zerstörerischen Charakter und stellt die Existenz der Kultur in Frage. Meyer hat deutliche Parallelen zwischen Antike und Gegenwart gesehen, wie seine Hinweise zum Niedergang des deutschen Bauerntums in den ostelbischen Gebieten zeigen. Die Analyse der antiken Wirtschaft und politisches Denken stehen bei Meyer in einer engen wechselseitigen Beziehung: Da Meyers Auffassung nach das zerstörerische Potential des Kapitalismus den Zusammenbruch der antiken Kultur bewirkt hat, ist er gezwungen, die Fortschrittsidee als inadäquate Theorie der welthistorischen Entwicklung zu verwerfen und auf die Diskontinuität zivilisatorischer Entwicklung zu insistieren.[145] Meyers Thesen stellen sich so als ein konservativer Protest gegen die Transformation traditionaler Strukturen im Modernisierungsprozeß dar.[146]

IV

Die Kenntnis der Rezeption eines Textes trägt oft zum Verständnis seiner Aussage bei; so macht die Resonanz von Meyers Vortrag in der Presse seine politischen Implikationen noch einmal deutlich. Die Zeitungsberichte über das Frankfurter Referat sind vor allem ein Beleg dafür, daß die Zeitgenossen die politischen Anspielungen Meyers als solche erkannt

---

[144] Meyer, Wirtschaftl. Entwicklung 110.132 f. 154 f.157.

[145] Es ist bemerkenswert, daß Meyer die Kontinuität vor allem im Bereich der Ideengeschichte sieht. Die "Idee einer allgemeinen Kirche und des einen allgemeinen Staats" existierte nicht zu Beginn der Antike wie im christlich-germanischen Mittelalter. Vgl. Wirtschaftl. Entwicklung 89 Anm. 1.

[146] Die gilt auch für die Bemerkungen über die Verflachung einer Kultur, die eine allgemeine Verbreitung findet. Vgl. Wirtschaftl. Entwicklung 147.

haben; die Parallelen zur Gegenwart, zur "allerneuesten Zeit," wurden
wahrgenommen und durchaus als Warnung verstanden.[147]

L.M. Hartmann hatte den Eindruck, daß Meyer kaum Unterschiede
zwischen antiker und moderner Wirtschaft gesehen hat.[148] In seiner
glänzenden Rezension zählt Hartmann daher eine Reihe von Faktoren
auf, die seiner Meinung nach bei einer differenzierten Analyse der antiken Wirtschaft zu berücksichtigen seien: Wegen der Transportverhält-
nisse konnten Massengüter nur zur See transportiert werden; Getreide
etwa wurde vom römischen Staat als Steuer eingezogen und aus den
Provinzen importiert. Die Differenz zwischen den Importen in der Antike
und in der Moderne veranschaulicht Hartmann am Beispiel von Kaffee
und Baumwollstoffen aus Übersee, die im 19. Jahrhundert für die über-
wiegende Masse der Bevölkerung erschwinglich waren und nicht nur
Luxusprodukte für eine kleine Minderheit darstellten. Der "größte Teil
von Griechenland" besaß nach Hartmann zudem "eine fast ausschließlich landwirtschaftliche Bevölkerung;" Korinth und Athen können nicht
als charakteristische Poleis gewertet werden. Die Rezension schließt mit
der Bemerkung, daß man in der Antike "ein Nebeneinander und ein
Nacheinander verschiedener wirtschaftlicher Typen" beobachten kann,
daß gleichwohl aber die "große Masse der Bevölkerung ... noch im
Banne der Eigenproduktion und Hauswirtschaft" lebte.

Die Replik Büchers, erstmals 1901 in der Festschrift für A. Schäffle und
dann in erweiterter Form 1922 erschienen, hatte auf den Gang der Diskussion keinen Einfluß mehr. Meyer qualifizierte sie in einer Anmerkung
zu einer späteren Fassung seines Vortrags als "Phantasien" ab, und die
Entgegnung von Beloch, der energisch für Meyer Partei ergriff, geht auf
die entscheidenden Probleme nicht ein.[149] Tatsächlich hat Bücher in
seinem Aufsatz zur griechischen Wirtschaftsgeschichte einige Thesen formuliert, die sich als unhaltbar erwiesen und gegen die bereits Beloch Einwände erhob.[150] Immerhin ist beachtlich, daß Bücher nicht einfach die
theoretische Diskussion über die Hauswirtschaft fortführt, sondern auf
die Argumentation von Meyer eingeht und diese sehr genau prüft, wobei
er auch die Quellenlage erörtert und nachweisen kann, daß viele Aus-

---

[147] Vgl. hierzu Schumann, Historikertage 59 f. Schumann wertet hier die Kölnische
Zeitung vom 23.4.1895 und die Frankfurter Zeitung vom 20.4.1895 aus.

[148] L.M. Hartmann, Zeitschrift für Sozial- und Wirtschaftsgesch. IV 1896, 153–157.

[149] K. Bücher, Zur griechischen Wirtschaftsgeschichte, in: ders., Beiträge zur Wirtschaftsgeschichte, Tübingen 1922, 1–97 (ND bei Finley, The Bücher-Meyer Controversy). Meyer, Wirtschaftl. Entwicklung 87 Anm. Beloch, Zur griech. Wirtschaftsge-
schich. 95 ff.169 ff.

[150] Dies gilt einerseits für die Besteuerung von Sklaven in der Begleitung von Reisen-
den (Bücher, Zur griech. Wirtschaftsgesch. 24 ff.) und andererseits für die Herkunft der
Keramik (aaO 65 ff.).

sagen Meyers über die Gewerbezentren der griechischen Welt in den antiken Texten nicht zu belegen sind.[151] Bücher hat so den Versuch unternommen, den man von den Althistorikern hätte erwarten sollen, den Versuch einer Begründung wirtschaftshistorischer Theorie durch eine präzise Analyse der Quellen.

Meyer stellte Büchers Theorie der antiken Hauswirtschaft das Bild einer modernen Antike, der Fortschrittsidee die Vorstellung des Kreislaufs in der Geschichte gegenüber. Die Position Meyers war der Büchers wissenschaftlich keineswegs überlegen. Will man das Verdienst Eduard Meyers im Bereich der antiken Wirtschaftsgeschichte charakterisieren, kann dies vielleicht am besten mit dem folgenden Aphorismus von Ludwig Wittgenstein getan werden: "Ist ein falscher Gedanke nur einmal kühn und klar ausgedrückt, so ist damit schon viel gewonnen."[152]

---

[151] Bücher, Zur griech. Wirtschaftsgesch. 39 ff.
[152] L. Wittgenstein, Vermischte Bemerkungen, Hg. G.H. von Wright, Frankfurt 1987, 146.

BERND SÖSEMANN

"DER KÜHNSTE ENTSCHLUSS FÜHRT AM SICHERSTEN ZUM ZIEL." EDUARD MEYER UND DIE POLITIK

Engagement hatte Eduard Meyer genug für seinen Ausflug in die Politik[1]—dennoch endete dieser Weg in einer Sackgasse.[2] Zumindest hat sich Meyer die Ergebnislosigkeit seiner hartnäckigen Bemühungen zum Wohl von Volk und Regierung rückblickend offen eingestanden. Seine Erfahrungen mit der Parteipolitik in der Weimarer Republik erhöhten sein Verständnis für konzessionsbereite Haltungen und korrigierten seine Vorstellung, daß mit dem "kühnsten Entschluß"[3] und auf der Grund-

---

[1] Der Beitrag "Eduard Meyer und die Politik" für das Wissenschaftliche Colloquium "Der Universalhistoriker Eduard Meyer. Werk und Wirkung" kann hier in einer erweiterten Fassung erscheinen, weil mir nachträglich noch der Hauptnachlaß Meyers in dem "Zentralen Archiv" der "Akademie der Wissenschaften der DDR" in Ostberlin zugänglich gemacht und etliche Zeitungsartikel aus auswärtigen Archiven und Bibliotheken zugesandt wurden. Nicht unbedeutende Aufschlüsse ergaben sich außerdem bei der Durchsicht des jüngst durch die Vermittlung Alexander Demandts in die "Staatsbibliothek Preußischer Kulturbesitz", Berlin, gelangten Teilnachlasses Eduard Meyers über seine Beziehungen zu Wilhelm II. und über den "Fall Nicolai". Für den Nachweis von weiteren Korrespondenzen danke ich den Kollegen Jürgen von Ungern-Sternberg (Basel) und Edgar Pack (Köln) sowie Herrn Michael May für die Mithilfe bei der Suche nach den publizistischen Quellen.
[2] Das öffentliche politische Wirken Eduard Meyers hat Heinrich Marohl nahezu vollständig bibliographisch erfaßt. Ich stütze mich hierbei auf knapp einhundert Veröffentlichungen unterschiedlichen Umfangs und Anspruchs. Über die Mitgliedschaft und das Wirken Eduard Meyers in Organisationen und Verbänden, in der Universität und der Berliner Akademie der Wissenschaften sind wir aufgrund der bisherigen Forschungen wenigstens in großen Zügen, für einzelne Vorgänge sogar sehr gut unterrichtet. Hier sind in erster Linie zu nennen: Böhme, K. (Hg.): Aufrufe und Reden deutscher Professoren im Ersten Weltkrieg. Stuttgart 1975; Brocke, Bernhard vom: Wissenschaft und Militarismus. In: W.M. Calder et al. (Hgg.), Wilamowitz nach 50 Jahren, Darmstadt 1985, S. 649–719; Döring, Herbert: Der Weimarer Kreis. Studien zum politischen Bewußtsein verfassungstreuer Hochschullehrer in der Weimarer Republik (Mannheimer Sozialwissenschaftliche Studien, Bd. 10). Meisenheim/Glan 1975; Grau, Conrad (Hg.): Die Berliner Akademie der Wissenschaften in der Zeit des Imperialismus, Teil 1 (Studien zur Geschichte der Akademie der Wissenschaften der DDR, Bd. II/1). Berlin (Ost) 1975; Schröder-Gudehus, Brigitte: Deutsche Wissenschaft und Internationale Zusammenarbeit 1914–1928. Ein Beitrag zum Studium kultureller Beziehungen in politischen Krisenzeiten. Genf 1966; Schwabe, Klaus: Wissenschaft und Kriegsmoral. Die deutschen Hochschullehrer und die politischen Grundfragen des Ersten Weltkrieges. Göttingen 1969. In den meisten Arbeiten stehen Eduard Meyers Aktivitäten allerdings nicht im Mittelpunkt.
[3] Die zitatähnliche Feststellung des Titels verkürzt eine Formulierung Meyers vom 14. Februar 1917 im Vorwort zu seinem Werk "Der amerikanische Kongreß und der Weltkrieg", S. XI, die lautet: "Wie immer in allen großen Krisen der Weltgeschichte [Entschluß zum uneingeschränkten U-Boot-Krieg in Deutschland und drohende Kriegs-

lage eines unerschütterlichen Willens die als richtig erkannten Ziele sicher zu erreichen seien. Die Enttäuschung über die Unfähigkeit der deutschen Regierungen während des Ersten Weltkriegs, über das "Versagen" des deutschen Volkes und die heftige Verbitterung über seine Entscheidung, der Wissenschaft Zeit und Kraft zu entziehen, ließen Meyer in einer späteren autobiographischen Aufzeichnung scharfe Worte wählen: Sein rücksichtsloser Kampf für die vaterländische Sache im Krieg und gegen die "vaterlandslose Gesinnung" in den Nachkriegsjahren sei ohne das erhoffte Ergebnis geblieben. Doch führte dieses 1923 resignativ vorgetragene Resümee[4] keineswegs zur Abstinenz von der Politik. Im Bereich der politischen Publizistik blieb Meyer ein scharf attackierender Befürworter konservativer Politik. Als Mitglied der "Deutschnationalen Volkspartei" trieben ihn seine auf ausgedehnten Reisen gewonnenen Erfahrungen und seine geistige Unabhängigkeit wiederholt in die schärfste Kritik an dem Kurs der Partei.[5]

Das Thema umschließt Überlegungen und Aktivitäten Meyers auf drei Ebenen. Den ersten Bereich bilden die Reden und Vorträge, Aufrufe und Korrespondenzen Meyers. Sie kulminieren in den sechs Jahren nach 1915, in denen "neben dem Streit der Waffen doch auch die literarische Diskussion in Presse und Flugschriften nicht ohne Wert" war und ihre "Sachwalter" verlangte, wie der junge Franz Schnabel in seiner Rezension zu Meyers Aufsatzsammlung "Weltgeschichte und Weltkrieg" schrieb.[6] Der zweite Bereich umfaßt die politischen Aktivitäten Meyers

---

erklärung der USA], so zeigt sich auch hier, daß der kühnste Entschluß, wenn er die verfügbaren Mittel richtig abschätzt und wenn er von einem klaren, unerschütterlichen Willen getragen wird, zugleich der beste ist und am sichersten zum Ziele führt."

[4] Unter der Überschrift "Eduard Meyer", und datiert auf den 10. Juni 1923: "Im übrigen habe ich mich seither vom öffentlichen Leben nach Möglichkeit zurückgezogen, da bei der gegenwärtigen Lage der Dinge eine Wirksamkeit aussichtslos ist und es vielmehr geboten ist, sich möglichst ruhig zu halten und abzuwarten, und im übrigen alle Kraft auf gewissenhafte Arbeit in seinem Fachgebiet zu konzentrieren" (Meyer, Eduard [autobiographische Notizen]. In: Almanach der Akademie der Wissenschaften, Wien 82 (1932), S. 211).

[5] Brief von E. Meyer an A. v. Tirpitz (handschriftlicher Entwurf) vom 20.V.1926: "Die so überaus kläglichen unpolitischen Vorgänge der letzten Wochen [Völkerbundsfrage, Fürstenenteignungsproblem, Flaggenverordnung, Sturz der Regierung Luther, Diktaturpläne der Rechtsradikalen] und das mir gänzlich unbegreifliche Verhalten der Deutschnationalen Partei [Austritt aus der Regierung, Stimmenenthaltung im Reichstag bei der Flaggen-Frage] lassen mir keine Ruhe [...]." Die DNVP übersehe die wahrhaft nationalen Fragen und versinke "noch tiefer in dem kläglichsten Parteisumpf." In: Akademie der Wissenschaften der DDR, Zentrales Akademie-Archiv, Berlin (Ost), Nachlaß Eduard Meyer (im folgenden abgekürzt: AkadWissDDR, NL Ed. Meyer), Nr. 1413; Meyers erster Briefentwurf datiert übrigens auf den 9. Mai 1926 und lautet: "Die traurigen politischen Vorgänge der letzten Tage und das mir vollständig unbegreifliche Verhalten [...]."

[6] Franz Schnabel. In: Zeitschrift für Politik 10 (1917), S. 160 f.

in Vereinen und Organisationen und schließt seine Arbeit in den akademischen Gremien und wissenschaftlichen Institutionen mit ein. Meyers
Position läßt sich auch den von ihm mit verfaßten oder wenigstens mit
getragenen Verlautbarungen, Denkschriften oder Aufrufen entnehmen.
Unter den Bedingungen der Militärzensur während des Ersten Weltkriegs[7] richteten sie sich größtenteils nicht an die Öffentlichkeit, sondern
an Politiker, Parteien und Regierungen, die im alldeutschen oder konservativen Sinn beeinflußt werden sollten. Der dritte Bereich hat mit Politik
in einem weitläufigeren Sinn zu tun. Er betrifft sowohl die Inhalte als
auch die Rezeptionsgeschichte des wissenschaftlichen Oeuvres, doch geht
es dabei in erster Linie um die Wirkungen außerhalb des fachwissenschaftlichen Diskurses.

Ulrich von Wilamowitz-Moellendorff weist in seiner Laudatio zum
siebzigsten Geburtstag Eduard Meyers in den "Süddeutschen Monatsheften" zu Recht darauf hin, daß, "so staunenswert die Leistungen des
Gelehrten" auch seien, mit ihnen bei weitem nicht die Persönlichkeit erfaßt
werden könne. Unverblümt habe Meyer auch in der Politik jederzeit das
von ihm als richtig Erkannte ausgesprochen. Wilamowitz-Moellendorff
bezieht somit die politische Publizistik[8] ausdrücklich in das Werk mit
ein, wenn er feststellt, daß Meyer durch seine politischen Aktivitäten zu
dem "bestgehaßten deutschen Gelehrten" seiner Zeit geworden sei.[9] Zu
dieser Ansicht haben in einem nicht geringen Maß die Schriften Meyers
über die USA und Großbritannien beigetragen, seine Äußerungen über
die internationale Gelehrtenrepublik, über den Rang der deutschen Kultur sowie sein publizistisch ausgetragener Kampf für einen "Siegfrieden"[10] und gegen innenpolitische Reformen in Preußen und im Reich.

---

[7] Vgl. dazu Huber, Ernst Rudolf: Deutsche Verfassungsgeschichte der Neuzeit,
Bd. 5, Stuttgart 1978, S. 39–73.

[8] Eine gewisse Distanz zum eigenen tagespolitischen Schaffen und die selbstkritische
Bewertung seiner Äußerungen auf diesem Terrain ergibt sich wohl bereits aus der Entscheidung Meyers, nur drei derartige Beiträge in seine "Kleinen Schriften" aufzu-
nehmen.

[9] Wilamowitz-Moellendorff, Ulrich von: Eduard Meyer. In: Süddeutsche Monatshefte 22 (Januar 1925), S. 58.

[10] "Der Krieg, der jetzt geführt wird, ist ein Kampf nicht nur um politische Fragen,
um die Behauptung der Machtstellung des Deutschen Reiches und der ihm eng verbündeten Österreichisch-Ungarischen Monarchie, sondern um unendlich viel mehr: es handelt sich um das Sein oder Nichtsein des deutschen Volkes. Wir wissen, was wir zu erwarten haben, wenn wir unterliegen; unsere Feinde haben uns den Untergang geschworen.
Zusammengeführt hat sie der Haß gegen den deutschen Namen, der Neid auf den steigenden Wohlstand Deutschlands, den wir unserer gewaltigen staatlichen und wirtschaftlichen
Ordnung, unserer geistigen und militärischen Erziehung, unserem festen Zusammenhalten verdanken, die ohnmächtige Wut darüber, daß sie nicht mehr nach Belieben in der
Welt schalten können wie ehemals, sondern Deutschland berücksichtigen müssen, die Erbitterung darüber, daß wir, in festem, unauflöslichem Bunde mit Österreich-Ungarn, sie
gezwungen haben, dreiundvierzig Jahre hindurch Frieden zu halten, während sie in

Eduard Meyers Verständnis von Politik, Staat und Gesellschaft hat erst
mit dem Ausbruch des Ersten Weltkriegs eine inhaltliche Klärung, eine
Präzisierung und schließlich auch eine parteipolitische Ausrichtung erfahren, die sein weiteres Leben prägen sollten. Das sogenannte August-
Erlebnis[11] und die Diskussionen über die Ideen von 1914[12] führten auch
bei ihm zu der Bereitschaft, zukünftig die politische Entwicklung mitbe-
einflussen zu wollen. Er tat es in der Überzeugung, daß der Ausgang des
Weltkriegs nicht nur die militärische Überlegenheit Deutschlands dokumentieren, sondern auch die politische Ordnung des Deutschen Reichs
stabilisieren und das monarchische System legitimieren werde. Die wohl-
vorbereitete Äußerung des Kaisers vor dem Reichstag, er kenne keine
Parteien mehr, sondern nur noch Deutsche, das Gelöbnis der Parteivor-
stände, die Unterstützung der Kriegskredite und des Ermächtigungs-
gesetzes vom 4. August durch die bislang als reichsfeindlich angesehene
Sozialdemokratie weckten entsprechende Hoffnungen in breiten Kreisen

---

früheren Zeiten ihre Streitigkeiten bequem auf deutschem Boden hatten ausfechten können. Diese Zeiten, da Deutschland zerrissen und machtlos war, wollen sie wieder herstellen; sollten sie siegen, so werden sie alle Mittel ergreifen, um Deutschland zu zertrüm-
mern, um uns nicht nur jede Möglichkeit zu nehmen, wieder zu staatlicher Macht zu
gelangen, sondern um uns national zu vernichten. Dann möchten wir wieder ein Volk von
Träumern werden [...], um die Dinge dieser Welt sollen wir uns nicht mehr kümmern,
die sollen wir den anderen Nationen zu freiem Schalten überlassen. Zu einem solchen
Volk von Kastraten will man uns erniedrigen'' (Meyer, Eduard: Deutschland und der
Krieg. In: Unterm Eisernen Kreuz. Kriegsschriften des Kaiser-Wilhelm-Dank (Verein
der Soldatenfreunde Bd. 3). September 1914, S. 6 f.).
11 ''Deutschland schien vom Parteihader, von religiösen, politischen, sozialen Gegen-
sätzen zerrissen; aber in dem Augenblick, wo der Krieg erklärt und der Mobilmachungs-
befehl erlassen war, war das alles verschwunden und vergessen, als sei es nie gewesen.
[...] Wer die ersten Augusttage des Jahres 1914 in Deutschland erlebt hat, der hat etwas
erlebt, was er sein Leben lang nicht vergessen wird, und was kein anderer Eindruck jemals
überbieten kann. [...] Und dieser Geist tiefen sittlichen Ernstes, er ging und geht durch
die gesamte Bevölkerung [...]. Nirgends voreiliger Siegesrausch oder eitle Überhebung;
wohl aber überall das Bewußtsein, daß wir für die heilige Sache des Vaterlandes siegen
oder sterben müssen. Das ist ja die große sittliche Gewalt des Krieges, daß der Einzelne,
sei er hoch oder gering, sich bewußt wird, daß er nur ein Atom ist in dem großen Ganzen,
das sich zu einheitlichem Willen, zu einheitlicher Kraftentfaltung zusammenschließt, daß
es gar keine andere Aufgabe, gar keine andere Betätigung mehr gibt als die eine, die
höchste und alleinige, seine Pflicht zu tun!'' (ebd., S. 17).
12 Vgl. dazu Koester, Eckart: Literatur und Weltkriegsideologie. Positionen und
Begründungszusammenhänge des publizistischen Engagements deutscher Schriftsteller
im Ersten Weltkrieg. Kronberg/Taunus 1977; Lübbe, Hermann: Die philosophischen
Ideen von 1914. In: ders., Politische Philosophie in Deutschland. Basel 1963, S. 173–238;
Rürup, Reinhard: Der ''Geist von 1914'' in Deutschland. Kriegsbegeisterung und Ideo-
logisierung des Krieges im Ersten Weltkrieg, in: Hüppauf, Bernd (Hg.): Ansichten vom
Krieg. Vergleichende Studien zum Ersten Weltkrieg in Literatur und Gesellschaft. Kron-
berg/Taunus 1984, S. 1–30; Schwarte, Max (Hg.): Der Weltkrieg in seiner Einwirkung
auf das deutsche Volk. Leipzig 1918; Vondung, Klaus (Hg.): Das Wilhelminische Bildungsbürgertum. Zur Sozialgeschichte seiner Ideen. Göttingen 1967.

des deutschen Volkes. Des weiteren verhießen Bethmann Hollwegs Idee
des "Burgfriedens" und des Kanzlers Politik der "nationalen Einheitsfront"[13] innerpolitische Integration, die Milderung klassenpolitischer
Gegensätze und die Stärkung des patriotischen Gefühls.

Eduard Meyer hat als Dreiundzwanzigjähriger die inneren Gegensätze
des Deutschen Kaiserreichs und die sich in der zweiten Hälfte der sieb-
ziger Jahre verschärfenden parteipolitischen Konfrontationen zwar wahrgenommen, hat jedoch keine wohl durchdachte und fest umrissene politische Position vertreten. Erst beim Kriegsausbruch, mit dem Gefühl, in
einer belagerten Festung gegen eine Welt von Feinden solidarisch ausharren zu müssen, ergab sich die klare parteipolitische Präferenz. Aus
vereinzelten Äußerungen und Berichten aus der Vorkriegszeit könnte auf
eine gewisse Vertrautheit Meyers mit liberaler Politik—Freundschaft mit
Friedberg bei gleichzeitiger Ablehnung des "schrankenlosen Individualismus[14]—und eine Sympathie für sozialdemokratische bzw. sozialistische Positionen geschlossen werden. Hatte Meyer doch in einem Privat-
brief den Wahlerfolg der SPD bereits im Winter 1877 begrüßt und seine
Zustimmung mit zwei verhaltenen Bemerkungen erläutert. Er bekannte
einem Freund, "daß er im allgemeinen mit ihnen [den Sozialdemokraten]
sympathisiere" und daß er es für "etwas wünschenswertes betrachte, daß
die Gesellschaft sich im Laufe der Jahrhunderte auf socialistischer Basis
umgestalte." Dieser Einstellung dürfte jedoch weniger eine nüchterne
politische Analyse als vielmehr eine emotional motivierte Fürsprache für
die Fraktion des Außenministers zugrunde gelegen haben, wenn man einmal bedenkt, daß die SPD im Januar 1877 mit vier zusätzlichen Abgeord-
neten in den Reichstag hatte einziehen können. Auch die Argumentation
Meyers gegen den Widerspruch seines Korrespondenzpartners läßt keine
fundierte Kenntnis "sozialistischer" Programmatik erkennen. Und
schließlich ist Meyers Hinweis, die gesellschaftliche Entwicklung laufe auf
eine "Emancipation der Individualität" hinaus, "die den modernen
Menschen von vielen Fesseln der Vergangenheit" befreie, eher in einem
liberalen als in einem "sozialistischen" Sinn zu deuten.[15] Man sollte also
diesen vagen Andeutungen[16] nicht durch eine direkte parteipolitische

---

[13] Huber, Verfassungsgeschichte (wie Anm. 7), S. 117–129.
 [14] Meyer, Eduard: Humanistische und geschichtliche Bildung. Vortrag, gehalten in
der Vereinigung der Freunde des humanistischen Gymnasiums in Berlin und der Provinz
Brandenburg am 27. November 1906. Berlin 1907, S. 38.
 [15] Die Korrespondenz mit Pietschmann weist Christhard Hoffmanns Beitrag in diesem
Band nach.
 [16] Vgl. auch den bewundernden Hinweis Meyers, daß die Sozialdemokratie, also die
"größte von allen politischen Parteien, die wir in Deutschland habe [...], auf eine
Geschichtstheorie aufgebaut" sei, "die einer der großen deutschen Denker des neunzehnten Jahrhunderts, Karl Marx, geschaffen" habe (Meyer, Humanistische und geschichtliche Bildung [wie Anm. 14], S. 27).

Zuordnung einen unangebrachten Akzent verleihen.[17] Den englischen Parlamentarismus betrachtete Meyer bereits zu dieser Zeit als nicht erstrebenswert für das Deutsche Reich. In den neunziger Jahren soll er, auf der Seite der "Flottenprofessoren" stehend, den entschiedenen Ausbau der deutschen Kriegsmarine begrüßt haben.[18] In einer Rezension dieser Jahre nennt er den "Socialismus" in einem Atem mit dem "moderne[n] Communismus," die beide "von Hause aus eine negative Erscheinung" seien und verargt "der heutigen Socialdemokratie das Rütteln an dem, was vaterländisch geschichtliche Größe heißt."[19]

Seit dem August 1914 war Meyers politisches Denken, wie das der meisten Zeitgenossen, von den vier Grundüberzeugungen geprägt, die die öffentliche Diskussion im Deutschen Reich so weitgehend bestimmten, daß von einer "quasi-plebiszitären Gesamtstimmung" gesprochen werden kann: Dem Deutschen Reich sei der Krieg aufgezwungen worden; es befinde sich in einem Verteidigungskampf; es verfolge begrenzte Kriegsziele und es erstrebe keineswegs die absolute Weltmacht, sondern nutze eine nicht unwillkommene Gelegenheit, sich günstigere Voraussetzungen für eine gesicherte Position im imperialen Weltstaatensystem zu schaffen. Die innere Politik des Deutschen Reichs müsse sich nunmehr auf ein "verwandeltes" Volk ausrichten. Sie habe mit der Erfahrung des patriotischen August-Erlebnisses und einer ungeahnten nationalen Solidarität die einmalige Chance, die soziale Frage losgelöst von partei-, konfessions- und verbandspolitischen Partialinteressen angehen zu können. Und schließlich gehörte noch zur allgemein verbreiteten Überzeugung hinzu, daß der Krieg wie 1870/71 wegen der begrenzten Ziele und der deutschen wirtschaftlichen und militärischen Stärke nach einem kurzen "Waffengang" vorüber sein werde.[20]

---

[17] Das gilt m.E. auch für die Behauptung Meyers in einem Brief an Victor Ehrenberg vom 10.V.1917, er "habe übrigens in den innerpolitischen Fragen niemals auf dem Standpunkt der Conservativen gestanden, sondern auf dem der Nationalliberalen, für die ich gelegentlich auch thätig gewesen bin" (Mitteilung des Kollegen von Ungern-Sternberg, der die Edition dieser Korrespondenz vorbereitet). Die Nationalliberalen akzeptierten nicht allein den Parlamentarismus, sondern beteiligten sich mit Stresemann, van Calker, Richthofen, Junck und Schiffer entscheidend an den Bemühungen des Interfraktionellen Ausschusses, in der Wahlrechts-, Friedens- und insbesondere in der Parlamentarisierungsfrage weiter voranzukommen. Öffentlich hat Meyer diese Politik nie vertreten.

[18] Nach Bruch, Rüdiger vom: Wissenschaft, Politik und öffentliche Meinung. Gelehrtenpolitik im Wilhelminischen Deutschland, 1890–1914 (Historische Studien, Bd. 435). Husum 1980, S. 66–91, 428–432.

[19] Meyer, Eduard: Communismus und Socialismus im Alterthum. In: Beilagen Nrr. 165 + 166 zur "Allgemeinen Zeitung", Nr. 198 (1894).

[20] S. dazu den Leitartikel von Theodor Wolff im "Berliner Tageblatt", Nr. 388, 3.VIII.1914, und das Geleitwort zu der Flugschriftenreihe "Zwischen Krieg und Frieden," Heft 1, Leipzig 1914.

Meyers geändertes Verhalten, die Entschiedenheit seiner Forderungen und sogar seine Diktion lassen sich auf diese allgemeinen Umstände ebenso zurückführen wie auf die Zensur- und Pressepolitik der politischen und militärischen Behörden. Während des Kriegs waren nämlich die Informations- und Kommunikationsverhältnisse uneinheitlich, kaum kalkulierbar und führten zu paradox anmutenden Erscheinungen. Die öffentliche Diskussion der Kriegsziele blieb bis zum Sommer 1916 grundsätzlich verboten; dennoch setzte sie hinter den Kulissen im Frühjahr 1915 mit der Denkschrift der sechs Verbände und ähnlichen Petitionen intensiv und auch relativ stark verbreitet ein. Abschriften wurden postalisch gezielt versandt, Klubs und Vereine von Annexionisten sowie von ihren pazifistischen, liberalen oder sozialdemokratischen Gegnern begründet. Das politisch-atmosphärische Umfeld wurde durch freiverkäufliche Broschüren und Flugschriften vorbereitet, die in Aufmachung und Argumentation versuchten, knapp unterhalb der Verbotschwelle zu bleiben. Allein die rein militärische Zensur griff rigoros durch. So erfuhr die Öffentlichkeit über die sich im Winter 1914/15 abzeichnende prekäre deutsche Lage nichts. Bis zum November 1918 hat für den deutschen Zeitungsleser die Marneschlacht nicht stattgefunden. Der verzerrende, zumindest jedoch beschönigende Hurra-Patriotismus der Berichterstattung beherrschte die offiziellen Verlautbarungen und die Publizistik, in der Abweichler wie das ''Berliner Tageblatt'' mit Rücksicht auf propagandistische oder außenpolitische Erwägungen geduldet wurden.[21]

1914 gehörte Meyer also zu dem großen Kreis jener Zeitgenossen in Deutschland, Frankreich oder Großbritannien, die aus nationaler Leidenschaft den Krieg begrüßten. Franzosen fuhren mit Taxis an die Front; ein Jahr später jubelten Italiener beim Kriegseintritt; und im April 1917 gab es im amerikanischen Kongreß bereits auf die entsprechende Ankündigung hin stürmischen Beifall. Meyer beteiligte sich an Kundgebungen und Aufrufen, an Vortragsveranstaltungen und Erklärungen, an Eingaben, Petitionen oder Adressen, formulierte Vorträge, Aufsätze und Artikel, die an Eindeutigkeit und Einseitigkeit der politischen Aussage nichts zu wünschen übrig ließen. Er trat dabei in der Rolle des Initiators ebenso auf wie in der des Mitunterzeichners und kollegial Unterstützen-

---

[21] Einen Einblick in die Thematik und eine Vorstellung von der Intensität und den Wirkungen der Auseinandersetzungen vermitteln die kontinuierlich vorgenommenen Aufzeichnungen eines gut informierten und distanziert beobachtenden Zeitgenossen: Vgl. Wolff, Theodor: Tagebücher 1914–1919. Der Erste Weltkrieg und die Entstehung der Weimarer Republik in Tagebüchern, Leitartikeln und Briefen des Chefredakteurs am ''Berliner Tageblatt'' und Mitbegründers der ''Deutschen Demokratischen Partei''. Vorwort und Einleitung von Bernd Sösemann (Deutsche Geschichtsquellen des 19. und 20. Jahrhunderts, Bd. 54). 2 Bde. Boppard am Rhein 1984, passim.

den. Zu den wichtigsten Berliner Foren gehörten die Universität, die
Akademie der Wissenschaften, der ''Unabhängige Ausschuß für einen
deutschen Frieden'', das ''Direktionskomitee der deutschen Vaterlandspartei'' und der ''Hauptausschuß für die deutschen Hochschulen'' der
Deutschnationalen Volkspartei Berlins. Er sprach aber auch mehrmals
vor der Ortsgruppe des ''Deutsch-evangelischen Frauenbundes'' oder
vor dem ''Zentralinstitut für Erziehung und Unterricht''. Seine Artikel
erschienen in der ''Vossischen Zeitung'', in den ''Süddeutschen Monatsheften'', den ''Zeit- und Streitfragen'', der ''Leipziger Illustrierten
Zeitung'', den ''Eisernen Blättern'' oder in den ''Kriegsschriften des
Kaiser-Wilhelm-Dank''.

Für Meyer lieferte der Krieg aller Welt den Beweis, daß der Machtstaat
alle Lebensverhältnisse beherrsche:[22] ''Wohl sind die wirtschaftlichen,
sozialen, kulturellen Kräfte vorhanden [. . .], aber sie finden die Möglichkeit ihrer Bestätigung nur durch den Staat innerhalb des Rahmens, den
er ihnen zuweist, auch wenn er ihnen gestattet, zeitweilig über seine
Grenzen in freier Betätigung hinauszugreifen.'' Die alles beherrschende
Position des Staats könne nur so lange angemessen gewahrt bleiben, wie
seine Hauptaufgabe darin gesehen werde, die Macht zu organisieren und
zu festigen. Die demokratische conditio sine qua non ''Gleiches Recht für
Alle'' widerspreche der Idee der Gerechtigkeit, weil sie ''eine Abstufung
der politischen Rechte nach der Individualität des Einzelnen'' ablehne.
Nur wenn sich das ''wilde anarchische Treiben der Demokratie und die
Beherrschung und Ausbeutung des Staats durch die Parteien und ihre
Führer'' verhindern lassen, könne der Staat seine höchste Aufgabe auch
nach außen erfüllen, nämlich ''sein Dasein in der Welt unabhängig gegen
alle rivalisierenden und feindlichen Mächte zu behaupten''.[23]

Die größte Aufmerksamkeit im In- und Ausland erzielte Eduard Meyer
mit seiner Zustimmung zu dem Aufruf ''An die Kulturwelt'', also zu dem
sogenannten ''Aufruf der 93''. Er erschien am 4. Oktober 1914 in allen
großen deutschen Tageszeitungen, wurde mit der privaten Korrespondenz breit ins Ausland gestreut, in zehn Sprachen übersetzt und wegen
seiner sechs apodiktischen Leitsätze in Frankreich, Rußland, Portugal,
Großbritannien oder in den USA scharf kritisiert. Als ''Vertreter
deutscher Wissenschaft und Kunst'' erhoben in ihm 53 Professoren, zahl-

---

[22] Hier und im folgenden nach: Meyer, Eduard: Der Staat, sein Wesen und seine
Organisation. Vortrag, gehalten am 9. Februar 1916 in Berlin für die Ortsgruppe des
Deutsch-Evangelischen Frauenbundes und die kirchlich-soziale Frauengruppe. In: Süd-
deutsche Monatshefte 13 (März 1916), S. 999–1016. Wiederveröffentlicht in: Meyer,
Weltgeschichte, S. 132–168.
[23] Ebd., S. 1009.

reiche Künstler, Politiker und Dichter "vor der gesamten Kulturwelt Protest gegen die Lügen und Verleumdungen" der Entente:

> "Es ist nicht wahr, daß Deutschland diesen Krieg verschuldet hat [. . .], daß wir freventlich die Neutralität Belgiens verletzt haben [. . .], daß unsere Kriegsführung die Gesetze des Völkerrechts mißachtet. Sie kennt keine zuchtlose Grausamkeit. Im Osten aber tränkt das Blut der von russischen Horden hingeschlachteten Frauen und Kinder die Erde, und im Westen zerreißen Dum-Dum-Geschosse unseren Kriegern die Brust. Sich als Verteidiger europäischer Zivilisation zu gebärden, haben die am wenigsten das Recht, die sich mit Russen und Serben verbünden und der Welt das schmachvolle Schauspiel bieten, Mongolen und Neger auf die weiße Rasse zu hetzen. Es ist nicht wahr, daß der Kampf gegen unseren sogenannten Militarismus kein Kampf gegen unsere Kultur ist, wie unsere Feinde heuchlerisch vorgeben. Ohne den deutschen Militarismus wäre die deutsche Kultur längst vom Erdboden getilgt."[24]

Diese Feststellung wiederholte Meyer in den eigenen Publikationen fast wörtlich.[25] Am 16. Oktober 1914 unterschrieb er auch die "Erklärung der Hochschullehrer des Deutschen Reiches", in der es u.a. hieß: "Unser Glaube ist, daß für die ganze Kultur Europas das Heil an dem Siege hängt, den der deutsche 'Militarismus' erkämpfen wird, die Manneszucht, die Treue, der Opfermut des einträchtigen freien deutschen Volkes". Mehr als 4000 Kollegen schlossen sich diesem Aufruf an. Ulrich von Wilamowitz-Moellendorff hatte ihn verfaßt; der Meyer freundschaftlich verbundene Historiker Dietrich Schäfer ließ ihn in kürzester Zeit verbreiten.[26] Weil dieser Aufruf weniger aggressiv formuliert war, stand er in der öffentlichen Polemik hinter dem "Aufruf der 93" zurück, der nicht nur sogleich Zurückweisungen provoziert hatte—sie waren übrigens ebenfalls nicht unerheblich von nationalem Hochmut bestimmt—, sondern noch nach Kriegsende die Atmosphäre vergiftete. Eine Rundfrage der "Deutschen Liga für Völkerbund" im Frühjahr 1919 erwies jedoch,

---

[24] Siehe dazu Marienfeld, Wolfgang: Wissenschaft und Schlachtflottenbau in Deutschland 1897–1906 (Marine Rundschau, Beiheft 2). Berlin/Frankfurt am Main 1957, S. 110–114.

[25] "Da können blutige Strafgerichte und Repressalien nicht ausbleiben, und furchtbare Szenen werden uns nicht erspart werden. Aber daß unsere Soldaten, trotz alles gerechten Ingrimms, dadurch verwildern und die Menschenwürde vergessen sollten, das brauchen wir nicht zu befürchten: dazu sind sie nicht nur zu diszipliniert, sondern vor allem zu gewissenhaft, zu ernst und zu gottesfürchtig. Es gibt auf Erden kein Heer, das humaner wäre als das deutsche" (Meyer, Deutschland und der Krieg [wie Anm. 10], S. 20).

[26] Vgl. hierzu und in diesem Zusammenhang Kellermann, Hermann (Ed.): Der Krieg der Geister. Eine Auslese deutscher und ausländischer Stimmen zum Weltkrieg 1914. Dresden 1915; Grumbauch, S[alomon] (Ed.): Das annexionistische Deutschland. Eine Sammlung von Dokumenten, die seit dem 4. August 1914 in Deutschland öffentlich oder geheim verbreitet wurden. Lausanne 1917.

daß sich nur noch 16 Unterzeichner vorbehaltlos zum Text bekannten.[27]

In der Historiographie wird zumeist ausdrücklich darauf hingewiesen, daß Eduard Meyer zu diesen Unverbesserlichen gezählt habe. Dabei wird der Situation zu wenig Beachtung geschenkt, in der diese Rundfrage vorgenommen wurde. Meyers Temperament, seine Kenntnis ausländischer Hetzreden[28] und Broschüren und seine tiefe Erbitterung über das Verhalten der Siegermächte in Versailles legen zumindest für das Frühjahr 1919 den Gedanken an eine politische Trotzreaktion auf die Anfrage nahe. Diese Vermutung findet eine zusätzliche Stütze in der bislang übersehenen Tatsache, daß es eine differenzierende Stellungnahme Meyers zum ''Aufruf der 93'' gibt. Sie wurde schon vier Monate nach der Unterzeichnung in der ''Leipziger Illustrirten Zeitung'' in Meyers Artikel ''Das Verhalten Nordamerikas gegen Deutschland im Weltkriege'' veröffentlicht.[29] Darin erklärt Meyer, daß die Erregung der Ersten Stunde die Feder geführt habe. Der Appell sei ''nicht besonders geschickt abgefaßt'' gewesen, doch in tödlicher Gefahr könne es passieren, daß ''nicht immer die richtigen Worte'' gewählt werden.[30]

Die im Frühjahr 1915 sich verbreitende Einsicht, daß der Krieg nicht in wenigen Wochen gewonnen werden könne, und die sukzessive Aufkündigung der Burgfriedenspolitik durch die Konservativen und die radikale Linke veranlaßten Meyer, sich mit Bethmann Hollwegs ''Politik der Diagonalen'' auseinanderzusetzen. Diese innenpolitische ''Neuorientierung'' sollte der ''Schützengraben-Generation'' die verdiente politische Anerkennung verschaffen. Dazu gehörten vorrangig die volle Rechtsgleichheit, ein reformiertes preußisches Wahlrecht, eine konsequent fortentwickelte Parlamentarisierung, die Förderung der Gewerkschaften und Berufsverbände, ein ''soziales Kaisertum'' in einem ausgebauten Sozialstaat und somit auch die stärkere Integration der Arbeiterschaft in Staat und Gesellschaft.[31]

Bis zum Sturz Bethmann Hollwegs wandte sich Meyer nicht expres-

---

[27] Diese Umfrage veranstaltete der Pazifist Hans Wehberg. Das Ergebnis veröffentlichte das ''Berliner Tageblatt'', Nr. 510, 28.X.1919 (Morgenausgabe); vgl. dazu Schröder-Gudehus, Deutsche Wissenschaft (wie Anm. 2), S. 201 f., und Wehberg, Hans: Wider den Aufruf der 93! Berlin 1920.

[28] Von einem Fall berichtet er voller Empörung in ''Die Vereinigten Staaten von Amerika. Geschichte der Kultur, Verfassung und Politik'' (Meyer, Nordamerika, S. 181).

[29] Vgl. Meyer, Eduard: Das Verhalten Nordamerikas gegen Deutschland im Weltkriege. In: Leipziger Illustrirte Zeitung, Nr. 3738, 18.II.1915, S. 178 f.; wiederveröffentlicht in: Meyer, Nordamerika, S. 7–22.

[30] Ebd., S. 12.

[31] Miller, Susanne: Burgfrieden und Klassenkampf. Die deutsche Sozialdemokratie im Ersten Weltkrieg (Beiträge zur Geschichte des Parlamentarismus und der politischen Parteien, Bd. 53). Düsseldorf 1974, S. 254–267.

sis verbis gegen dieses Reformkonzept. Doch lehnte er das Ziel dieser Politik der "Neuorientierung" deshalb ab, weil sie für ihn zur verstärkten Parlamentarisierung und der dann nicht mehr zu verhindernden Demokratisierung führen mußte. Gegen diese westlichen Ideen von 1789 galt es die deutsche Kultur, den Geist und die "Ideen von 1914" zu verteidigen. Es müsse im deutschen Staatsleben die "innere, sittliche Verantwortung" erhalten bleiben. Die Demokratie beseitige sie zugunsten einer "rein äußere[n], in rechtliche Formeln gefaßte[n] Verantwortung". Das Gegenteil sei anzustreben, nämlich der Appell "an die einzelne Persönlichkeit und ihr Pflichtgefühl".[32] Für die "Gestaltung der Kultur und für die Zukunft der Nation" könne allein eine "Geistesaristokratie" maßgebend sein.[33] Nicht Bethmann Hollwegs bedachtsame Umgestaltung hatte Meyer im Sinn, sondern eine "innere Gestaltung", die die Grundlagen nicht antastete: die militärischen und wirtschaftlichen Strukturen ebenso wenig wie die ungeschwächte, zu schöpferischer Gestaltung befähigte Monarchie.[34]

Meyers politische Haltung wurde jedoch nicht allein von der Ansicht bestimmt, daß die Monarchie und das deutsche Beamtentum die bessere Staatsform verkörperten, sondern auch durch die auf Reisen gewonnene und durch Lektüre vertiefte Kenntnis der englischen und amerikanischen

---

[32] Meyer, Eduard: Die Aufgaben der höheren Schulen und die Gestaltung des Geschichtsunterrichts. Leipzig 1918, S. 27. Ähnlich in seiner Rede "Staat und Universität". "Wo dagegen eine derartige beherrschende, schöpferische Persönlichkeit fehlt, da haben die untergeordneten Kräfte freien Spielraum, da waltet der anarchische Zufall des blinden Ungefährs. Es ist das schwerste Verhängnis unseres Volkes gewesen, daß uns in unserer Schicksalsstunde, als der Schrei nach einer überragenden Persönlichkeit durch das ganze Volk ging, eine solche nicht beschieden war, oder daß ihr, falls sie vorhanden war, die volle Wirkung versagt wurde; und es ist ein schlechter Trost, daß es um die übrige Welt nicht besser bestellt ist, vielmehr ist das ein deutliches Symptom dafür, daß die europäische Kultur in ihrer innersten Lebenskraft gebrochen ist und sich dem Niedergang zugewendet hat" (Meyer, Eduard: Staat und Universität. Auszug aus der am Friedrich-Wilhelmstag der Berliner Universität gehaltenen Festrede des derzeitigen Rektors. In: Velhagen & Klasings Monatshefte 35 [November 1920], S. 267).

[33] Meyer, Die Aufgaben (wie Anm. 32), S. 88.

[34] "Nicht jedem das Gleiche, wie die demokratische Theorie fordert, und noch weniger jedem das, was er erraffen kann, wie überall in der demokratischen Praxis, sondern jedem das, was ihm gebührt, suum cuique. [...] An Stelle der Forderung stetig weiter ausgedehnter Rechte dominieren der Begriff der Pflicht, die Umsetzung des gesetzlichen Zwanges in den freien Willen und damit in eine sittliche Tat. An Stelle der Herrschaft der Majorität und damit der Zerreißung des Volks in sich ununterbrochen bekämpfende, lediglich ihre Sonderziele verfolgende Parteien, eine unabhängige Regierung, die nicht den Schwankungen und Irrgängen der öffentlichen Meinung folgt, sondern führt, in engster, befruchtender Fühlung mit allen lebendigen und gesunden Kräften des Volks, denen sie den Raum schafft zu voller Entfaltung; und an der Spitze, als der feste Tragstein des Baus, eine starke Monarchie" (Meyer, Eduard: Preußen und Athen. Rede, gehalten bei der Übernahme des Rektorats der Universität Berlin am 15. Oktober 1919. Berlin 1920, S. 21 f.).

Verhältnisse. Für seine Mitstreiter war er wegen seiner Auslandsaufenthalte eine hoch gewürdigte landeskundige Autorität. Ein Vergleich der Publikationen zeigt jedoch ein diffuses und von den politischen Opportunitäten nicht unbeeinflußtes Bild. Veränderungen in der englischen und insbesondere in der amerikanischen Politik würdigt Meyer seit dem Kriegsausbruch nicht mehr angemessen. Die USA sind imperialistisch und kriegslüstern, aber auch pazifistisch und ängstlich. Ein entschiedenes, ja rücksichtsloses Verhalten des Deutschen Reiches könne keinen Schaden hervorrufen, da die USA militärisch schwach seien und in Europa nicht kriegsentscheidend eingreifen könnten. Eine harte Linie werde außerdem Wilsons Wiederwahl gefährden. Als der Erfolg dann eintrat und Wilson Vermittlungsangebote formulierte, hielt Meyer nunmehr diese pazifistische Anwandlung für die größte Gefahr.[35]

In der Vorkriegszeit hatte Meyer 1904 und 1909/10 auf seinen Reisen quer durch die Vereinigten Staaten, während seiner Lehrtätigkeit im Rahmen des Austauschprogramms, bei seinen zahllosen Gesprächen und gelegentlich seiner Vorträge die gern und intensiv genutzte Möglichkeit, sich nicht allein über wissenschaftliche Themen zu verständigen.[36] Die Lektüre seiner Schilderungen, Berichte und Analysen[37] zeigt, wie stark Meyer sich für die Probleme des Landes, für seine politischen Verhältnisse und für soziale Fragen interessierte. ''Vor allem aber'', schrieb er 1919, ''ist es unmöglich, für all diese zahllosen Ämter wirklich geeignete Kandidaten aufzutreiben, zumal für die unteren, schlecht besoldeten Stellen. So ist man doch immer wieder auf die Politiker angewiesen, die daraus ein Gewerbe machen.''[38] Im einzelnen ist er entweder zu sehr

---

[35] ''Da hat unser Volk, in wahnsinniger Veblendung, den gleisnerischen Verheißungen Amerikas und seines Präsidenten Glauben geschenkt und sich ihm vertrauensvoll zu Füßen geworfen und damit selbst sein Geschick besiegelt; die Folge war, daß der Präsident mit seinen Verbündeten zusammen unter dem erlogenen Namen eines Friedens Bedingungen diktierte, die allen von ihm so feierlich der Welt als Grundlagen eines ewigen Völkerfriedens verkündeten Grundsätzen ins Gesicht schlugen und in Wirklichkeit den Krieg und die Selbstzerfleischung Europas nicht beendet, sondern verewigt haben'' (Meyer, Eduard: *Kl. Schr.* I Vorwort).

[36] Die drei Teile dieses Werks ''Die Vereinigten Staaten von Amerika'' (wie Anm. 35) sind überschrieben ''Geschichte der Vereinigten Staaten'', ''Wirtschaft, Kultur und Nationalcharakter'' sowie ''Verfassung und Politik''. Zu dem ''Austauschprogramm'' s. Brocke, Bernhard vom: Der deutsch-amerikanische Professorenaustausch. In: Zeitschrift für Kulturaustausch 31 (1981), S. 128–182.

[37] 1915: Das Verhalten Nordamerikas gegen Deutschland im Weltkriege; Nordamerika und Deutschland; Der Geist von Harvard; Die neue Politik Amerikas; 1916: Amerika und unser Krieg; 1917: Der amerikanische Kongreß und der Weltkrieg; Die Lage in Amerika; Das Wesen der amerikanischen Demokratie und Präsident Wilson; 1920: Die Vereinigten Staaten von Amerika; Die Amerikaner über den Zusammenbruch Deutschlands.

[38] Meyer, Die Vereinigten Staaten (wie Anm. 36), S. 234.

fasziniert, als daß er als ein objektiver Berichterstatter gelten könne oder
zu stark voreingenommen, um die verfassungsrechtlichen Einzelheiten
angemessen würdigen zu können. Mit beeindruckender Genauigkeit und
mit einem klaren Blick auf die "Frag-Würdigkeit" hat Meyer jedoch die
starke Position des Präsidenten, die Einflußnahme der Presse auf Öffentlichkeit[39] und Politik und die aktuelle Lage der Schwarzen[40] abgehandelt.
Als er 1919 sein Werk "Die Vereinigten Staaten von Amerika" vorlegt,
versichert er, daß er sich bemüht habe, "völlig unparteiisch zu schreiben.
Die persönlichen Bande, die mich an Amerika und an zahlreiche Amerikaner knüpften, sind zerrissen. Aber auf das Buch habe ich der durch den
Krieg erzeugten Stimmung keine Einwirkung gewährt [...]."[41]

Doch bei Kriegsausbruch galt Meyers Haßliebe vorerst nicht den USA,
sondern Großbritannien in voller Stärke, weil es aus Herrschsucht und
Handelseifersucht Deutschlands volle Vernichtung wünsche[42] und die
europäische Friedens- und Rechtsordnung leichtfertig zerbrochen habe.
Bereits während des Kriegs merkte ein Rezensent an, daß sich bei Meyer
Worte "patriotischer Leidenschaft" vernehmen ließen, "wie man sie
selbst in dieser Stunde des Schicksals von einem historischen Forscher zu
vernehmen erstaunt ist: so fanatisch sind sie oft und so einseitig."[43] Mit
einem "Todfeind" könne es keine Versöhnung geben. "Das ganze Volk
weiß", verkündete er im November 1916 in den "Süddeutschen Monatsheften", "daß England der Feind ist, daß sein Verhalten den Krieg her-

---

[39] "Wer tagtäglich in seiner Zeitung von denselben Dingen liest und sie immer wieder
in der gleichen Weise behandelt sieht, der wird gezwungen, sich in seinen Gedanken
wenigstens zeitweise damit zu beschäftigen, und er bildet sich ein, sich ein eigenes Urteil
zu bilden [...]. Aber daß in ihnen [den Vorgängen um Einflußnahme auf die Presse] die
materiellen Interessen ausschlaggebend sind, daß die Drahtzieher vorwiegend in den
Magnaten der Industrie und des Geldes zu suchen sind, bedarf keiner Ausführung. Die
öffentliche Meinung ist für sie eines der Mittel, und vielleicht das stärkste von allen, durch
die sie ihre Ziele erreichen und den Staat beherrschen" (ebd., S. 238).
[40] "Zwar ist ihnen die Bewegungsfreiheit und die Möglichkeit, vorwärts zu kommen,
gewährt, aber überall haben die Befähigteren, die an sich dazu das Zeug haben, mit den
schwersten sozialen und wirtschaftlichen Hindernissen zu kämpfen, während die Masse
im wesentlichen in den alten Verhältnissen lebt, nur daß an die Stelle des alten, mit ihnen
verwachsenen nur zu oft ein fremder Grundherr getreten ist, der möglichst viel Geld einnehmen will, häufig ein jüdischer Spekulant, der weit härtere Anforderungen stellt, als
jener. Trotzdem haben die Neger zweifellos beträchtliche Fortschritte gemacht und sich
keineswegs sämtlich entwicklungsunfähig erwiesen. [...] Es [die Lösung des Rassen-
problems] ist nur um so schwerer, weil der Gegensatz der Rassen immer akuter wird und
eine Lösung hoffnunslos erscheint, so daß nicht nur die Regierung, sondern auch die
führenden Männer dem Gang der Dinge ratlos zuschauen und nicht wissen, wo und wie
sie eingreifen könnten" (ebd., S. 94, 96).
[41] Ebd., S. VII.
[42] In Meyers Vorwort zur Volksausgabe "England", S. XIII.
[43] Fischer zu Meyers Aufsatzsammlung "Weltgeschichte und Weltkrieg". In: Das
größere Deutschland. Dresden 1916, S. 829 f.

beigeführt hat und daß es die Seele des Krieges ist und ihm die Ziele setzt.''[44] In diesem Zusammenhang traten bei Meyer Überlegungen in den Vordergrund, die im weiteren Verlauf des Kriegs zumindest öffentlich von ihm nicht wieder ausgesprochen werden sollten. Sie zeigen einen zaudernden, skeptisch-abwägenden Meyer, das Bild eines verantwortungsbewußten, pessimistischen und von Untergangsstimmungen geängstigten Beobachters; im deutlichen Gegensatz zu dem allgemein verbreiteten Bild des nationalistischen Scharfmachers, des selbstgerechten alldeutschen Annexionisten, des überheblichen, weltfremd-unpolitischen Professors, der zum schmähenden Demagogen, zum Chauvinisten und Militaristen wird.

Meyer geht von der bedrückenden Prämisse aus, daß mit dem August 1914 eine Welt- und Rechtsordnung zusammengebrochen sei, die friedlich nicht so schnell wieder zu ordnen sei. Er bezweifelt, ob am Ende eines mit großer Anspannung geführten Vernichtungskriegs ein gleichartiges Staatensystem stehen könne. Man müsse sogar auf eine weitere Reihe von Kriegen mit England gefaßt sein.[45] Zahlreiche Ideale seien in der im August 1914 total umgewandelten Weltlage unwiederbringlich verloren gegangen, so daß es eine Versöhnungspolitik schlechterdings nicht mehr geben könne.[46] Als ''Satire auf ihre Zeit'' hätten sich die Haager Konferenzen und der Friedenspalast entlarvt. ''Statt des ewigen Friedens wird eine Folge langer, blutiger Kriege die Signatur des neuen Jahrhunderts sein [. . .].'' Es sei zumindest nicht sicher, ''daß Deutschland schon jetzt den vollen Sieg davontrage'' werde.[47] An die sich daraus ergebende Verantwortung für die Regierung und jeden einzelnen im Staat könne ''man nur mit bangem Zagen'' denken.[48] Unter der ''Steigerung der

---

[44] Meyer, Eduard: Zur Vorgeschichte des Weltkrieges. In: Kriegshefte der Süddeutschen Monatshefte 13, November 1916, S. 178.

[45] Vgl. Meyer, England (Volksausgabe), S. XV.

[46] ''Aber der schwerste Verlust, den die Zivilisation durch den Krieg erleidet, ist der Bruch zwischen England und Deutschland. Nicht nur durch die Blutsverwandtschaft und durch die Überlieferung langjähriger geschichtlicher Verbindung, sondern mehr noch durch die enge Berührung und den regen Austausch ihrer Kultur schienen die beiden Völker berufen zu dauernder Gemeinschaft und zu gegenseitiger Ergänzung in dem Aufbau der menschlichen Kultur, in engster Verbindung und Wechselwirkung mit der amerikanischen Nation, in der englisches und deutsches Blut untrennbar zu einer neuen dritten Gestaltung germanischen Volkstums verschmolzen sind. Dieser Zusammenhang ist jetzt jäh und furchtbar für alle absehbare Zukunft zerrissen. [. . .] eins ist sicher: die alten Beziehungen zwischen Deutschland und England werden sich nicht wiederherstellen lassen, an Stelle der engen Verbindung wird auf viele, viele Jahrzehnte hinaus ein erbitterter, unüberbrückbarer Gegensatz treten'' (Meyer, Deutschland und der Krieg [wie Anm. 10], S. 20 f.).

[47] Meyer, England, S. 207.

[48] Ebd., S. 203.

nationalen Gegensätze'' würden Wissenschaft und Kunst aufs Schwerste zu leiden haben.[49] Eine einzige schwache Hoffnung sah Meyer: "Persönliche Beziehungen zwischen einzelnen Gelehrten [...] werden sich [...] wieder herstellen lassen'', doch er fügte sogleich hinzu, "aber darüber hinauszugehen [,] ist auf alle absehbare Zeit jede Möglichkeit ausgeschlossen. Die Kluft, die sich hier geöffnet hat, läßt sich für die jetzt lebende Generation nicht wieder füllen.''[50]

Die weltpolitischen Konsequenzen glaubte er wie so häufig zu einem Vorgang der antiken Geschichte in Beziehung setzen zu können: "Die unmittelbare und zugleich die verhängnisvolle Folge des Hannibalischen Krieges und der aus ihm hervorgehenden Kriege Roms mit den makedonischen Reichen im Osten des Mittelmeers war die Emanzipation des Orients.''[51] Für die Nachkriegszeit befürchtete Meyer nämlich Konflikte in und um Asien, das sich von Europa losreißen werde. Er rechnet mit dem Untergang der abendländischen, europäischen Zivilisation, dem Aufstieg der Flügelmächte Japan,[52] Rußland und USA sowie mit einem erheblich wachsenden Gewicht des Islams in der Türkei und in Persien: "aber das ist sicher, daß [...] damit nicht nur für Vorderasien und Ägypten eine ganz neue Epoche der Weltgeschichte beginnt.''[53] Meyer schloß 1915 mit einem verhalten negativen Resümee, wie es sich in dieser Form in keiner seiner späteren Publikationen findet. Er diktierte darin Großbritannien die Schuld an diesem "unsühnbaren Verbrechen'' zu und

---

[49] Eine Auswirkung für deutsche Wissenschaftler in ihren Beziehungen zu amerikanischen Kollegen sah er folgendermaßen: "[...] die Harvarduniversität [...] nimmt jetzt in der antideutschen Agitation eine führende Stelle ein. [...] Für Deutschland aber ist das Ergebnis, daß der Professorenaustausch mit Harvard aufhören muß, jetzt und für alle Zukunft. Sollte doch der Versuch gemacht werden, ihn wieder ins Leben zu rufen, so hoffen und vertrauen wir, daß sich kein deutscher Gelehrter so erniedrigen wird, der Aufforderung, an dieser Universität zu lesen, Folge zu leisten'' (Meyer, Eduard: Der Geist von Harvard. In: Vossische Zeitung, Nr. 121, 7.III.1915).—In der Berliner Akademie der Wissenschaften gehörte Meyer zu der unter der Führung Roethes agierenden Gruppe in der Philosophisch-historischen Klasse, die etliche der ausländischen Mitglieder wegen antideutscher Äußerungen ausschließen wollte (s. Grau, Die Berliner Akademie [wie Anm. 2], S. 170–193).

[50] Meyer, England, S. 208 f. In diesem Zusammenhang verstärkt Meyer seinen Appell für eine imperialistische Politik durch eine historische Analogie, wenn er die Situation Roms nach dem Hannibalischen Krieg, dem "Wendepunkt der Geschichte des Altertums'', beschwört (Meyer, *Kl. Schr.*, S. 537).

[51] Meyer, England, S. 209.

[52] "Inzwischen hat nun auch Japan seine Stellung völlig demaskiert; es streckt offen seine Hände nach China aus [...]. Wohl aber ist jetzt die große Frage an die Zukunft gestellt, nicht nur ob es nach einem Jahrhundert noch europäische Besitzungen in Ostasien, in der Welt der Südsee und auf Australien geben wird, sondern ob alsdann überhaupt noch auch nur ein Mensch europäischer Abkunft in diesen Gebieten anzutreffen sein wird'' (Meyer, England, S. VII).

[53] Ebd., S. 211.

hielt es für ausgeschlossen, daß die verhängnisvollen weltpolitischen Machtverschiebungen und der Substanzverlust Europas durch die nationale Solidarität und Selbstbesinnung des Augusts 1914 aufgewogen werden könnten. "Die Gefahren, denen wir entgegengehn, sind vielleicht noch größer als die, mit denen wir jetzt ringen", meinte er in einer wissenschaftlichen Festrede[54] im Januar 1918.[55]

Eine herausragende Position nahm Meyer in den Auseinandersetzungen um den uneingeschränkten U-Boot-Krieg ein. Er berief sich auf das Urteil von Fachleuten, die eine Ausweitung dieses Seekriegs nicht nur für zwingend notwendig hielten, sondern auch für das entscheidende militärische Mittel zur Verkürzung des Kriegs. Daneben sah Meyer darin eine weitere Möglichkeit, die gegenüber Liberalen und Sozialdemokraten konzessionsbereite Reformpolitik des Kanzlers vernichtend zu treffen.

> "Die Möglichkeit, daß es mit Amerika zum Krieg kommt, müssen wir hinnehmen; dadurch wird unsere Lage nicht wesentlich schlimmer [...]. Gegen den U-Bootkrieg wird die Verantwortung angeführt, die damit übernommen werde, weil er vielleicht zu dem Eintritt bisher sei es dem Namen nach (wie Amerika) sei es tatsächlich neutraler Staaten in den Krieg führen kann. Dem steht aber die noch weit wuchtigere Verantwortung gegenüber, die eine ablehnende Entscheidung in sich enthält. Denn alsdann erhebt sich die Frage, ob wirklich alle Mittel ergriffen sind, die die Frist verkürzt hätten, in der der Sieg errungen werden konnte; [...] ob nicht diese Entscheidung, dieser Mangel an festem Willen und kühner Entschlußkraft die Schuld trägt, daß die Ergebnisse des Krieges den furchtbaren uns auferlegten Opfern nicht entsprechen, und daß der Friede eine Gestaltung bringt, welche die Zukunft Deutschlands nicht sicherstellt, wohl aber weitere furchtbare Gefahren und Kämpfe herbeiführt, denen wir schließlich erliegen müssen, auch wenn wir diesmal noch nicht zu Boden geworfen werden."[56]

Meyer neigt bei seinem Plädoyer für den "totalen" Einsatz, für die massive und "rücksichtslose" Anwendung aller Mittel im Krieg, dazu, das neue Kriegsmittel U-Boot in dilettantischer Faszination zu über-

---

[54] Meyer, Eduard: Vorläufer des Weltkrieges im Altertum. Wissenschaftliche Festrede, gehalten in der öffentlichen Sitzung der Preußischen Akademie der Wissenschaften am 24. Januar 1918 zur Feier des Geburtstages Sr. Majestät des Kaisers und Königs und des Jahrestages König Friedrichs II.; wiederveröffentlicht in: Meyer, *Kl. Schr.*, S. 507–538; Zitat auf S. 538.

[55] Diesen Gedanken hatte Meyer genau zwei Jahre zuvor Victor Ehrenberg gegenüber geäußert (handschriftliche Postkarte; Berlin, 8.I.1916: Im Zusammenhang mit Naumanns Mitteleuropa-Vorstellungen heißt es: "[...] die Schwierigkeiten, die sich dem entgegenthürmen, sind allerdings doch gewaltig und werden noch anwachsen. Aber so liegt es im Grunde überall; und doch müssen wir vorwärts" (Mitteilung des Kollegen Ungern-Sternberg [wie Anm. 17]).

[56] Meyer, Eduard: Amerika und unser Krieg. In: Unabhängiger Ausschuß für einen deutschen Frieden Nr. 38 (1916).

schätzen.[57] Deshalb konnte es ihm, der noch dazu das militärische Potential der USA unterschätzte, nicht darauf ankommen, die Verkündigung des uneingeschränkten U-Boot-Kriegs diplomatisch vorzubereiten. Ein entschiedenes Auftreten imponiere und sei deshalb opportun.[58] Rücksichtnahme signalisiere nur Schwäche und vermindere den "gewaltigen, enthusiastischen Aufschwung der Stimmung" in der deutschen Öffentlichkeit. Der verschärfte U-Boot-Krieg sei demnach allein schon deshalb anzuordnen, um nicht eines Tages dem Vorwurf ausgesetzt zu sein, leichtfertig auf ein wirksames Instrument verzichtet zu haben.[59] Habe Wilson "keinen Erfolg, bleiben wir fest, so ist aller Voraussicht nach sein Spiel verloren; [...] die letzte Konsequenz zu ziehen, das heißt Deutschland den Krieg zu erklären, dazu ist er gar nicht imstande, selbst wenn er den Wunsch hätte, da die friedliche Strömung viel zu stark ist, als daß er die Mehrheit des Kongresses für eine Kriegspolitik gewinnen könnte."[60] In der Ergänzung des "Vorworts" zu seiner Schrift "Der amerikanische Kongreß und der Weltkrieg" verhehlt Meyer nicht seine Genugtuung über die Eskalation im Februar 1917. Mit den Entscheidungen für den uneingeschränkten Unterwasserkrieg und für den Abbruch der diplomatischen Beziehungen sei die erlösende Situation eingetreten, die er mit seiner Broschüre herbeizuführen wünschte.[61]

Der Kampf um die "Politik der Diagonalen" Bethmann Hollwegs[62]

---

[57] Meyer berief sich dabei auf die "fachmännischen Autoritäten", die von der vollen Wirksamkeit des U-Bootkrieges überzeugt seien (ders.: Denkschrift über den U-Bootkrieg vom 25.VI. 1916).

[58] "Es wäre ein verhängnisvoller Wahn, wenn wir glaubten, durch Verhandlungen und durch Nachgiebigkeit irgend etwas erreichen zu können: wir würden dadurch nur ihre Anmaßung steigern. Je deutlicher wir ihnen zeigen, daß nicht wir sie nötig haben, wohl aber sie uns garnicht entbehren können, umso eher wird sich, soweit es überhaupt möglich ist, eine Annäherung erreichen lassen [...]" (Eduard Meyer in seinem Vorwort zu: Hall, Thomas C.: Licht und Schatten im amerikanischen Leben. Eine kulturgeschichtliche Betrachtung. Berlin 1916, S. 8).

[59] Vgl. Meyer, Denkschrift über den U-Bootkrieg (wie Anm. 57).

[60] Meyer, Eduard: Die neue Politik Amerikas. In: Vossische Zeitung, Nr. 380, 28.VII.1915.

[61] Vgl. Meyer, Der amerikanische Kongreß (wie Anm. 3), S. VIII.

[62] "Aber inzwischen sind wir von einer Krisis zur anderen getaumelt, die zersetzenden Kräfte erhoben, von der Regierung gefördert, immer höher ihr Haupt. So ist der Augenblick gekommen, wo jede Rücksicht schwinden muß. Die Gefahren, die unser Dasein und die gesamte Zukunft des deutschen Volkes bedrohen, sind so furchtbar, und zugleich ist der innere Zwiespalt, der durch unser Volk geht, so offenkundig, daß längeres Schweigen zum Verbrechen, und offenes Bekenntnis zur sittlichen Pflicht wird. Wir klagen den Reichskanzler, Herrn v. Bethmann Hollweg an, daß er alles getan hat, um die Stimmung im Volk und das Vertrauen auf einen glücklichen Ausgang des Krieges zu lähmen, daß er durch Parteinahme die Bestrebungen, welche auf die Zerstörung des deutschen Staates hinarbeiten, gefördert [...] hat. [...] Als Lohn für den Heroismus, mit dem unsere Heere die furchtbarsten Opfer gebracht haben und im feindlichen

kulminierte in der Ablehnung jeglicher Wahlrechtsreform in Preußen und sozialpolitischer Zugeständnisse von größerer Bedeutung. Bethmann Hollwegs Reformversuche, die offenkundige Schwierigkeit, gegen alldeutsche Stimmung im Staat zu einem ''Siegfrieden'' zu kommen, und das wachsende Gewicht einer antiannexionistisch eingestellten Fronde im Reichstag[63] ließen Meyer einen zunehmend härteren politischen Kurs verfolgen.[64] Er unterschrieb die Erklärung der ''deutschen Hochschullehrer gegen die Reichstagsmehrheit'', die dem ''Vorkriegs-Parlament'' im Oktober 1917 entschieden die Kompetenz absprach, ''über die heute zur Entscheidung stehenden Lebensfragen den Volkswillen in unzweifelhafter Weise zum Ausdruck zu bringen.''[65] Damit waren sowohl das Konzept einer ''nationalen Einheitsfront'' als auch die Burgfriedenspolitik gescheitert, denn Wahlrechts-, Parlamentarisierungs- und Friedensfrage standen in engen Wechselbeziehungen zueinander und waren direkt mit der Amtsführung Bethmann Hollwegs verknüpft: die Demission des Reichskanzlers stellte die aus unterschiedlichen Motiven erstrebte Lösung

Ansturm unerschütterlich und siegreich ausharren, für die Hingebung, mit der die Bevölkerung daheim alle Nöte willig und freudig erträgt, soll unser Volk den Umsturz der Grundlagen erhalten, auf denen unser Staat erwachsen ist und unsere organisierte Kraft beruht'' (Meyer, Eduard: Die Politik Bethmann Hollwegs. In: Tägliche Rundschau, Nr. 360, 17.VII.1917).
[63] Rauh, Manfred: Die Parlamentarisierung des Deutschen Reiches (Beiträge zur Geschichte des Parlamentarismus und der politischen Parteien, Bd. 60). Düsseldorf 1977, S. 325–362.
[64] Vorherrschende Begriffe wurden dabei ''rücksichtslos'', ''gebieterisch'', ''unerbittlich'', ''entschlossen'' und ''total''.
[65] So im Wortlaut der Erklärung, die die Zuversicht ausspricht, ''daß es den berufenen Leitern von Heer und Staat gelingen wird, allen äußeren und inneren Widerständen zum Trotz einen Frieden zu erringen, wie ihn Deutschland für sein Leben und Gedeihen braucht.'' Die Veröffentlichung in der ''Täglichen Rundschau'' (Nr. 510, 6.X.1917) schließt übrigens mit einer Erläuterung, die weitgehend Meyers Einschätzung umreißt: ''Diese Erklärung, die dank der in solchen Fällen leider üblichen Indiskretion schon geraume Zeit vor ihrem Erscheinen in der Presse der Linken in der dort ebenfalls leider üblichen Weise erörtert werden konnte, dürfte nunmehr, wo sie mit der stattlichen Zahl von 906 Unterschriften, darunter die angesehensten Namen unserer Hochschulwelt, ans Licht tritt, zu den eindrucksvollsten Kundgebungen der wahren öffentlichen Meinung zählen. [...] Wie wir hören, liegt es den Unterzeichnern fern, eine bestimmte praktische Maßregel wie etwa die Auflösung des Reichstages, herbeiführen zu wollen. Ihre Absicht ist vielmehr nur, dahin zu wirken, daß die Verantwortung für die zu fassenden Entschlüsse uneingeschränkt den Stellen bleibe, auf denen sie nach der geltenden Reichsverfassung nach der Natur der Dinge zu liegen hat.''
Ähnlich äußert sich Meyer in seiner Rede ''Preußen und Athen'': ''[...] die Entscheidung [über den Staat] hängt, und das ist das furchtbarste, keineswegs allein von unserem Willen, von einer Wiederaufrichtung des gebrochenen Volksgeistes ab, sondern in weitestem Umfang von dem herrischen Machtgebot unserer Todfeinde, die jedes Mittel ergreifen, um die deutsche Nation nicht wieder zu neuem gesunden Leben, zu einer selbständigen Stellung im Kreise der Völker erstehen lassen'' (Meyer, Preußen und Athen [wie Anm. 34], S. 6).

des Konflikts für die Alldeutschen, Konservativen und Militärs dar.

Der Sturz Bethmann Hollwegs im Sommer 1917 war also mit dem Scheitern seiner Friedenspolitik und dem Erfolg der Kampagne für den uneingeschränkten U-Boot-Krieg verknüpft.[66] Die Militarisierung der deutschen Politik, der Triumph des militärischen Denkens über die Erwägungen des geschwächten politischen Parts, bildete die Voraussetzung für eine dramatische Wende der deutschen Politik. Sie war allgemein durch eine Überhöhung und Überschätzung des Soldatischen gekennzeichnet, die dazu führte, daß auch im politischen Bereich einseitig das Kämpferische, das Technisch-Organisatorische und die generelle Prävalenz militärischer Erwägungen betont wurden. Meyer reflektierte diese Entwicklung höchst unzulänglich. In seinen Publikationen reduziert er das Phänomen ''Militarismus'' auf die Ebene des Institutionellen, des im Krieg Notwendigen und Nützlichen. Er berichtete deshalb seinen Lesern von dem eindrucksvollen Vorlesungsprogramm der ''Feld-Universität'' Tournai,[67] von den Hochschulkursen in Warschau[68] oder den ''Vorträgen deutscher Gelehrter über deutsches Geistesleben'', die das Oberkommando der 8. Armee in Reval gestaltete.[69] Des weiteren beschrieb er die Schutzmaßnahmen für die Kulturgüter in den eroberten Gebieten und die wirtschaftlichen Aufbauprogramme der Militärs hinter den Fronten.[70].

---

[66] Vgl. dazu auch den Briefwechsel zwischen Cossmann (''Süddeutsche Monatshefte''), Gebsattel (''Gäa'') und Meyer aus den Jahren 1916 und 1927 im AkadWissDDR, NL Ed. Meyer, Nr. 287. Zur deutschen Friedenspolitik siehe die Untersuchungen und Editionen von Steglich, Wolfgang (Hg.): Die Friedensversuche der kriegführenden Mächte im Sommer und Herbst 1917. Quellenkritische Untersuchungen, Akten und Vernehmungsprotokolle (Quellen und Studien zu den Friedensversuchen des Ersten Weltkrieges, Bd. 4). Wiesbaden 1984, und ders.: Die Friedenspolitik der Mittelmächte 1917/18. Bd. 1. Wiesbaden 1964.

[67] ''Da [im Schützengraben] steigert sich die Hingabe, die in den befriedeten Heimatgauen von der Höhe des August 1914 nur zu oft so traurig herabgesunken ist. [...] Aber das bewunderungswürdigste was geschaffen ist, sind doch die Hochschulkurse von Tournai. In ihnen offenbart sich der wahre Geist des deutschen Militarismus, und er ist kein anderer als der Geist des deutschen Volkes und der deutschen Kultur'' (Meyer, Eduard: Vom deutschen Militarismus. In: Süddeutsche Monatshefte 15 (September 1918), S. 428,430). Zum Thema ''Militarismus'' s. den Überblick bei Berghahn, Volker R.: Militarismus. Die Geschichte einer Internationalen Debatte. Hamburg 1986.

[68] Meyer las z.B. jeweils zweistündig über ''Die Entwicklung der römischen Weltherrschaft'' und über ''Die Vereinigten Staaten Amerikas''—mit diesem Thema waren die Militärs anfangs nicht einverstanden, da sie eine unzulässige Politisierung ihres ''literarisch-historischen Kursus'' befürchteten—, Gustav Roethe über ''Die wichtigsten Denkmale der mitteldeutschen Dichtung'', Heinrich Morf über die ''Französische Romantik'', Robert Holtzmann über ''Polnische Geschichte'' und Max Friedländer über ''Beethovens Leben und Wirken''.

[69] Zu den Einzelheiten dieser Reisen und den Programmen vgl. die Materialien im AkadWissDDR, NL Ed. Meyer, Nr. 338.

[70] Meyer, Militarismus (wie Anm. 67), S. 430.

Eduard Meyer führte seinen innenpolitischen Kampf vor allem zusammen mit Dietrich Schäfer und Otto Hoetzsch—es beteiligten sich hieran übrigens relativ wenige Professoren aktiv[71]—auf der institutionellen Grundlage des am 22. Juli 1916 gegründeten, aber bereits seit 1915 aktiven "Unabhängigen Ausschusses für einen deutschen Frieden". Er vereinigte unter Schäfers Vorsitz die Wortführer der sog. nationalen Kriegszielbewegung.[72] Meyer hat sich nicht mit klaren Annexionsforderungen an der Diskussion beteiligt, doch verbarg er nicht, daß seine Vorstellungen in einzelnen Fällen noch jenseits der Maximalforderungen liegen könnten. Denn der Friede müsse Deutschland eine Sicherung und Erweiterung seines Machtbereichs gewähren, die eine Wiederkehr der gegenwärtigen Lage zukünftig unmöglich machen und dem Deutschen Reich "für seine Weltstellung ein weit größeres Gebiet" eröffnen, als es bisher vorhanden war.[73] Nach einem siegreich beendeten Krieg sah Meyer weltweit territoriale, wirtschaftliche und politische Neuordnungsforderungen auf das Deutsche Reich zukommen. Im Fall der islamischen Welt warnte er nachdrücklich davor, sich diesen Aufgaben entziehen zu wollen.[74] Gerade in dieser Region müsse der Einfluß Großbritanniens ausgeschaltet werden.[75]

---

[71] Vgl. Schwabe, Klaus: Wissenschaft (wie Anm. 2), S. 98.

[72] Es war ihm eine "heilige Pflicht [...], immer von neuem gegen die Schuldlügen des sogenannten Friedensvertrages zu protestieren, und offen aus[zu]sprechen, daß von irgendwelcher Annäherung nicht die Rede sein kann, solange noch ein Stück deutschen Bodens vom Feinde besetzt ist" (Meyer, Eduard: Zur Einführung. In: Edouard Dujardin: Geistige Zusammenarbeit zwischen Deutschland und Frankreich [Süddeutsche Monatshefte 26 (April 1928)]; vgl. auch das Vorwort zur ergänzten Neuauflage der "Kleinen Schriften" (1924 in 2 Bden.), in dem sich Meyer gleichzeitig gegen "das eitle Geschwätz der Friedensschwärmer von Völkerversöhnung" wendet (separat gedruckt u.d.T. "Eduard Meyer über die Vereinigten Staaten". In: Süddeutsche Monatshefte 22 (Dezember 1924), S. 48 f.).

[73] Meyer, Weltgeschichte, S. 168.

[74] "Es sind ungeheure Aufgaben, die der Weltkrieg hier [in der islamischen Welt] wie überall unserer militärischen und politischen Leitung gestellt hat und ununterbrochen in stets gesteigertem Umfang stellt; und wohl mag der Blick schwindlich werden und die Phantasie versagen, wenn diese unermeßliche Welt sich vor uns öffnet. Und doch können wir diese Aufgaben gar nicht von uns weisen, [...] die Stellung, die wir gegenwärtig hier einnehmen, geht weit über die kühnsten Kriegsziele hinaus, welche die von felsenfestem Glauben an den Sieg Deutschlands beseelten Gruppen aufzustellen wagten, und noch ist auch hier gar nicht abzusehen, wohin uns der Zwang der Verhältnisse noch weiter treiben wird, wir mögen wollen oder nicht" (Meyer, Eduard: Deutschland und die islamische Welt. In: Süddeutsche Monatshefte 15 (Juli 1918), S. 272).

[75] "Das Widerwärtigste von allem jedoch ist das Lügensystem, zu dem die Engländer gegriffen und mit dem sie die ganze Welt überschwemmt haben: da tritt eine sittliche Verworfenheit zutage, von der man sich mit Ekel abwendet. Keine Verleumdung ist ihnen zu niedrig, keine Lüge zu sinnlos, um davor zurückzuscheuen. [...] Zugleich tritt dabei ihre tiefe Unbildung und die völlige Unfähigkeit, andere Völker zu verstehen, drastisch zutage" (Meyer, England, S. 199).

An der innnenpolitischen Agitation des "Unabhängigen Ausschusses"
beteiligte sich Meyer in führender Position. Am 17. März 1918 veröffentlichte er im Auftrag der Kanzlerfronde eine scharfe Abrechnung mit dem
zurückgetretenen Bethmann Hollweg. Wegen dessen "schlaffe[r] Nachgiebigkeit" sei es zu einem gravierenden Vertrauensverlust in der deutschen Öffentlichkeit und zu Siegeshoffnungen in den Entente-Ländern
gekommen. Bethmann Hollwegs Unfähigkeit habe sich schon vor dem
Kriegsausbruch bezeugt, und seit 1915 habe er die wahrhaft nationalen
Kräfte durch die Mißachtung der "Burgfriedens"-Verabredungen konsequent unterdrückt. Meyers Anklage gipfelt in den Behauptungen, des
Reichskanzlers Politik der Ablehnung eines "kraftvollen deutschen
Frieden[s]" habe den Krieg verlängert, auf einen "faulen Frieden [. . .]"
gezielt und mit der intendierten verfassungspolitischen Neuordnung die
Position des Kaisers schwächen wollen.[76]

Meyer erkannte weder die starke Aushöhlung des monarchischen Gedankens während des Kriegs noch die Bedeutung einer zunehmenden
Militarisierung des politischen und gesellschaftlichen Lebens.[77] Gegen
die ausländischen Angriffe auf den deutschen "Militarismus" und gegen
die Ideen der Französischen Revolution, des Liberalismus und Parlamentarismus setzte er die "Ideen von 1914";[78] denn die politische Freiheit
im Sinne des radikalen Liberalismus sei nicht das Ideal der Deutschen.[79]
Die Oktober-Reformen des Prinzen Max von Baden mußten in den
Augen Meyers das Ende des Kriegs und des Reichs beschleunigen, denn
sie knüpften an die Politik Bethmann Hollwegs an und setzten sie entschieden fort. Der "Neunte November" 1918 wurde für ihn zum Symbol
des politischen, geistigen und moralischen Niedergangs des deutschen
Volks. Seine düsteren Ahnungen von 1915 hielt Meyer nach dem Zusammenbruch der Monarchie für erfüllt.[80]

---

[76] Vgl. Meyer, Bethmann Hollweg (wie Anm. 62).

[77] Dazu Sösemann, Bernd: Der Verfall des Kaisergedankens im Ersten Weltkrieg. In:
Röhl, John (Hg.). ERSCHEINT DEMNÄCHST!

[78] Vgl. dazu Plenge, Johann: 1789 und 1914. Die symbolischen Jahre in der Geschichte des politischen Geistes. Berlin 1916; Sösemann, Bernd: Das "erneuerte Deutschland". Ernst Troeltschs politisches Engagement im Ersten Weltkrieg (Troeltsch-Studien,
Bd. 3). Gütersloh 1984, S. 120–144, insbesondere S. 133–135.

[79] "[. . .] er [der Deutsche] will regiert sein, und zwar in allen Schichten des Volks,
nicht selbst regieren. Die Regierung aber soll die Interessen der Gesamtheit vertreten, und
eben darum unparteiisch und mit gefesteter Autorität über den einzelnen und über den
Gruppen stehn. Der Pflichtbegriff steht dem Deutschen höher als der der politischen
Rechte, die Hingabe für ein über den einzelnen und sein Wohlergehn, über die 'Er-
strebung der Glückseligkeit' hinausgehendes Ziel, für eine Idee ist ihm das Ideal, mag sie
in Wirklichkeit auch noch so verschwommen und unhaltbar sein" (Meyer, Die Vereinigten Staaten [wie Anm. 36], S. 245).

[80] "Der *Sieg der Umstürzler* vom 9. November war nur möglich durch die *Lauheit und*

Das Deutsche Reich war seiner entscheidenden politischen und militärischen Grundlagen beraubt, die Weltstellung der europäischen Kultur vernichtet. Ob ein geistiger und moralischer Wiederaufbau Deutschlands nach diesem jähen Zusammenbruch und dem ''plötzliche[n] und vollständige[n] Versagen des Volks'' in diesem Jahrhundert überhaupt jemals würde wieder zu erreichen sein, schien ihm fraglich.[81] Den Gesamtvorgang sah er als einmalig in der Weltgeschichte an.[82] Eine unfähige Regierung habe nicht alle Kriegsmittel rücksichtslos eingesetzt und sich von den Verheißungen einer feindlichen Regierung, gemeint sind die Vorschläge Wilsons, blenden lassen. Der deutsche Verteidigungswille sei schließlich von außen und innen her zersetzt worden. Ohne daß hier der Begriff auftaucht, kulminiert die Argumentation im Bild des ''Dolchstoßes''.[83]

Da Meyer nicht, wie z.B. Troeltsch oder Meinecke,[84] eine Chance in der Republik und der Demokratie sah, blieb ihm allein die Hoffnung auf eine Verfassungsänderung und die Jugend. Der kommenden Generation müsse die Verantwortung für das erniedrigte Volk auferlegt, sie müsse für die Zukunft gewonnen werden. Denn momentan habe Deutschland ausschließlich die ''Gebrechen der amerikanischen Demokratie'' als eilfertiger gründlicher Schüler übernommen: Selbstsucht, Begehrlichkeit, Unterschleif und Mißwirtschaft in den Verwaltungsämtern, ''die gedankenlose Unterordnung unter die Majorität, die inhaltslose Phraseologie, die Tyrannis der gerissenen Politiker und Parteigrößen'', den Mißbrauch des Strafrechts und sogar die Lynchjustiz.[85] Hiermit formulierte Meyer in der Geburtsstunde Weimars, nämlich am Tag nach der Verkündung der Verfassung, seinen schärfsten Angriff auf das Weimarer System. Seine politische Strategie schien damit klar zu sein:

Mutlosigkeit des Bürgertums [...].'' Aus dem von Meyer mit unterzeichneten ''Aufruf deutscher Wissenschaftler. Wählt deutschnational!'' In: Deutsche Tageszeitung, Nr. 574, 6.XII.1924 (Abendausgabe); alle Hervorhebungen im Original.

[81] Meyer, Eduard: Deutschlands Lage in der Gegenwart und unsere Aufgaben für die Zukunft. Vortrag, gehalten in der Deutschnationalen Volkspartei in Berlin-Lichterfelde am 27.II.1919. Berlin 1919, S. 3.

[82] Vgl. Meyer, Eduard: Rede zur Gedächtnisfeier des Stifters der Berliner Universität König Friedrich Wilhelm III. in der Aula am 3. August 1920. Berlin 1920, S. 6; ders., Deutschlands Lage (wie Anm. 81), S. 3.

[83] Ebd., S. 8; vgl. ders.: Der 9. November, ein Mahnruf an das deutsche Volk. In: Berliner Hochschul-Nachrichten, Nr. 1, 16.IX.1919, S. 2. Siehe dazu auch die Flugschrift Koester, Adolf: Fort mit der Dolchstoßlegende. Warum wir 1918 nicht weiterkämpfen konnten. Berlin 1922, und das in mehreren Auflagen erschienene Heft ''Der Dolchstoß'' der Zeitschrift ''Süddeutsche Monatshefte''; vgl. auch die Leitartikel Theodor Wolffs im ''Berliner Tageblatt'' zu diesem Problem, Nr. 490, 25.IX.1918, und Nr. 80, 20.II.1919.

[84] Döring, Kreis (wie Anm. 2), insbesondere die Übersichten im Anhang; Sösemann, Das ''erneuerte Deutschland'' (wie Anm. 78), S. 141–144.

[85] Meyer, Die Vereinigten Staaten (wie Anm. 36), S. VII.

"Wenn nichts anderes, so zwingen uns in unserer jetzigen furchtbaren Lage
unsere Feinde zum Zusammenhalten gerade durch die Ketten, mit denen
sie uns in Fesseln zu schlagen und in dauernder Ohnmacht zu halten versuchen; eben diese Hammerschläge des Versailler Vertrags, die uns zer-
trümmern sollen, müssen und werden uns zusammenhämmern zu fest-
geschlossener innerer Einheit."[86]

Doch derartig negativ und grundsätzlich äußerte sich Meyer trotz seiner
anhaltenden Abneigung gegenüber einem zu mächtig agierenden Parlamentarismus in den folgenden Jahren nicht mehr.[87] Er trat der DNVP
bei und verkündete in mehreren Reden, daß das deutsche Volk in die
eigentliche Katastrophe erst jetzt nach dem Kriegsschluß hineingehe. Die
Sieger hätten den seiner Souveränität beraubten deutschen Staat mit
einem Diktatfrieden geknebelt und ihn durch eine aufgezwungene, ver-
derbliche Demokratie geschwächt, bedrohten ihn durch wirtschaftliche
Ausbeutung und handelten damit in ähnlicher Weise wie seinerzeit Rom
gegenüber Karthago:[88] Der Vernichtung der nationalen Existenz folge
ein "kümmerliches Fortvegetieren in elendem Sklavendasein".[89] Der
9. November müsse deshalb zur inneren Einkehr mahnen, zur Besinnung auf das Verantwortungs- und Pflichtgefühl des einzelnen. "Aus der
Reihe der Gedenktage der deutschen Nation kann er [der 9. November]
niemals ausgestrichen werden; aber aus einem Festtag wird der Tag, an
dem unser Volk sich selbst entmannt und in den Abgrund gestürzt hat,
sich umwandeln in einen großen nationalen Bußtag. Der Krieg ist nun
einmal die große Prüfung [. . .]. Und da hilft uns kein Sträuben, wir müssen das Verdikt der Geschichte anerkennen; wir sind gewogen und zu
leicht befunden."[90] Die Kraft für den "Entscheidungskampf zwischen
dem Geist vom 9. November und dem Geist Friedrichs des Großen,
Goethes, eines Freiherrn vom Stein"[91] suchte Meyer in der Landbevölkerung. Die notwendige Energie könne nicht von dem "zersetzenden"
städtischen Element ausgehen.[92] Deshalb engagierte Meyer sich stärker

---

[86] Meyer, Preußen und Athen (wie Anm. 34), S. 25.

[87] Am 12. August 1919 hieß es: "Falls die zukünftige Gestaltung Deutschlands wirklich dauernd eine demokratische Republik bleiben wird, ist es dringend geboten, bei
Amerika in die Lehre zu gehen und die neue Verfassung unter Benutzung des dort gebotenen Vorbildes von Grund auf umzugestalten, wenn die deutsche Nation überhaupt noch
eine Zukunft haben soll" (Meyer, Die Vereinigten Staaten [wie Anm. 36], S. VII).

[88] Vgl. Meyer, Der 9. November (wie Anm. 83), S. 4.

[89] Meyer, Preußen und Athen (wie Anm. 34), S. 20; zum Kampf Meyers gegen den
Versailler Vertrag s. die Planungen, Programme und Mitgliederlisten des Ausschusses,
der die "Vorläufige Leitung der Protest-Aktion gegen den Versailler Frieden" bildete
(AkadWissDDR, NL Ed. Meyer, Nr. 342).

[90] Meyer, Der 9. November (wie Anm. 83), S. 2.

[91] Meyer, Der Aufruf deutscher Wissenschaftler (wie Anm. 80).

[92] Im einzelnen bemerkt Meyer dazu: "Wenn wir in die Zustände zurückgedrängt

in Adolf Damaschkes "Heimstättenbewegung"—man hatte ihn bereits während des Kriegs als lebenslanges Mitglied aufgenommen[93]—, die für die Masse des Volkes Grundbesitz sichern wollte, da nur so ein Gegengewicht gegenüber den "die Volkskraft aufsaugenden Industriezentren" errichtet werden könne.[94] Wie in dem amerikanischen Verfassungsleben müsse auch in Deutschland die gutwillige, aber energielose Regierung von einer Persönlichkeit wie Themistokles oder Bismarck abgelöst werden, denn "die wirkliche Verantwortung der politischen Leitung" könne "immer nur von einem Einzelnen getragen werden, nie von einer Körperschaft."[95]

In der DNVP bzw. in deren "Hauptausschuß für die deutschen Hochschulen" arbeitete Meyer wieder mit den Kollegen Otto von Giercke, Lubarsch, Roethe, Schäfer, Schiemann, Seeberg und Wilamowitz-Moellendorff zusammen. Die Namen dieser kleinen Gruppe finden sich unter nahezu allen Kundgebungen, Petitionen und Aufrufen entschieden konservativen oder deutschnationalen Zuschnitts.[96] Sie vereinten sich öffentlich anläßlich der von Meyer konzipierten "Erklärung deutscher Hochschullehrer zur Auslieferungsfrage". In Meyers Lichterfelder Privatwohnung liefen die Unterschriftensammlungen zusammen. "Für Ehre, Wahrheit und Recht", gegen "die Auslieferung und Aburteilung des Kaisers", lautete die Parole, und für ein selbstbewußtes Deutschland nach neun Monaten der "armselige[n] Selbsterniedrigung".[97] Die

---

werden, wie sie vor einem halben und einem ganzen Jahrhundert bestanden, wenn unsere Großstädte wieder zu mittleren Städten zusammenschrumpfen, wenn die Grundlage wieder agrarisch wird und sich eine gesunde Landbevölkerung wieder entwickelt, die aus eigener Kraft leben kann, dann läßt sich die deutsche Nation auch in Zukunft noch einmal wieder aufbauen, dann ist die Möglichkeit eines neuen Aufstiegs ähnlich wie vor einem Jahrhundert nicht ganz ausgeschlossen." (Meyer, Deutschlands Lage [wie Anm 81], S. 13).
[93] Vgl. die Korrespondenz zwischen Adolf Damaschke und Eduard Meyer in Akad-WissDDR, NL Ed. Meyer, Nr. 518, hier insbesondere die Briefe Damaschkes vom 2.VIII. und 22.XI.1918.
[94] Meyer, Heimstätten, S. 52.
[95] Meyer, Deutschlands Lage (wie Anm. 81), S. 17.
[96] Vgl. die folgenden Aufrufe: Eine konservative Erklärung zum Wahlrechtserlaß (Berliner Professorenkundgebung für die Verschiebung der preußischen Wahlreform auf die Zeit nach dem Krieg). In: Germania, Nr. 314, 13.VIII.1917; Aufruf deutscher Hochschullehrer (für die DNVP zur Nationalversammlungswahl am 19.I.1919). In: Deutsche Tages-Zeitung, Nr. 15, 27.I.1919; Aufruf (deutschnationaler Professoren vor der preußischen Kommunalwahl am 23.II.1919). In: Ebd., Nr. 95, 21.II.1919; Ein Aufruf deutscher Wissenschaftler. Wählt deutschnational! (für die DNVP anläßlich der Dezemberwahl 1924). In: Ebd., Nr. 574, 6.XII.1924.
[97] Meyer, Eduard: Für Ehre, Wahrheit und Recht. Erklärung deutscher Hochschullehrer zur Auslieferungsfrage. Berlin 1919, S. 7.—Aus der Fülle der Korrespondenz, die Meyer im Sommer 1919 erreichte, seien die Briefe von A. von Harnack (20.VII.) und E. Norden (10.VII.) herausgehoben (Staats- und Universitätsbibliothek Hamburg,

"Berliner Hochschul-Nachrichten" verbreiteten am 16. Februar 1920 Meyers zusätzliche Erklärung, daß er "an dem Tage, an dem die Auslieferungsforderung amtlich" gestellt werde, "den Universitäten Oxford, Liverpool, St. Andrews, der Universität von Chicago und der Harvarduniversität", die ihm "in besseren Tagen die Doktorwürde verliehen" hatten, seine Diplome zerrissen zurückgeben werde. Dieses Nachrichtenblatt verbreitete in derselben Ausgabe auch den Text einer Rede des Rektors Eduard Meyer an die Berliner Studentenschaft:

> "In der schwersten Zeit deutscher Geschichte sind wir heute hier versammelt. [...] Und nun wird das Furchtbarste von uns verlangt, eine Forderung von einer Brutalität, von einer Unmenschlichkeit, wie sie noch nie an ein Volk gestellt worden ist. Mit Schaudern empfinden wir den Abgrund sittlichen Empfindens, der uns von unseren Feinden trennt. Undenkbar, daß je von deutscher Seite eine ähnliche Forderung an besiegte Feinde gestellt worden wäre, wie sie an uns gestellt ist: daß wir selbst die Hand dazu bieten sollen, uns für alle Ewigkeit zu schänden und auszustreichen aus den Nationen, aus den lebenskräftigen Völkern der Welt, daß wir die tiefste Schmach selbst an uns vollziehen und uns zu ihr bekennen sollen! Was wird von uns verlangt? Daß wir an tausend deutsche Bürger ihres Bürgerrechts berauben, sie rachsüchtigen Feinden ausliefern sollen zur Hinschlachtung, zur Mißhandlung ohne jede Spur von Recht und Gerechtigkeit [...]. Daß wir uns das nicht gefallen lassen wollen, daß der nationale Geist wieder erwacht in Deutschland, das ist ein Zeichen, daß wir noch nicht ganz verloren sind. Es geht ein Wehen durch unser Volk, welches wieder von fernher erinnert an den herrlichsten Tag, den das deutsche Volk erlebt hat: an den 4. August des Jahres 1914. Etwas von der Stimmung dieser gewaltigen Zeit, die uns zu den größten Taten geführt hat, die die Weltgeschichte aufzuweisen hat, geht wieder durch die Gegenwart. Es ist wieder ein Aufatmen, ein Wiederbesinnen auf die nationale Pflicht und die nationale Würde, und der nationale Stolz, er muß wieder erwachen [...]."[98]

Meyer ist nicht zu den Monarchisten zu zählen, die sich für eine Restauration dieser Staatsform einsetzten. Er hielt dies nicht für möglich, denn "eine gefallene Monarchie [lasse] sich nicht wieder aufrichten."[99] In diesem Zusammenhang erwähnt Meyer in seiner Rektoratsrede am 15. Oktober 1919 wie auch schon zuvor niemals Wilhelm II. Für ihn war

---

Handschriftenabteilung, Nachlaß Eduard Meyer, I 17; freundliche Mitteilung von Dr. Edgar Pack, der eine Edition vorbereitet), die beide ablehnen, den Aufruf zu unterzeichnen, da er "nach Innen u. nach Außen schädigen wird" (Harnack).

[98] Meyer, Eduard: Gegen die Auslieferung! In: Berliner Hochschul-Nachrichten, Nr. 4, 16.II.1920. Vgl. auch das von Meyer formulierte Rundschreiben an "sämtliche deutsche Hochschulen"; Berlin, 4.II.1920, und das Schreiben Edwin Emersons, "Vereinigung Vergewaltigter Völker," an Meyer o.D. (AkadWissDDR, NL Ed. Meyer, Nr. 336).

[99] Meyer, Preußen und Athen (wie Anm. 34), S. 23.

Wilhelm I. "der letzte wahre König [...], den die Erde gesehn hat."[100]
Offenkundig rechnete er den ins Exil gegangenen Kaiser zu denen, die
"ihrer Aufgabe nicht voll gewachsen" gewesen waren.

Der Kapp-Lüttwitz-Putsch brachte ihm einen kurzen Hoffnungsschim-
mer, es werde zu einem erfolgreichen politischen Umsturz kommen. In
der praktischen politischen Arbeit der deutschen Sozialdemokratie und in
einigen ihrer Repräsentanten, wie Friedrich Ebert oder Philipp
Scheidemann, hatte er zwar einen "gewaltigen, echt deutschen Idealismus"[101] entdecken können, jedoch nicht die notwendige Härte gegenüber der bolschewistischen Gefahr.[102] Kapp hielt er vielleicht für die
ersehnte starke Persönlichkeit, die seiner Ansicht nach dem Staat allein
die Gewähr dafür bot, die Krise oder den Ausnahmezustand zu bewältigen.[103] Jedenfalls beeilte er sich, den Wünschen eines studentischen
Anführers entschieden rechter Couleur weitgehend zu folgen[104] und
auch den Hochschulerlaß Kapps—es war die Anordnung über Schlies-
sung der Universitäten—ausdrücklich als "Wunsch des Herrn Reichskanzlers" an sämtliche Dozenten weiterzuleiten.[105]

Der "Fall Nicolai", die Auseinandersetzungen um den Berliner Extra-
ordinarius und Pazifisten, mußte für ihn schlagartig die eigenen politischen Niederlagen der Kriegszeit und den "Krieg der Geister"[106] im
Reich und die Angriffe aus dem Ausland ins Gedächtnis rufen.[107] Georg

---

[100] Ebd.

[101] Ebd., S. 24.

[102] Vgl. den "Bericht über die Sitzung" vom 10.X.1918 zwischen "Vertretern des
Unabhängigen Ausschusses für einen deutschen Frieden, der Deutschen Vaterlandspartei
und des Volksbundes für Freiheit und Vaterland unter dem Vorsitz von Professor Harnack", an der auch Gewerkschaftler und Sozialdemokraten teilnahmen (15 S.), in: Akad-
WissDDR, NL Ed. Meyer, Nr. 341.

[103] In den entscheidenden Stunden hat Meyer sich aus der Perspektive demokratischer Politiker nicht zweifelsfrei verhalten. In einem erklärenden Schreiben vom
15.III.1920 (eigenhändig unterzeichneter Entwurf mit handschriftlichen Zusätzen) räumt
er Versäumnisse in der Ausübung seines Amts als Rektor ein: er habe sich nicht selbst
informiert, auf Auskünfte aus zweiter Hand verlassen und sei erst verspätet in der Universität erschienen (AkadWissDDR, NL Ed. Meyer, Nr. 285).

[104] Vgl. den Artikel "Dies ater academicus" in den Berliner Hochschul-Nachrichten,
Nr. 4, 16.II.1920 (wie Anm. 98).

[105] Vgl. den Artikel "Rektor Eduard Meyer", in: Berliner Tageblatt, Nr. 157,
6.IV.1920; E.J. Gumbel, Vier Jahre politischer Mord (Berlin 1921), Nachdruck Heidelberg 1980, S. 99 verzeichnet auf einer "Kabinettsliste" Kapps auch Eduard Meyer.

[106] S. Anm. 26 und Brocke, Bernhard vom: "An die Europäer." Der Fall Nicolai und
die Biologie des Krieges, in: Historische Zeitschrift 240 (1985), S. 363–375; ders., Wissenschaft versus Militarismus: Nicolai, Einstein und die "Biologie des Krieges", in:
Annali dell'istituto storico italogermanico in Trento 10 (1984), Bologna 1985, S. 405–508
(mit Dokumentation); Zuelzer, Wolf: Der Fall Nicolai. Frankfurt/M. 1981.

[107] Meyer, Das Verhalten Nordamerika (wie Anm. 29); ders., Der Geist von Harvard
(wie Anm. 49); vgl. auch Dietz, Carl: Die deutsche Kultur im Spiegel englischer Urteile,
in: Preußische Jahrbücher 160 (April 1915), S. 100–124.

Friedrich Nicolai hatte nicht nur gegen den von Meyer mitunterzeich-
neten "Aufruf der 93" protestiert, sondern das Gegenmanifest "Aufruf
an die Europäer" verfaßt und seine Vorstellungen in seinem Buch "Die
Biologie des Krieges"[108] in der Schweiz erstmals publiziert. Im Deutschen Reich ließ es der Zensor beschlagnahmen; im Ausland erregte es die
größte Aufmerksamkeit. Sein Verfasser wurde im Sommersemester 1915
an der Abhaltung seiner Vorlesung gehindert, als Arzt strafversetzt und
schließlich wegen "antinationaler" Äußerungen sogar gefangengenom-
men. Nach seiner Degradierung und mehreren Prozessen floh Nicolai im
Sommer 1918, weil er als Arzt und Pazifist nicht mit der Waffe hatte
dienen wollen, mit einem Militärflugzeug nach Dänemark.[109]

1920 hetzten Tageszeitungen des rechten Flügels gegen die Wiederaufnahme der Nicolaischen Vorlesungen, und mit ihnen sympathisierten
nicht wenige Studenten der Friedrich Wilhelm-Universität. Meyer ließ es
als Rektor zu, daß der Akademische Senat die Angelegenheit Nicolai auch
unter politischen Fragestellungen untersuchte. Meyer ging gegen die
gewaltätig störenden Studenten nicht disziplinarisch vor und stritt sich
mit dem sozialdemokratischen Kultusminister Haenisch und dessen
Staatssekretär Carl Heinrich Becker darüber, ob der Akademische Senat
rechtmäßig gehandelt habe, als er Nicolai die venia legendi wegen Un-
würdigkeit entzog. Der Kultusminister hob zwar das Urteil wieder auf,
doch war er ebensowenig wie die angerufenen Gerichte dazu bereit,
Nicolai die Lehrfreiheit wieder zu verschaffen.[110]

Die bisher vorliegenden Studien[111] können nicht ganz befriedigen,
weil die Akten bislang nicht vollständig zugänglich waren oder in verengt-
er Perspektive interpretiert wurden. Meyers Rolle ist zwar auch jetzt
noch nicht in allen Einzelheiten klar erkennbar, doch zeichnet sich aufgrund der Nachlässe ein Bild ab, in dem Meyer zumindest zeitweise von
einem schwankend agierenden Kultusministerium bewußt im Unklaren
gelassen wurde. Aus dem Bericht Meyers "über meine persönlichen Erlebnisse der Verhandlungen in der Angelegenheit Nicolai" ergeben sich
im Detail Abweichungen zum bisher Bekannten.[112] Der Staatssekretär

---

[108] Nicolai, Georg Friedrich: Die Biologie des Krieges. Betrachtungen eines Natur-
forschers, den Deutschen zur Besinnung. Zürich 1917.

[109] Chronologische Übersicht in Zuelzer, Der Fall Nicolai (wie Anm. 106), S. 432–
435.

[110] Vgl. dazu die Korrespondenz zwischen dem Kultusminister Haenisch, seinem
Staatssekretär Becker einerseits und Meyer bzw. der Universität andererseits, in: Staatsbibliothek Preußischer Kulturbesitz, Berlin, Nachlaß Eduard Meyer (im folgenden abgekürzt: SB, NL Ed. Meyer), Nr. 213.

[111] Zuelzer (s. Anm. 106) hat viel Material zusammengetragen, ohne es jedoch in
quellenkritischer Hinsicht befriedigend auszuwerten.

[112] SB, NL Ed. Meyer, Nr. 213.

Becker habe bedauert, heißt es dort, "für Nicolai Stellung nehmen zu müssen." Aus den Marginalien Meyers zu einem Schreiben des Kultusministers, in dem ihm eine "ernste Missbilligung" ausgesprochen wird, weil Meyer "das selbstverständlichste Gebot amtlicher Disziplin schwer verletzt" habe, ist Meyers Reaktion gegenüber Haenisch deutlich zu entnehmen. "Diese ganze Darstellung ist völlig schief. [...] Das ist völlig unwahr! [...] Das ist [...] gelogen." Meyer urteilt ungewöhnlich scharf: "der Minister resp. Becker, der die Schriftstücke verfaßt hat, geht daher mit Stillschweigen darüber hinweg und wiederholt seine frühere unwahre Behauptung, in der er seine uns gegebenen Weisungen [...] mit kühler Stirn ableugnet, obwohl [der Universitätsrichter] Wollenberg und ich diese Tatsache eidlich zu bekräftigen jederzeit bereit sind."[113]

Meyer sandte den gedruckten Beschluß des Akademischen Senats und diesbezügliche Dokumente an alle deutschen Universitäten und informierte die Presse. Selbst das "Berliner Tageblatt" und die übrige liberale Publizistik wandten sich in keiner Phase der Auseinandersetzungen entschieden gegen seine Verfahrensweise. Das Verhalten der Siegermächte hatte offensichtlich die Stimmung verstärkt, die in Ricarda Huchs Ablehnung des Aufrufs Nicolais "Für die Unabhängigkeit des Geistes" ankling: Wie "die Hände zur Versöhnung ausstrecken, während sie uns mit den Füßen treten."[114]

Es ist opinio communis, daß Meyers wissenschaftliches Oeuvre von den politischen Ansichten und Fragestellungen des Verfassers partiell nicht unerheblich beeinflußt wurde. Als 1918 seine Untersuchung über die "Innere Geschichte Roms von 66 bis 44 vor Christus" unter dem Titel "Cäsars Monarchie und das Principat des Pompejus" erschien, wurde es von seinen Rezensenten sogleich als "seine Kriegsgabe"[115] angesehen, die aus den politischen Kämpfen seiner Zeit entstanden sei, der "Parteisumpf" von "politische[n] Narren und Verbrechern, konservative[n] Starrköpfen und revolutionäre[n] Feuerseelen, Dilettanten und Konjunkturpolitiker[n]" sei offenkundig derselbe gewesen.[116] Meyers Werk fand nicht zuletzt wegen dieser Bezüge einen besonders prominen-

---

[113] Ebd.
[114] Abgedruckt zusammen mit weiteren ("Absage"-) Briefen, in: Nicolai, Georg Friedrich: Romain Rollands Manifest und die deutschen Antworten. Berlin o.J. [1920].
[115] So Erich Kronemann in seiner Rezension, in: Literarisches Zentralblatt 70 (1918), S. 805.
[116] Mertel, H.: Caesar und Pompejus. In: Süddeutsche Monatshefte 17 (1919/20), S. 418–426.—Hielten Mertel (ebd., S. 421, 423) und Georg Schröder, Führer und Führungsschicht, in: Der Ring 3 (1930), S. 303 f., die Anspielungen auf zeitgenössische englische und amerikanische Staatsmänner für besonders erhellend, so wandte sich E. Hohl in einer Fußnote (Hohl, E.: Caesars Monarchie. In: Berliner Philologisches

ten Leser.[117] Es erstaunt rückblickend, daß Wilhelm II. die ersten Wochen des Exils auch dazu nutzte, ein über sechshundert Seiten starkes wissenschaftliches Werk aufmerksam mit dem Bleistift durchzulesen. Eine Fülle von Marginalien und zahlreiche Unterstreichungen dokumentieren das Interesse des Kaisers an historischen Vorgängen und an politischen Anspielungen. Meyers Kollege und politischer Mitstreiter, der Ordinarius für osteuropäische Geschichte, Theodor Schiemann, dürfte dieses Exemplar von ''Caesars Monarchie'' seinerzeit nach Doorn geschickt haben; jedenfalls erhielt Meyer am 22. April 1919 das Exemplar Wilhelms II. mit einem auf den 31. März datierten Billet zurück: ''Mit vielem Interesse gelesen! Wie ähnlich sind diese Zustände in der verkommenen Republik Rom denjenigen in der dreckigen Republik in Berlin!''[118]

Damit ist der Gesamttenor der Marginalien in ''Caesars Monarchie'' skizziert. Wilhelm II. überträgt Meyers kritische Bemerkungen zum römischen Adel direkt auf den deutschen; dieser lasse die Monarchie zu Grunde gehen, sei treulos und unfähig: ''wegen alten Adels erblich belastet und Lesens u. Schreibens unkundig.''[119] Wilhelm II. sieht hinter jeder Perfidie oder Rebellion der Catilinarier Scheidemann, Liebknecht, Spartakisten, Proletarier, Bolschewisten, Engländer oder Juden wirken.[120] Meyers positive Einschätzung des Wahlkönigtums der Römer wird mit dem Hinweis gerügt, im deutschen Mittelalter habe dieses Verfahren nicht zur Herrschaft der Besten und Weisesten geführt.[121] In Meyers Werk sind alle Sätze dick unterstrichen, die sich auf die Stellung des Princeps und die Eroberung bzw. Sicherung von Herrschaft und Macht beziehen.[122] Zustimmend entnimmt Wilhelm II. die Auffassung, die Diskussion der Machtfrage habe der der Verfassungsfrage vorauszugehen. In den von Meyer als ''militärisch völlig urteilslos'' eingeschätzten Senatoren sieht Wilhelm II. ''Unsere Parlamentarier.''[123] Sie seien

---

Wochenblatt 39 [1919], S. 867) ausdrücklich gegen derartige aktuelle Anspielungen. Vgl. dazu Meyer, Caesar, S. 186, S. 396, S. 417, Anm. 113.

[117] Es gibt ein Exemplar des Buches mit handschriftlichen Notizen und Unterstreichungen Wilhelms II. im Teilnachlaß Meyer (s. Anm. 1).

[118] Handschriftliche Notiz Wilhelms II. vom 31.III.1919. In: SB, NL Ed. Meyer, Nr. 213, unfol.

[119] Meyer, Caesar, S. 135 des von Wilhelm II. benutzten Exemplars.

[120] Dasselbe ebd., S. 113, S. 131, S. 144, S. 185, S. 216, S. 234, S. 240, S. 299, S. 332, S. 257, S. 497, S. 532.

[121] Dasselbe ebd., S. 179.

[122] Unterstreichungen Wilhelms II., vgl. ebd., S. 52, S. 135, S. 165, S. 171, S. 179, S. 185, S. 186 f., S. 240, S. 327, S. 328 f., S. 332, S. 356 f., S. 403, S. 415, S. 513, S. 532, S. 536.

[123] Handschriftliche Notiz Wilhelms II., ebd., S. 299.

in der gleichen Weise wie das aristokratische Regiment Roms den Aufgaben eines Weltregiments (Meyer) nicht gewachsen gewesen: "wie
bei uns die Continentalpolitik im Gegensatz zur Weltpolitik", schreibt
Wilhelm II.[124] neben die Feststellung Meyers, daß die Politik "den Intri-
ganten schlimmster Sorte [...] und damit einem wüsten Koterietreiben"
den weitesten Spielraum gegeben habe.[125] Ebenso streicht Wilhelm II.
Meyers Satz an: "Eine wirkliche Volksherrschaft ist ebenso unmöglich
geworden wie ein wahrhaft kollegiales Regiment der Nobilität; über
beiden erhebt sich übermächtig [...] die Einzelpersönlichkeit [...]."[126]
Wenn Meyer schließlich erklärt, man vergesse leicht, "daß oft gerade die
unheilvollsten Taten aus reinen Motiven hervorgegangen" seien, erinnert die Marginalie daran, daß Prinz Max von Baden "den Sattler Ebert
'den Mann mit dem reinen Willen!'" genannt habe.[127] Weiteren Textstellen unterlegt Wilhelm II. Ausfälle gegen die Entente und den politisch
naiven "modernen demokratischen, sozialistischen Liberalismus", der
per Gesetzgebung eine radikale Umwandlung erzwingen zu können
gedachte.[128]

Sind auch einige dieser Hervorhebungen und Interpretationen
Wilhelms II. allzu vordergründig ausgefallen, so bleibt doch zu konstatieren, daß Meyers Werk mit Urteilen über die Gesellschaft und über Prinzipien des Verfassungs- und Staatswesens geradezu übersät ist, die nicht
selten der aktuellen Situation entnommen sind. Diese profilierten Ansichten verweisen mit Nachdruck auf Meyers politische Publizistik. Einzelne Sätze aus "Caesars Monarchie und das Principat des Pompejus"
lesen sich deshalb wie der Streit um eine "Politik der Diagonalen" in
Rom. Meyers Urteile über Volksherrschaft und Monarchie könnten aus
seinen Artikeln gegen Bethmann Hollwegs "Neuorientierung" stammen.[129] Vor diesem Hintergrund kann man in Meyers Urteil über den
von ihm wissenschaftlich bewunderten, politisch jedoch mit großer Distanz betrachteten Theodor Mommsen ein Selbstporträt mit umgekehrten
politischen Vorzeichen sehen. Stellt doch Meyer bei dem Altliberalen
Mommsen fest, wie weit wissenschaftlicher Kenntnisreichtum bzw. eine
differenzierte Auseinandersetzung mit dem Forschungsstand und tieferes
politisches Verständnis bzw. verantwortungsbewußtes Handeln ausein-
anderklaffen können. Mommsen beurteile die Gegenwart unangemessen,
ja einseitig und von einer offenkundig der Vergangenheit zuzurechnenden

---

124 Dasselbe ebd., S. 327.
125 Ebd.; Wilhelm II. unterstrich hier das Wort "Koterietreiben."
126 Unterstreichung Wilhelms II., ebd., S. 356.
127 Handschriftliche Notiz Wilhelms II., ebd., S. 532.
128 Dasselbe ebd., S. 415.
129 Vgl. Meyer, Bethmann Hollweg (wie Anm. 62).

Anschauung her.[130] In ''Caesars Monarchie und das Principat des
Pompejus'' führt Meyer Mommsens negatives Urteil über die Patricier
und die Senatoren auf dessen ''Haß gegen das 'Junkertum', mit anderen
Worten: gegen die geschichtliche Gestaltung des preußischen Staats''
zurück, auf: ''ein[en] Haß, der Mommsens ganzes Empfinden und
Handeln'' beherrscht habe.[131]

Das liberale ''Berliner Tageblatt''[132] hob in seinem fairen Nachruf auf
Eduard Meyer die ihm weltweit gezollte Anerkennung als Universalhistoriker hervor. Nicht so bald wieder werde es wohl einem Wissenschaftler gelingen, Detailforschung und Universalgeschichte in einem
ähnlichen Umfang und mit diesem hohen Anspruch zu verbinden. Der
positiven Gesamteinschätzung schloß sich die eindeutig negative Bewertung seines politischen Wirkens an. In der Frage nach der Kriegs-
schuld habe er einen ''intransigenten Standpunkt'' eingenommen und
seine Auffassung der jüngsten Entwicklung sei ''von einem einseitigen
deutschnationalen Standpunkt diktiert'' gewesen. Hier ist eine Korrektur
nötig. Es kann keineswegs davon ausgegangen werden, daß Meyer sich
der deutschnationalen Parteilinie vorbehaltlos angeschlossen habe.
Einem sorgfältig redigierten Briefkonzept vom 20. Mai 1926 an Tirpitz
ist nämlich zu entnehmen:

> ''[. . .] Da ist es mir als ein schwerer Fehler erschienen, dass die DN. Partei
> aus der Regierung ausgetreten ist und es sich damit selbst unmöglich
> gemacht hat, auf die Gestaltung der Verhandlungen in Locarno einzuwir-
> ken. Statt dessen hat sie den bequemen Standpunkt einer in schönen Reden
> sich ergehenden aber eben darum völlig wirkungslosen Opposition vorgezo-
> gen. Scheinbar war ihr dadurch alle Verantwortung abgenommen, in Wirk-
> lichkeit aber liegt diese durch ihr rein negatives Verhalten nur um so stärker
> auf ihr, da sie dadurch das Gewicht der Linken wesentlich verstärkt und das
> Schwergewicht dorthin verschoben hat.
> Dass wir ohne Kompromisse und ohne eine Koalition bei der inneren Zer-
> splitterung niemals durchkommen können, dass daher keine Partei ohne
> Konzessionen irgendetwas erreichen kann, liegt doch auf der Hand. Hier
> aber handelt es sich vollends garnicht um einzelne Parteifragen, sondern um
> die Aufgaben einer nationalen Politik. Dafür galt es, alles Persönliche und

---

[130] ''Bei vielen haben seine Äußerungen lebendigen Widerhall, bei anderen scharfe
Opposition geweckt; gar manche aber mögen es bedauert haben, daß der Mann, zu dem
sie voll Verehrung aufblickten, sich so gänzlich mit einer Anschauung identifizierte, die
ihnen der Vergangenheit anzugehören und für die Beurteilung der Gegenwart und ihrer
großen Aufgaben nicht mehr den berechtigten Maßstab abzugeben schien. Daß man so
dachte, wußte er wohl; aber es konnte ihn nicht irre machen. Wohl aber mischte sich in
seine privaten und öffentlichen Außerungen [!] gar oft eine elegische Stimmung [. . .]''
(Meyer, Eduard: Theodor Mommsen. In: Meyer, *Kl. Schr.*, S. 549).

[131] Meyer, Caesar, S. 325.

[132] Vgl. Berliner Tageblatt, Nr. 411, 1.IX.1930.

Parteiinteressen hintan zu setzen und auf einen Zusammenschluss aller national gesinnten Kreise, also der gesamten Rechten, hinzuarbeiten, wenigstens den Versuch zu machen, uns aus dem Elend des kleinlichen Parteitreibens zu erlösen. [. . .] Und nun kommt der Flaggenerlass—eine absolut notwendige Maasregel, wie jeder zugeben wird, der die Verhältnisse im Ausland gesehen hat, und zugleich eine eminent nationale Maasregel, für die der von den nationalen Kreisen gewählte Reichspräsident sich persönlich einsetzt. Dass die Linksparteien dagegen auftreten, ist selbstverständlich; vor allem aber benutzt es das Häuflein der Demokraten, um hier im Trüben zu fischen und zu versuchen, ob sie durch eine mit allen Mitteln rücksichtslos betriebene Agitation nicht wieder einigen Gewinn für sich herausschlagen können. Und da, in dieser eminent nationalen Frage, läßt die Deutschnationale Partei den Präsidenten und die Regierung im Stich und führt durch ihre Stimmenthaltung im harmonischen Zusammenwirken mit Sozialisten, Kommunisten und Demokraten den Sturz der Regierung herbei [. . .].''[133]

Dieses Verhalten der DNVP interpretierte Meyer als politische Unfähigkeit, die sich im kleinlichsten Parteihader verstricke, statt ''auf eine Geschlossenheit der Nationalgesinnten hin[zu]arbeiten'', die den Reichspräsidenten Hindenburg entschieden zu stützen hätten, statt ihn zu desavouieren.

Alle Untersuchungen zur politischen Haltung deutscher Hochschullehrer oder zur politischen Kultur im Ersten Weltkrieg und in der Weimarer Republik zitierten mit Recht aus Meyers politischer Publizistik, um zugleich die nationalistisch-alldeutsche, republikfeindliche und antidemokratische Einstellung und Agitation eines nicht geringen Teils der deutschen Professorenschaft eindrucksvoll belegen zu können. Meyer gehörte zu den entschieden und durchgehend kämpferisch, zeitweise undifferenziert, emotional und mit auffallend geringem Feingefühl operierenden politischen Professoren.[134] In der Weimarer Republik bekämpfte er nachdrücklich den Versailler Vertrag. Dieser Beurteilung und Einstellung lag ein weitreichender parteipolitischer Konsens zu Grunde. Bei den Konservativen entstand er aus anderen Motiven als bei den liberalen und einem Teil der Sozialdemokraten, die zu Recht eine tiefgehende Belastung für die noch ungefestigte Demokratie befürchteten. Meyer verharrte jedoch nicht in Fundamentalopposition zu der ungeliebten Republik. Er läßt sich keineswegs als ''Totengräber der Republik'' oder sogar ''geistiger Vorbereiter'' des Nationalsozialismus einstufen.[135] 1926

---

[133] AkadWissDDR, NL Ed. Meyer, Nr. 1413.
[134] Vgl. Böhme, Aufrufe (wie Anm. 2), passim.
[135] In seiner Rezension des Spenglerschen Hauptwerks (Meyer, Eduard: Spenglers Untergang des Abendlandes. In: Deutsche Literaturzeitung 25 [1924], Sp. 1760–1780) lassen sich Inhalt und Umfang seiner Vorbehalte am klarsten aufzeigen: ''Gerade diese

beantwortete er in der "Deutschen Zukunft" die Frage nach seiner Einschätzung der aktuellen Situation durchgehend positiv. In Staat und
Gesellschaft seien bei der Jugend weder ein Leistungsrückgang noch eine
pessimistische Grundhaltung zu erkennen. Deutschland habe seine Position gefestigt und sein Ansehen im Ausland sei so deutlich gewachsen—
im Orient in einem außerordentlichen Maß—, daß Stolz auf die jüngsten
Leistungen angebracht sei. Kühle Ruhe und Souveränität im Parteien-
streit halte er für die besten Voraussetzungen für "ein ständiges Vor-
wärtsschreiten bei besonnener Haltung."[136]

In dieser Zeit rückten die Veränderungen in der Sowjetunion in
Meyers Blickfeld. Sein großes Interesse an diesem Land ist vor dem Hintergrund der Politik der Westmächte in Versailles und im Zusammenhang mit der alsbald einsetzenden außenpolitischen Offensive der deutschen Regierungen gegenüber der Sowjetunion zu beurteilen. Außerdem
sah er in der wissenschaftlichen Kontaktaufnahme die Chance, Deutschlands Wiedereinbindung in die internationale Gelehrtenwelt voran-
zutreiben. Der Besuch von Leningrad und Moskau im September 1925—
die "Akademie der Wissenschaften von Rußland" feierte ihr zweihun-
dertjähriges Jubiläum—verschaffte ihm erste Einblicke, über die er in der
"Deutschen Rundschau" berichtete.[137] In seinem Artikel versucht
Meyer, dem "neuen Rußland" vor dem Hintergrund "des alten, innerlich verrotteten zaristischen Regiments" gerecht zu werden, wie es ihm
"hochgebildete Männer, die sich ein unabhängiges Urteil über den Par-

---

Momente der inneren Zersetzung hat Spengler in den der Kritik der jetzt zur Herrschaft
gelangten Anschauungen gewidmeten Abschnitten, den Kapiteln über Staat und Politik,
über Demokratie und Parlamentarismus mit seinem wüsten Parteitreiben, über die
Allmacht der Presse, über das Wesen der Großstadt, über das Wirtschaftsleben, Geld und
Maschine in glänzender Weise geschildert. Sein vernichtendes Urteil teile ich durchaus
[...]" (Sp. 1779).

[136] Auf einem einzigen Gebiet, im Bereich der höheren Schulen, glaubt er "die
verhängnisvolle Wirkung des Experimentierens" entdecken zu können, "wodurch das
Niveau der Vorbildung sehr stark herabgedrückt und dadurch der Wahnglaube großgezo-
gen ist, man könne durch Intuition und Einfühlen die nötigen Kenntnisse und die Urteilsfähigkeit im Fluge erhaschen." (Meyer, Eduard: Deutsche Zukunft. In: Süddeutsche
Monatshefte 24 (Dezember 1926), S. 196.) Die Einstellung überrascht vor dem Hintergrund der dezidierten Stellungnahmen Meyers im allgemeinen und zum Geschichtsunterricht im besonderen; vgl. Meyer, Eduard: Der neue Geschichtsunterricht. In: Deutsches
Philologenblatt 23 (1915), S. 569 f.; Meyer, Aufgaben der höheren Schulen (wie Anm.
32).—Meyers Resümee zu der Rundfrage der Zeitschrift spiegelt sich in dem Satz "Es
wäre dringend zu wünschen, man könnte alle Pessimisten und Trübsalbläser einmal ins
Ausland schicken, damit sie sähen, wie unsere Stellung in Wirklichkeit ist, und dadurch
loskämen von dem Zerrbild, das das elende Parteitreiben im Inneren schafft, das überall
lähmend auf uns lastet" (Meyer, Deutsche Zukunft, S. 196).

[137] Meyer, Eduard: Das neue Rußland. Eindrücke von der Jubiläumsfeier der russischen Akademie der Wissenschaften. In: Deutsche Rundschau 52 (November 1925),
S. 101–118.

teien'' bewahrt hätten, geschildert hatten.[138] Daraus ergibt sich die Tendenz, die Zustände in dem Meyer bislang fremden, durch eine jahrelange
antirevolutionäre und antibolschewistische Propaganda weithin einseitig
gekennzeichneten Staat, in einem freundlich-wohlwollenden Licht erscheinen zu lassen: Rußland bot ihm ''ein ganz anderes Bild'' als er erwartet hatte: ''Die Verhältnisse haben sich gesetzt, die Zeit der Not ist
überwunden, das Leben ist wieder im Gange und kehrt in die gewohnten
Gleise zurück. Und dabei besteht durchweg Ruhe und Ordnung, die
polizeilichen Vorschriften werden vom Volk willig befolgt'', zu einer
prinzipiellen Religionsverfolgung sei es trotz der vollen Trennung von
Staat und Kirche nicht gekommen. Das altgläubige Volk habe sich ge-
fügt, weil es zugleich ''durch die materiellen Interessen abgelenkt'' worden sei. In dem Kreis der Wissenschaften habe die anfängliche Mißachtung geistiger und die überzogen starke Würdigung physischer Arbeit
die Geisteswissenschaften ruiniert, doch ließen sich Konsequenzen eines
Umdenkens deutlich erkenen.[139]

Die positiven Züge dieses Rußlandbilds sind zu einem nicht unerheb-
lichen Teil politisch motiviert und aus der Rapallo-Locarno-Situation zu
erklären. Die Hinwendung der deutschen Außenpolitik zum Osten, zu
der international in vergleichbarer Situation operierenden UdSSR, schuf
beiden Staaten außenpolitische Bewegungsmöglichkeiten in Verhandlungen mit den Westmächten.[140] Den Lenin-Kult und die Anstrengungen
der Agitations- und Propaganda-Kampagnen beschreibt Meyer zwar
amüsiert bis distanziert, doch verkennt er keineswegs die überragende
''Führerpersönlichkeit'' Lenins, des ''enthusiastische[n] Idealist[en]'',
der mit der Einführung der ''Neuen Ökonomischen Politik'' bewiesen
habe, daß er marxistische Theorien nicht sklavisch zu befolgen gedenke.
Meyer feiert Lenin als einen der wenigen neuen Politiker, ''die seit
Bismarck die Geschicke der Völker zu leiten versucht haben, vielleicht der
einzige, der den Namen eines Staatsmannes in vollem Sinne verdient''
habe.[141] Andererseits übersieht er keineswegs die ''schonungslose Bruta-
lität'' des ''Schreckensregiment[s], das noch weit hinausgeht über das der

---

[138] Ebd., S. 102.
[139] Vgl. ebd., S. 108, 110 und 111.
[140] Meyer zitiert hierzu zustimmend aus der Ansprache des deutschen Botschafters in
Moskau, Ulrich Graf von Brockdorff-Rantzau, der in ''knappen, vortrefflich formulierten
Sätzen'' ausgeführt habe, daß zwar in den grundsätzlichen Fragen die deutschen
Anschauungen vielfach sehr andere seien als die russischen und eine ihnen entgegengesetzte Stimmung erzeugten, daß aber die Lage der beiden Völker und die großen Aufgaben, die sie bewältigen müssen, trotzdem eine Interessengemeinschaft geschaffen hätten, die ein ehrliches Zusammengehen ermögliche, das beiden zum Segen gereichen
werde (ebd., S. 116).
[141] Ebd., S. 106.

französischen Revolution'' und seine Machtmittel auch in Zukunft zur
''rücksichtslose[n] Vernichtung und Ausmordung aller Gegner und
schonungslose[n] Durchführung der als Dogma verkündeten Grundsätze'' einsetzen werde.[142] Meyers positives Gesamturteil ergibt sich aus
der Notwendigkeit und ''fundamentalen Bedeutung'' guter politischer
und wirtschaftlicher Beziehungen zwischen Deutschland und Rußland.
Zugunsten dieses Zieles tilgte er z.b. vor der Drucklegung seines Berichts
den im Manuskript zu findenden Zusatz ''Massenmörder'' bei Sinowjew,
dem Präsidenten des Exekutiv-Komitees der III. Internationalen.[143]

Die Untersuchung sollte andeuten, daß Eduard Meyers verstärkte
Teilnahme an dem tagespolitischen Meinungsstreit sich wie bei vielen
anderen Zeitgenossen—man denke nur an Gerhart Hauptmanns oder
Nahum Goldmanns Nationalismus—auf das August-Erlebnis zurückführen läßt. Von etlichen seiner Mitstreiter unterschied er sich durch eine
relativ unflexible, entschieden konservativ-nationalistische Haltung,
durch den erheblichen Umfang seines publizistischen und verbands- bzw.
parteipolitischen Engagements und nicht zuletzt durch seine weltweit
anerkannte fachliche Autorität.

Mit dem August 1914 war für Meyer eine von ihm für stabil gehaltene
Welt- und Rechtsordnung zusammengebrochen—wie er bereits während
des Kriegs mit skeptischem Blick auf die Zukunft geäußert hatte.[144] Die
neue, sich an westlich-demokratischen Idealen orientierende Ordnung
der Weimarer Republik schien ihm für das Deutsche Reich in Anbetracht
der weltweit wachsenden Verpflichtungen ungeeignet.[145] Er traue es einer
demokratischen Staatsform nicht zu, sich verschärfende soziale Konflikte
lösen oder außenpolitisch die Einflußminderung Europas aufhalten zu
können, hatte er während des Kriegs erklärt, und diese Grundeinschätz-

---

[142] Ebd., S. 103–105; Zitate auf S. 103.

[143] Ebd., S. 111, 3. Zeile v.u.; zu den ''Abweichungen des Manuskriptes vom gedruckten Text'' vgl. die entsprechende Übersicht von Werner Hartke im Nachlaß (Akad-
WissDDR, NL Ed. Meyer, Nr. 309).

[144] ''Die Welt, in der wir gelebt haben, ist am 1. August 1914 versunken. Was vorher
liegt, erscheint schon jetzt in unendlich weite Ferne gerückt, so daß wir uns kaum noch
hineindenken können; wir haben vollständig umlernen und all unsere Gedanken gewaltsam in eine ganz neue Welt hineinzwängen müssen. Zu den neuen Problemen, die durch
den Krieg aufgeworfen sind, sind zahlreiche alte wieder aufgetaucht, die längst erledigt
zu sein und friedlich zu schlummern schienen, und die jetzt dringend eine Beantwortung
erheischen. Die Verantwortung, die uns damit auferlegt ist, der Staatsleitung wie jedem
Einzelnen und dem gesamten Volke, mögen wir nun siegen oder erliegen, ist eine ungeheure, an die man nur mit bangem Zagen zu denken vermag'' (Meyer, England, S. 203).

[145] Im Vortrag vor Mitgliedern und Sympathisanten der DNVP in Lichterfelde erklärte er am 27.II.1919 lapidar: ''Von allen modernen Staatsformen halte ich die parlamentarische Verfassung für die unglückseligste und verderblichste'' (Meyer, Eduard:
Deutschlands Lage in der Gegenwart und unsere Aufgaben für die Zukunft [als Flugschrift gedruckt], Berlin 1919, S. 16).

ung behielt er bei—trotz einiger Modifikationen in den späteren Jahren:

> "Von der anderen Seite kam [. . .] die anwachsende demokratische Strömung [. . .], welche dem einzelnen die Verantwortung abnimmt und sie durch Uniformierung und Reglementierung zu ersetzen sucht. Dadurch ist die freie Selbstbetätigung, die nur bei eigener Verantwortung gedeihen und schöpferisch wirken kann, lahmgelegt."[146] Denn "[. . .] nicht umsonst betrachteten die Griechen wie die Römer die radikale Demokratie als im Grunde identisch mit dem absoluten Königtum oder der Tyrannis, als die Herrschaft eines einzelnen Mannes, die die republikanische Freiheit aufhebt. Die Schwärmer für die Demokratie sind ja, wie alle Doktrinäre, unbelehrbar [. . .]."[147] Und Meyer resümiert für sich: "So zeigt sich überall, wie unendlich hoch unsere Staatsform und unsere Monarchie von Gottes Gnaden über der Machtergreifung steht, die uns immer wieder als ein begehrenswertes Ideal vorgehalten wird."[148]

Im Rahmen dieser weitgespannten welt- und kulturpolitischen Betrachtungsweise sind die von tiefer Emotion bestimmten Aufrufe, Reden und Broschüren der Kriegszeit als Überreaktion in einer Ausnahmesituation zu verstehen.[149] Hiermit ist kein national, parteipolitisch oder sozial scharf abzugrenzendes Phänomen und damit also kein deutsches Spezifikum angesprochen.[150]

Meyer hat sich 1914 mit nicht geringen Ambitionen und Ansprüchen in die politische Arena gestürzt. Die Publizistik und die Handlungen zeigen keinen kenntnisreich, geschickt, umsichtig oder nüchtern Agierenden. Historische Beispiele—stammen sie nun aus der Antike oder der

---

[146] Vgl. Meyer, Eduard: Der neue Geschichtsunterricht. In: Deutsches Philologenblatt, Nr. 23, 1915, S. 570. Ähnlich die folgende Bemerkung: "Die Demokratie dehnt die Forderung 'gleiches Recht für Alle' auch auf die Gestaltung des Staats aus [. . .]. Weiter aber ist für die Gestaltung der Demokratie entscheidend, daß die Massen ihrer Natur nach unfähig sind, dem Ideal zu entsprechen und die Leitung des Staats wirklich selbst in die Hand zu nehmen" (Meyer, Weltgeschichte, S. 161).
[147] Meyer, Eduard: Das Wesen der amerikanischen Demokratie und Präsident Wilson. In: Zeit- und Streitfragen 19, 29.V.1917.
[148] Ebd.
[149] "Nirgends ist dieser Deutschenhaß zugleich mächtiger und für uns überraschender zutage getreten, als in den Vereinigten Staaten von Nordamerika. [. . .] Der von zahlreichen deutschen Schriftstellern und Gelehrten unterzeichnete Appell 'An die Kulturwelt' und ähnliche Aufrufe waren gewiß nicht besonders geschickt abgefaßt—wer in tödlicher Gefahr um sein Leben ringt, wird nicht immer die richtigen Worte wählen—; die Antworten, die aus Amerika darauf gekommen sind, bringen nichts als überlegene Ablehnung oder gar kalten Hohn" (Meyer, Nordamerika, S. 9, 12).
[150] Diese Vorgänge im Ausland sind noch nicht mit derselben Akribie wie für Deutschland untersucht worden—aufgrund der bisherigen Forschung scheint es direkte Parallelen zu geben; insgesamt dürften die Reaktionen langfristig moderater abgelaufen sein, ohne daß sich der Nationalismus oder Chauvinismus französischer, britischer oder amerikanischer Professoren nennenswert von dem der deutschen Kollegen unterschied. Vgl. dazu Thimme, Heinrich: Weltkrieg ohne Waffen. Die Propaganda der Westmächte gegen Deutschland, ihre Wirkung und ihre Abwehr. Stuttgart 1932.

jüngsten Geschichte—bleiben bei ihm nicht selten ohne den Beigeschmack
des aparten Aperçus und sind zumeist zu sehr dem Vordergründigen
verhaftet—einmal steht Rom, das andere Mal Karthago für das Deutsche
Reich[151]—oder verlieren das erhellend Pointierte in der vorschnell formulierten Übertragung.[152] Spätestens hier ist jedoch daran zu erinnern,
daß sich Meyer zumindest in einem Teil seiner Publizistik auf eine Zuhö-
rer- oder Leserschaft mit durchschnittlichem Bildungshorizont einstellte.

    Meyer war ein überzeugter Monarchist, Annexionist und Nationalist.
Die Weimarer Republik hielt er anfangs für ein Verhängnis, später
jedoch, als sie ihm Leistungsfähigkeit und Stärke in einem beachtlichen
Ausmaß bewiesen hatte, vermochte er mit positiven Erwartungen in die
Zukunft zu blicken.[153] Als verheerend schätzte Meyer die Politik der
Siegermächte in Versailles und die flauen deutschen Reaktionen auf
deren politische und wirtschaftliche Diktate ein. Von seiner Unterschrift
unter den ''Aufruf der 93'' konnte er deshalb während des Kriegs sogleich
abrücken, nicht jedoch nach dem Friedensschluß. Die Monarchie wiederherzustellen, schien ihm nach den Erfahrungen des Wilhelminismus und

---

[151] Zum Problem derartiger Analogien hat sich Meyer klar und mit deutlicher Skepsis
in einer Rezension geäußert: neben dem ''Fünkchen Wahrheit'' stecke doch zumeist nur
Verwirrendes in diesen Vergleichen (vgl. Meyers Rezension zu Ernst Renans
''Geschichte des Volkes Israel'', in: Literarisches Zentralblatt 7 [1895], S. 212–214.) In
seiner Festrede vom 24. Januar 1918 über ''Vorläufer des Weltkrieges im Altertum''
(Meyer, Kl. Schr., S. 507–538) verwendet er an herausragenden Stellen wiederholt
Analogien (S. 515 f. Anm., S. 517 f. Anm., S. 522 Anm., S. 525 Anm., S. 536); im Fall
der römischen und deutschen Flotte konnte er in einer nach Kriegsschluß hinzugefügten
Fußnote nur bedauern, daß sich seine Hoffnung auf eine falsche Analogie gegründet habe
(ebd., S. 533 f. und Anm.).
    [152] ''Als im Jahre 264 v. Chr. der Krieg zwischen Rom und Karthago um Sizilien aus-
brach [. . .]. Das ist dieselbe Situation, in der sich Deutschland England gegenüber befindet, abgesehen davon, daß im Kriege um Sizilien Rom der Angreifer war, während gegenwärtig Deutschland wider seinen Willen zum Kriege gezwungen ist. [. . .] Polybios
[: '. . .] In Karthago war für die meisten Entschlüsse bereits das Volk ausschlaggebend
geworden (also die Demokratie durchgeführt), in Rom regierte der aus den besten Männern gebildete Senat. Daher waren die Beschlüsse und Maßnahmen der Römer der kar-
thagischen überlegen, und dadurch wurden sie schließlich der Karthager Herr.' [. . .] Es
ist nicht nötig, die Parallele im einzelnen durchzuführen. Die Unterschiede [. . .] liegen
auf der Hand; aber eben so deutlich ist, daß die entscheidenden Momente auch in dem
gegenwärtigen Krieg die gleichen sind. [. . .] die bange Frage, ob die Analogie mit den
Punischen Kriegen nicht noch viel weiter reicht, ob mit dem Ausbruch des Kriegs nicht
auch die moderne Kulturentwicklung ihren Höhepunkt überschritten hat und fortan dem
Niedergang sich entgegenneigt. In der Tat liegen die Symptome dafür offen zutage, wohin
immer der Blick sich wendet. Das gesamte Völkerrecht ist durch England vernichtet
[. . .]'' (Meyer, England, S. 200–202, S. 206).
    [153] ''Wir dürfen es voll Stolz aussprechen, daß wie auf militärischem Gebiet so auch
auf diesem kulturellen Gebiet (und ebenso in dem Wiederaufbau der deutschen Währung
und in der Bekämpfung der Arbeitslosigkeit) Deutschland geleistet hat, was kein anderes
Volk leistet und zu leisten imstande wäre'' (Meyer, Deutsche Zukunft [wie Anm. 135],
S. 196).

dem Versagen Wilhelms II. abwegig. Ebenso fern mußte ihm der Gedanke liegen, die Weimarer Republik nachdrücklich zu unterstützen. Deren innen- und außenpolitische Erfolge erkannte Meyer zwar an, doch die Herrschaft der Mittelmäßigkeiten und ''Zufallsmehrheiten'' im ''kläglichsten Parteisumpf'' stießen ihn ab. Der Parlamentarismus in Deutschland stellte für ihn die ''Karikatur der Demokratie''[154] dar, weil er eine starke Regierung verhindere, ja prinzipiell nicht erlaube.

---

[154] Meyer, Die Vereinigten Staaten (wie Anm. 36), S. VII.

JÜRGEN VON UNGERN – STERNBERG

POLITIK UND GESCHICHTE. DER ALTHISTORIKER EDUARD MEYER IM ERSTEN WELTKRIEG*

I

Eduard Meyers intensive Beteiligung an der militärischen und politischen Diskussion deutscher Professoren während des Ersten Weltkrieges braucht hier nicht eingehend dargestellt zu werden. Schon vor dem Krieg ein Befürworter des Flottenprogramms gehörte er zu den Erstunterzeichnern des fatalen Aufrufs der 93 'An die Kulturwelt!'—und distanzierte sich auch nach der Niederlage nicht von seiner Unterschrift—; war er mit Dietrich Schäfer führend am 'Unabhängigen Ausschuss für einen deutschen Frieden' beteiligt und setzte sich für deutsche Annexionen in West und Ost sowie für den unbeschränkten U-Boot-Krieg ein; lehnte er als Mitglied des Direktions-Komitees der 'Deutschen Vaterlandspartei' noch im Oktober 1918 entschieden die Wahlrechtsreform in Preussen ab. Er hat seine Haltung auch später nicht geändert. Die Niederlage vermochte er schon 1919 nur als Selbstpreisgabe des deutschen Volkes zu verstehen; als Rektor der Berliner Universität hat er beim 'Fall Nicolai' wie beim Kapp-Putsch eine durchaus angreifbare Rolle gespielt; er gehörte dem Reichsausschuss deutschnationaler Hochschullehrer an.[1]

---

* Das Referat wurde zu einem grossen Teil in der Fondation Hardt, Vandœuvres bei Genf, niedergeschrieben, deren grosszügig—internationale Atmosphäre einen wohltuenden Konstrast zu seinem Inhalt bildete. Als Vortrag wurde es auch der Kommission für Alte Geschichte und Epigraphik in München präsentiert.

[1] S. jetzt vor allem den Beitrag von B. Sösemann; vgl. L. Canfora, Wilamowitz e Meyer tra la sconfitta e la "Repubblica di Novembre," Quaderni di storia 2, H.3, 1976, 69 ff. Grundlegend: K. Schwabe, Wissenschaft und Kriegsmoral. Die deutschen Hochschullehrer und die politischen Grundfragen des Ersten Weltkrieges, Göttingen 1969; ferner: K. Fischer, Die politische und publizistische Tätigkeit Eduard Meyers im Ersten Weltkrieg und in den ersten Jahren der Weimarer Republik (1914–1920) Potsdam 1963 [Masch. schr.]; F. Klein, Die deutschen Historiker im ersten Weltkrieg, in: J. Streisand (Hg.), Studien über die deutsche Geschichtswissenschaft 2, Berlin 1969, 227 ff.; K. Thiessenhusen, Politische Kommentare deutscher Historiker zur Revolution und Neuordnung 1918/19, in: aus politik und zeitgeschichte B 45/1969; K. Böhme, Kriegsdienst mit der Feder. Der Erste Weltkrieg im politischen Urteil deutscher Professoren, Quaderni di storia 2, H.3, 1976, 49 ff.; L. Canfora, Intelletuali in Germania tra reazione e rivoluzione, Bari 1979; B. vom Brocke, 'Wissenschaft und Militarismus.' Der Aufruf der 93 'An die Kulturwelt!' und der Zusammenbruch der internationale Gelehrtenrepublik im Ersten Weltkrieg, in: Wilamowitz nach 50 Jahren, hg. W.M. Calder III u.a., Darmstadt 1985, 649 ff.; B. vom Brocke, Wissenschaft versus Militarismus: Nicolai, Einstein und die "Biologie des Krieges," Jb. des italienisch-deutschen historischen Instituts in Trient 10, 1984,

All dies ist gewiss ein—kleiner![2]—Mosaikstein zur deutschen Geschichte des 20. Jahrhunderts, es macht uns auch die Grenzen der politischen Urteilsfähigkeit Eduard Meyers deutlich.[3] Aber was hat das mit
dem Wissenschaftler Eduard Meyer zu tun, der doch gerade von seiner
fachlichen Kompetenz her den Anspruch auf Gehör erhoben hat? Welche
Rolle haben seine althistorischen Einsichten für seine Stellungnahme zur
Gegenwart gespielt? Die Frage ist bislang für ihn so wenig wie für irgend-
einen anderen der beteiligten Historiker gestellt worden, wiewohl gerade
Eduard Meyer wieder und wieder Vorgänge der Alten Geschichte als
Analogien zu gegenwärtigen Ereignissen und Entwicklungen herangezogen hat.[4] Ein Prüfstein par excellence für das altbekannte Problem, ob
sich aus der Geschichte etwas lernen lasse.

II

Während der vier Kriegsjahre hat Meyer mit dem sehr viel jüngeren
Althistoriker Victor Ehrenberg (1891 – 1976) korrespondiert, der damals

---

405 ff.; L. Canfora, Die Kritik der bürgerlichen Demokratie durch Eduard Meyer, in:
R.W. Müller u.a. (Hg.), Arthur Rosenberg zwischen Alter Geschichte und Zeitgeschichte, Politik und politischer Bildung, Göttingen 1986, 46 ff.
   [2] Zu denken gibt, dass z.B. F. Fischer, Griff nach der Weltmacht, 4. Aufl., Düsseldorf
1967; ders., Krieg der Illusionen, Düsseldorf 1969; B. Mann, Die baltischen Länder in
der deutschen Kriegszielpublizistik, Tübingen 1965 Eduard Meyer überhaupt nicht erwähnen. Auch bei R. vom Bruch, Wissenschaft, Politik und öffentliche Meinung, Husum
1980 spielt er kaum eine Rolle. Allerdings galt Meyer der damaligen öffentlichen
Meinung als repräsentativ für die Gruppe der Professoren (Hinweis von B. Sösemann).
   [3] Insbesondere von seinen Werken über England und die USA distanzieren sich
bereits die Nachrufe der Fachgenossen recht klar; die Gedächtnisrede von U. Wilcken,
in: Eduard Meyer. Bibliographie, hg. H. Marohl, Stuttgart 1941, 123 ebenso wie V.
Ehrenberg, HZ 143, 1930, 501 ff.; M. Gelzer, Gnomon 6, 1930, 622 ff. (= *Kl. Schr.* III,
Wiesbaden 1964, 329 ff.); E. Täubler, ZRG 51, 1931, 604 ff. (= Ausgewählte Schriften
zur alten Geschichte, Stuttgart 1987, 299 ff.). Scharfe Kritik übt E. Fraenkel, Das
deutsche Wilsonbild, Jb. f. Amerikastudien 5, 1960, 99 ff.; sehr zurückhaltend K. Christ,
Von Gibbon zu Rostovtzeff, Darmstadt 1972, 327 ff. (Irrtümlich lässt K. Christ, aO. 333
die politische Tätigkeit Meyers im Herbst 1919 enden, hierin wohl dessen 'Autobiographischer Skizze'—bei H. Marohl, 12—folgend, die freilich auf die Vorgänge des
Jahres 1920 noch recht deutlich anspielt: S. 11).
   [4] Zum wissenschaftlichen Werk grundlegend: K. Christ, Von Gibbon zu Rostovtzeff,
286 ff.; vgl. A. Demandt, Alte Geschichte an der Berliner Universität 1810–1960. Erg.
bd. zum Katalog der Ausstellung ''Berlin und die Antike,'' Berlin 1979, 84 ff.; A.
Momigliano, Premesse per una discussione su Eduard Meyer (1981), in: Settimo Contributo alla storia degli studi classici e del mondo antico, Rom 1984, 215 ff.; K. Christ,
Römische Geschichte und deutsche Geschichtswissenschaft, München 1982, 93 ff.;
E. Gabba, Caesare e Augusto nell' interpretazione di Ed. Meyer, RIS 94, 1982, 581 ff.;
B. Näf, Von Perikles zu Hitler? Die athenische Demokratie und die deutsche Althistorie
bis 1945, Bern 1986, 63 ff.; Chr. Hoffmann, Juden und Judentum im Werk deutscher
Althistoriker des 19. und 20. Jahrhunderts, Leiden 1988. Einige Hinweise verdanke ich
der Erlanger Staatsexamensarbeit von A. Künzl, Der Gegensatz Rom—Karthago im
Spiegel historisch-politischer Aeusserungen der Zeit um den ersten Weltkrieg (1977).

als Soldat an der Westfront stand. Der sehr inhaltsreiche Briefwechsel befindet sich teils im Nachlass Ehrenbergs in England, teils bei der Akademie der Wissenschaften der DDR in Berlin und soll demnächst ediert werden.[5] In seinem Brief vom 10. Oktober 1915 skizziert Meyer kurz seine bekannte Haltung in der Kriegszielfrage—er selbst spricht freilich von "Friedenszielen": Annexionen im Osten; Festhalten Belgiens als Vasallenstaat; Revision der Grenzen gegen Frankreich "rücksichtslos nach unseren Bedürfnissen." Aber dann fährt er fort:

"Dass wir damit über die Nationale Basis unseres Staats hinausgreifen, ist schmerzlich, aber nicht zu ändern: wir haben es nicht gewollt, aber unsere Feinde haben uns in eine Politik hineingezwungen, wie es die römische seit dem hannibalischen Kriege gewesen ist. Je fester und klarer wir dieser Lage ins Auge schauen, um so besser ist es, und um so eher werden wir die Fehler vermeiden können, die Rom damals begangen hat."

Das Unbehagen Meyers an seiner eigenen Position resultiert aus einer historischen Parallele, der Lage Roms um 200 v. Chr. nach dem Sieg über Hannibal, als es sich anschickte, über Italien hinaus die gesamte Mittelmeerwelt zu unterwerfen. Meyer spricht von "Notwendigkeiten, denen wir uns gar nicht entziehen können," von "Fehlern" Roms, ohne diese näher auszuführen. Deutlich ist aber, dass die Analogie für ihn ganz selbstverständlich und zugleich von eminenter Wichtigkeit ist.

Sie kehrt denn auch in dem Brief vom 6. April 1918 wieder. Dort spricht Meyer von der Friedensresolution des Reichstags vom 19. Juli 1917 und weiteren Friedensangeboten, die die deutsche Position bei den Verhandlungen in Brest-Litowsk sehr belastet hätten "und uns auch jetzt noch immer eine klare, ehrliche Politik und ein offenes Bekenntnis zu den Notwendigkeiten, aus denen wir gar nicht herauskönnen ... erschwert und vielfach unmöglich macht." Und dann folgt der Verweis auf die Situation um 200:

"Zugleich werden wir dadurch nur noch viel mehr auf die Wege Roms gedrängt: wir sind jetzt überall dabei, eine Masse von Vasallenstaaten zu schaffen, die nur durch uns eine gesicherte Existenz haben, und werden so in die Welthändel nur noch immer mehr hineingezogen. Das ist nun einmal unser Schicksal, und wenn wir versuchen, dem aus dem Wege zu gehen, wird es nur schlimmer, nicht besser." 'Hurra-Patriotismus' kann man das gewiss nicht nennen;[6] es herrscht eine düstere Grundstimmung vor, eine Art von 'Nibelungen-Trotz' in auswegloser Lage. Ehrenberg

---

[5] G. Audring—Chr. Hoffmann—J. v. Ungern-Sternberg (Hg.), Eduard Meyer—Victor Ehrenberg. Ein Briefwechsel. 1914–1930, Berlin-Stuttgart 1990. Zu Ehrenberg s. den Nachruf von J. Vogt, Gnomon 48, 1976, 423 ff.

[6] Nüchternheit bestimmt auch die Aeusserungen zur Innenpolitik; vgl. vor allem den Brief vom 10. April 1917 zur Wahlrechtsreform in Preussen.

hatte Meyer in seinem Brief vom 10. September 1915 in einer heute noch bewundernswerten Klarsicht die Problematik der deutschen Kriegsziel-politik dargelegt: Ihre Realisierung werde das Verhältnis Deutschlands zu allen Nachbarn aufs schwerste belasten, ja eine Verständigung auch in der weiteren Zukunft geradezu verhindern. Meyer hält den Einwänden in dem bereits zitierten Brief vom 10. Oktober 1915 nur entgegen:

"Wir müssen uns aber in die neue Weltlage finden; die Anschauungen, denen wir uns früher hingeben konnten, sind definitiv zusammenge-brochen und gehören einer fernen Vergangenheit an."

III

Etwa gleichzeitig—am 20. Oktober 1915—hat Eduard Meyer seinen Vortrag 'Die Einwirkungen des Weltkrieges auf die Kultur und die Kul-turaufgaben der deutschen Zukunft' gehalten.[7] Im Zentrum der Betrachtung stehen die Begriffe 'Staat' und 'Kultur', die beide zur welt-weiten Ausdehnung, zur 'Weltherrschaft' bzw. 'Weltkultur' tendierten. Im Altertum sei das weitgehend verwirklicht worden (2), anders im neu-zeitlichen Europa, wo sich feste Nationalitäten ausgebildet hätten:

"Eben durch die Rivalität der Nationen wird zugleich der Reichtum der Kultur gesteigert und ihre Erhaltung und Fortentwicklung gesichert: der Reihe nach lösen sich die Völker in der führenden Stellung ab, Italien, Frankreich, Holland, England, Deutschland, und ein jedes steuert von seiner Eigenart etwas Besonderes zu der allgemeinen Kultur der euro-päischen Menschheit bei" (7 f.).

Gerade der niemals endgültig entschiedene Wettkampf der Nationen habe die "universelle Kultur" Europas "gegen eine Stagnation, gegen ein inneres Absterben, *wie in der antiken Kultur,* gesichert" (13 f.). Mit den ersten Augusttagen des Jahres 1914 sei das alles aber schlagartig anders geworden. Die Gegner, insbesondere England, verneinten rundweg das Lebensrecht Deutschlands, von dem "höchstens ein paar völlig gekne-belte und politisch ohnmächtige Kleinstaaten übrig bleiben" dürften (17). Deutschland, das sich bislang bewusst in seinem Nationalstaat be-schränkt habe, dem viele Deutsche ferngeblieben seien, während anderer-seits unter dem "Zwang der geographischen und geschichtlichen Verhält-nisse" nur in Polen, Elsass-Lothringen und Nordschleswig "fremdes Volkstum" einbezogen worden sei (12), müsse nunmehr "hinausgreifen ... über die bisherigen Grenzen, nicht nur unseres Staats, sondern auch unseres Volkstums" (22).

Glücklich ist Meyer bei dem Gedanken an ein 'grösseres', in seiner nationalen Basis gefährdetes Deutschland keineswegs. Er findet Trost nur

---

[7] Weltgeschichte und Weltkrieg, Stuttgart-Berlin 1916, 1–38.

in der Gewissheit, dass "die grossen Nationen der Gegenwart . . . sich nicht absorbieren, die grossen fremden Nationalstaaten so wenig politisch vernichten (liessen) wie das Deutsche Reich; so wird sich die Gefahr vermeiden lassen, dass die moderne Kultur wie die des Altertums in die Einförmigkeit eines entnationalisierten Weltreichs ausmündet, in dem eben deshalb das selbständige Leben und die freie Bewegung und damit aller weitere Fortschritt erstickt wird" (23).

Das Altertum dient Meyer hier nur als Folie für seine Position zu den gegenwärtigen Fragen. In Wahrheit war es freilich für sein Denken konstitutiv. Das lehren sein Aufsatz 'Italien und die Entstehung der italischen Nation im Altertum' vom Juni 1915[8] und der am 27. November 1915 gehaltene Vortrag 'Die Entwicklung der römischen Weltherrschaft,'[9] die sich vielfach ergänzen und überschneiden. Dreh- und Angelpunkte der Ueberlegung sind in beiden Arbeiten der Beginn des Ersten Punischen Krieges und der Sieg Roms im Zweiten Punischen Krieg. Im Jahre 264 habe Rom mit dem Uebergang nach Sizilien den unwiderruflichen Schritt in die Weltpolitik getan, ein Ereignis, das Meyer mit der Eroberung Schlesiens durch Preussen, der Kubas und der Philippinen durch die USA vergleicht (Italien, 98). Nach der Ueberwindung der tödlichen Bedrohung durch Hannibal sei Rom präventiv jeder noch so entfernten Machtbildung entgegengetreten, bis es zuletzt—um 165 v. Chr. —die absolute Vorherrschaft in der damaligen Welt errungen habe (Italien, 100; Weltherrschaft, 66 f.). Beide Entwicklungen hält Meyer für verhängnisvoll. Mit dem Erwerb Siziliens habe Rom die nationale Basis verlassen, weshalb die von ihm eben erst geschaffene "italische Nation . . . nicht zur Perfektion gekommen" sei (Italien, 98). Vollends habe dann die "Weltstellung . . . auf die Masse des italischen Volks ihre zersetzende Wirkung ausgeübt" (Italien, 101 ff.; Weltherrschaft, 70).

Im Endergebnis sieht Meyer also den Nationalstaat Italien als Opfer des römischen Weltreichs. Mindestens ebenso fatal ist ihm aber auch die Vernichtung des hellenistischen Staatensystems durch Rom. Indem fortan sein Wille allein gegolten habe, sei "alles selbständige politische Leben . . . immer mehr erstickt" worden (Weltherrschaft, 43), darüber hinaus der Osten jenseits des Euphrats der hellenistischen Kultur allmählich verloren gegangen, die "orientalische Reaktion" auch im übrigen Orient entscheidend gefördert worden (44). Das Jahr 200 bezeichnet somit die Wende in der Geschichte der Alten Welt. Ihr Untergang war besiegelt, mochte er sich auch noch lange hinziehen.

Mehrmals unterstreicht Meyer die Parallelen zur Gegenwart. "Die

---

[8] Weltgeschichte und Weltkrieg, 81–131 (= Italien).
[9] Weltgeschichte und Weltkrieg, 39–80 (= Weltherrschaft).

Krisis, die wir durchleben, ist die des Hannibalischen Kriegs ... Wie Hannibal die gesamte Mittelmeerwelt in den Kampf gegen Rom zu führen suchte, so hat England bei allen Völkern und Staaten der Erde gegen uns geworben ..." (Weltherrschaft, 77). Deutschland befindet sich also in der Lage Roms. Im Moment ist die ungeheure Bedrohung durch seine Feinde vergleichbar, bald aber werden es die neuen Aufgaben und Herausforderungen sein, die auf den Sieger zukommen. "Auch wir werden hinausgreifen müssen über die Grenzen unseres Volkstums, wir müssen in ganz anderer Weise als bisher Stellung nehmen zu den Vorgängen, die sich ausserhalb unseres Reichs abspielen, und bereit sein, wo es nötig ist, rechtzeitig in sie einzugreifen, ehe die Gefahr zu mächtig anschwillt" (Weltherrschaft, 78).

Meyer interpretiert Roms Politik zwischen 200 und 165 v. Chr. rein defensiv-präventiv, ohne den bewussten Willen zur Weltherrschaft. Gerade darin aber sieht er ein verhängnisvolles Versäumnis Roms. Der Welt wäre seiner Ansicht nach viel Leid erspart geblieben, wenn es das Unvermeidliche als Aufgabe akzeptiert und in Angriff genommen hätte (Italien, 101). Der Gedanke der dira necessitas, die unbedingten Gehorsam fordert, ist für Meyers politisches Weltbild konstitutiv. Noch stärker als in den Briefen an Ehrenberg wird aber sein Unbehagen bei einer künftigen deutschen Weltpolitik formuliert:

"Das mag uns bitter ankommen und unser Gefühl mag sich dagegen sträuben; aber auf Gefühle kommt es nicht mehr an, es ist kein Entschluss, der von unserem freien Willen abhängt, sondern eine gebieterische Notwendigkeit, der sich weder unser Volk als Ganzes noch seine Leiter fortan entziehen können, auch wenn sie wollten" (Weltherrschaft, 78).

Wir dürfen Meyers Unbehagen ruhig ernst nehmen, nicht nur weil er es wiederholt mit ganz ähnlichen Worten formuliert hat.[10] Er sah noch nicht einmal die "Gefahr (!), dass wir in die Bahnen der römischen Weltherrschaft einmünden werden" wegen der grossen Stabilität der Nationen und Nationalstaaten der Gegenwart (Weltherrschaft, 78 f.). Erst recht sah er darin überhaupt nichts Verlockendes. Die deutschen Annexionspläne waren ja auch keineswegs so weit gespannt, dass sie das Kräfteverhältnis in der Welt grundlegend verändert hätten. Deutschlands Lage blieb allemal prekär und jeder Gewinn wurde von der damit verbundenen Problematik im Grunde weit überwogen.

Meyers historisch begründete Einsicht in die Fragwürdigkeit seiner

---

[10] Vgl. Weltgeschichte und Weltkrieg, 22: "Wohl mag sich bei manchem das Gefühl dagegen sträuben, dass wir damit hinausgehen müssen über die Basis des nationalen Staats ...."

politischen Position wird aber gerade durch die historische Parallele auch wieder ausser Kraft gesetzt: die Wiederholung des Gleichen ist unvermeidlich und wird immer noch besser vollzogen als erlitten. Allenfalls lassen sich die Fehler Roms vermeiden, indem Deutschland nach dem Vorbild Bismarcks 1879 (Beginn der Schutzzollpolitik zugunsten von Agrariern und Schwerindustrie) und Kardorffs 1902 (Zolltarifgesetz) anders als Rom seine agrarische Basis erhält und pflegt und indem es an der kraftvollen Monarchie festhält, die Rom so lange gefehlt hat (Weltherrschaft, 79 f.). Genau betrachtet sind das aber nur erleichternde Modifikationen. Das Grundgefühl Meyers bleibt die Ausweglosigkeit der Situation, zumal er durchaus sieht, dass der gegenwärtige Krieg die Weltstellung der europäischen Kultur insgesamt infragestelle.[11]

IV

Eduard Meyer hat mehrfach betont, dass sich seine Anschauungen über den Verlauf der Alten Geschichte geraume Zeit vor dem Weltkrieg herausgebildet hätten. U.a. spricht er von wiederholten Seminarübungen zum Zweiten Punischen Krieg.[12] In der Tat zeichnen sich seine Aeusserungen über die Jahrzehnte hin durch eine bemerkenswerte Konstanz, ja durch vielfache wörtliche Wiederholungen aus. Umso mehr gilt es, auf die Nuancierungen und Verschiebungen zu achten.

Im Jahre 1895 hielt Meyer seinen berühmten Vortrag über 'die wirtschaftliche Entwicklung des Altertums.'[13] Einer Darstellung der griechischen Verhältnisse folgt ein äusserst knapper Blick auf die Krise der römischen Republik (47 f.), dann sogleich das römische Kaiserreich. Es wird zunächst als eine Zeit weitverbreiteter Kultur (48), des Friedens (49), der Gerechtigkeit und Humanität (50) gewürdigt;[14] ja sogar der Spätantike gewinnt Meyer positive Aspekte ab: die grossen sakralen Bauten, vor allem aber die konsequent aufgebaute diokletianische Monarchie, die er zu der "Halbheit des augusteischen Prinzipats," dessen

---

[11] Weltgeschichte und Weltkrieg, 23; vgl. Vorläufer des Weltkriegs im Altertum (1918), *Kl. Schr.* II, 510.
[12] Weltgeschichte und Weltkrieg, 81 Anm. 1; *Kl. Schr.* II, Halle 1924, 423 Anm. 1; u.a. hielt er einen solchen Kurs im Winter 1909/10 in Harvard (s. den Beitrag von M. Chambers). Vgl. auch die Aeusserung *GdA* III², VI, er habe—anders als Wilamowitz—nur ganz wenige seiner wissenschaftlichen Thesen zurücknehmen müssen.
[13] Jena 1895 = Kl. Schr. I, Halle 1910, 79 ff. Seitenangaben nach der Erstauflage.
[14] Vgl. *GdA* II, Stuttgart 1893, 28: "Von der Cultur des Hellenismus und der Kaiserzeit wandte man sich mit Geringschätzung ab, hier vermochte man nur Verfall und Entartung zu erblicken, ihre weltgeschichtlich der classischen Zeit mindestens gleichstehende Bedeutung, die ungeheure Wirkung, welche diese Epochen auf alle Folgezeit ausgeübt haben und noch üben, blieben so gut wie unbeachtet."

"innere(r) Unwahrheit" in Kontrast setzt (51 Anm. 1). Aber im Ganzen überwiegt doch die Frage nach den Gründen des Verfalls. Meyer lehnt die Katastrophentheorie, die Zerstörung des Reiches durch die Barbaren, entschieden ab (50 f.). Für ihn handelt es sich um einen Prozess der inneren Auflösung, der Zersetzung, für den allgemein die allzu weite Ausdehnung, und damit Verflachung, der antiken Kultur (52) verantwortlich zu machen ist, spezieller das antike Städtewesen, das auf die Dauer das flache Land ruiniert habe (56 f. 60 f.), während andererseits—nicht ganz konsequent—auch der Verfall der städtischen Selbstverwaltung beklagt wird (54 f.). Sehr präzise ist das alles nicht. Meyer beschreibt mehr die Krise, wie er sie sieht, als dass er sie erklären kann.

Ganz anders ist die Gewichtsverteilung in der 1902 verfassten Abhandlung über den 'Gang der alten Geschichte: Hellas und Rom.'[15] Der erste Satz ist programmatisch: "Das Zentrum der Geschichte des Altertums bildet die Geschichte der griechischen Kultur" (233). Als Träger der Kultur aber stellt sich sogleich die Nation, als deren letztlich unentbehrlicher organisatorischer Rahmen wiederum der Nationalstaat dar. Allein diesem gilt Meyers eigentliches Interesse.[15a] Auf je 25 Seiten wird aufgezeigt, wie die Griechen die Ausbildung eines kräftigen Nationalstaates verfehlten, dann wie die Römer das Ziel zwar erreichten, das Erreichte jedoch durch die Aufrichtung der Weltherrschaft wieder verspielten. Die Darstellung bricht in der Mitte des 2. Jh. v. Chr. ab—aus äusseren Gründen, wie uns E. Badian anhand der von ihm wiederentdeckten amerikanischen Erstpublikation gezeigt hat. Aber doch nicht ohne tiefere Berechtigung: alles Weitere ist für Meyer nur noch die Konsequenz dieser Entwicklung, Verfallszeit. Das römische Kaiserreich und der Untergang der alten Welt kommen also nicht zur Sprache, und doch sind sie das Ziel aller Betrachtungen, läuft alles darauf hinaus zu erklären, warum der antiken Kultur keine ewige Dauer beschieden war. Insofern ist diese Abhandlung durchaus komplementär zu der von 1895.

Zunächst die Griechen. Erstmals haben sie nach dem Sieg über die Perser die Chance verfehlt, "die Herrschaft über die ganze Mittelmeerwelt (zu) gewinnen und dauernd (zu) behaupten und ihr für alle Zukunft das Gepräge ihres Volkstums auf(zu)drücken," da sie es nicht verstanden, "alle Kräfte zu einer einzigen festgefügten Grossmacht zusammen-

---

15 *Kl. Schr.* I, 231 ff. Einige der Grundgedanken finden sich bereits in dem ungedruckten Manuskript 'Der Untergang des Alterthums' (1871); dazu das Referat von Chr. Hoffmann.
15a S. dazu L. Canfora (Anm. 1) und im weiteren Rahmen der deutschen Geschichtswissenschaft vor dem Ersten Weltkrieg: J. v. Ungern-Sternberg, Einleitung zu E. Täubler, Der römische Staat, Stuttgart 1985; Chr. Simon, Staat und Geschichtswissenschaft in Deutschland und Frankreich 1871–1914, 2 Bde., Bern 1988.

zufassen'' (238). Auch später verfehlten sie immer wieder ihre ''nationale Aufgabe,'' selbst der äusserst positiv gesehene Dionysios I. von Syrakus vermochte daran nichts zu ändern (243 f.), allenfalls ein Philipp II. von Makedonien hätte Erfolg haben können. Durch die Beschränkung auf Kleinasien hätte er das makedonische Reich konsolidiert und zugleich der europäisch-griechischen Welt eine feste Gestalt gegeben. Indem Alexander aber die von Darius III. angebotene Reichsteilung ablehnte, brachte er letztlich das nationale Interesse und mit ihm die hellenische Kultur dem Gedanken der Weltherrschaft zum Opfer (246. 249). Sie konnte sich zwar nunmehr bis tief nach Asien ausbreiten—Meyer beurteilt insbesondere das Wirken der Seleukiden sehr positiv (253 ff.), würdigt auch das ''lebensvolle hellenistische Staatensystem'' des 3. Jh. (256)—ihr dauernder Geburtsfehler aber blieb das Fehlen ''ein(es) naturwüchsige(n) Staat(es)'' (257), da die einzelnen Staaten keine feste nationale Basis besassen. Vielleicht hätte im Verlauf von Jahrhunderten ''die Macht der Gewohnheit ihnen ein festeres Gefüge zu verleihen vermocht'' (257)— analog zur österreichisch-ungarischen Monarchie—, aber diese Zeit war ihnen nicht vergönnt.

Ganz anders Rom, das es verstanden hat, die Völker Italiens nicht zu Untertanen zu machen (261), sondern zu einer Nation zusammenzuschmieden (264), im Inneren dominiert von dem bäuerlichen Element unter der Führung der grossen Familien (262). Positiv vergleicht Meyer die Vereinigten Staaten, wo zwar das aristokratische Element in der Regierung fast vollständig fehle, aber wie in Rom die Autorität der höchsten Magistratur erhalten sei, ganz anders als in den parlamentarischen Staaten Europas (262). Aber auch Rom sah sich alsbald vor einer neuen Herausforderung. Das städtische Element der nunmehrigen Grossstadt machte sich politisch geltend, vor allem aber die Kapitalisten, die vornehmlich in den Ritterzenturien organisiert, weit über Italien hinaus blickten (264):

''Die Interessen der städtischen Elemente, der Kapitalisten, dagegen reichten über die See hinaus: das Schwergewicht des Staats jetzt auch in der Welt geltend zu machen, ringsum die Verhältnisse nach den eigenen Interessen zu ordnen, Italien vom fremden Handel, vor allem von Karthago zu emanzipieren erschien hier als die nächste Aufgabe'' (265).

Konsequent interpretiert Meyer die römische Politik des 3. Jh. v. Chr. als einen Kampf zwischen der agrarischen, italisch orientierten Partei und der kapitalistischen, überseeisch orientierten,[16] wobei die agrarische

---

[16] Ausführlich später nochmals in: Die römische Politik vom ersten bis zum Ausbruch des zweiten punischen Kriegs, *Kl. Schr.* II, 375 ff. (geschrieben *nach* dem Ersten Weltkrieg!).

Partei nach dem Ersten Punischen Krieg in C. Flaminius noch einmal einen fähigen Führer fand, der aber die Entwicklung nur noch zu hemmen, nicht zu ändern vermochte. Indem Rom im Jahre 264 den Kampf um Sizilien aufnahm, tat es einen "Schritt, der sich niemals wieder zurücknehmen liess, ein(en) Schritt von gleicher unabsehbarer Tragweite, wie die Besetzung Schlesiens für Preussen oder wie für Nordamerika der Krieg gegen Spanien und die Besetzung Cubas und der Philippinen" (265 f.).

Dass Meyers Sicht der römischen Geschichte die Auseinandersetzungen im wilhelminischen Deutschland um Agrar- und Schutzzollpolitik einerseits, Fernhandel andererseits widerspiegelt, ist offenkundig[17]— vollends bewiesen wird es durch seinen späteren Verweis auf die Politik Bismarcks 1879 und Kardorffs 1902,[18] gerade in dem Jahr also, in dem Meyer seine Abhandlung verfasst hat. Offenkundig ist aber auch, wo Meyers Sympathien angesiedelt waren in einer Zeit, in der viele von deutscher Weltpolitik und Weltgeltung träumten, eine starke Flotte, ein Kolonial- und Handelsimperium forderten. Nichts dergleichen ist bei Meyer positiv konnotiert. Er sieht nur die Gefahren einer Politik, die sich von den nationalen Grundlagen entfernt.

Aber das Deutschland seiner Zeit kommt expressis verbis so gut wie gar nicht vor. Genannt werden einige Male die USA—und nicht nur als Zugeständnis an die ursprünglich ins Auge gefassten amerikanischen Leser (232)—, einmal wird sogar das mangelnde Interesse für die amerikanische Geschichte des 19. Jh. in Europa beklagt (273 Anm. 1). Der Eintritt der USA, und der Japans, in die Weltpolitik erscheint Meyer als das gewichtigste Ereignis seiner Gegenwart, in unmittelbarer Parallele zur Weltlage zur Zeit des hannibalischen Krieges. Beide Mächte, vor allem aber doch die USA, befinden sich dabei in der Rolle Roms.[18a] Demgegenüber sieht Meyer die europäischen Staaten *gemeinsam* in ihrer bisherigen Weltstellung bedroht, ohne dass sie praktische Möglichkeiten zur Gegenwehr hätten (274 Anm. 1). Er vergleicht ihre Lage also mit der Karthagos.

Eine Gegenwehr versuchte in der Antike Hannibal durch seinen Prä-

---

[17] Vgl. F. Hampl, Zur Vorgeschichte des ersten und zweiten Punischen Krieges, ANRW I 1, 1972, 433.

[18] Weltgeschichte und Weltkrieg, 79. Der Gegensatz zwischen Kaufleuten— Industriellen und 'Agrariern' findet sich schon in der Abhandlung von 1898 'Die Sklaverei im Altertum' (*Kl. Schr.* I, 193 ff.), dagegen nicht in der z.T. parallelen Passage von 'Die wirtschaftliche Entwicklung des Altertums' (*Kl. Schr.* I, 121 ff.); vgl. das Referat von H. Schneider.

[18a] Vor dem Harvard Graduate Club bezeichnete Meyer am 15. Januar 1910 die USA als "the greatest conquering nation of the nineteenth century, as a glance at a map will show" (s. den Beitrag von M. Chambers).

ventivangriff auf "den übermächtigen Staat, der durch seine blosse Existenz allen anderen Staaten die freie Bewegung unmöglich machte" (270). Fern von eigenen Welteroberungsplänen ging es ihm allein um "die Erhaltung des bisherigen Staatensystems und der Unabhängigkeit der einzelnen Staaten" (269 Anm. 1), wobei er sich—letztlich vergeblich—darum bemühte, "die übrigen Staaten der Welt in den Krieg zu ziehen und zu einem entscheidenden Angriff auf Rom mit sich fortzureissen" (271). Sein Scheitern besiegelte die absolute Vormachtstellung Roms und hat zugleich dem Verlauf der Geschichte des Altertums die letzte fatale Wendung gegeben.

Die darauf bezüglichen Ausführungen Meyers können getrost als *die* zentrale Passage für sein Geschichtsdenken bezeichnet werden. Sie müssen daher in voller Länge vorgeführt werden:

"Der Krieg Hannibals gegen Rom ist der Höhepunkt der alten Geschichte: wenn bisher die Entwicklung der alten Welt und die der christlich-germanischen Völker des Mittelalters und der Neuzeit in den Grundzügen in parallelen Bahnen verläuft, von hier an scheiden sich die Wege. In der neueren Geschichte sind seit dem sechzehnten Jahrhundert alle Versuche, die Universalherrschaft eines Volkes aufzurichten, immer von neuem gescheitert; die einzelnen Völker haben sich selbständig behauptet, die politischen Staatengebilde sind in diesen Kämpfen zu nationalen Staaten erwachsen, denen die volle Kraft ihres Gebiets in demselben Umfang zu Gebote steht, wie im Altertum Rom allein. Auf diesem Gleichgewicht der Staaten und der in ihnen organisierten Nationen, auf ihrem ununterbrochenen Wettkampf auf allen Gebieten des staatlichen und kulturellen Lebens, der sie zwingt, wenn sie sich behaupten wollen, in jedem Moment ihre volle Kraft mit höchster Anspannung einzusetzen, beruht die moderne Gestaltung der Welt; auf ihr beruht es, dass die universelle Kultur der Neuzeit sich zu behaupten vermag und, bis jetzt wenigstens, ständig fortschreitet, während die Führung in dem fortwährenden Ringen immer aufs neue von einem Volk zum andern übergeht. Im Altertum dagegen ist der Versuch, ein Gleichgewicht der Staaten zu erhalten, im hannibalischen Kriege gescheitert; seitdem gibt es nur noch *eine* Macht, die in der Welt etwas zu sagen hat, den römischen Staat—und eben deshalb beginnt in demselben Moment zunächst der Stillstand und dann der Rückgang der Kultur. Ein einziger grosser Kulturstaat, in dem alle Nationalitäten aufgehoben sind, das ist das letzte Ergebnis, das in den folgenden Jahrhunderten aus dieser Gestaltung herauswächst. Damit ist aber der Wettkampf und das Lebenselement der Kultur aufgehoben: der Anreiz fehlt, weiter vorzuschreiten, die Rivalen zu überflügeln, man strebt nur noch, das gewonnene zu behaupten, und das bedeutet hier wie überall den Rückgang und den Tod der Kultur.
Auch Rom selbst und mit ihm ganz Italien hat, indem es den Gewinn des Sieges sicher zu stellen suchte, zugleich die verderblichen Folgen desselben in voller Schwere an sich erfahren müssen. Es ist hineingerissen in die Weltpolitik und kann aus derselben nicht mehr heraus, so gern es möchte; eine Rückkehr zu der alten italischen Politik mit ihren begrenzten bäuerlichen Tendenzen ist unmöglich geworden. Daher kommt es, dass die Verheerung,

welche der hannibalische Krieg Italien gebracht hat, bis auf den heutigen Tag niemals wieder gut gemacht ist, dass die Wunden, welche er der Volkskraft geschlagen hat, niemals vernarbt und verwachsen sind: der italische Staat und die werdende italische Nation sind nicht zur Perfektion gelangt, weil das nivellierende römische Weltreich ihnen über den Kopf wuchs'' (275 ff.).

Die einzelnen Motive sind uns bereits bekannt: Die Nationalstaaten als Träger der Kultur, ihr ständiger, niemals entschiedener Wettkampf als Garantie der lebendigen Weiterentwicklung. Scharf unterscheidet Meyer hier aber zwischen dem Altertum und der Gegenwart. Der damalige Betriebsunfall—die Monopolisierung der Macht durch Rom, ermöglicht durch das politische Versagen des Griechentums—kann sich nicht wiederholen, dazu sind die modernen Staaten in sich zu gefestigt und gleichwertig. Nichts anderes erscheint Meyer als wünschenswert. 'Der Griff nach der Weltmacht' ist für Täter und Opfer gleich verhängnisvoll, mag er, wie im Falle Roms, noch so widerwillig vollzogen werden.

Immer wieder betont Meyer im Folgenden, wie sehr Rom allein auf seine Sicherheit bedacht war, als es seine Macht über den gesamten Mittelmeerraum ausweitete. Manchmal für uns durchaus merkwürdig, wenn er etwa den Fortbestand der römischen Herrschaft in Spanien damit motiviert, dass niemand dagewesen sei, dem man es hätte übergeben können (277)—im Zeitalter des Kolonialismus freilich durchaus einsichtig. Er unterstreicht, dass es ''für Rom selbst wie für die Welt . . . sehr viel besser gewesen (wäre), Rom wäre systematisch auf die Welteroberung ausgegangen'' (280) und geisselt insbesondere die ''perfide Politik'' gegenüber dem Seleukidenreich (281).

V

Zurück zum Ersten Weltkrieg! Meyer schrieb am 10. April 1917 an Ehrenberg:

> ''Meine Ueberzeugung, dass 1914 den Wendepunkt der modernen Entwicklung bildet, und dass es von da aus bergab geht, festigt sich immer mehr.''

Immer wieder finden wir in seinen Aeusserungen während und nach dem Weltkrieg den Verweis auf die ersten Augusttage, spezieller den 4. August 1914: den Tag der Kriegserklärung Englands an Deutschland. Für Eduard Meyer bedeutete er den Zusammenbruch seines bisherigen Weltbildes. Er hatte fest an den friedlichen Wettbewerb der Nationen geglaubt, der bisher verhindert habe und in aller Zukunft verhindern werde, dass die europäische Kultur in einer dem römischen Kaiserreich gleichen Monotonie zum Stillstand kommen und schliesslich enden werde. Nun musste er feststellen: "Diese Auffassung und diese Erwartung ist durch den Krieg als Illusion erwiesen worden."[19]

Es handelt sich dabei schlichtweg um eine traumatische Erfahrung. Eduard Meyer jedenfalls hatte für Deutschland niemals mehr gewollt als das, was auch jeder der anderen grossen Nationen zustand:

". . . wir wollten von dem Glauben nicht lassen, dass, wenn wir dabei die Rechte und die berechtigten Interessen der anderen achteten, diese auch unsere Rechte anerkennen und achten und uns den Platz an der Sonne gönnen würden, der uns ebensogut zukam wie jenen. Gerade in dieser Konkurrenz der Nationen, in dem Zwange, der dadurch für eine jede gegeben war, ihr Bestes zu leisten und keinen Moment zu erschlaffen, erblickten wir das Mittel zur Aufrechterhaltung und fortschreitenden Steigerung der universellen Kultur, die dadurch gegen eine Stagnation, gegen ein inneres Absterben, wie in der antiken Kultur, gesichert war. Zugleich erschien eben die Höhe dieser Kultur . . . als ein Gegengewicht gegen die immer drohende Gefahr eines Krieges: die ungeheuren Verluste, die er bringen musste, schienen die Verantwortung so gewaltig zu steigern, dass ein jeder Staatsmann und ein jedes Volk davor zurückscheuen müsse."[20]

In diesem ehrlichen Glauben sah sich Meyer nunmehr brutal getäuscht. Er sah Deutschland auf einmal einer Welt von Feinden gegenüber, die ihm das Mitspracherecht in der Welt verweigern wollten,[21] ja die sogar sich anschickten, seine nationale Existenz zu vernichten.[22] Schlimmer noch, er musste feststellen, wie wenig beliebt Deutschland auch bei vielen neutralen Völkern, insbesondere in den Vereinigten Staaten, war, wie sehr die feindliche Propaganda Glauben fand, die Deutschland als autoritären Militärstaat zeichnete und das deutsche Heer in Belgien als plündernde und mordende Barbarenhorden.[23] In diesen Karikaturen vermochte sich Meyer nicht wiederzuerkennen. Im Bewusstsein seines eigenen wissenschaftlichen Werkes, der wissenschaftlichen und kulturellen Leistungen Deutschlands schlechthin, ebenso wie im Bewusstsein seiner friedlichen Absichten war er zutiefst verletzt und ausserstande, nach Elementen der deutschen Politik und des deutschen Auftretens vor 1914 zu fragen—bis hin zur Problematik des Einmarsches in Belgien—, die der gegnerischen Propaganda immerhin die Anhaltungspunkte boten,

---

[19] Weltgeschichte und Weltkrieg, XV; vgl. ebd., 19.170; *Kl. Schr.* I², Halle 1924, IV ff.; *Kl. Schr.* II, 507; Spenglers Untergang des Abendlandes, Berlin 1925, 4; Brief an Spengler vom 25.6.1922 (Oswald Spengler, Briefe 1913–1936, München 1963).

[20] Weltgeschichte und Weltkrieg, 13 f.

[21] Weltgeschichte und Weltkrieg, 15.

[22] z.B. *Kl. Schr.* II, 509.

[23] S. etwa Weltgeschichte und Weltkrieg, 19 f. und die Schriften über die USA.

die sie für viele Neutrale erst akzeptabel machten. Er reagierte wie fast alle seine Kollegen, völlig unpolitisch, ehrlich empört, ja eben: zutiefst verletzt.[24] Diese traumatische Erfahrung wird m.E. bei den bisherigen Arbeiten über das Verhalten der deutschen Professoren im Ersten Weltkrieg, etwa auch zu dem unglückseligen 'Aufruf der 93,' viel zu wenig in Rechnung gestellt. Aber nicht nur bei ihnen, man denke etwa an Thomas Mann! Die fast unvermeidliche Reaktion war Trotz—das Herauskehren und Beharren auf der 'deutschen Eigenart.' Es wäre doch genauer zu prüfen, wieviel von der Konzeption des deutschen 'Sonderwegs' schlichte Reaktion auf die Situation von 1914 ist. Nur wenigen deutschen Gelehrten gelang es im Verlauf des Ersten Weltkrieges zu einer klareren Beurteilung der innen- wie der aussenpolitischen Problematik vorzudringen.[25] Zu ihnen gehörte Eduard Meyer nicht.

VI

Er versuchte nunmehr, die Tatsache des Weltkriegs in sein geschichtliches Weltbild einzuordnen. Das schien nicht besonders schwierig. Der Zweite Punische Krieg war für ihn schon zuvor eine Art antiker Weltkrieg gewesen,[26] zugleich die entscheidende Wende im Verlauf der Geschichte des Altertums—der 1914 ausgebrochene weltweite Krieg bot dazu die perfekte Analogie. Aber wer war nun wer? Auch das schien nicht schwer zu beantworten. War es nicht England, das wie einst Hannibal Rom, so

---

[24] Die gleichen Reaktionen und die gleiche Unfähigkeit zu einer genaueren politischen Analyse finden sich freilich bereits 1870. Am 30. August 1870 schrieb der bekannte Berliner Aegyptologe Richard Lepsius (1810–1884) an seinen Genfer Schüler und Kollegen Edouard Naville (1844–1926) inmitten einer rein ägyptologischen Korrespondenz einen hochemotionalen Brief zum deutsch-französischen Krieg. Der Ton ist ernst und hebt, wie auch ein beigelegtes Gedicht von Ernst Curtius, die Verluste des Krieges hervor. Zur Reaktion der Umwelt auf den Krieg bemerkt Lepsius: ''Dass dann keine der Europäischen Mächte für uns das Schwert zog, war begreiflich, aber dass keine, auch England nicht, einen missbilligenden Ausdruck für diesen Ueberfall fand, zeigt, dass das sogenannte Gleichgewicht der Grossmächte nur auf gegenseitiger Furcht, ohne jegliche Beimischung von Gerechtigkeitsgefühl und öffentlicher Scham beruht. Wahre ethische und moralische Principien, soweit auch die an sich egoistische Völkerpolitik sie befolgen soll und kann, finden sich in der That zur Zeit unter den Grossmächten nur in Deutschland ....'' Bemerkenswert sind die territorialen Verschiebungen, die Lepsius für notwendig hält. An Deutschland sollen selbstverständlich Elsass und Lothringen fallen, auch wenn ''beide Länder ... für die nächsten 10 Jahre ein schwieriger und kein beneidenswerter Besitz'' sind, an die Schweiz oder Italien Savoyen, das Département du Nord an Belgien. Es gilt, das 'celtische' ''Frankreich so viel als möglich zu schwächen, und Deutschland nicht mehr zuzuweisen, als es sich assimilieren kann.'' (Bibliothèque publique et universitaire de Genève Ms. 2527, Blätter 60–66; freundlicher Hinweis von Denis van Berchem).

[25] Vgl. die Arbeiten von K. Schwabe (Anm. 1); B. vom Brocke, Wissenschaft versus Militarismus (Anm. 1).

[26] *Kl. Schr.* I, 271.

jetzt Deutschland durch eine grosse Koalition 'einzukreisen' und nieder-
werfen bestrebt war?[27] Für Meyer waren die Gleichungen evident; er hat
sie nie eigens begründet, sondern Elemente der Analogie hinüber und
herüber stets ganz selbstverständlich argumentativ und illustrativ eingesetzt.

Er setzte sich dabei grosszügig darüber hinweg, dass er 1902 die
Parallele ganz anders gezogen hatte. Damals hatte er ja die USA und
Japan mit Rom verglichen, Deutschland aber zusammen mit den übrigen
europäischen Staaten in die Lage Karthagos versetzt. Wie immer es sich
damit verhalten hatte—die neue Analogie jedenfalls war inhaltlich sehr
wenig ergiebig, ja geradezu irreführend. Deutschlands Macht entsprach
keineswegs der römischen im Jahre 218 v. Chr., die 'Weltherrschaft'
würde ihm selbst im Falle eines Sieges nicht zufallen—nirgends spricht
Meyer davon, dass Deutschland sie anstreben solle. Sie erschien ihm ja
auch weiterhin, darin blieb er konsequent, weder wünschenswert noch,
angesichts der Stabilität der Nationalstaaten, erreichbar.

Vergleichbar war allenfalls ganz allgemein die existentielle Gefahr,
die wie für Rom vom Angriff Hannibals, so nun für Deutschland vom
Angriff Englands ausging. Wie Hannibal ''die Organisation, die Rom
der italischen Welt gegeben hatte, ... zersprengen'' wollte, so sollte nun
das Deutsche Reich wieder in seine Bestandteile aufgelöst werden.[28]
Schlimmer noch, es handelte sich um einen ''Vernichtungskrieg, bei dem
nicht nur die Selbständigkeit und die staatliche Macht, sondern geradezu
die Existenz ganzer Nationen auf dem Spiel steht. Denn das deutsche
Volk in seinem Mark zu treffen, es für alle Zukunft aus der Geschichte
auszustreichen und in seiner Eigenart und seiner selbständigen, den
anderen Nationen gleichberechtigten Entwicklung vom Erdboden zu ver-
tilgen, es zu einem Volk von Heloten zu erniedrigen, ist das Ziel, das
England und seine Bundesgenossen erstreben und immer von neuem
offen verkünden ....''[29]

Vorherrschend bei Meyer war also ein Gefühl der—die realen Kriegsziele der Entente weit übersteigenden—totalen Bedrohung. Und dahinter
die zurückgedrängte, und doch immer wieder durchbrechende Erkenntnis, dass eigentlich England die weltweit herrschende, überlegene Macht
sei. Im Vorwort zur Volkausgabe seines Englandbuches hat Meyer un-
umwunden formuliert:

''Unser Volk weiss seit dem 4. August 1914, dass England unser Todfeind
ist, mit dem es eine Versöhnung nicht geben kann und nicht geben darf, ehe

---

[27] Etwa *Kl. Schr.* II, 510 ff.
[28] Weltgeschichte und Weltkrieg, IX f.
[29] *Kl. Schr.* II, 509.

Englands Anspruch auf Weltherrschaft gebrochen und es gezwungen ist, sich in ein neues Staatensystem zu fügen, das uns den nötigen Raum auf der Erde gibt.''[30]

Das würde an sich Deutschland den Part Hannibals im Weltkrieg zuweisen, wie Meyer doch vor dem Krieg Hannibal mit viel Sympathie gezeichnet und diese auch später nie verloren hat![31] Aber diese Konsequenz zieht Meyer im gleichen Werke nicht (200 ff.), wiewohl er dann wieder davon spricht, es gelte ''Englands Seeherrschaft und Tyrannei zu brechen'' (203). Und 1918 zur Vorgeschichte des Krieges bemerkte: ''Entscheidend steht im Mittelpunkt die Erhaltung und Erweiterung der englischen Weltherrschaft, die sich durch die selbständige Entwicklung Deutschlands in ihren Fundamenten bedroht glaubte.''[32]

War aber die Analogie schon in sich reichlich widersprüchlich, dann konnte sie natürlich auch keine wirklichen geschichtlichen Lehren vermitteln. In der Tat vermochte Meyer ihr nicht allzuviel Konkretes zu entnehmen. Wichtig war ihm der Selbstbehauptungswille Roms, der es durch alle Katastrophen des Zweiten Punischen Kriegs hindurch zum Siege geführt hat. Dabei wusste Meyer durchaus, dass Rom stets über das grössere Kräftepotential verfügt hat;[33] für Deutschland hingegen begnügte er sich mit moralischen Kategorien. Ein Abwägen der Stärkeverhältnisse findet sich nicht bei ihm, weswegen er noch im Oktober 1918 für eine Fortführung des Krieges eintreten und bereits 1919 die Niederlage allein aus dem moralische Versagen des deutschen Volkes erklären konnte, nahezu bereits in den Formulierungen der 'Dolchstosslegende.'[34] Und die Entschlossenheit Karthagos im Jahre 149, wie Athens 406, lobte, den Kampf bis zum Letzten zu führen.[35]

Wichtig waren für Meyer aber vor allem die Vorstellungen des 'Präventiven' wie des 'rechtzeitigen Vollzugs des ohnehin geschichtlich Notwendigen,' die er aus der Geschichte Roms nach 200 in die deutsche

---

[30] England. Volksausgabe, Stuttgart—Berlin 1915, XV.

[31] Vgl. das warme Lob Hannibals, der von den Römern mit ebensolchen Schauergeschichten verleumdet worden sei, ''wie sie jetzt unsere Feinde von uns erfinden'': Hannibal und Scipio, in: Meister der Politik, hg. E. Marcks—K.A. von Müller, Stuttgart—Berlin 1922, 79 f. Ebd. spricht Meyer freilich im übrigen von ''punischer Art'' und ''dem semitischen Wesen,'' was er zuvor in diesem Zusammenhang nie getan hatte; dazu im grösseren Rahmen. Chr. Hoffmann (Anm. 4).

[32] *Kl. Schr.* II, 510.

[33] *Kl. Schr.* I, 270 ff.

[34] *Kl. Schr.* II, 542; vgl. 570; besonders deutlich: Hannibal und Scipio (Anm. 31), 101 Anm. 1; dazu L. Canfora, Quaderni di storia 2, H.3, (Anm. 1).

[35] *Kl. Schr.* II, 543 f.546 f.; vgl. allgemein die Ueberlegungen Meyers, wie weit sich der Feldherr selbst in der Schlacht exponieren solle: *Kl. Schr.* II, 111 f. mit charakteristischem Tadel an dem Rationalisten Polybios (112 Anm. 1); ferner ebd., 493 f. (Perseus bei Pydna).

Gegenwart des Weltkriegs übertrug. "Wir haben die Bahn, die wir be-
schreiten müssen, nicht selbst gewählt, wir wollten Frieden halten; das
Streben nach Unterdrückung fremder Völker, und gar nach Weltherrschaft, lag uns völlig fern. Aber sie haben uns gezwungen, das wahr zu
machen, was *sie* befürchteten und *wir* nicht wollten. Fortan müssen alle
Bedenken schwinden; wir müssen in ganz anderer Weise als bisher unsere
Interessen vertreten und durchsetzen, und dürfen nicht dulden, dass
wieder eine Verschwörung gegen uns, wie die von England angezettelte,
sich bilden kann; und wenn dies doch geschehen sollte, dürfen wir nicht
wieder abwarten, sondern müssen rechtzeitig zugreifen und die Pläne im
Entstehen ersticken."[36]

Nur, wie war das in ein politisches Programm umzusetzen? Meyer hat
das nie recht gewusst; daher sein Unbehagen, seine düstere Grundstimmung. Sie wurde auch genährt durch seine Einsicht in die Fragwürdigkeit
der politischen Führung Deutschlands, vor allem der Machtverschiebung
hin zur Obersten Heeresleitung. Eine Einsicht, die er charakteristischer-
weise auch wieder nicht wahrhaben wollte. Er hebt einmal die Bedeutung
des Themistokles für den griechischen Sieg über die Perser hervor. "Die
Entscheidung (habe) sich in einer überragenden Persönlichkeit zusam-
mengefasst." "Eine solche Persönlichkeit," fährt er fort, "besitzen wir
jetzt in unserem genialen Feldherrn,"—gemeint ist Hindenburg—"der
eben dadurch auch der Ausschlag gebende Staatsmann geworden ist."
Der Vergleich drängt sich Meyer auf; er sucht ja nach einem Grund zur
Hoffnung für Deutschlands Zukunft. Und zugleich fühlt er das Unpas-
sende des Vergleichs, ja sogar das fatal Enthüllende, daher die ebenso
sophistische wie doch wieder zutreffende Fortsetzung: "denn auch wenn
er ein Eingreifen ablehnen sollte, würde er damit die Entscheidung geben;
die Verantwortung ist, er mag wollen oder nicht, allein auf seine
Schultern gelegt."[37]

Nach der Niederlage hat Meyer lapidar festgestellt, dass Deutschland
seit dem Sturze Bismarcks keinen wirklichen Staatsmann mehr gehabt
habe,[38] und zuletzt in seiner 'Autobiographischen Skizze' davon gesprochen, er habe während des Krieges "in die Unfähigkeit der Regierung ... einen sehr lebendigen Einblick gewonnen." Gelegentlich sah er
dafür sogar strukturelle Gründe. Der deutsche Staatsaufbau habe "eine
überlegene Persönlichkeit nicht aufkommen" lassen, dagegen: "unsere
Feinde haben mit ihrer improvisierten Organisation, bei der die befähig-
ten Persönlichkeiten frei und grosszügig schalten konnten ... schliesslich

---

[36] Weltgeschichte und Weltkrieg, 21 f.
[37] *Kl. Schr.* II, 516 f.
[38] *Kl. Schr.* II, 545.

weit mehr zu leisten vermocht als wir.''[39] Meyer kommt zu dieser Erkenntnis nicht zufällig im Rahmen seines Vergleichs zwischen den
Niederlagen Athens und Deutschlands. Seine Worte sind ein unmittelbarer Nachklang der Lobrede, die Thukydides den Perikles auf die attische Demokratie halten lässt: dem rigorosen System Spartas wird die
freie, und doch so erfolgreiche Initiative der Athener gegenübergestellt
(II 39).

Wie er hier der Wahrheit nahe kam, ohne doch daraus die nötigen
Konsequenzen zu ziehen, so ahnte er auch hinsichtlich der Notwendigkeit
eines rechtzeitigen Friedensschlusses durchaus das Richtige. Schon vor
dem Weltkrieg war es für ihn ein Problem, warum Karthago nicht im
Jahre 205 noch rechtzeitig Frieden geschlossen habe.[40] Später stellte er
sich die gleiche Frage für Athen,[41] den Vergleich mit Deutschland aber
zog er nur in der Weise, dass es dort die 'Systemveränderer' gewesen
seien, die den Versöhnungsfrieden gewollt hätten![42]

VII

In seiner nach dem Zusammenbruch Deutschlands am 15. Oktober 1919
gehaltenen Rektoratsrede stellt sich Meyer der Vergleich mit Rom und
Karthago in ganz neuem Lichte dar. Jetzt ist es ''der römische Senat'',
der ''mit derselben satanischen Politik gegen sie (Karthago) vorging, die
unsere Feinde bei den Friedensverhandlungen gegen uns angewandt
haben.'' Und wird Karthago gerühmt, weil ''es den genialen Feldherrn,
der den Krieg herbeigeführt und so viele Siege erfochten hatte, das Vorbild, an das Hindenburg und Ludendorff unmittelbar anknüpfen, nicht
etwa von sich gestossen, verleumdet und verfolgt, sondern ihm die Leitung
des Staates übertragen habe.''[43] Das Problem der geschichtlichen Analogie wird hier besonders gut sichtbar. Sie illustriert einfach in beliebiger
Auswahl und Isolierung des einzelnen Faktums den jeweiligen Gedanken.

Bei seiner Suche nach vergleichbaren Katastrophen in der Antike stösst
Meyer im übrigen auf die Niederlage Athens im Peloponnesischen Krieg
und auf ihre Darstellung im Werk des Thukydides. Eine insofern glück-
lichere Parallele, als Deutschland wie Athen nach erstaunlichen Anstrengungen und grossen zeitweiligen Erfolgen wesentlich an den eigenen
Fehlern, an einer aus politischer Blindheit resultierenden Ueberspannung

---

[39] *Kl. Schr.* II, 556; etwas anders 576.
[40] *Kl. Schr.* II, 353 Anm. 2.
[41] *Kl. Schr.* II, 526.
[42] *Kl. Schr.* II, 546 (vgl. 576 zu Friedrich dem Grossen); Hannibal und Scipio (Anm.
31), 101.
[43] *Kl. Schr.* II, 543.

seiner Kräfte, gescheitert war. Meyer sieht dies freilich nicht. Ihm gibt die Parallele als einem Thucydides redivivus Gelegenheit zu einem der perikleischen Leichenrede analogen Nachruf, den, wie kein Geringerer als Arnaldo Momigliano gesagt hat, ''si legge anche ora con il più grande rispetto come singolare documento di fedeltà alla vecchia Prussia.''[44]

Der Zweite Punische Krieg hingegen hat seine aktuelle Bedeutung für Meyer gänzlich eingebüsst. Der moderne Weltkrieg hatte ja ganz andere Folgen gehabt, als er erwartet hatte. Deutschland hatte nicht gesiegt, damit entfielen die von ihm vorausgesagten Probleme. Andererseits war es vom Frieden von Versailles zwar schwer getroffen, aber doch nicht vernichtet worden. Auch das Staatssystem hatte sich zwar in seiner Zusammensetzung sehr gewandelt, war aber grundsätzlich weiterhin durch das Neben- und Gegeneinander mehrerer grosser Mächte charakterisiert, nicht durch ein Rom analoges Monopol.

Nur in einem Punkt hatte Meyer richtig gesehen: der Weltkrieg hatte die Weltgeltung der europäischen Mächte insgesamt geschwächt. Aber dafür hätte er—wenn schon die Antike bemüht werden musste—eine sehr viel bessere Analogie im Peloponnesischen Krieg finden können, dessen Wirkung es letztlich gewesen ist, dass die Führung der griechischen Politik von Athen und Sparta an die Peripherie, an Makedonien, überging.

Hinsichtlich des Verlaufs der antiken Geschichte freilich hat Meyer an seinen früheren Ansichten festgehalten. Ganz ebenso wie im Jahre 1902 hat er in dem biographischen Abriss 'Hannibal und Scipio' (Anm. 31) die römische Parteiungen des 3. Jh. v. Chr. und das Ringen zwischen Rom und Karthago geschildert; wie schon 1902 bedeutet für ihn in seiner Abhandlung 'Blüte und Niedergang des Hellenismus in Asien' (Berlin 1925) das Angebot des Perserkönigs Darius, sein Reich mit Alexander zu teilen, ''die Schicksalsfrage für die antike Welt'' (7). So aber ist der Hellenismus, bei aller Anerkennung seiner weltgeschichtlichen Bedeutung, ''wesentlich daran verblutet, dass er nicht auf ein geschlossenes Gebiet beschränkt blieb, das auch politisch zu einer Einheit hätte verwachsen können'' (14). Agent des Schicksals ist wiederum Rom, nachdem es die tötliche Gefahr des Hannibalkrieges siegreich bestanden hatte (62 f.). ''Analogien mit der gegenwärtigen Weltlage'' aufzuzeigen, vermeidet Meyer aber dieses Mal, in der Annahme, dass sie ''sich dem Leser überall aufdrängen'' werden (Vorwort).

Einmal indes tut Meyer doch einen Seitenblick auf die Neuzeit:

> ''Setzen wir uns in die Zeit um die Wende vom dritten zum zweiten Jahrhundert v. Chr. zurück, so musste, wer die Weltlage überblickte, den Ein-

---

[44] A. Momigliano (Anm. 4), 230.

druck gewinnen, dass die Weltstellung des Hellenismus fest begründet und für alle Zukunft gesichert sei, etwa in derselben Weise, wie zu Ende des vergangenen Jahrhunderts die Herrschaft der europäischen Völker und ihrer Kultur über alle fünf Weltteile als das Endergebnis der geschichtlichen Entwicklung erschien'' (60).

Hier spricht Meyer durchaus in eigenem Namen. Er selbst war von der endgültig errungenen Vormachtstellung Europas überzeugt gewesen, bis dann der Eintritt Japans und der USA in die Weltpolitik in ihm Zweifel erregt hatten. Der—menschlich so begreiflichen!—Versuchung, den gegenwärtigen Zustand für den dauernd bleibenden zu halten, ist Meyer aber auch sonst nur allzu häufig erlegen. Etwa wenn er im nachhinein festellen muss, "dass das deutsche Kaiserreich nicht, wie wir geglaubt haben, ein Abschluss, sondern nur ein Durchgangspunkt der Entwicklung gewesen ist.''[45] Vieles von seinen Aeusserungen während des Weltkrieges ist einfach Fortschreibung der gegenwärtigen Kampfsituation in alle ferne Zukunft; so etwa wenn er die künftige Wiederaufnahme wissenschaftlicher Beziehungen mit dem feindlichen Ausland kategorisch ablehnt.[46] Im Grunde hat Meyer seltsam ungeschichtlich gedacht, ohne Sinn für den ständigen Wandel, der neue Konstellationen schafft, neue Chancen bietet.

Um 1900 charakterisierte Meyer rückblickend das dem Liberalismus verpflichtete Werk Georg Grote's 'A History of Greece.' "Aus der Geschichte glaubte sie den Massstab gewinnen zu können, nach dem die moderne Entwicklung zu messen sei, hier suchte sie die Principien, deren Sieg allein der Gegenwart ein gedeihliches Fortschreiten sichern könne. Aber thatsächlich entnahm sie den Massstab der Gegenwart selbst, und zwar nicht in einer unparteiischen Auffassung, die in dem harten Ringen der Gegensätze überhaupt nicht zu gewinnen war, sondern der eigenen Partei: die Berechtigung ihrer eigenen Anschauungen und Forderungen und die absolute Verwerflichkeit des gegnerischen Standpunktes wollte sie historisch erweisen ....'' Nicht anders ist man versucht auch über Meyers eigenes Verfahren zu urteilen. Er selbst hat das vorausschauend z.T. getan, aber eben nur teilweise: "Die Einseitigkeiten, die Abhängigkeit von ephemeren Erscheinungen der Gegenwart, die zweifellos auch unserer Auffassung anhaften, wird erst eine spätere Generation richtig zu erkennen vermögen; dass wir in politischen Fragen unparteiischer geworden und dadurch zu einem richtigeren und umfassenderen historischen Urtheil gelangt sind, wird schwerlich in Abrede gestellt werden können.''[47]

---

[45] *Kl. Schr.* II, 584.
[46] Weltgeschichte und Weltkrieg, 23 ff.
[47] *GdA* III, Stuttgart 1901, 292 f. (= *GdA* IV 1³, 1939, 274 f.); vgl. auch die Bemer-

Der Optimismus war wenig berechtigt. Theoretisch war sich Meyer über die Gefahren der historischen Analogie durchaus im klaren,[48] in seiner Praxis aber hat er seinen Erkenntnissen keine Rechnung getragen.[49]

---

kung zu den Werken über die späte römische Republik: Caesars Monarchie und das Principat des Pompeius, 3. Aufl., Stuttgart—Berlin 1922, VI.

[48] Grundsätzlich äussert er sich dazu in *GdA* I[3], Stuttgart 1910, 203 ff.: "Allerdings ist diese Versenkung in vergangene Zeiten immer nur relativ, weil der Betrachtende aus seiner eigenen Gegenwart und zugleich aus seiner eigenen Individualität niemals heraus kann, sondern deren Bedingungen, mögen sie durch Kritik noch so sehr unter Kontrolle gehalten werden, doch immer in sich trägt" (206 f.). S. dazu auch die Referate von J. Deininger und A. Demandt; methodisch wichtig nun: L. Canfora, Analogia e storia. L'uso politico dei paradigmi storici, Mailand 1982.

[49] In jedem Fall aber sollte man Meyers Verfahren positiv abheben von der Oberflächlichkeit und Effekthascherei, mit der damals andere die Vorgänge der Alten Geschichte mit solchen der Gegenwart in Parallele gesetzt haben; etwa ein Th. Birt—Klassenkamerad Meyers (Hinweis von E. Pack): Römische Charakterköpfe, 2. Aufl., Leipzig 1916 (6. Aufl., 1924); Charakterbilder Spätroms, 2. Aufl., Leipzig 1919 (beide nochmals in: Das römisch Weltreich, Berlin 1941).

WOLFHART UNTE

EDUARD MEYER UND DIE NOTGEMEINSCHAFT
DER DEUTSCHEN WISSENSCHAFT

Der Teil des Lebenswerkes Eduard Meyers, mit dem sich der vorliegende
Beitrag befaßt, ist zeitlich auf das letzte Lebensjahrzehnt des großen
Historikers beschränkt; es soll hier an Meyers Aktivitäten bei der Unterstützung der deutschen Wissenschaft in den Jahren nach dem Ersten
Weltkrieg und an seine Mitarbeit in der 1920 gegründeten Notgemeinschaft der Deutschen Wissenschaft erinnert werden, Tätigkeiten, die er
größtenteils als schon von seinen Amtspflichten entbundener Hochschullehrer ausübte
    Der katastrophale wirtschaftliche Niedergang Deutschlands nach dem
verlorenen Krieg wurde ebenso wie in allen Lebensbereichen auch in der
Wissenschaft spürbar. Um ihre Existenz und die ihrer Institutionen zu
sichern, mußte die deutsche Wissenschaft selbst initiativ werden. Das
führte bekanntlich zur Gründung der "Notgemeinschaft der Deutschen
Wissenschaft," einer von staatlicher, jedoch auch von Seiten der
Wirtschaft[1] finanziell getragenen Organisation, die sich zum Ziel gesetzt
hatte, durch Bereitstellung der notwendigen Geldmittel die Aufrechterhaltung wichtiger Forschungsvorhaben und eine kontinuierlich weiter-
geführte Forschungstätigkeit auf allen Wissenschaftsgebieten zu sichern
und somit den Anschluß der isolierten deutschen Forschung an das Ausland zu erhalten. In der Gründungsgeschichte der Notgemeinschaft[2]
spielten der ehemalige preußische Kultusminister Friedrich Schmidt-Ott
und der Chemiker und Nobelpreisträger Fritz Haber eine entscheidende
Rolle; ihren Initiativen und ihrem Einsatz hat die Notgemeinschaft ihre
Entstehung zu verdanken; beide haben, jeder in seiner Weise, die Arbeit
der Gemeinschaft im ersten Jahrzehnt bestimmt.
    Der Name Eduard Meyer begegnet im Ablauf der Gründungsgeschich-
te der Notgemeinschaft recht früh. Am 29. März 1920 beantragte Haber

---

[1] Sie war im "Stifterverband der Notgemeinschaft der Deutschen Wissenschaft"
vereinigt.
[2] K. Zierold, Forschungsförderung in drei Epochen. Deutsche Forschungsgemeinschaft. Geschichte, Arbeitsweise, Kommentar. Wiesbaden 1968; Th. Nipperdey u. L.
Schmugge, 50 Jahre Forschungsförderung in Deutschland. Ein Abriß der Geschichte der
Deutschen Forschungsgemeinschaft. 1920–1970. Berlin 1970; W. Schlicker u. L. Stern,
Die Berliner Akademie der Wissenschaften in der Zeit des Imperialismus. II: Von der
großen sozialistischen Oktoberrevolution bis 1933. Berlin 1975, 125–130.

bei Meyer als damaligem Rektor der Berliner Friedrich-Wilhelms-Universität "den Beitritt der hiesigen Universität zu einer Notgemeinschaft der Deutschen Wissenschaft unter Führung des Staatsministers Dr. Friedrich Schmidt herbeizuführen."[3] Zugleich sollte die Berliner Universität auf die anderen deutschen Hochschulen einwirken, sich ebenfalls in dem genannten Sinne zu beteiligen.

Die weiteren Initiativen gingen dann überwiegend von der Preußischen Akademie der Wissenschaften aus, an die Haber ein Schreiben gleichen Inhalts gesandt hatte. Sie führten am 24. Juni 1920 zur Konstituierung eines Gründungsausschusses und am 30. Oktober zur Gründungssitzung der Notgemeinschaft.

Eduard Meyers Name taucht dann in der weiteren Entwicklung der Notgemeinschaft im Zusammenhang mit der Gründung der Fachausschüsse auf, die "die Richtlinien für die zweckmäßige Verwendung der Mittel zu entwerfen und unter Berücksichtigung der vorliegenden Anträge den Verteilungsplan aufzustellen" hatten. Diesen Ausschüssen kam bei der Entscheidung über eine Unterstützung und der Festlegung von deren Höhe eine nicht unbedeutende Rolle zu. Die ersten Fachausschüsse wurden aufgrund eines Beschlusses des Gründungsausschusses von Präsidium und Hauptausschuß bestimmt.

In einem Brief vom 2. März 1921[4] erging die offizielle Aufforderung an Meyer, den Vorsitz im "Fachausschuß für alte und orientalische Philologie" zu übernehmen. Über das Verfahren bei der Benennung des Vorsitzenden und der Ausschußmitglieder ist dort zu lesen: "Infolge der in der Gründungssitzung der Notgemeinschaft der Deutschen Wissenschaft erteilten Ermächtigung haben Präsident und Hauptausschuß am 23. November v. J. beschlossen, die vorläufige Berufung der Fachausschüsse (§ 9 der Satzungen) in die Hände der Akademien der Wissenschaften und des Hochschulverbandes zu legen. Die Zusammensetzung des Fachausschusses für alte und orientalische Philologie wurde der Preußischen Akademie der Wissenschaften übertragen." Bei der Auswahl der Ausschußmitglieder wurden alle altertumswissenschaftlichen Disziplinen berücksichtigt,[5] wenn auch das klassische Altertum ein Übergewicht hatte; das änderte sich später, als zusätzlich für Assy-

---

³ Zierold, 10.

⁴ Akademie d. Wissenschaften d. DDR. Archiv: NL Ed. Meyer 274.—Neben dieser Funktion übte er in der Notgemeinschaft seit dem Anfang die Aufgabe des "Vertrauensmannes" der Berliner Universität in der Notgemeinschaft aus. Solche Vertrauensmänner wurden an den wissenschaftlichen Hochschulen, Akademien und bei der Kaiser-Wilhelm-Gesellschaft bestimmt und sollten die Verbindung der jeweiligen Institution zur Notgemeinschaft erleichtern (vgl. Zierold, 63–66).

⁵ Benannt wurden neben Meyer, der für die Alte Geschichte zuständig war, der

rologie und Sinologie eigene Gutachter berufen wurden.[6]

Die Nominierung der Ausschußmitglieder[7] und die Wahl Meyers zum Vorsitzenden wurde von derjenigen Institution bestimmt, bei der Meyer in einer Vielzahl von Kommissionen und Ausschüssen mitarbeitete;[8] in der Orientalischen Kommission führte er den Vorsitz.[9] Bei der Wahl Meyers spielte gewiß seine langjährige und vielfältige Tätigkeit in der Akademie eine Rolle, wo er sich durch seine Mitarbeit in den verschiedensten Bereichen als Ratgeber in fachlichen Fragen und in der Organisation bewährt hatte und einen starken Einfluß besaß.[10] Hinzukam sein wissenschaftlicher Rang, der zu seiner Nominierung beitrug, zumal er durch seine universalhistorische Betrachtung des Altertums und seine Vertrautheit mit klassischer Antike und Altem Orient eine Gelehrtenpersönlichkeit war, die wegen ihres umfassenden Wissens die zu erwartenden Anträge der verschiedenen im Fachausschuß zusammengeschlossenen Disziplinen sachkundig und kritisch zu beurteilen und im Ausschuß integrierend zu wirken vermochte. Sehr wertvoll für die Arbeit gerade in diesem Ausschuß war vor allem Meyers intime Kenntnis nicht nur der klassischen, sondern auch der orientalischen Sprachen und Literaturen sowie der von der Archäologie gebotenen materiellen Hinterlassenschaft des Altertums. Andererseits mag vielleicht Meyers Berufung in einen vorwiegend philologisch orientierten Ausschuß überraschen: Der Historiker Meyer, der in seiner wissenschaftstheoretischen Konzeption die Alte Geschichte mehr im Rahmen der Gesamtheit menschlichen Geschehens und nicht beschränkt unter altertumswissenschaftlichem Aspekt in Verbindung mit Philologie und Archäologie betrachtet wissen wollte,[11] hätte

---

Gräzist Franz Boll (Heidelberg), der Latinist Georg Wissowa (Halle), der Archäologe Paul Wolters (München), der Semitist Enno Littmann (Bonn), der Ägyptologe Hermann Ranke (Heidelberg) und der Indologe Heinrich Lüders (Berlin). Für Wissowa trat später Richard Heinze ein, dem 1929 Johannes Stroux folgte; nach Bolls Tod 1924 nahm Werner Jaeger dessen Platz ein.

[6] Für Assyrologie trat 1928/29 Bruno Meißner, für ostasiatische Kultur der Sinologe Otto Franke hinzu.

[7] Die Preußische Akademie der Wissenschaften bestätigte Meyer seine Nominierung in einem Brief vom 18. Januar 1921 (Akademie d. Wissenschaften d. DDR. Archiv: NL Ed. Meyer 277).

[8] Der Berliner Akademie gehörte Meyer seit 1903/04 an (vgl. Die Altertumswissenschaften an der Berliner Akademie. Wahlvorschläge zur Aufnahme von Mitgliedern von F.A. Wolf bis G. Rodenwaldt. 1799–1932. Hg. von Chr. Kirsten. Berlin 1985, 125; seine Antrittsrede in der Akademie hielt Meyer am 30. Juni 1904 (SB Berlin, Phil.-hist. Kl. 1904, 1012–1015).

[9] Seit 1913, vgl. dazu seine Jahresberichte in den SB Berlin, Phil.-hist. Kl. 1913–1930.

[10] Meyers wissenschaftsorganisatorische Tätigkeit in der Berliner Akademie könnte das Thema eines gesonderten Beitrages sein.

[11] Dazu K. Christ, Von Gibbon bis Rostovtzeff. Darmstadt 1972, 298.

mit nicht geringerer Berechtigung in den Fachausschuß Geschichte
berufen werden können, dem die Alte Geschichte, im wesentlichen
begrenzt auf die politische Geschichte Griechenlands und Roms,
zugeordnet worden war.[12] Im Fachausschuß für alte und orientalische
Philologie verstand Meyer Alte Geschichte als "Antike Kultur;" ab
1928/29 fand das in den Jahresberichten der Notgemeinschaft durch diese
Bezeichnung des Ressorts seinen Niederschlag.

Meyer entzog sich trotz seines Alters nicht der an ihn ergangenen
Aufforderung. Die Motive für seine Bereitschaft zur Mitarbeit sind
hauptsächlich in seiner patriotisch geprägten Gesinnung und seinen Vorstellungen von Kultur- und Wissenschaftspolitik in der schwierigen Situation Deutschlands nach dem verlorenen Kriege zu suchen. Von seiner
politisch-publizistischen Tätigkeit oder—wie er es in seiner autobiographischen Skizze selbst ausdrückte—"vom öffentlichen Leben"[13] hatte er
sich resignierend zurückgezogen, um so stärker galt sein Interesse den
nach seiner Aussage noch unversehrten Werten von Kultur und Wissenschaft, dem geistigen Leben, dessen Erhaltung und Förderung er sich
nunmehr neben der fachwissenschaftlichen Arbeit zum wichtigsten Ziel
machte. Hier ging es darum, dem Boykott deutscher Wissenschaft durch
das feindliche Ausland sowie der durch die fortschreitende Geldentwer-
tung bestehenden materiellen Not entgegenzuwirken[14] und sich beim
Aufbau wirksamer finanzieller Hilfe für die bedrängte Wissenschaft von
der organisatorischen Seite her zu beteiligen.

Meyers Vorstellungen über die Struktur und Organisation der Wissenschaft in der Verwaltung, in die solche Hilfsmaßnahmen einzubinden
waren, wurden dabei trotz seines Verständnisses für soziale Fragen und
seiner Aufgeschlossenheit für die Einführung von Neuerungen[15] dennoch im Einklang mit seiner monarchistischen Grundeinstellung[16] stark
von den Gegebenheiten der Vorkriegszeit bestimmt, wo die Wissenschaftspflege überwiegend einer mit obrigkeitlichen Befugnissen ausge-

---

[12] Fachvertreter in diesem Ausschuß war Konrad Cichorius, später Matthias Gelzer.

[13] Marohl, 12.—Meyers politisches Engagement entsprang einer nationalen Grundhaltung, die von Lauterkeit und hohem Idealismus geprägt war. Dieses in der damaligen
Zeit in Deutschland verbreitete Empfinden wird heutzutage vielfach völlig unhistorisch
unter Voraussetzung der später durch den Nationalsozialismus entstandenen Hypothek
sehr subjektiv und tendenziös betrachtet und abgewertet.

[14] Vgl. u.a. E. Meyer, Preußen und Athen. Rede gehalten bei der Übernahme des
Rektorats der Universität Berlin am 15. Oktober 1919; ders., Rede zum Stiftungstag der
Berliner Universität am 3. August 1920. Berlin 1920; ders., Korreferat zur Hochschulreform. In: Mitteilungen des Verbandes Deutscher Hochschulen. Sonderheft Juli 1920,
48–57.

[15] Unter Meyers Rektorat wurde beispielsweise an der Berliner Universität eine offizielle Studentenvertretung geschaffen und die Mensa eingerichtet.

[16] Dazu Christ, Von Gibbon bis Rostovtzeff, 307–308.

statteten Verwaltung oblag. Gesellschaftliche Gruppen, wie Parteien oder Interessenverbände, hatten wenig Einfluß, ebenso die Parlamente.[17] Der monarchistische Staat hatte im allgemeinen ausreichende Etatmittel zur Verfügung gestellt und dennoch der Wissenschaft und ihren Institutionen beträchtliche Freiheit gewährt, die vor allem in einer Verwaltung bestand, in die von übergeordneter Stelle verhältnismäßig wenig hineinregiert wurde. Hinzukam, daß die Wissenschaftler meistens aus dem wohlhabenden Bürgertum stammten; sie steuerten neben persönlicher Initiative viel Opferbereitschaft bei, auch in materieller Hinsicht, Faktoren, die für die Erfolge deutscher Forschung, gerade in den Geisteswissenschaften, nicht unerheblich waren. So konnten Wissenschaft und Wissenschaftler von einer recht gesicherten Warte aus ihren Aufgaben nachgehen und nahmen in der Skala des gesellschaftlichen Ansehens einen hohen Rang ein, der auf Leistung begründet war.

Mit dem Ende des Wohlstandes dieser gesellschaftlichen Mittelschicht war auch der wissenschaftlichen Arbeit ein wesentliches Fundament genommen. Eine weitere Folge der einsetzenden sozialen Veränderungen war die Beseitigung von Privilegien dieser gesellschaftlichen Gruppe und die Öffnung der wissenschaftlichen Berufe für alle Bevölkerungsschichten. Diese nun im neuen demokratischen Staat einsetzenden Umstrukturierungen, bei denen die Wissenschaft und besonders die Hochschulen einer starken Politisierung unterworfen wurden und Parteien und Interessengruppen ein nicht unerhebliches Mitspracherecht erhielten, stießen bei Meyer wie bei vielen seiner Generation auf entschiedene Ablehnung.[18] Meyer sah darin eine Gefährdung der Freiheit von Lehre und Forschung und damit eine zusätzliche Gefahr für die Weltgeltung der deutschen Wissenschaft, die schon durch den Boykott seitens des Auslandes und die Inflation zur Genüge in Not war.

Den Schwierigkeiten war nach Meyers Vorstellungen auf zweierlei Weise zu begegnen. Ideell sollten bewährte Traditionen, soweit wie möglich, erhalten und fortgeführt werden, gerade was die Organisation und Verwaltung der Wissenschaft und die Struktur der Hochschulen und Forschungseinrichtungen betraf, die auf dem Prinzip staatlichen Schutzes und zugleich einer Unabhängigkeit in Lehre und Forschung begründet war, einer Freiheit, die den einzelnen zu selbständiger Arbeit und wissen-

---

[17] Hierzu und zum Folgenden Nipperdey-Schmugge, 9–12. Zur politischen und gesellschaftlichen Orientierung der deutschen Gelehrten auch: F.K. Ring, The decline of the German mandarins. The German academic community. 1890–1933. Cambridge, Mass. 1969; dt. Ausg.: Die Gelehrten. Stuttgart 1983.

[18] Vgl. u.a. die Rede zum Stiftungstag der Berliner Universität 1920, 30–33; ders., Die Privatdozenten und die Zukunft der deutschen Universitäten. In: Preuß. Jahrbücher 175. 1919, 37; ders., Korreferat zur Hochschulreform, 30.

schaftlichem Engagement anregte.[19] Materiell sollten Forschungspro-
jekte unterstützt und der Not der Studenten, von denen viele—gerade
auch Kriegsteilnehmer—in einer finanziell sehr prekären Lage waren,
entgegengewirkt werden.[20] Institutioncll suchte Meyer seinen Beitrag
hauptsächlich auf zwei Wegen zu leisten, durch seinen Einsatz bei der von
ihm organisierten "Studentenhilfe"[21] und durch die Aufgaben, die er im
Rahmen der Notgemeinschaft der Deutschen Wissenschaft übernahm.

Von der Notgemeinschaft erhoffte Meyer gewiß vor allem deshalb eine
gute Möglichkeit effektiver Wissenschaftsförderung, weil sich dort führende Repräsentanten aller Wissenschaftsgebiete zusammengefunden
hatten. Auch die Person ihres Präsidenten Schmidt-Ott ließ eine mit
Sachkenntnis nach bewährtem Muster bisheriger Wissenschaftspflege
vorgenommene Arbeitsweise erwarten. Schmidt-Ott, wie Meyer Anhänger der Monarchie[22] und der von ihr vorgegebenen Form staatlicher
Administration, wirkte als enger Mitarbeiter Friedrich Althoffs jahrzehntelang in der Kultur- und Wissenschaftsverwaltung und bekleidete als
Höhepunkt seiner beruflichen Laufbahn in den letzten Jahren des Kaiser-
reiches das Amt des preußischen Kultusministers.

Die Fachausschüsse nahmen sofort nach ihrer Konstituierung die Arbeit auf, um die dringendsten Bedürfnisse der Wissenschaften zu erfüllen.
In den Geisteswissenschaften waren das die Fortführung wichtiger Zeitschriften, die Aufrechterhaltung langfristiger Großunternehmungen
sowie die Veröffentlichung bedeutender Forschungsarbeiten. Ferner
sollten die durch den Krieg und seine Folgen verursachten Lücken im
Bestand ausländischer Zeitschriften in den Bibliotheken geschlossen wer-

---

[19] Dazu E. Meyer, Über das Gymnasium. In: Das Gymnasium und die neue Zeit.
Leipzig 1919, 114; ders., Preußen und Athen, 28; ders., Die Privatdozenten, 28–29.—
Unter diesem Aspekt hat Meyer auch die Aufgabe des Gymnasiums gesehen, das für ihn
Ausbildungsstätte einer Elite war und in seiner bewährten Form mit den alten klassischen
Lehrplänen erhalten werden mußte.
[20] Soziales Engagement war für Meyer ein Merkmal konservativer Politik, vgl. E.
Meyer, Deutschlands Lage in der Gegenwart und unsere Aufgaben für die Zukunft.
Berlin-Lichterfelde 1919, 15.
[21] Zur Studentenhilfe: E. Meyer, Die soziale Not der deutschen Studentenschaft. In:
Berliner Hochschulnachrichten 2. 1920, 141–142; ders., Studentenhilfe. In: Der Tag. Jg
20. Ausg. A. Nr. 501/241 vom 31.10.1920; ders., in: Berliner Lokalanzeiger Jg 38,
Nr. 501 vom 31.10.1920; ders., Studentenhilfe. In: Berliner Hochschulnachrichten
5.1921,41; vgl. auch L. Canfora, Wilamowitz e Meyer tra la sconfitta e la "Repubblica
di Novembre." In: Quaderni di storia 3. 1976, 80–81.
[22] Die Verbundenheit zwischen Meyer und Schmidt-Ott in politischer Hinsicht zeigte
sich auch in dem fortbestehenden Kontakt beider zum Kaiser und im Austausch von
Nachrichten aus Doorn.—Zu Schmidt-Ott: W. Treue, Friedrich Schmidt-Ott. In: Berlinische Lebensbilder. Wissenschaftspolitik in Berlin. Hg. von W. Treue u. K. Gründer.
Berlin 1987, 235–250.

den. Neben diesen an höchster Priorität stehenden Aufgaben waren als
weitere Hilfsmaßnahmen Forschungs- und Reisestipendien vorgesehen.
Die Fachausschüsse hatten für jeden einzelnen Antrag das entscheidende
Gutachten vom fachwissenschaftlichen Standpunkt abzugeben[23] und
somit das "Schwergewicht der Arbeit" zu leisten. Die Aufgaben waren
vielseitig, aufwendig und entsagungsvoll.[24] Schmidt-Ott hat das noch im
Rückblick gerade bezüglich der Mitarbeit bedeutender Fachvertreter der
Geisteswissenschaften gewürdigt:[25] "Sicher war es etwas Großes, daß
Meister der Geisteswissenschaften wie Adolf v. Harnack, Eduard Meyer,
Paul Kehr, Seeberg oder auf archäologischem Gebiet Theodor Wiegand
sich uneingeschränkt in den Dienst der Arbeit gestellt haben."

Es war großenteils Klein- und Detailarbeit zu leisten; ihre gewissenhafte Erledigung war jedoch für das Gelingen dieser Wissenschaftsförderung von entscheidender Bedeutung; aus dieser Tätigkeit Meyers seien
im Folgenden einige ausgewählte Beispiele aufgeführt.

Im Aufgabenkatalog der Fachausschüsse nahm das Problem der wissenschaftlichen Zeitschriften einen besonders wichtigen Platz ein.
Schmidt-Ott richtete in dieser Angelegenheit bereits vor der offiziellen
Berufung der Fachausschußvorsitzenden an diese am 16. und 26. Februar
1921 zwei Schreiben. Im ersten Brief bat er für einen vorgesehenen
Tausch deutscher gegen ausländische Zeitschriften, vor allem mit Ländern hoher Valuta, um ein "Verzeichnis der wichtigen vorhandenen
Zeitschriften und zwar in der Reihenfolge ihrer Bedeutung" unter An-
gabe der Bezugspreise. Im zweiten Brief ging es um die Erhaltung und
Unterstützung deutscher Zeitschriften. Dafür sollten kurzfristig "die
unentbehrlichen wissenschaftlichen Zeitschriften der einzelnen Fachgebiete" ebenfalls in Abstufung ihrer Wichtigkeit zusammengestellt werden.

Bereits am 28. Februar übersandte Meyer den Entwurf einer von ihm
erstellten Zeitschriftenliste an die Mitglieder des Fachausschusses mit der
Bitte um Berichtigung und Ergänzung. Diese nach Prioritäten geordnete
Liste enthielt im wesentlichen die in der endgültigen Aufstellung für eine
Förderung vorgesehenen Zeitschriften, die er nochmals in einem Bericht

---

[23] Neben dem fachlichen Gutachten waren bei den Anträgen außerdem der Verlags-
ausschuß, wenn es um Druckkostenzuschüsse ging, oder der Bibliotheksausschuß, wenn
Fragen der Literaturversorgung zu entscheiden waren, einzuschalten.—Als Arbeits-
grundlage für die Fachausschüsse galt die "Anweisung für die Fachausschüsse der Notgemeinschaft" (In: Mitteilungen des Verbandes der Deutschen Hochschulen 2. 1922,
156–160).
[24] F. Schmidt-Ott, Aus vergangenen Tagen deutscher Wissenschaftspflege. Ansprache beim Wochenendfrühstück der Förderer der Deutschen Akademie im Kaiserhof
in Berlin am 4. April 1933. Berlin 1935, 13.
[25] Ebd., 14.

an die Mitglieder seines Fachausschusses vom 25. Oktober 1921[26] er-
läuterte.

Danach sollten in der Orientalistik die Publikationsorgane der Deutschen Morgenländischen Gesellschaft unterstützt werden. Voraussetzung
war allerdings eine Neuorganisation der Gesellschaft und ihres Veröffent-
lichungswesens; beides sollte auf der im gleichen Jahr in Leipzig statt-
findenden Mitgliederversammlung beschlossen werden.[27] Meyer hat
hier sowohl als Mitglied der Gesellschaft als auch als Vertreter der Notgemeinschaft mitgewirkt. Im Zuge der Rationalisierungsmaßnahmen
sollte die Gesellschaft die Aufgabe der Gesamtvertretung der deutschen
Orientalistik übernehmen[28] und das Zentrum und die Koordinierungs-
stelle für die Herausgabe der wissenschaftlichen Zeitschriften in der Orientalistik sein, um Überschneidungen von Fachgebieten bei den verschiedenen Publikationsorganen auszuschließen. Die Gesellschaft gab
nach der Neugliederung folgende von der Notgemeinschaft unterstützte
Veröffentlichungen heraus: Die "Zeitschrift der Deutschen Morgenländischen Gesellschaft," die "Abhandlungen für die Kunde des Morgen-
landes," die "Zeitschrift für Indologie und Iranistik," und die "Zeitschrift für Semitistik und verwandte Gebiete."[29] Zur Konzentrierung
der Forschung und ebenfalls zur Vermeidung von Überschneidungen
wurden "Konzerne" mit anderen benachbarten Publikationsorganen
gebildet, mit dem "Islam", der "Orientalistischen Literaturzeitung,"
der "Ostasiatischen Zeitung," der "Zeitschrift für ägyptische Sprache
und Altertumskunde" und der "Zeitschrift für Assyrologie und verwandte Gebiete."[30]

Durch diese Maßnahmen wurde ein Rahmen geschaffen, der sich auf
die allernotwendigsten Hilfsmittel für den Fortgang der Forschung beschränkte[31] und keine weiteren Reduzierungen zuließ. Meyer wies
darauf ein Jahr später in einem Brief vom 10. September 1922[32] an

---

[26] Akademie d. Wissenschaften d. DDR. Archiv: NL Ed. Meyer 274.

[27] Vgl. den "Protokollarischen Bericht" in: Zeitschrift d. Deutschen Morgenländischen Gesellschaft 76. 1922, S. III. Meyer berichtete dort über die Arbeit seines
Fachausschusses und die Hilfsmaßnahmen.

[28] Die Ausgrabungstätigkeit nahm jedoch weiterhin die Deutsche Orient-Gesellschaft
wahr; auch sie erhielt Zuschüsse; wir kommen darauf zurück.

[29] Die beiden letztgenannten Organe mußten offensichtlich unter politischem Druck
1935 ihr Erscheinen einstellen.

[30] Hinzukommen sollte die "Orientalistische Bibliographie;" sie erschien aber für die
Literatur des Jahres 1911 verspätet 1917–22 und danach in einem Band 1926; damit
wurde ihr Erscheinen eingestellt.

[31] Vgl. Fünfter Bericht d. Notgemeinschaft d. Deutschen Wissenschaft 1925/26, 145
= Deutsche Forschung. Aus d. Arbeit d. Notgemeinschaft d. Deutschen Wissenschaft
1. 1928, 26–26.

[32] Akademie d. Wissenschaften d. DDR. Archiv: NL Ed. Meyer 277.

Schmidt-Ott hin, womit er zwei Schreiben der Notgemeinschaft vom 1. und 4. September[33] beantwortete, in denen der Präsident wegen der fortschreitenden Inflation noch strengere Auswahlkriterien aufstellte.

Auch die Auswahl der Zeitschriften in der Klassischen Philologie war auf das Notwendigste eingeschränkt. Meyer gab hierzu ebenfalls Erläuterungen: Die Förderung von "Hermes" und "Rheinischem Museum" war selbstverständlich. Der "Philologus" wurde wegen seiner parallelen Zielsetzung zunächst zurückgestellt, danach aber, als das "Rheinische Museum" durch Krankheit und Tod des Herausgebers August Brinkmann auf Zeit sein Erscheinen eingestellt hatte, für dieses in die Förderung einbezogen, und zwar auf ausdrückliche Empfehlung Meyers hin.

Bedenken hatte Meyer bei der Unterstützung der "Neuen Jahrbücher für das Klassische Altertum, Geschichte und Literatur und für Pädagogik," da ihre Abonnentenzahl schrumpfte und es fraglich war, ob der Verlag Teubner sie weiter erscheinen lassen würde. Meyer war der Ansicht, daß die Zeitschrift "in zweiter Linie eigentlich wissenschaftlichen Zwecken" diente, sondern auf das "wissenschaftliche Leben der höheren Schule" zugeschnitten war und daher auch in die Zuständigkeit des Fachausschusses Pädagogik fiel. In der verschärften Situation von 1922 war er hier am ehesten zu einer Streichung bereit, ohne daß er es ausdrücklich aussprach. In dieser Frage stand Meyer im Gegensatz zu seinem Fachausschußkollegen Franz Boll, der Meyers Standpunkt in einem langen Brief kritisierte.[34] Boll argumentierte unter anderem damit, daß die Zeitschrift" seit einer langen Reihe von Jahren eine Fülle von wichtigen Beiträgen aus dem Gebiete der klassischen Philologie" enthalte, "für die sich gerade, weil sie nicht bloss einzelne Fragen behandeln, anderweitig gar kein geeignetes Unterkommen denken" ließe. Außerdem war für Boll die Bedeutung der Neuen Jahrbücher für die höhere Schule gerade ein Argument, sie zu fördern.

Am Ende waren offenbar die Argumente für eine Förderung stärker; die Zeitschrift erhielt ihren jährlichen Zuschuß.

Für unbedingt erforderlich hielt Meyer die Erhaltung der Spezialzeitschriften, "die in den umfassenden Zeitschriften nur ungenügend oder auch gar nicht berücksichtigt werden" könnten. Die Unterstützung des "Archivs für Papyrusforschung" und der "Byzantinischen Zeitschrift" stand für ihn diskussionslos fest. Beim "Archiv für Religionswissenschaft" machte er geltend, daß es sich um das Organ einer "werdenden Wissenschaft" handele, "in der es gärt und der vor allem jüngere Talente

---

[33] Ebd.
[34] Akademie d. Wissenschaften d. DDR. Archiv: NL Ed. Meyer 277, Brief vom 31. Oktober 1922.

sich zuwenden.'' Auch wenn ''Unzureichendes und Unhaltbares'' dort erscheine, müsse diese zentrale Zeitschrift erhalten bleiben, schon wegen der ''orientierenden Übersichten und Bibliographien.'' Um Einsparungen zu erreichen, schlug Meyer vor, das ''Archiv für Religionswissenschaft,'' wie es schon immer beim ''Archiv für Papyrusforschung'' der Fall war, in zwangloser Folge erscheinen zu lassen.[35]

Von offenbar besonderem Interesse war für Meyer die Erhaltung der ''Deutschen Literaturzeitung'' (DLZ), die er als ''allgemein wissenschaftliches Referateorgan'' für wichtig hielt. Voraussetzung dafür war jedoch eine Neuorganisation in der Redaktion, da nach dem Urteil vieler Fachgelehrter das Niveau der Zeitschrift sehr gesunken war. In einem Brief an Schmidt-Ott vom 5. Mai 1922[36] ergriff er die Initiative und sprach sich für die Gründung eines Kontrollgremiums aus, das aus Gelehrten verschiedener Wissenschaftsgebiete bestehen und beratend neben den bisherigen Schriftleiter Paul Hinneberg treten sollte; mit einigen Männern, die seiner Ansicht nach dafür in Frage kamen, war er bereits in Kontakt getreten.[37]

Die Angelegenheit wurde auf der Sitzung von Präsidium und Hauptausschuß am 30. Juni 1922 behandelt.[38] In der Diskussion widersetzten sich Eduard Schwartz, Mitglied des Hauptausschusses, und Josef Partsch, der Vorsitzende des Verlagsausschusses, Meyers Vorschlag. Sie warfen als Argumente den ''gesunkenen Wert'' der Zeitschrift und die Schwierigkeit der Kontrolle durch ein Gremium in die Debatte; außerdem sei die DLZ ein vorwiegend ''Berliner Organ.'' Wie aus dem ''Zweiten Bericht der Notgemeinschaft'' hervorgeht, setzte sich Meyer mit seinen Vorstellungen durch.[39] Die Redaktion der DLZ wurde reorganisiert und die

---

[35] Im weiteren seiner Ausführungen äußerte sich Meyer zu den Zeitschriften der Archäologie, Sprachwissenschaft und Alten Geschichte, die nicht eigentlich in die Zuständigkeit seines Ausschusses fielen. Er unterstrich die Unentbehrlichkeit dieser Publikationsorgane. Die ''Glotta'' wurde in den Kreis der über seinen Ausschuß geförderten Zeitschriften aufgenommen. In der Alten Geschichte hielt er Einschränkungen bei der ''Klio'' am ehesten für möglich wegen der Überschneidungen mit Hermes und Rheinischem Museum. Die Zeitschrift sollte in zwangloser Folge erscheinen.

[36] Zentralarchiv d. DDR, Merseburg: Rep. 92 Schmidt-Ott D 1, Bl. 32.

[37] Es waren der Indologe Heinrich Lüders, der Germanist Gustav Roethe, der Sprachwissenschaftler Wilhelm Schulze, der Geograph Albrecht Penck und Max Planck (vgl. auch Schlicker-Stern, 281).

[38] Akademie d. Wissenschaft d. DDR. Archiv: NL Ed. Meyer 275, Protokoll der Sitzung, Bl. 5.

[39] Weniger Erfolg hatte Meyer mit seinem Plan, im ''Sokrates'', der zum Kreis der von ihm zur Förderung vorgeschlagenen Zeitschriften gehörte, jährliche Übersichten über die Fortschritte in einzelnen Teilgebieten der klassischen Altertumswissenschaft zu geben. Wissowa, Latinist im Fachausschuß, hatte von Anfang an Bedenken gegen das Vorhaben. Bis 1923/24 erschienen einige Berichte; dann jedoch stellte der ''Sokrates'' sein Erscheinen ein.

Zeitschrift ab 1924 in einer neuen Folge vom "Verbande der deutschen Akademien der Wissenschaften Deutschlands und Österreichs" herausgegeben. Hinneberg blieb Schriftleiter, ihm stand jedoch ein "Redaktionsausschuß" namhafter Gelehrter verschiedener Fachgebiete zur Seite.[40]

In der durch die fortschreitende Inflation verschärften Lage von 1922 schlug Meyer in dem erwähnten Schreiben vom 10. September 1922 statt einer nochmaligen strengeren Selektion unter den bislang geförderten Zeitschriften Sparmaßnahmen in den Redaktionen vor. Diese sollten nicht unbedingt den ihnen zugestandenen Umfang ausschöpfen. Sie sollten bei den Manuskripten, besonders bei den umfangreichen, drastisch kürzen. Schließlich sollten die Anforderungen für die Annahme von Beiträgen erhöht und möglicherweise generell auf ein jährliches Erscheinen der Zeitschriften verzichtet werden.

In der Liste seiner Fachzeitschriften hat Meyer keine weiteren Streichungen hinnehmen müssen, jedoch hat er auf Einsparungen bei den Redaktionen offensichtlich streng geachtet, beispielsweise erschienen die "Byzantinische Zeitschrift" und das "Archiv für Religionswissenschaft" 1923/24 in einem Zweijahresband. Auch später noch wandte sich Meyer gegen die überflüssige Neugründung von Zeitschriften.[41]

Gemäß dem Auftrag des Präsidiums der Notgemeinschaft hatte sich Meyer zusammen mit den Mitgliedern seines Fachausschusses sofort um die Probleme der wissenschaftlichen Zeitschriften intensiv bemüht und ist dafür während der ganzen Zeit seiner Tätigkeit mit besonderer Entschiedenheit eingetreten. Noch im Rückblick unterstrich er die Wichtigkeit des Zeitschriftenproblems; es heißt im Protokoll der Hauptausschußsitzung vom 20. April 1929:[42] "Geheimrat Meyer findet die großartigste Leistung der Notgemeinschaft darin, daß sie in den Jahren nach der Inflation die Zeitschriften über Wasser gehalten habe. Auf weitere Betätigung zugunsten der Zeitschriften könne in keinem Falle verzichtet werden." Bestätigt wird das im Protokoll der Hauptausschußsitzung vom 12. April 1930. Danach setzte sich Meyer für eine Erhöhung des Bogenzuschusses der Zeitschriften ein, da die frühere Finanzierung durch Staatsmittel de facto durch die Notgemeinschaft ersetzt worden sei und die Zeitschriften ohne Hilfe nicht existieren könnten. Dieser Forderung schloß sich der

---

[40] Den Vorsitz hatte Julius Petersen, neben Meyer gehörten dem Gremium u.a. an: Adolf v. Harnack, Paul Kehr, Heinrich Lüders, Walter Nernst, Albrecht Penck und Ulrich v. Wilamowitz-Moellendorff (vgl. auch Wissenschaft in Berlin. Leitung: H. Laitko. Berlin 1987, 480).

[41] Akademie d. Wissenschaften d. DDR. Archiv: NL Ed. Meyer 275, Protokoll d. Hauptausschußsitzung vom 23.3.1927.

[42] Akademie d. Wissenschaften d. DDR. Archiv: NL Ed. Meyer 275, Protokoll, Bl. 16.

Geschäftsführer des Verlagsausschusses Karl Siegismund an. Trotzdem wurden 1930 im Zuge der Etatkürzungen auch die Druckbeihilfen für die Zeitschriften beträchtlich reduziert.[43]

Ebenso wie für die Zeitschriften hatte Meyer seine Zielsetzungen zur Unterstützung monographischer Veröffentlichungen formuliert.[44] Generell befürwortete er eine "Förderung aller bisher nicht oder ungenügend bearbeiteten Gebiete." Beispielsweise waren das grundlegende Textausgaben klassischer und orientalischer Autoren. Wenn sich hier ernstgemeinte Vorhaben zeigten, müßte nach Möglichkeiten einer Förderung gesucht werden; freilich müßte aber "eine strenge Prüfung und Einschränkung auf das wirklich Wesentliche und wissenschaftlich Fördernde in noch grösserem Masse stattfinden als bislang."

In der zugespitzten Situation im Herbst 1922 sah Meyer jedoch die Notwendigkeit der Eingrenzung der Hilfe auf Unternehmungen, "die bereits in Angriff genommen" waren und "die unbedingt fortgeführt werden" mußten. Er definierte diese Arbeiten im Sinne des Briefes der Notgemeinschaft vom 4. September 1922 als Vorhaben, die "neben den Zeitschriften in erster Linie in Betracht" kämen und "im Zweifelsfall auch sonst tüchtigen Einzelarbeiten voranzustellen" seien. Meyer gab zur Orientierung eine Auflistung solcher Werke, von denen ein großer Teil bei den Förderungsmaßnahmen dann auch berücksichtigt wurden.

Auf orientalistischem Gebiet nannte Meyer die Bearbeitung der hethitischen Texte von Boghazköi, die Turfantexte und die Veröffentlichung der Ausgrabungen der Deutschen Orient-Gesellschaft (D.O.G.) in Babylon, Assur und Ägypten (Tell el-Amarna). Die Grabungsberichte sollten sich auf das Notwendigste beschränken; in vielen Fällen sollte "bei den Veröffentlichungen ein im wesentlichen registrierendes Verfahren und eine Bekanntgabe des Wesentlichen" genügen, alles weitere im Manuskript für den Spezialforscher deponiert werden.

In der Ägyptologie hielt Meyer die Unterstützung des ägyptischen Wörterbuches von Adolf Erman und die Bearbeitung der Pyramidentexte durch Kurt Sethe für vordringlich, das letztgenannte Werk als "grundsätzliche Arbeit für die weitere Erforschung des Ägyptischen."[45]

Allgemein prognostizierte er weitere derartige Publikationen mit gleich hoher Priorität; auch "auf indischem, ostasiatischem, semitischem und islamischem Gebiet" sah er solche Projekte voraus, die schon wegen der Weltgeltung der deutschen Orientalistik aufgegriffen werden müßten.

---

[43] Zierold, 84–85.

[44] Brief vom 10. September 1922, s.o. Anm. 32.

[45] Der Band 3/4. 1922 erschien jedoch ohne Unterstützung der Notgemeinschaft, sondern mit amerikanischer Hilfe (vgl. Vorwort).

In der Klassischen Philologie hatte für Meyer die Fortführung der von der Preußischen Akademie der Wissenschaften herausgegebenen Inschriftencorpora eine besonders hohe Priorität. Er konnte schon mit Genugtuung vermerken, daß für die "grundlegende Neubearbeitung des ersten Bandes der ältern attischen Inschriften" eine Förderungszusage vorlag,[46] für das "Corpus Inscriptionum Latinarum" (CIL) stände sie in bescheidenerem Umfang bevor.[47] Nicht anders sprach er sich für die Unterstützung des von der Berliner Akademie in Verbindung mit der Dänischen Akademie der Wissenschaften herausgegebenen "Corpus medicorum Graecorum"[48] aus, dessen Leiter, Hermann Diels gerade verstorben war. An weiteren umfänglichen Unternehmungen führte er die Bearbeitung der Papyri an.[49]

Schließlich hob er paradigmatisch zwei Großvorhaben von Einzelgelehrten heraus, Wilhelm Crönerts Neubearbeitung von Passows griechischem Wörterbuch,[50] die "in ganz vortrefflicher, geradezu mustergültiger Weise" begonnen worden sei, sowie Felix Jacobys Sammlung der griechischen Historikerfragmente, die "eines der am peinlichsten empfundenen Bedürfnisse der Altertumsforschung" erfüllte.[51]

Ein instruktives Beispiel für Meyers Bemühungen bei der Hilfe für große wissenschaftliche Gemeinschaftsunternehmungen, die in Existenznot geraten waren, bietet der "Thesaurus linguae Latinae," der ein gemeinsames Projekt der deutschen Akademien der Wissenschaften war und hauptsächlich von Bayern und Preußen finanziert wurde. Die von den finanziellen Trägern in den Nachkriegsjahren bereitgestellten Mittel waren infolge der Inflation viel zu gering und reichten für die Drucklegung fertiggestellter Faszikel und die Deckung der Personal- und Sachkosten nicht aus.[52]

---

[46] Gefördert wurde IG. Ed. minor. Vol. I. Berolini 1924, vgl. W. Unte, Wilamowitz als wissenschaftlicher Organisator. In: Wilamowitz nach 50 Jahren. Darmstadt 1985, 753.

[47] Die in dieser Zeit herausgekommenen Bände des CIL 6,6,1 und 11,1,2 wurden jedoch ohne Hilfe der Notgemeinschaft veröffentlicht.

[48] Das Projekt erhielt 1926/27 und 1927/28 Druckkostenzuschüsse.

[49] Gefördert wurden u.a. in den ersten Jahren: Ägyptische Urkunden aus den Staatl. Museen Berlin; die von der Heidelberger Akademie betreute Veröffentlichung der badischen Papyrussammlungen; F. Preisigke, Sammelbuch griechischer Urkunden aus Ägypten; U. Wilcken, Urkunden der Ptolemäerzeit; P. Viereck, Staßburger Ostraka.

[50] Lfg 1–3. Göttingen 1912; die Neuarbeitung wurde nicht fortgesetzt; das Wörterbuch ist auch in der Liste der Förderungen in den Jahresberichten nicht aufgeführt.

[51] Neben den griechischen Historikerfragmenten wurden letztlich in den ersten Jahren u.a. folgende Vorhaben unterstützt: O. Kerns Orphikerfragmente; W. Camphausen, Romani Sophistae; Ed. Fraenkel, Plautinisches im Plautus; G. Goetz, Corpus Glossariorum Latinorum; Chr. Jensen, Philodemos, Über die Dichtungen; F. Vollmer, Poetae Latinae minores; E. Diehl, Inscriptiones Latinae Christianae veteres.

[52] Nach Meyers Bericht vom 25. Oktober 1921 wurden 50000 M bewilligt.

In einem mit dem 11. April 1923 datierten Bericht, der im Entwurf erhalten ist,[53] hat Meyer die wirtschaftliche Lage des Thesaurusunternehmens detailliert dargestellt,[54] um auf eine dringend erforderliche erweiterte Unterstützung durch die verantwortlichen Länderregierungen und durch die Notgemeinschaft aufmerksamzumachen. Nach Meyers Darstellung war ein wirkliches Vorankommen des Unternehmens nur erreichbar, wenn die Personalstärke der Vorkriegszeit wiederhergestellt würde. An den Hinweis auf die schleppende Fertigstellung des sechsten Bandes, an dem bereits zehn Jahre gearbeitet würde, schloß er die Befürchtung an, daß das Ende der noch veranschlagten weiteren sechs Bände nicht abzusehen sei. Er wandte sich strikt gegen die Forderung, durch ''eine Änderung der bisher befolgten Anlage'' des Werkes Einsparungen zu erzielen, da eine ''Zusammendrängung des Materials mit der erforderlichen peinlichen Sichtung'' weit mehr Arbeit und Zeit erfordern würde ''als eine breite Behandlung, wenn das Werk nicht flüchtig gearbeitet werden'' sollte und somit seinen Zweck verfehlte.

Meyer trat für eine Weiterführung des Thesaurus nach den bisherigen Grundsätzen und für eine Vermehrung des Personals ein. Neben einer weiteren Redaktorstelle waren nach seiner Ansicht fünf Mitarbeiterstellen zu schaffen. Die Kosten dafür wie auch für die erforderlichen Sachausgaben und die Druckkostenzuschüsse veranschlagte er auf 30–35 Millionen Mark (oder nach dem damaligen Valutastand auf 1500–1700 Dollar). Er fügte hinzu, daß diese Etatforderungen nur einen Bruchteil des Vorkriegsetats ausmachten; die damaligen 55000 Mark ergäben auf die Verhältnisse der Inflationszeit umgerechnet 275 Millionen Mark.

Meyers Stellungnahme, die unter Berücksichtigung der wissenschaftlichen Konzeption des Thesaurus und seiner Brauchbarkeit als Instrument für die Forschung praxis- und realitätsbezogen die für die Weiterführung des Unternehmens entscheidenden wirtschaftlichen und organisatorischen Probleme ansprach und Lösungen aufzeigte, läßt eine gründliche

---

[53] Akademie d. Wissenschaften d. DDR. Archiv: NL Ed. Meyer 274; dazu auch E. Norden, Bericht der Kommission für den Thesaurus linguae Latinae über die Zeit vom 1. April 1922 bis 31. März 1924. In: SB Berlin, Phil.-hist. Kl. 1924, 152–155.—Zur Geschichte des Thesaurus generell: G. Polara, Il ''Thesaurus linguae Latinae.'' In: Omaggio a B.G. Teubner. Napoli 1983, 77–111.

[54] Danach war die Zahl der Mitarbeiter von zwölf im Jahre 1913 auf sieben zurückgegangen; deren Finanzierung war zwar gedeckt, nicht jedoch die Fortführung des Projektes insgesamt. Meyer zeigte in Zahlen das Anschwellen der Ausgabe. Die Personalkosten betrugen im März 1922 monatlich 15 594 M, im Dezember 643 370 M, im März 1923 2 226 546 M. Die Kosten für Druck und Papier waren nach Meyers Bericht in der Zeit der Inflation überhaupt nicht abschätzbar. Die sachlichen Ausgaben für Miete, Heizung, Licht, die Bibliothek und Materialien veranschlagte er auf fünf Millionen Mark.

Beschäftigung mit dem Projekt erkennen. Die Einzelheiten und die genauen Zahlen zeigen eine enge Zusammenarbeit mit der Thesauruskommission. Vermutlich hat Meyer vor allem mit seinem Berliner Kollegen Eduard Norden, der kurze Zeit nach diesem Bericht am 1. Oktober 1923 interimistisch den Vorsitz in der Thesauruskommission übernahm,[55] jedoch auch schon vorher an der Leitung des Unternehmens beteiligt war, die Probleme des Thesaurus besprochen.

Meyers Forderungen wurden erwartungsgemäß nicht erfüllt. Die Existenz des Thesaurus wurde jedoch gesichert, da die Regierungen Bayerns und Preußens in den schwierigen Jahren 1922/23 die Personalkosten für die noch tätigen sieben Mitarbeiter übernahmen; außerdem flossen dem Projekt ansehnliche Mittel aus dem Ausland zu.[56] Die Notgemeinschaft war bei der Hilfsaktion in Form der Vermittlung einer Unterstützung durch die Milwaukee Emergency Society beteiligt.[57] Selbst trug sie sofort nach der Inflation 9000 Reichsmark und zwei Forschungsstipendien von 1200 Reichsmark zum Erhalt des Thesaurus bei.[58]

Aus den Beispielen über Meyers Fachausschußtätigkeit der ersten Jahre ergibt sich, daß er die beschränkten Mittel sinnvoll und wirkungsvoll für grundlegende Vorhaben und Hilfsmittel der Altertumswissenschaften eingesetzt hat;[59] bei den Wissenschaften drang er auf Selbstbeschränkung, Rationalisierung und Sparsamkeit. Andererseits befürwortete er dringend erforderliche Unterstützungen, wie die des

---

[55] E. Norden. Bericht 1922–24, 152.

[56] Ebd., 153.

[57] Zur damaligen Auslandshilfe s. Dritter Bericht d. Notgemeinschaft 1923/24, 57–59.

[58] E. Norden, Bericht der Kommission für den Thesaurus linguae Latinae über die Zeit vom 1. April 1924 bis 31. März 1925. In: SB Berlin, Phil.-hist. Kl. 1925, 262–264.—Auch in den Jahren 1926–1930 unterstützte die Notgemeinschaft den Thesaurus durch Druckkostenzuschüsse und Forschungsstipendien.

[59] Das wird auch aus einigen in seinem Bericht vom 25. Oktober 1922 genannten Ablehnungen ersichtlich. So war Meyer gegen eine Finanzierung der Neuauflage von Otto Kellers Horazausgabe; er folgte hier der Empfehlung Nordens und anderer Klassischer Philologen. In der Begründung heißt es: "In der gegenwärtigen Notlage erscheint es unzulässig, für den Wiederabdruck des riesigen Wustes an Varianten größere Summen auszugeben und wichtigeren Aufgaben zu entziehen." Meyer schlug vor, das Manuskript in einer Bibliothek für den Spezialbenutzer zu deponieren. Mit derselben Begründung lehnte er die Unterstützung des "Riesenindex" von Ernst Lommatzsch zum CIL I ab; er hielt den Druck dieses Index sogar in normalen Zeiten für überflüssig; in Betracht käme nur ein Index der Eigennamen, aber nicht ein erschöpfendes grammatisches und lexikalisches Register. Jeder auf dem Gebiet Arbeitende müsse sich das Material aus dem Text selbst zusammensuchen. In ähnlicher Weise drang Meyer bei dem von Eberhard Richtsteig vorbereiteten Index zur Libaniosausgabe Richard Foersters auf äußerste Knappheit, grundsätzlich befürwortete er aber den Druck, auch als Karl Siegismund, der Geschäftsführer des Verlagsausschusses in der Sache nochmals vorstellig wurde.—Zu den Kriterien für die Ablehnung von Anträgen vgl. auch Zierold, 79–80.

"Thesaurus linguae Latinae," nicht nur in der Notgemeinschaft, sondern auch bei den zuständigen Unterhaltsträgern in vollem Umfang. Schon Meyers oben skizzierte erste Zusammenstellung förderungswürdiger Forschungsvorhaben verrät ein wohlüberlegtes Konzept, das, wenn auch im einzelnen modifiziert, die Grundlage für die Maßnahmen der ersten Jahre bildete.

Während die Notgemeinschaft in den Anfangsjahren nur die allerdringendsten wissenschaftlichen Unternehmungen durch Zuschüsse unterstützen konnte, gelang es nach dem Ende der Inflation, den Kreis wichtiger Vorhaben erheblich zu erweitern; das galt besonders für die Druckkostenzuschüsse,[60] doch auch für andere Unterstützungen, so für die der deutschen Ausgrabungen im Ausland und der Veröffentlichung ihrer Ergebnisse. Die archäologische Forschung war von der wirtschaftlichen Not und dem Boykott deutscher Wissenschaft durch das feindliche Ausland besonders betroffen.

Innerhalb der Notgemeinschaft oblag die Betreuung der archäologischen Forschungsvorhaben nicht allein Meyer und seinem Fachausschuß für alte und orientalische Philologie, wo Paul Wolters Ausschußmitglied für Archäologie war, sondern viele Angelegenheiten waren in enger Zusammenarbeit mit Theodor Wiegand zu lösen, der den Fachausschuß für Kunstwissenschaften leitete. Meyer und Wiegand, die weltanschaulich und politisch harmonierten,[61] haben auch bei den wissenschaftsorganisatorischen Aufgaben innerhalb der Notgemeinschaft eng zusammengearbeitet.

Trotz der widrigen Umstände, die die archäologische Forschung belasteten, konnte Meyer im Fünften Bericht der Notgemeinschaft 1925/26[62] eine Reihe erfolgreich fortgesetzter Ausgrabungen aufzählen, zu deren Gelingen die Notgemeinschaft finanziell beigetragen hatte. Es waren die Unternehmungen in Didyma, Milet, Kos, Tiryns, bei den Pyramiden von Gizeh, in Sichem (Palästina), im Gebiet nördlich von Hebron und in Ephesos.

Mit Genugtuung äußerte er sich drei Jahre später auf der Mitgliederversammlung der Notgemeinschaft vom 1. Dezember 1928[63] zu der seither weiterhin positiv verlaufenen Entwicklung der Auslandsbeziehungen, die gerade auch die Ausgrabungstätigkeit betrafen. Er erinnerte an die

---

60 Vgl. dazu die Aufstellungen geförderter Werke im Fünften, Sechsten und Siebenten Bericht der Notgemeinschaft für die Jahre 1925–1928.

61 C. Watzinger, Theodor Wiegand. München 1944, 436.

62 Fünfter Bericht d. Notgemeinschaft 1925/26, 147–148 = Deutsche Forschung 1, 28–29.

63 Deutsche Forschung 7. 1929. Bericht über die Mitgliederversammlung vom 1. Dezember 1928, 43–47.

führen und zudem bestände die Aussicht auf Zuwendungen von privater Seite.

In Kleinasien befürwortete Meyer eine Fortsetzung der hethitischen Forschungen, die bisher eine deutsche Domäne gewesen seien. Da hier von amerikanischer Seite mit reichlicheren Mitteln Einfluß genommen würde, hielt er eine Wiederaufnahme für besonders wünschenswert. Freigelegt werden sollte vor allem Boghazköi; mögliche Schwierigkeiten mit den türkischen Archäologen sollten ausgeräumt werden.

In Mesopotamien plädierte Meyer für die Aufnahme von Grabungen in Warka (Uruk) oder Ktesiphon. Bei dem letztgenannten Vorhaben betonte er dessen Bedeutung für die Kenntnis der gesamten Epoche von Alexander dem Großen bis zum Beginn des Islam ''mit ihrem frühchristlichen Einschlag und ihrer wichtigen jüdischen Kolonie in Seleukia;'' auch ''für die Kenntnis der römischen Architektur böten sich Möglichkeiten.'' Neben den Grabungen schlug er eine topographische Aufnahme vor, so an der berühmten Straße nach Ekbatana, so daß mit den Ausgrabungen Forschungen zur antiken Geographie verknüpft würden. Meyer riet zunächst zu einer Vorexpedition,[70] 1928 sollte dann die volle Arbeit beginnen. Die Kosten für die Kampagnen (ihre Anzahl ließ er offen) setzte er mit 70–80000 Reichsmark an.

Die von Meyer vor allem bezüglich Seleukia-Ktesiphon vorgetragenen Vorschläge wurden angenommen. 1928/29 wurde bekanntlich eine Kampagne durchgeführt;[71] für sie wurden je 40000 Reichsmark von der D.O.G. und der Notgemeinschaft bereitgestellt.[72] Infolge der Etatkürzungen von 1929 konnten die Forschungen erst 1931/32 mit einer zweiten Kampagne fortgesetzt werden.

In den Jahren 1928/29 erreichten die Ausgrabungsförderungen der Nachkriegszeit einen Höhepunkt. Von den in diesem Zeitraum für Forschungsreisen, Expeditionen und ähnliche Zwecke bereitgestellten Mitteln von 866268,15 Reichsmark entfielen auf die Ausgrabungen in Asien und Griechenland 182500,—Reichsmark und auf andere altertumswissenschaftliche Forschungsvorhaben 84823,32 Reichsmark,[73] also fast ein

---

[70] Als Leiter nannte Meyer Oscar Reuther oder Julius Jordan, möglicherweise auch Theodor Dombart, alle drei auf dem Gebiet erfahrene Wissenschaftler. Im Zusammenhang mit der Benennung von Projektleitern für die mesopotamischen Vorhaben äußerte sich Meyer über das Potential der deutschen Assyriologie, die nach seiner Ansicht überwiegend philologisch ausgerichtet war. Er regte an, daß die Notgemeinschaft durch Vergabe von Stipendien geeignete Nachwuchskräfte mit archäologischem Schwerpunkt fördern sollte.

[71] Einen Bericht über diese Kampagne gab Meyer am 28. Februar 1929 in einem Vortrag vor der D.O.G. (In: Mitteilungen d. D.O.G., Nr. 67, April 1929, 1–26).

[72] Protokoll der Besprechung vom 17. Januar 1928.

[73] Achter Bericht d. Notgemeinschaft 1928/29, 163.

Drittel auf Fachgebiete, an deren Förderungsentscheidungen Meyer beteiligt war.

Die verstärkte deutsche Ausgrabungstätigkeit im Orient und ihre Unterstützung durch die Notgemeinschaft brachten Meyer in seiner Fachausschußarbeit neue, zusätzliche Aufgaben, besonders organisatorischer Art. Er war nicht nur für die Expeditionsfonds verantwortlich und zusammen mit Wiegand zeichnungsberechtigt,[74] sondern auch maßgeblich an der Auswahl der Projektleiter und ihres wissenschaftlichen Mitarbeiterstabes beteiligt,[75] Aufgaben, die vielfältige, teilweise schwierige Verhandlungen mit den vorgesehenen Wissenschaftlern und mit Verwaltungsstellen und Behörden erforderten.[76] Ebenso hatte er sich um geschäftliche Angelegenheiten wie Vertragsabschlüsse oder Versicherungen bei den Expeditionen zu kümmern. Zuweilen kamen Schwierigkeiten hinzu, die sich aus der Zusammenarbeit der für ein Projekt verantwortlichen Wissenschaftler ergaben, wie beispielsweise die Auseinandersetzungen zwischen Ernst Sellin und Gabriel Welter bei dem Unternehmen in Sichem.[77]

---

[74] Für die Grabungen in Seleukia-Ktesiphon war Meyer Vorsitzender der dafür eingerichteten Sonderkommission und hinsichtlich der Finanzen zusammen mit Wiegand für das Sonderkonto zeichnungsberechtigt. Ebenso war er für die Warka-Expedition Verwalter des Etats, wie sich aus einem Schreiben Oscar Reuthers vom 14.7.1928 ergibt, in dem dieser um die Überweisung von 10000 Reichmark bat und außerdem die Frage nach der Versicherung bei der Expedition stellte.

[75] Vgl. Anm. 70; bisweilen waren solche langwierigen Verhandlungen auch ergebnislos, wie im Falle von Julius Lewy, der als Assyrologe an dem Unternehmen in Warka (Uruk) teilnehmen sollte. Zu Meyers Beurteilung von Thesen Lewys in der Assyrologie vgl. H.E. Stier, Vorwort zu GdA III, S. VI, Anm. 1.

[76] So bat beispielsweise Walter Andrae in einem Brief vom 14. Juni 1928 Meyer darum, wegen der Freigabe von Julius Jordan und Konrad Preußer für die Grabungen in Warka (Uruk) mit der D.O.G. zu verhandeln; beide waren mit der Veröffentlichung alter Grabungsergebnisse der D.O.G. beschäftigt.

[77] Die Streitigkeiten führten zu einem Akten füllenden Vorgang, der den Verantwortlichen beim Archäologischen Institut des Deutschen Reiches und der Notgemeinschaft nicht geringe Mühen bereitete. Beide Forscher hatten die Leitung der Unternehmung in Sichem, wobei dem Theologen Sellin die Auswertung des Materials, Welter die archäologische Feldforschung oblag. Die schon lange schwelenden Eifersüchteleien, die vor allem von Sellin ausgingen, der wohl Welters archäologische Überlegenheit empfand, entwickelten sich zu einem offenen Streit in der unterschiedlichen Deutung archäologischer Denkmäler, die Sellin fälschlicherweise als "Masseben" ansah und "ohne Rücksprache und Korrespondenz mit dem für die archäologische Arbeit verantwortlichen Archäologen veröffentlichte" (Welter: Erklärung vom 31. Januar 1929). Welter seinerseits vergriff sich dem Älteren gegenüber teilweise im Ton. Die Frage der Erneuerung der am 31.12.1928 ablaufenden Grabungskonzessionen und Welters alleinige Verhandlungen dabei—wozu er als Grabungsleiter berechtigt war—schufen bei Sellin neue Verstimmung. Am 18.12.1928 fand in der Notgemeinschaft eine Besprechung statt, an der neben dem Präsidenten Meyer, Rodenwaldt, Wolters, Wiegand, Adolf Deissmann (Vorsitzender des Fachausschusses Theologie) und andere teilnahmen. Zweck der Unterredung war, durch eine Schlichtung des Streites die Ausgrabungen für die deutsche Wissenschaft zu retten, zumal von niederländischer Seite ein Interesse an ihnen bestand; hierauf wies besonders

Die Belege für die zahlreichen Vorgänge im einzelnen sind recht bruch-
stückhaft, so daß vieles in seiner Gesamtheit nicht rekonstuierbar ist.
Grund dafür ist, daß Meyers anstehende Fragen der Notgemeinschaft,
soweit die Ansprechpartner in Berlin saßen—und das war häufig der
Fall—, überwiegend telephonisch oder persönlich erledigte. Sowohl dieses
Faktum als auch einige Beispiele alltäglicher Arbeit für die Notgemeinschaft veranschaulicht ein Brief Meyers an Wiegand vom 21. Mai 1928;[78]
das Schreiben ist eines der wenigen schriftlichen Zeugnisse dafür, wie
Meyer derartige Angelegenheiten abwickelte:

Sehr geehrter Herr Kollege!

Da ich Sie weder am Sonnabend noch heute morgen (wo auf zahlreiche
Anrufe von der Notgem. aus kein Anschluss zu erhalten war) habe erreichen können, muss ich mich schriftlich an Sie wenden. Reuther[79] hat
mir den beiliegenden Brief über die Verpflichtung Wachsmuths für Ktesiphon[80] geschickt. Die darin vorgeschlagenen Bedingungen erscheinen
mir durchaus sachgemäss und billig; auch Schäfer[81] und Güterbock,[82]
mit denen ich darüber gesprochen habe, waren der gleichen Ansicht. So
bitte ich um Ihre Äusserung darüber. Ansonsten darf ich, da Sie in
solchen Dingen reiche Erfahrung haben, ich aber gar keine, Sie wohl um
die Freundlichkeit bitten, den Vertrag in Korrekturweise aufzusetzen

---

Meyer hin. Bekanntlich gelang es nochmals eine Einigung herzustellen; Welter setzte im
Sommer 1931 die Grabungen fort. Nach Sellins Ansicht gingen sie jedoch zu schleppend
voran. Er wandte sich daher gegen Welter an die Öffentlichkeit, wurde jedoch seinerseits
wegen seiner wissenschaftlichen Auswertungen von Hermann Thiersch kritisiert. Dennoch gelang es Sellin, daß ihm das Archäologische Institut des Deutschen Reiches 1933
die Arbeit zusammen mit Hans Steckeweh weiterhin übertrug. Vgl. zu den Vorgängen
auch K. Jaroš, Sichem. Göttingen 1976 (Orbis biblicus orientalis 11.), 18–19.

[78] Deutsches Archäologisches Institut. Archiv: Nachlaß Theodor Wiegand 35.

[79] Oscar Reuther (1880–1954), Professor für Bau- u. Kunstgeschichte an der Technischen Hochschule Dresden. Er war Leiter der Expedition nach Seleukia-Ktesiphon, vgl.
auch Anm. 70.

[80] Friedrich Wachsmuth (1883–1975), Bau- und Kunsthistoriker, war damals Privat-
dozent an der Technischen Hochschule Darmstadt und der Universität Marburg (vgl.
Kürschners Gelehrtenkalender 1931); er wurde Mitglied beider Expeditionen nach
Seleukia-Ktesiphon 1928/29 und 1931/32.

[81] Heinrich Schäfer (1868–1957) war von 1914–1935 Direktor der ägyptischen
Sammlung der Staatlichen Museen in Berlin; zu seiner Biographie s. Zeitschrift f. ägyptische Sprache 75. 1939, 1–16.

[82] Der Altorientalist Bruno Güterbock (1858–1940) war Schriftführer der D.O.G.
und damals Herausgeber der Wissenschaftlichen Veröffentlichungen und der Mitteilungen der Gesellschaft (vgl. E. v. Schuler, Siebzig Jahre Deutsche Orient-Gesellschaft.
In: Mitteilungen der D.O.G. 100. 1968, 10–13; J. Renger, Die Geschichte der Altorien-
talistik und der Vorderasiatischen Archäologie in Berlin. In: Berlin und die Antike. Aufsätze. Hg. von W. Arenhövel u. Chr. Schreiber. Berlin 1979, 179; 188 f.

und mir zur Unterschrift und Weitersendung zuzuschicken. Ist dazu ein Stempel erforderlich?

Über das Forschungsstipendium Wachsmuths habe ich mich heute bei der Notgem. erkundigt. Es ist zur Fertigstellung seiner Arbeit gewährt und läuft im December ab;[83] so scheint es mir richtig, es nicht zu berücksichtigen und seine Bezüge dadurch zu kürzen. Den Antrag auf Beurlaubung an die Fakultät werde ich selbst stellen; es handelt sich dabei ja um eine reine Formalität, um derentwillen es überflüssig wäre, die Notgem. zu bemühen.

Dass Heydenreich[84] zugesagt hat, hat mir Rodenwaldt[85] bestätigt; er will sich aber nochmals wegen der Verzögerung seiner Antwort erkundigen, die wohl dadurch veranlasst ist, dass er auf der Reise ist. Heute morgen hat mich Schmidt-Ott auffordern lassen, morgen (Dienstag) um 12 Uhr zu einer Besprechung mit Sellin zu ihm zu kommen. Ob auch Sie dabei sind, weiß ich nicht; sollte das der Fall sein, so könnten wir ja dort alles erledigen. Im übrigen komme ich morgen um 2 Uhr zu Schäfer ins Museum, und könnte Sie dann vielleicht auch dort aufsuchen; geben Sie ihm bitte eventuell Bescheid. Worum es sich bei der Besprechung mit Sellin handeln soll, weiß ich nicht. Wissen Sie, ob Welter nach Sichem gegangen ist und wie es dort steht?[86] In Frankfurt bei unserer Sitzung vor acht Tagen wusste man nichts darüber. Den Brief von Reuther darf ich bitten mir wieder zuzustellen.

Mit besten Grüssen
Ihr
Eduard Meyer

Mögen die alltäglichen Arbeiten im Gesamtbild von Meyers Wirken in der Notgemeinschaft weniger bedeutend erscheinen; wegen der Fülle der Zeit, die sie kosteten und die Meyer offensichtlich aus Überzeugung für die Sache opferte, verdienen sie erwähnt zu werden, zumal er in den letzten Lebensjahren mit seiner Zeit hauszuhalten suchte, um sein

---

[83] Für die Arbeit "Der Raum, Raumgestaltung und Raumwirkung" (vgl. Achter Bericht d. Notgemeinschaft 1928/29, 61).

[84] Robert Heidenreich (geb. 1899), 1931 Privatdozent, später Professor in Jena und Leipzig, war ebenfalls Mitglied des Ausgrabungsteams der beiden Kampagnen nach Seleukia-Ktesiphon (vgl. die Widmung bei J. Kröger, Sasanidischer Stuckdekor. Mainz 1982, Bagdader Forschungen 5).

[85] Gerhart Rodenwaldt (1886–1945) war bekanntlich ab 1922 Generalsekretär, 1929–1932 Präsident des Archäologischen Instituts des Deutschen Reiches (s.a. das Sammelheft: Rodenwaldts Beitrag zur Klassischen Archäologie. In: Wissenschaftl. Zeitschrift d. Humboldt-Universität zu Berlin 35, 8. 1986).

[86] Siehe Anm. 77.

Lebenswerk, seine Geschichte des Altertums, zum gewünschten Abschluß zu bringen.[87]

Der hoffnungsvolle Aufschwung in der Wissenschaftsförderung kam 1929 vorerst zum Stillstand, als im Zuge der wirtschaftlichen Rezession auch die Frage der Reduzierung des Etats der Notgemeinschaft zur Debatte stand und dabei eine lange schwelende Kritik an der Struktur der Gemeinschaft, ihrer Führungsspitze und ihrer Arbeitsweise offen zutagetrat.[88] Die Einwände kamen hauptsächlich vom preußischen Kultusministerium und richteten sich gegen den ganz auf das Prinzip der Selbstverwaltung abgestellten Modus der Bearbeitung der Anträge,[89] der der Staatsseite wenig Einblick gewährte. Bereits 1922 befolgte die Preußische Akademie der Wissenschaften auf ausdrückliches Votum Meyers hin nicht den Erlaß des Ministeriums, alle eingehenden Gesuche ihm zur Kenntnis zu geben.[90] Nun monierte das Ministerium erneut, daß Länder und Reich als finanzielle Träger der Notgemeinschaft zu wenig Einfluß auf die dort gefällten Entscheidungen besäßen, andererseits aber das Ministerium ständig mit Beschwerden und Anträgen überschüttet würde. Kritisiert wurde vor allem Schmidt-Otts Führung der Notgemeinschaft, seine ''Autokratie'', und die ''Clique von alten Herren'' mit einem ''Durchschnittsalter von 68½ Jahren,'' die den Präsidenten umgab und keine neuen Kräfte aufkommen ließ;[91] gemeint war die Zusammensetzung des Präsidiums, des Hauptausschusses, aber auch der Fachausschüsse. Bemängelt wurde ferner die Arbeit des Verlagsausschusses; er käme den Verlegern über Gebühr entgegen und ließe zu, daß fast jedes wissenschaftliche Buch gefördert würde. Schließlich gab es in einem Punkt Einwände, der Meyer vom Fach her besonders berührte, bei den Ausgrabungen, deren Kosten nach Ansicht der Kritiker in einer Zeit, in der Deutschland noch Reparationen zu zahlen hatte, die Verhältnisse von Reich und Ländern überstiegen.

Die Kritik war nicht völlig unberechtigt. Der Führungsstil Schmidt-Otts war tatsächlich teilweise ''patriarchalisch'', und der Kreis der mitwirkenden Gelehrten hatte sich seit der Gründung der Notgemeinschaft

---

[87] So äußerte er sich beispielsweise im Dankesbrief vom 27. Januar 1930 für die Glückwünsche zum 75. Geburtstag an Carl Heinrich Becker (Geheimes Staatsarchiv Berlin: Nachlaß C.H. Becker): ''Ich hoffe, dass es mir vergönnt sein wird, auch weiter, soweit Leben und Kraft reichen, meine Arbeiten fortzuführen und noch wenigstens einiges, vor allem die Geschichte des Orients und Griechenlands bis zu den Perserkriegen zum Abschluß zu bringen.''

[88] Zur Krise der Notgemeinschaft s. Zierold, 108–137.

[89] Ausführlich zu den Auseinandersetzungen Zierold, 109–110; 114–115.

[90] Zierold, 27.

[91] Aus der Niederschrift Salomonsohns über eine Unterredung mit dem preußischen Kultusminister und seinem Ministerialdirektor Werner Richter (Zierold, 110).

verhältnismäßig wenig verändert, in den Fachausschüssen meistens nur
durch das Ausscheiden bei Krankheit oder Tod.[92] Er bestand teilweise
aus emeritierten Hochschullehrern, Meyer war ein Beispiel dafür. Jüngere Gelehrte hatten wenig Chancen, in die Ausschüsse der Notgemeinschaft berufen zu werden, was zu Recht Unwillen hervorrief. Das ausgeprägte "Führungsprinzip" Schmidt-Otts wurde auch von seinem
Stellvertreter Fritz Haber nicht gutgeheißen, der mehrfach versuchte,
den Präsidenten zur Änderung seines Führungsstiles zu bewegen.

Andererseits hatten Schmidt-Ott und die auf seiner Linie liegenden
Mitarbeiter, zu denen Meyer gehörte, ihre Argumente. Man sträubte
sich mit Recht aus organisatorischen und arbeitsökonomischen Gründen
gegen Wahlen, weil durch einen zu häufigen Wechsel der Ausschußmitglieder und durch die Umständlichkeit eines solchen Verfahrens die Kontinuität der sehr umfangreichen und aufwendigen Arbeit nicht gewähr-
leistet war.

Das Unbehagen gegenüber Fachausschußwahlen bestand bei Teilen
der Notgemeinschaft seit den Anfängen. Nach den Vorstellungen, vor
allem von staatlicher Seite, sollten die Mitglieder der Fachausschüsse,
deren erste Zusammensetzung von wissenschaftlichen Institutionen, wie
den Akademien, oder vom Präsidium der Notgemeinschaft selbst vorgenommen worden war, künftig in demokratischem Verfahren von der
Gesamtheit der Gelehrten eines Faches gewählt werden.

Meyer hielt nichts von diesem Verfahren, wie er in einem Bericht vom
25. Oktober 1921 an die Mitglieder seines Fachausschusses[93] zum Ausdruck brachte: "Die Sache wird viel unnötige Arbeit machen und viel
Geld kosten; aber wie sie gestaltet wird, darf man wenigstens hoffen, dass
sie, wie so viele glorreiche Erfindungen der Demokratie, auf eine Farce
hinauskommen wird." Er fügte hinzu, auf der Mitgliederversammlung
der Notgemeinschaft am 12. Oktober 1921 in Baden-Baden habe er sich
den Forderungen nach Wahlen "auf breitester demokratischer Grundlage" mit "Gegengründen, die auf der Hand liegen," widersetzt. Man
habe sich jedoch den Befürwortern von Wahlen fügen müssen, da sowohl
der Staatssekretär Heinrich Schulz als auch das Mitglied der Budgetkom-
mission im Reichstag, Prälat Georg Schreiber,[94] deutlich zu verstehen
gegeben hätten, daß die "Wiederbewilligung und vollends die gehoffte
Erhöhung der Reichsunterstützung" sonst fraglich wären.

---

[92] Das traf auch für Meyers Fachausschuß zu, vgl. Anm. 5 u. 6.
[93] Akademie d. Wissenschaften d. DDR. Archiv: NL Ed. Meyer 274, Bericht, Bl. 5.
[94] Professor der katholischen Theologie und Kirchengeschichte in Münster, als Zen-
trumsabgeordneter Mitglied des Reichstages; er spielte als parlamentarischer Vertreter in
der Notgemeinschaft eine große Rolle. Zweifellos hat er sich um die Notgemeinschaft

Die konservativ gesinnte Gruppe innerhalb der Notgemeinschaft mußte zunächst nachgeben und sich den "demokratischen Grundsätzen" beugen. Meyer wurde sogar in die Kommission berufen, die eine Wahlordnung in einer von Haber vorgeschlagenen demokratischen Form erarbeiten sollte.[95] Diese Wahlordnung existierte in der Folgezeit jedoch nur auf dem Papier, wenn man von den Wahlen im Winter 1921/22 absieht.[96] Satzungsgemäß erforderliche Neuwahlen in den Jahren 1924, 1926 und 1928 fanden nicht statt; sie wurden offensichtlich durch die wiederholte Verlängerung des Mandats der bisherigen Ausschußmitglieder seitens des Präsidiums und des Hauptausschusses unterlaufen. Das Unbehagen führender Repräsentanten der Notgemeinschaft vor einem solchen demokratischen Verfahren spielte dabei sicherlich keine unwesentliche Rolle.

Meyers Vorstellungen über die Arbeit und Funktion der Fachausschüsse lassen sich auch an einem anderen Beispiel veranschaulichen. In dem oben genannten Bericht an die Mitglieder seines Fachausschusses vom 25. Oktober 1922 bat Meyer um Zustimmung, daß die Gutachtertätigkeit nicht allein von Ausschußmitgliedern übernommen wurde, sondern daß er von sich aus "andere Gelehrte, deren Sachkenntnis und Autorität auf dem betreffenden Fachgebiet außer Frage steht," hinzuziehen könne. Dieses Verfahren, das Meyer mit Erfolg erprobte und das gewiß zur Objektivität und Ausgewogenheit bei den von seinem Ausschuß befürworteten Forschungsunterstützungen beigetragen hat, hob er nochmals in der Hauptausschußsitzung vom 14. Juli 1927 als einen seiner Grundsätze hervor; im Protokoll heißt es:[97] "Er [Meyer] habe sich als Fachausschuß-Vorsitzender niemals an die Zugehörigkeit zum Fachausschuß gebunden, sondern im Einvernehmen mit dem Präsidenten stets geeignete Referenten herangezogen." Meyer sprach sich also für eine von Sachlichkeit und Kooperationsbereitschaft bestimmte Arbeitsweise aus; zu ihr gehörte das Kollegialprinzip in der Zusammenarbeit mit den Mitgliedern seines Ausschusses, aber auch die letztliche Verantwortung des Vorsitzenden. Er betrachtete—das geht aus seinen Äußerungen hervor—

---

große Verdienste erworben, andererseits hat er seinen Einfluß mit einer gewissen persönlichen Eitelkeit zu nutzen gewußt. Schmidt-Ott mußte ihm häufiger gegen seine Überzeugung nachgeben (vgl. Zierold, 21 ff.). Zu Schreiber auch: R. Morsey, Georg Schreiber. In: Berlinische Lebensbilder (wie Anm. 22), 269–284.

[95] Der Kommission gehörten außerdem Walter von Dyck, Fritz Haber, Paul Kehr, Friedrich von Müller und Georg Schreiber an (vgl. Zierold, 59).

[96] Die Wahlen wurden über die Fachverbände abgewickelt; für die Klassische Philologie fanden sie auf der Versammlung der Philologen und Schulmänner in Jena statt. Überwiegend wurde die bisherige Zusammensetzung der Fachausschüsse bestätigt, auch in Meyers Ausschuß.

[97] Akademie d. Wissenschaften d. DDR. Archiv: NL Ed. Meyer 275.

den Ausschuß als Arbeitsgruppe, nicht als parlamentarisches Gremium.

Kehren wir zu den Vorgängen im Jahre 1929 zurück. Ihr Ergebnis war, daß begrenzte Reformen in der Struktur der Notgemeinschaft und eine Umbildung des Hauptausschusses vorgenommen wurden.[98] Außerdem fanden die lange verschobenen Neuwahlen zu den Fachausschüssen statt.

Während der Wahlen wurden die unterschiedlichen Auffassungen zum Wahlverfahren und ebenso zu anderen Fragen in der Notgemeinschaft selbst nochmals auf einer Sitzung des Hauptausschusses am 16. Februar 1929[99] deutlich. Die Sitzung gibt auch für Meyers Standpunkte einige weitere Aufschlüsse. Denn in der Diskussion äußerte er sich zu zwei Streitpunkten des Wahlverfahrens, der Nominierung der Kandidaten und der Festlegung des Kreises der Wahlberechtigten. Aufgrund eigener Erfahrungen trug er die Schwierigkeiten vor, eine "Liste der anerkannten Forscher" für die Wahlen aufzustellen. Dahinter steckte das Bemühen seitens der Führung der Notgemeinschaft, deren Linie Meyer vertrat, der geforderten Nominierung der Fachausschußkandidaten auf der Grundlage breitester Mitbestimmung im Forum der einzelnen Wissenschaftsgebiete selbst durch eine eigene dem Präsidium und den Verantwortlichen der Notgemeinschaft vertrauenswürdige Liste entgegenzuwirken. In der Gemeinschaft bestand die Sorge, den Einfluß darauf zu verlieren, wirklich anerkannte Wissenschaftler für die Mitarbeit in den Fachausschüssen zu gewinnen. Bei einigen Wissenschaftsgebieten bestand andererseits eine merkliche Gleichgültigkeit, sich an der Arbeit der Notgemeinschaft zu beteiligen, so daß eine gewisse Hilfestellung durch eine vorgegebene Liste von Kandidaten sogar notwendig war. Aus diesen Gründen plädierte Meyer "für unverbindliche Vorschläge von seiten des Präsidiums."

Bedenken trug Meyer ferner gegen Bestrebungen vor, die Wahlberechtigung auf wissenschaftlich tätige Berufsgruppen außerhalb der Hochschulen und wissenschaftlichen Institutionen auszudehnen, eine solche Forderung hatten die Museumsbeamten erhoben. Er wies auf die Schwierigkeiten hin, eindeutige Richtlinien dafür zu finden, wer einzubeziehen sei oder nicht. Neben der rein praktischen Unmöglichkeit einer sinnvollen Abgrenzung spielte auch hier gewiß die Sorge mit, daß durch eine allzu große Ausweitung des Anspruches auf Wissenschaftlichkeit einer Nivellierung des wissenschaftlichen Niveaus Vorschub geleistet würde.

Bei der Frage der Kandidatenauswahl zeigte sich zusätzlich ein be-

[98] Dazu Zierold, 128–131.
[99] Akademie d. Wissenschaften d. DDR. Archiv: NL Ed. Meyer 275, Protokoll der Sitzung.

trächtlicher Unterschied in der Organisation und Kommunikation zwischen Geistes- und Naturwissenschaften. Er offenbarte zugleich einen recht schroffen Gegensatz zwischen Meyer und Haber. Dieser begründete die geringe Wahlbeteiligung in den Naturwissenschaften damit, daß "das wissenschaftliche Leben" dort in den großen Vereinen läge, und folgerte daraus, daß sie daher "kein wissenschaftliches Leben der Fachausschüsse" brauchten. "Vertrauensvolle Vorschläge" kämen von den Vereinen, solche der Notgemeinschaft seien bedeutungslos. Hinter dieser Aussage stand der Wunsch, die Kandidaten für die Fachausschüsse auf breiter Ebene über die wissenschaftlichen Vereine zu rekrutieren. Meyer hielt dem entgegen, daß in den Geisteswissenschaften keine derartigen Organisationen beständen. Für ihn waren daher Entscheidungshilfen durch die Notgemeinschaft bei der Auswahl der Kandidaten sinnvoll und wichtig.

Auch in der damals besonders aktuellen Frage der Mittelvergabe wurde der Gegensatz zwischen Meyer und Haber deutlich. Haber differenzierte zwischen den Belangen der Naturwissenschaften und denen der Geisteswissenschaften und unterstrich das mit den etwas herausfordernden Worten: "Wenn Herr Meyer mehr Druckkostenzuschüsse braucht, so brauchen sie mehr Forschungsstipendien und Apparate." Entschieden wandte er sich, solange die Mittel der Notgemeinschaft nicht aufgestockt würden, gegen die Erhöhung der Druckkostenzuschüsse, die Meyer wegen der nicht ausreichenden Unterstützung, besonders bei den Zeitschriften, trotz der schlechten Etatlage gefordert hatte.

Im Zusammenhang mit der Diskussion um die Stellung der Fachausschüsse wandte sich Meyer gegen die auf der Sitzung vorgetragene Idee, gemeinsame Sitzungen dieser Ausschüsse abzuhalten und dafür die Stelle eines "Sekretars" einzurichten. Er begrüßte zwar eine Kooperation der Ausschüsse, jedoch kein zusätzliches Gremium mit einem neuen Funktionsträger. Auch das verdeutlicht, daß Meyer die Fachausschüsse als Arbeitsgruppen verstand, die unter der gutachterlichen Tätigkeit von Fachwissenschaftlern die Förderungsmaßnahmen für die einzelnen Wissenschaften bestimmten und lenkten, nicht als Gremien, die auf parlamentarischer Grundlage die Funktion von Vertretungsorganen der einzelnen Fachwissenschaften in der Notgemeinschaft einnahmen.

Die personellen Veränderungen, die sich bei den Neuwahlen von 1929 für den Hauptausschuß und die Fachausschüsse ergaben, waren nicht umwälzend; vor allem in den Fachausschüssen behielten viele der bisherigen Mitglieder ihr Mandat. Auch Meyer wurde im Vorsitz seines Fachausschusses bestätigt. Seine Position in der Notgemeinschaft wurde noch gestärkt; denn er wurde—und vielleicht ist das etwas überraschend—trotz seines Alters zusätzlich zu seiner bisherigen Aufgabe in den

Hauptausschuß berufen. Doch auch diese Wahl war durchaus begründet. Meyer hatte seit Jahren über die eigentliche Fachausschußarbeit hinaus in den verschiedenen Organen der Notgemeinschaft, gerade auch im Hauptausschuß, mitgearbeitet; an dessen Sitzungen nahm er als Vertreter der Fachausschüsse teil. Seine Nominierung war die Folge seiner bisherigen Mitarbeit; auf die intime Kenntnis vieler Probleme, die der Vorsitzende des Fachausschusses für alte und orientalische Philologie hatte, wollte Schmidt-Ott nicht verzichten.

Weit schwerwiegender als die Auseinandersetzungen um die Struktur und Arbeitsweise der Notgemeinschaft sowie die Wahl der Ausschußmitglieder mußten sich die Etatkürzungen um eine Million Reichsmark auswirken, wie sie von staatlicher Seite vorgesehen waren. Aus dieser Sorge heraus wandte sich die Preußische Akademie der Wissenschaften in offensichtlicher Absprache mit der Notgemeinschaft mit einer Denkschrift vom 14. Mai 1929[100] an den Reichstag. Verfasser war Meyer, dessen persönliche Vorstellungen über die Wissenschaftspflege auch hier durchklangen.

Die Schrift begann mit einem kurzen Rückblick auf die erfolgreiche Hilfe, die die Notgemeinschaft für die Erhaltung der ''Leistungsfähigkeit'' und ''Schaffenskraft'' der deutschen Wissenschaft sowie ihrer Konkurrenzfähigkeit in der Welt geleistet hat. Besonders positiv bewertet wurde die Einigkeit bei diesem Ziel über ''Länder- und Parteieninteressen'' hinweg. Mochten diese Worte in erster Linie den offiziellen von der Akademie als Institution vertretenen Standpunkt wiedergeben, sie beschrieben zugleich die Verwirklichung eines Wunsches, der tief im Denken des Verfassers der Schrift verwurzelt war.

Als wichtige Faktoren für die sinnvolle Arbeit der Notgemeinschaft nannte Meyer die ''Selbstverwaltung'' und die ''freiwillige Mitarbeit aller führend anerkannten Persönlichkeiten.'' Selbstverwaltung war für ihn das bisher praktizierte Verfahren der Bearbeitung eingehender Anträge sowie die autonome Entscheidung ohne Einwirkung übergeordneter Stellen oder gar parlamentarischer Gremien. Diese Arbeitsweise war an den recht liberalen Prinzipien der Wissenschaftsverwaltung der Vorkriegszeit orientiert; zu ihnen gehörte im Sinne des mit diesen Grundsätzen verankerten Leistungsprinzips, daß führende Fachleute an den Aufgaben beteiligt waren.

Ein wichtiger Punkt der Denkschrift war, Tendenzen entgegenzutreten, nach denen die Notgemeinschaft nur für solche Forschungsvorhaben Mittel bereitstellen sollte, die einen praktischen Nutzen brächten. Die

---

[100] Denkschrift der Preußischen Akademie der Wissenschaften. Mai 1929. Berlin 1929.

Schrift richtete sich daher gegen Vorwürfe, wie den der "unproduktiven Ausgaben," und hielt dem entgegen, diese seien "in Wirklichkeit für die wissenschaftliche Arbeit so produktiv wie keine andern;" die deutsche Wissenschaft brauche "ihre freie Bewegung," sonst würde sie "verkümmern" und ihre Weltgeltung verlieren. Zur Stellung der deutschen Wissenschaft in der Welt hatte sich Meyer in den ersten Nachkriegsjahren besonders im Rahmen der Diskussion um die Hochschulreform eingehend geäußert und dabei die Wichtigkeit einer gediegenen Ausbildung des akademischen Nachwuchses betont. Seinerzeit hatte er die Überlegenheit der zu freier selbständiger Arbeit anregenden Lehrweise an den deutschen Universitäten gegenüber dem Schulbetrieb im anglo-amerikanischen Hochschulsystem deutlichgemacht.[101] Jetzt erinnerte er daran, daß es ein Verdienst der Notgemeinschaft sei, die materielle Grundlage für eine freie Forschungstätigkeit mitgeschaffen zu haben. Als nicht unerhebliche Kraft für die Leistungsfähigkeit der deutschen Wissenschaft führte er die "Anspruchslosigkeit" des deutschen Gelehrten an, ebenfalls ein Charakteristikum der Vorkriegszeit, das zu den Idealen des Verfassers gehörte.

Unter dem Gesichtspunkt ihrer kulturellen Bedeutung wurden in der Denkschrift die wegen ihrer hohen Kosten namentlich kritisierten Ausgrabungen verteidigt: "Daher darf auch die Fortführung der Ausgrabungen nicht unterbrochen werden, wenn wir nicht selbst unsere Kultur untergraben und damit unsere Betätigung und Bewegungsfreiheit auf demjenigen Gebiet aufgeben wollen, auf dem auch in unserer gegenwärtigen Lage keine Macht von außen imstande ist, sie zu hemmen und einzuschnüren, auf dem der freien wissenschaftlichen Arbeit."[102] Diese mit einem gewissen Pathos gesprochenen Worte sind für Meyer typische Formulierungen, wie sie aus seinen Reden und Schriften der ersten Nachkriegsjahre hinreichend bekannt sind.

Die Denkschrift läßt erkennen, daß Meyer in der Arbeit der Notgemeinschaft seine eigenen Vorstellungen der Wissenschaftspflege in vielem verwirklicht sah und daß es darum ging, diese bewährte Form der Wissenschaftsförderung in ganzem Umfang zu erhalten. Zu tiefgreifenden Reformen war er, wie auch viele andere seiner Kollegen in Akademie und Notgemeinschaft, nicht bereit.

Die Etatkürzungen waren 1929/30 trotz der Einwände von Wissenschaft und Notgemeinschaft nicht zu umgehen. Die Einschränkungen, die alle Bereiche, und somit auch die Ausgrabungen betrafen, wurden dadurch im Erträglichen gehalten, daß nach festem Plan Einsparungen

---

[101] Vgl. Meyer, Preußen und Athen, 27–28.
[102] Zur Notwendigkeit der Auslandsforschung und der Ausgrabungen s.a. Neunter Bericht d. Notgemeinschaft 1929/30, 166–167.

vorgenommen wurden, jedoch dort weitergearbeitet wurde, wo "eine Unterbrechung der Arbeit die weitere Verfügung über die Ausgrabungsstätten"[103] gefährdete und dadurch das "wissenschaftliche Ansehen im Ausland geschädigt" wurde. So wurden die großen Ausgrabungen von Warka (Uruk), Sichem, Pergamon, Ephesos und Aigina fortgesetzt. Unterbrochen wurden die Grabungen in Seleukia-Ktesiphon, da auch die D.O.G. ihren Beitrag nicht leisten konnte.

Die Aufrechterhaltung der großen Ausgrabungen war ganz gewiß auch ein Verdienst Meyers, der sich zusammen mit Schmidt-Ott, Wiegand und anderen gerade hierfür besonders eingesetzt und immer wieder auf den Schaden hingewiesen hatte, den der Abbruch dieser Forschungen für das Ansehen der deutschen Wissenschaft bringen würde. Ebenso sträubte man sich gegen die weitgehende Streichung der Forschungsreisen;[104] vor allem für jüngere, weniger begüterte Gelehrte müßte diese Möglichkeit der Finanzierung solcher Reisen erhalten bleiben, während wirtschaftlich besser gestellte Forscher die Mittel selbst aufbringen sollten. Dieser Vorschlag mit seiner sozialen Komponente hatte ebenfalls wieder sein Vorbild in den Verhältnissen der Vorkriegszeit, der Anspruchslosigkeit und Opferbereitschaft des Gelehrten für die Wissenschaft.

Meyers Sorge um die Erhaltung dessen, was in den Jahren nach dem Kriege mühevoll aufgebaut worden war, und sein engagierter Einsatz für die Belange der Altertumswissenschaften zeigen sich auch in seinem damaligen Vorstoß zugunsten der D.O.G., die nicht nur hinsichtlich der Fortsetzung ihrer Ausgrabungsprojekte, sondern auch der Veröffentlichung alter Grabungsergebnisse durch die drohende Mittelkürzung in Schwierigkeiten geraten war.

In einem an das Präsidium der Notgemeinschaft gerichteten Schreiben appellierte Meyer an die "moralischen Pflichten" der Gemeinschaft gegenüber der D.O.G. Auf einer durch seinen Brief veranlaßten Sitzung von Vertretern der Notgemeinschaft, des preußischen Kultusministeriums und der D.O.G. am 25. Juli 1929[105] wandte sich Schmidt-Ott gegen diesen etwas überspitzt formulierten Appell. Er, der wie Meyer langjähriges Mitglied der Gesellschaft war, wies darauf hin, daß die Notgemeinschaft nur Jahr für Jahr ihre Beträge bewilligen könne und die D.O.G. versuchen müsse, von anderer Seite, vor allem vom preußischen Kultusministerium, größere Mittel zu erlangen. In der Aussprache über die Aufarbeitung der alten Grabungsergebnisse der D.O.G. waren sich

---

[103] Ebd., 170.

[104] Ebd., 165–166.

[105] Akademie d. Wissenschaften d. DDR. Archiv: NL Ed. Meyer 277, Protokoll der Besprechung.

die Gesprächsteilnehmer über die Notwendigkeit der Fortsetzung dieser Aufgabe einig. Jedoch war allen, auch Meyer, bewußt, daß die Veröffentlichung nur in eingeschränkter und verkürzter Form erfolgen konnte.[106] Ergebnis der Besprechung war, daß die Notgemeinschaft jährlich einen Betrag von 20000 Reichsmark an Druckkostenzuschüssen zur Verfügung stellte; für die restlichen 12000 Reichsmark erhoffte man sich eine Hilfe "von den Ministerien." Mit dem ihm bisweilen in solchen Angelegenheiten eigenen Optimismus erklärte sich Meyer bereit, "dem Kultusminister die Lage in einer persönlichen Besprechung vorzustellen." Über das Zustandekommen eines solchen Gespräches mit dem damaligen Minister Carl Heinrich Becker—er war vom Fach her Orientalist, und Meyer kannte ihn gut—fehlen die Informationen, ebenso über die Bewilligung zusätzlicher Mittel durch das Ministerium; immerhin wurden in den folgenden Jahren eine Reihe von älteren Grabungsergebnissen der D.O.G. veröffentlicht.

Am 31. August 1930 starb Eduard Meyer; fast zur gleichen Zeit verlor die Notgemeinschaft zwei weitere verdiente Männer, Adolf von Harnack, den langjährigen Vorsitzenden des Hauptausschusses, und Arthur Salomonsohn, den Schatzmeister der Notgemeinschaft und ihres Stifterverbandes. Auf der Mitgliederversammlung am 31. Oktober 1930[107] würdigte Schmidt-Ott die Verdienste aller drei, die ihm auch persönlich sehr nahestanden. Das Menschliche und Persönliche, das in seinen Worten zum Gedenken Meyers zum Ausdruck kam, war zweifellos ein nicht unbedeutender Faktor für Meyers erfolgreiche Arbeit in der Notgemeinschaft. Die langjährigen gemeinsamen Aufgaben schufen Bindungen, die auf Vertrauen, Kollegialität und einem Gefühl der Zusammengehörigkeit gegründet waren. Meyer fiel von seinem Wesen her offenbar diese Form der Zusammenarbeit nicht schwer. Trotz der klaren Standpunkte, die er vertrat, war er dennoch ein Mann, der Kompromisse eingehen konnte, wenn es die Gegebenheiten erforderten. So fügte er sich im Interesse des für ihn vorrangigen Zieles der Hilfe für die bedrängte deutsche Wissenschaft den von ihm abgelehnten demokratischen Grundsätzen. Er war kooperationsbereit und in gewissem Grade anpassungsfähig, anders als etwa Eduard Schwartz, der 1929 im Zuge der Bestrebungen, dem Reichsministerium des Inneren stärkere Kompetenzen einzuräumen, kompromißlos seinen Sitz im Hauptausschuß niederlegte.

---

[106] Auf Einschränkungen bei den Veröffentlichungen der D.O.G. hatte Meyer schon früher hingewiesen vgl. Meyer, Fünfundzwanzig Jahre Deutsche Orient-Gesellschaft. Rede gehalten in der Festsitzung am 24. Februar 1923. In: Mitteilungen d. D.O.G., Nr. 62, April 1923, 22).

[107] Immerhin wurden in den folgenden Jahren eine Reihe von Grabungsergebnissen der D.O.G. veröffentlicht.

Meyers Eigenschaften waren Umgänglichkeit, "Urwüchsigkeit" und eine ihm zugeschriebene "Fröhlichkeit".[108] Sie erleichterten ihm die Kontakte, und diese Gabe hat er dadurch genutzt, daß er das persönliche Gespräch in vielen Geschäften für die Notgemeinschaft bevorzugte. Hinzukam die "Begeisterung" für die Sache im Kreise für das gleiche Ziel tätiger Kollegen. Mögen Meyers Motive für seine Beteiligung an der Wissenschaftsförderung ursprünglich von der Idee der Hilfe für die bedrängte Wissenschaft bestimmt gewesen sein, im Laufe der Zeit trat die Freude an der zwar aufwendigen,[109] aber erfolgreichen Arbeit hinzu. Schmidt-Ott veranschaulichte diesen freudigen und überzeugten Einsatz für die Notgemeinschaft durch die bewegende Schilderung der letzten gemeinsam erledigten Angelegenheit: "... und es ist mir eine rührende Erinnerung, wenn ich an das letzte Schriftstück denke, das wir kaum noch lesen konnten, in dem er sich auf dem Kranken- und Sterbebette mit der Notgemeinschaft beschäftigt hat. Es ist ihm—und ich muß das ja auch mit einer gewissen Beschämung sagen—oft vorgehalten worden, daß sein Leben der wissenschaftlichen Forschung gehörte, und er hat dann immer mit dem ihm eigenen fröhlichen Mute geantworte: «Nein, die Notgemeinschaft lasse ich mir nicht nehmen!»" In diesen Sätzen suchte Schmidt-Ott ein auch neuerdings wiederholtes Pauschalurteil über Meyer[110] mit Recht zu revidieren, das, was dessen Einsatz für die Notgemeinschaft angeht, nicht aufrechtzuerhalten ist.

In seiner 1923 geschriebenen autobiographischen Skizze äußerte Meyer über seine bis dahin geleistete Arbeit in der Notgemeinschaft, er habe "als Vorsitzender des Fachausschusses für alte und orientalische Philologie nicht ohne Erfolg wirken können."[111] Aus den zahlreichen, freilich vielfach sehr bruchstückhaften Unterlagen, die erhalten sind, läßt sich das für die gesamte Zeit seiner Tätigkeit voll bestätigen. Meyer fand sich in schwerer Zeit trotz fortgeschrittenen Alters zur Mitarbeit bei der Erhaltung der Arbeitsfähigkeit der deutschen Wissenschaft bereit. Er traf gleich am Anfang zusammen mit seinem Fachausschuß eine wohldurchdachte und ausgewogene Auswahl unentbehrlicher altertumswissenschaftlicher

---

108 Schmidt-Ott, Erlebtes u. Erstrebtes, 181; G. Karo, Eduard Meyer zum Gedächtnis. In: Süddeutsche Monatshefte 28. 1930, 41; M. Gelzer, Eduard Meyer †. In: Gnomon 6. 1930, 624.

109 Wieviel Zeit und Kraft Meyer für die Notgemeinschaft aufbrachte, veranschaulichte Schmidt-Ott in seinem Nachruf durch die Bemerkung, Meyer habe "sein Telephon aufgegeben, weil es einen Zwangsmieter hatte, der es zu stark benutzte; infolgedessen mußte er immer von Lichterfelde nach Berlin kommen, selbst um geringfügige Angelegenheiten zu erledigen."

110 Vgl. K. Christ, Römische Geschichte und deutsche Geschichtswissenschaft. München 1982, 99.

111 Marohl, 11.

Arbeiten und Projekte, deren Finanzierung durch die Notgemeinschaft den Fortbestand deutscher Forschung auf diesen Gebieten sicherte. So gelang es, die bedeutenden Zeitschriften und große wissenschaftliche Gemeinschaftsunternehmungen weiterzuführen sowie grundlegende Forschungsergebnisse zu veröffentlichen. Ebenso hatte Meyer nicht geringen Anteil an der erfolgreichen Fortsetzung deutscher Ausgrabungstätigkeit im Ausland, die nicht unerheblich dazu beitrug, daß die deutsche Wissenschaft sich nach und nach aus ihrer Isolierung lösen konnte. Er hat somit in dem Jahrzehnt seiner Tätigkeit in der Notgemeinschaft mit großem Engagement entscheidend zum Fortbestand der deutschen Altertumswissenschaft beigetragen. Wilamowitz schrieb zum Tode Meyers in einem Brief an Eduard Schwartz,[112] Meyer sei für die Notgemeinschaft ''unersetzlich'', ein Urteil, dem aus der Sicht der Zeitgenossen nur zuzustimmen ist. Auch die heutige Wissenschaft profitiert davon, daß durch die damaligen Hilfsmaßnahmen, deren Gestaltung in der Altertumswissenschaft Meyer wesentlich mitbestimmt hat, wichtige wissenschaftliche Aufgaben erfüllt werden konnten und die Kontinuität der deutschen Forschung nach dem Ersten Weltkrieg nicht unterbrochen wurde.

---

[112] W.M. Calder III and R.L. Fowler, The preserved letters of Ulrich von Wilamowitz-Moellendorff to Eduard Schwartz. Ed. with introd. and commentary. München 1986 (SB d. Bayerischen Akademie d. Wissenschaften. Phil.-hist. Kl. 1986, 1), 101.